A Frequency Dictionary of Mandarin Chinese

A Frequency Dictionary of Mandarin Chinese is an invaluable tool for all learners of Mandarin Chinese, providing a list of the 5,000 words and the 2,000 Chinese characters most commonly used in the language. Based on a 50-million-word corpus composed of spoken, fiction, non-fiction and news texts in current use, the dictionary provides the user with a detailed frequency-based list, as well as alphabetical and part-of-speech indexes.

All entries in the frequency list feature the English equivalent and a sample sentence with English translation. The dictionary also contains 30 thematically organised lists of frequently used words on a variety of topics such as food, weather, travel and time expressions.

A Frequency Dictionary of Mandarin Chinese enables students of all levels to maximise their study of Mandarin vocabulary in an efficient and engaging way. It also represents an excellent resource for teachers of the language.

Richard Xiao is Senior Lecturer and Programme Leader in Chinese Studies at Edge Hill University. **Paul Rayson** is Director of the University Centre for Computer Corpus Research on Language and a teaching fellow at Lancaster University. **Tony McEnery** is Professor of English Language and Linguistics at Lancaster University.

Routledge Frequency Dictionaries

General Editors:

Paul Rayson, *Lancaster University, UK*

Mark Davies, *Brigham Young University, USA*

Editorial Board:

Michael Barlow, *University of Auckland, New Zealand*

Geoffrey Leech, *Lancaster University, UK*

Barbara Lewandowska-Tomaszczyk, *University of Lodz, Poland*

Josef Schmied, *Chemnitz University of Technology, Germany*

Andrew Wilson, *Lancaster University, UK*

Adam Kilgarriff, *Lexicography MasterClass Ltd and University of Sussex, UK*

Hongying Tao, *University of California at Los Angeles*

Chris Tribble, *King's College London, UK*

Other books in the series:

A Frequency Dictionary of German

A Frequency Dictionary of Portuguese

A Frequency Dictionary of Spanish

A Frequency Dictionary of French (forthcoming)

A Frequency Dictionary of Arabic (forthcoming)

A Frequency Dictionary
of Mandarin Chinese

Core vocabulary for learners

Richard Xiao, Paul Rayson and Tony McEnery

 Routledge
Taylor & Francis Group

LONDON AND NEW YORK

First published 2009
by Routledge
2 Park Square, Milton Park, Abingdon, OX14 4RN

Simultaneously published in the USA and Canada
by Routledge
711 Third Ave, New York, NY 10017

Routledge is an imprint of the Taylor & Francis Group, an informa business

Typeset in Parisine by Graphicraft Limited, Hong Kong

British Library Cataloguing in Publication Data
A catalogue record for this book is available from the British Library

Library of Congress Cataloging-in-Publication Data
Xiao, Richard.
   A frequency dictionary of Mandarin Chinese : core vocabulary for learners / Richard Xiao,
   Paul Rayson, Tony McEnery.
      p. cm.
   Includes index.
   1. Chinese language—Dictionaries—English.   I. Rayson, Paul.   II. McEnery, Tony, 1964–
   III. Title.
   PL1455.X537 2008
   495.1'321—dc22

                                                                2008030172

ISBN13: 978-0-415-45586-2 (pbk)
ISBN13: 978-0-203-88307-5 (ebk)

Contents

Thematic vocabulary lists

Series preface

Frequency information has a central role to play in learning a language. Nation (1990) showed that the 4,000–5,000 most frequent words account for up to 95 per cent of a written text and the 1,000 most frequent words account for 85 per cent of speech. Although Nation's results were only for English, they do provide clear evidence that, when employing frequency as a general guide for vocabulary learning, it is possible to acquire a lexicon which will serve a learner well most of the time. There are two caveats to bear in mind here. First, counting words is not as straightforward as it might seem. Gardner (2007) highlights the problems that multiple word meanings, the presence of multiword items, and grouping words into families or lemmas, have on counting and analysing words. Second, frequency data contained in frequency dictionaries should never act as the only information source to guide a learner. Frequency information is nonetheless a very good starting point, and one which may produce rapid benefits. It therefore seems rational to prioritise learning the words that you are likely to hear and read most often. That is the philosophy behind this series of dictionaries.

Lists of words and their frequencies have long been available for teachers and learners of language. For example, Thorndike (1921, 1932) and Thorndike and Lorge (1944) produced word frequency books with counts of word occurrences in texts used in the education of American children. Michael West's *General Service List of English Words* (1953) was primarily aimed at foreign learners of English. More recently, with the aid of efficient computer software and very large bodies of language data (called corpora), researchers have been able to provide more sophisticated frequency counts from both written text and transcribed speech. One important feature of the resulting frequencies presented in this series is that they are derived from recently collected language data. The earlier lists for English included samples from, for example, Austen's *Pride and Prejudice* and Defoe's *Robinson Crusoe*, thus they could no longer represent present-day language in any sense.

Frequency data derived from a large representative corpus of a language brings students closer to language as it is used in real life as opposed to textbook language (which often distorts the frequencies of features in a language, see Ljung, 1990). The information in these dictionaries is presented in a number of formats to allow users to access the data in different ways. So, for example, if you would prefer not to simply drill down through the word frequency list, but would rather focus on verbs for example, the part of speech index will allow you to focus on just the most frequent verbs. Given that verbs typically account for 20 per cent of all words in a language, this may be a good strategy. Also, a focus on function words may be equally rewarding – 60 per cent of speech in English is composed of a mere 50 function words. The series also provides information of use to the language teacher. The idea that frequency information may have a role to play in syllabus design is not new (see, for example, Sinclair and Renouf, 1988). However, to date it has been difficult for those teaching languages other than English to use frequency information in syllabus design because of a lack of data.

Frequency information should not be studied to the exclusion of other contextual and situational knowledge about language use and we may even doubt the validity of frequency information derived from large corpora. It is interesting to note that Alderson (2007) found that corpus frequencies may not match a native speaker's intuition about estimates of word frequency and that a set of estimates of word frequencies collected from language experts varied widely. Thus corpus-derived frequencies are still the best current estimate of a word's importance that a learner will come across. Around the time of the construction of the first machine-readable corpora, Halliday (1971: 344) stated that "a rough indication of frequencies is often just what is needed". Our aim in this series is to provide as accurate as possible estimates of word frequencies.

Paul Rayson and Mark Davies
Lancaster and Provo, 2008

References

Alderson, J.C. (2008) Judging the frequency of English words. *Applied Linguistics*, 28(3): 383–409.

Gardner, D. (2007) Validating the construct of Word in applied corpus-based vocabulary research: a critical survey. *Applied Linguistics,* 28, pp. 241–265.

Halliday, M.A.K. (1971) Linguistic functions and literary style. In S. Chatman (ed.) Style: A Symposium. Oxford University Press, pp. 330–365.

Ljung, M. (1990) *A Study of TEFL Vocabulary*. Almqvist & Wiksell International, Stokholm.

Nation, I.S.P. (1990) *Teaching and learning vocabulary*. Heinle & Heinle, Boston.

Sinclair, J.M., and Renouf, A. (1988) "A lexical syllabus for language learning", in R. Carter & M. McCarthy (eds) *Vocabulary and Language Teaching*. Longman, London, pp. 140–158.

Thorndike, E. (1921) *Teacher's Word Book*. Columbia Teachers College, New York.

Thorndike, E. (1932) *A Teacher's Word Book of 20,000 Words*. Columbia University Press, New York.

Thorndike, E. and Lorge, I. (1944) *The Teacher's Word Book of 30,000 Words*. Columbia University Press, New York.

West, M. (1953) *A General Service List of English Words*. Longman, London.

Abbreviations

Abbreviation	Word class	Example
adj	adjective	**0028 好** [好] /hǎo/ (1) *adj* good, well 我认为她唱得很好。 She sang well, I thought. 11951 | 0.8 | 9535
adv	adverb	**0006 不** [不] /bù/ (1) *adv* no, not 这条街不准停车。 You can't park in this street. 50589 | 0.8 | 40245
aux	auxiliary	**0005 了** [了] /le/ (1) *aux* [aspect marker indicating realisation of a situation] 她从马上摔了下来。 She fell off her horse. 51296 | 0.9 | 46283
clas	classifier	**0008 个** [個] /gè/ (1) *clas* [generalised measure word used for nouns without a specific measure term] 山那边有一个村庄。 There is a village beyond the hill. 36612 | 0.83 | 30504
conj	conjunction	**0099 因为** [因為] /yīnwéi/ (1) *conj* because 她需要一把伞，因为天在下雨。 She needs an umbrella because it's raining. 4520 | 0.75 | 3378
idiom	idiomatic and formulaic expressions	**2675 可不** [可不] /kěbu/ *idiom* [same as 可不是 or 可不是吗] sure enough, exactly 她是个十足的美人，可不是吗？ She's a regular beauty, isn't she? 181 | 0.62 | 112
interj	interjection	**0820 嗯** [嗯] /ēn, ńg, ňg, ǹg/ (1) *interj* [interjection used for questioning, surprise, disapproval, or agreement] well, eh, hey, m-hm, uh-huh 嗯，他们是天生一对嘛。 Well, they seem to make a good couple. 2525 | 0.18 | 449 | S
loc	direction and locality	**0015 上** [上] /shàng/ (1) *loc* up, on, in 孩子的新毛衣上勾了一个洞。 The child has picked a hole in his new jumper. 22041 | 0.92 | 20201
n	noun	**0014 人** [人] /rén/ (1) *n* person, human, man 我尊重他这位作家，也尊重他这个人。 I respect him as a writer and as a man. 24724 | 0.86 | 21225
num	numeral	**0003 一** [一] /yī/ (1) *num* one, a, an 市政大厅前有一群人。 There is a crowd of people in front of the town hall. 69925 | 0.89 | 62263
ono	onomatopoeia	**3135 呀** [呀] /yā/ *ono* the sound of a creak 门呀的一声开了。 The door opened with a creak. 223 | 0.41 | 90 | S

Abbreviation	Word class	Example
part	particle	**0116** 吗 [嗎] /ma/ (1) *part* [question tag] 你的家人都好吗？ How's your family? 4440 | 0.64 | 2848
place	place word	**0587** 家里 [家里] /jiāli/ *space* home 我顺便拜访他们的时候，他们都在家里。 They were all at home when I stopped by. 841 | 0.7 | 590
pref	prefix	**1093** 前 [前] /qián/ *pref* ex-, former 这是美国前总统尼克松谈话的一部分。 This is an excerpt from a talk by the former President Nixon. 434 | 0.75 | 326
prep	preposition	**0004** 在 [在] /zài/ (1) *prep* [indicating location or time, etc.] at, in 她坐在窗旁。 She sat at the window. 52774 | 0.94 | 49460
pron	pronoun	**0010** 他 [他] /tā/ (1) *pron* he, him 目前，他正在度假。 At present, he is on holiday. 36234 | 0.76 | 27619
suf	suffix	**0111** 们 [們] /men/ (1) *suf* [plural marker for pronouns and some animate nouns] 朋友们舞会后就分开了。 The friends separated after the party. 3199 | 0.92 | 2930
time	time word	**0094** 现在 [現在] /xiànzài/ (1) *time* now 现在正在预报飞机的起飞时间。 Now it is broadcasting the take-off time for the planes. 4942 | 0.71 | 3484
v	verb	**0002** 是 [是] /shì/ (1) *v* be 你是哪里人呢？ Where are you from? 81965 | 0.83 | 67954

Introduction

The need for a frequency dictionary

A good dictionary is indispensable for language learning. This is particularly true when learning a second or foreign language. There are many kinds of dictionaries, designed for different purposes and having different values for different readers. For instance, a dictionary in multiple volumes that incorporates encyclopaedic or etymological knowledge may not be terribly relevant for language learners unless they are at very advanced levels. Different types of dictionaries can benefit different types of learners. Of those dictionaries that are specifically created for language learners, the focus is usually on providing basic information such as definitions, glosses and word classes illustrated by suitable examples. Such dictionaries typically follow the lexicographic convention of arranging words in alphabetic order so that, while providing an effective and convenient way of looking up a specific word, they do not tell learners which words are more commonly used – that is, which words learners are more likely to encounter at different stages of learning. Neither can a conventional dictionary tell learners which words they are more likely to encounter in different registers such as speech, news, imaginative or informative writing.

It is in these regards that a frequency dictionary as an innovative type of dictionary proves valuable. While it is clearly naïve to state simply and boldly that the most frequent words are the most important to learn, frequency ranking is nonetheless "a parameter for sequencing and grading learning materials" because frequency is "a measure of *probability* of usefulness" and "high-frequency words constitute a core vocabulary that is useful above the incidental choice of text of one teacher or textbook author" (Goethals 2003: 424). As Leech (1997: 16) argues: "Whatever the imperfections of the simple equation 'most frequent' = 'most important to learn', it is difficult to deny that frequency information derived from large collections of

text (corpora) has an important empirical input to language learning materials."

With that said, one should not assume that there is an irreconcilable conflict between the frequency and more conventional dictionary. Rather they have different focuses and are complementary to each other. In this dictionary, for example, we have provided just one illustrative example for each word included, even though the word can have different meanings. Readers seeking a broader range of illustrative examples may refer to a different type of dictionary. In addition, for a small number of words included in this dictionary where the word can have different pronunciations for its different senses, we have not indicated which pronunciation corresponds to which word sense. Again, a different dictionary can help with that issue. These decisions were motivated largely by considerations such as the levels of intended readership, the size of the dictionary (see section 5 for further discussion) and, crucially, what was readily available elsewhere. We did not want to unhelpfully replicate what other dictionaries could provide. This dictionary should be used with a conventional learner dictionary – not instead of one.

Like other volumes in the Routledge Frequency Dictionary series, *A Frequency Dictionary of Mandarin Chinese* furnishes a list of core vocabulary for learners of Mandarin Chinese as a second or foreign language, especially learners whose first or second language is English. This dictionary will prove useful for such learners, whether they are instructed in the classroom or are independent learners. It should also prove of benefit to teachers.

How might classroom learners use this dictionary? Classroom learners normally rely on a selected textbook, which is typically organised around a variety of themes (e.g. shopping, eating out). Thematically related words are surely of benefit in vocabulary acquisition, but a textbook rarely if ever tells learners which of these words are more likely to appear in their actual reading or conversation. In fact, it is very likely that some of those words, which they have learnt with painstaking effort, never occur beyond the classroom situations invented specifically for the sake of language learning. In other words, learners will not find a chance to employ those words in real communication contexts, unless they are talking about a specialised topic. As you will see in the callout boxes for themed vocabulary embedded in the main frequency index of common words, some words are infrequent in the language, but can be potentially useful when discussing specific topics. That's why we have decided to include 30 thematically related lists (see section 5). These thematically related lists are one resource that classroom learners should want to draw upon.

What of the independent learner? They tend to have needs somewhat distinct from those of the classroom learner. They may pick up a piece of text, e.g. a work of fiction or a newspaper, and step through it word by word, consulting a dictionary to check on words which are new to them. While such independent learners work on authentic texts, they may often suspect that their learning could be more effective if they knew at the outset that they were learning the most common words in general Mandarin, as these would be the words which they are most likely to encounter in a wide variety of contexts. They would then work towards specialised and infrequent vocabulary. A frequency dictionary should make an ideal companion for such learners.

Finally, how might teachers use a dictionary such as this? Language teachers should find a frequency dictionary a very helpful source of information. On the one hand, the frequency dictionary provides a graded list of vocabulary with authentic examples, which is valuable supplementary material to complement a textbook. On the other hand, the teacher may find it frustrating that some students entering intermediate level are deficient in vocabulary. In such cases, a frequency dictionary will be an advantage as it affords a structured remedy in this regard. Last but not least, the frequency information contained in this dictionary, which is based on a large balanced collection of data (see

section 2), will prove a valuable resource in guiding and informing the development of a language teaching curriculum.

The corpus

Given that the frequencies presented in this dictionary are derived from a large collection of Chinese language, a so-called *corpus*, it is clearly important to present the corpus data used in this dictionary. For a dictionary that aims to provide a frequency-based core vocabulary for learners, a well-composed corpus is essential. We think that such a corpus must satisfy four requirements for the intended purpose. First of all, it must be large enough to yield a basis for reliable quantification; second, it must achieve a reasonably wide coverage of registers so that learners are exposed to commonly used words in different communication contexts. Third, the language contained in the corpus must be current. Finally, in addition to the quality of data *per se*, corpus processing must be sufficiently reliable, and this is particularly important for a Chinese frequency dictionary because running texts in Chinese must first of all be segmented into legitimate tokens (a computational process known as segmentation or tokenisation, see below) before they can be annotated with word class information.

The corpus in this dictionary is composed of written and spoken texts from four broad categories as shown in Table 1, totalling roughly 50 million word tokens (or 73 million Chinese characters). The spoken component contains 3.4 million words, covering face-to-face conversations, telephone calls, cross-talks, movie and play scripts, interviews, storytelling, public lectures, radio broadcasts, and public debates, which were mostly produced in the 1990s and 2000–2006.[1] The news component comprises 16 million words of newswire texts released in 1995 by the Xinhua News Agency and newspaper texts published by the *People's Daily* in 1998 and 2000, in addition to the news categories in the Lancaster Corpus of Mandarin Chinese (LCMC)[2] and the UCLA Written Chinese Corpus.[3] The fiction component amounts to 15 million words, including all fiction categories in LCMC and UCLA Chinese corpora in addition to novels and short stories sampled from various periods in the twentieth

Table 1 Structure of the corpus

Register	Word tokens	Chinese characters
Spoken	3,400,883	4,679,991
News	16,081,928	26,277,906
Fiction	15,150,797	19,962,277
Non-fiction	15,115,904	22,158,904
Total	49,749,512	73,079,078

century, with the majority published in the 1980s – 1990s. The non-fiction component is composed of all informative categories in LCMC and UCLA corpora, together with various non-literary texts of different genres such as official documents, academic prose, applied writing and popular lore, which were sampled from different periods in the second half of the twentieth century, totalling 15 million words.

While the majority of our corpus data introduced above are monolingual Chinese texts, we have also used a parallel corpus composed of Chinese fictional and non-fictional texts with their English versions, which has allowed us to extract, for each of the selected words included in this dictionary, an illustrative example with English translation.[4]

Once the texts (including transcripts of spoken data) were collected, the next step was to segment the running strings of characters in these texts into word tokens. For alphabetical languages like English, word tokens in a written text are normally separated by white spaces so that the one-to-one correspondence between orthographic and morpho-syntactic word tokens can be considered as a default with a few exceptions: multiwords (e.g. *so that* and *in spite of*), mergers (e.g. *can't* and *gonna*) and variably spelt compounds (e.g. *noticeboard, notice-board, notice board*). In Chinese, however, since a written text contains running strings of characters with no delimiting spaces, one has to determine where the words are in the data. More specifically, as it is the computer that is analysing the data, a process must be run which allows the computer to determine where the words are. This process is called word segmentation. Word segmentation

requires complex computer processing, which generally involves lexicon matching and the use of a statistical model (cf. McEnery, Xiao and Tono 2006: 35).

The segmentation tool we engaged to process our Chinese corpus is ICTCLAS, an acronym for the Chinese Lexical Analysis System developed by the Institute of Computing Technology, Chinese Academy of Sciences. The core of the system lexicon incorporates a lexicon of 80,000 words with part of speech information. The system is based on a multi-layer hidden Markov model and integrates modules for word segmentation, part of speech analysis, so called part of speech tagging, and unknown word recognition (cf. Zhang, Liu, Zhang and Cheng 2002). The rough segmentation module of the system is based on the n-shortest paths method (Zhang and Liu 2002). The model, based on 2-shortest-paths, achieves a precision rate of 97.58 per cent, with a recall rate as high as 99.94 per cent (ibid.). In addition the average number of segmentation candidates is reduced by 64 times compared to the full segmentation method. The unknown word recognition module of the system is based on role tagging. The module applies the Viterbi algorithm to determine the sequence of roles (e.g. internal constituents and context) with the greatest probability in a sentence, on the basis of which template matching is carried out. The integrated ICTCLAS system is reported to achieve a precision rate of 97.16 per cent for tagging, with a recall rate of over 90 per cent for unknown words and 98 per cent for Chinese person names (ibid.).

ICTCLAS applies a very fine-grained part of speech annotation scheme, or tagset, (see Appendix) to corpus data. A *tagset* is the list of part of speech distinctions made by the programme, while *tagging* is the process whereby the machine decides which part of speech applies to each word and a *tag* is the individual mnemonic assigned to each word in the corpus by the computer when the tagging has determined which tag each word should have.

For the purpose of a frequency dictionary, we think that a less fine-grained tagset than that provided by ICTCLAS is more helpful as this can have a boosting effect on words of the same form but with minor difference in usage. Hence we decided to merge subcategories and similar part of speech categories. Our decision to combine those subcategories was also motivated by the fact that Chinese does not have a very strong link between word classes and grammatical functions. For example, adjectives can be used directly as adverbial (tagged as *ad* by ICTCLAS) while a verb can behave syntactically like a noun (tagged as *vn*) or adverb (tagged as *vd*). In addition, non-predicate adjectives

(tagged as *b*) and descriptive adjectives (tagged as *z*) are also merged into the broad category of adjectives. As it is not always possible to differentiate between idioms (tagged as *i*) and fixed expressions (tagged as *l*), the two categories are combined into the category for idiomatic and formulaic expressions. These manipulations resulted in a tagset for use in this dictionary, which consists of 20 part of speech tags as shown in Table 2.

When the texts were tokenised and annotated with part of speech information, the corpus was converted from the local character encoding GB2312 into Unicode (UTF-8), with register information and linguistic annotation marked up in the extensible mark-up language (XML) so that the corpus could be used with our PERL (Practical Extraction and Retrieval Language) scripts to build frequency indexes for use in this dictionary. This will be discussed in section 4. But before that, let us have a look at the previous frequency dictionaries and lists of words and characters in Chinese.

Table 2 Part of speech tags annotated in our corpus

Code	Word class	Abbreviation	ICTCLAS tags
a	adjective	adj	a, ad, ag, an b, z
c	conjunction	conj	c
d	adverb	adv	d, dg
e	interjection	interj	e
f	direction and locality	loc	f
g	non-word morpheme	morph	g
h	prefix	pref	h
k	suffix	suf	k
l	idiomatic and formulaic expressions	idiom	i, l
m	numeral	num	m
n	noun	n	n, ng, nr, ns, nt, nx, nz
o	onomatopoeia	ono	o
p	preposition	prep	p
q	classifier	clas	q
r	pronoun	pron	r
s	place word	place	s
t	time word	time	t
u	auxiliary	aux	u
v	verb	v	v, vd, vg, vn
y	particle	part	y

Previous frequency dictionaries of Chinese

Ours is not the first frequency dictionary of Chinese. It is, however, quite distinctive, as can be demonstrated by considering the other frequency dictionaries of Chinese that have been created.

Because of the large inventory of characters in Chinese, there has been a long tradition of teaching Chinese characters on basis of frequency, though the research of word frequency on the basis of large collections of text only became possible in the 1990s, with the advent of more powerful computers and specialised computer software for word segmentation. There are at least a dozen frequency lists or dictionaries of Chinese characters and words including, for example:

- Chen's (1928) *Yutiwen Yingyong Zi Hui* (The Applied Glossary of Modern Chinese): listing 4,261 distinct Chinese characters on the basis of six corpora (children's books, newspapers, women's magazines, after-class work of schoolchildren, classic and modern fiction, and miscellaneous) totalling 554,478 Chinese character tokens;
- Liu's (1973) *Frequency Dictionary of Chinese Words*: giving statistics such as frequency, dispersion index and usage rate for 3,059 most frequently used words in Chinese on the basis of a 0.25-million-word corpus covering five registers (fiction, drama, essays, newspapers and periodicals, technical writing);
- *Xiandai Hanzi Zonghe Shiyong Pindu Biao* (A Comprehensive Frequency Table of Character Usage in Modern Chinese), established on Project Code 748 (1976): listing 4,152 frequently used characters on the basis of a corpus of 21 million characters;
- Beijing Aeronautical University (1985) *Xiandai Hanyu Yong Zi Pindu Biao* (A Frequency Table of Character Usage in Modern Chinese): listing frequently used characters for ten genres and technical domains on the basis of samples totalling 11.08 million characters;
- Beijing Language and Culture University (1986) *Xiandai Hanyu Pinlü Cidian* (A Frequency Dictionary of Modern Chinese): listing 16,593 commonly used words extracted from 1,315,752 word tokens (or 1.82 million characters);

- National Language Committee (1988) *Xiandai Hanyu Changyong Zi Biao* (Commonly Used Characters in Modern Chinese): listing the most commonly used 2,500 characters and 1,000 commonly used characters on the basis of data collected by Beijing Aeronautic University covering the period 1928–1986;
- Hong Kong Polytechnic University (1991–1997) *Zhongguo Dalu, Taiwan, Xianggang Hanyu Ciku* (A Chinese Word Bank from Mainland China, Taiwan, and Hong Kong): listing 68,011 entries based on a 6-million-character corpus of news texts published during 1990–1992 in the three Chinese speech communities.

With the exception of Liu (1973), all other character and word frequency lists and dictionaries are published in Chinese. All of them are targeted either at native speakers of Mandarin learning their mother tongue (e.g. Chen 1928; National Language Committee 1988), or at language engineers (e.g. the frequency list by Project Code 738) and expert Chinese linguists (e.g. the word bank by Hong Kong Polytechnic University for studying language variation).[5] And with the exception of Liu (1973), all of the existing frequency dictionaries of Chinese characters and words were published and distributed in China, which makes it difficult for learners of Chinese as a second or foreign language outside China to get access to them.

Liu (1973) was published by Mouton and released worldwide, but it also suffers from a number of drawbacks. Like nearly all existing Chinese frequency dictionaries, it is based exclusively on written Mandarin; the data on which the dictionary is based are quite outdated, with texts published during the period 1910–1960; with a total of 0.25 million word tokens, the corpus is also rather small by today's standards; the word class categories featuring in the book are quite obsolete nowadays; no actual Chinese characters are used in the dictionary, these being replaced by a kind of Romanisation system which is no longer widely used; and most importantly, no English gloss or translation, no illustrative example, and no information related to usage are given, making the dictionary almost useless for today's learners of Chinese as a second or foreign language.

Table 3 HSK graded lists and words and characters in Chinese

HSK level	Words	Characters
Level 1	1033	800
Level 2	2019	803
Level 3	2205	591
Level 4	3583	671
Levels 1–3	5257	2194
Levels 1–4	8840	2865

Last but not least, we should not fail to mention the *Syllabus of Graded Words and Characters for Chinese Proficiency* compiled by the Chinese government's *Hanyu Shuiping Kaoshi* (the Chinese Proficiency Test, HSK) Committee, which was published in 1992 and revised in 2001. The HSK lexical syllabus lists the words and characters required of learners of Mandarin Chinese as a second or foreign language to pass the Chinese proficiency test HSK, as indicated in Table 3. While the lexical syllabus is undoubtedly instructive for learners of Mandarin – we have made special effort to include as many words as possible from the syllabus, especially Level 1 and 2 items (see section 4 for further discussion) – it serves a different purpose from a frequency list. The words in the syllabus are arranged conventionally in alphabetical order for each level rather than in the order of frequency, and no actual frequency or frequency ranking is given.

The compilation of the lexical syllabus, which was corpus-based, started in 1988 and the latest texts covered were produced in 1991. Unsurprisingly, most "new words" included in the syllabus are from the early 1980s while some words that were common in the 1970s–1980s, e.g. 少先队 "young pioneer" will not be common enough to merit a place on the list nowadays. On the other hand, many well-established vocabulary items which are commonly used today as a result of technological and social development are not covered in the syllabus, for example: 网络 "network", 手机 "mobile phone", 媒体 "media", 客户 "client", 机制 "mechanism", 市场经济 "market economy", 出国 "go abroad", 品牌 "brand", 消费者 "consumer", 上网 "go online", 总裁 "CEO", 董事长 "chair of the Board of Directors", 打工 "do odd jobs", 上市 "put on market", 开发区 "development zone", 股市 "stock market", 超市 "supermarket", 出租车 "taxi", 荧幕 "screen", 证券 "stock, share", 下岗 "get laid off", and 网站 "website".

A comparison of the HSK graded vocabulary and the frequency index in our dictionary appears to suggest that the corpus on which the HSK vocabulary is based relies too heavily on the Beijing dialect, as evidenced by dialectal usage like 半拉 "half" (Level 2) and words ending with the retroflective suffix 儿, including Level 1 words such as 小孩儿 "child", 面条儿 "noodle, pasta", Level 2 words such as 聊天儿 "chat" and 墨水儿 "ink", and Level 3 words such as 拐弯儿 "turn a corner, make a turn" and 药水儿 "liquid medicine". Words like these are normally listed in a dictionary without the retroflective 儿, which is tagged in our corpus as a suffix.

Selection of words and characters

According to the HSK lexical syllabus, learners of Chinese as a foreign language who have learnt about 5,000 words will be able to express their ideas on general issues in Chinese. As can be seen in Table 3, this vocabulary is approximate to the total of HSK Levels 1–3 words. The number of words we have decided to include in this dictionary is roughly comparable. While it is certainly true that the larger your vocabulary the better it is, it is nonetheless increasingly more difficult to learn new words as your vocabulary grows. This is because, according to Zipf's law, the frequency of a word is reversely proportional to its rank in the frequency table. As such, there is a 9.27 per cent increase in coverage from top 1,000 to top 2,000 words, whereas the

Table 4 Coverage of top N words

Top N words	Coverage (%)	Increase (%)
1,000	66.24	–
2,000	75.51	9.27
3,000	80.53	5.02
4,000	83.81	3.28
5,000	86.17	3.07
6,000	87.94	1.77
7,000	89.33	1.39
8,000	90.47	1.14
9,000	91.42	0.94

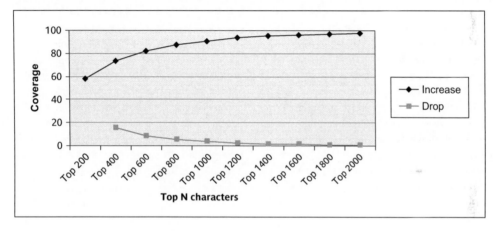

Figure 1 Coverage of top N characters

increase in coverage drops to 0.94 per cent from top 8,000 to top 9,000 words (see Table 4). In addition to the reference to the HSK syllabus, our decision to include 5,000 words was also empirically based by the sharp drop in coverage (from 3.07 per cent to 1.77 per cent) from top 5,000 to top 6,000 words.

As can be seen in Figure 1, which shows the increase and drop in coverage resulting from each additional block of 200 characters, Zipf's law also applies to characters. Coverage grows very slowly after the top 1,200 characters. The top 2,000 characters cover nearly 98 per cent of our whole corpus, with 4,839 characters accounting for the remaining 2 per cent of coverage.

We would like to point out that the above distribution statistics are based on a valid lexicon that we created from the corpus. By "valid lexicon",

we mean the frequency lists of words and characters that exclude items that are "uninteresting" from the perspective of vocabulary acquisition, e.g. symbols and punctuations, Arabic numerals (written in either full- or half-length), and non-Chinese character strings. We have also excluded abbreviations, numeral characters indicating years, person names, place names, organisation names, as well as other proper nouns such as names of countries, nationalities and languages, as well as brand names. Table 5 indicates the size of our valid lexicon.

While a frequency dictionary could be arranged simply in the order of raw frequencies, i.e. actual occurrences of words and characters, we have enlisted a more scientific way to decide which words and characters to include, which takes account of

Table 5 The valid lexicon

Register	Word tokens	Chinese characters
Spoken	2,692,315	3,824,579
News	12,147,572	20,185,322
Fiction	11,973,365	16,424,649
Non-fiction	11,900,160	17,954,729
Total	38,713,412	58,389,279

their frequencies as well as their distribution in different registers. Words and characters which are frequently used in more registers are clearly more useful than those that are frequent in fewer registers. In this dictionary, we have adopted the same hierarchy composed of three coefficients as established in Juilland and Chang-Rodriguez (1964), namely frequency, dispersion index and usage rate, which are explained as follows.

There are two types of frequency data. Raw frequency refers to the actual occurrence of a word or character in a corpus while normalised frequency means the frequency that has been adjusted to a common base, for example, in this case, the occurrences per million tokens so that the four registers covered in our corpus can be compared even if they are of different sizes. We have used normalised frequencies in different registers to compute dispersion index and usage rate, while the overall normalised frequency is also given in the entry for a headword so that the reader can easily compare the frequencies of different words on a common basis of per million words. Dispersion coefficient (D) is computed according to Juilland and Chang-Rodriguez's formula:

$$D = 1 - (n\Sigma\ x_i^2 - T^2)^{1/2}/2T$$

In this formula, n stands for the number of word types and T for the number of word tokens. This formula reduces dispersion to a coefficient ranging from 0–1, regardless of frequency. Words with a higher dispersion coefficient are more evenly distributed in different registers. The usage rate (U) takes account of both frequency and dispersion, which can be taken as a dispersion (D) percentage of frequency (F) or vice versa according to the following formula:

$$U = F \times D\ /100$$

This means that when D = 1 the usage rate equals frequency, and when D = 0.5 the usage rate is half of frequency. Hence, a more frequent word with a lower dispersion index can have a lower usage rate. For example, as the word 说 "say" is distributed fairly evenly in the four registers (9,383 instances per million words in spoken, 9,998 in fiction, 4,658 in non-fiction, 3,753 in news), it has a large dispersion index (0.80). If the word has an overall frequency of 27,792, then its usage rate will be 22,252. In contrast, the interjection 哎 has an overall frequency of 1,821 instances in our corpus, but it is distributed unevenly in the four registers (1,697 in spoken, 119 in fiction, 5 in non-fiction and 0 in news). Its dispersion index is much smaller (0.21), and its usage rate is 383 in spite of its high overall frequency.

We wrote PERL scripts that automatically computed the overall normalised frequency, normalised frequency in each of the four registers (i.e. spoken, news, fiction and non-fiction), the dispersion index, and usage rate for each word and character in our valid lexicon. We have used a combination of these statistics, while also taking account of basic vocabulary in the HSK syllabus as well as our intuitive knowledge of the Chinese language, to decide which words and characters to include in this dictionary.

- All words with a dispersion index below 0.25 are excluded unless they have a usage rate above 100 or a normalised frequency above 1,000 in any of the four registers.
- All items with a usage rate below 45 are excluded unless they are on the Levels 1 and 2 lists in the HSK syllabus.[6]

- All words with an overall normalised frequency below 55 are excluded unless they are on the Levels 1 and 2 lists in the HSK syllabus.
- All words with a normalised frequency below three per million words in the register of fiction are excluded unless they have a usage rate above 100 or are on the Levels 1 and 2 lists in the HSK syllabus.

These operations helped to establish a core list of top 5,004 words from a total of 30,922 words from our valid lexicon. Out list covers 95.61 per cent of Level 1 words, 80.43 per cent of Level 2 words, 44.22 per cent of Level 3 words, and 18.12 per cent of Level 4 words in the HSK syllabus. In addition to many advancement-related new words like those mentioned earlier, our word list includes many commonly used compound words which are missing in the HSK syllabus, for example: 看到 "see", 很多 "many", 提出 "put forward", 有人 "someone", 受到 "come in for", 家里 "home", 说话 "speak", 造成 "cause", 父母 "parents", 来到 "come to", 带来 "bring", 想到 "think of", 找到 "find", 实际上 "in fact", 回到 "return to", 留下 "leave behind, remain", 加上 "add, include", 关注 "follow an issue with interest", 回家 "go home", 哪儿 "where", 吃饭 "eat a meal, eat", 见到 "see", 不再 "no longer", 很快 "fast; soon", and 听到 "hear" among many others. Such new additions are obviously more helpful to learners than some dialectal or outdated items in the HSK syllabus such as 半拉 "half" and 反动 "reactionary" and 少先队 "young pioneer".

We have followed a similar procedure to establish a core list of commonly used Chinese characters. The following cutoff points are used:

- an overall normalised frequency of 70 instances per million tokens;
- a usage of 50 instances per million tokens;
- a dispersion index of 0.35;
- a minimal frequency of ten in each of the four registers.

These operations produced a list of 2,015 most commonly used characters. In order to include as many basic characters required in the HSK syllabus, the final criterion above was not strictly applied to Level 1 and 2 characters in the syllabus. As a result,

14 additional Level 1 characters and 83 additional Level 2 characters are included in our character list, thus pushing the total number of characters included in this dictionary to 2,112, which covers 99.3 per cent of Level 1 characters, and 96.64 per cent of Level 2 character in the HSK syllabus. Our character index also covers 81.56 per cent of the 2,500 common characters published in China by the Ministry of Education for native speakers of Mandarin.

Organisation of the dictionary

Following this introductory chapter are a number of indexes of the 5,004 most commonly used words, which are arranged in frequency rank order, in alphabetical order, in frequency rank order as per word classes, as well as a list of the 2,112 most commonly used Chinese characters mapping each character onto the top 5,004 words. The frequency index of the book also features a series of embedded callout boxes that show thematically related vocabulary. The remainder of this chapter will give more details of each of these indexes.

Frequency index

This section lists the 5,004 most commonly used words in the descending order of frequency rank. The following information is given for each of the listed headwords:

- frequency rank (in descending order of usage rate);
- headword in Simplified Chinese;
- headword in Traditional Chinese;
- Pinyin gloss of the headword;
- HSK Level (if the word is listed in the HSK syllabus);
- an illustrative example in Simplified Chinese (authentic example cited from our Chinese–English parallel corpus);
- English translation of the example (from our Chinese–English parallel corpus);
- normalised frequency per million words;
- dispersion index;
- usage rate;
- register code (i.e. S or W indicating whether the word is exceptionally common in speech or writing).

A typical entry looks like the following:

Frequency rank Headword in Simplified Chinese [Headword in Traditional Chinese] /*Pinyin*/ (Optional HSK Level) Part of speech English gloss
Illustrative example in Simplified Chinese and English translation of the example
Normalised frequency | Dispersion index | Usage rate | Optional register code

---

Here we show a concrete example of an entry:

0263 **然后** [然後] /*ránhòu*/ (1) adv afterwards, then
你走到第二个十字路口，然后向左拐。 You go ahead to the second crossing and then turn left.
1887 | 0.66 | 1241 | S

In this example, the headword with the frequency rank of 0263 (i.e. the 263rd most commonly used word in our corpus) is 然后, which is written as 然後 in Traditional Chinese. The Pinyin gloss of the word is *ránhòu*. It is listed as a Level 1 word in the HSK graded vocabulary. This is an adverb, meaning "afterwards, then", as exemplified in 你走到第二个十字路口，然后向左拐。"You go ahead to the second crossing and then turn left." This headword has an overall normalised frequency of 1,887 instances per million tokens and a dispersion index of 0.66 in our corpus, and thus a usage rate of 1,241 instances per million tokens. It is exceptionally common in spoken Mandarin.

At this point, we would like to remind the reader that when a headword has more than one sense, these senses are separated by a comma or a semi-colon, with the former for similar senses and the latter for different sense groups. However, when an orthographic word has different senses for different word classes, they are listed separately. For example, the orthographic word 会 can function as a verb (0035) meaning "can, know how to do; meet; be likely to, be sure to", or as a noun (0864) meaning "meeting, conference; moment". The two homonymous words are kept separate. Nevertheless, as our corpus is only tagged with part of speech information but not annotated with word senses, it is impossible to find out the frequencies of different word senses of a homonymous or polysemous word if these senses belong to the same part of speech.

Consequently similar and different word senses of the same word class are simply grouped together with the appropriate punctuation mark indicated above. It is also important to note that different senses of a word may have different Pinyin glosses and thus be pronounced differently. In such cases we simply insert commas to separate different Pinyin glosses without mapping Pinyin glosses to word senses,[7] and would like to advise the reader to consult a traditional dictionary to ascertain how a word is pronounced for a particular word sense.

Of the information given for each headword, HSK Level and register code are optional. A label for the HSK Level (i.e. 1–3) is only shown if the word is listed in the HSK graded vocabulary, while a register code (S or W) is available only if the word is exceptionally common in speech or writing. Please note that some words may have more than one meaning that belong to different HSK Levels, which are separated by a comma. For register code, two criteria were employed to determine whether a word is exceptionally common in speech or writing. If a chi-square test indicates that the difference in frequencies of the word in speech (i.e. the spoken register) and writing (e.g. fiction, non-fiction and news) is significant at the probability level $p < 0.0000001$ while at the same time the S/W ratio (or the W/S ratio) is greater than 3, the word carries the register code S (or W). Of the 5,004 most common words covered in this dictionary, 103 words are exceptionally common in speech while 203 are exceptionally common in writing.

This frequency index constitutes the meaty part of the book, which gives you all the essential information about each of the listed words. In addition, 30 callout boxes are embedded in this main frequency index, which feature thematically related vocabulary. They are organised along themes closely related to people's life, e.g. fruits, drinks and beverages, food (flavours, main food, meat, vegetables, food preparation, seasoning), clothing, weather and equipment, city facilities and stores, travel, directions and locations, cities, house and room, home electronics, computers and the Internet, school life and subjects, professions, sports, animals, and human body (physical appearance, body parts, parts on the head, senses). In addition, we have included a number of lists that help readers understand the Chinese language and culture, including the number system, time expressions, colours, Chinese festivals, Chinese zodiac signs, kinship and family relations, English loanwords in Mandarin, special vocabulary in language learning (terms for sentence analysis and punctuation marks), and commonly used words in various registers covered in our corpus (spoken, fiction, non-fiction and news). For most of the lists, frequency ranks are included, with frequent items on top of the lists unless stated otherwise in our comments. For example, the four lists of common words across registers are arranged by statistical salience. There are also a number of lists where no frequency ranks are given, which happens when a list shows an almost closed set of vocabulary items, or when few of the items on a list are covered in our valid lexicon (see section 4). When a themed list includes both items with a frequency rank and those without one, the list is arranged with most frequent words on the top, and then in the alphabetical order of words without a frequency rank. These thematic vocabulary lists are an important complement to frequency indexes in this dictionary because, as you will see, some words are important when you talk about a particular topic, yet they would only be included in a frequency list that covers top 20,000 common words. In other words, those words are infrequent in the language as a whole.

Alphabetical index

This section lists the 5,004 most common words in alphabetical order of the Pinyin glosses of headwords. A typical entry for the alphabetical index looks like:

> **Headword in Simplified Chinese** */Pinyin/*
> *Part of speech code* English gloss Frequency rank

Here is a concrete example:

> 已经 */yǐjīng/ adv* already 0101

In addition to providing the reader with a quick view of an entry, this alphabetical index also helps the reader to locate the entry in the main frequency index quickly and easily.

Part of speech index

This section gives a frequency index which shows, for each part of speech category, commonly used members in that group, covering all of the top 5,004 words in the main frequency and alphabetical indexes. For each entry in this part of speech index, the following information is included: frequency rank, headword in Simplified Chinese, Pinyin gloss, part of speech code, and English gloss.

This index helps readers to build up vocabulary while studying Chinese grammar. It also allows them to refer back quickly to the related items in the main frequency index.

Character frequency index

This frequency index lists the 2,112 most commonly used Chinese characters. We decided not to include part of speech information or English gloss, nor to give illustrative examples in this chapter. There are a number of reasons for this decision. First, as many characters in Chinese are meaningless unless they combine to form a word, it is not always possible to give an English gloss; second, as many of the common monosyllabic words have already been included in the three earlier indexes, it would be redundant to repeat their details here; third, as a focus on characters is different from the notion of words and parts of speech, English glosses and examples for headwords would be less instructive; finally, since the meaning of a Chinese word is not necessarily the aggregation of its constituent characters, learners are encouraged to build vocabulary "words" instead of characters. For each of the 2,112 commonly used characters included in this index, the following information is given:

> **Frequency rank Simplified Chinese**
> **[Traditional Chinese]** */Pinyin/* **(Optional HSK**
> **Level) List of headwords in word frequency**
> **index containing the character and word**
> **frequency ranks**

An example entry is as follows:

> 0017 们 [們] */men/* (1) 我们 0026 他们 0041
> 们 0111 你们 0179 人们 0237 它们 0535 咱们 0540
> 她们 0567

Each Chinese character in this index is linked to the words in the main frequency index. The frequency ranks of the linked words are given to enable readers to make cross-references easily. If no headword is included in the word frequency index (i.e. the headword is not in the top 5,004 list) for a certain character included in this index, only the character in Simplified Chinese, its Traditional Chinese version, and its Pinyin gloss (and the HSK Level if available) are given. The index of the top 2,112 characters is of help to readers when they decide which characters to learn first; it can also enable learners to switch smoothly between Pinyin and characters, and between Simplified Chinese and Traditional Chinese. In addition, the commonly used words containing the same characters which are mapped from the main frequency index are particularly useful in vocabulary building.

One must remember, however, that a dictionary is not simply a repository of information of use to learners of a language – it is also an embodiment of the language to some degree. As the language encodes in part a worldview and history, the dictionary also stands as a cultural artefact. The background of the language represented here thus deserves some consideration.

A brief introduction to Mandarin Chinese

Chinese belongs to the Sino-Tibetan languages. It is spoken by a total of 1.3 billion speakers. Of these, the majority are native speakers of Mandarin (i.e. Standard Chinese based on the Beijing dialect) as opposed to another variety of Chinese such as Cantonese. Mandarin Chinese has a total of 1,052 million speakers, more than twice as many as speak English, the language with the second highest total of speakers, at 508 million (see Ostler 2005). Mandarin Chinese is the official language of Mainland China and Taiwan; it is also one of the official languages of Singapore and the United Nations.

There are currently more than 30 million people in the world who are learning Mandarin Chinese as a foreign language.[8] The popularity of Chinese as a second language is growing. For example in the United States, the number of Chinese learners is growing fastest in comparison to learners of other foreign languages. In Britain, Mandarin is studied by more children than German and Russian (only French and Spanish are presently more popular); and Mandarin is expected to overtake Spanish in three years if the rate of growth continues.[9]

Probably the most striking difference between Chinese and most other languages is purely visual – its written form. English, and many other languages, employ an alphabetical system. Chinese uses a logographic system, i.e. roughly speaking, the symbols of English encode sounds, whereas those in Chinese either singly or in combination encode words, with each character being a syllable. As a result the Chinese writing system is relatively complex – English has only 26 alphabetical characters (i.e. letters) that can be arranged in different combinations to form tens of thousands of different words, Chinese has tens of thousands of individual characters that represent words. What makes it even more difficult for learners to build up their Chinese vocabulary is that, while some Chinese characters represent single words, it is more common for characters to function in combination to form words, many of which have a different meaning than the simple aggregation of the meanings of constituent characters (see below for further discussion). To make things yet more complex, since Chinese does not use white spaces to delimit words in writing, learners have to decide for themselves which characters in the running text form a word when they read, though word boundaries can be inferred in spoken Chinese on the basis of spoken features such as pauses and repetitions. Given the huge number of Chinese characters, and of words, it is not only quite impossible, but totally unnecessary as well, for learners (or average native Chinese speakers) to know tens of thousands of Chinese characters and words (see section 4). This explains why a frequency dictionary of Chinese, which provides core lists of characters and words in this language, can be of particular advantage as a guide to vocabulary teaching and learning.

As noted earlier, some Chinese characters can serve as words; they can also combine with other characters to form new words. In terms of word types, the overwhelming majority of Chinese words are disyllabic, as illustrated in Figure 2, which shows

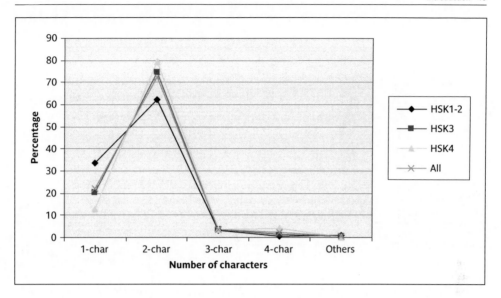

Figure 2 Words of varying lengths in the HSK syllabus

the proportions of words at different levels as required in the HSK syllabus. As can be seen, disyllabic words account for 72 per cent on average while the proportion of monosyllabic words is roughly 22 per cent. Words composed of three characters or more are relatively infrequent. It is also interesting to note that, as the HSK Level increases, disyllabic words increase in number while the proportion of monosyllabic words drops. This is probably because many high-frequency function words, which are more likely to be monosyllabic words, are typically required at HSK Level 1. For the same reason, monosyllabic words are expected to make up a large proportion of Chinese texts in terms of word tokens.

This expectation is in fact borne out in our corpus data. The "valid lexicon" (see section 4) which furnishes a quantitative basis for this dictionary comprises 38,713,412 word tokens (running words in the text) in 84,883 word types (different words). Of these, there are 6,413 monosyllabic words (7.56 per cent of the total), yet they account for 54.08 per cent of total tokens. In contrast, while 46,670 disyllabic words take up the largest proportion in terms of word types (54.98 per cent), they account for 42.33 per cent of total word tokens. Although three-character (22.35 per cent)

and four-character words (13.24 per cent) are also very frequent, they do not contribute much in terms of word tokens, as shown in Figure 3.

A character corresponds to a syllable in spoken Chinese (cf. Li and Thompson 1980: 13). While classical Chinese can be classified as a monosyllabic language, this is no longer true of modern Chinese. As we have noted, monosyllabic words only account for 22 per cent of the graded vocabulary in the HSK syllabus, while the proportion of monosyllabic words in Mandarin as a whole is much lower (see Figure 3). Some characters can be used directly as words, e.g. 有 "have", 来 "come", and 新 "new"; some characters can serve directly as words or as parts of a word, the meaning of which may or may not be related to the meanings of individual constituent characters (e.g. 我 "I, me", 们 "plural suffix" and 我们 "we, us" versus 东 "east", 西 "west" and 东西 "stuff"); some characters cannot stand alone as words (e.g. 蝴蝶 "butterfly" and 葡萄 "grape").

Words in Chinese can be simplex or compound. A simplex word has one morpheme, which can be monosyllabic (e.g. 天 "sky", 去 "go", 他 "he, him") or polysyllabic (仿佛 "as if", 往往 "often, frequently", 咖啡 "coffee"). In contrast, a word made of more than one morpheme is called a compound word.

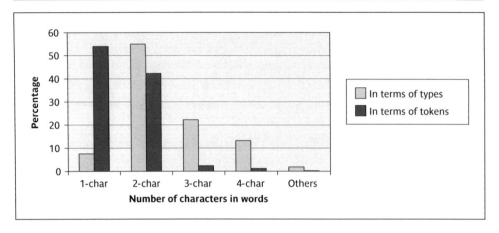

Figure 3 Words of varying lengths in our corpus

There are different types of compound words in Chinese according to their internal structures, namely, coordinate (e.g. 寒冷 "cold"), endocentric (e.g. 冰箱 "ice-box, refrigerator"), verb-complement (e.g. 提高 "raise, improve"), verb-object (洗澡 "take a bath or shower"), subject-predicate (e.g. 地震 "earthquake"), affixed (e.g. 刀子 "knife"), and reduplication (姐姐 "elder sister").

While the discussion above appears to suggest that "wordhood" is easy to define in Chinese, it is nevertheless not always easy or even possible to make a distinction between morphemes and words on the one hand and between words and phrases on the other hand (cf. Wu 2003: 3). In fact, a whole range of criteria have been proposed to define wordhood of various types, e.g. orthographical word, morphological word, lexical word, syntactic word, grammatical word, semantic word, sociological word, psychological word, phonological word, prosodic word (see Di Sciullo and Williams 1987; Dai 1998; Duanmu 1998; Packard 2000; Feng 2001a). On the basis of a review of such criteria, Dixon and Aikhenvald (2002) propose to maintain a distinction between phonological and grammatical words, which may or may not coincide. While the authors concede that the criteria that they engage to define a phonological word do not apply in every language, they offer three "universal criteria" that define a grammatical word: "A grammatical word consists of a number of grammatical elements which (a) always occur together, rather than scattered through the clause (the criterion of cohesiveness); (b) occur in a

fixed order; (c) have a conventionalised coherence and meaning" (ibid.: 19).

Unfortunately, the so-called "split words" in Chinese satisfy none of these criteria. The morphemes that make up a split word can not only scatter through the clause instead of occurring together (e.g. 睡觉 "sleep": 睡了一天觉 "slept for a whole day"), they can even occur in a reversed rather than fixed order (e.g. 上学 "go to school": 学，我爱上就上，不爱上就不上，谁管得着。 "School, I'll go if I like and won't if I don't. Who has the right to interfere?"). Dixon and Aikhenvald (ibid.: 20) comment that criterion (c) means that as a word has its own coherence and meaning, speakers of the language "may talk about a word (but are unlikely to talk about a morpheme)." This criterion does not apply in Chinese either, not only because morphemes in Chinese can be coherent and meaningful (a monosyllabic word consists of one morpheme) but also because even bound morphemes in split words such as 请客 "invite/ treat guest(s)" can be "talked about", e.g. 请了 三桌客 "invited/treated three tablefuls of guests". According to Dixon and Aikhenvald (ibid.: 6), "the (grammatical) word forms the interface between morphology and syntax. Morphology deals with the composition of words while syntax deals with the combination of words". In Chinese, however, word-internal structures are similar to syntactic structures (Dai 1998; Wu 2003: 3), as can be seen in the types of Chinese compound words discussed above.

As far as split words are concerned the difficulty lies in the fuzzy distinction between words and phrases. Many competing criteria have been proposed to differentiate (compound) words from phrases, e.g. conjunction reduction, freedom of parts, semantic composition, syllable count, insertion, exocentric structure, adverbial modification, XP substitution, productivity, and intuition (see Duanmu 1998 for a review). However, while each of these tests "may work in certain areas for certain cases, there is no overall generalisation and constraint on what is a compound and what must be a phrase" (Feng 2001b). By grammatical criteria such as splitability and insertion, disyllabic split words such as 吃饭 "eat", 睡觉 "sleep", 走路 "walk", 跑步 "jog", 关心 "care for", and 担心 "worry about" are phrases, but they are generally accepted as words by native speakers whereas those that can be judged as words by grammatical criteria (e.g. 多弹头分导重返大气层运载工具 "multiple independently targeted reentry vehicle, MIRV") may not be accepted as words. This is not only because "the morphological system of Chinese is strongly sensitive to prosodic foot" (Feng 1997: 135), but also because the "word sense" of a native speaker of Chinese is based on prosody (cf. Feng 2001a). Duanmu (1998) also observes that "there is a rich body of phonological evidence, especially metrical and tonal evidence, for the distinction between words and phrases in both Mandarin and other Chinese dialects". This view of wordhood is line with Matthews's (1991: 209) statement that "the word tends to be a unit of phonology as well as grammar".

Because of the multidimensional properties of wordhood in Chinese (cf. Feng 2001a), we decided to take a less rigid approach to what counts as a word. As noted in section 2, some of the "words" included in this dictionary can be more appropriately called formulaic expressions, e.g. 不得不 "have to", 也就是说 "that is to say", 与此同时 "meanwhile", 忍不住 "cannot help but", and 有意思 "interesting". We think that such commonly occurring formulaic expressions acting as larger "building blocks" of language are equally useful for learners, if not more so.

There are currently two sets of characters for the Chinese writing system: Simplified Chinese and Traditional Chinese. The former is officially used in

Mainland China, Singapore and Malaysia while the latter is officially used in Taiwan, Hong Kong and Macau. Overseas Chinese-speaking communities generally opt for Traditional Chinese characters, but Simplified Chinese characters are gradually becoming popular. In this dictionary, we have given both Simplified and Traditional Chinese versions for each entry of word and character, but illustrative examples are shown only in Simplified Chinese as they appear in our corpus.

In addition to Chinese characters for the writing system, a commonly used alphabetical system known as *Pinyin* has been employed to Romanise the Chinese script. Pinyin uses the Latin alphabet to represent sounds in Mandarin. It is not only beneficial in helping native children and foreign learners to learn spoken Chinese before they start to learn Chinese characters, but it is also a popular method of inputting Chinese characters into a computer. There are four tones in the Pinyin system, with each syllable of every word characterised by one of them, except for a few syllables which are considered toneless. The tones, which are marked on one of the vowels (a, e, i, o, u) in a syllable, are first or "high" (ā, ē, ī, ō, ū), second or "rising" (á, é, í, ó, ú), third or "falling-rising" (ǎ, ě, ǐ, ǒ, ǔ), and fourth or "falling" (à, è, ì, ò, ù). In this dictionary, toned Pinyin glosses are given for all entries of words and characters. It is important to note, however, that the same words can have different Pinyin glosses for different word senses (see section 5). Also the tones for the same characters in the word index and the character index may be different because of "tone sandhi", i.e. the change of tone that occurs when different tones come together in a word.

Notes

1 We thank Professor Hongyin Tao of the University of California, Los Angeles for permitting us to use part of the data he collected in the Lancaster Los Angeles Spoken Chinese Corpus (LLSCC, http://www.ling.lancs.ac.uk/corplang/llscc/). We are also grateful to Dr Jiajin Xu of Beijing Foreign Studies University for allowing us to use his corpus of Spoken Chinese of Urban Teenagers (SCOUT).
2 See http://www.elda.org/catalogue/en/text/W0039.html for more information about the LCMC corpus.
3 See http://www.ling.lancs.ac.uk/corplang/ucla/ for more information about the UCLA Written Chinese Corpus.

4 We would like to thank Professor Kefei Wang for granting us permission to use part of the data from the Chinese–English parallel corpus created by his team at Beijing Foreign Studies University.

5 The current national standard in China for Chinese Information Processing GB2312-80 (*Character Set for Chinese Character Encoding in Information Exchange – Basic Set*) is based on the frequency list established on Project Code 748.

6 The HSK Level 2 words 反动 "reactionary" and 红旗 "red flag" are excluded from our word list as they are not so common nowadays (ranking 5781 and 6004 respectively in our corpus) as they were during the so-called "Cultural Revolution".

7 This decision was motivated by the fact that in computer programming we had to keep the same kind of information (e.g. Pinyin gloss, or word sense) together in one field instead of mixing information of different kinds (e.g. Pinyin glosses and word senses).

8 See BBC News on 9 January 2007 (http://news.bbc.co.uk/2/hi/asia-pacific/6244763.stm).

9 See http://www.britishcouncil.org/china-aboutuk-trenduk-mandarin.htm.

References

Beijing Aeronautical University (1985)
《现代汉语用字频度表》 (A Frequency Table of Character Usage in Modern Chinese). Beijing: Beijing Aeronautical University.

Beijing Language and Culture University (1986)
《现代汉语频率词典》 (A Frequency Dictionary of Modern Chinese). Beijing: Beijing Language and Culture University Press.

Chen, H. (1928)
《语体文应用字汇》 (The Applied Glossary of Modern Chinese). Beijing: Commercial Printing House.

Dai, J.X.L. (1998)
"Syntactic, morphological and phonological words in Chinese". In J. Packard (ed.) *New Approaches to Chinese Word Formation*, pp. 103–134. Berlin: Mouton de Gruyter.

Di Sciullo, A.M. and Williams, E. (1987)
On the Definition of Word. Cambridge, MA: MIT Press.

Dixon, R.M.W. and Aikhenvald, A.Y. (2002)
Word: A Cross-Linguistic Typology. Cambridge: CUP.

Duanmu, S. (1998)
"Wordhood in Chinese". In J. Packard (ed.) *New Approaches to Chinese Word Formation*, pp. 135–196. Berlin: Mouton de Gruyter.

Feng, S. (1997)
"Prosodically determined word-formation in Mandarin Chinese". *Social Sciences in China*, Winter issue: 120–137.

Feng, S. (2001a)
《论汉语"词"的多维性》 ("The multidimensional properties of 'word' in Chinese"). *Contemporary Linguistics*, 3(3): 161–174.

Feng, S. (2001b)
"Minimal Word in Mandarin Chinese". Ms, University of Kansas.

Goethals, M. (2003)
"E.E.T.: the European English Teaching vocabulary-list". In B. Lewandowska-Tomaszczyk (ed.) *Practical Applications in Language and Computers*, pp. 417–427. Frankfurt: Peter Lang.

Hong Kong Polytechnic University (1991–1997)
《中国大陆、台湾、香港汉语词库》 (A Chinese Word Bank from Mainland China, Taiwan, and Hong Kong). Hong Kong: Hong Kong Polytechnic University.

Juilland, A. and Chang-Rodríguez, E. (1964)
Frequency Dictionary of Spanish Words. The Hague: Mouton.

Leech, G. (1997)
"Teaching and language corpora: A convergence". In A. Wichmann, S. Fligelstone, A. McEnery and G. Knowles (eds) *Teaching and Language Corpora*, pp. 1–23. London: Longman.

Li, N. and Thompson, S. (1980)
Mandarin Chinese. Berkeley: University of California Press.

Liu, E. (1973)
Frequency Dictionary of Chinese Words. The Hague: Mouton.

Matthews, P.H. (1991)
Morphology (2nd edn). Cambridge: Cambridge University Press.

McEnery, T., Xiao, R. and Tono, Y. (2006)
Corpus-Based Language Studies: An Advanced Resource Book. London and New York: Routledge.

National Language Committee (1988)

《现代汉语常用字表》 (Commonly Used Characters in Modern Chinese). Beijing: National Language Committee.

Ostler, Nicholas (2005)

Empires of the World. London: HarperCollins.

Packard, J. (2000)

The Morphology of Chinese. Cambridge: CUP.

Project Code 748 (1976)

《现代汉字综合使用频度表》 (A Comprehensive Frequency Table of Character Usage in Modern Chinese). Beijing.

Wu, A. (2003)

"Customisable segmentation of morphologically derived words in Chinese". *Computational Linguistics and Chinese Language Processing*, 8(1): 1–28.

Zhang, H. and Liu, Q. (2002)

"Model of Chinese words rough segmentation based on N-shortest-paths method". *Journal of Chinese Information Processing*, 16(5): 1–7.

Zhang, H., Liu, Q., Zhang, H. and Cheng, X. (2002)

"Automatic recognition of Chinese unknown words based on role tagging". In *Proceedings of the 1st SIGHAN Workshop, COLING 2002*, pp. 71–7. Taipei.

The ICTCLAS part of speech annotation scheme

Level 1 tag	Level 2 tag	Gloss
a	a	adjective
	ad	adjective as adverbial
	ag	adjective morpheme
	an	adjective with nominal function
b	b	non-predicate adjective
c	c	conjunction
d	d	adverb
	dg	adverb morpheme
e	e	interjection
f	f	direction and locality
g	g	morpheme
h	h	prefix
i	i	idiom
j	j	abbreviation
k	k	suffix
l	l	fixed expression
m	m	numeral
n	n	common noun
	ng	noun morpheme
	nr	personal name
	ns	place name
	nt	organisation name
	nx	nominal character string
	nz	other proper noun
o	o	onomatopoeia
p	p	preposition
q	q	classifier
r	r	pronoun
s	s	place word
t	t	time word
u	u	auxiliary
v	v	verb
	vd	verb as adverbial
	vg	verb morpheme
	vn	verb with nominal function
w	w	punctuation
x	x	non-morpheme symbol
y	y	modal particle
z	z	descriptive

Frequency index

0001 的 [的] /*de*/ (1) *aux* [structural particle used after an attribute]
非洲是一块非常大的大陆。Africa is a very large continent.
236106 | 0.95 | 223484

0002 是 [是] /*shì*/ (1) *v* be
你是哪里人呢？Where are you from?
81965 | 0.83 | 67954

0003 一 [一] /*yī*/ (1) *num* one, a, an
市政大厅前有一群人。There is a crowd of people in front of the town hall.
69925 | 0.89 | 62263

0004 在 [在] /*zài*/ (1) *prep* [indicating location or time, etc.] at, in
她坐在窗旁。She sat at the window.
52774 | 0.94 | 49460

0005 了 [了] /*le*/ (1) *aux* [aspect marker indicating realisation of a situation]
她从马上摔了下来。She fell off her horse.
51296 | 0.9 | 46283

0006 不 [不] /*bù*/ (1) *adv* no, not
这条街不准停车。You can't park in this street.
50589 | 0.8 | 40245

0007 我 [我] /*wǒ*/ (1) *pron* I, me
咖啡和茶使我感到兴奋。Coffee and tea stimulate me.
51365 | 0.71 | 36653

0008 个 [個] /*gè*/ (1) *clas* [generalised measure word used for nouns without a specific measure term]
山那边有一个村庄。There is a village beyond the hill.
36612 | 0.83 | 30504

1. Fruits

Simplified Chinese	Traditional Chinese	Pinyin	Gloss	Frequency rank
苹果	蘋果	*píngguǒ*	apple	3251
西瓜	西瓜	*xīguā*	watermelon	4644
葡萄	葡萄	*pútao*	grape	4858
桃	桃	*táo*	peach	6390
梨	梨	*lí*	pear	7564
香蕉	香蕉	*xiāngjiāo*	banana	8905
樱桃	櫻桃	*yīngtáo*	cherry	10789
荔枝	荔枝	*lìzhī*	litchi, lychee	12982
柿子	柿子	*shìzi*	persimmon	13269
石榴	石榴	*shíliu*	pomegranate	16967
芒果	芒果	*mángguǒ*	mango	17697
李子	李子	*lǐzi*	plum	18120
桔子	桔子	*júzi*	tangerine	18351
草莓	草莓	*cǎoméi*	strawberry	20407
橘子	橘子	*júzi*	orange	21757
椰子	椰子	*yēzi*	coconut	22864
龙眼	龍眼	*lóngyǎn*	longan fruit	24871
菠萝	菠蘿	*bōluó*	pineapple	26494
山楂	山楂	*shānzhā*	hawthorn	28271
猕猴桃	獼猴桃	*míhóutáo*	Chinese gooseberry	28302
柠檬	檸檬	*níngméng*	lemon	29335

0009 有 [有] /yǒu/ (1) v have, there be
我希望我有更多的时间。 I wish I had more time.
33648 | 0.87 | 29434

0010 他 [他] /tā/ (1) pron he, him
目前，他正在度假。 At present, he is on holiday.
36234 | 0.76 | 27619

0011 这 [這] /zhè/ (1) pron this
你想看这个电视节目吗？ Do you want to watch this TV programme?
31412 | 0.85 | 26678

0012 说 [說] /shuō/ (1) v say, speak, tell
除非他亲口对我说，否则我决不相信。 I will not believe it unless and until he tells me so.
27792 | 0.8 | 22252

0013 就 [就] /jiù/ (1) adv [used for emphasis] just; then; at once
法国客人就住在那边的旅馆。 The French are staying in the hotel just over there.
29964 | 0.72 | 21596

0014 人 [人] /rén/ (1) n person, human, man
我尊重他这位作家，也尊重他这个人。 I respect him as a writer and as a man.
24724 | 0.86 | 21225

0015 上 [上] /shàng/ (1) loc up, on, in
孩子的新毛衣上勾了一个洞。 The child has picked a hole in his new jumper.
22041 | 0.92 | 20201

0016 和 [和] /hé/ (1) conj and
二十世纪的经验和教训 the experience and lessons of the twentieth century
27438 | 0.7 | 19292

0017 也 [也] /yě/ (1) adv also
但他们也会带来欢乐。 But they will also give delight.
22338 | 0.85 | 19093

0018 你 [你] /nǐ/ (1) pron you
你也不错。 You're looking good yourself.
28592 | 0.64 | 18249

0019 了 [了] /le/ (1) part [sentence final particle indicating change of state or current relevance]
我累死了。 I am worn out.
26451 | 0.69 | 18204

0020 要 [要] /yào/ (1) v want; order
我就要份牛排。 I will take the beefsteak.
17290 | 0.92 | 15835

0021 到 [到] /dào/ (1) v go to, reach, arrive
他到了那里就可能不回来了。 Chances are that he won't come back when he gets there.
16955 | 0.9 | 15280

0022 对 [對] /duì/ (1) prep for, to, with regard to
她必须对她的行为负责。 She must answer for her actions.
15402 | 0.91 | 14018

0023 还 [還] /hái/ (1) adv still, yet
后面还有座位。 There are still vacant seats at the back.
16416 | 0.85 | 13957

0024 都 [都] /dōu/ (1) adv all
所有的家具都已处理了。 All the furniture has been disposed of.
16480 | 0.84 | 13809

0025 大 [大] /dà/ (1) adj big, large
一个大浪把小船卷走了。 A huge wave swept the boat away.
11795 | 0.98 | 11525

0026 我们 [我們] /wǒmen/ (1) pron we, us
我们早上很早就出发了。 We made an early start in the morning.
15065 | 0.74 | 11115

0027 着 [著] /zhe/ (1) aux [aspect marker indicating a durative or ongoing situation]
花园里的花正开着。 The flower in the garden is blooming.
15188 | 0.66 | 10015

0028 好 [好] /hǎo/ (1) adj good, well
我认为她唱得很好。 She sang well, I thought.
11951 | 0.8 | 9535

0029 种 [種] /zhǒng/ (1) clas [indicating species] kind, type
你提供这种服务吗？ Do you provide this kind of service?
11206 | 0.85 | 9528

0030 中 [中] /zhōng/ (1) loc in, within
数字写在背后的表中。 The figures are set out in the table at the back of the book.
12127 | 0.78 | 9457

0031 能 [能] /néng/ (1) v can
你自以为每次都能赢，未免太自大了。 It's arrogant of you to assume that you can win every time.
10434 | 0.89 | 9273

0032 她 [她] /tā/ (1) pron she, her
她各种音乐都喜爱，和我一样。 She enjoys all kinds of music, as I do.
17222 | 0.52 | 8954

0033 两 [兩] /liǎng/ (1) num two
这两幅画差别很小。 The differences between the two pictures are very slight.
9635 | 0.88 | 8523

0034 把 [把] /bǎ/ (1) prep [ba-structure preposing the object]
把嘴张开，说"啊"。 Open your mouth and say "ah".
9906 | 0.86 | 8485

0035 会 [會] /huì/ (1) v can, know how to do
谁说我不会做饭？ Who said that I cannot cook?
10178 | 0.83 | 8476

0036 地 [地] /de/ (1) aux [structural particle introducing an adverbial modifier]
你得认真地打每一个球。 You should be serious about each stroke.
10092 | 0.82 | 8256

0037 那 [那] /nà/ (1) *pron* that
那是一派胡言！That's total nonsense!
13126 | 0.62 | 8152 | S

0038 很 [很] /hěn/ (1) *adv* very
火车很可能要晚点。It's very likely that the
train will be delayed.
9533 | 0.82 | 7811

0039 看 [看] /kàn, kān/ (1, 3) *v* look, view;
look after
顺便问一下，现在看看房间方便吗？By the
way, will it be convenient to see the room now?
11068 | 0.7 | 7734

0040 去 [去] /qù/ (1) *v* go
你去哪？Where are you going?
10516 | 0.72 | 7589

0041 他们 [他們] /tāmen/ (1) *pron* they, them
他们刚刚到达。They've just arrived.
8394 | 0.88 | 7415

0042 从 [從] /cóng/ (1) *prep* from
河流从西到东穿过这座城市。The river flows
through the city from west to east.
7876 | 0.94 | 7402

0043 自己 [自己] /zìjǐ/ (1) *pron* self
你最好自己做这事。You'd better do it
yourself.
8896 | 0.8 | 7083

0044 得 [得] /de/ (1) *aux* [structural particle used
after a verb that introduces a complement
showing effect]
他吓得发抖。He is trembling from fear.
9147 | 0.74 | 6803

0045 什么 [什麼] /shénme/ (1) *pron* what
您要什么样的房间？What kind of room do
you want?
9952 | 0.67 | 6623

0046 又 [又] /yòu/ (1) *adv* again, once again
电梯又坏了。The elevator's out again.
7998 | 0.83 | 6612

0047 第 [第] /dì/ (1) *pref* [numeral prefix forming
ordinal numbers]
谁在四分钟内第一个跑完了一英里？Who was
the first man to run a mile in four minutes?
7829 | 0.83 | 6491

0048 年 [年] /nián/ (1) *n* year
这家公司创办于1724年。This company was
founded in the year 1724.
7501 | 0.86 | 6416

0049 而 [而] /ér/ (2) *conj* and, yet
我们耻于罪而不耻于犯罪。We are ashamed
of sin and yet not ashamed to sin.
7652 | 0.8 | 6151

0050 出 [出] /chū/ (1) *v* out; produce; happen
这儿出了什么事？What's happened here?
7051 | 0.85 | 6004

0051 这个 [這個] /zhège/ (1) *pron* this
在这个问题上有着各种不同的意见。There is
a wide spectrum of opinions on this
question.
10042 | 0.59 | 5896 | S

0052 三 [三] /sān/ (1) *num* three
三年内我有两次假期。I've had two holidays
in three years.
6511 | 0.87 | 5665

0053 来 [來] /lái/ (2) *aux* [preceding a verb to
indicate the intended or suggested action]
我找到这个小玩意儿来做开瓶器。I found this
gadget that will serve as a bottle opener.
6516 | 0.86 | 5604

0054 次 [次] /cì/ (1) *clas* [measure word indicating
number of repetitions or count of actions or
events] times
这种药每天喝三次。Take this medicine three
times a day.
6398 | 0.86 | 5516

0055 多 [多] /duō/ (1) *adj* many, much, plentiful
他的钱多得足够买下那个岛。He had enough
money to buy out the island.
5823 | 0.94 | 5485

0056 想 [想] /xiǎng/ (1) *v* think
对不起，我想她出去购物了。Sorry, I think
she's gone shopping.
7999 | 0.68 | 5411

0057 被 [被] /bèi/ (1) *prep* [passive marker]
他被一颗子弹射中心脏而死亡。He was killed
by a single bullet in the heart.
6059 | 0.88 | 5339

0058 最 [最] /zuì/ (1) *adv* [superlative degree] most
上海是世界上最大的城市之一。Shanghai is
among the largest cities in the world.
6011 | 0.88 | 5318

0059 里 [裏] /lǐ/ (1) *loc* in, inside
她知道这幢大楼里所有房间的号码。
She knows all the rooms in the building
by number.
6869 | 0.77 | 5295

0060 给 [給] /gěi/ (1) *prep* to
我昨天给她写了一封信。I wrote a letter to
her yesterday.
6847 | 0.76 | 5220

0061 但 [但] /dàn/ (2) *conj* but
请两边及后脑修一修，但前面保持原样。
Trim the sides and the back, but leave the
front as it is, please.
6224 | 0.82 | 5106

0062 几 [幾] /jǐ/ (1) *num* several; how much
我要离开几天。I am going away for a few
days.
5632 | 0.88 | 4952

0063 来 [來] /lái/ (1) *v* come
早点儿来。Do come early.
6357 | 0.77 | 4925

0064 下 [下] /xià/ (1) *loc* under, below
它们在我床下。They're under my bed.
5505 | 0.89 | 4916

0065 为 [為] /wèi/ (1) *prep* [introducing purpose,
reason, beneficiary, etc.] for, because of
你能为我弄到两张音乐会的票吗？Can you
secure me two good tickets for the concert?
7039 | 0.7 | 4915

0066 小 [小] /xiǎo/ (1) *adj* small, little
电梯很小，只容得下三个人。The lift was so small that only three people could fit in.
5892 | 0.83 | 4877

0067 后 [後] /hòu/ (1) *loc* behind; after, later
三天后您可以来试衣。You can come for a fitting three days later.
5706 | 0.85 | 4868

0068 用 [用] /yòng/ (1) *v* use
你会用筷子吗？Do you know how to use chopsticks?
5523 | 0.87 | 4788

0069 多 [多] /duō/ (1) *num* many, much, numerous
我们已试过多次了。We have tried many times.
5996 | 0.78 | 4684

0070 可以 [可以] /kěyǐ/ (1) *v* may, can
您可以到百老汇街乘 20 路公共汽车或乘地铁。You can catch bus 20 or the subway on Broadway.
5614 | 0.82 | 4608

0071 只 [只] /zhǐ/ (1) *adv* only
此警报按钮只在紧急情况下使用。This alarm button is only to be used in emergency.
5825 | 0.79 | 4606

0072 问题 [問題] /wèntí/ (1) *n* question, problem, issue
很抱歉我无法回答这个问题。I am sorry that I cannot answer the question.
5973 | 0.77 | 4596

0073 等 [等] /děng/ (1) *aux* et cetera
她的听觉、触觉等很灵敏。She's got very sensitive hearing, skin, etc.
6830 | 0.67 | 4567

0074 没有 [沒有] /méiyǒu/ *v* have not, there be not
他没有资金来实施他的计划。He does not have the funds to carry out his plan.
5737 | 0.78 | 4496

0075 过 [過] /guo/ (1) *aux* [aspect marker indicating experience]
你去过迪斯尼乐园吗？Have you ever been to Disneyland?
5631 | 0.79 | 4464

0076 做 [做] /zuò/ (1) *v* do, make
你看见她在做什么？What do you see her do?
5372 | 0.82 | 4423

0077 以 [以] /yǐ/ (2) *prep* by means of, with, in (some way); according to; because of
我不想以任何方式限制你的自由。I don't want to tie you down in any way.
6072 | 0.72 | 4384

0078 时 [時] /shí/ *n* time when . . .
过马路时要小心。Take care when crossing the road.
5430 | 0.8 | 4332

0079 让 [讓] /ràng/ (1) *v* give way; let, make; allow
让我说完。Let me finish.
5555 | 0.77 | 4278

0080 二 [二] /èr/ (1) *num* two
双方踢成二平。The two teams tied at 2:2.
4499 | 0.91 | 4105

0081 这样 [這樣] /zhèyàng/ (1) *pron* this (kind of, sort of); so
这样做影响不好。This would create a bad impression.
5318 | 0.77 | 4092

0082 可 [可] /kě/ (2) *conj* but, yet
我事先跟他说过，可他就是不听。I tried to warn him, but he wouldn't listen.
4663 | 0.86 | 4003

0083 更 [更] /gèng/ (1) *adv* [comparative degree] more
我无法跑得更快了。I can't run any faster.
4509 | 0.88 | 3988

0084 之 [之] /zhī/ (3) *aux* [archaic equivalent of structural particle 的]
他们做得对还是错，这是争议之处。It is a matter of dispute whether they did the right thing.
5125 | 0.77 | 3951

0085 走 [走] /zǒu/ (1) *v* walk; leave
他一句话都没说走就了。He left without a word.
5527 | 0.71 | 3939

0086 它 [它] /tā/ (1) *pron* [used for non-human things] it
我不要它。I don't want it.
6504 | 0.6 | 3928 | S

0087 再 [再] /zài/ (1) *adv* again
请再出来一下。Come out again, please!
4822 | 0.79 | 3813

0088 与 [與] /yǔ/ (2) *prep* [indicating involvement or relationship] with
此事与你无关。It has nothing to do with you.
4940 | 0.76 | 3741 | W

0089 呢 [呢] /ne/ (1) *part* [particle used at the end of a question or declarative sentence to indicate mood]
你为什么不回家去呢？Why didn't you go home?
6522 | 0.56 | 3677 | S

0090 知道 [知道] /zhīdào/ (1) *v* know
照理他应该知道她的地址。He ought to know her address.
5179 | 0.68 | 3510

0091 天 [天] /tiān/ (1) *clas* [measure word for time] day
实际工作时间只有 4 天。The actual work only lasted for four days.
4162 | 0.84 | 3501

0092 位 [位] /wèi/ (1) *clas* [measure word for respectable people]
是的，我找了一位好的外科医师进行手术。Yes, I got a good surgeon to perform the operation.
3860 | 0.91 | 3499

0093 才 [才] /cái/ (3) adv just
节目才开始。The performance has just started.
4291 | 0.81 | 3493

0094 现在 [現在] /xiànzài/ (1) time now
现在正在预报飞机的起飞时间。Now it is broadcasting the take-off time for the planes.
4942 | 0.71 | 3484

0095 于 [於] /yú/ (2) prep [indicating time, location, direction, etc.] in, at
他们将于下周出发到香港去。They will set out for Hong Kong next week.
4435 | 0.78 | 3452

0096 各 [各] /gè/ (1) pron each
各场比赛按现行国际规则进行。Each match is played to current international rules.
5532 | 0.62 | 3416

0097 为 [為] /wéi/ (1) v be, act as
学生和计算机的比例在全国范围内为 16 比 1 。The national ratio of students to computers is 16 to 1.
4486 | 0.76 | 3415

0098 工作 [工作] /gōngzuò/ (1) v work, do a job
你在哪里工作？Where do you work?
5298 | 0.64 | 3396

0099 因为 [因為] /yīnwéi/ (1) conj because
她需要一把伞，因为天在下雨。She needs an umbrella because it's raining.
4520 | 0.75 | 3378

0100 向 [向] /xiàng/ (1) prep [indicating direction] to, towards
那孩子向我跑来。The child came running towards me.
4141 | 0.81 | 3353

0101 已经 [已經] /yǐjīng/ (1) adv already
史密斯已经学两年汉语了。Smith has already studied Chinese for two years.
3781 | 0.86 | 3269

0102 并 [並] /bìng/ (2) conj and, besides
请把你的东西放入这信封并封闭好。Please put your articles in this envelope and seal it.
4453 | 0.7 | 3128

0103 时候 [時候] /shíhou/ (1) n when, time when . . .
我读书的时候不要打断我。Don't interrupt me when I'm reading.
4922 | 0.63 | 3105 | S

0104 这些 [這些] /zhèxiē/ (1) pron these
这些片剂一天吃三次。Please take these tablets three times a day.
3429 | 0.9 | 3089

0105 国 [國] /guó/ (1) n country, nation
各国人民都要和平。All nations want peace.
6889 | 0.45 | 3084 | W

0106 高 [高] /gāo/ (1) adj tall, high
多高的大楼啊！What a tall building it is!
3623 | 0.85 | 3074

0107 没有 [沒有] /méiyǒu/ (1) adv not
她一晚上都没有吃东西。She didn't touch her food all night.
3638 | 0.84 | 3052

0108 事 [事] /shì/ (1) n matter, thing
出了什么事？What's the matter?
4258 | 0.71 | 3035

0109 发展 [發展] /fāzhǎn/ (1) v develop
这有助于发展地区经济。This helps to develop local economies.
6387 | 0.46 | 2963

0110 成 [成] /chéng/ (1) v become, turn into; succeed
她成了医生。She became a doctor.
3332 | 0.88 | 2932

0111 们 [們] /men/ (1) suf [plural marker for pronouns and some animate nouns]
朋友们舞会后就分开了。The friends separated after the party.
3199 | 0.92 | 2930

0112 新 [新] /xīn/ (1) adj new
新货很快就到。The new order is coming soon.
4702 | 0.62 | 2925

0113 所 [所] /suǒ/ (2) aux [particle preceding a verb to form a nominal structure]
这本词典正是我所需要的。This dictionary is exactly what I need.
3646 | 0.8 | 2906

0114 社会 [社會] /shèhuì/ (1) n society
很多艺术家都感到与社会脱节。Many artists feel alienated from society.
4071 | 0.71 | 2894

0115 一些 [一些] /yìxiē/ (1) num some
我有一些科目得了高分。I got some high marks in some subjects.
3320 | 0.87 | 2876

0116 吗 [嗎] /ma/ (1) part [question tag]
你的家人都好吗？How's your family?
4440 | 0.64 | 2848

0117 与 [與] /yǔ/ (2) conj and
请问您的姓名与班机号码？What's your name and flight number?
4075 | 0.7 | 2842 | W

0118 没 [沒] /méi/ (1) adv not
你为什么没去呢？Why didn't you go?
4469 | 0.64 | 2838

0119 吧 [吧] /ba/ (1) part [modal particle indicating a suggestion or request; marking a question requesting confirmation, or a pause after alternatives]
这次我们各付各的吧。Let's go Dutch this time.
4772 | 0.59 | 2836

0120 打 [打] /dǎ/ (1) v beat, hit, strike; play; typewrite
他用拳头打我。He hit me with his fist.
3643 | 0.78 | 2828

0121 前 [前] /qián/ (1) *loc* before;
in front of
一定要在九点前赶到这儿！ Be sure
to get here before nine!
3029 | 0.93 | 2816

0122 如果 [如果] /rúguǒ/ (2) *conj* if
如果您要什么，就打电话给服务台。
If you want anything, just call the
desk.
3488 | 0.8 | 2806

0123 已 [已] /yǐ/ (2) *adv* already
这项工作已完成了一半。 Half the work is
already finished.
4351 | 0.63 | 2759 | W

0124 使 [使] /shǐ/ (2) *v* [often used in serial
verb constructions] make, cause,
enable
这消息使我很难过。 The news made me
feel very sad.
3549 | 0.76 | 2713

0125 话 [話] /huà/ (1) *n* word, talk, utterance
你说那种话，太不够聪明了。
You are not very smart to say that.
3653 | 0.73 | 2678

0126 世界 [世界] /shìjiè/ (1) *n* world
英国的咖啡是世界上最好的咖啡。
English coffee is the best in the
world.
3919 | 0.68 | 2674

0127 生活 [生活] /shēnghuó/ *v* live
我们想一起生活。 We want to live together in
the future.
3039 | 0.87 | 2644

0128 四 [四] /sì/ (1) *num* four
房间里有四张单人床。 There are four single
beds in the room.
2981 | 0.89 | 2641

0129 怎么 [怎麼] /zěnme/ (1) *pron* how
我怎么会知道呢？ How can I know?
4224 | 0.62 | 2635

0130 比 [比] /bǐ/ (1) *prep* [used for comparison]
than
电影院在路的另一端，比我原来想的还远。
The cinema is farther down the road than
I thought.
2718 | 0.97 | 2624

0131 将 [將] /jiāng/ (2) *adv* [indicating a future
happening] will, be going to
我们将尽快留意这个问题。 We will attend to
this matter as soon as possible.
4888 | 0.53 | 2604

0132 家 [家] /jiā/ (1) *clas* [measure word for families
or businesses]
你住在哪一家饭店啊？ Which hotel are you
staying at?
2855 | 0.91 | 2601

0133 像 [像] /xiàng/ (1) *v* look like, resemble;
look as if
她打扮得像个公主一样去参加宴会。
She dressed up like a princess for the party.
3502 | 0.72 | 2532

0134 叫 [叫] /jiào/ (1, 1) *v* name, call; shout; order
(somebody to do something); order (meal, taxi,
etc.)
你的父母叫你什么？ What do your parents call
you?
3944 | 0.63 | 2501

0135 国家 [國家] /guójiā/ (1) *n* country
儿童是国家和社会的未来。 Children are the
future of the country and society.
4533 | 0.55 | 2497

0136 起 [起] /qǐ/ (1) *v* get up, rise; up
我通常起得很早。 I usually get up early.
3000 | 0.83 | 2494

0137 吃 [吃] /chī/ (1) *v* eat
你吃过午饭了没有？ Did you have lunch?
3326 | 0.75 | 2480

0138 月 [月] /yuè/ (1) *n* moon; month
下个月我空得很。 I'll be quite free next month.
3391 | 0.73 | 2476

0139 开始 [開始] /kāishǐ/ (1) *v* begin, start
学校八点开始上课。 Classes begin at eight at
school.
2614 | 0.94 | 2465

0140 全 [全] /quán/ (1) *adj* whole, entire, complete
最为重要的一点是，全家人团聚在一起。 Most
important, the entire family was together.
4569 | 0.53 | 2415

0141 完 [完] /wán/ (1) *v* finish, be over; (use) up
我刚看完第3章。 I've just finished reading
Chapter 3.
3434 | 0.7 | 2388

0142 时间 [時間] /shíjiān/ (1) *n* time
剩下时间不多了。 There is little time left.
2634 | 0.9 | 2375

0143 起来 [起來] /qǐlái/ (1) *v* get up, rise; [following
a verb to indicate the beginning of a situation]
start to; [following a verb to indicate
completedeness or effectiveness]
她哭起来了。 She started crying.
3113 | 0.75 | 2340

0144 今天 [今天] /jīntiān/ (1) *time* today
今天上午我们有两节课。 We have two classes
this morning.
3271 | 0.71 | 2332

0145 和 [和] /hé/ (1) *prep* [indicating relationship or
comparison] with
他正愉快地和她交谈。 He is talking with her
pleasantly.
2732 | 0.84 | 2303

0146 听 [聽] /tīng/ (1) *v* listen
先生，请听我说！ Now listen to me, mister!
3435 | 0.67 | 2302

0147 老 [老] /lǎo/ (1) *adj* old, veteran
房子前面的那棵树很老了。 The tree in front
of the house is very old.
2817 | 0.81 | 2274

0148 可能 [可能] /kěnéng/ (1) *v* might (happen)
他可能明天来。 He may come tomorrow.
2849 | 0.78 | 2217

0149 孩子 [孩子] /háizi/ (1) *n* child, children
有孩子吗？Do you have any children?
2839 | 0.78 | 2213

0150 却 [卻] /què/ (2) *adv* but
人会说话，而动物却不会。Human beings can
talk, but animals can't.
3050 | 0.72 | 2188 | W

0151 太 [太] /tài/ (1) *adv* too, excessively;
very
恐怕对我来说这颜色太亮了。
I'm afraid the colour is a bit too
bright for me.
2917 | 0.75 | 2177

0152 十 [十] /shí/ (1) *num* ten
屋子里有十个人。There are ten people in the
room.
2468 | 0.88 | 2169

0153 地方 [地方] /dìfang, dìfāng/ (1, 2) *n* place,
space, room; locality (in relation to central
administration)
伦敦是个奢侈的地方。London was an
extravagant place.
2487 | 0.87 | 2157

0154 由 [由] /yóu/ (2) *prep* by, from
他是由他奶奶带大的。He was brought up by
his grandmother.
3000 | 0.72 | 2149

0155 但是 [但是] /dànshì/ (1) *conj* but
我明天要走，但是我还没有收拾衣箱。I am
leaving tomorrow, but I have not packed my
suitcase yet.
3276 | 0.65 | 2134 | S

0156 所以 [所以] /suǒyǐ/ (1) *conj* so, therefore
我要赶不上火车了，所以得跑着去。I was late
for the train so I had to run.
3720 | 0.57 | 2129 | S

0157 条 [條] /tiáo/ (1) *clas* [measure word for
things of a long and thin shape (e.g. string
and river), pieces of writing (e.g. news,
suggestions and regulations), or human
life]
这条裤子非常合身。The trousers fit
perfectly.
2268 | 0.94 | 2122

0158 钱 [錢] /qián/ (1) *n* money
我身上没有带钱。I didn't bring any money
with me.
2950 | 0.72 | 2114

0159 每 [每] /měi/ (1) *pron* each
她给我们每人一杯冷饮。She offered us each
a cold drink.
2398 | 0.88 | 2112

0160 认为 [認為] /rènwéi/ (1) *v* think, believe
我认为那部电影不怎么样。I do not think
much of the film.
2520 | 0.81 | 2036

0161 经济 [經濟] /jīngjì/ (1) *n* economy
现在我们一心一意地搞经济建设。We are now
devoting ourselves wholeheartedly to
economic development
4534 | 0.45 | 2019 | W

0162 公司 [公司] /gōngsī/ (2) *n* (business) company
这家公司创办于一八六零年。The company
was established in 1860.
2924 | 0.69 | 2010

0163 文化 [文化] /wénhuà/ (1) *n* culture
美国是个多文化的国家。The US is a country
with many different cultures.
2726 | 0.74 | 2007

0164 问 [問] /wèn/ (1) *v* ask
如果他来这儿，我将问他几个问题。If he
comes here, I shall ask him some questions.
3080 | 0.65 | 2004

0165 关系 [關係] /guānxì/ (1) *n* relation,
relationship; connections, ties
亲密的关系会使人的生活丰富多彩。
Intimate relationships enrich people's lives.
2967 | 0.67 | 2001

0166 觉得 [覺得] /juéde/ (1) *v* think, feel
你觉得怎么样？What do you feel?
2933 | 0.68 | 1999

0167 点 [點] /diǎn/ (1) *clas* [measure word for
point, item, etc.]; [measure word for small
quantities]
我只想简单讲两点。I shall only mention two
things in brief.
2479 | 0.79 | 1953

0168 谁 [誰] /shéi/ (1) *pron* who
我知道他是谁。I know who he is.
2736 | 0.71 | 1952

0169 出来 [出來] /chūlái/ (1) *v* come out
他出来时向人群挥舞着文件。He came out
waving the document at the crowd.
2651 | 0.73 | 1944

0170 进行 [進行] /jìnxíng/ (1) *v* go on, last; be under
way; carry on, carry out, perform
比赛进行了两个小时。The game lasted two
hours.
3383 | 0.57 | 1938

0171 重要 [重要] /zhòngyào/ (1) *adj* important,
vital
合理安排很重要。It is vital that rational
arrangements be made.
2718 | 0.71 | 1924

0172 五 [五] /wǔ/ (1) *num* five
他们五个人都很努力。All five of them are
hard workers.
2239 | 0.86 | 1923

0173 长 [長] /cháng/ (1) *adj* long
到城里要走很长的路程。It is a long walk to
the town.
2183 | 0.88 | 1919

0174 正 [正] /zhèng/ (1) *adv* just, precisely; just
(in progress)
我正准备打电话给你。I was just about to call
you.
2222 | 0.86 | 1917

0175 这么 [這麼] /zhème/ (1) *pron* so, such, like
this
我吃不下这么多。I can't eat so much.
3066 | 0.61 | 1879

2. Drinks and beverages

水	水	*shuǐ*	water	**206**
酒	酒	*jiǔ*	wine, liquor, spirit	**634**
茶	茶	*chá*	tea	**1812**
咖啡	咖啡	*kāfēi*	coffee	**3500**
啤酒	啤酒	*píjiǔ*	beer	**3702**
牛奶	牛奶	*niúnǎi*	milk	**4983**
矿泉水	礦泉水	*kuàngquán shuǐ*	mineral water	**8642**
葡萄酒	葡萄酒	*pútao jiǔ*	(grape) wine	**11122**
果汁	果汁	*guǒzhī*	(fruit) juice	**15707**
汽水	汽水	*qìshuǐ*	soda water, pop	**19292**
可乐	可樂	*kělè*	Coke	**21019**
红茶	紅茶	*hóngchá*	black tea	**24237**
绿茶	綠茶	*lǜchá*	green tea	**24319**
香槟	香檳	*xiāngbīn*	champagne	**25892**
白酒	白酒	*báijiǔ*	white spirit	
白兰地	白蘭地	*báilándì*	brandy	
白葡萄酒	白葡萄酒	*bái pútaojiǔ*	white wine	
百事可乐	百事可樂	*bǎi shì kělè*	Pepsi, Pepsi-Cola	
冰咖啡	冰咖啡	*bīng kāfēi*	ice coffee	
冰水	冰水	*bīng shuǐ*	ice water	
橙汁	橙汁	*chéngzhī*	orange juice	
纯净水	純淨水	*chúnjìng shuǐ*	purified water	
杜松子酒	杜松子酒	*dùsōngzǐjiǔ*	gin	
伏特加	伏特加	*fútèjiā*	vodka	
果酒	果酒	*guǒjiǔ*	cider	
红酒	紅酒	*hóngjiǔ*	red wine	
红葡萄酒	紅葡萄酒	*hóng pútaojiǔ*	red wine	
花茶	花茶	*huāchá*	scented tea	
鸡尾酒	雞尾酒	*jīwěijiǔ*	cocktail	
桔子汁	桔子汁	*júzi zhī*	orange juice	
可口可乐	可口可樂	*kěkǒu kělè*	Coca-Cola, Coke	
麦酒	麥酒	*màijiǔ*	ale	
茅台酒	茅臺酒	*máotái jiǔ*	maotai	
柠檬水	檸檬水	*níngméng shuǐ*	lemonade	
苹果汁	蘋果汁	*píngguǒ zhī*	apple juice	
热巧克力	熱巧克力	*rè qiǎokèlì*	hot chocolate	
威士忌	威士忌	*wēishìjì*	whisky	
雪碧	雪碧	*xuěbì*	Sprite	

0176 情况 [情況] /*qíngkuàng*/ (1) *n* situation, condition, circumstance
那得看具体情况。Well, it all depends on the situation.
2213 | 0.85 | 1875

0177 写 [寫] /*xiě*/ (1) *v* write
我写字总用钢笔。When I write, I always use a pen.
2808 | 0.66 | 1856

0178 这里 [這裏] /*zhèlǐ*/ (1) *pron* here
他现在不在这里。He is not here now.
1888 | 0.97 | 1834

0179 你们 [你們] /*nǐmen*/ (1) *pron* [plural] you
对不起，给你们找麻烦了。I'm sorry to have caused you so much trouble.
2859 | 0.64 | 1832

0180 找 [找] /zhǎo/ (1) v look for
你在找什么？What are you looking for?
2560 | 0.7 | 1795

0181 跟 [跟] /gēn/ (1) prep [indicating relationship, involvement, or comparison] with
我有点要紧的事跟他商量。I have something urgent to discuss with him.
3142 | 0.57 | 1786 | S

0182 儿 [兒] /ér, r/ suf [nonsyllabic suffix for retroflection, especially in the Beijing dialect]
这两张画儿不太一样。The two pictures are not quite the same.
3795 | 0.47 | 1778 | S

0183 讲 [講] /jiǎng/ (1) v speak, tell
我要跟你讲一个真实的故事。I want to tell you a true story.
2538 | 0.7 | 1776 | S

0184 女 [女] /nǚ/ (1) adj female, woman
门外是两个女鬼！Outside were two female ghosts.
2007 | 0.88 | 1761

0185 而且 [而且] /érqiě/ (1) conj (not only . . .) but also
这不仅省事而且省钱。This will save not only labour but also money.
2043 | 0.86 | 1761

0186 开 [開] /kāi/ (1) v open; operate, drive (car), turn on (light); start (business); hold (meeting, party, etc.); (water) boil; write (cheque); (flower) blossom
门是朝里开的。The door opened inwards.
2205 | 0.8 | 1760

0187 点 [點] /diǎn/ (1) n dot, point
夜空中，星星象无数的小亮点。Stars resemble innumerable dots of light in the night sky.
2199 | 0.79 | 1726

0188 其 [其] /qí/ (3) pron [third person singular or plural] his, her, its, their; that, such
他刚一收到支票即将其存入银行。He banked the cheque as soon as he received it.
2595 | 0.66 | 1724 | W

0189 企业 [企業] /qǐyè/ (2) n business establishment, enterprise
我认为他的企业成功的可能性很小。I think there is little probability of his success in the enterprise.
3807 | 0.45 | 1715 | W

0190 进 [進] /jìn/ (1) v enter; advance
他进了教室。He entered the classroom.
2071 | 0.82 | 1695

0191 没 [沒] /méi/ (1) v have not, there be not
我根本没时间给你写信。I have no time at all to write to you.
2756 | 0.61 | 1693

0192 名 [名] /míng/ (2) clas [measure word for persons in general]
你知道要成为一名记者我们应该做什么吗？Do you know what we should do to become a reporter?
2570 | 0.66 | 1692

0193 方面 [方面] /fāngmiàn/ (1) n aspect, respect, side
这是成功的第一个方面。This is the first aspect of the success.
2424 | 0.7 | 1690

0194 拿 [拿] /ná/ (1) v hold; take
谁会把它拿走呢？Who could have taken it?
2298 | 0.73 | 1683

0195 那么 [那麼] /nàme/ (1) pron so, that; in that way
怎么那么贵呢？Why is it so expensive?
3316 | 0.51 | 1680 | S

0196 应该 [應該] /yīnggāi/ (1) v ought to, should
高峰期间应该多开几趟公共汽车。There ought to be more buses during the rush hour.
2015 | 0.82 | 1654

0197 发现 [發現] /fāxiàn/ (1) v find
我发现那盒子空了。I find that box empty.
1850 | 0.89 | 1647

0198 当 [當] /dāng/ (1) prep just at (time or place)
当消息有进展时及时报道。Report the news as it develops.
1968 | 0.83 | 1630

0199 大家 [大家] /dàjiā/ (1) pron all, everyone
他衷心地感谢我们大家。He thanked us all warmly.
2341 | 0.7 | 1630

0200 住 [住] /zhù/ (1) v live, stay
你住在几号房间？先生。What room are you staying in, sir?
2375 | 0.69 | 1628

0201 见 [見] /jiàn/ (1) v see, meet
我不想见他。I don't feel like meeting him.
2399 | 0.68 | 1626

0202 将 [將] /jiāng/ (2) prep [equivalent of the object preposer 把]
晚上将贵重物品存入饭店的保险箱内。Items of value can be deposited in the hotel safe overnight.
2090 | 0.78 | 1622 | W

0203 岁 [歲] /suì/ (1) clas year (of age)
学生的平均年龄是 19 岁。The average age of the students is 19.
1795 | 0.9 | 1607

0204 带 [帶] /dài/ (1) v carry, bring, take
请务必随时随身带着钥匙。Please make sure that you take the key with you at all times.
2008 | 0.8 | 1607

0205 元 [元] /yuán/ (1) clas [Chinese currency unit] yuan
入场费 6 元。The admission fee is six yuan.
2860 | 0.56 | 1602 | W

0206 水 [水] /shuǐ/ (1) n water
我可以再要一杯水吗？Can I get another glass of water?
1789 | 0.89 | 1593

0207 为了 [為了] /wèile/ (1) *prep* for the sake of; in order to
为了买那本书，我不得不在吃的方面省俭。
I have to pinch on food in order to buy that book.
1760 | 0.91 | 1592

0208 东西 [東西] /dōngxi/ (1) *n* stuff, thing
这东西可真美！The thing is magnificent!
2345 | 0.68 | 1587

0209 您 [您] /nín/ (1) *pron* [honorific, no plural form] you
我们可以请您一起进餐吗？May we have the pleasure of your company at dinner?
2762 | 0.57 | 1576 | S

0210 地 [地] /dì/ (1) *n* earth, ground, field
地上有很多树叶。There are a lot of leaves on the ground.
1757 | 0.9 | 1572

0211 看到 [看到] /kàndào/ *v* see
我很希望将来能再看到你。I do hope I will see you again.
1838 | 0.86 | 1571

0212 同 [同] /tóng/ (2) *prep* [indicating relationship, involvement, comparison] with
在绘画方面，杰克不能同她相比。
Jack is no match for her in painting.
2059 | 0.76 | 1570

0213 干 [幹] /gàn/ (1) *v* work, do (a job)
干得很好！Well done!
2172 | 0.72 | 1557

0214 历史 [歷史] /lìshǐ/ (1) *n* history
研究历史时去伪存真是很重要的。It is important to sift the true from the false in the study of history.
2065 | 0.75 | 1556

0215 家 [家] /jiā/ (1) *n* home; family, household
今晚请到我家来。Come round to my home this evening.
1947 | 0.79 | 1546

0216 张 [張] /zhāng/ (1) *clas* [measure word for flat objects and things with a flat surface, and also for bows and mouths]
如果你愿意，我就给你弄一张票。If you like, I'll get a ticket for you.
1881 | 0.82 | 1546

0217 非常 [非常] /fēicháng/ (1) *adv* very, unusually
非常感谢你的好意。Thank you very much for your kindness.
2403 | 0.64 | 1535 | S

0218 回 [回] /huí/ (1) *v* return; reply; decline (invitation)
速去速回。Go and return quickly.
2128 | 0.72 | 1534

0219 件 [件] /jiàn/ (1) *clas* [measure word for clothes, furniture, affairs, etc.] item, article
她脱下旧连衣裙，穿上一件新的。
She took off the old dress and put on a new one.
1679 | 0.91 | 1530

0220 那个 [那個] /nèige/ (1) *pron* that one
她就是你在机场遇见的那个女孩。She is the girl whom you met at the airport.
2682 | 0.57 | 1523 | S

0221 真 [真] /zhēn/ (1) *adv* really
真漂亮。It's really beautiful.
2256 | 0.67 | 1521

0222 啊 [啊] /a/ (1) *part* [modal particle showing affirmation, approval, or consent]
多么美丽的地方啊。What a beautiful place it is!
4509 | 0.34 | 1518 | S

0223 或 [或] /huò/ (2) *conj* or
请给我一本杂志或是其他东西好吗？
May I have a magazine or something?
2484 | 0.61 | 1517 | W

0224 无 [無] /wú/ (2) *v* have no, there be no
目前我们无货供应。We have no stock available at the moment.
1846 | 0.82 | 1516

0225 此 [此] /cǐ/ (2) *pron* this
请对此多加关注。Please give this your attention.
1998 | 0.73 | 1465

0226 成为 [成為] /chéngwéi/ (2) *v* become
人们离开城市去度周末已成为习惯。
It has become the custom for people to go out of town for the weekend.
2034 | 0.72 | 1456

0227 最后 [最後] /zuìhòu/ (1) *adj* final, last
谁笑到最后谁笑得最好。Who laughs last laughs longest.
1609 | 0.9 | 1452

0228 人民 [人民] /rénmín/ (1) *n* (the) people
人民是文艺工作者的母亲。It is the people who nurture our writers and artists.
2754 | 0.53 | 1447

0229 手 [手] /shǒu/ (1) *n* hand
握住瓶子，用另一只手拔瓶塞。Hold the bottle and pull the cork out with the other hand.
2300 | 0.63 | 1447

0230 爱 [愛] /ài/ (1) *v* love, like
我最爱喝滚热的茶。I love my tea very hot.
1887 | 0.77 | 1445

0231 之后 [之後] /zhīhòu/ (2) *loc* after, afterwards
他做完家庭作业之后便到运动场上去了。
After finishing his homework, he went to the sports field.
1695 | 0.83 | 1413

0232 研究 [研究] /yánjiù/ (1) *v* do research, study
她研究过东方各国的文化。She has studied the cultures of Oriental countries.
1958 | 0.72 | 1413

0233 政府 [政府] /zhèngfǔ/ (1) *n* government
这篇文章展示了政府的政策。The article revealed the policies of the government.
2810 | 0.5 | 1396

0234 先生 [先生] /xiānsheng/ (1) *n* Mr; mister, sir
您需要什么？先生。What would you like, sir?
1748 | 0.8 | 1396

0235 内 [內] /nèi/ (1) *loc* inside, within
场内禁烟！No smoking within these walls!
1824 | 0.76 | 1379

0236 外 [外] /wài/ (1) *loc* outside
可能是我把手提袋遗留在博物馆外了。
Most probably I left my bag outside the museum.
1463 | 0.93 | 1367

0237 人们 [人們] /rénmen/ (1) *n* people
她有礼貌地回答了人们的问题。She politely answered people's questions.
1677 | 0.82 | 1366

0238 半 [半] /bàn/ (1) *num* half
我也许会迟到半个小时。I may be half an hour late.
1632 | 0.84 | 1365

0239 死 [死] /sǐ/ (1) *v* die
很明显她快要死了。It became apparent that she was going to die.
1938 | 0.7 | 1364

0240 一直 [一直] /yìzhí/ (1) *adv* straight (in a straight line); always, all along
一直往前走。Go straight ahead.
1554 | 0.88 | 1363

0241 书 [書] /shū/ (1) *n* book
这本书是我的。This book is mine.
1675 | 0.81 | 1363

0242 放 [放] /fàng/ (1) *v* put, place; let go, let off; lay aside; show, play (movies, etc.)
药品不应放在孩子们拿得到的地方。Medicine should not be put where it is accessible to children.
1736 | 0.79 | 1363

0243 特别 [特別] /tèbié/ (1) *adv* especially, particularly
在北京，您特别感兴趣的名胜有什么地方？
What are you particularly interested in seeing in Beijing?
1661 | 0.82 | 1362

0244 记者 [記者] /jìzhě/ (2) *n* reporter, journalist
我们认为她是我们最好的记者。We reckon her among our best reporters.
3607 | 0.38 | 1354

0245 谈 [談] /tán/ (1) *v* talk
我们换一下话题，谈谈你的工作吧。
Let's change the subject, and talk about your job.
1480 | 0.92 | 1354

0246 头 [頭] /tóu/ (1) *n* head; end
那球打在她头上了。The ball hit her on the head.
2009 | 0.67 | 1337

0247 需要 [需要] /xūyào/ (1) *v* need
您还需要别的吗？Do you need anything else?
1578 | 0.84 | 1326

0248 以后 [以後] /yǐhòu/ (1) *loc* after; afterwards
我到学校以后就给他打电话。I'll call him after I get to the school.
2070 | 0.64 | 1322 | S

0249 发生 [發生] /fāshēng/ (1) *v* happen, take place
事实上，这种事情以前也发生过。
In fact, this kind of thing had happened before.
1538 | 0.86 | 1320

0250 出现 [出現] /chūxiàn/ (1) *v* appear
得了这种病，腿上会出现斑点。In this disease spots appear on the legs.
1502 | 0.87 | 1313

0251 先 [先] /xiān/ (1) *adv* first, earlier
汤先上。Soup is served first.
1610 | 0.8 | 1293

0252 一起 [一起] /yìqǐ/ (1) *adv* together
我们常在一起散步。We often go for walks together.
1545 | 0.83 | 1286

0253 国际 [國際] /guójì/ (2) *n* international
国际驾驶执照行吗？Is an international driver's licence OK?
2762 | 0.46 | 1284

0254 一定 [一定] /yídìng/ (1) *adv* certainly
这一定会是一场精彩的比赛。It will certainly be a wonderful game.
1467 | 0.86 | 1267

0255 如 [如] /rú/ (2) *v* like, as, as if; such as
四季如春。It's like spring all the year round.
1751 | 0.72 | 1267

0256 句 [句] /jù/ (1) *clas* [measure word for sentences, poems or spoken words] word, sentence
警察把她说的每句话都记了下来。
The policeman noted down every word that she said.
1714 | 0.74 | 1264

0257 许多 [許多] /xǔduō/ (1) *num* many, plenty of
该系有许多教授和研究生。There are many professors and postgraduate students in the department.
1628 | 0.78 | 1261

0258 少 [少] /shǎo/ (1) *adj* few, rare
很少人知道他的名字。Few people know his name.
1414 | 0.89 | 1258

0259 希望 [希望] /xīwàng/ (1) *v* hope, wish for
希望孩子们都好。I hope that the children are okay.
1499 | 0.84 | 1256

0260 大学 [大學] /dàxué/ (1) *n* university
我终于在大学图书馆找到了那本书。I finally found the book in the university library.
1620 | 0.77 | 1255

0261 心 [心] /xīn/ (1) *n* heart; mind; core, centre
别把它放在心上。Do not take it to heart.
1773 | 0.7 | 1244

0262 作 [作] /zuò/ (1) v do
其中的一个成员被指定作记录。 One of the members was assigned to do the minutes.
1470 | 0.85 | 1244

0263 然后 [然後] /ránhòu/ (1) adv afterwards, then
你走到第二个十字路口，然后向左拐。 You go ahead to the second crossing and then turn left.
1887 | 0.66 | 1241 | S

0264 必须 [必須] /bìxū/ (1) v must, have to
我必须立即跟他说话。 I must talk to him immediately.
1627 | 0.76 | 1235

0265 事情 [事情] /shìqíng/ (1) n matter, thing
你怎么能做出这种事情？ How can you do such a thing?
1654 | 0.75 | 1232

0266 买 [買] /mǎi/ (1) v buy
我去买票。 I'll buy the tickets.
1642 | 0.75 | 1231

0267 为什么 [為什麼] /wèishénme/ (1) pron why
你为什么不打电话给我呢？ Why didn't you call me?
1673 | 0.73 | 1224

0268 请 [請] /qǐng/ (1) v please (do something); ask (somebody to do something); invite
请告诉我怎样拼。 How do you spell it, please?
1562 | 0.78 | 1224

0269 办 [辦] /bàn/ (1) v do
你要是我，你会怎么办？ What would you do if you were me?
1389 | 0.88 | 1218

0270 教育 [教育] /jiàoyù/ (1) v educate
教育儿童须要耐心。 It takes patience to educate children.
2039 | 0.6 | 1216

0271 者 [者] /zhě/ (3) suf [suffix for nouns denoting persons] -ist, -er
医生应说服吸烟者戒烟。 Doctors should try to persuade smokers to kick the habit.
1795 | 0.67 | 1211

0272 难 [難] /nán/ (1) adj difficult
汉语很难学吗？ Is Chinese difficult to learn?
1332 | 0.91 | 1205

0273 当时 [當時] /dāngshí/ (2) time then, at that time
你当时在哪里呢？ Where were you at that time?
1687 | 0.71 | 1205

0274 就 [就] /jiù/ (1) conj [as in 一 . . . 就 . . .] (no sooner . . .) than, at once
她一到就马上告诉我。 Tell me as soon as she arrives.
1630 | 0.73 | 1195

0275 之间 [之間] /zhījiān/ (1) loc between
不要在两顿饭之间吃糖果，以免吃不下饭。 Don't spoil your appetite by eating sweets between meals.
1335 | 0.89 | 1191

0276 当然 [當然] /dāngrán/ (1) adv of course, naturally, only natural
当然想了，我想马上知道。 Of course, I'd like to know at once.
1588 | 0.75 | 1188

0277 学 [學] /xué/ (1) v learn, study
这周我们学了10个句型。 We have learnt ten sentence patterns this week.
1443 | 0.82 | 1182

0278 学校 [學校] /xuéxiào/ (1) n school
你是哪个学校毕业的？ Which school did you graduate from?
1256 | 0.94 | 1181

0279 坐 [坐] /zuò/ (1) v sit
他坐在旁边一声不吭。 He sat there without saying a word.
1845 | 0.64 | 1177

0280 告诉 [告訴] /gàosù/ (1) v tell
告诉我你有何打算。 Tell me what you are driving at.
1494 | 0.79 | 1177

0281 间 [間] /jiān/ (1) clas [measure word for rooms]
我想要订一间房住两个星期。 I'd like to book a room for two weeks.
1282 | 0.92 | 1176

0282 本 [本] /běn/ (2) pron (one's) own; this, current
对不起，本星期天我另有约会。 I am sorry, I have another appointment this Sunday.
2154 | 0.55 | 1175

0283 该 [該] /gāi/ (2) pron this, that, the mentioned
已成立工作组调查该问题。 A working party has been set up to look into this problem.
1440 | 0.81 | 1169

0284 下 [下] /xià/ (1) v come down; alight; rain, snow; get off (from class, work, etc.); give (order, definition, conclusion, etc.); play (chess)
和我一起下楼去吃午饭。 Go downstairs with me to have lunch.
1469 | 0.8 | 1169

0285 便 [便] /biàn/ (2) adv [similar to 就] soon afterwards, just
跟着，我便到一间餐厅。 Then I went to a restaurant.
1744 | 0.67 | 1168 | W

0286 八 [八] /bā/ (1) num eight
三加五等于八。 Three plus five makes eight.
1443 | 0.81 | 1165

0287 自 [自] /zì/ (2) prep from
自北京起飞的中国航空公司123班机误点了。 CAAC Flight 123 from Beijing has been delayed.
1316 | 0.88 | 1162

0288 搞 [搞] /gǎo/ (1) v do
我知道你不是故意的，但确实是你搞的。 I know you didn't mean to, but you did do it.
1349 | 0.86 | 1161

0289 过 [過] /guò/ (1) v cross (road); spend (holiday, etc.); go beyond (time); go through; exceed
过马路要小心。 Be careful when crossing the street.
1511 | 0.77 | 1161

0290 所有 [所有] /suǒyǒu/ (1) pron all
所有的位子都可提前预订。 All seats are bookable in advance.
1258 | 0.92 | 1155

0291 活动 [活動] /huódòng/ (1) v move about for exercise
我真想到户外去活动活动。 I feel like exercising outside.
1961 | 0.59 | 1154

0292 就 [就] /jiù/ (2) prep regarding, as far as . . . is concerned
就我所知，这是真实情况。 This is the truth as far as I know it.
1355 | 0.84 | 1139

0293 呀 [呀] /ya/ (1) part [sentence final particle]
哇，他多帅呀！ Wow, how smart he is!
2304 | 0.49 | 1135 | S

0294 学生 [學生] /xuésheng/ (1) n student
我是学美术的学生，我画许多画。 I am an art student and I paint a lot of pictures.
1414 | 0.8 | 1134

0295 那些 [那些] /nàxiē/ (1) pron those
那些新鞋子弄痛了我。 Those new shoes are killing me!
1397 | 0.81 | 1124

0296 副 [副] /fù/ (2) adj deputy, associate, vice-
我们的副经理是公司的实际负责人。 Our deputy manager is the virtual head of the business.
1938 | 0.58 | 1123

0297 路 [路] /lù/ (1) n road; distance
沿这条路一直走，你就能到广场。 Walk straight down the road and you'll get to the square.
1275 | 0.88 | 1117

0298 不同 [不同] /bùtóng/ (1) adj different
我的想法跟你的不同。 My idea is different from yours.
1440 | 0.77 | 1114

0299 通过 [通過] /tōngguò/ (1) prep by means of, through, via
水通过这根水管流出去。 Water flows out through this pipe.
1623 | 0.68 | 1109

0300 虽然 [雖然] /suīrán/ (1) conj although
虽然他老了，他像小伙子那样努力工作。 Old as he is, he works as hard as a young man.
1299 | 0.85 | 1106

0301 也 [也] /yě/ (2) conj [as in 既 . . . 也] and also, (not) either
我既没有钱也没有朋友。 I have neither money nor friends.
1390 | 0.8 | 1106

0302 发 [發] /fā/ (1) v send out, give out, distribute
请把练习册发下去。 Give the workbooks out, please.
1269 | 0.87 | 1106

0303 朋友 [朋友] /péngyou/ (1) n friend
我的朋友都不吸烟。 None of my friends smoke.
1366 | 0.8 | 1098

0304 市场 [市場] /shìchǎng/ (2) n market
她在股票市场上大发了一笔财。 She's made a killing on the stock market.
2296 | 0.48 | 1096 | W

0305 得到 [得到] /dédào/ (1) v get
任何能得到的帮助他都需要。 He will need any help he can get.
1369 | 0.8 | 1096

0306 受 [受] /shòu/ (2) v receive; be subject to, suffer; endure, bear
无疑，你受了一次打击。 No doubt you have suffered a shock.
1217 | 0.9 | 1095

0307 块 [塊] /kuài/ (1) clas [measure word for thick pieces] lump; [spoken equivalent of the Chinese currency unit 元] yuan
把肉切成一块一块的。 Cut the meat into cubes.
1486 | 0.73 | 1089

0308 政治 [政治] /zhèngzhì/ (1) n politics
是那个事件激起了她对政治的兴趣。 It was that incident that sparked her interest in politics.
1720 | 0.63 | 1087

0309 些 [些] /xiē/ (1) clas some, an amount of
我买了些辣椒。 I have bought some peppers.
1491 | 0.73 | 1085

0310 段 [段] /duàn/ (1) clas section, part; length (of time or distance); paragraph
上山是一段长长的艰难的路。 It is a long hard slog up the mountain.
1184 | 0.91 | 1082

0311 过去 [過去] /guòqù/ (1) time (in the) past, before
现在我们总比过去好得多。 Anyway, things are much better than before.
1204 | 0.9 | 1080

0312 地区 [地區] /dìqū/ (2) n area, region, district
这个地区有许多住宅待售。 Many houses in the area are for sale.
2398 | 0.45 | 1078

0313 思想 [思想] /sīxiǎng/ (1) n thought, idea
每个人都有自己的思想。 Everybody has his own thoughts.
1607 | 0.67 | 1076

0314 很多 [很多] /hěnduō/ num very many, a large number or amount of
那儿有很多人。 There are many people.
1653 | 0.65 | 1074 | S

0315 下 [下] /xià/ (1) *clas* [measure word for counting actions] one stroke, (do) once
我要去一下银行。 I am just going to run down to the bank.
1600 | 0.67 | 1071

0316 精神 [精神] /jīngshén/ (1) *n* spirit, mind, mental state; essence; vigour, vitality
事故发生后她精神十分紧张。 She was in a very overwrought state after the accident.
1392 | 0.77 | 1070

0317 参加 [參加] /cānjiā/ (1) *v* take part in, participate; join
你经常参加什么活动项目？ Which kinds of activities do you often take part in?
1667 | 0.64 | 1061

0318 及 [及] /jí/ (2) *conj* and
这家商店销售自行车及零件。 This shop sells bicycles and spare parts.
1857 | 0.57 | 1056 | W

0319 就是 [就是] /jiùshì/ (2) *v* [emphasising that something is precisely or exactly what is stated] be exactly
我要的就是这一个。 What I want is exactly this one.
1776 | 0.59 | 1052 | S

0320 早 [早] /zǎo/ (1) *adj* early
我每天起得很早。 I get up early every day.
1190 | 0.88 | 1049

0321 比较 [比較] /bǐjiào/ (1) *adv* comparatively, relatively
我要比较好一点的东西。 I want something better.
1574 | 0.67 | 1049 | S

0322 场 [場] /cháng, chǎng/ (1) *clas* [measure word for processes or courses of occurrence such as rain, snow, illness, etc.] period, spell; [measure word for recreational or sports activities] show, match
关于这场比赛的最新消息是什么？ What's the latest news about the match?
1188 | 0.88 | 1049

0323 其他 [其他] /qítā/ (2) *pron* other
我们中一些人学习俄语，其他人学习英语。 Some of us study Russian, others English.
1308 | 0.8 | 1049

0324 送 [送] /sòng/ (1) *v* deliver; give as a gift; see off; escort
我们在 4 小时内将衣服给您送来。 We'll deliver your clothes within four hours.
1255 | 0.83 | 1047

0325 变 [變] /biàn/ (1) *v* change
你知道这儿的天气会很快变的。 You know, the weather here can change very quickly.
1199 | 0.87 | 1045

0326 完全 [完全] /wánquán/ (1) *adj* complete, whole
然而，科学家如今认为，情况并非完全如此。 Today, however, scientists say this is not the whole story.
1154 | 0.9 | 1044

0327 由于 [由於] /yóuyú/ (2) *prep* due to
由于事故这一条路不得不封闭几小时。 Due to the accident, the road had to be closed for several hours.
1405 | 0.74 | 1042

0328 别 [別] /bié/ (1) *adv* [negative imperative] don't, had better not
别再烦我。 Stop bothering me.
1740 | 0.59 | 1035

0329 字 [字] /zì/ (1) *n* (Chinese) character
信中有几个字已涂掉了。 Several characters in the letter had been blotted out.
1305 | 0.79 | 1033

0330 能够 [能夠] /nénggòu/ (1) *v* be able to, be capable of
我完全能够独自处理。 I'm well able to manage on my own.
1381 | 0.75 | 1033

0331 后来 [後來] /hòulái/ (2) *time* afterwards
后来怎么样？ What happened afterwards?
1461 | 0.71 | 1032

0332 六 [六] /liù/ (1) *num* six
他已失业六个月了。 He's been out of work for six months.
1194 | 0.86 | 1025

0333 影响 [影響] /yǐngxiǎng/ (1) *v* influence
他不想说什么来影响我的决定。 He did not want to say anything to influence my decision.
1345 | 0.76 | 1025

0334 领导 [領導] /lǐngdǎo/ (1) *n* leader, leadership
国家对国防活动实行统一的领导。 The state exercises unified leadership over defence-related activities.
1679 | 0.61 | 1024

0335 得 [得] /dé, děi/ (1, 1) *v* get, gain; must, have to; need
我得听他那些没完没了的牢骚。 I had to listen to a long recital of all his complaints.
1433 | 0.71 | 1023

0336 任何 [任何] /rènhé/ (1) *pron* any
我已经没有任何亲人了。 I no longer have any relatives.
1149 | 0.89 | 1021

0337 准备 [準備] /zhǔnbèi/ (1) *v* prepare, get ready
我们正在准备装箱单。 We are preparing the packing list.
1138 | 0.9 | 1020

0338 电话 [電話] /diànhuà/ (1) *n* telephone, telephone call
你不能使用长途电话。 You can't make a long-distance telephone call.
1180 | 0.86 | 1016

0339 其实 [其實] /qíshí/ (3) *adv* actually
别看她批评你，她其实很喜欢你。 Despite her criticism, she is actually very fond of you.
1354 | 0.75 | 1015

0340 车 [車] /chē/ (1) *n* car, vehicle; cart
要是我们有一辆车多好啊。 I wish we had a car.
1219 | 0.83 | 1013

3. Food

Flavour:

香	香	*xiāng*	tasty, appetising	1348
苦	苦	*kǔ*	bitter	1366
甜	甜	*tián*	sweet	3774
鲜	鮮	*xiān*	tasty, delicious	4415
酸	酸	*suān*	sour	4624
辣	辣	*là*	hot, spicy	6994
咸	咸	*xián*	salty	8236
麻	麻	*má*	hot, spicy	11495

Main food:

粥	粥	*zhōu*	congee	4134
面包	麵包	*miànbāo*	bread	4639
饺子	餃子	*jiǎozi*	dumpling	4640
饼	餅	*bǐng*	cake, pastry	5934
馒头	饅頭	*mántou*	steamed bread	6222
大米	大米	*dàmǐ*	rice	8340
面粉	麵粉	*miànfěn*	(wheat) flour	8703
包子	包子	*bāozi*	steamed bun	9309
米饭	米飯	*mǐfàn*	boiled rice	16645
馄饨	餛飩	*húntun*	wonton	21741
米粉	米粉	*mǐfěn*	rice flour	23647

Meat and fish:

鱼	魚	*yú*	fish	885
鸡	雞	*jī*	chicken	1353
鸭	鴨	*yā*	duck	4088
猪肉	豬肉	*zhūròu*	pork	5684
虾	蝦	*xiā*	shrimp, prawn	6576
牛肉	牛肉	*niúròu*	beef	6765
鹅	鵝	*é*	goose	6890
螃蟹	螃蟹	*pángxiè*	crab	7988
羊肉	羊肉	*yángròu*	mutton	9946
鲤鱼	鯉魚	*lǐyú*	carp	20863
比目鱼	比目魚	*bǐmùyú*	flatfish	30009
八带鱼	八帶魚	*bādàiyú*	octopus	
鲍鱼	鮑魚	*bàoyú*	abalone	
鳊鱼	鯿魚	*biānyú*	bream	
鲑鱼	鮭魚	*guīyú*	salmon	
蚝	蚝	*háo*	oyster	
黄鱼	黃魚	*huángyú*	yellow croaker	
鳗鱼	鰻魚	*mányú*	eel	
青鱼	青魚	*qīngyú*	herring	
沙丁鱼	沙丁魚	*shādīngyú*	sardine	
鳟鱼	鱒魚	*zūnyú*	trout	

Vegetables:

豆腐	豆腐	*dòufu*	tofu, bean curd	**6880**
葱	蔥	*cōng*	spring onions	**7355**
白菜	白菜	*báicài*	Chinese leaf	**8427**
西红柿	西紅柿	*xīhóngshì*	tomato	**9060**
黄瓜	黃瓜	*huángguā*	cucumber	**9148**
茄子	茄子	*qiézi*	eggplant, aubergine	**9911**
蘑菇	蘑菇	*mógu*	mushroom	**10160**
青菜	青菜	*qīngcài*	Chinese cabbage	**13101**
番茄	番茄	*fānqié*	tomato	**14718**
胡萝卜	胡蘿蔔	*húluóbo*	carrot	**16499**
菠菜	菠菜	*bōcài*	spinach	**23673**
洋葱	洋蔥	*yángcōng*	onion	**23798**
木耳	木耳	*mù'ěr*	edible tree fungus	**24881**
青椒	青椒	*qīngjiāo*	green pepper	**26964**

Food preparation:

Cooking:

烧	燒	*shāo*	cook, stew	**1134**
炸	炸	*zhá*	deep fry	**2191**
炒	炒	*chǎo*	sauté, stir fry	**2570**
烤	烤	*kǎo*	roast, bake	**3680**
蒸	蒸	*zhēng*	steam	**6805**
涮	涮	*shuàn*	boil in liquid	**11754**
红烧	紅燒	*hóngshāo*	braise in soy sauce	**19288**
煎	煎	*jiān*	pan fry	**29515**

Cutting:

块	塊	*kuài*	lump, cube	**307**
片	片	*piàn*	slice	**381**
球	球	*qiú*	ball	**1376**
丝	絲	*sī*	thread	**2951**
丁	丁	*dīng*	dice	**30720**

Seasoning:

糖	糖	*táng*	sugar	**2638**
盐	鹽	*yán*	salt	**3304**
醋	醋	*cù*	vinegar	**4915**
姜	薑	*jiāng*	ginger	**5268**
辣椒	辣椒	*làjiāo*	chilli, hot pepper	**7634**
酱油	醬油	*jiàngyóu*	soy sauce	**8485**
芝麻	芝麻	*zhīma*	sesame	**8604**
蒜	蒜	*suàn*	garlic	**8896**
味精	味精	*wèijīng*	monosodium glutamate	**16732**
胡椒粉	胡椒粉	*hújiāofěn*	pepper powder	**27311**

0341 啊 [啊] /ā, á, ǎ/ (1) *interj* [interjection expressing surprise, admiration, etc.] oh
啊！太贵了。 Oh, it's so expensive.
2418 | 0.42 | 1008 | S

0342 往 [往] /wǎng/ (1) *prep* towards
请你们往后挪。 Will you move towards the back please?
1466 | 0.69 | 1006

0343 其中 [其中] /qízhōng/ (2) *pron* among them, in it
他就是其中之一。 He was one of them.
1435 | 0.7 | 1004

0344 城市 [城市] /chéngshì/ (1) *n* city
世界上最大的城市是哪个？ Which is the largest city in the world?
1392 | 0.72 | 1001

0345 办法 [辦法] /bànfǎ/ (1) *n* method, means
一切办法都试过了。 All possible means have been tried.
1077 | 0.93 | 1001

0346 管理 [管理] /guǎnlǐ/ (2) *v* manage
老板不在时谁来管理？ Who will manage while the boss is away?
1997 | 0.5 | 999 | W

0347 越 [越] /yuè/ (2) *adv* [as in 越 . . . 越] (the more . . .) the more
你付出的越多，你得到的也就越多。 The more you give, the more you get.
1151 | 0.87 | 996

0348 下来 [下來] /xiàlái/ (1) *v* come down, descend
快点下来，你的朋友在门口等你呢。 Hurry down, your friend's at the door.
1345 | 0.73 | 985

0349 解决 [解決] /jiějué/ (1) *v* solve (a problem), settle (a dispute)
要研究解决这个问题。 We should investigate this problem and solve it.
1567 | 0.63 | 985

0350 技术 [技術] /jìshù/ (1) *n* technology
科学技术是第一生产力。 Science and technology are a primary productive force.
2050 | 0.48 | 983

0351 学习 [學習] /xuéxí/ (1) *v* learn, study
读书是学习，使用也是学习。 Reading is learning, but applying is also learning.
1254 | 0.78 | 980

0352 当 [當] /dāng, dàng/ (1, 2) *v* work as; regard as
我当了厨师五年了。 I've worked as a cook for five years.
1219 | 0.8 | 980

0353 喜欢 [喜歡] /xǐhuān/ (1) *v* like, enjoy
人们不喜欢有这么多广告。 People don't like so much advertising.
1319 | 0.74 | 976

0354 身 [身] /shēn/ (2) *n* body
身心一致。 Body and soul are in harmony.
1472 | 0.66 | 975

0355 着 [著] /zhāo/ (2) *n* move (in chess), step, trick
一着不慎，满盘皆输。 One careless move loses the whole game.
1888 | 0.52 | 975

0356 作为 [作為] /zuòwéi/ (2) *v* as, take as, regard as
我们把钢作为主要的工程材料。 We take steel as the leading engineering material.
1303 | 0.75 | 974

0357 曾 [曾] /céng/ (2) *adv* [referring to something that happened previously] once
我曾想给你打电话。 I once thought of ringing you.
1244 | 0.78 | 965

0358 快 [快] /kuài/ (1) *adj* fast, quick
他走路走不快。 He cannot walk very fast.
1108 | 0.87 | 962

0359 对于 [對於] /duìyú/ (2) *prep* regarding, as to, for, about
他对于人生充满着幻想。 He is very romantic about life.
1255 | 0.77 | 960

0360 生 [生] /shēng/ (2) *v* give birth to, bear; become (rusty, ill, etc.); light (a fire)
他生于1970年。 He was born in 1970.
1215 | 0.79 | 960

0361 应 [應] /yīng, yìng/ (2, 3) *v* ought to, should; answer, respond, echo; comply with
公共汽车司机应对旅客的安全负责。 The bus driver should answer for the safety of the passengers.
1475 | 0.65 | 955 | W

0362 近 [近] /jìn/ (1) *adj* near
邮局离学校很近。 The post office is very near to the school.
1421 | 0.67 | 954

0363 决定 [決定] /juédìng/ (1) *v* decide
你们决定去哪个国家了吗？ Have you decided which country to go to?
1172 | 0.8 | 940

0364 知 [知] /zhī/ (3) *v* know
他对这计划略有所知。 He knows a little about the plan.
1240 | 0.76 | 940

0365 连 [連] /lián/ (1) *prep* [as in 连 . . . 都(也) . . .] even
他小气极了，连自己的那份钱也不付。 He's too mean even to pay his share.
1190 | 0.79 | 939

0366 一切 [一切] /yíqiè/ (1) *pron* everything, all
一切都会安排妥当的。 Everything will be taken care of.
1126 | 0.83 | 934

0367 或者 [或者] /huòzhě/ (1) *conj* or
他想当医生或者经商。 He wants to be a doctor or go into business.
1372 | 0.68 | 931

0368 则 [則] /zé/ (2) conj [indicating cause, condition, contrast, etc.] then
物体受热则膨胀。When matter is heated, it expands.
1417 | 0.66 | 931

0369 同时 [同時] /tóngshí/ (1) conj at the same time, simultaneously; besides, moreover
我们必须努力工作，但同时也要有足够的休息。We must work hard, but we must get sufficient rest at the same time.
1284 | 0.72 | 926

0370 提出 [提出] /tíchū/ v raise (an issue), propose, suggest
你竟提出这种事，真荒唐。It is absurd of you to suggest such a thing.
1453 | 0.64 | 926

0371 了解 [瞭解] /liǎojiě/ (1) v get to know, understand
让我们进一步相互了解吧。Let's get better acquainted.
1119 | 0.83 | 924

0372 别人 [別人] /biérén/ (1) pron other people
我们难免要和别人竞争。We cannot avoid competing with others.
1237 | 0.75 | 921

0373 如何 [如何] /rúhé/ (2) pron how
你近况如何？How are you getting along?
1075 | 0.85 | 918

0374 个人 [個人] /gèrén/ (2) n individual
这侵害了我个人的权利。This impinges on my rights as an individual.
1079 | 0.85 | 912

0375 百 [百] /bǎi/ (1) num hundred
工业经济到现在已经有三百多年。It has been 300 years since the industrial economy started.
1131 | 0.8 | 909

0376 站 [站] /zhàn/ (1) v stand
他正站在窗口看着我们呢。He was standing by the window and looking at us.
1339 | 0.67 | 898

0377 算 [算] /suàn/ (1) v calculate; regard as
你算出假期得花多少钱了吗？Have you calculated how much the holiday will cost?
1295 | 0.69 | 897

0378 啦 [啦] /la/ (1) part [sentence final particle combining 了 and 啊]
你怎么啦？What's the matter with you?
2357 | 0.38 | 895 | S

0379 给 [給] /gěi/ (1) v give
他给了她一个深情的吻。He gave her a loving kiss.
1094 | 0.81 | 891

0380 方式 [方式] /fāngshì/ (2) n way, pattern or style of doing things
我不习惯他们的生活方式。I am not used to their way of living.
1163 | 0.77 | 890

0381 片 [片] /piàn/ (1) clas [measure word for flat and thin pieces] slice; [with 一 as in 一片 used for a vast expanse of something such as land and water]; [measure word for scene, sound, atmosphere, speech, intention, etc.]
她正读着书，一片树叶落到她的书上。A leaf came upon her book as she was reading.
1030 | 0.86 | 886

0382 至 [至] /zhì/ (2) v arrive, reach
她的连衣裙垂至脚踝。Her dress reached down to her ankles.
1511 | 0.59 | 886 | W

0383 以及 [以及] /yǐjí/ (2) conj and, as well as, along with
她显然丝毫也不顾及别人以及别人的感情。She shows a total disregard for other people and their feelings.
1347 | 0.66 | 885

0384 有些 [有些] /yǒuxiē/ (1) pron some
有些学生做了作业，但大多数都没做。Some of the students have done their homework but most haven't.
1111 | 0.8 | 884

0385 环境 [環境] /huánjìng/ (2) n environment
你在新的环境中交朋友了吗？Have you made friends yet in your new environment?
1426 | 0.62 | 881

0386 老师 [老師] /lǎoshī/ (1) n teacher
老师进来时他们停止了谈话。When the teacher came in, they stopped talking.
1162 | 0.75 | 876

0387 笑 [笑] /xiào/ (1) v laugh, smile
她母亲向她笑了笑。Her mother smiled at her.
2161 | 0.4 | 874

0388 七 [七] /qī/ (1) num seven
一个星期有七天。There are seven days in a week.
1046 | 0.83 | 873

0389 因此 [因此] /yīncǐ/ (2) conj as such, so, therefore, as a result
因此让我们重新开始。So let us begin anew.
1172 | 0.74 | 872

0390 结果 [結果] /jiéguǒ/ (3) n result, outcome
他总结了得到的结果。He summed up his results.
995 | 0.87 | 869

0391 有人 [有人] /yǒurén/ pron someone
如果有人打扰他，他就会生气。If someone interrupted him he got angry.
1046 | 0.83 | 868

0392 一般 [一般] /yìbān/ (1) adv generally, as a rule
对于这种商品，我们一般不给折扣。As a rule, we do not allow any discount for this commodity.
1106 | 0.78 | 867

0393 方 [方] /fāng/ (3) n side, party; square; direction
老师来的时候，孩子们向各方散开了。The children scattered in all directions when the teacher approached.
1032 | 0.84 | 862

0394 包括 [包括] /bāokuò/ (2) v include, comprise
租金已包括管理费。The management fee is included in the rent.
1176 | 0.73 | 862

0395 分 [分] /fēn/ (1) v divide, separate, differentiate; distribute
我分不清这两个双胞胎的女孩子。I can't tell the twin girls apart.
943 | 0.91 | 857

0396 继续 [繼續] /jìxù/ (1) v continue
我母亲的鼓励使我决心继续学业。My mum's encouragement made me determined to continue with my study.
1285 | 0.66 | 854

0397 回来 [回來] /huílái/ (1) v return
假若一切顺利，我天黑之前就回来。If everything goes according to the plan, I shall return before dark.
1344 | 0.63 | 851

0398 表示 [表示] /biǎoshì/ (1) v express
我谨表示我的谢意。I should like to express my appreciation.
1575 | 0.54 | 850

0399 跑 [跑] /pǎo/ (1) v run
他越跑越快。He ran faster and faster.
1195 | 0.71 | 849

0400 会议 [會議] /huìyì/ (2) n meeting
会议在混乱中结束了。The meeting broke up amid rowdy scenes.
1800 | 0.47 | 848 | W

0401 成功 [成功] /chénggōng/ (2) adj successful
这一产品非常成功，其名称已经家喻户晓。The product is so successful that its name has become a household word.
1111 | 0.76 | 845

0402 一样 [一樣] /yíyàng/ (1) aux [usually occurring in 像... 一样] like
时间的流逝像流水一样。Time flows away like running water.
1045 | 0.81 | 845

0403 能力 [能力] /nénglì/ (2) n ability, capability
她相信他有能力照料她。She trusted in his ability to look after her.
1117 | 0.75 | 843

0404 可是 [可是] /kěshì/ (1) conj but
我本来要写信的，可是把你的地址弄丢了。I was going to write, but I lost your address.
1228 | 0.69 | 842

0405 机会 [機會] /jīhuì/ (1) n opportunity
机会带来成功。Opportunity brings success.
963 | 0.87 | 842

0406 同志 [同志] /tóngzhì/ (1) n comrade; [more recent usage] someone who is homosexual
对于这种同志，我们应给予热情的鼓励和欢迎。We should warmly encourage and welcome such comrades.
1136 | 0.74 | 841

0407 因 [因] /yīn/ prep because of, as a result of, according to
比赛因雨而推迟举行。The match was put off because of rain.
1097 | 0.76 | 838

0408 有的 [有的] /yǒude/ (1) pron some
有的赞成，有的反对。Some are in favour of it, some are against it.
1008 | 0.83 | 838

0409 强 [強] /qiáng/ (2) adj strong, powerful, better
我们的生活条件一年比一年强。Our living conditions are getting better each year.
942 | 0.89 | 837

0410 民族 [民族] /mínzú/ (1) n nationality
中国是一个统一的多民族国家，有56个民族。China is a unified, multinational country, with 56 ethnic nationalities in all.
1287 | 0.65 | 836

0411 天 [天] /tiān/ (1) n day; sky, air; heaven; time of day; weather
天很可能要下雨了。It will probably rain.
1051 | 0.78 | 823

0412 部 [部] /bù/ (2) clas [measure word for machines and vehicles, etc.]; [measure word for books and films, etc.]
我要租一部汽车。I want to rent a car.
999 | 0.82 | 818

0413 多少 [多少] /duōshǎo/ (1) pron how many, how much; an unspecified number or amount
人口中男女的比例是多少？What is the proportion of men to women in the population?
1087 | 0.75 | 818

0414 整个 [整個] /zhěnggè/ (2) adj whole, entire, all
整个上午我们都在买新衣服。We shopped all morning for new coats.
891 | 0.92 | 816

0415 过程 [過程] /guòchéng/ (2) n process, course of actions
工程师必须学习各种工艺过程。Engineers must study various industrial processes.
1062 | 0.77 | 816

0416 改革 [改革] /gǎigé/ (2) v reform
改革经济体制，最重要的是人才。In reforming the economic structure, what matters most is capable people.
1809 | 0.45 | 815 | W

0417 相 [相] /xiāng/ (2) adv each other
学生和老师相混合。Teachers and students blended with each other.
890 | 0.91 | 807

0418 家庭 [家庭] /jiātíng/ (1) n family
她无钱养活一个大家庭。She lacks the means to support a large family.
945 | 0.85 | 807

0419 穿 [穿] /chuān/ (1) v wear, put on; bore a hole; cross
穿上你的雨衣，外面下着大雨。Put on your raincoat; it's pouring outside!
1097 | 0.73 | 805

0420 条件 [條件] /tiáojiàn/ (1) *n* condition
她同意了我的所有的条件。 She agreed to all
my conditions.
1124 | 0.72 | 804

0421 认识 [認識] /rènshí/ (1) *v* know, understand;
recognise
我不认识他。 I do not know him.
862 | 0.93 | 804

0422 目前 [目前] /mùqián/ (1) *time* currently,
at the present time
目前他正在度假。 At present he is on holiday.
1711 | 0.47 | 802

0423 人员 [人員] /rényuán/ (2) *n* staff,
personnel
我们雇佣临时工以弥补人员不足。
We employ part-timers to make up
for staff shortage.
1388 | 0.58 | 800 | W

0424 要求 [要求] /yāoqiú/ (1) *v* ask for, request,
demand
我停了下来，他要求搭便车。 I stopped and
he asked me for a lift.
1111 | 0.72 | 800

0425 另 [另] /lìng/ (2) *adj* other, another
一些客户在另一房间等候。 Several clients are
waiting in the other room.
940 | 0.85 | 799

0426 进入 [進入] /jìnrù/ (2) *v* enter, get into
我进入车内。 I got into the car.
1077 | 0.74 | 798

0427 作用 [作用] /zuòyòng/ (2) *n* action, effect; role,
function
这药起作用了。 The medicine took effect.
1217 | 0.65 | 795

0428 敢 [敢] /gǎn/ (1) *v* dare
她敢来吗？ Dare she come?
1177 | 0.68 | 795

0429 金 [金] /jīn/ (2) *n* gold, golden; metal;
money
我们有14K和18K的金项链、手链和耳环。
We have 14K and 18K gold necklaces,
chains and earrings.
853 | 0.92 | 784

0430 甚至 [甚至] /shènzhì/ (3) *adv* even
她的发音甚至比她老师的还要好。 Her
pronunciation is even better than that of her
teacher.
976 | 0.8 | 783

0431 掉 [掉] /diào/ (1) *v* drop
不要把烟灰掉在地毯上。 Don't drop cigarette
ash on the carpet.
1042 | 0.75 | 783

0432 一样 [一樣] /yíyàng/ (1) *adj* same
成本还是一样。 The costs would still be the
same.
1097 | 0.71 | 779

0433 万 [萬] /wàn/ (1) *num* 10,000
观众总计达两万人。 The audience totalled
20,000.
1099 | 0.71 | 776

0434 拉 [拉] /lā/ (1) *v* pull
如果你拉猫的尾巴，它会把你抓伤。
The cat will scratch you if you pull
her tail.
1039 | 0.75 | 774

0435 人类 [人類] /rénlèi/ (2) *n* human being,
mankind, man
人类正在与污染作斗争。 Man is fighting a
battle against pollution.
976 | 0.79 | 770

0436 表现 [表現] /biǎoxiàn/ (1) *v* manifest, show;
behave
孩子们都表现得很好。 The children all
behaved well.
921 | 0.84 | 770

0437 份 [份] /fèn/ (2) *clas* [measure word for
meals, gifts, newspapers, etc.] portion, part,
share
请给我两份火腿三明治。 Two ham
sandwiches, please.
843 | 0.91 | 766

0438 对 [對] /duì/ (1) *adj* right, correct; opposite
(in direction)
你看我的判断对吗？ Do you think my
judgement is correct?
836 | 0.91 | 764 | S

0439 起 [起] /qǐ/ (1) *loc* [usually occurring with 从
as in 从 . . . 起] starting from
从哪天起放假？ When does the vacation
begin?
873 | 0.88 | 764

0440 项 [項] /xiàng/ (2) *clas* [measure word for
items stipulated, planned, enumerated, or for
an account of facts or events]
他刚开始一项新工作。 He's just started a new
job.
1679 | 0.45 | 762 | W

0441 原因 [原因] /yuányīn/ (2) *n* cause, reason
我知道他生气的原因。 I know the reason why
he was angry.
905 | 0.84 | 759

0442 建设 [建設] /jiànshè/ (1) *v* build, construct
我要努力工作建设祖国。 I wanted to work
hard to build up my country.
2470 | 0.31 | 755 | W

0443 边 [邊] /biān/ (1) *n* side; edge
正方形有四条边，而圆形没有边。
A square has four sides but a circle has
no sides.
1039 | 0.72 | 753

0444 管 [管] /guǎn/ (2) *v* manage, run, administer;
take care (of), care about
市场要管好。 Markets must be managed
properly.
963 | 0.78 | 753

0445 感到 [感到] /gǎndào/ (1) *v* feel
我感到晕船。 I feel seasick.
969 | 0.78 | 752

0446 感觉 [感覺] /gǎnjué/ (2) *n* feeling
我很喜欢这种感觉。 I love this feeling.
994 | 0.76 | 750

0447 入 [入] /rù/ (2) v enter
严禁入内！No admittance!
934 | 0.8 | 749

0448 不要 [不要] /búyào/ (1) adv [negative imperative] don't
不要拖延时间！Don't hold up the game!
970 | 0.77 | 747

0449 十分 [十分] /shífēn/ (1) adv very, fully
若要我帮忙，我十分乐意相助。If you would like me to help you, I would be very glad to.
943 | 0.79 | 745

0450 部队 [部隊] /bùduì/ (2) n army, troops
短暂的战斗之后部队攻占了这个城镇。The troops carried the town after a brief fight.
947 | 0.79 | 745

0451 有关 [有關] /yǒuguān/ (2) v have something to do with
这跟她今天去银行有关吗？Does this have anything to do with her being at the bank today?
1454 | 0.51 | 741

0452 父亲 [父親] /fùqīn/ (1) n father
你父亲在哪儿？Where is your father?
996 | 0.74 | 738

0453 怕 [怕] /pà/ (1) v be afraid, fear
大多数人都怕痛。Most people fear pain.
1109 | 0.67 | 738

0454 远 [遠] /yuǎn/ (1) adj far
海滨离这儿不远。The beach is not far from here.
925 | 0.8 | 737

0455 不断 [不斷] /búduàn/ (2) adv unceasingly, always
汽车业总是不断推出新型汽车。The car industry is always producing new models.
1098 | 0.67 | 736

0456 儿子 [兒子] /érzi/ (1) n son
看到她的儿子，她非常高兴。She was filled with joy on seeing her son.
976 | 0.75 | 736

0457 按 [按] /àn/ (2) prep according to
他按老规矩办事。He does everything according to old rules and regulations.
835 | 0.88 | 736

0458 接受 [接受] /jiēshòu/ (2) v accept
此时，我只能请您接受我的歉意。Meanwhile, I can only ask you to accept my apology.
915 | 0.81 | 736

0459 面 [面] /miàn/ (2) n face, surface; side; (wheat) flour
卡片是面向上的。The cards were face upward.
954 | 0.77 | 735

0460 米 [米] /mǐ/ (1) clas [standard measure term] metre
这两所房子相距500米。The two houses are 500 metres apart.
983 | 0.75 | 734

0461 注意 [注意] /zhùyì/ (1) v pay attention to; take notice of, note
请注意这些问题。Please pay attention to these issues.
878 | 0.84 | 734

0462 年代 [年代] /niándài/ (2) n a decade of a century; years, time
这种机器是七十年代发明的。This kind of machine was invented in the 1970s.
956 | 0.77 | 733

0463 世纪 [世紀] /shìjì/ (2) n century
21世纪是高科技发展的世纪。The twenty-first century will see rapid development of high technology.
1174 | 0.62 | 733

0464 哪 [哪] /nǎ/ (1) pron what, which, where, how
哪个是你的？Which one is yours?
1140 | 0.64 | 733

0465 不过 [不過] /búguò/ (2) conj only; but
不过我很忙。But I'm busy.
993 | 0.74 | 731

0466 主要 [主要] /zhǔyào/ (1) adj main, major
健美运动已成为人们现代生活的主要内容之一。Body building has become one of the main parts of man's modern life.
1087 | 0.67 | 730

0467 存在 [存在] /cúnzài/ (2) v exist
那样的事只存在于幻想中。Such things exist only in fancy.
916 | 0.8 | 730

0468 男 [男] /nán/ (1) adj male, man
那个男青年是谁？Who's that young man?
832 | 0.88 | 728

0469 建立 [建立] /jiànlì/ (2) v establish, set up
这家公司在25年前就建立了。The company was established 25 years ago.
1402 | 0.52 | 726

0470 靠 [靠] /kào/ (2) v depend upon; be due to; lean against; come up to
他的成功主要靠运气。His success was largely due to luck.
751 | 0.97 | 725

0471 座 [座] /zuò/ (1) clas [measure word used for mountains, buildings, bridges, structures, and statues, etc.]
树丛中有一座漂亮的建筑物。There is a beautiful building among the trees.
810 | 0.89 | 723

0472 努力 [努力] /nǔlì/ (1) v strive to, try one's best to; make efforts to
我会努力去解决这个困难的。I'll try to tackle this difficult task.
1139 | 0.63 | 721

0473 门 [門] /mén/ (1) n door, gate
如果门开不开的话，就踢它一脚。If the door won't open, give it a kick.
1038 | 0.69 | 719

0474 相信 [相信] /xiāngxìn/ (1) v believe, trust, be convinced
有充分的理由相信那个人是无辜的。There is ample reason to believe that the man is innocent.
831 | 0.87 | 719

0475 组织 [組織] /zǔzhī/ (1) n organisation
他们加入了这个组织。They affiliated themselves with the organisation.
1267 | 0.57 | 718

0476 仍 [仍] /réng/ (2) adv still
伤口仍在渗血。Blood was still oozing from the wound.
945 | 0.76 | 715 | W

0477 处 [處] /chù/ (2) n place; department
无处可像家，在家千日好。There is no place like home.
807 | 0.88 | 710

0478 介绍 [介紹] /jièshào/ (1) v introduce
我可以自我介绍吗？May I introduce myself?
1059 | 0.67 | 708

0479 只 [只] /zhī/ (1) clas [measure word for one of a pair, birds and some animals, or boats, boxes, etc.]
狗在追一只兔子。The dog was running after a rabbit.
921 | 0.77 | 706

0480 某 [某] /mǒu/ (2) pron some, certain
他为某个金融公司工作。He works for some finance outfit.
953 | 0.74 | 705

0481 清楚 [清楚] /qīngchǔ/ (1) adj clear
证据确凿，事实清楚。The evidence is certain and the facts are clear.
1268 | 0.56 | 704 | S

0482 刚 [剛] /gāng/ (1) adv just, barely; just now
她刚登上公共汽车，汽车就开动了。She got on the bus just as it was leaving.
907 | 0.78 | 703

0483 母亲 [母親] /mǔqīn/ (1) n mother
孩子们跟着母亲进了房间。The children followed their mother into the room.
918 | 0.77 | 703

4. Clothing

帽子	帽子	*màozi*	hat, cap	**3172**
裤子	褲子	*kùzi*	trousers, pants	**4641**
西装	西裝	*xīzhuāng*	(Western-style) suit	**6476**
裙子	裙子	*qúnzi*	skirt	**6997**
袜子	襪子	*wàzi*	socks, stockings	**7760**
鞋子	鞋子	*xiézi*	shoes	**8337**
衬衫	襯衫	*chènshān*	shirt, blouse	**8436**
大衣	大衣	*dàyī*	coat, overcoat	**9491**
领带	領帶	*lǐngdài*	tie, necktie	**9964**
西服	西服	*xīfú*	(Western-style) suit	**10026**
毛衣	毛衣	*máoyī*	sweater	**12676**
手套	手套	*shǒutào*	glove, mitten	**13245**
牛仔裤	牛仔褲	*niúzǎikù*	jeans	**14090**
拖鞋	拖鞋	*tuōxié*	slippers	**14209**
皮带	皮帶	*pídài*	belt	**15133**
睡衣	睡衣	*shuìyī*	pyjamas	**17150**
围巾	圍巾	*wéijīn*	scarf, shawl	**17849**
内裤	內褲	*nèikù*	underwear	**19771**
外套	外套	*wàitào*	coat	**21147**
胸罩	胸罩	*xiōngzhào*	brassiere	**28924**
T恤衫	T恤衫	*tīxùshān*	T-shirt	
休闲服	休閒服	*xiūxián fú*	casual clothing	
泳衣	泳衣	*yǒngyì*	swimsuit, bathing suit	
雨衣	雨衣	*yǔyī*	raincoat	
浴袍	浴袍	*yùpáo*	bathrobe	

0484 代表 [代表] /dàibiǎo/ (1) *n* representative, delegate
工人们选出了几位代表。 The workers elected several representatives.
1299 | 0.54 | 703

0485 只要 [只要] /zhǐyào/ (2) *conj* if
当然可以，只要你愿意。 You may, if you like.
816 | 0.86 | 700

0486 于是 [於是] /yúshì/ (2) *conj* thereupon, and so, then
于是他出去了。 And then he took his departure.
922 | 0.76 | 700

0487 来说 [來說] /láishuō/ (3) *aux* [equivalent of 来讲, interpreting a topic from a particular viewpoint]
这对我来说是个谜。 It's a mystery to me.
848 | 0.82 | 698

0488 内容 [内容] /nèiróng/ (1) *n* content
读者要对原文中的内容批判地使用。 The reader must quote the content in the source article critically.
904 | 0.77 | 695

0489 山 [山] /shān/ (1) *n* mountain, hill
我们在山上一个小屋里度假。 We spend our holidays in a small house in the mountains.
733 | 0.95 | 695

0490 跟 [跟] /gēn/ *v* follow
跟着感觉走。 Follow your instincts.
1065 | 0.65 | 693

0491 既 [既] /jì/ (2) *conj* since, now that; as well as
她既漂亮又聪明。 She is both pretty and smart.
854 | 0.81 | 691

0492 艺术 [藝術] /yìshù/ (1) *n* art
使你的学生接触艺术。 Expose your students to art.
959 | 0.72 | 688

0493 产生 [產生] /chǎnshēng/ (2) *v* arise, generate
煤燃烧时产生热量。 When coal burns, it generates heat.
890 | 0.77 | 688

0494 反 [反] /fǎn/ (3) *v* oppose, combat; reverse; turn against
市长确信反犯罪活动之战争必定胜利。 The mayor is confident the war against crime will be won.
830 | 0.83 | 687

0495 满 [滿] /mǎn/ (1) *adj* full
所有桌子都坐满了。 All our tables are full now.
869 | 0.79 | 686

0496 女人 [女人] /nǚrén/ (2) *n* woman
他用一块木头雕了一个女人像。 He carved the figure of a woman from a piece of wood.
1217 | 0.56 | 684

0497 卖 [賣] /mài/ (1) *v* sell
书卖完了。 The book is sold out.
879 | 0.78 | 682

0498 干部 [幹部] /gànbù/ (1) *n* cadre
虽然他是位领导干部，却相当谦虚。 He is quite modest though he is a leading cadre.
1366 | 0.5 | 681 | W

0499 主席 [主席] /zhǔxí/ (2) *n* chairman, chairperson
发言的人在主席的左边。 The speaker is on the left of the chairman.
1342 | 0.51 | 678

0500 生产 [生產] /shēngchǎn/ (1) *v* produce
他们生产的钢质量很好。 The steel they produce is of excellent quality.
1368 | 0.5 | 678 | W

0501 对方 [對方] /duìfāng/ (2) *n* the opposite side or party, counterpart
对方很容易就把我们打败了。 We were simply taken apart by the opposition.
925 | 0.73 | 676

0502 生命 [生命] /shēngmìng/ (2) *n* life
人们总是在寻找延长生命的方法。 All the time people are seeking to prolong life.
776 | 0.87 | 675

0503 具有 [具有] /jùyǒu/ (2) *v* possess, have
中国具有五千年悠久历史。 China has a long history of 5,000 years.
1047 | 0.65 | 675

0504 低 [低] /dī/ (1) *adj* low
我的收入很低。 I have a very low income.
736 | 0.91 | 673

0505 基本 [基本] /jīběn/ (1) *adj* basic
告诉我一些关于网球的基本知识吧。 Tell me something basic about tennis.
1055 | 0.63 | 669

0506 那样 [那樣] /nàyàng/ (1) *pron* like that, in that way
不，那样做没用。 No, it is useless trying that way.
835 | 0.8 | 669

0507 传统 [傳統] /chuántǒng/ (2) *n* tradition
要把这个好的传统继承起来。 We should carry on this fine tradition.
936 | 0.71 | 666

0508 提高 [提高] /tígāo/ (1) *v* raise, improve
学汉字有助提高智商。 Learning Chinese characters helps improve IQ.
1494 | 0.45 | 665 | W

0509 农民 [農民] /nóngmín/ (1) *n* peasant, farmer
农民要靠丰收才能活命。 Peasants depend on a good harvest for their very existence.
1129 | 0.59 | 663

0510 时代 [時代] /shídài/ (2) *n* age, times; a period in one's life
你还能回忆起你的学生时代吗？ Can you recall your schooldays?
854 | 0.78 | 663

0511 子 [子] /zǐ/ (3) *n* son, child
地产的所有权已转给长子。 The estate was made over to the eldest son.
869 | 0.76 | 662

0512 主要 [主要] /zhǔyào/ (1) *adv* mainly, primarily, principally
该方言主要通行于农村地区。 The dialect is spoken principally in the rural areas.
862 | 0.76 | 658

0513 男人 [男人] /nánrén/ (2) *n* man
她与一个在假日认识的男人同居。 She's living with some man she picked up on holiday.
1138 | 0.58 | 658

0514 意义 [意義] /yìyì/ (1) *n* meaning, significance
意义上有微妙的差别。 There are subtle differences in meaning.
837 | 0.78 | 655

0515 队 [隊] /duì/ (2) *n* team; queue
什么队在比赛呢？ What teams are playing?
1034 | 0.63 | 655

0516 单位 [單位] /dānwèi/ (2) *n* (working or administrative) unit, institution; unit (of measurement)
工厂应该与科研单位挂钩。 Factories should establish close contact with institutes of scientific research.
1024 | 0.64 | 655

0517 军 [軍] /jūn/ (2) *n* army
实现这个胜负，依靠两军的决战。 To bring about victory or defeat a decisive battle between the two armies is necessary.
887 | 0.74 | 653 | W

0518 今年 [今年] /jīnnián/ (1) *time* this year
今年上半年生意清淡。 Business was slow in the first half of this year.
1588 | 0.41 | 653

0519 喝 [喝] /hē/ (1) *v* drink
您要喝点什么？ What will you have to drink?
962 | 0.68 | 653

0520 直接 [直接] /zhíjiē/ (2) *adj* direct
放学后，我直接去他家。 I will go to his house directly after school is over.
796 | 0.82 | 651

0521 党 [黨] /dǎng/ (2) *n* (political) party
要达到这种目的，党内的民主是必要的。 To attain this aim, inner-Party democracy is essential.
1298 | 0.5 | 651 | W

0522 心里 [心裏] /xīnli/ *place* in one's heart (mind)
他心里直冒火。 He was burning with anger in his heart.
1220 | 0.53 | 651

0523 真 [真] /zhēn/ *adj* real, true, genuine
这不可能是真的。 It cannot be true.
965 | 0.67 | 650

0524 总 [總] /zǒng/ (1) *adv* always; anyway, certainly; sooner or later
他总想某一天回去。 He always meant to go back one day.
908 | 0.72 | 650

0525 水平 [水平] /shuǐpíng/ (1) *n* level (of achievement, etc.)
那所学校的教学水平很高。 That school has a very high academic level.
1194 | 0.54 | 650

0526 号 [號] /hào/ (1) *clas* [measure word for workmen]; kind, sort
他是个懒汉，而我不喜欢这号人。 He's an indolent man and I don't like this kind of people.
748 | 0.87 | 650

0527 令 [令] /lìng/ (3) *v* order, command; cause, make
那情景令我毛骨悚然。 The sight made my flesh creep.
801 | 0.81 | 649

0528 关于 [關於] /guānyú/ (2) *prep* about, regarding, pertaining to
关于这件事他一无所知。 He knew nothing regarding the case.
965 | 0.67 | 648

0529 行为 [行為] /xíngwéi/ (3) *n* action, behaviour
这种行为说明了他的本质。 This behaviour shows his true nature.
818 | 0.79 | 647

0530 经过 [經過] /jīngguò/ (1) *prep* through, by; via; as a result of
油经过这根管子流入机器。 Oil feeds into the machine through this tubing.
843 | 0.77 | 646

0531 嘛 [嘛] /ma/ (1) *part* [sentence final modal particle indicating that something is obvious or expressing a hope, advice, etc.]
听起来挺好的嘛。 That sounds pretty good.
1366 | 0.47 | 645 | S

0532 红 [紅] /hóng/ (1) *adj* red; popular
她的眼睛哭红了。 Her eyes were red with weeping.
848 | 0.76 | 642

0533 未 [未] /wèi/ (2) *adv* [archaic] not (yet)
双方未能取得一致意见。 The two sides failed to reach agreement.
828 | 0.78 | 642

0534 部门 [部門] /bùmén/ (2) *n* department
我相信各部门都会有这样的人。 I believe that such people can be found in all departments.
1399 | 0.46 | 641 | W

0535 它们 [它們] /tāmen/ (1) *pron* [for inanimate objects] they, them
我把它们都搞混了。 I get them mixed up.
760 | 0.84 | 640

0536 指 [指] /zhǐ/ (1) *v* mean, refer to; point to
你是指这个吗？ Do you mean this?
799 | 0.8 | 636

0537 保护 [保護] /bǎohù/ (2) *v* protect
国家制定了保护儿童的法律和法规。 The state has formulated laws and regulations to protect children.
1021 | 0.62 | 636

0538 支持 [支持] /zhīchí/ (2) *v* support
你必须用行动支持，不能空口说白话。 You must show your support by deeds, not words.
1085 | 0.59 | 636

0539 较 [較] /jiào/ (2) *adv* [preceding an adjective or adverb to form a comparison] relatively
哪一个较便宜？Which is cheaper?
1066 | 0.59 | 634 | W

0540 咱们 [咱們] /zánmen/ (1) *pron* [including the addressee(s)] we
咱们去散散步吧！Let's go for a walk.
1123 | 0.56 | 633 | S

0541 中央 [中央] /zhōngyāng/ (2) *n* middle, centre; central authorities
房间的中央有一张桌子。There is a table in the centre of the room.
1119 | 0.56 | 632 | W

0542 提供 [提供] /tígòng/ (2) *v* provide, supply
他们只能提供实验证据。They can only provide experimental evidence.
1136 | 0.56 | 632

0543 据 [據] /jù/ *prep* according to
据他说下星期有个会。According to him, there will be a meeting next week.
1723 | 0.37 | 631 | W

0544 抓 [抓] /zhuā/ (2) *v* grab, grasp; arrest
小女孩把钱牢牢抓在手中。The girl clenched her money in her hand.
731 | 0.86 | 631

0545 脸 [臉] /liǎn/ (1) *n* face, cheek
她的脸胖起来了。Her cheeks began to fill out.
1527 | 0.41 | 629

0546 呀 [呀] /yā/ (1) *interj* [interjection expressing surprise] ah, oh
呀，好漂亮的房子！Ah, what a nice house!
1197 | 0.53 | 628 | S

0547 套 [套] /tào/ (2) *clas* [measure word for a group of associated things] set; suit; suite
他买了一套盘子。He bought a set of plates.
657 | 0.96 | 628

0548 受到 [受到] /shòudào/ *v* come in for
他的画受到了广泛的注意。His paintings come in for a great deal of attention.
812 | 0.77 | 626

0549 根据 [根據] /gēnjù/ *prep* according to
根据天气预报，今天下午将很冷。According to the weather forecast, it will be chilly this afternoon.
924 | 0.67 | 622

0550 下去 [下去] /xiàqù/ (1) *v* go down, descend
从这个坡下去。Walk down this hill.
841 | 0.74 | 622

0551 形成 [形成] /xíngchéng/ (2) *v* form, make
空气流动便形成了风。The movements of air make winds.
952 | 0.65 | 620

0552 全 [全] /quán/ *adv* all, fully
对不起，我全搞错了。Sorry, I got it all wrong.
912 | 0.68 | 618

0553 基础 [基礎] /jīchǔ/ (1) *n* base, basis
许多语言都以拉丁语为基础。Many languages have Latin as their base.
1213 | 0.51 | 618

0554 愿意 [願意] /yuànyì/ (1) *v* be willing to
您愿意坐在靠近门的地方吗？Would you like to sit over there close to the door?
697 | 0.88 | 616

0555 知识 [知識] /zhīshí/ (1) *n* knowledge
实践是获得知识的源泉。Practice is the fountain of knowledge.
837 | 0.74 | 615

0556 合作 [合作] /hézuò/ (2) *v* cooperate, collaborate
也许我们可以合作。Maybe we can cooperate.
1809 | 0.34 | 614 | W

0557 首先 [首先] /shǒuxiān/ (2) *adv* first, first of all
首先，画个圆圈。First, draw a circle.
774 | 0.79 | 613

0558 政策 [政策] /zhèngcè/ (2) *n* policy
对于当前存在的问题，要有明确的政策。Clear-cut policies should be worked out for tackling existing problems.
1235 | 0.5 | 613 | W

0559 晚上 [晚上] /wǎnshang/ (1) *time* (in the) evening
我宁愿等到晚上。I prefer to wait until evening.
795 | 0.77 | 613

0560 九 [九] /jiǔ/ (1) *num* nine
钟敲了九下。The clock struck nine.
915 | 0.67 | 612

0561 那里 [那裏] /nàli/ (1) *pron* there
要用很长时间才能到达那里。It takes a long time to get there.
777 | 0.79 | 612

0562 几乎 [幾乎] /jīhū/ (2) *adv* almost, nearly
她母亲高兴得几乎要晕倒了。Her mother nearly fainted with happiness.
740 | 0.82 | 609

0563 小时 [小時] /xiǎoshí/ (1) *n* hour
手术最多需要三小时。The operation will be completed in three hours at most.
678 | 0.9 | 608

0564 变化 [變化] /biànhuà/ (1) *v* change
世界在变化。The world is changing.
758 | 0.8 | 605

0565 步 [步] /bù/ *clas* pace; step
退一步才能进两步。We must take one step back in order to take two steps forward.
721 | 0.84 | 604

0566 报 [報] /bào/ (1) *n* newspaper
我在报上看到了有关此事的报导。I read about it in the newspaper.
1384 | 0.44 | 603 | W

0567 她们 [她們] /tāmen/ (1) *pron* [for female] they, them
是的，她们吸引了很多人。Yes, they attracted many people.
793 | 0.76 | 603

0568 之一 [之一] /zhīyī/ (2) *pron* one of
污染问题是当今世界上最重要的问题之一。Pollution is one of the most important issues in the world today.
827 | 0.73 | 603

0569 容易 [容易] /róngyì/ (1) *adj* easy
工作不象你想像的那么容易。The work is not so easy as you imagine.
777 | 0.77 | 602

0570 而是 [而是] /érshì/ (3) *conj* but, rather
我不是个教师，而是个学生。I am not a teacher, but a student.
763 | 0.79 | 602

0571 经验 [經驗] /jīngyàn/ (1) *n* experience
他不但有丰富经验，而且有知识。He has not only rich experience but also knowledge.
828 | 0.73 | 602

0572 身体 [身體] /shēntǐ/ (1) *n* (human) body, health
健康的身体是首要的。Good health is primary.
739 | 0.81 | 601

0573 妈妈 [媽媽] /māma/ (1) *n* mama, mum
提醒我给妈妈打电话。Remind me to call mum.
821 | 0.73 | 601

0574 即 [即] /jí/ (2) *v* is; that is
时间即金钱这句话说得很恰当。It is rightly said that time is money.
1000 | 0.6 | 601 | W

0575 计划 [計劃] /jìhuá/ (1) *n* plan
要讨论我们的工作计划。Our work plan is going to be discussed then.
973 | 0.62 | 599 | W

0576 不仅 [不僅] /bùjǐn/ (2) *conj* not only
莎士比亚不仅是位作家，而且也是一位演员。Shakespeare was not only a writer but an actor as well.
848 | 0.71 | 598

0577 方法 [方法] /fāngfǎ/ (1) *n* method, way
除了坐出租车外还有其他别的方法吗？Is there any other way to go besides taxi?
845 | 0.71 | 598

0578 制度 [制度] /zhìdù/ (2) *n* (political or administrative) system, institution
人民法院实行公开审判制度。The people's courts carry out a public trial system.
1064 | 0.56 | 597

0579 气 [氣] /qì/ (3) *n* air; breath; gas
我跑得喘不过气来。I ran out of breath.
930 | 0.64 | 597

0580 选择 [選擇] /xuǎnzé/ (2) *v* choose, select
选择这样的时间可真怪。It was a strange time to choose.
790 | 0.76 | 597

0581 中心 [中心] /zhōngxīn/ (2) *n* centre
他的事务所位于市中心。His practice is in the centre of the city.
1089 | 0.55 | 595

0582 改变 [改變] /gǎibiàn/ (1) *v* change, alter
诡辩改变不了事实。Sophistry won't alter facts.
717 | 0.83 | 592

0583 占 [占] /zhàn/ (1) *v* take; take up, occupy
你占了我的座位。You've taken my seat.
990 | 0.6 | 592

0584 考虑 [考慮] /kǎolù/ (2) *v* think over, consider
我需要好好考虑考虑。I need to think it over.
637 | 0.93 | 591

0585 高兴 [高興] /gāoxìng/ (1) *adj* happy, joyous
使他最高兴的是，他获得了第一名。He was very happy that he won the first prize.
706 | 0.84 | 590

0586 信 [信] /xìn/ (1) *n* letter, mail
我得去寄封信。I need to post a letter.
748 | 0.79 | 590

0587 家里 [家裏] /jiāli/ *place* home
我顺便拜访他们的时候，他们都在家里。They were all at home when I stopped by.
841 | 0.7 | 590

0588 同学 [同學] /tóngxué/ (1) *n* (fellow) classmate, student
考试前一天晚上同学们在举行晚会。The students were partying all night before the exam.
763 | 0.77 | 589

0589 作品 [作品] /zuòpǐn/ (2) *n* work (of art)
这部小说是优秀作品。This novel is a work of excellence.
814 | 0.72 | 589

0590 时期 [時期] /shíqī/ (2) *n* a particular period of time (especially in history)
一月份总是萧条时期。January is always a slack period.
802 | 0.73 | 588

0591 定 [定] /dìng/ (2) *v* set, fix, decide; subscribe to (newspapers and periodicals, etc.)
招待会的日期定在十月十日。The date for the reception has been fixed for 10 October.
686 | 0.85 | 586

0592 实现 [實現] /shíxiàn/ (1) *v* realise, fulfil, achieve
现在看，实现我们确定的宏伟目标有希望。I think it will be possible for us to achieve that magnificent goal.
1279 | 0.46 | 585 | W

0593 以前 [以前] /yǐqián/ (1) *time* before
现在的生活比以前好。The present life is better than before.
707 | 0.83 | 584

0594 法律 [法律] /fǎlǜ/ (2) *n* law
新法律将在下一个月生效。The new law will take effect next month.
996 | 0.59 | 583

0595 类 [類] /lèi/ (2) *clas* [measure word for a class of similar persons or things] category, kind, sort
世界上这类的国际争端还不少。There are many international disputes of this kind.
751 | 0.78 | 582

0596 每天 [每天] /měitiān/ *time* every day
她几乎每天上班都迟到。She's practically late for work every day.
660 | 0.88 | 582

0597 战争 [戰爭] /zhànzhēng/ (2) n war
他重新体验了战争的恐怖。He relived the horrors of war.
745 | 0.78 | 581

0598 清 [清] /qīng/ (2) adj clear
小河的水很清。The water in the river is very clear.
676 | 0.86 | 580

0599 利益 [利益] /lìyì/ (2) n benefit
每个人都得着眼于自己的利益。Everybody has an eye to his own benefit.
860 | 0.68 | 580

0600 病 [病] /bìng/ (1) n illness, ailment
他患了场大病。He suffered from a serious illness.
667 | 0.87 | 579

0601 接 [接] /jiē/ (1) v put together, join; receive, answer (call, letter, etc.); meet, pick up (somebody); extend, connect; catch (a ball, etc.)
我会去接你。I will pick you up.
808 | 0.72 | 579

0602 获得 [獲得] /huòdé/ (2) v obtain
想获得贷款需要什么手续？What does it require to obtain a loan?
948 | 0.61 | 579

0603 楼 [樓] /lóu/ (1) n building
突然楼里所有的灯都亮了。Suddenly all the lights in the building were turned on.
772 | 0.75 | 578

0604 越来越 [越來越] /yuèláiyuè/ (2) adv more and more
随着炉火逐渐减弱，房间越来越冷。The room grew colder as the fire burnt down.
636 | 0.91 | 577

0605 力量 [力量] /lìliàng/ (2) n strength, power
这是力量与技巧的结合。It's a combination of strength and skill.
748 | 0.77 | 576

0606 如此 [如此] /rúcǐ/ (3) pron such, like this, in this way
如此举动将会损害你的名誉。Such conduct will compromise your reputation.
755 | 0.76 | 576

0607 读 [讀] /dú/ (1) v read
你读这篇文章时可略去第二节。You can skip the second section of the article while reading it.
786 | 0.73 | 575

0608 深 [深] /shēn/ (1) adj deep
这河有一人深。The river is a man deep.
647 | 0.89 | 574

0609 处理 [處理] /chǔlǐ/ (2) v handle, deal with; take disciplinary action against; dispose of, sell at a reduced price
要怎样处理，你自己看着办好了。It's best for you to deal with them yourself.
767 | 0.75 | 574

0610 极 [極] /jí/ (2) adv extremely
他获奖的可能性极小。He has only an extremely small chance of winning the prize.
674 | 0.85 | 572

0611 项目 [項目] /xiàngmù/ (2) n project, item
进行这个项目的钱还没有着落。Money for the project is still lacking.
1415 | 0.4 | 572 | W

0612 全部 [全部] /quánbù/ (1) adj all, whole, full, entire, total
我们全部的努力都白费了。All our efforts were wasted.
692 | 0.83 | 572

0613 批 [批] /pī/ (2) clas batch, lot, group
这批活儿做得很好。This batch of products is well made.
889 | 0.64 | 570

0614 达 [達] /dá/ (3) v attain, reach; amount to
他们的旅费共达700美元。Their travelling expenses amount to $700.
1229 | 0.46 | 570 | W

0615 并 [並] /bìng/ (2) adv [typically occurring in negation] actually, definitely
请不要误解我，我并不是批评你。Please don't get me wrong; I'm not criticising you.
720 | 0.79 | 569

0616 城 [城] /chéng/ (1) n town, city; city wall
该城已落到敌人手中。The town fell into enemy hands.
609 | 0.93 | 567

0617 道 [道] /dào/ (1) clas [measure word for long and narrow objects, doors, orders, questions, dishes in a meal, and steps in a process, etc.]
我们有三道菜：汤、肉和蔬菜，还有水果。We had three courses: soup, meat and vegetables, and fruit.
1043 | 0.54 | 567

0618 完成 [完成] /wánchéng/ (1) v complete, accomplish
工作完成前别松劲。Don't slacken your efforts till the work is completed.
872 | 0.65 | 567

0619 目标 [目標] /mùbiāo/ (2) n target, goal
要把我们的目标和我们的能力协调起来。We should harmonise our goals with our abilities.
910 | 0.62 | 566

0620 又 [又] /yòu/ (2) conj [as in 既 . . . 又] (both . . .) and
她走后生活显得既单调又无意义。Life seemed grey and pointless after she'd gone.
734 | 0.77 | 563

0621 意思 [意思] /yìsi/ (1) n meaning, idea, opinion; trace, hint; gift, token of gratitude, etc.
我不明白你的意思。I don't catch your meaning.
839 | 0.67 | 563

0622 群众 [群眾] /qúnzhòng/ (2) *n* the masses
而这种文化运动和实践运动，都是群众的。
Both the cultural and practical movements must be of the masses.
1319 | 0.43 | 563 | W

0623 变成 [變成] /biànchéng/ (1) *v* become, turn into
我母亲的愿望变成了现实。 My mother's hope has become a reality.
672 | 0.84 | 561

0624 结束 [結束] /jiéshù/ (1) *v* be over, end, terminate
我们到达时，会议已结束了。 By the time we arrived the meeting was over.
798 | 0.7 | 557

0625 故事 [故事] /gùshì/ (1) *n* story
故事发生在战时巴黎的一家旅馆里。 The setting of the story is a hotel in Paris during the war.
709 | 0.78 | 555

0626 理解 [理解] /lǐjiě/ (2) *v* understand, apprehend
我未能理解他的意图。 I failed to understand his motives.
655 | 0.85 | 554

0627 意见 [意見] /yìjiàn/ (1) *n* opinion, comment; objection, complaint
调查结果表明各种意见差别很大。 The survey revealed a wide spread of opinions.
772 | 0.72 | 553

0628 不少 [不少] /bùshǎo/ (2) *adj* a good few
不少人认为这种想法是胡说八道。 A good few people dismiss the idea as sheer nonsense.
648 | 0.85 | 552

0629 区 [區] /qū/ (2) *n* area, district
能给我在禁烟区的位子吗？ Could you please put me in the non-smoking area?
931 | 0.59 | 552

0630 行 [行] /xíng/ (2) *n* trip; behaviour
他兴高采烈地谈了他的香港之行。 He talked of his trip to Hong Kong in a cheerful voice.
688 | 0.8 | 552

0631 出去 [出去] /chūqù/ (1) *v* go out
这种天气我们不能出去。 We cannot go out in this weather.
798 | 0.69 | 552

0632 帮助 [幫助] /bāngzhù/ (1) *v* help, assist
非常感激你帮助了我们。 I'm much obliged to you for helping us.
735 | 0.75 | 551

0633 白 [白] /bái/ (1) *adj* white
岁月染白了她的头发。 The years have silvered her hair.
777 | 0.71 | 550

0634 酒 [酒] /jiǔ/ (1) *n* wine, alcohol
这酒尝起来很酸。 The wine tastes sour.
755 | 0.73 | 550

0635 医院 [醫院] /yīyuàn/ (1) *n* hospital
医院在哪里？ Where is the hospital?
645 | 0.85 | 550

0636 地位 [地位] /dìwèi/ (2) *n* status, position
我们需要提高医生的工资和地位。
We need to upgrade the pay and status of doctors.
754 | 0.73 | 550

0637 说话 [説話] /shuōhuà/ *v* speak, talk
我想跟经理说话。 I'd like to speak to the manager.
831 | 0.66 | 549

0638 达到 [達到] /dádào/ (2) *v* reach, attain, be up to
这批货没有达到你们自己的标准。 This shipment is not up to your own standard.
888 | 0.62 | 548

0639 尤其 [尤其] /yóuqí/ (1) *adv* especially
她总是为我们一家人祈祷，尤其是有人出门在外时。 She always prays for our family, especially when one of us is away.
601 | 0.91 | 547

0640 电 [電] /diàn/ (1) *n* electricity, power; telegram, cable
我们这里刚停了电。 We've just had a power failure.
2476 | 0.22 | 547 | W

0641 省 [省] /shěng/ (1) *n* province
加拿大有十个省。 Canada has ten provinces.
1078 | 0.51 | 546

0642 投资 [投資] /tóuzī/ *v* invest
要想使生意扩大，必须投资。 You must invest if you want your business to grow.
1352 | 0.4 | 546 | W

0643 突然 [突然] /tūrán/ (1) *adj* sudden
他的突然到来使她很惊讶。 His sudden appearance surprised her.
867 | 0.62 | 541

0644 报告 [報告] /bàogào/ (2) *n* report
我们应该再写一份报告。 We should write another report.
770 | 0.7 | 541

0645 也许 [也許] /yěxǔ/ (1) *adv* perhaps
他也许是对的。 He's perhaps right.
750 | 0.72 | 540

0646 动 [動] /dòng/ (1) *v* move; arouse; change; use
我觉得我看到角落里有什么东西在动。 I fancied I saw something moving in the corner.
774 | 0.7 | 540

0647 产品 [產品] /chǎnpǐn/ (2) *n* product
该目录介绍了我们的各种产品。
The catalogue contains illustrations and descriptions of the large variety of our products.
1125 | 0.48 | 539 | W

0648 事业 [事業] /shìyè/ (2) *n* cause, career, undertaking
他 41 岁时到达事业的顶峰。 At 41 he'd reached the apex of his career.
903 | 0.6 | 539

0649 报道 [報導] /bàodào/ (2) v report
许多报纸和电视台报导了他们的发现。
Many newspapers and television stations reported their finding.
981 | 0.55 | 539

0650 青年 [青年] /qīngnián/ (1) n youth, young people
都市对农村青年具有一种诱惑力。Cities have a lure for young people from the country.
739 | 0.73 | 538

0651 台 [台] /tái/ (2) clas [measure word for machines, and also performances, etc.]
房间里有一台电视机。There is a television in the room.
650 | 0.83 | 538

0652 服务 [服務] /fúwù/ (1) v serve
我们期待着为您服务。We look forward to serving you.
1166 | 0.46 | 538 | W

0653 之前 [之前] /zhīqián/ (2) loc before
在采取任何行动之前，你必须仔细想清楚。You must think it through before you take any action.
603 | 0.89 | 536

0654 行 [行] /xíng/ (1) v be all right; travel
他的决定行吗？Is his decision all right?
851 | 0.63 | 536 | S

0655 责任 [責任] /zérèn/ (2) n responsibility
我们要负担什么责任呢？What responsibilities do we have?
676 | 0.79 | 535

0656 造成 [造成] /zàochéng/ v cause, result in
是什么原因造成了这条裂缝？What caused this crack?
720 | 0.74 | 534

0657 态度 [態度] /tàidu/ (1) n attitude
他态度坚定。His attitude is inflexible.
628 | 0.85 | 533

0658 电影 [電影] /diànyǐng/ (1) n movie
电影结束后我们回家了。After the movie, we went home.
728 | 0.73 | 533

0659 过来 [過來] /guòlái/ (1) v come over; manage to do something
过来帮我一下。Come over here and give me a hand.
879 | 0.61 | 533

0660 花 [花] /huā/ (1) v spend
我两天就花完了零用钱。I spent my pocket money in two days.
640 | 0.83 | 533

0661 使用 [使用] /shǐyòng/ (1) v use
你使用电吹风吗？Do you use a hairdryer?
819 | 0.65 | 533 | W

0662 以上 [以上] /yǐshàng/ (2) loc above; more than
你必须注意以上问题。You have to pay attention to the above question.
899 | 0.59 | 532

0663 文学 [文學] /wénxué/ (1) n literature
我不懂古典文学。I can't understand classical literature.
751 | 0.71 | 532

0664 信息 [信息] /xìnxī/ (3) n information
信息技术在现代工业中有十分重要的地位。Information technology occupies a very important position in modern industry.
882 | 0.6 | 532

0665 离开 [離開] /líkāi/ (1) v leave, depart
我们离开时天开始亮了。Day was breaking as we left.
669 | 0.8 | 532

0666 千 [千] /qiān/ (1) num 1,000
学校里有一千名学生。There are 1,000 students in the school.
594 | 0.89 | 531

0667 数 [數] /shù/ num several
在非洲艾滋病杀死了数千人。AIDS has killed several thousands in Africa.
583 | 0.91 | 531

0668 妇女 [婦女] /fùnǚ/ (2) n woman
应该让妇女有选举权吗？Should women have the vote?
1032 | 0.52 | 531

0669 转 [轉] /zhuǎn, zhuàn/ (2, 2) v change, shift; pass on; rotate, resolve; turn
往左拐弯，再往左转。Turn left and left again.
659 | 0.81 | 531

0670 约 [約] /yuē/ (2) adv approximately, about
步行约5分钟。It's about five minutes' walk.
738 | 0.72 | 530 | W

0671 帮 [幫] /bāng/ (2) v help, assist, do somebody a favour
请你帮帮我好吗？Will you do me a favour?
779 | 0.68 | 530

0672 分 [分] /fēn/ (1) clas minute; [Chinese monetary unit] fen; mark, score; [partitive measure for one-tenth of the whole]
我得了多少分？What's my score?
557 | 0.95 | 529

0673 严重 [嚴重] /yánzhòng/ (2) adj severe, serious
旱情严重。The drought is serious.
799 | 0.66 | 528

0674 妈 [媽] /mā/ n ma, mum
妈和爸从来没有对任何一件事有一致的看法。Mum and dad never see eye to eye on anything.
937 | 0.56 | 528

0675 人物 [人物] /rénwù/ (2) n personage, distinguished individual; characters in literary works
他在这么多的重要人物中间感到不安。He felt strange among so many important people.
666 | 0.79 | 526

0676 留 [留] /liú/ (1) v remain, stay; reserve, save for future use; leave behind
你们要留在这里等我回来。You are to stay here till I get back.
643 | 0.82 | 525

5. Colours

红色	紅色	*hóngsè*	red	2263
绿色	綠色	*lǜsè*	green	2778
黑色	黑色	*hēisè*	black	3026
白色	白色	*báisè*	white	3471
黄色	黃色	*huángsè*	yellow	4085
蓝色	藍色	*lánsè*	blue	4087
灰色	灰色	*huīsè*	grey	6278
紫色	紫色	*zǐsè*	purple, violet	13607
褐色	褐色	*hésè*	brown	15917
棕色	棕色	*zōngsè*	brown	22656
咖啡色	咖啡色	*kāfēisè*	brown	24356
粉红色	粉紅色	*fěnhóngsè*	pink	18621
乳白色	乳白色	*rǔbáisè*	oyster-white	21817
橙色	橙色	*chéngsè*	orange	22089
青色	青色	*qīngsè*	cyan	25327

0677 无法 [無法] /wúfǎ/ (3) v be unable to, can't
痛得很厉害，无法再忍受了。 It hurts so much I can't stand it any longer.
700 | 0.75 | 524

0678 终于 [終於] /zhōngyú/ (2) adv finally, at last
好啦，我们终于到了！ Well, here we are at last!
682 | 0.77 | 523

0679 理论 [理論] /lǐlùn/ (2) n theory
我们认为理论联系实际很重要。 We think it important that theory should be combined with practice.
729 | 0.72 | 523

0680 革命 [革命] /gémìng/ (2) n (political) revolution
无数同志为革命献出了他们的生命。 Countless comrades gave their lives for the revolution.
629 | 0.83 | 523

0681 面对 [面對] /miànduì/ (3) v face, confront
不管他面对什么困难，他从来不泄气。 He is never discouraged, no matter what difficulty he may face.
600 | 0.87 | 523

0682 换 [換] /huàn/ (1) v change; exchange
如果我换座位，你介意吗？ Do you mind if I change seats?
650 | 0.8 | 522

0683 行动 [行動] /xíngdòng/ (2) v act, take action; move about
人们在盛怒之下，很少理智地行动。 When people are very angry, they seldom act in a rational way.
787 | 0.66 | 521

0684 象 [象] /xiàng/ (2) n elephant; image, shape
下一步就是把象送到驯象基地。 The next stage is to get the elephant to the training establishment.
807 | 0.64 | 520

0685 父母 [父母] /fùmǔ/ n father and mother, parent
在我父母的心目中，我永远是个孩子。 In the eyes of my parents, I am forever a child.
687 | 0.76 | 520

0686 加 [加] /jiā/ (1) v add, increase; put in
如果茶太浓，请加点开水。 If the tea is too strong, add some more hot water.
575 | 0.91 | 520

0687 年轻 [年輕] /niánqīng/ (1) adj young
我年轻时常凭盲目的冲动行事。 I used to act out of blind impulse when I was young.
554 | 0.94 | 518

0688 大 [大] /dà/ adv greatly, a lot
你的意见对我大有帮助。 Your advice helped a lot.
630 | 0.82 | 517

0689 海 [海] /hǎi/ (1) n sea
风、沙和海的结合的确迷人。 The combination of wind, sand and sea is really fascinating.
539 | 0.96 | 517

0690 性 [性] /xìng/ (2) n property, disposition; sex
我们女人并不是两性中的弱者。 We women are not the weaker sex.
738 | 0.7 | 517

0691 增加 [增加] /zēngjiā/ (1) v increase
学校的学生人数不断增加。 The number of students of the school keeps increasing.
1032 | 0.5 | 517 | W

0692 坚持 [堅持] /jiānchí/ (1) v insist, persist, stick to
坚持你的原则。 Stick to your principles.
928 | 0.56 | 516 | W

0693 常 [常] /cháng/ (1) adv often, usually
我们常去那儿。 We often go there.
670 | 0.77 | 515

0694 收 [收] /shōu/ (1) v receive, collect; accept
我们不收小费。We don't accept tips.
562 | 0.92 | 515

0695 然而 [然而] /rán'ér/ (2) conj however
然而情况并非总是如此。However this is not always the case.
665 | 0.77 | 514

0696 电视 [電視] /diànshì/ (1) n television, TV
电视扼杀了交谈的艺术。Television has killed the art of conversation.
591 | 0.87 | 513

0697 明白 [明白] /míngbái/ (3) v realise, understand
你明白吗？Do you understand?
790 | 0.65 | 513

0698 离 [離] /lí/ (1) v leave, be away
他暂离一会去喝咖啡了。He was away for a quick coffee break.
602 | 0.85 | 511

0699 发表 [發表] /fābiǎo/ (2) v publish, issue
我选了其中 7 封将在此陆续发表。I have selected seven of these letters for publication.
791 | 0.65 | 510

0700 市 [市] /shì/ (1) n city, town; market
我认为他是本市最杰出的人才之一。I believe that he is one of the most remarkable talents in our city.
1147 | 0.44 | 509 | W

0701 困难 [困難] /kùnnán/ (1) adj difficult
要做到这一些, 应该说并不很困难。This should not be terribly difficult to do.
697 | 0.73 | 508

0702 非 [非] /fēi/ (3) adj non-
我们不容许非成员进入我们的俱乐部。We cannot admit non-members into our club.
597 | 0.85 | 507

0703 这儿 [這兒] /zhèr/ (1) pron here
我能坐这儿吗？May I sit here?
960 | 0.53 | 507 | S

0704 保持 [保持] /bǎochí/ (2) v keep, maintain
请保持安静。Please keep quiet.
794 | 0.64 | 507

0705 风 [風] /fēng/ (1) n wind
似乎明天要起风。It looks as if it will be windy tomorrow.
607 | 0.83 | 505

0706 取得 [取得] /qǔdé/ (1) v acquire, obtain, achieve; reach (an agreement)
他取得了惊人的成功。He has achieved amazing success.
1085 | 0.46 | 504

0707 双方 [雙方] /shuāngfāng/ (2) n both parties, the two sides
双方商定了谈判日期。The two sides have agreed on the date of negotiations.
964 | 0.52 | 503

0708 差 [差] /chà/ (1) adj short of; poor, not up to standard; wrong
这种材料质量很差。This material is of very poor quality.
578 | 0.87 | 502

0709 结构 [結構] /jiégòu/ (2) n structure
我碰到过在结构上与这个相似的句子。I came across a sentence similar to this one in structure.
856 | 0.58 | 499

0710 好像 [好像] /hǎoxiàng/ (1) v seem, look like, look as if
今天你好像不太高兴。You do not seem to be quite yourself today.
738 | 0.68 | 499

0711 教授 [教授] /jiàoshòu/ (2) n professor
这家公司聘请了一位退休教授担任顾问。The firm employed a retired professor as adviser.
604 | 0.83 | 498

0712 同意 [同意] /tóngyì/ (1) v agree
她的笑表示她同意了。Her smile denoted that she agreed.
515 | 0.97 | 498

0713 举行 [舉行] /jǔxíng/ (2) v hold (meeting, etc.)
下届奥运会在什么时候举行？When will the next Olympic Games be held?
1401 | 0.36 | 498

0714 来到 [來到] /láidào/ v come to
这是我来到北京后所遇到的最热的一天。This is the hottest day I have had since I came to Beijing.
531 | 0.94 | 498

0715 农村 [農村] /nóngcūn/ (1) n countryside, rural area
我想起了我在农村的那些日子。I thought of those days when I was in the countryside.
916 | 0.54 | 497

0716 弄 [弄] /nòng/ (2) v play with; do, get (ready)
别把我的头发弄乱, 我刚梳好。Don't mess up my hair, I've just combed it.
734 | 0.68 | 497

0717 引起 [引起] /yǐnqǐ/ (2) v evoke, give rise to, lead to
她的讲话引起了极大愤慨。Her speech evoked great anger.
632 | 0.79 | 497

0718 汽车 [汽車] /qìchē/ (1) n automobile, motor vehicle, car
他招认偷了那辆汽车。He admitted having stolen the car.
737 | 0.67 | 496

0719 晚 [晚] /wǎn/ (1) adj late
我们该走了, 天越来越晚了。We must go now; it's getting late.
523 | 0.95 | 495

0720 挺 [挺] /tǐng/ (1) adv very, rather
您学得挺快呀。You learn very quickly.
940 | 0.53 | 495 | S

0721 共 [共] /gòng/ (2) adv all together
这本教科书共有十六课。 This textbook contains 16 lessons all together.
886 | 0.56 | 495

0722 曾经 [曾經] /céngjīng/ (2) adv [referring to something that happened previously]
我曾经去过颐和园两次。 I have been to the Summer Palace twice.
609 | 0.81 | 495

0723 和平 [和平] /hépíng/ (2) n peace
中国是个爱好和平的国家。 China is a peace-loving country.
1090 | 0.45 | 495

0724 规定 [規定] /guīdìng/ (2) n regulation, stipulation, provision
现在有了这一条规定，就可以防止这种现象发生。 Now with this regulation we can check such a practice.
864 | 0.57 | 495

0725 利用 [利用] /lìyòng/ (1) v make use of, exploit
学生应当充分利用课堂上的时间。 Students should make good use of their time in class.
867 | 0.57 | 495

0726 重 [重] /zhòng/ (1) adj heavy
这个担子比那个更重。 This load is heavier than that one.
535 | 0.93 | 494

0727 女儿 [女兒] /nǚ'ér/ (1) n daughter
她为女儿的成就感到非常自豪。 She felt a glow of pride at her daughter's achievements.
675 | 0.73 | 494

0728 目的 [目的] /mùdì/ (2) n purpose, aim, end
你的来访目的是什么？ What's the purpose of your visit?
604 | 0.82 | 494

0729 情 [情] /qíng/ (3) n feeling, passion, sentiment; condition, situation
他掩盖不住对我无知的轻蔑之情。 He could hardly veil his contempt at my ignorance.
576 | 0.86 | 493

0730 提 [提] /tí/ (1) v carry; put forward, raise; mention, ask; lift; promote
我可以向您提个问题吗？ May I ask you a question?
595 | 0.83 | 492

0731 首 [首] /shǒu/ (2) n head
她名列全班之首。 She is head of her class.
814 | 0.6 | 491

0732 记 [記] /jì/ (1) v keep in mind, memorise, remember; take note, write down
等一下，让我记下来。 Wait a minute, let me write it down.
575 | 0.85 | 490

0733 共同 [共同] /gòngtóng/ (2) adj common
共同目标可缩小分歧。 A common goal can downplay differences.
931 | 0.52 | 488

0734 东 [東] /dōng/ (1) loc east
河水从东向西流去。 The river flows from east to west.
550 | 0.89 | 488

0735 届 [屆] /jiè/ (2) clas [measure word used for regular conferences, meetings, graduating classes, sports games, etc.]
第21届奥林匹克运动会是在蒙特利尔举行的。 The 21st Olympiad took place in Montreal.
1226 | 0.4 | 488

0736 眼睛 [眼睛] /yǎnjīng/ (1) n eye
长时间阅读后应该让眼睛休息一下。 You should rest your eyes after a lot of reading.
913 | 0.53 | 487

0737 倒 [倒] /dào/ (2) adv [indicating unexpectedness, contrast or concession] but
屋间不大，收拾得倒还整洁。 The room is small, but it's kept quite tidy.
732 | 0.66 | 486

0738 要求 [要求] /yāoqiú/ (1) n requirement, request
它看来很符合你的要求。 It seems to fit your requirements fairly well.
746 | 0.65 | 485

0739 爸爸 [爸爸] /bàba/ (1) n dad, father
我想去见她爸爸。 I want to visit her father.
691 | 0.7 | 484

0740 价值 [價值] /jiàzhí/ (2) n value
人们直到失去健康才知道它的价值。 People do not know the value of health till they lose it.
655 | 0.74 | 484

0741 文 [文] /wén/ n script, language; essay, writing
我们发表此文得到了他的同意。 We carry this essay with his permission.
580 | 0.84 | 484

0742 以来 [以來] /yǐlái/ (2) time since (a previous event)
自从他离开以来已经有六年了。 It is six years since he left.
939 | 0.52 | 484

0743 具体 [具體] /jùtǐ/ (2) adj concrete, specific
现在说几个具体问题。 Now I would like to discuss some specific questions.
626 | 0.77 | 483

0744 总 [總] /zǒng/ (3) adj overall, total; general, chief
他的总成绩是多少？ What are his total results?
739 | 0.65 | 483

0745 那么 [那麼] /nàme/ (1) conj then
那么，我希望不会使他们失望。 Then I hope I don't disappoint them.
957 | 0.5 | 482 | S

0746 过去 [過去] /guòqu/ (1) v go over, pass by; [used as verb complement in a resulative construction to indicate result]
请让我过去。 Please let me pass.
584 | 0.83 | 482

0747 比赛 [比賽] /bǐsài/ (1) n competition, contest, match, game
这一定会是一场精彩的比赛。 It must be a wonderful game.
1140 | 0.42 | 482

0748 飞 [飛] /fēi/ (1) v fly
企鹅不会飞。 Penguins cannot fly.
614 | 0.78 | 481

0749 部分 [部分] /bùfen/ (1) n part
系统由四个部分组成。 The system consists of four parts.
660 | 0.73 | 480

0750 联系 [聯係] /liánxì/ (1) v contact, get in touch
如果你需要协助，请随时和我联系。 If you need further help, please feel free to contact me.
592 | 0.81 | 480

0751 主任 [主任] /zhǔrèn/ (2) n director
主任对他有成见。 The director is biased against him.
665 | 0.72 | 478

0752 怎样 [怎樣] /zěnyàng/ (1) pron how
你打算怎样处理这个问题？ How are we going to deal with this problem?
577 | 0.83 | 478

0753 玩 [玩] /wán/ (1) v play, amuse oneself
孩子们在外面玩呢。 The children are playing outside.
658 | 0.73 | 478

0754 黑 [黑] /hēi/ (1) adj black; dark
冬天里，六点钟时天就黑了。 In winter it is dark at six o'clock.
653 | 0.73 | 477

0755 银行 [銀行] /yínháng/ (1) n bank
银行什么时候开门？ What time does the bank open?
1011 | 0.47 | 477 | W

0756 梦 [夢] /mèng/ (2) n dream
她做了一个可怕的梦。 She had a frightful dream.
784 | 0.61 | 477

0757 分析 [分析] /fēnxī/ (2) v analyse
下面就来分析这几点。 These points are analysed below.
652 | 0.73 | 477

0758 控制 [控制] /kòngzhì/ (2) v control
你要控制自己的物欲。 You should control your material desire.
638 | 0.75 | 477

0759 带来 [帶來] /dàilái/ v bring
春雨带来了夏日的百花。 Spring rains bring summer flowers.
599 | 0.8 | 477

0760 简单 [簡單] /jiǎndān/ (1) adj simple, easy
答案很简单。 The answer is simple.
601 | 0.79 | 476

0761 经常 [經常] /jīngcháng/ (1) adv often, frequently
夏天我经常吃西瓜。 I often eat watermelons in summer.
594 | 0.8 | 475

0762 系 [系] /xì/ (1) n (academic) department; system, series
这个新的系属文学院吗？ Should the new department form part of the Faculty of Arts?
556 | 0.86 | 475

0763 国内 [國內] /guónèi/ place domestic, home
国内市场销售相对平稳。 Domestic market sales remained stable.
815 | 0.58 | 475

0764 下午 [下午] /xiàwǔ/ (1) time (in the) afternoon
今天下午有篮球比赛吗？ Is there going to be a basketball match this afternoon?
602 | 0.79 | 474

0765 现 [現] /xiàn/ (3) time now
风势现已减弱。 The wind has dropped now.
545 | 0.87 | 474

0766 一定 [一定] /yídìng/ (1) adj definite, regular; given, certain; fixed, specified
在一定条件下，坏事可以变为好事。 In given conditions a bad thing can be turned into a good one.
583 | 0.81 | 473

0767 到 [到] /dào/ (1) prep to (a place); up until (time)
他从早到晚写东西。 He wrote from morning to night.
574 | 0.82 | 471

0768 篇 [篇] /piān/ (1) clas [measure word for essays and papers] piece (of writing)
这篇新闻报导是完全根据实际情况写成的。 This news report is based entirely on fact.
626 | 0.75 | 471

0769 派 [派] /pài/ (1) v send, dispatch
我们会派人去修理的。 We'll send someone to repair it.
522 | 0.9 | 471

0770 调查 [調查] /diàochá/ (2) v investigate, look into
我们正在调查，请稍等一下。 Please wait for a moment while we are investigating.
685 | 0.69 | 471

0771 底 [底] /dǐ/ (3) n bottom, base; end (of month or year); draft copy, duplicate copy for file; background
警方在湖底发现了一具尸体。 The police found a body at the bottom of the lake.
551 | 0.85 | 470

0772 想到 [想到] /xiǎngdào/ v think of
这一点我是应当想到的。 I should have thought of that.
670 | 0.7 | 470

0773 过 [過] /guò/ (3) adv excessively, unduly, too
用洗发剂不要过多。 Don't use too much shampoo.
626 | 0.75 | 468

0774 现象 [現象] /xiànxiàng/ (2) n appearance; phenomenon
这种现象是很不正常的。 This phenomenon is abnormal.
633 | 0.74 | 468

0775 落 [落] /luò/ (2) v fall, drop; lower; fall behind
树枝从树上落下了。 The branch fell from the tree.
611 | 0.77 | 468

0776 标准 [標準] /biāozhǔn/ (2) n standard, criterion
实践是检验真理的唯一标准。 Practice is the sole criterion of truth.
639 | 0.73 | 467

0777 安全 [安全] /ānquán/ (2) adj safe, secure
我要住一处既安全又清洁的地方。 I'd like to stay in a safe and clean place.
814 | 0.57 | 466

0778 小说 [小說] /xiǎoshuō/ (2) n novel, story
读那本小说花费很多时间。 A lot of time has been spent in reading that novel.
736 | 0.63 | 466

0779 创造 [創造] /chuàngzào/ (2) v create
生活的意义在于创造。 The meaning of life lies in creating.
701 | 0.67 | 466

0780 现代 [現代] /xiàndài/ (1) time modern times
现代科学技术正在经历着一场伟大的革命。 Modern science and technology are now undergoing a great revolution.
638 | 0.73 | 465

0781 最近 [最近] /zuìjìn/ (1) time recently
你最近有他的消息吗？ Have you heard from him recently?
626 | 0.74 | 465

0782 改 [改] /gǎi/ (1) v change, revise, modify
我们可以改到其他时间吗？ Can we change to another time?
529 | 0.88 | 465

0783 称 [稱] /chēng/ (2) v call; say, state; weigh
孩子们称他是老神仙。 The children call him old god.
596 | 0.78 | 464

0784 似乎 [似乎] /sìhū/ (2) adv apparently
似乎出错了。 Apparently something is wrong.
694 | 0.67 | 463 | W

0785 安排 [安排] /ānpái/ (1) v arrange, schedule
我下周已安排了一个音乐会。 I've scheduled a concert next week.
532 | 0.87 | 462

0786 采取 [採取] /cǎiqǔ/ (2) v adopt, carry out (policies, course of action, etc.); take (actions, measures)
采取措施避免出现不良后果。 Precautions must be taken to avoid any unwanted consequences.
832 | 0.56 | 462

0787 心理 [心理] /xīnlǐ/ (3) n mentality, psychology
我无法理解那个人的心理。 I can't understand that man's psychology.
646 | 0.72 | 461

0788 林 [林] /lín/ n woods, forest
林中有一些鹿。 There are some deer in the woods.
529 | 0.87 | 461

0789 回答 [回答] /huídá/ (1) v reply, answer, respond
她发现这个问题很难回答。 She found it very difficult to answer this question.
581 | 0.79 | 461

0790 脚 [腳] /jiǎo/ (1) n foot, feet; foot (of walls, mountains)
在长途跋涉中她的脚起泡了。 Her feet blistered during the long hike.
659 | 0.7 | 460

0791 口 [口] /kǒu/ (1) clas [measure word for people in a family or village, and also for pigs, etc.]; [measure word for tool or instrument with an edge such as a sword]; [measure word for the amount held in mouth] mouthful
他吸了一口清香的乡村空气。 He took a mouthful of sweet country air.
654 | 0.7 | 460

0792 所谓 [所謂] /suǒwèi/ (2) adj so-called
这种所谓的大减价不过是个骗局！ This so-called bargain is just a con!
614 | 0.75 | 459

0793 支 [支] /zhī/ (1) clas [measure word used for long and inflexible objects such as pens, arrows, cigarettes]; [measure word for troops and fleets]; [measure word for songs and melodies]; [measure word for brightness of electric bulbs, equivalent of watt]
好好一支笔丢了，真可惜！ What a pity to have lost such a nice pen!
562 | 0.82 | 458

0794 更加 [更加] /gèngjiā/ (2) adv more, further
如果我们不帮助他，他的处境会更加艰苦。 It will go even harder with him if we don't help him.
587 | 0.78 | 456

0795 按照 [按照] /ànzhào/ (2) prep according to
他们按照原先的计划行事。 They acted according to the original plan.
631 | 0.72 | 456

0796 分钟 [分鐘] /fēnzhōng/ (1) clas minute
这钟快了一分钟。 The clock is a minute fast.
492 | 0.93 | 456

0797 文章 [文章] /wénzhāng/ (1) n article, essay
这篇文章写得很糟糕，不宜发表。 The article is too badly written to be printable.
578 | 0.79 | 455

0798 新闻 [新聞] /xīnwén/ (1) n news
人要是咬了狗，那才是新闻！ When a man bites a dog, that is news!
679 | 0.67 | 455

0799 成立 [成立] /chénglì/ (2) v establish, set up
上星期我们成立了一个业余学习小组。 We established a spare time study group last week.
774 | 0.59 | 455

0800 余 [餘] /yú/ (3) num [following a number] more than, over
后来，我奔走外面，十余年没有回过家乡。 I later left the village and did not return for over ten years.
694 | 0.66 | 454

6. Weather and equipment

Weather:

风	風	*fēng*	wind	**705**
热	熱	*rè*	hot	**868**
雪	雪	*xuě*	snow	**1350**
雨	雨	*yǔ*	rain	**1406**
云	雲	*yún*	cloud	**1566**
冷	冷	*lěng*	cold	**1697**
天气	天氣	*tiānqì*	weather	**1883**
度	度	*dù*	degree	**1926**
冰	冰	*bīng*	ice	**2341**
气候	氣候	*qìhòu*	climate	**2654**
阴	陰	*yīn*	overcast, cloudy	**3015**
雷	雷	*léi*	thunder	**3872**
雾	霧	*wù*	fog, mist	**4914**
预报	預報	*yùbào*	forecast	**5637**
下雨	下雨	*xiàyǔ*	rain	**6262**
台风	颱風	*táifēng*	typhoon	**10280**
潮湿	潮濕	*cháoshī*	damp, moist	**10768**
暖和	暖和	*nuǎnhuo*	warm	**11485**
凉快	涼快	*liángkuai*	pleasantly cool	**13850**
闷	悶	*mēn*	stuffy	**16452**
摄氏	攝氏	*shèshì*	Celsius, centigrade	**18932**
闪电	閃電	*shǎndiàn*	lightning	**20217**

Equipment:

空调	空調	*kōngtiáo*	air conditioner	**4252**
伞	傘	*sǎn*	umbrella	**6108**
雨伞	雨傘	*yǔsǎn*	umbrella	**10668**
暖气	暖氣	*nuǎnqì*	heater	**11107**
电风扇	電風扇	*diànfēngshàn*	electric fan	**20151**
电扇	電扇	*diànshàn*	electric fan	**21138**

0801 口 [口] /kǒu/ (1) *n* mouth, opening, entrance; cut, hole
她用汤匙把牛奶舀入婴儿口中。She spooned milk into the baby's mouth.
700 | 0.65 | 454

0802 程度 [程度] /chéngdù/ (2) *n* degree, level, extent
在某种程度上你是正确的。To some extent you are correct.
571 | 0.8 | 454

0803 专家 [專家] /zhuānjiā/ (2) *n* expert, specialist
我决不自命为经济学专家。I lay no claim to being an expert economist.
830 | 0.55 | 454

0804 健康 [健康] /jiànkāng/ (1) *adj* healthy
在乡下两年后，她更健康了。After two years in the countryside, she is more healthy.
643 | 0.7 | 453

0805 尽管 [儘管] /jǐn'guǎn/ (2) *conj* although, despite
尽管下雨，我们还是去散步了。We went for a walk although it was raining.
522 | 0.87 | 453

0806 声 [聲] /shēng/ (1) *n* sound, noise; voice
爆炸声把我惊醒。The noise of the explosion awoke me.
800 | 0.57 | 453

0807 人家 [人家] /rénjia/ (2) *pron* other people
人家能做到的，我们也能做到。If other people can do it, so can we.
746 | 0.61 | 453 | S

0808 经营 [經營] /jīngyíng/ (3) *v* run a business, engage in (a business activity)
我们不经营此业。We are not engaged in this line of business.
811 | 0.56 | 453 | W

0809 著名 [著名] /zhùmíng/ (2) adj famous, well known
西湖以其风景而著名。 The West Lake is noted for its scenery.
615 | 0.74 | 452

0810 原则 [原則] /yuánzé/ (2) n principle
如实地答复孩子们的询问对她来说是原则问题。 It is a matter of principle with her to answer her children's questions honestly.
781 | 0.58 | 452

0811 当年 [當年] /dāngnián, dàngnián/ (2) time in those days, past; that very year, current year
好汉不提当年勇。 A hero is silent about his past glories.
482 | 0.94 | 452

0812 冲 [沖] /chōng/ (2, 3) v dash against, rush; rinse, flush; develop (a film)
他们冲到楼上。 They rushed up the stairs.
709 | 0.64 | 452

0813 找到 [找到] /zhǎodào/ v find
失踪的孩子还没找到。 The missing child has not been found yet.
517 | 0.87 | 452

0814 声音 [聲音] /shēngyīn/ (1) n sound, noise; voice
他的声音呈现出一种悲伤的情调。 His voice took on a sad tone.
779 | 0.58 | 451

0815 菜 [菜] /cài/ (1) n food; dish, course; vegetable
你喜欢吃中国菜吗？ Do you like Chinese food?
535 | 0.84 | 450

0816 说明 [説明] /shuōmíng/ (1) v explain
我要再说明一下吗？ Shall I explain it again?
539 | 0.84 | 450

0817 懂 [懂] /dǒng/ (1) v understand
我不懂。 I don't understand.
641 | 0.7 | 450

0818 反对 [反對] /fǎnduì/ (1) v oppose, object to, fight against
我们反对这个提议。 We object to the proposal.
589 | 0.76 | 450

0819 讨论 [討論] /tǎolùn/ (1) v discuss
研制的任务由委员会讨论。 The research task will be discussed by the committee.
592 | 0.76 | 450

0820 嗯 [嗯] /ēn, ńg, ňg, ǹg/ (1) interj [interjection used for questioning, surprise, disapproval, or agreement] well, eh, hey, m-hm, uh-huh
嗯，他们是天生一对嘛。 Well, they seem to make a good couple.
2525 | 0.18 | 449 | S

0821 系统 [系統] /xìtǒng/ (2) n system
修改后的系统使人比较满意。 The revised system is satisfactory.
720 | 0.62 | 449

0822 感情 [感情] /gǎnqíng/ (2) n feeling
我决不会有意伤害你的感情。 I would never intentionally hurt your feelings.
546 | 0.82 | 449

0823 组织 [組織] /zǔzhī/ (1) v organise
大家要我组织这次旅游，可是我把事情搞糟了。 I was asked to organise the trip, but I messed it up.
781 | 0.57 | 448

0824 仍然 [仍然] /réngrán/ (2) adv still
有些人仍然相信魔法。 Some people still believe in magic.
530 | 0.84 | 447

0825 性 [性] /xìng/ (2) suf [nominal suffix indicating a specified quality or property]
现在流行的运动几乎都是竞争性的。 Nearly all the sports practised nowadays are competitive.
610 | 0.73 | 445

0826 土地 [土地] /tǔdì/ (2) n land
也有自己全无土地，全部土地都是租入的。 Others have no land of their own at all and rent all their land.
652 | 0.68 | 445

0827 任务 [任務] /rènwù/ (2) n task, mission
虽然这个任务困难，他们还是设法按时完成了。 Though this task was difficult, they managed to accomplish it in time.
711 | 0.63 | 445

0828 代 [代] /dài/ (3) n generation; historical period, dynasty
一代更比一代强。 Each generation surpasses the preceding one.
529 | 0.84 | 445

0829 认真 [認真] /rènzhēn/ (1) adj earnest, serious
我是说着玩儿的，他就认真了。 I was only joking, but he took it seriously.
648 | 0.68 | 442

0830 样子 [樣子] /yàngzi/ (1) n look, appearance, manner
他显出惊异的样子。 He looked astonished.
698 | 0.63 | 442

0831 农业 [農業] /nóngyè/ (1) n agriculture
发展我们的农业是必要的。 It is necessary to develop our agriculture.
1130 | 0.39 | 442 | W

0832 工程 [工程] /gōngchéng/ (2) n engineering, project
你得雇个人监督这一工程。 You must employ someone to oversee the project.
1159 | 0.38 | 442 | W

0833 成绩 [成績] /chéngjī/ (1) n result, academic performance; achievement
今年的成绩要好于去年。 This year's result is better than last year's.
737 | 0.6 | 441

0834 老人 [老人] /lǎorén/ (2) n the aged, old people
她骗走了老人所有的钱。 She fooled the old man out of all his money.
469 | 0.94 | 441

0835 随着 [隨著] /suízhe/ prep along with
随着年龄的增长，人们就不那么喜欢幻想了。 People tend to become disillusioned as they grow older.
583 | 0.76 | 441

0836 加强 [加強] /jiāqiáng/ (2) v reinforce, intensify
要做到这一点，就要加强师资培训工作。
To enable them to do so, teacher training must be intensified.
1437 | 0.31 | 441 | W

0837 拍 [拍] /pāi/ (1) v clap, pat, strike; take (a picture), shoot (a film)
有人在我背上轻轻地拍了一下。Someone patted me on the back.
598 | 0.74 | 440

0838 不行 [不行] /bùxíng/ (2) adj won't do, no good, poor
你对衣着的鉴赏力不行。You have poor taste in dress.
704 | 0.62 | 439 | S

0839 节目 [節目] /jiémù/ (1) n programme; item of performance
我每周都看这个节目。I watch this programme every week.
702 | 0.63 | 439

0840 真正 [真正] /zhēnzhèng/ (1) adv really, truly, genuinely
现在真正干实际工作的还是那些年轻人。It's the younger people who are doing the real work today.
497 | 0.88 | 438

0841 自由 [自由] /zìyóu/ (2) adj free
这是一个自由的国家。This is a free country.
539 | 0.81 | 437

0842 直 [直] /zhí/ (2) adv straight, directly; keep (doing something), continuously
他们紧张得直哆嗦。They kept shivering with nervousness.
619 | 0.71 | 436

0843 来自 [來自] /láizì/ (2) v come from
我来自西南部。I come from the southwest.
665 | 0.66 | 435

0844 除了 [除了] /chúle/ (1) prep besides, in addition to; except
除了这个包裹外，还有12封挂号信也需投寄。There are twelve registered letters to be sent in addition to this parcel.
501 | 0.87 | 434

0845 县 [縣] /xiàn/ (2) n county
这个省由20个县组成。The province comprises twenty counties.
796 | 0.54 | 432

0846 人才 [人才] /réncái/ (2) n talented person, talent, qualified personnel
要尊重劳动，尊重人才。Labour must be valued and so must able personnel.
688 | 0.63 | 431

0847 教 [教] /jiào/ (1) v teach
下星期的什么时候教我好吗？Can you teach me sometime next week?
536 | 0.81 | 431

0848 重新 [重新] /chóngxīn/ (2) adv again; anew, afresh
我明天早晨重新开始工作。I'll start work again tomorrow morning.
472 | 0.91 | 430

0849 总统 [總統] /zǒngtǒng/ (2) n president (of a country)
总统演说由全国电视网联播。The president's speech is broadcast on a national television network.
987 | 0.44 | 430

0850 军队 [軍隊] /jūnduì/ (2) n army, troops
军队撤退了。The army withdrew.
569 | 0.76 | 430

0851 并且 [並且] /bìngqiě/ (2) conj and
然后填写这张表并且把它送到下一个窗口。Please fill out this form and take it to the next window.
549 | 0.78 | 428

0852 方向 [方向] /fāngxiàng/ (1) n direction
闪电向不同的方向扩散了。The lightning bolt forked in several directions.
504 | 0.85 | 428

0853 形式 [形式] /xíngshì/ (2) n form
主要是内容，其次才是形式。Content comes first, form second.
623 | 0.69 | 427

0854 意识 [意識] /yìshí/ (3) n consciousness
我们在睡眠期间没有意识。We have no consciousness during sleep.
531 | 0.8 | 427

0855 紧张 [緊張] /jǐnzhāng/ (1) adj nervous, strained
当她问问题的时候她的声音很紧张。Her voice was strained as she asked the question.
454 | 0.94 | 426

0856 科技 [科技] /kējì/ (3) n science and technology
现在要进一步解决科技和经济结合的问题。We should go a step further to integrate science and technology with economic development.
1210 | 0.35 | 426

0857 社会主义 [社會主義] /shèhuìzhǔyì/ (3) n socialism
贫穷绝不是社会主义。Socialism is certainly not poverty.
877 | 0.49 | 425 | W

0858 村 [村] /cūn/ n village
我们沿着村内一条主要街道走去。We walked down the main street of the village.
596 | 0.71 | 425

0859 看见 [看見] /kànjiàn/ (1) v see
我一看见她就立刻认出她来了。I recognised her immediately when I saw her.
705 | 0.6 | 425

0860 忙 [忙] /máng/ (1) adj busy
虽然他很忙，但从未缺过课。Although he is very busy, he has never been absent from class.
688 | 0.62 | 424

0861 事实 [事實] /shìshí/ (2) n fact
吸烟危害健康，这是事实。It is a fact that smoking is a danger to health.
483 | 0.88 | 424

0862 女性 [女性] /nǚxìng/ *n* female, woman
女性通常比男性长寿。 Women live longer than men in general.
591 | 0.72 | 423

0863 巨大 [巨大] /jùdà/ (2) *adj* huge
这部电视剧取得了巨大的成功。 The TV play was a huge success.
569 | 0.74 | 422

0864 会 [會] /huì/ (1) *n* meeting, conference; [also as 会儿] moment
我还有个会要开。 I still have a meeting to go to.
554 | 0.76 | 422

0865 背 [背] /bēi, bèi/ (2) *v* carry on one's back; learn by heart
她背着孩子。 She carried her child on her back.
593 | 0.71 | 421

0866 集团 [集團] /jítuán/ (3) *n* group
鼓励组建医疗服务集团。 The establishment of medical service groups is encouraged.
776 | 0.54 | 420 | W

0867 本 [本] /běn/ (2) *clas* [measure word for books, etc.]
学生们每人有十本书。 The students have ten books each.
497 | 0.85 | 420

0868 热 [熱] /rè/ (1) *adj* hot
人家说今年夏天很热。 They say we are going to have a hot summer.
499 | 0.84 | 419

0869 杀 [殺] /shā/ (2) *v* kill
如果我有一把剑，我就会杀了他。 If I had had a sword, I would have killed him.
561 | 0.75 | 419

0870 正常 [正常] /zhèngcháng/ (2) *adj* normal, regular
两国关系已恢复正常。 Relations between the two countries have been restored to normal.
476 | 0.88 | 418

0871 的话 [的話] /dehuà/ (2) *aux* [particle used at the end of a clause (. . . 的话) to express a condition] if
如果你同意的话我就来。 I will come if you agree.
604 | 0.69 | 418

0872 积极 [積極] /jījí/ (2) *adj* active; positive
中国政府对此作出了积极反应。 The Chinese government's response was positive.
1010 | 0.41 | 417 | W

0873 面前 [面前] /miànqián/ (2) *loc* before, in front of
那景色展现在我们面前。 The landscape unfolded before us.
621 | 0.67 | 417

0874 初 [初] /chū/ (2) *adj* elementary, just beginning; first
初雪来临。 The first snow came.
491 | 0.85 | 416

0875 以为 [以為] /yǐwéi/ (1) *v* think, believe
你真以为他喝醉了吗？ Did you think he was really drunk?
623 | 0.67 | 416

0876 还是 [還是] /háishì/ (1) *conj* or
你要茶还是要咖啡？ Would you prefer tea or coffee?
491 | 0.85 | 415

0877 消息 [消息] /xiāoxi/ (1) *n* news
当她听到这个好消息时，她的精神振奋了。 Her spirits rose when she heard the good news.
478 | 0.87 | 415

0878 科学 [科學] /kēxué/ (1) *adj* scientific
这些问题目前还没有科学的答案。 There are no scientific answers to these questions at present.
645 | 0.64 | 414

0879 船 [船] /chuán/ (1) *n* boat, ship
河中有一条船。 There is a boat in the river.
487 | 0.85 | 414

0880 机构 [機構] /jīgòu/ (3) *n* organisation, institution
公立医疗机构在管理和运行上缺乏活力。 The public medical institutions have poor capacity in management and operation.
857 | 0.48 | 414 | W

0881 跳 [跳] /tiào/ (1) *v* jump
他兴奋得跳来跳去。 He jumped up and down in excitement.
674 | 0.62 | 414

0882 倒 [倒] /dǎo, dào/ (1, 2) *v* fall, collapse; (business) close down; reverse, swap; dump (rubbish); move backwards; pour (tea)
他受到重击而倒下。 He collapsed under the full impact of the blow.
588 | 0.7 | 414

0883 运动 [運動] /yùndòng/ (1) *n* motion, movement; sports, exercise; (political) campaign
能推荐一些有当地特色的运动吗？ Could you recommend some local exercise classes to me?
513 | 0.8 | 412

0884 事件 [事件] /shìjiàn/ (2) *n* event, affair
新闻报导肆意夸大了整个事件。 The press exaggerated the whole affair wildly.
523 | 0.79 | 412

0885 鱼 [魚] /yú/ (1) *n* fish
鱼在水中，自得其所。 A fish in water is in its natural medium.
497 | 0.83 | 411

0886 采访 [採訪] /cǎifǎng/ *v* interview
如果你要采访市长，我可以安排。 If you want to interview the mayor, I can fix it.
581 | 0.71 | 411

0887 正是 [正是] /zhèngshì/ *v* be exactly
这正是我的想法。 That's exactly my intention.
503 | 0.82 | 411

0888 兴趣 [興趣] /xìngqù/ (2) *n* interest
他生活中有两大兴趣：音乐和绘画。 He has two great interests in life: music and painting.
469 | 0.88 | 410

0889 阶段 [階段] /jiēduàn/ (2) *n* stage
中国农村改革分为四个阶段。 China's rural reform may be divided into four stages.
593 | 0.69 | 410

0890 厂 [廠] /chǎng/ *n* factory
一个大厂就可以带动周围一片。 A big factory will be able to help the entire surrounding area.
566 | 0.72 | 410

0891 去年 [去年] /qùnián/ (1) *time* last year
这张照片是去年拍的。 This picture was taken last year.
1253 | 0.33 | 410 | W

0892 负责 [負責] /fùzé/ (1) *v* be in charge of; be responsible for
她是我的孩子，我对她负责。 She is my child, and I am responsible for her.
532 | 0.77 | 410

0893 充满 [充滿] /chōngmǎn/ (2) *v* be full of, be filled with
前途看来充满希望。 The future seems to be full of hope.
447 | 0.92 | 410

0894 人生 [人生] /rénshēng/ *n* (human) life
人生好比航海。 Life is compared to a voyage.
538 | 0.76 | 408

0895 装 [裝] /zhuāng/ (1) *v* pack, load; fix, install; pretend; play the role of
除了几件零星物品，所有的东西都装在盒子里了。 Everything has been packed in boxes except a few odds and ends.
502 | 0.81 | 407

0896 比如 [比如] /bǐrú/ (2) *v* take, for example
我想吃点特别的，比如北京烤鸭。 I'd like to eat something different, for example, Beijing roast duck.
604 | 0.67 | 407

0897 坏 [壞] /huài/ (1) *adj* bad
坏书比坏朋友害处更大。 Bad books do more harm than bad companions.
554 | 0.73 | 405

0898 眼 [眼] /yǎn/ (2) *n* eye
他眼露凶光。 He had a nasty look in his eye.
736 | 0.55 | 405

0899 饭 [飯] /fàn/ (1) *n* food, meal
是你做的饭吗？ Did you cook this food?
566 | 0.71 | 403

0900 经 [經] /jīng/ *prep* through, by means of; by way of, via
他们经伦敦去法国。 They are travelling to France by way of London.
578 | 0.7 | 403 | W

0901 商品 [商品] /shāngpǐn/ (2) *n* goods, commodity, article, item
很抱歉，这种商品暂时无货可供。 We are sorry that this item is out of stock for the time being.
665 | 0.61 | 402

0902 等等 [等等] /děngděng/ *aux* et cetera, and so on
我们学习政治、内科、外科等等。 We study politics, medicine, surgery and so forth.
520 | 0.77 | 402

0903 错 [錯] /cuò/ (1) *adj* wrong, mistaken
对不起，你打错号码了。 Sorry, but you have the wrong number.
557 | 0.72 | 401

0904 仅 [僅] /jǐn/ (2) *adv* just, only
这两次测试仅在一方面不同。 These two tests differ in only one respect.
646 | 0.62 | 401 | W

0905 现实 [現實] /xiànshí/ (2) *n* reality
他无法改变现实。 He cannot change the reality.
494 | 0.81 | 401

0906 证明 [證明] /zhèngmíng/ (2) *v* prove
时间会证明我是对的。 Time will prove me right.
459 | 0.87 | 401

0907 培养 [培養] /péiyǎng/ (3) *v* train, foster, rear, develop, cultivate
我不赞成她培养孩子的方法。 I disapprove of her child-rearing methods.
555 | 0.72 | 401

0908 另外 [另外] /lìngwài/ (2) *conj* in addition, by the way
另外，我还有点问题。 By the way, I might have a problem here.
585 | 0.69 | 400

0909 不管 [不管] /bùguǎn/ (2) *conj* no matter (what, how, etc.)
不管买哪个都有六个月的保修期。 Whichever you buy, there is a six-month guarantee.
497 | 0.81 | 400

0910 永远 [永遠] /yǒngyuǎn/ (1) *adv* forever
我永远不会忘记你。 I will never forget you.
503 | 0.8 | 400

0911 原来 [原來] /yuánlái/ (1) *adv* [meaning often implied in the past tense] originally, formerly; so, as a matter of fact
那原来是一家玩具工厂。 It was originally a toy factory.
534 | 0.75 | 399

0912 总理 [總理] /zǒnglǐ/ (2) *n* premier
周总理是一生勤勤恳恳、任劳任怨工作的人。 Premier Zhou was a man who worked hard and uncomplainingly all his life.
866 | 0.46 | 398

0913 作家 [作家] /zuòjiā/ (2) *n* writer
许多学生都喜欢阅读名作家的著作。 Many students like to read the works by the famous writers.
542 | 0.73 | 396

0914 西方 [西方] /xīfāng/ (2) *place* west; the West
希腊是西方文明的摇篮。 Greece was the cradle of Western culture.
539 | 0.74 | 396

0915 保证 [保證] /bǎozhèng/ (2) *v* guarantee
我向你保证按时完成工作。 You have my guarantee that I'll finish the job on time.
605 | 0.66 | 396

0916 立即 [立即] /lìjí/ (2) *adv* immediately
我立即派一辆去。 I'll send one at once.
514 | 0.77 | 395 | W

0917 飞机 [飛機] /fēijī/ (1) *n* airplane
我们在做一个飞机模型。 We are making a plane model.
469 | 0.84 | 395

0918 龙 [龍] /lóng/ (2) *n* dragon
龙的嘴里射出烟花火焰来。 The dragon shot fumes and flames out of its mouth.
510 | 0.78 | 395

0919 总是 [總是] /zǒngshì/ (1) *adv* always
油和水总是分开的。 Oil and water always separate out.
527 | 0.75 | 394

0920 医生 [醫生] /yīshēng/ (1) *n* doctor
我认不得医生的字迹。 I can't read the doctor's writing.
457 | 0.86 | 394

0921 名字 [名字] /míngzì/ (1) *n* name
我没有听清你的名字。 I didn't catch your name.
505 | 0.78 | 394

0922 班 [班] /bān/ (1) *n* class, team; shift, duty; squad
谁是你班最年轻的学生？ Who is the youngest in your class?
484 | 0.81 | 393

0923 层 [層] /céng/ (1) *clas* layer, tier; floor, storey
蛋糕中间有一层果酱。 The cake has a layer of jam in the middle.
467 | 0.84 | 393

0924 辆 [輛] /liàng/ (1) *clas* [measure word for vehicles]
一辆自行车比一辆小汽车便宜多了。 A bicycle is much cheaper than a car.
464 | 0.85 | 393

0925 开发 [開發] /kāifā/ (3) *v* develop, open up, exploit
科学家必须开发出新型能源。 Scientists must develop new forms of energy.
1287 | 0.31 | 393 | W

0926 平 [平] /píng/ (2) *adj* flat, level, even; calm; average, common
认为地球是平的的观念是错的。 That the earth is flat is an erroneous concept.
492 | 0.8 | 392

0927 至少 [至少] /zhìshǎo/ (2) *adv* at least
回家休息至少三四天。 Go home and rest for at least three or four days.
459 | 0.85 | 392

0928 实际上 [實際上] /shíjìshàng/ *adv* actually, in fact, as a matter of fact
实际上，增长知识是我们共同的愿望。 Actually, to gain more knowledge is our common interest.
628 | 0.62 | 392

0929 唱 [唱] /chàng/ (1) *v* sing
她唱得走调了。 Her singing was off key.
654 | 0.6 | 392

0930 之中 [之中] /zhīzhōng/ (2) *loc* in, inside, within
全镇沉浸在节日的气氛之中。 The whole town is in festive mood.
451 | 0.87 | 391

0931 里面 [裏面] /lǐmian/ (2) *loc* inside, in
里面没人。 There is nobody inside.
698 | 0.56 | 391 | S

0932 街 [街] /jiē/ (1) *n* street
沿这条街一直走两个街区。 Keep straight along this street for two blocks.
463 | 0.85 | 391

0933 矛盾 [矛盾] /máodùn/ (2) *adj* contradictory
那与存在的事实相矛盾。 It was contradictory to the existing facts.
475 | 0.82 | 390

0934 人口 [人口] /rénkǒu/ (2) *n* population
该市人口已增加到五百万。 The population of the city has risen to 5 million.
671 | 0.58 | 390

0935 是否 [是否] /shìfǒu/ (3) *v* whether (or not)
我去看看她是否在家。 I'll find out whether she's at home.
542 | 0.72 | 390

0936 明 [明] /míng/ *adj* bright, light, clear; open, overt, explicit
真理愈辩愈明。 The more truth is debated, the clearer it becomes.
458 | 0.85 | 389

0937 线 [線] /xiàn/ (2) *n* line; thread
从A到B画一条线。 Draw a line from A to B.
455 | 0.85 | 388

0938 委员会 [委員會] /wěiyuánhuì/ *n* committee
委员会由所有三个政党的成员组成。 The committee is composed of members of all three parties.
860 | 0.45 | 386 | W

0939 反映 [反映] /fǎnyìng/ (2) *v* reflect, mirror; report
这一举动反映出了他真正的信仰。 This action reflects his true beliefs.
536 | 0.72 | 386

0940 承认 [承認] /chéngrèn/ (2) *v* admit
他犯了严重的错误却不肯承认。 He made a gross mistake but refused to admit it.
423 | 0.91 | 386

0941 美元 [美元] /měiyuán/ (2) *n* US dollar
我想要100美元金额的旅行支票。 I'd like $100 worth of traveller's cheques.
1094 | 0.35 | 385 | W

0942 观众 [觀眾] /guānzhòng/ (2) *n* spectator, audience
电视节目有数以百万计的观众。TV programmes have an audience of several million.
534 | 0.72 | 385

0943 书记 [書記] /shūjì/ (2) *n* (party) secretary
第一书记不点头是不行的呀。Approval by the first secretary is a must.
586 | 0.66 | 385 | W

0944 旧 [舊] /jiù/ (1) *adj* old, used
把那辆旧车脱手了，我们很高兴。We are glad to get shot of that old car.
438 | 0.88 | 384

0945 关心 [關心] /guānxīn/ (1) *v* care for, be concerned about
国际国内都很关心这个问题。People both in China and abroad are concerned about this question.
498 | 0.77 | 384

0946 哎 [哎] /āi/ (2) *interj* [interjection expressing surprise, disapproval, reminder, etc.]
哎，这段时间我只得呆在这里了。Well, I'm stuck here for the duration.
1821 | 0.21 | 383 | S

0947 状态 [狀態] /zhuàngtài/ (2) *n* state of affairs, condition
不能改变这种状态。This state of affairs must not change.
467 | 0.82 | 383

0948 驻 [駐] /zhù/ (3) *v* be stationed
他受政府之命将担任驻日本的新大使。He is to be the new ambassador to Japan by decree of the government.
597 | 0.64 | 383

0949 解释 [解釋] /jiěshì/ (2) *v* explain
我们仍不能令人满意地解释宇宙的起源。We cannot yet satisfactorily explain the genesis of the universe.
460 | 0.83 | 382

0950 资源 [資源] /zīyuán/ (2) *n* resource
我国资源丰富。Our country is wealthy in resources.
768 | 0.5 | 381 | W

0951 俩 [倆] /liǎ/ (1) *num* the two of, both
你俩能来我很高兴。I am so glad the two of you can come.
612 | 0.62 | 380

0952 左右 [左右] /zuǒyòu/ (2) *num* [following a quantifier] about, or so
到那儿要 15 分钟左右。It'll take you about 15 minutes to get there.
469 | 0.81 | 380

0953 专业 [專業] /zhuānyè/ (2) *n* speciality, specialised field of study, major
他的专业是农业经济。His major is agricultural economy.
492 | 0.77 | 379

0954 若 [若] /ruò/ (3) *conj* if
你若那样做，就是自讨苦吃。If you do that, you're just asking for trouble.
552 | 0.69 | 378

0955 刚刚 [剛剛] /gānggang/ (2) *adv* just now, a short while ago; barely, just
他刚刚来。He has just come.
403 | 0.94 | 378

0956 工人 [工人] /gōngrén/ (1) *n* worker
这位工人正在逐个检查机器。The worker is checking one machine after another.
463 | 0.82 | 378

0957 回到 [回到] /huídào/ *v* come back, go back, return to
她平安地回到了家。She came back home safe and sound.
459 | 0.82 | 378

0958 双 [雙] /shuāng/ (3) *adj* double; even (as opposed to odd)
中国人喜欢双数。The Chinese people like even numbers.
449 | 0.84 | 377

0959 相当 [相當] /xiāngdāng/ (2) *adv* very, quite, considerably
这似乎是个相当不错的主意。It seems a very good idea.
443 | 0.85 | 377

0960 西 [西] /xī/ (1) *loc* west
这条小河折向西流。The stream bends to the west.
404 | 0.93 | 377

0961 师 [師] /shī/ *n* teacher; person with a particular professional skill; division
验光师说我需要配新眼镜。The optician said that I needed new glasses.
572 | 0.66 | 377 | W

0962 尽 [盡] /jìn, jǐn/ (2, 2) *v* exhaust; do one's best; give priority to
我们已尽了最大的努力。We have tried our best.
430 | 0.88 | 376

0963 别的 [別的] /biéde/ (1) *pron* other, else
先生，还要别的吗？Will there be anything else, sir?
528 | 0.71 | 375

0964 睡 [睡] /shuì/ (1) *v* sleep
他睡了四个多钟头。He slept more than four hours.
614 | 0.61 | 375

0965 收入 [收入] /shōurù/ (2) *n* income, revenue
她靠写作那点微薄的收入生活。She lives on the meagre income from her writing.
650 | 0.58 | 374

0966 位置 [位置] /wèizhi/ (2) *n* position, location
请把座位靠背转到垂直位置。Please put the back of your seat in an upright position.
414 | 0.9 | 374

0967 根本 [根本] /gēnběn/ *adv* [usually in negative sentences] at all; radically, thoroughly
这一夜她根本就没有睡。She didn't sleep at all that night.
487 | 0.77 | 373

7. City facilities and stores

学校	學校	*xuéxiào*	school	278
市场	市場	*shìchǎng*	market	304
医院	醫院	*yīyuàn*	hospital	635
银行	銀行	*yínháng*	bank	755
办公室	辦公室	*bàn'gōngshì*	office	1023
饭店	飯店	*fàndiàn*	hotel	1824
电视台	電視臺	*diànshìtái*	television station	1825
图书馆	圖書館	*túshūguǎn*	library	2156
商店	商店	*shāngdiàn*	store, shop	2408
电台	電臺	*diàntái*	radio station	2950
博物馆	博物館	*bówùguǎn*	museum	3209
车站	車站	*chēzhàn*	bus stop, station	3252
酒店	酒店	*jiǔdiàn*	hotel	3308
旅馆	旅館	*lǚguǎn*	guesthouse, hotel	3839
超市	超市	*chāoshì*	supermarket	4140
码头	碼頭	*mǎtóu*	harbour, wharf	4176
火车站	火車站	*huǒchēzhàn*	railway station	4188
书店	書店	*shūdiàn*	bookstore	4579
餐馆	餐館	*cān'guǎn*	restaurant	4815
饭馆	飯館	*fàn'guǎn*	restaurant	5957
动物园	動物園	*dòngwùyuán*	zoo	5992
剧院	劇院	*jùyuàn*	theatre	6897
教堂	教堂	*jiàotáng*	church, chapel	7098
旅行社	旅行社	*lǚxíngshè*	travel agency	7966
邮局	郵局	*yóujú*	post office	8498
酒吧	酒吧	*jiǔbā*	bar	8553
电影院	電影院	*diànyǐngyuàn*	cinema	8916
茶馆	茶館	*cháguǎn*	teahouse	9140
体育场	體育場	*tǐyùchǎng*	stadium	9707
美术馆	美術館	*měishù guǎn*	art gallery	10132
停车场	停車場	*tíngchēchǎng*	parking lot	10868
体育馆	體育館	*tǐyùguǎn*	gym	11212
警察局	警察局	*jǐngchájú*	police station	11777
药店	藥店	*yàodiàn*	pharmacy	14950
戏院	戲院	*xìyuàn*	theatre	15605
超级市场	超級市場	*chāojí shìchǎng*	supermarket	15676
咖啡馆	咖啡館	*kāfēi guǎn*	cafe	16610
药房	藥房	*yàofáng*	pharmacy	17350
飞机场	飛機場	*fēijīchǎng*	airport	18787
机场	機場	*jīchǎng*	airport	18787
植物园	植物園	*zhíwùyuán*	botanical garden	19868
音乐厅	音樂廳	*yīnyuètīng*	concert hall	24930
花店	花店	*huādiàn*	florist shop	28636

0968 不可 [不可] /bùkě/ (3) v cannot
一心不可二用。 No man can do two things at once.
450 | 0.83 | 372

0969 确实 [確實] /quèshí/ (1) adv truly, really
我确实得走了。 I really must go.
464 | 0.8 | 371

0970 点儿 [點兒] /diǎnr/ clas [measure word that often follows numeral 一] a little, a bit
要不要在茶里加点儿牛奶？ Would you like some milk in your tea?
742 | 0.5 | 371 | S

0971 够 [夠] /gòu/ (1) adj enough, sufficient
写这封信十分钟就够了。 Ten minutes is enough to write this letter.
519 | 0.72 | 371

0972 即使 [即使] /jíshǐ/ (3) conj even if
即使我们能去度假，我们可能也不想去。 Even if we could have taken a vacation, we may not have wanted to.
487 | 0.76 | 370

0973 工业 [工業] /gōngyè/ (1) n industry
贸易促进工业的发展。 Trade helps the development of industry.
911 | 0.41 | 370 | W

0974 重视 [重視] /zhòngshì/ (2) v take something seriously, attach importance to
中国对此同样十分重视。 China also attaches great importance to this issue.
653 | 0.57 | 370

0975 追求 [追求] /zhuīqiú/ (3) v seek, pursue; court, woo
他为了追求享乐而白白虚度了一生。 He wasted his life in the vain pursuit of pleasure.
425 | 0.87 | 370

0976 动物 [動物] /dòngwù/ (1) n animal
虎是一种凶猛的动物。 The tiger is a fierce animal.
487 | 0.76 | 369

0977 封 [封] /fēng/ (1) clas [measure word for letters, telegrams, etc.]
我昨天给她写了一封信。 I wrote a letter to her yesterday.
472 | 0.78 | 369

0978 指出 [指出] /zhǐchū/ (2) v point out
假如我指出你的错，请别见怪。 Please don't take it amiss, if I point out your errors.
932 | 0.4 | 369 | W

0979 道 [道] /dào/ (2) v [archaic, usually following communication verbs such as 说, 笑, 喊 and 叫] say, talk, speak
刘小姐道："不知道谁会哭！" Miss Liu said, "Who does the crying?"
616 | 0.6 | 369

0980 哭 [哭] /kū/ (1) v cry, sob, weep
这小孩从来不哭，除非生病。 The child never cried unless sick.
663 | 0.56 | 368

0981 衣服 [衣服] /yīfu/ (1) n clothes, dress
汗水浸透了他们的衣服。 Sweat soaked their clothes.
567 | 0.65 | 367

0982 图 [圖] /tú/ (2) n picture, drawing, chart, diagram, graph
他在图上画了一条线。 He drew a line on the chart.
479 | 0.77 | 366

0983 公里 [公里] /gōnglǐ/ (1) clas kilometre, km
光一秒钟传播的距离约30万公里。 The distance light travels in one second is about 300,000 kilometres.
566 | 0.65 | 366

0984 借 [借] /jiè/ (1) v borrow, lend; take advantage of, make use of
我可以借一下你的照相机吗？ Can I borrow your camera?
442 | 0.83 | 366

0985 拥有 [擁有] /yōngyǒu/ v have, possess, own
他拥有一家小型旅游公司。 He owns a small travel business.
510 | 0.72 | 366

0986 官 [官] /guān/ (2) n official, officer
清官难断家务事。 Even an upright official finds it hard to settle a family quarrel.
456 | 0.8 | 365

0987 那儿 [那兒] /nàr/ (1) pron there
那儿有两辆公共汽车。 There are two buses over there.
775 | 0.47 | 365 | S

0988 试 [試] /shì/ (1) v test, try
给我一个机会来试一试这个工作。 Give me a chance to try the job.
450 | 0.81 | 365

0989 回去 [回去] /huíqù/ (1) v return, go back
一小时后他们遛跶着回去工作。 They wandered back to work an hour later.
590 | 0.62 | 365

0990 军事 [軍事] /jūnshì/ (2) n military affairs
军事干涉极不相宜。 Military intervention is highly undesirable.
523 | 0.7 | 364

0991 团 [團] /tuán/ (2) n something with a round shape, ball, wad; group; regiment; [short form for 共青团] the League
噪声很大，她用棉花团把耳朵堵上了。 The noise was so loud that she put a wad of cotton wool in her ear.
391 | 0.93 | 364

0992 应当 [應當] /yīngdāng/ (2) v should, ought to
你应当多锻炼以保持精力充沛。 You should exercise more so as to keep energetic.
515 | 0.71 | 364

0993 明显 [明顯] /míngxiǎn/ (2) adj obvious, notable, clear
中国发生了明显的变化。 Notable changes have taken place in China.
534 | 0.68 | 363

0994 语言 [語言] /yǔyán/ (1) *n* language
掌握一门语言要花好几年。 It takes years to master a language.
538 | 0.68 | 363

0995 丈夫 [丈夫] /zhàngfu/ (2) *n* husband
我丈夫已经教三十年书了。 My husband has taught for 30 years.
491 | 0.74 | 363

0996 画 [畫] /huà/ (1) *v* draw, paint (a picture)
她画了一张我的肖像。 She drew a portrait of me.
451 | 0.81 | 363

0997 主 [主] /zhǔ/ *adj* main, primary, principal
主甲板被淹没了。 The main deck was afloat.
410 | 0.88 | 362

0998 日子 [日子] /rìzi/ (1) *n* date; day, time; life
人们记得这是一个难忘的日子。 Everyone remembers the day that is a memorable day.
481 | 0.75 | 362

0999 留下 [留下] /liúxià/ *v* leave behind, remain
那么请留下车子和车钥匙？ Then would you leave your car and keys here?
401 | 0.9 | 362

1000 家 [家] /jiā/ (1) *suf* [nominal suffix indicating a specialist in a particular field] -ist, -ian
统计学家应是多面手。 A statistician has to be something of a generalist.
420 | 0.86 | 361

1001 大量 [大量] /dàliàng/ (2) *num* a great deal of, plenty of
他有大量信件要处理。 He had a great deal of correspondence to deal with.
532 | 0.68 | 360

1002 未来 [未來] /wèilái/ (2) *time* the future
我尽量不去想未来。 I try not to think of the future.
482 | 0.75 | 360

1003 毕业 [畢業] /bìyè/ (2) *v* graduate
你哪一年毕业的? When did you graduate?
433 | 0.83 | 360

1004 刚才 [剛才] /gāngcái/ (1) *adv* just now, a moment ago
他刚才睡了一会儿。 He slept a little just now.
657 | 0.55 | 359 | S

1005 遇到 [遇到] /yùdào/ (1) *v* encounter, meet, come across, run into
我在星期二遇到了他。 I met him on Tuesday.
405 | 0.89 | 359

1006 不错 [不錯] /búcuò/ (1) *adj* not bad, pretty good; correct, right
这幅画不错。 This picture is not bad.
502 | 0.71 | 358

1007 愿 [願] /yuàn/ (3) *v* hope, wish; will, be willing to
我愿尽全力帮助你。 I'll do my best to help you.
425 | 0.84 | 358

1008 马 [馬] /mǎ/ (1) *n* horse
她从来没骑过马。 She never sat on a horse.
458 | 0.78 | 357

1009 结婚 [結婚] /jiéhūn/ (2) *v* marry
你要结婚是真的吗？ Is it true you're getting married?
534 | 0.67 | 357

1010 交 [交] /jiāo/ (1) *v* hand in, submit, deliver
我们今天必须交练习吗？ Must we hand in the exercise today?
390 | 0.91 | 356

1011 充分 [充分] /chōngfèn/ (2) *adj* full, abundant, ample, sufficient
没有充分的证据证明他有罪。 There wasn't sufficient evidence to prove him guilty.
649 | 0.55 | 355 | W

1012 北 [北] /běi/ (1) *loc* north
一大群鸟向北飞去。 A flock of birds flew to the north.
392 | 0.91 | 355

1013 级 [級] /jí/ *clas* [measure word for levels, grades and ranks, etc.]; [measure word for stairs, and steps, etc.]
国际风力等级把风分为从 0 级到 12 级的 12 个等级。 Wind is divided into 12 levels ranging from 0 to 12 on the international scale of wind force.
738 | 0.48 | 355 | W

1014 哪里 [哪裡] /nǎli/ (1) *pron* where; wherever; [often used (in repetition) as a modest reply to a compliment]; [used in a rhetorical question for negation]
你去哪里了？ Where did you go?
478 | 0.74 | 355

1015 嘴 [嘴] /zuǐ/ (1) *n* mouth
张开嘴好吗？ Open your mouth wide, will you?
574 | 0.62 | 354

1016 诗 [詩] /shī/ (2) *n* poem, poetry
她创作了一首诗。 She composed a poem.
515 | 0.69 | 354

1017 质量 [質量] /zhìliàng/ (2) *n* quality
我们对产品做例行质量检查。 We conduct regular checks on the quality of our product.
702 | 0.51 | 354

1018 那时 [那時] /nàshí/ *pron* at that time
她那时正在做家庭作业。 She was doing her homework at that time.
466 | 0.76 | 354

1019 明天 [明天] /míngtiān/ (1) *time* tomorrow
今日可做的事不要拖到明天。 Don't put off until tomorrow what can be done today.
454 | 0.78 | 354

1020 欢迎 [歡迎] /huānyíng/ (1) *v* welcome
我很高兴今天在这里欢迎你们。 It is my pleasure to welcome you all here today.
517 | 0.69 | 354

1021 交流 [交流] /jiāoliú/ (2) *v* exchange, interchange
他们经常交流经验。 They exchange experience from time to time.
645 | 0.55 | 353

1022 形象 [形象] /xíngxiàng/ (2) *n* image
她的形象在我眼前出现了。Her image rose before my eyes.
431 | 0.82 | 352

1023 办公室 [辦公室] /bàngōngshì/ (1) *n* office
会议将在我们办公室召开。The meeting will take place in our office.
420 | 0.84 | 351

1024 增长 [增長] /zēngzhǎng/ (2) *v* grow, increase
今年国家的国民生产总值增长了10%。The country's GNP has risen by 10 per cent this year.
1150 | 0.31 | 351 | W

1025 强调 [強調] /qiángdiào/ (2) *v* emphasise, stress
厂长特别强调了那一点。The director stressed that point in particular.
713 | 0.49 | 351

1026 全面 [全面] /quánmiàn/ (2) *adj* all-around, overall
业界最新的变化将有助于带来全面的改进。Recent changes in the industry will help bring about overall improvements.
754 | 0.46 | 350 | W

1027 言 [言] /yán/ *n* speech, word
他言行不一。His word is not in agreement with his deed.
441 | 0.79 | 350

1028 迅速 [迅速] /xùnsù/ (2) *adv* rapidly
业务正在迅速发展。Business is developing rapidly.
494 | 0.71 | 349 | W

1029 网 [網] /wǎng/ *n* net; web, internet
这网是用来捕鱼的。This net is used to catch fish.
496 | 0.7 | 349 | W

1030 加上 [加上] /jiāshàng/ *v* add, include
请在名单上加上我的名字。Please add my name to the list.
375 | 0.93 | 349

1031 房 [房] /fáng/ *n* room
这间房多少钱？What is the price of the room?
456 | 0.76 | 348

1032 开放 [開放] /kāifàng/ (2) *v* open, open up; (flower) blossom
阅览室今天不开放是吗？The reading room won't open today, will it?
737 | 0.47 | 348 | W

1033 关注 [關注] /guānzhù/ *v* follow (an issue) closely with interest
请对此多加关注。Please give it your attention.
487 | 0.71 | 348

1034 观念 [觀念] /guānniàn/ (3) *n* idea, notion, view
这项新的发现对传统观念提出了挑战。This new discovery challenges traditional beliefs.
468 | 0.74 | 347

1035 群 [群] /qún/ (2) *clas* [measure word for people or things gathered, also for some birds and animals] crowd, flock, herd
我们在那里看到一群群的牛在草地上吃草。There we saw herds of cows grazing on the pasture.
414 | 0.84 | 347

1036 正式 [正式] /zhèngshì/ (2) *adj* formal, official
这家店下周正式开张。The official opening of the store will take place next week.
586 | 0.59 | 346

1037 长期 [長期] /chángqī/ (2) *adj* long-term
改革开放是我国长期的战略方针。The reform and open policy is the long-term strategy of our country.
539 | 0.64 | 346

1038 重大 [重大] /zhòngdà/ (2) *adj* great, major, important, significant
这一发现意义重大。This is a significant finding.
686 | 0.5 | 346

1039 实在 [實在] /shízài/ (2) *adv* indeed, really
我实在不喜欢它。I really hate it.
492 | 0.7 | 346

1040 女子 [女子] /nǚzǐ/ (3) *n* woman
任何女子都忍受不了这种情况。It's more than a woman can tolerate.
494 | 0.7 | 346

1041 快 [快] /kuài/ *adv* fast, quickly; soon
我很快就睡着了。I went to sleep quickly.
557 | 0.62 | 345

1042 照片 [照片] /zhàopiàn/ (2) *n* photo
我们在公园里拍了一些照片。We took several photos in the park.
398 | 0.87 | 345

1043 古 [古] /gǔ/ (2) *adj* ancient, old
她是一位古钱币专家。She is an expert in old coins.
396 | 0.87 | 344

1044 本来 [本來] /běnlái/ (2) *adv* originally
她本来从哪儿来的？Where did she come from originally?
449 | 0.77 | 344

1045 发挥 [發揮] /fāhuī/ (2) *v* bring into play, give play to
我想找一份能让我发挥所长的工作。I'm looking for a job that gives me an opportunity to do what I'm good at.
719 | 0.48 | 344

1046 姑娘 [姑娘] /gūniáng/ (1) *n* girl
姑娘们穿着漂亮、时髦。The girls were well turned out and smart.
487 | 0.71 | 343

1047 感 [感] /gǎn/ *v* feel
她无礼的言词使他深感受辱。He felt deeply insulted by her rude words.
413 | 0.83 | 343

1048 看来 [看來] /kànlái/ (2) *conj* it appears, it looks as if
看来今天将会变热。It looks as if it's going to get hot today.
456 | 0.75 | 342

1049 年 [年] /nián/ clas year
她的第一次婚姻维持了五年。Her first
marriage ended after five years.
413 | 0.83 | 342

1050 式 [式] /shì/ suf type, style
我们要一份美式早餐。We'd like an American-
style breakfast.
445 | 0.77 | 341

1051 音乐 [音樂] /yīnyuè/ (1) n music
人们称音乐为世界的语言。Music has been
called the universal language.
400 | 0.85 | 341

1052 停 [停] /tíng/ (1) v stop
幸亏在我们出发前雨停了。Fortunately the
rain stopped before we started.
531 | 0.64 | 341

1053 结合 [結合] /jiéhé/ (2) v combine, integrate;
be united in wedlock
我们必须把理论与实践相结合。We must
combine theory with practice.
613 | 0.56 | 341

1054 竞争 [競爭] /jìngzhēng/ (3) v compete, rival
说到美，没有哪个城市能与威尼斯竞争。
No city can rival Venice in beauty.
562 | 0.61 | 341

1055 进一步 [進一步] /jìnyíbù/ (2) adv further
妇女受教育的权利得到进一步保障。Women's
rights to receive education have been further
protected.
962 | 0.35 | 340 | W

1056 当地 [當地] /dāngdì/ (2) place local, in the
locality
上星期二他接到当地警察局的来信。
Last Tuesday he received a letter from the
local police.
513 | 0.66 | 340

1057 立 [立] /lì/ (2) v stand; erect, set up;
establish
那颗老松树仍然立在那儿，像一把雨伞
盖住了入口。The old pine tree still stood
there like an umbrella covering the
entrance.
392 | 0.87 | 340

1058 伟大 [偉大] /wěidà/ (1) adj great
谁是最伟大的活着的诗人？Who is the
greatest living poet?
426 | 0.8 | 339

1059 特点 [特點] /tèdiǎn/ (2) n characteristic
(feature)
她最为突出的特点是诚实。Her predominant
characteristic is honesty.
454 | 0.75 | 338

1060 房子 [房子] /fángzi/ (2) n house
他们住在路右边一所小房子里。They live
in a small house on the right side of the
road.
471 | 0.72 | 338

1061 超过 [超過] /chāoguò/ (2) v surpass, exceed
所用的时间从不超过一小时。It never takes
more than an hour.
526 | 0.64 | 338

1062 力 [力] /lì/ (2) n power, strength
她个子虽小但力大惊人。For a small woman
she has surprising strength.
430 | 0.79 | 337

1063 每年 [每年] /měinián/ time every year
我每年都到那里去。I go there every year.
536 | 0.63 | 337

1064 范围 [範圍] /fànwéi/ (2) n range, scope
你们的经营范围是什么？What's your business
scope?
480 | 0.7 | 336

1065 求 [求] /qiú/ (2) v beg, request, strike for,
seek
放开他吧，我求求你！Set him free, I beg you!
385 | 0.87 | 336

1066 儿童 [兒童] /értóng/ (2) n child, children
他把大量时间花在设法帮助弱智儿童上。
He invested a lot of time in trying to help
retarded children.
470 | 0.71 | 335

1067 洗 [洗] /xǐ/ (1) v wash
我在洗杯子。I was washing cups.
453 | 0.74 | 335

1068 上面 [上面] /shàngmian/ (2) loc on top of,
above, over; aforesaid
我要烤个蛋糕，并在上面插上蜡烛。I'll bake a
cake and put candles on it.
452 | 0.74 | 334

1069 任 [任] /rèn/ (3) v appoint, occupy or take up a
post; give free rein to
我姐姐在该部门任要职。My sister
occupies an important position in that
department.
407 | 0.82 | 334

1070 回家 [回家] /huíjiā/ v go home, come
home
他昨天回家了。He went home yesterday.
458 | 0.73 | 334

1071 急 [急] /jí/ (1) adj anxious; annoyed; urgent;
hurried
我比你还急嘛！I am actually more anxious
than you are!
526 | 0.63 | 332

1072 学院 [學院] /xuéyuàn/ (1) n college
她从一所美国的学院毕业。She graduated
from an American college.
443 | 0.75 | 332

1073 烟 [煙] /yān/ (3) n smoke; cigarette
烟熏得他咳嗽起来。The smoke made him
cough.
503 | 0.66 | 332

1074 商业 [商業] /shāngyè/ (2) n business,
commerce
他通过卑鄙的手段来达到商业上的成功。
He achieved success in business only by
underhand methods.
471 | 0.7 | 331

1075 兵 [兵] /bīng/ (2) n soldier
您当过兵吗？You have been a soldier?
389 | 0.85 | 331

1076 材料 [材料] /cáiliào/ (2) *n* material
现在塑胶已代替了许多传统材料。Nowadays plastics have taken the place of many conventional materials.
411 | 0.81 | 331

1077 火 [火] /huǒ/ (2) *n* fire
无火不起烟。There is no smoke without fire.
409 | 0.81 | 331

1078 战略 [戰略] /zhànlüè/ (3) *n* strategy
我们的战略战术根据自己球队情况而定。We base our strategy and tactics on the conditions of our team.
666 | 0.5 | 331 | W

1079 听说 [聽説] /tīngshuō/ (1) *v* hear of, be told
我从未听说有人做那种事。I've never heard of anyone doing that.
473 | 0.7 | 331

1080 上 [上] /shàng/ (1) *v* go up, ascend; board; leave for; go ahead; be engaged in (class, work, etc.); serve (tea, food, etc.)
我们通常下午上两节课。We usually have two classes in the afternoon.
388 | 0.85 | 331

1081 恢复 [恢復] /huīfù/ (2) *v* resume, renew; recover, restore
网站恢复了。The websites were restored.
452 | 0.73 | 331

1082 强烈 [強烈] /qiángliè/ (2) *adj* intense, strong
这是一个强烈的对比。This is a strong contrast.
409 | 0.81 | 330

1083 挂 [掛] /guà/ (1) *v* hang
钥匙挂在门边的一根绳子上。The key is hanging on a string by the door.
419 | 0.79 | 330

1084 反正 [反正] /fǎnzhèng/ (2) *adv* anyway
反正要去一个人，就让我去吧。Since someone has to go anyway, let me go.
723 | 0.46 | 329 | S

1085 肯定 [肯定] /kěndìng/ (2) *v* be certain; affirm
我敢肯定您会喜欢的。I'm sure you will enjoy it.
375 | 0.88 | 329

1086 特殊 [特殊] /tèshū/ (2) *adj* special
守门是一项特殊的技能。Goalkeeping is a special skill.
405 | 0.81 | 328

1087 中间 [中間] /zhōngjiān/ (1) *loc* middle, between
我的自行车被两辆汽车夹在中间。My bicycle was caught between two cars.
382 | 0.86 | 328

1088 教师 [教師] /jiàoshī/ (2) *n* teacher
我想要做一名教师。I want to be a teacher.
406 | 0.81 | 328

1089 包 [包] /bāo/ (2) *v* pack, wrap; assure, guarantee; undertake the whole thing; hire
给我把这包裹包好。Wrap this package for me.
414 | 0.79 | 328

1090 道理 [道理] /dàolǐ/ (1) *n* reason
道理很简单。The reason is very simple.
401 | 0.82 | 327

1091 世 [世] /shì/ *n* the world; lifetime; era, age
桂林以山水著称于世。Guilin is known throughout the world for its scenery.
361 | 0.91 | 327

1092 批评 [批評] /pīpíng/ (1) *v* criticise
他严厉地批评了我。He criticised me sharply.
414 | 0.79 | 327

1093 前 [前] /qián/ *pref* ex-, former
这是美国前总统尼克松谈话的一部分。This is an excerpt from a talk by the former President Nixon.
434 | 0.75 | 326

1094 何 [何] /hé/ *pron* what, how, when, where, why
中国经济发展从何入手？Where shall we begin developing China's economy?
399 | 0.82 | 326

1095 如今 [如今] /rújīn/ (2) *time* nowadays, today
如今，电影越来越让位于电视了。Today, films are losing more and more ground to TV shows.
395 | 0.83 | 326

1096 实行 [實行] /shíxíng/ (2) *v* implement, carry out, bring into effect
下周将实行夏日作息表。The summer schedule comes into effect next week.
686 | 0.48 | 326 | W

1097 短 [短] /duǎn/ (1) *adj* short, brief
随着冬天来临，白天越来越短了。The days get shorter as winter approaches.
381 | 0.85 | 325

1098 优秀 [優秀] /yōuxiù/ (2) *adj* excellent
她是优秀的网球选手。She's an excellent tennis player.
462 | 0.7 | 325

1099 因素 [因素] /yīnsù/ (2) *n* element, factor
贫穷是引发犯罪的一个因素。Poverty is a causative factor in crime.
459 | 0.71 | 325

1100 哪儿 [哪兒] /nǎr/ *pron* where
打扰了，这车是去哪儿的？Excuse me, where does this bus go?
577 | 0.56 | 325 | S

1101 忘 [忘] /wàng/ (1) *v* forget
忘了它吧！Forget it!
472 | 0.69 | 325

1102 失去 [失去] /shīqù/ (2) *v* lose
在激烈的争论中，他失去了控制。In the heat of the argument he lost his self-control.
399 | 0.82 | 325

1103 正确 [正確] /zhèngquè/ (1) *adj* correct
所述的每一细节都正确无误。The account is correct in every particular.
490 | 0.66 | 324

1104 手段 [手段] /shǒuduàn/ (2) n means, method; measure, step; trick
什么也不能诱使他采用那样的手段。Nothing could tempt him to take such a step.
431 | 0.75 | 324

1105 翻 [翻] /fān/ (1) v open (a book); turn over; look through; get over, cross; translate
你在我的书桌里乱翻什么呀？What are you doing rooting around in my desk?
428 | 0.76 | 324

1106 吃饭 [吃飯] /chīfàn/ v eat (a meal)
一起去吃饭好吗？Shall we go out to dinner?
446 | 0.73 | 324

1107 期间 [期間] /qījiān/ (2) time period of time, course
在整个表演期间，我们不得不站着！We had to stand for the entire performance!
604 | 0.54 | 323

1108 断 [斷] /duàn/ (2) v break
我的腿断了。I've broken my leg.
367 | 0.88 | 323

1109 无论 [無論] /wúlùn/ (2) conj no matter (what, how)
无论怎样劝说，她也总是我行我素。Whatever you suggest, she will always go her own way.
414 | 0.78 | 322

1110 往往 [往往] /wǎngwǎng/ (2) adv often, frequently
业余演员往往表演过火。Amateur actors often overact.
491 | 0.66 | 322

1111 店 [店] /diàn/ (2) n shop, store; inn
在本店购买的商品七天内可以退换。Goods purchased in this store are refundable within seven days.
381 | 0.85 | 322

1112 人家 [人家] /rénjiā/ (3) n household, family
这儿有一家穷苦的人家。There is a needy family.
490 | 0.66 | 322

1113 黄 [黃] /huáng/ (1) adj yellow; pornographic
秋天树叶由绿变黄。In autumn the leaves change from green to yellow.
415 | 0.77 | 321

1114 光 [光] /guāng/ (2) n light, brightness; glory, honour
声音比光传播得慢些。Sound travels more slowly than light.
405 | 0.79 | 321

1115 老板 [老闆] /lǎobǎn/ (2) n boss
我和老板相处得很好。My boss and I get along very well.
473 | 0.68 | 321

1116 学者 [學者] /xuézhě/ (3) n scholar
他是一位经验丰富的学者。He is an experienced scholar.
440 | 0.73 | 321

1117 死 [死] /sǐ/ (3) adj dead
我在花园里看见了一只死鸟。I saw a dead bird in the garden.
449 | 0.71 | 320

1118 电脑 [電腦] /diànnǎo/ (3) n computer
房间里有一台电脑。There is a computer in the room.
442 | 0.73 | 320 | W

1119 见到 [見到] /jiàndào/ v see
我见到你很高兴。I'm very glad to see you.
420 | 0.76 | 320

1120 丰富 [豐富] /fēngfù/ (1) adj rich, abundant, plentiful
孩子们有丰富的想象力。The children have rich imaginations.
432 | 0.74 | 319

1121 大概 [大概] /dàgài/ (1) adv roughly
我大概在今晚8点会到达饭店。I'll be at the hotel at around eight tonight.
506 | 0.63 | 318 | S

1122 作者 [作者] /zuòzhě/ (2) n author
喜剧的作者是一位年轻人。The author of the comedy is a young man.
423 | 0.75 | 318

1123 检查 [檢查] /jiǎnchá/ (1) v check up, examine, inspect
请检查刹车。Please check the brakes.
486 | 0.66 | 318

1124 一边 [一邊] /yìbiān/ (1) adv at the same time, simultaneously
她一边等着一边翻阅杂志。She flicked through a magazine while she waited.
525 | 0.61 | 317

1125 合同 [合同] /hétóng/ (2) n contract
合同第三款规定了付款的时间。The third clause of the contract specifies when the payment is due.
418 | 0.76 | 317

1126 稳定 [穩定] /wěndìng/ (2) adj stable
物价稳定。Prices remain stable.
766 | 0.41 | 316 | W

1127 药 [藥] /yào/ (1) n medicine, drug
如果及时服用，这药是很有效的。If taken in time, the medicine will be effective.
355 | 0.89 | 316

1128 歌 [歌] /gē/ (1) n song
你喜欢那首歌吗？Do you like the song?
370 | 0.86 | 316

1129 退 [退] /tuì/ (1) v move back, retreat; return, refund; withdraw; (of tide) recede
潮退了。The tide is out.
350 | 0.9 | 316

1130 活 [活] /huó/ (1) v live, survive
我们没有食物和饮料就活不了多久。We cannot survive for long without food and drink.
434 | 0.73 | 316

1131 合 [合] /hé/ (2) v shut; suit, agree; combine; add up to
他然后合上了盒子，把它放回桌子上。He shut the box then, and put it back on the table.
370 | 0.85 | 316

8. Travel

路	路	*lù*	road	297
汽车	汽車	*qìchē*	car, bus	718
船	船	*chuán*	a boat, ship	879
飞机	飛機	*fēijī*	airplane	917
街	街	*jiē*	street	932
票	票	*piào*	ticket	1375
桥	橋	*qiáo*	bridge	1555
机场	機場	*jīchǎng*	airport	1801
公园	公園	*gōngyuán*	park	1998
火车	火車	*huǒchē*	train	2129
自行车	自行車	*zìxíngchē*	bicycle	2298
大街	大街	*dàjiē*	street, avenue	2398
街道	街道	*jiēdào*	street	2508
广场	廣場	*guǎngchǎng*	square	2580
马路	馬路	*mǎlù*	street, road	3043
旅馆	旅館	*lǚguǎn*	hotel	3839
摩托车	摩托車	*mótuōchē*	motorcycle	4086
码头	碼頭	*mǎtóu*	harbour, dock	4176
火车站	火車站	*huǒchēzhàn*	railway station	4188
出租车	出租車	*chūzūchē*	taxi, cab	4248
卡车	卡車	*kǎchē*	truck, lorry	4466
行李	行李	*xíngli*	baggage, luggage	4799
海关	海關	*hǎiguān*	customs	4984
签证	簽證	*qiānzhèng*	visa	5827
路口	路口	*lùkǒu*	crossing	6712
护照	護照	*hùzhào*	passport	6807
大道	大道	*dàdào*	main street	7061
隧道	隧道	*suìdào*	tunnel, underpass	7604
机票	機票	*jīpiào*	airline ticket	7671
旅行社	旅行社	*lǚxíngshè*	travel agency	7966
市中心	市中心	*shì zhōngxīn*	city centre, downtown	8320
导游	導遊	*dǎoyóu*	tour guide	8551
轮船	輪船	*lúnchuán*	ship	8737
地铁	地鐵	*dìtiě*	subway	8810
停车场	停車場	*tíngchēchǎng*	parking lot	10868
日程	日程	*rìchéng*	itinerary	11085
天桥	天橋	*tiānqiáo*	overpass	12108
电车	電車	*diànchē*	trolley bus	13494
十字路口	十字路口	*shízìlùkǒu*	cross street	14442
加油站	加油站	*jiāyóu zhàn*	petrol station	16714
飞机场	飛機場	*fēijīchǎng*	airport	18787
出租汽车	出租汽車	*chūzū qìchē*	taxi, cab	22042
登机	登機	*dēngjī*	board	22619
汽车站	汽車站	*qìchēzhàn*	bus stop, bus station	22716
安全带	安全帶	*ānquándài*	seat belt	26798

1132 复杂 [複雜] /fùzá/ (1) *adj* complicated
我觉得情节太复杂了。 The plot was too complicated for me.
357 | 0.88 | 315

1133 养 [養] /yǎng/ (2) *v* keep, raise (animals, etc.); provide for, support (a family); give birth to; develop (a habit); rest, maintain
我这里养了许多宠物。 I keep many pets here.
380 | 0.83 | 315

1134 烧 [燒] /shāo/ (2) *v* burn; cook, have a fever
那房子烧成了灰烬。 The house burnt to ashes.
414 | 0.76 | 315

1135 不再 [不再] /búzài/ *adv* no longer
他不再做生意了。 He is no longer in business.
401 | 0.78 | 314

1136 外国 [外國] /wàiguó/ (1) *n* foreign country
该课程是专为外国学生开的。 The course was orientated towards foreign students.
423 | 0.74 | 314

1137 警察 [警察] /jǐngchá/ (2) *n* police
警察取缔了违法药品。 The police clamped down on illegal drugs.
352 | 0.89 | 314

1138 狗 [狗] /gǒu/ (2) *n* dog
狗摇着尾巴迎接主人。 The dog greeted its master with a wag of its tail.
448 | 0.7 | 314

1139 资金 [資金] /zījīn/ (3) *n* fund, capital
他们面临的最大困难是资金不足。 Lack of funds was the main difficulty that faced them.
740 | 0.42 | 314 | W

1140 会儿 [會兒] /huìr/ *clas* [usually following the numeral 一] a moment, a while
您能等一会儿吗? Would you mind waiting for a while?
536 | 0.59 | 314

1141 摆 [擺] /bǎi/ (1) *v* put, place, arrange; put on (airs); sway
她把拖鞋整齐地摆在床下。 She put the slippers under the bed neatly.
364 | 0.86 | 314

1142 必要 [必要] /bìyào/ (2) *adj* necessary
睡眠对健康是必要的。 Sleep is necessary to health.
387 | 0.81 | 313

1143 训练 [訓練] /xùnliàn/ (2) *v* train
受过特殊训练的狗能嗅出毒品。 Specially trained dogs can sniff out drugs.
411 | 0.76 | 313

1144 资料 [資料] /zīliào/ (2) *n* data, material
这儿有一些产品目录和技术资料。 Here are some catalogues and technical data.
414 | 0.75 | 312

1145 属于 [屬於] /shǔyú/ *v* belong to, be classified as
他属于哪一组? What group does he belong to?
380 | 0.82 | 312

1146 分别 [分別] /fēnbié/ (2) *adv* respectively, separately
你们必须分别登记。 You'll have to register separately.
672 | 0.46 | 311 | W

1147 体育 [體育] /tǐyù/ (1) *n* sport; physical education, PE
中国拥有自己的体育传统。 China has its own sporting legends.
584 | 0.53 | 311

1148 建筑 [建築] /jiànzhù/ (2) *n* architecture; building
这些古老的建筑应该保存。 These ancient buildings must be preserved.
407 | 0.76 | 311

1149 宣布 [宣佈] /xuānbù/ (2) *v* announce, declare
宣布比赛什么时候开始了吗? Have they announced when the race will begin?
549 | 0.57 | 311

1150 值得 [值得] /zhídé/ (2) *v* deserve, be worth
国家博物馆值得一看,对吗? The national museum is worth visiting, isn't it?
361 | 0.86 | 311

1151 始终 [始終] /shǐzhōng/ (2) *adv* from beginning to end, all along, always
对我来说他始终是一个兄长。 I have always looked upon him as my elder brother.
386 | 0.81 | 310

1152 权 [權] /quán/ *n* power, authority; right
买方保留了索赔权。 The buyer reserved their right to claim.
401 | 0.77 | 310

1153 参与 [參與] /cānyù/ *v* participate, take part in, be involved in
我敢说他一定参与了此事。 I bet he had a hand in it.
555 | 0.56 | 310

1154 河 [河] /hé/ (1) *n* river
河中心的水流最急。 The current is strongest in the middle of the river.
342 | 0.9 | 309

1155 价格 [價格] /jiàgé/ (2) *n* price
食品价格下跌了。 The price of food has fallen.
546 | 0.57 | 309 | W

1156 怎么样 [怎麼樣] /zěnmeyàng/ (1) *pron* how
你们产品的质量怎么样? How is the quality of your product?
600 | 0.52 | 309 | S

1157 喊 [喊] /hǎn/ (1) *v* call, shout, yell
我把他们喊来了。 They came at my call.
620 | 0.5 | 309

1158 推 [推] /tuī/ (1) *v* push
用力推门。 Give the door a hard push.
417 | 0.74 | 309

1159 发出 [發出] /fāchū/ (2) *v* send out; give out
请贴发出了吗? Have you sent out the invitations?
360 | 0.86 | 309

1160 只有 [只有] /zhǐyǒu/ (2) *conj* only if
我们双方只有摊开来说才能达成协议。 We can only reach an agreement if we both put our cards on the table.
359 | 0.86 | 308

1161 很快 [很快] /hěnkuài/ *adv* quickly, soon
她休息了几天，身体很快复元了。 Her health soon picked up after a few days' rest.
357 | 0.86 | 308

1162 花 [花] /huā/ (1) *n* flower
这朵花是真的。 The flower is real.
375 | 0.82 | 308

1163 小姐 [小姐] /xiǎojie/ (1) *n* miss; young lady; [more recent usage] waitress; prostitute
小姐，你还要别的吗？ Do you need anything else, miss?
606 | 0.51 | 308

1164 似的 [似的] /sìde/ (3) *aux* seem, as if
他看来像失去知觉似的。 He looked as if he lost consciousness.
593 | 0.52 | 308

1165 设计 [設計] /shèjì/ (2) *v* design
这个房间不是为工作而设计的。 This room is not designed for work.
418 | 0.74 | 308

1166 真正 [真正] /zhēnzhèng/ (1) *adj* genuine, true, real
青蛙并非真正的爬行动物。 The frog is not a true reptile.
366 | 0.84 | 307

1167 爱情 [愛情] /àiqíng/ (2) *n* love
爱情不论门第。 Love makes all equal.
428 | 0.72 | 307

1168 民 [民] /mín/ *n* the people; civilian
一定要取信于民。 We must win the trust of the people.
366 | 0.84 | 307

1169 事儿 [事兒] /shìr/ *n* business, matter, affair
他老是想自己的事儿。 He is always full of his own affairs.
569 | 0.54 | 307 | S

1170 原 [原] /yuán/ *adj* former, original
他重任原公司的职务。 He resumed his former position with the company.
400 | 0.77 | 306

1171 队伍 [隊伍] /duìwǔ/ (2) *n* ranks, line, procession, parade; contingent
那年轻人走在游行队伍最前面。 The young man walked at the head of the parade.
468 | 0.65 | 306

1172 神 [神] /shén/ (2) *n* god
许多地方有神的庙宇。 There are temples of the gods in many places.
374 | 0.82 | 306

1173 领域 [領域] /lǐngyù/ (3) *n* domain, area, field
第一章阐明了她的研究领域。 The first chapter delimits her area of research.
677 | 0.45 | 306 | W

1174 般 [般] /bān/ (3) *aux* same as, just like
对他说话时，她明亮的眼睛充满了姊妹般的爱。 Her bright eyes were full of sisterly affection when she spoke to him.
408 | 0.75 | 306

1175 劳动 [勞動] /láodòng/ (1) *v* work; do physical labour
新中国妇女享有与男子同等的劳动权利。 In New China, women enjoy the same right to work as men.
418 | 0.73 | 306

1176 假 [假] /jiǎ/ (2) *adj* fake, false; artificial
这钻石是假的。 This diamond is a fake.
357 | 0.86 | 305

1177 部 [部] /bù/ (2) *n* part, section; department; ministry
我在找国际商务部。 I'm looking for the International Business Section.
369 | 0.83 | 304

1178 进步 [進步] /jìnbù/ (2) *v* make progress
虚心使人进步，骄傲使人落后。 Modesty helps one to go forward, conceit makes one lag behind.
475 | 0.64 | 304

1179 普通 [普通] /pǔtōng/ (2) *adj* common, ordinary
游泳是最普通的水上体育项目。 Swimming is the most common water sport.
349 | 0.87 | 303

1180 常常 [常常] /chángcháng/ (1) *adv* often, frequently
生活常常是不公平的。 Life is ofen unfair.
413 | 0.74 | 303

1181 掌握 [掌握] /zhǎngwò/ (1) *v* grasp, master
对我们来说，掌握两门外语是可能的。 It is not impossible for us to master two foreign languages.
372 | 0.81 | 303

1182 实施 [實施] /shíshī/ (3) *v* implement, carry out
实施网络安全是一个四阶段的过程。 Implementing network security is a four-stage process.
825 | 0.37 | 303 | W

1183 制 [制] /zhì/ (3) *v* make, manufacture
制冰机的声音淹没了音乐。 The noise from the ice-making machine drowned out the music.
387 | 0.78 | 303

1184 周围 [周圍] /zhōuwéi/ (1) *loc* around, round
如果我是你，我会在房子周围种一些树。 If I were you I would plant some trees round the house.
328 | 0.92 | 302

1185 妻子 [妻子] /qīzi/ (2) *n* wife
对我妻子所做的一切，我认为我不能负责。 I don't hold myself responsible for what my wife did.
413 | 0.73 | 302

1186 扩大 [擴大] /kuòdà/ (2) *v* enlarge, expand
书使我的知识面扩大了。 Books helped me to broaden my knowledge.
637 | 0.48 | 302 | W

1187 肉 [肉] /ròu/ (1) *n* meat
这肉似乎坏了。The meat smells as if it is tainted.
383 | 0.79 | 301

1188 自然 [自然] /zìrán/ *adv* naturally
她很自然地依恋这个地方。Naturally she is attached to the place.
391 | 0.77 | 300

1189 墙 [牆] /qiáng/ (1) *n* wall
请你把它放在那边的墙边好吗？Would you please put it over there by the wall?
371 | 0.81 | 300

1190 压力 [壓力] /yālì/ (3) *n* pressure
工作的压力把她的身体弄垮了。Her health broke down under the pressure of work.
359 | 0.84 | 300

1191 网络 [網絡] /wǎngluò/ *n* network
中国已建成遍及全国城乡的妇幼保健服务网络。China has set up healthcare networks for women and children all over the country.
532 | 0.56 | 299 | W

1192 斗争 [鬥爭] /dòuzhēng/ (2) *v* struggle, fight; strive for
人民更大规模地起来为救亡而斗争。More and more people have risen to fight for national salvation.
424 | 0.71 | 299

1193 建 [建] /jiàn/ (2) *v* establish; construct, build
这所房子的一侧建有一个车库。There is a garage built onto the side of the house.
442 | 0.68 | 299

1194 确定 [確定] /quèdìng/ (2) *v* determine, fix
我们来确定一个会议日期吧。Let's fix upon a date for the meeting.
438 | 0.68 | 299

1195 听到 [聽到] /tīngdào/ *v* hear
你听到老鼠吱吱叫吗？Can you hear the mice squeaking?
401 | 0.75 | 299

1196 销售 [銷售] /xiāoshòu/ *v* sell
我们还销售文具。We also sell stationery.
524 | 0.57 | 299 | W

1197 词 [詞] /cí/ (1) *n* word, term; speech, statement; [a kind of Chinese poetry]
你能从它的上下文说出这个词的意思吗？Can you tell the meaning of this word from its context?
421 | 0.71 | 298

1198 速度 [速度] /sùdù/ (2) *n* speed
火车加快了速度。The train picked up speed.
416 | 0.72 | 298

1199 通 [通] /tōng/ (1) *v* open up by poking; understand, know; connect, communicate; lead to
这条街道通哪儿？Where does this street lead?
321 | 0.93 | 298

1200 型 [型] /xíng/ *suf* model, type
本产品须提供三相接地型插头。The product is provided with a three-wire, grounding-type plug.
444 | 0.67 | 297

1201 报纸 [報紙] /bàozhǐ/ (2) *n* newspaper
我所知道的一切，都是从报纸上看来的。All I know is what I read in the newspapers.
325 | 0.92 | 297

1202 抓住 [抓住] /zhuāzhù/ *v* grab, grip; catch hold of; catch; seize (an opportunity)
她又抓住我抽烟了。She caught me smoking again.
362 | 0.82 | 297

1203 感受 [感受] /gǎnshòu/ (3) *v* sense, feel
我们感受到了通货膨胀的影响。We felt the effects of inflation.
344 | 0.86 | 296

1204 根本 [根本] /gēnběn/ (2) *adj* basic, fundamental
在这个根本问题上没有任何付价还价的余地。On this fundamental issue there is no room for haggling.
457 | 0.64 | 294

1205 夫人 [夫人] /fūrén/ (1) *n* lady; Mrs; wife
夫人，能告诉我发生什么事了吗？Would you please tell me what has happened, madam?
330 | 0.89 | 294

1206 番 [番] /fān/ (3) *clas* [measure word for a course of actions and events]; [measure word indicating species] kind; [measure word indicating multiplication] times, -fold
我们要把房子彻底打扫一番。We'll give the house a thorough cleaning.
342 | 0.86 | 294

1207 这时 [這時] /zhèshí/ *pron* at this time
这时下课铃响了。At this moment the bell rang announcing the end of class.
467 | 0.63 | 294 | W

1208 抱 [抱] /bào/ (1) *v* hold in arms
她抱着婴儿。She was holding the baby in her arms.
483 | 0.61 | 294

1209 钟 [鐘] /zhōng/ (1) *n* clock, bell
钟停了。The clock stopped.
435 | 0.68 | 293

1210 咱 [咱] /zán/ (1) *pron* [including the addressee] we, us
咱俩一道走吧。Let's go together.
525 | 0.56 | 293 | S

1211 热情 [熱情] /rèqíng/ (1) *adj* enthusiastic, cordial, warm
谢谢你们热情的接待。Thanks for your warm reception.
329 | 0.89 | 292

1212 语 [語] /yǔ/ *n* language, word
恶语伤人似利刃。One hurtful word wounds like a sharp sword.
385 | 0.76 | 292

1213 到底 [到底] /dàodǐ/ (2) *adv* to the end; at last, finally; after all; [used for emphasis]
他们到底在干什么？What on earth are they doing?
406 | 0.72 | 291

1214 措施 [措施] /cuòshī/ (2) n measure
我毫无保留地支持这一措施。 I support this measure without reservation.
707 | 0.41 | 291 | W

1215 建议 [建議] /jiànyì/ (2) n suggestion, proposal
我的建议遭到很多反对意见。 My proposal met with much opposition.
502 | 0.58 | 291 | W

1216 局 [局] /jú/ (3) n bureau, office; state of affairs
他在这个局工作过。 He worked in this bureau.
501 | 0.58 | 291

1217 工 [工] /gōng/ n work, labour; industry; project
你这样做既省工，又省料，一举两得。 You'll save both labour and material in this way.
313 | 0.93 | 291

1218 待 [待] /dāi, dài/ (2) v stay; wait for; deal with, treat; entertain
我们何不待在家里呢？ Why don't we stay at home?
358 | 0.81 | 291

1219 做出 [做出] /zuòchū/ v make, put out
我们经过长时间考虑后最终做出了决定。 We finally made the decision after lengthy deliberations.
347 | 0.84 | 291

1220 美丽 [美麗] /měilì/ (2) adj beautiful
西北是一个美丽的地方。 The northwest is a beautiful place.
383 | 0.76 | 290

1221 同时 [同時] /tóngshí/ (1) n meanwhile, the moment
他到达的同时房子塌了。 The building collapsed the moment he arrived.
415 | 0.7 | 290

1222 选 [選] /xuǎn/ (2) v choose
他选了块很好的带有花卉图案的料子做窗帘。 He chose a nice material with a floral pattern for the curtain.
319 | 0.91 | 290

1223 调整 [調整] /tiáozhěng/ (2) v adjust
我们准备按照你方要求调整报价。 We are ready to adjust our offer according to your request.
652 | 0.45 | 290 | W

1224 左 [左] /zuǒ/ (1) loc left
回头走，到第一条横马路往左拐。 Turn round and take the first on the left.
345 | 0.84 | 289

1225 贡献 [貢獻] /gòngxiàn/ (2) n contribution
爱因斯坦对科学作出了伟大的贡献。 Einstein made a great contribution to science.
510 | 0.57 | 289

1226 调 [調] /diào, tiáo/ (2) v transfer, shift; adjust, turn; harmonise
把收音机的声音调小点好吗？ Would you mind turning the radio down?
332 | 0.87 | 289

1227 漂亮 [漂亮] /piàoliang/ (1) adj beautiful, pretty, handsome; brilliant, remarkable
所有的晚礼服都很漂亮。 All the evening dresses were beautiful.
396 | 0.73 | 288

1228 还是 [還是] /háishì/ (1) adv still, yet; [indicating a preferred alternative]
还是太贵了。 That's still much too expensive.
374 | 0.77 | 288

1229 情绪 [情緒] /qíngxù/ (2) n feeling, emotion; mood, sentiment, morale; moodiness
这是一种正常的情绪，正常的反映。 That is a normal feeling and a normal reaction.
361 | 0.8 | 288

1230 意 [意] /yì/ n meaning, idea; intention, desire
"先生"的称谓则透着尊敬之意。 The addressing of "Mister" reveals the meaning of respect.
366 | 0.79 | 288

1231 颗 [顆] /kē/ (2) clas [measure word for small roundish objects such as grains]
他的衬衫少了三颗钮扣。 Three buttons were missing from his shirt.
360 | 0.8 | 288

1232 乱 [亂] /luàn/ adv at random, arbitrarily, disorderly
孩子们到处乱闯。 The children were rushing about.
328 | 0.88 | 287

1233 贸易 [貿易] /màoyì/ (2) n trade
冬季贸易不景气。 Trade is slack in winter.
749 | 0.38 | 287 | W

1234 接触 [接觸] /jiēchù/ (2) v contact, expose to
这些孩子从来没有接触过西方文化。 These children have never been exposed to Western culture.
328 | 0.88 | 287

1235 担心 [擔心] /dānxīn/ (2) v worry
你不必为她担心。 You do not need to be worrying about her.
378 | 0.76 | 287

1236 之外 [之外] /zhīwài/ (3) loc outside; except
那是在我的计划之外。 This is outside my plan.
331 | 0.87 | 286

1237 腿 [腿] /tuǐ/ (1) n leg
我的腿受伤了。 My leg hurts.
416 | 0.69 | 286

1238 幸福 [幸福] /xìngfú/ (1) adj happy, blessed
富人未必总是幸福的。 The rich are not always happy.
376 | 0.76 | 285

1239 胜利 [勝利] /shènglì/ (1) v be victorious
只要这两点做到了，我们就胜利了。 If we get these two points, we shall be victorious.
403 | 0.71 | 285

1240 特别 [特別] /tèbié/ (1) adj special, particular
您有什么特别的东西要报关吗？ Do you have anything particular to declare?
326 | 0.87 | 284

1241 肯定 [肯定] /kěndìng/ adv certainly, for
sure
他肯定是对的。 He is certainly right.
374 | 0.76 | 284

1242 女孩 [女孩] /nǚhái/ n girl
正在采花的那个女孩是我的妹妹。 The
girl gathering flowers is my younger
sister.
423 | 0.67 | 284

1243 头 [頭] /tóu/ (1) clas [measure word for
some animals such as pigs and cattle, also for
garlics]
河边有十二头公牛。 There are 12 oxen by the
stream.
351 | 0.81 | 284

1244 样 [樣] /yàng/ (2) clas [measure word for
material objects] type, sort
这三样东西哪样最贵？ Which of the three
costs most?
386 | 0.74 | 284

1245 反应 [反應] /fǎnyìng/ (2) n reaction; response
他对这消息的反应如何？ What was his
reaction to the news?
303 | 0.94 | 284

1246 投入 [投入] /tóurù/ (2) v throw (oneself) into
(work); put into (operation)
这个系统已经投入运行。 This system has
been put into operation.
532 | 0.54 | 284

1247 习惯 [習慣] /xíguàn/ (1) n habit
睡懒觉不是我的习惯。 It's not my habit to
sleep late.
376 | 0.75 | 283

1248 戏 [戲] /xì/ (2) n drama, play, show
这出戏是现实与虚构的混合物。 The play is a
composite of reality and fiction.
416 | 0.68 | 283

1249 回 [回] /huí/ (1) clas [measure word for actions
and events] times; [measure word for old-style
Chinese novels] chapter
这件事我们谈过好几回了。 We have talked it
over several times already.
430 | 0.66 | 283

1250 自我 [自我] /zìwǒ/ (2) pron oneself, self
思考是自我交谈。 To think is to converse with
oneself.
376 | 0.75 | 283

1251 心中 [心中] /xīnzhōng/ place in one's heart,
in one's mind
这个欲望深藏在他心中。 The desire was
deeply implanted in his heart.
440 | 0.64 | 283

1252 促进 [促進] /cùjìn/ (2) v promote, advance
我们必须促进与邻国的贸易。 We must
promote commerce with neighbouring
countries.
823 | 0.34 | 282 | W

1253 属 [屬] /shǔ/ v belong, be
他们不属同一级别。 They're not in the same
league.
335 | 0.84 | 282

1254 自然 [自然] /zìrán/ (2) adj natural
这小孩演得很自然。 The acting of the little
girl is natural and free from affectations.
332 | 0.85 | 281

1255 虽 [雖] /suī/ (3) conj although, though
文章虽短，但很有说服力。 The article is very
convincing though it is short.
366 | 0.77 | 281 | W

1256 业务 [業務] /yèwù/ (2) n business; professional
work
我公司业务已转向出口方面。 Our firm is
orientated towards the export side of the
business.
474 | 0.59 | 281 | W

1257 显得 [顯得] /xiǎnde/ (2) v appear, seem,
look
我跟她讲话时她始终显得心事重重。
She seemed preoccupied all the time I was
talking to her.
395 | 0.71 | 281

1258 记得 [記得] /jìde/ (2) v remember
我记得在我年轻的时候读了这本书三次。
I remember reading the book three times
when I was young.
372 | 0.76 | 281

1259 痛苦 [痛苦] /tòngkǔ/ (2) adj painful
他忘不了那种痛苦的回忆。 He could not rid
himself of the painful memories.
361 | 0.78 | 280

1260 满意 [滿意] /mǎnyì/ (1) adj satisfied,
satisfactory
亲眼看一看，便会满意的。 Yes, seeing for
yourself is the most satisfactory evidence.
338 | 0.83 | 279

1261 够 [夠] /gòu/ (1) v reach
在病人伸手可够得着的地方有个电铃。
There is a bell within the patient's reach.
297 | 0.94 | 279

1262 深刻 [深刻] /shēnkè/ (2) adj profound
这句话含义深刻。 This remark has profound
implications.
344 | 0.81 | 279

1263 唯一 [唯一] /wéiyī/ adj [equivalent of 惟一] only
她是唯一能做那事的人。 She was the only
person able to do it.
333 | 0.84 | 279

1264 兄弟 [兄弟] /xiōngdì/ (2) n brother
她有兄弟姐妹吗？ Does she have any brothers
or sisters?
362 | 0.77 | 279

1265 院 [院] /yuàn/ (2) n courtyard; academy,
institute, hospital
他因轻度烧伤而入院。 He was admitted to
hospital with minor burns.
313 | 0.89 | 279

1266 骂 [罵] /mà/ (2) v scold, tell off; call names,
curse; condemn
那些男孩子很吵闹，我把他们骂了一顿。 I told
the boys off for making so much
noise.
464 | 0.6 | 279

1267 传 [傳] /chuán/ (2) v pass on, spread; hand down
请把球传给我。 Pass me the basketball, please.
342 | 0.82 | 279

1268 尊重 [尊重] /zūnzhòng/ (3) v respect, value
我们必须尊重他的意愿。 We must respect his wishes.
363 | 0.77 | 279

1269 有点 [有點] /yǒudiǎn/ adv somewhat, a bit
裤子有点长。 The pants are a bit too long.
429 | 0.65 | 278

1270 机关 [機關] /jīguān/ (2) n organ, office
公安机关依法具有拘留权。 According to law, public security organs have the authority to detain.
521 | 0.54 | 278 | W

9. Directions and locations

近	近	jìn	near	362
远	遠	yuǎn	far	454
东	東	dōng	east	734
里面	裏面	lǐmian	inside	931
西	西	xī	west	960
北	北	běi	north	1012
上面	上面	shàngmian	above	1068
中间	中間	zhōngjiān	middle, between	1087
前面	前面	qiánmian	front	1328
下面	下面	xiàmian	below, under	1340
附近	附近	fùjìn	nearby	1361
后面	後面	hòumian	behind	1418
南	南	nán	south	1521
旁边	旁邊	pángbiān	beside	1572
外面	外面	wàimian	outside	1597
东北	東北	dōngběi	northeast	1693
西北	西北	xīběi	northwest	2636
里边	里邊	lǐbian	inside	3496
里头	裡頭	lǐtou	inside	3835
西南	西南	xī'nán	southwest	3880
东南	東南	dōngnán	southeast	3934
外边	外邊	wàibian	outside	4742
左边	左邊	zuǒbian	left	7498
右边	右邊	yòubian	right	8271
外头	外頭	wàitou	outside	8394
后边	後邊	hòubian	behind	8655
右面	右面	yòumiàn	right	8655
上边	上邊	shàngbian	above	8870
下边	下邊	xiàbian	below, under	9347
前边	前邊	qiánbian	front	9444
东边	東邊	dōngbian	east	10311
西边	西邊	xībian	west	10583
北面	北面	běimiàn	north	12616
北边	北邊	běibian	north	13489
南面	南面	nánmiàn	south	13718
南边	南邊	nánbian	south	14986
西面	西面	xīmiàn	west	16123
楼上	樓上	lóushàng	upstairs	22225
楼下	樓下	lóuxià	downstairs	30710

1271 对象 [對象] /duìxiàng/ (2) n target, object; boy or girl friend
这种广告的对象是孩子们。The target of this type of advertising is children.
332 | 0.84 | 278

1272 道路 [道路] /dàolù/ (2) n road
有些道路因积雪而封闭。Some roads are closed owing to drifting snow.
393 | 0.71 | 278

1273 共产党 [共產黨] /gòngchǎndǎng/ (2) n Communist Party
这份报纸是共产党的官方喉舌。This paper is the official organ of the Communist Party.
372 | 0.75 | 278

1274 本身 [本身] /běnshēn/ (3) pron (in) itself, per se
这主意本身并不错。This is not a bad idea in itself.
384 | 0.73 | 278

1275 进去 [進去] /jìnqù/ (1) v go in
每个人都可以进去看看。Everybody can go in and have a look.
420 | 0.66 | 278

1276 原来 [原來] /yuánlái/ (1) adj original, former
我认为你原来的计划比这个好。I prefer your original plan to this one.
308 | 0.9 | 277

1277 慢慢 [慢慢] /mànman/ adv slowly
她慢慢地走下楼来。She came slowly down the stairs.
403 | 0.69 | 277

1278 关键 [關鍵] /guānjiàn/ (2) n key, crux
在投资上取得成功的关键，是跑在市场的前端。The key to any successful investments is to lead the whole market.
383 | 0.72 | 277

1279 血 [血] /xuè/ (2) n blood
伤口流出了血。The wound streamed blood.
364 | 0.76 | 277

1280 体制 [體制] /tǐzhì/ n institutional system, structure
这是我讲的经济体制改革。So much for reform of the economic structure.
548 | 0.51 | 277

1281 正在 [正在] /zhèngzài/ (1) adv be under way, be in progress
你们正在谈论什么？What are you talking about?
451 | 0.61 | 276

1282 互相 [互相] /hùxiāng/ (1) adv each other
他们互相拥抱。They embraced each other.
297 | 0.93 | 276

1283 朝 [朝] /cháo/ (1) prep towards; facing
他们朝我冲过来。They rushed towards me.
402 | 0.69 | 276

1284 流 [流] /liú/ (1) v flow
水从管道里通畅地流了出来。Water flowed freely from the pipe.
337 | 0.82 | 276

1285 排 [排] /pái/ (2) v arrange, line, put in order; exclude, discharge
把玻璃杯排好，我来斟酒。Line up the glasses, and I'll fill them.
293 | 0.94 | 276

1286 执行 [執行] /zhíxíng/ (2) v implement, carry out
不管你遇到什么困难，都要执行计划。No matter what difficulty you meet, carry out your plan.
474 | 0.58 | 276 | W

1287 真实 [真實] /zhēnshí/ (2) adj true, real, authentic
一个人的真实感情必然在他的言行中表现出来。One's true feelings cannot but come through in what one says and does.
327 | 0.84 | 275

1288 有时 [有時] /yǒushí/ (2) adv sometimes
她有时来访问我们。She comes to visit us sometimes.
408 | 0.68 | 275

1289 空间 [空間] /kōngjiān/ (2) n space, room
发展空间十分巨大。There is enormous room for growth.
332 | 0.83 | 275

1290 状况 [狀況] /zhuàngkuàng/ (2) n condition, state of affairs
儿童健康状况显著改善。The physical conditions of children have improved noticeably.
409 | 0.67 | 274

1291 举 [舉] /jǔ/ (1) v lift, raise; enumerate, give (an example)
你可以把你的手举过头顶。You can hold your hand up over your head.
333 | 0.82 | 274

1292 只好 [只好] /zhǐhǎo/ (1) adv have to, have no alternative but to
如果这样，我们只好把会议推迟。If so, we'll have to put the meeting off.
395 | 0.69 | 273

1293 形势 [形勢] /xíngshì/ (2) n situation
我觉得形势很令人担忧。I find the situation very worrying.
545 | 0.5 | 273

1294 利 [利] /lì/ (3) n advantage; benefit, profit, gain
有利必有弊。Every advantage has its disadvantages.
333 | 0.82 | 273

1295 法 [法] /fǎ/ n law; method, way, how-to
请告诉我如何穿法。Please tell me how to put it on.
472 | 0.58 | 273

1296 声 [聲] /shēng/ (1) clas [measure word for sound, shout, cry, laugh, yell, etc.]
我们到那儿的时候，请告诉我一声可以吗？Could you please tell me when we get there?
556 | 0.49 | 273

1297 着 [着] /zháo/ v touch (the ground, land); catch (cold); (fire) be lit, catch fire; succeed in
那干草着了火，不过我们已将它扑灭了。
The dry grass caught fire, but we beat it out.
411 | 0.67 | 273

1298 床 [床] /chuáng/ (1) n bed
他从床上跳了起来。He sprang out of the bed.
533 | 0.51 | 272

1299 草 [草] /cǎo/ (1) n grass; straw
草变绿了。The grass is turning green.
339 | 0.8 | 272

1300 效果 [效果] /xiàoguǒ/ (2) n effect, (positive) result
这一政策已开始有些效果。This policy has already shown some positive results.
364 | 0.75 | 272

1301 印象 [印象] /yìnxiàng/ (2) n impression
这给了我很深的印象。It has had a deep impression on me.
325 | 0.84 | 272

1302 昨天 [昨天] /zuótiān/ (1) time yesterday
他们昨天去钓鱼了。They went fishing yesterday.
343 | 0.79 | 272

1303 危险 [危險] /wēixiǎn/ (1) adj dangerous
高速转弯很危险。It's dangerous to turn a corner at high speed.
308 | 0.88 | 271

1304 竟 [竟] /jìng/ (3) adv [expressing unexpectedness] actually
她竟有脸那样说吗？Did she have the nerve to say that?
380 | 0.72 | 271 | W

1305 难以 [難以] /nányǐ/ (3) adv hard to, difficult to; hardly
我们激动的心情难以用笔墨来形容。Words can hardly describe how excited we were.
345 | 0.79 | 271

1306 讲话 [講話] /jiǎnghuà/ (2) n speech, talk
他的讲话非常感人。His speech was very moving.
484 | 0.56 | 271

1307 量 [量] /liàng/ (3) n quantity, amount, capacity
如果我们的订货量大，佣金率会高些吗？Can we get a higher commission rate if we order a larger quantity?
356 | 0.76 | 271

1308 创作 [創作] /chuàngzuò/ (2) v create (especially literary works), write
他创作了四部小说。He wrote four novels.
372 | 0.73 | 271

1309 拒绝 [拒絕] /jùjué/ (2) v refuse, reject, decline
他拒绝服从。They refused to obey.
328 | 0.83 | 271

1310 体现 [體現] /tǐxiàn/ (3) v embody, show
而且，丝绸服装更能体现出女性的身材。What's more, the silk dress can better show off women's beautiful figures.
394 | 0.69 | 271

1311 粮食 [糧食] /liángshí/ (2) n foodstuff, grain, cereals
粮食调剂今年有了不少的成绩。Much has been accomplished this year in the regulation of food supplies.
445 | 0.61 | 270

1312 工资 [工資] /gōngzī/ (2) n salary, wage, pay
他是家中唯一挣工资的人。He is the sole wage earner in his family.
339 | 0.8 | 270

1313 读者 [讀者] /dúzhě/ (2) n reader
他的作品受到读者的赞许。His works won the enthusiastic approval of his readers.
368 | 0.74 | 270

1314 史 [史] /shǐ/ n history
它是当代艺术史上的里程碑。It is a landmark in the history of modern art.
344 | 0.79 | 270

1315 除 [除] /chú/ (3) prep except, besides
除这些以外还有什么？Anything else besides these?
380 | 0.71 | 270

1316 死亡 [死亡] /sǐwáng/ (3) v die
他因服药过量而死亡。He died by taking an overdose.
306 | 0.88 | 270

1317 香 [香] /xiāng/ (1) adj fragrant, sweet-scented; sound (sleep); appetising, (eat) with relish
这花闻起来真香。The flower smells sweet.
381 | 0.71 | 269

1318 存 [存] /cún/ (2) v exist; deposit; accumulate; check (luggage), leave something with someone
您想怎样存钱？How would you like to deposit your money?
306 | 0.88 | 269

1319 否则 [否則] /fǒuzé/ (2) conj otherwise
照所吩咐的做，否则你就会受罚。Do what you have been told, otherwise you will be punished.
334 | 0.8 | 268

1320 交通 [交通] /jiāotōng/ (2) n traffic
街道交通受阻。The street is blocked to traffic.
483 | 0.56 | 268

1321 权力 [權力] /quánlì/ (3) n power, authority
真正的权力属于人民。The real power resides in the people.
345 | 0.78 | 268

1322 权利 [權利] /quánlì/ (3) n right
你一定要维护自己的权利。You must stand up for your rights.
345 | 0.78 | 268

1323 向 [向] /xiàng/ (1) v side with, be partial to, favour
父母往往向着最小的孩子。Parents usually favour their youngest child.
341 | 0.79 | 268

1324 打开 [打開] /dǎkāi/ v open
我打开窗户好吗？Shall I open the window?
365 | 0.73 | 268

1325 方 [方] /fāng/ (2) adj square
古时候人们以为地球是方的。In ancient times people conceived of the earth as square.
318 | 0.84 | 267

1326 从来 [從來] /cónglái/ (2) adv always, all along
这样做肯定是对的，因为从来就是这样。It must be right. It's always been like that.
359 | 0.75 | 267

1327 观点 [觀點] /guāndiǎn/ (2) n point of view, viewpoint, opinion
关于那个问题，他倾向于你的观点。He inclined to your opinion on that matter.
380 | 0.71 | 267

1328 前面 [前面] /qiánmian/ (2) n front; ahead
前面有一些空位。There are some vacant seats at the front.
351 | 0.76 | 267

1329 明确 [明確] /míngquè/ (2) adj clear-cut, explicit, unequivocal
他对此事的态度十分明确。He was quite explicit about the matter.
396 | 0.67 | 266

1330 大会 [大會] /dàhuì/ (2) n congress, assembly, meeting
这项动议已提交给大会了。The motion was put to the assembly.
589 | 0.45 | 266

1331 里 [里] /lǐ/ (1) clas [measure word for distance in Chinese local unit] li (0.5 km)
车站离海边有十里。The station is ten li from the seaside.
280 | 0.95 | 266

1332 取 [取] /qǔ/ (2) v get, take, fetch
我取下隐形眼镜。I took out my contact lens.
328 | 0.81 | 266

1333 吹 [吹] /chuī/ (1) v blow, puff; play (flute, etc.); boast; (lovers) break up, (plan, etc.) fall through
风将我的帽子吹掉了。The wind blew my hat off.
367 | 0.72 | 265

1334 准 [准] /zhǔn/ (2) v allow, permit
外国访客只准逗留一个月。Foreign visitors are only allowed one month's residence.
276 | 0.96 | 265

1335 治 [治] /zhì/ (2) v rule, govern; treat, cure; control, harness; punish
心无杂念治百病。To cure bad health, think nothing unclean.
314 | 0.85 | 265

1336 一旦 [一旦] /yídàn/ conj once, in case
一旦他了解了情况，他什么都会原谅的。Once he understands, he will forgive everything.
328 | 0.81 | 264

1337 右 [右] /yòu/ (1) loc right
从这里往右拐走环行道可以避开闹市中心。To avoid the city centre, we may turn right here and take the highway.
311 | 0.85 | 264

1338 看法 [看法] /kànfǎ/ (2) n opinion, view; unfavourable view
你的看法如何？What's your opinion?
314 | 0.84 | 264

1339 文字 [文字] /wénzì/ (2) n character, script, writing; style of writing; word
你不要玩文字游戏，我不懂。Don't play on words, I can't catch the meaning.
357 | 0.74 | 264

1340 下面 [下面] /xiàmian/ (2) n the following, below; next; lower level
把你的答案写在下面。Write your answers below.
405 | 0.65 | 264 | S

1341 职工 [職工] /zhígōng/ (2) n staff, staff member, worker
职工的生活水平迅速提高。The living standard of the workers has been improved rapidly.
641 | 0.41 | 263

1342 心情 [心情] /xīnqíng/ (2) n feeling, state of mind, mood
我知道你的心情。I know how you feel.
374 | 0.7 | 263

1343 道德 [道德] /dàodé/ (2) n morals, morality, ethics
他失去了信仰，没丧失道德。He lost his faith but not his morality.
363 | 0.73 | 263

1344 男子 [男子] /nánzǐ/ (3) n man, male
女子比男子的直觉力更强吗？Are women more intuitive than men?
407 | 0.65 | 263 | W

1345 章 [章] /zhāng/ (2) clas chapter
这部著作只完成了五章。Only five chapters of the book were completed.
428 | 0.62 | 263 | W

1346 追 [追] /zhuī/ (2) v chase, pursue; court, woo
他赤着脚在草地上追她。He chased her barefoot across the meadow.
388 | 0.68 | 263

1347 信 [信] /xìn/ (2) v believe, believe in
信不信由你，这才只是冰山的一角。Believe it or not, this is just the tip of the iceberg.
348 | 0.76 | 263

1348 以 [以] /yǐ/ (2) conj in order to, so as to
他喝下一杯浓茶以使自己清醒过来。He drank a cup of strong tea so as to sober himself up.
341 | 0.77 | 262

1349 边 [邊] /biān/ (2) adv [as in 边 ... 边 ... indicating simultaneous progression of two events] while
她边做饭边唱歌。She was singing while she was cooking.
383 | 0.68 | 262

1350 雪 [雪] /xuě/ (1) n snow
下雪天外出要穿上暖和的衣服。Put on your warm clothes before you go out in the snow.
366 | 0.72 | 262

1351 满足 [滿足] /mǎnzú/ (2) v satisfy
我们一定要设法满足广大民众的要求。We must try to satisfy the needs of the multitude.
319 | 0.82 | 262

1352 作出 [作出] /zuòchū/ v make
他们权衡利弊之后才作出决定。They weighed the advantages and disadvantages before making the decision.
612 | 0.43 | 262 | W

1353 鸡 [雞] /jī/ (1) n chicken
我想尝尝这鸡。I'd like to try the chicken.
348 | 0.75 | 261

1354 优势 [優勢] /yōushì/ (3) n advantage, strength
我的优势正是在这儿。Just here lies my advantage.
541 | 0.48 | 261 | W

1355 破坏 [破壞] /pòhuài/ (2) v wreck, destroy, damage
地震使一些建筑受到了破坏。The earthquake damaged several buildings.
330 | 0.79 | 261

1356 吸引 [吸引] /xīyǐn/ (2) v attract
音乐会吸引了许多人。The concert attracted a great number of people.
345 | 0.76 | 261

1357 再次 [再次] /zàicì/ adv once again
还需要我再次提醒你吗？Do I have to remind you yet again?
348 | 0.75 | 260

1358 物质 [物質] /wùzhì/ (2) n substance, matter; material
这两种物质间似乎有些区别。There seems to be some difference between the two substances.
343 | 0.76 | 260

1359 重点 [重點] /zhòngdiǎn/ (2) n emphasis, focus point
只是教学重点不同罢了。It's only a question of different emphases in teaching.
591 | 0.44 | 260 | W

1360 命运 [命運] /mìngyùn/ (2) n fate
他只得甘心服从他的命运。He resigned himself to his fate.
303 | 0.86 | 259

1361 附近 [附近] /fùjìn/ (1) loc nearby, (in the) vicinity
她住在附近。She lives nearby.
297 | 0.87 | 258

1362 铁路 [鐵路] /tiělù/ (2) n railway
全国铁路现已电气化了。The national railways have now been electrified.
426 | 0.61 | 258

1363 春 [春] /chūn/ (1) time spring
四季如春。It's like spring all the year round.
297 | 0.87 | 258

1364 今后 [今後] /jīnhòu/ (2) time from now on, hereafter, in future
我今后一定要加小心。I should be careful in future.
456 | 0.57 | 258

1365 把 [把] /bǎ/ (3) v guard; hold
两个侦探把住了门口。Two detectives kept guard at the door.
398 | 0.65 | 258

1366 苦 [苦] /kǔ/ (1) adj bitter; hard (times), tough
他的日子过得很苦。He led a hard life.
329 | 0.78 | 257

1367 彻底 [徹底] /chèdǐ/ (2) adj thorough
你应该进行一次彻底检查。You should go and have a thorough checkup.
296 | 0.87 | 257

1368 设备 [設備] /shèbèi/ (2) n equipment
我们酒店是一家设备齐全，服务优秀的五星级酒店。Our hotel is a five-star hotel with good facilities and excellent service standards.
445 | 0.58 | 257

1369 笔 [筆] /bǐ/ (1) clas [measure word for handwritings or drawings]; [measure word for a sum of money or a transaction]
三笔帐归并起来，一共二百元。The three entries put together come to 200 yuan.
278 | 0.93 | 257

1370 宣传 [宣傳] /xuānchuán/ (2) v propagate, publicise, promote
他在城里宣传他的新书。He was in town to promote his new book.
432 | 0.6 | 257

1371 导致 [導致] /dǎozhì/ (3) v cause, lead to, result in
大雨是导致洪水产生的原因。The heavy rain caused the flood.
365 | 0.71 | 257

1372 交往 [交往] /jiāowǎng/ v associate with, consort with
不要与这种人交往。Never consort with such people.
311 | 0.83 | 257

1373 那 [那] /nà/ (1) conj then, in that case
那你要我们怎么办呢？Then what would you like us to do?
399 | 0.64 | 256

1374 其它 [其它] /qítā/ (2) pron other
你去过其它的国家吗？Have you ever visited any other countries?
324 | 0.79 | 256

1375 票 [票] /piào/ (1) *n* ticket
你弄到音乐会的票了吗？ Did you manage to get tickets for the concert?
295 | 0.87 | 255

1376 球 [球] /qiú/ (1) *n* ball
那个球把一块窗玻璃打碎了。 The ball smashed a window.
320 | 0.8 | 255

1377 职业 [職業] /zhíyè/ (2) *n* occupation, profession
请说明姓名、年龄和职业。 Please state your name, age and occupation.
366 | 0.7 | 255

1378 犯 [犯] /fàn/ (2) *v* commit (crime, mistake, etc.); violate, offend (rule, etc.); have a recurrence of (illness, bad habit, etc.)
他后悔犯了这样的错误。 He regretted having made such a mistake.
308 | 0.83 | 255

1379 有效 [有效] /yǒuxiào/ (2) *adj* effective, valid
旅行支票只有会签后才有效。 A traveller's cheque is not valid until it is countersigned.
500 | 0.51 | 254 | W

1380 良好 [良好] /liánghǎo/ (2) *adj* good
运动和良好的健康使得她显得更美。 Exercise and good health have enhanced her beauty.
507 | 0.5 | 254 | W

1381 依然 [依然] /yīrán/ (3) *adv* still
在新年这一天下决心是一个依然流行的习俗。 Making resolutions on New Year's Day is a custom that still prevails.
326 | 0.78 | 254

1382 日 [日] /rì/ (1) *n* day; the sun
二十年前大多数人干的是八小时工作日。 Most people worked an eight-hour day 20 years ago.
319 | 0.8 | 254

1383 年龄 [年齡] /niánlíng/ (2) *n* age
成年的法定年龄是 18 岁。 The age of majority is 18.
274 | 0.93 | 254

1384 动作 [動作] /dòngzuò/ (2) *n* movement, motion, action
他们注视着她的每一个动作。 They were watching her every movement.
279 | 0.91 | 254

1385 物 [物] /wù/ *n* thing
物以稀为贵。 When a thing is scarce, it is precious.
325 | 0.78 | 254

1386 该 [該] /gāi/ (1) *v* should, ought to
问题是我们该怎样去找到好的销路。 The problem is how we should make a good sale.
411 | 0.62 | 254

1387 实践 [實踐] /shíjiàn/ (1) *v* practise
你实践越多，你就懂得越多。 The more you practise, the more you know.
444 | 0.57 | 254

1388 最终 [最終] /zuìzhōng/ *adv* finally, eventually
她最终实现了戒烟的诺言。 She has finally carried out her promise to quit smoking.
324 | 0.78 | 253

1389 太阳 [太陽] /tàiyáng/ (1) *n* the sun
太阳一出来，雾就会消失。 As soon as the sun comes out, the mist will pass away.
382 | 0.66 | 253

1390 客人 [客人] /kèren/ (2) *n* guest
他喜欢客人守时。 He likes his guests to be punctual.
289 | 0.88 | 253

1391 家长 [家長] /jiāzhǎng/ *n* parent; head of a family
有些家长允许孩子自己做决定。 Some parents allow their children to make their own decisions.
333 | 0.76 | 253

1392 主动 [主動] /zhǔdòng/ (2) *adj* on one's own initiative, active
有人责怪我们凡事不主动。 The charge against us is that we have no initiative.
306 | 0.83 | 252

1393 啥 [啥] /shà/ *pron* [dialect] what
爸爸，你看，那边跑的是啥？ What is that running over there, daddy?
479 | 0.53 | 252

1394 考 [考] /kǎo/ (2) *v* take an examination, test or quiz, test
用这个测验来考考你的知识。 Test your knowledge with this quiz.
382 | 0.66 | 252

1395 表达 [表達] /biǎodá/ (2) *v* express, voice (one's opinion)
我无法表达我的谢意。 I can't express my thanks.
328 | 0.77 | 252

1396 冲突 [衝突] /chōngtū/ (3) *v* conflict, clash with
你们的聚会和我要去参加的婚礼时间上有冲突。 Your party clashes with a wedding I'm going to.
361 | 0.7 | 252

1397 民主 [民主] /mínzhǔ/ (2) *adj* democratic
只能采取民主手段，不能采取压制、打击的手段。 We must use democratic means and not resort to coercion or attack.
429 | 0.58 | 250 | W

1398 中学 [中學] /zhōngxué/ (1) *n* middle school, secondary school, high school
他在一所中学教英语。 He teaches English in a middle school.
291 | 0.86 | 250

1399 田 [田] /tián/ (2) *n* field, farmland
田里竖起了几个稻草人。 A few scarecrows were set up in the field.
280 | 0.89 | 250

1400 牌 [牌] /pái/ (2) *n* cards; brand; (number) plate
我得到的牌非常好。 The run of the cards favoured me.
283 | 0.89 | 250

1401 那天 [那天] /nàtiān/ *pron* that day
那天相当冷。It was rather chilly that day.
368 | 0.68 | 250

1402 望 [望] /wàng/ (2) *v* have a look; hope
他同情地望着她。He was looking at her
sympathetically.
496 | 0.5 | 250 | W

1403 旅游 [旅遊] /lǚyóu/ (3) *v* travel, take a tour, go
sightseeing
他陪我一起旅游。He accompanied me
travelling.
580 | 0.43 | 250

1404 实际 [實際] /shíjì/ (2) *adj* practical, actual
这个问题很实际又很紧迫。This is a very
practical and pressing issue.
376 | 0.66 | 249

1405 既然 [既然] /jìrán/ (2) *conj* since, now that
既然你已来了，我们开始吧。Now that you
have arrived, let's begin.
344 | 0.72 | 249

1406 雨 [雨] /yǔ/ (1) *n* rain
他的衣服被雨淋湿了。His clothes were
soaked through by the rain.
381 | 0.66 | 249

1407 规模 [規模] /guīmó/ (2) *n* scale, size
这个公司具有中等规模。The company is of
medium size.
474 | 0.53 | 249

1408 官员 [官員] /guānyuán/ *n* official
移民局的官员将要求你出示证件。Immigration
officials will ask to see your papers.
405 | 0.62 | 249

1409 享受 [享受] /xiǎngshòu/ (2) *v* lead a life of
pleasure; enjoy (rights, benefits, etc.)
在这个城市可以享受什么娱乐活动呢？What
entertainments can we enjoy in this city?
276 | 0.9 | 249

1410 消费 [消費] /xiāofèi/ (2) *v* consume
该消费还是该节约？Should we consume or
conserve?
415 | 0.6 | 249

1411 游 [遊] /yóu/ (3) *v* swim; travel around
我游过了河。I swam across the river.
256 | 0.98 | 249

1412 了 [了] /liǎo/ *v* finish, settle; [occurring in the
structure of verb + 得/不 + 了 to express
possibility]
很抱歉，我来不了。I am sorry, I am afraid
I cannot come.
373 | 0.67 | 249

1413 究竟 [究竟] /jiūjìng/ (2) *adv* [used for
emphasis] actually, exactly
她究竟在哪里呢？Where on earth can she
be?
311 | 0.8 | 248

1414 行业 [行業] /hángyè/ (3) *n* trade, industry,
profession
在服装贸易行业她很有名气。She is very well
known in the clothing trade.
462 | 0.54 | 248 | W

1415 爸 [爸] /bà/ *n* dad, father
在许多人中她没有找到她爸。Among many
people she has not found her father.
432 | 0.57 | 248

1416 股 [股] /gǔ/ (3) *clas* [measure word for a
stream of strength, water, air or smell, and also
for long narrow things]
这个烟囱冒出一股浓烟。The chimney
exhaled a thick smoke.
315 | 0.79 | 248

1417 一致 [一致] /yízhì/ (2) *adj* identical;
unanimous; consistent
第二份声明与第一份声明不一致。The second
statement is not consistent with the first one.
350 | 0.71 | 247

1418 后面 [後面] /hòumian/ (2) *n* rear, back
请大点儿声说，我们在后面听不见。Please
speak up; we cannot hear you at the back.
363 | 0.68 | 247

1419 地球 [地球] /dìqiú/ (2) *n* the earth, the
globe
月球是地球的卫星。The moon is the earth's
satellite.
405 | 0.61 | 247

1420 开展 [開展] /kāizhǎn/ (2) *v* develop, launch (a
campaign), carry out
工厂很愿意开展这方面的研究。The factory
is willing to carry out research work in this
field.
762 | 0.33 | 247 | W

1421 处于 [處於] /chǔyú/ (3) *v* be (in a certain state,
position, or condition)
灯突然熄灭了，我们处于黑暗中。The lights
suddenly went out and we were in the
dark.
345 | 0.72 | 247

1422 感谢 [感謝] /gǎnxiè/ (1) *v* thank, be grateful,
express gratitude
非常感谢您！Thank you very much.
295 | 0.84 | 246

1423 表明 [表明] /biǎomíng/ (2) *v* make known or
clear; state clearly; show
如果你什么也不说，就表明你没有不同意。
If you say nothing you are showing that you
do not disagree.
430 | 0.57 | 246

1424 正 [正] /zhèng/ (2) *adj* principal (as opposed to
vice-); straight, upright; right (side); regular
(shape)
你的帽子没戴正。Your hat's not on
straight.
290 | 0.85 | 245

1425 学术 [學術] /xuéshù/ (2) *n* scholarly learning
大学的目标应是促进学术。The aim of a
university should be the advancement of
learning.
340 | 0.72 | 245

1426 符合 [符合] /fúhé/ (2) *v* accord with, be in
keeping with
这种做法不符合我们的政策。Such an act will
not be in accord with our policy.
374 | 0.66 | 245

1427 打电话 [打電話] /dǎdiànhuà/ v make a telephone call
请今晚给我打电话。 Please call me this evening.
320 | 0.77 | 245

1428 内部 [內部] /nèibù/ (2) loc inside, within
她负责确定该公司内部的工资水准。 She is responsible for the determination of wage levels within this company.
355 | 0.69 | 244

1429 生意 [生意] /shēngyì/ (2) n business, trade
您的生意如何？ How is your business getting along?
311 | 0.79 | 244

1430 作为 [作為] /zuòwéi/ (2) prep as
作为推销员，他有很好的工作阅历。 He has a good track record as a salesman.
348 | 0.7 | 244

1431 加入 [加入] /jiārù/ (3) v join, become a member; add (in)
你有资格加入这个俱乐部吗？ Are you eligible to join this club?
381 | 0.64 | 244 | W

1432 次 [次] /cì/ (3) adj inferior
我们不能发运比样品质料次的皮货。 We can't send leather goods inferior to the samples.
281 | 0.87 | 243

1433 部长 [部長] /bùzhǎng/ (2) n minister; head of department
这个部长上个月才被任命。 The minister was ordained only last month.
541 | 0.45 | 243 | W

1434 想法 [想法] /xiǎngfǎ/ (2) n idea, opinion
他向我们提出一个想法。 He suggested an idea to us.
310 | 0.78 | 243

1435 思考 [思考] /sīkǎo/ (3) v think, ponder over, reflect on
人是唯一的会思考的动物。 Man is the only creature that thinks.
324 | 0.75 | 243

1436 先进 [先進] /xiānjìn/ (2) adj advanced
设计师采用了最先进的设计技术。 The designer adopted the most advanced technique.
543 | 0.45 | 242

1437 不但 [不但] /búdàn/ (1) conj not only (. . . but also . . .), as well as
她不但聪明，而且漂亮。 She's clever as well as good-looking.
313 | 0.77 | 242

1438 减少 [減少] /jiǎnshǎo/ (2) v reduce, lessen, decrease
夏天那小河水量减少，成了涓涓细流。 The stream is reduced to a mere trickle in summer.
413 | 0.59 | 242

1439 评价 [評價] /píngjià/ (3) v evaluate, assess
你对自己怎么评价？ How would you assess yourself?
323 | 0.75 | 242

1440 国有 [國有] /guóyǒu/ adj state-owned
我们对搞好国有企业是有信心的。 We are quite confident in the success of state-owned enterprises.
689 | 0.35 | 242 | W

1441 久 [久] /jiǔ/ (1) adj long (time); of a specified duration
我们等公共汽车等了很久。 We had a long wait for the bus.
335 | 0.72 | 241

1442 合理 [合理] /hélǐ/ (2) adj reasonable, rational
合理安排很重要。 It is vital that rational arrangements be made.
373 | 0.65 | 241

1443 念 [念] /niàn/ (1) v read aloud; think of, miss; attend school
要我念课文吗？ Shall I read the text?
380 | 0.64 | 241 | S

1444 轻 [輕] /qīng/ (1) adj light
海绵是一种软而轻的物质。 Sponge is a soft and light substance.
349 | 0.69 | 240

1445 一半 [一半] /yíbàn/ (2) num half
二等票的价格是头等票的一半。 The price of a second-class ticket is half that of a first-class.
264 | 0.91 | 240

1446 需要 [需要] /xūyào/ (1) n need
引进的技术必须先进而且适合中国的需要。 The technology to be imported should be advanced and appropriate to China's needs.
332 | 0.72 | 240

1447 距离 [距離] /jùlí/ (2) n distance
超市离这儿只有很短的一段距离。 The supermarket is only a short distance away.
275 | 0.88 | 240

1448 在于 [在於] /zàiyú/ (3) v lie in, consist in, depend on
成功在于毅力。 Success depends on perseverance.
329 | 0.73 | 240

1449 子 [子] /zi/ suf [nominal suffix to form a disyllabic word]
他们用筐子往高处运土。 They lifted earth in baskets.
328 | 0.73 | 239

1450 理由 [理由] /lǐyóu/ (2) n reason
确实没有理由担心。 There's really no reason to be worried.
301 | 0.79 | 239

1451 统一 [統一] /tǒngyī/ (2) v unify, unite; standardise
德国在 1990 年正式统一了。 Germany officially unified in 1990.
586 | 0.41 | 239 | W

1452 闹 [鬧] /nào/ (2) v make noise or disturbance; give vent to (anger, etc.); be troubled with; go in for
小狗都正在花园里又叫又闹。 All the pups were having a rough and tumble in the garden.
362 | 0.66 | 239

10. Cities

澳门	澳門	*Àomén*	Macao
北京	北京	*Běijīng*	Beijing
长沙	長沙	*Chángshā*	Changsha
成都	成都	*Chéngdū*	Chengdu
重庆	重慶	*Chóngqìng*	Chongqing
广州	廣州	*Guǎngzhōu*	Guangzhou
桂林	桂林	*Guìlín*	Guilin
哈尔滨	哈爾濱	*Hā'ěrbīn*	Harbin
杭州	杭州	*Hángzhōu*	Hangzhou
昆明	昆明	*Kūnmíng*	Kunming
拉萨	拉薩	*Lāsà*	Lhasa
南京	南京	*Nánjīng*	Nanjing
青岛	青島	*Qīngdǎo*	Qingdao
三亚	三亞	*Sānyà*	Sanya
上海	上海	*Shànghǎi*	Shanghai
石家庄	石家莊	*Shíjiāzhuāng*	Shijiazhuang
苏州	蘇州	*Sūzhōu*	Suzhou
台北	臺北	*Táiběi*	Taipei
天津	天津	*Tiānjīn*	Tianjin
武汉	武漢	*Wǔhàn*	Wuhan
西安	西安	*Xī'ān*	Xi'an
香港	香港	*Xiānggǎng*	Hong Kong

1453 功能 [功能] */gōngnéng/* (3) *n* function
这一程序有哪些功能？What functions can this programme perform?
342 | 0.7 | 238

1454 成员 [成員] */chéngyuán/* (3) *n* member
她绝对是我们组最活跃的成员。She is easily the most active member in our group.
391 | 0.61 | 238

1455 身边 [身邊] */shēnbiān/* (2) *place* at one's side, within reach
她坐丈夫的身边。She was sitting beside her husband.
404 | 0.59 | 238

1456 寻找 [尋找] */xúnzhǎo/* (2) *v* look for, seek
我焦急地寻找起来。I started looking for it hurriedly.
292 | 0.82 | 238

1457 美好 [美好] */měihǎo/* (2) *adj* happy, glorious, good, beautiful
我们在海边度过了美好的一天。We had a super day at the seaside.
251 | 0.95 | 237

1458 连 [連] */lián/* (2) *adv* continuously, repeatedly
他连连敲门，直到有人应声。He hammered away on the door until he got an answer.
319 | 0.74 | 237

1459 英雄 [英雄] */yīngxióng/* (2) *n* hero
时势造英雄。The times produce their heroes.
263 | 0.9 | 237

1460 一生 [一生] */yìshēng/* (2) *n* all one's life
那是我一生中最愉快的一天。That was the happiest day of my life.
288 | 0.82 | 237

1461 美 [美] */měi/* (2) *adj* beautiful, pretty
你的发型很美。That's a very beautiful hair-style you have.
290 | 0.82 | 236

1462 身份 [身份] */shēnfèn/* (3) *n* identity
他不得不公开自己的身份。He had to make his identity public.
266 | 0.89 | 236

1463 进来 [進來] */jìnlái/* (1) *v* come in
我可以进来吗？May I come in?
411 | 0.57 | 236

1464 伤 [傷] */shāng/* (2) *v* injure, hurt; do harm to
你要小心不要伤了自己。You must take care not to hurt yourself.
308 | 0.77 | 236

1465 专门 [專門] /zhuānmén/ (2) *adv* specifically, for a particular purpose, occasion, etc.
这些是专门为老年人设计的房子。These are the houses specifically designed for old people.
267 | 0.88 | 235

1466 机 [機] /jī/ (3) *n* machine
你能给我解释一下人机接口吗？Can you give me an explanation of the man–machine interface?
282 | 0.84 | 235

1467 寄 [寄] /jì/ (1) *v* send, post; check (luggage), leave with
您希望寄平信还是挂号信？Do you wish to send it as an ordinary or a registered letter?
368 | 0.64 | 235

1468 压 [壓] /yā/ (2) *v* press
他轻轻地压下手柄。He pressed lightly on the handle.
290 | 0.81 | 235

1469 全球 [全球] /quánqiú/ *n* the whole world
我们应当放眼全球。We should keep the whole world in view.
366 | 0.64 | 234

1470 星 [星] /xīng/ *n* star
这颗星肉眼看不见。This star is not visible to the naked eye.
280 | 0.84 | 234

1471 产业 [產業] /chǎnyè/ *n* industry
纺织工业是中国传统的支柱产业。The textile industry is a traditional pillar industry in China.
731 | 0.32 | 234 | W

1472 倍 [倍] /bèi/ (1) *clas* (two, three, etc.) -fold; times
亚洲有欧洲的四倍大。Asia is four times as large as Europe.
339 | 0.69 | 234

1473 面 [面] /miàn/ (2) *clas* [measure word for something with a flat surface such as a mirror and flag]
生活是一面镜子。Life is like a mirror.
276 | 0.85 | 234

1474 上午 [上午] /shàngwǔ/ (1) *time* (in the) morning
今天上午我们有两节课。We have two classes this morning.
372 | 0.63 | 234

1475 费 [費] /fèi/ (2) *v* expend; consume too much, be wasteful
他们费尽全力想爬出来。They expended all their strength in trying to climb out.
251 | 0.94 | 234

1476 普遍 [普遍] /pǔbiàn/ (2) *adj* common, widespread
这些观点在知识份子中很普遍。These views were common among intellectuals.
350 | 0.67 | 233

1477 小学 [小學] /xiǎoxué/ (2) *n* primary school
现在小学教员的工资太低。Today, salaries for primary school teachers are too low.
267 | 0.87 | 233

1478 夜 [夜] /yè/ *time* night
夜已消逝。Night had fled.
320 | 0.73 | 233

1479 戴 [戴] /dài/ (1) *v* put on, wear
请戴上安全帽！Put on the helmet, please.
289 | 0.81 | 233

1480 失败 [失敗] /shībài/ (2) *v* fail, be defeated
如果你不帮助我，我就失败了。Had you not helped me, I should have failed.
309 | 0.76 | 233

1481 相互 [相互] /xiānghù/ (2) *adv* each other, mutually
双方应该相互学习，相互支持。Both sides should learn from each other and support each other.
391 | 0.6 | 232

1482 纸 [紙] /zhǐ/ (1) *n* paper
他把房子的轮廓画在纸上。He drew the outline of a house on the paper.
292 | 0.79 | 232

1483 校长 [校長] /xiàozhǎng/ (2) *n* headmaster; president, chancellor
校长说他无法出席这次会议。The schoolmaster said that he was unable to attend this meeting.
305 | 0.76 | 232

1484 集体 [集體] /jítǐ/ (2) *n* collective
个人是集体的一分子。Any individual is a member of the collective.
331 | 0.7 | 232

1485 访问 [訪問] /fǎngwèn/ (1) *v* visit, pay a visit (to)
他们此时正在南方访问。They are visiting some places in the south at this time.
649 | 0.36 | 232

1486 解放 [解放] /jiěfàng/ (2) *v* liberate; emancipate
林肯解放了奴隶。Lincoln liberated the slaves.
292 | 0.8 | 232

1487 生存 [生存] /shēngcún/ (3) *v* subsist, live
我们没有水就不能生存。We cannot live without water.
297 | 0.78 | 232

1488 快乐 [快樂] /kuàilè/ (2) *adj* happy
新年快乐！Happy New Year!
328 | 0.71 | 231

1489 允许 [允許] /yǔnxǔ/ (2) *v* permit, allow
请允许我向您表示祝贺。Allow me to heartily congratulate you.
279 | 0.83 | 231

1490 抢 [搶] /qiǎng/ (2) *v* rob, loot; snatch, grab; vie for; rush
在饭店前我的钱包被抢了。I had my wallet robbed in front of the hotel.
309 | 0.75 | 231

1491 制定 [制定] /zhìdìng/ (2) *v* draw up, make, set forth
我们制定了长期计划。We made long-term plans.
515 | 0.45 | 231 | W

1492 古代 [古代] /gǔdài/ (2) *time* ancient times
这座宫殿建筑代表着中国古代的建筑式样。
This palace is an example of ancient Chinese architecture.
349 | 0.66 | 230

1493 演出 [演出] /yǎnchū/ (1) *v* perform, put on a show
你们在哪个剧场演出的? At what theatre did you perform?
335 | 0.69 | 230

1494 组成 [組成] /zǔchéng/ (3) *v* form, make up, constitute; consist of
新西兰由两个大的岛和一些小岛组成。
New Zealand consists of two large islands and some smaller ones.
365 | 0.63 | 230

1495 从而 [從而] /cóng'ér/ (2) *conj* thus, so
关税提供了保护,从而促进了国内的生产。
Tariffs provide protection and thus stimulate domestic production.
381 | 0.6 | 229

1496 文件 [文件] /wénjiàn/ (2) *n* document
他终于读完了那份长长的文件。He finished reading the long documents at last.
311 | 0.74 | 229

1497 经历 [經歷] /jīnglì/ (2) *n* experiences
这些经历能使存钱成为终身的习惯。These experiences can help make saving money a lifetime habit.
287 | 0.8 | 229

1498 素质 [素質] /sùzhì/ *n* inner quality, making
她具备当个好律师的素质。She has the makings of a good lawyer.
454 | 0.51 | 229 | W

1499 代表 [代表] /dàibiǎo/ (1) *v* represent, stand for, act on one's behalf
他无权代表我们做事。He has no authority to act on our behalf.
313 | 0.73 | 229

1500 放弃 [放棄] /fàngqì/ (2) *v* give up, quit
他因病被迫放弃学业。He is compelled by illness to give up his study.
279 | 0.82 | 229

1501 修 [修] /xiū/ (2) *v* repair, mend, fix; build; trim, prune
你要是不会修就别胡来。If you don't know how to repair it, don't fool with it.
290 | 0.79 | 229

1502 严格 [嚴格] /yángé/ (2) *adj* strict
他对你们运动员要求严格吗? Is he strict with you athletes?
397 | 0.57 | 228

1503 刀 [刀] /dāo/ (1) *n* knife
别玩弄那把刀! Do not play with that knife!
286 | 0.8 | 228

1504 科学 [科學] /kēxué/ (1) *n* science
她专攻计算机科学。She specialises in computer science.
333 | 0.69 | 228

1505 出口 [出口] /chūkǒu/ (2) *n* exit; export
丝绸是中国的传统出口产品之一。Silk is one of China's traditional exports.
536 | 0.43 | 228 | W

1506 土 [土] /tǔ/ (2) *n* earth, soil
他往土里掺沙子以提高渗水性能。He added sand to the soil to make it more porous.
249 | 0.92 | 228

1507 经理 [經理] /jīnglǐ/ (2) *n* manager
请把我的电话接到经理那儿。Please put my call through to the manager.
273 | 0.84 | 228

1508 末 [末] /mò/ (3) *n* end, tip; minor details; powder
这个学期末不考试。There will be no exam at the end of this term.
302 | 0.76 | 228

1509 熟悉 [熟悉] /shúxī/ (2) *v* be familiar with
我们熟悉了新的环境。We familiarised ourselves with the new surroundings.
260 | 0.88 | 228

1510 绝对 [絕對] /juéduì/ (2) *adv* absolutely
这一点,我认为绝对没有疑义。I hold this as absolutely beyond doubt.
284 | 0.8 | 227

1511 性格 [性格] /xìnggé/ (2) *n* disposition, nature, personality
他性格坚强。He has a strong personality.
306 | 0.74 | 227

1512 照 [照] /zhào/ (2) *v* shine, beam, light up; reflect, mirror
火光照在他们脸上。The fire beamed on their faces.
299 | 0.76 | 227

1513 同样 [同樣] /tóngyàng/ (2) *adv* likewise, similarly, by the same token
其他文化活动也同样吸引了不少人参加。Other cultural events similarly drew in the crowds.
299 | 0.76 | 226

1514 恐怕 [恐怕] /kǒngpà/ (2) *adv* (I'm) afraid (that)
夫人,恐怕不行。I'm afraid not, madam.
285 | 0.79 | 226

1515 敌人 [敵人] /dírén/ (2) *n* enemy
敌人把他俘房了。The enemy took him prisoner.
303 | 0.75 | 226

1516 国外 [國外] /guówài/ *place* abroad
他每年都到国外去。He goes abroad every year.
331 | 0.68 | 226

1517 从事 [從事] /cóngshì/ (2) *v* go in for, be engaged in
他从事教学工作。He is engaged in teaching.
329 | 0.69 | 226

1518 做到 [做到] /zuòdào/ *v* accomplish, achieve, manage to do something
那种工作不可能做到十全十美。Perfection is impossible to achieve in that kind of work.
304 | 0.75 | 226

1519 亲自 [親自] /qīnzì/ (2) *adv* in person, personally, (do) oneself
他亲自动手修理他的自行车。He repaired his bike himself.
248 | 0.91 | 225

1520 均 [均] /jūn/ (3) *adv* all, with no exception
各项准备工作均已就绪。All the preparatory work has been completed.
434 | 0.52 | 225 | W

1521 南 [南] /nán/ (1) *loc* south
这房子坐北朝南。The house faces south.
258 | 0.87 | 225

1522 号 [號] /hào/ (1) *n* date; number; size
你的房间号是多少？What's your room number?
314 | 0.72 | 225

1523 枪 [槍] /qiāng/ (2) *n* gun, rifle
快逃吧！他带着枪呢。Run for it; he's got a gun!
325 | 0.69 | 225

1524 赢 [贏] /yíng/ (1) *v* win, gain; beat
哪个队赢了？Which team won?
297 | 0.76 | 225

1525 登 [登] /dēng/ (2) *v* ascend, mount, climb; board; print, publish
你登过泰山吗？Have you ever climbed Mount Tai?
274 | 0.82 | 225

1526 改造 [改造] /gǎizào/ (2) *v* change, transform, reform, reclaim; remodel, convert
我们正在改造这些房子。We are remodelling these rooms.
396 | 0.57 | 225

1527 召开 [召開] /zhāokāi/ (2) *v* convene (a conference or meeting), hold
会议是按预定的时间召开吗？Will the meeting be held as scheduled?
510 | 0.44 | 225 | W

1528 出版 [出版] /chūbǎn/ (2) *v* publish
她的新书出版了。Her new book is published.
354 | 0.64 | 225

1529 哪 [哪] /na/ (1) *part* [sentence final particle similar to 啊，following words ending with the consonant n]
我的天哪！My goodness!
593 | 0.38 | 225 | S

1530 成熟 [成熟] /chéngshú/ (2) *adj* mature
竹子最终将占到成熟大熊猫食物的 98 %。Bamboo eventually forms 98 per cent of the mature panda's diet.
262 | 0.85 | 223

1531 油 [油] /yóu/ (2) *n* oil, petrol, gas
我车上的汽油表显示剩下的油不多了。My car's gas gauge indicated that there was little gas left.
288 | 0.78 | 223

1532 角度 [角度] /jiǎodù/ (3) *n* angle, viewpoint
试从另一角度来看这件事。Try looking at the affair from a different angle.
303 | 0.74 | 223

1533 指导 [指導] /zhǐdǎo/ (2) *v* guide, direct
他们逐步取得了指导这项工作的经验。Gradually they acquired experience in how to guide the work.
389 | 0.57 | 223

1534 争 [爭] /zhēng/ (2) *v* contend for, vie for; argue
男孩子们争着炫耀自己。The boys vied with each other in showing off.
243 | 0.92 | 223

1535 结 [結] /jié, jiē/ (3) *v* form; settle; tie, knit, knot; bear (fruit)
地面结了霜。Frost has formed on the ground.
261 | 0.86 | 223

1536 绿 [綠] /lǜ/ (1) *adj* green
树叶变绿了。Leaves of trees became green.
233 | 0.95 | 222

1537 色 [色] /sè/ (2) *n* colour; countenance, look; type; female charm
他的话使她面露失望之色。His word brought a cloud of disappointment to her face.
290 | 0.77 | 222

1538 文明 [文明] /wénmíng/ (2) *n* civilisation; manners
研究成果将对人类文明有重大作用。The achievements of the research will be of great importance for human civilisation.
309 | 0.72 | 222

1539 大陆 [大陸] /dàlù/ (2) *n* mainland, continent
岛上有座桥与大陆相连。The island is joined to the mainland by a bridge.
304 | 0.73 | 222

1540 功 [功] /gōng/ *n* merit, achievement; skill
要做到功过分明。Clear differentiation must be made between merits and demerits.
324 | 0.69 | 222

1541 估计 [估計] /gūjì/ (2) *v* estimate
对他的能力无法估计。It is impossible to estimate his abilities yet.
238 | 0.93 | 222

1542 制造 [製造] /zhìzào/ (2) *v* make, manufacture
许多人都参观过他制造的机器人。Many people visited the robot that he had made.
314 | 0.71 | 222

1543 战 [戰] /zhàn/ *v* fight
他们不战而降。They gave up without a fight.
282 | 0.79 | 222

1544 乱 [亂] /luàn/ (1) *adj* messy, in disorder; confused
你的房间那么乱，收拾一下吧。Your room is in a mess, please tidy it up.
255 | 0.87 | 221

1545 特 [特] /tè/ (3) *adj* special, unusual
今天的特餐是什么？What's today's special?
246 | 0.9 | 221

1546 皇帝 [皇帝] /huángdì/ (2) *n* emperor
当时的许多作家都谴责该皇帝的行径。Many contemporary writers condemned the emperor's actions.
474 | 0.47 | 221

1547 架 [架] /jià/ (2) *clas* [measure word for machines and instruments resting on a stand such as airplanes, pianos, cameras, etc.]
它一定是一架直升飞机。 It must be a helicopter.
278 | 0.8 | 221

1548 查 [查] /chá/ (1) *v* look up, consult; check, examine; investigate, look into
我必须查一下你乘坐的火车的时间。 I must look up the time of your train.
253 | 0.88 | 221

1549 维护 [維護] /wéihù/ (2) *v* defend, safeguard; uphold, maintain
一个生意人也该注意维护自己的名声。 A businessman should also be careful to maintain his reputation.
478 | 0.46 | 221

1550 适应 [適應] /shìyìng/ (2) *v* suit; adapt to
她很快地适应了这种新的气候。 She adapted herself quickly to the new climate.
354 | 0.62 | 221

1551 根 [根] /gēn/ (1) *clas* [measure word for long and slender objects]
我发现轮胎上扎着一根钉子。 I found a nail stuck in the tyre.
301 | 0.73 | 220

1552 联合 [聯合] /liánhé/ (2) *v* join forces, unite, band together; combine
他们联合起来为和平而战。 They joined forces to fight for peace.
516 | 0.43 | 220 | W

1553 盖 [蓋] /gài/ (2) *v* cover; build (a house); affix (a seal); surpass
请你把盖子盖好。 Can you fix this lid on?
263 | 0.84 | 220

1554 显然 [顯然] /xiǎnrán/ (2) *adv* clearly, obviously
显然他很紧张。 He was obviously very nervous.
286 | 0.77 | 219

1555 桥 [橋] /qiáo/ (1) *n* bridge
河上有座桥。 There is a bridge over the river.
248 | 0.88 | 219

1556 题 [題] /tí/ (2) *n* title; topic, subject; problem (in exam)
我算不出那道题。 I can't work out the problem.
275 | 0.8 | 219

1557 体系 [體系] /tǐxì/ (2) *n* system
英国于1971年改行十进制货币体系。 Britain converted to a decimal currency system in 1971.
431 | 0.51 | 219 | W

1558 读书 [讀書] /dúshū/ (2) *v* read, study; attend school
孩子们正在学习读书写字。 The children are learning to read and write.
296 | 0.74 | 219

1559 负 [負] /fù/ (3) *v* bear; take (responsibility); fail; lose (a match)
如果装船货与样品不符，贵公司须负责任。 Shipment unequal to sample will hold you responsible.
284 | 0.77 | 219

1560 病人 [病人] /bìngrén/ (2) *n* sick person, patient
病人情况稳定。 The patient's condition is stable.
241 | 0.91 | 218

1561 案 [案] /àn/ *n* (legal or criminal) case; proposal; long narrow table
纠正错案这很有必要。 It is necessary that all wrong cases should be corrected.
280 | 0.78 | 218

1562 兼 [兼] /jiān/ (3) *v* hold (different posts) concurrently
她兼做导师工作和研究工作。 Her work was divided between tutoring and research.
316 | 0.69 | 218

1563 监督 [監督] /jiāndū/ (3) *v* supervise, control
我方人员有权监督产品的包装和质量。 We have the right to supervise the quality and the packing of the product.
545 | 0.4 | 218 | W

1564 显示 [顯示] /xiǎnshì/ (3) *v* show
这张图显示了工厂的布局。 This map shows the layout of the plant.
318 | 0.69 | 218

1565 至今 [至今] /zhìjīn/ (2) *adv* until now, so far
我至今没有得到她的答复。 I have had no reply from her so far.
269 | 0.81 | 217

1566 云 [雲] /yún/ (1) *n* cloud
云开始散开。 The clouds began to break.
294 | 0.74 | 217

1567 演员 [演員] /yǎnyuán/ (2) *n* actor or actress
演那教授的演员是谁？ Who is the actor playing the professor?
283 | 0.77 | 217

1568 奖 [獎] /jiǎng/ (2) *n* prize, award
获此奖标志着舞台生涯成就的顶峰。 This award has set the seal on a successful stage career.
306 | 0.71 | 217

1569 观察 [觀察] /guānchá/ (2) *v* observe
请观察这两种化学成分的反应。 Please observe the reaction of these two chemicals.
288 | 0.76 | 217

1570 坚决 [堅決] /jiānjué/ (2) *adj* firm, resolute, determined
她的眼睛里盈满了泪水，但是她的语气却很坚决。 She had tears in her eyes, but her voice was firm.
332 | 0.65 | 216

1571 毕竟 [畢竟] /bìjìng/ (3) *adv* after all
他毕竟还是来了！ He did come after all!
287 | 0.75 | 216

1572 旁边 [旁邊] /pángbiān/ (1) *loc* side
如果你坐在司机的旁边，就会看到更好的
景色。 If you sit beside the driver, you will
get a better view.
324 | 0.67 | 216

1573 室 [室] /shì/ (2) *n* room
我们去样品室看看好吗？ Shall we go to the
sample room?
276 | 0.78 | 216

1574 话题 [話題] /huàtí/ *n* topic, subject
他试图改变话题。 He tried to change the
subject.
248 | 0.87 | 216

1575 关 [關] /guān/ (1) *v* close, shut; turn off;
concern, involve; shut in, lock up; (business)
close down
请别忘了关灯。 Please do not forget to turn
off the light.
298 | 0.73 | 216

1576 等 [等] /děng/ (1) *v* wait
您能等一会儿吗？ Would you mind waiting
for a while?
335 | 0.65 | 216

1577 鼓励 [鼓勵] /gǔlì/ (2) *v* encourage
要鼓励他把心中的一切讲出来，以便大家
帮助。 You should encourage him to speak
his mind so that other people can help
him.
329 | 0.66 | 216

1578 非 [非] /fēi/ (3) *adv* not; simply (must)
实际上你非来不可。 You simply must
come.
263 | 0.82 | 215

1579 树 [樹] /shù/ (1) *n* tree
这棵树很高。 This tree is very tall.
248 | 0.87 | 215

1580 含 [含] /hán/ (2) *v* keep in mouth; contain,
include
租金含水电费吗？ Does the rent include
bills?
338 | 0.64 | 215 | W

1581 解 [解] /jiě/ (2) *v* untie, undo; explain, solve
这个结系得那么紧，根本解不开。 The knot is
fastened in such a way that it is impossible to
undo.
256 | 0.84 | 215

1582 方便 [方便] /fāngbiàn/ (1) *adj* convenient
我今天下午去看你方便吗？ Will it be
convenient to see you this afternoon?
238 | 0.9 | 214

1583 高级 [高級] /gāojí/ (3) *adj* high quality; high
grade, advanced; senior, high level
他们住在高级住宅区。 They live in a posh
part of town.
314 | 0.68 | 214

1584 广告 [廣告] /guǎnggào/ (2) *n* advertisement,
advert
谁也不能避免受到广告的影响。 No one
can avoid being influenced by
advertisments.
273 | 0.78 | 214

1585 婚姻 [婚姻] /hūnyīn/ (2) *n* marriage,
matrimony
很多妇女都能做到婚姻、事业两不误。
Many women successfully mix marriage and
a career.
280 | 0.76 | 214

1586 说法 [説法] /shuōfa/ (3) *n* statement,
argument; wording, version
这种说法对不对呢？ Is this statement correct?
299 | 0.72 | 214

1587 自身 [自身] /zìshēn/ (3) *pron* self, oneself
蜡烛照他人，不顾焚自身。 A candle lights
others and consumes itself.
321 | 0.67 | 214

1588 争取 [爭取] /zhēngqǔ/ (2) *v* strive for, fight for
怎样争取最后胜利？ How shall we strive for
final victory?
297 | 0.72 | 214

1589 收到 [收到] /shōudào/ *v* receive
她今天收到了一个邮包。 She received a parcel
by post today.
246 | 0.87 | 214

1590 卫生 [衛生] /wèishēng/ (2) *n* hygiene,
sanitation, public health
同文化教育相联系的还有卫生问题。 Related
to culture and education is the question of
public health.
349 | 0.61 | 213

1591 足 [足] /zú/ (3) *adj* enough, adequate,
sufficient
这个轮胎没气了；你并没打足气。 This tyre is
flat; you did not pump enough air in.
261 | 0.82 | 213

1592 且 [且] /qiě/ (2) *conj* (both . . .) and; even,
furthermore
因为天气温暖且阳光充足，橘子在这里生长得
很好。 Because of the warm and sunny
weather, oranges grow very well here.
288 | 0.74 | 213

1593 旁 [旁] /páng/ (2) *loc* beside, by
他坐在火炉旁他常坐的座位上。 He took his
accustomed seat by the fire.
273 | 0.78 | 213

1594 模式 [模式] /móshì/ *n* mode, pattern; way
世界上的问题不可能都用一个模式解决。
The world's problems cannot all be solved
in the same way.
311 | 0.69 | 213

1595 好好 [好好] /hǎohǎo/ *adv* all out, good
您得好好休息一下。 You'd better have a good
rest.
313 | 0.68 | 212

1596 损失 [損失] /sǔnshī/ (2) *n* loss
她的离去对公司将是一个巨大的损失。
Her leaving will be a great loss to the
company.
297 | 0.72 | 212

1597 外面 [外面] /wàimian/ (2) *n* outside
这盒子外面是红的，里面是绿的。 The box
had a red outside and a green inside.
328 | 0.65 | 212

11. House and room

墙	牆	qiáng	wall	1189
房间	房間	fángjiān	room	1744
门	門	mén	door, gate	2136
厕所	廁所	cèsuǒ	toilet, lavatory	3155
窗户	窗戶	chuānghù	window	3836
厨房	廚房	chúfáng	kitchen	3837
客厅	客廳	kètīng	sitting room	4854
公寓	公寓	gōngyù	apartment, flat	4871
地毯	地毯	dìtǎn	carpet, rug	6854
楼梯	樓梯	lóutī	stair, staircase	6956
卧室	臥室	wòshì	bedroom	7205
书房	書房	shūfáng	study	7919
窗子	窗子	chuāngzi	window	10077
地下室	地下室	dìxiàshì	basement, cellar	10837
浴室	浴室	yùshì	bathroom	11723
卫生间	衛生間	wèishēngjiān	bathroom	12979
车库	車庫	chēkù	garage	22190
楼上	樓上	lóushàng	upstairs	22225
门厅	門廳	méntīng	doorway	22370
阁楼	閣樓	gélóu	attic	23286
饭厅	飯廳	fàntīng	dining room	24289
楼下	樓下	lóuxià	downstairs	30710
卧房	臥房	wòfáng	bedroom	30861

1598 皮 [皮] /pí/ (2) *n* skin; leather; peel (of fruit)
我们说桔子皮，苹果皮，土豆皮。 One speaks of orange peel, and apple peel, and tomato skin.
314 | 0.68 | 212

1599 人士 [人士] /rénshì/ (3) *n* person, personage, public figure
好几位社会知名人士出席了这位政治家的追悼仪式。 Several noted public figures were present at the statesman's memorial service.
442 | 0.48 | 212 | W

1600 集中 [集中] /jízhōng/ (2) *v* concentrate, focus on
你做事精神要再集中些。 Try and concentrate more on your work.
305 | 0.7 | 212

1601 归 [歸] /guī/ (3) *v* return, go back; be in one's charge; group (together)
你就可以满载而归。 You can return home with your pockets full.
266 | 0.8 | 212

1602 面临 [面臨] /miànlín/ (3) *v* face, be faced with
我深切地了解我们所面临的困难。 I am acutely aware of the difficulty we face.
356 | 0.6 | 212

1603 广泛 [廣泛] /guǎngfàn/ (2) *adj* extensive
电视上对选举作了广泛的报导。 The election was given extensive coverage on TV.
405 | 0.52 | 211

1604 纷纷 [紛紛] /fēnfēn/ (2) *adv* one after another
亲朋好友纷纷向新娘新郎祝福。 Relatives and friends showered good wishes on the bride and bridegroom.
279 | 0.76 | 211

1605 难道 [難道] /nándào/ (2) *adv* [used to reinforce a rhetorical question]
难道你不应该再考虑一下你的决定吗？ Won't you reconsider your decision?
300 | 0.71 | 211

1606 反而 [反而] /fǎn'ér/ (3) *adv* instead, on the contrary
他不但不承认，反而支吾其词。 Instead of admitting his guilt, he prevaricated.
257 | 0.82 | 211

1607 必 [必] /bì/ (3) *adv* must, certainly
二者必居其一，其他的道路是没有的。 They must do one or the other, for there is no third choice.
276 | 0.77 | 211

1608 课 [課] /kè/ (1) *n* class; subject, course; lesson
学校里每星期有多少节课？How many lessons are there in the school week?
257 | 0.82 | 211

1609 成果 [成果] /chéngguǒ/ (2) *n* result, outcome, achievement
科技战线取得了很多突出的成果。Large numbers of outstanding achievements have been registered in the field of science and technology.
486 | 0.43 | 211

1610 期 [期] /qī/ (2) *clas* [measure word for things arranged by periods] issue (of a periodical)
短训班办了两期。The short-term training class has been run twice.
278 | 0.76 | 211

1611 采用 [採用] /cǎiyòng/ (2) *v* use, make use of, adopt
内包装通常采用一些防水材料。Waterproof material is normally used for inner packing.
327 | 0.65 | 211

1612 现代化 [現代化] /xiàndàihuà/ *n* modernisation
这有助于我们实现现代化。This will help us achieve modernisation.
452 | 0.47 | 211 | W

1613 颇 [頗] /pō/ *adv* quite, rather
她头痛，颇感不适。She has a headache and is rather indisposed.
269 | 0.78 | 210

1614 成就 [成就] /chéngjiù/ (2) *n* accomplishment, achievement
你有理由为自己的成就而自豪。You can be justly proud of your achievements.
319 | 0.66 | 210

1615 协议 [協議] /xiéyì/ *n* agreement
双方都应按照协议条款办事。Both sides have to act according to the provisions of the agreement.
535 | 0.39 | 210

1616 眼 [眼] /yǎn/ *clas* [measure word for the action of look or glance]; [measure word for wells]
他冷冷地看了我一眼。He gave me an icy look.
516 | 0.41 | 210 | W

1617 处 [處] /chù/ *clas* [measure word for places occupied]
有一道栅栏隔着这两处房产。A fence divides the two properties.
246 | 0.85 | 210

1618 当中 [當中] /dāngzhōng/ (3) *place* in the middle or centre; among
在他们当中他讲英语最流利。He speaks English the most fluently of them all.
570 | 0.37 | 210 | S

1619 谈判 [談判] /tánpàn/ (2) *v* negotiate
当局拒绝与恐怖分子谈判。The government refuses to negotiate with terrorists.
412 | 0.51 | 210

1620 赶 [趕] /gǎn/ (2) *v* catch up with; drive away; rush through; try to catch (train, bus, etc.); rush for
我只好拚命跑去赶公共汽车。I had to run like anything to catch the bus.
270 | 0.78 | 210

1621 富 [富] /fù/ (2) *adj* rich, wealthy
但愿我很富。If only I were rich.
253 | 0.83 | 209

1622 平衡 [平衡] /pínghéng/ (3) *adj* balanced
账目看起来是平衡的。The books looked balanced.
263 | 0.8 | 209

1623 以下 [以下] /yǐxià/ (2) *loc* below, following, as follows
120 公分以下的小孩不必买票。Children below 120 cm needn't pay any fare.
319 | 0.66 | 209

1624 方案 [方案] /fāng'àn/ (2) *n* scheme, plan
这个方案被压下来了。The scheme has been pigeonholed.
314 | 0.67 | 209

1625 气氛 [氣氛] /qìfēn/ (3) *n* atmosphere
她一进来气氛就变了。The atmosphere changed as soon as she walked in.
245 | 0.86 | 209

1626 年轻人 [年輕人] /niánqīngrén/ *n* young people
你们年轻人都有无限光明的前途。There is an infinitely bright future ahead of you young people.
257 | 0.82 | 209

1627 通过 [通過] /tōngguò/ (1) *v* go through; get past; pass, approve
他这次考试通过了。He passed the examination this time.
353 | 0.59 | 209

1628 接近 [接近] /jiējìn/ (2) *v* be close to, approach
这里是禁区，不许接近。It is not allowed to approach the forbidden area.
243 | 0.86 | 209

1629 威胁 [威脅] /wēixié/ (3) *v* threaten
不要威胁我。Don't try to threaten me.
261 | 0.8 | 209

1630 及时 [及時] /jíshí/ (2) *adj* in time
为了及时赶到那里，他跑得很快。He ran very fast in order to get there in time.
335 | 0.62 | 208 | W

1631 穷 [窮] /qióng/ (2) *adj* poor
假如我们将那笔钱全部花光，我们又将变穷了。If we spend all that money, we shall be poor again.
244 | 0.85 | 208

1632 有所 [有所] /yǒusuǒ/ *adv* somewhat, slightly
贸易差额方面有所改善。The balance of trade has improved slightly.
266 | 0.78 | 208

1633 至于 [至於] /zhìyú/ (3) *prep* as regards
至于应该穿什么衣服，并没有硬性规定。There are no special rules as regards what clothes you should wear.
274 | 0.76 | 208

1634 搬 [搬] /bān/ (1) v move, remove
下月初我就可以搬进来。I can move in early next month.
271 | 0.77 | 208

1635 瞧 [瞧] /qiáo/ (2) v look
瞧那些乌云，眼看要有暴风雨了。Look at those black clouds; there is going to be a storm.
379 | 0.55 | 208 | S

1636 小 [小] /xiǎo/ (1) pref [usually preceding a family name or given name as a title of address to show affection]
小刘一下课就钻到图书馆去了。Xiao Liu got into the library as soon as the class was over.
253 | 0.82 | 207

1637 祖国 [祖國] /zǔguó/ (1) n motherland
为祖国争光！Win glory for our motherland!
550 | 0.38 | 207 | W

1638 工厂 [工廠] /gōngchǎng/ (1) n factory
今年这家工厂的产量提高不少。There has been a great increase in the factory's turnout this year.
269 | 0.77 | 207

1639 现场 [現場] /xiànchǎng/ place scene (of event or incident), site, spot
立即派了医生和护士急忙赶到事故现场。Doctors and nurses were rushed to the accident spot.
265 | 0.78 | 207

1640 造 [造] /zào/ (2) v make, build; make up
这是他们造的桥。This is the bridge that they built.
274 | 0.76 | 207

1641 顶 [頂] /dǐng/ (2) v carry on one's head; go against; prop up; stand up to; retort
妇女能顶半边天。Women hold up half the sky.
250 | 0.83 | 207

1642 统计 [統計] /tǒngjì/ (3) n statistics
他很仔细地检查了统计数字。He examined the statistical figures precisely.
464 | 0.45 | 207 | W

1643 想起 [想起] /xiǎngqǐ/ v remember, recollect
你要是想起什么来，就告诉我们。If you remember anything at all, please let us know.
355 | 0.58 | 207

1644 站 [站] /zhàn/ (1) n station, (bus) stop
您乘过站了。You have missed your stop.
290 | 0.71 | 206

1645 博士 [博士] /bóshì/ (3) n doctor, Ph.D.
她正在攻读博士学位。She's studying for her doctorate.
249 | 0.83 | 206

1646 谢谢 [謝謝] /xièxie/ (1) v thank
谢谢你的光临。Thank you for coming.
374 | 0.55 | 206 | S

1647 使得 [使得] /shǐde/ (3) v cause, make; [dialect] be usable or workable
洪水使得很多人无家可归。The flood made many people homeless.
244 | 0.85 | 206

1648 打击 [打擊] /dǎjī/ (3) v strike, attack; crack down; dampen
这会不会打击其他人的积极性？But will this practice dampen others' initiative?
320 | 0.65 | 206

1649 麻烦 [麻煩] /máfán/ (1) adj troublesome
这就很麻烦了。This is rather troublesome.
270 | 0.76 | 205

1650 差不多 [差不多] /chàbuduō/ (2) adj almost the same; just about right; more or less
我差不多已经把这本书看完了。I've more or less finished reading the book.
304 | 0.68 | 205

1651 数字 [數字] /shùzì/ (2) n number, figure
我需要确实的数字，不要估计的。I need the actual figures, not an estimate.
291 | 0.71 | 205

1652 致 [致] /zhì/ (3) v cause, result in; send, deliver (a speech)
这次事故是由于疏忽所致。The accident was caused by negligence.
241 | 0.85 | 205

1653 称为 [稱為] /chēngwéi/ v call, refer to . . . as
那些在办公室工作的人被称为"白领工人"。People who work in offices are usually referred to as "white collar workers".
281 | 0.73 | 205

1654 简直 [簡直] /jiǎnzhí/ (3) adv simply
他的发音简直太糟糕了。His pronunciation is simply terrible.
312 | 0.66 | 204

1655 战士 [戰士] /zhànshì/ (2) n soldier, fighter
从战士到干部都要苦练。Everybody, from soldiers to cadres, should undergo such training.
266 | 0.77 | 204

1656 保险 [保險] /bǎoxiǎn/ (3) n insurance
你买的保险够不够？Have you got adequate insurance?
393 | 0.52 | 204

1657 特色 [特色] /tèsè/ n characteristic, unique feature
它们各有特色。They are unique in different ways.
380 | 0.54 | 204

1658 幅 [幅] /fú/ (2) clas [measure word for pictures, paintings, calligraphies, maps and cloth, etc.]
你要是在墙上挂几幅画，这个房间就更有生气。If you put some pictures on the wall the room will look brighter.
227 | 0.9 | 204

1659 周 [周] /zhōu/ clas week; cycle
这任务竟然在一周内就完成了。To my surprise, the task was finished in only one week.
243 | 0.84 | 204

1660 东方 [東方] /dōngfāng/ place east; the East
太阳在东方升起。The sun rises in the east.
248 | 0.82 | 204

1661 爬 [爬] /pá/ (1) v crawl; climb
爬了十层楼，他已上气不接下气了。He was breathless after climbing ten floors.
308 | 0.66 | 204

1662 代 [代] /dài/ (2) v replace, substitute; (do) on one's behalf
请代我向我父亲求情。Please intercede with my father on my behalf.
218 | 0.94 | 204

1663 怀疑 [懷疑] /huáiyí/ (3) v doubt; suspect
我怀疑借这么一大笔钱是否明智。I doubt the wisdom of borrowing such a large sum of money.
264 | 0.77 | 204

1664 相关 [相關] /xiāngguān/ v be interrelated
梦与睡眠紧密相关。Dreams have close ties with sleep.
293 | 0.7 | 204

1665 顺利 [順利] /shùnlì/ (2) adj smooth, successful
工作不象我们想象的那样进展顺利。The work did not go as smoothly as we wished.
332 | 0.61 | 203

1666 逐渐 [逐漸] /zhújiàn/ (2) adv gradually
他们的希望逐渐破灭了。Their hopes gradually withered away.
251 | 0.81 | 203

1667 原 [原] /yuán/ adv [short form of 原来, meaning often implied in the past tense] originally, formerly
我原以为你是诚实的人。I took you to be an honest man.
239 | 0.85 | 203

1668 领导人 [領導人] /lǐngdǎorén/ n leader
工会领导人当场作出罢工的决定。The union leader made a spot decision to stage a strike.
473 | 0.43 | 203

1669 对 [對] /duì/ (2) clas pair, couple
餐具架上有一对花瓶。There are a pair of vases on the sideboard.
222 | 0.92 | 203

1670 算是 [算是] /suànshì/ (3) v be considered to be
他可算是个音乐家。He is somewhat of a musician.
291 | 0.7 | 203

1671 承担 [承擔] /chéngdān/ (3) v undertake, bear (cost, responsibility, etc.)
展览会的费用将由该公司承担。The cost of the exhibition will be borne by the company.
277 | 0.73 | 203

1672 设 [設] /shè/ (3) v set up, establish
他在集贸市场上设了个摊床。He set up a stand on the pedlars' market.
274 | 0.74 | 203

1673 广大 [廣大] /guǎngdà/ (2) adj vast, broad, extensive
同时，广大的妇女群众参加了生产工作。Moreover, women are taking part in production in great numbers.
488 | 0.41 | 202 | W

1674 突出 [突出] /tūchū/ (2) adj outstanding, prominent
她最为突出的特点是诚实。Her predominant characteristic is honesty.
348 | 0.58 | 202

1675 哦 [哦] /ò/ (3) interj [interjection expressing realisation] ah
哦，是的，我真傻！Oh, yes how silly of me!
415 | 0.49 | 202 | S

1676 宗教 [宗教] /zōngjiào/ (3) n religion
公民享有宗教信仰自由。Citizens enjoy freedom of religious belief.
305 | 0.66 | 202

1677 样 [樣] /yàng/ n appearance; sample
凭样交货。Shipment per sample.
288 | 0.7 | 202

1678 玉 [玉] /yù/ n jade
我还想买一只玉手镯。And I want a jade bracelet, too.
286 | 0.71 | 202

1679 将来 [將來] /jiānglái/ (1) time future
这些地方将来会怎么样呢？What does the future hold for these places?
240 | 0.84 | 202

1680 表演 [表演] /biǎoyǎn/ (1) v perform
孩子们要表演自己的节目。The children will perform their own programmes.
255 | 0.8 | 202

1681 丢 [丟] /diū/ (1) v lose
她到处找那本丢了的书。She looked all over for the book that she had lost.
304 | 0.67 | 202

1682 考察 [考察] /kǎochá/ (3) v inspect
他下个月起程去中国考察。He is leaving for China on an inspection tour next month.
333 | 0.61 | 202

1683 规律 [規律] /guīlǜ/ (2) n law, rule; regularity
不按客观规律办事，非失败不可。We will fail if we do not follow the practical rules.
264 | 0.76 | 201

1684 分子 [分子] /fènzi, fēnzǐ/ (3, 3) n member of a class or group; numerator (in a fractional number); molecule
恐怖分子在这里找不到安身之处。Terrorists will not find a safe haven here.
277 | 0.73 | 201

1685 上去 [上去] /shàngqù/ (1) v go up; [used as a resultative verb complement] up
怎样才能把国民经济搞上去？How can we give the economy a boost?
283 | 0.71 | 201

1686 广播 [廣播] /guǎngbō/ (1) v broadcast
这家电台用三种不同的周率广播。This radio station broadcasts on three different frequencies.
301 | 0.67 | 201

1687 输 [輸] /shū/ (1) v lose, be defeated; transport
这场争论他输了。He lost the argument.
218 | 0.92 | 201

1688 分配 [分配] /fēnpèi/ (2) v assign; distribute
这两间大教室已经分配给我们了。The two large classrooms have been assigned to us.
267 | 0.76 | 201

1689 缺乏 [缺乏] /quēfá/ (2) v lack, be short of
我承认由于缺乏经验，犯了错误。I admit that due to lack of experience, I have made a mistake.
289 | 0.7 | 201

1690 平等 [平等] /píngděng/ (2) adj equal
最理想的是，人人都能有平等的机会。Ideally, everyone would be given equal opportunities.
295 | 0.68 | 200

1691 独立 [獨立] /dúlì/ adj independent
政府奉行独立的外交政策。The government acts on an independent foreign policy.
289 | 0.69 | 200

1692 到处 [到處] /dàochù/ (2) adv everywhere, in all places
我们一直到处找你。We've been looking for you everywhere.
237 | 0.85 | 200

1693 东北 [東北] /dōngběi/ (2) loc northeast
你能想起一个家在东北的人吗？Can you think of anyone whose home is in the northeast?
253 | 0.79 | 200

1694 岸 [岸] /àn/ (2) n bank
河水溢过两岸。The river overflowed its banks.
567 | 0.35 | 200 | W

1695 担任 [擔任] /dānrèn/ (2) v hold (a government office or post), act as
她担任我的辩护律师。She acted as my defence lawyer.
294 | 0.68 | 200

1696 替 [替] /tì/ (2) v take the place of, substitute for
他替那个生病司机的班。He substituted for the driver who was ill.
350 | 0.57 | 200

1697 冷 [冷] /lěng/ (1) adj cold
我的房间很冷。My room is very cold.
284 | 0.7 | 199

1698 细 [細] /xì/ (1) adj thin, fine; exquisite; careful
那条绳子上有一处磨细了。The rope was wearing thin in one place.
243 | 0.82 | 199

1699 化 [化] /huà/ (2) suf [verb suffix] -ise, -ify
让我们把危险减少到最小化。Let's minimise the risk.
268 | 0.75 | 199

1700 猪 [豬] /zhū/ (1) n pig, hog
去年他们饲养了三十头猪。They raised 30 pigs last year.
237 | 0.84 | 199

1701 命令 [命令] /mìnglìng/ (2) n order, command
这种人需要的只是一道命令。All these men needed was the order.
295 | 0.68 | 199

1702 面积 [面積] /miànjī/ (2) n (surface) area
厨房的面积是12平方米。The kitchen has an area of 12 square metres.
434 | 0.46 | 199

1703 危机 [危機] /wēijī/ (2) n crisis
当时他们面临着很多危机。They were facing a variety of crises at that time.
297 | 0.67 | 199

1704 市长 [市長] /shìzhǎng/ (3) n mayor
他们选他当市长了吗？Did they elect him mayor?
285 | 0.7 | 199

1705 手机 [手機] /shǒujī/ n mobile phone, cell phone
使用手机对健康有害吗？Is the health hazard from cell phones real?
227 | 0.88 | 199

1706 推动 [推動] /tuīdòng/ (2) v promote, push forward
这种推动作用，将是很大的。The effect of such pushing will be very great.
525 | 0.38 | 199 | W

1707 软 [軟] /ruǎn/ (2) adj soft
这种料子摸上去很软。This material feels soft.
229 | 0.87 | 198

1708 重 [重] /chóng/ (2) adv again, once more
我愿意重做一次。I would do the same again.
224 | 0.89 | 198

1709 天天 [天天] /tiāntiān/ adv every day; day by day
几乎天天下雨。It rained practically every day.
270 | 0.73 | 198

1710 老百姓 [老百姓] /lǎobǎixìng/ (2) n ordinary people; civilians
老百姓渴望和平。The people were anxious to have peace.
257 | 0.77 | 198

1711 实际 [實際] /shíjì/ (2) n reality
合不合乎实际？Does this conform to the reality?
345 | 0.57 | 198

1712 凭 [憑] /píng/ (3) prep by, (taking) as the basis
凭请柬入场。Admission is by invitation only.
245 | 0.81 | 198

1713 挖 [挖] /wā/ (2) v dig
别偷懒，继续挖！Stop slacking and get on with that digging!
226 | 0.88 | 198

1714 队员 [隊員] /duìyuán/ (3) n team member
我为能成为一个队员感到骄傲。I am proud to be a member of the team.
315 | 0.63 | 197 | W

1715 宫 [宮] /gōng/ (3) n palace
武士们冲进宫里保护国王。The cavaliers rushed into the palace to protect the king.
276 | 0.71 | 197

1716 民间 [民間] /mínjiān/ (3) n among the people, folk
我教中国的民间舞蹈。I taught Chinese folk dancing.
269 | 0.74 | 197

1717 需求 [需求] /xūqiú/ n demand
对计算机有稳定的需求。There is a steady demand for computers.
337 | 0.59 | 197

1718 成长 [成長] /chéngzhǎng/ (2) v grow up
随着孩子不断成长，他们便开始偏离其父母的观点。As children grow up, they drift away from their parents' views.
277 | 0.71 | 197

1719 运 [運] /yùn/ (2) v transport
他们用卡车运砖。They transported the bricks in a lorry.
242 | 0.81 | 197

1720 守 [守] /shǒu/ (3) v guard; keep watch; abide by
是谁守的球门？Who kept the goal?
247 | 0.8 | 197

1721 大约 [大約] /dàyuē/ (2) adv approximately, about
这花园的面积大约是 200 平方米。The garden is about 200 square metres in area.
245 | 0.8 | 196

1722 仅仅 [僅僅] /jǐnjǐn/ (2) adv only, merely
但我仅仅是个业余爱好者。But I'm only an amateur.
237 | 0.83 | 196

1723 上来 [上來] /shànglái/ (1) v come up; [used as a resultative verb complement indicating the upward direction or success of doing something]
突然，他的信心上来了，而我的却下降了。All of a sudden, his confidence went up and mine went down.
257 | 0.77 | 196

1724 胜 [勝] /shèng/ (2) v win, defeat
校队先后胜了五场球。The school team won five games successively.
314 | 0.63 | 196

1725 投 [投] /tóu/ (2) v throw; project, cast
落日投下长长的余晖。The setting sun threw long shadows.
219 | 0.9 | 196

1726 视 [視] /shì/ v look; regard (. . . as)
久而久之，我竟视它为知己了。I gradually regarded it as my best friend.
226 | 0.87 | 196

1727 不足 [不足] /bùzú/ (3) adj insufficient, inadequate
电池充电不足。The battery has insufficient charge.
290 | 0.67 | 195

1728 乐 [樂] /lè/ adj happy, joyful
她乐得嘴也合不上了。She was so happy that she couldn't keep her mouth shut.
229 | 0.85 | 195

1729 界 [界] /jiè/ suf the circle or world of
他的画将他推荐进了艺术界。His paintings commended him to the artistic world.
247 | 0.79 | 195

1730 立场 [立場] /lìchǎng/ (2) n stand, position
在采取行动前他试图先摸清双方的立场。He tried to feel out the positions of both sides before committing himself.
319 | 0.61 | 195

1731 某些 [某些] /mǒuxiē/ (3) pron some, certain
我们做某些事都有自己爱用的办法。We all have our favourite ways of doing certain things.
282 | 0.69 | 195

1732 平时 [平時] /píngshí/ (2) time in normal times
你平时下班几点到家？When do you normally get home from work?
242 | 0.81 | 195

1733 考试 [考試] /kǎoshì/ (1) n examination, test, quiz
他有信心通过考试。He is confident that he will pass the exams.
233 | 0.84 | 195

1734 正好 [正好] /zhènghǎo/ (2) adv just (in time); as it happens, exactly
现在正好是7点。It's exactly seven o'clock.
281 | 0.69 | 194

1735 早已 [早已] /zǎoyǐ/ (3) adv for a long time, long ago; already
我打电话时，她早已走了。She had already left when I phoned.
267 | 0.73 | 194

1736 阿 [阿] /ā/ (2) pref [nominal prefix used before a personal name for endearment]
今天是阿新生日吗？Is it Ah Xin's birthday today?
283 | 0.69 | 194

1737 足球 [足球] /zúqiú/ (1) n football
我不怎么喜欢足球。I don't like football very much.
313 | 0.62 | 194

1738 文艺 [文藝] /wényì/ (1) n literature and art
我们的文艺属于人民。Our literature and art belong to the people.
265 | 0.73 | 194

1739 基地 [基地] /jīdì/ (3) n base
这是海军基地。This is a naval base.
428 | 0.46 | 194 | W

1740 实力 [實力] /shílì/ n strength
我们的实力不断壮大。We have grown from strength to strength.
318 | 0.61 | 194

1741 下子 [下子] /xiàzi/ clas [measure word for occurrences of an action or event]; [occurring in the fixed expression 一下子 "suddenly"]
他用大剪刀几下子就把灌木给修剪好了。With a few quick snips of the shear he pruned the bush.
269 | 0.72 | 194

1742 休息 [休息] /xiūxi/ (1) v rest
他们在小山的顶部停下来休息。At the top of the hill they paused for a rest.
248 | 0.79 | 194

1743 可以 [可以] /kěyǐ/ (2) adj not bad, pretty good; passable
这份家庭作业还算可以，其实你可以做得更好。This homework is all right but you could do better.
245 | 0.79 | 193

1744 房间 [房間] /fángjiān/ (1) n room
一张床占去了房间的一角。A bed occupied a corner of the room.
364 | 0.53 | 193

1745 小孩 [小孩] /xiǎohái/ n child
她把小孩抱在怀里。She held the child to her bosom.
258 | 0.75 | 193

1746 各自 [各自] /gèzì/ (3) pron each
我们各自关在自己的小办公室里。Each of us is boxed off in his own little office.
237 | 0.82 | 193

1747 领 [領] /lǐng/ (2) v lead
导游把游客领进旅游车里。A guide guided the tourists into the coach.
244 | 0.79 | 193

1748 信任 [信任] /xìnrèn/ (3) v trust
她对他绝对信任。She has complete faith in him.
225 | 0.86 | 193

1749 奇怪 [奇怪] /qíguài/ (2) adj strange
他有一些奇怪的想法。He has some very strange ideas.
288 | 0.67 | 192

1750 将军 [將軍] /jiāngjūn/ (3) n (army) general
将军制定出了新的进攻方案。The general worked out a new plan of attack.
246 | 0.78 | 192

1751 所 [所] /suǒ/ (2) clas [measure word for houses, schools and hospitals, etc.]
村里新办了一所中学。A new middle school has been set up in the village.
268 | 0.72 | 192

1752 贴 [貼] /tiē/ (2) v stick, paste; keep close to; subsidise
你把邮票贴上好吗？Will you stick the stamps on?
239 | 0.8 | 192

12. Home electronics

电话	電話	diànhuà	telephone	338
电视	電視	diànshì	TV, television	696
电脑	電腦	diànnǎo	computer	1118
手机	手機	shǒujī	mobile phone	1705
电视机	電視機	diànshìjī	television set	4336
照相机	照相機	zhàoxiàngjī	camera	7023
洗衣机	洗衣機	xǐyījī	washing machine	8729
摄像机	攝像機	shèxiàngjī	video camera	10286
收音机	收音機	shōuyīnjī	radio	10470
录音机	錄音機	lùyīnjī	audio recorder	10750
电池	電池	diànchí	battery	10875
录像带	錄像帶	lùxiàngdài	video cassette	12893
电冰箱	電冰箱	diànbīngxiāng	refrigerator	13089
录音带	錄音帶	lùyīndài	audio tape	16743
传真机	傳真機	chuánzhēnjī	fax machine	18288
录像机	錄像機	lùxiàngjī	video recorder, VCR	18778
打印机	打印機	dǎyìnjī	printer	22522
有线电视	有線電視	yǒuxiàn diànshì	cable television	27586
打字机	打字機	dǎzìjī	typewriter	29640

1753 给予 [給予] /jǐyǔ/ (3) v give, afford
只要我们给予，就会得到赐福。As long as we gave, we were blessed.
339 | 0.57 | 192

1754 保障 [保障] /bǎozhàng/ (3) v safeguard, guarantee
工会要努力保障工人的福利。Unions must be active in protecting the workers' welfare.
420 | 0.46 | 192 | W

1755 早就 [早就] /zǎojiù/ adv for a long time, long ago, early
如果我们走了另外一条路，可能早就到了。If we had taken the other road we might have arrived earlier.
259 | 0.74 | 191

1756 之下 [之下] /zhīxià/ (2) loc under, below
在光天化日之下竟发生绑架事件。The kidnapping occurred under the sun.
232 | 0.82 | 191

1757 大事 [大事] /dàshì/ n a major event; the overall situation
其实没有发生什么大事，我们很快就解决了。Actually it was no big problem, and we solved it quickly.
210 | 0.91 | 191

1758 轮 [輪] /lún/ clas round (of competitions and talks, etc.); [measure word for the sun and the full moon]
我们队在最后一轮中被淘汰。Our team went out in the last round.
436 | 0.44 | 191 | W

1759 系列 [系列] /xìliè/ clas series
实际传送中要涉及一系列的中间站。The actual delivery may involve a series of intermediate staging points.
356 | 0.54 | 191

1760 化 [化] /huà/ (2) v melt, dissolve; transform, make into
雪化了。The snow has melted.
230 | 0.83 | 191

1761 率 [率] /shuài/ v lead
一九六三年我率代表团去莫斯科，会谈破裂。In 1963 I led a delegation to Moscow. The negotiations broke up.
300 | 0.64 | 191

1762 贵 [貴] /guì/ (1) adj expensive
为什么饮料要这么贵？Why is the drink so expensive?
250 | 0.76 | 190

1763 激烈 [激烈] /jīliè/ (2) adj intense, fierce
我觉得竞争非常激烈。It's my impression that competition is fierce.
248 | 0.77 | 190

1764 概念 [概念] /gàiniàn/ (2) n concept
知识管理是一种概念。Knowledge management is a concept.
278 | 0.68 | 190

1765 计算机 [計算機] /jìsuànjī/ (3) n computer
这台计算机需要修理。This computer needs repairing.
306 | 0.62 | 190

1766 背景 [背景] /bèijǐng/ (3) n background
这背景有点单调。The background is a bit dull.
237 | 0.8 | 190

1767 卷 [卷] /juǎn, juàn/ (3) clas [measure word for things made into the shape of a cylinder] roll; [measure word for book] volume
这是前三卷，第四卷于下个月出版。Here are the first three volumes, the fourth one to come out next month.
213 | 0.89 | 190

1768 见面 [見面] /jiànmiàn/ (1) v meet
我很高兴有机会同您见面。I am very glad to have the opportunity to meet you.
231 | 0.82 | 190

1769 保 [保] /bǎo/ (2) v protect, defend; guarantee; preserve, maintain; bail
但是三件事可保住他的性命。There are three things you can do to ensure his survival.
215 | 0.89 | 190

1770 指挥 [指揮] /zhǐhuī/ (2) v command, direct; (music) conduct
我用它来指挥我的猎狗。I commanded my hounds with it.
238 | 0.8 | 190

1771 持续 [持續] /chíxù/ v last, continue; sustain
干旱持续了许多星期。Week after week the drought continued.
385 | 0.5 | 190 | W

1772 安 [安] /ān/ (3) adj calm, at ease
她安于现状。She is content with things as they are.
205 | 0.93 | 189

1773 牛 [牛] /niú/ adj [a popular compliment among young people] great, excellent, matchless
你太牛了！You rule!
246 | 0.77 | 189

1774 多么 [多麼] /duōme/ (1) adv [used in exclamations] how; [occurring in a clause of concession to indicate an unspecified high degree] however, (no matter) how
她的记忆力多么惊人啊！What a wonderful memory she has!
254 | 0.75 | 189

1775 武器 [武器] /wǔqì/ (2) n weapon
藏在山洞里的武器被敌人发现了。The weapons hidden in the cave were discovered by the enemy.
258 | 0.74 | 189

1776 做法 [做法] /zuòfǎ/ (2) n practice, measure
这个公司采取了一系列使用户满意的做法。The company has adopted a series of measures which satisfy the users.
263 | 0.72 | 189

1777 阳光 [陽光] /yángguāng/ (2) n sunshine
暴风雨过后出现了灿烂的阳光。The storm gave way to bright sunshine.
259 | 0.73 | 189

1778 哪个 [哪個] /nǎge/ (2) pron which
你喜欢哪个就挑哪个。You can pick whichever one you like.
258 | 0.73 | 189

1779 运用 [運用] /yùnyòng/ (2) v use, apply
计算机目前广泛运用于商业。Computers are now widely used in business.
269 | 0.7 | 189

1780 马上 [馬上] /mǎshàng/ (1) adv at once, immediately
先生，我会马上让人把它换掉。I'll see that it's changed straight away, sir.
264 | 0.71 | 188

1781 灯 [燈] /dēng/ (1) n lamp, light
因停电所有的灯都熄灭了。There was a power cut and all the lights went out.
267 | 0.71 | 188

1782 信心 [信心] /xìnxīn/ (2) n confidence
我对他们完全有信心。I have complete confidence in them.
270 | 0.7 | 188

1783 改善 [改善] /gǎishàn/ (2) v improve
大多数行业效益改善。Most sectors improved their profitability.
447 | 0.42 | 188 | W

1784 交给 [交給] /jiāogěi/ v hand over to, give
信已经交给他了。I've handed the letter to him.
236 | 0.8 | 188

1785 居然 [居然] /jūrán/ (3) adv [expressing surprise] unexpectedly, actually
我花了那么多钱，这东西居然不能用。I pay all that money and the thing doesn't actually work!
336 | 0.56 | 187

1786 工作 [工作] /gōngzuò/ (1) n job, work
这就有大量的工作要做。This will involve a great deal of work.
273 | 0.69 | 187

1787 货 [貨] /huò/ (2) n goods
我想让这批货尽早上市。I want these goods on our market at the earliest possible date.
244 | 0.77 | 187

1788 罪 [罪] /zuì/ (3) n crime, offence; guilt; suffering
他因偷窃罪被传讯。He was arraigned for theft.
205 | 0.91 | 187

1789 门口 [門口] /ménkǒu/ (1) place doorway, gate
明晨七时在门口会齐。We'll assemble at the gate at seven o'clock tomorrow morning.
339 | 0.55 | 187

1790 激动 [激動] /jīdòng/ (2) adj excited
他们非常激动。They're very excited.
252 | 0.74 | 187

1791 肯 [肯] /kěn/ (2) v be content, agree, be willing to
我想跟你补习英文，你肯不肯？Would you be willing to help me review my English?
299 | 0.63 | 187

1792 摸 [摸] /mō/ (2) v touch, feel with the hand
他刚要摸她的手，她一下子就把手缩了回去。She jerked her hand away when he tried to touch it.
287 | 0.65 | 187

1793 慢 [慢] /màn/ (1) adj slow
我的表大约慢3分钟。My watch is about three minutes slow.
224 | 0.83 | 186

1794 聪明 [聰明] /cōngmíng/ (2) adj clever, smart, witty
她出奇地聪明。She's amazingly clever.
251 | 0.74 | 186

1795 自然 [自然] /zìrán/ (2) n nature
人能够征服自然。Human beings can subdue nature.
232 | 0.8 | 186

1796 冠军 [冠軍] /guànjūn/ (2) n champion
他是去年的游泳世界冠军。He was the world champion of swimming last year.
472 | 0.4 | 186

1797 把握 [把握] /bǎwò/ (3) n grasp, confidence, certainty, probability
你认为你获得成功有多大把握？How do you view your chances of success?
230 | 0.81 | 186

1798 辩 [辯] /biàn/ v argue, debate
和他辩也是白搭。It's no use arguing with him.
483 | 0.39 | 186

1799 文明 [文明] /wénmíng/ (2) adj civilised, civil
我相信文明的人必定行为举止有礼貌。I believe a civilised man has good manners.
274 | 0.68 | 185

1800 忽然 [忽然] /hūrán/ (1) adv suddenly
他们忽然发现他们花在衣物上的钱太多了。They suddenly found out that they had spent a disproportionate amount of their money on clothing.
319 | 0.58 | 185

1801 机场 [機場] /jīchǎng/ (1) n airport
我该什么时候到达机场？When should I get to the airport?
313 | 0.59 | 185 | W

1802 乡 [鄉] /xiāng/ (2) n township; country, countryside
以乡为分配土地的单位。The township is taken as the unit for land distribution.
284 | 0.65 | 185

1803 院长 [院長] /yuànzhǎng/ (2) n [head of a hospital, school, faculty, college or university, etc.] director, dean, president
院长要求医生们立即到医院。The president asked all the doctors to be in the hospital at once.
218 | 0.85 | 185

1804 行政 [行政] /xíngzhèng/ (3) n administration
她一直在管日常的行政工作。She has been looking after the day-to-day administration.
370 | 0.5 | 185 | W

1805 甲 [甲] /jiǎ/ (3) n [used for the first of enumerated items] first; shell
计划甲每次赔偿可达五万元。Plan A covers a total of $50,000 dollars per claim.
236 | 0.79 | 185

1806 那边 [那邊] /nàbian/ (2) *pron* there
孩子们在那边玩。 The children are playing over there.
348 | 0.53 | 185 | S

1807 许 [許] /xǔ/ (2) *v* allow
只许前进，不许后退。 No retreat is allowed, only advance.
236 | 0.79 | 185

1808 谈话 [談話] /tánhuà/ (2) *v* talk
你在同谁谈话？ Who were you talking to?
231 | 0.8 | 185

1809 想象 [想象] /xiǎngxiàng/ (2) *v* imagine
我无法想象会让人骗了。 I can't imagine myself allowing people to cheat me.
226 | 0.82 | 185

1810 不得 [不得] /bùdé, bude/ *v* must not
迅速办理，不得违误。 This must be acted upon without delay.
225 | 0.82 | 185

1811 单 [單] /dān/ (2) *adj* single, solitary; odd
这是单号座位入口。 This entrance is for odd numbers.
198 | 0.93 | 184

1812 茶 [茶] /chá/ (1) *n* tea
我自己沏了一杯茶。 I made myself a cup of tea.
245 | 0.75 | 184

1813 鸟 [鳥] /niǎo/ (2) *n* bird
那声音把鸟吓飞了。 Alarmed by the noise, the birds flew away.
219 | 0.84 | 184

1814 命 [命] /mìng/ (3) *n* life; fate, destiny; order
你救了我的命，我永远感恩不尽。
You saved my life; I am forever in your debt.
276 | 0.67 | 184

1815 内心 [內心] /nèixīn/ *n* heart
她的内心充满了耻辱和犯罪的心情。 Her heart was filled with shame and guilt.
243 | 0.76 | 184

1816 辈子 [輩子] /bèizi/ *clas* [typically occurring with — "one"] all one's life, lifetime
我愿意服侍你一辈子。 I'll serve you all my life.
316 | 0.58 | 184

1817 照顾 [照顧] /zhàogù/ (1) *v* take care of, look after
当他生病时，他的儿子照顾他。 His son took care of him when he was ill.
220 | 0.84 | 184

1818 破 [破] /pò/ (1) *v* break
我的购物袋破了，东西纷纷都掉了出来。
My shopping bag broke and everything tumbled out.
225 | 0.82 | 184

1819 告 [告] /gào/ (2) *v* tell, make known; sue
详情容后再告。 Permit me to tell the details later.
222 | 0.83 | 184

1820 呆 [呆] /dāi/ (2) *v* stay; look like a dummy
你能呆多久？ How long can you stay?
296 | 0.62 | 184

1821 补 [補] /bǔ/ (2) *v* mend, repair; make up for
他那双靴子的底该补了。 The soles of his boots needed repairing.
245 | 0.75 | 184

1822 犯罪 [犯罪] /fànzuì/ (3) *v* commit a crime
驱使他犯罪的并非贪婪而是野心。 It was not greed but ambition that drove him to crime.
362 | 0.51 | 184

1823 引 [引] /yǐn/ (3) *v* cause, make; guide, lead; quote, cite
我不该引你讲起这些话。 I shouldn't have led you to talk about it.
232 | 0.8 | 184

1824 饭店 [飯店] /fàndiàn/ (1) *n* hotel, restaurant
当你离开饭店时，不要忘记交回房门钥匙。
Do not forget to give back your door key when you leave the hotel.
194 | 0.94 | 183

1825 电视台 [電視臺] /diànshìtái/ (2) *n* television station
那你还在电视台工作过一段时间。 And you worked at a television station for a time too.
246 | 0.75 | 183

1826 感动 [感動] /gǎndòng/ (2) *v* move
在场的每一个人都深受感动。 Everybody present was deeply moved.
232 | 0.79 | 183

1827 科 [科] /kē/ (2) *n* branch of study; division, section
他太太是人事科科长。 His wife was the head of the personnel division.
211 | 0.87 | 182

1828 米 [米] /mǐ/ (2) *n* rice
这种米出饭。 This kind of rice rises well when it's cooked.
207 | 0.88 | 182

1829 在 [在] /zài/ (1) *v* be available or present; exist; consist in
人都在吗？ Is everyone here?
225 | 0.81 | 182

1830 停止 [停止] /tíngzhǐ/ (2) *v* stop, put an end to
现在的确该停止这场争论了。 It is high time that we put an end to this controversy.
224 | 0.82 | 182

1831 端 [端] /duān/ (2) *v* hold or carry something level
端一杯茶给他。 Take him a cup of tea.
317 | 0.57 | 182

1832 等于 [等於] /děngyú/ (2) *v* equal
波速等于频率乘以波长。 Wave speed equals frequency times wavelength.
265 | 0.69 | 182 | S

1833 适合 [適合] /shìhé/ (2) *v* fit, suit
这样的天气不适合旅行。 This weather is not fit for travel.
224 | 0.81 | 182

1834 公开 [公開] /gōngkāi/ (2) *adj* open, public
他们的交易公开而坦诚。 Their business was open and above board.
300 | 0.6 | 181

1835 本 [本] /běn/ (1) *adv* originally, formerly
我本以为她会赢得这场比赛。 I originally thought she was going to win this match.
218 | 0.83 | 181

1836 屋 [屋] /wū/ (2) *n* house, room
我们屋有八台计算机。 There are eight computers in our room.
265 | 0.69 | 181

1837 体 [體] /tǐ/ *n* body; style; system
他久病体弱。 His body was wasted by long illness.
226 | 0.81 | 181

1838 大学生 [大學生] /dàxuéshēng/ *n* college or university student
我们很惊奇这小男孩是大学生。 We wonder that the little boy is a university student.
228 | 0.8 | 181

1839 升 [升] /shēng/ (2) *v* rise, raise; promote
飞机慢慢地升到云里去了。 The plane slowly rose into the air.
190 | 0.96 | 181

1840 总结 [總結] /zǒngjié/ (2) *v* summarise, sum up
他简单总结了讲话。 He gave a brief summary of this speech.
263 | 0.69 | 181

1841 容 [容] /róng/ (3) *v* hold, contain; tolerate; allow, permit
这个礼堂可容 2000 人。 This auditorium can hold 2,000 persons.
219 | 0.83 | 181

1842 强大 [強大] /qiángdà/ (2) *adj* strong, powerful
他们的阵容十分强大。 They have a really strong team.
231 | 0.78 | 180

1843 外交 [外交] /wàijiāo/ (2) *n* diplomacy
两国间的边界之争导致了外交关系的断绝。 The frontier dispute between the two countries resulted in the rupture of diplomatic relations.
294 | 0.61 | 180

1844 电子 [電子] /diànzǐ/ (3) *n* electronics
通讯和电子系统的建设已经完成。 The construction of the communication and electronic system has been completed.
389 | 0.46 | 180 | W

1845 遍 [遍] /biàn/ (1) *clas* [measure word for the course of actions] time; once through
咱们再检查一遍数字，好吗？ Let's go over the figures again, OK?
242 | 0.75 | 180

1846 姓 [姓] /xìng/ (1) *v* be surnamed
您姓什么？ What is your family name?
275 | 0.65 | 180

1847 需 [需] /xū/ (3) *v* need, require
这艘船需用两艘拖船把它拖进港。 The ship needed two tugs to tow it into port.
271 | 0.67 | 180

1848 硬 [硬] /yìng/ (2) *adj* hard
我喜欢在硬场地上打球。 I like to play on the hard court.
201 | 0.89 | 179

1849 头 [頭] /tóu/ (2) *num* first
他竟然获得了头等奖！ He's won the first prize!
244 | 0.74 | 179

1850 司机 [司機] /sījī/ (2) *n* driver, chauffeur
我请公共汽车司机在快到市中心时让我下车。 I asked the bus driver to put me off near the town centre.
204 | 0.88 | 179

1851 情感 [情感] /qínggǎn/ *n* feeling, emotion
我在寻找恰当的字眼来表达我的情感。 I'm groping for the right words to express my feelings.
227 | 0.79 | 179

1852 堆 [堆] /duī/ (3) *clas* pile, heap
他是在一堆旧书中找到它的。 He found it among a pile of old books.
260 | 0.69 | 179

1853 手里 [手裏] /shǒuli/ *place* in hand, at hand
她把信塞进他的手里。 She thrust the letter into his hand.
303 | 0.59 | 179

1854 秋 [秋] /qiū/ (1) *time* autumn, fall; a period of (troubled) time
叶落于秋。 Trees lose their leaves in autumn.
233 | 0.77 | 179

1855 团结 [團結] /tuánjié/ (1) *v* unite
团结一切可以团结的力量。 Unite with all the forces that can be united.
348 | 0.52 | 179 | W

1856 进攻 [進攻] /jìn'gōng/ (2) *v* attack, take the offensive
决不可无故进攻人家。 We must never attack others without provocation.
309 | 0.58 | 179

1857 牺牲 [犧牲] /xīshēng/ (2) *v* sacrifice
他牺牲性命去拯救快要溺死的孩子。 He sacrificed his life in order to save the drowning child.
194 | 0.93 | 179

1858 练 [練] /liàn/ (2) *v* practise
她是从学校里学的，她练得多。 She learnt it in school and practised a lot.
224 | 0.8 | 179

1859 围 [圍] /wéi/ (2) *v* gather round; wrap round; surround, enclose
一会儿，全家就围在一起开始包饺子。 In no time, all had gathered around the table to make dumplings.
227 | 0.79 | 179

1860 回忆 [回憶] /huíyì/ (2) *v* recall, recollect, bring to mind
这张照片让我回忆起过去的好时光。 This photo took me back to the good old days.
213 | 0.84 | 179

1861 公共 [公共] /gōnggòng/ (2) adj public
这是我第一次在公共场合发言。 It is the first time that I have spoken in public.
220 | 0.81 | 178

1862 哥哥 [哥哥] /gēge/ (1) n elder brother
我哥哥比我大一岁。 My elder brother is one year older than I.
274 | 0.65 | 178

1863 医学 [醫學] /yīxué/ (2) n medicine, medical science
这个发现几乎被医学界忽视了。 This discovery is largely ignored by the medical world.
235 | 0.76 | 178

1864 协会 [協會] /xiéhuì/ (3) n association, society
他给动物保护协会捐了一大笔钱。 He donated a large sum to an animal protection society.
390 | 0.46 | 178

1865 同事 [同事] /tóngshì/ n colleague
她是我们的同事。 She is our colleague.
230 | 0.78 | 178

1866 对待 [對待] /duìdài/ (2) v treat
你对待自己的员工可好？ Do you treat your employees well?
212 | 0.84 | 178

1867 基本上 [基本上] /jīběnshàng/ adv basically, in the main
结果基本上是令人满意的。 The results are, in the main, satisfactory.
246 | 0.72 | 177

1868 羊 [羊] /yáng/ (1) n sheep
房屋前面有一只羊。 There was a sheep in front of the house.
211 | 0.84 | 177

1869 空气 [空氣] /kōngqì/ (1) n air
空气和水是生命所必需的东西。 Air and water are indispensable to life.
200 | 0.89 | 177

1870 女士 [女士] /nǚshì/ (2) n lady
女士们、先生们，请往这边走。 Kindly step this way, ladies and gentlemen.
217 | 0.82 | 177

1871 食品 [食品] /shípǐn/ (2) n foodstuff, food
食品价格下跌了。 The price of food has fallen.
280 | 0.63 | 177

1872 海洋 [海洋] /hǎiyáng/ (2) n ocean
科学家过去认为海洋深处没有生物。 Scientists used to believe that there was no life in the depth of the ocean.
242 | 0.74 | 177

1873 资格 [資格] /zīgé/ (3) n qualification
做这项工作需要什么资格？ What sort of qualifications do you need for the job?
227 | 0.78 | 177

1874 核心 [核心] /héxīn/ n core
金融很重要，是现代经济的核心。 Finance is very important, because it is the core of the modern economy.
285 | 0.62 | 177

1875 手中 [手中] /shǒuzhōng/ place in hand
她手中有一盒糖果。 There is a box of candy in her hand.
235 | 0.76 | 177

1876 配合 [配合] /pèihé/ (2) v coordinate, cooperate
要做好这项工作，必须配合各方面的努力。 To do well in this endeavour, coordination among the various fields is essential.
241 | 0.74 | 177

1877 陪 [陪] /péi/ (2) v accompany, escort
他陪她回家。 He escorted her back home.
309 | 0.58 | 177

1878 乘 [乘] /chéng/ (2) v ride, travel by; take advantage of; multiply
我想乘第一班飞机。 I'd like to take the first available flight.
201 | 0.88 | 177

1879 大型 [大型] /dàxíng/ (2) adj large-scale
北京具有举办大型运动会的经验。 Beijing has the experience of hosting many large-scale sporting competitions.
377 | 0.47 | 176

1880 此外 [此外] /cǐwài/ (2) conj besides, in addition
此外，支持和维护也简化了。 In addition, support and maintenance are simplified.
310 | 0.57 | 176

1881 尚 [尚] /shàng/ adv still, yet
这事尚未确定。 It has not yet been definitely decided.
234 | 0.76 | 176

1882 一部分 [一部分] /yíbùfen/ num a part of
一部分费用可报销。 Part of the expenses will be refunded.
229 | 0.77 | 176

1883 天气 [天氣] /tiānqì/ (1) n weather
这天气真好。 Isn't this lovely weather?
196 | 0.9 | 176

1884 教学 [教學] /jiàoxué/ (2) n teaching
她从事教学有年头了。 She has been teaching for years.
251 | 0.7 | 176

1885 少年 [少年] /shàonián/ (2) n teenager, early youth
他是个英俊的少年。 He was a handsome boy.
208 | 0.85 | 176

1886 天下 [天下] /tiānxià/ (3) n land under heaven, the world; the country
她依然是天下最美的女人。 She was still the most beautiful woman in the world.
221 | 0.8 | 176

1887 吓 [嚇] /xià, hè/ (2) v frighten, scare; threaten
我被吓得魂飞魄散。 I was scared to death.
346 | 0.51 | 176

1888 缺 [缺] /quē/ (2) v lack; be absent, be missing
什么也不缺。 Nothing is lacking.
200 | 0.88 | 176

1889 赚 [赚] /zhuàn/ (3) v earn, make a profit
你做这笔交易准能赚很多钱。You stand to make a lot of money from this deal.
216 | 0.82 | 176

1890 培训 [培訓] /péixùn/ v train
年轻的工人都必须受培训。The young workers must be trained.
344 | 0.51 | 176 | W

1891 严肃 [嚴肅] /yánsù/ (2) adj serious, solemn
别开玩笑了，严肃一会儿吧！Stop jesting and be serious for a moment!
206 | 0.85 | 175

1892 完整 [完整] /wánzhěng/ (2) adj complete, intact
事实上，这种观点既不完整也不科学。In fact, this view is neither complete nor scientific.
232 | 0.76 | 175

1893 整 [整] /zhěng/ (3) adj whole, entire
我很快入睡而且整晚睡得非常好。I went to sleep immediately and slept soundly all night.
201 | 0.87 | 175

1894 名 [名] /míng/ adj famous, renowned
那些是名画。They're famous paintings.
223 | 0.78 | 175

1895 结果 [結果] /jiéguǒ/ (1) conj as a result, consequently
结果他辞职了。As a result, he resigned the job.
205 | 0.86 | 175

1896 只是 [只是] /zhǐshì/ (2) adv merely, only
我只是看看而已，谢谢你。I am just looking around, thank you.
238 | 0.74 | 175

1897 千万 [千萬] /qiānwàn/ (2) adv [usually occurring in negative imperatives] be sure to, must
千万注意看好自己的行李。Never leave your luggage unattended.
214 | 0.82 | 175

1898 居民 [居民] /jūmín/ (3) n resident, inhabitant; citizen
但我不是本地居民。But I'm not a resident here.
386 | 0.46 | 175 | W

1899 关 [關] /guān/ (3) n customs; barrier, obstacle; pass
谁也不能永远逃避这一关。It was an obstacle that no one could avoid forever.
189 | 0.93 | 175

1900 此时 [此時] /cǐshí/ pron at this moment
每天在此时市中心将会非常拥挤。Downtown will be very crowded at this time of day.
251 | 0.7 | 175

1901 运动 [運動] /yùndòng/ (1) v move; do sports activities
她经常运动。She plays a lot of sport.
234 | 0.75 | 175

1902 综合 [綜合] /zōnghé/ (2) adj comprehensive, synthetic
综合治理人口问题。The population issue is to be solved in a comprehensive way.
356 | 0.49 | 175

1903 势力 [勢力] /shìlì/ (3) n power, force
对对立的两个势力都忠实是不可能的。It is impossible to give allegiance to two opposing forces.
231 | 0.75 | 174

1904 对手 [對手] /duìshǒu/ n opponent; competitor
他是我比赛中的对手。He is my competitor in the game.
241 | 0.72 | 174

1905 石 [石] /shí/ n rock, stone
水滴石穿。A continual dripping will wear a hollow even in a stone.
217 | 0.8 | 174

1906 金融 [金融] /jīnróng/ n finance
在海外工作期间他积累了许多金融方面的经验。He accumulated a lot of experience in finance while working abroad.
584 | 0.3 | 174 | W

1907 随 [隨] /suí/ (2) prep along with
那何不随我同行呢？Why not come along with me?
199 | 0.87 | 174

1908 夏 [夏] /xià/ (1) time summer
谷子秋冬便宜，春夏又贵得厉害。Rice is cheap in the autumn and winter, but it becomes terribly dear in spring and summer.
299 | 0.58 | 174 | W

1909 出发 [出發] /chūfā/ (1) v start out
他们即将出发。They are about to start.
242 | 0.72 | 174

1910 邀请 [邀請] /yāoqǐng/ (2) v invite
如果你邀请他的话，他会来的。He will come if you invite him.
301 | 0.58 | 174

1911 观 [觀] /guān/ v watch, look at
公司提出一个小规模实验方案以观设想的生产体系是否有效。The company set up a pilot project to see if the proposed manufacturing system is efficient.
184 | 0.95 | 174

1912 仔细 [仔細] /zǐxì/ (2) adj careful
他仔细选择了问题。He made a careful choice of the question.
228 | 0.76 | 173

1913 一方面 [一方面] /yìfāngmiàn/ (2) conj on the one hand, while
他们一方面鼓吹和平，一方面准备战争。They preach peace while preparing for war.
215 | 0.81 | 173

1914 圈 [圈] /quān/ clas circle, round
他用螺丝刀把螺丝拧了几圈。He turned the screws round and round with a screwdriver.
209 | 0.83 | 173

1915 中午 [中午] /zhōngwǔ/ (1) time noon
我中午在办公室吃午饭。I have lunch in the office at noon.
206 | 0.84 | 173

1916 放心 [放心] /fàngxīn/ (2) v rest assured, feel relieved, set one's mind at rest
你放心好啦。You can rest assured.
255 | 0.68 | 173

1917 恨 [恨] /hèn/ (2) v hate
由于他对我家的所作所为，我才恨他。
After what he did to my family, I hate him.
261 | 0.66 | 173

1918 获 [獲] /huò/ (3) v win, obtain, reap
她在百米赛跑中获头奖。She won
the first prize in the 100 metres race.
340 | 0.51 | 173

1919 制作 [製作] /zhìzuò/ (3) v make
这双鞋是手工制作的。This pair of shoes is
handmade.
232 | 0.75 | 173

1920 活 [活] /huó/ (3) adj living, alive; lively;
movable, flexible
活的东西离开空气是不能生存的。
Living things cannot survive without air.
202 | 0.85 | 172

1921 如 [如] /rú/ (2) conj if, in case of; as, as if
如遇火警，立即停止手头的一切工作，马上离开
建筑物。In case of a fire alarm, drop whatever
you are doing and leave the building at once.
238 | 0.72 | 172

1922 从此 [從此] /cóngcǐ/ (2) adv since then,
after that
从此，我学习十分努力。After that, I studied
very hard.
216 | 0.8 | 172

1923 连续 [連續] /liánxù/ (2) adv continuously,
in succession
天气连续低温多雨。The weather continued
cold and wet.
287 | 0.6 | 172

1924 以外 [以外] /yǐwài/ (2) loc beyond,
outside; other than
她除了兄弟姐妹以外没有真正的
朋友。She has no real friends
other than her brothers and
sisters.
204 | 0.85 | 172

1925 科学家 [科學家] /kēxuéjiā/ (2) n
scientist
他在科学家中是杰出的。He is eminent
among scientists.
247 | 0.7 | 172

13. Computers and the internet

电脑	電腦	diànnǎo	computer	**1118**
网络	網絡	wǎngluò	network	**1191**
文件	文件	wénjiàn	file	**1496**
计算机	計算機	jìsuànjī	computer	**1765**
软件	軟件	ruǎnjiàn	software	**2530**
上网	上網	shàngwǎng	go online	**2916**
网站	網站	wǎngzhàn	website	**4592**
硬件	硬件	yìngjiàn	hardware	**7773**
密码	密碼	mìmǎ	password	**8044**
光盘	光盤	guāngpán	CD, compact disc	**8453**
目录	目錄	mùlù	directory	**8615**
网页	網頁	wǎngyè	webpage	**10845**
键盘	鍵盤	jiànpán	keyboard	**11580**
鼠标	鼠標	shǔbiāo	mouse	**12539**
显示器	顯示器	xiǎnshìqì	monitor	**13237**
口令	口令	kǒulìng	password	**13392**
因特网	因特網	yīntèwǎng	Internet	**15236**
网吧	網吧	wǎngbā	Internet cafe	**15665**
服务器	服務器	fúwùqì	server	**17164**
下载	下載	xiàzǎi	download	**18654**
打印机	打印機	dǎyìnjī	printer	**22522**
内存	內存	nèicún	memory	**24195**
工作站	工作站	gōngzuò zhàn	workstation	**24834**
浏览器	瀏覽器	liúlǎn qì	browser	**26350**
网址	網址	wǎngzhǐ	web address, URL	**26892**
磁盘	磁盤	cípán	disk	**27964**
光碟	光碟	guāngdié	CD, compact disc	**30021**

1926 度 [度] /dù/ (2) *clas* [measure word for temperature, angle, electricity, etc.] degree; kwh
温度是零下十五度。 The temperature is 15 degrees below zero.
196 | 0.88 | 172

1927 而言 [而言] /éryán/ *aux* [as in 就... 而言] as far as ... is concerned
对我而言没什么差别。 It does not make any difference to me.
229 | 0.75 | 172

1928 逼 [逼] /bī/ (2) *v* force, press; close in on
别在这问题上逼我。 Do not press me on this point.
230 | 0.75 | 172

1929 害怕 [害怕] /hàipà/ (2) *v* be afraid, be scared
他今天起得很早，因为他害怕迟到。 He got up very early this morning, because he was afraid of being late.
245 | 0.7 | 172

1930 出生 [出生] /chūshēng/ (2) *v* be born
我是1972年出生的。 I was born in 1972.
218 | 0.79 | 172

1931 配 [配] /pèi/ (3) *v* match; deserve; fit; mix; join
这顶帽子与外衣很相配。 The hat is a match for the coat.
198 | 0.87 | 172

1932 欣赏 [欣賞] /xīnshǎng/ (3) *v* appreciate, enjoy
你最欣赏的是什么？ What did you enjoy most?
201 | 0.86 | 172

1933 涉及 [涉及] /shèjí/ *v* involve, concern, cover
他的报告涉及很多课题。 His talk covered many subjects.
268 | 0.64 | 172

1934 一面 [一面] /yímiàn/ (3) *adv* [as in 一面... 一面..., equivalent of 一边... 一边...] simultaneously, at the same time
他一面按铃，一面想，该死！该死！As he pressed the bell, he thought, "Hell!"
226 | 0.76 | 171

1935 唉 [唉] /āi, ài/ (3) *interj* [interjection expressing sadness, disappointment, weariness, etc.] alas, oh, well; [as a response to calling, etc.]
唉，这件事就我们无能为力了。 Oh well, there's nothing we can do about it.
316 | 0.54 | 171 | S

1936 好处 [好處] /hǎochù/ (1) *n* benefit, good
空谈没有好处。 Empty talk is no good.
203 | 0.85 | 171

1937 不久 [不久] /bùjiǔ/ (1) *n* soon, before long, soon after
我们分手不久就相会了。 We met each other soon after we parted.
231 | 0.74 | 171

1938 智慧 [智慧] /zhìhuì/ (3) *n* wisdom
智慧是成熟的标识。 Wisdom is the badge of maturity.
236 | 0.72 | 171

1939 枚 [枚] /méi/ *clas* [measure word for small objects such as medals, badges, stamps, and also for round-shaped objects like missiles]
他在奥运会上得了一枚金牌。 He won a gold medal in the Olympic Games.
305 | 0.56 | 171

1940 忘记 [忘記] /wàngjì/ (2) *v* forget
你一旦学会了就永远不会忘记的。 Once you have learnt it, you'll never forget it.
204 | 0.84 | 171

1941 构成 [構成] /gòuchéng/ (2) *v* constitute, comprise
他们的生活由日常生存的平凡活动所构成。 Their life consisted of the humdrum activities of everyday existence.
231 | 0.74 | 171

1942 救 [救] /jiù/ (2) *v* save, rescue
警方救出了人质。 Police rescued the hostages.
230 | 0.74 | 171

1943 作战 [作戰] /zuòzhàn/ (3) *v* fight, conduct military operations
后来我们的作战原则有了进一步的发展。 Later our operational principles were developed a step further.
258 | 0.66 | 171 | W

1944 理想 [理想] /lǐxiǎng/ *adj* ideal, desirable
香港是理想的购物之处。 Hong Kong is an ideal place for shopping.
209 | 0.82 | 170

1945 先后 [先後] /xiānhòu/ (2) *adv* one after another, successively
这里先后住过24个皇帝。 They housed the courts of a succession of 24 emperors.
364 | 0.47 | 170

1946 活 [活] /huó/ (1) *n* work; job
我将给他找个活干。 I'll find a job for him.
218 | 0.78 | 170

1947 头发 [頭髮] /tóufà/ (2) *n* hair
她想把她的头发修剪得短一点。 She wanted her hair cropped short.
264 | 0.65 | 170

1948 吨 [噸] /dūn/ (2) *clas* ton
我们已收到两吨煤的定单。 We've received an order for two tons of coal.
444 | 0.38 | 170 | W

1949 组 [組] /zǔ/ *clas* group; set
谈判人员提出了一组新数字。 The negotiators produced a new set of figures.
216 | 0.79 | 170

1950 混 [混] /hùn/ (2) *v* mix, confuse; muddle along
在英国，很多不同种族的人混在一起。 In Britain, many different races of people are mixed together.
238 | 0.71 | 170

1951 供 [供] /gōng, gòng/ (2) *v* supply, offer; confess; enshrine
有两个航班可供他们选择。 They are offered the choice of two alternative flights.
204 | 0.84 | 170

1952 举办 [舉辦] /jǔbàn/ (3) v conduct, hold
他们举办了一次音乐会，把收入捐给了慈善机构。 They gave a concert and donated the proceeds to charity.
416 | 0.41 | 170

1953 为主 [為主] /wéizhǔ/ v give priority to, form the main part
亚裔科学家以华族和印族为主。 Chinese and Indians form the bulk of the Asian scientists.
277 | 0.62 | 170

1954 宽 [寬] /kuān/ (2) adj wide, broad; well off
她束了一条宽腰带。 She wore a wide belt round her waist.
198 | 0.86 | 169

1955 接着 [接著] /jiēzhe/ (1) adv follow, carry on
咱们接着打电话吧。 Let's go on with this phone call.
247 | 0.69 | 169

1956 没什么 [沒什麼] /méishénme/ (2) idiom [idiomatic expression] nothing serious, it's nothing, it's alright
你去不去对我来说没什么大不了。 It does not matter much to me whether you go or not.
271 | 0.63 | 169

1957 运动员 [運動員] /yùndòngyuán/ (2) n athlete, sportsman
大家认为他是一个全能运动员。 By all accounts he is an all-round athlete.
321 | 0.53 | 169

1958 国民党 [國民黨] /guómíndǎng/ (2) n Kuomintang, nationalist party
三民主义为国民党所奉行之主义。 The Three People's Principles are the platform of the Kuomintang.
260 | 0.65 | 169

1959 组 [組] /zǔ/ (2) n group
他是我们组的笔杆子。 He is one of the most effective writers in our group.
268 | 0.63 | 169

1960 进程 [進程] /jìnchéng/ n process
运用你的知识你可以促进这一进程。 You could facilitate the process by sharing your knowledge.
354 | 0.48 | 169

1961 哥 [哥] /gē/ n elder brother
你哥是干什么的？ What does your brother do?
301 | 0.56 | 169

1962 设施 [設施] /shèshī/ n facility
请问你们有哪些设施？ Could you tell me what facilities you have?
443 | 0.38 | 169

1963 经历 [經歷] /jīnglì/ (2) v experience, live through
只有经历过悲痛的人才能了解幸福的滋味。 To know happiness one must first experience sadness.
205 | 0.83 | 169

1964 搭 [搭] /dā/ (2) v build, put up; travel by; come into contact
我想搭电车去。 I want to go by streetcar.
225 | 0.75 | 169

1965 产 [產] /chǎn/ v produce, yield; reproduce
苏州产蚕丝。 Silk is produced in Suzhou.
309 | 0.55 | 169 | W

1966 么 [麼] /me/ part [interrogative particle]
这个日期对你合适么？ Will the date suit you?
372 | 0.46 | 169

1967 呃 [呃] /e/ part [particle used for a pause or to express wonder or admiration] er, oh
那么谁看马呢，呃？ And who is to look after the horses, eh?
1266 | 0.13 | 169 | S

1968 蓝 [藍] /lán/ (1) adj blue
你偏向蓝队还是红队？ Do you favour the team in blue or in red?
227 | 0.74 | 168

1969 贫困 [貧困] /pínkùn/ adj poor, impoverished
他们虽然贫困，但很慷慨。 They are generous though they are poor.
356 | 0.47 | 168 | W

1970 亦 [亦] /yì/ adv also
样品亦附于内。 Samples are also enclosed here.
263 | 0.64 | 168

1971 方针 [方針] /fāngzhēn/ (2) n policy, directive
这就是我们的根本方针。 This is our basic policy.
347 | 0.49 | 168 | W

1972 记忆 [記憶] /jìyì/ (2) n memory
那件事唤起他对学生时代的记忆。 The incident evoked a memory of his schooldays.
217 | 0.78 | 168

1973 理 [理] /lǐ/ (3) n reason; natural science (in relation to humanities)
万无此理。 There is no such reason.
202 | 0.84 | 168

1974 士兵 [士兵] /shìbīng/ (3) n soldier
四名士兵将负责守护。 Four soldiers will keep watch.
212 | 0.8 | 168

1975 媒体 [媒體] /méitǐ/ n media
电视媒体地位如何？ What is the importance of television media?
264 | 0.64 | 168

1976 相同 [相同] /xiāngtóng/ (2) adj identical, same, common
我们有许多相同之处。 We have something in common.
224 | 0.75 | 167

1977 一时 [一時] /yìshí/ (2) adv for the moment, temporarily, for a short while
我一时想不起他的名字。 I can't think of his name for the moment.
251 | 0.67 | 167

1978 就要 [就要] /jiùyào/ adv (be) about to
我就要出去了。 I'm about to leave.
212 | 0.79 | 167

1979 好几 [好幾] /hǎojǐ/ num several, quite a few, many a
这家旅馆里有好几个酒吧。 There are several bars in the hotel.
231 | 0.72 | 167

1980 抽 [抽] /chōu/ (1) v draw, take out
发动机将水沿管道抽来。The engine drew water along the pipe.
272 | 0.62 | 167

1981 答应 [答應] /dāying/ (2) v answer, reply; agree, promise
我答应帮助你。I promise I will help you.
267 | 0.63 | 167

1982 撞 [撞] /zhuàng/ (2) v bump against, collide; run into
他没看好路猛然撞在一棵树上。He wasn't looking and ran straight into a tree.
238 | 0.7 | 167

1983 治疗 [治療] /zhìliáo/ (3) v treat
我要治疗这颗牙齿。I want to have the tooth treated.
222 | 0.75 | 167

1984 错误 [錯誤] /cuòwù/ adj wrong, mistaken
我开始觉得我作出了一个错误的决定。I am beginning to think I have made a wrong decision.
231 | 0.72 | 166

1985 通知 [通知] /tōngzhī/ (1) n note, notice, announcement
我可以通过内部通讯系统给他发个通知。I can send him a note via the internal mail system.
226 | 0.74 | 166

1986 数量 [數量] /shùliàng/ (2) n quantity, amount
请告知贵方可供货数量及最早交货期。Please inform us of the quantity you can supply and the earliest delivery as well.
254 | 0.66 | 166

1987 风格 [風格] /fēnggé/ (3) n style
他以通俗的风格写作。He wrote in a familiar style.
213 | 0.78 | 166

1988 武 [武] /wǔ/ n martial arts
六大舞又分为"文"、"武"两类。The six major dances were also categorised into the "civil" and "martial" types.
243 | 0.69 | 166

1989 挑 [挑] /tiāo, tiǎo/ (2) v carry on a pole, shoulder; choose, select; push up, stir up
你喜欢哪个就挑哪个。You can pick whichever one you like.
234 | 0.71 | 166

1990 嫁 [嫁] /jià/ (3) v marry, take as husband
要相信你的直觉，就嫁给他吧！Trust your instincts and marry him!
281 | 0.59 | 166

1991 维持 [維持] /wéichí/ (3) v maintain, keep; continue, last; sustain
食物是维持生命所必需的。Food is necessary to maintain life.
199 | 0.84 | 166

1992 哲学 [哲學] /zhéxué/ (2) n philosophy
他在寻求一种他可以相信的哲学。He is looking for a philosophy he can believe in.
216 | 0.77 | 165

1993 形 [形] /xíng/ n shape, form
她买了一面心形镜子。She bought a heart-shaped mirror.
216 | 0.77 | 165

1994 风险 [風險] /fēngxiǎn/ n risk
我清楚地知道其中的风险。I'm well aware of the risks.
259 | 0.64 | 165

1995 挤 [擠] /jǐ/ (1) v squeeze, press, push; crowd
公共汽车挤得满满的。The bus was jammed full.
211 | 0.79 | 165

1996 夺 [奪] /duó/ (2) v seize, take by force; contend for
没有东西可以夺去我们这样甜蜜的记忆。Nothing can rob us of such sweet memories.
177 | 0.93 | 165

1997 紧 [緊] /jǐn/ (1) adj tight
我们的日程安排很紧。We have a tight schedule.
238 | 0.69 | 164

1998 公园 [公園] /gōngyuán/ (1) n park
晚饭后我去公园。I'll go to the park after supper.
205 | 0.8 | 164

1999 台 [台] /tái/ (2) n platform, stage; desk, table; (TV or radio) station
他几乎整出戏都在台上。He was on stage for most of the play.
190 | 0.87 | 164

2000 猫 [貓] /māo/ (2) n cat
她非常喜欢那只猫。She's crazy about that cat.
222 | 0.74 | 164

2001 价 [價] /jià/ (3) n price
现在你们卖什么价？What price do you ask for it now?
190 | 0.87 | 164

2002 目光 [目光] /mùguāng/ (3) n sight, vision; gaze
很多赞许的目光向她投来。She received many approving glances.
323 | 0.51 | 164

2003 发言 [發言] /fāyán/ (2) v make a speech, make a statement, take the floor
下一个该谁发言？Who's the next speaker?
236 | 0.7 | 164

2004 行 [行] /xíng/ (1) adj OK, all right
什么时间都行。Any time will be all right.
196 | 0.84 | 163

2005 公平 [公平] /gōngpíng/ adj fair
这种评估是不公平的。The evaluation is unfair.
186 | 0.88 | 163

2006 部分 [部分] /bùfen/ num part of
部分工人正在加班干活。Part of the workforce is on overtime.
245 | 0.67 | 163

2007 资本 [資本] /zīběn/ (3) n capital; advantage
影响发展的主要障碍是缺乏资本。 The main impediment to growth was a lack of capital.
273 | 0.6 | 163 | W

2008 地震 [地震] /dìzhèn/ (3) n earthquake
地震延续了三天。 The earthquake lasted for three days.
283 | 0.58 | 163

2009 交 [交] /jiāo/ n an act of falling over; friendship, acquaintance
差点儿绊了我一交。 I tripped and almost fell.
180 | 0.91 | 163

2010 躺 [躺] /tǎng/ (1) v lie, recline
病人躺在床上。 The patient is lying in bed.
314 | 0.52 | 163

2011 脱 [脱] /tuō/ (1) v take off (clothes, shoes, etc.); shed, come off
入室必须脱鞋。 It is obligatory to remove your shoes before entering.
224 | 0.73 | 163

2012 展开 [展開] /zhǎnkāi/ (2) v unfold, launch, set off; spread
他们对这个问题展开了辩论。 They set off a debate about the problem.
239 | 0.68 | 163

2013 懂得 [懂得] /dǒngde/ (2) v understand
起先我不懂得这是为什么，但现在我懂了。 At first I did not understand why, but now I do.
213 | 0.77 | 163

2014 主持 [主持] /zhǔchí/ (3) v preside over
那次专题研讨会是由一位著名的科学家主持的。 The special workshop was presided over by a famous scientist.
254 | 0.65 | 163

2015 之所以 [之所以] /zhīsuǒyǐ/ conj [as in 之所以 ... 是因为] the reason that ...
我之所以做这件事，是因为我喜欢。 I do it because I like it.
203 | 0.8 | 162

2016 大部分 [大部分] /dàbùfen/ num a large part of, the majority of
我们大部分知识都是间接得来的。 Most of our knowledge is second-hand.
203 | 0.8 | 162

2017 客 [客] /kè/ (3) n guest; customer
客随主便。 A guest should suit the convenience of the host.
204 | 0.8 | 162

2018 局面 [局面] /júmiàn/ (3) n situation, aspect
应付这一局面需要一个坚决果断的人。 A decisive person is needed to deal with the situation.
251 | 0.65 | 162

2019 舞台 [舞臺] /wǔtái/ (3) n stage; arena
我在舞台上忘了台词。 I forgot my lines on stage.
206 | 0.79 | 162

2020 堂 [堂] /táng/ n hall, room
四世同堂。 Four generations live under one roof.
204 | 0.8 | 162

2021 除 [除] /chú/ (2) v remove, get rid of; divide
我们可以从通讯录上将他的名字除掉。 We can remove his name from the mailing list.
184 | 0.88 | 162

2022 暗 [暗] /àn/ (2) adj dark, unclear
喔，这房间太暗了一点。 Oh, this room is a little too dark.
246 | 0.66 | 161

2023 脑 [腦] /nǎo/ n brain, head
她把头发盘在脑后。 She coiled her hair at the back of her head.
194 | 0.83 | 161

2024 据说 [據說] /jùshuō/ (2) v it is said that
据说他失踪了。 He is said to be missing.
203 | 0.79 | 161

2025 避免 [避免] /bìmiǎn/ (2) v avoid, avert
尽量避免人身攻击。 Try to avoid making personal comments.
239 | 0.68 | 161

2026 战斗 [戰鬥] /zhàndòu/ (2) v fight, combat
这场战斗持续了一星期。 The fighting continued for a week.
210 | 0.77 | 161

2027 发动 [發動] /fādòng/ (2) v start, launch; mobilise
我们不能发动这辆汽车。 We couldn't start the car.
209 | 0.77 | 161

2028 体会 [體會] /tǐhuì/ (2) v know (through learning or by experience)
我可以体会"面子"在东亚是非常重要的。 I appreciate that "face" is very important in East Asia.
182 | 0.89 | 161

2029 降 [降] /jiàng/ (2) v drop, fall, decline, decrease, lower
温度降到零摄氏度以下。 The temperature fell below zero degrees centigrade.
217 | 0.74 | 161

2030 合适 [合適] /héshì/ (1) adj suitable
我看我们星期六下午见面不太合适。 I think Saturday afternoon is not quite suitable for us to meet.
209 | 0.77 | 160

2031 严 [嚴] /yán/ (3) adj strict, stern; (air- or water-) tight
他待子女很严。 He is very strict with his children.
239 | 0.67 | 160

2032 绝 [絕] /jué/ (3) adv [usually occurring in negative sentences] definitely, absolutely; extremely; by (no) means
你绝不能出去。 You are in no condition to be outside.
181 | 0.89 | 160

2033 笔 [筆] /bǐ/ (1) n pen
这支笔使起来很得劲。 This pen writes easily.
189 | 0.85 | 160

2034 整体 [整體] /zhěngtǐ/ (3) n whole, entirety, overall
从整体上来说，要轻视它。Regarding it as a whole, we must despise it.
260 | 0.62 | 160

2035 杂志 [雜誌] /zázhì/ (3) n magazine
我不知道把那本新杂志放到哪儿去了。I have mislaid the new magazine.
214 | 0.75 | 160

2036 帐 [帳] /zhàng/ (3) n account, account book; bill; (mosquito) net
你最好记住是谁付的帐。You would do well to remember who is paying the bill.
190 | 0.84 | 160

2037 礼 [禮] /lǐ/ (3) n gift; courtesy; ceremony
礼多人不怪。One never loses anything by politeness.
206 | 0.78 | 160

2038 人人 [人人] /rénrén/ pron everyone
人人都难免有错。Everybody is fallible.
185 | 0.87 | 160

2039 长 [長] /zhǎng/ (1) v grow, develop; increase
这个园子里长了许多野草。The garden is overgrown with weeds.
187 | 0.86 | 160

2040 剩下 [剩下] /shèngxià/ v remain, be left over
剩下的时间不多了。There is not much time left.
214 | 0.75 | 160

2041 挑战 [挑戰] /tiǎozhàn/ v challenge
你向他挑战是自讨苦吃。You are asking for trouble if you challenge him.
271 | 0.59 | 160

2042 石头 [石頭] /shítou/ (2) n rock, stone
这块石头上的字迹很模糊。The writing on the stone was very faint.
212 | 0.75 | 159

2043 镇 [鎮] /zhèn/ (3) n town, township
他一辈子都住在这个镇上。He has lived in this town all his life.
245 | 0.65 | 159

2044 成本 [成本] /chéngběn/ (3) n cost
实际成本比我们预料的高得多。The actual cost was much higher than we had expected.
271 | 0.59 | 159 | W

2045 主义 [主義] /zhǔyì/ n doctrine, -ism
我从来不赞同政治上的极端主义。I have never associated myself with political extremism.
243 | 0.66 | 159

2046 盘 [盤] /pán/ (2) clas [measure word for food contained in a plate]; [measure word for objects of shallow, and usually circular, almost flat shape such as tapes] coil; [measure word for a game of chess, etc.]
这盘菜尝起来很咸。This dish tastes salty.
184 | 0.87 | 159

2047 当天 [當天] /dàngtiān/ time the same day
我们的帽子在进货的当天就卖掉了。Our caps sold out the same day they came in.
192 | 0.83 | 159

2048 逃 [逃] /táo/ (2) v escape, flee, run away
什么也逃不过他的注意。Nothing escaped his attention.
220 | 0.72 | 159

2049 攻击 [攻擊] /gōngjī/ (3) v attack
那个政客攻击他的敌手。The politician attacked his rival.
223 | 0.72 | 159

2050 提到 [提到] /tídào/ v mention
这是老师昨天提到的那本书。Here is the book which the teacher mentioned yesterday.
204 | 0.78 | 159

2051 轻松 [輕鬆] /qīngsōng/ (2) adj light, relaxed
可以想见，这是一次轻松而和谐的聚会。Apparently it was a cosy meeting.
191 | 0.83 | 159

2052 热烈 [熱烈] /rèliè/ (2) adj warm, cordial; lively, enthusiastic
她获得了观众热烈的欢迎。She received an enthusiastic ovation from the audience.
235 | 0.67 | 158

2053 姐姐 [姐姐] /jiějie/ (1) n older sister
他是我姐姐的一个朋友。He is a friend of my sister's.
222 | 0.71 | 158

2054 拖 [拖] /tuō/ (2) v drag, haul; delay, put off; mop (the floor)
今天可以做的事情不要拖到明天做。Do not put off until tomorrow what can be done today.
210 | 0.75 | 158

2055 付出 [付出] /fùchū/ v pay, give . . . as a price
他为自己粗心的失误付出了巨大的代价。He paid dearly for his careless slip.
184 | 0.86 | 158

2056 欲 [欲] /yù/ v desire, want, wish; (be) about to
己所不欲，勿施与人。Do not do to others what you would not want done to yourself.
218 | 0.73 | 158

2057 厉害 [厲害] /lìhài/ (2) adj intense, severe; harsh, stern; fierce, terrible
我病得很厉害。I've been terribly sick.
252 | 0.63 | 157

2058 空 [空] /kōng, kòng/ (2, 3) adj empty, hollow; blank; vacant
在吸烟区有空座位吗？Is there a vacant seat in the smoking area?
202 | 0.78 | 157

2059 赶紧 [趕緊] /gǎnjǐn/ (2) adv hurriedly
我赶紧回家告诉家人这一好消息。I hastened home to tell my family the good news.
244 | 0.65 | 157

2060 道 [道] /dào/ (2) n road, path; method, way; line
看来你的汽车挡着道了。 I'm afraid your car is in the way.
203 | 0.78 | 157

2061 比例 [比例] /bǐlì/ (2) n proportion, ratio
她的头部与身体大小不成比例。 Her head is out of proportion to the size of her body.
249 | 0.63 | 157

2062 资产 [資產] /zīchǎn/ n asset
商誉是一种无形资产。 Business reputation is an intangible asset.
353 | 0.45 | 157 | W

2063 开始 [開始] /kāishǐ/ n beginning, start
这个新生在数学课上有一个好的开始。 The freshman got off to a good start in his math class.
169 | 0.93 | 157

2064 心灵 [心靈] /xīnlíng/ n internal spirit, heart, soul, mind
美德是心灵美。 Virtue is the beauty of the mind.
198 | 0.8 | 157

2065 爷 [爺] /yé/ n [usually taking the suffix 儿] father, grandfather; [used as a polite term of address for an old man] uncle
爷儿俩在同一个公司工作。 Father and son work in the same company.
297 | 0.53 | 157

2066 彼此 [彼此] /bǐcǐ/ (3) pron each other
他们彼此相爱了。 They fell in love with each other.
200 | 0.79 | 157

2067 隔 [隔] /gé/ (2) v separate; be apart; partition
这两个国家远隔重洋。 The two countries are separated by vast oceans.
203 | 0.78 | 157

2068 赛 [賽] /sài/ (2) v compete; surpass
年轻人在气力上赛过老年人。 Young people surpass old men in strength.
292 | 0.54 | 157

2069 批准 [批准] /pīzhǔn/ (2) v approve
董事会批准了此项建议。 The proposal is approved by the board.
338 | 0.47 | 157 | W

2070 离婚 [離婚] /líhūn/ (2) v divorce
这对夫妻结婚六个月就离婚了。 The couple divorced after only six months.
222 | 0.71 | 157

2071 多数 [多數] /duōshù/ num most, the majority
多数人这么想。 Most people think so.
206 | 0.76 | 156

2072 场 [場] /chǎng/ (1) n field, court; ground
他把球踢出了场外。 He drove the ball out of the court.
185 | 0.85 | 156

2073 板 [板] /bǎn/ (2) n board, plank
两块板夹在一起。 Two boards were clamped together.
166 | 0.94 | 156

2074 局长 [局長] /júzhǎng/ (2) n chief of a bureau
他被任命为警察局局长。 He was nominated as the police chief.
231 | 0.68 | 156

2075 鬼 [鬼] /guǐ/ (2) n ghost, spook
你怕不怕鬼？ Are you afraid of ghosts?
251 | 0.62 | 156

2076 虎 [虎] /hǔ/ n tiger
虎是肉食动物。 Tigers are flesh-eating animals.
194 | 0.81 | 156

2077 主题 [主題] /zhǔtí/ n theme, keynote
会议的主题是失业问题。 Unemployment has been the keynote of the conference.
222 | 0.71 | 156

2078 今 [今] /jīn/ time today, now
从今以后你不用再来了。 You need not come again from now on.
184 | 0.85 | 156

2079 叫做 [叫做] /jiàozuò/ (2) v be called
水的固体状态叫做冰。 The solid state of water is called ice.
334 | 0.47 | 156 | S

2080 创新 [創新] /chuàngxīn/ (3) v innovate, be creative
鼓励创新或许比发展高科技更重要。 Perhaps being creative is more important than the development of high technology.
352 | 0.45 | 156 | W

2081 兴 [興] /xīng/ v prevail, be in fashion; promote; permit, allow
这种衣服式样已经不兴了。 This clothes style is out of fashion.
178 | 0.88 | 156

2082 光 [光] /guāng/ (2) adv only, alone
光说不做，当然不行。 Only talk and no action, naturally that won't do.
198 | 0.78 | 155

2083 凡 [凡] /fán/ (2) adv [equivalent of 凡是] all (that meets the specified requirements); altogether
凡我所有都是你的。 All that I have is yours.
199 | 0.78 | 155

2084 全体 [全體] /quántǐ/ (1) n all, whole
司令进来时，全体起立。 Everyone stood up when the commander came in.
239 | 0.65 | 155

2085 腰 [腰] /yāo/ (2) n waist
草已长得齐腰高了。 The grass had grown waist-high.
243 | 0.64 | 155

2086 路线 [路線] /lùxiàn/ (2) n route, line; itinerary
这条公共汽车路线通到博物馆。 The bus line comes to the museum.
230 | 0.67 | 155

2087 味 [味] /wèi/ (3) n taste, smell
这里确有很强烈的煤气味。 There is a strong smell of gas here.
221 | 0.71 | 155

2088 财产 [財產] /cáichǎn/ (3) n wealth, property
谁也不知道她的财产是怎么来的。 Nobody knew how she had acquired her wealth.
205 | 0.76 | 155

2089 思维 [思維] /sīwéi/ (3) n (way of) thinking, (line of) thought, mind
人的思维机制是十分复杂的。 People's thought processes are extremely complicated.
212 | 0.73 | 155

2090 市民 [市民] /shìmín/ n city resident; citizen
市民可以自由使用图书馆。 Citizens may have free access to the library.
245 | 0.63 | 155

2091 客户 [客戶] /kèhù/ n client, customer
我们打算给潜在的客户寄一些广告资料。
We are going to send advertising materials to the prospective clients.
362 | 0.43 | 155 | W

2092 杯 [杯] /bēi/ (1) clas [measure word for drinks] cup, mug, glass
你要再来一杯茶吗？ Would you like another cup of tea?
237 | 0.66 | 155

2093 曲 [曲] /qǔ/ clas [measure word for tunes, songs and melodies, etc.]
他用长笛吹出一曲优美的旋律。 He played a delightful melody on his flute.
188 | 0.83 | 155

2094 居 [居] /jū/ v live, reside; rank
中国纺织品服装出口居世界第一位。 China's exports of textiles and garments rank first in the world.
247 | 0.63 | 155

2095 不用 [不用] /búyòng/ (1) adv need not
不用麻烦了。 Don't bother about it.
205 | 0.75 | 154

2096 随时 [隨時] /suíshí/ (2) adv at any time
我随时听候你的吩咐。 I'm at your disposal any time.
179 | 0.87 | 154

2097 金牌 [金牌] /jīnpái/ n gold medal
他在滑雪比赛中得了金牌。 He won the gold medal in skating.
347 | 0.45 | 154

2098 角色 [角色] /juésè/ n role, part
这个角色他扮演得十分出色。 He was very good in the part.
207 | 0.75 | 154

2099 选举 [選舉] /xuǎnjǔ/ (2) v elect
我们选举他为董事会主席。 We elected him chairman of the board.
302 | 0.51 | 154

2100 提醒 [提醒] /tíxǐng/ (3) v remind
谢谢你提醒我。 Thanks for reminding me.
186 | 0.83 | 154

2101 做好 [做好] /zuòhǎo/ v do well
不管你做什么工作都要把工作做好。
No matter what you do, you should do it well.
294 | 0.53 | 154

2102 竟然 [竟然] /jìngrán/ (3) adv unexpectedly, actually
她一气之下竟然将信撕碎了。 She was so angry that she actually tore up the letter.
227 | 0.68 | 153

2103 鞋 [鞋] /xié/ (1) n shoe
这双鞋比那双穿着舒服。 These shoes are more comfortable than those.
188 | 0.82 | 153

2104 人民币 [人民幣] /rénmínbì/ (2) n Chinese currency, RMB
你们收美元吗？我身边带的人民币不够了。
Do you take dollars, because I haven't got enough Chinese currency on me?
381 | 0.4 | 153

2105 奶奶 [奶奶] /nǎinai/ (2) n (paternal) grandmother
奶奶年事日高，不象从前那样常出门了。
Grandma's getting on a bit and doesn't go out as much as she used to.
230 | 0.67 | 153

2106 夫妻 [夫妻] /fūqī/ (3) n man and wife, couple
他们是一对好夫妻。 They are a nice couple.
205 | 0.75 | 153

2107 小组 [小組] /xiǎozǔ/ (3) n group
所有的调查员将被分为三个小组。 The investigators will be divided into three groups.
364 | 0.42 | 153 | W

2108 仪式 [儀式] /yíshì/ (3) n ceremony
所有这些仪式都是不必要的。 All these ceremonies were uncalled for.
279 | 0.55 | 153

2109 骑 [騎] /qí/ (1) v ride (a bike, horse, etc.); straddle
我不敢骑摩托车。 I dare not ride a motorbike.
195 | 0.79 | 153

2110 睡觉 [睡覺] /shuìjiào/ (1) v go to bed, sleep
你来电话时我正要睡觉。 I was on the point of going to bed when you rang.
220 | 0.7 | 153

2111 上班 [上班] /shàngbān/ (2) v go to work
我今天不舒服，不能上班。 I don't feel up to going to work today.
211 | 0.73 | 153

2112 答 [答] /dá/ (2) v answer, reply
这些题目，我一个也答不出来。 I cannot answer any of these.
159 | 0.96 | 153

2113 消失 [消失] /xiāoshī/ (2) v disappear
然后它就消失了。 Then it disappeared.
220 | 0.7 | 153

2114 集 [集] /jí/ v gather, collect; centre on
美德和财富很少集于一人之身。 Virtue and riches seldom settle on one man.
188 | 0.82 | 153

2115 错 [錯] /cuò/ (1) n fault, mistake
谁的错最少？ Who has the fewest mistakes?
214 | 0.71 | 152

14. School life and subjects

School life:

报告	報告	*bàogào*	report, talk, lecture	**644**
教授	教授	*jiàoshòu*	professor	**711**
校长	校長	*xiàozhǎng*	chancellor, schoolmaster	**1483**
课	課	*kè*	class, lesson	**1608**
博士	博士	*bóshì*	doctor, Ph.D.	**1645**
考试	考試	*kǎoshì*	exam	**1733**
年级	年級	*niánjí*	grade	**2486**
宿舍	宿舍	*sùshè*	dormitory	**2617**
硕士	碩士	*shuòshì*	master's degree	**3807**
课程	課程	*kèchéng*	course	**3838**
餐厅	餐廳	*cāntīng*	canteen	**4851**
学期	學期	*xuéqī*	term, semester	**4965**
讲座	講座	*jiǎngzuò*	lecture	**4998**
暑假	暑假	*shǔjià*	summer vacation	**6583**
寒假	寒假	*hánjià*	winter vacation	**8919**
学士	學士	*xuéshì*	bachelor degree	**11038**
本科生	本科生	*běnkēshēng*	undergraduate	**13353**

Subjects:

历史	歷史	*lìshǐ*	history	**214**
艺术	藝術	*yìshù*	art	**492**
文学	文學	*wénxué*	literature	**663**
音乐	音樂	*yīnyuè*	music	**1051**
体育	體育	*tǐyù*	physical education	**1147**
医学	醫學	*yīxué*	medicine, medical science	**1863**
哲学	哲學	*zhéxué*	philosophy	**1992**
摄影	攝影	*shèyǐng*	photography	**2757**
数学	數學	*shùxué*	mathematics	**2790**
化学	化學	*huàxué*	chemistry	**2919**
美术	美術	*měishù*	fine arts, art	**4084**
心理学	心理學	*xīnlǐ xué*	psychology	**4390**
经济学	經濟學	*jīngjì xué*	economics	**6985**
社会学	社會學	*shèhuì xué*	sociology	**7172**
法学	法學	*fǎ xué*	legal studies	**8649**
物理学	物理學	*wùlǐ xué*	physics	**10285**
文科	文科	*wénkē*	humanities	**10496**
生物学	生物學	*shēngwù xué*	biology	**11652**
人类学	人類學	*rénlèi xué*	anthropology	**13738**
理科	理科	*lǐkē*	science	**15832**
天文学	天文學	*tiānwén xué*	astronomy	**16312**
政治学	政治學	*zhèngzhì xué*	political science	**19370**
语言学	語言學	*yǔyán xué*	linguistics	**20235**
动物学	動物學	*dòngwù xué*	zoology	**21154**
解剖学	解剖學	*jiěpōu xué*	anatomy	**22235**
工科	工科	*gōngkē*	engineering	**24198**
神学	神學	*shén xué*	theology	**24395**
教育学	教育學	*jiàoyù xué*	pedagogy	**24401**
地理学	地理學	*dìlǐ xué*	geography	**24547**
植物学	植物學	*zhíwù xué*	botany	**25019**
地质学	地質學	*dìzhì xué*	geology	**25838**
管理学	管理學	*guǎnlǐ xué*	management	**29760**

2116 错误 [錯誤] /cuòwù/ (1) *n* mistake, error
他承认了他的错误。He admitted his mistake.
229 | 0.67 | 152

2117 工具 [工具] /gōngjù/ (2) *n* tool
我将随身带来那些工具。I'll bring the tools with me.
203 | 0.75 | 152

2118 锅 [鍋] /guō/ (2) *n* pot, pan, wok
她在平锅里煎鸡蛋。She fried the eggs in a frying pan.
239 | 0.64 | 152

2119 岛 [島] /dǎo/ (2) *n* island
木材和石头是这个岛上仅有的原材料。Wood and stone are the only raw materials on the island.
191 | 0.8 | 152

2120 机制 [機制] /jīzhì/ *n* mechanism
让竞争机制发挥应有的作用。Enable competition mechanisms to play their due role.
378 | 0.4 | 152 | W

2121 眼前 [眼前] /yǎnqián/ (2) *place* before one's eyes; the present
眼前我们看到一片开阔的田野。In front of us we saw a stretch of open field.
252 | 0.61 | 152

2122 抬 [抬] /tái/ (1) *v* lift, raise; carry
你能帮助我抬走这张桌子吗? Can you help me carry this table?
285 | 0.53 | 152

2123 斗 [鬥] /dòu/ (3) *v* fight; contend with
不要和穷人斗。Don't fight the poor.
197 | 0.78 | 152

2124 随便 [隨便] /suíbiàn/ (2) *adj* casual, careless; informal
他试图显得随便一点。He tried to appear casual.
213 | 0.71 | 151

2125 亲 [親] /qīn/ (3) *adj* close, intimate
她一向待我亲如姐妹。She has been as close as a sister to me.
203 | 0.75 | 151

2126 深入 [深入] /shēnrù/ *adj* thorough, deep, in depth
需要深入探索新的主题。The new subject needs to be explored in depth.
290 | 0.52 | 151

2127 不必 [不必] /búbì/ (2) *adv* need not, no need
不必惊慌。There's no need to panic.
245 | 0.62 | 151

2128 确 [確] /què/ *adv* indeed, really
这个你们比我们更清楚,确是很不容易。You know this better than we do; it is exceedingly difficult.
182 | 0.83 | 151

2129 火车 [火車] /huǒchē/ (1) *n* train
火车晚点一个小时。The trains are running an hour late.
182 | 0.83 | 151

2130 费用 [費用] /fèiyòng/ (2) *n* expense, charge
费用多少呢? How much is the charge?
230 | 0.66 | 151

2131 教训 [教訓] /jiàoxùn/ (2) *n* lesson
这正是我们的历史教训。These are historical lessons for us.
176 | 0.86 | 151

2132 源 [源] /yuán/ *n* source
懒惰为万恶之源。Idleness is the parent of all vice.
172 | 0.88 | 151

2133 员工 [員工] /yuángōng/ *n* staff, personnel, employee
那家公司有多少员工? How many employees are there in the company?
434 | 0.35 | 151 | W

2134 层次 [層次] /céngcì/ *n* level, layer, hierarchy
我从两个层次上来回答这个问题。Let me answer that on two levels.
232 | 0.65 | 151

2135 选手 [選手] /xuǎnshǒu/ *n* (selected) contestant, player
她是优秀的网球选手。She's an excellent tennis player.
569 | 0.27 | 151 | W

2136 门 [門] /mén/ *clas* [measure word for subjects of study]; [measure word for cannons]
下周要上一门新课。A new subject is going to be given next week.
167 | 0.91 | 151

2137 本人 [本人] /běnrén/ (3) *pron* I; oneself
关于那件事本人感到很抱歉。I'm so sorry about that.
182 | 0.83 | 151

2138 地下 [地下] /dìxià/ *place* underground
矿工在地下工作。Miners work underground.
161 | 0.94 | 151

2139 演 [演] /yǎn/ (2) *v* perform, play, show
你演哪一个角色? Which part do you play?
201 | 0.76 | 151

2140 咬 [咬] /yǎo/ (2) *v* bite
爱叫的狗很少咬人。Barking dogs seldom bite.
246 | 0.61 | 151

2141 限制 [限制] /xiànzhì/ (2) *v* restrict
新法律将限制政府开支。The new law will put a lid on government spending.
214 | 0.71 | 151

2142 意味着 [意味著] /yìwèizhe/ (3) *v* mean, imply
沉默意味着同意。Silence means consent.
193 | 0.78 | 151

2143 树 [樹] /shù/ *v* set, set up; uphold
她的成功为我们树了一个好榜样。Her success sets a good example to us.
161 | 0.94 | 151

2144 干 [幹] /gān/ (2) *adj* dry
水塘快干了。The pond is running dry.
200 | 0.75 | 150

2145 立刻 [立刻] /lìkè/ (1) *adv* at once, immediately
我一看见她就立刻认出她来了。I recognised her immediately when I saw her.
295 | 0.51 | 150

2146 不得不 [不得不] /bùdébù/ (2) *adv* have to
她不得不依她父亲说的去做。She had to do what her father said.
188 | 0.8 | 150

2147 真的 [真的] /zhēnde/ *adv* really
我真的很感激。I really appreciate it.
239 | 0.63 | 150

2148 画 [畫] /huà/ (1) *n* drawing, painting
他们默默地欣赏着那幅画。They looked in silent admiration at the painting.
189 | 0.8 | 150

2149 老婆 [老婆] /lǎopo/ (3) *n* [informal] wife
他怕老婆。He was afraid of his wife.
261 | 0.58 | 150

2150 案件 [案件] /ànjiàn/ *n* case
他公正地判决了那个案件。He decided the case disinterestedly.
312 | 0.48 | 150

2151 夜 [夜] /yè/ *clas* night
两夜未睡我已筋疲力尽了。Two nights without sleep have worn me out.
210 | 0.72 | 150

2152 青 [青] /qīng/ (2) *adj* blue, green, cyan
他被打得鼻青脸肿。He was beaten black and blue.
187 | 0.8 | 149

2153 尽量 [儘量] /jìnliàng/ (2) *adv* as far as possible, to the greatest extent
我尽量避开他。I avoided him as much as possible.
180 | 0.83 | 149

2154 远远 [遠遠] /yuǎnyuǎn/ *adv* by far; far away
他的工作远远没有做完。He's fallen far behind in his work.
170 | 0.88 | 149

2155 事实上 [事實上] /shìshíshàng/ *idiom* in fact
事实上，我认为有一辆旧车总比没车强。In fact, I think an old car is better than none.
207 | 0.72 | 149

2156 图书馆 [圖書館] /túshūguǎn/ (1) *n* library
这个城市有三个图书馆。There are three libraries in the city.
185 | 0.81 | 149

2157 导演 [導演] /dǎoyǎn/ (3) *n* (film) director
剧本已提前送交导演了。The script was delivered to the director ahead of schedule.
195 | 0.77 | 149

2158 阵 [陣] /zhèn/ (2) *clas* [measure word for a short period of time or action] gust, spell
凉爽的微风一阵阵地吹过河面。A fresh breeze puffed across the river.
298 | 0.5 | 149

2159 射 [射] /shè/ (2) *v* shoot, spout; send out
猎人射了一只兔子。The hunter shot a hare.
174 | 0.86 | 149

2160 认 [認] /rèn/ (2) *v* recognise; admit; resign oneself to
我简直认不出她来了。I can scarcely recognise her.
214 | 0.7 | 149

2161 值 [值] /zhí/ (3) *v* be worth; be on duty
这值多少钱？What's its worth?
171 | 0.87 | 149

2162 挣 [掙] /zhèng, zhēng/ (3) *v* earn; struggle to get free
他靠演戏挣了大笔的钱。He earned large sums of money by acting.
231 | 0.65 | 149 | S

2163 友好 [友好] /yǒuhǎo/ (1) *adj* friendly
他对我们大家都很友好。He is friendly to us all.
535 | 0.28 | 148 | W

2164 相当 [相當] /xiāngdāng/ (2) *adj* matching, commensurate with; suitable, appropriate; considerable
妇女在高知识领域已占有相当比例。Women accounted for a considerable proportion in the field of advanced knowledge.
178 | 0.83 | 148

2165 恶 [惡] /è/ (3) *adj* bad, evil, wicked; fierce
恶事传千里。Bad news spreads everywhere.
200 | 0.74 | 148

2166 妹妹 [妹妹] /mèimei/ (1) *n* younger sister
她留在家里陪伴她妹妹。She stayed at home to keep her younger sister company.
222 | 0.67 | 148

2167 结论 [結論] /jiélùn/ (2) *n* conclusion
你怎么得出那个结论的？How did you reach that conclusion?
184 | 0.81 | 148

2168 校 [校] /xiào/ *n* school
几个学生因患病而没有来校上课。Several children are away from school because of illness.
187 | 0.79 | 148

2169 斤 [斤] /jīn/ (1) *clas* [measure term for weight in Chinese local unit] jin (half a kilo)
我每种要1斤。I'll take half a kilo each of these.
215 | 0.69 | 148 | S

2170 上学 [上學] /shàngxué/ (1) *v* go to school
我每天走路上学。I walk to school every day.
178 | 0.83 | 148

2171 冒 [冒] /mào/ (2) *v* emit, give off; risk, brave
开水正冒着蒸汽。The boiling water is giving off steam.
186 | 0.8 | 148

2172 猜 [猜] /cāi/ (2) *v* guess
是的，你猜得很对。Yes, that's a good guess.
222 | 0.67 | 148

2173 厚 [厚] /hòu/ (2) *adj* thick
地上积了厚厚的雪。Snow lay thick on the ground.
237 | 0.62 | 147

2174 落后 [落後] /luòhòu/ (2) *adj* backward, outdated, behind the times
我们不能安于落后。We must not be content to remain backward.
220 | 0.67 | 147

2175 平均 [平均] /píngjūn/ (2) *adj* average, mean
一个班的学生平均人数是30。The average number of students in a class is 30.
267 | 0.55 | 147

2176 秩序 [秩序] /zhìxù/ (2) *n* order
学校的教学秩序非常好。The teaching order in the school is very good.
246 | 0.6 | 147

2177 市场经济 [市場經濟] /shìchǎngjīngjì/ *n* market economy
社会主义和市场经济之间不存在根本矛盾。There is no fundamental contradiction between socialism and a market economy.
336 | 0.44 | 147 | W

2178 带 [帶] /dài/ *n* ribbon, belt; zone, area
这一带的一些小路只有晴天才能走。Some of the walks in this area are only possible in dry weather.
184 | 0.8 | 147

2179 气 [氣] /qì/ (2) *v* get angry; make angry
我气得不得了，就打了他。I was so furious I couldn't control myself, and I hit him.
263 | 0.56 | 147

2180 爆发 [爆發] /bàofā/ (3) *v* break out
第二次世界大战是1939年爆发的。The Second World War broke out in 1939.
167 | 0.88 | 147

2181 众多 [眾多] /zhòngduō/ *num* numerous, many
游客可观赏众多名胜古迹。Visitors will get chances to visit many places of natural beauty and historical relics.
199 | 0.74 | 146

2182 湖 [湖] /hú/ (1) *n* lake
夏天我们在湖上泛舟。We sail on the lake in summer.
171 | 0.86 | 146

2183 大人 [大人] /dàrén/ (2) *n* adult, grown-up
大人尚且举不起来，何况小孩子。Grown-ups can't lift it, let alone children.
205 | 0.71 | 146

2184 游戏 [遊戲] /yóuxì/ (3) *n* game
现在我可以去玩电子游戏吗？May I go to play a video game now?
266 | 0.55 | 146

2185 福 [福] /fú/ *n* good fortune, happiness, blessing
他可说是因病得福，他后来娶了他的护士。His illness became a blessing in disguise, when he married his nurse.
175 | 0.84 | 146

2186 子女 [子女] /zǐnǚ/ *n* child, children
父母应当关心子女的教育。Parents must attend to the education of their children.
174 | 0.84 | 146

2187 劝 [勸] /quàn/ (2) *v* persuade; comfort
他劝她努力学习。He persuaded her to study hard.
213 | 0.69 | 146

2188 上升 [上升] /shàngshēng/ (3) *v* rise, go up
气温在上升。The temperature is going up.
260 | 0.56 | 146

2189 转移 [轉移] /zhuǎnyí/ (3) *v* transfer, shift, move
由于战争难民被迫转移。The refugees were displaced by the war.
194 | 0.76 | 146

2190 突破 [突破] /tūpò/ (3) *v* break through; surmount
愤怒的人群突破了警方的封锁线走到街上。An angry crowd burst through the line of police and into the street.
259 | 0.57 | 146

2191 炸 [炸] /zhá, zhà/ (3, 3) *v* fry; explode
房子被炸得粉碎。The house was ripped asunder by the explosion.
199 | 0.74 | 146

2192 熟 [熟] /shú, shóu/ (1) *adj* ripe; (food) cooked, done; familiar; skilled; sound (sleep)
牛肉熟了。The beef is done.
201 | 0.72 | 145

2193 的确 [的確] /díquè/ (2) *adv* indeed, really
我听到这消息的确很高兴。I was indeed very glad to hear the news.
185 | 0.79 | 145

2194 希望 [希望] /xīwàng/ (1) *n* hope
我们的希望破灭了。Our hopes were defeated.
171 | 0.85 | 145

2195 主人 [主人] /zhǔrén/ (2) *n* master; host; owner
这家餐馆去年换了两次主人。This restaurant changed owners twice last year.
177 | 0.82 | 145

2196 婚 [婚] /hūn/ *n* marriage
希望你婚后生活事事顺心。I hope everything goes well with your married life.
210 | 0.69 | 145

2197 吸 [吸] /xī/ (2) *v* inhale, draw; suck, suck up; attract
她深深地吸了一口烟。She took a long pull at her cigarette.
203 | 0.72 | 145

2198 躲 [躲] /duǒ/ (2) *v* hide; dodge, avoid
她的原来的朋友现在躲着她。Her former friends now avoid her.
248 | 0.59 | 145

2199 骗 [騙] /piàn/ (2) *v* take in, cheat
想来他是不会骗你的。I assume that he won't cheat you.
212 | 0.69 | 145

2200 塞 [塞] /sāi/ (3) *v* squeeze in; stop up
他把衣服塞进袋子。He jammed the clothes into a bag.
173 | 0.84 | 145

2201 具 [具] /jù/ v possess, have
我对自己颇具信心。I have confidence in myself.
191 | 0.76 | 145

2202 准确 [準確] /zhǔnquè/ (2) adj accurate, exact
权威人士不愿提供准确数位。Authorities hesitated to quote exact figures.
184 | 0.79 | 144

2203 遗憾 [遺憾] /yíhàn/ (3) adj sorry, pitiful, regretful
听说他考试不及格我很遗憾。I am sorry to hear about his failure in the examination.
159 | 0.91 | 144

2204 灵 [靈] /líng/ adj effective; quick-minded
大脑越用越灵。The more you use your head, the more quick-witted you will be.
192 | 0.75 | 144

2205 认识 [認識] /rènshí/ (1) n understanding, knowledge, awareness
他们对这个问题缺乏清楚的认识。They lacked a clear understanding of the problem.
181 | 0.8 | 144

2206 井 [井] /jǐng/ (2) n well
院子里有一眼井。There is a well in the yard.
159 | 0.91 | 144

2207 法院 [法院] /fǎyuàn/ (3) n court of law
法院判定她有罪。The court found her guilty.
250 | 0.58 | 144

2208 桌 [桌] /zhuō/ n table, desk
请给我一张两人桌。I'd like a table for two, please.
254 | 0.57 | 144

2209 顿 [頓] /dùn/ (1) clas [measure word for regular meals]; [measure word for unpleasant events such as criticising, abusing, reprimanding, etc.]
跟我们一块儿吃顿便饭吧。Come along and take potluck with us.
212 | 0.68 | 144

2210 首 [首] /shǒu/ (2) clas [measure word for songs and poems]
你喜欢那首歌吗？Do you like the song?
194 | 0.74 | 144

2211 加以 [加以] /jiāyǐ/ (2) v [normally preceding a disyllabic verb to prepose the object before the verb]
所以事物都要加以具体分析。We need to make a concrete analysis of everything.
204 | 0.71 | 144

2212 依靠 [依靠] /yīkào/ (2) v depend on, rely on
盲人在很大程度上依靠触觉。Blind people rely a lot on touch.
227 | 0.64 | 144

2213 申请 [申請] /shēnqǐng/ (3) v apply
我想申请驾驶执照。I'd like to apply for a driver's licence.
200 | 0.72 | 144

2214 写作 [寫作] /xiězuò/ (3) n writing
我其实是个教师，写作只是我的兼职。I'm a teacher really; my writing is just a sideline.
213 | 0.68 | 144

2215 相比 [相比] /xiāngbǐ/ v compare
二者不能相比。There is no comparison between the two.
207 | 0.7 | 144

2216 而已 [而已] /éryǐ/ part [sentence final particle, equivalent of 罢了 nothing more, that is all
我只不过是做着玩而已。I only do it for amusement.
211 | 0.68 | 144

2217 牛 [牛] /niú/ (1) n ox, cow, cattle; beef
这块土地每亩可喂养十头牛。This land will carry ten cows to the acre.
182 | 0.79 | 143

2218 委员 [委員] /wěiyuán/ (2) n committee member
委员们意愿不一，发生了冲突。There was a clash of wills among committee members.
410 | 0.35 | 143 | W

2219 人数 [人數] /rénshù/ n number of people
学生人数增多。The number of students increased.
236 | 0.61 | 143

2220 应用 [應用] /yìngyòng/ (2) v use, apply
这项研究成果能应用于新的技术开发方面。The results of this research can be applied to new developments in technology.
242 | 0.59 | 143

2221 商量 [商量] /shāngliang/ (2) v consult, discuss
你还是与他商量一下这件事为好。You will do well to discuss the matter with him.
210 | 0.68 | 143

2222 伤害 [傷害] /shānghài/ (3) v harm, injure, offend
我们必须小心，不要伤害读者的感情。We have to be careful not to offend our readers' sensibilities.
187 | 0.77 | 143

2223 北方 [北方] /běifāng/ (2) place north
听她的口音，她一定是北方人。Judging by her accent, she must be from the north.
169 | 0.84 | 142

2224 大多数 [大多數] /dàduōshù/ (2) num most, the majority
大多数节目都不合我的胃口。Most of the programs are not to my taste.
201 | 0.71 | 142

2225 程序 [程序] /chéngxù/ (3) n procedure; (computer) program
他们采取了一种反复试验的程序。They adopted a trial-and-error procedure.
217 | 0.66 | 142

2226 眼光 [眼光] /yǎn'guāng/ (3) n eye, sight; foresight
她以怀疑的眼光注视着我。She stared at me with unbelieving eyes.
241 | 0.59 | 142

2227 大门 [大門] /dàmén/ n gate, (main) entrance
大门没锁上。The gate wasn't locked.
177 | 0.8 | 142

2228 亩 [畝] /mǔ/ (2) clas [measure term for area of land in Chinese local unit] mu (equal to 0.165 acres)
我们村没有一亩荒废的土地。Not a single hectare of land is left uncultivated in our village.
355 | 0.4 | 142 | W

2229 划 [劃] /huá, huà/ (2) v row, paddle; scratch, strike; delimit, differentiate; assign
我们在湖上划船划了一个下午。We spent the whole afternoon rowing on the lake.
167 | 0.86 | 142

2230 毫无 [毫無] /háowú/ (2) v not have at all
这报告毫无真实性可言。There is not a vestige of truth in the report.
202 | 0.71 | 142

2231 编 [編] /biān/ (2) v compile, edit; make up; weave, plait
他提出的缺席理由显然是瞎编的。The reason he gave for his absence was obviously fabricated.
171 | 0.83 | 142

2232 探索 [探索] /tànsuǒ/ (3) v explore
我们已经探索过了各种途径。We have explored every avenue.
264 | 0.54 | 142

2233 失 [失] /shī/ v lose
原稿已失，这是副本。The original manuscript has been lost; this is a copy.
170 | 0.84 | 142

2234 累 [累] /lèi/ (1) adj tired, weary
你是累了不是？You're tired, aren't you?
195 | 0.73 | 141

2235 发达 [發達] /fādá/ (2) adj developed, advanced; flourishing
美国是一个发达的工业国家 The United States is a developed industrial country.
192 | 0.74 | 141

2236 颜色 [顏色] /yánsè/ (1) n colour
衬衫的颜色与领带不相配。The colour of the shirt does not match that of the tie.
186 | 0.76 | 141

2237 证据 [證據] /zhèngjù/ (3) n evidence, proof
我能给你好几个证据证明它的真实性。I can give you more than one proof that it is true.
181 | 0.78 | 141

2238 医疗 [醫療] /yīliáo/ (3) n medicine, medical treatment
请你送我去最近的医疗中心好吗？Could you take me to the nearest medical centre?
263 | 0.54 | 141

2239 总经理 [總經理] /zǒngjīnglǐ/ n general manager
重大问题由总经理亲自处理。Matter of great weight is handled by the general manager himself.
187 | 0.76 | 141

2240 势 [勢] /shì/ n power, influence; momentum, tendency; situation
杂草越来越多，有取代其他植物之势。Weeds tend to displace other plants.
173 | 0.82 | 141

2241 代表团 [代表團] /dàibiǎotuán/ n delegation
代表团将于星期一上午到达。The delegation will arrive on Monday morning.
375 | 0.38 | 141

2242 遇 [遇] /yù/ (2) v meet with, encounter
我们在路上相遇了。We met on the road.
173 | 0.82 | 141

2243 闻 [聞] /wén/ (2) v smell; hear
牛奶闻起来完全变味了。The milk smells decidedly off.
184 | 0.77 | 141

2244 辩论 [辯論] /biànlùn/ (3) v debate, argue
辩论这个问题是没用的。It is useless arguing about this problem.
257 | 0.55 | 141

2245 位于 [位於] /wèiyú/ (3) v be located, be situated
这家饭店位于高速公路旁，交通十分便利。The hotel is conveniently located near the motorway.
223 | 0.64 | 141

2246 展示 [展示] /zhǎnshì/ v demonstrate, reveal, open up before one's eyes
从来没有机会展示她的技能。There was never an occasion for her to demonstrate her skills.
210 | 0.67 | 141

2247 热闹 [熱鬧] /rènao/ (2) adj busy, bustling with noise and excitement
人来人往，好不热闹！What a busy place, with so many people coming and going.
179 | 0.79 | 140

2248 新鲜 [新鮮] /xīnxiān/ (2) adj fresh
新鲜空气有利于健康。Fresh air is conducive to health.
171 | 0.82 | 140

2249 根 [根] /gēn/ (1) n root
这些根扎得很深。The roots go a long way down.
173 | 0.81 | 140

2250 杯 [杯] /bēi/ (1) n cup, mug, glass
啤酒杯里有些啤酒。There's some beer in the glass.
195 | 0.72 | 140

2251 洞 [洞] /dòng/ (2) n hole, cavity, cave
躲进洞里去，那他们就看不到你了。Go into the cave, then they won't see you.
167 | 0.84 | 140

2252 老太太 [老太太] /lǎotàitai/ (2) n old lady
客车上坐满了老太太。The coach is full of elderly ladies.
235 | 0.6 | 140 | S

2253 厅 [廳] /tīng/ (3) *n* hall, foyer, lounge;
[a provincial-level government department]
department
营业厅挤满了人。 The crowd filled the
business hall.
181 | 0.77 | 140

2254 生态 [生態] /shēngtài/ *n* ecology
全区生态环境不断得到改善。 The region's
ecological environment has improved
steadily.
345 | 0.41 | 140

2255 运输 [運輸] /yùnshū/ (2) *v* transport
这种货物我们只能用卡车来运输。 We can
only use trucks for the transport of this kind
of goods.
253 | 0.56 | 140

2256 独特 [獨特] /dútè/ (3) *adj* unique
这座城市的美在于它建筑物的独特风格。
The beauty of the city consists in the unique
style of its buildings.
182 | 0.77 | 139

2257 逐步 [逐步] /zhúbù/ (2) *adv* step by step,
gradually
城市空气质量逐步提高。 The air quality in the
urban areas picked up gradually.
343 | 0.41 | 139 | W

2258 星期 [星期] /xīngqī/ (1) *n* week
你这星期以来在干什么？ What have you been
doing this week?
169 | 0.83 | 139

2259 性质 [性質] /xìngzhì/ (2) *n* nature, character
这两个问题的性质完全不同。 The two issues
are entirely different in nature.
191 | 0.73 | 139

2260 时刻 [時刻] /shíkè/ (2) *n* moment; timetable
这是一个激动人心的时刻。 It was an exciting
moment!
155 | 0.9 | 139

2261 区域 [區域] /qūyù/ (3) *n* region, area
军队在进入敌军的区域之前进行了伪装。
The troops camouflaged themselves before
they went into enemy territory.
252 | 0.55 | 139

2262 负责人 [負責人] /fùzérén/ *n* person in charge,
director
这项工作从一开始他就是负责人。 He has
been director of the project since its
inception.
324 | 0.43 | 139 | W

2263 红色 [紅色] /hóngsè/ *n* red
这毯子是红色的。 The blanket is red.
169 | 0.82 | 139

2264 当初 [當初] /dāngchū/ (3) *time* at the
beginning, in the first place
他当初真不该娶我。 He shouldn't have
married me in the first place.
185 | 0.75 | 139

2265 扔 [扔] /rēng/ (2) *v* toss, throw (away)
他把书扔在桌子上。 He tossed the book down
on the table.
223 | 0.63 | 139

2266 遭到 [遭到] /zāodào/ (2) *v* suffer; encounter,
meet with
她的建议遭到了强烈反对。 Her proposal met
with strong opposition.
195 | 0.71 | 139

2267 统一 [統一] /tǒngyī/ (2) *adj* unified, uniform;
centralised
不能设想我们国家可以没有统一的中学教材。
It is inconceivable that our country has no set
of unified teaching materials for secondary
schools.
240 | 0.58 | 138

2268 跟 [跟] /gēn/ (1) *conj* and
窗帘跟墙是同一个颜色。 The curtains and
walls are the same colour.
230 | 0.6 | 138

2269 单 [單] /dān/ (2) *adv* only, alone
毕竟人不能单靠面包生活！ After all, man
does not live by bread alone!
158 | 0.88 | 138

2270 决定 [決定] /juédìng/ (1) *n* decision
我对这一决定不十分满意。 I am not
altogether happy about the decision.
204 | 0.68 | 138

2271 生活 [生活] /shēnghuó/ (1) *n* life
这些东西正在影响着人们的生活和行为。
These things are affecting people's lives and
behaviours.
170 | 0.82 | 138

2272 精力 [精力] /jīnglì/ (2) *n* energy, vigour
她精力充沛。 She's full of energy.
163 | 0.85 | 138

2273 编辑 [編輯] /biānjí/ (3) *n* editor; editing
编辑把整段全删掉了。 The editor struck out
the whole paragraph.
201 | 0.69 | 138

2274 服装 [服裝] /fúzhuāng/ *n* clothing, garment,
wear
她开设了一家妇女服装商店。 She opened a
women's clothing shop.
194 | 0.72 | 138

2275 志 [志] /zhì/ *n* ambition, aspiration; will;
records
人穷志不穷。 One may be poor but never
cease to have ambition.
188 | 0.74 | 138

2276 之类 [之類] /zhīlèi/ (3) *pron* and so on, and
the like
你难道没有集邮之类的爱好吗？ Don't you
have any habits like stamp collection and
so on?
186 | 0.74 | 138

2277 春天 [春天] /chūntiān/ (1) *time* spring
树在春天长出新叶子。 The trees send out
new leaves in spring.
153 | 0.91 | 138

2278 经过 [經過] /jīngguò/ (1) *v* pass, go
through
在路上，我经过一所小学。 On the way I
passed a primary school.
148 | 0.93 | 138

15. Professions

老师	老師	*lǎoshī*	teacher	386
农民	農民	*nóngmín*	farmer, peasant	509
教授	教授	*jiàoshòu*	professor	711
作家	作家	*zuòjiā*	writer	913
医生	醫生	*yīshēng*	doctor	920
工人	工人	*gōngrén*	factory worker	956
教师	教師	*jiàoshī*	teacher	1088
警察	警察	*jǐngchá*	police	1137
校长	校長	*xiàozhǎng*	chancellor, schoolmaster	1483
演员	演員	*yǎnyuán*	actor, actress	1567
院长	院長	*yuànzhǎng*	dean, director	1803
军人	軍人	*jūnrén*	soldier	2313
律师	律師	*lǜshī*	lawyer	2426
明星	明星	*míngxīng*	star, celebrity	2683
会计	會計	*kuàijì*	accountant	2730
教练	教練	*jiàoliàn*	coach	2816
工程师	工程師	*gōngchéngshī*	engineer	3789
法官	法官	*fǎguān*	judge	4244
服务员	服務員	*fúwùyuán*	waiter, waitress	4524
护士	護士	*hùshi*	nurse	4995
教员	教員	*jiàoyuán*	teacher, instructor	7083
翻译	翻譯	*fānyì*	translator, interpreter	7979
营业员	營業員	*yíngyèyuán*	shop assistant	9625
售货员	售貨員	*shòuhuò yuán*	salesperson	10030
系主任	系主任	*xì zhǔrèn*	head of department	10404
书法家	書法家	*shūfǎ jiā*	calligrapher	11439
建筑师	建築師	*jiànzhú shī*	architect	14698
海员	海員	*hǎiyuán*	sailor	20276

2279 加工 [加工] /*jiāgōng*/ (2) *v* process
请放心，这些原材料将会得到认真仔细的加工。We can assure you that the raw material will be carefully processed.
277 | 0.5 | 138

2280 完善 [完善] /*wánshàn*/ (3) *v* improve, make perfect
完善失业保险制度。We need to improve the unemployment insurance system.
336 | 0.41 | 138 | W

2281 推进 [推進] /*tuījìn*/ (3) *v* boost, advance, push on
减税将会推进经济的增长。The tax cut will boost the economy.
395 | 0.35 | 138 | W

2282 密切 [密切] /*mìqiē*/ (2) *adj* close
他们和我保持密切联系。They keep close touch with me.
222 | 0.62 | 137

2283 腐败 [腐敗] /*fǔbài*/ *n* corruption
腐败危害社会。Corruption damages the society.
255 | 0.54 | 137

2284 因而 [因而] /*yīn'ér*/ (2) *conj* so, therefore, hence
因而你必须小心。So you must be careful.
221 | 0.62 | 137

2285 研究所 [研究所] /*yánjiùsuǒ*/ (2) *n* research institute
考虑到便于研究，我们建立了研究所。We have established the institute with a view to facilitating the research.
217 | 0.63 | 137

2286 铁 [鐵] /*tiě*/ (2) *n* iron
这把铲子是用铁做的。This spade is made of iron.
156 | 0.88 | 137

2287 公路 [公路] /gōnglù/ (2) *n* road, highway
公路交通费已经上涨。Road transport costs have risen.
277 | 0.5 | 137

2288 趋势 [趨勢] /qūshì/ *n* trend, tendency
这个趋势将继续下去。This trend will continue.
232 | 0.59 | 137

2289 卡 [卡] /kǎ/ *n* card
我想取消那张卡。I'd like to cancel my card.
174 | 0.79 | 137

2290 营 [營] /yíng/ *n* camp; battalion
我们回营去吧。Let's go back to the camp.
176 | 0.78 | 137

2291 衣 [衣] /yī/ *n* clothes, clothing
你应该穿上保暖衣。You had better put on warm clothes.
189 | 0.73 | 137

2292 当代 [當代] /dāngdài/ (3) *time* the present age
他是当代最伟大的科学家之一。He is one of the greatest scientists of our age.
185 | 0.74 | 137

2293 开会 [開會] /kāihuì/ (2) *v* have a meeting
星期一开会怎样？How about having a meeting on Monday?
159 | 0.87 | 137

2294 论 [論] /lùn/ (3) *v* discuss, talk about, expound; decide on
所论各点可以归为三个主要方面。The points to be discussed can be brought under three main headings.
176 | 0.78 | 137

2295 生 [生] /shēng/ (2) *adj* raw; unripe; unfamiliar; alive, living
大部分的水果是生吃的。Most fruits are eaten raw.
167 | 0.82 | 136

2296 有限 [有限] /yǒuxiàn/ (3) *adj* limited
他的社交范围非常有限。His social sphere is limited.
169 | 0.81 | 136

2297 随后 [隨後] /suíhòu/ (3) *adv* soon afterwards
我们随后就到了。We arrived soon after.
165 | 0.83 | 136

2298 自行车 [自行車] /zìxíngchē/ (1) *n* bicycle, bike
你在骑自行车之前应该检查一下。You should check your bicycle before you ride it.
155 | 0.88 | 136

2299 期 [期] /qī/ (2) *n* a period of time, phase, stage; schedule time
保护期越长，付的费就越多。The longer the protection period, the more they have to pay.
200 | 0.68 | 136

2300 真理 [真理] /zhēnlǐ/ (2) *n* truth
真理永恒；谬误短暂。Truth is immortal; error is mortal.
195 | 0.7 | 136

2301 表面 [表面] /biǎomiàn/ (2) *n* surface, outside
她表面很镇静，但我知道她实际上很不安。She seems calm on the outside but I know how worried she really is.
174 | 0.79 | 136

2302 负担 [負擔] /fùdān/ (3) *n* burden, load
学生负担太重是不好的。It is not good to put too heavy a load on students.
226 | 0.6 | 136

2303 知识份子 [知識份子] /zhīshìfènzi/ (3) *n* intellectual
要发挥知识份子的专长。We must take full advantage of the specialised knowledge of intellectuals.
191 | 0.72 | 136

2304 早晨 [早晨] /zǎochén/ (1) *time* early morning
我在早晨八点出发。I start at eight in the morning.
169 | 0.81 | 136

2305 增强 [增强] /zēngqiáng/ (3) *v* enhance, strengthen
他一反对反而增强了我们的决心。His opposition served only to strengthen our resolve.
367 | 0.37 | 136 | W

2306 同样 [同樣] /tóngyàng/ (2) *adj* same
我一直在另一家公司里做同样的工作。I have been doing the same job in another company.
191 | 0.71 | 135

2307 渐渐 [漸漸] /jiànjiàn/ (2) *adv* gradually
月亮渐渐地升高了。The moon is rising gradually.
221 | 0.61 | 135

2308 西部 [西部] /xībù/ (2) *loc* west, western part
西部经常多雨，而南部有时是温暖的。It's often wet in the west and sometimes warm in the south.
576 | 0.24 | 135 | W

2309 理想 [理想] /lǐxiǎng/ (2) *n* ideal, dream
有了理想，还要有纪律才能实现。Ideals cannot be realised without discipline.
154 | 0.88 | 135

2310 情形 [情形] /qíngxíng/ (2) *n* circumstance, situation
这又是一种情形。That is another aspect of the situation.
179 | 0.76 | 135

2311 解放军 [解放軍] /jiěfàngjūn/ (3) *n* liberation army (specifically referring to the Chinese army known as the People's Liberation Army), the PLA; PLA soldier
就在这时候，一位解放军从旁边走过。Just at the moment a PLA man passed by.
207 | 0.65 | 135

2312 武装 [武裝] /wǔzhuāng/ (3) *n* arms
这两国间有可能发生武装冲突。Armed conflict is likely to break out between the two countries.
235 | 0.58 | 135

2313 军人 [軍人] /jūnrén/ (3) n serviceman, soldier
孩子们玩着当军人的游戏。The children were playing at soldiers.
172 | 0.79 | 135

2314 他人 [他人] /tārén/ pron other people
我们不该打听他人的私事。We should not spy into other people's affairs.
192 | 0.7 | 135

2315 当前 [當前] /dāngqián/ (2) time currently, presently
这些地区当前正面临严峻的问题。These areas are currently facing severe problems.
329 | 0.41 | 135 | W

2316 醒 [醒] /xǐng/ (2) v wake up
我夜里醒过两次。I woke up twice in the night.
217 | 0.63 | 135

2317 托 [托] /tuō/ (2) v hold in one's hand; entrust
我不在家时把猫托给朋友照料。I entrust my cat to a friend while I am away.
172 | 0.79 | 135

2318 刺激 [刺激] /cìjī/ (3) v stimulate, provoke
这本书刺激了她的想像。The book stimulated her imagination.
165 | 0.82 | 135

2319 达成 [達成] /dáchéng/ (3) v reach (an agreement)
还要有一番讨价还价才能达成协定。There will be a lot of wheeling and dealing before an agreement can be reached.
272 | 0.5 | 135

2320 可怕 [可怕] /kěpà/ (2) adj frightful, terrible
那是一次可怕的风暴。It was a frightful storm.
181 | 0.74 | 134

2321 接着 [接著] /jiēzhe/ (1) conj then, next
接着,他们七嘴八舌地说起话来。Then they all started talking at once.
180 | 0.75 | 134

2322 食物 [食物] /shíwù/ (2) n food
他把盘子里盛满了食物。He heaped his plate with food.
209 | 0.64 | 134

2323 公 [公] /gōng/ (3) n public; official business; father-in-law
我是因公而来的。I've come here on business.
169 | 0.8 | 134

2324 舆论 [輿論] /yúlùn/ n public opinion
电视能影响舆论。Television moulds public opinion.
193 | 0.7 | 134

2325 今日 [今日] /jīnrì/ (3) time today
今日盘点,明日照常营业。Stock-taking today. Business as usual tomorrow.
191 | 0.71 | 134

2326 锻炼 [鍛煉] /duànliàn/ (1) v exercise; temper
他每天锻炼两次。He exercises twice a day.
167 | 0.8 | 134

2327 付 [付] /fù/ (2) v pay; commit to
我们在哪儿付车费?Where shall we pay the fare?
157 | 0.86 | 134

2328 具备 [具備] /jùbèi/ (2) v have, possess
你具备领导者的才能。You have the necessary equipment for leadership.
191 | 0.71 | 134

2329 等待 [等待] /děngdài/ (2) v wait
他们等待暴风雨过去。They waited for the storm to pass.
182 | 0.74 | 134

2330 前进 [前進] /qiánjìn/ (2) v advance, move forward
我在大雪中努力前进。I pushed on through the snow.
198 | 0.68 | 134

2331 购买 [購買] /gòumǎi/ (3) v buy, purchase
越来越多的家庭和公司购买个人电脑。More and more people are buying PCs for their home and office.
212 | 0.63 | 134

2332 下降 [下降] /xiàjiàng/ (3) v decline, drop
市场价格总水平继续下降。The general level of market prices continued to drop.
287 | 0.47 | 134 | W

2333 持 [持] /chí/ v hold, maintain
他们持相反意见。They hold converse opinions.
177 | 0.76 | 134

2334 认定 [認定] /rèndìng/ v maintain, hold, affirm
我认定这是错的。I maintained that it was wrong.
153 | 0.88 | 134

2335 用于 [用於] /yòngyú/ v use in, use for
1941 年,这种药物被宣布可安全用于人体。In 1941 the drug was declared safe for use on humans.
251 | 0.53 | 134

2336 设立 [設立] /shèlì/ v establish, set up
设立中文学院正是时候。It's time for a School of Chinese Studies.
270 | 0.5 | 134

2337 赴 [赴] /fù/ v leave for, go to
他们还将赴杭州访问。They will also go to Hangzhou for a visit.
218 | 0.62 | 134

2338 恐怖 [恐怖] /kǒngbù/ (3) adj horrible, terrifying
她发出恐怖的叫喊。She let out a scream of terror.
153 | 0.87 | 133

2339 及其 [及其] /jíqí/ conj and (its, their)
警察抓获了小偷及其赃物。The thieves were caught with their loot by the police.
235 | 0.57 | 133

2340 快速 [快速] /kuàisù/ adv fast, at high speed, rapidly
我们加快了脚步,向那条小溪快速走去。We quickened our pace and made our way rapidly towards the stream.
241 | 0.55 | 133

2341 冰 [冰] /bīng/ (2) *n* ice
美国人喜欢在饮料里加冰。Americans like ice in their drinks.
164 | 0.81 | 133

2342 太太 [太太] /tàitai/ (2) *n* Mrs, madam, lady; wife
不要忘记和你太太一起来。Don't forget to bring your wife.
213 | 0.63 | 133

2343 个体 [個體] /gètǐ/ (2) *n* individual; unit
她总是把每个客户视为不同的个体。She always treated her clients as individuals.
181 | 0.74 | 133

2344 沟 [溝] /gōu/ (3) *n* ditch, channel, trench
小河在沙地上冲出了一条沟。The stream had washed out a channel in the sand.
148 | 0.9 | 133

2345 诗人 [詩人] /shīrén/ (3) *n* poet, bard
诗人是天生的，不是造成的。A poet is born, not made.
180 | 0.74 | 133

2346 男性 [男性] /nánxìng/ *n* male
男性的嗓音比女性的低沉。The male voice is deeper than the female.
186 | 0.72 | 133

2347 群体 [群體] /qúntǐ/ *n* group
这两个群体中有 60％的人做义工。Sixty per cent of both groups do volunteer work.
193 | 0.69 | 133

2348 状 [狀] /zhuàng/ *n* condition; form; plaint
有些生物分子呈螺旋状。Some biological molecules have the form of a helix.
180 | 0.74 | 133

2349 精 [精] /jīng/ (3) *adj* clever, shrewd; refined; exquisite; adept, skilled
他特别精于绘画。He's exceptionally skilled in painting.
154 | 0.86 | 132

2350 深 [深] /shēn/ *adv* deeply, profoundly
听众深为感动。The audience was deeply affected.
161 | 0.83 | 132

2351 蛋 [蛋] /dàn/ (2) *n* egg
窝里有个蛋。There is an egg in that nest.
156 | 0.85 | 132

2352 所在 [所在] /suǒzài/ (3) *n* place, locus, whereabouts
那就是我们意见分歧所在。That's where we differ.
157 | 0.85 | 132

2353 少数民族 [少數民族] /shǎoshùmínzú/ *n* ethnic minority
少数民族占人口的6％。The minority nationalities account for 6 per cent of the population.
219 | 0.61 | 132

2354 前提 [前提] /qiántí/ *n* premise
我怀疑整个前提是否正确。I wonder whether the whole premise is right.
184 | 0.72 | 132

2355 夫妇 [夫婦] /fūfù/ *n* a (married) couple
邻居夫妇总吵架。The couple next door are always arguing.
142 | 0.93 | 132

2356 早上 [早上] /zǎoshang/ (1) *time* (early) morning
他早上迟到了。He came late in the morning.
174 | 0.76 | 132

2357 夏天 [夏天] /xiàtiān/ (1) *time* summer
你家乡夏天很热吗？Is it very hot in summer in your hometown?
164 | 0.81 | 132

2358 对不起 [對不起] /duìbuqǐ/ (1) *v* sorry, excuse me; let somebody down
对不起，她不在。Sorry, she's not in.
228 | 0.58 | 132

2359 闭 [閉] /bì/ (2) *v* close
他闭着眼睛安静地坐着。He sat quietly with closed eyes.
228 | 0.58 | 132

2360 转变 [轉變] /zhuǎnbiàn/ (2) *v* transform, change
电能能转变为光能。Electric energy can be changed into light energy.
246 | 0.54 | 132

2361 打破 [打破] /dǎpò/ (3) *v* break
小心别打破杯子。Be careful not to break the cup.
178 | 0.74 | 132

2362 长大 [長大] /zhǎngdà/ *v* grow up
当你长大后，你想要做什么？What do you want to be when you grow up?
171 | 0.78 | 132

2363 极大 [極大] /jídà/ *adv* enormously; greatly
那丑闻极大地损害了他的形象。The scandal took away greatly from his public image.
186 | 0.7 | 131

2364 家乡 [家鄉] /jiāxiāng/ (2) *n* hometown
我家乡春天多风。It's quite windy in spring in my hometown.
143 | 0.92 | 131

2365 空军 [空軍] /kōngjūn/ (3) *n* air force
空军轰炸了两个城镇。The air force bombed two towns.
170 | 0.77 | 131

2366 掌声 [掌聲] /zhǎngshēng/ (3) *n* applause
他们的表演赢得一阵阵掌声。Their performance brought round after round of applause.
227 | 0.58 | 131

2367 上述 [上述] /shàngshù/ (3) *adj* above mentioned
然而这是不可能的，因此上述结论是不正确的。But this is impossible, hence the above conclusions are not correct.
263 | 0.5 | 131 | W

2368 患者 [患者] /huànzhě/ *n* patient
我们必须考虑到患者的年龄。We must take account of the patient's age.
202 | 0.65 | 131

2369 旗 [旗] /qí/ *n* flag, banner
船长命令在船首船尾都挂旗。The captain ordered two flags to be placed fore and aft.
197 | 0.67 | 131

2370 户 [戶] /hù/ *clas* [measure word for households]
他借住在一户人家里。He's staying with a family.
250 | 0.53 | 131

2371 另外 [另外] /lìngwài/ (2) *adj* another, other, extra
这是另外一种误解。Here is another misunderstanding.
192 | 0.68 | 131 | S

2372 以往 [以往] /yǐwǎng/ *time* before, the past
他以往从没迟到过。He was never ever late before.
158 | 0.83 | 131

2373 钻 [鑽] /zuān, zuàn/ (2) *v* get into, get through; dig into; bore or drill (a hole)
老鼠钻进了洞里。The rat got into the hole.
175 | 0.75 | 131

2374 纪念 [紀念] /jìniàn/ (2) *v* honour the memory of, commemorate
他们将建造一座纪念碑来纪念这位民族英雄。They will build a monument in memory of the national hero.
252 | 0.52 | 131

2375 日常 [日常] /rìcháng/ (2) *adj* daily
淡水对于我们日常生活很重要。Fresh water is important to our daily life.
179 | 0.73 | 130

2376 艰难 [艱難] /jiānnán/ (3) *adj* difficult, hard
需要进行艰难的谈判。Some hard bargaining is called for.
147 | 0.89 | 130

2377 神秘 [神秘] /shénmì/ (3) *adj* mysterious
她向我使个神秘的眼色。She gave me a mysterious look.
161 | 0.81 | 130

2378 必然 [必然] /bìrán/ (2) *adv* necessarily, inevitably
做坏事必然会暴露。Wrongdoing inevitably trips itself up.
163 | 0.8 | 130

2379 情景 [情景] /qíngjǐng/ (2) *n* scene, sight, situation
她可以想像出那种情景。She could picture the situation.
147 | 0.89 | 130

2380 规则 [規則] /guīzé/ (3) *n* rule
这些规则并非总能行得通。These rules don't always apply.
175 | 0.75 | 130

2381 公民 [公民] /gōngmín/ (3) *n* citizen
公民在法律和制度面前人人平等。All citizens are equal before the law.
193 | 0.67 | 130

2382 青少年 [青少年] /qīngshàonián/ *n* adolescent, teenager
这种衣服在青少年中间很畅销。This clothing sells well to the teenage market.
246 | 0.53 | 130

2383 姐 [姐] /jiě/ *n* elder sister
但这一双是我姐上个月买的。But my sister bought this pair last month.
239 | 0.55 | 130 | S

2384 棵 [棵] /kē/ (1) *clas* [measure word for plants]
种了多少棵果树？How many fruit trees have been planted?
152 | 0.86 | 130

2385 规定 [規定] /guīdìng/ (2) *v* stipulate, provide
合同规定每年增加费用。The contract provides for an annual increase in charges.
201 | 0.65 | 130

2386 顾 [顧] /gù/ (2) *v* look after, help, attend to; have consideration for
我自顾不暇，又怎么能帮助他们呢？How could I help them, who could so little help myself?
179 | 0.73 | 130

2387 污染 [污染] /wūrǎn/ (2) *v* pollute
工业废物污染了湖泊。The industrial wastes polluted the lake.
249 | 0.52 | 130

2388 降低 [降低] /jiàngdī/ (2) *v* lower, reduce
竞争迫使旅游公司降低了价格。Competition has forced the tour company to lower its price.
218 | 0.6 | 130

2389 毁 [毀] /huǐ/ (3) *v* destroy, ruin
他毁了我的生活。He ruined my life.
135 | 0.96 | 130

2390 占领 [佔領] /zhànlǐng/ (3) *v* occupy
恐怖分子占领了大使馆。The terrorists have occupied the embassy.
194 | 0.67 | 130

2391 陷入 [陷入] /xiànrù/ *v* fall into; be deep in
他陷入了沉思中。He was deep in thought.
160 | 0.81 | 130

2392 出国 [出國] /chūguó/ *v* go abroad
她最近就要出国。She'll be going abroad soon.
147 | 0.89 | 130

2393 便宜 [便宜] /piányi/ (1) *adj* cheap, inexpensive
乘火车旅行要比乘飞机便宜。Rail travel is cheaper than air travel.
173 | 0.75 | 129

2394 阳 [陽] /yáng/ *adj* positive; Yang (positive)
阴阳是自然中两对立的本源：阴为负，阳为正。Yin and Yang are two opposing principles in nature, the former negative, the latter positive.
156 | 0.83 | 129

2395 弟弟 [弟弟] /dìdi/ (1) *n* younger brother
我得在家照顾我的小弟弟。I should take care of my brother at home.
190 | 0.68 | 129

2396 科研 [科研] /kēyán/ (2) *n* (scientific) research
科研工作要有耐心和奉献精神。 Patience and devotion are essential to scientific research work.
303 | 0.43 | 129

2397 森林 [森林] /sēnlín/ (2) *n* forest
这片森林出产各种木材。 There are many kinds of wood growing in this forest.
200 | 0.65 | 129

2398 大街 [大街] /dàjiē/ (2) *n* avenue, street
这幢房子的前门通大街。 The front door of the house opens on the street.
144 | 0.9 | 129

2399 人群 [人群] /rénqún/ (3) *n* crowd (of people)
他从人群中认出了他的朋友。 He spotted his friend in the crowd.
187 | 0.69 | 129

2400 财政 [財政] /cáizhèng/ (3) *n* finance
这不是个简单的财政集中分散的问题。 This is not simply a problem of financial centralisation or decentralisation.
398 | 0.33 | 129 | W

2401 州 [州] /zhōu/ *n* prefecture; state; [often used as part of place names in China]
每个州有自己的办学标准。 Each state sets its own accrediting criteria.
177 | 0.73 | 129

2402 明年 [明年] /míngnián/ (1) *time* next year
你有明年的日历吗？ Do you have next year's calendar?
204 | 0.64 | 129

2403 移 [移] /yí/ (2) *v* move, remove; change
请把这些盒子移到角落。 Move those boxes into the corner, please.
150 | 0.86 | 129

2404 败 [敗] /bài/ (2) *v* be defeated, fail
事情可能就败在他手里。 He may spoil the whole show.
148 | 0.88 | 129

2405 沉重 [沉重] /chénzhòng/ (3) *adj* heavy; serious
我的心情非常沉重。 My heart was very heavy.
159 | 0.81 | 128

2406 神 [神] /shén/ *adj* magic, miraculous; smart; supernatural
这家伙神了！ This fellow is incredible!
145 | 0.88 | 128

2407 众 [眾] /zhòng/ *adj* numerous
众说不一。 There are many different versions of a story.
150 | 0.85 | 128

2408 商店 [商店] /shāngdiàn/ (1) *n* shop, store
这旅馆里有商店吗？ Is there a shop in the hotel?
142 | 0.91 | 128

2409 爷爷 [爺爺] /yéye/ (2) *n* (paternal) grandpa
我爷爷擅长京剧。 My grandpa is good at Beijing Opera.
174 | 0.74 | 128

2410 脑子 [腦子] /nǎozi/ (2) *n* brain, mind
这事我已记在脑子里了。 I have got it right in my mind.
203 | 0.63 | 128

2411 脑袋 [腦袋] /nǎodài/ (2) *n* head
那男孩儿有一个大脑袋。 The boy has a big head.
238 | 0.54 | 128

2412 生物 [生物] /shēngwù/ (2) *n* living thing; biology
太阳给地球热量，这对地球上的生物很重要。 The sun heats the earth, which is very important to living things.
193 | 0.67 | 128

2413 色彩 [色彩] /sècǎi/ (3) *n* colour
这房间的色彩很调和。 The colours in the room harmonised.
170 | 0.76 | 128

2414 娘 [娘] /niáng/ (3) *n* mother, mum
娘，你气它干么？ Mother, what's the use of getting upset about it?
247 | 0.52 | 128

2415 自治区 [自治區] /zìzhìqū/ (3) *n* autonomous region
西藏自治区成立于 1965 年 9 月。 The Tibet Autonomous Region was founded in September 1965.
363 | 0.35 | 128

2416 场面 [場面] /chǎngmiàn/ (3) *n* scene, spectacle
这是个动人的场面。 This is a moving spectacle.
140 | 0.92 | 128

2417 剑 [劍] /jiàn/ *n* sword
这把剑是他曾祖父传下来的。 The sword has descended from his great-grandfather.
229 | 0.56 | 128

2418 大师 [大師] /dàshī/ *n* great master
她师从这位著名的大师当学徒。 She apprenticed with the great master.
171 | 0.75 | 128

2419 扎 [紮] /zā, zhā/ (2) *v* tie or bind (with a string or ribbon); prick; plunge into
她的头发用一条丝带扎着。 Her hair was tied up with a ribbon.
157 | 0.82 | 128

2420 有力 [有力] /yǒulì/ (2) *adj* powerful
事实是对造谣者最有力的回答。 Facts are the most powerful rebuff to rumour mongers.
208 | 0.61 | 127

2421 偏 [偏] /piān/ (2) *adv* simply, wilfully, deliberately
他偏不听。 He simply wouldn't listen.
141 | 0.9 | 127

2422 即将 [即將] /jíjiāng/ (3) *adv* (be) about to, soon
我们即将动身。 We're about to start.
200 | 0.64 | 127

2423 无数 [無數] /wúshù/ (2) *num* countless, innumerable
无数的星星点缀着夜空。 The night sky was set with countless stars.
160 | 0.8 | 127

16. Sports

足球	足球	zúqiú	football	1737
游泳	游泳	yóuyǒng	swimming	2908
篮球	籃球	lánqiú	basketball	3359
乒乓球	乒乓球	pīngpāngqiú	table tennis	4286
散步	散步	sànbù	taking a walk	6533
体操	體操	tǐcāo	gymnastics	8154
网球	網球	wǎngqiú	tennis	9336
羽毛球	羽毛球	yǔmáoqiú	badminton	9397
跑步	跑步	pǎobù	running, jogging	10283
排球	排球	páiqiú	volleyball	10455
太极拳	太極拳	tàijíquán	tai chi chuan	13273
滑冰	滑冰	huábīng	skating	14158
滑雪	滑雪	huáxuě	skiing	15492
高尔夫球	高爾夫球	gāo'ěrfū qiú	golf	17172
举重	舉重	jǔzhòng	weightlifting	18559
冰球	冰球	bīngqiú	ice hockey	20367
橄榄球	橄欖球	gǎnlǎnqiú	soccer	22451

2424 例子 [例子] /lìzi/ (2) n example, case
我给你举个例子。 I'll give you an example.
242 | 0.52 | 127

2425 规划 [規劃] /guīhuá/ (3) n scheme, plan
反对该规划的意见不太多。 There's not much opposition to the scheme.
261 | 0.49 | 127

2426 律师 [律師] /lǜshī/ n lawyer
我父亲原本希望我当一名律师。 My father had hoped that I would be a lawyer.
171 | 0.75 | 127

2427 恋爱 [戀愛] /liàn'ài/ (2) v love, be in love
他们在恋爱。 They are in love.
182 | 0.7 | 127

2428 铺 [鋪] /pū/ (2) v spread; pave; make (bed)
她将地板铺上地毯。 She spread the floor with rugs.
143 | 0.89 | 127

2429 流行 [流行] /liúxíng/ (3) v be in fashion, prevail; spread
今年流行粉红色。 Pink is quite in fashion this year.
164 | 0.78 | 127

2430 退休 [退休] /tuìxiū/ (3) v retire
他最好还是立刻退休。 It is expedient that he should retire at once.
172 | 0.74 | 127

2431 清醒 [清醒] /qīngxǐng/ (3) adj sober, clear-headed
你应该清醒冷静。 You should be clear-headed and calm.
151 | 0.84 | 126

2432 大大 [大大] /dàdà/ (3) adv greatly
人民的健康水平大大提高。 The people's health has greatly improved.
203 | 0.62 | 126

2433 相对 [相對] /xiāngduì/ adv relatively
但这一类极端的情况相对罕见。 But such extremes are relatively rare.
170 | 0.74 | 126

2434 少数 [少數] /shǎoshù/ (2) num a small number of; minority
这里只有少数人知道他的名字。 Only a few people here know his name.
189 | 0.67 | 126

2435 眼泪 [眼淚] /yǎnlèi/ (2) n tear
眼泪顺着她的脸流下。 Tears ran down her face.
233 | 0.54 | 126

2436 团长 [團長] /tuánzhǎng/ (3) n head of a delegation or troupe; regimental commander
政府贸易代表团团长由贸易部部长担任。 The government trade delegation was headed by the Minister of Trade.
171 | 0.74 | 126

2437 园 [園] /yuán/ n garden
鲜花满园。 The garden is bright with flowers.
157 | 0.8 | 126

2438 男孩 [男孩] /nánhái/ n boy
两个男孩打了一架。 The two boys had a fight.
198 | 0.64 | 126

2439 擦 [擦] /cā/ (1) v wipe, clean; rub; spread
你每月都叫人擦窗户吗？ Do you have your windows cleaned every month?
215 | 0.59 | 126

2440 沟通 [溝通] /gōutōng/ v communicate
我能轻松地和外国人沟通。 I can communicate with foreigners easily.
211 | 0.6 | 126

2441 温暖 [溫暖] /wēnnuǎn/ (2) adj warm
此地景色宜人而温暖。 This place is nice and warm.
151 | 0.83 | 125

2442 齐 [齊] /qí/ (2) adj neat, even; all ready
我想是否东西全带齐了？ I wonder if I have got everything in order?
169 | 0.74 | 125

2443 出色 [出色] /chūsè/ adj remarkable, brilliant
他们取得了出色的成绩。 They have had a brilliant success.
141 | 0.89 | 125

2444 生日 [生日] /shēngrì/ (1) n birthday
我打算去买生日礼物。 I am going to buy a birthday present.
151 | 0.83 | 125

2445 主意 [主意] /zhǔyì/ (1) n idea
这是谁的主意？ Whose idea is it?
193 | 0.65 | 125

2446 商场 [商場] /shāngchǎng/ (2) n shopping mall
附近有商场吗？ Are there any shopping malls nearby?
153 | 0.82 | 125

2447 愿望 [願望] /yuànwàng/ (2) n wish
她的愿望实现了。 Her wish came true.
184 | 0.68 | 125

2448 毒品 [毒品] /dúpǐn/ n drug
两国达成协议控制毒品走私。 The two nations made a compact to control drug traffic.
170 | 0.74 | 125

2449 招 [招] /zhāo/ n move, trick
你这一招可真高。 That was really a brilliant stroke of yours.
151 | 0.83 | 125

2450 出版社 [出版社] /chūbǎnshè/ n press, publisher, publishing company
我在一家出版社工作。 I'm working for a publishing company.
181 | 0.69 | 125

2451 人格 [人格] /réngé/ n personality, character; integrity
伟人能以人格的力量支配他人。 A great man can dominate others by force of character.
188 | 0.67 | 125

2452 品牌 [品牌] /pǐnpái/ n brand
我们这里有许多品牌。 We have lots of brands here.
184 | 0.68 | 125

2453 心态 [心態] /xīntài/ n state of mind, mindset
我再也不能忍受他们自私自利的心态了。 I can't take their selfish mindset any more.
176 | 0.71 | 125

2454 毛 [毛] /máo/ (1) clas [measure term for the Chinese currency, less formal than 角] mao (one-tenth of yuan), ten cents
她到这时候，才摸出来一毛钱。 It was only at this point that she managed to find ten cents.
205 | 0.61 | 125

2455 周年 [周年] /zhōunián/ (3) clas full year, anniversary
再过五天，就是一周年了。 In five more days it'll be the anniversary.
310 | 0.41 | 125

2456 自 [自] /zì/ pron self
他自认为很走运。 He counted himself lucky.
161 | 0.78 | 125

2457 冬天 [冬天] /dōngtiān/ (1) time winter
在冬天许多动物进入冬眠状态。 Many animals are in a dormant state during winter.
151 | 0.83 | 125

2458 春节 [春節] /chūnjié/ (2) time Spring Festival (Chinese New Year)
你到哪里去过春节？ Where are you going to celebrate your Spring Festival?
248 | 0.5 | 125

2459 白天 [白天] /báitiān/ (2) time day, daytime
白天变得越来越短。 The days are getting shorter and shorter.
157 | 0.8 | 125

2460 醉 [醉] /zuì/ (2) v be drunk
他显然是醉了。 He was obviously drunk.
179 | 0.7 | 125

2461 传播 [傳播] /chuánbō/ (2) v disseminate, spread
传染病可以通过不同途径传播。 Infections may be spread in a variety of ways.
172 | 0.73 | 125

2462 理 [理] /lǐ/ (3) v pay attention to; put in order
别理他，他很奇怪。 Pay no attention to him. He is strange.
177 | 0.71 | 125

2463 说道 [說道] /shuōdào/ v say
"我累了。" 他说道。"I'm tired," he said.
293 | 0.43 | 125 | W

2464 赶到 [趕到] /gǎndào/ v rush to, arrive (in a hurry)
你能设法在六点钟赶到那儿吗？ Can you contrive to be there by six?
146 | 0.86 | 125

2465 愉快 [愉快] /yúkuài/ (1) adj cheerful, joyful, happy
你在这里过得愉快，我们很高兴。 We are glad you have been happy here.
145 | 0.86 | 124

2466 详细 [詳細] /xiángxì/ (2) adj detailed
她把事件向警方作了详细叙述。 She gave the police a detailed account of the incident.
139 | 0.89 | 124

2467 尽快 [儘快] /jìnkuài/ adv as soon as possible
你要尽快来。Come as soon as you can.
220 | 0.57 | 124

2468 微 [微] /wēi/ adv slightly
灯光里她睫毛微动。Her eyelashes seemed to flutter slightly in the lamplight.
157 | 0.79 | 124

2469 馆 [館] /guǎn/ (1) n [house for business or public service such as tea house, hotel, library, museum or embassy] hall, house
这个馆陈列的是玉器和陶器。This hall exhibits jadeware and ceramics.
160 | 0.78 | 124

2470 木 [木] /mù/ (2) n wood
桌子多为木制的。Tables are usually made of wood.
139 | 0.9 | 124

2471 前途 [前途] /qiántú/ (2) n future, prospect
作为一个剧作家，他前途光明。He has a bright future as a dramatist.
140 | 0.89 | 124

2472 寺 [寺] /sì/ n temple
该寺在战争期间未受到损害。The temple remained untouched in the war.
141 | 0.88 | 124

2473 贷款 [貸款] /dàikuǎn/ n loan
我们提前三年还清了贷款。We paid back the loans three years earlier.
340 | 0.37 | 124 | W

2474 海外 [海外] /hǎiwài/ place overseas
他在海外生活了多年。He lived overseas for many years.
272 | 0.46 | 124

2475 饿 [餓] /è/ (1) v be hungry
我快饿死了。I am starving.
192 | 0.65 | 124

2476 娶 [娶] /qǔ/ (3) v take a wife, marry
你打算娶她吗？Do you plan to marry her?
225 | 0.56 | 124

2477 继承 [繼承] /jìchéng/ (3) v inherit
她从父亲那儿继承了一所房子。She inherited a house from her father.
182 | 0.68 | 124

2478 操作 [操作] /cāozuò/ v operate
他似乎不能操作计算机。He seemed unable to operate a computer.
166 | 0.75 | 124

2479 落实 [落實] /luòshí/ v implement, fulfil
目前，这两点意见已基本得到落实。At present, the two recommendations have basically been implemented.
377 | 0.33 | 124 | W

2480 也好 [也好] /yěhǎo/ part may as well
我们明天再来也好。We may as well come back tomorrow.
211 | 0.59 | 124 | S

2481 洋 [洋] /yáng/ (3) adj foreign
古为今用，洋为中用。Make the past serve the present and foreign things serve China.
140 | 0.88 | 123

2482 合法 [合法] /héfǎ/ (3) adj lawful, legal
他是那份遗产的合法继承人。He is the lawful heir to that property.
199 | 0.62 | 123

2483 有时候 [有時候] /yǒushíhou/ (1) adv sometimes
冬天有时候下很大的雪。Sometimes it snows a lot in winter.
188 | 0.66 | 123 | S

2484 稍 [稍] /shāo/ (2) adv slightly, a little
请稍等。Just a moment, please.
165 | 0.75 | 123

2485 作业 [作業] /zuòyè/ (1) n assignment, homework
你做完作业了吗？Have you done your homework?
136 | 0.91 | 123

2486 年级 [年級] /niánjí/ (1) n grade, year
三个年级有十八个班。There are 18 classes in three grades.
152 | 0.81 | 123

2487 特征 [特徵] /tèzhēng/ (3) n characteristic
这是他的特征。It's characteristic of him.
196 | 0.63 | 123

2488 青春 [青春] /qīngchūn/ (3) n youth, youthfulness
健康使人焕发青春。He who has good health is young.
135 | 0.91 | 123

2489 大哥 [大哥] /dàgē/ (3) n eldest brother; [also used as a polite address for a man of about one's own age]
我的大哥在印度。My eldest brother is in India.
222 | 0.55 | 123

2490 职务 [職務] /zhíwù/ n post, position
他适合担任此职务。He is fitted for the post.
185 | 0.67 | 123

2491 趟 [趟] /tàng/ (2) clas [measure word for a return trip]; [measure word for a single trip of train]
你最好亲自去跑一趟。You had better go by yourself.
178 | 0.69 | 123

2492 聊 [聊] /liáo/ (2) v chat
我和她聊了很久。I had a long chat with her.
185 | 0.67 | 123

2493 计算 [計算] /jìsuàn/ (2) v calculate, compute
我在计算时，别跟我说话。Do not talk to me while I am in the middle of calculating.
174 | 0.71 | 123

2494 吸收 [吸收] /xīshōu/ (2) v absorb, draw; enroll, recruit
吸墨纸吸收墨水。A blotter absorbs ink.
168 | 0.73 | 123

2495 防止 [防止] /fángzhǐ/ (2) v prevent
这对防止事故有帮助。This will help to prevent accidents.
202 | 0.61 | 123

2496 会见 [會見] /huìjiàn/ (2) v meet with (somebody who is paying a visit for official business)
他避免会见那些人。He avoided meeting those people.
549 | 0.23 | 123 | W

2497 汇报 [彙報] /huìbào/ (3) v report
这个小组汇报了他们在调查中取得的重大进展。The team reported significant advances in their investigation.
154 | 0.8 | 123

2498 加快 [加快] /jiākuài/ v quicken, expedite, speed up
我们加快了脚步。We quickened our steps.
439 | 0.28 | 123 | W

2499 意外 [意外] /yìwài/ (2) adj unexpected
这意外的消息他相当吃惊。The unexpected news fairly knocked him down.
172 | 0.71 | 122

2500 可惜 [可惜] /kěxī/ (3) adj pitiful
多可惜呀！What a pity it is!
174 | 0.7 | 122

2501 雅 [雅] /yǎ/ adj elegant, refined
样式不雅。The model is not elegant.
198 | 0.62 | 122

2502 只不过 [只不過] /zhǐbúguò/ adv merely
她只不过是个孩子。She's a mere child.
167 | 0.73 | 122

2503 无疑 [無疑] /wúyí/ (3) adv undoubtedly
这部电影无疑是今年最好的一部。It is undoubtedly the best film of the year.
164 | 0.75 | 122

2504 专 [專] /zhuān/ adv specially, specifically
这些牛仔裤是专为妇女设计的。These jeans are designed specifically for women.
145 | 0.84 | 122

2505 皆 [皆] /jiē/ adv all
所有会议皆不得缺席。Attendance is mandatory at all meetings.
174 | 0.71 | 122

2506 勇气 [勇氣] /yǒngqì/ (2) n courage
他缺乏说实话的勇气。He wants the courage to speak the truth.
155 | 0.79 | 122

2507 地面 [地面] /dìmiàn/ (2) n ground
下雨时，地面变得很泥泞。When it rains the ground becomes very muddy.
135 | 0.91 | 122

2508 街道 [街道] /jiēdào/ (2) n street
横过街道时你得左右看看。You have to look around when you cross the street.
159 | 0.77 | 122

2509 证 [證] /zhèng/ n certificate, papers; proof, evidence
有何为证？Can you prove it?
142 | 0.86 | 122

2510 魅力 [魅力] /mèilì/ n charm
她有不可抗拒的魅力。She has an irresistible charm.
143 | 0.85 | 122

2511 股票 [股票] /gǔpiào/ n share, stock
我不敢买股票，怕赔钱。I'm wary of buying shares, in case I lose money.
163 | 0.75 | 122

2512 消费者 [消費者] /xiāofèizhě/ n consumer
消费者究竟需要什么？What do consumers really want?
224 | 0.55 | 122

2513 身 [身] /shēn/ clas [measure word for clothes] suit; [preceded by the numeral 一 as a temporary measure for things covering somebody, like water, mud, sweat, etc.]
她突然冒一身冷汗。She broke into a cold sweat.
196 | 0.62 | 122

2514 打算 [打算] /dǎsuàn/ (1) v plan, intend
您打算住多久？How long will you be staying?
219 | 0.56 | 122

2515 绕 [繞] /rào/ (2) v move around, make a detour; wind, make (wire, cable, etc.) into a coil or ball
线已经绕成球了。The threads are wound into a ball.
158 | 0.78 | 122

2516 批判 [批判] /pīpàn/ (2) v criticise
这种观点应当批判。Such views are to be criticised.
181 | 0.67 | 122

2517 害 [害] /hài/ (2) v do harm to; suffer from (illness); cause trouble to
我们没想到他会害我们。We little believed that he would harm us.
170 | 0.72 | 122

2518 减 [減] /jiǎn/ (2) v subtract, minus; reduce, cut
到 1999 年，这一数字已减至 35 类。By 1999, the number had been reduced to 35.
165 | 0.74 | 122

2519 摆脱 [擺脱] /bǎituō/ (3) v get rid of, break away from
请告诉我如何摆脱它。Please tell me how to get rid of it.
149 | 0.82 | 122

2520 恋 [戀] /liàn/ v love, feel attached to
他深深爱恋着他的女朋友。He is deeply in love with his girlfriend.
206 | 0.59 | 122

2521 足够 [足夠] /zúgòu/ adj enough, sufficient
我有足够的钱买这些书。I have enough money to buy these books.
149 | 0.82 | 122

2522 列 [列] /liè/ v list, itemise
这儿所列的物品都要缴税。All the articles listed here incur duty.
162 | 0.76 | 122

2523 干净 [乾淨] /gānjìng/ (1) adj clean
杯子是干净的。The cup is clean.
164 | 0.74 | 121

2524 集中 [集中] /jízhōng/ (2) *adj* concentrated, focused; centralised
紧张和疲劳常使人精神不集中。Stress and tiredness often result in a lack of concentration.
206 | 0.59 | 121

2525 可见 [可見] /kějiàn/ (3) *conj* it can be seen
可见经济利益对学习语文的影响有多大！What a great influence money has on language learning!
154 | 0.79 | 121

2526 节 [節] /jié, jiē/ (1) *n* festival, holiday; section, division; node, joint; critical juncture
学完本节后，你应能够：... When you have completed this unit, you will be able to: ...
173 | 0.7 | 121

2527 高中 [高中] /gāozhōng/ (3) *n* high school
她离婚之后又和高中时的恋人再婚了。After her divorce, she got remarried, to her high school sweetheart.
139 | 0.88 | 121

2528 来源 [來源] /láiyuán/ (3) *n* source
这消息来源可靠。The news comes from a reliable source.
177 | 0.69 | 121

2529 头脑 [頭腦] /tóunǎo/ (3) *n* brain, head
这种场合需要冷静的头脑。The occasion calls for a cool head.
144 | 0.85 | 121

2530 软件 [軟件] /ruǎnjiàn/ *n* software
一个办法是用硬件而不是软件，来消除这个瓶颈。One solution is to use hardware, rather than software, to eliminate this bottleneck.
216 | 0.56 | 121

2531 跨 [跨] /kuà/ (2) *v* step across, stride, step forward; overarch
小溪很窄，我们能很容易跨过去。The stream was so narrow that we could easily stride over it.
203 | 0.6 | 121

2532 修改 [修改] /xiūgǎi/ (2) *v* revise, amend
这条裙子要修改一下了。This dress needs to be altered.
192 | 0.63 | 121

2533 砸 [砸] /zá/ (3) *v* smash
瓶子被砸碎了。The bottle was shattered into pieces.
172 | 0.71 | 121

2534 甚至 [甚至] /shènzhì/ (3) *conj* so much so that, so far as to
他们对自己的产品十分有信心，甚至没有做广告。They had so much faith in their product that they did not even advertise.
163 | 0.74 | 120

2535 也就是说 [也就是說] /yějiùshìshuō/ *idiom* that is to say, namely
三天之后，也就是说星期五。Three days from now, that is to say Friday.
208 | 0.58 | 120 | S

2536 疾病 [疾病] /jíbìng/ (3) *n* disease, illness
很多疾病是由于不清洁而引起的。Many diseases are attributable to lack of cleanliness.
180 | 0.67 | 120

2537 华人 [華人] /huárén/ (3) *n* Chinese
华人占新加坡人口的大多数。Chinese make up the overwhelming majority of the population in Singapore.
200 | 0.6 | 120

2538 事务 [事務] /shìwù/ (3) *n* affairs
我度假时我的代理人将负责我的事务。My deputy will attend to my affairs while I am on vacation.
246 | 0.49 | 120

2539 障碍 [障礙] /zhàng'ài/ (3) *n* barrier, obstacle
她有决心克服通往成功路上的一切障碍。She has the determination to overcome all the obstacles to success.
163 | 0.74 | 120

2540 近年来 [近年來] /jìnniánlái/ *time* in recent years
我国的对外贸易近年来已有极大发展。Our foreign trade has expanded greatly in recent years.
359 | 0.34 | 120 | W

2541 到达 [到達] /dàodá/ (2) *v* arrive, reach
若无交通阻塞，我们半小时后可到达。We should arrive in half an hour, barring hold-ups.
163 | 0.74 | 120

2542 提前 [提前] /tíqián/ (2) *v* advance (to an earlier date or time); do something in advance or ahead of time
会议时间提前了一个钟头。The time of the meeting was brought forward an hour.
159 | 0.76 | 120

2543 为止 [為止] /wéizhǐ/ (3) *v* until, up to; that's all for ...
顺这条路一直走到一家旅馆为止。Continue on down this road until you come to a hotel.
140 | 0.86 | 120

2544 似 [似] /sì/ *v* seem, appear
这样看似聪明而实则不然。It appears to be wisdom and yet it is not.
164 | 0.74 | 120

2545 弱 [弱] /ruò/ (2) *adj* weak
那段日子里，我感到很弱，也很内疚。I felt weak in those days. And guilty.
134 | 0.89 | 119

2546 怪 [怪] /guài/ (2) *adj* strange
谁弄出的那种怪声？Who's making those strange noises?
166 | 0.72 | 119

2547 自觉 [自覺] /zìjué/ (2) *adj* conscious, conscientious; on one's own initiative
他学习很自觉。He studies on his own initiative.
168 | 0.71 | 119

2548 高度 [高度] /gāodù/ (2) adv highly
在那个国家，医生受到高度重视。Doctors are highly appreciated in that country.
265 | 0.45 | 119

2549 无 [無] /wú/ (2) adv not
没有订购的货物就无须付款。You're under no obligation to pay for goods which you did not order.
154 | 0.78 | 119

2550 内外 [內外] /nèiwài/ loc inside and outside; home and abroad
房子内外都油漆过了。The house has been painted inside and out.
231 | 0.52 | 119

2551 首都 [首都] /shǒudū/ (1) n capital
北京是中国的首都。Beijing is the capital of China.
269 | 0.45 | 119

2552 利润 [利潤] /lìrùn/ (3) n profit
我们的一半利润来自国外的销售额。
Half of our profit comes from sales abroad.
175 | 0.68 | 119

2553 天地 [天地] /tiāndì/ n heaven and earth; world
别有一番天地。There seems to be a different world.
131 | 0.92 | 119

2554 小子 [小子] /xiǎozi/ n boy, young fellow; [derogatory] bloke; chap
你这小子不懂好歹！You don't know when you're well off, young fellow!
230 | 0.52 | 119

2555 踢 [踢] /tī/ (1) v kick
我被他踢了一脚。I was kicked by him.
175 | 0.68 | 119

2556 少 [少] /shǎo/ (1) v be short, lack; [usually in imperatives] stop, quit
这批货少了3件。The shipment is three items short.
144 | 0.83 | 119

2557 保留 [保留] /bǎoliú/ (2) v keep, retain
两张表格保留哪张都行。Keep either one of the forms.
139 | 0.86 | 119

2558 超 [超] /chāo/ (2) v exceed, surpass, go beyond; overtake
她加把劲儿，一下子又超了过去。
She redoubled her efforts again and soon overtook him.
162 | 0.74 | 119

2559 插 [插] /chā/ (2) v insert, plug
洗衣机只有插上电源才能运行。
The washing machine won't go unless it's plugged in.
165 | 0.72 | 119

2560 假如 [假如] /jiǎrú/ (3) conj if, in the event of
假如你愿意的话，你就来。You may come if you wish.
157 | 0.75 | 118

17. Human body

Physical appearance:

高	高	gāo	tall	106
美丽	美麗	měilì	pretty, beautiful	1220
漂亮	漂亮	piàoliang	pretty, beautiful	1227
美	美	měi	beautiful	1461
可爱	可愛	kě'ài	lovely	2808
好看	好看	hǎokàn	good-looking	3410
瘦	瘦	shòu	thin, skinny	3433
胖	胖	pàng	fat, plump	3771
矮	矮	ǎi	short	6213
丑	醜	chǒu	ugly	7796
难看	難看	nánkàn	ugly	8082
酷	酷	kù	cool	8301
帅	帥	shuài	handsome	17130
苗条	苗條	miáotiáo	slender, slim	17983

Body parts:

手	手	shǒu	hand	229
头	頭	tóu	head	246
脸	臉	liǎn	face, cheek	545

脚	腳	jiǎo	foot	790
腿	腿	tuǐ	leg	1237
头发	頭髮	tóufa	hair	1947
腰	腰	yāo	waist	2085
肚子	肚子	dùzi	stomach, belly	2754
脖子	脖子	bózi	neck	3228
皮肤	皮膚	pífū	skin	3440
屁股	屁股	pìgu	buttock, bottom	3670
手指	手指	shǒuzhǐ	finger	4082
肩膀	肩膀	jiānbǎng	shoulder	4701
胳膊	胳膊	gēbo	arm	4746
手腕	手腕	shǒuwàn	wrist	8833
指甲	指甲	zhǐjia	fingernail	9326
膝盖	膝蓋	xīgài	knee	9548
腕	腕	wàn	wrist	9750
喉咙	喉嚨	hóulóng	throat	10112
手掌	手掌	shǒuzhǎng	palm	10331
大腿	大腿	dàtuǐ	thigh	12333
肘	肘	zhǒu	elbow	15345
肩头	肩頭	jiāntóu	shoulder	16937
胸部	胸部	xiōngbù	chest	17422
脚趾	腳趾	jiǎozhǐ	toe	24470
颈项	頸項	jǐngxiàng	neck	26483

Parts of the head:

眼睛	眼睛	yǎnjing	eye	736
声音	聲音	shēngyīn	voice, sound	814
嘴	嘴	zuǐ	mouth	1015
鼻子	鼻子	bízi	nose	2679
耳朵	耳朵	ěrduo	ear	2698
胡子	鬍子	húzi	beard, moustache	4329
牙齿	牙齒	yáchǐ	tooth	4477
嘴唇	嘴唇	zuǐchún	lip	6025
舌头	舌頭	shétou	tongue	6610
舌	舌	shé	tongue	9202
眉毛	眉毛	méimao	eyebrow	9418
脸颊	臉頰	liǎnjiá	cheek	13011
眼皮	眼皮	yǎnpí	eyelid	13508
鼻孔	鼻孔	bíkǒng	nostril	14320
下巴	下巴	xiàba	chin	14522
睫毛	睫毛	jiémao	eyelash	17316
前额	前額	qián'è	forehead	21812

Senses:

视觉	視覺	shìjué	sense of vision, sight	6128
嗅觉	嗅覺	xiùjué	sense of smell	14096
听觉	聽覺	tīngjué	sense of hearing	14902
触觉	觸覺	chùjué	sense of touch, feel	20870
味觉	味覺	wèijué	sense of taste	28336

2561 文物 [文物] /wénwù/ (2) *n* cultural relic
大批珍贵文物得到全面保护。 Large numbers of rare cultural relics have been put under full protection.
233 | 0.51 | 118

2562 论文 [論文] /lùnwén/ (2) *n* paper, dissertation, thesis
他正在写博士论文。 He is writing his doctoral thesis.
152 | 0.78 | 118

2563 灵魂 [靈魂] /línghún/ (3) *n* soul
忏悔可能对灵魂有好处，但对声誉则有损无益。 Confessions may be good for the soul but they are bad for the reputation.
154 | 0.77 | 118

2564 个性 [個性] /gèxìng/ (3) *n* individuality, (individual) character
她个性很强。 She is a woman of strong character.
160 | 0.74 | 118

2565 针对 [針對] /zhēnduì/ (2) *prep* at, against, for
批评不是针对你的。 The criticism was not aimed at you.
205 | 0.58 | 118

2566 空中 [空中] /kōngzhōng/ (2) *place* in the air
一个测风气球被放入空中。 A pilot balloon was sent into the air.
139 | 0.86 | 118

2567 补充 [補充] /bǔchōng/ (2) *v* add; complement; replenish
我对我先前说的话，没有什么补充的。 I have nothing to add to my earlier statement.
151 | 0.79 | 118

2568 伸 [伸] /shēn/ (2) *v* stretch, extend
小孩伸手拿点心。 The child stretched out for the cookie.
182 | 0.65 | 118

2569 企图 [企圖] /qǐtú/ (2) *v* attempt
囚犯企图逃跑，但是失败了。 The prisoners attempted to escape but failed.
155 | 0.77 | 118

2570 炒 [炒] /chǎo/ (3) *v* stir fry; speculate, drive up (value or price through manipulation)
这是青椒洋葱炒牛肉。 Here is the fried beef with green pepper and onion.
217 | 0.55 | 118

2571 居住 [居住] /jūzhù/ (3) *v* live, reside, inhabit
这个镇上居住的是渔民。 The town is inhabited by fishermen.
154 | 0.77 | 118

2572 思 [思] /sī/ *v* think
寡言多思。 Say nothing but think the more.
145 | 0.81 | 118

2573 碰到 [碰到] /pèngdào/ *v* come across, meet with
我在十字路口碰到了他。 I met him at the junction of the street.
157 | 0.75 | 118

2574 主管 [主管] /zhǔguǎn/ *v* take charge of, head
谁主管这个部门？ Who headed the department?
190 | 0.63 | 118

2575 幽默 [幽默] /yōumò/ *adj* humorous
这部电影既幽默又动人。 The film is both humorous and moving.
231 | 0.51 | 117

2576 奇 [奇] /qí, jī/ *adj* strange; odd (number)
这真奇了，自己的，究竟是谁的呢？ This is truly a strange question. "Our own?" But whose dialect is it really?
158 | 0.75 | 117

2577 向前 [向前] /xiàngqián/ *adv* forward
这是向前迈出的很大的一步。 This has been a great step forward.
141 | 0.83 | 117

2578 之内 [之內] /zhīnèi/ (3) *loc* within
这在两个月之内有效。 It is valid within two months.
130 | 0.9 | 117

2579 品种 [品種] /pǐnzhǒng/ (2) *n* variety, assortment
很难将不同品种区分开来。 It's hard to differentiate one variety from another.
204 | 0.58 | 117

2580 广场 [廣場] /guǎngchǎng/ (2) *n* square
广场上人山人海。 The square was a sea of people.
182 | 0.64 | 117

2581 指示 [指示] /zhǐshì/ (2) *n* directive, instruction
这是上面的指示。 These are the instructions from above.
146 | 0.8 | 117

2582 这边 [這邊] /zhèbian/ (2) *pron* this side, this way, over here
你们坐到这边来好吗？ Do you mind sitting over here?
271 | 0.43 | 117 | S

2583 奋斗 [奮鬥] /fèndòu/ (2) *v* strive, struggle
他们为谋求和平而奋斗。 They have striven for peace.
194 | 0.61 | 117

2584 对话 [對話] /duìhuà/ (2) *n* dialogue
大多数戏剧都是用对话体写的。 Most plays are written in dialogue.
170 | 0.69 | 117

2585 连 [連] /lián/ (2) *v* join, link, connect
打个结，把这两根绳子连上。 Tie a knot to join those two pieces of rope.
146 | 0.8 | 117

2586 试验 [試驗] /shìyàn/ (2) *n* test, experiment
直到做完试验你才能离开房间。 Don't leave the room until you have finished the test.
165 | 0.71 | 117

2587 创 [創] /chuàng/ (2) *v* achieve, set (a record)
在这次锦标赛上创了许多新的世界纪录。 Many new world records were set at this championship.
200 | 0.59 | 117

2588 砍 [砍] /kǎn/ (2) v chop, cut
他从树上砍下一根树枝。He chopped a branch off the tree.
148 | 0.79 | 117

2589 公布 [公佈] /gōngbù/ (3) v announce, publicise
他公布了开会日期。He announced the date of the meeting.
234 | 0.5 | 117

2590 进展 [進展] /jìnzhǎn/ v make progress
工作进展得十分顺利。The work progressed very successfully.
288 | 0.41 | 117

2591 着急 [着急] /zháojí/ (1) adj anxious, worried
飞机上的人都很着急。Everybody on board was worried.
177 | 0.66 | 116

2592 通 [通] /tōng/ (1) adj unblocked, open, through; (of writing) smooth
水管不通了。The waterpipe is blocked.
136 | 0.86 | 116

2593 另一方面 [另一方面] /lìng yìfāngmiàn/ conj on the other hand
的确，不过从另一方面说这很花时间。True enough, but on the other hand, it's time-consuming.
159 | 0.73 | 116

2594 从小 [從小] /cóngxiǎo/ adv since childhood, from an early age
她从小就想当演员。She has wanted to go on the stage from an early age.
142 | 0.82 | 116

2595 极为 [極為] /jíwèi/ adv extremely
颜色和式样极为适合您。Both the colour and shape fit you admirably.
149 | 0.78 | 116

2596 研究 [研究] /yánjiù/ (1) n research
这本书对你的研究工作很有价值。This book will be of great value to you in your research.
163 | 0.72 | 116

2597 机器 [機器] /jīqì/ (1) n machine
工厂里有很多机器。There are many machines in the factory.
149 | 0.78 | 116

2598 泥 [泥] /ní/ (2) n mud
整日下雨，我们的鞋上粘满了泥。It had rained all day and the mud stuck to our shoes.
145 | 0.8 | 116

2599 小伙子 [小伙子] /xiǎohuǒzi/ (2) n young man
你的眼力好吗，小伙子？Do you have good eyesight, young man?
156 | 0.75 | 116

2600 数据 [數據] /shùjù/ (3) n data
如何保护数据？How to protect your data?
191 | 0.61 | 116

2601 司令 [司令] /sīlìng/ (3) n commander
总统的职责包括担任总司令。The President's official duties include being Commander in Chief.
152 | 0.77 | 116

2602 战场 [戰場] /zhànchǎng/ (3) n battlefield
他在战场上表现很勇敢。He acquitted himself bravely on the battlefield.
143 | 0.81 | 116

2603 表情 [表情] /biǎoqíng/ (3) n (facial) expression
他脸上有种紧张的表情。He had a tense expression on his face.
274 | 0.43 | 116

2604 团体 [團體] /tuántǐ/ (3) n group, organisation, society
该团体的成员之间有牢固的友情。There are strong ties of friendship between the members of the society.
234 | 0.5 | 116

2605 艾滋病 [艾滋病] /àizībìng/ n AIDS
我们迄今尚未找到治疗艾滋病的有效办法。So far we have not found an effective way to cure AIDS.
165 | 0.7 | 116

2606 好事 [好事] /hǎoshì/ n good deed; good thing; [sometimes used ironically] bad deed
然而，这是件好事。Nevertheless, it is a good thing.
126 | 0.93 | 116

2607 差距 [差距] /chājù/ n disparity, gap
男女实际收入尚有一定差距。Some real income gaps still exist between men and women.
189 | 0.62 | 116

2608 骨 [骨] /gǔ, gú/ n bone
一根鱼骨卡在他喉咙里。A fish bone lodged in his throat.
147 | 0.8 | 116

2609 判断 [判斷] /pànduàn/ (2) v judge
据我判断，他们都有责任。As far as I can judge, they are all to blame.
177 | 0.66 | 116

2610 拍摄 [拍攝] /pāishè/ (3) v take (a picture), shoot (a film)
她把她的孩子在花园嬉戏的镜头拍摄了下来。She filmed her children playing in the garden.
163 | 0.72 | 116

2611 平静 [平靜] /píngjìng/ (2) adj calm, tranquil
岛上的生活是多么平静啊！How calm life on the island is!
178 | 0.65 | 115

2612 客观 [客觀] /kèguān/ (3) adj objective
这是谁也无法否认的客观事实。This is an objective fact that no one can deny.
151 | 0.77 | 115

2613 公正 [公正] /gōngzhèng/ adj just, fair, impartial
那是公正的评价。That's a fair comment.
186 | 0.62 | 115

2614 果然 [果然] /guǒrán/ (2) adv sure enough, as expected
事情果然办得很快。Sure enough, everything was fixed up very quickly.
171 | 0.68 | 115

2615 仿佛 [仿佛] /fǎngfó/ (2) adv as though, apparently
他仿佛觉得有人看见他了。It seemed to him as though he might be seen.
200 | 0.58 | 115

2616 初 [初] /chū/ (2) pref [prefix preceding a numeral to indicate dates on the lunar calendar, and also for grades or years in the junior high school]
为什么大年初一不可以穿黑色？Why is black not allowed on the first day of Chinese New Year?
147 | 0.78 | 115

2617 宿舍 [宿舍] /sùshè/ (1) n dormitory
宿舍前面有个花园。There is a garden in front of the dormitory.
164 | 0.7 | 115

2618 牙 [牙] /yá/ (2) n tooth
这婴儿已长了八颗牙。The baby has eight teeth.
168 | 0.69 | 115

2619 后果 [後果] /hòuguǒ/ (3) n consequence
你必须对你行动的后果负责。You must accept the consequences of your action.
139 | 0.83 | 115

2620 财富 [財富] /cáifù/ (3) n wealth
他的成功与他的财富无关。His success has nothing to do with his wealth.
192 | 0.6 | 115

2621 氏 [氏] /shì/ n person surnamed; family, clan
我的大家族叫黄氏家族！My big family has a name. The Huang family!
135 | 0.86 | 115

2622 食 [食] /shí/ n food, meal; animal feed; eclipse
洪水过后，当地的人丧失了一切，无衣无食，一无所有。After the floods, the local people lost everything; that is, they had no food, no clothing, nothing.
176 | 0.66 | 115

2623 父 [父] /fù/ n father
这些孩子因丧父而悲伤不已。The children were inconsolable when their father died.
159 | 0.73 | 115

2624 人性 [人性] /rénxìng/ n human nature, humanity
他的残忍表示他没有人性。His cruelty suggests that he is less than human.
188 | 0.62 | 115

2625 柳 [柳] /liǔ/ n willow
花园中花红柳绿，春意盎然。Bright red flowers and green willows are in the garden, and spring is in the air.
181 | 0.64 | 115

2626 百姓 [百姓] /bǎixìng/ n [also written as 老百姓] common people, civilian
百姓被从城里疏散到了农庄。The civilians were evacuated from the city to farms.
136 | 0.85 | 115

2627 碗 [碗] /wǎn/ (1) clas [measure word for food contained in a bowl] bowl
那个男孩今天早上吃了三碗米饭。The boy ate three bowls of rice this morning.
160 | 0.72 | 115

2628 听见 [聽見] /tīngjiàn/ (1) v hear
你听见有人在敲门吗？Do you hear someone knocking at the door?
218 | 0.53 | 115

2629 摔 [摔] /shuāi/ (2) v fall; break, cause to fall and break; throw, fling
我几乎从自行车上摔了下来。I nearly fell off my bike.
179 | 0.64 | 115

2630 出身 [出身] /chūshēn/ (3) v come from (a particular family background)
我出身贫寒。I sprang from a poor family.
150 | 0.77 | 115

2631 引进 [引進] /yǐnjìn/ (3) v introduce from elsewhere, import; bring in
他引进了更有效的生产方法。He introduced more efficient methods of production.
288 | 0.4 | 115

2632 舒服 [舒服] /shūfú/ (1) adj comfortable; (physically) well
我觉得不舒服。I do not feel well.
171 | 0.67 | 114

2633 亲切 [親切] /qīnqiè/ (2) adj amiable, kind, intimate
是的，他总是很亲切，很耐心。Yes, he is always kind and patient.
177 | 0.64 | 114

2634 不利 [不利] /búlì/ (3) adj unfavourable, harmful
抽烟对你的健康不利。Smoking is bad for your health.
147 | 0.78 | 114

2635 哼 [哼] /hng/ (2) interj [interjection expressing disapproval] humph
哼，你信他的！Humph, don't tell me you take him at his word!
289 | 0.39 | 114 | S

2636 西北 [西北] /xīběi/ (2) loc northwest
冷风从西北方向吹来。A cold wind blew from the northwest.
163 | 0.7 | 114

2637 年纪 [年紀] /niánjì/ (1) n age
她看来没有那么大年纪。She does not look her age.
168 | 0.68 | 114

2638 糖 [糖] /táng/ (1) n sugar, sweets
她在蛋糕上洒了一点糖。She sprinkled sugar on top of her cake.
167 | 0.68 | 114

2639 蔬菜 [蔬菜] /shūcài/ (2) n vegetable
我的意见是，我们要多吃蔬菜。My idea is that we should eat more vegetables.
186 | 0.62 | 114

2640 宇宙 [宇宙] /yǔzhòu/ (3) n universe
很难想像宇宙有多大。It is hard to imagine the scale of the universe.
211 | 0.54 | 114

2641 舞蹈 [舞蹈] /wǔdǎo/ (3) *n* dance
你喜欢那个舞蹈吗？ Did you like the dance?
197 | 0.58 | 114

2642 族 [族] /zú/ *n* race; group
蒙古族向来以能歌善舞著称。 The Mongolians are renowned for their singing and dancing.
147 | 0.78 | 114

2643 佛 [佛] /fó/ *n* Buddha
许多人都信佛。 Many people believe in Buddha.
130 | 0.88 | 114

2644 埋 [埋] /mái/ (2) *v* cover up, bury
这根柱子的末端埋在地下。 The end of the post was buried in the ground.
152 | 0.76 | 114

2645 交换 [交換] /jiāohuàn/ (2) *v* change, exchange
你可以跟我交换一下座位吗？ Would you change places with me?
199 | 0.58 | 114

2646 掏 [掏] /tāo/ (2) *v* take out, produce (from pocket)
他从口袋里掏出一条绳子。 He took a length of string out of his pocket.
198 | 0.58 | 114

2647 报 [報] /bào/ (3) *v* report; announce; recompense, reclaim; repay (one's kindness); revenge
于是他们报了警。 They filed a report at the police station.
125 | 0.92 | 114

2648 再说 [再説] /zàishuō/ (3) *v* put off for future decision
我们等到天气好些再说。 We're waiting until the weather picks up a bit.
180 | 0.63 | 114

2649 发行 [發行] /fāxíng/ (3) *v* publish, issue, release, distribute
下个月将发行许多新影片。 A number of new films are to be released next month.
217 | 0.53 | 114

2650 期待 [期待] /qīdài/ *v* look forward to, long for
我期待您再次光临。 I'm looking forward to seeing you again.
133 | 0.86 | 114

2651 有利 [有利] /yǒulì/ (2) *adj* advantageous, beneficial
协议对我们有利。 The agreement works to our advantage.
171 | 0.67 | 113

2652 最佳 [最佳] /zuìjiā/ *adj* best, optimal
毫无疑问他是这项工作的最佳人选。 He is, beyond question, the best man for the job.
171 | 0.66 | 113

2653 表 [表] /biǎo/ (1) *n* watch; form, table
对不起，你的表几点了？ Excuse me, what does your watch say?
134 | 0.85 | 113

2654 气候 [氣候] /qìhòu/ (2) *n* climate
那潮湿的气候对他不合适。 The humid climate didn't agree with him.
155 | 0.74 | 113

2655 本质 [本質] /běnzhì/ (2) *n* essence; true nature
这种行为说明了他的本质。 This behaviour shows his true nature.
151 | 0.75 | 113

2656 私人 [私人] /sīrén/ (2) *adj* private, personal
在上班时间，工作人员不准打私人电话。 Staff are not allowed to make personal calls during office hours.
126 | 0.9 | 113

2657 政权 [政權] /zhèngquán/ (3) *n* regime; power
军队夺取了政权。 The army has seized power.
162 | 0.7 | 113

2658 妻 [妻] /qī/ *n* wife
他娶她为妻。 He got her for his wife.
147 | 0.77 | 113

2659 欲望 [欲望] /yùwàng/ *n* desire
这取决于你求知的欲望。 It depends on your desire for knowledge.
156 | 0.73 | 113

2660 自从 [自從] /zìcóng/ (2) *prep* since
自从你们离开这儿以来，事情变化很大。 Things have changed very much since you left here.
152 | 0.75 | 113

2661 村里 [村里] /cūnli/ *place* in the village
村里有一个露天市场。 There is an open market in the village.
157 | 0.73 | 113

2662 参观 [參觀] /cānguān/ (1) *v* visit
你喜欢参观历史名胜吗？ Do you like visiting historical spots?
195 | 0.58 | 113

2663 碰 [碰] /pèng/ (1) *v* touch
别碰那个！ Do not touch that!
178 | 0.64 | 113

2664 接待 [接待] /jiēdài/ (2) *v* receive (a guest)
我们热情地接待了他们。 We received them warmly.
179 | 0.64 | 113

2665 娱乐 [娛樂] /yúlè/ (3) *n* entertainment, recreation
打牌是一种娱乐。 Playing cards is an entertainment.
152 | 0.75 | 113

2666 引导 [引導] /yǐndǎo/ (3) *v* guide, lead
那会把我们引导到什么地方去呢？ Where would that lead us?
211 | 0.54 | 113

2667 就业 [就業] /jiùyè/ *n* employment
旅游业会带来新的就业机会。 Tourism generates new job opportunities.
267 | 0.42 | 113 | W

2668 推出 [推出] /tuīchū/ *v* present, introduce
下面是即将推出的有关这方面的规则。 The following are the related rules to be introduced.
238 | 0.48 | 113

2669 相反 [相反] /xiāngfǎn/ adj opposite, contrary
我们要去的方向刚好相反。We're going in the opposite direction.
165 | 0.69 | 113

2670 破 [破] /pò/ (1) adj broken, worn out; lousy
我的袜子穿破了。I have worn holes in my socks.
154 | 0.73 | 112

2671 暂时 [暫時] /zànshí/ (2) adj temporary
差距是暂时的。The difference is only temporary.
136 | 0.83 | 112

2672 当 [當] /dàng/ (3) adj appropriate
你做的方法不当。You're not doing it in an appropriate way.
162 | 0.7 | 112

2673 要是 [要是] /yàoshi/ (1) conj if, in case
要是这样的话，那就换一种试试吧。If so, I'll try another brand.
193 | 0.58 | 112

2674 全都 [全都] /quándōu/ adv all, with no exception
我把我学的新词全都记在一个笔记本上了。I have jotted down all the new words I have learnt in a notebook.
162 | 0.69 | 112

2675 可不 [可不] /kěbu/ idiom [same as 可不是 or 可不是吗] sure enough, exactly
她是个十足的美人，可不是吗？She's a regular beauty, isn't she?
181 | 0.62 | 112

2676 汤 [湯] /tāng/ (1) n soup
这个汤你觉得怎么样？What do you think of the soup?
168 | 0.67 | 112

2677 大小 [大小] /dàxiǎo/ (2) n size
这个我穿着大小正好。It's my size.
137 | 0.82 | 112

2678 石油 [石油] /shíyóu/ (2) n oil
石油通过输油管输送到炼油厂。The oil is carried to the oil refinery by pipelines.
300 | 0.38 | 112

2679 鼻子 [鼻子] /bízi/ (2) n nose
只是我的鼻子很痒，不停流鼻涕。It's just that my nose feels itchy and it keeps running.
175 | 0.64 | 112

2680 传说 [傳說] /chuánshuō/ (3) n legend
这些传说是从十五世纪流传下来的。These legends came down to us from the fifteenth century.
155 | 0.73 | 112

2681 宝 [寶] /bǎo/ (3) n treasure
这是一件希世之宝。This is an extremely rare treasure.
148 | 0.76 | 112

2682 总部 [總部] /zǒngbù/ n headquarters
他们用无线电跟总部联络上了。They made contact with the headquarters by radio.
152 | 0.74 | 112

2683 明星 [明星] /míngxīng/ n star
她很有希望成为网球明星。She has been spotted as a likely tennis star of the future.
140 | 0.8 | 112

2684 企业家 [企業家] /qǐyèjiā/ n entrepreneur
他是一位精明强干的企业家。He is a clever entrepreneur.
197 | 0.57 | 112

2685 住房 [住房] /zhùfáng/ n house, housing
你们镇上现在住房情况如何？What are housing conditions like in your town now?
232 | 0.49 | 112

2686 扣 [扣] /kòu/ (2) v button up, buckle; deduct; detain
这件衬衫扣起来不太容易。The shirt does not button up very easily.
129 | 0.87 | 112

2687 盯 [盯] /dīng/ (3) v stare, keep an eye on
他透过厚厚的眼镜片盯着看我。He stared at me through thick glasses.
243 | 0.46 | 112

2688 迎 [迎] /yíng/ (3) v welcome; go to meet; move against
因此我们就能迎着困难上。Therefore we are able to look difficulties squarely in the face.
160 | 0.7 | 112

2689 爆炸 [爆炸] /bàozhà/ (3) v explode
工厂的一个车间爆炸了。A workshop of the factory exploded.
141 | 0.8 | 112

2690 有利于 [有利於] /yǒulìyú/ v be beneficial to, be helpful to
这有利于健康。This is helpful to health.
260 | 0.43 | 112 | W

2691 著 [著] /zhù/ v write
他已发表了很多文章，并著有数本专著。He has published many articles and written several monographs.
217 | 0.52 | 112

2692 签 [簽] /qiān/ v sign
我被迫违心地在协议上签了字。I was forced to sign the agreement against my will.
127 | 0.88 | 112

2693 出于 [出於] /chūyú/ v start from, stem from; come out of
她说的话是出于妒嫉。What she has said stems from envy.
139 | 0.81 | 112

2694 亮 [亮] /liàng/ (1) adj bright, light; enlightened
蜡烛烧得更亮了。The candles flamed brighter.
166 | 0.67 | 111

2695 易 [易] /yì/ (3) adj easy
这问题绝非易事。The problem is far from easy.
174 | 0.64 | 111

2696 难得 [難得] /nándé/ (3) adj rare
你应该好好利用这一次难得的机会。You should make good use of this rare opportunity.
129 | 0.86 | 111

2697 总之 [總之] /zǒngzhī/ (3) conj in sum, in a word
总之，计划告吹了。 In sum, the plan failed.
144 | 0.78 | 111

2698 耳朵 [耳朵] /ěrduo/ (2) n ear
我在他耳朵上狠狠打了一拳。 I gave him a good box on the ear.
170 | 0.65 | 111

2699 焦点 [焦點] /jiāodiǎn/ n focus
住房问题一直是公众兴趣的焦点。 The housing problem has always been the focus of pubic interest.
244 | 0.46 | 111

2700 景 [景] /jǐng/ n scene, sight, view
从这儿看到的塔景美极了。 The view of the tower from here is great.
122 | 0.92 | 111

2701 怎 [怎] /zěn/ pron how, why
你怎不早点告诉他们呀？ Why didn't you tell them earlier?
203 | 0.55 | 111

2702 内地 [內地] /nèidì/ place inland
沿海如何帮助内地，这是一个大问题。 It is a big problem to find ways for the coastal areas to assist the inland areas.
219 | 0.51 | 111

2703 今晚 [今晚] /jīnwǎn/ time tonight
我想预定今晚的席位。 I'd like to reserve a table for tonight, please.
175 | 0.63 | 111

2704 同情 [同情] /tóngqíng/ (2) v show pity or compassion
我完全同情这些孤儿。 I pity the orphans with all my heart.
137 | 0.81 | 111

2705 订 [訂] /dìng/ (2) v book, order, reserve; draw up, conclude; subscribe; staple
我想订个房间，住两天。 I'd like to reserve a room for two days.
129 | 0.86 | 111

2706 出席 [出席] /chūxí/ (2) v attend
如果你要出席宴会，你会穿什么？ If you are to attend the banquet, what will you wear?
345 | 0.32 | 111 | W

2707 送给 [送給] /sònggěi/ v give
这些书他们送给我了。 These books were given to me by them.
137 | 0.81 | 111

2708 喝酒 [喝酒] /hējiǔ/ v drink (alcohol)
你应该少喝酒。 You should drink less.
160 | 0.7 | 111

2709 回国 [回國] /huíguó/ v return to one's country
他回国两个月了。 He has been back from abroad for two months.
139 | 0.8 | 111

2710 哇 [哇] /wa/ (2) part [sentence final particle replacing 啊 where the preceding word ends with the vowel u or ao]
要是雨能停，该多好哇！ If only the rain would stop!
285 | 0.39 | 111 | S

2711 精彩 [精彩] /jīngcǎi/ (1) adj brilliant, splendid, wonderful
这一定会是一场精彩的比赛。 It must be a wonderful game.
142 | 0.78 | 110

2712 反复 [反復] /fǎnfù/ (2) adv repeatedly, again and again
为什么电视台要反复播放这样的镜头？ Why did the TV station play the scene over and over again?
149 | 0.74 | 110

2713 零 [零] /líng/ (1) num zero
气温是零度以下。 The temperature is below zero.
158 | 0.7 | 110

2714 味道 [味道] /wèidào/ (2) n taste, flavour
味道好极了。 It's delicious.
163 | 0.68 | 110

2715 功夫 [功夫] /gōngfū/ (2) n kung fu, martial arts; workmanship, skill
这是部非常好的功夫片。 This was a very good kung fu movie.
136 | 0.81 | 110

2716 条约 [條約] /tiáoyuē/ (2) n treaty
国会批准了该条约。 The treaty was ratified by the congress.
212 | 0.52 | 110

2717 公安 [公安] /gōng'ān/ (3) n police
公安机关在全国搜捕逃犯。 The police scoured the country for the fugitives.
236 | 0.47 | 110

2718 主持人 [主持人] /zhǔchírén/ n (TV or radio) presenter, host; (of meeting) chairperson
作为一个主持人应该幽默且健谈。 To be a host one should be humorous and talkative.
168 | 0.66 | 110

2719 黄金 [黃金] /huángjīn/ n gold
他们到处寻找黄金。 They travelled in search of gold.
137 | 0.81 | 110

2720 听 [聽] /tīng/ clas [measure word for stuff contained in a tin or can] tin, can
我拿了一听啤酒。 I took a can of beer.
172 | 0.64 | 110

2721 公斤 [公斤] /gōngjīn/ (1) clas kilo, kilogram
您的行李超重6公斤。 You've got six kilos of excess baggage.
322 | 0.34 | 110

2722 哪些 [哪些] /nǎxiē/ (2) pron which, what
你们有哪些海味？ What kinds of seafood do you have?
142 | 0.78 | 110

2723 偷 [偷] /tōu/ (2) v steal
他招认偷了那辆汽车。 He admitted having stolen the car.
168 | 0.66 | 110

2724 整理 [整理] /zhěnglǐ/ (2) v sort
我能帮你整理一下吗？ Can I help you sort it?
134 | 0.82 | 110

2725 显 [顯] /xiǎn/ v show, display; be apparent or obvious
深色衣服不显脏。 Dark clothes do not show the dirt.
120 | 0.92 | 110

2726 一块 [一塊] /yíkuài/ adv together
咱们一块做些事好了。 Let's do something together.
146 | 0.75 | 109

2727 发现 [發現] /fāxiàn/ (1) n finding, discovery
这项新的发现对传统观念提出了异议。 This new discovery challenges traditional beliefs.
131 | 0.83 | 109

2728 事物 [事物] /shìwù/ (2) n thing
许多新事物正在涌现。 Many new things are springing up.
168 | 0.65 | 109

2729 秘书 [秘書] /mìshū/ (3) n secretary
公司给我配备了一名秘书。 The firm put a secretary at my disposal.
165 | 0.66 | 109

2730 会计 [會計] /kuàijì/ n accountant; accounting
会计迅速地审核了这堆发票。 The accountant quickly looked through the pile of invoices.
142 | 0.77 | 109

---

18. The number system in Chinese

Basic numbers:

O（零）	O（零）	líng	0
一	一	yī	1
二	二	èr	2
三	三	sān	3
四	四	sì	4
五	五	wǔ	5
六	六	liù	6
七	七	qī	7
八	八	bā	8
九	九	jiǔ	9
十	十	shí	10
百	百	bǎi	100
千	千	qiān	1,000
万	萬	wàn	10,000
亿	億	yì	100,000,000

Numbers in words:

零	零	líng	zero
壹	壹	yī	one
贰	貳	èr	two
叁	叁	sān	three
肆	肆	sì	four
伍	伍	wǔ	five
陆	陸	liù	six
柒	柒	qī	seven
捌	捌	bā	eight
玖	玖	jiǔ	nine
拾	拾	shí	ten
佰	佰	bǎi	hundred
仟	仟	qiān	thousand
萬	萬	wàn	ten thousand
億	億	yì	hundred million

Examples of number combinations

十一	*shí-yī*	11
十二	*shí-èr*	12
十三	*shí-sān*	13
十四	*shí-sì*	14
十五	*shí-wǔ*	15
十六	*shí-liù*	16
十七	*shí-qī*	17
十八	*shí-bā*	18
十九	*shí-jiǔ*	19
二十	*èr-shí*	20
二十一	*èr-shí-yī*	21
九十九	*jiǔ-shí-jiǔ*	99
一百	*yì-bǎi*	100
一百〇一	*yì-bǎi-líng-yī*	101
一百一十	*yì-bǎi-yì-shí*	110
一百一十一	*yì-bǎi-yì-shí-yī*	111
二百	*èr-bǎi*	200
三百	*sān-bǎi*	300
一千	*yì-qiān*	1,000
一千〇一	*yì-qiān-líng-yī*	1,001
二千〇八十	*èr-qiān-líng-bā-shí*	2,080
九千九百九十九	*jiǔ-qiān-jiǔ-bǎi-jiǔ-shí-jiǔ*	9,999
一万	*yí-wàn*	10,000
一万〇一	*yí-wàn-líng-yī*	10,001
二万	*èr-wàn*	20,000
十万	*shí-wàn*	100,000
二十万	*èr-shí-wàn*	200,000
一百万	*yì-bǎi-wàn*	1,000,000
一千万	*yì-qiān-wàn*	10,000,000
一亿	*yí-yì*	100,000,000

Comments:

1 For numbers above 100, 〇 (零) *líng* must be used to make a difference between numbers such as 一百〇一 (101) and 一百一 *yì-bǎi-yī* (110).

2 There are two ways to read or write a single unit of tens i.e. 一十 *yì-shí* (e.g. 一百一十 *yì-bǎi-yì-shí* for 110) or just 十 *shí* (e.g. 一百十 *yì-bǎi-shí* for 110).

3 Chinese has an additional unit of number unit 万 *wàn* (10,000), which is not available in languages like English.

4 Ordinal numbers are prefixed with the prefix 第 as in 第一 "first".

5 半 *bàn* in Chinese means "half".

6 With the exception of 零 *líng* "zero", numbers in words are rarely used for purposes other than to prevent fraud (e.g. for banknotes, cheques and contracts).

2731 境界 [境界] /jìngjiè/ n realm, level or extent reached
他的思想境界非常崇高。 His realm of thought is lofty.
140 | 0.78 | 109

2732 悲剧 [悲劇] /bēijù/ n tragedy
他是一个悲剧演员。 He is a tragic actor.
181 | 0.6 | 109

2733 运行 [運行] /yùnxíng/ v move, be in motion; run, operate
地球环绕太阳运行。 The earth revolves round the sun.
216 | 0.51 | 109

2734 寒 [寒] /hán/ adj cold
这个棚子可以避寒。 The shelter was proof against the cold weather.
174 | 0.62 | 108

2735 上下 [上下] /shàngxià/ (3) loc up and down, high and low; about, approximately
老人把不速之客上下打量了一番。 The old man looked the uninvited guest up and down.
118 | 0.92 | 108

2736 汗 [汗] /hàn/ (2) n perspiration, sweat
他脸上淌着汗。 His face was streaming with sweat.
154 | 0.71 | 108

2737 毛病 [毛病] /máobìng/ (2) n fault, shortcoming, defect; ailment, illness
电话一定出毛病了。 There must be something wrong with the telephone.
141 | 0.77 | 108

2738 人间 [人間] /rénjiān/ (3) n human world, the world
人间若有天堂，非此莫属！ If there is a heaven on earth, this is it!
132 | 0.82 | 108

2739 学会 [學會] /xuéhuì/ (3) n professional or academic association, society
你是哪个专业学会的？ Do you belong to any professional associations?
140 | 0.77 | 108

2740 官兵 [官兵] /guānbīng/ n officers and men (in the army)
舰长统率舰上全体官兵。 The ship's captain commands all the officers and men.
171 | 0.63 | 108

2741 有关 [有關] /yǒuguān/ prep concerning, related to
他对有关这计划的想法怎样？ What about his ideas concerning this plan?
181 | 0.6 | 108

2742 疼 [疼] /téng/ (1) v ache, have a pain, hurt; love dearly
你疼不疼？ Did you have any pain?
191 | 0.57 | 108

2743 吵 [吵] /chǎo/ (2) v quarrel, have a row
她和父母大吵一场就离开了家。 She had a dreadful row with her parents and left home.
178 | 0.61 | 108

2744 赞成 [贊成] /zànchéng/ (2) v support, approve, be in favour of
哦，好，我非常赞成你的建议。 Oh, good, I am very much in favour of your proposal.
123 | 0.88 | 108

2745 聚 [聚] /jù/ (3) v gather together
他们聚在火炉周围取暖。 They gathered around the stove to soak up warmth.
121 | 0.9 | 108

2746 渴望 [渴望] /kěwàng/ (3) v be eager to, long for
她渴望成功。 She is eager for success.
137 | 0.79 | 108

2747 到来 [到來] /dàolái/ v arrive
他们设法坚持住直到有救援到来。 They managed to hold on until help arrived.
139 | 0.78 | 108

2748 承受 [承受] /chéngshòu/ v bear, endure
浩繁的开支，使他难以承受。 He cannot bear the heavy expenditure.
123 | 0.88 | 108

2749 辉煌 [輝煌] /huīhuáng/ (3) adj splendid, glorious
他们赢得了辉煌的胜利。 They had won a glorious victory.
139 | 0.77 | 107

2750 单纯 [單純] /dānchún/ (3) adj simple
与其说她善良不如说她单纯。 She is not kind so much as simple.
125 | 0.86 | 107

2751 敏感 [敏感] /mǐn'gǎn/ adj sensitive
她是个敏感的艺术家。 She is a sensitive artist.
130 | 0.82 | 107

2752 同时 [同時] /tóngshí/ (1) adv at the same time, at once
我无法同时做两件事。 I can't do two things at once.
129 | 0.83 | 107

2753 可能 [可能] /kěnéng/ (1) n possibility, chance
他获奖的可能极小。 He has only a slight chance of winning the prize.
131 | 0.82 | 107

2754 肚子 [肚子] /dùzi/ (2) n stomach, belly
我能空着肚子跑吗？ Do you think I can run on an empty stomach?
193 | 0.56 | 107

2755 手术 [手術] /shǒushù/ (2) n (surgical) operation
他做了一个高难度的外科手术。 He performed a difficult surgical operation.
126 | 0.85 | 107

2756 大使 [大使] /dàshǐ/ (3) n ambassador
他被任命为驻英大使。 He was appointed ambassador to Great Britain.
220 | 0.49 | 107

2757 摄影 [攝影] /shèyǐng/ (3) n photography
你喜欢摄影吗？ Do you like photography?
189 | 0.57 | 107

2758 当今 [當今] /dāngjīn/ *time* today, nowadays
保健是当今的热门话题。 Physical fitness is today's hot topic.
152 | 0.71 | 107

2759 微笑 [微笑] /wēixiào/ (2) *v* smile
她向我微笑。 She smiled at me.
211 | 0.51 | 107

2760 浪费 [浪費] /làngfèi/ (2) *v* waste
我们为修汽车浪费了整个下午。 We wasted a whole afternoon trying to repair the car.
125 | 0.86 | 107

2761 战胜 [戰勝] /zhànshèng/ (2) *v* beat, defeat, triumph over; overcome, surmount
正义必将战胜非正义。 Justice will triumph over injustice.
230 | 0.47 | 107

2762 攻 [攻] /gōng/ (3) *v* attack; specialise in
我的头刚伸出门，他们就对我群起而攻之。 As soon as I stuck my head out the door, they all attacked me.
140 | 0.77 | 107

2763 记住 [記住] /jìzhù/ *v* remember
我们将永远记住它。 We will remember it forever.
138 | 0.78 | 107

2764 舞 [舞] /wǔ/ *v* dance; wield
只剩下柳枝随着风狂舞。 Only willow branches remained, dancing madly in the wind.
123 | 0.88 | 107

2765 协调 [協調] /xiétiáo/ *adj* matching, coordinated, in keeping
那条领带不十分协调。 That tie is not quite in keeping.
191 | 0.56 | 107

2766 建成 [建成] /jiànchéng/ *v* complete, finish building
我们的新图书馆是1992年建成的。 Our new library was completed in 1992.
328 | 0.33 | 107 | W

2767 联 [聯] /lián/ *v* ally, join
命运使他们联在一起。 Destiny brought them together.
141 | 0.77 | 107

2768 广 [廣] /guǎng/ (3) *adj* wide, broad, extensive
这本简史涉及的话题范围很广。 The survey covered a broad spectrum of topics.
132 | 0.81 | 106

2769 莫 [莫] /mò/ *adv* not, do not
非公莫入。 No admittance except on business.
161 | 0.66 | 106

2770 好多 [好多] /hǎoduō/ *num* a good deal, a lot
我们有好多事要办。 We have a lot to do.
170 | 0.63 | 106 | S

2771 本 [本] /běn/ (2) *n* root, origin, foundation, basis; edition, version
谦逊是美德之本。 Humility is the solid foundation of all virtues.
135 | 0.79 | 106

2772 亲戚 [親戚] /qīnqī/ (2) *n* relative
附近的朋友胜过远方的亲戚。 A near friend is better than a far-away relative.
145 | 0.73 | 106

2773 玻璃 [玻璃] /bōlí/ (2) *n* glass
玻璃必须小心轻放。 Glass must be handled with care.
136 | 0.79 | 106

2774 主张 [主張] /zhǔzhāng/ (2) *n* advocacy, proposition
这一主张得到普遍的赞同。 This proposition met with general approval.
179 | 0.59 | 106

2775 标志 [標誌] /biāozhì/ (3) *n* sign, symbol
机动车辆驾驶员必须能看懂交通标志。 A motorist must be able to read traffic signs.
149 | 0.71 | 106

2776 公众 [公眾] /gōngzhòng/ *n* the public
这座花园向公众开放。 This garden is open to the public.
146 | 0.73 | 106

2777 沙 [沙] /shā/ *n* sand
这种土壤含沙很多。 This soil is very sandy.
126 | 0.85 | 106

2778 绿色 [綠色] /lǜsè/ *n* green; (of food) organic
那吉普车是绿色的。 That jeep is green.
174 | 0.61 | 106

2779 义 [義] /yì/ *n* meaning, sense; justice, righteousness
这个词不能按本义去理解。 This word should not be taken in its literal sense.
132 | 0.81 | 106

2780 平方米 [平方米] /píngfāngmǐ/ *clas* square metre
厨房的面积是12平方米。 The kitchen has an area of 12 square metres.
217 | 0.49 | 106

2781 会谈 [會談] /huìtán/ (2) *n* talks
他们在和平会谈中采取了强硬的态度。 They took an uncompromising stance in the peace talks.
355 | 0.3 | 106 | W

2782 带有 [帶有] /dàiyǒu/ *v* have, carry, bear
您带有多少外币？ How much foreign currency are you carrying?
129 | 0.82 | 106

2783 响 [響] /xiǎng/ (1) *adj* loud; noisy
收音机太响了。 The radio is too noisy.
185 | 0.57 | 105

2784 干脆 [乾脆] /gāncuì/ (2) *adj* straightforward, clear-cut
他办事喜欢干脆。 He likes to be straightforward in doing things.
139 | 0.76 | 105

2785 适当 [適當] /shìdàng/ (2) *adj* suitable, proper
这个问题你在适当的时候问问她吧。 Ask her about it when a suitable moment offers itself.
170 | 0.62 | 105

2786 密 [密] /mì/ (2) adj thick, dense; close, intimate; secret
小径旁边的玫瑰长得很密。 The rose grew thick along the path.
113 | 0.93 | 105

2787 巧 [巧] /qiǎo/ (2) adj opportune, by chance; skilful, clever
巧得很，我们正好坐同一列火车。 By a strange coincidence we happened to be travelling on the same train.
144 | 0.73 | 105

2788 或是 [或是] /huòshì/ conj or
她仅有的娱乐活动或是看电视，或是去看电影。 Her only recreation is watching TV or going to the movies.
141 | 0.75 | 105

2789 紧 [緊] /jǐn/ adv tightly, closely; (rain, firing, etc.) heavily
有人看到那女子紧跟着他. The woman was observed to follow him closely.
152 | 0.7 | 105

2790 数学 [數學] /shùxué/ (1) n mathematics, maths
他因数学成绩优异而获奖。 The prize was awarded to him for excellence in maths.
158 | 0.67 | 105

2791 宾馆 [賓館] /bīn'guǎn/ (2) n guesthouse, hotel
在宾馆前面他停下汽车。 He pulled the car up in front of the hotel.
120 | 0.88 | 105

2792 账 [賬] /zhàng/ (3) n account, account book; bill
我们会记在您的账上的。 We'll add it to your bill.
115 | 0.92 | 105

2793 稿 [稿] /gǎo/ (3) n script, manuscript, contribution
他为报纸写稿。 He writes for a newspaper.
123 | 0.86 | 105

2794 交易 [交易] /jiāoyì/ (3) n deal, transaction
如果双方各让一步，便可谈成交易。 If we can meet each other halfway, we may be able to conclude the business.
156 | 0.67 | 105

2795 女孩子 [女孩子] /nǚháizi/ n girl
这女孩子的模样很讨人喜欢。 The girl has a pleasing appearance.
164 | 0.65 | 105

2796 耳 [耳] /ěr/ n ear
她在我耳边低语了几句。 She whispered something in my ear.
129 | 0.82 | 105

2797 艘 [艘] /sōu/ (3) clas [measure word for boats and ships, etc.]
这艘船载重多少？ What's the carrying capacity of this ship?
146 | 0.72 | 105

2798 屋里 [屋裏] /wūli/ place indoors, in the house or room
屋里冷清清的。 The house looked deserted.
192 | 0.55 | 105

2799 侵略 [侵略] /qīnlüè/ (2) v invade
他们侵略了我们的领海。 They invaded our territorial waters.
155 | 0.68 | 105

2800 临 [臨] /lín/ (2) v face, overlook; be present; be about to
我想订一个临湖的房间。 I'd like to reserve a room facing the lake.
126 | 0.84 | 105

2801 防 [防] /fáng/ (2) v prevent, guard against; defend
那么我就防着她。 I'll be on my guard against her, then.
137 | 0.77 | 105

2802 直到 [直到] /zhídào/ (2) prep until, up to
直到你告诉我，我才知道这事。 I remained in ignorance of it until you told me.
132 | 0.8 | 105

2803 消除 [消除] /xiāochú/ (3) v eliminate, remove
他无法消除他的恐惧。 He couldn't remove his fears.
179 | 0.59 | 105

2804 遭 [遭] /zāo/ (3) v [sometimes written as 遭到] suffer, encounter
整个小镇已遭地震摧毁。 The whole town was destroyed by the earthquake.
129 | 0.82 | 105

2805 分布 [分佈] /fēnbù/ (3) v distribute, spread
这种蝴蝶在我国分布很广。 This species of butterfly is widely distributed over our country.
146 | 0.72 | 105

2806 来看 [來看] /láikàn/ v judge from
根据以往的经验来看，他得迟到。 Judging from previous experience, he will be late.
128 | 0.82 | 105

2807 看出 [看出] /kànchū/ v make out, see, find
我能看出他是一位医生。 I can see that he is a physician.
127 | 0.83 | 105

2808 可爱 [可愛] /kě'ài/ (2) adj lovely
她女儿多么可爱呀！ How lovely her daughter is!
148 | 0.71 | 104

2809 关键 [關鍵] /guānjiàn/ adj key, crucial, critical
她在关键时刻分散了我的注意力。 She distracted my attention at the crucial moment.
136 | 0.77 | 104

2810 不论 [不論] /búlùn/ (2) conj no matter (what, who, how, etc.), irrespective of
不论走哪条路都要三小时。 It takes three hours, whichever route you take.
122 | 0.85 | 104

2811 甚 [甚] /shèn/ adv very, quite
这个地区的新房子天花板甚高。 The new houses in this locality have very high ceilings.
151 | 0.69 | 104

2812 地点 [地點] /dìdiǎn/ (2) n venue, location, place
我们必须安排一个合适的时间和地点开会。 We must arrange a convenient time and place for the meeting.
126 | 0.83 | 104

2813 狼 [狼] /láng/ (2) n wolf
狼并不常常袭击人。 Wolves will not usually attack humans.
178 | 0.59 | 104

2814 答案 [答案] /dá'àn/ (2) n answer
答案错了。 The answer was wrong.
145 | 0.72 | 104

2815 决心 [決心] /juéxīn/ (2) n determination, resolution
他的决心是不可动摇的。 His resolution is not to be shaken by anything.
136 | 0.77 | 104

2816 教练 [教練] /jiàoliàn/ (3) n coach
他已当了三十五年的教练了。 He has been a coach for 35 years.
182 | 0.58 | 104

2817 研究生 [研究生] /yánjiùshēng/ (3) n graduate, postgraduate
研究生一般年龄较大。 Generally speaking, the graduate students are older.
131 | 0.8 | 104

2818 目 [目] /mù/ n eye; list
他一目失明。 He is blind in one eye.
126 | 0.83 | 104

2819 线 [線] /xiàn/ clas [measure word for slim things such as rays and hopes]
哪怕只有一线希望我也不会放弃。 I will not give up even if there is only a gleam of hope.
131 | 0.8 | 104

2820 城里 [城裏] /chénglǐ/ place in town or city
乡下比城里空气新鲜。 The air is fresher in the countryside than in the city.
133 | 0.79 | 104

2821 推广 [推廣] /tuīguǎng/ (2) v popularise, promote
推广这种新方法不是一件容易的工作。 Popularising this new method was not an easy job.
241 | 0.43 | 104

2822 止 [止] /zhǐ/ (2) v stop, end
恨永远无法止恨，只有爱可以止恨。 Hatred is never ended by hatred but by love.
127 | 0.82 | 104

2823 拨 [撥] /bō/ (3) v move; dial (a phone number); allocate
很抱歉，您拨错电话号码了。 I'm afraid you've got the wrong number.
120 | 0.87 | 104

2824 交谈 [交談] /jiāotán/ (3) v talk, converse
近来我不太有机会与她交谈。 I haven't had many chances to talk to her recently.
129 | 0.81 | 104

2825 全球化 [全球化] /quánqiúhuà/ n globalisation
经济全球化势不可挡。 The trend of economic globalisation is irresistible.
180 | 0.58 | 104

2826 拉开 [拉開] /lākāi/ v draw open; space out
拉开抽屉你就会找到钱。 Open the drawer and you will find the money.
137 | 0.76 | 104

2827 个别 [個別] /gèbié/ (2) adj very few
只有个别人请假。 Only one or two people asked for leave.
131 | 0.79 | 103

2828 大胆 [大膽] /dàdǎn/ (2) adj bold, courageous, daring
这是个大胆的计划。 It was a daring plan.
121 | 0.85 | 103

2829 大力 [大力] /dàlì/ (3) adv vigorously, greatly
大力推进优质服务。 Quality services should be greatly promoted.
318 | 0.33 | 103 | W

2830 略 [略] /lüè/ adv slightly; briefly
市场物价略有回升。 Market prices picked up slightly.
138 | 0.75 | 103

2831 媳妇 [媳婦] /xífù/ (3) n daughter-in-law; wife
她未做到一个好媳妇应尽的义务。 She failed in her obligations as a good daughter-in-law.
169 | 0.61 | 103

2832 艺术家 [藝術家] /yìshùjiā/ n artist
她是真正的艺术家。 She is an artist to her fingertips.
142 | 0.73 | 103

2833 权益 [權益] /quányì/ n rights and interests
它们是维护妇女权益的重要力量。 They are an important force in safeguarding the rights and interests of women.
199 | 0.52 | 103

2834 镜头 [鏡頭] /jìngtóu/ n (camera) lens; scene, shot (in a movie, etc.)
有两个镜头被审查员剪掉了。 Two scenes were cut by the censor.
138 | 0.75 | 103

2835 激情 [激情] /jīqíng/ n enthusiasm; passion, fervour
我带着同样的激情渴求知识。 With equal passion I have sought knowledge.
133 | 0.78 | 103

2836 沿 [沿] /yán/ (2) prep along
他沿街漫步。 He strolled along the street.
135 | 0.77 | 103

2837 双 [雙] /shuāng/ (1) clas pair
我想买一双运动鞋。 I want to buy a pair of sports shoes.
163 | 0.64 | 103

2838 一日 [一日] /yírì/ time one day
一日，他来到一个小镇。 One day, he went to a small town.
160 | 0.65 | 103

2839 亮 [亮] /liàng/ (1) v get light, show, reveal; shine; lift (one's voice)
天渐渐亮了。It's beginning to get light.
151 | 0.68 | 103

2840 统治 [統治] /tǒngzhì/ (2) v rule over, reign; dominate
亨利八世统治了很长一段时间。Henry VIII reigned for a long time.
147 | 0.7 | 103

2841 欠 [欠] /qiàn/ (2) v owe; lack, be short
他欠她的情永远也还不了。The debt that he owed her can never be paid.
126 | 0.82 | 103

2842 缺少 [缺少] /quēshǎo/ (2) v lack, be short of
我们缺少人手。We are short of men.
135 | 0.76 | 103

2843 捧 [捧] /pěng/ (2) v hold (in both hands); give somebody a boost
这次我接住了它，并且捧着让她看。This time I caught it and held it up for her to see.
153 | 0.68 | 103

2844 取消 [取消] /qǔxiāo/ (2) v cancel
请告诉我如何取消。Please tell me how to cancel it.
168 | 0.62 | 103

2845 重复 [重複] /chóngfù/ (2) v repeat
请你再重复一遍好吗？Will you please repeat it?
125 | 0.83 | 103

2846 奔 [奔] /bēn, bèn/ (3, 3) v rush, run quickly; head for; approach
她以轻快优雅的步子奔上楼去。She ran up the stairs with a light graceful step.
148 | 0.7 | 103

2847 对外 [對外] /duìwài/ adj external, foreign
我们把争取和平作为对外政策的首要任务。Peace is the prime objective of our foreign policy.
224 | 0.46 | 103

2848 圆 [圓] /yuán/ (1) adj round
地球是圆的。The earth is round.
124 | 0.83 | 102

2849 准 [准] /zhǔn/ (2) adj accurate; quasi-
我的手表走得很准。My watch keeps good time.
111 | 0.92 | 102

2850 类似 [類似] /lèisì/ (3) adj similar
他以前也听说过类似的情况。He had heard similar tales before.
132 | 0.78 | 102

2851 其次 [其次] /qícì/ (2) adv next, secondly
其次就是付款的问题。Next comes the question of payment.
147 | 0.7 | 102

2852 日益 [日益] /rìyì/ (3) adv day by day
他们的组织日益壮大。Their organisation is getting more powerful day by day.
205 | 0.5 | 102

2853 更为 [更為] /gèngwéi/ adv even more, all the more
健康的丧失比金钱的损失更为严重。Loss of health is more serious than loss of money.
142 | 0.72 | 102

2854 尚未 [尚未] /shàngwèi/ adv not yet
银行尚未开始营业。The bank isn't open yet.
145 | 0.7 | 102

2855 噢 [噢] /ō/ (3) interj [interjection expressing mental realisation] oh
噢，这张桌子空着。Well, this table is free.
256 | 0.4 | 102 | S

2856 友谊 [友誼] /yǒuyì/ (1) n friendship
他们之间的友谊日益亲密。A close friendship gradually grew up between them.
184 | 0.56 | 102

2857 秘密 [秘密] /mìmì/ (2) n secret
这是一个秘密。This is a secret.
119 | 0.86 | 102

2858 评论 [評論] /pínglùn/ (3) n comment; review
你明白他的评论是什么意思吗？What did you take his comments to mean?
138 | 0.74 | 102

2859 基层 [基層] /jīcéng/ (3) n grassroots, basic level, lower level; base
工作总是离不开基层。Our work must be done by grassroots organisations.
279 | 0.37 | 102 | W

2860 义务 [義務] /yìwù/ (3) n obligation, duty; volunteer, voluntary
没有购买的义务。There is no obligation to buy.
139 | 0.74 | 102

2861 海军 [海軍] /hǎijūn/ (3) n navy
它是海军和空军的联合行动。It was a joint operation of the navy and air force.
151 | 0.68 | 102

2862 类型 [類型] /lèixíng/ (3) n kind, type
你们有什么类型的车呢？What kinds of cars do you have?
142 | 0.72 | 102

2863 职 [職] /zhí/ n post, position, appointment
他因健康欠佳而被迫辞去此职。He was constrained by ill health to give up this appointment.
128 | 0.8 | 102

2864 活力 [活力] /huólì/ n vigour, vitality
她充满活力。She is full of vitality.
160 | 0.64 | 102

2865 暴力 [暴力] /bàolì/ n violence
人们不能宽恕使用凶残的暴力。People cannot condone the use of extreme violence.
145 | 0.71 | 102

2866 泪 [淚] /lèi/ n tear
他流着泪跑回家去找妈妈。He ran home in tears to his mother.
173 | 0.59 | 102

2867 总体 [總體] /zǒngtǐ/ *adj* overall, total
我的总体印象是很好的。My overall impression was favourable.
183 | 0.56 | 102

2868 司 [司] /sī/ *n* department (in a ministry); firm, company
对该司的询价信，我们已经回复。We have answered the inquiry received from the firm.
125 | 0.82 | 102

2869 己 [己] /jǐ/ *pron* self
他们总是以损人开始，以害己告终。They invariably start by doing others harm but end by ruining themselves.
131 | 0.78 | 102

2870 眼里 [眼裏] /yǎnli/ *place* in one's eyes, in one's view
她的眼里流露出受委屈的神情。Her eyes took on a hurt expression.
160 | 0.64 | 102

2871 例如 [例如] /lìrú/ (1) *v* take . . . for example
我有很多业余爱好，例如钓鱼。I have many hobbies – fishing, for example.
211 | 0.49 | 102

2872 忍 [忍] /rěn/ (2) *v* bear, endure, stand, put up with
我不能再忍了。I can't stand it any more.
162 | 0.63 | 102

2873 善于 [善於] /shànyú/ (2) *v* be good at
他善于发表即席演说。He is good at making impromptu speeches.
148 | 0.69 | 102

2874 办事 [辦事] /bànshì/ (2) *v* attend to (a matter); act
你要凭良心办事。You should act according to your conscience.
138 | 0.74 | 102

2875 对付 [對付] /duìfu/ (2) *v* deal with, cope with; make do with
恐怕我对付不了这些麻烦。I am afraid I cannot cope with those troubles.
123 | 0.84 | 102

2876 冲击 [衝擊] /chōngjī/ (3) *v* charge, attack, assault; lash
波浪冲击着岸边。The waves lashed the shore.
130 | 0.79 | 102

2877 露 [露] /lù, lòu/ (2, 3) *v* show, reveal
这条裙子腿露得太多了。This skirt shows too much leg.
132 | 0.77 | 102

2878 买卖 [買賣] /mǎimài/ *n* buying and selling, (business) transaction, deal
在这笔买卖中他赚了二百元。He gained 200 yuan by this deal.
126 | 0.82 | 102

2879 傻 [傻] /shǎ/ (2) *adj* foolish
我太傻了，竟会相信他的话。I have been foolish enough to believe what he said.
190 | 0.53 | 101

2880 闲 [閑] /xián/ (2) *adj* free, idle
我今天闲着。I am free today.
145 | 0.7 | 101

2881 净 [淨] /jìng/ (3) *adj* clean; net
净工资是工资总额减去税收并扣除国民保险。Net salary is gross salary minus tax and national insurance deduction.
143 | 0.71 | 101

2882 极其 [極其] /jíqí/ (2) *adv* extremely
我居住的那个城市极其美丽。The city where I live is extremely beautiful.
127 | 0.8 | 101

2883 特 [特] /tè/ *adv* specially, especially
他篮球打得特好。He is especially good at basketball.
109 | 0.93 | 101

2884 绝不 [絕不] /juébù/ *adv* never
我绝不会忘记这一天。I shall never forget this day.
115 | 0.88 | 101

2885 队长 [隊長] /duìzhǎng/ (2) *n* team leader, captain
他是我们的队长。He is our captain.
133 | 0.76 | 101

2886 号码 [號碼] /hàomǎ/ (2) *n* number
航班号码是多少？What's the flight number?
110 | 0.93 | 101

2887 老虎 [老虎] /lǎohǔ/ (2) *n* tiger
老虎向山羊扑去。The tiger sprang on the goat.
134 | 0.75 | 101

2888 美女 [美女] /měinǚ/ *n* beauty
她是上一世纪有名的美女之一。She was one of the famous beauties of the last century.
199 | 0.51 | 101

2889 君 [君] /jūn/ *n* monarch; [used as a formal title of addressing a man] Mr
他们被控欺君谋反、知情不举。They were accused of being privy to the plot against the king.
138 | 0.74 | 101

2890 情节 [情節] /qíngjié/ *n* plot; circumstances
我喜欢这个小说的情节，但不喜欢它的语言。I like the plot of the novel, but not the language.
143 | 0.71 | 101

2891 画面 [畫面] /huàmiàn/ *n* (picture) image; (video) frame
电视画面模糊不清。The television picture is fuzzy.
128 | 0.79 | 101

2892 德 [德] /dé/ *n* virtue; moral character
女子无才便是德。Ignorance is a woman's virtue.
110 | 0.92 | 101

2893 比 [比] /bǐ/ (1) *v* compare; match, liken to
跟我比起来，他算是有钱人了。Compared with me, he is rich.
131 | 0.77 | 101

2894 切 [切] /qiē/ (2) v cut, carve
请再给我切一片。 Please carve me another slice.
182 | 0.56 | 101

2895 生气 [生氣] /shēngqì/ (2) v be angry
他生气时不免有些失礼。 He was rather curt when he was angry.
172 | 0.59 | 101

2896 踏 [踏] /tà/ (3) v step on
你脚踏线啦！ You stepped on the foul line.
129 | 0.79 | 101

2897 专门 [專門] /zhuānmén/ (2) adj special, specialised
该公司是专门的计算机公司。 This is a specialised computer company.
150 | 0.67 | 100

2898 混乱 [混亂] /hùnluàn/ (3) adj confused
混乱不清的思绪掠过他的心头。 Confused ideas floated through his mind.
120 | 0.83 | 100

2899 喜 [喜] /xǐ/ adj happy, delighted, joyful
她转喜为悲。 She swung from happiness to tears.
142 | 0.71 | 100

2900 或许 [或許] /huòxǔ/ adv perhaps
或许那封信今天能到。 Perhaps the letter will come today.
153 | 0.66 | 100

2901 大多 [大多] /dàduō/ adv mostly
街上的人大多是游客。 The people in the streets were mostly tourists.
136 | 0.74 | 100

2902 著作 [著作] /zhùzuò/ (2) n book, writing, work
许多学生都喜欢阅读名作家的著作。 Most students like to read the works of famous writers.
140 | 0.72 | 100

2903 顾客 [顧客] /gùkè/ (2) n customer
这样对顾客很方便。 It is quite convenient for customers.
171 | 0.58 | 100

2904 毒 [毒] /dú/ (3) n poison; drug
他终于戒了毒了。 He's finally off drugs.
125 | 0.8 | 100

2905 声明 [聲明] /shēngmíng/ (3) n statement
这是一篇充满火药味的声明。 This statement has a strong smell of gunpowder.
226 | 0.44 | 100

2906 遗址 [遺址] /yízhǐ/ n ancient ruins
我们在导游的陪同下游览了那里的遗址。 We had a guided tour of the ruins.
201 | 0.5 | 100

2907 空 [空] /kōng, kòng/ n air, sky; empty space, blank space; spare time, free time
风筝升入空中。 The kite rose into the air.
118 | 0.85 | 100

2908 游泳 [游泳] /yóuyǒng/ (1) v swim
在这条河里游泳是非常危险的。 It is dangerous to swim in this river.
131 | 0.77 | 100

2909 克服 [克服] /kèfú/ (2) v overcome
我们完全相信我们能够克服这些困难。 We are fully confident that we can overcome these difficulties.
154 | 0.66 | 100

2910 跪 [跪] /guì/ (2) v kneel down, fall to one's knees
他感激万分，跪倒地上。 Overwhelmed with gratitude, he fell to his knees.
164 | 0.62 | 100

2911 保存 [保存] /bǎocún/ (2) v preserve; save (a computer file, etc.)
这栋旧建筑保存得很好。 The old building is well preserved.
130 | 0.77 | 100

2912 消灭 [消滅] /xiāomiè/ (2) v perish, eliminate
不可能完全消灭贫穷。 It will not be able to eliminate poverty completely.
134 | 0.75 | 100

2913 记录 [記錄] /jìlù/ (2) v record, put down
把你的花费都记录下来。 Keep a tally of how much you spend.
125 | 0.8 | 100

2914 富有 [富有] /fùyǒu/ (3) v be wealthy; be rich in
他富有教学经验。 He is rich in teaching experience.
130 | 0.77 | 100

2915 载 [載] /zǎi, zài/ (3) v record; carry (in a vehicle)
这架飞机可以载多少旅客？ How many passengers does the plane accommodate?
136 | 0.74 | 100

2916 上网 [上網] /shàngwǎng/ v get on the internet, go online
我能上网吗？ Can I get on the internet?
141 | 0.71 | 100

2917 一再 [一再] /yízài/ (3) adv repeatedly
他一再缺课令人担忧。 His repeated absence is worrying.
105 | 0.95 | 99

2918 水果 [水果] /shuǐguǒ/ (1) n fruit
我吃很多水果。 I eat a lot of fruit.
125 | 0.8 | 99

2919 化学 [化學] /huàxué/ (1) n chemistry
她主修化学。 She majors in chemistry.
127 | 0.78 | 99

2920 桌子 [桌子] /zhuōzi/ (1) n table, desk
把书放在桌子上。 Put the book on the table.
164 | 0.6 | 99

2921 营养 [營養] /yíngyǎng/ (2) n nutrition
他因为营养不良，身体越来越虚弱。 Because of his poor nutrition, he has grown weaker and weaker.
148 | 0.67 | 99

2922 意志 [意志] /yìzhì/ (2) n will
他是具有钢铁意志的汉子。 He is a man of iron will.
127 | 0.78 | 99

2923 指标 [指標] /zhǐbiāo/ (3) *n* target; quota
这个指标偏低。 The target is on the low side.
165 | 0.6 | 99

2924 待遇 [待遇] /dàiyù/ (3) *n* treatment; remuneration
他对于自己所受到的待遇感到不满。 He was dissatisfied with his treatment.
125 | 0.8 | 99

2925 夫 [夫] /fū/ *n* husband; manual labourer
她选他为夫。 She chose him for her husband.
123 | 0.81 | 99

2926 思路 [思路] /sīlù/ *n* line of thought, thinking
我得整理一下思路。 I have to tidy my thoughts.
153 | 0.65 | 99

2927 业 [業] /yè/ *n* trade, line of business; profession, occupation; estate, property; undertaking
我们不经营此业。 We are not engaged in this line of business.
136 | 0.73 | 99

2928 竹 [竹] /zhú/ *n* bamboo
而且房内的陈设也都是竹制的。 Nearly everything inside their houses is made of bamboo, too.
115 | 0.87 | 99

2929 粮 [糧] /liáng/ *n* grain; food
由于干旱少雨，缺粮问题更加严重。 The lack of rain aggravated the serious lack of food.
128 | 0.78 | 99

2930 外地 [外地] /wàidì/ (2) *place* non-local place
他现在到外地度假去了。 He is at present away on his holidays.
116 | 0.86 | 99

2931 家中 [家中] /jiāzhōng/ *place* at home
现在呢，家中还有谁？ Who else do you have at home now?
126 | 0.79 | 99

2932 接到 [接到] /jiēdào/ (2) *v* receive, get
我刚接到一笔大的订单。 I've just received a big order.
111 | 0.9 | 99

2933 违反 [違反] /wéifǎn/ (2) *v* violate
那是违反合同的。 That's a violation of the contract.
161 | 0.62 | 99

2934 袭击 [襲擊] /xíjī/ (3) *v* assault, hit; surprise
暴徒袭击了过路人。 The mob assaulted a passer-by.
133 | 0.75 | 99

2935 放松 [放鬆] /fàngsōng/ (3) *v* relax; loosen
有些人即使在家也不能很好地放松。 Some people can't even relax when they are at home.
108 | 0.92 | 99

2936 体验 [體驗] /tǐyàn/ *v* experience
你体验过真正的饥饿吗？ Have you experienced real hunger?
131 | 0.76 | 99

2937 转向 [轉向] /zhuǎnxiàng/ *v* change direction
风转向了。 The wind changed.
112 | 0.88 | 99

2938 名叫 [名叫] /míngjiào/ *v* be called
这个乐队名叫"四合一"。 The band is called "Four and One".
113 | 0.88 | 99

2939 咨询 [諮詢] /zīxún/ *v* consult
但是，我还得咨询一下本部。 But I'll have to consult my home office.
177 | 0.56 | 99

2940 能否 [能否] /néngfǒu/ *v* whether or not one can
能否给我提些建议？ Can you give me some suggestions?
144 | 0.69 | 99

2941 故意 [故意] /gùyì/ (2) *adj* deliberate, intentional
请相信我，这不是故意的。 I assure you it was not deliberate.
145 | 0.68 | 98

2942 生动 [生動] /shēngdòng/ (2) *adj* vivid, lively
他生动地讲述了那次经历。 He recalled the experience vividly.
126 | 0.78 | 98

2943 大规模 [大規模] /dàguīmó/ *adj* large-scale
逐步的变化比突然的、大规模的变化更好。 Gradual change is preferable to sudden, large-scale change.
160 | 0.62 | 98

2944 真是 [真是] /zhēnshì/ (3) *adv* really, actually; [equivalent of 真是的, expressing dissatisfaction] well, really
真是岂有此理！ It's really outrageous!
153 | 0.64 | 98

2945 永 [永] /yǒng/ *adv* forever
烈士的英雄业绩永存。 The heroic deeds of the martyr live forever.
135 | 0.73 | 99

2946 题目 [題目] /tímù/ (2) *n* title, topic, subject; question in examination
现在让我们看看下一个题目。 Let us now pass on to the next subject.
166 | 0.59 | 98

2947 圈 [圈] /quān, juàn/ (2) *n* circle, ring; fold, sty
他把这根铁丝紧系在金属圈上。 He made the wire fast to the metal ring.
121 | 0.81 | 98

2948 盘 [盤] /pán/ (2) *n* plate, dish; tray; (chess) board
水果盘里没有葡萄，对吗？ There are no grapes in the fruit bowl, are there?
123 | 0.8 | 98

2949 学问 [學問] /xuéwèn/ (2) *n* scholarly learning
他很有学问，可是好忘事。 He's very learned but rather absent-minded.
139 | 0.71 | 98

19. Time expressions

Days of the week:

星期天	星期天	*xīngqītiān*	Sunday
星期日	星期日	*xīngqīrì*	Sunday
星期一	星期一	*xīngqīyī*	Monday
星期二	星期二	*xīngqīèr*	Tuesday
星期三	星期三	*xīngqīsān*	Wednesday
星期四	星期四	*xīngqīsì*	Thursday
星期五	星期五	*xīngqīwǔ*	Friday
星期六	星期六	*xīngqīliù*	Saturday
周日	週日	*zhōurì*	Sunday
周末	週末	*zhōumò*	weekend
周一	週一	*zhōuyī*	Monday
周二	週二	*zhōuèr*	Tuesday
周三	週三	*zhōusān*	Wednesday
周四	週四	*zhōusì*	Thursday
周五	週五	*zhōuwǔ*	Friday
周六	週六	*zhōuliù*	Saturday

Months:

一月	一月	*yīyuè*	January
二月	二月	*èryuè*	February
三月	三月	*sānyuè*	March
四月	四月	*sìyuè*	April
五月	五月	*wǔyuè*	May
六月	六月	*liùyuè*	June
七月	七月	*qīyuè*	July
八月	八月	*bāyuè*	August
九月	九月	*jiǔyuè*	September
十月	十月	*shíyuè*	October
十一月	十一月	*shíyīyuè*	November
十二月	十二月	*shí'èryuè*	December

Seasons:

春天	春天	*chūntiān*	spring
春季	春季	*chūnjì*	spring
夏天	夏天	*xiàtiān*	summer
夏季	夏季	*xiàjì*	summer
秋天	秋天	*qiūtiān*	autumn
秋季	秋季	*qiūjì*	autumn
冬天	冬天	*dōngtiān*	winter
冬季	冬季	*dōngjì*	winter

Time of the day:

凌晨	凌晨	*língchén*	early morning
清晨	清晨	*qīngchén*	early morning
早晨	早晨	*zǎochén*	morning
早上	早上	*zǎoshang*	morning
上午	上午	*shàngwǔ*	morning
中午	中午	*zhōngwǔ*	noon
下午	下午	*xiàwǔ*	afternoon
傍晚	傍晚	*bàngwǎn*	early evening
晚上	晚上	*wǎnshang*	evening
夜里	夜裏	*yèli*	night
深夜	深夜	*shēnyè*	late night
午夜	午夜	*wǔyè*	middle night

2950 电台 [電臺] /diàntái/ (2) *n* transmitter-receiver, transceiver; radio station
我刚按电台的报时信号拨了表。I have just set my watch by the radio time signal.
158 | 0.62 | 98

2951 丝 [絲] /sī/ (2) *n* silk, thread
这种纸摸起来像丝。This paper feels like silk.
170 | 0.58 | 98

2952 效率 [效率] /xiàolǜ/ (2) *n* efficiency
目前我们主要的任务是提高效率。Our main task at present is to raise our efficiency.
156 | 0.63 | 98

2953 银 [銀] /yín/ (2) *n* silver
铜和银都是电的良导体。Both copper and silver are good conductors of electricity.
105 | 0.93 | 98

2954 阵地 [陣地] /zhèndì/ (3) *n* position, front
他们向敌人阵地发起冲击。They assaulted the enemy position.
156 | 0.63 | 98

2955 音 [音] /yīn/ (3) *n* sound; news
这个音怎么发? How do you pronounce this sound?
117 | 0.84 | 98

2956 代价 [代價] /dàijià/ (3) *n* price, cost
当然，对这种灵活性是要付出代价的。There's a price to that flexibility, of course.
127 | 0.77 | 98

2957 轨道 [軌道] /guǐdào/ (3) *n* orbit; track
工作已走上轨道。The work has got onto the right track.
146 | 0.67 | 98

2958 天空 [天空] /tiānkōng/ (3) *n* sky
夕阳映红了天空。The sky was aglow with the setting sun.
158 | 0.62 | 98

2959 叶 [葉] /yè/ *n* leaf; part of a historical period
判断树优劣，看果不看叶。A tree is known by the fruit, not by the leaves.
124 | 0.79 | 98

2960 沿着 [沿著] /yánzhe/ *prep* along
那我建议您最好沿着大路走。I suggest you walk only along the main road.
116 | 0.85 | 98

2961 剩 [剩] /shèng/ (1) *v* leave over, remain
只剩一点儿时间了。There's a little bit of time left.
132 | 0.74 | 98

2962 煮 [煮] /zhǔ/ (2) *v* cook, boil
你早饭要吃煮鸡蛋吗? Do you want a boiled egg for breakfast?
162 | 0.61 | 98

2963 否定 [否定] /fǒudìng/ (2) *v* negate
这些事实否定了你的理论。These facts negate your theory.
130 | 0.76 | 98

2964 添 [添] /tiān/ (2) *v* add
几句笑话会给你的演说添些生气。A few jokes will add a final fillip to your speech.
119 | 0.83 | 98

2965 商 [商] /shāng/ *v* discuss, consult
有要事相商。I have important matters to discuss with you.
149 | 0.66 | 98

2966 喜 [喜] /xǐ/ *v* like, be fond of
猴子性喜攀缘。Monkeys have a natural inclination for climbing.
144 | 0.69 | 98

2967 顺 [順] /shùn/ (3) *adj* smooth, without a hitch
车子不仅开得很顺而且很快。The car is not only smooth but also fast.
121 | 0.81 | 97

2968 科学院 [科學院] /kēxuéyuàn/ (2) *n* academy of sciences
他在中国科学院工作。He works in the Chinese Academy of Sciences.
158 | 0.62 | 97

2969 大爷 [大爺] /dàyé/ (2) *n* grandpa, elder uncle; [often used as a respectful term for an elderly man, equivalent of 老大爷] uncle
王大爷的话还在她脑中回响。Uncle Wang's words still rang in her head.
178 | 0.55 | 97

2970 脾气 [脾氣] /píqì/ (2) *n* disposition, temperament
要控制住自己，不要发脾气。Don't let your temper run away with you.
152 | 0.64 | 97

2971 家属 [家屬] /jiāshǔ/ (3) *n* family member
被告家属在审讯时旁听。The defendant's family were present at the hearing.
118 | 0.82 | 97

2972 岗位 [崗位] /gǎngwèi/ (3) *n* post, position
他被派到了新的工作岗位。He has been assigned to a new post.
157 | 0.62 | 97

2973 灰 [灰] /huī/ (3) *adj* grey
他是个长着灰胡子的高个子男人。He's a tall man with a grey beard.
148 | 0.66 | 97

2974 途径 [途徑] /tújìng/ (3) *n* means, pathway
应当通过各种途径宣传它。It should be publicised by all means.
173 | 0.56 | 97

2975 农场 [農場] /nóngchǎng/ (3) *n* farm
他住在一个农场里。He lives on a farm.
106 | 0.92 | 97

2976 事故 [事故] /shìgù/ (3) *n* accident
这对防止事故有帮助。This will help to prevent accidents.
185 | 0.53 | 97

2977 儿女 [兒女] /érnǚ/ (3) *n* children
他们有儿女吗? Do they have any children?
101 | 0.96 | 97

2978 和尚 [和尚] /héshang/ *n* monk
妻子死后他出家当了和尚。He went to a temple to be a monk after his wife died.
150 | 0.65 | 97

2979 陆 [陸] /lù/ *n* land
大象是现有的最大的陆上动物。 The elephant is the largest land animal in existence.
147 | 0.66 | 97

2980 国民 [國民] /guómín/ *n* national, citizen
国家的职责是保护它的国民。 The state's duty is to protect its nationals.
171 | 0.57 | 97

2981 校园 [校園] /xiàoyuán/ *n* campus
我们的校园很安静。 Our campus is a very quiet place.
130 | 0.75 | 97

2982 家族 [家族] /jiāzú/ *n* clan, family
我家族的人大都相当长寿。 My family tend to be quite long-lived.
121 | 0.81 | 97

2983 友 [友] /yǒu/ *n* friend
他不能辨别敌友。 He never knows a friend from an enemy.
255 | 0.38 | 97

2984 支援 [支援] /zhīyuán/ (2) *v* support, aid
另一个方面是工业支援农业。 The other is to have industry support agriculture.
126 | 0.77 | 97

2985 踩 [踩] /cǎi/ (2) *v* step on, tread on
我一踩冰就裂了。 The ice cracked as I stepped onto it.
141 | 0.69 | 97

2986 涌 [湧] /yǒng/ (3) *v* gush, surge; rush
音乐会结束后乐迷涌向舞台。 Fans rushed to the stage after the concert.
142 | 0.69 | 97

2987 流动 [流動] /liúdòng/ (3) *v* flow, surge
洪水沿着山谷滚滚流动。 The floods surged along the valley.
158 | 0.62 | 97

2988 返回 [返回] /fǎnhuí/ *v* return
您当天就返回吗？ Are you returning on the same day?
117 | 0.83 | 97

2989 臭 [臭] /chòu/ (2) *adj* stinking, smelly; disgraceful, discredited
谁要你的臭钱！ Who wants your stinking money?
140 | 0.69 | 96

2990 不满 [不滿] /bùmǎn/ (3) *adj* dissatisfied, discontented, resentful
他对自己的薪水感到不满。 He was discontented with his salary.
113 | 0.85 | 96

2991 秘密 [秘密] /mìmì/ *adj* secret
他们与其主要竞争者签了一份秘密协议。 They signed a secret deal with their main rival.
104 | 0.92 | 96

2992 善 [善] /shàn/ *adj* virtuous, good; kind, friendly
来者不善，善者不来。 Those who have come are not friendly; those who are friendly have not come.
133 | 0.73 | 96

2993 赶快 [趕快] /gǎnkuài/ (2) *adv* hurriedly, quickly
请赶快过来。 Please come quickly!
151 | 0.64 | 96

2994 由此 [由此] /yóucǐ/ *adv* from this, hereby; hence
由此可能产生严重后果。 Serious consequences may arise from this.
140 | 0.69 | 96

2995 并非 [並非] /bìngfēi/ *adv* actually not
这些规则并非总能行得通。 These rules do not always apply.
146 | 0.66 | 96

2996 喂 [喂] /wèi/ (1) *interj* hello, hey
喂，你上哪儿去？ Hey, where are you going?
167 | 0.58 | 96

2997 通讯 [通訊] /tōngxùn/ (2) *n* communication, telecommunication; correspondence, news report
卫星是重要的通讯工具。 The satellite is an important means of communication.
166 | 0.58 | 96

2998 党员 [黨員] /dǎngyuán/ (2) *n* Party member
据说他已经成为一名党员了。 It is said that he has become a Party member.
218 | 0.44 | 96

2999 浪 [浪] /làng/ (2) *n* wave
风吹浪高。 The wind blew the waves into great peaks.
110 | 0.88 | 96

3000 县城 [縣城] /xiànchéng/ (3) *n* county seat, county town
县城离这有百儿八十里。 The county town is 100 li or so away from here.
110 | 0.88 | 96

3001 依据 [依據] /yījù/ (3) *n* basis, foundation, evidence
他以事实作为他主张的依据。 His claim had a foundation in facts.
146 | 0.66 | 96

3002 社 [社] /shè/ *n* society, club; agency
我想所有的网球社都一样吧！ I guess all tennis clubs are about the same.
133 | 0.73 | 96

3003 额 [額] /é/ *n* amount, volume; forehead
销售额令人失望。 The sales volume is disappointing.
130 | 0.74 | 96

3004 权威 [權威] /quánwēi/ *n* authority
他的意见具有权威性。 His opinion carries authority.
136 | 0.71 | 96

3005 外国人 [外國人] /wàiguórén/ *n* foreigner
他与一外国人结婚了。 He is married to a foreigner.
116 | 0.83 | 96

3006 页 [頁] /yè/ *clas* page
这本书有120页。 The book has 120 pages.
152 | 0.63 | 96

3007 比较 [比較] /bǐjiào/ (1) v compare
让我们把译文和原文比较一下。Let's compare the translation with the original.
123 | 0.78 | 96

3008 患 [患] /huàn/ (3) v suffer from, fall ill with, catch
昨天我患了重感冒。I caught a bad cold yesterday.
137 | 0.71 | 96

3009 须 [須] /xū/ (3) v must, have to
他的判断是否正确尚须验证。The soundness of his judgement has yet to be tested.
128 | 0.75 | 96

3010 如同 [如同] /rútóng/ (3) v like, as
这条消息如同一个炸弹。The news came like a bombshell.
136 | 0.71 | 96

3011 挨 [挨] /āi, ái/ (2, 3) v be next to; get close to; suffer, endure
他因为上班迟到而挨了一顿骂。He got quite a blowing up for being late for work.
145 | 0.67 | 96

3012 探讨 [探討] /tàntǎo/ v explore, approach, investigate
本文探讨两者的关系。This article examines the relationship between the two.
146 | 0.66 | 96

3013 呈现 [呈現] /chéngxiàn/ v show, appear
雾一消散景色就呈现在我们眼前了。The view opened out in front of us as the fog cleared.
126 | 0.76 | 96

3014 前往 [前往] /qiánwǎng/ v go to, leave for
她经过住院治疗后，前往海滨养病。She went to the seaside to convalesce after her stay in hospital.
166 | 0.58 | 96

3015 阴 [陰] /yīn/ (1) adj (of weather) overcast; negative; Yin (negative)
天气又冷又阴。It was cold and cloudy.
125 | 0.76 | 95

3016 古老 [古老] /gǔlǎo/ (2) adj ancient, old, time-honoured
这是一个古老的习俗。This is a time-honoured custom.
123 | 0.77 | 95

3017 坚定 [堅定] /jiāndìng/ (2) adj firm, steadfast
中国是维护世界和平的坚定力量。China is a steadfast force for safeguarding world peace.
133 | 0.72 | 95

3018 清晰 [清晰] /qīngxī/ (3) adj clear, distinct
你的电视机图像清晰吗？Do you get a clear picture on your TV?
115 | 0.83 | 95

3019 便 [便] /biàn/ adj convenient; informal, ordinary
穿便装就行。An ordinary suit will do.
149 | 0.64 | 95

3020 同一 [同一] /tóngyī/ adj same, identical
我们在同一个城市里住了好几年。We dwelt in the same town for years.
123 | 0.78 | 95

3021 屋子 [屋子] /wūzi/ (1) n house
屋子乱得一塌糊涂。The house was in a mess.
158 | 0.6 | 95

3022 阵 [陣] /zhèn/ (2) n (military) front, field; battle array
他错过了机会，而且临阵脱逃。He let the opportunity slip and fled the field.
131 | 0.73 | 95

3023 监狱 [監獄] /jiānyù/ (3) n prison, jail
他从监狱里逃跑了。He escaped from prison.
107 | 0.89 | 95

3024 家伙 [傢伙] /jiāhuo/ (3) n guy, fellow; tool, weapon
你最好不要惹那个家伙。You'd better not bother that guy.
218 | 0.44 | 95

3025 乙 [乙] /yǐ/ (3) n [used for the second of enumerated items] second
甲真的打败了乙。A really whipped B.
142 | 0.67 | 95

3026 黑色 [黑色] /hēisè/ n black
他的小汽车是黑色的。He has a black car.
134 | 0.71 | 95

3027 热爱 [熱愛] /rè'ài/ (2) v love
他非常热爱他的事业。He loves his career very much.
114 | 0.84 | 95

3028 握 [握] /wò/ (2) v hold, grasp
她把那小鸟握在掌心里。She held the small bird in the hollow of her hand.
153 | 0.62 | 95

3029 生长 [生長] /shēngzhǎng/ (2) v grow
这种植物能在地球上许多地方生长。This plant can grow in many parts of the globe.
120 | 0.8 | 95

3030 透 [透] /tòu/ (2) v penetrate, pass through; reveal, let out
从钥匙孔透出一线亮光。A thread of light emerged from the keyhole.
147 | 0.65 | 95

3031 租 [租] /zū/ (3) v rent, hire
我想租一辆车。I'd like to rent a car.
111 | 0.86 | 95

3032 评 [評] /píng/ (3) v comment, review; judge, appraise; choose
你评评理看。You can be the judge as to who is right.
119 | 0.8 | 95

3033 不见 [不見] /bújiàn/ (3) v disappear, miss; not meet
客人报告说她房间里的钱包不见了。The guest reported that her wallet was missing from her room.
137 | 0.69 | 95

3034 去世 [去世] /qùshì/ v die, pass away
她活到高龄才去世。She died at an advanced age.
127 | 0.76 | 95

3035 呈 [呈] /chéng/ v assume (shape, colour, property, etc.); submit, present
满月呈圆形。 The full moon has a circular shape.
138 | 0.69 | 95

3036 确保 [確保] /quèbǎo/ v ensure, make sure
我们检查了每一批货以确保准确无误。
We have checked each batch to make sure it is perfect.
237 | 0.4 | 95

3037 表 [表] /biǎo/ v express, show
对他的逝世，我们深表哀悼。 We express our deepest condolences over his death.
122 | 0.79 | 95

3038 打断 [打斷] /dǎduàn/ v interrupt, cut short
我正要告诉你，你把话打断了。 I was just about to tell you when you interrupted.
167 | 0.57 | 95

3039 指责 [指責] /zhǐzé/ v criticise, accuse
要先掌握实据才可公开指责。 One must be sure of one's facts before making a public accusation.
117 | 0.82 | 95

3040 花 [花] /huā/ (1) adj coloured; flowery, fancy; (of eyes) blurred
这件衣服我穿太花了。 The dress is too loud for me.
116 | 0.81 | 94

3041 一路 [一路] /yílù/ adv all the way
我从家里一路走到图书馆，不料已经关门了。
I walked all the way from home to the library, only to find it closed.
133 | 0.71 | 94

3042 最初 [最初] /zuìchū/ (1) adj initial, first
你对北京的最初印象如何？ What were your first impressions of Beijing?
124 | 0.76 | 94

3043 马路 [馬路] /mǎlù/ (2) n road, highway
请用地下通道穿越马路。 Use the underpass to cross the road.
132 | 0.72 | 94

3044 款 [款] /kuǎn/ (2) n money, fund; pattern, style
你想他会不会付不起款？ Do you think he may not be able to make payment?
132 | 0.71 | 94

3045 风景 [風景] /fēngjǐng/ (2) n scenery
那风景美丽得难以形容。 The scenery was beautiful beyond description.
110 | 0.86 | 94

3046 例 [例] /lì/ (2) n example, case
为给您这方面的实证，我们以现代绘画为例。
To give you an example of this, take modern painting for instance.
137 | 0.69 | 94

3047 手续 [手續] /shǒuxù/ (2) n formalities, procedure
请问海关的手续办完了吗？ Well, is that it for customs formalities?
122 | 0.78 | 94

3048 棋 [棋] /qí/ (3) n chess, board game
她下什么棋都比他强。 She outrivals him at all board games.
118 | 0.8 | 94

3049 渠道 [渠道] /qúdào/ (3) n channel
大部分消息我们是通过那个渠道得到的。
Most information we get through that channel.
175 | 0.54 | 94

3050 章 [章] /zhāng/ n seal, stamp; badge
海关官员在该文件上盖了章。 The document was stamped by the customs officer.
139 | 0.68 | 94

3051 场所 [場所] /chǎngsuǒ/ n place, venue
你不可在公共场所做那事。 You mustn't do that in a public place.
140 | 0.68 | 94

3052 术 [術] /shù/ n way, practice; (surgical) operation
货源落实，是商家未雨绸缪的经营之术。
To make sure of the sources of goods is a businessman's way of operation.
119 | 0.79 | 94

3053 主张 [主張] /zhǔzhāng/ (2) v advocate, maintain, argue for
他主张继续进行搜查。 He argued for a continuation of the search.
136 | 0.69 | 94

3054 实验 [實驗] /shíyàn/ (2) n experiment, test
学生们在老师指导下做实验。 The students are doing their experiments with the help of their teacher.
131 | 0.72 | 94

3055 签订 [簽訂] /qiāndìng/ (2) v sign (an agreement, contract and treaty, etc.)
他们签订了一项代理协议。 They signed an agency agreement.
181 | 0.52 | 94

3056 印 [印] /yìn/ (2) v print
那景象深深印在我的记忆中。 The scene is printed in my memory.
96 | 0.99 | 94

3057 探 [探] /tàn/ (2) v explore; visit; stretch forward
请勿探身。 Don't lean out.
126 | 0.75 | 94

3058 惊 [驚] /jīng/ (3) v surprise, shock
这条消息使我们惊得目瞪口呆。 The news struck us all dumb.
171 | 0.55 | 94

3059 损害 [損害] /sǔnhài/ (3) v harm
如此举动将会损害你的名誉。
Such conduct will compromise your reputation.
137 | 0.69 | 94

3060 注重 [注重] /zhùzhòng/ v lay stress on, take pains with
她很注重自己的外表。 She always takes pains with her appearance.
162 | 0.58 | 94

20. Chinese festivals

元旦	元旦	*yuándàn*	New Year's Day	1 January
春节	春節	*chūnjié*	Spring Festival	Lunar 1 January
元宵节	元宵節	*yuánxiāo jié*	Lantern Festival	Lunar 15 January
清明节	清明節	*qīngmíng jié*	Tomb-sweeping Festival	Lunar 5 April
端午节	端午節	*duānwǔ jié*	Dragon Boat Festival	Lunar 5 May
中秋节	中秋節	*zhōngqiū jié*	Mid-autumn Festival	Lunar 15 August
教师节	教師節	*jiàoshī jié*	Teachers' Day	10 September
重阳节	重陽節	*chóngyang jié*	Double-ninth Day	Lunar 9 September
国庆节	國慶日	*guóqìng jié*	National Day	1 October
除夕	除夕	*chúxī*	Chinese New Year's Eve	Lunar 31 December

3061 露出 [露出] /*lùchū*/ v show, reveal
他眼里露出恐惧的目光。His fear showed in his eyes.
195 | 0.48 | 94

3062 私 [私] /*sī*/ (2) adj personal, private; illicit
那是一家公私合营企业。That is a state–private joint enterprise.
104 | 0.9 | 93

3063 不仅仅 [不僅僅] /*bùjǐnjǐn*/ adv not merely, more than
新经济不仅仅是科技。New economy is not merely an economy of technology.
121 | 0.77 | 93

3064 报道 [報導] /*bàodào*/ (2) n (news) report
咱们看的一定是同一份报导。We must have read the same report.
174 | 0.54 | 93

3065 决议 [決議] /*juéyì*/ (3) n resolution, motion
他投票赞成这项决议。He voted for the motion.
168 | 0.56 | 93

3066 环节 [環節] /*huánjié*/ n link
分析的结果，当前的薄弱环节是铁路。Analysis shows that the weak link at the moment is the railways.
148 | 0.63 | 93

3067 嘴里 [嘴裏] /*zuǐli*/ place in mouth
嘴里有东西时不要说话。Don't talk with your mouth full.
187 | 0.5 | 93

3068 窗口 [窗口] /*chuāngkǒu*/ n window
这是卖邮票的窗口吗？Is this the right window for stamps?
116 | 0.81 | 93

3069 移动 [移動] /*yídòng*/ (2) v move
你能把车座向前移动吗？Can you move the car seat forward?
157 | 0.59 | 93

3070 填 [填] /*tián*/ (2) v fill; fill in, complete (a form)
告诉我如何填这张表。Tell me how to fill out this form.
105 | 0.89 | 93

3071 拆 [拆] /*chāi*/ (2) v dismantle, take apart, pull down
要修理这部发动机，我得拆下里面的部件。To repair this engine I'll have to have its innards out.
108 | 0.86 | 93

3072 夹 [夾] /*jiā*/ (2) v hold between, put in between; carry under one's arm; mingle, mix
她胳膊下夹着一包书。She is carrying a parcel of books under her arm.
138 | 0.68 | 93

3073 发起 [發起] /*fāqǐ*/ v initiate, sponsor, launch
这次会议是由二十二所院校发起的。The meeting was sponsored by 22 colleges.
137 | 0.68 | 93

3074 相应 [相應] /*xiāngyìng*/ adj corresponding, relevant
他们在利润方面获得相应的增长。They achieved a corresponding rise in profits.
158 | 0.59 | 93

3075 前来 [前來] /*qiánlái*/ v come over
那场大雪使他未能前来参加我们的宴会。The heavy snow stopped him from coming to our party.
148 | 0.63 | 93

3076 附 [附] /*fù*/ v enclose, attach
请在里面附一个写着你自己地址的信封。Please enclose a self-addressed envelope.
193 | 0.48 | 93

3077 否认 [否認] /*fǒurèn*/ v deny
这些指责遭到了断然否认。The allegations were all flatly denied.
107 | 0.87 | 93

3078 不能 [不能] /*bùnéng*/ v can't
恐怕我们不能来。I'm afraid we can't come.
114 | 0.82 | 93

3079 有趣 [有趣] /*yǒuqù*/ (2) adj interesting
你所说的非常有趣。What you have said is most interesting.
119 | 0.78 | 92

3080 紧紧 [緊緊] /jǐnjǐn/ *adv* tightly, closely
这一对情侣紧紧地搂抱着。The lovers held each other tight.
141 | 0.66 | 92

3081 比如说 [比如說] /bǐrúshuō/ *idiom* for example, say
留点小费，比如说，10 元也可以。Leave a small tip, say, ten dollars.
372 | 0.25 | 92 | S

3082 若干 [若干] /ruògān/ (3) *num* a number of, several; how many, how much
笔者认为有若干至关重要的因素。I think there are several crucial factors.
133 | 0.7 | 92

3083 瓶 [瓶] /píng/ (1) *n* bottle
请把空牛奶瓶全部退回。Please return all empty milk bottles.
97 | 0.96 | 92

3084 俱乐部 [俱樂部] /jùlèbù/ (2) *n* club
要加入俱乐部必须有一位会员介绍人。To join the club you have to be put up by an existing member.
149 | 0.62 | 92

3085 根本 [根本] /gēnběn/ (2) *n* base, root, fundamental, core
只有亲自参加实践，才能了解问题的根本。Only through taking part in practice ourselves can we know the core of the problem.
118 | 0.78 | 92

3086 角 [角] /jiǎo/ (2) *n* corner; horn; angle, cape
我的胳膊肘撞着桌子角了。I banged my elbow on the corner of the table.
112 | 0.82 | 92

3087 场合 [場合] /chǎnghé/ (3) *n* occasion
你的演说适合这种场合。Your speech is suitable for this occasion.
118 | 0.79 | 92

3088 地质 [地質] /dìzhì/ (3) *n* geology
然而，他对植物、动物和地质却很感兴趣。However, he was very interested in plants, animals and geology.
146 | 0.63 | 92

3089 基因 [基因] /jīyīn/ *n* gene
如今我们对基因的结构有了较多的了解。We know a lot about the structure of the gene now.
133 | 0.69 | 92

3090 细节 [細節] /xìjié/ *n* detail
每个细节都已经想透了。Every detail has been thought out.
122 | 0.76 | 92

3091 姐妹 [姐妹] /jiěmèi/ *n* sister
她是三个姐妹中最年轻的。She is the youngest of the three sisters.
98 | 0.95 | 92

3092 丝 [絲] /sī/ *clas* [measure word for tiny bits] a thread of, a trace of
她脸上闪过一丝微笑。A faint smile flickered across her face.
156 | 0.59 | 92

3093 贯彻 [貫徹] /guànchè/ (2) *v* implement, carry out
其职责就是贯彻落实这一计划。It is their duty to carry out this programme.
298 | 0.31 | 92 | W

3094 捞 [撈] /lāo/ (2) *v* take something out of water, fish for; gain, get (money or benefits) by improper means
他没有捞到任何好处。He has gained nothing.
122 | 0.76 | 92

3095 提倡 [提倡] /tíchàng/ (2) *v* advocate, promote
要提倡学术交流。Academic exchanges should be promoted.
125 | 0.74 | 92

3096 独立 [獨立] /dúlì/ (2) *v* be independent
国家不能独立，人民的生命就没有保障。Without national independence, there would be no guarantee for the people's lives.
128 | 0.72 | 92

3097 禁止 [禁止] /jìnzhǐ/ (2) *v* prohibit, ban
公共场所禁止吸烟。Smoking is banned in public places.
143 | 0.65 | 92

3098 闯 [闖] /chuǎng/ (2) *v* rush, dash; break in
他闯入商店。He broke into the shop.
98 | 0.95 | 92

3099 推荐 [推薦] /tuījiàn/ (3) *v* recommend
我毫无保留地推荐这家餐馆！I can unreservedly recommend this restaurant!
122 | 0.76 | 92

3100 演讲 [演講] /yǎnjiǎng/ *n* speech, lecture
人们对她的演讲反应如何？How did her speech go over?
127 | 0.72 | 92

3101 严厉 [嚴厲] /yánlì/ (3) *adj* severe, stern
我们的老师没有他们的严厉。Our teacher is less strict than theirs.
122 | 0.75 | 91

3102 灿烂 [燦爛] /cànlàn/ (3) *adj* bright; brilliant
花园里阳光灿烂。The garden is bright with sunshine.
96 | 0.96 | 91

3103 冷静 [冷靜] /lěngjìng/ (3) *adj* calm
他很冷静，很沉着。He was calm and collected.
124 | 0.74 | 91

3104 真诚 [真誠] /zhēnchéng/ *adj* sincere, true
她的话听起来是真诚的。Her words rang true.
108 | 0.85 | 91

3105 不良 [不良] /bùliáng/ *adj* bad, harmful
他的不良行为超出了开玩笑的范围。His bad behaviour was beyond a joke.
124 | 0.74 | 91

3106 前后 [前後] /qiánhòu/ (3) *loc* in front and behind; before and after, around; from beginning to end
这事将在圣诞节前后完成。It will be finished around Christmas.
106 | 0.86 | 91

3107 亿 [億] /yì/ (1) num 100 million
我们大概要筹集 2 亿 5 千万美元。We need to raise about $250 million.
189 | 0.48 | 91

3108 庙 [廟] /miào/ (2) n temple
此庙由粗大的柱子支撑。The temple is supported by massive columns.
111 | 0.82 | 91

3109 伙伴 [伙伴] /huǒbàn/ (3) n partner (for an activity); pal, mate
他是我儿时的游戏夥伴。He was my playmate when I was a child.
162 | 0.56 | 91

3110 人体 [人體] /réntǐ/ (3) n human, human body
这种药尚未经过人体试验。The drug has not been tried out on humans yet.
148 | 0.62 | 91

3111 可能性 [可能性] /kěnéngxìng/ n possibility, chance
你晋升的可能性如何？What are your chances of being promoted?
108 | 0.85 | 91

3112 大楼 [大樓] /dàlóu/ n building
他们住在这座大楼内。They live in this building.
100 | 0.91 | 91

3113 局势 [局勢] /júshì/ n situation
局势现已失控。The situation is now out of control.
151 | 0.61 | 91

3114 为何 [為何] /wèihé/ pron why
你下午为何缺课？Why did you cut the afternoon classes?
111 | 0.83 | 91

3115 南方 [南方] /nánfāng/ place south
他习惯于南方温暖的气候。He is used to the soft climate of the south.
113 | 0.81 | 91

3116 凌晨 [凌晨] /língchén/ time early morning before dawn, small hours
每夜的电视节目现在持续到了凌晨 3 点或者 4 点。Nightly television now goes on until 3 or 4 am.
108 | 0.85 | 91

3117 喜爱 [喜愛] /xǐ'ài/ (3) v like, love
我喜爱海味。I love seafood.
102 | 0.9 | 91

3118 罚 [罰] /fá/ (3) v penalise, punish
老师警告他们说谁要不守规矩就罚谁。The teacher warned them that she would punish anyone who stepped out of line.
115 | 0.79 | 91

3119 诞生 [誕生] /dànshēng/ (3) v be born
我极想看看那国王诞生的房子。I am curious to see the house where the king was born.
119 | 0.77 | 91

3120 加大 [加大] /jiādà/ v increase, enlarge
国家要加大对中西部地区的支持力度。The state will increase its support for the central and western parts.
283 | 0.32 | 91 | W

3121 得知 [得知] /dézhī/ v learn, hear, get to know
我得知他回来了。I heard of his return.
108 | 0.85 | 91

3122 承诺 [承諾] /chéngnuò/ v undertake, promise
他们书面承诺他们将不侵犯我们的专利。They have given us a written undertaking that they will not infringe our patent.
158 | 0.58 | 91

3123 顿 [頓] /dùn/ adv suddenly, immediately
几口饭下肚，五人精神顿振。After a few mouthfuls of food, their spirits picked up immediately.
130 | 0.7 | 90

3124 原本 [原本] /yuánběn/ adv originally, formerly
他原本名叫庄士顿。He was originally named Johnston.
135 | 0.67 | 90

3125 不能不 [不能不] /bùnéngbù/ adv have to, cannot but
这不能不防备！One had to be prepared.
107 | 0.84 | 90

3126 流 [流] /liú/ (1) n flow, stream of water or air, current
没有压差，就没有水流。No flow of water occurs unless there is a difference in pressure.
111 | 0.82 | 90

3127 来信 [來信] /láixìn/ (2) n (incoming) letter
谢谢你的来信。Thank you for your letter.
101 | 0.89 | 90

3128 高度 [高度] /gāodù/ (2) n height
飞机爬到一万米的高度。The plane climbed to a height of 10,000 metres.
138 | 0.65 | 90

3129 户 [戶] /hù/ (2) n family, household; door; (bank) account
天堂里各家各户各得其所。In paradise each family has a place of its own.
131 | 0.69 | 90

3130 动力 [動力] /dònglì/ (3) n drive, motivation; power
他有追求成功的强烈的动力。He has a strong drive for success.
138 | 0.66 | 90

3131 公安局 [公安局] /gōng'ānjú/ n public security bureau, police station
护照遗失或失窃，应立即向当地公安局报告。In the case of a lost or stolen passport, the loss must be immediately reported to the local public security bureau.
123 | 0.74 | 90

3132 版 [版] /bǎn/ n edition; (of newspaper) page
这一版限出二万册。The edition is limited to 20,000 copies.
117 | 0.77 | 90

3133 尊严 [尊嚴] /zūnyán/ n dignity
人的尊严不应该被忽视。Man's dignity should not be ignored.
100 | 0.9 | 90

3134 小时候 [小時候] /xiǎoshíhou/ *n* (in) one's childhood
我小时候经常在小河边玩。 I often played by the river in my childhood.
128 | 0.71 | 90

3135 呀 [呀] /yā/ *ono* [the sound of a creak]
门呀的一声开了。 The door opened with a creak.
223 | 0.41 | 90 | S

3136 在内 [在內] /zàinèi/ *aux* including, included
伙食费也包括在内。 Meals are also included.
159 | 0.57 | 90

3137 围绕 [圍繞] /wéirào/ (2) *v* revolve around; surround
无限的空间围绕着地球。 Infinite space surrounds the earth.
187 | 0.49 | 90

3138 摘 [摘] /zhāi/ (2) *v* pick, pluck, take off; make a summary
他摘下眼镜，把它放进口袋里。 He took off his glasses and put them into his pocket.
111 | 0.81 | 90

3139 不顾 [不顧] /búgù/ (3) *v* have no regard for, neglect
她不顾儿女。 She neglected her children.
103 | 0.88 | 90

3140 占有 [佔有] /zhànyǒu/ (3) *v* have, possess; occupy, hold
他在竞争中占有轻微的优势。 He had an edge on the competition.
118 | 0.77 | 90

3141 整 [整] /zhěng/ (3) *v* put in order; punish
我迟早要整他一下。 I'll fix him sooner or later.
115 | 0.79 | 90

3142 怀 [懷] /huái/ (3) *v* cherish, keep in mind; be pregnant
多年来她怀着她儿子会回来的希望。 For many years she cherished the hope that her son would return.
124 | 0.73 | 90

3143 聊天 [聊天] /liáotiān/ *v* chat
我们一边喝茶一边愉快地聊天。 We had a pleasant chat over a cup of tea.
129 | 0.7 | 90

3144 学会 [學會] /xuéhuì/ *v* learn
你学会游泳了吗？ Have you learnt to swim?
120 | 0.76 | 90

3145 当作 [當作] /dàngzuò/ *v* treat as, regard as
他们把那个小女孩当作自己的孩子。 They regard the little girl as one of their own children.
124 | 0.73 | 90

3146 响 [響] /xiǎng/ *v* sound, make a sound, (of applause) break out, (of telephone) ring
她正要出去，电话铃响了。 She was on the point of going out when the telephone rang.
160 | 0.56 | 90

3147 庆 [慶] /qìng/ *v* celebrate
我建议让我们两家俱乐部一起搞庆新年的活动。 I suggest that our two clubs celebrate New Year together.
153 | 0.59 | 90

3148 紧急 [緊急] /jǐnjí/ (3) *adj* urgent
我从她声音中察觉到情况紧急。 I detected a note of urgency in her voice.
130 | 0.69 | 89

3149 实 [實] /shí/ *adj* solid, firm; true, real, actual
打夯机用来将地面打实。 A ramming machine is used to make the ground firm.
104 | 0.86 | 89

3150 善良 [善良] /shànliáng/ *adj* kind-hearted, good and honest
我姑母是一个善良的女人。 My aunt is a kind woman.
115 | 0.78 | 89

3151 岂 [豈] /qǐ/ *adv* [used formally in rhetorical questions] how can it be possible that . . .
这样岂不更好些？ Wouldn't that be better?
123 | 0.72 | 89

3152 物理 [物理] /wùlǐ/ (1) *n* physics
我喜欢物理和化学。 I like both physics and chemistry.
111 | 0.81 | 89

3153 花园 [花園] /huāyuán/ (2) *n* garden
街的对面有个花园。 There is a garden on the opposite side of the street.
100 | 0.9 | 89

3154 植物 [植物] /zhíwù/ (2) *n* plant
许多植物具有药性。 Many plants have medicinal properties.
121 | 0.74 | 89

3155 厕所 [廁所] /cèsuǒ/ (2) *n* toilet, WC
男厕所在哪儿？ Where's the men's room?
118 | 0.76 | 89

3156 遗产 [遺產] /yíchǎn/ (3) *n* heritage, inheritance, legacy
他继承了一大笔遗产。 He received a large inheritance.
204 | 0.44 | 89

3157 档案 [檔案] /dàng'àn/ (3) *n* files, archive
他弄了一份档案的复制品。 He made a duplicate for the files.
113 | 0.79 | 89

3158 名义 [名義] /míngyì/ *n* name
他以他父亲的名义参加了聚会。 He attended the party in the name of his father.
104 | 0.86 | 89

3159 机遇 [機遇] /jīyù/ *n* opportunity, favourable circumstances
中国对外经贸机遇和挑战并存。 China's foreign trade faces both opportunities and challenges.
196 | 0.46 | 89

3160 总裁 [總裁] /zǒngcái/ *n* president, CEO (chief executive officer)
他担任了两届总裁。 He served two terms as president.
144 | 0.62 | 89

3161 依 [依] /yī/ *prep* according to, by
他们生活宽裕，甚至依某些标准来说是富有的。 They were comfortable or even wealthy by some standards.
111 | 0.81 | 89

3162 习惯 [習慣] /xíguàn/ (1) *v* be used to, be accustomed to
你很快就会习惯的。 You'll soon get used to it.
120 | 0.75 | 89

3163 涨 [漲] /zhǎng, zhàng/ (2) *v* (of prices, rivers, etc.) rise; swell
从长远看，物价肯定要涨。 In the long run prices are bound to rise.
111 | 0.8 | 89

3164 摇 [搖] /yáo/ (2) *v* shake, rock, wave, wag
她把它摇了摇以确定里面没有东西。 She shook it to make certain there was nothing inside.
162 | 0.55 | 89

3165 暴露 [暴露] /bàolù/ (3) *v* expose, reveal
沉住气，千万别暴露你的身份。 Hold your horses and take care not to reveal your identity.
101 | 0.89 | 89

3166 吐 [吐] /tǔ, tù/ (2, 2) *v* spit, disgorge; vomit, throw up
她拚命想把鱼刺吐出来。 She was trying hard to disgorge a fish bone.
147 | 0.61 | 89

3167 得以 [得以] /déyǐ/ *v* be able to
掌声停止后演员们才得以继续演出。 The applause died down and the actors were able to continue.
121 | 0.74 | 89

3168 繁荣 [繁榮] /fánróng/ (2) *adj* prosperous, booming
生意日趋繁荣。 Business is booming.
193 | 0.46 | 88

3169 过分 [過分] /guòfèn/ (3) *adj* excessive, too much
她对孩子要求太过分了。 She is asking too much of a child.
113 | 0.79 | 88

3170 另 [另] /lìng/ (2) *adv* in addition; separately
对不起，本星期天我另有约会。 I am sorry, I have another appointment this Sunday.
107 | 0.83 | 88

3171 愈 [愈] /yù/ (3) *adv* [as in 愈...愈...] the more (the more...)
她愈想愈伤心。 The more she thought, the worse she felt.
137 | 0.65 | 88

3172 帽子 [帽子] /màozi/ (1) *n* hat, cap; label
你戴的那顶帽子很可笑。 That's a comical hat you're wearing.
113 | 0.79 | 88

3173 机械 [機械] /jīxiè/ (2) *n* machinery
我对机械一窍不通。 I have little mechanical knowledge.
152 | 0.59 | 88

3174 学位 [學位] /xuéwèi/ (3) *n* (academic) degree
我打算申请硕士学位。 My intention is to apply for an MA degree.
111 | 0.79 | 88

3175 大地 [大地] /dàdì/ (3) *n* earth, ground
雪覆盖着大地。 Snow covered the ground.
105 | 0.84 | 88

3176 画家 [畫家] /huàjiā/ (3) *n* painter
他是位著名的画家。 He is eminent as a painter.
104 | 0.85 | 88

3177 坑 [坑] /kēng/ (3) *n* hole, pit
他险些儿掉到坑里去了。 He came near to falling into the pit.
109 | 0.81 | 88

3178 典型 [典型] /diǎnxíng/ (3) *n* typical example, exemplar
还要注意抓典型，总结先进经验，加以推广。 It should also grasp typical examples, review advanced experience and disseminate it.
127 | 0.7 | 88

3179 房屋 [房屋] /fángwū/ (3) *n* house
车库在房屋后面。 The garage is at the back of the house.
117 | 0.76 | 88

3180 人心 [人心] /rénxīn/ (3) *n* public feeling, public sentiment
人心大快。 The public sentiment is satisfied.
103 | 0.86 | 88

3181 作风 [作風] /zuòfēng/ (3) *n* style
他的作风民主。 He has a democratic work style.
151 | 0.58 | 88

3182 决策 [決策] /juécè/ *n* policy decision; decision making
优秀的领导者必须善于决策。 A good excutive must be good at decision making.
154 | 0.57 | 88

3183 移民 [移民] /yímín/ *n* migrant, immigrant, emigrant; immigration
英国人占澳洲移民人口的14%。 The British account for 14 per cent of the immigrant population in Australia.
146 | 0.6 | 88

3184 劲儿 [勁兒] /jìnr/ *n* strength; drive, vigour, zeal
他使出浑身劲儿来推。 He pushed with all his strength.
140 | 0.63 | 88

3185 面子 [面子] /miànzi/ *n* face, reputation; sensibilities
他怕丢面子。 He was afraid of losing face.
138 | 0.64 | 88

3186 尾 [尾] /wěi/ *n* tail; end
在书尾有一个索引。 There is an index at the end of the book.
108 | 0.82 | 88

3187 对 [對] /duì/ (1) *v* answer; counter; be directed at; compare; suit, agree; match
现在来对答案。 Now, we'll check the answers.
197 | 0.45 | 88

3188 扶 [扶] /fú/ (2) v support or hold with hand
队友们扶着那位受伤的队员。Teammates supported the injured player.
157 | 0.57 | 88

3189 积累 [積累] /jīlěi/ (2) v accumulate
他积累起了大量财富。He accumulated great wealth.
129 | 0.69 | 88

3190 敲 [敲] /qiāo/ (2) v knock, tap; strike; fleece
谁在敲窗户？Who's that tapping at the window?
135 | 0.66 | 88

3191 描写 [描寫] /miáoxiě/ (2) v describe, portray
父亲在这部戏剧里被描写成一个懦弱的人。The father is portrayed as a coward in this play.
147 | 0.6 | 88

3192 进口 [進口] /jìnkǒu/ (2) v import
我们已经进口了很多技术。Many techniques have been imported.
198 | 0.45 | 88

3193 蒙 [蒙] /mēng, méng/ (3) v deceive, take in; be shocked; make a wild guess; cover
我简直蒙了。I got a terrible shock.
103 | 0.86 | 88

3194 服 [服] /fú/ (3) v take (medicine); be convinced, obey
这种药每日服两次。Take this medicine twice a day.
114 | 0.77 | 88

3195 拼 [拼] /pīn/ (3) v piece together, join; spell; go all out
这个帘子是用两幅布料拼成的。Two widths of cloth were joined to make the curtain.
102 | 0.87 | 88

3196 预防 [預防] /yùfáng/ (3) v prevent, secure against
联合国如何预防冲突？What is the UN doing to prevent conflicts?
141 | 0.63 | 88

3197 讲究 [講究] /jiǎngjiù/ (3) v be careful about; strive for
他十分讲究外表。He is extremely careful about his appearance.
122 | 0.73 | 88

3198 证实 [證實] /zhèngshí/ (3) v confirm, prove
这已为经验所证实。It is confirmed by experience.
104 | 0.85 | 88

3199 受伤 [受傷] /shòushāng/ v hurt, be wounded, be injured
我的腿受伤了。My leg hurts.
111 | 0.8 | 88

3200 命 [命] /mìng/ v command, order
随即命人抬来一口大瓮。He then ordered his subordinates to bring a big vat.
120 | 0.74 | 88

3201 不幸 [不幸] /búxìng/ (2) adj unfortunate, unlucky
我多不幸啊！How unfortunate I was!
104 | 0.84 | 87

3202 老实 [老實] /lǎoshí/ (2) adj honest
他一向忠诚老实。He is always honest.
194 | 0.45 | 87

3203 艰苦 [艱苦] /jiānkǔ/ (2) adj difficult, hard
看来他不愿做艰苦的工作。He seems to be averse to hard work.
121 | 0.73 | 87

3204 只是 [只是] /zhǐshì/ (2) conj except that, but
它可以用，只是太长了。That will do except that it is too long.
117 | 0.75 | 87

3205 与此同时 [與此同時] /yǔcǐtóngshí/ conj meanwhile
与此同时我们继续进行调查。Meanwhile we continued our investigations.
157 | 0.56 | 87

3206 渐 [漸] /jiàn/ (3) adv gradually
天色渐暗。It was gradually getting dark.
176 | 0.5 | 87

3207 布 [布] /bù/ (1) n cloth
这块布摸上去毛茸茸的。This cloth has a warm, woolly feel.
109 | 0.8 | 87

3208 师傅 [師傅] /shīfu/ (1) n master worker, teacher; [used as a respectful term of address for a skilled worker, or as a polite form of address for a stranger]
为恶不用师傅教。Vice is learnt without a master.
126 | 0.7 | 87

3209 博物馆 [博物館] /bówùguǎn/ (3) n museum
博物馆还展出了中国特有的珍奇动、植物。The museum also shows rare plants and animals found only in China.
137 | 0.64 | 87

3210 怀 [懷] /huái/ (3) n (in) one's arms, bosom; mind
她对着怀里的孩子轻声低语。She murmured softly to the baby in her arms.
179 | 0.49 | 87

3211 上帝 [上帝] /shàngdì/ (3) n God
在上帝面前我发誓我是无辜的。Before God I swear I am innocent.
124 | 0.7 | 87

3212 戏剧 [戲劇] /xìjù/ (3) n drama, play
他正在学习戏剧。He is studying drama.
141 | 0.62 | 87

3213 同胞 [同胞] /tóngbāo/ (3) n fellow countryman, compatriot
我愿与更多的同胞分享这份喜悦之情。I'd like to share the happiness with more of my fellow countrymen.
240 | 0.36 | 87

3214 差异 [差異] /chāyì/ n difference
他的早期作品和后期作品之间有明显的差异。There is a notable difference between his earlier and later writing.
132 | 0.66 | 87

3215 请问 [請問] /qǐngwèn/ (1) v [used as a polite expression when asking for information] may I ask ...
请问，我到市商业区乘哪辆车？Could you please tell me which bus I should take to go downtown?
152 | 0.57 | 87 | S

3216 搁 [擱] /gē/ (2) v place, put; put aside
就把它们搁在那处的墙边。Just put them there against the wall.
151 | 0.58 | 87 | S

3217 保卫 [保衛] /bǎowèi/ (2) v guard, defend
许多年青人服兵役保卫国家。Many young men enter the service to defend the country.
114 | 0.77 | 87

3218 议论 [議論] /yìlùn/ (2) v remark on, comment on
议论一位女士的外貌是不礼貌的。It would be rude to remark on a lady's appearance.
105 | 0.83 | 87

3219 迎接 [迎接] /yíngjiē/ (2) v meet, welcome, usher in
她热情地迎接客人。She welcomed the visitors warmly.
158 | 0.55 | 87

3220 动员 [動員] /dòngyuán/ (2) v mobilise
学生们很快就动员起来了。The students mobilised quickly.
125 | 0.7 | 87

3221 联络 [聯絡] /liánluò/ (3) v get or keep in contact or liaison
我昨天无法和你联络上。I was not able to get in touch with you yesterday.
124 | 0.71 | 87

3222 传来 [傳來] /chuánlái/ v (news, sound, etc.) come
这声音是从哪儿传来的？Where did that voice come from?
174 | 0.51 | 87

3223 超越 [超越] /chāoyuè/ v surmount, surpass; overtake
那辆汽车一加速就超越了我。The car accelerated as it overtook me.
112 | 0.78 | 87

3224 明白 [明白] /míngbái/ (3) adj clear, explicit; sensible
答案是很明白的。The answer is obvious.
124 | 0.7 | 86

3225 荣 [榮] /róng/ adj proud; glorious; prosperous
你以你的行为为荣吗？Are you proud of your deed?
146 | 0.59 | 86

3226 一向 [一向] /yíxiàng/ (3) adv all along, always
你一向用左手写字吗？Do you always write left-handed?
134 | 0.64 | 86

3227 最为 [最為] /zuìwéi/ adv most
这是最为要紧的一点。That was the most important thing.
127 | 0.68 | 86

3228 脖子 [脖子] /bózi/ (2) n neck
把围巾围在你的脖子上。Wrap a scarf round your neck.
159 | 0.55 | 86

3229 上级 [上級] /shàngjí/ (2) n higher authorities, superior; upper level
她对上级非常谦恭。She is very humble towards her superiors.
105 | 0.83 | 86

3230 洪水 [洪水] /hóngshuǐ/ (3) n flood
我们为避开洪水得绕道而行。We had to make a detour round the floods.
132 | 0.66 | 86

3231 影片 [影片] /yǐngpiàn/ (3) n film, movie
影片的构思相当巧妙。The plot of the film is ingeniously conceived.
119 | 0.73 | 86

3232 料 [料] /liào/ (3) n material; (animal) feed
这件上衣连工带料合多少钱？How much will this coat cost, including material and tailoring?
112 | 0.77 | 86

3233 主角 [主角] /zhǔjué/ n leading role
这位女主角似乎有点呆板。The leading lady seems a little stiff.
101 | 0.86 | 86

3234 双手 [雙手] /shuāngshǒu/ n both hands
他紧紧地握住我的双手。He held my hands firmly.
201 | 0.43 | 86

3235 福利 [福利] /fúlì/ n welfare, benefit
这些都是涉及社会福利的问题。These are matters that bear on the welfare of the community.
132 | 0.66 | 86

3236 扫 [掃] /sǎo/ (2) v sweep (away), brush; pass quickly, glance
她的长裙扫过地板。Her long skirt brushed the floor.
139 | 0.62 | 86

3237 灭 [滅] /miè/ (2) v (of fire, light) go off; extinguish, put out, wipe out
风把腊烛吹灭了。The wind blew the candles out.
110 | 0.78 | 86

3238 脱离 [脫離] /tuōlí/ (2) v leave, separate; break away from, divorce
他现在已经脱离危险了。He is now out of danger.
105 | 0.83 | 86

3239 出门 [出門] /chūmén/ (3) v go out, be away from home
她出门之前仔细地整了整衣服和头发。She carefully adjusted her clothes and her hair before going out.
139 | 0.62 | 86

3240 调动 [調動] /diàodòng/ (3) v transfer, shift, move; bring ... into play
我弟弟要求调动工作。My brother has asked for a transfer.
130 | 0.67 | 86

21. Chinese zodiac signs

1	鼠	鼠	*shǔ*	rat
2	牛	牛	*niú*	ox
3	虎	虎	*hǔ*	tiger
4	兔	兔	*tù*	rabbit
5	龙	龍	*lóng*	dragon
6	蛇	蛇	*shé*	snake
7	马	馬	*mǎ*	horse
8	羊	羊	*yáng*	sheep
9	猴	猴	*hóu*	monkey
10	鸡	雞	*jī*	rooster
11	狗	狗	*gǒu*	dog
12	猪	豬	*zhū*	pig

3241 扬 [揚] /*yáng*/ (3) *v* raise; spread
汽车开过时扬起一阵尘土。 The car raised a cloud of dust as it rushed past.
211 | 0.41 | 86

3242 判 [判] /*pàn*/ *v* sentence; judge
抢劫犯被判十年监禁。 The robber was sentenced to ten years' imprisonment.
96 | 0.9 | 86

3243 饱 [飽] /*bǎo*/ (1) *adj* full
不用，谢谢，我已经吃饱了。 No, thanks, I'm full.
110 | 0.78 | 85

3244 光 [光] /*guāng*/ (2) *adj* used up; (of surface) smooth, polished; bare, naked
水漏光了。 All the water has leaked out.
116 | 0.74 | 85

3245 原始 [原始] /*yuánshǐ*/ (3) *adj* primitive, primeval; (of data) original, firsthand
因为有些原始数据丢了，必须重做实验。 It was necessary to repeat the experiments because some of the original data had been lost.
126 | 0.68 | 85

3246 陌生 [陌生] /*mòshēng*/ (3) *adj* strange, unfamiliar
他站在一条陌生的街道上。 He stood in a strange street.
123 | 0.69 | 85

3247 一级 [一級] /*yìjí*/ *adj* first rate, first class, first degree
大气环境质量达到国家环境质量一级标准。 The atmospheric environment there has attained the state's first-level quality.
117 | 0.73 | 85

3248 哪怕 [哪怕] /*nǎpà*/ (2) *conj* even if, even though
哪怕是一个很小的缺点，我们也得注意改正。 Even if it is a small mistake, we should try to correct it.
115 | 0.75 | 85

3249 哟 [喲] /*yo*/ (3) *interj* [interjection expressing surprise] oh, well
哟，你真吓了我一跳！ Well, you do surprise me!
173 | 0.5 | 85 | S

3250 大批 [大批] /*dàpī*/ (2) *num* large quantities
那项比赛吸引了大批观众。 The match attracted a large crowd.
121 | 0.71 | 85

3251 苹果 [蘋果] /*píngguǒ*/ (1) *n* apple
她挑了一个最好的苹果。 She picked out the best apple.
97 | 0.88 | 85

3252 车站 [車站] /*chēzhàn*/ (1) *n* (bus or railway) station
他住在车站附近的旅馆里。 He lived in a hotel near the station.
91 | 0.94 | 85

3253 口号 [口號] /*kǒuhào*/ (2) *n* slogan
这个口号应当宣传。 This slogan should be publicised.
111 | 0.77 | 85

3254 季节 [季節] /*jìjié*/ (2) *n* season
秋天是收获的季节。 Autumn is a reaping season.
104 | 0.83 | 85

3255 奖金 [獎金] /*jiǎngjīn*/ (3) *n* bonus
奖金与生产率挂钩。 Bonus payment is linked to productivity.
118 | 0.73 | 85

3256 梦想 [夢想] /*mèngxiǎng*/ (3) *n* dream, dream hope; vain hope
我的梦想在不久的将来会成为现实的。 My dream will be realised in the near future.
132 | 0.65 | 85

3257 村民 [村民] /*cūnmín*/ *n* villager
该村村民吃井水。 The villagers get their water from a well.
190 | 0.45 | 85 | W

3258 台阶 [臺階] /táijiē/ n step; [figuratively] way out
你走到地下室去时要当心台阶。Mind the steps when you go down into the cellar.
106 | 0.81 | 85

3259 岁月 [歲月] /suìyuè/ n time; years (of one's life)
岁月冲淡了他的忧伤。Time had dulled the edge of his grief.
99 | 0.87 | 85

3260 纪录 [紀錄] /jìlù/ n record
她决心要打破世界纪录。She will attempt to beat the world record.
232 | 0.37 | 85

3261 此后 [此後] /cǐhòu/ time hence, hereafter
此后，我们成了好朋友。Hence we became good friends.
121 | 0.71 | 85

3262 争论 [爭論] /zhēnglùn/ (2) v argue, debate
两个人在激烈地争论。Two men were deep in argument.
110 | 0.78 | 85

3263 藏 [藏] /cáng/ (2) v hide
你这个小淘气，把我的书藏到哪里去了？Where have you hidden my book, you little mischief?
103 | 0.83 | 85

3264 抄 [抄] /chāo/ (2) v copy
请你把这个材料照抄一份。Please make a copy of this material.
133 | 0.64 | 85

3265 深入 [深入] /shēnrù/ (2) v penetrate deeply, go deep into
我实在没机会深入你们的社会。I don't really have a chance to go deep into your society.
183 | 0.47 | 85

3266 喂 [喂] /wèi/ (2) v feed
你喂喂猫好吗？Can you feed the cat?
144 | 0.59 | 85 | S

3267 寻求 [尋求] /xúnqiú/ v seek, look for
谈判双方正寻求和平解决争端的办法。Negotiators are looking for a peaceful settlement to the dispute.
125 | 0.68 | 85

3268 退出 [退出] /tuìchū/ v withdraw, drop out of
他不能继续下去而退出了比赛。He could not keep up and dropped out of the race.
102 | 0.84 | 85

3269 自杀 [自殺] /zìshā/ v commit suicide
他差点自杀了。He came close to committing suicide.
112 | 0.77 | 85

3270 开车 [開車] /kāichē/ v drive (a car)
他酩酊大醉，没法开车回家。He was too drunk to drive home.
114 | 0.75 | 85

3271 脏 [髒] /zāng/ (1) adj dirty
我的鞋子脏了。My shoes were dirty.
114 | 0.74 | 85

3272 平常 [平常] /píngcháng/ (2) adj ordinary, common
我不过是一个平常的人，跟你一样的人。I'm just an ordinary person, the same as everyone else.
109 | 0.77 | 84

3273 失望 [失望] /shīwàng/ (2) adj disappointed
他拒绝参加我们的聚会，令人非常失望。His refusal to come to our party was most disappointing.
128 | 0.66 | 84

3274 兴奋 [興奮] /xīngfèn/ (2) adj excited
我们都为这消息感到兴奋。We were all excited by the news.
125 | 0.68 | 84

3275 完美 [完美] /wánměi/ adj perfect, flawless
这幅画并非完美无缺。The painting isn't flawless.
112 | 0.76 | 84

3276 通常 [通常] /tōngcháng/ (3) adv usually
晚上我通常在家。I am usually at home in the evening.
136 | 0.62 | 84

3277 整天 [整天] /zhěngtiān/ adv all day long
我整天不停地打喷嚏。I can't help sneezing all day.
112 | 0.75 | 84

3278 叔叔 [叔叔] /shūshu/ (2) n uncle; [also used as a polite term of address for men of one's parents' age]
她从她叔叔那儿得到很多油画。She got a lot of paintings from her uncle.
150 | 0.56 | 84

3279 奇迹 [奇跡] /qíjī/ (3) n miracle
我们能够及时赶到，这简直是奇迹。It was a positive miracle that we arrived on time.
106 | 0.8 | 84

3280 列车 [列車] /lièchē/ (3) n train
76 次列车是在哪个站台？Which platform is it for train 76?
124 | 0.68 | 84

3281 正义 [正義] /zhèngyì/ (3) n justice
让正义作我们奋斗的目标吧。Let justice be our objective.
103 | 0.82 | 84

3282 传 [傳] /zhuàn/ n biography
所以就我个人来说，我从来不赞成给我写传。Personally, I have all along rejected offers to write my biography.
101 | 0.84 | 84

3283 同行 [同行] /tóngháng/ n peer; profession
她是同行的光荣。She is an honour to her profession.
98 | 0.86 | 84

3284 老年人 [老年人] /lǎoniánrén/ n old people, the aged
帮助老年人是一种美德。Helping the old is a virtue.
114 | 0.74 | 84

3285 行 [行] /háng/ (3) *clas* [measure word for things arranged in a line or row] line; row
站成三行。Stand in three lines.
91 | 0.93 | 84

3286 咋 [咋] /ză/ *pron* how, why
你咋不知道呢？Why don't you know?
196 | 0.43 | 84

3287 度过 [度過] /dùguò/ (2) *v* pass, spend (time)
她平静地度过了晚年。She lived the remainder of her life in peace.
97 | 0.87 | 84

3288 想像 [想像] /xiăngxiàng/ (2) *v* imagine
谁能想像得到？Who would have imagined it?
122 | 0.69 | 84

3289 告别 [告別] /gàobié/ (2) *v* leave, say goodbye to
他们挥手告别。They waved farewell.
101 | 0.83 | 84

3290 感染 [感染] /gănrăn/ *v* infect; affect
男子更容易感染疾病。Males are affected more by disease.
104 | 0.81 | 84

3291 决 [決] /jué/ *v* decide; (of a dam or dyke) burst
我们打了一场决胜负的战争。We fought a decisive battle.
107 | 0.79 | 84

3292 施 [施] /shī/ *v* impose, exert, carry out; use, apply; give, bestow
我们断定他对汽车施了魔法。We came to the conclusion that he had put a hex on the cars.
99 | 0.86 | 84

3293 有名 [有名] /yŏumíng/ (1) *adj* famous
她年轻时是个有名的美人。She was a famous beauty in her youth.
115 | 0.73 | 83

3294 直 [直] /zhí/ (2) *adj* straight; straightforward, frank
他弄直了一段铁丝。He straightened a piece of wire.
113 | 0.74 | 83

3295 富裕 [富裕] /fùyù/ (3) *adj* affluent, well off
他家不太富裕。His family is not very well off.
119 | 0.7 | 83

3296 佳 [佳] /jiā/ (3) *adj* good, excellent
钓鱼是一种极佳的休假方式。Fishing is a marvellous way of spending a day off.
120 | 0.69 | 83

3297 不安 [不安] /bù'ān/ (3) *adj* uneasy
我很不安。I feel very uneasy.
130 | 0.64 | 83

3298 浪漫 [浪漫] /làngmàn/ *adj* romantic
这真是个浪漫的假期。This was a really romantic holiday.
120 | 0.7 | 83

3299 不然 [不然] /bùrán/ (2) *conj* otherwise, or
快点儿吧，不然就要迟到了。Come along or we'll be late.
149 | 0.56 | 83

3300 大声 [大聲] /dàshēng/ (1) *adv* loudly
他大声地读课文。He read the text loudly.
162 | 0.52 | 83

3301 窗 [窗] /chuāng/ (1) *n* window
我们可以坐在靠窗的位置吗？Can we sit by the window?
143 | 0.58 | 83

3302 笑话 [笑話] /xiàohuà/ (2) *n* joke
我认为他讲的笑话太粗俗了。I thought his jokes were in very poor taste.
117 | 0.72 | 83

3303 山区 [山區] /shānqū/ (2) *n* mountain area
他住在山区。He lives in a mountainous district.
168 | 0.5 | 83

3304 盐 [鹽] /yán/ (2) *n* salt
请把盐和胡椒递给我。Please pass me the salt and pepper.
177 | 0.47 | 83

3305 逻辑 [邏輯] /luóji/ (3) *n* logic
这种逻辑是十分荒谬的。This kind of logic is quite ridiculous.
130 | 0.64 | 83

3306 经费 [經費] /jīngfèi/ (3) *n* funding
学校经费不足。The schools are short of funding.
141 | 0.59 | 83

3307 潮 [潮] /cháo/ (3) *n* tide; moist
潮退了。The tide ebbed away.
98 | 0.85 | 83

3308 酒店 [酒店] /jiŭdiàn/ (3) *n* hotel
旅游车可否到酒店接我？Can the bus pick me up at my hotel?
108 | 0.78 | 83

3309 主力 [主力] /zhŭlì/ (3) *n* main force, backbone
地方小团体是该党的主力。The small local groups are the backbone of the party.
123 | 0.68 | 83

3310 才能 [才能] /cáinéng/ (3) *n* talent
她显示了她烹饪的才能。She showed her talent for cooking.
113 | 0.74 | 83

3311 初中 [初中] /chūzhōng/ (3) *n* junior high school, secondary school
我当时在镇上读初中。I was studying in a secondary school in our town at that time.
98 | 0.86 | 83

3312 名称 [名稱] /míngchēng/ *n* name
这一产品非常成功，其名称已经家喻户晓。The product is so successful that its name has become a household word.
120 | 0.7 | 83

3313 团 [團] /tuán/ (2) *clas* [measure word for objects made into the shape of a ball] a ball of
一团泥糊在了他的肩上。A ball of mud caught him on the shoulder.
159 | 0.53 | 83

3314 深处 [深處] /shēnchù/ *place* depth; deepest or most distant part
有朝一日人类也许能在海洋深处生活。Humans may be able to live in the depth of the ocean some day.
106 | 0.79 | 83

3315 刮 [刮] /guā/ (1) *v* scrape; shave; (of wind) blow
进屋前先把鞋上的泥刮掉。Scrape all the mud off your shoes before you come in.
107 | 0.78 | 83

3316 上课 [上課] /shàngkè/ (1) *v* (of students) attend class; (of teachers) give a lesson
咱们快点走，免得上课迟到。Let's hurry so as not to be late for the class.
106 | 0.79 | 83

3317 带领 [帶領] /dàilǐng/ (3) *v* lead, guide
她带领人们游览这座城市。She guides people around the city.
128 | 0.65 | 83

3318 警告 [警告] /jǐnggào/ (3) *v* warn
我警告他不要走太远。I warned him not to go too far.
100 | 0.83 | 83

3319 置 [置] /zhì/ *v* put, place; buy
我们必须把过去的争论置于脑后。We must put the arguments of the past behind us.
107 | 0.78 | 83

3320 包装 [包裝] /bāozhuāng/ *v* pack, wrap up
请把它好好地包装起来。Please wrap it up carefully.
124 | 0.67 | 83

3321 看待 [看待] /kàndài/ *v* regard, view
他宁愿被当成普通工人看待。He preferred to be regarded as an ordinary worker.
97 | 0.86 | 83

3322 杀人 [殺人] /shārén/ *v* commit manslaughter, murder, kill
诽谤如暗箭，远处可杀人。Slander is compared to an arrow because it kills at a distance.
105 | 0.79 | 83

3323 引发 [引發] /yǐnfā/ *v* trigger, evoke
不慎重的政治行动能引发一场战争。Careless political action can trigger off a war.
109 | 0.77 | 83

3324 食 [食] /shí/ *v* eat
不劳动者不得食。Those who do not work will not eat.
129 | 0.65 | 83

3325 没事 [沒事] /méishì/ *v* be free; it's nothing, it's all right
我希望她没事。I hope she's all right.
146 | 0.57 | 83

3326 相似 [相似] /xiāngsì/ (2) *adj* similar
他们自己就曾有过相似的经历。They themselves have had a similar experience.
108 | 0.76 | 82

3327 乃至 [乃至] /nǎizhì/ *conj* even
他在性格上阴沉乃至抑郁。He is grave or even gloomy in character.
129 | 0.64 | 82

3328 即便 [即便] /jíbiàn/ *conj* even if
我即便听了他的解释，仍然不明白。Even after listening to his explanation I'm none the wiser.
114 | 0.72 | 82

3329 事先 [事先] /shìxiān/ (2) *adv* beforehand, in advance
哦，我非常感激你事先让我们知道此事。Well, I appreciate your letting us know this in advance.
97 | 0.85 | 82

3330 是的 [是的] /shìde/ (3) *idiom* yes
是的，你在终点站下车。Yes, you'll get off at the terminal.
140 | 0.59 | 82

3331 大夫 [大夫] /dàifu/ (1) *n* doctor, physician
你不请大夫来，他就要死了。He will certainly die if you don't call a doctor.
116 | 0.71 | 82

3332 阶级 [階級] /jiējí/ (2) *n* (social) class
我们现在就来分析一下中国社会的各阶级。Let us now analyse the different classes in Chinese society.
179 | 0.46 | 82

3333 邻居 [鄰居] /línjū/ (2) *n* neighbour
他一向是个好邻居。He has always been a good neighbour.
98 | 0.84 | 82

3334 沙漠 [沙漠] /shāmò/ (2) *n* desert
沙漠里植物稀少。There is little vegetation in the desert.
122 | 0.68 | 82

3335 垃圾 [垃圾] /lājī/ (2) *n* rubbish, waste, trash; junk
废物和垃圾不许倒在公路上。No waste or garbage is to be emptied on highways.
105 | 0.78 | 82

3336 纪律 [紀律] /jìlǜ/ (2) *n* discipline
这就是不守纪律！This is a violation of discipline.
133 | 0.62 | 82

3337 党委 [黨委] /dǎngwěi/ (3) *n* Party committee
这是各级党委的中心工作。This should be the central task of Party committees at all levels.
211 | 0.39 | 82 | W

3338 时机 [時機] /shíjī/ (3) *n* opportunity, time, moment
你得等候适当的时机。You'll have to watch for the right moment.
108 | 0.76 | 82

3339 差别 [差別] /chābié/ (3) n difference
这种差别即使存在也是微不足道的。
The difference, if it exists, is extremely tenuous.
104 | 0.8 | 82

3340 货物 [貨物] /huòwù/ (3) n goods
这些货物与我的订货单不符。These goods do not correspond with my order.
161 | 0.51 | 82

3341 岩 [岩] /yán/ n rock, cliff
攀岩运动能考验人的勇气和技巧。Rock-climbing is a test of nerve and skill.
115 | 0.71 | 82

3342 联邦 [聯邦] /liánbāng/ n federation, commonwealth
联邦赤字会引起通货膨胀。Federal deficits can cause inflation.
177 | 0.47 | 82

3343 理性 [理性] /lǐxìng/ n reason
理性是人的特点。Reason defines man.
133 | 0.62 | 82

3344 客气 [客氣] /kèqi/ (1) v be polite; be courteous; act politely; be modest
请不要客气。Please don't stand on ceremony.
153 | 0.54 | 82

3345 采购 [採購] /cǎigòu/ (2) v purchase; do shopping
我们星期六去采购东西。We do our shopping on Saturdays.
183 | 0.45 | 82 | W

3346 刻 [刻] /kè/ (2) v cut, carve, inscribe
我认不出刻在柱子上的是什么。
I can't decipher what is inscribed on the pillar.
93 | 0.89 | 82

3347 考验 [考驗] /kǎoyàn/ (3) v try, test, put to test
事业造就人，也能考验人。Business makes a man as well as tries him.
106 | 0.78 | 82

3348 转化 [轉化] /zhuǎnhuà/ (3) v transform, change into
电能可以转化为光能。Electric energy can be changed into light energy.
147 | 0.56 | 82

3349 撤 [撤] /chè/ (3) v remove; withdraw, evacuate, retreat
火山爆发处附近已迅速撤空。The region near the erupting volcano was rapidly evacuated.
98 | 0.84 | 82

3350 承包 [承包] /chéngbāo/ (3) v contract
这个村的农民今年承包了 5,000 亩农田。
The farmers of this village have contracted for 5,000 mu of farmland.
126 | 0.66 | 82

3351 予以 [予以] /yǔyǐ/ v give, bestow
敬请及早予以安排。Please give the matter your early attention.
148 | 0.55 | 82

3352 讨厌 [討厭] /tǎoyàn/ v dislike, hate
我实在讨厌让我等着。I really hate being kept waiting.
142 | 0.58 | 82

3353 光荣 [光榮] /guāngróng/ (2) adj glorious, honoured, proud
这是一项光荣的任务。It is a glorious task.
101 | 0.81 | 81

3354 纯 [純] /chún/ (3) adj pure
另外，这是纯羊毛的，手感柔和。Besides, it's made of pure wool, very soft.
97 | 0.84 | 81

3355 偶然 [偶然] /ǒurán/ (3) adv incidentally, by chance; occasionally
我偶然遇到了他。I met him by chance.
108 | 0.76 | 81

3356 系统 [系統] /xìtǒng/ adj systematic
对公众关心的事件作了系统的调查。
A systematic investigation was made into matters of public interest.
129 | 0.63 | 81

3357 良 [良] /liáng/ adj good
金属是热的良导体，因为热容易通过。
Metals are good heat conductors because heat goes through them easily.
111 | 0.73 | 81

3358 南部 [南部] /nánbù/ (2) loc southern part, south
中国南部多雨。The south of China is rainy.
142 | 0.58 | 81

3359 篮球 [籃球] /lánqiú/ (1) n basketball
她也会打篮球，也会打网球。She can play tennis as well as basketball.
110 | 0.74 | 81

3360 记录 [記錄] /jìlù/ (2) n record; (of meeting) minutes
他以创记录的时间跑完100米。He ran the 100 metres in record time.
105 | 0.77 | 81

3361 母 [母] /mǔ/ (2) n mother, parent
失败为成功之母。Failure is the mother of success.
108 | 0.75 | 81

3362 故乡 [故鄉] /gùxiāng/ (2) n hometown, native place
她一生从未离开过故乡。She passed her life within the confines of her native place.
91 | 0.9 | 81

3363 劲 [勁] /jìn/ (2) n [often as 劲儿] strength; effort; drive, vigour, zeal; interest, relish
这时他浑身是劲。At the moment he was all energy.
119 | 0.69 | 81

3364 信念 [信念] /xìnniàn/ (3) n faith, belief
他按照自己的信念行事。He acted in accordance with his beliefs.
124 | 0.65 | 81

3365 难题 [難題] /nántí/ (3) n difficult problem
他们的确有难题。They have quite a problem.
113 | 0.72 | 81

3366 胡同 [胡同] /hútóng/ (3) *n* lane, alley
这条胡同不通。 This is a blind alley.
121 | 0.67 | 81

3367 技巧 [技巧] /jìqiǎo/ (3) *n* skill, technique
技巧有时可以弥补力量的不足。 Skill sometimes compensates for lack of strength.
136 | 0.6 | 81

3368 规矩 [規矩] /guīju/ (3) *n* rule, custom; manners
请您别忘了规矩。 Please remember your manners.
115 | 0.71 | 81

3369 气质 [氣質] /qìzhì/ *n* temperament; quality
他是个有艺术家气质的男子。 He is a man with an artistic temperament.
118 | 0.69 | 81

3370 论坛 [論壇] /lùntán/ *n* forum, tribune
这份报纸的读者来信栏是公众意见的论坛。 The letters page of this newspaper is a forum for public argument.
182 | 0.45 | 81

3371 当局 [當局] /dāngjú/ *n* the authorities
我们应该看看当局怎么说。 We must see what the authorities have to say.
178 | 0.46 | 81

3372 智力 [智力] /zhìlì/ *n* intelligence
这些儿童在智力上大致相同。 In intelligence, the children are about equal.
105 | 0.77 | 81

3373 尸体 [屍體] /shītǐ/ *n* body, corpse
那具尸体已冲到海里。 The body was washed out to sea.
91 | 0.9 | 81

3374 董事长 [董事長] /dǒngshìzhǎng/ *n* chairperson of the board (of directors)
董事长有决定性的一票。 The chairman has the casting vote.
127 | 0.64 | 81

3375 首脑 [首腦] /shǒunǎo/ *n* head (of state or government); summit (meeting)
他已经就任该党首脑。 He has got into office as the head of the party.
192 | 0.43 | 81

3376 彩 [彩] /cǎi/ *n* colour, coloured
她用彩纸把礼物包起来。 She wrapped the gift up in coloured paper.
93 | 0.88 | 81

3377 古人 [古人] /gǔrén/ *n* ancient people
今人能从古人的智慧中得到很多的启发。 Modern people can benefit greatly from the wisdom of the ancients.
125 | 0.65 | 81

3378 登记 [登記] /dēngjì/ (2) *v* register; check in (at hotel, etc.)
请把您所带的外币登记一下，好吗？ Will you please make a record of all your foreign currency?
121 | 0.67 | 81

3379 回头 [回頭] /huítóu/ (2) *v* turn round
回头走，到红绿灯右转弯。 Turn round and turn right at the traffic light.
145 | 0.56 | 81

3380 打听 [打聽] /dǎtīng/ (2) *v* ask about, enquire
最好是先去打听打听。 Better make some enquiries first.
120 | 0.68 | 81

3381 撒 [撒] /sā, sǎ/ (2) *v* sprinkle, spray, scatter, spread; cast, let go, let out; spill
她在胸前撒上了香水。 She sprayed perfume over her chest.
100 | 0.82 | 81

3382 锁 [鎖] /suǒ/ (3) *v* lock (up)
我把钥匙锁在房间里了。 I locked the keys in my room.
110 | 0.74 | 81

3383 寻 [尋] /xún/ (3) *v* look for, seek
他正在寻你。 He is looking for you.
111 | 0.74 | 81

3384 招 [招] /zhāo/ (3) *v* beckon; enrol, recruit; provoke; confess
别招他生气。 Don't provoke his anger.
112 | 0.73 | 81

3385 展现 [展現] /zhǎnxiàn/ *v* unfold, present
那景色展现在我们面前。 The landscape unfolded before us.
95 | 0.86 | 81

3386 启动 [啟動] /qǐdòng/ *v* start, initiate
我重新启动了汽车，直奔家中。 I started the car again, and we drove home.
155 | 0.52 | 81

3387 治理 [治理] /zhìlǐ/ *v* govern; harness
有人认为社会应该由精英分子治理。 It has been argued that society should be governed by an elite group of individuals.
219 | 0.37 | 81

3388 花钱 [花錢] /huāqián/ *v* spend money
那又得花钱。 That meant spending money.
101 | 0.81 | 81

3389 辛苦 [辛苦] /xīnkǔ/ (1) *adj* hard, painstaking
评阅试卷是一件很辛苦的工作。 Marking exam papers was quite a job.
103 | 0.79 | 80

3390 骄傲 [驕傲] /jiāo'ào/ (2) *adj* proud; arrogant
我们并没有什么东西值得骄傲。 We have nothing to be proud of.
101 | 0.8 | 80

3391 显著 [顯著] /xiǎnzhù/ (2) *adj* remarkable, outstanding
科学有了显著的进步。 Science has made remarkable progress.
185 | 0.44 | 80

3392 遥远 [遙遠] /yáoyuǎn/ (3) *adj* far away, remote, distant
星星太遥远了。 The stars are too far away.
89 | 0.91 | 80

3393 随意 [隨意] /suíyì/ *adj* random, arbitrary; voluntary, as one pleases
我的选择相当随意。 My choice was quite arbitrary.
94 | 0.85 | 80

3394 周 [周] /zhōu/ adj considerate, thoughtful; careful
我考虑不周，没有给你写封信。It is very thoughtless of me; I should have written you a letter.
112 | 0.72 | 80

3395 精心 [精心] /jīngxīn/ adv with utmost care; meticulously
它们的食物得精心准备。Their food has to be prepared with great care.
111 | 0.73 | 80

3396 力气 [力氣] /lìqì/ (2) n strength
我没有力气抬这张桌子。I haven't the strength to lift this table.
118 | 0.68 | 80

3397 煤 [煤] /méi/ (2) n coal
煤燃烧时产生热量。When coal burns, it generates heat.
107 | 0.76 | 80

3398 军官 [軍官] /jūnguān/ (3) n (military) officer
士兵们必须执行军官的命令。The soldiers must follow the officer's orders.
110 | 0.73 | 80

3399 景象 [景象] /jǐngxiàng/ (3) n scene, sight
到处呈现一片兴旺景象。Everywhere is a scene of prosperity.
87 | 0.93 | 80

3400 力度 [力度] /lìdù/ n dynamism, vigour, strength
扩大内需必须加大力度。Expansion of domestic demand should be strengthened.
261 | 0.31 | 80

3401 荣誉 [榮譽] /róngyù/ n honour
军人应该视荣誉重于生命吗？Should a soldier value honour above life?
114 | 0.71 | 80

3402 遭受 [遭受] /zāoshòu/ (2) v suffer
我们如何补偿你所遭受的损害？How can we make up to you for what you have suffered?
114 | 0.71 | 80

3403 动手 [動手] /dòngshǒu/ (2) v set out, start; use hand (to fight or touch)
请勿动手！No touching!
113 | 0.71 | 80

3404 援助 [援助] /yuánzhù/ (3) v provide help, aid or support
他们投票建议援助亚洲的不发达国家。They voted aid for the underdeveloped countries in Asia.
176 | 0.46 | 80

3405 安 [安] /ān/ (3) v fix, install, set up; be contented
他在围墙的开口处安了一扇门。He put a gate across the opening in the fence.
93 | 0.86 | 80

3406 赶上 [趕上] /gǎnshàng/ (3) v catch up with
她决定努力学习以便赶上别人。She decided to work harder so as to catch up with the others.
111 | 0.73 | 80

3407 扯 [扯] /chě/ (3) v pull; tear (off, into pieces); chat
别扯我的头发！Don't pull my hair!
171 | 0.47 | 80

3408 打工 [打工] /dǎgōng/ v work (especially referring to doing odd jobs or manual labour)
我打算暑假去打工。I plan to find a part-time job this summer holiday.
88 | 0.91 | 80

3409 履行 [履行] /lǚxíng/ v fulfil
她不折不扣地履行了她的所有诺言。She carried out all her pledges to the letter.
154 | 0.52 | 80

3410 好看 [好看] /hǎokàn/ adj good-looking, beautiful
是的，它很好看。Yes, it is beautiful.
121 | 0.67 | 80

3411 设置 [設置] /shèzhì/ v set, set up
警察设置了路障捉拿逃犯。Roadblocks were set up by the police to catch the escaped prisoner.
123 | 0.65 | 80

3412 透露 [透露] /tòulù/ v reveal, disclose
我不想透露他们的姓名。I have no intention of disclosing their names.
160 | 0.51 | 80

3413 黑暗 [黑暗] /hēi'àn/ (2) adj dark
天空非常黑暗。The sky is very dark.
112 | 0.71 | 79

3414 痛 [痛] /tòng/ adv bitterly; severely, thoroughly
那位冠军痛击他的对手。The champion punished his opponent severely.
131 | 0.61 | 79

3415 鸡蛋 [雞蛋] /jīdàn/ (1) n (chicken) egg
我需要一个鸡蛋。I need an egg.
107 | 0.74 | 79

3416 顾问 [顧問] /gùwèn/ (3) n adviser, consultant
他被聘为顾问。He was invited as an adviser.
139 | 0.57 | 79

3417 灾难 [災難] /zāinàn/ (3) n disaster
在当时那就像是一场灾难。It seemed like a disaster at the time.
103 | 0.77 | 79

3418 倾向 [傾向] /qīngxiàng/ (3) n trend, tendency
这些倾向能不能克服呢？Can these tendencies be overcome?
119 | 0.67 | 79

3419 奶 [奶] /nǎi/ (3) n milk; breast
加糖和奶。With sugar and cream, please.
105 | 0.75 | 79

3420 爹 [爹] /diē/ (3) n dad, father
我爹也是教书的。My father was a teacher too.
169 | 0.47 | 79

3421 大厅 [大廳] /dàtīng/ n hall
她坐在大厅后排，听不清。She sat at the back of the hall and couldn't hear clearly.
98 | 0.81 | 79

22. Animals

龙	龍	*lóng*	dragon	918
马	馬	*mǎ*	horse	1008
狗	狗	*gǒu*	dog	1138
鸡	雞	*jī*	chicken, fowl	1353
猪	豬	*zhū*	hog, pig, swine	1700
羊	羊	*yáng*	sheep, goat	1868
猫	貓	*māo*	cat, kitty	2000
虎	虎	*hǔ*	tiger	2076
牛	牛	*niú*	ox, cow, bull	2217
狼	狼	*láng*	wolf	2813
蛇	蛇	*shé*	snake, serpent	3501
老鼠	老鼠	*lǎoshǔ*	rat, mouse	4049
鸭	鴨	*yā*	duck	4088
熊	熊	*xióng*	bear	4391
猴子	猴子	*hóuzi*	monkey	4468
狮子	獅子	*shīzi*	lion	4803
鹰	鷹	*yīng*	eagle, falcon, hawk	6799
长颈鹿	長頸鹿	*chángjǐnglù*	giraffe	6890
鹅	鵝	*é*	goose	6890
鸽子	鴿子	*gēzi*	pigeon	7530
鹿	鹿	*lù*	deer	7751
兔	兔	*tù*	rabbit	7998
鲨鱼	鯊魚	*shāyú*	shark	8016
龟	龜	*guī*	tortoise, turtle	8314
大象	大象	*dàxiàng*	elephant	9892
熊猫	熊貓	*xióngmāo*	panda	13622
大熊猫	大熊貓	*dà xióngmāo*	giant panda	14244
鹦鹉	鸚鵡	*yīngwǔ*	parrot	16968
黄牛	黃牛	*huángniú*	cow, ox	19653
金鱼	金魚	*jīnyú*	goldfish	21678
河马	河馬	*hémǎ*	hippopotamus	22406
驴子	驢子	*lǘzi*	ass, donkey	23581
鲸鱼	鯨魚	*jīngyú*	whale	25085
松鼠	松鼠	*sōngshǔ*	squirrel	27752
鳄鱼	鱷魚	*èyú*	crocodile	28107

3422 亲 [親] /*qīn*/ *n* parent, next of kin, relative; marriage
他们是我妈妈的双亲。 They are my mother's parents.
103 | 0.78 | 79

3423 影 [影] /*yǐng*/ *n* shadow, reflected image; trace; film
树影映在墙上。 The tree cast its shadow on the wall.
105 | 0.75 | 79

3424 家人 [家人] /*jiārén*/ *n* family member
还有比家人团聚更感人的场面吗？ Is there a sight more heartwarming than a family reunion?
94 | 0.84 | 79

3425 庄 [莊] /*zhuāng*/ *n* village, hamlet, farm; manor; place of business
庄上没有男孩子吗？ Are there no boys at the farm?
88 | 0.9 | 79

3426 刻 [刻] /kè/ (1) *clas* quarter (of an hour)
这样过了一刻钟。A quarter of an hour passed thus.
109 | 0.73 | 79

3427 收拾 [收拾] /shōushí/ (1) *v* sort out, put in order
请你先把办公桌收拾好再离开办公室。Please put your desk in order before you leave the office.
155 | 0.52 | 79

3428 闪 [閃] /shǎn/ (2) *v* flash, flicker; dodge
他心中仍闪出一线希望。A slender hope still flickered within him.
175 | 0.45 | 79

3429 痛 [痛] /tòng/ (2) *v* hurt, ache, pain
我在吃甜食时，我就感觉牙齿痛。When I eat sweet things I feel a pain in my teeth.
140 | 0.57 | 79

3430 跌 [跌] /diē/ (2) *v* fall; (price) drop
他脸朝下跌到沙子里。He fell face downwards in the sand.
109 | 0.73 | 79

3431 办理 [辦理] /bànlǐ/ (3) *v* handle
此事如何办理？How are we to handle this matter?
149 | 0.53 | 79

3432 描述 [描述] /miáoshù/ *v* describe, depict
这幅画描述了乡村生活。This scene depicts country life.
123 | 0.65 | 79

3433 瘦 [瘦] /shòu/ (2) *adj* thin, bony; (of clothes) tight; (of meat) lean
她现在比以前更瘦。She is thinner now than she was.
122 | 0.64 | 78

3434 静 [靜] /jìng/ (2) *adj* quiet; still, motionless
屋子里又黑又静。The room was dark and quiet.
111 | 0.71 | 78

3435 和谐 [和諧] /héxié/ *adj* harmonious, in harmony
这对夫妇生活得很和谐。The couple live together in harmony.
104 | 0.76 | 78

3436 虚 [虛] /xū/ *adj* empty; false; virtual; in poor health; timid
其结果证明是虚惊一场。It turned out to be a false alarm.
109 | 0.72 | 78

3437 最新 [最新] /zuìxīn/ *adj* latest
我想买一盘最新的流行歌带。I want to buy a tape of the latest pop songs.
144 | 0.55 | 78

3438 之际 [之際] /zhījì/ *loc* at the time when . . .
在弥留之际，他还想着孩子。When he was dying, he still thought of the children.
128 | 0.62 | 78

3439 绝大多数 [絕大多數] /juédàduōshù/ *num* vast majority
我想绝大多数人是拥护这个决定的。I think the overwhelming majority support this decision.
114 | 0.69 | 78

3440 皮肤 [皮膚] /pífū/ (2) *n* skin
她的皮肤像丝绸一样光滑。Her skin is as smooth as silk.
127 | 0.62 | 78

3441 地址 [地址] /dìzhǐ/ (2) *n* address
你知道这个地址在哪里？Do you know where this address is?
106 | 0.74 | 78

3442 粉 [粉] /fěn/ (3) *n* powder
该油漆以粉制品形式出售。The paint is sold in powdered form.
124 | 0.63 | 78

3443 阶层 [階層] /jiēcéng/ (3) *n* social stratum
他们代表各个社会阶层。They represent all social strata.
264 | 0.3 | 78 | W

3444 能量 [能量] /néngliàng/ (3) *n* energy
从风中可以吸取有用的能量。Usable energy can be extracted from winds.
98 | 0.8 | 78

3445 峰 [峰] /fēng/ *n* peak
黄山有著名的72峰。The Yellow Mountain has 72 famous peaks.
96 | 0.82 | 78

3446 民众 [民眾] /mínzhòng/ *n* populace, people
这封信声称是表达民众的意见。The letter purports to express people's opinion.
121 | 0.65 | 78

3447 老爷 [老爺] /lǎoye/ *n* lord, master; [equivalent of 姥爷] (maternal) grandfather; something old and worn out
总之，我们一些干部成了老爷就是了。In short, some of our cadres have become overlords.
139 | 0.57 | 78 | S

3448 基 [基] /jī/ *n* base, foundation
教育乃万业之基，这是毫无疑义的。There is no doubt that education is the foundation of all.
118 | 0.67 | 78

3449 幕 [幕] /mù/ *clas* [measure word for plays] act; scene
这是一部五幕剧。It's a play in five acts.
97 | 0.81 | 78

3450 周末 [週末] /zhōumò/ (3) *time* weekend
你周末都做什么？What do you do at the weekend?
84 | 0.93 | 78

3451 危害 [危害] /wēihài/ (2) *v* endanger, jeopardise
如果抽烟太多，会危害你的健康。You will endanger your health if you smoke too much.
120 | 0.65 | 78

3452 呼吸 [呼吸] /hūxī/ (2) *v* breathe
鱼离开水就不能呼吸。Fish cannot breathe
out of water.
109 | 0.72 | 78

3453 部署 [部署] /bùshǔ/ (3) *v* dispose, deploy
炮兵部署在西边。Artillery was deployed in
the west.
174 | 0.45 | 78

3454 抵 [抵] /dǐ/ (3) *v* reach, arrive; balance, be
equal to; make up for; resist
支出跟收入相抵。The expenses balance the
receipts.
101 | 0.78 | 78

3455 迷 [迷] /mí/ (3) *v* bewilder, confuse; be
fascinated by
他迷了路。He lost his way.
99 | 0.79 | 78

3456 播 [播] /bō/ (3) *v* sow, seed; broadcast
他们已经在油菜地里播了种。They seeded in
the field of rape.
103 | 0.76 | 78

3457 抗 [抗] /kàng/ *v* resist, fight; refuse, defy
他们制订了一个详细的抗旱计划。
They made a detailed plan to fight the
drought.
103 | 0.76 | 78

3458 期望 [期望] /qīwàng/ *v* expect, look forward
to
你期望有什么样的结果？What results did
you expect?
99 | 0.8 | 78

3459 拜 [拜] /bài/ *v* worship, pay respect; visit
她拜偶像吗？Does she worship idols?
90 | 0.87 | 78

3460 碎 [碎] /suì/ (2) *adj* broken
他们把玻璃窗打碎了。They broke the
window.
112 | 0.7 | 77

3461 之上 [之上] /zhīshàng/ (2) *loc* above
山峰在云层之上。The peak is above the
clouds.
98 | 0.79 | 77

3462 面貌 [面貌] /miànmào/ (2) *n* appearance,
feature; outlook, look
现在农村面貌一新。The countryside has
assumed a new look.
101 | 0.76 | 77

3463 领袖 [领袖] /lǐngxiù/ (2) *n* leader
大家都想让他当领袖。The people want him
as their leader.
105 | 0.74 | 77

3464 旅客 [旅客] /lǚkè/ (2) *n* passenger
她给旅客送水倒茶。She brought drinking
water and tea for the passengers.
136 | 0.57 | 77

3465 产量 [產量] /chǎnliàng/ (2) *n* output
由于需求量下降，公司削减了产量。
The company reduced output because of a
fall in demand.
182 | 0.42 | 77

3466 模样 [模樣] /múyàng/ (2) *n* appearance,
look; [used to indicate approximation]
about
他的模样显得是有罪的。His looks condemn
him.
133 | 0.58 | 77

3467 温度 [溫度] /wēndù/ (2) *n* temperature
明天的温度是多少？What's the temperature
going to be tomorrow?
106 | 0.73 | 77

3468 商人 [商人] /shāngrén/ (3) *n* business people,
merchant
他是镇上最有钱的商人。He is the richest
merchant in the town.
110 | 0.7 | 77

3469 地理 [地理] /dìlǐ/ (3) *n* geography
他地理学得很好。He is good at geography.
101 | 0.77 | 77

3470 浑身 [渾身] /húnshēn/ (3) *n* all over
比赛后我浑身疼痛。I'm aching all over after
the match.
140 | 0.56 | 77

3471 白色 [白色] /báisè/ *n* white colour
我们的厨房漆成了白色。Our kitchen is
painted white.
125 | 0.62 | 77

3472 眼神 [眼神] /yǎnshén/ *n* expression or emotion
shown in one's eyes
她以漫不经心的眼神打量他。She looked
through him with blank unseeing eyes.
152 | 0.51 | 77

3473 镜 [鏡] /jìng/ *n* mirror; glasses
湖平如镜。The lake is as smooth as a
mirror.
157 | 0.49 | 77

3474 节 [節] /jié/ (1) *clas* [measure word for a
section of things joined together such
as coaches of a train and sections of
a text]; [measure word for a period
of class time]
一天有几节课？How many classes do you
have every day?
94 | 0.82 | 77

3475 之 [之] /zhī/ (3) *pron* it, him, her, them
他不值得我与之较量。He's not worth my
while.
86 | 0.91 | 77

3476 翻译 [翻譯] /fānyì/ (1) *v* translate
他一字一句地翻译这篇文章。He translated
this article literally.
103 | 0.76 | 77

3477 不如 [不如] /bùrú/ (1) *v* be not as good as,
be inferior to
讲能力，我不如你。As to ability, I am not
your match.
99 | 0.79 | 77

3478 献 [獻] /xiàn/ (2) *v* offer, present;
dedicate
我要把这首歌献给我太太。I dedicate this
song to my wife.
97 | 0.8 | 77

3479 办公 [辦公] /bàn'gōng/ (2) v handle official business; open, work (in office)
银行星期日不办公。 Banks do not open on Sundays.
93 | 0.83 | 77

3480 拔 [拔] /bá/ (2) v pull up, pull out
那些钉子真难拔。 Those nails were real swines to pull out.
110 | 0.7 | 77

3481 庆祝 [慶祝] /qìngzhù/ (2) v celebrate
这需要庆祝一番。 This calls for a celebration.
134 | 0.58 | 77

3482 种 [種] /zhòng/ (2) v plant
山坡上种满了树。 The hillside was planted with trees.
86 | 0.9 | 77

3483 架 [架] /jià/ (3) v put up, set up; support
我们把帐篷架起来吧。 Let's set up the tent.
96 | 0.8 | 77

3484 泡 [泡] /pào/ (3) v steep, soak; dawdle
她喜欢泡在浴缸中。 She loves to soak in the bathtub.
102 | 0.76 | 77

3485 顺 [順] /shùn/ (3) v obey, yield to; put something in order
你不能一味顺着他。 You cannot just yield to him whatever it is that he desires.
124 | 0.63 | 77

3486 嫌 [嫌] /xián/ (3) v dislike, mind
你不嫌简陋，尽管来。 If you don't mind visiting a modest home, come by all means.
114 | 0.68 | 77

3487 撑 [撐] /chēng/ (3) v prop up, support; open (an umbrella, etc.); overfill; pole (a boat)
用这只箱子把门撑开。 Use this box to prop the door open.
112 | 0.69 | 77

3488 分开 [分開] /fēnkāi/ v separate
这两个分句由一个逗号分开。 The two clauses are separated by a comma.
89 | 0.87 | 77

3489 宝贵 [寶貴] /bǎoguì/ (2) adj valuable, precious
我们有许多宝贵的经验。 We have had much valuable experience.
104 | 0.73 | 76

3490 坚强 [堅強] /jiānqiáng/ (2) adj firm, strong
行动是坚强的人的性格。 Acting is the character of a strong person.
93 | 0.82 | 76

3491 绝 [絕] /jué/ (3) adj superb, matchless; uncompromising; desperate; exhausted
这双鞋配那条裙子真绝了。 Those shoes are deadly with that skirt.
99 | 0.78 | 76

3492 珍贵 [珍貴] /zhēnguì/ (3) adj precious
他把自己所有的珍贵图画都拿出来给朋友们看。 He showed all his precious pictures to his friends.
94 | 0.82 | 76

3493 孤独 [孤獨] /gūdú/ adj lonely
他总是很孤独。 He was always lonely.
105 | 0.73 | 76

3494 深深 [深深] /shēnshēn/ adv deeply, profoundly
他听到这故事时深深地感动了。 On hearing the story, he was deeply moved.
100 | 0.76 | 76

3495 哈 [哈] /hā/ interj [interjection expressing satisfaction] ha
哈！哈！哈！真好玩。 Ha! Ha! Ha! That was fun.
236 | 0.33 | 76 | S

3496 里边 [裏邊] /lǐbian/ (1) loc inside, within
这扇门是从里边栓上的。 This door bolts on the inside.
309 | 0.25 | 76 | S

3497 底下 [底下] /dǐxià/ (2) loc below, under
把这体温表放在舌头底下。 Put this thermometer under your tongue.
130 | 0.59 | 76 | S

3498 沿海 [沿海] /yánhǎi/ (3) place along the coast, coastal
台风侵袭沿海地区。 The typhoon hit the coastal areas.
153 | 0.5 | 76

3499 首 [首] /shǒu/ num first
这是该画首次公开展出。 It's the first time the painting has been displayed to the public.
97 | 0.79 | 76

3500 咖啡 [咖啡] /kāfēi/ (1) n coffee
他喜欢不加牛奶的咖啡。 He likes black coffee.
103 | 0.74 | 76

3501 蛇 [蛇] /shé/ (2) n snake
她讨厌蛇。 She dislikes the snakes.
97 | 0.79 | 76

3502 流域 [流域] /liúyù/ (3) n river basin, valley
黄河流域是中华民族灿烂文化的摇篮。 The Yellow River Valley is a cradle of splendid ancient Chinese civilisation.
126 | 0.6 | 76

3503 经典 [經典] /jīngdiǎn/ n classics
她喜欢读经典著作。 She enjoys reading the classics.
111 | 0.69 | 76

3504 标题 [標題] /biāotí/ n title, heading
这个标题看上去和正文关系不大。 The heading seemed to have little to do with the text.
279 | 0.27 | 76 | W

3505 游客 [遊客] /yóukè/ n tourist
暑假期间他们给游客提供住宿。 They lodge tourists during summer holidays.
154 | 0.49 | 76

3506 金钱 [金錢] /jīnqián/ n money
在生意场上，时间就是金钱。 In business, time is money.
103 | 0.75 | 76

3507 价值观 [價值觀] /jiàzhíguān/ n values, value judgement
亚洲人与西方人的价值观存在差别。 There are differences between Asian and Western values.
126 | 0.6 | 76

3508 冬 [冬] /dōng/ (1) time winter
他们一冬都在建这座楼。 They worked on the building all through the winter.
92 | 0.83 | 76

3509 干吗 [幹嗎] /gànmá/ (2) pron why, what to do; whatever for
干吗这么大规矩？ Why all this formality?
157 | 0.49 | 76 | S

3510 巩固 [鞏固] /gǒnggù/ (2) v consolidate, strengthen
究竟能不能巩固呢？ Is it possible to consolidate them?
151 | 0.51 | 76

3511 逛 [逛] /guàng/ (2) v stroll
各处溜溜逛逛一逛，看看景色怎么样？ How do you like to stroll around for a while and see the sights?
97 | 0.79 | 76

3512 随 [隨] /suí/ (2) v follow, comply with; allow one to do as one likes
请随我来。 Can you follow me, please?
85 | 0.9 | 76

3513 哼 [哼] /hēng/ (2) v hum
他一边走，一边哼着曲子。 He was humming a tune as he walked along.
201 | 0.38 | 76

3514 丧失 [喪失] /sàngshī/ (3) v lose
他们有理想，不会丧失信心。 They have high ideals and never lose confidence.
103 | 0.74 | 76

3515 乐 [樂] /lè/ (3) v be amused; find pleasure in, enjoy, be happy
听到这个消息，简直乐坏了我们。 On hearing the news, we became very happy.
96 | 0.79 | 76

3516 询问 [詢問] /xúnwèn/ (3) v enquire, question
警察询问了室内所有的人。 The police questioned everybody in the room.
100 | 0.77 | 76

3517 熬 [熬] /áo/ (3) v endure, get through; cook, boil
嗯，好歹总能熬过去的。 Well, I'll get through it somehow.
103 | 0.74 | 76

3518 通信 [通信] /tōngxìn/ (3) n correspondence, communication
请在所有通信中引用这个查询号。 Please quote this reference in all correspondence.
209 | 0.37 | 76 | W

3519 回避 [回避] /huíbì/ v evade, avoid, bypass
你不能回避这些规则！ You cannot bypass these rules!
83 | 0.92 | 76

3520 赢得 [贏得] /yíngdé/ v win
谁得分最多，谁就赢得比赛。 Whoever gains the most points wins the competition.
124 | 0.62 | 76

3521 演习 [演習] /yǎnxí/ v hold (military) exercises, manoeuvre
演习达到了预期目的，是成功的。 The exercises have achieved the anticipated results and have been a success.
139 | 0.55 | 76

3522 访 [访] /fǎng/ v visit, call on
时隔多年，旧地重访使人感到很新奇。 It felt strange to be visiting the place again after all these years.
162 | 0.47 | 76

3523 支撑 [支撐] /zhīchēng/ v prop up, support; sustain, hold
墙支撑着屋顶。 Walls hold up the roof.
90 | 0.84 | 76

3524 回报 [回報] /huíbào/ v return, repay
我无法回报她对我的许多帮助。 I can never repay her many kindnesses to me.
88 | 0.87 | 76

3525 绝对 [絕對] /juéduì/ (2) adj absolute
美是没有绝对的标准的。 There is no absolute standard for beauty.
96 | 0.78 | 75

3526 耐心 [耐心] /nàixīn/ (2) adj patient
她对孩子们很耐心。 She is very patient with the children.
91 | 0.83 | 75

3527 最终 [最終] /zuìzhōng/ adj final, ultimate
他的最终目标是组建自己的公司。 His ultimate goal is to set up his own company.
96 | 0.79 | 75

3528 威 [威] /wēi/ n power, prestige, honour
他的官威得到了维护。 His official honour is vindicated.
113 | 0.67 | 75

3529 恐惧 [恐懼] /kǒngjù/ n fear, dread
那封信又勾起了往日的恐惧。 The letter awoke old fears.
110 | 0.69 | 75

3530 何况 [何況] /hékuàng/ (3) conj let alone, needless to say; moreover, besides
我走还走不动，更何况跑呢！ I cannot even walk, let alone run.
125 | 0.6 | 75

3531 凡是 [凡是] /fánshì/ (3) adv [equivalent of 凡] all (that meets the specified requirements)
凡是值得做的事就值得把它做好。 Whatever is worth doing at all is worth doing well.
95 | 0.8 | 75

3532 回头 [回頭] /huítóu/ adv [colloquial] later
我回头找你算帐。 I will get even with you later.
129 | 0.59 | 75 | S

3533 先是 [先是] /xiānshì/ adv previously, originally, first
她先是同意跟我出去，后来又爽约了。
First she agreed to come out with me, then she stood me up.
97 | 0.78 | 75

3534 实 [實] /shí/ adv really, truly
本店经营各类玩具，实为儿童天地。Dealing in an assortment of toys, this shop is really a children's world.
88 | 0.85 | 75

3535 碗 [碗] /wǎn/ (1) n bowl
这只碗边上有个缺口。The bowl has a chipped edge.
121 | 0.62 | 75

3536 卫星 [衛星] /wèixīng/ (2) n satellite
这颗卫星正围绕着地球运行。The satellite is orbiting round the earth.
147 | 0.51 | 75

3537 武术 [武術] /wǔshù/ (2) n martial arts
她的武术练到家了。She is expert at martial arts.
134 | 0.57 | 75

3538 药物 [藥物] /yàowù/ (3) n medication, drug
有些药物能影响视力。Some drugs can affect your sight.
100 | 0.76 | 75

3539 资本主义 [資本主義] /zīběnzhǔyì/ (3) n capitalism
市场经济不等于资本主义。A market economy is not capitalism.
133 | 0.57 | 75

3540 质 [質] /zhì/ (3) n quality; substance
我方产品因质优价廉而著称。Our products are well known for their fine quality and low price.
110 | 0.68 | 75

3541 孙子 [孫子] /sūnzi/ (3) n grandson, grandchild
他的孙子很淘气。His grandson is very naughty.
97 | 0.78 | 75

3542 身子 [身子] /shēnzi/ (3) n body; pregnancy
你能动一下你的身子吗？Can you move your body?
224 | 0.34 | 75

3543 财务 [財務] /cáiwù/ n finance
你需要专业人士替你管理财务。You need a professional to sort out your finances.
130 | 0.58 | 75

3544 仙 [仙] /xiān/ n immortal being
八仙过海，各显神通。Like the Eight Immortals crossing the sea, each one shows his or her special prowess.
87 | 0.87 | 75

3545 仗 [仗] /zhàng/ n battle
他们打了一场漂亮仗。They fought a good battle.
112 | 0.67 | 75

3546 街头 [街頭] /jiētóu/ place street, street corner
人们开始在街头聚集。People began to assemble on the street.
94 | 0.8 | 75

3547 上次 [上次] /shàngcì/ time last time
我上次在伦敦见到了他。I saw him in London last time.
130 | 0.58 | 75

3548 蹲 [蹲] /dūn/ (2) v crouch, squat
我蹲在沙发后面。I crouched behind the sofa.
128 | 0.59 | 75

3549 感觉 [感覺] /gǎnjué/ (2) v feel
您感觉舒适吗？Do you feel comfortable?
100 | 0.76 | 75

3550 清 [清] /qīng/ (2) v clear up; settle
在他开始讲话前，他先清了清嗓子。He cleared his throat before he started to speak.
102 | 0.74 | 75

3551 染 [染] /rǎn/ (2) v catch (a disease), addict; dye
他染上了各种恶习。He was addicted to all sorts of vice.
97 | 0.77 | 75

3552 捡 [撿] /jiǎn/ (2) v pick up
他捡起课本开始阅读。He picked up the book and started to read.
106 | 0.71 | 75

3553 阻止 [阻止] /zǔzhǐ/ (3) v prevent, stop
任何事都无法阻止他去。Nothing will stop him going.
100 | 0.76 | 75

3554 留学 [留學] /liúxué/ (3) v study abroad
你哪一年出国留学的？When did you go abroad for study?
114 | 0.66 | 75

3555 交代 [交代] /jiāodài/ (3) v hand over; explain, make clear; confess
这一点在前面一段里已经交代过了。This point has been explained in the preceding paragraph.
100 | 0.76 | 75

3556 供应 [供應] /gōngyìng/ (3) v supply, serve (a meal)
早饭什么时间开始供应？What time will breakfast be served?
135 | 0.56 | 75

3557 关怀 [關懷] /guānhuái/ (3) v care for
关怀下一代是我们的责任。It's our responsibility to care for our young generation.
87 | 0.87 | 75

3558 放到 [放到] /fàngdào/ v put (something at a particular place)
他拾起烟灰缸，放到桌上。He picked up the ashtray and put it on the table.
90 | 0.84 | 75

3559 确认 [確認] /quèrèn/ v confirm
我们能确认下星期日有一个房间。We can confirm a room for next Sunday.
105 | 0.72 | 75

3560 预测 [預測] /yùcè/ v forecast
专家们预测游客人数会稳步增长。Experts have forecasted a steady rise in the number of tourists.
125 | 0.61 | 75

3561 免费 [免費] /miǎnfèi/ adj free, free of charge
毕竟，天下没有免费的午餐。After all, there is no free lunch in this world.
97 | 0.78 | 75

3562 试图 [試圖] /shìtú/ v attempt, try
科学家们现正试图探索这是否可能。Scientists are now trying to discover if this is possible.
102 | 0.74 | 75

3563 浅 [淺] /qiǎn/ (1) adj shallow; simple, easy; (of colour) light, pale
这条小河比那条浅。This stream is shallower than that one.
94 | 0.8 | 74

3564 浓 [濃] /nóng/ (2) adj thick, dense; strong
这咖啡太浓了。This coffee is too strong.
91 | 0.82 | 74

3565 格外 [格外] /géwài/ (3) adv especially, exceptionally
今日的天气格外晴朗。It's exceptionally fine today.
94 | 0.8 | 74

3566 礼物 [禮物] /lǐwù/ (1) n gift, present
这点礼物是我们大家的一点心意。This little gift is a token of our regard.
104 | 0.72 | 74

3567 成分 [成分] /chéngfèn/ (2) n ingredient, element
这是主要的成分。It is the basic ingredient.
116 | 0.64 | 74

3568 亲人 [親人] /qīnrén/ (3) n family, relative
我已经没有任何亲人了。I no longer have any relatives.
86 | 0.87 | 74

3569 品质 [品質] /pǐnzhì/ (3) n quality
你们有更好品质的吗？Do you have anything of better quality?
120 | 0.62 | 74

3570 少女 [少女] /shàonǚ/ (3) n young girl
少女站起来收拾东西。The girl got up to collect her things.
110 | 0.68 | 74

3571 听众 [聽眾] /tīngzhòng/ n audience
现在请听众向讲演者提问题。The audience are now invited to put questions to the speaker.
195 | 0.38 | 74 | S

3572 现状 [現狀] /xiànzhuàng/ n status quo, present conditions
该合同改变不了现状。The contract will not alter the status quo.
109 | 0.68 | 74

3573 前景 [前景] /qiánjǐng/ n prospect, outlook
经济前景不乐观。The economic outlook is not good.
178 | 0.42 | 74

3574 基金 [基金] /jījīn/ n fund
他捐赠一大笔钱给学院基金。He donated a large sum to the college fund.
216 | 0.34 | 74

3575 其余 [其餘] /qíyú/ (2) pron rest
班里只有十名女孩，其余都是男孩。There are only ten girls in the class, the rest are boys.
101 | 0.74 | 74

3576 夜里 [夜裏] /yèli/ (2) time night
夜里他听到一个可怕的声音。In the night he heard a fearful sound.
124 | 0.6 | 74

3577 赔 [賠] /péi/ (2) v compensate, make good (one's loss); lose in business, sustain a loss
损坏东西要赔。Pay for anything you damage.
97 | 0.76 | 74

3578 报复 [報復] /bàofù/ (3) v retaliate, pay back, put it across
她以同样的方式报复了他。She paid him back in kind.
81 | 0.92 | 74

3579 检验 [檢驗] /jiǎnyàn/ (3) v test, check, verify
这让他们来检验。This is for them to examine.
119 | 0.62 | 74

3580 抛 [拋] /pāo/ (3) v throw, toss, fling; leave behind
他把球抛给了我。He threw the ball to me.
99 | 0.75 | 74

3581 加速 [加速] /jiāsù/ (3) v accelerate; expedite, speed up
我们向您保证我们将尽全力加速装船。We assure you that we shall do our utmost to expedite shipment.
137 | 0.55 | 74

3582 凑 [湊] /còu/ (3) v put together, come together; move closer
凑近点儿。Come closer, please.
125 | 0.6 | 74

3583 审查 [審查] /shěnchá/ (3) v examine, look through
他逐一审查了各项建议才予以批准。He looked the proposals through before approving them.
116 | 0.64 | 74

3584 收购 [收購] /shōugòu/ v purchase, buy
纽约的一个商人把整个公司收购了。A New York businessman has bought up the entire company.
133 | 0.56 | 74

3585 上市 [上市] /shàngshì/ v put (goods and shares, etc.) on the market
随着这些产品开始上市，人们的期望值很高。Expectations are high as these products begin to hit the market.
142 | 0.52 | 74

3586 消 [消] /xiāo/ v disappear, cause to disappear
他的怒气一会儿就消了。His anger soon disappeared.
97 | 0.77 | 74

3587 违法 [違法] /wéifǎ/ *v* break the law, be against the law, be illegal
那是违法的。That's against the law.
171 | 0.44 | 74

3588 欢乐 [歡樂] /huānlè/ (3) *adj* joyous, cheerful
这个节日是个欢乐的时节。This festival is a cheerful occasion.
85 | 0.86 | 73

3589 惨 [慘] /cǎn/ (3) *adj* miserable, awful, tragic
我们的足球队踢输了，真惨。It was tragic when our football team lost the match.
114 | 0.65 | 73

3590 母 [母] /mǔ/ *adj* female
那是一只母狗。That is a female dog.
98 | 0.75 | 73

3591 一流 [一流] /yìliú/ *adj* first rate, first class
他是当今中国的一流画家。He is a first-class painter in China today.
111 | 0.66 | 73

3592 独 [獨] /dú/ *adv* alone; solely, only
她独居。She lived alone.
85 | 0.87 | 73

3593 当场 [當場] /dāngchǎng/ *adv* on the spot
困难当场解决了。The problem was solved on the spot.
81 | 0.91 | 73

3594 轻易 [輕易] /qīngyì/ *adv* easily, readily; lightly, rashly
我不轻易灰心。I don't discourage easily.
99 | 0.74 | 73

3595 嘿 [嘿] /hēi/ (2) *interj* hey, why
嘿，下雪了！Why, it's snowing!
229 | 0.32 | 73 | S

3596 江 [江] /jiāng/ (1) *n* river
我们打算去江边。We are going to the bank of the river.
90 | 0.81 | 73

3597 能源 [能源] /néngyuán/ (2) *n* energy
节省能源十分重要。It is important to conserve energy.
182 | 0.4 | 73

3598 胸 [胸] /xiōng/ (2) *n* chest, bosom; mind
她感到剧烈的胸痛。She felt acute chest pains.
102 | 0.72 | 73

3599 度 [度] /dù/ (2) *n* degree (of intensity), extent; capacity; limit
将玻璃管加热，以能弯曲为度。Heat the glass tube to the point that it can bend.
85 | 0.87 | 73

3600 航空 [航空] /hángkōng/ (2) *n* aviation, by air
公司提供航空货运服务。The company provides air cargo service.
196 | 0.38 | 73

3601 墓 [墓] /mù/ (3) *n* tomb, grave
他们站立在她的墓的周围向她默哀。They stood in silent homage round her grave.
100 | 0.74 | 73

3602 饮食 [飲食] /yǐnshí/ *n* food and drink, diet
你应该更加注意饮食。You should pay more attention to diet.
118 | 0.62 | 73

3603 纠纷 [糾紛] /jiūfēn/ *n* dispute
他调解了这场家庭纠纷。He interceded in the family dispute.
112 | 0.66 | 73

3604 众人 [眾人] /zhòngrén/ *n* everyone, crowd
警察驱散了众人。The policeman parted the crowd.
133 | 0.55 | 73

3605 法庭 [法庭] /fǎtíng/ *n* court
他的案子已送交法庭审理。His case was brought up before the court.
96 | 0.76 | 73

3606 工商 [工商] /gōngshāng/ *n* industry and commerce
严格注意保护工商业。Pay strict attention to the protection of industry and commerce.
162 | 0.45 | 73

3607 库 [庫] /kù/ *n* warehouse, store room, bank
我们的保险库建造得十分安全。The strong room is as secure as we can make it.
102 | 0.73 | 73

3608 政 [政] /zhèng/ *n* government, politics
党、政、军、经、财等事宜都自行管理。It will run its own party, political, military, economic and financial affairs.
87 | 0.84 | 73

3609 角 [角] /jiǎo/ (1) *clas* [measure term for the Chinese currency] jiao (one-tenth of yuan), ten cents
苹果每只八角钱。The apples cost 80 cents a piece.
86 | 0.85 | 73

3610 境内 [境內] /jìngnèi/ *place* within borders (of a country or province, etc.); internal, domestic
外方投资者在中国境内设有代表机构。The foreign investor has a representative office inside China.
128 | 0.57 | 73

3611 展览 [展覽] /zhǎnlǎn/ (1) *v* exhibit, put on display
我们正在展览生产线上增加的几种新产品。We are exhibiting several additions to our product line.
142 | 0.52 | 73

3612 发明 [發明] /fāmíng/ (2) *v* invent
你知道纸是谁发明的吗？Do you know who invented paper?
100 | 0.73 | 73

3613 觉 [覺] /jué/ (3) *v* feel; become aware
自选担子不觉沉。A burden of one's choice is not felt.
105 | 0.7 | 73

3614 记载 [記載] /jìzǎi/ (3) *v* record, write down
历史学家记载了罗马帝国衰亡的经过。Historians record how Rome fell.
116 | 0.63 | 73

3615 助 [助] /zhù/ (3) v help, aid, assist
他总是乐于助人，作为回报，大家都喜欢他。
He was always ready to help others, and in return, he was liked by everyone.
88 | 0.84 | 73

3616 建造 [建造] /jiànzào/ (3) v build, construct
这所房子是用木头建造的。 The house is built of wood.
97 | 0.75 | 73

3617 散 [散] /sǎn, sàn/ (3, 3) v fall apart, come loose; break up, disperse; spread, distribute
行李散了。 The luggage has come loose.
97 | 0.76 | 73

3618 执 [執] /zhí/ v hold, grasp
学生们手执彩旗欢迎外宾。 The students held colourful flags to greet the foreign guests.
85 | 0.86 | 73

23. Kinship and family relations

Simplified Chinese	Traditional Chinese	Gloss	Hierarchy
父亲，爸爸	父親，爸爸	father	parents
母亲，妈妈	母親，媽媽	mother	
儿子	兒子	son	offspring
女儿	女兒	daughter	
哥哥	哥哥	elder brother	siblings
弟弟	弟弟	younger brother	
姐姐	姐姐	elder sister	
妹妹	妹妹	younger sister	
丈夫，先生，老公	丈夫，先生，老公	husband	spouse
妻子，太太，老婆	妻子，太太，老婆	wife	
爷爷，祖父	爺爺，祖父	father's father	grandparents
奶奶，祖母	奶奶，祖母	father's mother	
外公，外祖父	外公，外祖父	mother's father	
外婆，外祖母	外婆，外祖母	mother's mother	
孙子	孫子	son's son	grandchildren
孙女	孫女	son's daughter	
外孙	外孫	daughter's son	
外孙女	外孫女	daughter's daughter	
堂哥/堂弟/堂姐/堂妹	堂哥/堂弟/堂姐/堂妹	cousins on father's side	cousins
表哥/表弟/表姐/表妹	表哥/表弟/表姐/表妹	cousins on mother's side	
伯伯，伯父	伯伯，伯父	father's elder brother	uncles
叔叔，叔父	叔叔，叔父	father's younger brother	
舅舅，舅父	舅舅，舅父	mother's brother	
姑姑，姑妈	姑姑，姑媽	father's sister	aunts
伯母	伯母	wife of father's elder brother	
婶婶	嬸嬸	wife of father's younger brother	
姨妈，阿姨	姨媽，阿姨	mother's sister	
舅妈	舅媽	wife of mother's brother	
侄儿，侄子	姪兒，姪子	brother's son	nephews
外甥	外甥	sister's son	
侄女	姪女	brother's daughter	nieces
外甥女，甥女	外甥女，甥女	sister's daughter	

Comments:

Kinship terms in Chinese are a reflection of the Chinese collectivist culture, which is family-centred. The family relations in Chinese, which differentiate not only between the elder and the younger but also between the paternal and maternal side, are much more complex than in English.

3619 叹 [嘆] /tàn/ v sigh
她在床上向后一躺，长叹了一声。 She sighed as she lay back on the bed.
192 | 0.38 | 73

3620 做人 [做人] /zuòrén/ v conduct oneself, behave; be an upright or decent person
从现在起，希望你规规矩矩做人。 From now on, I hope you'll behave yourself.
90 | 0.82 | 73

3621 依赖 [依賴] /yīlài/ v depend on, count on
在任何时候你都可以依赖我的帮助。 You can count on me to help you any time.
102 | 0.72 | 73

3622 跃 [躍] /yuè/ v leap, jump
他一跃跳过了围墙。 He went over the fence in one jump.
169 | 0.44 | 73

3623 讨 [討] /tǎo/ v ask for, beg; take (as wife)
我尽力讨她的欢心。 I tried to win her affections.
102 | 0.72 | 73

3624 辞职 [辭職] /cízhí/ v resign, quit
结果他辞职了。 As a result, he resigned the job.
98 | 0.75 | 73

3625 禁 [禁] /jìn, jīn/ v prohibit, ban; endure
地方保护主义屡禁不止。 Local protectionism remains a problem despite repeated orders to ban it.
81 | 0.91 | 73

3626 可靠 [可靠] /kěkào/ (2) adj reliable
这个公司生产的产品非常可靠。 The company makes a very reliable product.
88 | 0.83 | 72

3627 自动 [自動] /zìdòng/ (2) adj automatic
我的照相机是自动的。 My camera is automatic.
87 | 0.83 | 72

3628 稳 [穩] /wěn/ (2) adj steady; certain
这张桌子不稳。 This table is not steady.
89 | 0.81 | 72

3629 滑 [滑] /huá/ (2) adj slippery, smooth; crafty
只是道路太滑了一点。 It's just too slippery on the road.
91 | 0.8 | 72

3630 灵活 [靈活] /línghuó/ (2) adj flexible, elastic
我们的计划相当灵活。 Our plans are fairly elastic.
95 | 0.76 | 72

3631 烂 [爛] /làn/ (2) adj rotten, festering; overcooked; lousy, messy
这个梨烂透了。 The pear was rotten right through.
101 | 0.72 | 72

3632 陆续 [陸續] /lùxù/ (2) adv in turn, successively
客人们陆续来了。 The guests came one after another.
111 | 0.65 | 72

3633 京剧 [京劇] /jīngjù/ (2) n Beijing opera
他看京剧上瘾了。 He is crazy about Beijing opera.
129 | 0.56 | 72

3634 炮 [炮] /pào/ (2) n cannon, gun; firecracker
枪炮声整天响个不停。 The guns banged away all day.
90 | 0.81 | 72

3635 箭 [箭] /jiàn/ (2) n arrow
箭射中了目标。 The arrow found its mark.
83 | 0.87 | 72

3636 气息 [氣息] /qìxī/ n flavour, taste; smell, odour; breath
田野散发出春天的气息。 The fields give forth the scent of spring.
105 | 0.69 | 72

3637 玩具 [玩具] /wánjù/ n toy
请把玩具放入盒子里好吗？ Can you fit the toy into the box?
80 | 0.91 | 72

3638 高手 [高手] /gāoshǒu/ n master hand, top player
他是个高尔夫球高手。 He is a very good golf player.
79 | 0.91 | 72

3639 农 [農] /nóng/ n agriculture, farming
我父亲以农为生。 My father farms for a living.
100 | 0.73 | 72

3640 站 [站] /zhàn/ clas [measure word for sections of a bus or railway journey] stop
到博物馆有几站路？ How many stops are there to the museum?
90 | 0.8 | 72

3641 路 [路] /lù/ clas [measure word for groups of people] route
敌人兵分六路进行围攻。 The enemy forces were divided into six routes to make a converging attack.
87 | 0.83 | 72

3642 开玩笑 [開玩笑] /kāiwánxiào/ (1) v play a joke, make fun of
你在开玩笑。 You are kidding.
114 | 0.64 | 72

3643 率领 [率領] /shuàilǐng/ (2) v lead
代表团由市长亲自率领。 The visiting delegation was led by the mayor himself.
123 | 0.59 | 72

3644 采 [采] /cǎi/ (2) v pick, gather; mine
请为我采一些花。 Please gather me some flowers.
78 | 0.93 | 72

3645 干涉 [干涉] /gānshè/ (3) v meddle in
你老是要干涉我的事情。 You are always meddling in my affairs.
112 | 0.65 | 72

3646 投降 [投降] /tóuxiáng/ (3) v surrender, give in
叛乱者被迫投降。 The rebels were forced to give in.
97 | 0.75 | 72

3647 怪 [怪] /guài/ (3) v blame
这事应该怪谁？ Who is to blame for this?
127 | 0.57 | 72

3648 侵犯 [侵犯] /qīnfàn/ (3) v violate, infringe
当心不要侵犯别人的权利。 Be careful not to infringe the rights of other people.
101 | 0.71 | 72

3649 崇拜 [崇拜] /chóngbài/ v worship, adore
她看不起那些崇拜足球明星的女孩子。 She scorns the girls who worship football stars.
98 | 0.74 | 72

3650 留给 [留給] /liúgěi/ v leave, set aside for
那是她留给我的唯一的一本书。 That's the only book she has left me.
85 | 0.85 | 72

3651 兴奋 [興奮] /xīngfèn/ v be excited
他兴奋得满脸通红。 His face flushed red with excitement.
105 | 0.69 | 72

3652 转身 [轉身] /zhuǎnshēn/ v turn round
她飞快地转身接球。 She spun round to catch the ball.
199 | 0.36 | 72

3653 当成 [當成] /dàngchéng/ v take for, regard as
我们把你当成家里人。 We regard you as one of the family.
101 | 0.72 | 72

3654 善 [善] /shàn/ v be good at; be apt to
女人善编织。 Women are good at knitting.
95 | 0.77 | 72

3655 伤亡 [傷亡] /shāngwáng/ n casualties
可悲的是这次进攻结果造成重大伤亡。 Tragically, the attempt resulted in heavy casualties.
93 | 0.78 | 72

3656 注册 [註冊] /zhùcè/ v register
注册商标受到法律的保护。 A registered trademark is protected by the law.
126 | 0.57 | 72

3657 勇敢 [勇敢] /yǒnggǎn/ (2) adj brave
他真勇敢。 Truly, he is brave.
94 | 0.76 | 71

3658 封建 [封建] /fēngjiàn/ (2) adj feudal
他不再相信封建的老一套了。 He lost faith in feudal traditions.
103 | 0.69 | 71

3659 尴尬 [尷尬] /gān'gà/ adj embarrassed, embarrassing
他评论我的衣服使我很尴尬。 I was embarrassed by his comments about my clothes.
111 | 0.64 | 71

3660 最低 [最低] /zuìdī/ adj lowest, minimum
有最低消费吗？ Is there a minimum charge?
109 | 0.66 | 71

3661 硬 [硬] /yìng/ (3) adv obstinately, stubbornly; (do something) mechanically in spite of difficulties
他硬要我们重新开始。 He insisted that we should make a fresh start.
103 | 0.7 | 71

3662 处处 [處處] /chùchù/ (3) adv everywhere
人间处处有温情。 There is kindness to be found everywhere.
81 | 0.88 | 71

3663 终 [終] /zhōng/ adv finally
终有所成。 Perseverance finally pays off.
88 | 0.81 | 71

3664 从来不 [從來不] /cóngláibù/ adv never
他从来不和他的同事交际。 He never socialises with his colleagues.
101 | 0.71 | 71

3665 血液 [血液] /xuèyè/ (2) n blood
血液在她的膝盖伤口周围凝固了。 The blood had congealed round the cut on her knee.
91 | 0.78 | 71

3666 本事 [本事] /běnshi/ (2) n [equivalent of 本领] ability, skill
她们可真有本事。 They certainly had this ability.
105 | 0.68 | 71

3667 地图 [地圖] /dìtú/ (2) n map
跟着地图上的箭头走。 Follow the arrows on the map.
75 | 0.95 | 71

3668 阿姨 [阿姨] /āyí/ (2) n (maternal side) aunt, auntie; [also used as a polite term of address for a woman of one's parents' age]
我们去看你叔叔阿姨时你要听话。 Be good when we visit your uncle and aunt.
154 | 0.46 | 71

3669 草原 [草原] /cǎoyuán/ (2) n grassland, prairie
草原的浩瀚确是奇观。 The spread of the prairie is indeed a startling sight.
103 | 0.7 | 71

3670 屁股 [屁股] /pìgu/ (3) n buttocks, bottom; end, butt
她打了他屁股一巴掌。 She gave him a smack in the buttocks.
141 | 0.5 | 71

3671 物品 [物品] /wùpǐn/ (3) n article, item
你可以去看看免税物品一览表。 You can check the list of duty-free articles.
93 | 0.76 | 71

3672 幻想 [幻想] /huànxiǎng/ (3) n fantasy, illusion, delusion
他生活在幻想的世界里。 He lives in a world of fantasy.
99 | 0.72 | 71

3673 果 [果] /guǒ/ n fruit
什么样的树结什么样的果。 Different trees bear different fruits.
89 | 0.81 | 71

3674 大姐 [大姐] /dàjiě/ *n* eldest sister, elder sister; [also used as a polite term of address for a women of one's own age] big sister, sister
她在工厂里被叫作"大姐"。 She was called "Elder Sister" in the factory.
122 | 0.58 | 71

3675 手法 [手法] /shǒufǎ/ *n* technique, skill, way; trick
他们很佩服她处理这场危机的手法。 They admired the way she dealt with the crisis.
89 | 0.8 | 71

3676 病毒 [病毒] /bìngdú/ *n* virus
当心计算机病毒。 Beware of the computer virus.
99 | 0.72 | 71

3677 副 [副] /fù/ (2) *clas* [measure word for objects forming a set] pair, set; [measure word for one's facial expression]
你需要一副游泳镜。 You'll need a pair of goggles.
129 | 0.55 | 71

3678 起 [起] /qǐ/ *clas* [measure word for cases, incidents, accidents, etc.]
警方怀疑这两起谋杀案可能有关联。 Police suspect there might be a link between the two murders.
121 | 0.59 | 71

3679 尝 [嘗] /cháng/ (2) *v* taste
我伤风了，尝不出味儿来。 I have a bad cold and can't taste anything.
86 | 0.84 | 71

3680 烤 [烤] /kǎo/ (2) *v* roast, bake, toast; get warm or dry by the fire
我喜欢吃烤牛肉。 I like to eat roast beef.
91 | 0.79 | 71

3681 过年 [過年] /guònián/ (2) *v* celebrate the New Year
他今年回家过年。 He will go home for the New Year.
86 | 0.83 | 71

3682 沉 [沉] /chén/ (3) *v* sink, submerge
油船在去海湾的途中沉了。 The tanker sank when she was en route to the gulf.
116 | 0.61 | 71

3683 设想 [設想] /shèxiǎng/ (3) *v* imagine
设想有一所带大花园的房子。 Imagine a house with a big garden.
89 | 0.8 | 71

3684 收回 [收回] /shōuhuí/ *v* take back, recover; withdraw
期初投资根本没收回。 The initial investment was never recovered.
83 | 0.86 | 71

3685 推行 [推行] /tuīxíng/ *v* carry out, push on with
不管有什么困难，他都要继续推行他的计划。 He will push on with his project whatever the difficulty may be.
148 | 0.48 | 71

3686 尝试 [嘗試] /chángshì/ *v* try, attempt
我想问一下，您尝试过戒烟吗？ Now, may I ask if you have ever tried to give up smoking?
94 | 0.76 | 71

3687 考上 [考上] /kǎoshàng/ *v* be admitted by examination, pass
所以我一定能考上。 So I'll pass for sure.
95 | 0.75 | 71

3688 看上去 [看上去] /kànshàngqù/ *v* look, appear
我妹妹看上去总是很时髦。 My sister always looks smart.
101 | 0.71 | 71

3689 释放 [釋放] /shìfàng/ *v* set free, release
法庭宣布被告无罪，予以释放。 The court cleared the accused of any crime and set him free.
92 | 0.78 | 71

3690 呐 [吶] /na/ (1) *part* [sentence final particle, especially following words ending with the consonant n]
这些人多得很呐！ Indeed, there have been a great many of them!
242 | 0.3 | 71 | S

3691 粗 [粗] /cū/ (2) *adj* thick; coarse, rough; (of voice) husky; rude
导线越粗，电阻越小。 The thicker the wire, the smaller the resistance.
99 | 0.71 | 70

3692 业余 [業餘] /yèyú/ (2) *adj* spare-time; amateur
我仅仅是个业余爱好者。 I'm only an amateur.
101 | 0.69 | 70

3693 温 [溫] /wēn/ (3) *adj* warm
给婴儿吃的东西应该是温的，不能是烫的。 Food for a baby should be warm, not hot.
96 | 0.73 | 70

3694 疯 [瘋] /fēng/ (3) *adj* insane, crazy
他把车开得这样快，真是疯了。 He was crazy to drive his car so fast.
120 | 0.59 | 70

3695 杰出 [傑出] /jiéchū/ *adj* outstanding, distinguished
也许有一天他会成为一名杰出的艺术家。 One day he may become a distinguished artist.
98 | 0.72 | 70

3696 除非 [除非] /chúfēi/ (3) *conj* unless
除非他受到邀请，他是不会来的。 He will not come unless he is invited.
93 | 0.76 | 70

3697 从不 [從不] /cóngbù/ (2) *adv* [equivalent of 从来不] never
他们从不跳舞，也不唱歌。 They never dance or sing.
100 | 0.7 | 70

3698 北部 [北部] /běibù/ (2) *loc* north, northern part
英格兰北部到处都在下雪。 Snow is falling over the north of England.
115 | 0.61 | 70

3699 对了 [對了] /duìle/ (3) *idiom* right, correct, that's it; by the way
对了，你是不是自己洗衣服？ By the way, do you do your own laundry?
117 | 0.6 | 70 | S

3700 来 [來] /lái/ (2) *num* [following a round number to indicate approximation] a bit over
他有三十来岁。 He is in his early thirties.
96 | 0.74 | 70

3701 节日 [節日] /jiérì/ (1) *n* holiday, festival
我们在谈论即将到来的节日。 We are talking about the coming festival.
130 | 0.55 | 70

3702 啤酒 [啤酒] /píjiǔ/ (1) *n* beer
我不喜欢泡沫太多的啤酒。 I don't like beer with too much froth.
88 | 0.8 | 70

3703 胃 [胃] /wèi/ (2) *n* stomach
他胃痛。 He's got stomach ache.
99 | 0.72 | 70

3704 心脏 [心臟] /xīnzàng/ (2) *n* heart
我有心脏病。 I have heart trouble.
82 | 0.86 | 70

3705 院子 [院子] /yuànzi/ (2) *n* yard, courtyard
他把车停在院子里。 He parked his car in the yard.
127 | 0.55 | 70

3706 装备 [裝備] /zhuāngbèi/ (3) *n* equipment
现代露营装备变得越来越讲究。 The equipment of modern camping has become increasingly sophisticated.
119 | 0.6 | 70

3707 税 [税] /shuì/ (3) *n* tax, duty
小费是税前帐单的15%。 Tipping is 15 per cent based on the cost before tax.
107 | 0.66 | 70

3708 大队 [大隊] /dàduì/ (3) *n* brigade
几个大队合并成了一个村。 A couple of brigades entered a village.
83 | 0.85 | 70

3709 笑容 [笑容] /xiàoróng/ (3) *n* smile
难得看到她面带笑容。 It's rare to see her smile.
155 | 0.45 | 70

3710 医 [醫] /yī/ *n* medical science, medicine; doctor, physician
她医技高明。 She is a highly skilled doctor.
76 | 0.93 | 70

3711 财 [財] /cái/ *n* wealth, fortune
他发了一笔小财。 He cleaned up a small fortune.
77 | 0.92 | 70

3712 战役 [戰役] /zhànyì/ *n* (military) campaign
整个战役，共分三个阶段。 The campaign took place in three stages.
107 | 0.65 | 70

3713 笑声 [笑聲] /xiàoshēng/ *n* laughter
我们听到阵阵笑声。 We heard gales of laughter.
96 | 0.73 | 70

3714 当事人 [當事人] /dāngshìrén/ *n* person or party involved
经调解，双方当事人达成调解协定。 The two parties negotiated a settlement through mediation.
96 | 0.73 | 70

3715 题材 [題材] /tícái/ *n* subject matter, material
这是一个重大的题材。 It's a great subject.
98 | 0.72 | 70

3716 贵族 [貴族] /guìzú/ *n* noble, aristocrat, peer
她出身贵族。 She comes from an aristocratic family.
102 | 0.7 | 70

3717 潜力 [潛力] /qiánlì/ *n* potential, potentiality
它是一个有畅销潜力的新发明。 It is a new invention with big sales potential.
149 | 0.47 | 70

3718 婚礼 [婚禮] /hūnlǐ/ *n* wedding
他们至今对婚礼仍记忆犹新。 Their memory of the wedding is still fresh in their mind.
88 | 0.81 | 70

3719 名单 [名單] /míngdān/ *n* (name) list
他把名单匆匆地看了一遍。 He ran through the names on the list.
98 | 0.72 | 70

3720 平方公里 [平方公里] /píngfānggōnglǐ/ *clas* square kilometre
中国有960万平方公里的陆地国土。 China has a land area of 9.6 million square kilometres.
135 | 0.52 | 70

3721 门前 [門前] /ménqián/ *place* in front of the door or gate
门前禁止停车。 No parking in front of this gate.
91 | 0.78 | 70

3722 祝 [祝] /zhù/ (1) *v* wish
祝您幸福。 I wish you happiness.
78 | 0.9 | 70

3723 改进 [改進] /gǎijìn/ (2) *v* improve
他提出了一些改进这个计划的意见。 He offered a few ideas to improve the plan.
163 | 0.43 | 70

3724 牵 [牽] /qiān/ (2) *v* lead, lead along
你别想再牵着我的鼻子走！ You're not going to lead me by the nose again!
119 | 0.59 | 70

3725 帮忙 [幫忙] /bāngmáng/ (2) *v* help
他请邻居帮忙。 He asked his neighbour to help him.
120 | 0.59 | 70

3726 纠正 [糾正] /jiūzhèng/ (2) *v* correct, rectify
如果他们犯了错误，由他们自己去纠正。 If they have made mistakes, it is up to them to correct them.
99 | 0.71 | 70

3727 测 [測] /cè/ (3) *v* measure, gauge
这是用来测温度的仪表。 The instrument is used to measure temperature.
78 | 0.91 | 70

24. Moods and emotions

高兴	高興	gāoxìng	happy	585
担心	擔心	dānxīn	worried	1235
幸福	幸福	xìngfú	happy	1238
痛苦	痛苦	tòngkǔ	painful	1259
满意	滿意	mǎnyì	satisfied	1260
快乐	快樂	kuàilè	joyful	1488
激动	激動	jīdòng	excited	1790
感动	感動	gǎndòng	moved	1826
遗憾	遺憾	yíhàn	sorry, regretful	2203
平静	平靜	píngjìng	calm	2611
生气	生氣	shēngqì	angry	2895
不满	不滿	bùmǎn	dissatisfied	2990
冷静	冷靜	lěngjìng	calm	3103
失望	失望	shīwàng	disappointed	3273
兴奋	興奮	xīngfèn	excited	3274
不安	不安	bù'ān	uneasy	3297
骄傲	驕傲	jiāo'ào	proud	3390
孤独	孤獨	gūdú	lonely	3493
恐惧	恐懼	kǒngjù	terrified	3529
尴尬	尷尬	gāngà	embarrassed	3659
自豪	自豪	zìháo	proud	3734
愤怒	憤怒	fènnù	angry, indignant	3772
无奈	無奈	wúnài	utterly helpless	3779
惊讶	驚訝	jīngyà	surprised	3865
伤心	傷心	shāngxīn	sad	3980
难受	難受	nánshòu	unhappy, unwell	4025
寂寞	寂寞	jìmò	lonely	4026
得意	得意	déyì	proud, complacent	4058
悲哀	悲哀	bēiāi	sorrow	4218
感激	感激	gǎnjī	grateful	4550
痛快	痛快	tòngkuài	delighted, jolly	4690
绝望	絕望	juéwàng	desperate	4693
困惑	困惑	kùnhuò	perplexed	4736
满足	滿足	mǎnzú	satisfied, content	4737
烦恼	煩惱	fánnǎo	vexed, upset	4908

3728 伸手 [伸手] /shēnshǒu/ v hold out one's hand; ask for
他伸手去拿笔。 He reached out his hand for the pen.
181 | 0.39 | 70

3729 对抗 [對抗] /duìkàng/ v resist, act against, withstand
政府决心对抗那些示威者。 The government decided to react against the protesters.
84 | 0.84 | 70

3730 塑造 [塑造] /sùzào/ v shape, mould; portray (literary characters)
有些人认为环境塑造人的性格。 Some people think that environment shapes personality.
91 | 0.78 | 70

3731 支付 [支付] /zhīfù/ v pay, make a payment
工资每星期支付一次。 Wages are paid weekly.
125 | 0.56 | 70

3732 捐 [捐] /juān/ v donate, contribute
他们举办了一次音乐会，把收入捐给了慈善机构。They gave a concert and donated the proceeds to charity.
73 | 0.96 | 70

3733 乐观 [樂觀] /lèguān/ (2) adj optimistic
这个乐观的预言，不是没有根据的。This optimistic prediction is not groundless.
86 | 0.81 | 69

3734 自豪 [自豪] /zìháo/ (3) adj proud
他为自己的作品感到自豪。He was very proud of his work.
81 | 0.86 | 69

3735 固定 [固定] /gùdìng/ (3) adj fixed
对不起，我们的价格是固定的。Sorry, our prices are fixed.
86 | 0.8 | 69

3736 迟 [遲] /chí/ (3) adj late
现在就得做，否则就太迟了。Do it now, otherwise it will be too late.
84 | 0.82 | 69

3737 要么 [要麼] /yàome/ conj (either . . .) or
你要么遵守校规，要么离开学校。You must conform to the rules or leave the school.
84 | 0.83 | 69

3738 好 [好] /hǎo/ (1) adv very, rather
好暗呀！It's very dark, isn't it?
116 | 0.6 | 69

3739 四处 [四處] /sìchù/ (3) adv everywhere, all round
可以带我到市里四处看看吗？Would you please show me around the city?
103 | 0.67 | 69

3740 各种各样 [各種各樣] /gèzhǒnggèyàng/ idiom various, of all kinds
她喜欢参加各种各样的聚会。She is fond of all kinds of parties.
106 | 0.65 | 69

3741 你好 [你好] /nǐhǎo/ idiom hello
你好，你叫什么名字？Hello, what's your name?
122 | 0.57 | 69

3742 派 [派] /pài/ (1) n side, faction, group, school
你属于哪一派？Which side are you on?
82 | 0.85 | 69

3743 原料 [原料] /yuánliào/ (2) n raw material
许多天然原料越来越少。Many natural materials are becoming scarce.
122 | 0.57 | 69

3744 礼貌 [禮貌] /lǐmào/ (2) n politeness, courtesy; manner
他没礼貌。He has no manners.
91 | 0.76 | 69

3745 水泥 [水泥] /shuǐní/ (2) n cement
用水泥砌牢砖头。Bricks are bedded in cement.
87 | 0.79 | 69

3746 乡村 [鄉村] /xiāngcūn/ (3) n village, countryside
他怀念平静的乡村生活的种种乐趣。He missed the delight of the peaceful country life.
104 | 0.67 | 69

3747 领土 [領土] /lǐngtǔ/ (3) n territory
领土被侵占者瓜分。The territory was carved up by the occupying powers.
161 | 0.43 | 69

3748 瓜 [瓜] /guā/ (3) n melon
大约有一个瓜那么大。About the size of a melon.
75 | 0.93 | 69

3749 论 [論] /lùn/ (3) n theory; view, opinion
他转而信仰达尔文的进化论。He was converted to the Darwinian theory of evolution.
102 | 0.68 | 69

3750 初期 [初期] /chūqī/ (3) n initial stage, early days
此故事是以第二次世界大战初期为背景的。The story is set in the early days of the Second World War.
101 | 0.69 | 69

3751 华侨 [華僑] /huáqiáo/ (3) n overseas Chinese
国外华侨都思念他们的祖国。The Chinese living overseas are thinking of their motherland.
136 | 0.51 | 69

3752 结局 [結局] /jiéjú/ n ending, final upshot
喜剧通常有一个愉快的结局。A comedy usually has a happy ending.
90 | 0.77 | 69

3753 治安 [治安] /zhì'ān/ n public order
警方必须努力恢复治安。The police must try to restore order.
149 | 0.46 | 69

3754 分歧 [分歧] /fēnqí/ n difference, divergence
他们消除了分歧。They settled their differences.
119 | 0.58 | 69

3755 电视剧 [電視劇] /diànshìjù/ n TV play
这部电视剧取得了巨大的成功。The TV play was a huge success.
108 | 0.64 | 69

3756 医药 [醫藥] /yīyào/ n medicine
难民苦于缺少食物和医药用品。The refugees are suffering for want of food and medical supplies.
124 | 0.56 | 69

3757 处 [處] /chǔ/ (2) v be in; get along; sentence, punish
要是你处在他的位置，那么你会怎么办？If you were in his position, what would you do?
76 | 0.92 | 69

3758 下班 [下班] /xiàbān/ (2) v get off work
下午四点我们就下班了。We are off work at four o'clock in the afternoon.
95 | 0.73 | 69

3759 阅读 [閱讀] /yuèdú/ (2) v read
许多人抱怨他们太忙，找不到时间阅读。
Many people complain that they are too busy to find time for reading.
125 | 0.56 | 69

3760 如下 [如下] /rúxià/ (3) v as follows
他们的名字如下。Their names are as follows.
116 | 0.6 | 69

3761 盼 [盼] /pàn/ (3) v expect, long for, look forward to
我一直盼着你能打电话来。I've been expecting your call.
97 | 0.72 | 69

3762 抗议 [抗議] /kàngyì/ (3) v protest
工会抗议解雇工人。The union protested against the sacking.
85 | 0.82 | 69

3763 策划 [策劃] /cèhuá/ v plot, plan
他们精心策划了越狱计划。The breakout was carefully planned.
84 | 0.82 | 69

3764 旅 [旅] /lǚ/ n trip
这位作者吹嘘了他的异国之旅。
This author romanticised his trip to an exotic country.
97 | 0.71 | 69

3765 示 [示] /shì/ v show
她砰砰地走出门去，以示愤怒。She stormed out to show her anger.
88 | 0.79 | 69

3766 识 [識] /shí/ v know
对不起，我不识路。Sorry, I don't know the way.
88 | 0.79 | 69

3767 免 [免] /miǎn/ v excuse from, waive, exempt; dismiss; avoid
他身体不好，因而免服兵役。His bad health exempted him from military service.
72 | 0.97 | 69

3768 冲动 [衝動] /chōngdòng/ n impulse
他一时冲动买了这辆汽车。He bought the car on impulse.
105 | 0.66 | 69

3769 评估 [評估] /pínggū/ v evaluate, assess
评估股票的合理价值有许多方法。There are many ways to assess the fair value of a share.
115 | 0.61 | 69

3770 安静 [安靜] /ānjìng/ (1) adj quiet
孩子们很安静。The children are quiet.
114 | 0.6 | 68

3771 胖 [胖] /pàng/ (2) adj fat, stout, obese
她越来越胖了。She's growing fat.
117 | 0.59 | 68

3772 愤怒 [憤怒] /fènnù/ (2) adj angry, indignant
他愤怒得难以自持。He could scarcely keep in his indignation.
98 | 0.7 | 68

3773 紫 [紫] /zǐ/ (2) adj purple, violet
他的面孔气得发紫。He became purple with rage.
96 | 0.71 | 68

3774 甜 [甜] /tián/ (2) adj sweet
不够甜你再加点糖。Help yourself to some sugar if it's not sweet enough.
90 | 0.76 | 68

3775 无比 [無比] /wúbǐ/ (3) adj matchless, unsurpassed, immeasurable
在战斗中他们表现得无比英勇。They showed unsurpassed bravery in battle.
97 | 0.7 | 68

3776 精神 [精神] /jīngshén/ (3) adj lively, vigorous, smart, cute
实际上，你看起来也很精神。As a matter of fact, you look smart yourself.
83 | 0.83 | 68

3777 典型 [典型] /diǎnxíng/ (3) adj typical
这是传统建筑的一个典型例子。It is a typical example of traditional architecture.
89 | 0.77 | 68

3778 不对 [不對] /búduì/ (3) adj wrong, incorrect
你玩弄她的感情是不对的。It is wrong of you to trifle with her affections.
99 | 0.7 | 68

3779 无奈 [無奈] /wúnài/ adj having no choice, utterly helpless
他无奈地看着火车开出了车站。He helplessly watched the train pull out of the station.
101 | 0.68 | 68

3780 脆弱 [脆弱] /cuìruò/ adj frail, fragile
她太脆弱，太易生气了。She was still so fragile, so angry.
76 | 0.91 | 68

3781 重点 [重點] /zhòngdiǎn/ adj key, major
搞好重点项目建设。Efforts should be made to do a good job in key construction projects.
172 | 0.4 | 68

3782 决 [決] /jué/ (2) adv extremely, most; [usually in negative sentences] absolutely, at all
我决不能同意这种要求。I can never assent to such a request.
89 | 0.76 | 68

3783 许 [許] /xǔ/ (2) adv about, approximately; perhaps
清晨五时许，疏疏落落下了几点雨。About five o'clock in the morning there were a few drops of rain.
107 | 0.64 | 68

3784 恰恰 [恰恰] /qiàqià/ (3) adv exactly, just
恰恰在这个时候，电话铃响了。At exactly that moment, the telephone rang.
95 | 0.72 | 68

3785 越是 [越是] /yuèshì/ adv [as in 越是 ... 越是 ...] the more (... the more)
他情绪越低落越是借酒浇愁。The more depressed he got, the more he turned to drinking.
82 | 0.83 | 68

3786 整整 [整整] /zhěngzhěng/ *adj* whole, full
我们每人都喝了整整一瓶。We drank a whole bottle each.
82 | 0.83 | 68

3787 有意思 [有意思] /yǒuyìsi/ (1) *idiom* interesting
这听起来很有意思。This sounds interesting.
121 | 0.57 | 68 | S

3788 丝毫 [絲毫] /sīháo/ (3) *num* [normally occurring in negative sentences] at all, least
我们丝毫没费气力就找到了他。We did not have the least difficulty in finding him.
90 | 0.77 | 68

3789 工程师 [工程師] /gōngchéngshī/ (2) *n* engineer
我的朋友是一名工程师。My friend is an engineer.
80 | 0.86 | 68

3790 神经 [神經] /shénjīng/ (2) *n* nerve
我们长期处于紧张状态，神经已吃不消了。Constant stress has made our nerves brittle.
84 | 0.81 | 68

3791 沙发 [沙發] /shāfā/ (2) *n* sofa
我在沙发上躺了一会。I lay on the sofa for a while.
163 | 0.42 | 68

3792 积极性 [積極性] /jījíxìng/ (2) *n* enthusiasm, initiative, zeal
我们必须发挥群众的积极性。We must give play to the initiative of the masses.
140 | 0.49 | 68

3793 大妈 [大媽] /dàmā/ (2) *n* (paternal) aunt; [also used in northern dialects as a polite term of address for a woman of one's parents' age]
赵大妈从上个世纪 70 年代就住在这里了。Aunt Zhao has been living here since the 1970s.
127 | 0.54 | 68

3794 鲜花 [鮮花] /xiānhuā/ (2) *n* (fresh) flowers
她从花园里抱着一捧鲜花进来。She brought in an armful of fresh flowers from the garden.
87 | 0.78 | 68

3795 歌曲 [歌曲] /gēqǔ/ (3) *n* song
我听到那些旧歌曲就有些怀旧。Hearing those old songs takes me back a bit.
84 | 0.81 | 68

3796 出路 [出路] /chūlù/ (3) *n* way out, solution
那出路何在？What's the solution?
82 | 0.84 | 68

3797 象征 [象徵] /xiàngzhēng/ (3) *n* emblem, symbol, token
鸽子是和平的象征。The dove is the symbol of peace.
100 | 0.68 | 68

3798 车辆 [車輛] /chēliàng/ (3) *n* vehicle
那座旧桥只能通行轻型车辆。The old bridge can only be used by light vehicles.
114 | 0.6 | 68

3799 厂长 [廠長] /chǎngzhǎng/ (3) *n* factory manager, director
工人们对厂长的回答很满意。The workers were very satisfied with the factory manager's answers.
90 | 0.76 | 68

3800 住宅 [住宅] /zhùzhái/ (3) *n* residence
他们的住宅大楼坐落于公园旁。Their residential building is located next to the park.
122 | 0.56 | 68

3801 形态 [形態] /xíngtài/ (3) *n* shape, form
你能真正地看到大地的形态。You really see the shape of the land.
100 | 0.69 | 68

3802 借口 [藉口] /jièkǒu/ (3) *n* excuse
他们需要的是按时交货，而不是藉口。They want delivery on time, not excuses.
76 | 0.9 | 68

3803 体力 [體力] /tǐlì/ (3) *n* physical strength
这需要有高超的技术和体力。It takes a lot of skill and physical strength to do that.
82 | 0.84 | 68

3804 氛围 [氛圍] /fēnwéi/ *n* ambience, atmosphere, aura
家庭的融洽氛围是难能可贵的。The harmonising atmosphere of a family is valuable.
89 | 0.77 | 68

3805 老大 [老大] /lǎodà/ *n* eldest child (in a family); number one, leader of a team
我知道老大决不让我去的。I knew Eldest Brother would never let me go.
116 | 0.59 | 68

3806 策略 [策略] /cèlüè/ *n* strategy
我们的销售策略本该取得什么效果？What should our marketing strategy have achieved?
108 | 0.63 | 68

3807 硕士 [碩士] /shuòshì/ *n* master's degree
她完成了硕士学位的要求。She has completed the requirements for her master's degree.
83 | 0.82 | 68

3808 窝 [窩] /wō/ *n* nest
那个窝里没有蛋。There are no eggs in that nest.
94 | 0.72 | 68

3809 队 [隊] /duì/ *clas* [measure word for a group of people arranged in a line or file]
我随着一队游客混入了博物馆。I attached myself to a group of tourists entering the museum.
111 | 0.62 | 68

3810 眼中 [眼中] /yǎnzhōng/ *place* in one's eyes
泪珠在她眼中闪烁。Tears sparkled in her eyes.
135 | 0.51 | 68

3811 年底 [年底] /niándǐ/ *time* the end of the year
这房子的租约年底到期。The lease on this house expires at the end of the year.
103 | 0.66 | 68

3812 旅行 [旅行] /lǚxíng/ (1) v travel
没有汽车她怎样旅行？ How does she travel around without a car?
100 | 0.69 | 68

3813 惹 [惹] /rě/ (2) v provoke, cause, make; offend, get on one's nerves
她总惹麻烦。 She's always making trouble.
137 | 0.5 | 68

3814 应付 [應付] /yìngfu/ (3) v handle, deal with; do something perfunctorily, make do
他很难应付。 He is very hard to handle.
88 | 0.78 | 68

3815 协助 [協助] /xiézhù/ (3) v assist, help
那件事我可以协助你。 I can help you with that.
106 | 0.65 | 68

3816 抵抗 [抵抗] /dǐkàng/ (3) v resist
他再也抵抗不住了。 He could resist no longer.
98 | 0.7 | 68

3817 停留 [停留] /tíngliú/ (3) v (stop and) stay; remain
我们停留了一小时左右。 We stayed for an hour or so.
76 | 0.91 | 68

3818 视为 [視為] /shìwéi/ v deem, view as
很多人把车子视为地位的象征。 Many people view their car as a status symbol.
104 | 0.66 | 68

3819 收费 [收費] /shōufèi/ v charge
入场要收费吗？ Do they charge for admission?
187 | 0.37 | 68

3820 伸出 [伸出] /shēnchū/ v stretch out, extend
他伸出手臂去拿书。 He stretched out his arm to take the book.
131 | 0.53 | 68

3821 舍 [舍] /shě/ v abandon, give up, part with
不舍小利，难获厚利。 If small sums do not go out, large sums will not come in.
121 | 0.57 | 68

3822 清理 [清理] /qīnglǐ/ v clear, sort out
你能把这些文件清理掉吗？ Could you clear away these papers?
124 | 0.56 | 68

3823 琢磨 [琢磨] /zhuómó, zuómo/ v carve and polish, polish and refine; think over, ponder
好好琢磨一下再回答。 Think of the answers carefully.
97 | 0.71 | 68

3824 松 [松] /sōng/ (2) adj loose, slack, relaxed; soft and crisp
打包裹的绳很松。 The string around the parcel was slack.
81 | 0.83 | 68

3825 横 [橫] /héng, hèng/ (3) adj horizontal; unruly
先横后直。 First horizontal then vertical.
77 | 0.87 | 67

3826 散 [散] /sǎn/ (3) adj loose; leisurely; scattered, dispersive
绳子散了。 The string came untied.
91 | 0.74 | 67

3827 盲目 [盲目] /mángmù/ (3) adj blind
爱情是盲目的。 Love is blind.
89 | 0.76 | 67

3828 残酷 [殘酷] /cánkù/ (3) adj cruel
他对动物很残酷。 He is cruel to animals.
83 | 0.82 | 67

3829 爱国 [愛國] /àiguó/ adj patriotic
宗教界的爱国人士也是这样。 The same holds true for the patriotic people in religious circles.
111 | 0.6 | 67

3830 温柔 [溫柔] /wēnróu/ adj gentle and soft, amiable
她的性情温柔。 She has an amiable disposition.
134 | 0.5 | 67

3831 与其 [與其] /yǔqí/ (3) conj [used in pair with 不如 or 毋宁，etc.] rather than, better than
与其求人，何如自力更生。 It would be better to rely on oneself than on others.
94 | 0.72 | 67

3832 万一 [萬一] /wànyī/ conj just in case
万一下雨，他们就不能去了。 In case of rain they can't go.
102 | 0.66 | 67

3833 一律 [一律] /yílǜ/ adv all, with no exception
国家不分大小，应该一律平等。 Countries, big or small, should all be equal.
81 | 0.83 | 67

3834 互 [互] /hù/ adv mutually, each other
同学们要互帮互学。 Students should help and learn from each other.
85 | 0.79 | 67

3835 里头 [里頭] /lǐtou/ (3) loc inside
光剩了个空信封，里头什么也没有。 There's only an empty envelope with nothing in it.
221 | 0.3 | 67 | S

3836 窗户 [窗戶] /chuānghù/ (1) n window
起居室里有三扇窗户。 There are three windows in the sitting room.
106 | 0.64 | 67

3837 厨房 [廚房] /chúfáng/ (2) n kitchen
这厨房太脏了！ This kitchen's a mess!
126 | 0.53 | 67

3838 课程 [課程] /kèchéng/ (2) n course
我在夜校上汉语课程。 I'm taking courses on Chinese at a night school.
110 | 0.62 | 67

3839 旅馆 [旅館] /lǚguǎn/ (2) n guesthouse, hotel
该旅馆面向大海。 The hotel looks towards the sea.
80 | 0.85 | 67

3840 人力 [人力] /rénlì/ (3) *n* manpower
我们尽管缺少人力，仍力争按时完成任务。
We'll try to finish the work in time though we
are short of manpower.
112 | 0.6 | 67

3841 砖 [磚] /zhuān/ (3) *n* brick
这座房子的外墙是砖的。The outer walls of
the house were made of bricks.
78 | 0.87 | 67

3842 觉 [覺] /jiào, júe/ (3) *n* sleep; sense
我要的是好好睡一觉。What I need is a good
sleep.
99 | 0.68 | 67

3843 细胞 [細胞] /xìbāo/ (3) *n* cell
构成一切生物的细胞大部分是水。The cells of
which all living things are made are largely
water.
90 | 0.75 | 67

3844 职责 [職責] /zhízé/ *n* responsibility, duty
裁判员的职责是什么？What are the
responsibilities of a referee?
117 | 0.58 | 67

3845 风暴 [風暴] /fēngbào/ *n* storm
经过这场风暴后，大海平静下来了。The sea
was calm after the storm.
74 | 0.91 | 67

3846 年度 [年度] /niándù/ *n* year
你做的本年度预算数位十分准确。
Your budget figures were spot-on this year.
138 | 0.49 | 67

3847 派出所 [派出所] /pàichūsuǒ/ *n* local police
station
小偷被扭送到派出所了。The thief was seized
and turned over to a police station.
92 | 0.73 | 67

3848 难度 [難度] /nándù/ *n* (degree of) difficulty
考试的难度令我震惊。The difficulty of the
examination staggered me.
100 | 0.67 | 67

3849 心目 [心目] /xīnmù/ *n* mind
你心目中可有人选？Do you have someone in
mind?
84 | 0.81 | 67

3850 班 [班] /bān/ (1) *clas* [measure word for a
group of people] class, squad, team; [measure
word for regular transport services]
公共汽车多久一班？How often does this bus
run?
84 | 0.8 | 67

3851 册 [冊] /cè/ (2) *clas* [measure word for books]
copy
到1996年底，累计印刷发行《圣经》
达1800多万册。By the end of 1996
more than 18 million copies of the Bible
had been printed.
87 | 0.77 | 67

3852 桶 [桶] /tǒng/ *clas* [measure word] pail, bucket,
barrel
劳驾，我想来桶冰块。I'd like a bucket of ice,
please.
76 | 0.89 | 67

3853 练习 [練習] /liànxí/ (1) *v* practise
练习15分钟。Practise for 15 minutes.
93 | 0.73 | 67

3854 概括 [概括] /gàikuò/ (2) *v* recapitulate,
summarise, generalise
让我们来概括一下要点。Let's recapitulate the
main ideas.
90 | 0.75 | 67

3855 布置 [佈置] /bùzhì/ (2) *v* fix up, arrange,
decorate; assign (work, homework, etc.)
大家把会场布置得非常漂亮。The meeting
place is decorated beautifully.
87 | 0.77 | 67

3856 包含 [包含] /bāohán/ (3) *v* contain, include
小费包含在内吗？Are service charges
included?
94 | 0.71 | 67

3857 整顿 [整頓] /zhěngdùn/ (3) *v* rectify
他们必须整顿工作作风。They must rectify
the style of work.
123 | 0.55 | 67

3858 收集 [收集] /shōují/ (3) *v* gather, collect
收集古董突然盛行起来。Suddenly, collecting
antiques is all the fashion.
85 | 0.79 | 67

3859 问道 [問道] /wèndào/ *v* ask
他惊讶地问道。He asked in surprise.
162 | 0.42 | 67 | W

3860 迁 [遷] /qiān/ *v* move
他已经迁进新居了吗？Has he moved to his
new house yet?
88 | 0.77 | 67

3861 指定 [指定] /zhǐdìng/ *v* name, designate,
assign, appoint
他承认他没有读指定的书。He confessed
that he did not read the assigned books.
99 | 0.68 | 67

3862 抬头 [抬頭] /táitóu/ *v* raise one's head,
look up; hold one's head high; gain
ground
我不敢抬头望。I did not dare look up.
138 | 0.49 | 67

3863 震惊 [震驚] /zhènjīng/ *v* shock, astonish
这个事件震惊了世人。The event shocked the
world.
82 | 0.82 | 67

3864 暖 [暖] /nuǎn/ (2) *adj* warm
天气开始变暖了。The weather is starting to
turn warmer.
71 | 0.94 | 66

3865 惊讶 [驚訝] /jīngyà/ (3) *adj* surprised,
astonished
他万分惊讶。He was astonished beyond
measure.
103 | 0.65 | 66

3866 惊人 [驚人] /jīngrén/ (3) *adj* astonishing,
amazing
她的记忆力多么惊人啊！What an amazing
memory she has!
82 | 0.81 | 66

3867 最好 [最好] /zuìhǎo/ (2) *adv* had better, would better
你最好乘出租车。 You had better take a taxi.
81 | 0.82 | 66

3868 不已 [不已] /bùyǐ/ *adv* endlessly, incessantly
他懊悔不已。 He glutted himself with remorse.
93 | 0.71 | 66

3869 哎呀 [哎呀] /āiyā/ (2) *interj* [interjection expressing wonder, shock or complaint] ah, my god, damn
哎呀，多可怕呀！ Oh, how horrible!
227 | 0.3 | 66 | S

3870 优点 [優點] /yōudiǎn/ (2) *n* merit, strength, advantage
显然，电视有优点也有缺点。 Obviously, television has both advantages and disadvantages.
88 | 0.76 | 66

3871 区别 [區別] /qūbié/ (2) *n* difference
请注意下面两句话的区别。 Notice the difference between the following two sentences.
94 | 0.71 | 66

3872 雷 [雷] /léi/ (2) *n* thunder; mine
打了个响雷。 There was a loud crash of thunder.
115 | 0.58 | 66

3873 骆驼 [駱駝] /luòtuó/ (3) *n* camel
在动物园我看见了两只小骆驼。 I saw two small camels in the zoo.
80 | 0.83 | 66

3874 重要性 [重要性] /zhòngyàoxìng/ *n* importance
将来你会逐渐意识到节约的重要性。 Some day you will come to realise the importance of saving.
101 | 0.66 | 66

3875 风光 [風光] /fēngguāng/ *n* scene, scenery, view
西藏的风光无比优美。 The scenery in Tibet is magnificent.
71 | 0.94 | 66

3876 节奏 [節奏] /jiézòu/ *n* rhythm; tempo; pace
这部小说的节奏太慢。 This novel lacks pace.
72 | 0.92 | 66

3877 处长 [處長] /chùzhǎng/ *n* head of department
谁被任命为处长？ Who has been nominated head of the department?
95 | 0.7 | 66

3878 格局 [格局] /géjú/ *n* pattern, setup, layout
房子的格局如何？ What is the layout of this house like?
127 | 0.53 | 66

3879 真相 [真相] /zhēnxiàng/ *n* truth; the actual situation or facts
我想你不能不把真相告诉他。 I do not think you can avoid telling him the truth.
80 | 0.84 | 66

3880 西南 [西南] /xīnán/ *place* southwest
比方说，你要检查一下西南地区的销售结果。 Say you want to check out the sales results from the southwest region.
110 | 0.61 | 66

3881 秋天 [秋天] /qiūtiān/ (1) *time* autumn
你喜欢北京的秋天吗？ How do you like autumn in Beijing?
80 | 0.83 | 66

3882 反抗 [反抗] /fǎnkàng/ (2) *v* resist, revolt, rebel
谁受这样的对待都得反抗。 Such treatment would make anyone rebel.
91 | 0.73 | 66

3883 遵守 [遵守] /zūnshǒu/ (2) *v* abide by, observe
不管你在哪里你都要遵守法律。 Wherever you may be, you must observe the law.
101 | 0.65 | 66

3884 观看 [觀看] /guānkàn/ (3) *v* watch, see, view
有相当多的人来观看比赛。 A good few people came to watch the game.
102 | 0.65 | 66

3885 树立 [樹立] /shùlì/ (3) *v* set up, establish
他为我们树立了一个好榜样。 He set a fine example for us all.
147 | 0.45 | 66

3886 珍惜 [珍惜] /zhēnxī/ (3) *v* treasure, value, cherish
珍惜生命，拒绝毒品。 Cherish life, say no to drugs.
78 | 0.85 | 66

3887 制止 [制止] /zhìzhǐ/ (3) *v* stop, curb, prevent
此类活动必须予以制止。 We must put an end to this practice.
100 | 0.67 | 66

3888 争夺 [爭奪] /zhēngduó/ (3) *v* scramble for, contend for, contest
我们互相争夺那份奖品。 We contended with each other for the prize.
118 | 0.56 | 66

3889 被迫 [被迫] /bèipò/ (3) *v* be compelled to, be forced to
我被迫违心地在协议上签了字。 I was forced to sign the agreement against my will.
92 | 0.73 | 66

3890 迷信 [迷信] /míxìn/ (3) *v* have blind faith in
不要完全迷信这个。 Don't place blind faith in that.
84 | 0.79 | 66

3891 可谓 [可謂] /kěwèi/ *v* it may well be said, so to speak
他可谓一部活字典。 He is, so to speak, a walking dictionary.
88 | 0.75 | 66

3892 点头 [點頭] /diǎntóu/ *v* nod
他点了点头作为回答。 He replied with a nod.
197 | 0.34 | 66

3893 摄 [攝] /shè/ *v* take (a photograph)
这张照片摄于2002年4月。 This photograph was taken in April 2002.
206 | 0.32 | 66 | W

3894 极了 [極了] /jíle/ (1) adv extremely
真是美极了！It's so brilliantly beautiful!
102 | 0.65 | 66

3895 频繁 [頻繁] /pínfán/ adv frequently, often
你最好不要频繁地换工作。You'd better not change jobs so often.
90 | 0.73 | 65

3896 庞大 [龐大] /pángdà/ adj enormous, huge
大象是一种体积庞大的动物。Elephants are huge animals.
87 | 0.75 | 65

3897 毫不 [毫不] /háobù/ (2) adv not at all
她毫不迟疑立即作了回答。She answered without any hesitation.
87 | 0.75 | 65

3898 顿时 [頓時] /dùnshí/ (3) adv suddenly; immediately, at once
她听到这个消息顿时脸色苍白。She went as white as a sheet immediately when she heard the news.
129 | 0.51 | 65

3899 就算 [就算] /jiùsuàn/ conj granted that, even if
就算花我 10 年时间，我也决心完成这项工作。Even if it takes me ten years, I am determined to accomplish the job.
110 | 0.59 | 65

3900 故 [故] /gù/ adv on purpose, deliberately; pretentiously
他用神采奕奕的眼光看着人们，故作深沉。He pretended to be deep by staring into people's eyes.
110 | 0.59 | 65

3901 东部 [東部] /dōngbù/ (2) loc east, eastern part
医院在城市的东部。The hospital is in the east of the city.
152 | 0.43 | 65

3902 教室 [教室] /jiàoshì/ (1) n classroom
你在教室里找到她了吗？Did you find her in the classroom?
91 | 0.71 | 65

3903 姿态 [姿態] /zītài/ (3) n posture, manner; attitude, stance
行路的姿态是人的性格的表征。The way one walks gives an indication of one's character.
86 | 0.76 | 65

3904 药品 [藥品] /yàopǐn/ (3) n medicine, drug
药品不应放在孩子们拿得到的地方。Medicine should not be kept where it is accessible to children.
127 | 0.52 | 65

3905 钥匙 [鑰匙] /yàoshi/ (3) n key
他们用一把钥匙打开了锁。They opened the lock with a key.
93 | 0.71 | 65

3906 神话 [神話] /shénhuà/ (3) n fairy tale, myth
这不过是个神话。It's only a myth.
94 | 0.7 | 65

3907 小事 [小事] /xiǎoshì/ n trivial matter, triviality
他对她说不要为小事而烦扰他。He told her not to pester him with trivialities.
82 | 0.8 | 65

3908 开发区 [開發區] /kāifāqū/ n development district
我这次来要看看你们的开发区。During this visit I would like to see your development district.
168 | 0.39 | 65

3909 弹 [彈] /dàn/ n bullet, bomb
警方没费一枪一弹就擒住了罪犯。The police caught the criminal without firing a single shot.
86 | 0.76 | 65

25. English loanwords

米	米	*mǐ*	metre	**460**
幽默	幽默	*yōumò*	humour	**2575**
基因	基因	*jīyīn*	gene	**3089**
逻辑	邏輯	*luóji*	logic	**3305**
咖啡	咖啡	*kāfēi*	coffee	**3500**
沙发	沙發	*shāfā*	sofa	**3791**
坦克	坦克	*tǎnkè*	tank	**3943**
模特	模特	*mótè*	model	**4819**
马拉松	馬拉松	*mǎlāsōng*	marathon	**8095**
酷	酷	*kù*	cool	**8301**
酒吧	酒吧	*jiǔbā*	bar	**8553**
雷达	雷達	*léidá*	radar	**8912**
克隆	克隆	*kèlóng*	clone	**9327**

摩托	摩托	*mótuō*	motor	**10380**
吉普车	吉普車	*jípǔchē*	jeep	**10430**
沙拉	沙拉	*shālā*	salad	**11664**
芭蕾	芭蕾	*bālěi*	ballet	**11744**
巧克力	巧克力	*qiǎokèlì*	chocolate	**11968**
木乃伊	木乃伊	*mùnǎiyī*	mummy	**12158**
吉他	吉他	*jítā*	guitar	**13272**
沙龙	沙龍	*shālóng*	salon	**13602**
可可	可可	*kěkě*	cocoa	**14051**
卡通	卡通	*kǎtōng*	cartoon	**15886**
巴士	巴士	*bāshì*	bus	**16205**
迪斯科	迪斯科	*dísīkē*	disco	**16326**
磅	磅	*bàng*	pound	**16784**
保龄球	保齡球	*bǎolíngqiú*	bowling	**17553**
休克	休克	*xiūkè*	shock	**17961**
扑克	撲克	*pūkè*	poker	**20020**
引擎	引擎	*yǐnqíng*	engine	**20300**
尼龙	尼龍	*nílóng*	nylon	**20495**
可乐	可樂	*kělè*	cola	**21019**
摩登	摩登	*módēng*	modern	**21821**
歇斯底里	歇斯底里	*xiēsīdǐlǐ*	hysteria	**23284**
拷贝	拷貝	*kǎobèi*	copy	**23788**
香槟	香檳	*xiāngbīn*	champagne	**25892**
高尔夫	高爾夫	*gāo'ěrfū*	golf	**26797**
三明治	三明治	*sānmíngzhì*	sandwich	**26901**
雪茄	雪茄	*xuějiā*	cigar	**27524**
柠檬	檸檬	*níngméng*	lemon	**29335**
阿斯匹林	阿斯匹林	*āsīpǐlín*	aspirin	
爱滋	愛滋	*àizī*	AIDS	
奥林匹克	奧林匹克	*àolínpǐkè*	Olympics	
白兰地	白蘭地	*báilándì*	brandy	
比基尼	比基尼	*bǐjīní*	bikini	
比萨饼	比薩餅	*bǐsàbǐng*	pizza	
布丁	布丁	*bùdīng*	pudding	
伏特加	伏特加	*fútèjiā*	vodka	
汉堡包	漢堡包	*hànbǎobāo*	hamburger	
荷尔蒙	荷爾蒙	*hé'ěrméng*	hormone	
咖喱	咖喱	*gālí*	curry	
卡路里	卡路裡	*kǎlùlǐ*	calorie	
康乃馨	康乃馨	*kāngnǎixīn*	carnation	
来福枪	來福槍	*láifúqiāng*	rifle	
摩丝	摩絲	*mósī*	mousse	
尼古丁	尼古丁	*nígǔdīng*	nicotine	
苏打	蘇打	*sūdǎ*	soda	
探戈	探戈	*tàngē*	tango	
威士忌	威士忌	*wēishìjì*	whisky	
香波	香波	*xiāngbō*	shampoo	

3910 念头 [念頭] /niàntou/ n thought, idea
我突然有了一个奇怪的念头。A strange idea suddenly occurred to me.
111 | 0.59 | 65

3911 殿 [殿] /diàn/ n palace hall
请进殿内看一看。Step into the hall and have a look, please.
94 | 0.7 | 65

3912 使命 [使命] /shǐmìng/ n mission
照顾她兄弟的孩子似乎成了她一生的使命。It seems to be her mission to care for her brother's children.
103 | 0.64 | 65

3913 小孩子 [小孩子] /xiǎoháizi/ n child
小孩子最怕的是药。Children hate to take medicine.
93 | 0.7 | 65

3914 世人 [世人] /shìrén/ n (common) people, the world
但是世人对这一地区的实际情况仍然知之甚少。However, the world still knows very little about real developments in this region.
77 | 0.85 | 65

3915 火 [火] /huǒ/ (2) v get angry, be annoyed
你要再这样我就火了。If you do that again, I'll get angry.
89 | 0.74 | 65

3916 磨 [磨] /mó/ (2) v wear; rub; grind, polish; pester; dawdle
地毯渐渐磨坏了。The carpets are starting to wear.
80 | 0.82 | 65

3917 分裂 [分裂] /fēnliè/ (3) v split up, break apart
1989年以后南斯拉夫分裂了。Yugoslavia broke apart after 1989.
165 | 0.4 | 65

3918 游行 [遊行] /yóuxíng/ (3) v parade, march
失业的工人们在首都游行。Unemployed workers marched on the capital.
78 | 0.84 | 65

3919 自信 [自信] /zìxìn/ (3) v be confident
他自信能考及格。He feels confident he will pass the examination.
94 | 0.7 | 65

3920 高于 [高於] /gāoyú/ v be higher than, be above
健康高于财富。Good health is more important than wealth.
110 | 0.59 | 65

3921 解除 [解除] /jiěchú/ v remove, relieve
这些药片可以解除这病痛。These tablets should clear up the trouble.
96 | 0.68 | 65

3922 相处 [相處] /xiāngchǔ/ v get along
我觉得他极易相处。I found him quite easy to get along with.
92 | 0.71 | 65

3923 原有 [原有] /yuányǒu/ adj old, originally existing
她原有的恐惧再次向她袭来。Her old fears reassailed her.
98 | 0.67 | 65

3924 坐下 [坐下] /zuòxià/ v sit down
我要坐下歇歇腿。I need to sit down and rest my weary limbs.
154 | 0.42 | 65

3925 运作 [運作] /yùnzuò/ v operate
州代理机构运作方式相同。State agencies operate in a similar fashion.
110 | 0.59 | 65

3926 无限 [無限] /wúxiàn/ (2) adj unlimited, boundless
群众有无限的创造力。The masses have boundless creative power.
73 | 0.88 | 64

3927 漫长 [漫長] /màncháng/ (3) adj very long, endless
中国有漫长的海岸线。China has a very long coastline.
75 | 0.86 | 64

3928 鲜明 [鮮明] /xiānmíng/ (3) adj bright; distinct; striking
白色的墙壁与黑色的地毯形成了鲜明的对照。The white walls make a striking contrast with the black carpet.
84 | 0.76 | 64

3929 偷偷 [偷偷] /tōutōu/ (2) adv stealthily, secretly
一个男人偷偷地走进了加油站。A man stepped stealthily into the petrol station.
102 | 0.63 | 64

3930 大都 [大都] /dàdū/ (3) adv mostly, for the most part
旧房大都潮湿。Old houses are mostly damp.
83 | 0.78 | 64

3931 偶尔 [偶爾] /ǒu'ěr/ (3) adv occasionally
我偶尔晚上出去看看戏。I enjoy an occasional night out at the theatre.
103 | 0.63 | 64

3932 再也 [再也] /zàiyě/ adv [occurring in negative sentences] ever again
他发誓说再也不喝酒了。He vowed never to drink alcohol again.
105 | 0.62 | 64

3933 不时 [不時] /bùshí/ adv from time to time
她不时停下来休息。From time to time she would stop for a rest.
91 | 0.71 | 64

3934 东南 [東南] /dōngnán/ (2) loc southeast
飞机向东南方向飞去。The airplane flew towards the southeast.
80 | 0.8 | 64

3935 运动会 [運動會] /yùndònghuì/ (2) n sports meeting, games
我们举行了一场运动会。We had a sports meeting.
175 | 0.37 | 64

3936 费 [費] /fèi/ (2) n fee, expense
我应该付多少超重费？How much should I pay for the amount overweight?
73 | 0.88 | 64

3937 针 [針] /zhēn/ (2) *n* pin, needle; stitch; injection
一根针刺入我的手。A pin stuck me in the hand.
80 | 0.8 | 64

3938 电梯 [電梯] /diàntī/ (2) *n* elevator, lift, escalator
这是您的钥匙，电梯就在拐角处。Here's your key and the lift's just round the corner.
90 | 0.71 | 64

3939 平凡 [平凡] /píngfán/ (3) *adj* common, ordinary
他是一个平凡的人。He is just an ordinary person.
79 | 0.82 | 64

3940 协定 [協定] /xiédìng/ (3) *n* agreement
这个协定必须经董事会的正式批准。The agreement has to go to the board for ratification.
120 | 0.54 | 64

3941 宣言 [宣言] /xuānyán/ (3) *n* declaration, manifesto
他起草了独立宣言。He drew up the declaration of independence.
106 | 0.61 | 64

3942 行人 [行人] /xíngrén/ (3) *n* pedestrian
行人靠边走。Pedestrians keep to the side of the road.
77 | 0.84 | 64

3943 坦克 [坦克] /tǎnkè/ (3) *n* tank
坦克在那次进攻中打头阵。The tanks spearheaded the offensive.
114 | 0.56 | 64

3944 名牌 [名牌] /míngpái/ *n* famous brand or make
这是一台名牌洗衣机。This is a well-known brand of washing machine.
96 | 0.67 | 64

3945 历程 [歷程] /lìchéng/ *n* course, process
学习本身应该当作是创作的历程。Learning should become a process of creating.
88 | 0.73 | 64

3946 滋味 [滋味] /zīwèi/ *n* taste
这盘菜的滋味不错。This dish tastes good.
95 | 0.68 | 64

3947 毕业生 [畢業生] /bìyèshēng/ *n* graduate
我们的大多数毕业生都找到工作了。Most of our graduates are employed.
95 | 0.68 | 64

3948 爱心 [愛心] /àixīn/ *n* love, affection
这些教师都对学生具有爱心和耐心。All the teachers display an abundance of love and patience towards their students.
79 | 0.82 | 64

3949 人文 [人文] /rénwén/ *n* humanities
她学过人文学科。She has a background in humanities.
89 | 0.73 | 64

3950 人事 [人事] /rénshì/ *n* personnel affairs
他是那里的人事部主任。He is the director of the personnel department there.
88 | 0.74 | 64

3951 诗歌 [詩歌] /shīgē/ *n* poetry, poem
诗歌翻译不好。Poetry does not translate well.
106 | 0.61 | 64

3952 门外 [門外] /ménwài/ *place* outside the door
一群人站在门外聊天。A knot of people stood talking outside the door.
115 | 0.57 | 64

3953 夜晚 [夜晚] /yèwǎn/ (2) *time* night
这是个宁静的夜晚。It was a serene night.
88 | 0.73 | 64

3954 浮 [浮] /fú/ (2) *v* float
船静静地浮在水面上。The ship was floating silently on the water.
88 | 0.73 | 64

3955 堵 [堵] /dǔ/ (2) *v* stop up, block
下水道堵了。The drain is blocked.
79 | 0.81 | 64

3956 施工 [施工] /shīgōng/ (2) *v* be under construction
水库正在施工。The reservoir is under construction.
140 | 0.46 | 64

3957 报名 [報名] /bàomíng/ (2) *v* sign up, enrol
我想报名参加这烹饪课。I would like to enrol in this cooking class.
85 | 0.76 | 64

3958 折 [折] /zhé/ (2) *v* break, bend, fold; convert to
像这样把这边折上去。Fold this side up, like this.
82 | 0.78 | 64

3959 喷 [噴] /pēn/ (2) *v* spurt, squirt, spray, sprinkle
水喷了我一身。Water squirted all over me.
90 | 0.72 | 64

3960 抑制 [抑制] /yìzhì/ (3) *v* restrain, refrain
他抑制不住自己的好奇心。He couldn't restrain his curiosity.
86 | 0.75 | 64

3961 忽视 [忽視] /hūshì/ (3) *v* neglect, overlook
不应忽视困难。We should not overlook the difficulties.
99 | 0.65 | 64

3962 防御 [防禦] /fángyù/ (3) *v* defend, guard against
这个要塞无法防御来自空中的袭击。The fort cannot be defended against an air attack.
88 | 0.73 | 64

3963 沾 [沾] /zhān/ (3) *v* be stained with; touch, touch on
雪花沾手就化。The snowflakes melt the moment they touch one's hand.
97 | 0.66 | 64

3964 惯 [慣] /guàn/ (3) *v* be accustomed to; be in the habit of; spoil (a child)
他孤独惯了。He has become accustomed to loneliness.
88 | 0.73 | 64

3965 等到 [等到] /děngdào/ (3) *v* wait until
你在这儿等到他来再走。Wait here till he arrives.
85 | 0.76 | 64

3966 信仰 [信仰] /xìnyǎng/ n belief, faith
为何你有这么深的信仰？Why do you have
such strong faith?
86 | 0.76 | 64

3967 回归 [回歸] /huíguī/ v return
香港于 1997 年回归中国。Hong Kong was
returned to China in 1997.
121 | 0.53 | 64

3968 始 [始] /shǐ/ v begin, start
这场竞赛始于 1981 年。This race started in
1981.
86 | 0.75 | 64

3969 发布 [發佈] /fābù/ v issue, release, announce;
promulgate
这消息是由北京广播电台发布的。The news
was announced by Radio Beijing.
124 | 0.52 | 64

3970 度 [度] /dù/ v spend, pass (time)
望和你共度佳节。I hope we can spend the
holidays together.
80 | 0.81 | 64

3971 扮演 [扮演] /bànyǎn/ v play the role of, act as
这个角色他扮演得十分出色。He was very
good in the part.
78 | 0.83 | 64

3972 派出 [派出] /pàichū/ v send
他们立刻派出了医生。They sent the doctor
at once.
113 | 0.57 | 64

3973 任命 [任命] /rènmìng/ v appoint
她被任命为主任。She was appointed as the
director.
96 | 0.67 | 64

3974 讲述 [講述] /jiǎngshù/ v talk about, tell
我对你给我讲述的一切都感兴趣。I am
interested in all that you have told me.
81 | 0.79 | 64

3975 养老 [養老] /yǎnglǎo/ v provide for the elderly;
live out one's life in retirement
他努力工作为养老做准备。He worked hard to
provide for his old age.
104 | 0.62 | 64

3976 竞选 [競選] /jìngxuǎn/ v run for (an office)
他今年打算竞选市长。He is going to run for
mayor this year.
101 | 0.64 | 64

3977 临时 [臨時] /línshí/ (2) adj temporary
无家可归的家庭以活动房为临时住处。
Mobile homes are used as temporary housing
for homeless families.
82 | 0.78 | 63

3978 优美 [優美] /yōuměi/ (2) adj beautiful,
graceful
这座房屋四周的环境优美。The house is in
beautiful surroundings.
74 | 0.86 | 63

3979 雄 [雄] /xióng/ (2) adj male; heroic
雄火鸡既大又漂亮。The male turkey is big
and beautiful.
79 | 0.81 | 63

3980 伤心 [傷心] /shāngxīn/ (2) adj sad
你竟然欺骗了我，使我很伤心。That you
should cheat me made me sad.
116 | 0.55 | 63

3981 可怜 [可憐] /kělián/ (2) adj pitiful, poor
这个可怜的姑娘被当即解雇。The poor girl
was dismissed instantly.
115 | 0.56 | 63

3982 疯狂 [瘋狂] /fēngkuáng/ (3) adj crazy, mad
钱多使人疯狂。Too much money makes man
mad.
90 | 0.7 | 63

3983 惟一 [惟一] /wéiyī/ adj [equivalent of 唯一]
only, sole
我惟一喜欢的体育活动就是散步。The only
exercise I enjoy is taking walks.
98 | 0.65 | 63

3984 在 [在] /zài/ (1) adv [preceding a verb to
indicate an event in progress]
孩子们在玩。The children are playing.
144 | 0.44 | 63

3985 再度 [再度] /zàidù/ adv again, once more
不久，她再度离家出走。She left home again
before long.
90 | 0.71 | 63

3986 过于 [過於] /guòyú/ adv excessively, too
much
我们是否过于容忍？Are we too tolerant?
90 | 0.7 | 63

3987 以便 [以便] /yǐbiàn/ conj so that, in
order to
我把灯打开以便看得清楚些。I turned on
the light so that I could see clearly.
103 | 0.62 | 63

3988 诸多 [諸多] /zhūduō/ num a lot of
做我的工作，你要冒诸多风险。You have to
take a lot of risks in my job.
90 | 0.71 | 63

3989 钢 [鋼] /gāng/ (2) n steel
钢比铁更坚固。Steel is stronger than iron.
85 | 0.75 | 63

3990 国王 [國王] /guówáng/ (2) n king
他的行动证明了他对国王的一片忠心。
His action was a token of his loyalty to
the king.
96 | 0.66 | 63

3991 玉米 [玉米] /yùmǐ/ (2) n sweetcorn
玉米在这里不能成长。Corn doesn't grow
here.
88 | 0.72 | 63

3992 是非 [是非] /shìfēi/ (3) n right and wrong;
dispute
孩子们必须培养判断是非的能力。Children
must develop a sense of right and wrong.
78 | 0.82 | 63

3993 大众 [大眾] /dàzhòng/ (3) n the public, the
people
这个游泳池是开放给大众的。This swimming
pool is open to the general public.
90 | 0.71 | 63

3994 情报 [情報] /qíngbào/ (3) n intelligence, information
这情报证明很有用。 This information proved useful.
86 | 0.74 | 63

3995 高潮 [高潮] /gāocháo/ (3) n high tide, upsurge; climax; orgasm
这部小说有两个高潮。 There are two climaxes in this novel.
84 | 0.76 | 63

3996 线索 [線索] /xiànsuǒ/ n clue
上下文线索有助于了解意思。 Contextual clues can help one to find the meaning.
71 | 0.9 | 63

3997 学历 [學歷] /xuélì/ n academic qualification
你的最高学历是什么？ What is your highest academic qualification?
81 | 0.78 | 63

3998 轿车 [轎車] /jiàochē/ n car
小轿车比摩托车舒服。 A car is more comfortable than a motorcycle.
108 | 0.59 | 63

3999 平民 [平民] /píngmín/ n civilians, ordinary people
平民保有武器是不合法的。 It is illegal for civilians to keep weapons.
78 | 0.81 | 63

4000 打算 [打算] /dǎsuàn/ n plan
他想逃走的打算完全吹了。 His plan to escape came badly unstuck.
78 | 0.81 | 63

4001 步伐 [步伐] /bùfá/ n pace, step
他的步伐加快了。 His pace quickened.
156 | 0.41 | 63

4002 都市 [都市] /dūshì/ n city, metropolis
他习惯于都市生活。 He was accustomed to living in a big city.
73 | 0.87 | 63

4003 大厦 [大廈] /dàshà/ n building, mansion
这栋古老的大厦建于1850年。 The old mansion was built in 1850.
89 | 0.72 | 63

4004 实验室 [實驗室] /shíyànshì/ n lab, laboratory
实验室需要一些新设备。 The lab needs some new apparatus.
90 | 0.71 | 63

4005 通道 [通道] /tōngdào/ n passage, passageway; aisle
一条地下通道通到街对面的大楼。 An underground passage leads to the building across the street.
100 | 0.63 | 63

4006 内涵 [內涵] /nèihán/ n meaning, connotation
安全的内涵不断扩大。 The connotation of security is expanding continuously.
90 | 0.7 | 63

4007 俺 [俺] /ǎn/ pron [northern dialects] I, we, my, our, me, us
俺和你当时距离不算近，但是俺们的心的确是在一起的。 We were not near, yet we were together.
93 | 0.68 | 63

4008 失业 [失業] /shīyè/ (2) v become unemployed, be out of work
她已失业一年了。 She had been out of work for a year.
119 | 0.53 | 63

4009 称赞 [稱讚] /chēngzàn/ (2) v praise, speak well of
四周邻居都称赞他。 The whole neighbourhood speaks well of him.
81 | 0.79 | 63

4010 睁 [睜] /zhēng/ (2) v open (eyes)
她睁开了眼睛。 She opened her eyes.
163 | 0.39 | 63

4011 欺骗 [欺騙] /qīpiàn/ (2) v deceive, cheat
欺骗那女孩，真是不象话！ What a shame to deceive the girl!
75 | 0.84 | 63

4012 活跃 [活躍] /huóyuè/ (2) v be active, make . . . active
新的力量活跃在我们四周。 New forces are energising all about us.
89 | 0.72 | 63

4013 烫 [燙] /tàng/ (2) v scald, burn; iron, press; have one's hair permed
这条裙子我要烫一下。 I'd like to have this skirt pressed.
88 | 0.72 | 63

4014 流传 [流傳] /liúchuán/ (3) v spread, circulate, pass down
故事被一代代流传下来。 The story was passed down from father to son.
88 | 0.72 | 63

4015 飞行 [飛行] /fēixíng/ (3) v fly, make a flight
大型客机在云层上面飞行。 The airliner flew above the clouds.
98 | 0.64 | 63

4016 译 [譯] /yì/ v translate
这本小说被译成汉语了。 This novel has been translated into Chinese.
86 | 0.73 | 63

4017 提起 [提起] /tíqǐ/ v mention
你别向任何人提起这件事，好吗？ Would you mind not mentioning it to anyone?
71 | 0.89 | 63

4018 心想 [心想] /xīnxiǎng/ v think
我心想，一切都完了。 It was all over, I thought.
116 | 0.55 | 63

4019 怒 [怒] /nù/ adj angry, indignant
她满脸怒容。 She wore an angry expression.
113 | 0.56 | 63

4020 布 [佈] /bù/ v arrange, deploy; announce, declare
军队已布好阵势迎战。 The army is arranged for battle.
89 | 0.71 | 63

4021 注 [注] /zhù/ v annotate; pour, inject; concentrate
他汗流如注。 The sweat was pouring off him.
93 | 0.68 | 63

4022 糊涂 [糊塗] /hútu/ (2) *adj* muddled, confused; blurred
把我弄得更糊涂了！I am even more confused!
92 | 0.67 | 62

4023 湿 [濕] /shī/ (2) *adj* wet, sodden
我在雨里这么一跑，鞋全湿了。My shoes are sodden from walking in the rain.
92 | 0.68 | 62

4024 实在 [實在] /shízài/ (2) *adj* real; honest and trustworthy
他做生意很实在。He is honest in business.
82 | 0.76 | 62

4025 难受 [難受] /nánshòu/ (2) *adj* unwell; unhappy
我热得难受。I felt oppressed with the heat.
100 | 0.63 | 62

4026 寂寞 [寂寞] /jìmò/ (3) *adj* lonely
你有时候是否感到寂寞？Do you ever feel lonely?
93 | 0.67 | 62

4027 好奇 [好奇] /hàoqí/ (3) *adj* curious
他对新来的邻居很好奇。He felt curious about his new neighbour.
108 | 0.58 | 62

4028 知名 [知名] /zhīmíng/ *adj* renowned, well known
这是知名品牌。It's a well-known brand.
86 | 0.73 | 62

4029 单独 [單獨] /dāndú/ (3) *adv* alone
我要跟你单独谈一谈。I want to speak to you alone.
71 | 0.88 | 62

4030 南北 [南北] /nánběi/ *loc* north and south, from south to north
那条路是南北走向。The road runs from south to north.
89 | 0.71 | 62

4031 邮票 [郵票] /yóupiào/ (1) *n* stamp
那抽屉里有邮票吗？Are there any stamps in that drawer?
98 | 0.64 | 62

4032 椅子 [椅子] /yǐzi/ (1) *n* chair
这张椅子会摇晃。This chair wobbles.
126 | 0.49 | 62

4033 电报 [電報] /diànbào/ (2) *n* telegram, telegraph, cable
她给我拍了封电报。She sent me a telegram.
85 | 0.74 | 62

4034 家俱 [傢俱] /jiājù/ (2) *n* furniture
你是自己搬的这些家俱吗？Did you move all this furniture on your own?
70 | 0.9 | 62

4035 身材 [身材] /shēncái/ (3) *n* stature, figure, build
我中等身材。I am of average height.
89 | 0.7 | 62

4036 日报 [日報] /rìbào/ (3) *n* daily (newspaper)
你看了今天的体育日报没有？Have you read today's *Sports Daily*?
92 | 0.68 | 62

4037 一行 [一行] /yìxíng/ (3) *n* group, delegation
你们一行有多少人？How many people are in your group?
158 | 0.4 | 62

4038 中医 [中醫] /zhōngyī/ (3) *n* Chinese medicine; herb doctor
他不大相信中医。He has no great belief in Chinese medicine.
93 | 0.67 | 62

4039 共和国 [共和國] /gònghéguó/ (3) *n* republic
工人农民是这个共和国的基本群众。The workers and peasants are the basic masses of the republic.
98 | 0.64 | 62

4040 书法 [書法] /shūfǎ/ *n* calligraphy; handwriting
许多留学生对中国书法艺术感兴趣。Many foreign students are interested in Chinese calligraphy.
106 | 0.59 | 62

4041 老家 [老家] /lǎojiā/ *n* native place, hometown
你是问我的老家吗？Are you asking about my hometown?
77 | 0.81 | 62

4042 课题 [課題] /kètí/ *n* research topic, (research) project
他全力以赴地做这项研究课题。He bent his mind to the research project.
123 | 0.51 | 62

4043 江湖 [江湖] /jiānghú/ *n* rivers and lakes; the wide world; itinerant entertainer, quack
可别上当；他纯粹是江湖医生。Don't be taken in; he's just a quack.
81 | 0.77 | 62

4044 掌 [掌] /zhǎng/ *n* palm
魔术师把牌藏于掌中。The magician palmed the card.
91 | 0.69 | 62

4045 等级 [等級] /děngjí/ *n* class, grade, rank
我们现在急需这两种等级的货。We are in urgent need of these two grades.
84 | 0.74 | 62

4046 预算 [預算] /yùsuàn/ *n* budget
我们的预算需作重大修改。Our budget needs drastic revision.
167 | 0.38 | 62

4047 谷 [穀] /gǔ/ *n* grain, cereal; valley
早餐有多种谷类食物可供选用。There is a variety of different cereals for breakfast.
73 | 0.85 | 62

4048 首相 [首相] /shǒuxiàng/ *n* prime minister
首相出席了典礼。The prime minister attended the ceremony.
157 | 0.4 | 62

4049 老鼠 [老鼠] /lǎoshǔ/ *n* rat, mouse
老鼠传染疾病。Rats carry diseases.
82 | 0.76 | 62

4050 克 [克] /kè/ (1) *clas* [measure term for weight] gram
这封信超重 10 克。This letter is ten grams overweight.
152 | 0.41 | 62

26. Language learning

Simplified Chinese	Traditional Chinese	Pinyin	Gloss
Sentence analysis:			
宾语	賓語	*bīnyǔ*	object
补语	補語	*bǔyǔ*	complement
成语	成語	*chéngyǔ*	idiom
处所词	處所詞	*chùsuǒ cí*	place word
词	詞	*cí*	word
词汇	詞彙	*cíhuì*	vocabulary
词头	詞頭	*cítóu*	prefix
词尾	詞尾	*cíwěi*	suffix
代词	代詞	*dàicí*	pronoun
定语	定語	*dìngyǔ*	attributive
动词	動詞	*dòngcí*	verb
动态助词	動態助詞	*dòngtài zhùcí*	aspect particle
短语	短語	*duǎnyǔ*	phrase
方位词	方位詞	*fāngwèi cí*	locality word
副词	副詞	*fùcí*	adverb
感叹词	感嘆詞	*gǎntàncí*	interjection
惯用语	慣用語	*guànyòngyǔ*	fixed expression
结构助词	結構助詞	*jiégòu zhùcí*	structural particle
介词	介詞	*jiècí*	preposition
句子	句子	*jùzi*	sentence
连词	連詞	*liáncí*	conjunction
量词	量詞	*liàngcí*	measure word, classifier
名词	名詞	*míngcí*	noun
能愿动词	能願動詞	*néngyuàn dòngcí*	optative verb
时间词	時間詞	*shíjiāncí*	time word
述语	述語	*shùyǔ*	predicate
数词	數詞	*shùcí*	numeral
数量词	數量詞	*shùliàngcí*	numeral measure word
叹词	嘆詞	*tàncí*	interjection
谓语	謂語	*wèiyǔ*	predicate
习惯用语	習慣用語	*xíguàn yòngyǔ*	idiomatic expression
象声词	象聲詞	*xiàngshēngcí*	onomatopoeia
形容词	形容詞	*xíngróngcí*	adjective
谚语	諺語	*yànyǔ*	proverb
疑问代词	疑問代詞	*yíwèn dàicí*	question pronoun
疑问助词	疑問助詞	*yíwèn zhùcí*	question particle
语法术语	語法術語	*yǔfǎ shùyǔ*	grammatical term
语气助词	語氣助詞	*yǔqì zhùcí*	modal particle
主语	主語	*zhǔyǔ*	subject
助词	助詞	*zhùcí*	particle
专有名词	專有名詞	*zhuānyǒu míngcí*	proper noun
状语	狀語	*zhuàngyǔ*	adverbial
字	字	*zì*	character

Punctuation marks:

逗号	逗號	*dòuhào*	comma
顿号	頓號	*dùnhào*	enumeration comma
分号	分號	*fēnhào*	semicolon
感叹号	感嘆號	*gǎntànhào*	exclamation mark
句号	句號	*jùhào*	full stop
括号	括號	*kuòhào*	parenthesis, bracket
冒号	冒號	*màohào*	colon
破折号	破折號	*pòzhéhào*	dash
省略号	省略號	*shěnglüèhào*	ellipsis
书名号	書名號	*shūmínghào*	book title mark
双引号	雙引號	*shuāng yǐnhào*	double quotation mark
单引号	單引號	*dān yǐnhào*	single quotation mark
问号	問號	*wènhào*	question mark
星号	星號	*xīnghào*	asterisk
引号	引號	*yǐnhào*	quotation mark

4051 集 [集] /*jí*/ clas [measure word for TV plays, movies and books, etc.] episode, part, volume
把三集的内容压缩成了一个节目。 Three episodes have been telescoped into a single programme.
90 | 0.69 | 62

4052 本地 [本地] /*běndì*/ place [as opposed to 外地] local place
我在哪儿能吃到本地的风味儿？ Where can I enjoy the best local food?
88 | 0.71 | 62

4053 室内 [室內] /*shìnèi*/ place indoor
乒乓球是一项很好的室内运动。 Ping-pong is a good indoor sport.
81 | 0.77 | 62

4054 近日 [近日] /*jìnrì*/ time recently, in the past or next few days
希望近日内还能见面。 Hope to see you again soon.
225 | 0.28 | 62

4055 松 [松] /*sōng*/ (2) v loosen, unfasten
你的鞋带松了。 Your shoelace has come loose.
98 | 0.64 | 62

4056 割 [割] /*gē*/ (2) v cut
他割开袋子。 He cut the bag open.
78 | 0.8 | 62

4057 过渡 [過渡] /*guòdù*/ (3) n transition, interim
在过渡期间，没发生过任何事。 Nothing has happened in the interim.
116 | 0.54 | 62

4058 得意 [得意] /*déyì*/ (3) adj proud (of oneself), complacent
他脸上显出得意的神气。 He had an air of complacency.
115 | 0.54 | 62

4059 忍不住 [忍不住] /*rěnbuzhù*/ (3) v cannot help but
他忍不住笑了出来。 He couldn't help chuckling aloud.
181 | 0.34 | 62

4060 包围 [包圍] /*bāowéi*/ (3) v surround, encircle
警察把大楼包围起来了。 Police surrounded the building.
90 | 0.7 | 62

4061 罢 [罷] /*bà*/ (3) v stop, cease; dismiss; [used as a resultative verb complement indicating completion] finish
说罢，他就走了。 With these words he left.
98 | 0.64 | 62

4062 盛 [盛] /*chéng*/ (3) v fill (a bowl, etc.) with; hold, contain
那罐子能盛多少水？ How much water does the jug hold?
80 | 0.78 | 62

4063 积 [積] /*jī*/ v accumulate, collect
窗台上积了灰尘。 Dust had collected on the windowsill.
83 | 0.75 | 62

4064 谢 [謝] /*xiè*/ v thank; (of flowers) wither
我真不知怎么谢您才好。 I really do not know how I can thank you enough.
85 | 0.74 | 62

4065 购物 [購物] /*gòuwù*/ v do shopping
你可以在那儿购物。 You can do your shopping.
93 | 0.68 | 62

4066 走过 [走過] /*zǒuguò*/ v cross, go through, walk past
他从我身边走过，没说一句话。 He walked by me without speaking.
74 | 0.84 | 62

4067 聚会 [聚會] /jùhuì/ n gathering, meeting, party
你能来参加这次聚会吗？ Can you come to the party?
69 | 0.9 | 62

4068 尊 [尊] /zūn/ v respect
倡扬尊老爱幼的美德。 The virtue of respecting the old and loving the young should be advocated.
77 | 0.81 | 62

4069 收藏 [收藏] /shōucáng/ v collect
我收藏外国硬币。 I collect foreign coins.
75 | 0.83 | 62

4070 增 [增] /zēng/ v increase
她原先的投资额已增至两倍。 Her original investment has increased twofold.
119 | 0.53 | 62

4071 呗 [唄] /bei/ part [sentence final particle indicating something obvious or expressing resignation]
你要唱就唱呗。 Well, sing if you like.
134 | 0.47 | 62 | S

4072 薄 [薄] /báo, bó/ (2) adj thin; small, meagre
池塘上结了一层薄冰。 The pond is coated with thin ice.
77 | 0.79 | 61

4073 光明 [光明] /guāngmíng/ (2) adj bright
只要我们努力，我们的前途是光明的。 If we try hard, our future will be bright.
72 | 0.85 | 61

4074 古典 [古典] /gǔdiǎn/ (3) adj classical
她喜欢古典音乐。 She likes classical music.
102 | 0.6 | 61

4075 犹豫 [猶豫] /yóuyù/ (3) adj hesitant
她对是否接受邀请犹豫不决。 She was hesitant about accepting the invitation.
106 | 0.58 | 61

4076 旺 [旺] /wàng/ adj prosperous, flourishing, brisk; (of fire) blazing
购销两旺。 Both purchasing and marketing are brisk.
82 | 0.74 | 61

4077 神奇 [神奇] /shénqí/ adj magical, mystical, miraculous
这些书充满了神奇的故事。 These books are littered with miraculous stories.
72 | 0.86 | 61

4078 一手 [一手] /yìshǒu/ adv single-handedly, all along, all by oneself
他是由母亲一手抚养大的。 His mother brought him up single-handedly.
91 | 0.68 | 61

4079 身后 [身後] /shēnhòu/ loc behind somebody; after one's death
她把一大群摄影记者甩在身后。 She left a swarm of photographers behind her.
138 | 0.45 | 61

4080 热 [熱] /rè/ suf craze, fad
股票热降温了。 The stock craze has abated.
73 | 0.84 | 61

4081 高原 [高原] /gāoyuán/ (2) n plateau, highland
许多游客不适应高原气候。 Many tourists were not accustomed to the plateau climate.
114 | 0.54 | 61

4082 手指 [手指] /shǒuzhǐ/ (2) n finger
我手指扎了根刺。 I've got a splinter in my finger.
122 | 0.51 | 61

4083 工夫 [工夫] /gōngfu/ (2) n time; effort; workmanship, skill; [equivalent of 功夫] kung fu, martial arts
明天有工夫再来吧。 Come again tomorrow if you have time.
88 | 0.7 | 61

4084 美术 [美術] /měishù/ (2) n art, fine arts, painting
我是学美术的学生，我画许多画。 I am an art student and I paint a lot of pictures.
95 | 0.65 | 61

4085 黄色 [黃色] /huángsè/ (3) n yellow; pornography
我们把房间油漆成黄色。 We painted the rooms yellow.
76 | 0.81 | 61

4086 摩托车 [摩托車] /mótuōchē/ (3) n motorcycle, motorbike
我想骑摩托车去。 I want to go by motorbike.
95 | 0.65 | 61

4087 蓝色 [藍色] /lánsè/ n blue
我个人最喜欢蓝色。 Personally, I like blue best.
81 | 0.76 | 61

4088 鸭 [鴨] /yā/ n duck
鸡和鸭是两种类型的家禽。 Chicken and duck are two types of fowl.
84 | 0.73 | 61

4089 高考 [高考] /gāokǎo/ n college entrance examination
现行高考制度将终结？ Will the current system of college entrance examination end?
93 | 0.66 | 61

4090 时尚 [時尚] /shíshàng/ n fashion, vogue
时尚无处不在，它是不可回避的。 Fashion is everywhere, and it is unavoidable.
91 | 0.68 | 61

4091 兵力 [兵力] /bīnglì/ n troops, military strength; strength
而集中兵力，是首先的和主要的。 And of these, concentration of troops is the first and most essential.
107 | 0.57 | 61

4092 影视 [影視] /yǐngshì/ n film and video
她是舞台影视三栖明星。 She is a star of stage, screen and video.
105 | 0.59 | 61

4093 业绩 [業績] /yèjì/ n performance; achievement
公司业绩仅属一般。 The company's performance is only average.
103 | 0.6 | 61

4094 号召 [號召] /hàozhào/ (2) v call for
工会号召总罢工。The union call for an all-out strike.
82 | 0.76 | 61

4095 住院 [住院] /zhùyuàn/ (2) v be hospitalised
你必须立即住院。You must be hospitalised right now.
69 | 0.89 | 61

4096 服从 [服從] /fúcóng/ (2) v obey; be subordinate to
儿童应该服从他们的父母。Children should obey their parents.
78 | 0.79 | 61

4097 小心 [小心] /xiǎoxīn/ (2) v be careful, take care; guard against
她本该这么小心些。She ought to have been more careful.
98 | 0.63 | 61

4098 燃烧 [燃燒] /ránshāo/ (2) v burn
那所房子燃烧了数小时火才扑灭。The house burnt for hours before the blaze was put out.
70 | 0.88 | 61

4099 冻 [凍] /dòng/ (2) v freeze
我们几乎冻死了。We nearly froze to death.
76 | 0.81 | 61

4100 违背 [違背] /wéibèi/ (3) v violate, go against, be contrary to
我不会要你违背艺术良心。I wouldn't want you to violate your artistic conscience.
85 | 0.73 | 61

4101 返 [返] /fǎn/ (3) v return, go back
我计划重返校园。I plan to go back to school.
65 | 0.94 | 61

4102 促使 [促使] /cùshǐ/ (3) v impel, spur on, prompt
他父母促使他作出更大的努力。His parents impelled him to greater efforts.
101 | 0.61 | 61

4103 干扰 [幹擾] /gānrǎo/ (3) v disturb
把收音机开小点儿，别干扰人家。Turn down the radio, or you'll disturb people.
81 | 0.76 | 61

4104 委托 [委託] /wěituō/ (3) v entrust
我把事情委托给了一个有经验的律师。I trusted my affairs to an experienced lawyer.
100 | 0.61 | 61

4105 奉献 [奉獻] /fèngxiàn/ v dedicate, devote, consecrate
他将一生奉献给了音乐。He devoted himself entirely to music.
88 | 0.7 | 61

4106 审 [審] /shěn/ v try; examine, review
这个案子哪位法官来审？Which judge will try the case?
72 | 0.86 | 61

4107 传递 [傳遞] /chuándì/ v transmit, communicate, pass
你有什么话要我传递的吗？Is there any message you wish me to pass along?
75 | 0.81 | 61

4108 享有 [享有] /xiǎngyǒu/ v enjoy (rights, etc.)
妇女享有与男子平等的政治权利。Women enjoy equal political rights with men.
96 | 0.64 | 61

4109 延续 [延續] /yánxù/ v continue, last
面试延续了近一个小时。The interview lasted about an hour.
76 | 0.8 | 61

4110 挣钱 [掙錢] /zhèngqián/ v earn money
她为了挣钱而努力工作。She's working hard to earn money.
91 | 0.68 | 61

4111 全部 [全部] /quánbù/ n all, everything, entirety, totality
我们必须看事物的全部。We must view things in their totality.
72 | 0.84 | 60

4112 高尚 [高尚] /gāoshàng/ (3) adj noble, lofty
他是一个节操高尚的人。He's a noble man of moral integrity.
70 | 0.86 | 60

4113 恶劣 [惡劣] /èliè/ (3) adj bad, vile, abominable
多么恶劣的天气！What bad weather!
75 | 0.8 | 60

4114 顽强 [頑強] /wánqiáng/ (3) adj indomitable; tenacious
他们同干旱进行了顽强的斗争。They put up a tenacious fight against the drought.
81 | 0.74 | 60

4115 模糊 [模糊] /móhu/ (3) adj vague, faint, blurred
这块石头上的字迹很模糊。The writing on the stone was very faint.
82 | 0.74 | 60

4116 有益 [有益] /yǒuyì/ (3) adj beneficial, good
我认为运动对你有益。I think sports are good for you.
99 | 0.61 | 60

4117 异 [異] /yì/ adj different; strange, unusual
其表演技法也随之而异。The play is accordingly different.
80 | 0.76 | 60

4118 时刻 [時刻] /shíkè/ (2) adv at any moment, constantly
要时刻牢记自己在事业上的奋斗目标。Keep your career aims constantly in view.
70 | 0.87 | 60

4119 明明 [明明] /míngmíng/ (3) adv clearly, obviously, undoubtedly
这话明明是她说的。It is undoubtedly she who has said that.
84 | 0.72 | 60

4120 未必 [未必] /wèibì/ (3) adv not necessarily
有钱人未必快乐。The rich are not necessarily happy.
84 | 0.73 | 60

4121 尽可能 [盡可能] /jìnkěnéng/ adv as far as possible
请尽可能早些来。Please come as early as possible.
85 | 0.71 | 60

4122 从未 [從未] /cóngwèi/ adv never (before)
我从未见过这么大的钻石。I have never seen such a huge diamond.
79 | 0.77 | 60

4123 没关系 [沒關係] /méiguānxi/ (1) idiom it doesn't matter, it's all right, never mind
一点儿没关系。It does not matter at all.
109 | 0.55 | 60 | S

4124 有的是 [有的是] /yǒudeshì/ (2) idiom have plenty of, there's no lack of
我们有的是时间。We have got plenty of time.
79 | 0.76 | 60

4125 平原 [平原] /píngyuán/ (2) n plain
东部平原极其肥沃。The plains in the east are extremely fertile.
78 | 0.78 | 60

4126 眼镜 [眼鏡] /yǎnjìng/ (2) n glasses, spectacles
我的眼镜遗失了。I lost my glasses.
94 | 0.64 | 60

4127 坡 [坡] /pō/ (2) n slope
从这个坡下去。Walk down this slope.
72 | 0.83 | 60

4128 矿 [礦] /kuàng/ (2) n ore; mine
新矿正在开发。New mines are opening up.
85 | 0.71 | 60

4129 步骤 [步驟] /bùzhòu/ (3) n step, move
这一步骤目前正在准备中。This move is now in preparation.
92 | 0.66 | 60

4130 土壤 [土壤] /tǔrǎng/ (3) n soil
按时给植物浇水以保持土壤湿润。Water the plant regularly to keep the soil moist.
77 | 0.79 | 60

4131 面孔 [面孔] /miànkǒng/ (3) n face
她很有兴趣地打量着他的面孔。She studied his face with interest.
134 | 0.45 | 60

4132 脸色 [臉色] /liǎnsè/ (3) n complexion, look; facial expression
你脸色有点苍白。You look a bit pale.
193 | 0.31 | 60

4133 战术 [戰術] /zhànshù/ (3) n tactic
这是一个新战术。It's a new tactic.
80 | 0.76 | 60

4134 粥 [粥] /zhōu/ (3) n gruel, porridge, congee
粥有益于消化。Porridge is good for digestion.
80 | 0.76 | 60

4135 壁 [壁] /bì/ (3) n wall
他把壁上的油漆刮掉了。He scaled off the paint from the wall.
74 | 0.81 | 60

4136 嘴巴 [嘴巴] /zuǐba/ n mouth
请张开嘴巴。Please open your mouth.
100 | 0.6 | 60

4137 潮流 [潮流] /cháoliú/ n tide; trend
我们到底如何赶上这些变化和潮流？How do we then keep up with all these changes and trends?
87 | 0.7 | 60

4138 官方 [官方] /guānfāng/ adj official, of or from the government
他把一些官方文件留在车里。He left some official documents in his car.
86 | 0.7 | 60

4139 股市 [股市] /gǔshì/ n stock market
股市上的价格普遍上涨。Price generally advanced on the stock market.
103 | 0.59 | 60

4140 超市 [超市] /chāoshì/ n supermarket, superstore
欢迎光临我们超市。Welcome to our supermarket.
112 | 0.54 | 60

4141 投资 [投資] /tóuzī/ n investment
对外投资有了初步发展。Overseas investment witnessed initial development.
189 | 0.32 | 60

4142 泪水 [淚水] /lèishuǐ/ n tear, teardrop
她的眼里充满泪水。Her eyes were full of tears.
126 | 0.48 | 60

4143 扛 [扛] /káng/ (2) v carry on one's shoulder, shoulder
他把行李扛在肩上。He carried his luggage on his shoulder.
86 | 0.71 | 60

4144 呼 [呼] /hū/ (2) v exhale, breathe; shout; call
男子呼了口气，一副放下心头石的模样。The man breathed a sigh of relief, as if a heavy stone had been lifted from his heart.
87 | 0.69 | 60

4145 循环 [迴圈] /xúnhuán/ (3) v circle, circulate
锻炼帮助血液和其他体液循环。Exercise helps the blood and other body fluids to circulate.
87 | 0.7 | 60

4146 打架 [打架] /dǎjià/ (3) v fight
不可打架。Please stop fighting.
92 | 0.65 | 60

4147 瞪 [瞪] /dèng/ (3) v stare at
她严厉地瞪着我。She stared pointedly at me.
205 | 0.3 | 60

4148 计 [計] /jì/ (3) v count, calculate, number; haggle over
申请者数以千计。The applicants numbered in the thousands.
77 | 0.78 | 60

4149 写信 [寫信] /xiěxìn/ v write (a letter)
他写信说他很快就会来。He wrote that he would be coming soon.
82 | 0.73 | 60

4150 鼓 [鼓] /gǔ/ v rouse, pluck up (encourage); bulge
他的口袋由于装满糖果鼓起来了。 His pocket was bulging with sweets.
75 | 0.8 | 60

4151 跟踪 [跟蹤] /gēnzōng/ v follow one's tracks, tail
我不能摆脱跟踪我的那辆车。 I couldn't shake the car that was following me.
68 | 0.89 | 60

4152 面向 [面向] /miànxiàng/ v face
这座房子面向花园。 The house faces the park.
141 | 0.43 | 60

4153 占据 [佔據] /zhànjù/ v occupy, take up
空气虽然看不见，但它占据了空间。 Even though air is invisible, it takes up space.
80 | 0.76 | 60

4154 走路 [走路] /zǒulù/ v walk, go on foot
今天上午我不得不走路来上班。 I had to walk to work this morning.
81 | 0.75 | 60

4155 做事 [做事] /zuòshì/ v act, work, do one's work
他做事很莽撞。 He works rashly.
83 | 0.72 | 60

4156 继 [繼] /jì/ v continue, follow
老夫妻惊异之后，继以懊恼。 After the old couple got over their initial surprise, vexation followed.
78 | 0.78 | 60

4157 认可 [認可] /rènkě/ v approve of, accept
她父母不认可她的朋友。 Her parents don't approve of her friends.
77 | 0.79 | 60

4158 敬 [敬] /jìng/ v respect; offer politely
敬你一杯。 Here's to you.
81 | 0.74 | 60

4159 沉默 [沉默] /chénmò/ (2) adj silent
我认为你不应该保持沉默。 I do not think you should keep silent.
106 | 0.56 | 59

4160 异常 [異常] /yìcháng/ (2) adj unusual
这是一个相当异常的问题。 That is rather an unusual question.
72 | 0.83 | 59

4161 活泼 [活潑] /huópō/ (2) adj lively
这孩子既健康又活泼。 The child is lively as well as healthy.
67 | 0.89 | 59

4162 了不起 [了不起] /liǎobuqǐ/ (2) adj amazing, terrific
这真了不起！ That's terrific!
76 | 0.78 | 59

4163 神圣 [神聖] /shénshèng/ (3) adj holy, divine, sacred
婚姻制度是神圣的。 Marriage is a sacred institution.
73 | 0.82 | 59

4164 幸运 [幸運] /xìngyùn/ adj lucky, fortunate
我有你们在身边真是幸运。 It is very fortunate for me to have you around.
76 | 0.79 | 59

4165 优 [優] /yōu/ adj excellent, fine
质优价廉将有助于推销你们的产品。 Fine quality as well as low price will help push the sale of your product.
79 | 0.75 | 59

4166 素 [素] /sù/ adj plain
这幅画衬在素墙上就更加好看了。 The picture may be seen to its best advantage against a plain wall.
75 | 0.79 | 59

4167 不禁 [不禁] /bùjīn/ (3) adv can't help (doing something)
她不禁破涕为笑。 She couldn't refrain from smiling through tears.
112 | 0.53 | 59

4168 复 [複] /fù/ adv again
但它一去不复回！ But it never comes again!
83 | 0.71 | 59

4169 较为 [較為] /jiàowéi/ adv relatively, comparatively, more
下午6时至上午8时之间较为便宜。 It's cheaper between 6 pm and 8 am.
98 | 0.61 | 59

4170 一度 [一度] /yídù/ adv once, on one occasion, for a time
他一度住在我们隔壁的那栋房子里。 He used to live for a time in the house next to ours.
82 | 0.72 | 59

4171 外部 [外部] /wàibù/ (3) loc outside, exterior
房子的外部需要粉刷。 The outside of the house needs painting.
92 | 0.65 | 59

4172 无所谓 [無所謂] /wúsuǒwèi/ (3) idiom be indifferent; make no difference
这对我无所谓。 It makes no difference to me.
88 | 0.67 | 59

4173 受不了 [受不了] /shòubuliǎo/ idiom (somebody) cannot endure, (something) be intolerable
这样的痛苦几乎使他受不了。 The pain was almost more than he could bear.
92 | 0.65 | 59

4174 食堂 [食堂] /shítáng/ (1) n canteen, dining hall
这个学生食堂办得很好。 The students' dining room is well managed.
77 | 0.78 | 59

4175 晚会 [晚會] /wǎnhuì/ (1) n evening, evening party
参加晚会的人很多吗？ Were there many people at the party?
102 | 0.58 | 59

4176 码头 [碼頭] /mǎtóu/ (2) n harbour, dock, wharf, pier
船停在码头边。 Ships anchored alongside the dock.
87 | 0.68 | 59

4177 生气 [生氣] /shēngqi/ (2) *n* life, vigour, vitality
她给晚会带来了生气。 She breathed life into the party.
108 | 0.55 | 59

4178 学说 [學說] /xuéshuō/ (3) *n* theory, doctrine
他因提出该学说而获奖。 He won the prize by propounding the theory.
100 | 0.59 | 59

4179 书籍 [書籍] /shūjí/ (3) *n* (a general term for) books
图书馆里有各种不同种类的书籍。 There are different categories of books in a library.
82 | 0.72 | 59

4180 信号 [信號] /xìnhào/ (3) *n* signal
那艘船发出了无线电求救信号。 The ship sent a radio signal asking for help.
73 | 0.81 | 59

4181 赛 [賽] /sài/ *n* match, game, competition
赛前队员们的士气很高。 The team's morale was high before the match.
155 | 0.38 | 59

4182 水面 [水面] /shuǐmiàn/ *n* water, water surface
我们看见水面下有各种鱼。 We could see fishes under the water.
64 | 0.92 | 59

4183 高层 [高層] /gāocéng/ *n* high level, high tier; high-rise (building)
公司高层会议到半夜才结束。 The company top meeting didn't break up until midnight.
98 | 0.6 | 59

4184 虫 [蟲] /chóng/ *n* insect; worm
早起的鸟儿有虫吃。 The early bird gets the worm.
69 | 0.86 | 59

4185 钢铁 [鋼鐵] /gāngtiě/ *n* steel, iron
磁石能吸钢铁。 A magnet attracts steel.
105 | 0.56 | 59

4186 金额 [金額] /jīn'é/ *n* amount
未付金额为多少？ What is the amount outstanding?
123 | 0.48 | 59

4187 大气 [大氣] /dàqì/ *n* atmosphere; heavy breath
月球上没有大气。 The moon has no atmosphere.
87 | 0.69 | 59

4188 火车站 [火車站] /huǒchēzhàn/ *n* railway station
这条路直通火车站。 This road leads directly to the railway station.
63 | 0.94 | 59

4189 每当 [每當] /měidāng/ *prep* whenever, every time
每当她遇到困难时，就找他帮忙。 Whenever she is in a spot she turns to him for help.
76 | 0.78 | 59

4190 扇 [扇] /shàn/ *clas* [measure word for doors, windows, etc.]
那扇门半开着。 The door stood ajar.
81 | 0.73 | 59

4191 扑 [撲] /pū/ (2) *v* rush at; throw oneself into, be bent on; flap
他一心扑在这项工程上。 He is fully bent on the project.
115 | 0.52 | 59

4192 披 [披] /pī/ (2) *v* drape over one's shoulders
她的鬈发披在肩上。 Her hair fell over her shoulders in a mass of curls.
84 | 0.71 | 59

4193 飘 [飄] /piāo/ (2) *v* flutter or float (in the air)
树叶在秋天时随风而飘落。 Leaves flutter down in the light wind in autumn.
95 | 0.63 | 59

4194 晓得 [曉得] /xiǎode/ (2) *v* know
能做不能做，试过才晓得。 You never know what you can do till you try.
96 | 0.62 | 59

4195 挡 [擋] /dǎng/ (2) *v* keep off; block
这些树可以挡风。 The trees keep out the wind.
82 | 0.73 | 59

4196 晒 [曬] /shài/ (2) *v* dry in the sun; sunbathe
不宜提倡中午在海滩上晒太阳。 Sunbathing on the beach at midday is not advised.
80 | 0.74 | 59

4197 形容 [形容] /xíngróng/ (2) *v* describe
我们激动的心情难以用笔墨来形容。 Words can hardly describe how excited we were.
76 | 0.78 | 59

4198 震动 [震動] /zhèndòng/ (3) *v* shake, quake, vibrate; shock
这消息使她大为震动。 She was very much shocked by the news.
73 | 0.81 | 59

4199 规划 [規劃] /guīhuà/ (3) *v* plan
这个城市规划得很好。 The city is well planned.
124 | 0.48 | 59

4200 往来 [往來] /wǎnglái/ (3) *v* contact, exchange visits; travel between
我和她早不往来了。 I've long since stopped seeing her.
106 | 0.56 | 59

4201 射击 [射擊] /shèjī/ (3) *v* shoot, fire
恐怖分子向人群胡乱射击。 The terrorists fired into the crowd at random.
70 | 0.84 | 59

4202 赔偿 [賠償] /péicháng/ (3) *v* compensate
航空公司拒绝向他赔偿丢失的行李。 The airline refused to compensate him when his baggage was lost.
89 | 0.67 | 59

4203 修建 [修建] /xiūjiàn/ (3) *v* build
这是我们去年修建的水库。 This is the reservoir that we built last year.
93 | 0.64 | 59

4204 佩服 [佩服] /pèifú/ (3) *v* admire
我十分佩服他的勇气。 I have great admiration for his courage.
85 | 0.71 | 59

4205 抵达 [抵達] /dǐdá/ v arrive
他们约在七时抵达。They arrived around seven o'clock.
139 | 0.43 | 59

4206 在场 [在場] /zàichǎng/ v be present, be at the scene
宣布那消息时你在场吗？Were you present when the news was announced?
69 | 0.86 | 59

4207 得出 [得出] /déchū/ v obtain (results, conclusions, etc.)
用这种方法，将会得出较好的结论。A better conclusion will be arrived at in this way.
74 | 0.8 | 59

4208 认同 [認同] /rèntóng/ v identify with, accept, approve
或者，你也认同这样的观点？Or, do you share his observation?
115 | 0.52 | 59

4209 备 [備] /bèi/ v get ready; prepare against; be available, be equipped with
货物几日内便可备妥装运。The goods will be ready for shipment in a few days.
74 | 0.81 | 59

4210 回顾 [回顧] /huígù/ v look back, review
她骄傲地回顾了她所取得的成就。She reviewed her achievements with pride.
96 | 0.62 | 59

4211 下令 [下令] /xiàlìng/ v give an order
我不下令就藏着别动。Stay hidden until I give the word.
84 | 0.71 | 59

4212 放开 [放開] /fàngkāi/ v let go, release
他松手放开了绳子。He let go of the rope.
89 | 0.66 | 59

4213 击 [擊] /jī/ v hit, strike
用力击球。Hit the ball hard.
85 | 0.7 | 59

4214 分为 [分為] /fēnwéi/ v divide into
地球被分为二十四个时区。The earth is divided into 24 time zones.
91 | 0.65 | 59

4215 审美 [審美] /shěnměi/ n good taste; appreciation of beauty, aesthetics
她对服装有很好的审美眼光。She has good taste in clothes.
93 | 0.63 | 59

4216 偏 [偏] /piān/ (3) adj slanting, leaning; prejudiced, biased
画挂偏了一点。The picture hung off center.
67 | 0.88 | 58

4217 棒 [棒] /bàng/ (3) adj terrific, superb
演得太棒了。That was pretty superb acting.
74 | 0.79 | 58

4218 悲哀 [悲哀] /bēi'āi/ (3) adj sad, grieved, sorrowful
这个悲哀的场景结束了电影。This sad scene ended the movie.
78 | 0.75 | 58

4219 宜 [宜] /yí/ adj suitable
这里的气候恰好宜于种植水稻。The climate here is just suitable for planting rice.
136 | 0.43 | 58

4220 一道 [一道] /yídào/ (2) adv together
我们一道去吧。Let's all go together.
72 | 0.81 | 58

4221 从中 [從中] /cóngzhōng/ adv from it, therefrom
那么能从中学到些什么呢？What can we learn from it then?
77 | 0.76 | 58

4222 无论如何 [無論如何] /wúlùnrúhé/ (3) idiom anyhow, at any rate, by all means, whatever happens
无论如何要完成任务。We must complete the task, whatever happens.
83 | 0.71 | 58

4223 影子 [影子] /yǐngzi/ (2) n shadow
随着太阳落山，影子也逐渐伸长。The shadows lengthened with the approach of sunset.
91 | 0.65 | 58

4224 工会 [工會] /gōnghuì/ (2) n trade union
工会被迫缓和了其提出的要求。The union is forced to moderate its claim.
105 | 0.56 | 58

4225 口袋 [口袋] /kǒudài/ (2) n bag, pocket
他把手放在口袋里。He put his hands in his pockets.
91 | 0.64 | 58

4226 疑问 [疑問] /yíwèn/ (2) n doubt; query
有什么疑问吗？Is there any doubt?
68 | 0.86 | 58

4227 铜 [銅] /tóng/ (2) n copper
人类生产的第一种金属是铜。The first metal that was produced by man was copper.
69 | 0.85 | 58

4228 牌子 [牌子] /páizi/ (3) n sign, plate; brand
何不换种别的牌子试试？Why don't you choose another brand instead?
69 | 0.84 | 58

4229 墨 [墨] /mò/ (3) n ink, China ink, ink stick
他的衬衣上有一块墨迹。There is an ink mark on his shirt.
82 | 0.71 | 58

4230 地步 [地步] /dìbù/ (3) n degree, extent, plight
他的作品已达到炉火纯青的地步。His works have reached a high degree of excellence.
77 | 0.76 | 58

4231 边界 [邊界] /biānjiè/ (3) n boundary, border
中国是一个有着漫长陆地边界的国家。China is a country with extensive land borders.
103 | 0.57 | 58

4232 婴儿 [嬰兒] /yīng'ér/ (3) n infant, baby
这个婴儿才学着爬。The baby is just learning to crawl.
78 | 0.75 | 58

27. Commonly used words in the spoken register

Headword	POS	Gloss	Frequency rank
呃	part	[particle used for a pause or to express wonder or admiration] er, oh	1967
嗯	interj	[interjection used for questioning, surprise, disapproval, or agreement] well, eh, hey, m-hm, uh-huh	820
哎	interj	[interjection expressing surprise, disapproval, reminder, etc.]	946
比如说	idiom	for example, say	3081
里边	loc	inside, within	3496
呐	part	[sentence final particle, especially following words ending with the consonant *n*]	3690
哎呀	interj	[interjection expressing wonder, shock or complaint] ah, my god, damn	3869
里头	loc	inside	3835
哈	ono	[usually reduplicated to indicate the sound of laughing]	4338
哈	interj	[interjection expressing satisfaction] ha	3495
嘿	interj	hey, why	3595
啊	part	[modal particle showing affirmation, approval or consent]	222
会儿	time	[preceded by the demonstrative pronoun 这 or 那] (at this or that) moment	4394
当中	place	in the middle or centre; among	1618
甭	adv	don't, needn't	4795
哎哟	interj	[particle expressing astonishment or pain] hey, oh, ouch	4848
听众	n	audience	3571
啦	part	[sentence final particle combining 了 and 啊]	378
哪	part	[sentence final particle similar to 啊, following words ending with the consonant *n*]	1529
哇	part	[sentence final particle replacing 啊 where the preceding word ends with the vowel *u* or *ao*]	2710
头儿	n	head, chief, superior	4541
哼	interj	[interjection expressing disapproval] humph	2635
噢	interj	[interjection expressing mental realisation] oh	2855
呀	ono	[the sound of a creak]	3135
啊	interj	[interjection expressing surprise, admiration, etc.] oh	341
对	adj	right, correct; opposite (in direction)	438
这边	pron	this side, this way, over here	2582
嘿嘿	ono	[sound of laughing]	4392
来讲	aux	[equivalent of 来说] from one's viewpoint	4300
叫做	v	be called	2079
外边	loc	outside	4742
反正	adv	anyway	1084
呗	part	[sentence final particle indicating something obvious or expressing resignation]	4071
那儿	pron	there	987

儿	suf	[nonsyllabic suffix for retroflection, especially in the Beijing dialect]	182
嘛	part	[sentence final modal particle indicating that something is obvious or expressing a hope, advice, etc.]	531
哦	interj	[interjection expressing realisation] ah	1675
呀	part	[sentence final particle]	293
干吗	pron	why, what to do; whatever for	3509
呃	part	[particle used for a pause or to express wonder or admiration] er, oh	1967
嗯	interj	[interjection used for questioning, surprise, disapproval, or agreement] well, eh, hey, m-hm, uh-huh	820

Comments:

For each of the four registers:

1 Remove all items with a dispersion index equal to or greater than 0.5;

2 First sort by normalised frequency of the register under consideration;

3 Compute the ratio of the register with the other three (normalised frequency of register / (sum of the normalised frequencies of the other three registers);

4 Cut off where there is a significant drop in the ratio computed in (2);

5 Because of the topics covered in the public lectures and debates in the spoken registers, some words which may not be typically spoken appear on the list, which are removed by hand, e.g. 火山 "volcano" (4935), 友 "friend" (2983), 辩 "argue, debate" (1798), 遗产 "heritage, inheritance, legacy" (3156), 焦点 "focus" (2699), and 皇帝 "emperor" (1546);

6 The list is arranged by statistical salience instead of frequency ranks.

4233 刊物 [刊物] /kānwù/ (3) n publication, magazine, journal
这本刊物两个月出版一次。The journal makes its appearance once every two months.
84 | 0.69 | 58

4234 生理 [生理] /shēnglǐ/ (3) n physiology
无论在生理上或心理上，男孩都比女孩成熟得慢。Boys mature more slowly than girls both physically and psychologically.
88 | 0.67 | 58

4235 计 [計] /jì/ (3) n idea, plan; gauge, metre
一日之计在于晨。An idea in the morning is worth two in the evening.
74 | 0.79 | 58

4236 级别 [級別] /jíbié/ (3) n level, rank, scale
他的级别比我高。He is above me in rank.
85 | 0.69 | 58

4237 散文 [散文] /sǎnwén/ (3) n prose
他既写诗又写散文。He writes poetry and prose.
88 | 0.67 | 58

4238 资 [資] /zī/ n money, capital, investment; endowment; qualifications
该公司投入巨资购置新设备。The firm has made a huge investment in new plant.
72 | 0.82 | 58

4239 眉 [眉] /méi/ n eyebrow
她长着柳叶眉。Her eyebrow looked like a leaf.
159 | 0.37 | 58

4240 兄 [兄] /xiōng/ n elder brother; [preceded by a surname to be used as a courtesy term of address between male friends]
他把亡兄的孩子养育成人。He brought up his dead brother's children.
88 | 0.67 | 58

4241 举 [舉] /jǔ/ n act, move
正好在价格下跌前脱手，真是精明之举。It is an astute move to sell just before prices go down.
66 | 0.89 | 58

4242 展 [展] /zhǎn/ n exhibition, display
这么多的新产品参展，给我印象很深。I am much impressed by so many new products on display.
98 | 0.59 | 58

4243 全身 [全身] /quánshēn/ n the whole body, all over
我全身发痒。I itched all over.
97 | 0.61 | 58

4244 法官 [法官] /fǎguān/ n judge
那法官素以大公无私著称。The judge had a reputation for complete objectivity.
100 | 0.59 | 58

4245 敌 [敵] /dí/ n enemy
自满乃学习之敌。Complacency is the enemy of study.
83 | 0.71 | 58

4246 灯光 [燈光] /dēngguāng/ n light, lighting
远处闪烁着灯光。Lights glimmered in the distance.
102 | 0.57 | 58

4247 家园 [家園] /jiāyuán/ n home, homestead, homeland
火灾毁灭了我们的家园。Fire had devoured our home.
78 | 0.76 | 58

4248 出租车 [出租車] /chūzūchē/ n taxi
我们坐出租车吧。Let's take a taxi.
73 | 0.8 | 58

4249 名人 [名人] /míngrén/ n celebrity
她一下子成了名人了。She became a celebrity overnight.
77 | 0.76 | 58

4250 良心 [良心] /liángxīn/ n conscience
他的良心驱使他向警方认罪。His conscience pricked him on to admit his crime to the police.
80 | 0.73 | 58

4251 理念 [理念] /lǐniàn/ n idea, philosophy
公司的运营理念：走在竞争者的前列。Business Philosophy: Lead the pack of competitors.
99 | 0.59 | 58

4252 空调 [空調] /kōngtiáo/ n air conditioner
空调坏了。The air conditioner is out of order.
73 | 0.8 | 58

4253 冬季 [冬季] /dōngjì/ (3) time winter
冬季白天较短。Days are shorter in winter.
110 | 0.54 | 58

4254 祝贺 [祝賀] /zhùhè/ (2) v congratulate
请允许我向您表示祝贺。May I congratulate you?
112 | 0.53 | 58

4255 尊敬 [尊敬] /zūnjìng/ (2) v respect
她对她的父母很尊敬。She respects her parents.
72 | 0.81 | 58

4256 预备 [預備] /yùbèi/ (2) v prepare, get ready
你预备好圣诞礼物了吗？Have you got your Christmas presents ready?
66 | 0.89 | 58

4257 道歉 [道歉] /dàoqiàn/ (2) v apologise
更糟的是他拒不道歉。To make matters worse, he refused to apologise.
79 | 0.74 | 58

4258 递 [遞] /dì/ (2) v hand over, pass
我递给他绳子，他接住了。I passed him the rope and he took it.
104 | 0.57 | 58

4259 洒 [灑] /sǎ/ (2) v spray, sprinkle; spill
请给花洒些水。Please spray some water on the flower.
75 | 0.78 | 58

4260 愁 [愁] /chóu/ (2) v worry
我愁得睡不着了。I worried so much I couldn't sleep.
75 | 0.79 | 58

4261 提问 [提問] /tíwèn/ (3) v ask questions; (teacher) put a question to
请随便提问。Please feel free to ask questions.
80 | 0.73 | 58

4262 代理 [代理] /dàilǐ/ (3) n agent, agency; (computing) proxy
我们想把代理协议续订两年。We'd like to renew our agency agreement for another two years.
94 | 0.63 | 58

4263 怨 [怨] /yuàn/ (3) v blame; complain
怨来怨去只好怨她自己不好！She only has herself to blame!
95 | 0.61 | 58

4264 来往 [來往] /láiwǎng/ (3) v come and go, travel between; contact, associate with
他总是与大企业来往。He always associates with large enterprises.
72 | 0.81 | 58

4265 象征 [象徵] /xiàngzhēng/ (3) v stand for, symbolise, signify
自由女神象征着什么？What does the Statue of Liberty symbolise?
99 | 0.59 | 58

4266 耽误 [耽誤] /dānwù/ (3) v delay
他可能被大雾耽误了。He could have been delayed by fog.
78 | 0.75 | 58

4267 说服 [説服] /shuōfú/ (3) v convince, persuade
我们怎么才能说服他呢？How are we to convince him?
75 | 0.78 | 58

4268 伴 [伴] /bàn/ v accompany
闪电划过天边，伴着低沉的隆隆雷声。Lightning danced across the horizon, accompanied by low, rumbling thunder.
72 | 0.81 | 58

4269 提升 [提升] /tíshēng/ v promote
不久就把他提升为工程师了。Soon he was promoted to be an engineer.
88 | 0.67 | 58

4270 开门 [開門] /kāimén/ v open the door, open
邮局何时开门？What time does the post office open?
97 | 0.6 | 58

4271 惩罚 [懲罰] /chéngfá/ v punish, penalise
我们的目的是改造罪犯，而不是惩罚他们。Our purpose is to reform criminals rather than punish them.
72 | 0.81 | 58

4272 死去 [死去] /sǐqù/ v die
他在他出生的村子里死去了。He died in the village where he was born.
78 | 0.75 | 58

4273 排除 [排除] /páichú/ *v* exclude; remove, clear away
我们必须排除干扰。We have to clear away the obstacles.
77 | 0.76 | 58

4274 营业 [營業] /yíngyè/ *v* do business, be open
酒吧对外营业。The bar is open to non-residents.
81 | 0.72 | 58

4275 安置 [安置] /ānzhì/ *v* find a suitable place for, arrange for, help somebody to settle down; install, fix
在讲台上安置了一台电脑。A computer was installed on the platform.
108 | 0.54 | 58

4276 干活 [幹活] /gànhuó/ *v* work
干活去吧。Let's get to work.
85 | 0.69 | 58

4277 动人 [動人] /dòngrén/ (2) *adj* moving, touching
故事非常动人。The story is very moving.
66 | 0.88 | 57

4278 尖锐 [尖銳] /jiānruì/ (2) *adj* sharp, penetrating, piercing
他的评语非常尖锐。His remark was sharp and cutting.
66 | 0.87 | 57

4279 肯定 [肯定] /kěndìng/ (2) *adj* affirmative, positive; definite, sure
他作了肯定的回答。He answered in the affirmative.
64 | 0.9 | 57

4280 依旧 [依舊] /yījiù/ (3) *adv* as before, still
她依旧是那个老样子。She still looks her old self.
87 | 0.67 | 57

4281 倒霉 [倒黴] /dǎoméi/ (3) *adj* having bad luck
真倒霉！What lousy luck!
90 | 0.64 | 57

4282 永恒 [永恆] /yǒnghéng/ *adj* eternal, everlasting
我们的友谊是永恒的。Our friendship is everlasting.
65 | 0.88 | 57

4283 一同 [一同] /yìtóng/ (2) *adv* together
咱们一同走吧。Let's go together.
93 | 0.61 | 57

4284 器 [器] /qì/ *suf* [nominal suffix following a verb indicating the related device or instrument]
枪的瞄准器必须与射击目标对准成一线。The sights of the gun must be in alignment with the target.
77 | 0.75 | 57

4285 姓名 [姓名] /xìngmíng/ (2) *n* full name
请告诉我你的姓名和地址。Your name and address, please.
66 | 0.87 | 57

4286 乒乓球 [乒乓球] /pīngpāngqiú/ (2) *n* table tennis
乒乓球她比我打得好。She plays table tennis better than I.
126 | 0.46 | 57

4287 车间 [車間] /chējiān/ (2) *n* workshop
她是我们车间的主心骨。She is the mainstay of our workshop.
78 | 0.74 | 57

4288 口气 [口氣] /kǒuqì/ (3) *n* tone, manner of speaking
她用恼怒的口气说话。She spoke in an angry tone.
114 | 0.5 | 57

4289 一带 [一帶] /yídài/ (3) *n* area, region, part
这一带有时会很冷。It can be very cold in this region.
66 | 0.86 | 57

4290 物资 [物資] /wùzī/ (3) *n* goods and materials, supplies
飞机向灾区空投救灾物资。The planes dropped relief supplies to the stricken area.
111 | 0.52 | 57

4291 老子 [老子] /lǎozi/ *n* [informal] father; [referring to the speaker to take advantage of the addressee] I, me
你把老子吓死了！Are you trying to worry me to death?
87 | 0.67 | 57

4292 时光 [時光] /shíguāng/ *n* time; period of time
不要浪费你的大好时光。Don't idle away your precious time.
76 | 0.76 | 57

4293 点儿 [點兒] /diǎnr/ *n* point, spot, dot
她在纸上画了个点儿作记号。She marked the paper with a dot.
102 | 0.57 | 57

4294 大海 [大海] /dàhǎi/ *n* sea
大海在风暴中波涛汹涌。The sea was rough in the storm.
70 | 0.82 | 57

4295 困境 [困境] /kùnjìng/ *n* predicament, plight, dilemma
他陷入了困境。He was thrown into a dilemma.
82 | 0.7 | 57

4296 造型 [造型] /zàoxíng/ *n* shape, moulding
这些古代工艺品造型优美。These ancient art objects are beautifully shaped.
72 | 0.8 | 57

4297 朵 [朵] /duǒ/ (2) *clas* [measure word for flowers]
我想再要几朵红玫瑰。I'd like a few more red roses.
80 | 0.71 | 57

4298 刀 [刀] /dāo/ *clas* [measure word for meat] a cut of; [measure word for action of cutting with a knife]
好像我向他捅了一刀似的。It was as though I had sliced into him with a knife.
72 | 0.79 | 57

4299 瞬间 [瞬間] /shùnjiān/ *time* instant, moment
那是个真正令人喜悦但却飘然逝去的瞬间。It was a moment of pure joy, a buoyant moment.
89 | 0.65 | 57

4300 来讲 [來講] /láijiǎng/ aux [equivalent of 来说] from one's viewpoint
明星地位对于她来讲没有什么。Stardom meant nothing to her.
124 | 0.46 | 57 | S

4301 抓紧 [抓緊] /zhuājǐn/ (2) v grasp firmly; pay close attention; hurry
如果抓紧点，你会赶上下一班公共汽车。If you hurry, you can catch the next bus.
109 | 0.53 | 57

4302 代替 [代替] /dàitì/ (2) v substitute, replace
在这个食谱中，可用蜂蜜代替食糖。Honey can substitute for sugar in this recipe.
78 | 0.74 | 57

4303 聚集 [聚集] /jùjí/ (3) v assemble, gather
人群很快聚集在他周围。A crowd soon gathered round him.
75 | 0.77 | 57

4304 意识 [意識] /yìshí/ (3) v be conscious of, be aware of, realise
很少有人意识到这一发现的重要性。Few people realised the significance of the discovery.
66 | 0.87 | 57

4305 膨胀 [膨脹] /péngzhàng/ (3) v expand, inflate
液体通常随着温度上升而膨胀。Liquid usually expands with an increase in temperature.
82 | 0.7 | 57

4306 制约 [制約] /zhìyuē/ v constrain, condition, govern
供应受生产制约。Supply is conditioned by production.
106 | 0.55 | 57

4307 轮 [輪] /lún/ v take turns
现在轮到你发牌了。It's your turn to deal now.
73 | 0.79 | 57

4308 资助 [資助] /zīzhù/ v support, sponsor, finance
谁资助了这个展览？Who sponsored the exhibition?
92 | 0.63 | 57

4309 抢救 [搶救] /qiǎngjiù/ v rescue, save
他从桥上跳入水中去抢救那溺水儿童。He dived from the bridge to rescue the drowning child.
78 | 0.73 | 57

4310 取代 [取代] /qǔdài/ v replace, take the place of
什么都无法取代母爱。Nothing can replace a mother's love.
75 | 0.77 | 57

4311 分成 [分成] /fēnchéng/ v divide into
她把全班分成四组。She divided the class into four groups.
71 | 0.81 | 57

4312 暗示 [暗示] /ànshì/ v suggest, imply
这部电影暗示了什么？What does this movie imply?
75 | 0.77 | 57

4313 划分 [劃分] /huáfēn/ v divide
科学可划分为基础科学和应用科学。Science can be divided into basic and applied types.
82 | 0.71 | 57

4314 挖掘 [挖掘] /wājué/ v dig, excavate; tap (potentials, talents, etc.)
国有企业要积极挖掘内部潜力。State-owned enterprises should actively tap their own potential.
72 | 0.79 | 57

4315 亏 [虧] /kuī/ v lose money (in business); owe; treat unfairly
这多亏了我的朋友们，他们帮我很多忙。I owe it all to my friends who helped me so much.
75 | 0.77 | 57

4316 透 [透] /tòu/ (2) adv really, completely, thoroughly
他们真是坏透了。They're really vicious.
81 | 0.7 | 56

4317 紧密 [緊密] /jǐnmì/ (3) adv closely
只要我们紧密团结，我们一定会克服这些困难。We can surely overcome these difficulties so long as we are closely united.
115 | 0.49 | 56

4318 繁华 [繁華] /fánhuá/ adj flourishing and bustling, busy
这是这个城市最繁华的街道之一。This is one of the busiest streets in the city.
60 | 0.95 | 56

4319 短暂 [短暫] /duǎnzàn/ adj short, brief, transient
生命短暂，艺术永恒。Art is long, and life is short.
64 | 0.88 | 56

4320 照样 [照樣] /zhàoyàng/ (3) adv all the same
我不是照样付钱的？Don't I pay just the same as everyone else?
73 | 0.77 | 56

4321 原先 [原先] /yuánxiān/ (3) adv originally, formerly
这所学校原先很小。The school was originally quite small.
81 | 0.7 | 56

4322 特意 [特意] /tèyì/ adv specially
谢谢您为我特意准备如此丰盛的晚餐。Thank you very much for preparing such a splendid dinner specially for me.
74 | 0.76 | 56

4323 俱 [俱] /jù/ adv all
事实俱在。The facts are all there.
77 | 0.73 | 56

4324 起码 [起碼] /qǐmǎ/ adv at least
它起码也有100年历史了。It must be at least 100 years' old.
82 | 0.69 | 56

4325 影响 [影響] /yǐngxiǎng/ (1) n influence, impact
没有人能避免受广告的影响。No one can avoid being influenced by advertisements.
74 | 0.76 | 56

4326 级 [級] /jí/ (2) *n* level, rank, grade; step; degree
他属 54 公斤级的。He is in the 54 kg class.
103 | 0.55 | 56

4327 碑 [碑] /bēi/ (2) *n* monument
这座碑是为纪念我们的胜利而建的。
This monument commemorates our victory.
70 | 0.81 | 56

4328 伤 [傷] /shāng/ (2) *n* injury, wound
他的伤怎么样？What about his injuries?
85 | 0.66 | 56

4329 胡子 [鬍子] /húzi/ (2) *n* beard, moustache, whiskers
他留着长长的灰白胡子。He had a long grey beard.
83 | 0.68 | 56

4330 舅舅 [舅舅] /jiùjiu/ (3) *n* (maternal) uncle
当时带我坐车的人是我的舅舅。The man I travelled with was my uncle.
109 | 0.52 | 56

4331 实质 [實質] /shízhì/ (3) *n* essence, substance, crux
你的提问触及到了此事的实质。Your question got to the essence of the matter.
81 | 0.69 | 56

4332 记载 [記載] /jìzǎi/ *n* record
根据历史记载，这个大理石台阶重 300 吨。
Historical record has it that the marble ramp weighs about 300 tons.
90 | 0.63 | 56

4333 岗 [崗] /gǎng/ *n* post; sentry post; hillock, mound
那头驴负载过重，几乎爬不过岗。The donkey was so overloaded that it could hardly climb the hill.
69 | 0.82 | 56

4334 档 [檔] /dàng/ *n* files, archive
按编号顺序把这些发票入档。File these invoices in numerical order.
86 | 0.66 | 56

4335 支队 [支隊] /zhīduì/ *n* division, detachment
他在交警支队上班。He works in the traffic police division.
88 | 0.65 | 56

4336 电视机 [電視機] /diànshìjī/ *n* television (set)
电视机又出毛病了。The television has gone wrong again.
66 | 0.86 | 56

4337 车子 [車子] /chēzi/ *n* vehicle, car
车子进得来么？Can the car get in?
88 | 0.64 | 56

4338 哈 [哈] /hā/ *ono* [usually reduplicated to indicate the sound of laughing]
大家全哈哈地笑起来。They all roared with laughter.
178 | 0.31 | 56 | S

4339 基于 [基於] /jīyú/ *prep* based on; in view of, because of
多数可笑的故事是基于喜剧情景的。Most funny stories are based on comic situations.
81 | 0.69 | 56

4340 清晨 [清晨] /qīngchén/ (3) *time* early morning
这一天从清晨就风和日丽。From the early morning the day was bright and breezy.
73 | 0.78 | 56

4341 通知 [通知] /tōngzhī/ (1) *v* notify, inform, give notice
如果有什么消息，我会通知你。If anything turns up, I'll notify you.
69 | 0.81 | 56

4342 决心 [決心] /juéxīn/ (2) *v* pledge, resolve, be determined to
他决心再也不喝酒了。He resolved never to drink again.
74 | 0.76 | 56

4343 羡慕 [羨慕] /xiànmù/ (2) *v* admire, envy
我太羡慕他了。How I admire him.
79 | 0.71 | 56

4344 滚 [滾] /gǔn/ (2) *v* roll; fall; get away, get lost; (water) boil
他们跑上山坡，同时有些小石子滚了下来。
Small stones rolled down the hillside as they ran up.
101 | 0.56 | 56

4345 为首 [為首] /wéishǒu/ (3) *v* be led by, have . . . as the head
这项研究是由一个以约翰为首的科学家小组完成的。The research was done by a group of scientists headed by John.
78 | 0.73 | 56

4346 征 [征] /zhēng/ (3) *v* levy; solicit
政府已征15%的汽油税。The government has imposed a 15 per cent tax on petrol.
71 | 0.79 | 56

4347 着手 [着手] /zhuóshǒu/ (3) *v* set about, start
我该由哪儿着手？Where should I start?
78 | 0.73 | 56

4348 安装 [安裝] /ānzhuāng/ (3) *v* install
上周我们安装了一套新的电话系统。We had a new telephone system installed last week.
92 | 0.61 | 56

4349 分离 [分離] /fēnlí/ (3) *v* separate, part, split
他们发誓永不分离。They swore never to be separated.
81 | 0.7 | 56

4350 粉碎 [粉碎] /fěnsuì/ (3) *v* shatter, crush, smash
警方粉碎了贩毒集团。Police smashed the drug ring.
69 | 0.81 | 56

4351 种植 [種植] /zhòngzhí/ (3) *v* plant
我们在房子周围种植了果树。We planted fruit trees round the house.
140 | 0.4 | 56

4352 发射 [發射] /fāshè/ (3) *v* launch, fire
他们朝夜空发射了一颗照明弹。They fired a flare up into the night sky.
96 | 0.58 | 56

4353 饮 [飲] /yǐn/ *v* drink
你要先饮些红酒吗？Would you like to drink some red wine first?
79 | 0.72 | 56

4354 谴责 [譴責] /qiǎnzé/ *v* denounce, condemn
我谴责这种无谓的暴行。 I condemn this senseless violence.
85 | 0.66 | 56

4355 列入 [列入] /lièrù/ *v* put in on a list, include
我们宁愿不把这个列入议程。 We preferred not to put this on the agenda.
104 | 0.54 | 56

4356 谋 [謀] /móu/ *v* seek; consult; plan
一位朋友设法为我兄弟在银行里谋了个职位。 A friend procured a position in the bank for my brother.
74 | 0.77 | 56

4357 抱怨 [抱怨] /bàoyuàn/ *v* complain
你抱怨什么？ What are you complaining about?
80 | 0.71 | 56

4358 来临 [來臨] /láilín/ *v* come, arrive
看起来一场雷雨即将来临了。 It looks as if a thunderstorm is coming up.
70 | 0.81 | 56

4359 反省 [反省] /fǎnxǐng/ *v* reflect on; engage in introspection
请反省一下自己的行动吧。 Please reflect on your actions.
60 | 0.94 | 56

4360 走私 [走私] /zǒusī/ *v* smuggle
他因走私毒品而判刑。 He was jailed for smuggling drugs.
105 | 0.53 | 56

4361 控 [控] /kòng/ *v* control; accuse
她被控受贿。 She was accused of taking bribes.
67 | 0.85 | 56

4362 公认 [公認] /gōngrèn/ *v* recognise, accept, establish
他已被公认为著名的艺术家。 He is recognised as a famous artist.
74 | 0.77 | 56

4363 轰炸 [轟炸] /hōngzhà/ *v* bomb, bombard
敌机在一周内对这座城市轰炸了两次。 The enemy planes bombed the city twice in a week.
85 | 0.67 | 56

4364 妙 [妙] /miào/ (2) *adj* wonderful
妙极了！ It is simply wonderful!
74 | 0.75 | 55

4365 谨慎 [謹慎] /jǐnshèn/ (3) *adj* cautious, prudent
他措辞很谨慎。 He is cautious in his choice of words.
68 | 0.81 | 55

4366 合格 [合格] /hégé/ (3) *adj* qualified
她的愿望是成为一名合格的教师。 Her wish is to become a qualified teacher.
97 | 0.57 | 55

4367 邪 [邪] /xié/ *adj* evil, weird
邪不压正。 We can overcome evil with greater good.
69 | 0.81 | 55

4368 残 [殘] /cán/ *adj* disabled; incomplete; remnant
她身残志不残。 She was physically but not spiritually disabled.
64 | 0.87 | 55

4369 不如 [不如] /bùrú/ (1) *conj* might as well, not so much as
与其说他聪明倒不如说他勤奋。 He is not so much clever as diligent.
70 | 0.79 | 55

4370 临时 [臨時] /línshí/ (2) *adv* temporarily, for the time being
房子里的大房间被临时用来当教室。 The big room in the house is being temporarily used as a schoolroom.
58 | 0.95 | 55

4371 匆匆 [匆匆] /cōngcōng/ *adv* hastily, hurriedly, in a hurry
她给母亲匆匆写了一封信。 She hastily wrote a letter to her mother.
93 | 0.59 | 55

4372 没法 [沒法] /méifǎ/ *v* cannot, have no choice
他没法掩盖自己的窘态。 He could not hide his embarrassment.
85 | 0.65 | 55

4373 用不着 [用不着] /yòngbuzháo/ (2) *idiom* no need; have no use for
用不着谢我。 No need to thank me.
83 | 0.67 | 55

4374 姓 [姓] /xìng/ (1) *n* surname, last name
我想不起她的姓来了。 I can't think what her last name is.
78 | 0.71 | 55

4375 日记 [日記] /rìjì/ (2) *n* diary
日记显示了他那晚的悲伤。 The diary showed his distress that evening.
68 | 0.81 | 55

4376 公元 [公元] /gōngyuán/ (2) *n* the Christian era, AD
公元是从基督的生年算起的。 The Christian era is counted from the birth of Christ.
81 | 0.69 | 55

4377 流氓 [流氓] /liúmáng/ (3) *n* rogue, hoodlum, rascal, gangster
我要是逮住这个流氓，非狠狠揍他一顿不可！ If I ever catch the rascal I'll really wallop him!
92 | 0.61 | 55

4378 地主 [地主] /dìzhǔ/ (3) *n* landlord, landowner, squire; host
农民过去受地主的压迫。 Peasants used to be subject to the local landowner.
80 | 0.7 | 55

4379 痕迹 [痕跡] /hénjì/ (3) *n* track, trace
这房间里有搏斗过的痕迹。 The room bore traces of a struggle.
72 | 0.77 | 55

4380 魂 [魂] /hún/ *n* soul; spirit, mood
几乎把我魂都吓掉了。 It almost frightened me out of my senses.
70 | 0.79 | 55

28. Commonly used words in the fiction register

Headword	POS	Gloss	Frequency rank
瞪	v	stare at	4147
脸色	n	complexion, look; facial expression	4132
身子	n	body; pregnancy	3542
点头	v	nod	3892
忍不住	v	cannot help but	4059
转身	v	turn round	3652
眉	n	eyebrow	4239
摇头	v	shake one's head	4513
唇	n	lip	4873
叹	v	sigh	3619
伸手	v	hold out one's hand; ask for	3728
睁	v	open (eyes)	4010
笑	v	laugh, smile	387
眼	clas	[measure word for the action of look or glance]; [measure word for wells]	1616
扬	v	raise; spread	3241
脸	n	face, cheek	545
沙发	n	sofa	3791
开口	v	open one's mouth, start to talk	4402
双手	n	both hands	3234
坐下	v	sit down	3924
表情	n	(facial) expression	2603
客厅	n	sitting room, reception room	4854
咋	pron	how, why	3286
跃	v	leap, jump	3622
问道	v	ask	3859
家伙	n	guy, fellow; tool, weapon	3024
神情	n	look, facial expression	4753
窗外	place	out of the window	4824
身后	loc	behind somebody; after one's death	4079
低头	v	hang (one's) head; give in, submit, bend, bow	4780
肩膀	n	shoulder	4701
闪	v	flash, flicker; dodge	3428
老实	adj	honest	3202
面孔	n	face	4131
笑容	n	smile	3709
说道	v	say	2463
盯	v	stare, keep an eye on	2687
扯	v	pull; tear (off, into pieces); chat	3407
么	part	[interrogative particle]	1966
阿姨	n	(maternal side) aunt, auntie; [also used as a polite term of address for a woman of one's parent's age]	3668
怀	n	(in) one's arms, bosom; mind	3210

露出	v	show, reveal	3061
泪水	n	tear, teardrop	4142
抬头	v	raise one's head, look up; hold one's head high; gain ground	3862
镜	n	mirror; glasses	3473
声	clas	[measure word for sound, shout, cry, laugh, yell, etc.]	1296
心思	n	idea; thinking, thought	4530
椅子	n	chair	4032
爹	n	dad, father	3420

Comments

For each of the four registers:

1 Remove all items with a dispersion index equal to or greater than 0.5;

2 First sort by normalised frequency of the register under consideration;

3 Compute the ratio of the register with the other three (normalised frequency of register / (sum of the normalised frequencies of the other three registers);

4 Cut off where there is a significant drop in the ratio computed in (2);

5 The list is arranged by statistical salience instead of frequency ranks.

4381 歌声 [歌聲] /gēshēng/ n singing
她的歌声博得了热烈的喝采。 Her singing evoked warm acclamations.
61 | 0.91 | 55

4382 屏幕 [屏幕] /píngmù/ n screen
大字标题在屏幕上闪现了一下。 The headlines flashed on the screen.
66 | 0.83 | 55

4383 谈 [談] /tán/ n talk
一天，我和他作了一次长谈。 One day, I had a long talk with him.
69 | 0.8 | 55

4384 智 [智] /zhì/ n wisdom
吃一堑，长一智。 A fall into the pit, a gain in your wit.
68 | 0.81 | 55

4385 总数 [總數] /zǒngshù/ n total amount, sum
这些捐款很快就集少成多，总数相当可观。 These small contributions soon added up to a sizeable amount.
122 | 0.46 | 55

4386 文人 [文人] /wénrén/ n man of letters, scholar
这是文人的骄傲。 This is the pride of scholars.
81 | 0.68 | 55

4387 海湾 [海灣] /hǎiwān/ n gulf, bay
海湾向北方延伸。 The gulf extends northward.
92 | 0.6 | 55

4388 尿 [尿] /niào/ n urine, pee
小狗在地毯上撒了一泡尿。 The puppy has done a piddle on the carpet.
76 | 0.73 | 55

4389 谜 [謎] /mí/ n puzzle, mystery; riddle
他们为什么离开还是个谜。 Why they left is still a mystery.
77 | 0.73 | 55

4390 心理学 [心理學] /xīnlǐxué/ n psychology
那是一个心理学的问题。 It was a psychological question.
90 | 0.62 | 55

4391 熊 [熊] /xióng/ n bear
如果我们真遇到一头熊，该怎么办？ What if we should encounter a bear?
67 | 0.83 | 55

4392 嘿嘿 [嘿嘿] /hēihēi/ ono [sound of laughing]
我嘿嘿地笑着，后来就在篝火旁睡熟了。 I laughed too as I fell asleep by the campfire.
131 | 0.43 | 55 | S

4393 瓶 [瓶] /píng/ (1) clas [measure word for drink contained in a bottle] a bottle of
请给我一瓶矿泉水。 May I have a bottle of mineral water?
83 | 0.66 | 55

4394 会儿 [會兒] /huìr/ time [preceded by the demonstrative pronoun 这 or 那 (at this or that) moment
他这会儿出去了。 He is out at the moment.
161 | 0.34 | 55 | S

4395 减轻 [減輕] /jiǎnqīng/ (2) v lighten, ease, alleviate
医生给她注射以减轻疼痛。 The doctor gave her an injection to ease the pain.
113 | 0.49 | 55

4396 招呼 [招呼] /zhāohū/ (2) v call; greet
那边有人招呼你。 Someone over there is calling you.
110 | 0.5 | 55

4397 后悔 [後悔] /hòuhuǐ/ (2) v regret
他后悔犯了这样的错误。 He regretted having
made such a mistake.
96 | 0.58 | 55

4398 涂 [塗] /tú/ (2) v spread, smear; scribble;
cross out
他在面包上涂了厚厚的一层黄油。 He spread
the butter thickly on his bread.
79 | 0.7 | 55

4399 撕 [撕] /sī/ (2) v tear
这布料容易撕破。 This cloth tears easily.
82 | 0.68 | 55

4400 驾驶 [駕駛] /jiàshǐ/ (3) v drive
小心驾驶。 Drive with caution.
68 | 0.82 | 55

4401 折磨 [折磨] /zhémó/ (3) v torture
别让那事折磨你了。 Do not let that torture
you.
79 | 0.7 | 55

4402 开口 [開口] /kāikǒu/ (3) v open one's mouth,
start to talk
只要你开口，我就叫他走。 Just say the word,
and I'll ask him to leave.
133 | 0.42 | 55

4403 譬如 [譬如] /pìrú/ (3) v take . . . for example
譬如昨天晚上，我觉得鬼真可怕。 Like last
night, for instance, I thought ghosts were
really scary.
75 | 0.73 | 55

4404 靠近 [靠近] /kàojìn/ (3) v be close to; draw
near, approach
他的住宅靠近马路。 His house is close to the
highway.
66 | 0.84 | 55

4405 挣扎 [掙扎] /zhēngzhá/ (3) v struggle
他挣扎着要逃脱。 He struggled to get free.
94 | 0.59 | 55

4406 捏 [捏] /niē/ (3) v pinch, squeeze; knead;
make up
她握着我的手，轻轻捏了捏。 She gave my
hand a gentle squeeze.
99 | 0.56 | 55

4407 夸 [誇] /kuā/ (3) v praise; boast, exaggerate
大家都夸他很努力。 His efforts were much
appreciated.
70 | 0.79 | 55

4408 处在 [處在] /chǔzài/ v be (in a certain state,
position, or condition)
他正处在事业的颠峰状态。 He is at the zenith
of his career.
72 | 0.77 | 55

4409 称之为 [稱之為] /chēngzhīwéi/ v call it . . .
水遇冷凝结，称之为冰。 When water
freezes it becomes solid and we call
it ice.
79 | 0.7 | 55

4410 预计 [預計] /yùjì/ v estimate, expect
装船预计需要20天。 Shipment is expected to
take 20 days.
163 | 0.34 | 55

4411 掀起 [掀起] /xiānqǐ/ v lift; raise; set off, start
他们掀起一阵抢购浪潮。 They started a wave
of buying.
66 | 0.85 | 55

4412 预料 [預料] /yùliào/ v anticipate, expect
实际成本比我们预料的高得多。 The actual
cost was much higher than we had expected.
59 | 0.93 | 55

4413 组建 [組建] /zǔjiàn/ v put together, set up
兄弟几个组建了一个新公司。 The brothers
have set up a new company.
132 | 0.42 | 55

4414 好吃 [好吃] /hǎochī/ (1) adj tasty, delicious;
edible
她也许想要点好吃的东西。 She might like
something tasty.
74 | 0.74 | 54

4415 鲜 [鮮] /xiān/ (2) adj fresh; (of colour) bright;
(of food) tasty
请来一杯鲜橙汁。 A fresh orange, please.
83 | 0.66 | 54

4416 广阔 [廣闊] /guǎngkuò/ (2) adj wide, broad,
vast
国内市场广阔，这是中国最大的优势。
The vast domestic market is China's greatest
advantage.
112 | 0.49 | 54

4417 笨 [笨] /bèn/ (2) adj stupid
你怎么这么笨竟相信他的话？ How could you
be so stupid as to believe him?
87 | 0.63 | 54

4418 不易 [不易] /búyì/ adj not easy, difficult
像这样的包装方法不易携带。 It is rare
for packs like these to be so easy to
handle.
74 | 0.74 | 54

4419 贤 [賢] /xián/ adj virtuous and able; [used as
part of a term of respect]
福在子孙贤，子孙贤是福。 But if your
descendants are virtuous, this brings great
happiness.
62 | 0.87 | 54

4420 独自 [獨自] /dúzì/ (3) adv alone
你独自一人旅行吗？ Are you travelling
alone?
91 | 0.6 | 54

4421 相继 [相繼] /xiāngjì/ adv in succession; one
after another
他们三人一个个相继入睡了。 The three of
them fell asleep one after another.
106 | 0.52 | 54

4422 数十 [數十] /shùshí/ num tens of, dozens of
每一个人才都有数十个可供选择的工作机会。
Every qualified talent attracts dozens of job
offers.
80 | 0.68 | 54

4423 留学生 [留學生] /liúxuéshēng/ (1) n overseas
student, returned student
它描绘海外中国留学生的生活。 It portrays the
life of overseas Chinese students.
73 | 0.75 | 54

4424 肩 [肩] /jiān/ (2) *n* shoulder
朝你右肩后方看去。Look over your right shoulder.
87 | 0.62 | 54

4425 种子 [種子] /zhǒngzi/ (2) *n* seed
不要把不同的种子混杂在一起。Don't mix up different kinds of seeds.
113 | 0.49 | 54

4426 学费 [學費] /xuéfèi/ (2) *n* tuition fees
谁在付她的学费？Who's paying for her tuition?
67 | 0.82 | 54

4427 话剧 [話劇] /huàjù/ (3) *n* (stage) play
这出话剧改编自真人真事。The play is a dramatic representation of a real event.
85 | 0.64 | 54

4428 课堂 [課堂] /kètáng/ (3) *n* classroom
我们不仅在课堂上学，而且在课外学。We learn not only inside the classroom but also outside.
62 | 0.88 | 54

4429 大自然 [大自然] /dàzìrán/ (3) *n* nature
我们欣赏大自然的美。We enjoy the beauty of nature.
70 | 0.78 | 54

4430 局部 [局部] /júbù/ (3) *n* part, locality
局部服从整体。The part must be subordinate to the whole.
73 | 0.74 | 54

4431 风气 [風氣] /fēngqì/ (3) *n* general mood; atmosphere; common practice
这种好风气，要把它恢复起来。We should try to restore this healthy atmosphere.
74 | 0.73 | 54

4432 准则 [準則] /zhǔnzé/ *n* norm, rule, criterion
在社会中生活就要遵循社会行为准则。You must adapt to the norms of the society you live in.
75 | 0.73 | 54

4433 含义 [含義] /hányì/ *n* meaning, implication
你能领会这封信的含义吗？Do you comprehend the meaning of this letter?
73 | 0.75 | 54

4434 处境 [處境] /chǔjìng/ *n* (difficult) position, plight
你不了解我的处境有多困难。You don't understand what a difficult position I am in.
71 | 0.76 | 54

4435 绘画 [繪畫] /huìhuà/ *n* drawing, painting
我最喜欢的是绘画。What I most enjoy is painting.
72 | 0.75 | 54

4436 排 [排] /pái/ (2) *clas* [measure word for a line of persons or things] a line of, a row of
房间里有一排椅子。There are a row of chairs in the room.
79 | 0.69 | 54

4437 厘米 [釐米] /límǐ/ (2) *clas* [measure term for length] centimetre, cm
这带子有30厘米长。This piece of string is 30 centimetres long.
83 | 0.66 | 54

4438 两者 [兩者] /liǎngzhě/ *pron* the two, both
两者相差无几。There is little difference between the two.
75 | 0.73 | 54

4439 跳舞 [跳舞] /tiàowǔ/ (1) *v* dance
您跳舞吗？Can you dance?
77 | 0.7 | 54

4440 吸烟 [吸煙] /xīyān/ (2) *v* smoke
他素来不吸烟。He never smokes.
70 | 0.77 | 54

4441 挥 [揮] /huī/ (2) *v* wave, wield; scatter, disperse
他绝望地向他的伙伴挥了挥手。He waved desperately to his companion.
103 | 0.53 | 54

4442 对比 [對比] /duìbǐ/ (2) *v* contrast, compare
这位人类学家在讲座中将两种文化进行了对比。The anthropologist contrasted the two cultures in his lecture.
71 | 0.77 | 54

4443 甩 [甩] /shuǎi/ (2) *v* fling; throw off
她甩掉鞋子跑开了。She flung off her shoes and ran away.
93 | 0.58 | 54

4444 扭 [扭] /niǔ/ (2) *v* turn around; twist; strain
他扭了一下我的手臂。He gave my arm a twist.
107 | 0.51 | 54

4445 动摇 [動搖] /dòngyáo/ (3) *v* waver, shake
这一新证据动摇了她的理论。Her theory has been shaken by this new evidence.
69 | 0.78 | 54

4446 自愿 [自願] /zìyuàn/ (3) *adv* voluntarily
他自愿参了军。He joined the army voluntarily.
70 | 0.78 | 54

4447 护 [護] /hù/ (3) *v* protect; be partial to
我本能地抬起手臂护着脸。I instinctively raised my arm to protect my face.
69 | 0.8 | 54

4448 带动 [帶動] /dàidòng/ (3) *v* spur on, provide an impetus, drive, bring along
高新技术产业带动了经济结构的优化。Hi-tech industry has been driving the optimisation of the economic structure.
133 | 0.41 | 54

4449 谈论 [談論] /tánlùn/ (3) *v* talk about
他正在谈论他的作品。He is talking about his works.
71 | 0.76 | 54

4450 自治 [自治] /zìzhì/ (3) *n* autonomy, self-governing
分裂主义者在要求他们的州完全自治。The separatist is demanding full autonomy for their state.
116 | 0.47 | 54

4451 亡 [亡] /wáng/ v die, perish
猎人开了枪，野兔倒地而亡。The hunter fired and the rabbit fell dead.
67 | 0.82 | 54

4452 操 [操] /cāo/ v hold; speak (a language); drill
她操着北方口音问道。She asked in a northern accent.
78 | 0.7 | 54

4453 限 [限] /xiàn/ v limit, set a limit
人数不限。There is no limit on the number of people.
69 | 0.79 | 54

4454 诱惑 [誘惑] /yòuhuò/ v entice, tempt
她用色情来诱惑男人。She used sex appeal to entice men.
69 | 0.79 | 54

4455 衡量 [衡量] /héngliáng/ v weigh; measure
幸福令人向往而又难以衡量。Happiness is desirable but hard to measure.
69 | 0.78 | 54

4456 应有 [應有] /yīngyǒu/ adj proper, due, deserved
中医受到了应有的尊重。Doctors of Chinese traditional medicine are accorded due respect.
93 | 0.59 | 54

4457 封闭 [封閉] /fēngbì/ v close, seal off; seal
请把你的东西放入这信封并封闭好。Please put your articles in this envelope and seal it.
68 | 0.8 | 54

4458 弃 [棄] /qì/ v relinquish, abandon; discard
困难之际，它也不离不弃。It does not turn its back upon us in times of adversity or distress.
67 | 0.81 | 54

4459 深受 [深受] /shēnshòu/ v receive, [passive marker] be deeply -en (loved, moved, etc.)
观众深受感动。The audience was deeply affected.
71 | 0.77 | 54

4460 贫穷 [貧窮] /pínqióng/ (3) adj poor, impoverished
她父母很贫穷。Her parents were very poor.
74 | 0.72 | 53

4461 细致 [細緻] /xìzhì/ (3) adj delicate, fine; careful
可是后来，这个细致的工作总算做完了。But now the delicate work is finished.
65 | 0.82 | 53

4462 消极 [消極] /xiāojí/ (3) adj passive, inactive
他们的态度始终是消极的。They remain inactive throughout.
77 | 0.7 | 53

4463 低下 [低下] /dīxià/ adj low (status)
第二个原因是经济地位低下。The second reason is their low economic status.
76 | 0.7 | 53

4464 吉 [吉] /jí/ adj lucky
吉星高照。The lucky star shines bright.
64 | 0.84 | 53

4465 虽说 [雖説] /suīshuō/ (3) conj although, though
虽说她聪明，但她见识不高。Although she was intelligent, she had little insight.
74 | 0.72 | 53

4466 卡车 [卡車] /kǎchē/ (1) n truck, lorry
这辆卡车装着一车香蕉。The truck was carrying a load of bananas.
61 | 0.87 | 53

4467 物价 [物價] /wùjià/ (2) n price
物价仍在急剧上涨。Prices are still spiralling.
118 | 0.46 | 53

4468 猴子 [猴子] /hóuzi/ (2) n monkey
小孩最喜欢猴子。Children like monkeys best.
104 | 0.52 | 53

4469 地带 [地帶] /dìdài/ (2) n zone, region
在沙漠地带，绝大多数时间都是大晴天，下雨天极少。Sunny days predominate over rainy days in desert regions.
70 | 0.77 | 53

4470 环 [環] /huán/ (2) n ring; link
这是解决地下水问题的重要一环。This is the important link for problems of subsurface flow.
73 | 0.73 | 53

4471 塑料 [塑料] /sùliào/ (2) n plastics
塑料易于加工成各种不同的形状。Plastics can be easily made into different shapes.
59 | 0.91 | 53

4472 证书 [證書] /zhèngshū/ (3) n certificate, diploma
向毕业班学生颁发了毕业证书。Diplomas were conferred on members of the graduating class.
87 | 0.62 | 53

4473 角落 [角落] /jiǎoluò/ (3) n corner
你能让我们在那个角落下车吗？Could you drop us off on that corner?
81 | 0.66 | 53

4474 村子 [村子] /cūnzi/ (3) n village
村子在河那边。The village is beyond the river.
66 | 0.82 | 53

4475 谈话 [談話] /tánhuà/ (3) n talk
她打断了我们的谈话。She cut across our talk.
65 | 0.82 | 53

4476 穷人 [窮人] /qióngrén/ (3) n the poor, poor people
她年年送钱帮助穷人。She sent money year after year to help the poor.
70 | 0.76 | 53

4477 牙齿 [牙齒] /yáchǐ/ (3) n tooth
我要治疗这颗牙齿。I want to have the tooth treated.
71 | 0.75 | 53

4478 肌肉 [肌肉] /jīròu/ (3) n muscle
锻炼身体能使肌肉结实。Exercise will firm up your muscles.
70 | 0.76 | 53

4479 报刊 [報刊] /bàokān/ (3) *n* newspapers and periodicals, the press
它们受到报刊的公开赞扬。 They are complimented in the public press.
81 | 0.66 | 53

4480 工地 [工地] /gōngdì/ (3) *n* construction site
到建筑工地只有五公里路程。 It is only five kilometres to the construction site.
67 | 0.79 | 53

4481 肚 [肚] /dù, dǔ/ *n* stomach, belly; tripe
肚里有一种空空然的感觉。 His stomach felt empty.
81 | 0.66 | 53

4482 视野 [視野] /shìyě/ *n* field of view, vision
他们很快就消失在我们视野之外了。
They were soon out of view.
67 | 0.8 | 53

4483 陵 [陵] /líng/ *n* hill, mound; tomb
你去参观过十三陵水库吗？ Have you been to the Ming Tombs Reservoir?
66 | 0.82 | 53

4484 玩意 [玩意] /wányì/ *n* [often taking the suffix 儿] toy, plaything; thing
可别给我来那些花花哨哨的玩意儿！ None of these fancy bits for me!
87 | 0.61 | 53

4485 助理 [助理] /zhùlǐ/ *n* assistant
他是经理助理。 He is the manager's assistant.
79 | 0.67 | 53

4486 空白 [空白] /kòngbái/ *n* blank space; gap
我们的发现填补了这个空白。 Our findings filled the gap.
67 | 0.8 | 53

4487 女生 [女生] /nǚshēng/ *n* girl student
该校不收女生。 The school does not take girls.
98 | 0.55 | 53

4488 老头 [老頭] /lǎotóu/ *n* [disrespectful] old man, old chap
那个顽固老头就是不肯进医院。 The obstinate old man refused to go to hospital.
86 | 0.62 | 53

4489 本能 [本能] /běnnéng/ *n* instinct
他做这件好事是出于本能。 He does this good thing from instinct.
77 | 0.69 | 53

4490 坏人 [壞人] /huàirén/ *n* bad people, villain, evildoer
不要受坏人拉拢。 Don't get roped in by bad people.
76 | 0.7 | 53

4491 照 [照] /zhào/ (2) *prep* according to; in the direction of
照他们这一讲，都错了。 According to them, we are wrong in both.
71 | 0.76 | 53

4492 伙 [伙] /huǒ/ (3) *clas* [measure word for a crowd of people] a crowd of, a band of
他遭到一伙暴徒袭击。 He was attacked by a band of ruffians.
76 | 0.7 | 53

4493 开辟 [開闢] /kāipì/ (2) *v* open up
那项技术开辟了新的科学领域。 The technology opened up a new scientific field.
99 | 0.54 | 53

4494 避 [避] /bì/ (2) *v* avoid, evade
她对我的问题避而不答。 She avoided answering my questions.
70 | 0.77 | 53

4495 录 [錄] /lù/ (2) *v* record
这些歌曲是由广播公司录下的。 The songs were recorded by the radio company.
84 | 0.64 | 53

4496 拥护 [擁護] /yōnghù/ (2) *v* support, advocate
我拥护逐步改革的政策。 I advocate a policy of gradual reform.
81 | 0.66 | 53

4497 来不及 [來不及] /láibují/ (2) *v* it's too late for, there is not time for
要退缩已经来不及了。 It was too late to retreat.
92 | 0.58 | 53

4498 传达 [傳達] /chuándá/ (3) *v* convey, communicate
思想可由语言传达。 Ideas are communicated by words.
69 | 0.78 | 53

4499 不止 [不止] /bùzhǐ/ (3) *v* without end, incessantly; exceed, more than
他把自己割伤了，血流不止。 He cut himself and could not stop the bleeding.
66 | 0.81 | 53

4500 保密 [保密] /bǎomì/ (3) *v* keep something in secrecy, keep something secret
我们这儿讨论的事必须保密。 We must keep a secret of the things being discussed here.
58 | 0.92 | 53

4501 耐 [耐] /nài/ (3) *v* endure
这种玻璃很能耐热。 This kind of glass can endure much heat.
62 | 0.87 | 53

4502 揪 [揪] /jiū/ (3) *v* clutch, pull
别那么使劲揪绳子。 Don't pull so hard at the rope.
84 | 0.64 | 53

4503 抹 [抹] /mǒ/ (3) *v* smear, spread; wipe; erase
这盘子洗过后要抹一抹。 Wipe the dishes after they have been washed.
93 | 0.58 | 53

4504 创业 [創業] /chuàngyè/ *v* do pioneering work, start a business
他用房产押款创业。 He mortgaged his house in order to start a business.
95 | 0.56 | 53

4505 兴起 [興起] /xīngqǐ/ *v* rise, spring up, develop
一个建设的新高潮正在兴起。 A new upsurge in construction is in the making.
72 | 0.74 | 53

4506 抛弃 [拋棄] /pāoqì/ *v* discard, abandon
我觉得你是在抛弃我。 I feel like you're abandoning me.
62 | 0.86 | 53

4507 签字 [簽字] /qiānzì/ v sign
请您在这儿签字。Please sign your name here.
89 | 0.61 | 53

4508 现有 [現有] /xiànyǒu/ adj currently existing
他们决心使现有工厂现代化。They are determined to modernise the existing factories.
101 | 0.53 | 53

4509 碰上 [碰上] /pèngshàng/ v run into, come across
我正出门的时候碰上他了。I ran into him on the way out.
78 | 0.68 | 53

4510 追究 [追究] /zhuījiù/ v enquire into, take action against, penalise
我们必须追究此事。We must enquire into the matter.
85 | 0.63 | 53

4511 邀 [邀] /yāo/ v invite
我很荣幸被邀在这里讲话。It is an honour for me to be invited to speak here.
61 | 0.88 | 53

4512 犹如 [猶如] /yóurú/ v be just like, as if
生活无目标犹如航海没有指南针。Living without an aim is like sailing without a compass.
72 | 0.74 | 53

4513 摇头 [搖頭] /yáotóu/ v shake one's head
他摇了摇头表示反对。He shook his head in disapproval.
144 | 0.37 | 53

4514 难免 [難免] /nánmiǎn/ v it is hard to avoid
犯错误是难免的。It's hard to avoid mistakes.
74 | 0.72 | 53

4515 睡着 [睡着] /shuìzháo/ v go to sleep, fall asleep
她转过身就睡着了。She turned over and went to sleep.
99 | 0.54 | 53

4516 深厚 [深厚] /shēnhòu/ (2) adj deep, profound
两家人建立了深厚的情谊。The two families established a profound friendship.
69 | 0.75 | 52

4517 高大 [高大] /gāodà/ (2) adj tall; lofty
他像父亲一样高大。He is as tall as his father.
72 | 0.73 | 52

4518 狂 [狂] /kuáng/ (3) adj mad, crazy; conceited, arrogant; unrestrained, wild
他这么狂。He is such an arrogant man.
76 | 0.69 | 52

4519 长远 [長遠] /chángyuǎn/ (3) adj long-term
但这是长远计划。But that's a long-term plan.
104 | 0.51 | 52

4520 必定 [必定] /bìdìng/ (3) adv surely
他必定失败。He will surely fail.
70 | 0.75 | 52

4521 无非 [無非] /wúfēi/ adv only, nothing but, no more than
说穿了，无非是想推卸责任。To put it bluntly, this is only shifting responsibility.
68 | 0.78 | 52

4522 背后 [背後] /bèihòu/ (2) loc behind, at the back
在这些技术的背后是什么呢？So what's behind these techniques?
65 | 0.81 | 52

4523 月亮 [月亮] /yuèliang/ (1) n moon
月亮被云遮住了。The moon was obscured by clouds.
72 | 0.73 | 52

4524 服务员 [服務員] /fúwùyuán/ (1) n attendant, waiter, waitress
服务员，这张桌子空着吗？Is the table free, waiter?
69 | 0.76 | 52

4525 名 [名] /míng/ (2) n name; fame
他的第二部小说确立了他作家之名。His second novel established his fame as a writer.
63 | 0.83 | 52

4526 箱子 [箱子] /xiāngzi/ (2) n box, suitcase
请你把这只箱子打开，好吗？Would you mind unlocking this suitcase please?
80 | 0.65 | 52

4527 座位 [座位] /zuòwèi/ (2) n seat
后面有许多座位。There are plenty of seats in the rear.
71 | 0.74 | 52

4528 金属 [金屬] /jīnshǔ/ (2) n metal
金属受热则膨胀。Metals expand when they are heated.
61 | 0.86 | 52

4529 驴 [驢] /lǘ/ (3) n donkey
他有一头驴。He had a donkey.
85 | 0.62 | 52

4530 心思 [心思] /xīnsī/ (3) n idea; thinking, thought
他们看出了她的心思。They read her thoughts.
107 | 0.49 | 52

4531 价钱 [價錢] /jiàqián/ (3) n price
请问价钱多少？What is the price?
67 | 0.78 | 52

4532 学员 [學員] /xuéyuán/ (3) n learner, student
办学校的人要了解学员。Those in charge of the schools must know their students well.
81 | 0.65 | 52

4533 报社 [報社] /bàoshè/ (3) n newspaper, press
这条消息被泄露到了报社。The news was leaked to the press.
58 | 0.9 | 52

4534 导师 [導師] /dǎoshī/ (3) n tutor, supervisor
她的导师说她进步很大。Her tutor says she is making good progress.
76 | 0.69 | 52

4535 心眼 [心眼] /xīnyǎn/ n heart, mind; cleverness; tolerance
我不由打心眼里同情他。 I pitied him from the bottom of my heart.
86 | 0.6 | 52

4536 现金 [現金] /xiànjīn/ n cash
我宁愿付现金。 I'd rather pay by cash.
79 | 0.67 | 52

4537 皇家 [皇家] /huángjiā/ n royal family, imperial family
他们是皇家成员。 They are members of the royal family.
61 | 0.86 | 52

4538 婆 [婆] /pó/ n woman; matron; mother-in-law; grandma
她现在是个富婆，过着安逸的生活。 She is a rich woman now, and leads a life of ease.
81 | 0.65 | 52

4539 宗旨 [宗旨] /zōngzhǐ/ n aim, goal
这一慈善团体的宗旨是帮助人们实行自助。 This charity aims to help people to help themselves.
111 | 0.47 | 52

4540 证券 [證券] /zhèngquàn/ n securities, stock
证券市场进一步规范发展。 The stock market further developed with regulation.
143 | 0.37 | 52

4541 头儿 [頭兒] /tóur/ n head, chief, superior
那么你认识这位头儿了？ You know this chief, then?
131 | 0.4 | 52 | S

4542 边境 [邊境] /biānjìng/ n border, frontier
这一边境事件导致了两国交战。 The border incident led to war between the two countries.
93 | 0.56 | 52

4543 顶 [頂] /dǐng/ (3) clas [measure word for objects with a top such as hats, caps and sedan chairs]
我能试一下这顶帽子吗？ Can I try this hat on?
65 | 0.8 | 52

4544 栋 [棟] /dòng/ clas [measure word for houses and buildings]
我们看了几栋房子，但尚未买成。 We went over several houses, but have not bought one yet.
63 | 0.84 | 52

4545 从前 [從前] /cóngqián/ (1) time before, in the past
我们从前看过这部影片。 We have seen the film before.
68 | 0.78 | 52

4546 握手 [握手] /wòshǒu/ (1) v shake hands
他走过去与客人握手。 He went up and shook hands with the guests.
64 | 0.82 | 52

4547 捉 [捉] /zhuō/ (2) v clutch, seize; catch, capture
猫捉老鼠。 A cat catches mice.
75 | 0.71 | 52

4548 压迫 [壓迫] /yāpò/ (2) v oppress
一切受压迫的民族都要独立。 All oppressed nations want independence.
75 | 0.71 | 52

4549 抽烟 [抽煙] /chōuyān/ (2) v smoke
他用烟斗抽烟。 He smokes tobacco in his pipe.
77 | 0.68 | 52

4550 感激 [感激] /gǎnjī/ (2) v appreciate, be grateful, be obliged
非常感激你帮助了我们。 I'm much obliged to you for helping us.
85 | 0.62 | 52

4551 消耗 [消耗] /xiāohào/ (3) v consume, deplete
我们的食物储备已消耗殆尽。 Our stock of food is greatly depleted.
68 | 0.77 | 52

4552 打仗 [打仗] /dǎzhàng/ (3) v fight, fight a war
女人不适合打仗。 It does not become women to fight.
76 | 0.69 | 52

4553 连接 [連接] /liánjiē/ (3) v connect, join, link
铁路把这两个城市连接起来。 The railway line links the two cities together.
77 | 0.69 | 52

4554 叙述 [敘述] /xùshù/ (3) v give an account of, tell about
他如实叙述了发生的事。 He gave an unvarnished account of what happened.
68 | 0.78 | 52

4555 下岗 [下崗] /xiàgǎng/ v stand down; be laid off
国有企业职工大量下岗。 Large numbers of workers were laid off from state-owned enterprises.
144 | 0.37 | 52

4556 更新 [更新] /gèngxīn/ v update, renew
这些数字每年更新。 The figures are updated annually.
89 | 0.59 | 52

4557 定位 [定位] /dìngwèi/ v position, set on; locate
他们测试了他的空间定位能力。 They tested his ability to locate objects in space.
73 | 0.72 | 52

4558 响起 [響起] /xiǎngqǐ/ v sound, make a sound, break out
响起了一阵欢呼声。 A roar of cheering broke out.
91 | 0.57 | 52

4559 注定 [註定] /zhùdìng/ v be doomed, be destined
她注定是要成为一个伟大的钢琴家的。 She was destined to become a great pianist.
69 | 0.76 | 52

4560 组合 [組合] /zǔhé/ v assemble, combine
这些园林把山、水、建筑和草木巧妙地组合起来。 These gardens ingeniously combine hills, waters, buildings, trees and flowers.
71 | 0.73 | 52

29. Commonly used words in the non-fiction register

Headword	POS	Gloss	Frequency rank
阶层	n	social stratum	3443
员工	n	staff, personnel, employee	2133
克	clas	[measure term for weight] gram	4050
宜	adj	suitable	4219
客户	n	client, customer	2091
赌博	v	gamble	4899
阶级	n	(social) class	3332
盐	n	salt	3304
采购	v	purchase; do shopping	3345
夏季	time	summer	4766
例如	v	for example	2871
考核	v	examine, appraise, assess	4613
社会主义	n	socialism	857
金额	n	amount	4186
资产	n	asset	2062
说道	v	say	2463
网站	n	website	4592
问道	v	ask	3859
企业	n	business establishment, enterprise	189
方针	n	policy, directive	1971
产品	n	product	647
大使	n	ambassador	2756
有利于	v	be beneficial to, be helpful to	2690
下降	v	decline, drop	2332
机构	n	organisation, institution	880
潜力	n	potential, potentiality	3717
规划	n	scheme, plan	2425
总数	n	total amount, sum	4385
树立	v	set up, establish	3885
制定	v	draw up, make, set forth	1491
规划	v	plan	4199
辩	v	argue, debate	1798
机制	n	mechanism	2120
积极性	n	enthusiasm, initiative, zeal	3792
皇帝	n	emperor	1546
现代化	n	modernisation	1612
实行	v	implement, carry out, bring into effect	1096
推出	v	present, introduce	2668
股份	n	share, stock	4707
破产	v	go bankrupt; fail, fall through	4885
就业	n	employment	2667
自治	n	autonomy, self-governing	4450
保障	v	safeguard, guarantee	1754

战胜	v	beat, defeat, triumph over; overcome, surmount	2761
年度	n	year	3846
部门	n	department	534
显著	adj	remarkable, outstanding	3391
市场	n	market	304
综合	adj	comprehensive, synthetic	1902
创新	v	innovate, be creative	2080
窗外	place	out of the window	4824
批准	v	approve	2069
紧密	adv	closely	4317
生产	n	production	4993
市场经济	n	market economy	2177
椅子	n	chair	4032
改进	v	improve	3723
推行	v	carry out, push on with	3685
叫做	v	be called	2079
扩大	v	enlarge, expand	1186
优势	n	advantage, strength	1354
逐步	adv	step by step, gradually	2257
减轻	v	lighten, ease, alleviate	4395
村民	n	villager	3257
机遇	n	opportunity, favourable circumstances	3159
人士	n	person, personage, public figure	1599
开放	v	open, open up; (flower) blossom	1032
实现	v	realise, fulfil, achieve	592
调整	v	adjust	1223
技术	n	technology	350
进口	v	import	3192
领域	n	domain, area, field	1173
海外	place	overseas	2474
银行	n	bank	755
事务	n	affairs	2538
广阔	adj	wide, broad, vast	4416
改革	v	reform	416
全面	adj	all-around, overall	1026
居民	n	resident, inhabitant; citizen	1898

Comments:

For each of the four registers:

1 Remove all items with a dispersion index equal to or greater than 0.5;

2 First sort by normalised frequency of the register under consideration;

3 Compute the ratio of the register with the other three (normalised frequency of register / (sum of the normalised frequencies of the other three registers);

4 Cut off where there is a significant drop in the ratio computed in (2);

5 The list is arranged by statistical salience instead of frequency ranks.

4561 淘汰 [淘汰] /táotài/ v eliminate (through selection or competition); become obsolete
他在第四轮被淘汰。 He was eliminated in the fourth round.
92 | 0.57 | 52

4562 致使 [致使] /zhìshǐ/ v cause, result in
飞机猛然俯冲致使驾驶员昏厥。 The plane dived suddenly, causing the pilot to black out.
82 | 0.65 | 52

4563 散发 [散發] /sànfā/ v distribute, circulate; give off, emit
花儿散发着清香。 The flowers gave off a delicate fragrance.
68 | 0.77 | 52

4564 延伸 [延伸] /yánshēn/ v extend, stretch
我们的花园一直延伸到河边。 Our garden goes down as far as the river.
73 | 0.73 | 52

4565 融 [融] /róng/ v melt, thaw; fuse, mix together
快到中午时,雪融掉了。 The snow melted away at the approach of noon.
69 | 0.76 | 52

4566 赖 [賴] /lài/ v rely, depend; go back on one's word; hold on in a place
可他们赖着不走了。 But they overstayed their welcome.
96 | 0.55 | 52

4567 开拓 [開拓] /kāituò/ v open, open up
这一经验为他的思想开拓了新的境界。 This experience opened a new prospect to his mind.
126 | 0.42 | 52

4568 悠久 [悠久] /yōujiǔ/ (2) adj of long standing
这是一家历史悠久的商号。 This is a firm of long standing.
73 | 0.71 | 51

4569 不好意思 [不好意思] /bùhǎoyìsi/ (2) idiom feel embarrassed, find it embarrassing
我出了这种错误很不好意思。 I'm embarrassed about my mistake.
88 | 0.58 | 51

4570 正当 [正當] /zhèngdāng/ (3) adj proper
不要拘束她的正当活动。 Don't restrict her proper activities.
72 | 0.71 | 51

4571 猛 [猛] /měng/ (3) adj ferocious, hard
悠着点劲,别太猛了。 Take it easy! Don't go at it so hard!
81 | 0.64 | 51

4572 勇 [勇] /yǒng/ adj brave, courageous
他勇于改过。 He has the courage to correct his mistakes.
65 | 0.79 | 51

4573 丰 [豐] /fēng/ adj abundant, plentiful; good-looking
今年这煤矿产量甚丰。 This year's yield from the coal mine was very large.
64 | 0.81 | 51

4574 以此 [以此] /yǐcǐ/ adv hereby, by this, with this
还是让我们以此来作为一个小小的开端吧。 But let's make a small beginning with this.
76 | 0.68 | 51

4575 似 [似] /sì/ adv apparently, as if
他似乎把它给忘了。 He has apparently forgotten it.
94 | 0.55 | 51

4576 盆 [盆] /pén/ (2) n basin, tub; pot, bowl
她把盆里的衣服洗了。 She washed the clothes in the tub.
66 | 0.77 | 51

4577 语气 [語氣] /yǔqì/ (2) n tone, manner of speaking; (subjunctive, imperative, etc.) mood
他的语气使我吃惊。 I was surprised at his tone.
103 | 0.5 | 51

4578 尾巴 [尾巴] /wěiba/ (2) n tail
老鼠有条长尾巴。 A mouse has a long tail.
79 | 0.66 | 51

4579 书店 [書店] /shūdiàn/ (2) n bookstore
这家书店不经销医学类书藉。 This bookstore doesn't handle medical books.
66 | 0.78 | 51

4580 用品 [用品] /yòngpǐn/ (3) n articles for use, appliance
所有这些东西都是我的私人用品。 All these are my personal articles.
75 | 0.68 | 51

4581 幼儿园 [幼兒園] /yòu'éryuán/ (3) n kindergarten
孩子们在幼儿园受到很好的照看。 The children are well looked after in the kindergarten.
56 | 0.91 | 51

4582 树木 [樹木] /shùmù/ (3) n tree
树木秋天时落叶。 A tree sheds its leaves in autumn.
55 | 0.93 | 51

4583 摊 [攤] /tān/ (3) n stand, stall, vendor's booth
他母亲摆了个摊卖水果。 His mother set up a stall to sell fruit.
63 | 0.82 | 51

4584 战友 [戰友] /zhànyǒu/ (3) n comrade in arms, fellow soldier
他们是我的老战友。 They are my old comrades in arms.
69 | 0.75 | 51

4585 境 [境] /jìng/ (3) n border, boundary; condition, circumstance
毒品走私是跨境犯罪。 Drug smuggling is a cross-border crime.
66 | 0.78 | 51

4586 高峰 [高峰] /gāofēng/ (3) n peak, summit
因为现在是晚餐高峰时间。 Because this is the peak time for dinner orders.
74 | 0.7 | 51

4587 包袱 [包袱] /bāofu/ (3) *n* burden, weight (on one's mind); a bundle wrapped in cloth
你不要因此背包袱。Don't let it weigh on your mind.
63 | 0.82 | 51

4588 成人 [成人] /chéngrén/ *n* adult
这些电影只适宜成人观看。These films are suitable for adults only.
65 | 0.79 | 51

4589 阴影 [陰影] /yīnyǐng/ *n* shadow, shade; blight, spectre
一个阴影投在墙上。A shadow fell on the wall.
64 | 0.81 | 51

4590 钢琴 [鋼琴] /gāngqín/ *n* piano
这架钢琴把房间衬托得很有气派。The piano gives the room a touch of style.
63 | 0.82 | 51

4591 内阁 [內閣] /nèigé/ *n* cabinet
内阁成员是由首相挑选的。Members of the cabinet are chosen by the prime minister.
90 | 0.58 | 51

4592 网站 [網站] /wǎngzhàn/ *n* website
这个网站县至还提供医药和其他健康概念。The website even detailed pharmaceutical and other health issues.
116 | 0.45 | 51

4593 存款 [存款] /cúnkuǎn/ *n* deposit (in a bank), savings
储蓄存款的利率是多少？What's the interest rate for the savings account?
104 | 0.5 | 51

4594 股东 [股東] /gǔdōng/ *n* stockholder, shareholder
他开始做股东所要求的报告。He began to write the report requested by the shareholders.
77 | 0.66 | 51

4595 生涯 [生涯] /shēngyá/ *n* career
她 18 岁就开始了教书生涯。She began her teaching career when she was only 18.
70 | 0.73 | 51

4596 政治家 [政治家] /zhèngzhìjiā/ *n* politician, statesman
她得到有权力和有影响的政治家的支持。She had the support of powerful and influential politicians.
67 | 0.77 | 51

4597 例外 [例外] /lìwài/ *n* exception
这些规章制度不能有例外。These regulations permit no exception.
65 | 0.79 | 51

4598 举动 [舉動] /jǔdòng/ *n* act, movement, conduct, behaviour
她的举动未受怀疑。Her behaviour aroused no suspicion.
66 | 0.78 | 51

4599 新人 [新人] /xīnrén/ *n* new face, new people; newly wed, bride and bridegroom; people of a new age or a new generation
你将面对一些新人。You will face new people.
64 | 0.81 | 51

4600 蚂蚁 [螞蟻] /mǎyǐ/ *n* ant
蚂蚁喜欢吃甜食。Ants are fond of sweet food.
70 | 0.74 | 51

4601 顺着 [順着] /shùnzhe/ *prep* along
我要顺着河走一段路。I want to take a walk along the river.
77 | 0.67 | 51

4602 匹 [匹] /pǐ/ (2) *clas* [measure word for horses and mules, etc.]; [measure word for bolts of cloth]
你押的是哪匹马？Which horse are you backing?
72 | 0.71 | 51

4603 寸 [寸] /cùn/ (2) *clas* [measure term for length in Chinese local unit] Chinese inch, cun (equivalent of one-thirtieth of a metre)
地上积着一寸厚的白雪。There was an inch of snow on the ground.
65 | 0.8 | 51

4604 消化 [消化] /xiāohuà/ (2) *v* digest
这食物容易消化。This food is easily digested.
75 | 0.68 | 51

4605 催 [催] /cuī/ (2) *v* urge, rush, chase up
别催我。Don't rush me.
68 | 0.76 | 51

4606 拼命 [拼命] /pīnmìng/ (2) *adv* desperately
那些囚犯拼命企图逃亡。The prisoners became desperate in their attempts to escape.
99 | 0.52 | 51

4607 分工 [分工] /fēn'gōng/ (3) *v* divide up the work
我们之间得分分工。We'll have to divide the work between us.
70 | 0.73 | 51

4608 奖励 [獎勵] /jiǎnglì/ (3) *v* reward
为救那女孩的生命他受到奖励。He was rewarded for saving the girl's life.
83 | 0.62 | 51

4609 研制 [研製] /yánzhì/ (3) *v* develop
那两个公司已合作研制新型赛车。The two companies have teamed up to develop a new racing car.
143 | 0.36 | 51

4610 在座 [在座] /zàizuò/ (3) *v* be present
在座的有20个孩子。There are 20 children present.
76 | 0.68 | 51

4611 忍受 [忍受] /rěnshòu/ (3) *v* bear, tolerate, put up with
我再也不能忍受如此热的天气了。I cannot put up with such hot weather any longer.
74 | 0.7 | 51

4612 挺 [挺] /tǐng/ (3) *v* straighten up, stiffen; endure
他挺起胸膛。He squared his shoulders.
84 | 0.62 | 51

4613 考核 [考核] /kǎohé/ *v* examine, appraise, assess
我们祝贺他通过考核。We congratulated him on having passed the examination.
105 | 0.49 | 51

4614 伴随 [伴隨] /bànsuí/ v accompany, follow
它伴随着人们的生活。It accompanies them in their daily life.
65 | 0.79 | 51

4615 特有 [特有] /tèyǒu/ v be unique to or characteristic of
这是香蕉所特有的味道。It is the characteristic flavour of bananas.
62 | 0.83 | 51

4616 排名 [排名] /páimíng/ v rank
这位网球运动员排名世界第三。This tennis player was ranked third in the world.
107 | 0.48 | 51

4617 做饭 [做飯] /zuòfàn/ v cook
你会做饭吗？Can you cook?
73 | 0.7 | 51

4618 弥补 [彌補] /míbǔ/ v make up, compensate, remedy
你们必须设法来弥补它。You have to do something to make up for it.
63 | 0.82 | 51

4619 用人 [用人] /yòngrén/ v employ, make use of personnel
她一向善于用人。She always gets the best out of people.
96 | 0.53 | 51

4620 勒 [勒] /lēi, lè/ v tighten; strangle; rein in (the horse)
我得勒紧裤腰带了。I have to tighten my belt.
59 | 0.88 | 51

4621 接收 [接收] /jiēshōu/ v receive
卫星接收到信号，将其增强。The satellite receives the signal and makes it stronger.
63 | 0.81 | 51

4622 关闭 [關閉] /guānbì/ v close, shut; (of business) close down
剧院因为整修而关闭了。The theatre was closed for renovations.
76 | 0.68 | 51

4623 转换 [轉換] /zhuǎnhuàn/ v change, switch, convert, transform
热可以转换为电。Heat can be converted into electricity.
77 | 0.66 | 51

4624 酸 [酸] /suān/ (1) adj sour, tart; pedantic
这些橘子吃起来很酸。These oranges taste sour.
71 | 0.7 | 50

4625 天真 [天真] /tiānzhēn/ (2) adj naive, innocent
她带着天真的笑容。She was wearing an innocent smile.
73 | 0.7 | 50

4626 废 [廢] /fèi/ (3) adj waste, useless; disused, abandoned
他们用废报纸生起了火。They made a fire with waste newspaper.
66 | 0.77 | 50

4627 可笑 [可笑] /kěxiào/ (3) adj funny, ridiculous
你说可笑不可笑？Isn't that ridiculous?
72 | 0.7 | 50

4628 豪华 [豪華] /háohuá/ adj luxurious
这种汽车是我们最豪华的型号了。This car is our most luxurious model.
60 | 0.84 | 50

4629 单一 [單一] /dānyī/ adj single
再要提倡单一的欣赏标准已是不可能的了。No longer was it possible to promote a single standard of taste.
72 | 0.7 | 50

4630 俗 [俗] /sú/ adj vulgar
色彩夺目，迥然不俗。Colours are striking, yet not vulgar.
68 | 0.74 | 50

4631 接下来 [接下來] /jiēxiàlái/ conj after that, and then, next
接下来，我想简单介绍一下本厂的情况。Then I'll give you a brief account of our work.
72 | 0.71 | 50

4632 白 [白] /bái/ (2) adv in vain, for nothing; free of charge
她白等了。She waited, but in vain.
83 | 0.61 | 50

4633 净 [淨] /jìng/ (3) adv all, all the time; only, merely
你净胡说八道！You do talk a load of crap!
83 | 0.61 | 50

4634 无意 [無意] /wúyì/ adv inadvertently, accidentally
她无意中泄漏了答案。She gave the answer away accidentally.
65 | 0.77 | 50

4635 猛 [猛] /měng/ adv suddenly, abruptly; vigorously, fiercely
这时他才猛醒过来。Only at that moment, he woke up suddenly.
89 | 0.57 | 50

4636 实事求是 [實事求是] /shíshìqiúshì/ (2) idiom seek truth from facts, be practical and realistic
这种态度，就是实事求是的态度。To take such an attitude is to seek truth from facts.
87 | 0.58 | 50

4637 说不定 [說不定] /shuōbudìng/ (3) idiom maybe, perhaps
说不定他已经走了。Maybe he's already left.
82 | 0.62 | 50

4638 宴会 [宴會] /yànhuì/ (1) n banquet, dinner party
你在宴会上愉快吗？Did you enjoy yourself at the party?
63 | 0.81 | 50

4639 面包 [面包] /miànbāo/ (1) n bread
再来一点黄油面包好吗？Would you like some more bread and butter?
63 | 0.8 | 50

4640 饺子 [餃子] /jiǎozi/ (1) n dumpling
春节我们通常吃饺子。We usually eat dumplings during the Spring Festival.
58 | 0.87 | 50

4641 裤子 [褲子] /kùzi/ (2) *n* trousers
这条新裤子有点大。 These new trousers are a bit on the large side.
77 | 0.66 | 50

4642 本领 [本領] /běnlǐng/ (2) *n* [equivalent of 本事] ability, skill
她喜欢卖弄她的看家本领。 She likes to show off her special skill.
53 | 0.94 | 50

4643 镜子 [鏡子] /jìngzi/ (2) *n* mirror
那平静的水面十分象一面镜子。 The calm water surface is very much like a mirror.
81 | 0.62 | 50

4644 西瓜 [西瓜] /xīguā/ (2) *n* watermelon
你想要几个西瓜？ How many watermelons do you want?
61 | 0.83 | 50

4645 形状 [形狀] /xíngzhuàng/ (2) *n* shape
这茶壶把儿的形状真别扭。 The handle of this teapot has an awkward shape.
70 | 0.72 | 50

4646 日期 [日期] /rìqī/ (2) *n* date
信上的日期被涂掉了。 The date on the letter had been blacked out.
63 | 0.8 | 50

4647 骨干 [骨幹] /gǔgàn/ (3) *n* backbone, mainstay
他是队里的骨干。 He's the backbone of the team.
110 | 0.46 | 50

4648 大脑 [大腦] /dànǎo/ (3) *n* brain
酒精对大脑有影响。 Alcohol acts on the brain.
69 | 0.73 | 50

4649 功课 [功課] /gōngkè/ (3) *n* schoolwork, homework; school subject
我已做完功课。 I've finished my homework.
70 | 0.72 | 50

4650 语文 [語文] /yǔwén/ (3) *n* language, (specifically) Chinese (as a school subject)
这对他们语文能力的掌握和进步都有帮助。 This would help them to learn and improve their language skills.
64 | 0.79 | 50

4651 老年 [老年] /lǎonián/ (3) *n* old age
我们的体力、精力在老年时就衰退。 Our powers decline in old age.
76 | 0.67 | 50

4652 岭 [嶺] /lǐng/ *n* ridge; mountain range
我们雇了个向导带领我们翻山越岭。 We engaged a guide to show us the way across the mountains.
55 | 0.92 | 50

4653 罪犯 [罪犯] /zuìfàn/ *n* criminal
罪犯终于落入法网。 The criminal was finally caught in the net of justice.
75 | 0.67 | 50

4654 味儿 [味兒] /wèir/ *n* taste, flavour
这东西有洋葱味儿。 It tastes of onions.
86 | 0.59 | 50

4655 态 [態] /tài/ *n* form, appearance; state
物质被认为存在有三态。 Matter is thought of as existing in three states.
62 | 0.82 | 50

4656 麦 [麥] /mài/ *n* wheat
眼前是一片绿油油的麦田。 Before our eyes is a stretch of green wheat fields.
65 | 0.78 | 50

4657 起点 [起點] /qǐdiǎn/ *n* starting point
所有成就的起点，都是渴望。 The starting point of all achievements is desire.
70 | 0.72 | 50

4658 警方 [警方] /jǐngfāng/ *n* police
警方正在追捕杀害她的凶手。 The police are hunting her killer.
109 | 0.46 | 50

4659 谱 [譜] /pǔ/ *n* chart, list; music score; a fair amount of confidence, idea; spectrum
下一步该怎么做，我心里一点谱都没有。 I have no idea what to do next.
60 | 0.84 | 50

4660 臂 [臂] /bì, bei/ *n* arm
他两臂在胸前交叉坐着。 He sat with his arms across his chest.
59 | 0.85 | 50

4661 民警 [民警] /mínjǐng/ *n* (civilian) police
民警把走失的孩子带回了派出所。 The policeman took the lost child to the local police station.
95 | 0.53 | 50

4662 外汇 [外匯] /wàihuì/ *n* foreign exchange, foreign currency
强化外汇管理。 Foreign exchange control should be tightened.
157 | 0.32 | 50

4663 靠 [靠] /kào/ (2) *prep* by, against
靠墙放着一张旧方桌。 There is an old table by the wall.
57 | 0.89 | 50

4664 尺 [尺] /chǐ/ (2) *clas* [measure word for length in Chinese local unit] Chinese foot, chi (equivalent of ten cun or one-third of a metre)
这块桌布宽五尺。 The tablecloth is five feet wide.
67 | 0.75 | 50

4665 株 [株] /zhū/ (2) *clas* [measure word for plants]
这是一株西瓜苗。 It's a watermelon plant.
64 | 0.79 | 50

4666 串 [串] /chuàn/ (3) *clas* [measure word for things growing or attached together] string, bunch, cluster
那串珍珠是真的吗？ Is that a real string of pearls?
68 | 0.74 | 50

4667 路边 [路邊] /lùbiān/ *place* roadside
小汽车在路边停下来。 The car stopped at the roadside.
74 | 0.68 | 50

4668 原谅 [原諒] /yuánliàng/ (1) *v* forgive
请原谅我。 Forgive me, please.
98 | 0.51 | 50

30. Common words in the news register

Headword	POS	Gloss	Frequency rank
电	n	electricity, power; telegram, cable	640
会见	v	meet with (somebody who is paying a visit for official business)	2496
西部	loc	west, western part	2308
选手	n	(selected) contestant, player	2135
标题	n	title, heading	3504
近日	time	recently, in the past or next few days	4054
友好	adj	friendly	2163
加快	v	quicken, expedite, speed up	2498
金融	n	finance	1906
会谈	n	talks	2781
开发	v	develop, open up, exploit	925
加强	v	reinforce, intensify	836
增长	v	grow, increase	1024
建设	v	build, construct	442
力度	n	dynamism, vigour, strength	3400
海关	n	customs	4984
贯彻	v	implement, carry out	3093
投资	n	investment	4141
摄	v	take (a photograph)	3893
出席	v	attend	2706
外汇	n	foreign exchange, foreign currency	4662
加大	v	increase, enlarge	3120
大力	adv	vigorously, greatly	2829
产业	n	industry	1471
去年	time	last year	891
开展	v	develop, launch (a campaign), carry out	1420
建成	v	complete, finish building	2766
财政	n	finance	2400
落实	v	implement, fulfil	2479
预计	v	estimate, expect	4410
近年来	time	in recent years	2540
合作	v	cooperate, collaborate	556
公斤	clas	kilo, kilogram	2721
基金	n	fund	3574
促进	v	promote, advance	1252
委员	n	committee member	2218
岸	n	bank	1694
科技	n	science and technology	856
美元	n	US dollar	941
进一步	adv	further	1055
国有	adj	state-owned	1440
举行	v	hold (meeting, etc.)	713
推进	v	boost, advance, push on	2281

自治区	n	autonomous region	2415
研制	v	develop	4609
访问	v	visit, pay a visit (to)	1485
同胞	n	fellow countryman, compatriot	3213
搞好	v	do well, do a good job of	4722
听取	v	listen to, hear; follow (advice)	4896
下岗	v	stand down; be laid off	4555
证券	n	securities, stock	4540
贷款	n	loan	2473
初步	adj	preliminary, initial, tentative	4839
收费	v	charge	3819
据	prep	according to	543
基层	n	grassroots, basic level, lower level; base	2859
通信	n	correspondence, communication	3518
纪录	n	record	3260
实施	v	implement, carry out	1182
治理	v	govern; harness	3387
运动会	n	sports meeting, games	3935
祖国	n	motherland	1637
石油	n	oil	2678
航空	n	aviation, by air	3600
记者	n	reporter, journalist	244
增强	v	enhance, strengthen	2305
预算	n	budget	4046
代表团	n	delegation	2241
推动	v	promote, push forward	1706
国防	n	national defence	4860
工程	n	engineering, project	832
设施	n	facility	1962
赛	n	match, game, competition	4181
吨	clas	ton	1948
贸易	n	trade	1233
开发区	n	development district	3908
党委	n	Party committee	3337
一行	n	group, delegation	4037
协议	n	agreement	1615
农业	n	agriculture	831
分裂	v	split up, break apart	3917
冠军	n	champion	1796
重点	adj	key, major	3781
亩	clas	[measure term for area of land in Chinese local unit] mu (equal to 0.165 acres)	2228
指出	v	point out	978
首相	n	prime minister	4048
引进	v	introduce from elsewhere, import; bring in	2631
届	clas	[measure word used for regular conferences, meetings, graduating classes, sports games, etc.]	735
步伐	n	pace, step	4001

监督	v	supervise, control	1563
人民币	n	Chinese currency *yuan, RMB*	2104
进展	v	make progress	2590
确保	v	ensure, make sure	3036
生态	n	ecology	2254
带动	v	spur on, provide an impetus, drive, bring along	4448
项目	n	project, item	611
能源	n	energy	3597
周年	clas	full year, anniversary	2455
种植	v	plant	4351
投资	v	invest	642
工业	n	industry	973
统一	v	unify, unite; standardise	1451
职工	n	staff, staff member, worker	1341
举办	v	conduct, hold	1952
当前	time	currently, presently	2315
稳定	adj	stable	1126
今年	time	this year	518
前景	n	prospect, outlook	3573
措施	n	measure	1214
逐步	adv	step by step, gradually	2257
积极	adj	active; positive	872
广大	adj	vast, broad, extensive	1673
完善	v	improve, make perfect	2280
组建	v	put together, set up	4413
机制	n	mechanism	2120
小组	n	group	2107
开拓	v	open, open up	4567
比赛	n	competition, contest, match, game	747
出口	n	exit; export	1505
资金	n	fund, capital	1139
改善	v	improve	1783
联合	v	join forces, unite, band together; combine	1552
群众	n	the masses	622
产量	n	output	3465
抵达	v	arrive	4205
首脑	n	head (of state or government); summit (meeting)	3375
科研	n	(scientific) research	2396
领土	n	territory	3747
作出	v	make	1352
旅游	v	travel, take a tour, go sightseeing	1403
领导人	n	leader	1668
负责人	n	person in charge, director	2262
面向	v	face	4152
东部	loc	east, eastern part	3901
报	n	newspaper	566
轮	clas	round (of competitions and talks, etc.); [measure word for the sun and the full moon]	1758

早日	adv	at an earlier date, soon	4847
成果	n	result, outcome, achievement	1609
推广	v	popularise, promote	2821
就业	n	employment	2667
违法	v	break the law, be against the law, be illegal	3587
总统	n	president (of a country)	849
改进	v	improve	3723
市	n	city, town; market	700
党员	n	Party member	2998
重点	n	emphasis, focus point	1359
部长	n	minister; head of department	1433
声明	n	statement	2905
召开	v	convene (a conference or meeting), hold	1527
首都	n	capital	2551
显著	adj	remarkable, outstanding	3391
先进	adj	advanced	1436
市场经济	n	market economy	2177
提高	v	raise, improve	508
大会	n	congress, assembly, meeting	1330
国	n	country, nation	105
地区	n	area, region, district	312
经济	n	economy	161
论坛	n	forum, tribune	3370
调整	v	adjust	1223
有利于	v	be beneficial to, be helpful to	2690
委员会	n	committee	938
部署	v	dispose, deploy	3453
骨干	n	backbone, mainstay	4647
统计	n	statistics	1642
基地	n	base	1739
进口	v	import	3192
高度	adv	highly	2548
项	clas	[measure word for items stipulated, planned, enumerated, or for an account of facts or events]	440
工商	n	industry and commerce	3606
创新	v	innovate, be creative	2080
村民	n	villager	3257
警方	n	police	4658
和平	n	peace	723
施工	v	be under construction	3956
改革	v	reform	416
当局	n	the authorities	3371
领域	n	domain, area, field	1173
协会	n	association, society	1864
居民	n	resident, inhabitant; citizen	1898
物价	n	price	4467
金牌	n	gold medal	2097
治安	n	public order	3753

制定	v	draw up, make, set forth	1491
援助	v	provide help, aid or support	3404
繁荣	adj	prosperous, booming	3168
对外	adj	external, foreign	2847
面积	n	(surface) area	1702
海外	place	overseas	2474
达	v	attain, reach; amount to	614
电子	n	electronics	1844
机遇	n	opportunity, favourable circumstances	3159
股份	n	share, stock	4707
实现	v	realise, fulfil, achieve	592
分别	adv	respectively, separately	1146
目前	time	currently, at the present time	422
公安	n	police	2717
服务	v	serve	652
树立	v	set up, establish	3885
部门	n	department	534
问候	v	greet, give somebody one's respects	4977
大型	adj	large-scale	1879
总理	n	premier	912
取得	v	acquire, obtain, achieve; reach (an agreement)	706
维护	v	defend, safeguard; uphold, maintain	1549
深入	v	penetrate deeply, go deep into	3265
总数	n	total amount, sum	4385
保障	v	safeguard, guarantee	1754
全面	adj	all-around, overall	1026
发展	v	develop	109
访	v	visit, call on	3522
先后	adv	one after another, successively	1945
国际	n	international	253
宗旨	n	aim, goal	4539
贫困	adj	poor, impoverished	1969
批准	v	approve	2069
联邦	n	federation, commonwealth	3342
会议	n	meeting	400
战胜	v	beat, defeat, triumph over; overcome, surmount	2761
企业	n	business establishment, enterprise	189
银行	n	bank	755
自治	n	autonomy, self-governing	4450
网站	n	website	4592
生产	n	production	4993
气象	n	meteorology, weather; scene	4743
开放	v	open, open up; (flower) blossom	1032
现代化	n	modernisation	1612
附	v	enclose, attach	3076
资产	n	asset	2062
发挥	v	bring into play, give play to	1045
扩大	v	enlarge, expand	1186

级	clas	[measure word for levels, grades and ranks, etc.]; [measure word for stairs, and steps, etc.]	1013
亿	num	a hundred million	3107
排名	v	rank	4616
赞赏	v	appreciate	4950
潜力	n	potential, potentiality	3717
市场	n	market	304
种子	n	seed	4425
人士	n	person, personage, public figure	1599
下降	v	decline, drop	2332
围绕	v	revolve around; surround	3137
住房	n	house, housing	2685
实行	v	implement, carry out, bring into effect	1096
技术	n	technology	350
推行	v	carry out, push on with	3685
案件	n	case	2150
推出	v	present, introduce	2668
优势	n	advantage, strength	1354
广阔	adj	wide, broad, vast	4416
进程	n	process	1960
规划	v	plan	4199
破产	v	go bankrupt; fail, fall through	4885
事务	n	affairs	2538
乒乓球	n	table tennis	4286
平方米	clas	square metre	2780
游客	n	tourist	3505
减轻	v	lighten, ease, alleviate	4395
年度	n	year	3846
强调	v	emphasise, stress	1025
积极性	n	enthusiasm, initiative, zeal	3792
紧密	adv	closely	4317
产品	n	product	647
机构	n	organisation, institution	880
综合	adj	comprehensive, synthetic	1902
规划	n	scheme, plan	2425
大使	n	ambassador	2756
方针	n	policy, directive	1971
金额	n	amount	4186
社会主义	n	socialism	857
考核	v	examine, appraise, assess	4613

Comments

For each of the four registers:

1 Remove all items with a dispersion index equal to or greater than 0.5;
2 First sort by normalised frequency of the register under consideration;
3 Compute the ratio of the register with the other three (normalised frequency of register / (sum of the normalised frequencies of the other three registers);
4 Cut off where there is a significant drop in the ratio computed in (2);
5 The list is arranged by statistical salience instead of frequency ranks.

4669 接见 [接見] /jiējiàn/ (2) v receive, see
我只能接见你十分钟。 I can only see you for ten minutes.
57 | 0.88 | 50

4670 竞赛 [競賽] /jìngsài/ (2) n contest, competition, race
那是一场公平的竞赛。 It was a fair contest.
94 | 0.53 | 50

4671 建议 [建議] /jiànyì/ (2) v suggest, propose, advise
我建议你服用中药。 I suggest you take traditional Chinese medicine.
66 | 0.76 | 50

4672 缩 [縮] /suō/ (2) v shrink, contract; withdraw, draw back
蜗牛把触角缩了回去。 The snail drew in its feelers.
75 | 0.68 | 50

4673 漏 [漏] /lòu/ (2) v leak; be missing
水漏光了。 All the water has leaked out.
55 | 0.93 | 50

4674 宣告 [宣告] /xuān'gào/ (3) v declare, proclaim
该公司上月宣告破产。 The company declared bankruptcy last month.
62 | 0.82 | 50

4675 耍 [耍] /shuǎ/ (3) v play, play with
他不定在耍什么花招。 He's playing some sort of trick.
73 | 0.69 | 50

4676 吞 [吞] /tūn/ (3) v swallow, bolt, devour
不要囫囵吞下你的食物。 Don't bolt your food!
77 | 0.66 | 50

4677 夸张 [誇張] /kuāzhāng/ v exaggerate
人们不会相信老是夸张的人。 People will not believe a person who always exaggerates.
65 | 0.77 | 50

4678 判决 [判決] /pànjué/ v pass verdict, pronounce, judge
他判决该案十分公正。 He judged the case without partiality.
77 | 0.66 | 50

4679 超出 [超出] /chāochū/ v be beyond or outside, exceed
此事超出我的责任范围。 The matter is outside my area of responsibility.
64 | 0.79 | 50

4680 出差 [出差] /chūchāi/ v be on a business trip
他到香港出差去了。 He went to Hong Kong on business.
61 | 0.83 | 50

4681 忽略 [忽略] /hūlüè/ v neglect, ignore
他显然忽略了这个问题。 He pointedly ignored the question.
71 | 0.72 | 50

4682 重建 [重建] /chóngjiàn/ v reconstruct, rebuild
人们发现这个城市完全重建了。 The city is found completely rebuilt.
83 | 0.6 | 50

4683 赚钱 [賺錢] /zhuànqián/ v make money
要想赚钱就得贱买贵卖。 If you want to make money, buy cheap and sell dear.
63 | 0.81 | 50

4684 升起 [升起] /shēngqǐ/ v rise, ascend
我们看着薄雾从下面的山谷中升起。 We watched the mists ascending from the valley below.
57 | 0.88 | 50

4685 休 [休] /xiū/ v rest, take (leave); stop, cease
我上个月休了一星期的病假。 I took a week's sick leave last month.
62 | 0.82 | 50

4686 乃 [乃] /nǎi/ v be
你这样做乃轻率之举。 It's imprudent of you to have done such a thing.
79 | 0.64 | 50

4687 流血 [流血] /liúxuè/ v bleed, shed blood
他手指上的伤口在流血。 The cut on his finger was bleeding.
55 | 0.91 | 50

4688 失误 [失誤] /shīwù/ n error, mistake
这是一个重大失误。 That is a major mistake.
81 | 0.62 | 50

4689 罢了 [罷了] /bàle/ part [sentence final particle, equivalent of 而已] nothing more, merely, only
她只是装模作样罢了。 She's merely putting on an act.
87 | 0.58 | 50

4690 痛快 [痛快] /tòngkuài/ (1) adj delighted, jolly; straightforward; to one's heart's content
祝你玩得痛快。 Have a good time.
73 | 0.68 | 49

4691 扁 [扁] /biǎn/ (2) adj flat
那只箱子被压扁了。 The box was crushed flat.
71 | 0.7 | 49

4692 天然 [天然] /tiānrán/ (3) adj natural
有的人长着天然卷发。 Some people have naturally frizzy hair.
70 | 0.71 | 49

4693 绝望 [絕望] /juéwàng/ adj desperate
我感到绝望了。 I feel desperate.
80 | 0.62 | 49

4694 中等 [中等] /zhōngděng/ adj medium, medium-sized
这个公司具有中等规模。 The company is of medium size.
64 | 0.77 | 49

4695 有意 [有意] /yǒuyì/ (3) adv intentionally, deliberately
他有意地欺骗我们。 He has deliberately deceived us.
64 | 0.78 | 49

4696 偏偏 [偏偏] /piānpiān/ (3) adv wilfully, just, unluckily; contrary to what is expected
我倒是想答应的，不过那偏偏办不到。 I'd like to say yes, but that's just impossible.
83 | 0.59 | 49

4697 宁 [寧] /nìng/ adv (would) rather
我宁死不受辱。 I would rather die than disgrace myself.
78 | 0.64 | 49

4698 盒 [盒] /hé/ (2) n box
盒上印有装配模型的简要说明。 Simple directions for assembling the model are printed on the box.
65 | 0.76 | 49

4699 会场 [會場] /huìchǎng/ (2) n meeting place, conference site
会场始终充满了活跃的气氛。 The meeting room had a lively atmosphere.
62 | 0.79 | 49

4700 商 [商] /shāng/ n trade, commerce, business
国民经济，无商不活。 The national economy cannot be brisk without trade.
68 | 0.73 | 49

4701 肩膀 [肩膀] /jiānbǎng/ n shoulder
她感到了有人拍她的肩膀。 She felt someone tap her on the shoulder.
111 | 0.45 | 49

4702 家门 [家門] /jiāmén/ n gate of one's house, one's home; family
这是我第一次走出家门。 This is the first time I've been out.
68 | 0.72 | 49

4703 乐趣 [樂趣] /lèqù/ n joy, pleasure
他从学习中获得极大的乐趣。 He derived great pleasure from his study.
63 | 0.78 | 49

4704 反响 [反響] /fǎnxiǎng/ n repercussion, echo; impact, effect
到目前为止反响很不错。 We've seen a very positive effect thus far.
75 | 0.66 | 49

4705 户口 [戶口] /hùkǒu/ n household registration, registered residence
我现在的户口在北京。 Right now my household registration is in Beijing.
59 | 0.83 | 49

4706 往事 [往事] /wǎngshì/ n past events, the past
往事不堪回首。 It is too sad to recall the past.
67 | 0.73 | 49

4707 股份 [股份] /gǔfèn/ n share, stock
他们购买了该公司30％的股份。 They have purchased 30 per cent of the shares of the company.
110 | 0.45 | 49

4708 公主 [公主] /gōngzhǔ/ n princess
她打扮得像个公主一样去参加宴会。 She dressed up like a princess for the party.
68 | 0.72 | 49

4709 厂家 [廠家] /chǎngjiā/ n manufacturer
保证书还有效，所以厂家会给修理的。 It's still under guarantee, so the manufacturer will repair it.
77 | 0.64 | 49

4710 名气 [名氣] /míngqì/ n fame, reputation
杭州的名气主要在于风景如画的西湖。 Hangzhou's fame lies mainly in its picturesque West Lake.
58 | 0.84 | 49

4711 袋 [袋] /dài/ (2) clas [measure word for things contained in a bag, packet, sachet, etc.]
这是一袋普通的盐。 It is a pocket of common salt.
97 | 0.51 | 49

4712 拳 [拳] /quán/ clas [measure word for actions of hitting with one's fist]
他狠狠地还击了一拳。 He returned the blow smartly.
74 | 0.68 | 49

4713 周 [周] /zhōu/ (1) time week
本周咖啡大减价。 Coffee is on special this week.
54 | 0.91 | 49

4714 深夜 [深夜] /shēnyè/ (3) time late at night, far into the night
他一直工作到深夜。 He carried on working far into the night.
65 | 0.76 | 49

4715 往后 [往後] /wǎnghòu/ time from now on, afterwards
往后的天气越来越冷了。 It's going to get colder and colder from now on.
84 | 0.59 | 49

4716 吊 [吊] /diào/ (2) v hang, suspend (in the air); lift (with a rope); condole with; revoke
灯吊在天花板上。 The lamp was suspended from the ceiling.
66 | 0.74 | 49

4717 晃 [晃] /huǎng, huàng/ (3) v dazzle; flash past; shake, jerk, sway
拍照时照相机不要晃。 Try not to jerk the camera when taking a photograph.
91 | 0.54 | 49

4718 对立 [對立] /duìlì/ (3) v be opposed
工作不一定与玩耍对立。 Work is not always opposed to play.
65 | 0.77 | 49

4719 栽 [栽] /zāi/ (3) v plant; frame; fall
后院里栽了很多花。 Many flowers are planted in the backyard.
65 | 0.76 | 49

4720 损 [損] /sǔn/ v damage, harm; lose; deride, be sarcastic
他们总是以损人开始，以害己告终。 They invariably start by doing others harm but end by ruining themselves.
66 | 0.76 | 49

4721 融合 [融合] /rónghé/ v merge, mix together
我们把资源融合在一块。 We merged our resources.
65 | 0.76 | 49

4722 搞好 [搞好] /gǎohǎo/ v do well, do a good job
他要尽一切努力搞好学习。 He should make a good effort to study well.
135 | 0.36 | 49

4723 上车 [上車] /shàngchē/ v board, go aboard
请大家上车了。 All aboard, please.
68 | 0.72 | 49

4724 赏 [賞] /shǎng/ v award, bestow (a reward); feast one's eyes on; appreciate
应该赏什么人呢？ Who ought to be rewarded?
62 | 0.8 | 49

4725 倾 [傾] /qīng/ v lean, bend; pour out
我倾身向前，以便能听清楚些。 I leant forward to listen better.
70 | 0.71 | 49

4726 外出 [外出] /wàichū/ v go out, be away
我近来几乎从不外出。 I hardly ever go out these days.
67 | 0.74 | 49

4727 约束 [約束] /yuēshù/ v bind, restrain
公司受公司章程的约束。 The company is bound by its articles of association.
74 | 0.67 | 49

4728 命名 [命名] /mìngmíng/ v name
这个海峡是以它的发现者命名的。 The strait was named after its discoverer.
70 | 0.71 | 49

4729 得罪 [得罪] /dézuì/ v offend
我没有意识到得罪了他。 I was not conscious of having offended him.
64 | 0.77 | 49

4730 透过 [透過] /tòuguò/ prep through
我透过窗户看见他们了。 I saw them through the window.
60 | 0.83 | 49

4731 活跃 [活躍] /huóyuè/ (2) adj active, lively
讨论会开得很活跃。 The discussion was very lively.
65 | 0.75 | 48

4732 被动 [被動] /bèidòng/ (3) adj passive
它使经理处于被动地位。 It left the manager in a passive position.
65 | 0.75 | 48

4733 安定 [安定] /āndìng/ (3) adj stable
人民生活安定。 People lead a stable life.
65 | 0.74 | 48

4734 野 [野] /yě/ adj wild; rough, rude; unruly
他射中一只野鸭。 He shot a wild duck.
68 | 0.72 | 48

4735 主导 [主導] /zhǔdǎo/ adj leading, predominant
今年，这种主导作用依然非常突出。 This year, the leading role is still very prominent.
88 | 0.55 | 48

4736 困惑 [困惑] /kùnhuò/ adj perplexed, puzzled
她看起来很困惑。 She looked perplexed.
61 | 0.79 | 48

4737 满足 [滿足] /mǎnzú/ adj satisfied
一个人不应该只因一点小成就而感到满足。 One shouldn't be satisfied with only a little success.
61 | 0.8 | 48

4738 稍微 [稍微] /shāowēi/ (2) adv slightly, a little
他今天早晨稍微好了一些。 He was a little better this morning.
90 | 0.54 | 48

4739 难怪 [難怪] /nán'guài/ (3) adv no wonder
难怪你来晚了！ No wonder you were late!
68 | 0.71 | 48

4740 当即 [當即] /dāngjí/ adv at once, immediately
这个建议当即遭到了拒绝。 The proposal was rejected immediately.
59 | 0.83 | 48

4741 更是 [更是] /gèngshì/ adv even more, especially
在当前的形势下更是如此。 This is especially true in the current circumstances.
59 | 0.83 | 48

4742 外边 [外邊] /wàibian/ (1) loc outside
他们在外边玩。 They are playing outside.
105 | 0.46 | 48 | S

4743 气象 [氣象] /qìxiàng/ (2) n meteorology, weather; scene
有电话号码去询问气象资料吗？ Is there a number to call for weather information?
102 | 0.48 | 48

4744 集 [集] /jí/ (2) n collection, album; market, country fair; set, group
这是一部文学作品的选文集。 This is a collection of excerpts from literary works.
75 | 0.64 | 48

4745 棉花 [棉花] /miánhuā/ (2) n cotton
棉花摸上去很软。 Cotton feels soft.
96 | 0.51 | 48

4746 胳膊 [胳膊] /gēbo/ (2) n arm
他抓住了我的胳膊。 He seized me by the arm.
98 | 0.5 | 48

4747 组长 [組長] /zǔzhǎng/ (3) n group leader
我们赞成他当我们的组长。 We got behind him to be our group leader.
67 | 0.72 | 48

4748 边缘 [邊緣] /biānyuán/ (3) n edge, margin, brink
地震活动往往集中在板块的边缘。 Earthquakes tend to be concentrated along the margins of plates.
55 | 0.88 | 48

4749 季 [季] /jì/ (3) n season; quarter
按季收取电费。 Electricity is charged quarterly.
66 | 0.73 | 48

4750 香烟 [香煙] /xiāngyān/ (3) n cigarette; smoke from burning incense
请将香烟熄灭。 Please extinguish your cigarette.
61 | 0.8 | 48

4751 蝴蝶 [蝴蝶] /húdié/ (3) n butterfly
几只蝴蝶正在他身边飞舞。 Some butterflies fluttered around him.
62 | 0.78 | 48

4752 债 [債] /zhài/ (3) n debt
那么说，她还欠着债？So she had debts, then?
67 | 0.72 | 48

4753 神情 [神情] /shénqíng/ (3) n look, facial expression
他一脸吃惊的神情。He had a startled look on his face.
109 | 0.45 | 48

4754 仓库 [倉庫] /cāngkù/ (3) n warehouse
这些箱子堆放在仓库里。The boxes are stacked in the warehouse.
63 | 0.76 | 48

4755 参谋 [參謀] /cānmóu/ (3) v give advice
这事可以让他给你参谋一下。You might ask him for advice on this matter.
88 | 0.55 | 48

4756 车队 [車隊] /chēduì/ n motorcade, a queue of wagons or carts; fleet, vehicle service brigade
这家饭店拥有一个运送客人去机场的豪华车队。The hotel has a fleet of limousines to take guests to the airport.
61 | 0.8 | 48

4757 豆 [豆] /dòu/ n bean
种豆得豆。He who sows beans will reap beans.
57 | 0.85 | 48

4758 纹 [紋] /wén/ n stria, line
掌纹不变。The lines on a palm do not change.
66 | 0.74 | 48

4759 青年人 [青年人] /qīngniánrén/ n young people
青年人总是生气勃勃。The young are usually very active.
61 | 0.8 | 48

4760 婆婆 [婆婆] /pópo/ n husband's mother, mother-in-law; old woman
她对她的婆婆非常不好。She behaved badly towards her mother-in-law.
77 | 0.62 | 48

4761 年头 [年頭] /niántóu/ n year; days, times; long time
这年头人们不得不多加小心。One can't be too careful these days.
58 | 0.84 | 48

4762 修养 [修養] /xiūyǎng/ n culture, cultivation, self-possession
她是个文化修养很高的女子。She is a woman of considerable culture.
61 | 0.8 | 48

4763 活儿 [活兒] /huór/ n work, job
这活儿看来今天可以做完。It looks as if we'll be able to finish this job today.
89 | 0.55 | 48 | S

4764 后者 [後者] /hòuzhě/ pron the latter
如果你把木材同塑胶相比，后者较轻。If you compare wood with plastics, the latter is lighter.
84 | 0.58 | 48

4765 乡下 [鄉下] /xiāngxia/ (2) place country, countryside
我实际上是个乡下姑娘。I'm a country girl at heart.
65 | 0.74 | 48

4766 夏季 [夏季] /xiàjì/ (3) time summer
棉制品适于夏季穿用。Cotton is suitable for wear in summer.
100 | 0.48 | 48

4767 后期 [後期] /hòuqī/ time late stage, late period
20世纪70年代后期，他从企鹅出版社起步。His career began in the late 1970s at Penguin Books.
67 | 0.72 | 48

4768 洗澡 [洗澡] /xǐzǎo/ (1) v bathe, take a bath or shower
她每天早晨洗澡。She bathes in the morning.
64 | 0.76 | 48

4769 适用 [適用] /shìyòng/ (2) v apply
这个规则不适用。This rule does not apply.
87 | 0.56 | 48

4770 迈 [邁] /mài/ (2) v stride, take a step
他向门口迈了一步。He took a step towards the door.
52 | 0.94 | 48

4771 请求 [請求] /qǐngqiú/ (2) v request, ask
他请求经理准许他请假一天。He asked the manager's permission to take a day off.
64 | 0.76 | 48

4772 启发 [啟發] /qǐfā/ (2) v enlighten, inspire, illuminate
那句话突然启发了她。That sentence suddenly enlightened her.
64 | 0.76 | 48

4773 拥抱 [擁抱] /yōngbào/ (2) v embrace, hug
我拥抱了每个孩子。I hugged each child.
66 | 0.74 | 48

4774 打交道 [打交道] /dǎjiāodào/ (3) v deal with; hang out with; work with
我同海外客户打交道。I deal with overseas clients.
60 | 0.82 | 48

4775 参考 [參考] /cānkǎo/ (3) v consult, make reference to
详细资料请参考附后文献。Accompanying texts should be consulted for further details.
71 | 0.68 | 48

4776 发育 [發育] /fāyù/ (3) v grow, develop (physically or mentally)
他再不会正常发育。He will never grow normally.
68 | 0.72 | 48

4777 困扰 [困擾] /kùnrǎo/ v perplex, puzzle, bother
居民为飞机的噪声所困扰。The inhabitants are bothered by the noise of the planes.
62 | 0.78 | 48

4778 向往 [嚮往] /xiàngwǎng/ v yearn for, look forward to, dream of
人们向往更美好的未来。People dream of a better future.
56 | 0.86 | 48

4779 睡眠 [睡眠] /shuìmián/ *n* sleep
睡眠对健康是必要的。Sleep is necessary to health.
67 | 0.72 | 48

4780 低头 [低頭] /dītóu/ *v* hang (one's) head; give in, submit, bend, bow
他不愿向命运低头。He didn't want to bend to fate.
108 | 0.45 | 48

4781 出售 [出售] /chūshòu/ *v* sell
这个购物中心出售许多种商品。The shopping centre sells a variety of goods.
87 | 0.56 | 48

4782 毁灭 [毀滅] /huǐmiè/ *v* destroy, perish
火灾毁灭了我们的家园。Fire destroyed our home.
60 | 0.82 | 48

4783 审判 [審判] /shěnpàn/ *v* try, bring to trial
他因盗窃受到审判。He was tried for theft.
87 | 0.55 | 48

4784 共有 [共有] /gòngyǒu/ *v* total; share, have in common
汽车旅馆共有 16 个单元客房。The motel has a total of 16 units.
93 | 0.52 | 48

4785 视察 [視察] /shìchá/ *v* inspect
他们视察了该校的工作。They inspected the work of the school.
73 | 0.67 | 48

4786 处罚 [處罰] /chǔfá/ *v* punish, penalise
那教师布置额外的家庭作业来处罚学生。The teacher punished the class by giving them extra homework.
86 | 0.57 | 48

4787 窄 [窄] /zhǎi/ (2) *adj* narrow
这条河很窄。The river is narrow.
55 | 0.86 | 47

4788 寒冷 [寒冷] /hánlěng/ (2) *adj* cold
花在寒冷的天气里凋谢了。The flowers withered in the cold.
56 | 0.85 | 47

4789 喜悦 [喜悅] /xǐyuè/ (3) *n* happiness, joy
她眼睛里闪烁着喜悦。Her eyes shone with joy.
65 | 0.74 | 47

4790 透明 [透明] /tòumíng/ (3) *adj* transparent
玻璃是一种透明物。Glass is a transparent material.
60 | 0.8 | 47

4791 巨 [巨] /jù/ *adj* huge, enormous
一个巨浪淹没了那条船。The boat was swamped with a huge wave.
61 | 0.77 | 47

4792 孤 [孤] /gū/ *adj* lonely, solitary
孤岛上共有 15 个人。There were 15 people in all on the lonely island.
75 | 0.63 | 47

4793 孝 [孝] /xiào/ *adj* filial
孩子们都很孝。My children are very filial.
69 | 0.69 | 47

4794 悄悄 [悄悄] /qiāoqiāo/ (2) *adv* quietly
他悄悄地进来免得把小孩吵醒了。He came in quietly so that he would not wake the child.
83 | 0.57 | 47

4795 甭 [甭] /béng/ (3) *adv* don't, needn't
甭再说了。Don't say any more.
127 | 0.37 | 47 | S

4796 全力 [全力] /quánlì/ *adv* with all one's strength, all out, sparing no effort
我们全力支持你。We support you with all our strength.
74 | 0.64 | 47

4797 随之 [隨之] /suízhī/ *adv* along with it, following it; accordingly
报纸和电视台的采访随之而至。Newspaper and TV interviews followed.
59 | 0.8 | 47

4798 周边 [周邊] /zhōubiān/ *loc* periphery, vicinity, neighbouring, surrounding
工业区带动了周边地区的发展。The industrial district has promoted the development of surrounding areas.
75 | 0.63 | 47

4799 行李 [行李] /xínglǐ/ (2) *n* baggage, luggage
我能带多少行李？How much luggage can I take with me?
73 | 0.65 | 47

4800 嗓子 [嗓子] /sǎngzi/ (2) *n* throat
他清了清嗓子。He cleared his throat.
77 | 0.62 | 47

4801 班长 [班長] /bānzhǎng/ (2) *n* class monitor, captain; squad leader
他是我们的班长。He is our monitor.
73 | 0.65 | 47

4802 缺点 [缺點] /quēdiǎn/ (2) *n* shortcoming, weakness, defect
但她有一个重大的缺点。But she had one important weakness.
77 | 0.62 | 47

4803 狮子 [獅子] /shīzi/ (2) *n* lion
狮子被称为百兽之王。The lion is called the king of beasts.
61 | 0.78 | 47

4804 骨头 [骨頭] /gútou/ (2) *n* bone; moral character; bitterness
我把一根骨头扔给了狗。I threw a bone to the dog.
71 | 0.67 | 47

4805 收获 [收穫] /shōuhuò/ (2) *n* result, reward, gains; harvest
据说他此行得到了很大的收获。It was believed that he gained much benefit from his visit.
59 | 0.81 | 47

4806 彩色 [彩色] /cǎisè/ (2) *n* colour
打印机将会输出彩色图表。The printer will output colour charts.
58 | 0.83 | 47

4807 技能 [技能] /jìnéng/ (3) *n* skill
守门是一项特殊的技能。 Goalkeeping is a special skill.
78 | 0.61 | 47

4808 战线 [戰線] /zhànxiàn/ (3) *n* battle line; front
统一战线必须坚持下去。 The united front must be persevered in.
75 | 0.63 | 47

4809 中年 [中年] /zhōngnián/ (3) *n* middle age
我正接近中年。 I am getting onto middle age.
57 | 0.83 | 47

4810 终身 [終身] /zhōngshēn/ (3) *n* all one's life, lifelong
他终身残废。 He has been an invalid all his life.
56 | 0.85 | 47

4811 脚步 [腳步] /jiǎobù/ (3) *n* footstep
他们突然停住脚步。 They checked their steps.
85 | 0.56 | 47

4812 帽 [帽] /mào/ *n* hat, cap
注意一个戴黑帽的高个男人。 Watch out for a tall man in a black hat.
59 | 0.81 | 47

4813 君子 [君子] /jūnzi/ *n* gentleman, man of honour
君子动口不动手。 A gentleman uses his tongue, not his hands.
71 | 0.67 | 47

4814 令 [令] /lìng/ *n* order, command, decree
许多国家都实施了禁烟令。 There is a ban on smoking in many countries.
74 | 0.64 | 47

4815 餐馆 [餐館] /cān'guǎn/ *n* restaurant
这是我所知道的最好的一家餐馆。 This is the best restaurant I know.
62 | 0.77 | 47

4816 上司 [上司] /shàngsī/ *n* superior
她只对她的上司礼貌。 She is only polite to her superiors.
85 | 0.56 | 47

4817 望远镜 [望遠鏡] /wàngyuǎnjìng/ *n* telescope, binoculars
我有一副望远镜。 I've got a pair of binoculars.
91 | 0.52 | 47

4818 话语 [話語] /huàyǔ/ *n* what is said, words
那些话语意味深长。 Those words are of great significance.
71 | 0.67 | 47

4819 模特 [模特] /mótè/ *n* [often taking the suffix 儿] model
她是全国的顶尖模特儿。 She is one of the country's top models.
66 | 0.72 | 47

4820 天堂 [天堂] /tiāntáng/ *n* heaven, paradise
人间若有天堂，非此莫属！ If there is a heaven on earth, this is it!
62 | 0.77 | 47

4821 图案 [圖案] /tú'àn/ *n* design, pattern
两者在图案和颜色方面都有差别。 They're different in design and colour.
64 | 0.74 | 47

4822 帐篷 [帳篷] /zhàngpéng/ *n* tent
她走向一个大帐篷。 She walked to a big tent.
56 | 0.85 | 47

4823 籍 [籍] /jí/ *n* record; native place; membership; nationality
他是一位美籍华裔科学家。 He is a Chinese American scientist.
62 | 0.77 | 47

4824 窗外 [窗外] /chuāngwài/ *place* out of the window
她在朝着窗外做白日梦。 She looked out the window, daydreaming.
109 | 0.44 | 47

4825 下次 [下次] /xiàcì/ *time* next time
下次给您补偿。 I'll make it up to you next time.
61 | 0.78 | 47

4826 夺取 [奪取] /duóqǔ/ (3) *v* seize, capture; strive for, win
他们靠武装夺取了政权。 They seized power with the aid of the armed forces.
70 | 0.68 | 47

4827 思索 [思索] /sīsuǒ/ (3) *v* think deeply, ponder
我整天都在思索可还是找不到头绪。 I've been thinking all day and getting nowhere.
60 | 0.79 | 47

4828 缩小 [縮小] /suōxiǎo/ (3) *v* reduce; shrink
这台机器能把复印件缩小到原件的一半。 This machine can reduce copies of the original page to half size.
78 | 0.62 | 47

4829 较量 [較量] /jiàoliàng/ *v* compete, measure up against
他急于要和对手较量一番。 He was eager to measure swords with his competitors.
68 | 0.69 | 47

4830 覆盖 [覆蓋] /fùgài/ *v* cover
地上覆盖着一层皑皑积雪。 The ground was covered in a pristine layer of snow.
74 | 0.65 | 47

4831 看望 [看望] /kànwàng/ *v* call on, visit, see
在我生病时他来看望过我。 He came to see me during my illness.
78 | 0.62 | 47

4832 赋予 [賦予] /fùyǔ/ *v* give, bestow, entrust
谁赋予了他们这个权力？ Who gave them the power to do that?
76 | 0.63 | 47

4833 约定 [約定] /yuēdìng/ *v* agree on, arrange, fix
我们约定3点整吧。 Let's make it three o'clock sharp.
60 | 0.79 | 47

4834 营造 [營造] /yíngzào/ *v* build, construct
该监狱建150年前营造的。 The prison was built 150 years ago.
84 | 0.56 | 47

4835 休闲 [休閒] /xiūxián/ v enjoy leisure, relax
每周应该拨出一天时间休闲。 One day of the week should be set apart for relaxation.
79 | 0.6 | 47

4836 品 [品] /pǐn/ v taste, sample
是她第一个向我介绍了品酒的乐趣。 It was she who first introduced me to the pleasures of wine-tasting.
65 | 0.74 | 47

4837 歧视 [歧視] /qíshì/ v discriminate against
法律对穷人不予歧视。 The law does not discriminate against the poor.
63 | 0.75 | 47

4838 整齐 [整齊] /zhěngqí/ (1) adj neat, tidy
他衣着整齐。 He is neatly attired.
57 | 0.81 | 46

4839 初步 [初步] /chūbù/ (2) adj preliminary, initial, tentative
我们只是简单地提出以上初步的意见。 We only seek to offer some simple preliminary opinions.
128 | 0.36 | 46

4840 清洁 [清潔] /qīngjié/ (3) adj clean
一切都那么清洁和整齐。 Everything's so clean and tidy.
61 | 0.76 | 46

4841 缓慢 [緩慢] /huǎnmàn/ (3) adj slow
我们进展缓慢。 We are making slow progress.
61 | 0.76 | 46

4842 有钱 [有錢] /yǒuqián/ adj rich, wealthy
这是一个非常有钱的家庭。 This is a wealthy family.
70 | 0.67 | 46

4843 形象 [形象] /xíngxiàng/ adj vivid
每个山峰都有一个生动形象的名字。 Each peak has been given a vivid name.
60 | 0.78 | 46

4844 就是 [就是] /jiùshì/ (3) conj [as in 就是... 也] even if
就是下雨我们也要去。 We shall go even if it rains.
77 | 0.6 | 46

4845 一共 [一共] /yígòng/ (1) adv altogether, in all
我们一共十四个人。 We are 14 in all.
91 | 0.51 | 46 | S

4846 立 [立] /lì/ adv immediately, instantly
这所学校保证立见成效。 The school promised rapid results.
56 | 0.84 | 46

4847 早日 [早日] /zǎorì/ adv at an earlier date, soon
望早日回信。 I'm looking forward to hearing from you soon.
106 | 0.44 | 46

4848 哎哟 [哎喲] /āiyō/ (3) interj [particle expressing astonishment or pain] hey, oh, ouch
哎哟，你踩了我的脚了。 Ouch, you stepped on my foot.
127 | 0.37 | 46 | S

4849 表现 [表現] /biǎoxiàn/ (1) n behaviour
他的表现着实令我震惊。 His behaviour really threw me.
61 | 0.76 | 46

4850 晚饭 [晚飯] /wǎnfàn/ (1) n supper, dinner
今晚我带你出去吃晚饭。 I'd like to take you out to dinner this evening.
80 | 0.59 | 46

4851 餐厅 [餐廳] /cāntīng/ (2) n dining hall, dining room
餐厅什么时间开放呢？ When does the dining room open?
74 | 0.62 | 46

4852 气温 [氣溫] /qìwēn/ (2) n temperature
近来的气温一直比平均温度高。 The temperature has been above the average recently.
72 | 0.65 | 46

4853 小朋友 [小朋友] /xiǎopéngyou/ (2) n children
有些小朋友上课经常睡觉。 Some children often sleep in class.
57 | 0.82 | 46

4854 客厅 [客廳] /kètīng/ (3) n sitting room, reception room
她把我引进客厅。 She showed me into the sitting room.
106 | 0.44 | 46

4855 饮料 [飲料] /yǐnliào/ (3) n drink
你喜欢喝什么饮料？ What's your favourite drink?
58 | 0.8 | 46

4856 犯人 [犯人] /fànrén/ (3) n convict, prisoner
四名犯人被释放了。 Four prisoners were released.
56 | 0.82 | 46

4857 运气 [運氣] /yùnqi/ (3) n luck
我是靠运气赢的。 I only won by luck.
60 | 0.78 | 46

4858 葡萄 [葡萄] /pútao/ (3) n grape
我给了他一串葡萄。 I gave him a bunch of grapes.
59 | 0.8 | 46

4859 旗帜 [旗幟] /qízhì/ (3) n banner, flag; [figuratively] one's stand or position
那面旗帜在微风中随风飘扬。 The flag was flapping about in the light wind.
81 | 0.58 | 46

4860 国防 [國防] /guófáng/ (3) n national defence
国防方面的开支很大。 A lot of money is spent on defence.
124 | 0.37 | 46

4861 河流 [河流] /héliú/ (3) n river
长江是世界上最长的河流之一。 The Yangtze River is one of the longest rivers in the world.
56 | 0.82 | 46

4862 导弹 [導彈] /dǎodàn/ (3) n missile
他们的导弹发射井在地下。 Their missile silos are below ground.
89 | 0.52 | 46

4863 动机 [動機] /dòngjī/ (3) *n* motive, motivation
他犯罪的真正动机仍不清楚。His real motive for the crime remains obscure.
65 | 0.71 | 46

4864 废话 [廢話] /fèihuà/ (3) *n* nonsense
她说了一大堆的废话。She talked a lot of nonsense.
79 | 0.59 | 46

4865 琴 [琴] /qín/ (3) *n* [general term for some stringed musical instruments such as piano, violin] instrument, qin
这张琴弹起来果然非常好听。This musical instrument, when played, turned out to be extremely pleasant to the ear.
81 | 0.57 | 46

4866 身影 [身影] /shēnyǐng/ *n* figure, silhouette
突然，他看到一个熟悉的身影。Suddenly, a familiar figure came into his sight.
73 | 0.63 | 46

4867 责任感 [責任感] /zérèngǎn/ *n* sense of duty
他有强烈的责任感。He has a strong sense of duty.
68 | 0.69 | 46

4868 棉 [棉] /mián/ *n* cotton
全棉内衣，给您百般体贴。All-cotton underwear brings you every comfort.
60 | 0.78 | 46

4869 名片 [名片] /míngpiàn/ *n* (business) card
这是我的名片。Here's my card.
64 | 0.72 | 46

4870 期限 [期限] /qīxiàn/ *n* deadline, time limit, term
贷款期限为 15 年。The term of the loan is 15 years.
75 | 0.62 | 46

4871 公寓 [公寓] /gōngyù/ *n* flat, apartment
我觉得住在公寓很方便。I think it's very convenient living in a flat.
70 | 0.66 | 46

4872 短期 [短期] /duǎnqī/ *n* short term
他只是短期外出，至多一周。He's only away for short periods, a week at the longest.
76 | 0.61 | 46

4873 唇 [唇] /chún/ *n* lip
他的唇边徐徐地绽出了愉快的笑意。A pleasant smile broke quietly over his lips.
126 | 0.37 | 46

4874 银子 [銀子] /yínzi/ *n* silver; money
见有了这个银子，想来也就无话了。So the silver will shut their mouths.
84 | 0.55 | 46

4875 男朋友 [男朋友] /nánpéngyou/ *n* boyfriend
听说你男朋友也来了。I hear your boyfriend is also here.
82 | 0.56 | 46

4876 王国 [王國] /wángguó/ *n* kingdom
国王是一个王国中最重要的人物。The king is the most important person in a kingdom.
61 | 0.76 | 46

4877 伦理 [倫理] /lúnlǐ/ *n* ethics, moral principles
法律必须支持伦理。The law must support ethics.
75 | 0.62 | 46

4878 貌 [貌] /mào/ *n* appearance, look
不要以貌取人。Don't judge by appearances.
55 | 0.85 | 46

4879 多久 [多久] /duōjiǔ/ *pron* how long, how often
你们多久见一次面？How often do you meet?
76 | 0.61 | 46

4880 体内 [體內] /tǐnèi/ *place* inside the body
细菌可以通过嘴进入体内。Germs may get into the body by way of the mouth.
63 | 0.74 | 46

4881 前夕 [前夕] /qiánxì/ *time* (on) the eve of
他在考试前夕很紧张。He was nervous on the eve of the examination.
82 | 0.57 | 46

4882 生前 [生前] /shēngqián/ *time* during one's lifetime, before one's death
那是他生前写的最后一部小说。That was the last novel he wrote before he died.
57 | 0.82 | 46

4883 表扬 [表揚] /biǎoyáng/ (1) *v* praise
她应该得到表扬。She ought to be praised.
65 | 0.72 | 46

4884 渡 [渡] /dù/ (2) *v* cross; pull through
你们渡江花了多少时间？How long did it take you to cross the river?
58 | 0.8 | 46

4885 破产 [破產] /pòchǎn/ (3) *v* go bankrupt; fail, fall through
阴谋破产了。The plot has fallen through.
95 | 0.49 | 46

4886 强迫 [強迫] /qiǎngpò/ (3) *v* compel, force
你不应强迫他这样做。You mustn't force him to do it.
61 | 0.77 | 46

4887 烦 [煩] /fán/ (3) *v* be vexed or irritated; bother, pester; be tired of
不要烦我。Don't bother me.
81 | 0.57 | 46

4888 养成 [養成] /yǎngchéng/ (3) *v* cultivate, acquire, develop
自那以后，他养成了另一个坏习惯。Since then, he has developed another bad habit.
69 | 0.68 | 46

4889 趴 [趴] /pā/ (3) *v* to lie on one's stomach; bend over
我一定是趴在桌上睡着了。I must have nodded off over my desk.
89 | 0.52 | 46

4890 回想 [回想] /huíxiǎng/ (3) *v* think back, recall, recollect
回想一下你自己的经历。Think back on your own experience.
62 | 0.75 | 46

4891 生病 [生病] /shēngbìng/ (3) v be ill
她的小孩生病时，她很紧张。 She was nervous when her baby was ill.
60 | 0.77 | 46

4892 敢于 [敢於] /gǎnyú/ (3) v dare, venture, be bold to
我们要敢于同不良现象作斗争。 We should dare to combat unhealthy phenomena.
71 | 0.66 | 46

4893 旋转 [旋轉] /xuánzhuǎn/ (3) v rotate, revolve, spin
月亮围绕着地球旋转。 The moon revolves around the earth.
55 | 0.85 | 46

4894 挑选 [挑選] /tiāoxuǎn/ (3) v choose, select
你说我挑选哪一个好？ Which one will you advise me to choose?
58 | 0.8 | 46

4895 赞同 [贊同] /zàntóng/ v approve of, endorse, be in favour of
我赞同这个建议。 I'm in favour of the suggestion.
61 | 0.77 | 46

4896 听取 [聽取] /tīngqǔ/ v listen to, hear; follow (advice)
他们要求听取他们的意见。 They demanded that their voice be heard.
130 | 0.36 | 46

4897 猜测 [猜測] /cāicè/ v guess
我们只能猜测发生了什么事。 We can only guess what happened.
62 | 0.75 | 46

4898 爆 [爆] /bào/ v explore; burst
车胎爆了。 The tyre's burst.
57 | 0.81 | 46

4899 赌博 [賭博] /dǔbó/ v gamble
他赌博成瘾。 He was addicted to gambling.
107 | 0.43 | 46

4900 起草 [起草] /qǐcǎo/ v draft, draw up
那么我们起草合同，然后签字。 Now let's draft the contract and then sign it.
72 | 0.65 | 46

4901 悟 [悟] /wù/ v come to realise; awaken, enlighten
她已悟出人生的真谛。 She awoke to the realities of life.
63 | 0.74 | 46

4902 缠 [纏] /chán/ v wind; tangle; pester; deal with
她把毛线缠成了一个球。 She wound the yarn into a ball.
83 | 0.56 | 46

4903 淡 [淡] /dàn/ (2) adj bland, tasteless, mild; (of colour) pale; (of business) slack; indifferent
烟味很淡。 The tobacco is very mild.
67 | 0.68 | 45

4904 舒适 [舒適] /shūshì/ (2) adj comfortable, cosy
穿着舒适吗？ Do they feel comfortable?
53 | 0.86 | 45

4905 反 [反] /fǎn/ (3) adj reverse, wrong in direction; [used as a prefix] anti-, counter-
他把袜子穿反了。 He put his socks on inside out.
56 | 0.82 | 45

4906 圆满 [圓滿] /yuánmǎn/ (3) adj satisfactory, successful, happy
会议获得圆满成功。 The meeting was a complete success.
92 | 0.5 | 45

4907 严峻 [嚴峻] /yánjùn/ adj severe, serious, stern, grim
总而言之，形势很严峻。 In a word, the situation is serious.
90 | 0.51 | 45

4908 烦恼 [煩惱] /fánnǎo/ adj vexed, worried, upset
别为那件事太烦恼了。 Now don't get all upset about it.
68 | 0.67 | 45

4909 现行 [現行] /xiànxíng/ adj current, in effect, in operation
我们现行的有些做法非改不行。 Some current practices simply must be changed.
74 | 0.62 | 45

4910 就算 [就算] /jiùsuàn/ v count as, regard as
我们就算它五块钱好吗？ Shall we call it five dollars?
81 | 0.56 | 45

4911 每 [每] /měi/ (2) adv every time, on each occasion
不要每碰到一个不认识的单词或短语就停下来。 Don't stop every time you come to a word or phrase you don't know.
52 | 0.88 | 45

4912 老 [老] /lǎo/ (1) pref [used as an affix preceding or following the surname of a person or a numeral to indicate affection or familiarity, or to indicate the order of birth of the children in a family]
我是来看老李的。 I came to see Lao Li.
81 | 0.56 | 45

4913 灾 [災] /zāi/ (2) n disaster, calamity
幸未成灾。 Fortunately it didn't cause a disaster.
52 | 0.88 | 45

4914 雾 [霧] /wù/ (2) n fog, mist
小山隐没在浓雾之中。 The hills were wrapped in mist.
73 | 0.63 | 45

4915 醋 [醋] /cù/ (2) n vinegar; jealousy
我们要酱油和醋吗？ Do we need some soy sauce and vinegar?
77 | 0.6 | 45

4916 教材 [教材] /jiàocái/ (2) n teaching materials
关键是教材。 The important thing is the teaching materials we use.
67 | 0.68 | 45

4917 处分 [處分] /chǔfèn/ (2) n disciplinary action, punishment
他没受处分就过去了。 He was let off without punishment.
58 | 0.78 | 45

4918 不是 [不是] /bùshi/ (3) *n* fault, blame
我并非在说他们的不是。 I'm not blaming them.
60 | 0.76 | 45

4919 柜台 [櫃檯] /guìtái/ (3) *n* counter
您可以到那边的柜台换钱。 You can change your money at the counter over there.
55 | 0.82 | 45

4920 性别 [性別] /xìngbié/ (3) *n* gender, sex
不论年龄性别，人们都有相同的权利。 Irrespective of age and sex, people have the same rights.
59 | 0.76 | 45

4921 血管 [血管] /xuèguǎn/ (3) *n* vein
血液在我的血管里流动。 Blood flows in my veins.
56 | 0.82 | 45

4922 胆 [膽] /dǎn/ (3) *n* gall, gall bladder; guts, nerve, courage
他浑身是胆。 He abounds in courage.
64 | 0.72 | 45

4923 核 [核] /hé/ (3) *n* pit, stone; nucleus
数一下你盘子边的樱桃核。 Count the cherry stones on the side of your plate.
90 | 0.51 | 45

4924 陆军 [陸軍] /lùjūn/ (3) *n* army, land force
陆军的结构将发生变化。 Army structure will change.
79 | 0.57 | 45

4925 玩笑 [玩笑] /wánxiào/ (3) *n* joke
跟你开个玩笑你都受不了吗？ Can't you take a joke?
78 | 0.58 | 45

4926 大桥 [大橋] /dàqiáo/ *n* (grand) bridge
而她常常在大桥上陪伴着我。 Often she would join me on the bridge.
67 | 0.67 | 45

4927 限度 [限度] /xiàndù/ *n* limit, limitation
然而让步是有限度的。 Moreover, the concessions have limits.
68 | 0.68 | 45

4928 部位 [部位] /bùwèi/ *n* position, place, area
鲸鱼哪个部位是注射的最佳部位？ Which is the best place to inject the whale?
58 | 0.79 | 45

4929 息 [息] /xī/ *n* (bank) interest; breath; news
减租减息。 Reduce rent and interest.
55 | 0.82 | 45

4930 介绍 [介紹] /jièshào/ *n* introduction
有必要做一基本的介绍。 A brief introduction to these issues will prove useful.
61 | 0.74 | 45

4931 坏事 [壞事] /huàishì/ *n* bad thing, evil deed
这件坏事变成好事的可能性是有的。 It is possible for us to turn this bad thing to good account.
58 | 0.78 | 45

4932 场景 [場景] /chǎngjǐng/ *n* scene
剧中的第一个场景是王宫。 The first scene of the play is set in the king's palace.
55 | 0.83 | 45

4933 文凭 [文憑] /wénpíng/ *n* diploma, certificate, academic credentials
我没有大学文凭。 I don't have a university diploma.
65 | 0.71 | 45

4934 童年 [童年] /tóngnián/ *n* childhood
他童年时代没受到丝毫的疼爱。 Love was totally absent from his childhood.
66 | 0.7 | 45

4935 火山 [火山] /huǒshān/ *n* volcano
火山喷出了烟尘。 The volcano belched out smoke and ashes.
125 | 0.36 | 45

4936 古城 [古城] /gǔchéng/ *n* ancient city
这座古城有什么好玩的地方？ What interesting place is there in this ancient city?
64 | 0.71 | 45

4937 父子 [父子] /fùzǐ/ *n* father and son
父子俩对这部电影都不感兴趣。 Neither the father nor the son is interested in the film.
56 | 0.81 | 45

4938 丈 [丈] /zhàng/ (2) *clas* [measure term for length in Chinese local unit] zhang (equivalent of ten chi, or about 3.33 metres)
它的干呢，通常是丈把高。 Their trunks are usually over ten feet tall.
61 | 0.75 | 45

4939 市区 [市區] /shìqū/ *place* city proper, town, city; downtown
我去市区买点儿东西。 I'm going downtown to do some shopping.
82 | 0.56 | 45

4940 眼下 [眼下] /yǎnxià/ *time* at present, now, for the time being
眼下我不能告诉你那消息。 I cannot tell you the news for the time being.
71 | 0.64 | 45

4941 供给 [供給] /gōngjǐ/ (2) *v* supply
镇上的用水是由山里的一个水库供给的。 The town is supplied with water from a reservoir in the hills.
64 | 0.71 | 45

4942 逢 [逢] /féng/ (2) *v* meet by chance
他们多年后又相逢了。 They met again after an elapse of many years.
54 | 0.85 | 45

4943 讽刺 [諷刺] /fěngcì/ (3) *v* satirise, ridicule
作者讽刺了政治家的建议。 The writer satirised the politician's proposal.
59 | 0.78 | 45

4944 欺负 [欺負] /qīfu/ (3) *v* bully
她太欺负人了！ She is such a bully.
85 | 0.53 | 45

4945 答复 [答復] /dáfù/ (3) v reply
请尽早答复。Please reply at your earliest
convenience.
55 | 0.82 | 45

4946 测试 [測試] /cèshì/ (3) v test
系统已测试过了。The system has been
tested.
68 | 0.67 | 45

4947 空 [空] /kòng/ (3) v leave empty, leave blank
如果答不上来就空着。If you cannot answer
the question, leave a blank.
59 | 0.77 | 45

4948 垫 [墊] /diàn/ (3) v pad, fill up; pay on behalf
of somebody (for future repayment)
她说着坐了下来，把一本书垫在冰凉的铁踏板
上。She spoke, placing a book on the chilly
steel floor before sitting down.
58 | 0.78 | 45

4949 生育 [生育] /shēngyù/ v bear, give birth to
她给他生育了六个孩子。She's borne him six
children.
67 | 0.67 | 45

4950 赞赏 [讚賞] /zànshǎng/ v appreciate
对您在此事上的合作，深表赞赏。We
appreciate your cooperation in this matter.
94 | 0.49 | 45

4951 育 [育] /yù/ v give birth; raise, keep; educate
女人做的不仅仅是生儿育女。Women do
more than just give birth.
62 | 0.73 | 45

4952 销 [銷] /xiāo/ v sell; fasten (with a bolt)
你们打算把产品销往欧洲吗？Do you have
any plans to sell in Europe?
69 | 0.65 | 45

4953 列为 [列為] /lièwéi/ v be classified as,
be rated as
他被列为最佳小说家之列。He is rated among
the best novelists.
84 | 0.54 | 45

4954 拒 [拒] /jù/ v refuse; repel, resist
她拒不同意。She refused to give her
permission.
57 | 0.8 | 45

4955 描绘 [描繪] /miáohuì/ v depict, portray
这幅画描绘了落日的美景。The picture
portrays a beautiful sunset.
55 | 0.83 | 45

4956 无力 [無力] /wúlì/ v feel weak, lack strength or
power; be unable
我觉得浑身无力。My whole body feels weak.
66 | 0.69 | 45

4957 渗透 [滲透] /shèntòu/ v permeate, penetrate
雨水渗透了泥土。The rain permeated the
soil.
59 | 0.77 | 45

4958 吸毒 [吸毒] /xīdú/ v take drug
所以，吸毒会增加感染艾滋病的危险性。
So taking drugs can increase the danger of
catching AIDS.
70 | 0.65 | 45

4959 贪 [貪] /tān/ v be greedy
他们又贪又吝。They are all greedy and
avaricious.
59 | 0.77 | 45

4960 蹦 [蹦] /bèng/ v jump, leap
他使劲一蹦就过了沟。With one powerful leap
he crossed the ditch.
69 | 0.66 | 45

4961 变为 [變為] /biànwéi/ v become
假如海洋上升500英尺，印度将会变为孤岛。
If the sea were to rise 500 feet, India would
become an island.
65 | 0.7 | 45

4962 崇高 [崇高] /chónggāo/ (2) adj lofty, high
这些都是崇高的理想。These are lofty ideals.
69 | 0.64 | 44

4963 不大 [不大] /búdà/ (2) adv not very; not often
我觉得不大舒服。I am not feeling very well.
57 | 0.78 | 44

4964 变化 [變化] /biànhuà/ (1) n change
我的家乡发生了很大的变化。Great changes
have taken place in my hometown.
57 | 0.79 | 44

4965 学期 [學期] /xuéqī/ (2) n term, semester
这个学期期末有考试吗？Are there any exams
at the end of this term?
56 | 0.79 | 44

4966 郊区 [郊區] /jiāoqū/ (2) place suburbs, outskirts
我们喜欢住在郊区。We prefer to live in the
suburbs.
59 | 0.76 | 44

4967 拦 [攔] /lán/ (2) v block, stop, hold back, stand
in one's way
你要是想学医我们决不拦你。If you want to
study medicine, we won't stand in your way.
72 | 0.61 | 44

4968 平安 [平安] /píng'ān/ (2) adj safe and sound
知你平安无事才放下心来。It's a great relief
to know you're safe.
52 | 0.84 | 43

4969 反动 [反動] /fǎndòng/ (2) adj reactionary
我们决不向反动势力妥协。We'll never
compromise with the reactionary forces.
73 | 0.59 | 43

4970 保护 [保護] /bǎohù/ (2) n protection
西藏地区的文物受到了全面的保护。Cultural
relics in Tibet are put under full protection.
59 | 0.73 | 43

4971 星星 [星星] /xīngxing/ (2) n star
星星在天空中闪闪发光。Stars twinkled in the
sky.
57 | 0.76 | 43

4972 水稻 [水稻] /shuǐdào/ (2) n (paddy) rice
亚洲其他国家也种植水稻。Rice is also grown
in many other Asian countries.
73 | 0.59 | 43

4973 草地 [草地] /cǎodì/ (2) n grass, meadow, lawn
禁止踏草地。Keep off the grass.
62 | 0.71 | 43

4974 指挥 [指揮] /zhǐhuī/ (2) *n* command, direction; commander; (music) conductor
他们愿意服从他的指挥。They would put themselves under his command.
61 | 0.72 | 43

4975 滴 [滴] /dī/ (2) *clas* [measure word for a tiny amount of liquid] drop
我恐怕再喝一滴也不行了。I am afraid I cannot take a drop more.
67 | 0.64 | 43

4976 开学 [開學] /kāixué/ (1) *v* the school opens, a new term begins
新学期何时开学？When does the new semester start?
52 | 0.84 | 43

4977 问候 [問候] /wènhòu/ (2) *v* greet, give somebody one's respects
仪式结束后，教堂里的人们互相问候。
After the ceremony, people in the church started to greet each other.
92 | 0.47 | 43

4978 遇见 [遇見] /yùjiàn/ (2) *v* meet
我没有想到会在这里遇见你。I didn't expect to meet you here.
64 | 0.67 | 43

4979 杂 [雜] /zá/ (2) *adj* mixed, varied, miscellaneous
假期的工作又多又杂。Holiday jobs are many and varied.
55 | 0.76 | 42

4980 主观 [主觀] /zhǔguān/ (2) *adj* subjective
评论她的作品不要过于主观。Do not judge her work too subjectively.
62 | 0.69 | 42

4981 只有 [只有] /zhǐyǒu/ (2) *adv* only
只有我们在那里。We were the only people there.
52 | 0.82 | 42

4982 一边 [一邊] /yìbiān/ (2) *loc* one side
她叹了口气，将书放在一边。She sighed and put the book aside.
73 | 0.58 | 42

4983 牛奶 [牛奶] /niúnǎi/ (1) *n* milk
我不喜欢牛奶。I don't like milk.
56 | 0.77 | 42

4984 海关 [海關] /hǎiguān/ (2) *n* customs
他父亲是一位海关官员。His father is a customs officer.
137 | 0.31 | 42

4985 延长 [延長] /yáncháng/ (2) *v* extend, renew
你在申请延长签证时遇到什么困难了吗？
Did you have any difficulty in renewing your visa?
72 | 0.58 | 42

4986 区别 [區別] /qūbié/ (2) *v* differentiate, tell apart
你能将这两个品种区别开来吗？
Can you differentiate one variety from the other?
60 | 0.71 | 42

4987 节约 [節約] /jiéyuē/ (2) *v* practise thrift, save
政府正在鼓励各公司节约能源。
The government is encouraging companies to save energy.
63 | 0.67 | 42

4988 仰 [仰] /yǎng/ (2) *v* look up, face up, raise one's head
她仰着头恳求他。She pleaded, raising her head.
83 | 0.51 | 42

4989 困 [困] /kùn/ (2) *v* be sleepy; sleep; be stranded or trapped
有个姑娘困在里面了！There's a girl trapped in here!
55 | 0.77 | 42

4990 安慰 [安慰] /ānwèi/ (2) *v* comfort, console, solace, soothe
母亲在试图安慰泪水汪汪的小女孩。
The mother was trying to comfort the tearful little girl.
80 | 0.53 | 42

4991 尖 [尖] /jiān/ (2) *adj* pointed; shrill; sharp, acute
铅笔削尖了。The pencil is sharpened to a point.
60 | 0.7 | 41

4992 懒 [懶] /lǎn/ (2) *adj* lazy
她很懒，逃避工作。She was lazy and shunned work.
70 | 0.59 | 41

4993 生产 [生產] /shēngchǎn/ (1) *n* production
工业生产稳定增长。Industrial production grew steadily.
89 | 0.47 | 41

4994 外语 [外語] /wàiyǔ/ (1) *n* foreign language
学习外语离不开好的词典。A good dictionary is indispensable for learning a foreign language.
51 | 0.81 | 41

4995 护士 [護士] /hùshi/ (2) *n* nurse
他的母亲是个护士。His mother is a nurse.
66 | 0.64 | 41

4996 科长 [科長] /kēzhǎng/ (2) *n* section chief
你找科长请假了吗？Have you approached the section chief about taking the day off?
59 | 0.7 | 41

4997 仪器 [儀器] /yíqì/ (2) *n* instrument, apparatus
工厂决定生产这种仪器。The factory decided to produce this kind of instrument.
54 | 0.76 | 41

4998 讲座 [講座] /jiǎngzuò/ (2) *n* lecture
有些学生在听讲座时打瞌睡。Some students dozed off during the lecture.
61 | 0.67 | 41

4999 红旗 [紅旗] /hóngqí/ (2) *n* red flag
广场上红旗招展。The square was bedecked with red flags.
53 | 0.79 | 41

5000 打扮 [打扮] /dǎbàn/ (2) *v* dress up, make up; pretend to be, act as
孩子们都喜欢化装打扮。Children love dressing up.
69 | 0.6 | 41

5001 误会 [誤會] /wùhuì/ (2) v misunderstand, mistake
你一定误会了我的意思。 You must have misunderstood my meaning.
65 | 0.64 | 41

5002 明确 [明確] /míngquè/ (2) v make clear, clarify
我希望明确一下儿，这个决定是不可更改的。 I wish to make it clear that the decision is final.
65 | 0.64 | 41

5003 弹 [彈] /tán/ (2) v play (some musical instruments); bounce, spring; flick, flip
他弹钢琴弹得还不错。 He plays the piano tolerably well.
59 | 0.7 | 41

5004 一块儿 [一塊兒] /yíkuàir/ (1) adv together
我们一块儿去公园散散步吧。 Let's go and take a walk in the park together.
81 | 0.5 | 40 | S

Alphabetical index

Headword in Simplified Chinese */Pinyin/ Part of speech code* English gloss
Frequency rank

A

阿 /ā/ *pref* [nominal prefix used before a personal name for endearment] 1736

阿姨 /āyí/ *n* (maternal side) aunt, auntie; [also used as a polite term of address for a woman of one's parents' age] 3668

啊 /a/ *part* [modal particle showing affirmation, approval or consent] 0222

啊 /ā, á, ǎ/ *interj* [interjection expressing surprise, admiration, etc.] oh 0341

哎 /āi/ *interj* [interjection expressing surprise, disapproval, reminder, etc.] 0946

哎呀 /āiyā/ *interj* [interjection expressing wonder, shock or complaint] ah, my god, damn 3869

哎哟 /āiyō/ *interj* [particle expressing astonishment or pain] hey, oh, ouch 4848

唉 /āi, ài/ *interj* [interjection expressing sadness, disappointment, weariness, etc.] alas, oh, well; [as a response to calling, etc.] 1935

挨 /āi, ái/ *v* be next to; get close to; suffer, endure 3011

艾滋病 /àizībìng/ *n* AIDS 2605

爱 /ài/ *v* love, like 0230

爱国 /àiguó/ *adj* patriotic 3829

爱情 /àiqíng/ *n* love 1167

爱心 /àixīn/ *n* love, affection 3948

安 /ān/ *adj* calm, at ease 1772

安 /ān/ *v* fix, install, set up; be contented 3405

安定 /āndìng/ *adj* stable 4733

安静 /ānjìng/ *adj* quiet 3770

安排 /ānpái/ *v* arrange, schedule 0785

安全 /ānquán/ *adj* safe, secure 0777

安慰 /ānwèi/ *v* comfort, console, solace, soothe 4990

安置 /ānzhì/ *v* find a suitable place for, arrange for, help somebody to settle down; install, fix 4275

安装 /ānzhuāng/ *v* install 4348

俺 /ǎn/ *pron* [northern dialects] I, we, my, our, me, us 4007

岸 /àn/ *n* bank 1694

按 /àn/ *prep* according to 0457

按照 /ànzhào/ *prep* according to 0795

案 /àn/ *n* (legal or criminal) case; proposal; long narrow table 1561

案件 /ànjiàn/ *n* case 2150

暗 /àn/ *adj* dark, unclear 2022

暗示 /ànshì/ *v* suggest, imply 4312

熬 /áo/ *v* endure, get through; cook, boil 3517

B

八 /bā/ *num* eight 0286

吧 /ba/ *part* [modal particle indicating a suggestion or request; marking a question requesting confirmation, or a pause after alternatives] 0119

拔 /bá/ *v* pull up, pull out 3480

把 /bǎ/ *prep* [ba-structure preposing the object] 0034

把 /bǎ/ *v* guard; hold 1365

把握 /bǎwò/ *n* grasp, confidence, certainty, probability 1797

爸 /bà/ *n* dad, father 1415

爸爸 /bàba/ *n* dad, father 0739

罢 /bà/ *v* stop, cease; dismiss; [used as a resultative verb complement indicating completion] finish 4061

罢了 /bàle/ *part* [sentence final particle, equivalent of 而已] nothing more, merely, only 4689

白 /bái/ *adj* white 0633

白 /bái/ *adv* in vain, for nothing; free of charge 4632

白色 /báisè/ *n* white 3471

白天 /báitiān/ *time* day, daytime 2459

百 /bǎi/ *num* hundred 0375

百姓 /bǎixìng/ *n* [also written as 老百姓] common people, civilian 2626

摆 /bǎi/ *v* put, place, arrange; put on (airs); sway 1141

摆脱 /bǎituō/ *v* get rid of, break away from 2519

呗 /bei/ *part* [sentence final particle indicating something obvious or expressing resignation] 4071

败 /bài/ *v* be defeated, fail 2404

拜 /bài/ *v* worship, pay respect; visit 3459

班 /bān/ *n* class, team; shift, duty; squad 0922

班 /bān/ *clas* [measure word for a group of people] class, squad, team; [measure word for regular transport services] 3850

班长 /bānzhǎng/ n class monitor, captain; squad leader 4801

般 /bān/ aux same as, just like 1174

搬 /bān/ v move, remove 1634

板 /bǎn/ n board, plank 2073

版 /bǎn/ n edition; (of newspaper) page 3132

办 /bàn/ v do 0269

办法 /bànfǎ/ n method, means 0345

办公 /bàn'gōng/ v handle official business; open, work (in office) 3479

办公室 /bàngōngshì/ n office 1023

办理 /bànlǐ/ v handle 3431

办事 /bànshì/ v attend to (a matter); act 2874

半 /bàn/ num half 0238

伴 /bàn/ v accompany 4268

伴随 /bànsuí/ v accompany, follow 4614

扮演 /bànyǎn/ v play the role of, act as 3971

帮 /bāng/ v help, assist, do somebody a favour 0671

帮忙 /bāngmáng/ v help 3725

帮助 /bāngzhù/ v help, assist 0632

棒 /bàng/ adj terrific, superb 4217

包 /bāo/ v pack, wrap; assure, guarantee; undertake the whole thing; hire 1089

包袱 /bāofu/ n burden, weight (on one's mind); a bundle wrapped in cloth 4587

包含 /bāohán/ v contain, include 3856

包括 /bāokuò/ v include, comprise 0394

包围 /bāowéi/ v surround, encircle 4060

包装 /bāozhuāng/ v pack, wrap up 3320

薄 /báo, bó/ adj thin; small, meagre 4072

宝 /bǎo/ n treasure 2681

宝贵 /bǎoguì/ adj valuable, precious 3489

饱 /bǎo/ adj full 3243

保 /bǎo/ v protect, defend; guarantee; preserve, maintain; bail 1769

保持 /bǎochí/ v keep, maintain 0704

保存 /bǎocún/ v preserve; save (a computer file, etc.) 2911

保护 /bǎohù/ v protect 0537

保护 /bǎohù/ n protection 4970

保留 /bǎoliú/ v keep, retain 2557

保密 /bǎomì/ v keep something in secrecy, keep something secret 4500

保卫 /bǎowèi/ v guard, defend 3217

保险 /bǎoxiǎn/ n insurance 1656

保障 /bǎozhàng/ v safeguard, guarantee 1754

保证 /bǎozhèng/ v guarantee 0915

报 /bào/ n newspaper 0566

报 /bào/ v report; announce; recompense, reclaim; repay (one's kindness); revenge 2647

报道 /bàodào/ v report 0649

报道 /bàodào/ n (news) report 3064

报复 /bàofù/ v retaliate, pay back, put it across 3578

报告 /bàogào/ n report 0644

报刊 /bàokān/ n newspapers and periodicals, the press 4479

报名 /bàomíng/ v sign up, enroll 3957

报社 /bàoshè/ n newspaper, press 4533

报纸 /bàozhǐ/ n newspaper 1201

抱 /bào/ v hold in arms 1208

抱怨 /bàoyuàn/ v complain 4357

暴力 /bàolì/ n violence 2865

暴露 /bàolù/ v expose, reveal 3165

爆 /bào/ v explore; burst 4898

爆发 /bàofā/ v break out 2180

爆炸 /bàozhà/ v explode 2689

杯 /bēi/ clas [measure word for drinks] cup, mug, glass 2092

杯 /bēi/ n cup, mug, glass 2250

悲哀 /bēi'āi/ adj sad, grieved, sorrowful 4218

悲剧 /bēijù/ n tragedy 2732

碑 /bēi/ n monument 4327

北 /běi/ loc north 1012

北部 /běibù/ loc north, northern part 3698

北方 /běifāng/ place north 2223

备 /bèi/ v get ready; prepare against; be available, be equipped with 4209

背 /bēi, bèi/ v carry on one's back; learn by heart 0865

背后 /bèihòu/ loc behind, at the back 4522

背景 /bèijǐng/ n background 1766

倍 /bèi/ clas (two, three, etc.)-fold; times 1472

被 /bèi/ prep [passive marker] 0057

被动 /bèidòng/ adj passive 4732

被迫 /bèipò/ v be compelled to, be forced to 3889

辈子 /bèizi/ clas [typically occurring with 一 "one"] all one's life, lifetime 1816

奔 /bēn, bèn/ v rush, run quickly; head for; approach 2846

本 /běn/ pron (one's) own; this, current 0282

本 /běn/ clas [measure word for books, etc.] 0867

本 /běn/ adv originally, formerly 1835

本 /běn/ n root, origin, foundation, basis; edition, version 2771

本地 /běndì/ place [as opposed to 外地] local place 4052

本来 /běnlái/ adv originally 1044

本领 /běnlǐng/ n [equivalent of 本事] ability, skill 4642

本能 /běnnéng/ *n* instinct 4489

本人 /běnrén/ *pron* I; oneself 2137

本身 /běnshēn/ *pron* (in) itself, *per se* 1274

本事 /běnshi/ *n* [equivalent of 本领] ability, skill 3666

本质 /běnzhì/ *n* essence; true nature 2655

笨 /bèn/ *adj* stupid 4417

甭 /béng/ *adv* don't, needn't 4795

蹦 /bèng/ *v* jump, leap 4960

逼 /bī/ *v* force, press; close in on 1928

鼻子 /bízi/ *n* nose 2679

比 /bǐ/ *prep* [used for comparison] than 0130

比 /bǐ/ *v* compare; match, liken to 2893

比较 /bǐjiào/ *adv* comparatively, relatively 0321

比较 /bǐjiào/ *v* compare 3007

比例 /bǐlì/ *n* proportion, ratio 2061

比如 /bǐrú/ *v* take, for example 0896

比如说 /bǐrúshuō/ *idiom* for example, say 3081

比赛 /bǐsài/ *n* competition, contest, match, game 0747

彼此 /bǐcǐ/ *pron* each other 2066

笔 /bǐ/ *clas* [measure word for handwritings or drawings]; [measure word for a sum of money or a transaction] 1369

笔 /bǐ/ *n* pen 2033

必 /bì/ *adv* must, certainly 1607

必定 /bìdìng/ *adv* surely 4520

必然 /bìrán/ *adv* necessarily, inevitably 2378

必须 /bìxū/ *v* must, have to 0264

必要 /bìyào/ *adj* necessary 1142

毕竟 /bìjìng/ *adv* after all 1571

毕业 /bìyè/ *v* graduate 1003

毕业生 /bìyèshēng/ *n* graduate 3947

闭 /bì/ *v* close 2359

壁 /bì/ *n* wall 4135

避 /bì/ *v* avoid, evade 4494

避免 /bìmiǎn/ *v* avoid, avert 2025

臂 /bì, bei/ *n* arm 4660

边 /biān/ *n* side; edge 0443

边 /biān/ *adv* [as in 边 . . . 边 . . . indicating simultaneous progression of two events] while 1349

边界 /biānjiè/ *n* boundary, border 4231

边境 /biānjìng/ *n* border, frontier 4542

边缘 /biānyuán/ *n* edge, margin, brink 4748

编 /biān/ *v* compile, edit; make up; weave, plait 2231

编辑 /biānjí/ *n* editor; editing 2273

扁 /biǎn/ *adj* flat 4691

便 /biàn/ *adv* [similar to 就] soon afterwards, just 0285

便 /biàn/ *adj* convenient; informal, ordinary 3019

变 /biàn/ *v* change 0325

变成 /biànchéng/ *v* become, turn into 0623

变化 /biànhuà/ *v* change 0564

变化 /biànhuà/ *n* change 4964

变为 /biànwéi/ *v* become 4961

遍 /biàn/ *clas* [measure word for the course of actions] time; once through 1845

辩 /biàn/ *v* argue, debate 1798

辩论 /biànlùn/ *v* debate, argue 2244

标题 /biāotí/ *n* title, heading 3504

标志 /biāozhì/ *n* sign, symbol 2775

标准 /biāozhǔn/ *n* standard, criterion 0776

表 /biǎo/ *n* watch; form, table 2653

表 /biǎo/ *v* express, show 3037

表达 /biǎodá/ *v* express, voice (one's opinion) 1395

表面 /biǎomiàn/ *n* surface, outside 2301

表明 /biǎomíng/ *v* make known or clear; state clearly; show 1423

表情 /biǎoqíng/ *n* (facial) expression 2603

表示 /biǎoshì/ *v* express 0398

表现 /biǎoxiàn/ *v* manifest, show; behave 0436

表现 /biǎoxiàn/ *n* behaviour 4849

表演 /biǎoyǎn/ *v* perform 1680

表扬 /biǎoyáng/ *v* praise 4883

别 /bié/ *adv* [negative imperative] don't, had better not 0328

别的 /biéde/ *pron* other, else 0963

别人 /biérén/ *pron* other people 0372

宾馆 /bīn'guǎn/ *n* guesthouse, hotel 2791

冰 /bīng/ *n* ice 2341

兵 /bīng/ *n* soldier 1075

兵力 /bīnglì/ *n* troops, military strength; strength 4091

并 /bìng/ *conj* and, besides 0102

并 /bìng/ *adv* [typically occurring in negation] actually, definitely 0615

并非 /bìngfēi/ *adv* actually not 2995

并且 /bìngqiě/ *conj* and 0851

病 /bìng/ *n* illness, ailment 0600

病毒 /bìngdú/ *n* virus 3676

病人 /bìngrén/ *n* sick person, patient 1560

拨 /bō/ *v* move; dial (a phone number); allocate 2823

玻璃 /bōlí/ *n* glass 2773

脖子 /bózi/ *n* neck 3228

播 /bō/ *v* sow, seed; broadcast 3456

博士 /bóshì/ *n* doctor, Ph.D. 1645

博物馆 /bówùguǎn/ *n* museum 3209

补 /bǔ/ *v* mend, repair; make up for 1821

补充 /bǔchōng/ *v* add; complement; replenish 2567

不 /bù/ *adv* no, not 0006

不安 /bù'ān/ *adj* uneasy 3297

不必 /búbì/ adv need not, no need 2127

不错 /búcuò/ adj not bad, pretty good; correct, right 1006

不大 /búdà/ adv not very; not often 4963

不但 /búdàn/ conj not only (. . . but also . . .), as well as 1437

不得 /bùdé, bude/ v must not 1810

不得不 /bùdébù/ adv have to 2146

不断 /búduàn/ adv unceasingly, always 0455

不对 /búduì/ adj wrong, incorrect 3778

不顾 /búgù/ v have no regard for, neglect 3139

不管 /bùguǎn/ conj no matter (what, how, etc.) 0909

不过 /búguò/ conj only; but 0465

不好意思 /bùhǎoyìsi/ idiom feel embarrassed, find it embarrassing 4569

不见 /bújiàn/ v disappear, miss; not meet 3033

不仅 /bùjǐn/ conj not only 0576

不仅仅 /bùjǐnjǐn/ adv not merely, more than 3063

不禁 /bùjīn/ adv can't help (doing something) 4167

不久 /bùjiǔ/ n soon, before long, soon after 1937

不可 /bùkě/ v cannot 0968

不利 /búlì/ adj unfavourable, harmful 2634

不良 /bùliáng/ adj bad, harmful 3105

不论 /búlùn/ conj no matter (what, who, how, etc.), irrespective of 2810

不满 /bùmǎn/ adj dissatisfied, discontented, resentful 2990

不能 /bùnéng/ v can't 3078

不能不 /bùnéngbù/ adv have to, cannot but 3125

不然 /bùrán/ conj otherwise, or 3299

不如 /bùrú/ v be not as good as, be inferior to 3477

不如 /bùrú/ conj might as well, not so much as 4369

不少 /bùshǎo/ adj a good few 0628

不时 /bùshí/ adv from time to time 3933

不是 /bùshì/ n fault, blame 4918

不同 /bùtóng/ adj different 0298

不行 /bùxíng/ adj won't do, no good, poor 0838

不幸 /búxìng/ adj unfortunate, unlucky 3201

不要 /búyào/ adv [negative imperative] don't 0448

不已 /bùyǐ/ adv endlessly, incessantly 3868

不易 /búyì/ adj not easy, difficult 4418

不用 /búyòng/ adv need not 2095

不再 /búzài/ adv no longer 1135

不止 /bùzhǐ/ v without end, incessantly; exceed, more than 4499

不足 /bùzú/ adj insufficient, inadequate 1727

布 /bù/ n cloth 3207

布 /bù/ v arrange, deploy; announce, declare 4020

布置 /bùzhì/ v fix up, arrange, decorate; assign (work, homework, etc.) 3855

步 /bù/ clas pace; step 0565

步伐 /bùfá/ n pace, step 4001

步骤 /bùzhòu/ n step, move 4129

部 /bù/ clas [measure word for machines and vehicles, etc.]; [measure word for books and films, etc.] 0412

部 /bù/ n part, section; department; ministry 1177

部队 /bùduì/ n army, troops 0450

部分 /bùfen/ n part 0749

部分 /bùfen/ num part of 2006

部门 /bùmén/ n department 0534

部署 /bùshǔ/ v dispose, deploy 3453

部位 /bùwèi/ n position, place, area 4928

部长 /bùzhǎng/ n minister; head of department 1433

C

擦 /cā/ v wipe, clean; rub; spread 2439

猜 /cāi/ v guess 2172

猜测 /cāicè/ v guess 4897

才 /cái/ adv just 0093

才能 /cáinéng/ n talent 3310

材料 /cáiliào/ n material 1076

财 /cái/ n wealth, fortune 3711

财产 /cáichǎn/ n wealth, property 2088

财富 /cáifù/ n wealth 2620

财务 /cáiwù/ n finance 3543

财政 /cáizhèng/ n finance 2400

采 /cǎi/ v pick, gather; mine 3644

采访 /cǎifǎng/ v interview 0886

采购 /cǎigòu/ v purchase; do shopping 3345

采取 /cǎiqǔ/ v adopt, carry out (policies, course of action, etc.); take (actions, measures) 0786

采用 /cǎiyòng/ v use, make use of, adopt 1611

彩 /cǎi/ n colour, coloured 3376

彩色 /cǎisè/ n colour 4806

踩 /cǎi/ v step on, tread on 2985

菜 /cài/ n food; dish, course; vegetable 0815

参观 /cānguān/ v visit 2662

参加 /cānjiā/ v take part in, participate; join 0317

参考 /cānkǎo/ v consult, make reference to 4775

参谋 /cānmóu/ v give advice 4755

参与 /cānyù/ v participate, take part in, be involved in 1153

餐馆 /cān'guǎn/ n restaurant 4815

餐厅 /cāntīng/ n dining hall, dining room 4851

残 /cán/ adj disabled; incomplete; remnant 4368

残酷 /cánkù/ adj cruel 3828

惨 /cǎn/ adj miserable, awful, tragic 3589

灿烂 /cànlàn/ adj bright; brilliant 3102

仓库 /cāngkù/ n warehouse 4754

藏 /cáng/ v hide 3263

操 /cāo/ v hold; speak (a language); drill 4452

操作 /cāozuò/ v operate 2478

草 /cǎo/ n grass; straw 1299

草地 /cǎodì/ n grass, meadow, lawn 4973

草原 /cǎoyuán/ n grassland, prairie 3669

册 /cè/ clas [measure word for books] copy 3851

厕所 /cèsuǒ/ n toilet, WC 3155

测 /cè/ v measure, gauge 3727

测试 /cèshì/ v test 4946

策划 /cèhuá/ v plot, plan 3763

策略 /cèlüè/ n strategy 3806

层 /céng/ clas layer, tier; floor, storey 0923

层次 /céngcì/ n level, layer, hierarchy 2134

曾 /céng/ adv [referring to something that happened previously] once 0357

曾经 /céngjīng/ adv [referring to something that happened previously] 0722

插 /chā/ v insert, plug 2559

查 /chá/ v look up, consult; check, examine; investigate, look into 1548

茶 /chá/ n tea 1812

差 /chà/ adj short of; poor, not up to standard; wrong 0708

差别 /chābié/ n difference 3339

差不多 /chàbuduō/ adj almost the same; just about right; more or less 1650

差距 /chājù/ n disparity, gap 2607

差异 /chāyì/ n difference 3214

拆 /chāi/ v dismantle, take apart, pull down 3071

缠 /chán/ v wind; tangle; pester; deal with 4902

产 /chǎn/ v produce, yield; reproduce 1965

产量 /chǎnliàng/ n output 3465

产品 /chǎnpǐn/ n product 0647

产生 /chǎnshēng/ v arise, generate 0493

产业 /chǎnyè/ n industry 1471

长 /cháng/ adj long 0173

长期 /chángqī/ adj long-term 1037

长远 /chángyuǎn/ adj long-term 4519

尝 /cháng/ v taste 3679

尝试 /chángshì/ v try, attempt 3686

常 /cháng/ adv often, usually 0693

常常 /chángcháng/ adv often, frequently 1180

厂 /chǎng/ n factory 0890

厂长 /chǎngzhǎng/ n factory manager, director 3799

厂家 /chǎngjiā/ n manufacturer 4709

场 /cháng, chǎng/ clas [measure word for processes or courses of occurrence such as rain, snow, illness, etc.] period, spell; [measure word for recreational for sports activities] show, match 0322

场 /chǎng/ n field, court; ground 2072

场合 /chǎnghé/ n occasion 3087

场景 /chǎngjǐng/ n scene 4932

场面 /chǎngmiàn/ n scene, spectacle 2416

场所 /chǎngsuǒ/ n place, venue 3051

唱 /chàng/ v sing 0929

抄 /chāo/ v copy 3264

超 /chāo/ v exceed, surpass, go beyond; overtake 2558

超出 /chāochū/ v be beyond or outside, exceed 4679

超过 /chāoguò/ v surpass, exceed 1061

超市 /chāoshì/ n supermarket, superstore 4140

超越 /chāoyuè/ v surmount, surpass; overtake 3223

朝 /cháo/ prep towards; facing 1283

潮 /cháo/ n tide; moist 3307

潮流 /cháoliú/ n tide; trend 4137

吵 /chǎo/ v quarrel, have a row 2743

炒 /chǎo/ v stir fry; speculate, drive up (value or price through manipulation) 2570

车 /chē/ n car, vehicle; cart 0340

车队 /chēduì/ n motorcade, a queue of wagons or carts; fleet, vehicle service brigade 4756

车间 /chējiān/ n workshop 4287

车辆 /chēliàng/ n vehicle 3798

车站 /chēzhàn/ n (bus or railway) station 3252

车子 /chēzi/ n vehicle, car 4337

扯 /chě/ v pull; tear (off, into pieces); chat 3407

彻底 /chèdǐ/ adj thorough 1367

撤 /chè/ v remove; withdraw, evacuate, retreat 3349

沉 /chén/ v sink, submerge 3682

沉默 /chénmò/ adj silent 4159

沉重 /chénzhòng/ adj heavy; serious 2405

称 /chēng/ v call; say, state; weigh 0783

称为 /chēngwéi/ v call, refer to . . . as 1653

称赞 /chēngzàn/ v praise, speak well of 4009

称之为 /chēngzhīwéi/ v call it . . . 4409

撑 /chēng/ v prop up, support; open (an umbrella, etc.); overfill; pole (a boat) 3487

成 /chéng/ v become, turn into; succeed 0110

成本 /chéngběn/ n cost 2044

成分 /chéngfèn/ n ingredient, element 3567

成功 /chénggōng/ adj successful 0401

成果 /chéngguǒ/ n result, outcome, achievement 1609

成绩 /chéngjī/ n result, academic performance; achievement 0833

成就 /chéngjiù/ n accomplishment, achievement 1614

成立 /chénglì/ v establish, set up 0799

成人 /chéngrén/ n adult 4588

成熟 /chéngshú/ adj mature 1530

成为 /chéngwéi/ v become 0226

成员 /chéngyuán/ n member 1454

成长 /chéngzhǎng/ v grow up 1718

呈 /chéng/ v assume (shape, colour, property, etc.); submit, present 3035

呈现 /chéngxiàn/ v show, appear 3013

承包 /chéngbāo/ v contract 3350

承担 /chéngdān/ v undertake, bear (cost, responsibility, etc.) 1671

承诺 /chéngnuò/ v undertake, promise 3122

承认 /chéngrèn/ v admit 0940

承受 /chéngshòu/ v bear, endure 2748

城 /chéng/ n town, city; city wall 0616

城里 /chénglǐ/ place in town or city 2820

城市 /chéngshì/ n city 0344

乘 /chéng/ v ride, travel by; take advantage of; multiply 1878

惩罚 /chéngfá/ v punish, penalise 4271

程度 /chéngdù/ n degree, level, extent 0802

程序 /chéngxù/ n procedure; (computer) programme 2225

盛 /chéng/ v fill (a bowl, etc.) with; hold, contain 4062

吃 /chī/ v eat 0137

吃饭 /chīfàn/ v eat (a meal) 1106

迟 /chí/ adj late 3736

持 /chí/ v hold, maintain 2333

持续 /chíxù/ v last, continue; sustain 1771

尺 /chǐ/ clas [measure word for length in Chinese local unit] Chinese foot, chi (equivalent of ten cun or one-third of a metre) 4664

充分 /chōngfèn/ adj full, abundant, ample, sufficient 1011

充满 /chōngmǎn/ v be full of, be filled with 0893

冲 /chōng/ v dash against, rush; rinse, flush; develop (a film) 0812

冲动 /chōngdòng/ n impulse 3768

冲击 /chōngjī/ v charge, attack, assault; lash 2876

冲突 /chōngtū/ v conflict, clash with 1396

虫 /chóng/ n insect; worm 4184

重 /chóng/ adv again, once more 1708

重复 /chóngfù/ v repeat 2845

重建 /chóngjiàn/ v reconstruct, rebuild 4682

重新 /chóngxīn/ adv again; anew, afresh 0848

崇拜 /chóngbài/ v worship, adore 3649

崇高 /chónggāo/ adj lofty, high 4962

抽 /chōu/ v draw, take out 1980

抽烟 /chōuyān/ v smoke 4549

愁 /chóu/ v worry 4260

臭 /chòu/ adj stinking, smelly; disgraceful, discredited 2989

出 /chū/ v out; produce; happen 0050

出版 /chūbǎn/ v publish 1528

出版社 /chūbǎnshè/ n press, publisher, publishing company 2450

出差 /chūchāi/ v be on a business trip 4680

出发 /chūfā/ v start out 1909

出国 /chūguó/ v go abroad 2392

出口 /chūkǒu/ n exit; export 1505

出来 /chūlái/ v come out 0169

出路 /chūlù/ n way out, solution 3796

出门 /chūmén/ v go out, be away from home 3239

出去 /chūqù/ v go out 0631

出色 /chūsè/ adj remarkable, brilliant 2443

出身 /chūshēn/ v come from (a particular family background) 2630

出生 /chūshēng/ v be born 1930

出售 /chūshòu/ v sell 4781

出席 /chūxí/ v attend 2706

出现 /chūxiàn/ v appear 0250

出于 /chūyú/ v start from, stem from; come out of 2693

出租车 /chūzūchē/ n taxi 4248

初 /chū/ adj elementary, just beginning; first 0874

初 /chū/ pref [prefix preceding a numeral to indicate dates on the lunar calendar, and also for grades or years in the junior high school] 2616

初步 /chūbù/ adj preliminary, initial, tentative 4839

初期 /chūqī/ n initial stage, early days 3750

初中 /chūzhōng/ n junior high school, secondary school 3311

除 /chú/ prep except, besides 1315

除 /chú/ v remove, get rid of; divide 2021

除非 /chúfēi/ conj unless 3696

除了 /chúle/ prep besides, in addition to; except 0844

厨房 /chúfáng/ n kitchen 3837

处 /chù/ n place; department 0477

处 /chù/ clas [measure word for places occupied] 1617

处 /chǔ/ v be in; get along; sentence, punish 3757

处长 /chùzhǎng/ n head of department 3877

处处 /chùchù/ adv everywhere 3662

处罚 /chǔfá/ v punish, penalise 4786

处分 /chǔfèn/ n disciplinary action, punishment 4917

处境 /chǔjìng/ n (difficult) position, plight 4434

处理 /chǔlǐ/ v handle, deal with; take disciplinary action against; dispose of, sell at a reduced price 0609

处于 /chǔyú/ v be (in a certain state, position, or condition) 1421

处在 /chǔzài/ v be (in a certain state, position, or condition) 4408

穿 /chuān/ v wear, put on; bore a hole; cross 0419

传 /chuán/ v pass on, spread; hand down 1267

传播 /chuánbō/ v disseminate, spread 2461

传达 /chuándá/ v convey, communicate 4498

传递 /chuándì/ v transmit, communicate, pass 4107

传来 /chuánlái/ v (news, sound, etc.) come 3222

传说 /chuánshuō/ n legend 2680

传统 /chuántǒng/ n tradition 0507

船 /chuán/ n boat, ship 0879

串 /chuàn/ clas [measure word for things growing or attached together] string, bunch, cluster 4666

窗 /chuāng/ n window 3301

窗户 /chuānghù/ n window 3836

窗口 /chuāngkǒu/ n window 3068

窗外 /chuāngwài/ place out of the window 4824

床 /chuáng/ n bed 1298

闯 /chuǎng/ v rush, dash; break in 3098

创 /chuàng/ v achieve, set (a record) 2587

创新 /chuàngxīn/ v innovate, be creative 2080

创业 /chuàngyè/ v do pioneering work, start a business 4504

创造 /chuàngzào/ v create 0779

创作 /chuàngzuò/ v create (especially literary works), write 1308

吹 /chuī/ v blow, puff; play (flute, etc.); boast; (lovers) break up, (plan, etc.) fall through 1333

春 /chūn/ time spring 1363

春节 /chūnjié/ time Spring Festival (Chinese New Year) 2458

春天 /chūntiān/ time spring 2277

纯 /chún/ adj pure 3354

唇 /chún/ n lip 4873

词 /cí/ n word, term; speech, statement; [a kind of Chinese poetry] 1197

辞职 /cízhí/ v resign, quit 3624

此 /cǐ/ pron this 0225

此后 /cǐhòu/ time hence, hereafter 3261

此时 /cǐshí/ pron at this moment 1900

此外 /cǐwài/ conj besides, in addition 1880

次 /cì/ clas [measure word indicating number of repetitions or count of actions or events] times 0054

次 /cì/ adj inferior 1432

刺激 /cìjī/ v stimulate, provoke 2318

从 /cóng/ prep from 0042

从不 /cóngbù/ adv [equivalent of 从来不] never 3697

从此 /cóngcǐ/ adv since then, after that 1922

从而 /cóng'ér/ conj thus, so 1495

从来 /cónglái/ adv always, all along 1326

从来不 /cóngláibù/ adv never 3664

从前 /cóngqián/ time before, in the past 4545

从事 /cóngshì/ v go in for, be engaged in 1517

从未 /cóngwèi/ adv never (before) 4122

从小 /cóngxiǎo/ adv since childhood, from an early age 2594

从中 /cóngzhōng/ adv from it, therefrom 4221

匆匆 /cōngcōng/ adv hastily, hurriedly, in a hurry 4371

聪明 /cōngmíng/ adj clever, smart, witty 1794

凑 /còu/ v put together, come together; move closer 3582

粗 /cū/ adj thick; coarse, rough; (of voice) husky; rude 3691

促进 /cùjìn/ v promote, advance 1252

促使 /cùshǐ/ v impel, spur on, prompt 4102

醋 /cù/ n vinegar; jealousy 4915

催 /cuī/ v urge, rush, chase up 4605

脆弱 /cuìruò/ adj frail, fragile 3780

村 /cūn/ n village 0858

村里 /cūnli/ place in the village 2661

村民 /cūnmín/ n villager 3257

村子 /cūnzi/ n village 4474

存 /cún/ v exist; deposit; accumulate; check (luggage), leave something with someone 1318

存款 /cúnkuǎn/ n deposit (in a bank), savings 4593

存在 /cúnzài/ v exist 0467

寸 /cùn/ clas [measure term for length in Chinese local unit] Chinese inch, cun (equivalent of one-thirtieth of a metre) 4603

措施 /cuòshī/ n measure 1214

错 /cuò/ adj wrong, mistaken 0903

错 /cuò/ n fault, mistake 2115

错误 /cuòwù/ adj wrong, mistaken 1984

错误 /cuòwù/ n mistake, error 2116

D

搭 /dā/ v build, put up; travel by; come into contact 1964

达 /dá/ v attain, reach; amount to 0614

达成 /dáchéng/ v reach (an agreement) 2319

达到 /dádào/ v reach, attain, be up to 0638

答 /dá/ v answer, reply 2112

答案 /dá'àn/ n answer 2814

答复 /dáfù/ v reply 4945

答应 /dāying/ v answer, reply; agree, promise 1981

打 /dǎ/ v beat, hit, strike; play; typewrite 0120

打扮 /dǎbàn/ v dress up, make up; pretend to be, act as 5000

打电话 /dǎdiànhuà/ v make a telephone call 1427

打断 /dǎduàn/ v interrupt, cut short 3038

打工 /dǎgōng/ v work (especially referring to doing odd jobs or manual labour) 3408

打击 /dǎjī/ v strike, attack; crack down; dampen 1648

打架 /dǎjià/ v fight 4146

打交道 /dǎjiāodào/ v deal with; hang out with; work with 4774

打开 /dǎkāi/ v open 1324

打破 /dǎpò/ v break 2361

打算 /dǎsuàn/ v plan, intend 2514

打算 /dǎsuàn/ n plan 4000

打听 /dǎtīng/ v ask about, enquire 3380

打仗 /dǎzhàng/ v fight, fight a war 4552

大 /dà/ adj big, large 0025

大 /dà/ adv greatly, a lot 0688

大部分 /dàbùfen/ num a large part of, the majority of 2016

大大 /dàda/ adv greatly 2432

大胆 /dàdǎn/ adj bold, courageous, daring 2828

大地 /dàdì/ n earth, ground 3175

大都 /dàdū/ adv mostly, for the most part 3930

大队 /dàduì/ n brigade 3708

大多 /dàduō/ adv mostly 2901

大多数 /dàduōshù/ num most, the majority 2224

大概 /dàgài/ adv roughly 1121

大哥 /dàgē/ n eldest brother; [also used as a polite address for a man of about one's own age] 2489

大规模 /dàguīmó/ adj large-scale 2943

大海 /dàhǎi/ n sea 4294

大会 /dàhuì/ n congress, assembly, meeting 1330

大家 /dàjiā/ pron all, everyone 0199

大街 /dàjiē/ n avenue, street 2398

大姐 /dàjiě/ n eldest sister, elder sister; [also used as a polite term of address for a women of one's own age] big sister, sister 3674

大力 /dàlì/ adv vigorously, greatly 2829

大量 /dàliàng/ num a great deal of, plenty of 1001

大楼 /dàlóu/ n building 3112

大陆 /dàlù/ n mainland, continent 1539

大妈 /dàmā/ n (paternal) aunt; [also used in northern dialects as a polite term of address for a woman of one's parents' age] 3793

大门 /dàmén/ n gate, (main) entrance 2227

大脑 /dànǎo/ n brain 4648

大批 /dàpī/ num large quantities 3250

大气 /dàqì/ n atmosphere; heavy breath 4187

大桥 /dàqiáo/ n (grand) bridge 4926

大人 /dàrén/ n adult, grown-up 2183

大厦 /dàshà/ n building, mansion 4003

大声 /dàshēng/ adv loudly 3300

大师 /dàshī/ n great master 2418

大使 /dàshǐ/ n ambassador 2756

大事 /dàshì/ n a major event; the overall situation 1757

大厅 /dàtīng/ n hall 3421

大小 /dàxiǎo/ n size 2677

大型 /dàxíng/ adj large-scale 1879

大学 /dàxué/ n university 0260

大学生 /dàxuéshēng/ n college or university student 1838

大爷 /dàyé/ n grandpa, elder uncle; [often used as a respectful term of an elderly man, equivalent of 老大爷] uncle 2969

大约 /dàyuē/ adv approximately, about 1721

大众 /dàzhòng/ n the public, the people 3993

大自然 /dàzìrán/ n nature 4429

呆 /dāi/ v stay; look like a dummy 1820

大夫 /dàifu/ n doctor, physician 3331

代 /dài/ n generation; historical period, dynasty 0828

代 /dài/ v replace, substitute; (do) on one's behalf 1662

代表 /dàibiǎo/ n representative, delegate 0484

代表 /dàibiǎo/ v represent, stand for, act on one's behalf 1499

代表团 /dàibiǎotuán/ n delegation 2241

代价 /dàijià/ n price, cost 2956

代理 /dàilǐ/ n agent, agency; (computing) proxy 4262

代替 /dàitì/ v substitute, replace 4302

带 /dài/ v carry, bring, take 0204

带 /dài/ n ribbon, belt; zone, area 2178

带动 /dàidòng/ v spur on, provide an impetus, drive, bring along 4448

带来 /dàilái/ v bring 0759

带领 /dàilǐng/ v lead, guide 3317

带有 /dàiyǒu/ v have, carry, bear 2782

待 /dāi, dài/ v stay; wait for; deal with, treat; entertain 1218

待遇 /dàiyù/ n treatment; remuneration 2924

贷款 /dàikuǎn/ n loan 2473

袋 /dài/ clas [measure word for things contained in a bag, packet, sachet, etc.] 4711

戴 /dài/ *v* put on, wear 1479

单 /dān/ *adj* single, solitary; odd 1811

单 /dān/ *adv* only, alone 2269

单纯 /dānchún/ *adj* simple 2750

单独 /dāndú/ *adv* alone 4029

单位 /dānwèi/ *n* (working or administrative) unit, institution; unit (of measurement) 0516

单一 /dānyī/ *adj* single 4629

担任 /dānrèn/ *v* hold (a governmental office or post), act as 1695

担心 /dānxīn/ *v* worry 1235

耽误 /dānwù/ *v* delay 4266

胆 /dǎn/ *n* gall, gall bladder; guts, nerve, courage 4922

但 /dàn/ *conj* but 0061

但是 /dànshì/ *conj* but 0155

诞生 /dànshēng/ *v* be born 3119

弹 /dàn/ *n* bullet, bomb 3909

淡 /dàn/ *adj* bland, tasteless, mild; (of colour) pale; (of business) slack; indifferent 4903

蛋 /dàn/ *n* egg 2351

当 /dāng/ *prep* just at (time or place) 0198

当 /dāng, dàng/ *v* work as; regard as 0352

当 /dàng/ *adj* appropriate 2672

当场 /dāngchǎng/ *adv* on the spot 3593

当初 /dāngchū/ *time* at the beginning, in the first place 2264

当代 /dāngdài/ *time* the present age 2292

当地 /dāngdì/ *place* local, in the locality 1056

当即 /dāngjí/ *adv* at once, immediately 4740

当今 /dāngjīn/ *time* today, nowadays 2758

当局 /dāngjú/ *n* the authorities 3371

当年 /dāngnián, dàngnián/ *time* in those days, past; that very year, current year 0811

当前 /dāngqián/ *time* currently, presently 2315

当然 /dāngrán/ *adv* of course, naturally, only natural 0276

当时 /dāngshí/ *time* then, at that time 0273

当事人 /dāngshìrén/ *n* person or party involved 3714

当中 /dāngzhōng/ *place* in the middle or centre; among 1618

当成 /dàngchéng/ *v* take for, regard as 3653

当天 /dàngtiān/ *time* the same day 2047

当作 /dàngzuò/ *v* treat as, regard as 3145

挡 /dǎng/ *v* keep off; block 4195

党 /dǎng/ *n* (political) party 0521

党委 /dǎngwěi/ *n* Party committee 3337

党员 /dǎngyuán/ *n* Party member 2998

档 /dàng/ *n* files, archive 4334

档案 /dàng'àn/ *n* files, archive 3157

刀 /dāo/ *n* knife 1503

刀 /dāo/ *clas* [measure word for meat] a cut of; [measure word for action of cutting with a knife] 4298

导弹 /dǎodàn/ *n* missile 4862

导师 /dǎoshī/ *n* tutor, supervisor 4534

导演 /dǎoyǎn/ *n* (film) director 2157

导致 /dǎozhì/ *v* cause, lead to, result in 1371

岛 /dǎo/ *n* island 2119

倒 /dào/ *adv* [indicating unexpectedness, contrast or concession] but 0737

倒 /dǎo, dào/ *v* fall, collapse; (business) close down; reverse, swap; dump (rubbish); move backwards; pour (tea) 0882

倒霉 /dǎoméi/ *adj* having bad luck 4281

到 /dào/ *v* go to, reach, arrive 0021

到 /dào/ *prep* to (a place); up until (time) 0767

到处 /dàochù/ *adv* everywhere, in all places 1692

到达 /dàodá/ *v* arrive, reach 2541

到底 /dàodǐ/ *adv* to the end; at last, finally; after all; [used for emphasis] 1213

到来 /dàolái/ *v* arrive 2747

道 /dào/ *clas* [measure word for long and narrow objects, doors, orders, questions, dishes in a meal, and steps in a process, etc.] 0617

道 /dào/ *v* [archaic, usually following communication verbs such as 说，笑，喊 and 叫] say, talk, speak 0979

道 /dào/ *n* road, path; method, way; line 2060

道德 /dàodé/ *n* morals, morality, ethics 1343

道理 /dàolǐ/ *n* reason 1090

道路 /dàolù/ *n* road 1272

道歉 /dàoqiàn/ *v* apologise 4257

得 /de/ *aux* [structural particle used after a verb that introduces a complement showing effect] 0044

得 /dé, děi/ *v* get, gain; must, have to; need 0335

得出 /déchū/ *v* obtain (results, conclusions, etc.) 4207

得到 /dédào/ *v* get 0305

得以 /déyǐ/ *v* be able to 3167

得意 /déyì/ *adj* proud (of oneself), complacent 4058

得知 /dézhī/ *v* learn, hear, get to know 3121

得罪 /dézuì/ *v* offend 4729

德 /dé/ *n* virtue; moral character 2892

的 /de/ *aux* [structural particle used after an attribute] 0001

的话 /dehuà/ *aux* [particle used at the end of a clause (. . . 的话 to express a condition] if 0871

灯 /dēng/ *n* lamp, light 1781

灯光 /dēngguāng/ *n* light, lighting 4246

登 /dēng/ *v* ascend, mount, climb; board; print, publish 1525

登记 /dēngjì/ *v* register; check in (at hotel, etc.) 3378

等 /děng/ *aux* et cetera 0073

等 /děng/ *v* wait 1576

等待 /děngdài/ *v* wait 2329

等到 /děngdào/ *v* wait until 3965

等等 /děngděng/ *aux* et cetera, and so on 0902

等级 /děngjí/ *n* class, grade, rank 4045

等于 /děngyú/ *v* equal 1832

瞪 /dèng/ *v* stare at 4147

低 /dī/ *adj* low 0504

低头 /dītóu/ *v* hang (one's) head; give in, submit, bend, bow 4780

低下 /dīxià/ *adj* low (status) 4463

滴 /dī/ *clas* [measure word for a tiny amount of liquid] drop 4975

的确 /díquè/ *adv* indeed, really 2193

敌 /dí/ *n* enemy 4245

敌人 /dírén/ *n* enemy 1515

底 /dǐ/ *n* bottom, base; end (of month or year); draft copy, duplicate copy for file; background 0771

底下 /dǐxià/ *loc* below, under 3497

抵 /dǐ/ *v* reach, arrive; balance, be equal to; make up for; resist 3454

抵达 /dǐdá/ *v* arrive 4205

抵抗 /dǐkàng/ *v* resist 3816

地 /de/ *aux* [structural particle introducing an adverbial modifier] 0036

地 /dì/ *n* earth, ground, field 0210

地步 /dìbù/ *n* degree, extent, plight 4230

地带 /dìdài/ *n* zone, region 4469

地点 /dìdiǎn/ *n* venue, location, place 2812

地方 /dìfang, dìfāng/ *n* place, space, room; locality (in relation to central administration) 0153

地理 /dìlǐ/ *n* geography 3469

地面 /dìmiàn/ *n* ground 2507

地球 /dìqiú/ *n* the earth, the globe 1419

地区 /dìqū/ *n* area, region, district 0312

地图 /dìtú/ *n* map 3667

地位 /dìwèi/ *n* status, position 0636

地下 /dìxià/ *place* underground 2138

地震 /dìzhèn/ *n* earthquake 2008

地址 /dìzhǐ/ *n* address 3441

地质 /dìzhì/ *n* geology 3088

地主 /dìzhǔ/ *n* landlord, landowner, squire; host 4378

弟弟 /dìdi/ *n* younger brother 2395

递 /dì/ *v* hand over, pass 4258

第 /dì/ *pref* [numeral prefix forming ordinal numbers] 0047

典型 /diǎnxíng/ *n* typical example, exemplar 3178

典型 /diǎnxíng/ *adj* typical 3777

点 /diǎn/ *clas* [measure word for point, item, etc.]; [measure word for small quantities] 0167

点 /diǎn/ *n* dot, point 0187

点儿 /diǎnr/ *clas* [measure word that often follows numeral 一] a little, a bit 0970

点儿 /diǎnr/ *n* point, spot, dot 4293

点头 /diǎntóu/ *v* nod 3892

电 /diàn/ *n* electricity, power; telegram, cable 0640

电报 /diànbào/ *n* telegram, telegraph, cable 4033

电话 /diànhuà/ *n* telephone, telephone call 0338

电脑 /diànnǎo/ *n* computer 1118

电视 /diànshì/ *n* television, TV 0696

电视机 /diànshìjī/ *n* television (set) 4336

电视剧 /diànshìjù/ *n* TV play 3755

电视台 /diànshìtái/ *n* television station 1825

电台 /diàntái/ *n* transmitter-receiver, transceiver; radio station 2950

电梯 /diàntī/ *n* elevator, lift, escalator 3938

电影 /diànyǐng/ *n* movie 0658

电子 /diànzǐ/ *n* electronics 1844

店 /diàn/ *n* shop, store; inn 1111

垫 /diàn/ *v* pad, fill up; pay on behalf of somebody (for future repayment) 4948

殿 /diàn/ *n* palace hall 3911

吊 /diào/ *v* hang, suspend (in the air); lift (with a rope); condole with; revoke 4716

调 /diào, tiáo/ *v* transfer, shift; adjust, turn; harmonise 1226

调查 /diàochá/ *v* investigate, look into 0770

调动 /diàodòng/ *v* transfer, shift, move; bring . . . into play 3240

掉 /diào/ *v* drop 0431

爹 /diē/ *n* dad, father 3420

跌 /diē/ *v* fall; (price) drop 3430

盯 /dīng/ *v* stare, keep an eye on 2687

顶 /dǐng/ *v* carry on one's head; go against; prop up; stand up to; retort 1641

顶 /dǐng/ *clas* [measure word for objects with a top such as hats, caps and sedan chairs] 4543

订 /dìng/ *v* book, order, reserve; draw up, conclude; subscribe; staple 2705

定 /dìng/ *v* set, fix, decide; subscribe to (newspapers and periodicals, etc.) 0591

定位 /dìngwèi/ *v* position, set on; locate 4557

丢 /diū/ *v* lose 1681

东 /dōng/ *loc* east 0734

东北 /dōngběi/ *loc* northeast 1693

东部 /dōngbù/ *loc* east, eastern part 3901

东方 /dōngfāng/ *place* east; the East 1660

东南 /dōngnán/ *loc* southeast 3934

东西 /dōngxi/ *n* stuff, thing 0208

冬 /dōng/ *time* winter 3508

冬季 /dōngjì/ *time* winter 4253

冬天 /dōngtiān/ *time* winter 2457

董事长 /dǒngshìzhǎng/ *n* chairperson of the board (of directors) 3374

懂 /dǒng/ *v* understand 0817

懂得 /dǒngde/ *v* understand 2013

动 /dòng/ *v* move; arouse; change; use 0646

动机 /dòngjī/ *n* motive, motivation 4863

动力 /dònglì/ *n* drive, motivation; power 3130

动人 /dòngrén/ *adj* moving, touching 4277

动手 /dòngshǒu/ *v* set out, start; use hand (to fight or touch) 3403

动物 /dòngwù/ *n* animal 0976

动摇 /dòngyáo/ *v* waver, shake 4445

动员 /dòngyuán/ *v* mobilise 3220

动作 /dòngzuò/ *n* movement, motion, action 1384

冻 /dòng/ *v* freeze 4099

栋 /dòng/ *clas* [measure word for houses and buildings] 4544

洞 /dòng/ *n* hole, cavity, cave 2251

都 /dōu/ *adv* all 0024

都市 /dūshì/ *n* city, metropolis 4002

斗 /dòu/ *v* fight; contend with 2123

斗争 /dòuzhēng/ *v* struggle, fight; strive for 1192

豆 /dòu/ *n* bean 4757

毒 /dú/ *n* poison; drug 2904

毒品 /dúpǐn/ *n* drug 2448

读 /dú/ *v* read 0607

读书 /dúshū/ *v* read, study; attend school 1558

读者 /dúzhě/ *n* reader 1313

独 /dú/ *adv* alone; solely, only 3592

独立 /dúlì/ *adj* independent 1691

独立 /dúlì/ *v* be independent 3096

独特 /dútè/ *adj* unique 2256

独自 /dúzì/ *adv* alone 4420

堵 /dǔ/ *v* stop up, block 3955

赌博 /dǔbó/ *v* gamble 4899

肚 /dù, dǔ/ *n* stomach, belly; tripe 4481

肚子 /dùzi/ *n* stomach, belly 2754

度 /dù/ *clas* [measure word for temperature, angle, electricity, etc.] degree; kwh 1926

度 /dù/ *n* degree (of intensity), extent; capacity; limit 3599

度 /dù/ *v* spend, pass (time) 3970

度过 /dùguò/ *v* pass, spend (time) 3287

渡 /dù/ *v* cross; pull through 4884

端 /duān/ *v* hold or carry something level 1831

短 /duǎn/ *adj* short, brief 1097

短期 /duǎnqī/ *n* short term 4872

短暂 /duǎnzàn/ *adj* short, brief, transient 4319

段 /duàn/ *clas* section, part; length (of time or distance); paragraph 0310

断 /duàn/ *v* break 1108

锻炼 /duànliàn/ *v* exercise; temper 2326

堆 /duī/ *clas* pile, heap 1852

队 /duì/ *n* team; queue 0515

队 /duì/ *clas* [measure word for a group of people arranged in a line or file] 3809

队长 /duìzhǎng/ *n* team leader, captain 2885

队伍 /duìwǔ/ *n* ranks, line, procession, parade; contingent 1171

队员 /duìyuán/ *n* team member 1714

对 /duì/ *prep* for, to, with regard to 0022

对 /duì/ *adj* right, correct; opposite (in direction) 0438

对 /duì/ *clas* pair, couple 1669

对 /duì/ *v* answer; counter; be directed at; compare; suit, agree; match 3187

对比 /duìbǐ/ *v* contrast, compare 4442

对不起 /duìbuqǐ/ *v* sorry, excuse me; let somebody down 2358

对待 /duìdài/ *v* treat 1866

对方 /duìfāng/ *n* the opposite side or party, counterpart 0501

对付 /duìfu/ *v* deal with, cope with; make do with 2875

对话 /duìhuà/ *n* dialogue 2584

对抗 /duìkàng/ *v* resist, act against, withstand 3729

对立 /duìlì/ *v* be opposed 4718

对了 /duìle/ *idiom* right, correct, that's it; by the way 3699

对手 /duìshǒu/ *n* opponent; competitor 1904

对外 /duìwài/ *adj* external, foreign 2847

对象 /duìxiàng/ *n* target, object; boy or girl friend 1271

对于 /duìyú/ *prep* regarding, as to, for, about 0359

吨 /dūn/ *clas* ton 1948

蹲 /dūn/ *v* crouch, squat 3548

顿 /dùn/ *clas* [measure word for regular meals]; [measure word for unpleasant events such as criticising, abusing, reprimanding, etc.] 2209

顿 /dùn/ *adv* suddenly, immediately 3123

顿时 /dùnshí/ *adv* suddenly; immediately, at once 3898

多 /duō/ *adj* many, much, plentiful 0055

多 /duō/ *num* many, much, numerous 0069

多久 /duōjiǔ/ *pron* how long, how often 4879

多么 /duōme/ *adv* [used in exclamations] how; [occurring in a clause of concession to indicate an unspecified high degree] however, (no matter) how 1774

多少 /duōshǎo/ *pron* how many, how much; an unspecified number or amount 0413

多数 /duōshù/ *num* most, the majority 2071

夺 /duó/ *v* seize, take by force; contend for 1996

夺取 /duóqǔ/ *v* seize, capture; strive for, win 4826

朵 /duǒ/ *clas* [measure word for flowers] 4297

躲 /duǒ/ *v* hide; dodge, avoid 2198

E

额 /é/ *n* amount, volume; forehead 3003

呃 /e/ *part* [particle used for a pause or to express wonder or admiration] er, oh 1967

恶 /è/ *adj* bad, evil, wicked; fierce 2165

恶劣 /èliè/ *adj* bad, vile, abominable 4113

饿 /è/ *v* be hungry 2475

嗯 /ēn, ńg, ňg, ǹg/ *interj* [interjection used for questioning, surprise, disapproval, or agreement] well, eh, hey, m-hm, uh-huh 0820

儿 /ér, r/ *suf* [nonsyllabic suffix for retroflection, especially in the Beijing dialect] 0182

儿女 /érnǚ/ *n* children 2977

儿童 /értóng/ *n* child, children 1066

儿子 /érzi/ *n* son 0456

而 /ér/ *conj* and, yet 0049

而且 /érqiě/ *conj* (not only . . .) but also 0185

而是 /érshì/ *conj* but, rather 0570

而言 /éryán/ *aux* [as in 就 . . . 而言] as far as . . . is concerned 1927

而已 /éryǐ/ *part* [sentence final particle, equivalent of 罢了] nothing more, that is all 2216

耳 /ěr/ *n* ear 2796

耳朵 /ěrduo/ *n* ear 2698

二 /èr/ *num* two 0080

F

发 /fā/ *v* send out, give out, distribute 0302

发表 /fābiǎo/ *v* publish, issue 0699

发布 /fābù/ *v* issue, release, announce; promulgate 3969

发出 /fāchū/ *v* send out; give out 1159

发达 /fādá/ *adj* developed, advanced; flourishing 2235

发动 /fādòng/ *v* start, launch; mobilise 2027

发挥 /fāhuī/ *v* bring into play, give play to 1045

发明 /fāmíng/ *v* invent 3612

发起 /fāqǐ/ *v* initiate, sponsor, launch 3073

发射 /fāshè/ *v* launch, fire 4352

发生 /fāshēng/ *v* happen, take place 0249

发现 /fāxiàn/ *v* find 0197

发现 /fāxiàn/ *n* finding, discovery 2727

发行 /fāxíng/ *v* publish, issue, release, distribute 2649

发言 /fāyán/ *v* make a speech, make a statement, take the floor 2003

发育 /fāyù/ *v* grow, develop (physically or mentally) 4776

发展 /fāzhǎn/ *v* develop 0109

罚 /fá/ *v* penalise, punish 3118

法 /fǎ/ *n* law; method, way, how-to 1295

法官 /fǎguān/ *n* judge 4244

法律 /fǎlǜ/ *n* law 0594

法庭 /fǎtíng/ *n* court 3605

法院 /fǎyuàn/ *n* court of law 2207

番 /fān/ *clas* [measure word for a course of actions and events]; [measure word indicating species] kind; [measure word indicating multiplication] times, -fold 1206

翻 /fān/ *v* open (a book); turn over; look through; get over, cross; translate 1105

翻译 /fānyì/ *v* translate 3476

凡 /fán/ *adv* [equivalent of 凡是] all (that meets the specified requirements); altogether 2083

凡是 /fánshì/ *adv* [equivalent of 凡] all (that meets the specified requirements) 3531

烦 /fán/ *v* be vexed or irritated; bother, pester; be tired of 4887

烦恼 /fánnǎo/ *adj* vexed, worried, upset 4908

繁华 /fánhuá/ *adj* flourishing and bustling, busy 4318

繁荣 /fánróng/ *adj* prosperous, booming 3168

反 /fǎn/ *v* oppose, combat; reverse; turn against 0494

反 /fǎn/ *adj* reverse, wrong in direction; [used as a prefix] anti-, counter- 4905

反动 /fǎndòng/ *adj* reactionary 4969

反对 /fǎnduì/ *v* oppose, object to, fight against 0818

反而 /fǎn'ér/ *adv* instead, on the contrary 1606

反复 /fǎnfù/ *adv* repeatedly, again and again 2712

反抗 /fǎnkàng/ *v* resist, revolt, rebel 3882

反省 /fǎnxǐng/ *v* reflect on; engage in introspection 4359

反响 /fǎnxiǎng/ n repercussion, echo; impact, effect 4704

反应 /fǎnyìng/ n reaction; response 1245

反映 /fǎnyìng/ v reflect, mirror; report 0939

反正 /fǎnzhèng/ adv anyway 1084

返 /fǎn/ v return, go back 4101

返回 /fǎnhuí/ v return 2988

犯 /fàn/ v commit (crime, mistake, etc.); violate, offend (rule, etc.); have a recurrence of (illness, bad habit, etc.) 1378

犯人 /fànrén/ n convict, prisoner 4856

犯罪 /fànzuì/ v commit a crime 1822

饭 /fàn/ n food, meal 0899

饭店 /fàndiàn/ n hotel, restaurant 1824

范围 /fànwéi/ n range, scope 1064

方 /fāng/ n side, party; square; direction 0393

方 /fāng/ adj square 1325

方案 /fāng'àn/ n scheme, plan 1624

方便 /fāngbiàn/ adj convenient 1582

方法 /fāngfǎ/ n method, way 0577

方面 /fāngmiàn/ n aspect, respect, side 0193

方式 /fāngshì/ n way, pattern or style of doing things 0380

方向 /fāngxiàng/ n direction 0852

方针 /fāngzhēn/ n policy, directive 1971

防 /fáng/ v prevent, guard against; defend 2801

防御 /fángyù/ v defend, guard against 3962

防止 /fángzhǐ/ v prevent 2495

房 /fáng/ n room 1031

房间 /fángjiān/ n room 1744

房屋 /fángwū/ n house 3179

房子 /fángzi/ n house 1060

仿佛 /fǎngfó/ adv as though, apparently 2615

访 /fǎng/ v visit, call on 3522

访问 /fǎngwèn/ v visit, pay a visit (to) 1485

放 /fàng/ v put, place; let go, let off; lay aside; show, play (movies, etc.) 0242

放到 /fàngdào/ v put (something at a particular place) 3558

放开 /fàngkāi/ v let go, release 4212

放弃 /fàngqì/ v give up, quit 1500

放松 /fàngsōng/ v relax; loosen 2935

放心 /fàngxīn/ v rest assured, feel relieved, set one's mind at rest 1916

飞 /fēi/ v fly 0748

飞机 /fēijī/ n airplane 0917

飞行 /fēixíng/ v fly, make a flight 4015

非 /fēi/ adj non- 0702

非 /fēi/ adv not; simply (must) 1578

非常 /fēicháng/ adv very, unusually 0217

废 /fèi/ adj waste, useless; disused, abandoned 4626

废话 /fèihuà/ n nonsense 4864

费 /fèi/ v expend; consume too much, be wasteful 1475

费 /fèi/ n fee, expense 3936

费用 /fèiyòng/ n expense, charge 2130

分 /fēn/ v divide, separate, differentiate; distribute 0395

分 /fēn/ clas minute; [Chinese monetary unit] fen; mark, score; [partitive measure for one-tenth of the whole] 0672

分别 /fēnbié/ adv respectively, separately 1146

分布 /fēnbù/ v distribute, spread 2805

分成 /fēnchéng/ v divide into 4311

分工 /fēn'gōng/ v divide up the work 4607

分开 /fēnkāi/ v separate 3488

分离 /fēnlí/ v separate, part, split 4349

分裂 /fēnliè/ v split up, break apart 3917

分配 /fēnpèi/ v assign; distribute 1688

分歧 /fēnqí/ n difference, divergence 3754

分为 /fēnwéi/ v divide into 4214

分析 /fēnxī/ v analyse 0757

分钟 /fēnzhōng/ clas minute 0796

分子 /fènzi, fēnzǐ/ n member of a class or group; numerator (in a fractional number); molecule 1684

纷纷 /fēnfēn/ adv one after another 1604

氛围 /fēnwéi/ n ambience, atmosphere, aura 3804

粉 /fěn/ n powder 3442

粉碎 /fěnsuì/ v shatter, crush, smash 4350

份 /fèn/ clas [measure word for meals, gifts, newspapers, etc.] portion, part, share 0437

奋斗 /fèndòu/ v strive, struggle 2583

愤怒 /fènnù/ adj angry, indignant 3772

丰 /fēng/ adj abundant, plentiful; good-looking 4573

丰富 /fēngfù/ adj rich, abundant, plentiful 1120

风 /fēng/ n wind 0705

风暴 /fēngbào/ n storm 3845

风格 /fēnggé/ n style 1987

风光 /fēngguāng/ n scene, scenery, view 3875

风景 /fēngjǐng/ n scenery 3045

风气 /fēngqì/ n general mood; atmosphere; common practice 4431

风险 /fēngxiǎn/ n risk 1994

封 /fēng/ clas [measure word for letters, telegrams, etc.] 0977

封闭 /fēngbì/ v close, seal off; seal 4457

封建 /fēngjiàn/ adj feudal 3658

疯 /fēng/ *adj* insane, crazy 3694

疯狂 /fēngkuáng/ *adj* crazy, mad 3982

峰 /fēng/ *n* peak 3445

逢 /féng/ *v* meet by chance 4942

讽刺 /fěngcì/ *v* satirise, ridicule 4943

奉献 /fèngxiàn/ *v* dedicate, devote, consecrate 4105

佛 /fó/ *n* Buddha 2643

否定 /fǒudìng/ *v* negate 2963

否认 /fǒurèn/ *v* deny 3077

否则 /fǒuzé/ *conj* otherwise 1319

夫 /fū/ *n* husband; manual labourer 2925

夫妇 /fūfù/ *n* a (married) couple 2355

夫妻 /fūqī/ *n* man and wife, couple 2106

夫人 /fūrén/ *n* lady; Mrs; wife 1205

扶 /fú/ *v* support or hold with hand 3188

服 /fú/ *v* take (medicine); be convinced, obey 3194

服从 /fúcóng/ *v* obey; be subordinate to 4096

服务 /fúwù/ *v* serve 0652

服务员 /fúwùyuán/ *n* attendant, waiter, waitress 4524

服装 /fúzhuāng/ *n* clothing, garment, wear 2274

浮 /fú/ *v* float 3954

符合 /fúhé/ *v* accord with, be in keeping with 1426

幅 /fú/ *clas* [measure word for pictures, paintings, calligraphies, maps and cloth, etc.) 1658

福 /fú/ *n* good fortune, happiness, blessing 2185

福利 /fúlì/ *n* welfare, benefit 3235

腐败 /fǔbài/ *n* corruption 2283

父 /fù/ *n* father 2623

父母 /fùmǔ/ *n* father and mother, parent 0685

父亲 /fùqīn/ *n* father 0452

父子 /fùzǐ/ *n* father and son 4937

付 /fù/ *v* pay; commit to 2327

付出 /fùchū/ *v* pay, give . . . as a price 2055

妇女 /fùnǚ/ *n* woman 0668

负 /fù/ *v* bear; take (responsibility); fail; lose (a match) 1559

负担 /fùdān/ *n* burden, load 2302

负责 /fùzé/ *v* be in charge of; be responsible for 0892

负责人 /fùzérén/ *n* person in charge, director 2262

附 /fù/ *v* enclose, attach 3076

附近 /fùjìn/ *loc* nearby, (in the) vicinity 1361

复 /fù/ *adv* again 4168

复杂 /fùzá/ *adj* complicated 1132

赴 /fù/ *v* leave for, go to 2337

副 /fù/ *adj* deputy, associate, vice- 0296

副 /fù/ *clas* [measure word for objects forming a set] pair, set; [measure word for one's facial expression] 3677

富 /fù/ *adj* rich, wealthy 1621

富有 /fùyǒu/ *v* be wealthy; be rich in 2914

富裕 /fùyù/ *adj* affluent, well off 3295

赋予 /fùyǔ/ *v* give, bestow, entrust 4832

覆盖 /fùgài/ *v* cover 4830

G

该 /gāi/ *pron* this, that, the mentioned 0283

该 /gāi/ *v* should, ought to 1386

改 /gǎi/ *v* change, revise, modify 0782

改变 /gǎibiàn/ *v* change, alter 0582

改革 /gǎigé/ *v* reform 0416

改进 /gǎijìn/ *v* improve 3723

改善 /gǎishàn/ *v* improve 1783

改造 /gǎizào/ *v* change, transform, reform, reclaim; remodel, convert 1526

盖 /gài/ *v* cover; build (a house); affix (a seal); surpass 1553

概括 /gàikuò/ *v* recapitulate, summarise, generalise 3854

概念 /gàiniàn/ *n* concept 1764

干 /gàn/ *v* work, do (a job) 0213

干 /gān/ *adj* dry 2144

干部 /gànbù/ *n* cadre 0498

干脆 /gāncuì/ *adj* straightforward, clear-cut 2784

干活 /gànhuó/ *v* work 4276

干净 /gānjìng/ *adj* clean 2523

干吗 /gànmá/ *pron* why, what to do; whatever for 3509

干扰 /gānrǎo/ *v* disturb 4103

干涉 /gānshè/ *v* meddle in 3645

尴尬 /gān'gà/ *adj* embarrassed, embarrassing 3659

赶 /gǎn/ *v* catch up with; drive away; rush through; try to catch (train, bus, etc.); rush for 1620

赶到 /gǎndào/ *v* rush to, arrive (in a hurry) 2464

赶紧 /gǎnjǐn/ *adv* hurriedly 2059

赶快 /gǎnkuài/ *adv* hurriedly, quickly 2993

赶上 /gǎnshàng/ *v* catch up with 3406

敢 /gǎn/ *v* dare 0428

敢于 /gǎnyú/ *v* dare, venture, be bold to 4892

感 /gǎn/ *v* feel 1047

感到 /gǎndào/ *v* feel 0445

感动 /gǎndòng/ *v* move 1826

感激 /gǎnjī/ *v* appreciate, be grateful, be obliged 4550

感觉 /gǎnjué/ *n* feeling 0446

感觉 /gǎnjué/ *v* feel 3549

感情 /gǎnqíng/ *n* feeling 0822

感染 /gǎnrǎn/ *v* infect; affect 3290

感受 /gǎnshòu/ *v* sense, feel 1203

感谢 /gǎnxiè/ *v* thank, be grateful, express gratitude 1422

刚 /gāng/ *adv* just, barely; just now 0482

刚才 /gāngcái/ *adv* just now, a moment ago 1004

刚刚 /gānggang/ *adv* just now, a short while ago; barely, just 0955

岗 /gǎng/ *n* post; sentry post; hillock, mound 4333

岗位 /gǎngwèi/ *n* post, position 2972

钢 /gāng/ *n* steel 3989

钢琴 /gāngqín/ *n* piano 4590

钢铁 /gāngtiě/ *n* steel, iron 4185

高 /gāo/ *adj* tall, high 0106

高层 /gāocéng/ *n* high level, high tier; high-rise (building) 4183

高潮 /gāocháo/ *n* high tide, upsurge; climax; orgasm 3995

高大 /gāodà/ *adj* tall; lofty 4517

高度 /gāodù/ *adv* highly 2548

高度 /gāodù/ *n* height 3128

高峰 /gāofēng/ *n* peak, summit 4586

高级 /gāojí/ *adj* high quality; high grade, advanced; senior, high level 1583

高考 /gāokǎo/ *n* college entrance examination 4089

高尚 /gāoshàng/ *adj* noble, lofty 4112

高手 /gāoshǒu/ *n* master hand, top player 3638

高兴 /gāoxìng/ *adj* happy, joyous 0585

高于 /gāoyú/ *v* be higher than, be above 3920

高原 /gāoyuán/ *n* plateau, highland 4081

高中 /gāozhōng/ *n* high school 2527

搞 /gǎo/ *v* do 0288

搞好 /gǎohǎo/ *v* do well, do a good job of 4722

稿 /gǎo/ *n* script, manuscript, contribution 2793

告 /gào/ *v* tell, make known; sue 1819

告别 /gàobié/ *v* leave, say goodbye to 3289

告诉 /gàosù/ *v* tell 0280

哥 /gē/ *n* elder brother 1961

哥哥 /gēge/ *n* elder brother 1862

胳膊 /gēbo/ *n* arm 4746

割 /gē/ *v* cut 4056

搁 /gē/ *v* place, put; put aside 3216

歌 /gē/ *n* song 1128

歌曲 /gēqǔ/ *n* song 3795

歌声 /gēshēng/ *n* singing 4381

革命 /gémìng/ *n* (political) revolution 0680

格局 /géjú/ *n* pattern, setup, layout 3878

格外 /géwài/ *adv* especially, exceptionally 3565

隔 /gé/ *v* separate; be apart; partition 2067

个 /gè/ *clas* [generalised measure word used for nouns without a specific measure term] 0008

个别 /gèbié/ *adj* very few 2827

个人 /gèrén/ *n* individual 0374

个体 /gètǐ/ *n* individual; unit 2343

个性 /gèxìng/ *n* individuality, (individual) character 2564

各 /gè/ *pron* each 0096

各种各样 /gèzhǒnggèyàng/ *idiom* various, of all kinds 3740

各自 /gèzì/ *pron* each 1746

给 /gěi/ *prep* to 0060

给 /gěi/ *v* give 0379

根 /gēn/ *clas* [measure word for long and slender objects] 1551

根 /gēn/ *n* root 2249

根本 /gēnběn/ *adv* [usually in negative sentences] at all; radically, thoroughly 0967

根本 /gēnběn/ *adj* basic, fundamental 1204

根本 /gēnběn/ *n* base, root, fundamental, core 3085

根据 /gēnjù/ *prep* according to 0549

跟 /gēn/ *prep* [indicating relationship, involvement, or comparison] with 0181

跟 /gēn/ *v* follow 0490

跟 /gēn/ *conj* and 2268

跟踪 /gēnzōng/ *v* follow one's tracks, tail 4151

更 /gèng/ *adv* [comparative degree] more 0083

更加 /gèngjiā/ *adv* more, further 0794

更是 /gèngshì/ *adv* even more, especially 4741

更为 /gèngwéi/ *adv* even more, all the more 2853

更新 /gèngxīn/ *v* update, renew 4556

工 /gōng/ *n* work, labour; industry; project 1217

工厂 /gōngchǎng/ *n* factory 1638

工程 /gōngchéng/ *n* engineering, project 0832

工程师 /gōngchéngshī/ *n* engineer 3789

工地 /gōngdì/ *n* construction site 4480

工夫 /gōngfū/ *n* time; effort; workmanship, skill; [equivalent of 功夫] kung fu, martial arts 4083

工会 /gōnghuì/ *n* trade union 4224

工具 /gōngjù/ *n* tool 2117

工人 /gōngrén/ *n* worker 0956

工商 /gōngshāng/ *n* industry and commerce 3606

工业 /gōngyè/ *n* industry 0973

工资 /gōngzī/ *n* salary, wage, pay 1312

工作 /gōngzuò/ *v* work, do a job 0098

工作 /gōngzuò/ *n* job, work 1786

公 /gōng/ *n* public; official business; father-in-law 2323

公安 /gōng'ān/ *n* police 2717

公安局 /gōng'ānjú/ *n* public security bureau, police station 3131

公布 /gōngbù/ *v* announce, publicise 2589

公共 /gōnggòng/ *adj* public 1861

公斤 /gōngjīn/ *clas* kilo, kilogram 2721

公开 /gōngkāi/ *adj* open, public 1834

公里 /gōnglǐ/ *clas* kilometre, km 0983

公路 /gōnglù/ *n* road, highway 2287

公民 /gōngmín/ *n* citizen 2381

公平 /gōngpíng/ *adj* fair 2005

公认 /gōngrèn/ *v* recognise, accept, establish 4362

公司 /gōngsī/ *n* (business) company 0162

公寓 /gōngyù/ *n* flat, apartment 4871

公元 /gōngyuán/ *n* the Christian era, AD 4376

公园 /gōngyuán/ *n* park 1998

公正 /gōngzhèng/ *adj* just, fair, impartial 2613

公众 /gōngzhòng/ *n* the public 2776

公主 /gōngzhǔ/ *n* princess 4708

功 /gōng/ *n* merit, achievement; skill 1540

功夫 /gōngfū/ *n* kung fu, martial arts; workmanship, skill 2715

功课 /gōngkè/ *n* schoolwork, homework; school subject 4649

功能 /gōngnéng/ *n* function 1453

攻 /gōng/ *v* attack; specialise in 2762

攻击 /gōngjī/ *v* attack 2049

供 /gōng, gòng/ *v* supply, offer; confess; enshrine 1951

供给 /gōngjǐ/ *v* supply 4941

供应 /gōngyìng/ *v* supply, serve (a meal) 3556

宫 /gōng/ *n* palace 1715

巩固 /gǒnggù/ *v* consolidate, strengthen 3510

共 /gòng/ *adv* all together 0721

共产党 /gòngchǎndǎng/ *n* Communist Party 1273

共和国 /gònghéguó/ *n* republic 4039

共同 /gòngtóng/ *adj* common 0733

共有 /gòngyǒu/ *v* total; share, have in common 4784

贡献 /gòngxiàn/ *n* contribution 1225

沟 /gōu/ *n* ditch, channel, trench 2344

沟通 /gōutōng/ *v* communicate 2440

狗 /gǒu/ *n* dog 1138

构成 /gòuchéng/ *v* constitute, comprise 1941

购买 /gòumǎi/ *v* buy, purchase 2331

购物 /gòuwù/ *v* do shopping 4065

够 /gòu/ *adj* enough, sufficient 0971

够 /gòu/ *v* reach 1261

估计 /gūjì/ *v* estimate 1541

姑娘 /gūniáng/ *n* girl 1046

孤 /gū/ *adj* lonely, solitary 4792

孤独 /gūdú/ *adj* lonely 3493

古 /gǔ/ *adj* ancient, old 1043

古城 /gǔchéng/ *n* ancient city 4936

古代 /gǔdài/ *time* ancient times 1492

古典 /gǔdiǎn/ *adj* classical 4074

古老 /gǔlǎo/ *adj* ancient, old, time-honoured 3016

古人 /gǔrén/ *n* ancient people 3377

谷 /gǔ/ *n* grain, cereal; valley 4047

股 /gǔ/ *clas* [measure word for a stream of strength, water, air or smell, and also for long narrow things] 1416

股东 /gǔdōng/ *n* stockholder, shareholder 4594

股份 /gǔfèn/ *n* share, stock 4707

股票 /gǔpiào/ *n* share, stock 2511

股市 /gǔshì/ *n* stock market 4139

骨 /gǔ, gú/ *n* bone 2608

骨干 /gǔgàn/ *n* backbone, mainstay 4647

骨头 /gútou/ *n* bone; moral character; bitterness 4804

鼓 /gǔ/ *v* rouse, pluck up (encourage); bulge 4150

鼓励 /gǔlì/ *v* encourage 1577

固定 /gùdìng/ *adj* fixed 3735

故 /gù/ *adv* on purpose, deliberately; pretentiously 3900

故事 /gùshì/ *n* story 0625

故乡 /gùxiāng/ *n* hometown, native place 3362

故意 /gùyì/ *adj* deliberate, intentional 2941

顾 /gù/ *v* look after, help, attend to; have consideration for 2386

顾客 /gùkè/ *n* customer 2903

顾问 /gùwèn/ *n* adviser, consultant 3416

瓜 /guā/ *n* melon 3748

刮 /guā/ *v* scrape; shave; (of wind) blow 3315

挂 /guà/ *v* hang 1083

怪 /guài/ *adj* strange 2546

怪 /guài/ *v* blame 3647

关 /guān/ *v* close, shut; turn off; concern, involve; shut in, lock up; (business) close down 1575

关 /guān/ *n* customs; barrier, obstacle; pass 1899

关闭 /guānbì/ *v* close, shut; (of business) close down 4622

关怀 /guānhuái/ *v* care for 3557

关键 /guānjiàn/ *n* key, crux 1278

关键 /guānjiàn/ *adj* key, crucial, critical 2809

关系 /guānxì/ *n* relation, relationship; connections, ties 0165

关心 /guānxīn/ *v* care for, be concerned about 0945

关于 /guānyú/ *prep* about, regarding, pertaining to 0528

关注 /guānzhù/ *v* follow (an issue) closely with interest 1033

观 /guān/ *v* watch, look at 1911

观察 /guānchá/ *v* observe 1569

观点 /guāndiǎn/ *n* point of view, viewpoint, opinion 1327

观看 /guānkàn/ *v* watch, see, view 3884

观念 /guānniàn/ *n* idea, notion, view 1034

观众 /guānzhòng/ *n* spectator, audience 0942

官 /guān/ *n* official, officer 0986

官兵 /guānbīng/ *n* officers and men (in the army) 2740

官方 /guānfāng/ *adj* official, of or from the government 4138

官员 /guānyuán/ *n* official 1408

冠军 /guànjūn/ *n* champion 1796

馆 /guǎn/ *n* [house for business or public service such as tea house, hotel, library, museum or embassy] hall, house 2469

管 /guǎn/ *v* manage, run, administer; take care (of), care about 0444

管理 /guǎnlǐ/ *v* manage 0346

贯彻 /guànchè/ *v* implement, carry out 3093

惯 /guàn/ *v* be accustomed to; be in the habit of; spoil (a child) 3964

光 /guāng/ *n* light, brightness; glory, honour 1114

光 /guāng/ *adv* only, alone 2082

光 /guāng/ *adj* used up; (of surface) smooth, polished; bare, naked 3244

光明 /guāngmíng/ *adj* bright 4073

光荣 /guāngróng/ *adj* glorious, honoured, proud 3353

广 /guǎng/ *adj* wide, broad, extensive 2768

广播 /guǎngbō/ *v* broadcast 1686

广场 /guǎngchǎng/ *n* square 2580

广大 /guǎngdà/ *adj* vast, broad, extensive 1673

广泛 /guǎngfàn/ *adj* extensive 1603

广告 /guǎnggào/ *n* advertisement, advert 1584

广阔 /guǎngkuò/ *adj* wide, broad, vast 4416

逛 /guàng/ *v* stroll 3511

归 /guī/ *v* return, go back; be in one's charge; group (together) 1601

规定 /guīdìng/ *n* regulation, stipulation, providsion 0724

规定 /guīdìng/ *v* stipulate, provide 2385

规划 /guīhuá/ *n* scheme, plan 2425

规划 /guīhuà/ *v* plan 4199

规矩 /guīju/ *n* rule, custom; manners 3368

规律 /guīlǜ/ *n* law, rule; regularity 1683

规模 /guīmó/ *n* scale, size 1407

规则 /guīzé/ *n* rule 2380

轨道 /guǐdào/ *n* orbit; track 2957

鬼 /guǐ/ *n* ghost, spook 2075

柜台 /guìtái/ *n* counter 4919

贵 /guì/ *adj* expensive 1762

贵族 /guìzú/ *n* noble, aristocrat, peer 3716

跪 /guì/ *v* kneel down, fall to one's knees 2910

滚 /gǔn/ *v* roll; fall; get away, get lost; (water) boil 4344

锅 /guō/ *n* pot, pan, wok 2118

国 /guó/ *n* country, nation 0105

国防 /guófáng/ *n* national defence 4860

国际 /guójì/ *n* international 0253

国家 /guójiā/ *n* country 0135

国民 /guómín/ *n* national, citizen 2980

国民党 /guómíndǎng/ *n* Kuomintang, nationalist party 1958

国内 /guónèi/ *place* domestic, home 0763

国外 /guówài/ *place* abroad 1516

国王 /guówáng/ *n* king 3990

国有 /guóyǒu/ *adj* state-owned 1440

果 /guǒ/ *n* fruit 3673

果然 /guǒrán/ *adv* sure enough, as expected 2614

过 /guo/ *aux* [aspect marker indicating experience] 0075

过 /guò/ *v* cross (road); spend (holiday, etc.); go beyond (time); go through; exceed 0289

过 /guò/ *adv* excessively, unduly, too 0773

过程 /guòchéng/ *n* process, course of actions 0415

过渡 /guòdù/ *n* transition, interim 4057

过分 /guòfèn/ *adj* excessive, too much 3169

过来 /guòlái/ *v* come over; manage to do something 0659

过年 /guònián/ *v* celebrate the New Year 3681

过去 /guòqù/ *time* (in the) past, before 0311

过去 /guòqu/ *v* go over, pass by; [used as verb complement in a resultative construction to indicate result] 0746

过于 /guòyú/ *adv* excessively, too much 3986

H

哈 /hā/ *interj* [interjection expressing satisfaction] ha 3495

哈 /hā/ *ono* [usually reduplicated to indicate the sound of laughing] 4338

孩子 /háizi/ *n* child, children 0149

海 /hǎi/ *n* sea 0689

海关 /hǎiguān/ *n* customs 4984

海军 /hǎijūn/ *n* navy 2861

海外 /hǎiwài/ *place* overseas 2474

海湾 /hǎiwān/ *n* gulf, bay 4387

海洋 /hǎiyáng/ *n* ocean 1872

害 /hài/ *v* do harm to; suffer from (illness); cause trouble to 2517

害怕 /hàipà/ *v* be afraid, be scared 1929

含 /hán/ v keep in mouth; contain, include 1580

含义 /hányì/ n meaning, implication 4433

寒 /hán/ adj cold 2734

寒冷 /hánlěng/ adj cold 4788

喊 /hǎn/ v call, shout, yell 1157

汗 /hàn/ n perspiration, sweat 2736

行 /háng/ clas [measure word for things arranged in a line or row] line; row 3285

行业 /hángyè/ n trade, industry, profession 1414

航空 /hángkōng/ n aviation, by air 3600

毫不 /háobù/ adv not at all 3897

毫无 /háowú/ v not have at all 2230

豪华 /háohuá/ adj luxurious 4628

好 /hǎo/ adj good, well 0028

好 /hǎo/ adv very, rather 3738

好吃 /hǎochī/ adj tasty, delicious; edible 4414

好处 /hǎochù/ n benefit, good 1936

好多 /hǎoduō/ num a good deal, a lot 2770

好好 /hǎohǎo/ adv all out, good 1595

好几 /hǎojǐ/ num several, quite a few, many a 1979

好看 /hǎokàn/ adj good-looking, beautiful 3410

好事 /hǎoshì/ n good deed; good thing; [sometimes used ironically] bad deed 2606

好像 /hǎoxiàng/ v seem, look like, look as if 0710

好奇 /hàoqí/ adj curious 4027

号 /hào/ clas [measure word for workmen]; kind, sort 0526

号 /hào/ n date; number; size 1522

号码 /hàomǎ/ n number 2886

号召 /hàozhào/ v call for 4094

喝 /hē/ v drink 0519

喝酒 /hējiǔ/ v drink (alcohol) 2708

合 /hé/ v shut; suit, agree; combine; add up to 1131

合法 /héfǎ/ adj lawful, legal 2482

合格 /hégé/ adj qualified 4366

合理 /hélǐ/ adj reasonable, rational 1442

合适 /héshì/ adj suitable 2030

合同 /hétóng/ n contract 1125

合作 /hézuò/ v cooperate, collaborate 0556

何 /hé/ pron what, how, when, where, why 1094

何况 /hékuàng/ conj let alone, needless to say; moreover, besides 3530

和 /hé/ conj and 0016

和 /hé/ prep [indicating relationship or comparison] with 0145

和平 /hépíng/ n peace 0723

和尚 /héshang/ n monk 2978

和谐 /héxié/ adj harmonious, in harmony 3435

河 /hé/ n river 1154

河流 /héliú/ n river 4861

核 /hé/ n pit, stone; nucleus 4923

核心 /héxīn/ n core 1874

盒 /hé/ n box 4698

黑 /hēi/ adj black; dark 0754

黑暗 /hēi'àn/ adj dark 3413

黑色 /hēisè/ n black 3026

嘿 /hēi/ interj hey, why 3595

嘿嘿 /hēihēi/ ono [sound of laughing] 4392

痕迹 /hénjì/ n track, trace 4379

很 /hěn/ adv very 0038

很多 /hěnduō/ num very many, a large number or amount of 0314

很快 /hěnkuài/ adv quickly, soon 1161

恨 /hèn/ v hate 1917

哼 /hng/ interj [interjection expressing disapproval] humph 2635

哼 /hēng/ v hum 3513

横 /héng, hèng/ adj horizontal; unruly 3825

衡量 /héngliáng/ v weigh; measure 4455

轰炸 /hōngzhà/ v bomb, bombard 4363

红 /hóng/ adj red; popular 0532

红旗 /hóngqí/ n red flag 4999

红色 /hóngsè/ n red 2263

洪水 /hóngshuǐ/ n flood 3230

猴子 /hóuzi/ n monkey 4468

后 /hòu/ loc behind; after, later 0067

后果 /hòuguǒ/ n consequence 2619

后悔 /hòuhuǐ/ v regret 4397

后来 /hòulái/ time afterwards 0331

后面 /hòumian/ n rear, back 1418

后期 /hòuqī/ time late stage, late period 4767

后者 /hòuzhě/ pron the latter 4764

厚 /hòu/ adj thick 2173

呼 /hū/ v exhale, breathe; shout; call 4144

呼吸 /hūxī/ v breathe 3452

忽略 /hūlüè/ v neglect, ignore 4681

忽然 /hūrán/ adv suddenly 1800

忽视 /hūshì/ v neglect, overlook 3961

胡同 /hútóng/ n lane, alley 3366

胡子 /húzi/ n beard, moustache, whiskers 4329

湖 /hú/ n lake 2182

糊涂 /hútu/ adj muddled, confused; blurred 4022

蝴蝶 /húdié/ n butterfly 4751

虎 /hǔ/ n tiger 2076

互 /hù/ adv mutually, each other 3834

互相 /hùxiāng/ adv each other 1282

户 /hù/ clas [measure word for households] 2370

户 /hù/ n family, household; door; (bank) account 3129

户口 /hùkǒu/ n household registration, registered residence 4705

护 /hù/ v protect; be partial to 4447

护士 /hùshi/ n nurse 4995

花 /huā/ v spend 0660

花 /huā/ n flower 1162

花 /huā/ adj coloured; flowery, fancy; (of eyes) blurred 3040

花钱 /huāqián/ v spend money 3388

花园 /huāyuán/ n garden 3153

华侨 /huáqiáo/ n overseas Chinese 3751

华人 /huárén/ n Chinese 2537

滑 /huá/ adj slippery, smooth; crafty 3629

化 /huà/ suf [verb suffix] -ise, -ify 1699

化 /huà/ v melt, dissolve; transform, make into 1760

化学 /huàxué/ n chemistry 2919

划 /huá, huà/ v row, paddle; scratch, strike; delimit, differentiate; assign 2229

划分 /huàfēn/ v divide 4313

画 /huà/ v draw, paint (a picture) 0996

画 /huà/ n drawing, painting 2148

画家 /huàjiā/ n painter 3176

画面 /huàmiàn/ n (picture) image; (video) frame 2891

话 /huà/ n word, talk, utterance 0125

话剧 /huàjù/ n (stage) play 4427

话题 /huàtí/ n topic, subject 1574

话语 /huàyǔ/ n what is said, words 4818

怀 /huái/ v cherish, keep in mind; be pregnant 3142

怀 /huái/ n (in) one's arms, bosom; mind 3210

怀疑 /huáiyí/ v doubt; suspect 1663

坏 /huài/ adj bad 0897

坏人 /huàirén/ n bad people, villain, evildoer 4490

坏事 /huàishì/ n bad thing, evil deed 4931

欢乐 /huānlè/ adj joyous, cheerful 3588

欢迎 /huānyíng/ v welcome 1020

还 /hái/ adv still, yet 0023

还是 /háishì/ conj or 0876

还是 /háishì/ adv still, yet; [indicating a preferred alternative] 1228

环 /huán/ n ring; link 4470

环节 /huánjié/ n link 3066

环境 /huánjìng/ n environment 0385

缓慢 /huǎnmàn/ adj slow 4841

幻想 /huànxiǎng/ n fantasy, illusion, delusion 3672

换 /huàn/ v change; exchange 0682

患 /huàn/ v suffer from, fall ill with, catch 3008

患者 /huànzhě/ n patient 2368

皇帝 /huángdì/ n emperor 1546

皇家 /huángjiā/ n royal family, imperial family 4537

黄 /huáng/ adj yellow; pornographic 1113

黄金 /huángjīn/ n gold 2719

黄色 /huángsè/ n yellow; pornography 4085

晃 /huǎng, huàng/ v dazzle; flash past; shake, jerk, sway 4717

灰 /huī/ adj grey 2973

恢复 /huīfù/ v resume, renew; recover, restore 1081

挥 /huī/ v wave, wield; scatter, disperse 4441

辉煌 /huīhuáng/ adj splendid, glorious 2749

回 /huí/ v return; reply; decline (invitation) 0218

回 /huí/ clas [measure word for actions and events] times; [measure word for old-styled Chinese novels] chapter 1249

回报 /huíbào/ v return, repay 3524

回避 /huíbì/ v evade, avoid, bypass 3519

回答 /huídá/ v reply, answer, respond 0789

回到 /huídào/ v come back, go back, return to 0957

回顾 /huígù/ v look back, review 4210

回归 /huíguī/ v return 3967

回国 /huíguó/ v return to one's country 2709

回家 /huíjiā/ v go home, come home 1070

回来 /huílái/ v return 0397

回去 /huíqù/ v return, go back 0989

回头 /huítóu/ v turn round 3379

回头 /huítóu/ adv [colloquial] later 3532

回想 /huíxiǎng/ v think back, recall, recollect 4890

回忆 /huíyì/ v recall, recollect, bring to mind 1860

汇报 /huìbào/ v report 2497

会 /huì/ v can, know how to do 0035

会 /huì/ n meeting, conference; [also as 会儿] moment 0864

会场 /huìchǎng/ n meeting place, conference site 4699

会儿 /huìr/ clas [usually following the numeral 一] a moment, a while 1140

会儿 /huìr/ time [preceded by the demonstrative pronoun 这 or 那] (at this or that) moment 4394

会见 /huìjiàn/ v meet with (somebody who is paying a visit for official business) 2496

会谈 /huìtán/ n talks 2781

会议 /huìyì/ n meeting 0400

绘画 /huìhuà/ n drawing, painting 4435

毁 /huǐ/ v destroy, ruin 2389

毁灭 /huǐmiè/ v destroy, perish 4782

婚 /hūn/ n marriage 2196

婚礼 /hūnlǐ/ n wedding 3718

婚姻 /hūnyīn/ n marriage, matrimony 1585

浑身 /húnshēn/ n all over 3470

魂 /hún/ *n* soul; spirit, mood 4380

混 /hùn/ *v* mix, confuse; muddle along 1950

混乱 /hùnluàn/ *adj* confused 2898

活 /huó/ *v* live, survive 1130

活 /huó/ *adj* living, alive; lively; movable, flexible 1920

活 /huó/ *n* work; job 1946

活动 /huódòng/ *v* move about for exercise 0291

活力 /huólì/ *n* vigour, vitality 2864

活泼 /huópō/ *adj* lively 4161

活儿 /huór/ *n* work, job 4763

活跃 /huóyuè/ *v* be active, make . . . active 4012

活跃 /huóyuè/ *adj* active, lively 4731

火 /huǒ/ *n* fire 1077

火 /huǒ/ *v* get angry, be annoyed 3915

火车 /huǒchē/ *n* train 2129

火车站 /huǒchēzhàn/ *n* railway station 4188

火山 /huǒshān/ *n* volcano 4935

伙 /huǒ/ *clas* [measure word for a crowd of people] a crowd of, a band of 4492

伙伴 /huǒbàn/ *n* partner (for an activity); pal, mate 3109

或 /huò/ *conj* or 0223

或是 /huòshì/ *conj* or 2788

或许 /huòxǔ/ *adv* perhaps 2900

或者 /huòzhě/ *conj* or 0367

货 /huò/ *n* goods 1787

货物 /huòwù/ *n* goods 3340

获 /huò/ *v* win, obtain, reap 1918

获得 /huòdé/ *v* obtain 0602

J

击 /jī/ *v* hit, strike 4213

机 /jī/ *n* machine 1466

机场 /jīchǎng/ *n* airport 1801

机构 /jīgòu/ *n* organisation, institution 0880

机关 /jīguān/ *n* organ, office 1270

机会 /jīhuì/ *n* opportunity 0405

机器 /jīqì/ *n* machine 2597

机械 /jīxiè/ *n* machinery 3173

机遇 /jīyù/ *n* opportunity, favourable circumstances 3159

机制 /jīzhì/ *n* mechanism 2120

肌肉 /jīròu/ *n* muscle 4478

鸡 /jī/ *n* chicken 1353

鸡蛋 /jīdàn/ *n* (chicken) egg 3415

积 /jī/ *v* accumulate, collect 4063

积极 /jījí/ *adj* active; positive 0872

积极性 /jījíxìng/ *n* enthusiasm, initiative, zeal 3792

积累 /jīlěi/ *v* accumulate 3189

基 /jī/ *n* base, foundation 3448

基本 /jīběn/ *adj* basic 0505

基本上 /jīběnshàng/ *adv* basically, in the main 1867

基层 /jīcéng/ *n* grassroots, basic level, lower level; base 2859

基础 /jīchǔ/ *n* base, basis 0553

基地 /jīdì/ *n* base 1739

基金 /jījīn/ *n* fund 3574

基因 /jīyīn/ *n* gene 3089

基于 /jīyú/ *prep* based on; in view of, because of 4339

激动 /jīdòng/ *adj* excited 1790

激烈 /jīliè/ *adj* intense, fierce 1763

激情 /jīqíng/ *n* enthusiasm; passion, fervour 2835

及 /jí/ *conj* and 0318

及其 /jíqí/ *conj* and (its, their) 2339

及时 /jíshí/ *adj* in time 1630

吉 /jí/ *adj* lucky 4464

级 /jí/ *clas* [measure word for levels, grades and ranks, etc.]; [measure word for stairs, and steps, etc.] 1013

级 /jí/ *n* level, rank, grade; step; degree 4326

级别 /jíbié/ *n* level, rank, scale 4236

即 /jí/ *v* is; that is 0574

即便 /jíbiàn/ *conj* even if 3328

即将 /jíjiāng/ *adv* (be) about to, soon 2422

即使 /jíshǐ/ *conj* even if 0972

极 /jí/ *adv* extremely 0610

极大 /jídà/ *adv* enormously; greatly 2363

极了 /jíle/ *adv* extremely 3894

极其 /jíqí/ *adv* extremely 2882

极为 /jíwèi/ *adv* extremely 2595

急 /jí/ *adj* anxious; annoyed; urgent; hurried 1071

疾病 /jíbìng/ *n* disease, illness 2536

集 /jí/ *v* gather, collect; centre on 2114

集 /jí/ *clas* [measure word for TV plays, movies and books, etc.] episode, part, volume 4051

集 /jí/ *n* collection, album; market, country fair; set, group 4744

集体 /jítǐ/ *n* collective 1484

集团 /jítuán/ *n* group 0866

集中 /jízhōng/ *v* concentrate, focus on 1600

集中 /jízhōng/ *adj* concentrated, focused; centralised 2524

籍 /jí/ *n* record; native place; membership; nationality 4823

几乎 /jīhū/ *adv* almost, nearly 0562

几 /jǐ/ *num* several; how much 0062

己 /jǐ/ *pron* self 2869

挤 /jǐ/ v squeeze, press, push; crowd 1995

给予 /jǐyǔ/ v give, afford 1753

计 /jì/ v count, calculate, number; haggle over 4148

计 /jì/ n idea, plan; gauge, metre 4235

计划 /jìhuá/ n plan 0575

计算 /jìsuàn/ v calculate, compute 2493

计算机 /jìsuànjī/ n computer 1765

记 /jì/ v keep in mind, memorise, remember; take note, write down 0732

记得 /jìde/ v remember 1258

记录 /jìlù/ v record, put down 2913

记录 /jìlù/ n record; (of meeting) minutes 3360

记忆 /jìyì/ n memory 1972

记载 /jìzǎi/ v record, write down 3614

记载 /jìzǎi/ n record 4332

记者 /jìzhě/ n reporter, journalist 0244

记住 /jìzhù/ v remember 2763

纪录 /jìlù/ n record 3260

纪律 /jìlǜ/ n discipline 3336

纪念 /jìniàn/ v honour the memory of, commemorate 2374

技能 /jìnéng/ n skill 4807

技巧 /jìqiǎo/ n skill, technique 3367

技术 /jìshù/ n technology 0350

季 /jì/ n season; quarter 4749

季节 /jìjié/ n season 3254

既 /jì/ conj since, now that; as well as 0491

既然 /jìrán/ conj since, now that 1405

继 /jì/ v continue, follow 4156

继承 /jìchéng/ v inherit 2477

继续 /jìxù/ v continue 0396

寂寞 /jìmò/ adj lonely 4026

寄 /jì/ v send, post; check (luggage), leave with 1467

加 /jiā/ v add, increase; put in 0686

加大 /jiādà/ v increase, enlarge 3120

加工 /jiāgōng/ v process 2279

加快 /jiākuài/ v quicken, expedite, speed up 2498

加强 /jiāqiáng/ v reinforce, intensify 0836

加入 /jiārù/ v join, become a member; add (in) 1431

加上 /jiāshàng/ v add, include 1030

加速 /jiāsù/ v accelerate; expedite, speed up 3581

加以 /jiāyǐ/ v [normally preceding a disyllabic verb to prepose the object before the verb] 2211

夹 /jiā/ v hold between, put in between; carry under one's arm; mingle, mix 3072

佳 /jiā/ adj good, excellent 3296

家 /jiā/ clas [measure word for families or businesses] 0132

家 /jiā/ n home; family, household 0215

家 /jiā/ suf [nominal suffix indicating a specialist in a particular field] -ist, -ian 1000

家伙 /jiāhuo/ n guy, fellow; tool, weapon 3024

家具 /jiājù/ n furniture 4034

家里 /jiāli/ place home 0587

家门 /jiāmén/ n gate of one's house, one's home; family 4702

家人 /jiārén/ n family member 3424

家属 /jiāshǔ/ n family member 2971

家庭 /jiātíng/ n family 0418

家乡 /jiāxiāng/ n hometown 2364

家园 /jiāyuán/ n home, homestead, homeland 4247

家长 /jiāzhǎng/ n parent; head of a family 1391

家中 /jiāzhōng/ place at home 2931

家族 /jiāzú/ n clan, family 2982

甲 /jiǎ/ n [used for the first of enumerated items] first; shell 1805

价 /jià/ n price 2001

价格 /jiàgé/ n price 1155

价钱 /jiàqián/ n price 4531

价值 /jiàzhí/ n value 0740

价值观 /jiàzhíguān/ n values, value judgement 3507

驾驶 /jiàshǐ/ v drive 4400

架 /jià/ clas [measure word for machines and instruments resting on a stand such as airplanes, pianos, cameras, etc.] 1547

架 /jià/ v put up, set up; support 3483

假 /jiǎ/ adj fake, false; artificial 1176

假如 /jiǎrú/ conj if, in the event of 2560

嫁 /jià/ v marry, take as husband 1990

尖 /jiān/ adj pointed; shrill; sharp, acute 4991

尖锐 /jiānruì/ adj sharp, penetrating, piercing 4278

坚持 /jiānchí/ v insist, persist, stick to 0692

坚定 /jiāndìng/ adj firm, steadfast 3017

坚决 /jiānjué/ adj firm, resolute, determined 1570

坚强 /jiānqiáng/ adj firm, strong 3490

间 /jiān/ clas [measure word for rooms] 0281

肩 /jiān/ n shoulder 4424

肩膀 /jiānbǎng/ n shoulder 4701

艰苦 /jiānkǔ/ adj difficult, hard 3203

艰难 /jiānnán/ adj difficult, hard 2376

兼 /jiān/ v hold (different posts) concurrently 1562

监督 /jiāndū/ v supervise, control 1563

监狱 /jiānyù/ n prison, jail 3023

捡 /jiǎn/ v pick up 3552

减 /jiǎn/ v subtract, minus; reduce, cut 2518

减轻 /jiǎnqīng/ v lighten, ease, alleviate 4395

减少 /jiǎnshǎo/ v reduce, lessen, decrease 1438

检查 /jiǎnchá/ v check up, examine, inspect 1123

检验 /jiǎnyàn/ v test, check, verify 3579

简单 /jiǎndān/ adj simple, easy 0760

简直 /jiǎnzhí/ adv simply 1654

见 /jiàn/ v see, meet 0201

见到 /jiàndào/ v see 1119

见面 /jiànmiàn/ v meet 1768

件 /jiàn/ clas [measure word for clothes, furniture, affairs, etc.] item, article 0219

建 /jiàn/ v establish; construct, build 1193

建成 /jiànchéng/ v complete, finish building 2766

建立 /jiànlì/ v establish, set up 0469

建设 /jiànshè/ v build, construct 0442

建议 /jiànyì/ n suggestion, proposal 1215

建议 /jiànyì/ v suggest, propose, advise 4671

建造 /jiànzào/ v build, construct 3616

建筑 /jiànzhù/ n architecture; building 1148

剑 /jiàn/ n sword 2417

健康 /jiànkāng/ adj healthy 0804

渐 /jiàn/ adv gradually 3206

渐渐 /jiànjiàn/ adv gradually 2307

箭 /jiàn/ n arrow 3635

江 /jiāng/ n river 3596

江湖 /jiānghú/ n rivers and lakes; the wide world; itinerant entertainer, quack 4043

将 /jiāng/ adv [indicating a future happening] will, be going to 0131

将 /jiāng/ prep [equivalent of the object preposer 把] 0202

将军 /jiāngjūn/ n (army) general 1750

将来 /jiānglái/ time future 1679

讲 /jiǎng/ v speak, tell 0183

讲话 /jiǎnghuà/ n speech, talk 1306

讲究 /jiǎngjiù/ v be careful about; strive for 3197

讲述 /jiǎngshù/ v talk about, tell 3974

讲座 /jiǎngzuò/ n lecture 4998

奖 /jiǎng/ n prize, award 1568

奖金 /jiǎngjīn/ n bonus 3255

奖励 /jiǎnglì/ v reward 4608

降 /jiàng/ v drop, fall, decline, decrease, lower 2029

降低 /jiàngdī/ v lower, reduce 2388

交 /jiāo/ v hand in, submit, deliver 1010

交 /jiāo/ n an act of falling over; friendship, acquaintance 2009

交代 /jiāodài/ v hand over; explain, make clear; confess 3555

交给 /jiāogěi/ v hand over to, give 1784

交换 /jiāohuàn/ v change, exchange 2645

交流 /jiāoliú/ v exchange, interchange 1021

交谈 /jiāotán/ v talk, converse 2824

交通 /jiāotōng/ n traffic 1320

交往 /jiāowǎng/ v associate with, consort with 1372

交易 /jiāoyì/ n deal, transaction 2794

郊区 /jiāoqū/ place suburbs, outskirts 4966

骄傲 /jiāo'ào/ adj proud; arrogant 3390

焦点 /jiāodiǎn/ n focus 2699

角 /jiǎo/ n corner; horn; angle, cape 3086

角 /jiǎo/ clas [measure term for the Chinese currency] jiao (one-tenth of yuan), ten cents 3609

角度 /jiǎodù/ n angle, viewpoint 1532

角落 /jiǎoluò/ n corner 4473

饺子 /jiǎozi/ n dumpling 4640

脚 /jiǎo/ n foot, feet; foot (of walls, mountains) 0790

脚步 /jiǎobù/ n footstep 4811

觉 /jiào, júe/ n sleep; sense 3842

叫 /jiào/ v name, call; shout; order (somebody to do something); order (meal, taxi, etc.) 0134

叫做 /jiàozuò/ v be called 2079

轿车 /jiàochē/ n car 3998

较 /jiào/ adv [preceding an adjective or adverb to form a comparison] relatively 0539

较量 /jiàoliàng/ v compete, measure up against 4829

较为 /jiàowéi/ adv relatively, comparatively, more 4169

教 /jiào/ v teach 0847

教材 /jiàocái/ n teaching materials 4916

教练 /jiàoliàn/ n coach 2816

教师 /jiàoshī/ n teacher 1088

教室 /jiàoshì/ n classroom 3902

教授 /jiàoshòu/ n professor 0711

教学 /jiàoxué/ n teaching 1884

教训 /jiàoxùn/ n lesson 2131

教育 /jiàoyù/ v educate 0270

阶层 /jiēcéng/ n social stratum 3443

阶段 /jiēduàn/ n stage 0889

阶级 /jiējí/ n (social) class 3332

皆 /jiē/ adv all 2505

接 /jiē/ v put together, join; receive, answer (call, letter, etc.); meet, pick up (somebody); extend, connect; catch (a ball, etc.) 0601

接触 /jiēchù/ v contact, expose to 1234

接待 /jiēdài/ v receive (a guest) 2664

接到 /jiēdào/ v receive, get 2932

接见 /jiējiàn/ v receive, see 4669

接近 /jiējìn/ v be close to, approach 1628

接收 /jiēshōu/ v receive 4621

接受 /jiēshòu/ v accept 0458

接下来 /jiēxiàlái/ conj after that, and then, next 4631

接着 /jiēzhe/ *adv* follow, carry on 1955

接着 /jiēzhe/ *conj* then, next 2321

街 /jiē/ *n* street 0932

街道 /jiēdào/ *n* street 2508

街头 /jiētóu/ *place* street, street corner 3546

节 /jié, jiē/ *n* festival, holiday; section, division; node, joint; critical juncture 2526

节 /jié/ *clas* [measure word for a section of things joined together such as coaches of a train and sections of a text]; [measure word for a period of class time] 3474

节目 /jiémù/ *n* programme; item of performance 0839

节日 /jiérì/ *n* holiday, festival 3701

节约 /jiéyuē/ *v* practise thrift, save 4987

节奏 /jiézòu/ *n* rhythm; tempo; pace 3876

杰出 /jiéchū/ *adj* outstanding, distinguished 3695

结 /jié, jiē/ *v* form; settle; tie, knit, knot; bear (fruit) 1535

结构 /jiégòu/ *n* structure 0709

结果 /jiéguǒ/ *n* result, outcome 0390

结果 /jiéguǒ/ *conj* as a result, consequently 1895

结合 /jiéhé/ *v* combine, integrate; be united in wedlock 1053

结婚 /jiéhūn/ *v* marry 1009

结局 /jiéjú/ *n* ending, final upshot 3752

结论 /jiélùn/ *n* conclusion 2167

结束 /jiéshù/ *v* be over, end, terminate 0624

姐 /jiě/ *n* elder sister 2383

姐姐 /jiějie/ *n* older sister 2053

姐妹 /jiěmèi/ *n* sister 3091

解 /jiě/ *v* untie, undo; explain, solve 1581

解除 /jiěchú/ *v* remove, relieve 3921

解放 /jiěfàng/ *v* liberate; emancipate 1486

解放军 /jiěfàngjūn/ *n* liberation army (specifically referring to the Chinese army known as the People's Liberation Army), the PLA; PLA soldier 2311

解决 /jiějué/ *v* solve (a problem), settle (a dispute) 0349

解释 /jiěshì/ *v* explain 0949

介绍 /jièshào/ *v* introduce 0478

介绍 /jièshào/ *n* introduction 4930

届 /jiè/ *clas* [measure word used for regular conferences, meetings, graduating classes, sports games, etc.] 0735

界 /jiè/ *suf* the circle or world of 1729

借 /jiè/ *v* borrow, lend; take advantage of, make use of 0984

借口 /jièkǒu/ *n* excuse 3802

今 /jīn/ *time* today, now 2078

今后 /jīnhòu/ *time* from now on, hereafter, in future 1364

今年 /jīnnián/ *time* this year 0518

今日 /jīnrì/ *time* today 2325

今天 /jīntiān/ *time* today 0144

今晚 /jīnwǎn/ *time* tonight 2703

斤 /jīn/ *clas* [measure term for weight in Chinese local unit] jin (half a kilo) 2169

金 /jīn/ *n* gold, golden; metal; money 0429

金额 /jīn'é/ *n* amount 4186

金牌 /jīnpái/ *n* gold medal 2097

金钱 /jīnqián/ *n* money 3506

金融 /jīnróng/ *n* finance 1906

金属 /jīnshǔ/ *n* metal 4528

仅 /jǐn/ *adv* just, only 0904

仅仅 /jǐnjǐn/ *adv* only, merely 1722

紧 /jǐn/ *adj* tight 1997

紧 /jǐn/ *adv* tightly, closely; (rain, firing, etc.) heavily 2789

紧急 /jǐnjí/ *adj* urgent 3148

紧紧 /jǐnjǐn/ *adv* tightly, closely 3080

紧密 /jǐnmì/ *adv* closely 4317

紧张 /jǐnzhāng/ *adj* nervous, strained 0855

谨慎 /jǐnshèn/ *adj* cautious, prudent 4365

尽 /jìn, jǐn/ *v* exhaust; do one's best; give priority to 0962

尽管 /jǐn'guǎn/ *conj* although, despite 0805

尽可能 /jìnkěnéng/ *adv* as far as possible 4121

尽快 /jìnkuài/ *adv* as soon as possible 2467

尽量 /jìnliàng/ *adv* as far as possible, to the greatest extent 2153

劲 /jìn/ *n* [often as 劲儿] strength; effort; drive, vigour, zeal; interest, relish 3363

劲儿 /jìnr/ *n* strength; drive, vigour, zeal 3184

近 /jìn/ *adj* near 0362

近年来 /jìnniánlái/ *time* in recent years 2540

近日 /jìnrì/ *time* recently, in the past or next few days 4054

进 /jìn/ *v* enter; advance 0190

进步 /jìnbù/ *v* make progress 1178

进程 /jìnchéng/ *n* process 1960

进攻 /jìn'gōng/ *v* attack, take the offensive 1856

进口 /jìnkǒu/ *v* import 3192

进来 /jìnlái/ *v* come in 1463

进去 /jìnqù/ *v* go in 1275

进入 /jìnrù/ *v* enter, get into 0426

进行 /jìnxíng/ *v* go on, last; be under way; carry on, carry out, perform 0170

进一步 /jìnyíbù/ *adv* further 1055

进展 /jìnzhǎn/ *v* make progress 2590

禁 /jìn, jīn/ *v* prohibit, ban; endure 3625

禁止 /jìnzhǐ/ *v* prohibit, ban 3097

京剧 /jīngjù/ *n* Beijing opera 3633

经 /jīng/ *prep* through, by means of; by way of, via 0900

经常 /jīngcháng/ *adv* often, frequently 0761

经典 /jīngdiǎn/ *n* classics 3503

经费 /jīngfèi/ *n* funding 3306

经过 /jīngguò/ *prep* through, by; via; as a result of 0530

经过 /jīngguò/ *v* pass, go through 2278

经济 /jīngjì/ *n* economy 0161

经理 /jīnglǐ/ *n* manager 1507

经历 /jīnglì/ *n* experiences 1497

经历 /jīnglì/ *v* experience, live through 1963

经验 /jīngyàn/ *n* experience 0571

经营 /jīngyíng/ *v* run a business, engage in (a business activity) 0808

惊 /jīng/ *v* surprise, shock 3058

惊人 /jīngrén/ *adj* astonishing, amazing 3866

惊讶 /jīngyà/ *adj* surprised, astonished 3865

精 /jīng/ *adj* clever, shrewd; refined; exquisite; adept, skilled 2349

精彩 /jīngcǎi/ *adj* brilliant, splendid, wonderful 2711

精力 /jīnglì/ *n* energy, vigour 2272

精神 /jīngshén/ *n* spirit, mind, mental state; essence; vigour, vitality 0316

精神 /jīngshén/ *adj* lively, vigorous, smart, cute 3776

精心 /jīngxīn/ *adv* with utmost care; meticulously 3395

井 /jǐng/ *n* well 2206

景 /jǐng/ *n* scene, sight, view 2700

景象 /jǐngxiàng/ *n* scene, sight 3399

警察 /jǐngchá/ *n* police 1137

警方 /jǐngfāng/ *n* police 4658

警告 /jǐnggào/ *v* warn 3318

净 /jìng/ *adj* clean; net 2881

净 /jìng/ *adv* all, all the time; only, merely 4633

竞赛 /jìngsài/ *n* contest, competition, race 4670

竞选 /jìngxuǎn/ *v* run for (an office) 3976

竞争 /jìngzhēng/ *v* compete, rival 1054

竟 /jìng/ *adv* [expressing unexpectedness] actually 1304

竟然 /jìngrán/ *adv* unexpectedly, actually 2102

敬 /jìng/ *v* respect; offer politely 4158

境 /jìng/ *n* border, boundary; condition, circumstance 4585

境界 /jìngjiè/ *n* realm, level or extent reached 2731

境内 /jìngnèi/ *place* within borders (of a country or province, etc.); internal, domestic 3610

静 /jìng/ *adj* quiet; still, motionless 3434

镜 /jìng/ *n* mirror; glasses 3473

镜头 /jìngtóu/ *n* (camera) lens; scene, shot (in a movie, etc.) 2834

镜子 /jìngzi/ *n* mirror 4643

纠纷 /jiūfēn/ *n* dispute 3603

纠正 /jiūzhèng/ *v* correct, rectify 3726

究竟 /jiūjìng/ *adv* [used for emphasis] actually, exactly 1413

揪 /jiū/ *v* clutch, pull 4502

九 /jiǔ/ *num* nine 0560

久 /jiǔ/ *adj* long (time); of a specified duration 1441

酒 /jiǔ/ *n* wine, alcohol 0634

酒店 /jiǔdiàn/ *n* hotel 3308

旧 /jiù/ *adj* old, used 0944

救 /jiù/ *v* save, rescue 1942

就 /jiù/ *adv* [used for emphasis] just; then; at once 0013

就 /jiù/ *conj* [as in 一 . . . 就 . . .] (no sooner . . .) than, at once 0274

就 /jiù/ *prep* regarding, as far as . . . is concerned 0292

就是 /jiùshì/ *v* [emphasising that something is precisely or exactly what is stated] be exactly 0319

就是 /jiùshì/ *conj* [as in 就是 . . . 也] even if 4844

就算 /jiùsuàn/ *conj* granted that, even if 3899

就算 /jiùsuàn/ *v* count as, regard as 4910

就要 /jiùyào/ *adv* (be) about to 1978

就业 /jiùyè/ *n* employment 2667

舅舅 /jiùjiu/ *n* (maternal) uncle 4330

居 /jū/ *v* live, reside; rank 2094

居民 /jūmín/ *n* resident, inhabitant; citizen 1898

居然 /jūrán/ *adv* [expressing surprise] unexpectedly, actually 1785

居住 /jūzhù/ *v* live, reside, inhabit 2571

局 /jú/ *n* bureau, office; state of affairs 1216

局部 /júbù/ *n* part, locality 4430

局面 /júmiàn/ *n* situation, aspect 2018

局势 /júshì/ *n* situation 3113

局长 /júzhǎng/ *n* chief of a bureau 2074

举 /jǔ/ *v* lift, raise; enumerate, give (an example) 1291

举 /jǔ/ *n* act, move 4241

举办 /jǔbàn/ *v* conduct, hold 1952

举动 /jǔdòng/ *n* act, movement, conduct, behaviour 4598

举行 /jǔxíng/ *v* hold (meeting, etc.) 0713

句 /jù/ *clas* [measure word for sentences, poems or spoken words] word, sentence 0256

巨 /jù/ *adj* huge, enormous 4791

巨大 /jùdà/ *adj* huge 0863

拒 /jù/ *v* refuse; repel, resist 4954

拒绝 /jùjué/ *v* refuse, reject, decline 1309

具 /jù/ *v* possess, have 2201

具备 /jùbèi/ *v* have, possess 2328

具体 /jùtǐ/ *adj* concrete, specific 0743

具有 /jùyǒu/ *v* possess, have 0503

俱 /jù/ *adv* all 4323

俱乐部 /jùlèbù/ *n* club 3084

据 /jù/ *prep* according to 0543

据说 /jùshuō/ *v* it is said that 2024

距离 /jùlí/ *n* distance 1447

聚 /jù/ *v* gather together 2745

聚会 /jùhuì/ *n* gathering, meeting, party 4067

聚集 /jùjí/ *v* assemble, gather 4303

捐 /juān/ *v* donate, contribute 3732

卷 /juǎn, juàn/ *clas* [measure word for things made into the shape of a cylinder] roll; [measure word for book] volume 1767

决 /jué/ *v* decide; (of a dam or dyke) burst 3291

决 /jué/ *adv* extremely, most; [usually in negative sentences] absolutely, at all 3782

决策 /juécè/ *n* policy decision; decision making 3182

决定 /juédìng/ *v* decide 0363

决定 /juédìng/ *n* decision 2270

决心 /juéxīn/ *n* determination, resolution 2815

决心 /juéxīn/ *v* pledge, resolve, be determined to 4342

决议 /juéyì/ *n* resolution, motion 3065

角色 /juésè/ *n* role, part 2098

绝 /jué/ *adv* [usually occurring in negative sentences] definitely, absolutely; extremely; by (no) means 2032

绝 /jué/ *adj* superb, matchless; uncompromising; desperate; exhausted 3491

绝不 /juébù/ *adv* never 2884

绝大多数 /juédàduōshù/ *num* vast majority 3439

绝对 /juéduì/ *adv* absolutely 1510

绝对 /juéduì/ *adj* absolute 3525

绝望 /juéwàng/ *adj* desperate 4693

觉 /jué/ *v* feel; become aware 3613

觉得 /juéde/ *v* think, feel 0166

军 /jūn/ *n* army 0517

军队 /jūnduì/ *n* army, troops 0850

军官 /jūnguān/ *n* (military) officer 3398

军人 /jūnrén/ *n* serviceman, soldier 2313

军事 /jūnshì/ *n* military affairs 0990

君 /jūn/ *n* monarch; [used as a formal title of addressing a man] Mr 2889

君子 /jūnzǐ/ *n* gentleman, man of honour 4813

均 /jūn/ *adv* all, with no exception 1520

K

咖啡 /kāfēi/ *n* coffee 3500

卡 /kǎ/ *n* card 2289

卡车 /kǎchē/ *n* truck, lorry 4466

开 /kāi/ *v* open; operate, drive (car), turn on (light); start (business); hold (meeting, party, etc.); (water) boil; write (cheque); (flower) blossom 0186

开车 /kāichē/ *v* drive (a car) 3270

开发 /kāifā/ *v* develop, open up, exploit 0925

开发区 /kāifāqū/ *n* development district 3908

开放 /kāifàng/ *v* open, open up; (flower) blossom 1032

开会 /kāihuì/ *v* have a meeting 2293

开口 /kāikǒu/ *v* open one's mouth, start to talk 4402

开门 /kāimén/ *v* open the door, open 4270

开辟 /kāipì/ *v* open up 4493

开始 /kāishǐ/ *v* begin, start 0139

开始 /kāishǐ/ *n* beginning, start 2063

开拓 /kāituò/ *v* open, open up 4567

开玩笑 /kāiwánxiào/ *v* play a joke, make fun of 3642

开学 /kāixué/ *v* the school opens, a new term begins 4976

开展 /kāizhǎn/ *v* develop, launch (a campaign), carry out 1420

刊物 /kānwù/ *n* publication, magazine, journal 4233

砍 /kǎn/ *v* chop, cut 2588

看 /kàn, kān/ *v* look, view; look after 0039

看出 /kànchū/ *v* make out, see, find 2807

看待 /kàndài/ *v* regard, view 3321

看到 /kàndào/ *v* see 0211

看法 /kànfǎ/ *n* opinion, view; unfavourable view 1338

看见 /kànjiàn/ *v* see 0859

看来 /kànlái/ *conj* it appears, it looks as if 1048

看上去 /kànshàngqù/ *v* look, appear 3688

看望 /kànwàng/ *v* call on, visit, see 4831

扛 /káng/ *v* carry on one's shoulder, shoulder 4143

抗 /kàng/ *v* resist, fight; refuse, defy 3457

抗议 /kàngyì/ *v* protest 3762

考 /kǎo/ *v* take an examination, test or quiz, test 1394

考察 /kǎochá/ *v* inspect 1682

考核 /kǎohé/ *v* examine, appraise, assess 4613

考虑 /kǎolǜ/ *v* think over, consider 0584

考上 /kǎoshàng/ *v* be admitted by examination, pass 3687

考试 /kǎoshì/ *n* examination, test, quiz 1733

考验 /kǎoyàn/ *v* try, test, put to test 3347

烤 /kǎo/ v roast, bake, toast; get warm or dry by the fire 3680

靠 /kào/ v depend upon; be due to; lean against; come up to 0470

靠 /kào/ prep by, against 4663

靠近 /kàojìn/ v be close to; draw near, approach 4404

科 /kē/ n branch of study; division, section 1827

科技 /kējì/ n science and technology 0856

科学 /kēxué/ adj scientific 0878

科学 /kēxué/ n science 1504

科学家 /kēxuéjiā/ n scientist 1925

科学院 /kēxuéyuàn/ n academy of sciences 2968

科研 /kēyán/ n (scientific) research 2396

科长 /kēzhǎng/ n section chief 4996

棵 /kē/ clas [measure word for plants] 2384

颗 /kē/ clas [measure word for small roundish objects such as grains] 1231

可 /kě/ conj but, yet 0082

可爱 /kě'ài/ adj lovely 2808

可不 /kěbu/ idiom [same as 可不是 or 可不是吗] sure enough, exactly 2675

可见 /kějiàn/ conj it can be seen 2525

可靠 /kěkào/ adj reliable 3626

可怜 /kělián/ adj pitiful, poor 3981

可能 /kěnéng/ v might (happen) 0148

可能 /kěnéng/ n possibility, chance 2753

可能性 /kěnéngxìng/ n possibility, chance 3111

可怕 /kěpà/ adj frightful, terrible 2320

可是 /kěshì/ conj but 0404

可谓 /kěwèi/ v it may well be said, so to speak 3891

可惜 /kěxī/ adj pitiful 2500

可笑 /kěxiào/ adj funny, ridiculous 4627

可以 /kěyǐ/ v may, can 0070

可以 /kěyǐ/ adj not bad, pretty good; passable 1743

渴望 /kěwàng/ v be eager to, long for 2746

克 /kè/ clas [measure term for weight] gram 4050

克服 /kèfú/ v overcome 2909

刻 /kè/ v cut, carve, inscribe 3346

刻 /kè/ clas quarter (of an hour) 3426

客 /kè/ n guest; customer 2017

客观 /kèguān/ adj objective 2612

客户 /kèhù/ n client, customer 2091

客气 /kèqì/ v be polite; be courteous; act politely; be modest 3344

客人 /kèren/ n guest 1390

客厅 /kètīng/ n sitting room, reception room 4854

课 /kè/ n class; subject, course; lesson 1608

课程 /kèchéng/ n course 3838

课堂 /kètáng/ n classroom 4428

课题 /kètí/ n research topic, (research) project 4042

肯 /kěn/ v content, agree, be willing to 1791

肯定 /kěndìng/ v be certain; affirm 1085

肯定 /kěndìng/ adv certainly, for sure 1241

肯定 /kěndìng/ adj affirmative, positive; definite, sure 4279

坑 /kēng/ n hole, pit 3177

空 /kōng, kòng/ adj empty, hollow; blank; vacant 2058

空 /kōng, kòng/ n air, sky; empty space, blank space; spare time, free time 2907

空 /kòng/ v leave empty, leave blank 4947

空白 /kòngbái/ n blank space; gap 4486

空间 /kōngjiān/ n space, room 1289

空军 /kōngjūn/ n air force 2365

空气 /kōngqì/ n air 1869

空调 /kōngtiáo/ n air conditioner 4252

空中 /kōngzhōng/ place in the air 2566

恐怖 /kǒngbù/ adj horrible, terrifying 2338

恐惧 /kǒngjù/ n fear, dread 3529

恐怕 /kǒngpà/ adv (I'm) afraid (that) 1514

控 /kòng/ v control; accuse 4361

控制 /kòngzhì/ v control 0758

口 /kǒu/ clas [measure word for people in a family or village, and also for pigs, etc.]; [measure word for tool or instrument with an edge such as a sword]; [measure word for the amount held in mouth] mouthful 0791

口 /kǒu/ n mouth, opening, entrance; cut, hole 0801

口袋 /kǒudài/ n bag, pocket 4225

口号 /kǒuhào/ n slogan 3253

口气 /kǒuqì/ n tone, manner of speaking 4288

扣 /kòu/ v button up, buckle; deduct; detain 2686

哭 /kū/ v cry, sob, weep 0980

苦 /kǔ/ adj bitter; hard (times), tough 1366

库 /kù/ n warehouse, store room, bank 3607

裤子 /kùzi/ n trousers 4641

夸 /kuā/ v praise; boast, exaggerate 4407

夸张 /kuāzhāng/ v exaggerate 4677

跨 /kuà/ v step across, stride, step forward; overarch 2531

块 /kuài/ clas [measure word for thick pieces] lump; [spoken equivalent of the Chinese currency unit 元] yuan 0307

快 /kuài/ adj fast, quick 0358

快 /kuài/ adv fast, quickly; soon 1041

快乐 /kuàilè/ adj happy 1488

快速 /kuàisù/ adv fast, at high speed, rapidly 2340

会计 /kuàijì/ n accountant; accounting 2730

宽 /kuān/ adj wide, broad; well off 1954

款 /kuǎn/ n money, fund; pattern, style 3044

狂 /kuáng/ adj mad, crazy; conceited, arrogant; unrestrained, wild 4518

矿 /kuàng/ n ore; mine 4128

亏 /kuī/ v lose money (in business); owe; treat unfairly 4315

困 /kùn/ v be sleepy; sleep; be stranded or trapped 4989

困惑 /kùnhuò/ adj perplexed, puzzled 4736

困境 /kùnjìng/ n predicament, plight, dilemma 4295

困难 /kùnnán/ adj difficult 0701

困扰 /kùnrǎo/ v perplex, puzzle, bother 4777

扩大 /kuòdà/ v enlarge, expand 1186

L

垃圾 /lājī/ n rubbish, waste, trash; junk 3335

拉 /lā/ v pull 0434

拉开 /lākāi/ v draw open; space out 2826

啦 /la/ part [sentence final particle combining 了 and 啊] 0378

来 /lái/ aux [preceding a verb to indicate the intended or suggested action] 0053

来 /lái/ v come 0063

来 /lái/ num [following a round number to indicate approximation] a bit over 3700

来不及 /láibují/ v it's too late for, there is not time for 4497

来到 /láidào/ v come to 0714

来讲 /láijiǎng/ aux [equivalent of 来说] from one's viewpoint 4300

来看 /láikàn/ v judge from 2806

来临 /láilín/ v come, arrive 4358

来说 /láishuō/ aux [equivalent of 来讲, interpreting a topic from a particular viewpoint] 0487

来往 /láiwǎng/ v come and go, travel between; contact, associate with 4264

来信 /láixìn/ n (incoming) letter 3127

来源 /láiyuán/ n source 2528

来自 /láizì/ v come from 0843

赖 /lài/ v rely, depend; go back on one's word; hold on in a place 4566

拦 /lán/ v block, stop, hold back, stand in one's way 4967

蓝 /lán/ adj blue 1968

蓝色 /lánsè/ n blue 4087

篮球 /lánqiú/ n basketball 3359

懒 /lǎn/ adj lazy 4992

烂 /làn/ adj rotten, festering; overcooked; lousy, messy 3631

狼 /láng/ n wolf 2813

浪 /làng/ n wave 2999

浪费 /làngfèi/ v waste 2760

浪漫 /làngmàn/ adj romantic 3298

捞 /lāo/ v take something out of water, fish for; gain, get (money or benefits) by improper means 3094

劳动 /láodòng/ v work; do physical labour 1175

老 /lǎo/ adj old, veteran 0147

老 /lǎo/ pref [used as an affix preceding or following the surname of a person or a numeral to indicate affection or familiarity, or to indicate the order of birth of the children in a family] 4912

老百姓 /lǎobǎixìng/ n ordinary people; civilians 1710

老板 /lǎobǎn/ n boss 1115

老大 /lǎodà/ n eldest child (in a family); number one, leader of a team 3805

老虎 /lǎohǔ/ n tiger 2887

老家 /lǎojiā/ n native place, home town 4041

老年 /lǎonián/ n old age 4651

老年人 /lǎoniánrén/ n old people, the aged 3284

老婆 /lǎopo/ n [informal] wife 2149

老人 /lǎorén/ n the aged, old people 0834

老师 /lǎoshī/ n teacher 0386

老实 /lǎoshí/ adj honest 3202

老鼠 /lǎoshǔ/ n rat, mouse 4049

老太太 /lǎotàitai/ n old lady 2252

老头 /lǎotóu/ n [disrespectful] old man, old chap 4488

老爷 /lǎoye/ n lord, master; [equivalent of 姥爷] (maternal) grandfather; something old and worn out 3447

老子 /lǎozi/ n [informal] father; [referring to the speaker to take advantage of the addressee] I, me 4291

乐 /lè/ adj happy, joyful 1728

乐 /lè/ v be amused; find pleasure in, enjoy, be happy 3515

乐观 /lèguān/ adj optimistic 3733

乐趣 /lèqù/ n joy, pleasure 4703

勒 /lēi, lè/ v tighten; strangle; rein in (the horse) 4620

雷 /léi/ n thunder; mine 3872

泪 /lèi/ n tear 2866

泪水 /lèishuǐ/ n tear, teardrop 4142

类 /lèi/ clas [measure word for a class of similar persons or things] category, kind, sort 0595

类似 /lèisì/ adj similar 2850

类型 /lèixíng/ n kind, type 2862

累 /lèi/ adj tired, weary 2234

冷 /lěng/ adj cold 1697

冷静 /lěngjìng/ adj calm 3103

厘米 /lǐmǐ/ *clas* [measure term for length]
　　centimetre, cm 4437

离 /lí/ *v* leave, be away 0698

离婚 /líhūn/ *v* divorce 2070

离开 /líkāi/ *v* leave, depart 0665

礼 /lǐ/ *n* gift; courtesy; ceremony 2037

礼貌 /lǐmào/ *n* politeness, courtesy; manner 3744

礼物 /lǐwù/ *n* gift, present 3566

里 /lǐ/ *loc* in, inside 0059

里 /lǐ/ *clas* [measure word for distance in Chinese
　　local unit] li (0.5 km) 1331

里边 /lǐbian/ *loc* inside, within 3496

里面 /lǐmian/ *loc* inside, in 0931

里头 /lǐtou/ *loc* inside 3835

理 /lǐ/ *n* reason; natural science (in relation to
　　humanities) 1973

理 /lǐ/ *v* pay attention to; put in order 2462

理解 /lǐjiě/ *v* understand, apprehend 0626

理论 /lǐlùn/ *n* theory 0679

理念 /lǐniàn/ *n* idea, philosophy 4251

理想 /lǐxiǎng/ *adj* ideal, desirable 1944

理想 /lǐxiǎng/ *n* ideal, dream 2309

理性 /lǐxìng/ *n* reason 3343

理由 /lǐyóu/ *n* reason 1450

力 /lì/ *n* power, strength 1062

力度 /lìdù/ *n* dynamism, vigour, strength 3400

力量 /lìliàng/ *n* strength, power 0605

力气 /lìqì/ *n* strength 3396

历程 /lìchéng/ *n* course, process 3945

历史 /lìshǐ/ *n* history 0214

厉害 /lìhài/ *adj* intense, severe; harsh, stern; fierce,
　　terrible 2057

立 /lì/ *v* stand; erect, set up; establish 1057

立 /lì/ *adv* immediately, instantly 4846

立场 /lìchǎng/ *n* stand, position 1730

立即 /lìjí/ *adv* immediately 0916

立刻 /lìkè/ *adv* at once, immediately 2145

利 /lì/ *n* advantage; benefit, profit, gain 1294

利润 /lìrùn/ *n* profit 2552

利益 /lìyì/ *n* benefit 0599

利用 /lìyòng/ *v* make use of, exploit 0725

例 /lì/ *n* example, case 3046

例如 /lìrú/ *v* take . . . for example 2871

例外 /lìwài/ *n* exception 4597

例子 /lìzi/ *n* example, case 2424

俩 /liǎ/ *num* the two of, both 0951

连 /lián/ *prep* [as in 连 . . . 都(也) . . .] even 0365

连 /lián/ *adv* continuously, repeatedly 1458

连 /lián/ *v* join, link, connect 2585

连接 /liánjiē/ *v* connect, join, link 4553

连续 /liánxù/ *adv* continuously, in succession 1923

联 /lián/ *v* ally, join 2767

联邦 /liánbāng/ *n* federation, commonwealth 3342

联合 /liánhé/ *v* join forces, unite, band together;
　　combine 1552

联络 /liánluò/ *v* get or keep in contact or liaison 3221

联系 /liánxì/ *v* contact, get in touch 0750

脸 /liǎn/ *n* face, cheek 0545

脸色 /liǎnsè/ *n* complexion, look; facial expression
　　4132

练 /liàn/ *v* practise 1858

练习 /liànxí/ *v* practise 3853

恋 /liàn/ *v* love, feel attached to 2520

恋爱 /liàn'ài/ *v* love, be in love 2427

良 /liáng/ *adj* good 3357

良好 /liánghǎo/ *adj* good 1380

良心 /liángxīn/ *n* conscience 4250

粮 /liáng/ *n* grain; food 2929

粮食 /liángshí/ *n* foodstuff, grain, cereals 1311

两 /liǎng/ *num* two 0033

两者 /liǎngzhě/ *pron* the two, both 4438

亮 /liàng/ *adj* bright, light; enlightened 2694

亮 /liàng/ *v* get light, show, reveal; shine; lift (one's
　　voice) 2839

辆 /liàng/ *clas* [measure word for vehicles] 0924

量 /liàng/ *n* quantity, amount, capacity 1307

聊 /liáo/ *v* chat 2492

聊天 /liáotiān/ *v* chat 3143

了 /le/ *aux* [aspect marker indicating realisation of a
　　situation] 0005

了 /le/ *part* [sentence final particle indicating change
　　of state or current relevance] 0019

了 /liǎo/ *v* finish, settle; [occurring in the structure of
　　verb + 得/不 + 了 to express possibility] 1412

了不起 /liǎobuqǐ/ *adj* amazing, terrific 4162

了解 /liǎojiě/ *v* get to know, understand 0371

料 /liào/ *n* material; (animal) feed 3232

列 /liè/ *v* list, itemise 2522

列车 /lièchē/ *n* train 3280

列入 /lièrù/ *v* put in on a list, include 4355

列为 /lièwéi/ *v* be classified as, be rated as 4953

邻居 /línjū/ *n* neighbour 3333

林 /lín/ *n* woods, forest 0788

临 /lín/ *v* face, overlook; be present; be about to 2800

临时 /línshí/ *adj* temporary 3977

临时 /línshí/ *adv* temporarily, for the time being 4370

灵 /líng/ *adj* effective; quick-minded 2204

灵魂 /línghún/ *n* soul 2563

灵活 /línghuó/ *adj* flexible, elastic 3630

岭 /líng/ *n* ridge; mountain range 4652

凌晨 /língchén/ *time* early morning before dawn, small hours 3116

陵 /líng/ *n* hill, mound; tomb 4483

零 /líng/ *num* zero 2713

领 /lǐng/ *v* lead 1747

领导 /lǐngdǎo/ *n* leader, leadship 0334

领导人 /lǐngdǎorén/ *n* leader 1668

领土 /lǐngtǔ/ *n* territory 3747

领袖 /lǐngxiù/ *n* leader 3463

领域 /lǐngyù/ *n* domain, area, field 1173

令 /lìng/ *v* order, command; cause, make 0527

令 /lìng/ *n* order, command, decree 4814

另 /lìng/ *adj* other, another 0425

另 /lìng/ *adv* in addition; separately 3170

另外 /lìngwài/ *conj* in addition, by the way 0908

另外 /lìngwài/ *adj* another, other, extra 2371

另一方面 /lìng yìfāngmiàn/ *conj* on the other hand 2593

流 /liú/ *v* flow 1284

流 /liú/ *n* flow, stream of water or air, current 3126

流传 /liúchuán/ *v* spread, circulate, pass down 4014

流动 /liúdòng/ *v* flow, surge 2987

流氓 /liúmáng/ *n* rogue, hoodlum, rascal, gangster 4377

流行 /liúxíng/ *v* be in fashion, prevail; spread 2429

流血 /liúxuè/ *v* bleed, shed blood 4687

流域 /liúyù/ *n* river basin, valley 3502

留 /liú/ *v* remain, stay; reserve, save for future use; leave behind 0676

留给 /liúgěi/ *v* leave, set aside for 3650

留下 /liúxià/ *v* leave behind, remain 0999

留学 /liúxué/ *v* study abroad 3554

留学生 /liúxuéshēng/ *n* overseas student, returned student 4423

柳 /liǔ/ *n* willow 2625

六 /liù/ *num* six 0332

龙 /lóng/ *n* dragon 0918

楼 /lóu/ *n* building 0603

漏 /lòu/ *v* leak; be missing 4673

露 /lù, lòu/ *v* show, reveal 2877

露出 /lùchū/ *v* show, reveal 3061

陆 /lù/ *n* land 2979

陆军 /lùjūn/ *n* army, land force 4924

陆续 /lùxù/ *adv* in turn, successively 3632

录 /lù/ *v* record 4495

路 /lù/ *n* road; distance 0297

路 /lù/ *clas* [measure word for groups of people] route 3641

路边 /lùbiān/ *place* roadside 4667

路线 /lùxiàn/ *n* route, line; itinerary 2086

驴 /lǘ/ *n* donkey 4529

旅 /lǚ/ *n* trip 3764

旅馆 /lǚguǎn/ *n* guesthouse, hotel 3839

旅客 /lǚkè/ *n* passenger 3464

旅行 /lǚxíng/ *v* travel 3812

旅游 /lǚyóu/ *v* travel, take a tour, go sightseeing 1403

履行 /lǚxíng/ *v* fulfil 3409

律师 /lùshī/ *n* lawyer 2426

绿 /lù/ *adj* green 1536

绿色 /lùsè/ *n* green; (of food) organic 2778

乱 /luàn/ *adv* at random, arbitrarily, disorderly 1232

乱 /luàn/ *adj* messy, in disorder; confused 1544

略 /lüè/ *adv* slightly; briefly 2830

伦理 /lúnlǐ/ *n* ethics, moral principles 4877

轮 /lún/ *clas* round (of competitions and talks, etc.); [measure word for the sun and the full moon] 1758

轮 /lún/ *v* take turns 4307

论 /lùn/ *v* discuss, talk about, expound; decide on 2294

论 /lùn/ *n* theory; view, opinion 3749

论坛 /lùntán/ *n* forum, tribune 3370

论文 /lùnwén/ *n* paper, dissertation, thesis 2562

逻辑 /luóji/ *n* logic 3305

骆驼 /luòtuó/ *n* camel 3873

落 /luò/ *v* fall, drop; lower; fall behind 0775

落后 /luòhòu/ *adj* backward, outdated, behind the times 2174

落实 /luòshí/ *v* implement, fulfil 2479

M

妈 /mā/ *n* ma, mum 0674

妈妈 /māma/ *n* mama, mum 0573

麻烦 /máfán/ *adj* troublesome 1649

马 /mǎ/ *n* horse 1008

马路 /mǎlù/ *n* road, highway 3043

马上 /mǎshàng/ *adv* at once, immediately 1780

码头 /mǎtóu/ *n* harbour, dock, wharf, pier 4176

蚂蚁 /mǎyǐ/ *n* ant 4600

骂 /mà/ *v* scold, tell off; call names, curse; condemn 1266

吗 /ma/ *part* [question tag] 0116

嘛 /ma/ *part* [sentence final modal particle indicating that something is obvious or expressing a hope, advice, etc.] 0531

埋 /mái/ *v* cover up, bury 2644

买 /mǎi/ *v* buy 0266

买卖 /mǎimài/ *n* buying and selling, (business) transaction, deal 2878

迈 /mài/ *v* stride, take a step 4770

麦 /mài/ *n* wheat 4656

卖 /mài/ *v* sell 0497

满 /mǎn/ *adj* full 0495

满意 /mǎnyì/ *adj* satisfied, satisfactory 1260

满足 /mǎnzú/ *v* satisfy 1351

满足 /mǎnzú/ *adj* satisfied 4737

慢 /màn/ *adj* slow 1793

慢慢 /mànman/ *adv* slowly 1277

漫长 /màncháng/ *adj* very long, endless 3927

忙 /máng/ *adj* busy 0860

盲目 /mángmù/ *adj* blind 3827

猫 /māo/ *n* cat 2000

毛 /máo/ *clas* [measure term for the Chinese currency, less formal than 角] mao (one-tenth of yuan), ten cents 2454

毛病 /máobìng/ *n* fault, shortcoming, defect; ailment, illness 2737

矛盾 /máodùn/ *adj* contradictory 0933

冒 /mào/ *v* emit, give off; risk, brave 2171

贸易 /màoyì/ *n* trade 1233

帽 /mào/ *n* hat, cap 4812

帽子 /màozi/ *n* hat, cap; label 3172

貌 /mào/ *n* appearance, look 4878

么 /me/ *part* [interrogative particle] 1966

没 /méi/ *adv* not 0118

没 /méi/ *v* have not, there be not 0191

没法 /méifǎ/ *v* cannot, have no choice 4372

没关系 /méiguānxi/ *idiom* it doesn't matter, it's all right, never mind 4123

没什么 /méishénme/ *idiom* [idiomatic expression] nothing serious, it's nothing, it's all right 1956

没事 /méishì/ *v* be free; it's nothing, it's all right 3325

没有 /méiyǒu/ *v* have not, there be not 0074

没有 /méiyǒu/ *adv* not 0107

枚 /méi/ *clas* [measure word for small objects such as medals, badges, stamps, and also for round-shaped objects like missiles] 1939

眉 /méi/ *n* eyebrow 4239

媒体 /méitǐ/ *n* media 1975

煤 /méi/ *n* coal 3397

每 /měi/ *pron* each 0159

每 /měi/ *adv* every time, on each occasion 4911

每当 /měidāng/ *prep* whenever, every time 4189

每年 /měinián/ *time* every year 1063

每天 /měitiān/ *time* every day 0596

美 /měi/ *adj* beautiful, pretty 1461

美好 /měihǎo/ *adj* happy, glorious, good, beautiful 1457

美丽 /měilì/ *adj* beautiful 1220

美女 /měinǚ/ *n* beauty 2888

美术 /měishù/ *n* art, fine arts, painting 4084

美元 /měiyuán/ *n* US dollar 0941

妹妹 /mèimei/ *n* younger sister 2166

魅力 /mèilì/ *n* charm 2510

门 /mén/ *n* door, gate 0473

门 /mén/ *clas* [measure word for subjects of study]; [measure word for cannons] 2136

门口 /ménkǒu/ *place* doorway, gate 1789

门前 /ménqián/ *place* in front of the door or gate 3721

门外 /ménwài/ *place* outside the door 3952

们 /men/ *suf* [plural marker for pronouns and some animate nouns] 0111

猛 /měng/ *adj* ferocious, hard 4571

猛 /měng/ *adv* suddenly, abruptly; vigorously, fiercely 4635

蒙 /mēng, méng/ *v* deceive, take in; be shocked; make a wild guess; cover 3193

梦 /mèng/ *n* dream 0756

梦想 /mèngxiǎng/ *n* dream, dream hope; vain hope 3256

弥补 /míbǔ/ *v* make up, compensate, remedy 4618

迷 /mí/ *v* bewilder, confuse; be fascinated by 3455

迷信 /míxìn/ *v* have blind faith in 3890

谜 /mí/ *n* puzzle, mystery; riddle 4389

米 /mǐ/ *clas* [standard measure term] metre 0460

米 /mǐ/ *n* rice 1828

秘密 /mìmì/ *n* secret 2857

秘密 /mìmì/ *adj* secret 2991

秘书 /mìshū/ *n* secretary 2729

密 /mì/ *adj* thick, dense; close, intimate; secret 2786

密切 /mìqiè/ *adj* close 2282

棉 /mián/ *n* cotton 4868

棉花 /miánhuā/ *n* cotton 4745

免 /miǎn/ *v* excuse from, waive, exempt; dismiss; avoid 3767

免费 /miǎnfèi/ *adj* free, free of charge 3561

面 /miàn/ *n* face, surface; side; (wheat) flour 0459

面 /miàn/ *clas* [measure word for something with a flat surface such as a mirror and flag] 1473

面包 /miànbāo/ *n* bread 4639

面对 /miànduì/ *v* face, confront 0681

面积 /miànjī/ *n* (surface) area 1702

面孔 /miànkǒng/ *n* face 4131

面临 /miànlín/ *v* face, be faced with 1602

面貌 /miànmào/ *n* appearance, feature; outlook, look 3462

面前 /miànqián/ *loc* before, in front of 0873

面向 /miànxiàng/ *v* face 4152

面子 /miànzi/ *n* face, reputation; sensibilities 3185

描绘 /miáohuì/ *v* depict, portray 4955

描述 /miáoshù/ *v* describe, depict 3432

描写 /miáoxiě/ *v* describe, portray 3191

妙 /miào/ *adj* wonderful 4364

庙 /miào/ *n* temple 3108

灭 /miè/ *v* (of fire, light) go off; extinguish, put out, wipe out 3237

民 /mín/ *n* the people; civilian 1168

民间 /mínjiān/ *n* among the people, folk 1716

民警 /mínjǐng/ *n* (civilian) police 4661

民众 /mínzhòng/ *n* populace, people 3446

民主 /mínzhǔ/ *adj* democratic 1397

民族 /mínzú/ *n* nationality 0410

敏感 /mǐn'gǎn/ *adj* sensitive 2751

名 /míng/ *clas* [measure word for persons in general] 0192

名 /míng/ *adj* famous, renowned 1894

名 /míng/ *n* name; fame 4525

名称 /míngchēng/ *n* name 3312

名单 /míngdān/ *n* (name) list 3719

名叫 /míngjiào/ *v* be called 2938

名牌 /míngpái/ *n* famous brand or make 3944

名片 /míngpiàn/ *n* (business) card 4869

名气 /míngqì/ *n* fame, reputation 4710

名人 /míngrén/ *n* celebrity 4249

名义 /míngyì/ *n* name 3158

名字 /míngzì/ *n* name 0921

明 /míng/ *adj* bright, light, clear; open, overt, explicit 0936

明白 /míngbái/ *v* realise, understand 0697

明白 /míngbái/ *adj* clear, explicit; sensible 3224

明明 /míngmíng/ *adv* clearly, obviously, undoubtedly 4119

明年 /míngnián/ *time* next year 2402

明确 /míngquè/ *adj* clear-cut, explicit, unequivocal 1329

明确 /míngquè/ *v* make clear, clarify 5002

明天 /míngtiān/ *time* tomorrow 1019

明显 /míngxiǎn/ *adj* obvious, notable, clear 0993

明星 /míngxīng/ *n* star 2683

命 /mìng/ *n* life; fate, destiny; order 1814

命 /mìng/ *v* command, order 3200

命令 /mìnglìng/ *n* order, command 1701

命名 /mìngmíng/ *v* name 4728

命运 /mìngyùn/ *n* fate 1360

摸 /mō/ *v* touch, feel with the hand 1792

模糊 /móhu/ *adj* vague, faint, blurred 4115

模式 /móshì/ *n* mode, pattern; way 1594

模特 /mótè/ *n* [often taking the suffix 儿] model 4819

模样 /múyàng/ *n* appearance, look; [used to indicate approximation] about 3466

摩托车 /mótuōchē/ *n* motorcycle, motorbike 4086

磨 /mó/ *v* wear; rub; grind, polish; pester; dawdle 3916

抹 /mǒ/ *v* smear, spread; wipe; erase 4503

末 /mò/ *n* end, tip; minor details; powder 1508

陌生 /mòshēng/ *adj* strange, unfamiliar 3246

莫 /mò/ *adv* not, do not 2769

墨 /mò/ *n* ink, China ink, ink stick 4229

谋 /móu/ *v* seek; consult; plan 4356

某 /mǒu/ *pron* some, certain 0480

某些 /mǒuxiē/ *pron* some, certain 1731

母 /mǔ/ *n* mother, parent 3361

母 /mǔ/ *adj* female 3590

母亲 /mǔqīn/ *n* mother 0483

亩 /mǔ/ *clas* [measure term for area of land in Chinese local unit] mu (equal to 0.165 acres) 2228

木 /mù/ *n* wood 2470

目 /mù/ *n* eye; list 2818

目标 /mùbiāo/ *n* target, goal 0619

目的 /mùdì/ *n* purpose, aim, end 0728

目光 /mùguāng/ *n* sight, vision; gaze 2002

目前 /mùqián/ *time* currently, at the present time 0422

墓 /mù/ *n* tomb, grave 3601

幕 /mù/ *clas* [measure word for plays] act; scene 3449

N

拿 /ná/ *v* hold; take 0194

哪 /nǎ/ *pron* what, which, where, how 0464

哪 /na/ *part* [sentence final particle similar to 啊, following words ending with the consonant n] 1529

哪儿 /nǎr/ *pron* where 1100

哪个 /nǎge/ *pron* which 1778

哪里 /nǎli/ *pron* where; wherever; [often used (in repetition) as a modest reply to a compliment]; [used in a rhetorical question for negation] 1014

哪怕 /nǎpà/ *conj* even if, even though 3248

哪些 /nǎxiē/ *pron* which, what 2722

呐 /na/ *part* [sentence final particle, especially following words ending with the consonant n] 3690

内 /nèi/ *loc* inside, within 0235

内部 /nèibù/ *loc* inside, within 1428

内地 /nèidì/ *place* inland 2702

内阁 /nèigé/ *n* cabinet 4591

内涵 /nèihán/ *n* meaning, connotation 4006

内容 /nèiróng/ *n* content 0488

内外 /nèiwài/ *loc* inside and outside; home and abroad 2550

内心 /nèixīn/ *n* heart 1815

那 /nà/ *pron* that 0037

那 /nà/ *conj* then, in that case 1373

那边 /nàbian/ *pron* there 1806

那儿 /nàr/ *pron* there 0987

那个 /nèige/ *pron* that one 0220

那里 /nàli/ *pron* there 0561

那么 /nàme/ *pron* so, that; in that way 0195

那么 /nàme/ *conj* then 0745

那时 /nàshí/ *pron* at that time 1018

那天 /nàtiān/ *pron* that day 1401

那些 /nàxiē/ *pron* those 0295

那样 /nàyàng/ *pron* like that, in that way 0506

乃 /nǎi/ *v* be 4686

乃至 /nǎizhì/ *conj* even 3327

奶 /nǎi/ *n* milk; breast 3419

奶奶 /nǎinai/ *n* (paternal) grandmother 2105

耐 /nài/ *v* endure 4501

耐心 /nàixīn/ *adj* patient 3526

男 /nán/ *adj* male, man 0468

男孩 /nánhái/ *n* boy 2438

男朋友 /nánpéngyou/ *n* boyfriend 4875

男人 /nánrén/ *n* man 0513

男性 /nánxìng/ *n* male 2346

男子 /nánzǐ/ *n* man, male 1344

南 /nán/ *loc* south 1521

南北 /nánběi/ *loc* north and south, from south to north 4030

南部 /nánbù/ *loc* southern part, south 3358

南方 /nánfāng/ *place* south 3115

难 /nán/ *adj* difficult 0272

难道 /nándào/ *adv* [used to reinforce a rhetorical question] 1605

难得 /nándé/ *adj* rare 2696

难度 /nándù/ *n* (degree of) difficulty 3848

难怪 /nán'guài/ *adv* no wonder 4739

难免 /nánmiǎn/ *v* it is hard to avoid 4514

难受 /nánshòu/ *adj* unwell; unhappy 4025

难题 /nántí/ *n* difficult problem 3365

难以 /nányǐ/ *adv* hard to, difficult to; hardly 1305

脑 /nǎo/ *n* brain, head 2023

脑袋 /nǎodài/ *n* head 2411

脑子 /nǎozi/ *n* brain, mind 2410

闹 /nào/ *v* make noise or disturbance; give vent to (anger, etc.); be troubled with; go in for 1452

呢 /ne/ *part* [particle used at the end of a question or declarative sentence to indicate mood] 0089

能 /néng/ *v* can 0031

能否 /néngfǒu/ *v* whether or not one can 2940

能够 /nénggòu/ *v* be able to, be capable of 0330

能力 /nénglì/ *n* ability, capability 0403

能量 /néngliàng/ *n* energy 3444

能源 /néngyuán/ *n* energy 3597

泥 /ní/ *n* mud 2598

你 /nǐ/ *pron* you 0018

你好 /nǐhǎo/ *idiom* hello 3741

你们 /nǐmen/ *pron* [plural] you 0179

年 /nián/ *n* year 0048

年 /nián/ *clas* year 1049

年代 /niándài/ *n* a decade of a century; years, time 0462

年底 /niándǐ/ *time* the end of the year 3811

年度 /niándù/ *n* year 3846

年级 /niánjí/ *n* grade, year 2486

年纪 /niánjì/ *n* age 2637

年龄 /niánlíng/ *n* age 1383

年轻 /niánqīng/ *adj* young 0687

年轻人 /niánqīngrén/ *n* young people 1626

年头 /niántóu/ *n* year; days, times; long time 4761

念 /niàn/ *v* read aloud; think of, miss; attend school 1443

念头 /niàntou/ *n* thought, idea 3910

娘 /niáng/ *n* mother, mum 2414

鸟 /niǎo/ *n* bird 1813

尿 /niào/ *n* urine, pee 4388

捏 /niē/ *v* pinch, squeeze; knead; make up 4406

您 /nín/ *pron* [honorific, no plural form] you 0209

宁 /nìng/ *adv* (would) rather 4697

牛 /niú/ *adj* [a popular compliment among young people] great, excellent, matchless 1773

牛 /niú/ *n* ox, cow, cattle; beef 2217

牛奶 /niúnǎi/ *n* milk 4983

扭 /niǔ/ *v* turn around; twist; strain 4444

农 /nóng/ *n* agriculture, farming 3639

农场 /nóngchǎng/ *n* farm 2975

农村 /nóngcūn/ *n* countryside, rural area 0715

农民 /nóngmín/ *n* peasant, farmer 0509

农业 /nóngyè/ *n* agriculture 0831

浓 /nóng/ *adj* thick, dense; strong 3564

弄 /nòng/ *v* play with; do, get (ready) 0716

努力 /nǔlì/ *v* strive to, try one's best to; make efforts to 0472

怒 /nù/ *adj* angry, indignant 4019
女 /nǚ/ *adj* female, woman 0184
女儿 /nǚ'ér/ *n* daughter 0727
女孩 /nǚhái/ *n* girl 1242
女孩子 /nǚháizi/ *n* girl 2795
女人 /nǚrén/ *n* woman 0496
女生 /nǚshēng/ *n* girl student 4487
女士 /nǚshì/ *n* lady 1870
女性 /nǚxìng/ *n* female, woman 0862
女子 /nǚzǐ/ *n* woman 1040
暖 /nuǎn/ *adj* warm 3864

O

噢 /ō/ *interj* [interjection expressing mental realisation] oh 2855
哦 /ò/ *interj* [interjection expressing realisation] ah 1675
偶尔 /ǒu'ěr/ *adv* occasionally 3931
偶然 /ǒurán/ *adv* incidentally, by chance; occasionally 3355

P

趴 /pā/ *v* to lie on one's stomach; bend over 4889
爬 /pá/ *v* crawl; climb 1661
怕 /pà/ *v* be afraid, fear 0453
拍 /pāi/ *v* clap, pat, strike; take (a picture), shoot (a film) 0837
拍摄 /pāishè/ *v* take (a picture), shoot (a film) 2610
排 /pái/ *v* arrange, line, put in order; exclude, discharge 1285
排 /pái/ *clas* [measure word for a line of persons or things] a line of, a row of 4436
排除 /páichú/ *v* exclude; remove, clear away 4273
排名 /páimíng/ *v* rank 4616
牌 /pái/ *n* cards; brand; (number) plate 1400
牌子 /páizi/ *n* sign, plate; brand 4228
派 /pài/ *v* send, dispatch 0769
派 /pài/ *n* side, faction, group, school 3742
派出 /pàichū/ *v* send 3972
派出所 /pàichūsuǒ/ *n* local police station 3847
盘 /pán/ *clas* [measure word for food contained in a plate]; [measure word for objects of shallow, and usually circular, almost flat shape such as tapes] coil; [measure word for a game of chess, etc.] 2046
盘 /pán/ *n* plate, dish; tray; (chess) board 2948
判 /pàn/ *v* sentence; judge 3242
判断 /pànduàn/ *v* judge 2609
判决 /pànjué/ *v* pass verdict, pronounce, judge 4678
盼 /pàn/ *v* expect, long for, look forward to 3761

庞大 /pángdà/ *adj* enormous, huge 3896
旁 /páng/ *loc* beside, by 1593
旁边 /pángbiān/ *loc* side 1572
胖 /pàng/ *adj* fat, stout, obese 3771
抛 /pāo/ *v* throw, toss, fling; leave behind 3580
抛弃 /pāoqì/ *v* discard, abandon 4506
炮 /pào/ *n* cannon, gun; firecracker 3634
跑 /pǎo/ *v* run 0399
泡 /pào/ *v* steep, soak; dawdle 3484
陪 /péi/ *v* accompany, escort 1877
培训 /péixùn/ *v* train 1890
培养 /péiyǎng/ *v* train, foster, rear, develop, cultivate 0907
赔 /péi/ *v* compensate, make good (one's loss); lose in business, sustain a loss 3577
赔偿 /péicháng/ *v* compensate 4202
佩服 /pèifú/ *v* admire 4204
配 /pèi/ *v* match; deserve; fit; mix; join 1931
配合 /pèihé/ *v* coordinate, cooperate 1876
喷 /pēn/ *v* spurt, squirt, spray, sprinkle 3959
盆 /pén/ *n* basin, tub; pot, bowl 4576
朋友 /péngyou/ *n* friend 0303
膨胀 /péngzhàng/ *v* expand, inflate 4305
捧 /pěng/ *v* hold (in both hands); give somebody a boost 2843
碰 /pèng/ *v* touch 2663
碰到 /pèngdào/ *v* come across, meet with 2573
碰上 /pèngshàng/ *v* run into, come across 4509
批 /pī/ *clas* batch, lot, group 0613
批判 /pīpàn/ *v* criticise 2516
批评 /pīpíng/ *v* criticise 1092
批准 /pīzhǔn/ *v* approve 2069
披 /pī/ *v* drape over one's shoulders 4192
皮 /pí/ *n* skin; leather; peel (of fruit) 1598
皮肤 /pífū/ *n* skin 3440
啤酒 /píjiǔ/ *n* beer 3702
脾气 /píqì/ *n* disposition, temperament 2970
匹 /pǐ/ *clas* [measure word for horses and mules, etc.]; [measure word for bolts of cloth] 4602
屁股 /pìgu/ *n* buttocks, bottom; end, butt 3670
譬如 /pìrú/ *v* take . . . for example 4403
片 /piàn/ *clas* [measure word for flat and thin pieces] slice; [with 一 as in 一片 used for a vast expanse of something such as land and water]; [measure word for scene, sound, atmosphere, speech, intention, etc.] 0381
偏 /piān/ *adv* simply, wilfully, deliberately 2421
偏 /piān/ *adj* slanting, leaning; prejudiced, biased 4216

偏偏 /piānpiān/ adv wilfully, just, unluckily; contrary to what is expected 4696

篇 /piān/ clas [measure word for essays and papers] piece (of writing) 0768

便宜 /piányi/ adj cheap, inexpensive 2393

骗 /piàn/ v take in, cheat 2199

飘 /piāo/ v flutter or float (in the air) 4193

漂亮 /piàoliang/ adj beautiful, pretty, handsome; brilliant, remarkable 1227

票 /piào/ n ticket 1375

拼 /pīn/ v piece together, join; spell; go all out 3195

拼命 /pīnmìng/ adv desperately 4606

贫困 /pínkùn/ adj poor, impoverished 1969

贫穷 /pínqióng/ adj poor, impoverished 4460

频繁 /pínfán/ adv frequently, often 3895

品 /pǐn/ v taste, sample 4836

品牌 /pǐnpái/ n brand 2452

品质 /pǐnzhì/ n quality 3569

品种 /pǐnzhǒng/ n variety, assortment 2579

乒乓球 /pīngpāngqiú/ n table tennis 4286

平 /píng/ adj flat, level, even; calm; average, common 0926

平安 /píng'ān/ adj safe and sound 4968

平常 /píngcháng/ adj ordinary, common 3272

平等 /píngděng/ adj equal 1690

平凡 /píngfán/ adj common, ordinary 3939

平方公里 /píngfānggōnglǐ/ clas square kilometre 3720

平方米 /píngfāngmǐ/ clas square metre 2780

平衡 /pínghéng/ adj balanced 1622

平静 /píngjìng/ adj calm, tranquil 2611

平均 /píngjūn/ adj average, mean 2175

平民 /píngmín/ n civilians, ordinary people 3999

平时 /píngshí/ time in normal times 1732

平原 /píngyuán/ n plain 4125

评 /píng/ v comment, review; judge, appraise; choose 3032

评估 /pínggū/ v evaluate, assess 3769

评价 /píngjià/ v evaluate, assess 1439

评论 /pínglùn/ n comment; review 2858

凭 /píng/ prep by, (taking) as the basis 1712

苹果 /píngguǒ/ n apple 3251

屏幕 /píngmù/ n screen 4382

瓶 /píng/ n bottle 3083

瓶 /píng/ clas [measure word for drink contained in a bottle] a bottle of 4393

坡 /pō/ n slope 4127

颇 /pō/ adv quite, rather 1613

婆 /pó/ n woman; matron; mother-in-law; grandma 4538

婆婆 /pópo/ n husband's mother, mother-in-law; old woman 4760

破 /pò/ v break 1818

破 /pò/ adj broken, worn out; lousy 2670

破产 /pòchǎn/ v go bankrupt; fail, fall through 4885

破坏 /pòhuài/ v wreck, destroy, damage 1355

扑 /pū/ v rush at; throw oneself into, be bent on; flap 4191

铺 /pū/ v spread; pave; make (bed) 2428

葡萄 /pútao/ n grape 4858

普遍 /pǔbiàn/ adj common, widespread 1476

普通 /pǔtōng/ adj common, ordinary 1179

谱 /pǔ/ n chart, list; music score; a fair amount of confidence, idea; spectrum 4659

Q

七 /qī/ num seven 0388

妻 /qī/ n wife 2658

妻子 /qīzi/ n wife 1185

期 /qī/ clas [measure word for things arranged by periods] issue (of a periodical) 1610

期 /qī/ n a period of time, phase, stage; schedule time 2299

期待 /qīdài/ v look forward to, long for 2650

期间 /qījiān/ time period of time, course 1107

期望 /qīwàng/ v expect, look forward to 3458

期限 /qīxiàn/ n deadline, time limit, term 4870

欺负 /qīfu/ v bully 4944

欺骗 /qīpiàn/ v deceive, cheat 4011

齐 /qí/ adj neat, even; all ready 2442

其 /qí/ pron [third person singular or plural] his, her, its, their; that, such 0188

其次 /qícì/ adv next, secondly 2851

其实 /qíshí/ adv actually 0339

其他 /qítā/ pron other 0323

其它 /qítā/ pron other 1374

其余 /qíyú/ pron rest 3575

其中 /qízhōng/ pron among them, in it 0343

奇 /qí, jī/ adj strange; odd (number) 2576

奇怪 /qíguài/ adj strange 1749

奇迹 /qíjī/ n miracle 3279

歧视 /qíshì/ v discriminate against 4837

骑 /qí/ v ride (a bike, horse, etc.); straddle 2109

棋 /qí/ n chess, board game 3048

旗 /qí/ n flag, banner 2369

旗帜 /qízhì/ n banner, flag; [figuratively] one's stand or position 4859

企图 /qǐtú/ v attempt 2569

企业 /qǐyè/ n business establishment, enterprise 0189

企业家 /qǐyèjiā/ n entrepreneur 2684

岂 /qǐ/ adv [used formally in rhetorical questions] how can it be possible that . . . 3151

启动 /qǐdòng/ v start, initiate 3386

启发 /qǐfā/ v enlighten, inspire, illuminate 4772

起 /qǐ/ v get up, rise; up 0136

起 /qǐ/ loc [usually occurring with 从 as in 从 … 起] starting from 0439

起 /qǐ/ clas [measure word for cases, incidents, accidents, etc.] 3678

起草 /qǐcǎo/ v draft, draw up 4900

起点 /qǐdiǎn/ n starting point 4657

起来 /qǐlái/ v get up, rise; [following a verb to indicate the beginning of a situation] start to; [following a verb to indicate completedness or effectiveness] 0143

起码 /qǐmǎ/ adv at least 4324

气 /qì/ n air; breath; gas 0579

气 /qì/ v get angry; make angry 2179

气氛 /qìfēn/ n atmosphere 1625

气候 /qìhòu/ n climate 2654

气温 /qìwēn/ n temperature 4852

气息 /qìxī/ n flavour, taste; smell, odour; breath 3636

气象 /qìxiàng/ n meteorology, weather; scene 4743

气质 /qìzhì/ n temperament; quality 3369

弃 /qì/ v relinquish, abandon; discard 4458

汽车 /qìchē/ n automobile, motor vehicle, car 0718

器 /qì/ suf [nominal suffix following a verb indicating the related device or instrument] 4284

恰恰 /qiàqià/ adv exactly, just 3784

千 /qiān/ num thousand 0666

千万 /qiānwàn/ adv [usually occurring in negative imperatives] be sure to, must 1897

迁 /qiān/ v move 3860

牵 /qiān/ v lead, lead along 3724

签 /qiān/ v sign 2692

签订 /qiāndìng/ v sign (an agreement, contract and treaty, etc.) 3055

签字 /qiānzì/ v sign 4507

前 /qián/ loc before; in front of 0121

前 /qián/ pref ex-, former 1093

前后 /qiánhòu/ loc in front and behind; before and after, around; from beginning to end 3106

前进 /qiánjìn/ v advance, move forward 2330

前景 /qiánjǐng/ n prospect, outlook 3573

前来 /qiánlái/ v come over 3075

前面 /qiánmian/ n front; ahead 1328

前提 /qiántí/ n premise 2354

前途 /qiántú/ n future, prospect 2471

前往 /qiánwǎng/ v go to, leave for 3014

前夕 /qiánxì/ time (on) the eve of 4881

钱 /qián/ n money 0158

潜力 /qiánlì/ n potential, potentiality 3717

浅 /qiǎn/ adj shallow; simple, easy; (of colour) light, pale 3563

谴责 /qiǎnzé/ v denounce, condemn 4354

欠 /qiàn/ v owe; lack, be short 2841

枪 /qiāng/ n gun, rifle 1523

强 /qiáng/ adj strong, powerful, better 0409

强大 /qiángdà/ adj strong, powerful 1842

强调 /qiángdiào/ v emphasise, stress 1025

强烈 /qiángliè/ adj intense, strong 1082

强迫 /qiǎngpò/ v compel, force 4886

墙 /qiáng/ n wall 1189

抢 /qiǎng/ v rob, loot; snatch, grab; vie for; rush 1490

抢救 /qiǎngjiù/ v rescue, save 4309

悄悄 /qiāoqiāo/ adv quietly 4794

敲 /qiāo/ v knock, tap; strike; fleece 3190

桥 /qiáo/ n bridge 1555

瞧 /qiáo/ v look 1635

巧 /qiǎo/ adj opportune, by chance; skilful, clever 2787

切 /qiē/ v cut, carve 2894

且 /qiě/ conj (both . . .) and; even, furthermore 1592

亲 /qīn/ adj close, intimate 2125

亲 /qīn/ n parent, next of kin, relative; marriage 3422

亲戚 /qīnqī/ n relative 2772

亲切 /qīnqiè/ adj amiable, kind, intimate 2633

亲人 /qīnrén/ n family, relative 3568

亲自 /qīnzì/ adv in person, personally, (do) oneself 1519

侵犯 /qīnfàn/ v violate, infringe 3648

侵略 /qīnlüè/ v invade 2799

琴 /qín/ n [general term for some stringed musical instruments such as piano, violin] instrument, qin 4865

青 /qīng/ adj blue, green, cyan 2152

青春 /qīngchūn/ n youth, youthfulness 2488

青年 /qīngnián/ n youth, young people 0650

青年人 /qīngniánrén/ n young people 4759

青少年 /qīngshàonián/ n adolescent, teenager 2382

轻 /qīng/ adj light 1444

轻松 /qīngsōng/ adj light, relaxed 2051

轻易 /qīngyì/ adv easily, readily; lightly, rashly 3594

倾 /qīng/ v lean, bend; pour out 4725

倾向 /qīngxiàng/ n trend, tendency 3418

清 /qīng/ adj clear 0598

清 /qīng/ v clear up; settle 3550

清晨 /qīngchén/ *time* early morning 4340

清楚 /qīngchǔ/ *adj* clear 0481

清洁 /qīngjié/ *adj* clean 4840

清理 /qīnglǐ/ *v* clear, sort out 3822

清晰 /qīngxī/ *adj* clear, distinct 3018

清醒 /qīngxǐng/ *adj* sober, clear-headed 2431

情 /qíng/ *n* feeling, passion, sentiment; condition, situation 0729

情报 /qíngbào/ *n* intelligence, information 3994

情感 /qínggǎn/ *n* feeling, emotion 1851

情节 /qíngjié/ *n* plot; circumstances 2890

情景 /qíngjǐng/ *n* scene, sight, situation 2379

情况 /qíngkuàng/ *n* situation, condition, circumstance 0176

情形 /qíngxíng/ *n* circumstance, situation 2310

情绪 /qíngxù/ *n* feeling, emotion; mood, sentiment, morale; moodiness 1229

请 /qǐng/ *v* please (do something); ask (somebody to do something); invite 0268

请求 /qǐngqiú/ *v* request, ask 4771

请问 /qǐngwèn/ *v* [used as a polite expression when asking for information] may I ask . . . 3215

庆 /qìng/ *v* celebrate 3147

庆祝 /qìngzhù/ *v* celebrate 3481

穷 /qióng/ *adj* poor 1631

穷人 /qióngrén/ *n* the poor, poor people 4476

秋 /qiū/ *time* autumn, fall; a period of (troubled) time 1854

秋天 /qiūtiān/ *time* autumn 3881

求 /qiú/ *v* beg, request, strike for, seek 1065

球 /qiú/ *n* ball 1376

区 /qū/ *n* area, district 0629

区别 /qūbié/ *n* difference 3871

区别 /qūbié/ *v* differentiate, tell apart 4986

区域 /qūyù/ *n* region, area 2261

趋势 /qūshì/ *n* trend, tendency 2288

渠道 /qúdào/ *n* channel 3049

取 /qǔ/ *v* get, take, fetch 1332

取代 /qǔdài/ *v* replace, take the place of 4310

取得 /qǔdé/ *v* acquire, obtain, achieve; reach (an agreement) 0706

取消 /qǔxiāo/ *v* cancel 2844

曲 /qǔ/ *clas* [measure word for tunes, songs and melodies, etc.] 2093

娶 /qǔ/ *v* take a wife, marry 2476

去 /qù/ *v* go 0040

去年 /qùnián/ *time* last year 0891

去世 /qùshì/ *v* die, pass away 3034

圈 /quān/ *clas* circle, round 1914

圈 /quān, juàn/ *n* circle, ring; fold, sty 2947

全 /quán/ *adj* whole, entire, complete 0140

全 /quán/ *adv* all, fully 0552

全部 /quánbù/ *adj* all, whole, full, entire, total 0612

全部 /quánbù/ *n* all, everything, entirety, totality 4111

全都 /quándōu/ *adv* all, with no exception 2674

全力 /quánlì/ *adv* with all one's strength, all out, sparing no effort 4796

全面 /quánmiàn/ *adj* all-around, overall 1026

全球 /quánqiú/ *n* the whole world 1469

全球化 /quánqiúhuà/ *n* globalisation 2825

全身 /quánshēn/ *n* the whole body, all over 4243

全体 /quántǐ/ *n* all, whole 2084

权 /quán/ *n* power, authority; right 1152

权力 /quánlì/ *n* power, authority 1321

权利 /quánlì/ *n* right 1322

权威 /quánwēi/ *n* authority 3004

权益 /quányì/ *n* rights and interests 2833

拳 /quán/ *clas* [measure word for actions of hitting with one's fist] 4712

劝 /quàn/ *v* persuade; comfort 2187

缺 /quē/ *v* lack; be absent, be missing 1888

缺点 /quēdiǎn/ *n* shortcoming, weakness, defect 4802

缺乏 /quēfá/ *v* lack, be short of 1689

缺少 /quēshǎo/ *v* lack, be short of 2842

却 /què/ *adv* but 0150

确 /què/ *adv* indeed, really 2128

确保 /quèbǎo/ *v* ensure, make sure 3036

确定 /quèdìng/ *v* determine, fix 1194

确认 /quèrèn/ *v* confirm 3559

确实 /quèshí/ *adv* truly, really 0969

群 /qún/ *clas* [measure word for people or things gathered, also for some birds and animals] crowd, flock, herd 1035

群体 /qúntǐ/ *n* group 2347

群众 /qúnzhòng/ *n* the masses 0622

R

然而 /rán'ér/ *conj* however 0695

然后 /ránhòu/ *adv* afterwards, then 0263

燃烧 /ránshāo/ *v* burn 4098

染 /rǎn/ *v* catch (a disease), addict; dye 3551

让 /ràng/ *v* give way; let, make; allow 0079

绕 /rào/ *v* move around, make a detour; wind, make (wire, cable, etc.) into a coil or ball 2515

惹 /rě/ *v* provoke, cause, make; offend, get on one's nerves 3813

热 /rè/ *adj* hot 0868

热 /rè/ *suf* craze, fad 4080

热爱 /rè'ài/ *v* love 3027

热烈 /rèliè/ *adj* warm, cordial; lively, enthusiastic 2052

热闹 /rènao/ *adj* busy, bustling with noise and excitement 2247

热情 /rèqíng/ *adj* enthusiastic, cordial, warm 1211

人 /rén/ *n* person, human, man 0014

人才 /réncái/ *n* talented person, talent, qualified personnel 0846

人格 /réngé/ *n* personality, character; integrity 2451

人家 /rénjia/ *pron* other people 0807

人家 /rénjiā/ *n* household, family 1112

人间 /rénjiān/ *n* human world, the world 2738

人口 /rénkǒu/ *n* population 0934

人类 /rénlèi/ *n* human being, mankind, man 0435

人力 /rénlì/ *n* manpower 3840

人们 /rénmen/ *n* people 0237

人民 /rénmín/ *n* (the) people 0228

人民币 /rénmínbì/ *n* Chinese currency, RMB 2104

人群 /rénqún/ *n* crowd (of people) 2399

人人 /rénrén/ *pron* everyone 2038

人生 /rénshēng/ *n* (human) life 0894

人士 /rénshì/ *n* person, personage, public figure 1599

人事 /rénshì/ *n* personnel affairs 3950

人数 /rénshù/ *n* number of people 2219

人体 /réntǐ/ *n* human, human body 3110

人文 /rénwén/ *n* humanities 3949

人物 /rénwù/ *n* personage, distinguished individual; characters in literary works 0675

人心 /rénxīn/ *n* public feeling, public sentiment 3180

人性 /rénxìng/ *n* human nature, humanity 2624

人员 /rényuán/ *n* staff, personnel 0423

忍 /rěn/ *v* bear, endure, stand, put up with 2872

忍不住 /rěnbuzhù/ *v* cannot help but 4059

忍受 /rěnshòu/ *v* bear, tolerate, put up with 4611

认 /rèn/ *v* recognise; admit; resign oneself to 2160

认定 /rèndìng/ *v* maintain, hold, affirm 2334

认可 /rènkě/ *v* approve of, accept 4157

认识 /rènshí/ *v* know, understand; recognise 0421

认识 /rènshí/ *n* understanding, knowledge, awareness 2205

认同 /rèntóng/ *v* identify with, accept, approve 4208

认为 /rènwéi/ *v* think, believe 0160

认真 /rènzhēn/ *adj* earnest, serious 0829

任 /rèn/ *v* appoint, occupy or take up a post; give free rein to 1069

任何 /rènhé/ *pron* any 0336

任命 /rènmìng/ *v* appoint 3973

任务 /rènwù/ *n* task, mission 0827

扔 /rēng/ *v* toss, throw (away) 2265

仍 /réng/ *adv* still 0476

仍然 /réngrán/ *adv* still 0824

日 /rì/ *n* day; the sun 1382

日报 /rìbào/ *n* daily (newspaper) 4036

日常 /rìcháng/ *adj* daily 2375

日记 /rìjì/ *n* diary 4375

日期 /rìqī/ *n* date 4646

日益 /rìyì/ *adv* day by day 2852

日子 /rìzi/ *n* date; day, time; life 0998

荣 /róng/ *adj* proud; glorious; prosperous 3225

荣誉 /róngyù/ *n* honour 3401

容 /róng/ *v* hold, contain; tolerate; allow, permit 1841

容易 /róngyì/ *adj* easy 0569

融 /róng/ *v* melt, thaw; fuse, mix together 4565

融合 /rónghé/ *v* merge, mix together 4721

肉 /ròu/ *n* meat 1187

如 /rú/ *v* like, as, as if; such as 0255

如 /rú/ *conj* if, in case of; as, as if 1921

如此 /rúcǐ/ *pron* such, like this, in this way 0606

如果 /rúguǒ/ *conj* if 0122

如何 /rúhé/ *pron* how 0373

如今 /rújīn/ *time* nowadays, today 1095

如同 /rútóng/ *v* like, as 3010

如下 /rúxià/ *v* as follows 3760

入 /rù/ *v* enter 0447

软 /ruǎn/ *adj* soft 1707

软件 /ruǎnjiàn/ *n* software 2530

若 /ruò/ *conj* if 0954

若干 /ruògān/ *num* a number of, several; how many, how much 3082

弱 /ruò/ *adj* weak 2545

S

撒 /sā, sǎ/ *v* sprinkle, spray, scatter, spread; cast, let go, let out; spill 3381

洒 /sǎ/ *v* spray, sprinkle; spill 4259

塞 /sāi/ *v* squeeze in; stop up 2200

赛 /sài/ *v* compete; surpass 2068

赛 /sài/ *n* match, game, competition 4181

三 /sān/ *num* three 0052

散 /sǎn, sàn/ *v* fall apart, come loose; break up; disperse; spread, distribute 3617

散 /sǎn/ *adj* loose; leisurely; scattered, dispersive 3826

散发 /sànfā/ *v* distribute, circulate; give off, emit 4563

散文 /sǎnwén/ *n* prose 4237

嗓子 /sǎngzi/ *n* throat 4800

丧失 /sàngshī/ *v* lose 3514

扫 /sǎo/ *v* sweep (away), brush; pass quickly, glance 3236

色 /sè/ n colour; countenance, look; type; female charm 1537

色彩 /sècǎi/ n colour 2413

森林 /sēnlín/ n forest 2397

杀 /shā/ v kill 0869

杀人 /shārén/ v commit manslaughter, murder, kill 3322

沙 /shā/ n sand 2777

沙发 /shāfā/ n sofa 3791

沙漠 /shāmò/ n desert 3334

傻 /shǎ/ adj foolish 2879

啥 /shà/ pron [dialect] what 1393

晒 /shài/ v dry in the sun; sunbathe 4196

山 /shān/ n mountain, hill 0489

山区 /shānqū/ n mountain area 3303

闪 /shǎn/ v flash, flicker; dodge 3428

扇 /shàn/ clas [measure word for doors, windows, etc.] 4190

善 /shàn/ adj virtuous, good; kind, friendly 2992

善 /shàn/ v be good at; be apt to 3654

善良 /shànliáng/ adj kind-hearted, good and honest 3150

善于 /shànyú/ v be good at 2873

伤 /shāng/ v injure, hurt; do harm to 1464

伤 /shāng/ n injury, wound 4328

伤害 /shānghài/ v harm, injure, offend 2222

伤亡 /shāngwáng/ n casualties 3655

伤心 /shāngxīn/ adj sad 3980

商 /shāng/ v discuss, consult 2965

商 /shāng/ n trade, commerce, business 4700

商场 /shāngchǎng/ n shopping mall 2446

商店 /shāngdiàn/ n shop, store 2408

商量 /shāngliang/ v consult, discuss 2221

商品 /shāngpǐn/ n goods, commodity, article, item 0901

商人 /shāngrén/ n business people, merchant 3468

商业 /shāngyè/ n business, commerce 1074

赏 /shǎng/ v award, bestow (a reward); feast one's eyes on; appreciate 4724

上 /shàng/ loc up, on, in 0015

上 /shàng/ v go up, ascend; board; leave for; go ahead; be engaged in (class, work, etc.); serve (tea, food, etc.) 1080

上班 /shàngbān/ v go to work 2111

上车 /shàngchē/ v board, go aboard 4723

上次 /shàngcì/ time last time 3547

上帝 /shàngdì/ n God 3211

上级 /shàngjí/ n higher authorities, superior; upper level 3229

上课 /shàngkè/ v (of students) attend class; (of teachers) give a lesson 3316

上来 /shànglái/ v come up; [used as a resultative verb complement indicating the upward direction or success of doing something] 1723

上面 /shàngmian/ loc on top of, above, over; aforesaid 1068

上去 /shàngqù/ v go up; [used as a resultative verb complement] up 1685

上升 /shàngshēng/ v rise, go up 2188

上市 /shàngshì/ v put (goods and shares, etc.) on the market 3585

上述 /shàngshù/ adj above mentioned 2367

上司 /shàngsī/ n superior 4816

上网 /shàngwǎng/ v get on the internet, go online 2916

上午 /shàngwǔ/ time (in the) morning 1474

上下 /shàngxià/ loc up and down, high and low; about, approximately 2735

上学 /shàngxué/ v go to school 2170

尚 /shàng/ adv still, yet 1881

尚未 /shàngwèi/ adv not yet 2854

烧 /shāo/ v burn; cook, have a fever 1134

稍 /shāo/ adv slightly, a little 2484

稍微 /shāowēi/ adv slightly, a little 4738

少 /shǎo/ adj few, rare 0258

少 /shǎo/ v be short, lack; [usually in imperatives] stop, quit 2556

少数 /shǎoshù/ num a small number of; minority 2434

少数民族 /shǎoshùmínzú/ n ethnic minority 2353

少年 /shàonián/ n teenager, early youth 1885

少女 /shàonǚ/ n young girl 3570

蛇 /shé/ n snake 3501

舍 /shě/ v abandon, give up, part with 3821

设 /shè/ v set up, establish 1672

设备 /shèbèi/ n equipment 1368

设计 /shèjì/ v design 1165

设立 /shèlì/ v establish, set up 2336

设施 /shèshī/ n facility 1962

设想 /shèxiǎng/ v imagine 3683

设置 /shèzhì/ v set, set up 3411

社 /shè/ n society, club; agency 3002

社会 /shèhuì/ n society 0114

社会主义 /shèhuìzhǔyì/ n socialism 0857

射 /shè/ v shoot, spout; send out 2159

射击 /shèjī/ v shoot, fire 4201

涉及 /shèjí/ v involve, concern, cover 1933

摄 /shè/ v take (a photograph) 3893

摄影 /shèyǐng/ n photography 2757

谁 /shéi/ *pron* who 0168

申请 /shēnqǐng/ *v* apply 2213

伸 /shēn/ *v* stretch, extend 2568

伸出 /shēnchū/ *v* stretch out, extend 3820

伸手 /shēnshǒu/ *v* hold out one's hand; ask for 3728

身 /shēn/ *n* body 0354

身 /shēn/ *clas* [measure word for clothes] suit; [preceded by the numeral 一 as a temporary measure for things covering somebody like water, mud, sweat, etc.] 2513

身边 /shēnbiān/ *place* at one's side, within reach 1455

身材 /shēncái/ *n* stature, figure, build 4035

身份 /shēnfèn/ *n* identity 1462

身后 /shēnhòu/ *loc* behind somebody; after one's death 4079

身体 /shēntǐ/ *n* (human) body, health 0572

身影 /shēnyǐng/ *n* figure, silhouette 4866

身子 /shēnzi/ *n* body; pregnancy 3542

深 /shēn/ *adj* deep 0608

深 /shēn/ *adv* deeply, profoundly 2350

深处 /shēnchù/ *place* depth; deepest or most distant part 3314

深厚 /shēnhòu/ *adj* deep, profound 4516

深刻 /shēnkè/ *adj* profound 1262

深入 /shēnrù/ *adj* thorough, deep, in depth 2126

深入 /shēnrù/ *v* penetrate deeply, go deep into 3265

深深 /shēnshēn/ *adv* deeply, profoundly 3494

深受 /shēnshòu/ *v* receive, [passive marker] be deeply -en (loved, moved, etc.) 4459

深夜 /shēnyè/ *time* late at night, far into the night 4714

神 /shén/ *n* god 1172

神 /shén/ *adj* magic, miraculous; smart; supernatural 2406

神话 /shénhuà/ *n* fairy tale, myth 3906

神经 /shénjīng/ *n* nerve 3790

神秘 /shénmì/ *adj* mysterious 2377

神奇 /shénqí/ *adj* magical, mystical, miraculous 4077

神情 /shénqíng/ *n* look, facial expression 4753

神圣 /shénshèng/ *adj* holy, divine, sacred 4163

审 /shěn/ *v* try; examine, review 4106

审查 /shěnchá/ *v* examine, look through 3583

审美 /shěnměi/ *n* good taste; appreciation of beauty, aesthetics 4215

审判 /shěnpàn/ *v* try, bring to trial 4783

甚 /shèn/ *adv* very, quite 2811

甚至 /shènzhì/ *adv* even 0430

甚至 /shènzhì/ *conj* so much so that, so far as to 2534

渗透 /shèntòu/ *v* permeate, penetrate 4957

升 /shēng/ *v* rise, raise; promote 1839

升起 /shēngqǐ/ *v* rise, ascend 4684

生 /shēng/ *v* give birth to, bear; become (rusty, ill, etc.); light (a fire) 0360

生 /shēng/ *adj* raw; unripe; unfamiliar; alive, living 2295

生病 /shēngbìng/ *v* be ill 4891

生产 /shēngchǎn/ *v* produce 0500

生产 /shēngchǎn/ *n* production 4993

生存 /shēngcún/ *v* subsist, live 1487

生动 /shēngdòng/ *adj* vivid, lively 2942

生活 /shēnghuó/ *v* live 0127

生活 /shēnghuó/ *n* life 2271

生理 /shēnglǐ/ *n* physiology 4234

生命 /shēngmìng/ *n* life 0502

生气 /shēngqì/ *v* be angry 2895

生气 /shēngqi/ *n* life, vigour, vitality 4177

生前 /shēngqián/ *time* during one's lifetime, before one's death 4882

生日 /shēngrì/ *n* birthday 2444

生态 /shēngtài/ *n* ecology 2254

生物 /shēngwù/ *n* living thing; biology 2412

生涯 /shēngyá/ *n* career 4595

生意 /shēngyì/ *n* business, trade 1429

生育 /shēngyù/ *v* bear, give birth to 4949

生长 /shēngzhǎng/ *v* grow 3029

声 /shēng/ *n* sound, noise; voice 0806

声 /shēng/ *clas* [measure word for sound, shout, cry, laugh, yell, etc.] 1296

声明 /shēngmíng/ *n* statement 2905

声音 /shēngyīn/ *n* sound, noise; voice 0814

胜 /shèng/ *v* win, defeat 1724

胜利 /shènglì/ *v* win victory 1239

省 /shěng/ *n* province 0641

剩 /shèng/ *v* leave over, remain 2961

剩下 /shèngxià/ *v* remain, be left over 2040

尸体 /shītǐ/ *n* body, corpse 3373

失 /shī/ *v* lose 2233

失败 /shībài/ *v* fail, be defeated 1480

失去 /shīqù/ *v* lose 1102

失望 /shīwàng/ *adj* disappointed 3273

失误 /shīwù/ *n* error, mistake 4688

失业 /shīyè/ *v* become unemployed, be out of work 4008

师 /shī/ *n* teacher; person with a particular professional skill; division 0961

师傅 /shīfu/ *n* master worker, teacher; [used as a respectful term of address for a skilled worker, or as a polite form of address for a stranger] 3208

诗 /shī/ n poem, poetry 1016

诗歌 /shīgē/ n poetry, poem 3951

诗人 /shīrén/ n poet, bard 2345

施 /shī/ v impose, exert, carry out; use, apply; give, bestow 3292

施工 /shīgōng/ v be under construction 3956

狮子 /shīzi/ n lion 4803

湿 /shī/ adj wet, sodden 4023

十 /shí/ num ten 0152

十分 /shífēn/ adv very, fully 0449

什么 /shénme/ pron what 0045

石 /shí/ n rock, stone 1905

石头 /shítou/ n rock, stone 2042

石油 /shíyóu/ n oil 2678

时 /shí/ n time when . . . 0078

时代 /shídài/ n age, times; a period in one's life 0510

时光 /shíguāng/ n time; period of time 4292

时候 /shíhou/ n when, time when . . . 0103

时机 /shíjī/ n opportunity, time, moment 3338

时间 /shíjiān/ n time 0142

时刻 /shíkè/ n moment; timetable 2260

时刻 /shíkè/ adv at any moment, constantly 4118

时期 /shíqī/ n a particular period of time (especially in history) 0590

时尚 /shíshàng/ n fashion, vogue 4090

识 /shí/ v know 3766

实 /shí/ adj solid, firm; true, real, actual 3149

实 /shí/ adv really, truly 3534

实际 /shíjì/ adj practical, actual 1404

实际 /shíjì/ n reality 1711

实践 /shíjiàn/ v practise 1387

实际上 /shíjìshàng/ adv actually, in fact, as a matter of fact 0928

实力 /shílì/ n strength 1740

实施 /shíshī/ v implement, carry out 1182

实事求是 /shíshìqiúshì/ idiom seek truth from facts, be practical and realistic 4636

实现 /shíxiàn/ v realise, fulfil, achieve 0592

实行 /shíxíng/ v implement, carry out, bring into effect 1096

实验 /shíyàn/ n experiment, test 3054

实验室 /shíyànshì/ n lab, laboratory 4004

实在 /shízài/ adv indeed, really 1039

实在 /shízài/ adj real; honest and trustworthy 4024

实质 /shízhì/ n essence, substance, crux 4331

食 /shí/ n food, meal; animal feed; eclipse 2622

食 /shí/ v eat 3324

食品 /shípǐn/ n foodstuff, food 1871

食堂 /shítáng/ n canteen, dining hall 4174

食物 /shíwù/ n food 2322

史 /shǐ/ n history 1314

使 /shǐ/ v [often used in serial verb constructions] make, cause, enable 0124

使得 /shǐde/ v cause, make; [dialect] be usable or workable 1647

使命 /shǐmìng/ n mission 3912

使用 /shǐyòng/ v use 0661

始 /shǐ/ v begin, start 3968

始终 /shǐzhōng/ adv from beginning to end, all along, always 1151

士兵 /shìbīng/ n soldier 1974

氏 /shì/ n person surnamed; family, clan 2621

世 /shì/ n the world; lifetime; era, age 1091

世纪 /shìjì/ n century 0463

世界 /shìjiè/ n world 0126

世人 /shìrén/ n (common) people, the world 3914

市 /shì/ n city, town; market 0700

市场 /shìchǎng/ n market 0304

市场经济 /shìchǎngjīngjì/ n market economy 2177

市民 /shìmín/ n city resident; citizen 2090

市区 /shìqū/ place city proper, town, city; downtown 4939

市长 /shìzhǎng/ n mayor 1704

示 /shì/ v show 3765

式 /shì/ suf type, style 1050

事 /shì/ n matter, thing 0108

事儿 /shìr/ n business, matter, affair 1169

事故 /shìgù/ n accident 2976

事件 /shìjiàn/ n event, affair 0884

事情 /shìqíng/ n matter, thing 0265

事实 /shìshí/ n fact 0861

事实上 /shìshíshàng/ idiom in fact 2155

事务 /shìwù/ n affairs 2538

事物 /shìwù/ n thing 2728

事先 /shìxiān/ adv beforehand, in advance 3329

事业 /shìyè/ n cause, career, undertaking 0648

势 /shì/ n power, influence; momentum, tendency; situation 2240

势力 /shìlì/ n power, force 1903

视 /shì/ v look; regard (. . . as) 1726

视察 /shìchá/ v inspect 4785

视为 /shìwéi/ v deem, view as 3818

视野 /shìyě/ n field of view, vision 4482

试 /shì/ v test, try 0988

试图 /shìtú/ v attempt, try 3562

试验 /shìyàn/ n test, experiment 2586

室 /shì/ n room 1573

室内 /shìnèi/ place indoor 4053

是 /shì/ *v* be 0002

是的 /shìde/ *idiom* yes 3330

是非 /shìfēi/ *n* right and wrong; dispute 3992

是否 /shìfǒu/ *v* whether (or not) 0935

适当 /shìdàng/ *adj* suitable, proper 2785

适合 /shìhé/ *v* fit, suit 1833

适应 /shìyìng/ *v* suit; adapt to 1550

适用 /shìyòng/ *v* apply 4769

释放 /shìfàng/ *v* set free, release 3689

收 /shōu/ *v* receive, collect; accept 0694

收藏 /shōucáng/ *v* collect 4069

收到 /shōudào/ *v* receive 1589

收费 /shōufèi/ *v* charge 3819

收购 /shōugòu/ *v* purchase, buy 3584

收回 /shōuhuí/ *v* take back, recover; withdraw 3684

收获 /shōuhuò/ *n* result, reward, gains; harvest 4805

收集 /shōují/ *v* gather, collect 3858

收入 /shōurù/ *n* income, revenue 0965

收拾 /shōushí/ *v* sort out, put in order 3427

手 /shǒu/ *n* hand 0229

手段 /shǒuduàn/ *n* means, method; measure, step; trick 1104

手法 /shǒufǎ/ *n* technique, skill, way; trick 3675

手机 /shǒujī/ *n* mobile phone, cell phone 1705

手里 /shǒuli/ *place* in hand, at hand 1853

手术 /shǒushù/ *n* (surgical) operation 2755

手续 /shǒuxù/ *n* formalities, procedure 3047

手指 /shǒuzhǐ/ *n* finger 4082

手中 /shǒuzhōng/ *place* in hand 1875

守 /shǒu/ *v* guard; keep watch; abide by 1720

首 /shǒu/ *n* head 0731

首 /shǒu/ *clas* [measure word for songs and poems] 2210

首 /shǒu/ *num* first 3499

首都 /shǒudū/ *n* capital 2551

首脑 /shǒunǎo/ *n* head (of state or government); summit (meeting) 3375

首先 /shǒuxiān/ *adv* first, first of all 0557

首相 /shǒuxiàng/ *n* prime minister 4048

受 /shòu/ *v* receive; be subject to, suffer; endure, bear 0306

受不了 /shòubuliǎo/ *idiom* (somebody) cannot endure, (something) be intolerable 4173

受到 /shòudào/ *v* come in for 0548

受伤 /shòushāng/ *v* hurt, be wounded, be injured 3199

瘦 /shòu/ *adj* thin, bony; (of clothes) tight; (of meat) lean 3433

书 /shū/ *n* book 0241

书店 /shūdiàn/ *n* bookstore 4579

书法 /shūfǎ/ *n* calligraphy; handwriting 4040

书籍 /shūjí/ *n* (a general term for) books 4179

书记 /shūjì/ *n* (Party) secretary 0943

叔叔 /shūshu/ *n* uncle; [also used as a polite term of address for men of one's parents' age] 3278

舒服 /shūfú/ *adj* comfortable; (physically) well 2632

舒适 /shūshì/ *adj* comfortable, cosy 4904

输 /shū/ *v* lose, be defeated; transport 1687

蔬菜 /shūcài/ *n* vegetable 2639

熟 /shú, shóu/ *adj* ripe; (food) cooked, done; familiar; skilled; sound (sleep) 2192

熟悉 /shúxī/ *v* be familiar with 1509

属 /shǔ/ *v* belong, be 1253

属于 /shǔyú/ *v* belong to, be classified as 1145

术 /shù/ *n* way, practice; (surgical) operation 3052

树 /shù/ *n* tree 1579

树 /shù/ *v* set, set up; uphold 2143

树立 /shùlì/ *v* set up, establish 3885

树木 /shùmù/ *n* tree 4582

数 /shù/ *num* several 0667

数据 /shùjù/ *n* data 2600

数量 /shùliàng/ *n* quantity, amount 1986

数十 /shùshí/ *num* tens of, dozens of 4422

数学 /shùxué/ *n* mathematics, maths 2790

数字 /shùzì/ *n* number, figure 1651

耍 /shuǎ/ *v* play, play with 4675

摔 /shuāi/ *v* fall; break, cause to fall and break; throw, fling 2629

甩 /shuǎi/ *v* fling; throw off 4443

率 /shuài/ *v* lead 1761

率领 /shuàilǐng/ *v* lead 3643

双 /shuāng/ *adj* double; even (as opposed to odd) 0958

双 /shuāng/ *clas* pair 2837

双方 /shuāngfāng/ *n* both parties, the two sides 0707

双手 /shuāngshǒu/ *n* both hands 3234

水 /shuǐ/ *n* water 0206

水稻 /shuǐdào/ *n* (paddy) rice 4972

水果 /shuǐguǒ/ *n* fruit 2918

水面 /shuǐmiàn/ *n* water, water surface 4182

水泥 /shuǐní/ *n* cement 3745

水平 /shuǐpíng/ *n* level (of achievement, etc.) 0525

税 /shuì/ *n* tax, duty 3707

睡 /shuì/ *v* sleep 0964

睡觉 /shuìjiào/ *v* go to bed, sleep 2110

睡眠 /shuìmián/ *n* sleep 4779

睡着 /shuìzháo/ *v* go to sleep, fall asleep 4515

顺 /shùn/ *adj* smooth, without a hitch 2967

顺 /shùn/ *v* obey, yield to; put something in order 3485

顺利 /shùnlì/ *adj* smooth, successful 1665

顺着 /shùnzhe/ *prep* along 4601

瞬间 /shùnjiān/ *time* instant, moment 4299

说 /shuō/ *v* say, speak, tell 0012

说不定 /shuōbudìng/ *idiom* maybe, perhaps 4637

说道 /shuōdào/ *v* say 2463

说法 /shuōfa/ *n* statement, argument; wording, version 1586

说服 /shuōfú/ *v* convince, persuade 4267

说话 /shuōhuà/ *v* speak, talk 0637

说明 /shuōmíng/ *v* explain 0816

硕士 /shuòshì/ *n* master's degree 3807

丝 /sī/ *n* silk, thread 2951

丝 /sī/ *clas* [measure word for tiny bits] a thread of, a trace of 3092

丝毫 /sīháo/ *num* [normally occurring in negative sentences] at all, least 3788

司 /sī/ *n* department (in a ministry); firm, company 2868

司机 /sījī/ *n* driver, chauffeur 1850

司令 /sīlìng/ *n* commander 2601

私 /sī/ *adj* personal, private; illicit 3062

私人 /sīrén/ *adj* private, personal 2656

思 /sī/ *v* think 2572

思考 /sīkǎo/ *v* think, ponder over, reflect on 1435

思路 /sīlù/ *n* line of thought, thinking 2926

思索 /sīsuǒ/ *v* think deeply, ponder 4827

思维 /sīwéi/ *n* (way of) thinking, (line of) thought, mind 2089

思想 /sīxiǎng/ *n* thought, idea 0313

撕 /sī/ *v* tear 4399

死 /sǐ/ *v* die 0239

死 /sǐ/ *adj* dead 1117

死去 /sǐqù/ *v* die 4272

死亡 /sǐwáng/ *v* die 1316

四 /sì/ *num* four 0128

四处 /sìchù/ *adv* everywhere, all round 3739

寺 /sì/ *n* temple 2472

似 /sì/ *v* seem, appear 2544

似 /sì/ *adv* apparently, as if 4575

似的 /sìde/ *aux* seem, as if 1164

似乎 /sìhū/ *adv* apparently 0784

松 /sōng/ *adj* loose, slack, relaxed; soft and crisp 3824

松 /sōng/ *v* loosen, unfasten 4055

送 /sòng/ *v* deliver; give as a gift; see off; escort 0324

送给 /sònggěi/ *v* give 2707

艘 /sōu/ *clas* [measure word for boats and ships, etc.] 2797

俗 /sú/ *adj* vulgar 4630

素 /sù/ *adj* plain 4166

素质 /sùzhì/ *n* inner quality, making 1498

速度 /sùdù/ *n* speed 1198

宿舍 /sùshè/ *n* dormitory 2617

塑料 /sùliào/ *n* plastics 4471

塑造 /sùzào/ *v* shape, mould; portray (literary characters) 3730

酸 /suān/ *adj* sour, tart; pedantic 4624

算 /suàn/ *v* calculate; regard as 0377

算是 /suànshì/ *v* be considered to be 1670

虽 /suī/ *conj* although, though 1255

虽然 /suīrán/ *conj* although 0300

虽说 /suīshuō/ *conj* although, though 4465

随 /suí/ *prep* along with 1907

随 /suí/ *v* follow, comply with; allow one to do as one likes 3512

随便 /suíbiàn/ *adj* casual, careless; informal 2124

随后 /suíhòu/ *adv* soon afterwards 2297

随时 /suíshí/ *adv* at any time 2096

随意 /suíyì/ *adj* random, arbitrary; voluntary, as one pleases 3393

随之 /suízhī/ *adv* along with it, following it; accordingly 4797

随着 /suízhe/ *prep* along with 0835

岁 /suì/ *clas* year (of age) 0203

岁月 /suìyuè/ *n* time; years (of one's life) 3259

碎 /suì/ *adj* broken 3460

孙子 /sūnzi/ *n* grandson, grandchild 3541

损 /sǔn/ *v* damage, harm; lose; deride, be sarcastic 4720

损害 /sǔnhài/ *v* harm 3059

损失 /sǔnshī/ *n* loss 1596

缩 /suō/ *v* shrink, contract; withdraw, draw back 4672

缩小 /suōxiǎo/ *v* reduce; shrink 4828

所 /suǒ/ *aux* [particle preceding a verb to form a nominal structure] 0113

所 /suǒ/ *clas* [measure word for houses, schools and hospitals, etc.] 1751

所谓 /suǒwèi/ *adj* so-called 0792

所以 /suǒyǐ/ *conj* so, therefore 0156

所有 /suǒyǒu/ *pron* all 0290

所在 /suǒzài/ *n* place, locus, whereabouts 2352

锁 /suǒ/ *v* lock (up) 3382

T

他 /tā/ *pron* he, him 0010

他们 /tāmen/ *pron* they, them 0041

他人 /tārén/ *pron* other people 2314

她 /tā/ *pron* she, her 0032

她们 /tāmen/ *pron* [for female] they, them 0567

它 /tā/ *pron* [used for non-human things] it 0086

它们 /tāmen/ *pron* [for inanimate objects] they, them 0535

踏 /tà/ *v* step on 2896

台 /tái/ *clas* [measure word for machines, and also performances, etc.] 0651

台 /tái/ *n* platform, stage; desk, table; (TV or radio) station 1999

台阶 /táijiē/ *n* step; [figuratively] way out 3258

抬 /tái/ *v* lift, raise; carry 2122

抬头 /táitóu/ *v* raise one's head, look up; hold one's head high; gain ground 3862

太 /tài/ *adv* too, excessively; very 0151

太太 /tàitai/ *n* Mrs, madam, lady; wife 2342

太阳 /tàiyáng/ *n* the sun 1389

态 /tài/ *n* form, appearance; state 4655

态度 /tàidu/ *n* attitude 0657

贪 /tān/ *v* be greedy 4959

摊 /tān/ *n* stand, stall, vendor's booth 4583

弹 /tán/ *v* play (some musical instruments); bounce, spring; flick, flip 5003

谈 /tán/ *v* talk 0245

谈 /tán/ *n* talk 4383

谈话 /tánhuà/ *v* talk 1808

谈话 /tánhuà/ *n* talk 4475

谈论 /tánlùn/ *v* talk about 4449

谈判 /tánpàn/ *v* negotiate 1619

坦克 /tǎnkè/ *n* tank 3943

叹 /tàn/ *v* sigh 3619

探 /tàn/ *v* explore; visit; stretch forward 3057

探索 /tànsuǒ/ *v* explore 2232

探讨 /tàntǎo/ *v* explore, approach, investigate 3012

汤 /tāng/ *n* soup 2676

堂 /táng/ *n* hall, room 2020

糖 /táng/ *n* sugar, sweets 2638

躺 /tǎng/ *v* lie, recline 2010

烫 /tàng/ *v* scald, burn; iron, press; have one's hair permed 4013

趟 /tàng/ *clas* [measure word for a return trip]; [measure word for a single trip of train] 2491

掏 /tāo/ *v* take out, produce (from pocket) 2646

逃 /táo/ *v* escape, flee, run away 2048

淘汰 /táotài/ *v* eliminate (through selection or competition); become obsolete 4561

讨 /tǎo/ *v* ask for, beg; take (as wife) 3623

讨论 /tǎolùn/ *v* discuss 0819

讨厌 /tǎoyàn/ *v* dislike, hate 3352

套 /tào/ *clas* [measure word for a group of associated things] set; suit; suite 0547

特 /tè/ *adj* special, unusual 1545

特 /tè/ *adv* specially, especially 2883

特别 /tèbié/ *adv* especially, particularly 0243

特别 /tèbié/ *adj* special, particular 1240

特点 /tèdiǎn/ *n* characteristic (feature) 1059

特色 /tèsè/ *n* characteristic, unique feature 1657

特殊 /tèshū/ *adj* special 1086

特意 /tèyì/ *adv* specially 4322

特有 /tèyǒu/ *v* be unique to or characteristic of 4615

特征 /tèzhēng/ *n* characteristic 2487

疼 /téng/ *v* ache, have a pain, hurt; love dearly 2742

踢 /tī/ *v* kick 2555

提 /tí/ *v* carry; put forward, raise; mention, ask; lift; promote 0730

提倡 /tíchàng/ *v* advocate, promote 3095

提出 /tíchū/ *v* raise (an issue), propose, suggest 0370

提到 /tídào/ *v* mention 2050

提高 /tígāo/ *v* raise, improve 0508

提供 /tígòng/ *v* provide, supply 0542

提起 /tíqǐ/ *v* mention 4017

提前 /tíqián/ *v* advance (to an earlier date or time); do something in advance or ahead of time 2542

提升 /tíshēng/ *v* promote 4269

提问 /tíwèn/ *v* ask questions; (teacher) put a question to 4261

提醒 /tíxǐng/ *v* remind 2100

题 /tí/ *n* title; topic, subject; problem (in exam) 1556

题材 /tícái/ *n* subject matter, material 3715

题目 /tímù/ *n* title, topic, subject; question in examination 2946

体 /tǐ/ *n* body; style; system 1837

体会 /tǐhuì/ *v* know (through learning or by experience) 2028

体力 /tǐlì/ *n* physical strength 3803

体内 /tǐnèi/ *place* inside the body 4880

体系 /tǐxì/ *n* system 1557

体现 /tǐxiàn/ *v* embody, show 1310

体验 /tǐyàn/ *v* experience 2936

体育 /tǐyù/ *n* sport; physical education, PE 1147

体制 /tǐzhì/ *n* institutional system, structure 1280

替 /tì/ *v* take the place of, substitute for 1696

天 /tiān/ *clas* [measure word for time] day 0091

天 /tiān/ *n* day; sky, air; heaven; time of day; weather 0411

天地 /tiāndì/ *n* heaven and earth; world 2553

天空 /tiānkōng/ *n* sky 2958

天气 /tiānqì/ *n* weather 1883

天然 /tiānrán/ adj natural 4692

天堂 /tiāntáng/ n heaven, paradise 4820

天天 /tiāntiān/ adv every day; day by day 1709

天下 /tiānxià/ n land under heaven, the world; the country 1886

天真 /tiānzhēn/ adj naive, innocent 4625

添 /tiān/ v add 2964

田 /tián/ n field, farmland 1399

甜 /tián/ adj sweet 3774

填 /tián/ v fill; fill in, complete (a form) 3070

挑 /tiāo, tiǎo/ v carry on a pole, shoulder; choose, select; push up, stir up 1989

挑选 /tiāoxuǎn/ v choose, select 4894

挑战 /tiǎozhàn/ v challenge 2041

条 /tiáo/ clas [measure word for things of a long and thin shape (e.g. string and river), pieces of writing (e.g. news, suggestions and regulations) or human life] 0157

条件 /tiáojiàn/ n condition 0420

条约 /tiáoyuē/ n treaty 2716

调整 /tiáozhěng/ v adjust 1223

跳 /tiào/ v jump 0881

跳舞 /tiàowǔ/ v dance 4439

贴 /tiē/ v stick, paste; keep close to; subsidise 1752

铁 /tiě/ n iron 2286

铁路 /tiělù/ n railway 1362

厅 /tīng/ n hall, foyer, lounge; [a provincial-level government department] department 2253

听 /tīng/ v listen 0146

听 /tīng/ clas [measure word for stuff contained in a tin or can] tin, can 2720

听到 /tīngdào/ v hear 1195

听见 /tīngjiàn/ v hear 2628

听取 /tīngqǔ/ v listen to, hear; follow (advice) 4896

听说 /tīngshuō/ v hear of, be told 1079

听众 /tīngzhòng/ n audience 3571

停 /tíng/ v stop 1052

停留 /tíngliú/ v (stop and) stay; remain 3817

停止 /tíngzhǐ/ v stop, put an end to 1830

挺 /tǐng/ adv very, rather 0720

挺 /tǐng/ v straighten up, stiffen; endure 4612

通 /tōng/ v open up by poking; understand, know; connect, communicate; lead to 1199

通 /tōng/ adj unblocked, open, through; (of writing) smooth 2592

通常 /tōngcháng/ adv usually 3276

通道 /tōngdào/ n passage, passageway; aisle 4005

通过 /tōngguò/ prep by means of, through, via 0299

通过 /tōngguò/ v go through; get past; pass, approve 1627

通信 /tōngxìn/ n correspondence, communication 3518

通讯 /tōngxùn/ n communication, telecommunication; correspondence, news report 2997

通知 /tōngzhī/ n note, notice, announcement 1985

通知 /tōngzhī/ v notify, inform, give notice 4341

同 /tóng/ prep [indicating relationship, involvement, comparison] with 0212

同胞 /tóngbāo/ n fellow countryman, compatriot 3213

同行 /tónghẳng/ n peer; profession 3283

同情 /tóngqíng/ v show pity or compassion 2704

同时 /tóngshí/ conj at the same time, simultaneously; besides, moreover 0369

同时 /tóngshí/ n meanwhile, the moment 1221

同时 /tóngshí/ adv at the same time, at once 2752

同事 /tóngshì/ n colleague 1865

同学 /tóngxué/ n (fellow) classmate, student 0588

同样 /tóngyàng/ adv likewise, similarly, by the same token 1513

同样 /tóngyàng/ adj same 2306

同一 /tóngyī/ adj same, identical 3020

同意 /tóngyì/ v agree 0712

同志 /tóngzhì/ n comrade; [more recent usage] someone who is homosexual 0406

铜 /tóng/ n copper 4227

童年 /tóngnián/ n childhood 4934

统计 /tǒngjì/ n statistics 1642

统一 /tǒngyī/ v unify, unite; standardise 1451

统一 /tǒngyī/ adj unified, uniform; centralised 2267

统治 /tǒngzhì/ v rule over, reign; dominate 2840

桶 /tǒng/ clas [measure word] pail, bucket, barrel 3852

痛 /tòng/ adv bitterly; severely, thoroughly 3414

痛 /tòng/ v hurt, ache, pain 3429

痛苦 /tòngkǔ/ adj painful 1259

痛快 /tòngkuài/ adj delighted, jolly; straightforward; to one's heart's content 4690

偷 /tōu/ v steal 2723

偷偷 /tōutōu/ adv stealthily, secretly 3929

头 /tóu/ n head; end 0246

头 /tóu/ clas [measure word for some animals such as pigs and cattle, also for garlics] 1243

头 /tóu/ num first 1849

头发 /tóufā/ n hair 1947

头脑 /tóunǎo/ n brain, head 2529

头儿 /tóur/ n head, chief, superior 4541

投 /tóu/ v throw; project, cast 1725

投入 /tóurù/ v throw (oneself) into (work); put into (operation) 1246

投降 /tóuxiáng/ v surrender, give in 3646

投资 /tóuzī/ v invest 0642

投资 /tóuzī/ n investment 4141

透 /tòu/ v penetrate, pass through; reveal, let out 3030

透 /tòu/ adv really, completely, thoroughly 4316

透过 /tòuguò/ prep through 4730

透露 /tòulù/ v reveal, disclose 3412

透明 /tòumíng/ adj transparent 4790

突出 /tūchū/ adj outstanding, prominent 1674

突破 /tūpò/ v break through; surmount 2190

突然 /tūrán/ adj sudden 0643

图 /tú/ n picture, drawing, chart, diagram, graph 0982

图案 /tú'àn/ n design, pattern 4821

图书馆 /túshūguǎn/ n library 2156

涂 /tú/ v spread, smear; scribble; cross out 4398

途径 /tújìng/ n means, pathway 2974

土 /tǔ/ n earth, soil 1506

土地 /tǔdì/ n land 0826

土壤 /tǔrǎng/ n soil 4130

吐 /tǔ, tù/ v spit, disgorge; vomit, throw up 3166

团 /tuán/ n something with a round shape, ball, wad; group; regiment; [short form for 共青团] the League 0991

团 /tuán/ clas [measure word for objects made into the shape of a ball] a ball of 3313

团结 /tuánjié/ v unite 1855

团体 /tuántǐ/ n group, organisation, society 2604

团长 /tuánzhǎng/ n head of a delegation or troupe; regimental commander 2436

推 /tuī/ v push 1158

推出 /tuīchū/ v present, introduce 2668

推动 /tuīdòng/ v promote, push forward 1706

推广 /tuīguǎng/ v popularise, promote 2821

推荐 /tuījiàn/ v recommend 3099

推进 /tuījìn/ v boost, advance, push on 2281

推行 /tuīxíng/ v carry out, push on with 3685

腿 /tuǐ/ n leg 1237

退 /tuì/ v move back, retreat; return, refund; withdraw; (of tide) recede 1129

退出 /tuìchū/ v withdraw, drop out of 3268

退休 /tuìxiū/ v retire 2430

吞 /tūn/ v swallow, bolt, devour 4676

托 /tuō/ v hold in one's hand; entrust 2317

拖 /tuō/ v drag, haul; delay, put off; mop (the floor) 2054

脱 /tuō/ v take off (clothes, shoes, etc.); shed, come off 2011

脱离 /tuōlí/ v leave, separate; break away from, divorce 3238

W

哇 /wa/ part [sentence final particle replacing 啊 where the preceding word ends with the vowel u or ao] 2710

挖 /wā/ v dig 1713

挖掘 /wājué/ v dig, excavate; tap (potentials, talents, etc.) 4314

外 /wài/ loc outside 0236

外边 /wàibian/ loc outside 4742

外部 /wàibù/ loc outside, exterior 4171

外出 /wàichū/ v go out, be away 4726

外地 /wàidì/ place non-local place 2930

外国 /wàiguó/ n foreign country 1136

外国人 /wàiguórén/ n foreigner 3005

外汇 /wàihuì/ n foreign exchange, foreign currency 4662

外交 /wàijiāo/ n diplomacy 1843

外面 /wàimian/ n outside 1597

外语 /wàiyǔ/ n foreign language 4994

完 /wán/ v finish, be over; (use) up 0141

完成 /wánchéng/ v complete, accomplish 0618

完美 /wánměi/ adj perfect, flawless 3275

完全 /wánquán/ adj complete, whole 0326

完善 /wánshàn/ v improve, make perfect 2280

完整 /wánzhěng/ adj complete, intact 1892

玩 /wán/ v play, amuse oneself 0753

玩具 /wánjù/ n toy 3637

玩笑 /wánxiào/ n joke 4925

玩意 /wányì/ n [often taking the suffix 儿] toy, plaything; thing 4484

顽强 /wánqiáng/ adj indomitable; tenacious 4114

晚 /wǎn/ adj late 0719

晚饭 /wǎnfàn/ n supper, dinner 4850

晚会 /wǎnhuì/ n evening, evening party 4175

晚上 /wǎnshang/ time (in the) evening 0559

碗 /wǎn/ clas [measure word for food contained in a bowl] bowl 2627

碗 /wǎn/ n bowl 3535

万 /wàn/ num 10,000 0433

万一 /wànyī/ conj just in case 3832

亡 /wáng/ v die, perish 4451

王国 /wángguó/ n kingdom 4876

网 /wǎng/ n net; web, internet 1029

网络 /wǎngluò/ n network 1191

网站 /wǎngzhàn/ n website 4592

往 /wǎng/ prep towards 0342

往后 /wǎnghòu/ *time* from now on, afterwards 4715

往来 /wǎnglái/ *v* contact, exchange visits; travel between 4200

往事 /wǎngshì/ *n* past events, the past 4706

往往 /wǎngwǎng/ *adv* often, frequently 1110

忘 /wàng/ *v* forget 1101

忘记 /wàngjì/ *v* forget 1940

旺 /wàng/ *adj* prosperous, flourishing, brisk; (of fire) blazing 4076

望 /wàng/ *v* have a look; hope 1402

望远镜 /wàngyuǎnjìng/ *n* telescope, binoculars 4817

危害 /wēihài/ *v* endanger, jeopardise 3451

危机 /wēijī/ *n* crisis 1703

危险 /wēixiǎn/ *adj* dangerous 1303

威 /wēi/ *n* power, prestige, honour 3528

威胁 /wēixié/ *v* threaten 1629

微 /wēi/ *adv* slightly 2468

微笑 /wēixiào/ *v* smile 2759

为 /wéi/ *v* be, act as 0097

为首 /wéishǒu/ *v* be led by, have . . . as the head 4345

为止 /wéizhǐ/ *v* until, up to; that's all for . . . 2543

为主 /wéizhǔ/ *v* give priority to, form the main part 1953

为 /wèi/ *prep* [introducing purpose, reason, beneficiary, etc.] for, because of 0065

为何 /wèihé/ *pron* why 3114

为了 /wèile/ *prep* for the sake of; in order to 0207

为什么 /wèishénme/ *pron* why 0267

围 /wéi/ *v* gather round; wrap round; surround, enclose 1859

围绕 /wéirào/ *v* revolve around; surround 3137

违背 /wéibèi/ *v* violate, go against, be contrary to 4100

违法 /wéifǎ/ *v* break the law, be against the law, be illegal 3587

违反 /wéifǎn/ *v* violate 2933

唯一 /wéiyī/ *adj* [equivalent of 惟一] only 1263

惟一 /wéiyī/ *adj* [equivalent of 唯一] only, sole 3983

维持 /wéichí/ *v* maintain, keep; continue, last; sustain 1991

维护 /wéihù/ *v* defend, safeguard; uphold, maintain 1549

伟大 /wěidà/ *adj* great 1058

尾 /wěi/ *n* tail; end 3186

尾巴 /wěiba/ *n* tail 4578

委托 /wěituō/ *v* entrust 4104

委员 /wěiyuán/ *n* committee member 2218

委员会 /wěiyuánhuì/ *n* committee 0938

卫生 /wèishēng/ *n* hygiene, sanitation, public health 1590

卫星 /wèixīng/ *n* satellite 3536

未 /wèi/ *adv* [archaic] not (yet) 0533

未必 /wèibì/ *adv* not necessarily 4120

未来 /wèilái/ *time* the future 1002

位 /wèi/ *clas* [measure word for respectable people] 0092

位于 /wèiyú/ *v* be located, be situated 2245

位置 /wèizhì/ *n* position, location 0966

味 /wèi/ *n* taste, smell 2087

味道 /wèidào/ *n* taste, flavour 2714

味儿 /wèir/ *n* taste, flavour 4654

胃 /wèi/ *n* stomach 3703

喂 /wèi/ *interj* hello, hey 2996

喂 /wèi/ *v* feed 3266

温 /wēn/ *adj* warm 3693

温度 /wēndù/ *n* temperature 3467

温暖 /wēnnuǎn/ *adj* warm 2441

温柔 /wēnróu/ *adj* gentle and soft, amiable 3830

文 /wén/ *n* script, language; essay, writing 0741

文化 /wénhuà/ *n* culture 0163

文件 /wénjiàn/ *n* document 1496

文明 /wénmíng/ *n* civilisation; manners 1538

文明 /wénmíng/ *adj* civilised, civil 1799

文凭 /wénpíng/ *n* diploma, certificate, academic credentials 4933

文人 /wénrén/ *n* man of letters, scholar 4386

文物 /wénwù/ *n* cultural relic 2561

文学 /wénxué/ *n* literature 0663

文艺 /wényì/ *n* literature and art 1738

文章 /wénzhāng/ *n* article, essay 0797

文字 /wénzì/ *n* character, script, writing; style of writing; word 1339

纹 /wén/ *n* stria, line 4758

闻 /wén/ *v* smell; hear 2243

稳 /wěn/ *adj* steady; certain 3628

稳定 /wěndìng/ *adj* stable 1126

问 /wèn/ *v* ask 0164

问道 /wèndào/ *v* ask 3859

问候 /wènhòu/ *v* greet, give somebody one's respects 4977

问题 /wèntí/ *n* question, problem, issue 0072

窝 /wō/ *n* nest 3808

我 /wǒ/ *pron* I, me 0007

我们 /wǒmen/ *pron* we, us 0026

握 /wò/ *v* hold, grasp 3028

握手 /wòshǒu/ *v* shake hands 4546

污染 /wūrǎn/ *v* pollute 2387

屋 /wū/ *n* house, room 1836

屋里 /wūli/ *place* indoors, in the house or room 2798

屋子 /wūzi/ n house 3021

无 /wú/ v have no, there be no 0224

无 /wú/ adv not 2549

无比 /wúbǐ/ adj matchless, unsurpassed, immeasurable 3775

无法 /wúfǎ/ v be unable to, can't 0677

无非 /wúfēi/ adv only, nothing but, no more than 4521

无力 /wúlì/ v feel weak, lack strength or power; be unable 4956

无论 /wúlùn/ conj no matter (what, how) 1109

无论如何 /wúlùnrúhé/ idiom anyhow, at any rate, by all means, whatever happens 4222

无奈 /wúnài/ adj having no choice, utterly helpless 3779

无数 /wúshù/ num countless, innumerable 2423

无所谓 /wúsuǒwèi/ idiom be indifferent; make no difference 4172

无限 /wúxiàn/ adj unlimited, boundless 3926

无疑 /wúyí/ adv undoubtedly 2503

无意 /wúyì/ adv inadvertently, accidentally 4634

五 /wǔ/ num five 0172

武 /wǔ/ n martial arts 1988

武器 /wǔqì/ n weapon 1775

武术 /wǔshù/ n martial arts 3537

武装 /wǔzhuāng/ n arms 2312

舞 /wǔ/ v dance; wield 2764

舞蹈 /wǔdǎo/ n dance 2641

舞台 /wǔtái/ n stage; arena 2019

物 /wù/ n thing 1385

物价 /wùjià/ n price 4467

物理 /wùlǐ/ n physics 3152

物品 /wùpǐn/ n article, item 3671

物质 /wùzhì/ n substance, matter; material 1358

物资 /wùzī/ n goods and materials, supplies 4290

误会 /wùhuì/ v misunderstand, mistake 5001

悟 /wù/ v come to realise; awaken, enlighten 4901

雾 /wù/ n fog, mist 4914

X

西 /xī/ loc west 0960

西北 /xīběi/ loc northwest 2636

西部 /xībù/ loc west, western part 2308

西方 /xīfāng/ place west; the West 0914

西瓜 /xīguā/ n watermelon 4644

西南 /xīnán/ place southwest 3880

吸 /xī/ v inhale, draw; suck, suck up; attract 2197

吸毒 /xīdú/ v take drug 4958

吸收 /xīshōu/ v absorb, draw; enrol, recruit 2494

吸烟 /xīyān/ v smoke 4440

吸引 /xīyǐn/ v attract 1356

希望 /xīwàng/ v hope, wish for 0259

希望 /xīwàng/ n hope 2194

息 /xī/ n (bank) interest; breath; news 4929

牺牲 /xīshēng/ v sacrifice 1857

习惯 /xíguàn/ n habit 1247

习惯 /xíguàn/ v be used to, be accustomed to 3162

袭击 /xíjī/ v assault, hit; surprise 2934

媳妇 /xífù/ n daughter-in-law; wife 2831

洗 /xǐ/ v wash 1067

洗澡 /xǐzǎo/ v bathe, take a bath or shower 4768

喜 /xǐ/ adj happy, delighted, joyful 2899

喜 /xǐ/ v like, be fond of 2966

喜爱 /xǐ'ài/ v like, love 3117

喜欢 /xǐhuān/ v like, enjoy 0353

喜悦 /xǐyuè/ n happiness, joy 4789

戏 /xì/ n drama, play, show 1248

戏剧 /xìjù/ n drama, play 3212

系 /xì/ n (academic) department; system, series 0762

系列 /xìliè/ clas series 1759

系统 /xìtǒng/ n system 0821

系统 /xìtǒng/ adj systematic 3356

细 /xì/ adj thin, fine; exquisite; careful 1698

细胞 /xìbāo/ n cell 3843

细节 /xìjié/ n detail 3090

细致 /xìzhì/ adj delicate, fine; careful 4461

下 /xià/ loc under, below 0064

下 /xià/ v come down; alight; rain, snow; get off (from class, work, etc.); give (order, definition, conclusion, etc.); play (chess) 0284

下 /xià/ clas [measure word for counting actions] one stroke, (do) once 0315

下班 /xiàbān/ v get off work 3758

下次 /xiàcì/ time next time 4825

下岗 /xiàgǎng/ v stand down; be laid off 4555

下降 /xiàjiàng/ v decline, drop 2332

下来 /xiàlái/ v come down, descend 0348

下令 /xiàlìng/ v give an order 4211

下面 /xiàmian/ n the following, below; next; lower level 1340

下去 /xiàqù/ v go down, descend 0550

下午 /xiàwǔ/ time (in the) afternoon 0764

下子 /xiàzi/ clas [measure word for occurrences of an action or event]; [occurring in the fixed expression 一下子 "suddenly"] 1741

吓 /xià, hè/ v frighten, scare; threaten 1887

夏 /xià/ time summer 1908

夏季 /xiàjì/ *time* summer 4766

夏天 /xiàtiān/ *time* summer 2357

仙 /xiān/ *n* immortal being 3544

先 /xiān/ *adv* first, earlier 0251

先后 /xiānhòu/ *adv* one after another, successively 1945

先进 /xiānjìn/ *adj* advanced 1436

先生 /xiānsheng/ *n* Mr; mister, sir 0234

先是 /xiānshì/ *adv* previously, originally, first 3533

掀起 /xiānqǐ/ *v* lift; raise; set off, start 4411

鲜 /xiān/ *adj* fresh; (of colour) bright; (of food) tasty 4415

鲜花 /xiānhuā/ *n* (fresh) flowers 3794

鲜明 /xiānmíng/ *adj* bright; distinct; striking 3928

闲 /xián/ *adj* free, idle 2880

贤 /xián/ *adj* virtuous and able; [used as part of a term of respect] 4419

嫌 /xián/ *v* dislike, mind 3486

显 /xiǎn/ *v* show, display; be apparent or obvious 2725

显得 /xiǎnde/ *v* appear, seem, look 1257

显然 /xiǎnrán/ *adv* clearly, obviously 1554

显示 /xiǎnshì/ *v* show 1564

显著 /xiǎnzhù/ *adj* remarkable, outstanding 3391

县 /xiàn/ *n* county 0845

县城 /xiànchéng/ *n* county seat, county town 3000

现 /xiàn/ *time* now 0765

现场 /xiànchǎng/ *place* scene (of event or incident), site, spot 1639

现代 /xiàndài/ *time* modern times 0780

现代化 /xiàndàihuà/ *n* modernisation 1612

现金 /xiànjīn/ *n* cash 4536

现实 /xiànshí/ *n* reality 0905

现象 /xiànxiàng/ *n* appearance; phenomenon 0774

现行 /xiànxíng/ *adj* current, in effect, in operation 4909

现有 /xiànyǒu/ *adj* currently existing 4508

现在 /xiànzài/ *time* now 0094

现状 /xiànzhuàng/ *n* status quo, present conditions 3572

线 /xiàn/ *n* line; thread 0937

线 /xiàn/ *clas* [measure word for slim things such as rays and hopes] 2819

线索 /xiànsuǒ/ *n* clue 3996

限 /xiàn/ *v* limit, set a limit 4453

限度 /xiàndù/ *n* limit, limitation 4927

限制 /xiànzhì/ *v* restrict 2141

陷入 /xiànrù/ *v* fall into; be deep in 2391

羡慕 /xiànmù/ *v* admire, envy 4343

献 /xiàn/ *v* offer, present; dedicate 3478

乡 /xiāng/ *n* township; country, countryside 1802

乡村 /xiāngcūn/ *n* village, countryside 3746

乡下 /xiāngxia/ *place* country, countryside 4765

相 /xiāng/ *adv* each other 0417

相比 /xiāngbǐ/ *v* compare 2215

相处 /xiāngchǔ/ *v* get along 3922

相当 /xiāngdāng/ *adv* very, quite, considerably 0959

相当 /xiāngdāng/ *adj* matching, commensurate with; suitable, appropriate; considerable 2164

相对 /xiāngduì/ *adv* relatively 2433

相反 /xiāngfǎn/ *adj* opposite, contrary 2669

相关 /xiāngguān/ *v* be interrelated 1664

相互 /xiānghù/ *adv* each other, mutually 1481

相继 /xiāngjì/ *adv* in succession; one after another 4421

相似 /xiāngsì/ *adj* similar 3326

相同 /xiāngtóng/ *adj* identical, same, common 1976

相信 /xiāngxìn/ *v* believe, trust, be convinced 0474

相应 /xiāngyìng/ *adj* corresponding, relevant 3074

香 /xiāng/ *adj* fragrant, sweet-scented; sound (sleep); appetising, (eat) with relish 1317

香烟 /xiāngyān/ *n* cigarette; smoke from burning incense 4750

箱子 /xiāngzi/ *n* box, suitcase 4526

详细 /xiángxì/ *adj* detailed 2466

享受 /xiǎngshòu/ *v* lead a life of pleasure; enjoy (rights, benefits, etc.) 1409

享有 /xiǎngyǒu/ *v* enjoy (rights, etc.) 4108

响 /xiǎng/ *adj* loud; noisy 2783

响 /xiǎng/ *v* sound, make a sound, (of applause) break out, (of telephone) ring 3146

响起 /xiǎngqǐ/ *v* sound, make a sound, break out 4558

想 /xiǎng/ *v* think 0056

想到 /xiǎngdào/ *v* think of 0772

想法 /xiǎngfǎ/ *n* idea, opinion 1434

想起 /xiǎngqǐ/ *v* remember, recollect 1643

想象 /xiǎngxiàng/ *v* imagine 1809

想像 /xiǎngxiàng/ *v* imagine 3288

向 /xiàng/ *prep* [indicating direction] to, towards 0100

向 /xiàng/ *v* side with, be partial to, favour 1323

向前 /xiàngqián/ *adv* forward 2577

向往 /xiàngwǎng/ *v* yearn for, look forward to, dream of 4778

项 /xiàng/ *clas* [measure word for items stipulated, planned, enumerated, or for an account of facts or events] 0440

项目 /xiàngmù/ *n* project, item 0611

象 /xiàng/ *n* elephant; image, shape 0684

象征 /xiàngzhēng/ *n* emblem, symbol, token 3797

象征 /*xiàngzhēng*/ *v* stand for, symbolise, signify 4265

像 /*xiàng*/ *v* look like, resemble; look as if 0133

消 /*xiāo*/ *v* disappear, cause to disappear 3586

消除 /*xiāochú*/ *v* eliminate, remove 2803

消费 /*xiāofèi*/ *v* consume 1410

消费者 /*xiāofèizhě*/ *n* consumer 2512

消耗 /*xiāohào*/ *v* consume, deplete 4551

消化 /*xiāohuà*/ *v* digest 4604

消极 /*xiāojí*/ *adj* passive, inactive 4462

消灭 /*xiāomiè*/ *v* perish, eliminate 2912

消失 /*xiāoshī*/ *v* disappear 2113

消息 /*xiāoxi*/ *n* news 0877

销 /*xiāo*/ *v* sell; fasten (with a bolt) 4952

销售 /*xiāoshòu*/ *v* sell 1196

小 /*xiǎo*/ *adj* small, little 0066

小 /*xiǎo*/ *pref* [usually preceding a family name or given name as a title of address to show affection] 1636

小孩 /*xiǎohái*/ *n* child 1745

小孩子 /*xiǎoháizi*/ *n* child 3913

小伙子 /*xiǎohuǒzi*/ *n* young man 2599

小姐 /*xiǎojie*/ *n* miss; young lady; [more recent usage] waitress; prostitute 1163

小朋友 /*xiǎopéngyou*/ *n* children 4853

小时 /*xiǎoshí*/ *n* hour 0563

小时候 /*xiǎoshíhou*/ *n* (in) one's childhood 3134

小事 /*xiǎoshì*/ *n* trivial matter, triviality 3907

小说 /*xiǎoshuō*/ *n* novel, story 0778

小心 /*xiǎoxīn*/ *v* be careful, take care; guard against 4097

小学 /*xiǎoxué*/ *n* primary school 1477

小子 /*xiǎozi*/ *n* boy, young fellow; [derogatory] bloke; chap 2554

小组 /*xiǎozǔ*/ *n* group 2107

晓得 /*xiǎode*/ *v* know 4194

孝 /*xiào*/ *adj* filial 4793

效果 /*xiàoguǒ*/ *n* effect, (positive) result 1300

效率 /*xiàolǜ*/ *n* efficiency 2952

校 /*xiào*/ *n* school 2168

校园 /*xiàoyuán*/ *n* campus 2981

校长 /*xiàozhǎng*/ *n* headmaster; president, chancellor 1483

笑 /*xiào*/ *v* laugh, smile 0387

笑话 /*xiàohuà*/ *n* joke 3302

笑容 /*xiàoróng*/ *n* smile 3709

笑声 /*xiàoshēng*/ *n* laughter 3713

些 /*xiē*/ *clas* some, an amount of 0309

协定 /*xiédìng*/ *n* agreement 3940

协会 /*xiéhuì*/ *n* association, society 1864

协调 /*xiétiáo*/ *adj* matching, coordinated, in keeping 2765

协议 /*xiéyì*/ *n* agreement 1615

协助 /*xiézhù*/ *v* assist, help 3815

邪 /*xié*/ *adj* evil, weird 4367

鞋 /*xié*/ *n* shoe 2103

写 /*xiě*/ *v* write 0177

写信 /*xiěxìn*/ *v* write (a letter) 4149

写作 /*xiězuò*/ *n* writing 2214

谢 /*xiè*/ *v* thank; (of flowers) wither 4064

谢谢 /*xièxie*/ *v* thank 1646

心 /*xīn*/ *n* heart; mind; core, centre 0261

心里 /*xīnli*/ *place* in one's heart (mind) 0522

心理 /*xīnlǐ*/ *n* mentality, psychology 0787

心灵 /*xīnlíng*/ *n* internal spirit, heart, soul, mind 2064

心理学 /*xīnlǐxué*/ *n* psychology 4390

心目 /*xīnmù*/ *n* mind 3849

心情 /*xīnqíng*/ *n* feeling, state of mind, mood 1342

心思 /*xīnsī*/ *n* idea; thinking, thought 4530

心态 /*xīntài*/ *n* state of mind, mindset 2453

心想 /*xīnxiǎng*/ *v* think 4018

心眼 /*xīnyǎn*/ *n* heart, mind; cleverness; tolerance 4535

心脏 /*xīnzàng*/ *n* heart 3704

心中 /*xīnzhōng*/ *place* in one's heart, in one's mind 1251

辛苦 /*xīnkǔ*/ *adj* hard, painstaking 3389

欣赏 /*xīnshǎng*/ *v* appreciate, enjoy 1932

新 /*xīn*/ *adj* new 0112

新人 /*xīnrén*/ *n* new face, new people; newly wed, bride and bridegroom; people of a new age or a new generation 4599

新闻 /*xīnwén*/ *n* news 0798

新鲜 /*xīnxiān*/ *adj* fresh 2248

信 /*xìn*/ *n* letter, mail 0586

信 /*xìn*/ *v* believe, believe in 1347

信号 /*xìnhào*/ *n* signal 4180

信念 /*xìnniàn*/ *n* faith, belief 3364

信任 /*xìnrèn*/ *v* trust 1748

信息 /*xìnxī*/ *n* information 0664

信心 /*xìnxīn*/ *n* confidence 1782

信仰 /*xìnyǎng*/ *n* belief, faith 3966

兴 /*xīng*/ *v* prevail, be in fashion; promote; permit, allow 2081

兴奋 /*xīngfèn*/ *adj* excited 3274

兴奋 /*xīngfèn*/ *v* be excited 3651

兴起 /*xīngqǐ*/ *v* rise, spring up, develop 4505

兴趣 /*xìngqù*/ *n* interest 0888

星 /*xīng*/ *n* star 1470

星期 /*xīngqī*/ *n* week 2258

星星 /xīngxing/ *n* star 4971

行 /xíng/ *n* trip; behaviour 0630

行 /xíng/ *v* be all right; travel 0654

行 /xíng/ *adj* OK, all right 2004

行动 /xíngdòng/ *v* act, take action; move about 0683

行李 /xínglǐ/ *n* baggage, luggage 4799

行人 /xíngrén/ *n* pedestrian 3942

行为 /xíngwéi/ *n* action, behaviour 0529

行政 /xíngzhèng/ *n* administration 1804

形 /xíng/ *n* shape, form 1993

形成 /xíngchéng/ *v* form, make 0551

形容 /xíngróng/ *v* describe 4197

形式 /xíngshì/ *n* form 0853

形势 /xíngshì/ *n* situation 1293

形态 /xíngtài/ *n* shape, form 3801

形象 /xíngxiàng/ *n* image 1022

形象 /xíngxiàng/ *adj* vivid 4843

形状 /xíngzhuàng/ *n* shape 4645

型 /xíng/ *suf* model, type 1200

醒 /xǐng/ *v* wake up 2316

姓 /xìng/ *v* be surnamed 1846

姓 /xìng/ *n* surname, last name 4374

姓名 /xìngmíng/ *n* full name 4285

幸福 /xìngfú/ *adj* happy, blessed 1238

幸运 /xìngyùn/ *adj* lucky, fortunate 4164

性 /xìng/ *n* property, disposition; sex 0690

性 /xìng/ *suf* [nominal suffix indicating a specified quality or property] 0825

性别 /xìngbié/ *n* gender, sex 4920

性格 /xìnggé/ *n* disposition, nature, personality 1511

性质 /xìngzhì/ *n* nature, character 2259

兄 /xiōng/ *n* elder brother; [preceded by a surname to be used as a courtesy term of address between male friends] 4240

兄弟 /xiōngdì/ *n* brother 1264

胸 /xiōng/ *n* chest, bosom; mind 3598

雄 /xióng/ *adj* male; heroic 3979

熊 /xióng/ *n* bear 4391

休 /xiū/ *v* rest, take (leave); stop, cease 4685

休息 /xiūxi/ *v* rest 1742

休闲 /xiūxián/ *v* enjoy leisure, relax 4835

修 /xiū/ *v* repair, mend, fix; build; trim, prune 1501

修改 /xiūgǎi/ *v* revise, amend 2532

修建 /xiūjiàn/ *v* build 4203

修养 /xiūyǎng/ *n* culture, cultivation, self-possession 4762

须 /xū/ *v* must, have to 3009

虚 /xū/ *adj* empty; false; virtual; in poor health; timid 3436

需 /xū/ *v* need, require 1847

需求 /xūqiú/ *n* demand 1717

需要 /xūyào/ *v* need 0247

需要 /xūyào/ *n* need 1446

许 /xǔ/ *v* allow 1807

许 /xǔ/ *adv* about, approximately; perhaps 3783

许多 /xǔduō/ *num* many, plenty of 0257

叙述 /xùshù/ *v* give an account of, tell about 4554

宣布 /xuānbù/ *v* announce, declare 1149

宣传 /xuānchuán/ *v* propagate, publicise, promote 1370

宣告 /xuān'gào/ *v* declare, proclaim 4674

宣言 /xuānyán/ *n* declaration, manifesto 3941

旋转 /xuánzhuǎn/ *v* rotate, revolve, spin 4893

选 /xuǎn/ *v* choose 1222

选举 /xuǎnjǔ/ *v* elect 2099

选手 /xuǎnshǒu/ *n* (selected) contestant, player 2135

选择 /xuǎnzé/ *v* choose, select 0580

学 /xué/ *v* learn, study 0277

学费 /xuéfèi/ *n* tuition fees 4426

学会 /xuéhuì/ *n* professional or academic association, society 2739

学会 /xuéhuì/ *v* learn 3144

学历 /xuélì/ *n* academic qualification 3997

学期 /xuéqī/ *n* term, semester 4965

学生 /xuésheng/ *n* student 0294

学术 /xuéshù/ *n* scholarly learning 1425

学说 /xuéshuō/ *n* theory, doctrine 4178

学位 /xuéwèi/ *n* (academic) degree 3174

学问 /xuéwèn/ *n* scholarly learning 2949

学习 /xuéxí/ *v* learn, study 0351

学校 /xuéxiào/ *n* school 0278

学员 /xuéyuán/ *n* learner, student 4532

学院 /xuéyuàn/ *n* college 1072

学者 /xuézhě/ *n* scholar 1116

雪 /xuě/ *n* snow 1350

血 /xuè/ *n* blood 1279

血管 /xuèguǎn/ *n* vein 4921

血液 /xuèyè/ *n* blood 3665

寻 /xún/ *v* look for, seek 3383

寻求 /xúnqiú/ *v* seek, look for 3267

寻找 /xúnzhǎo/ *v* look for, seek 1456

询问 /xúnwèn/ *v* enquire, question 3516

循环 /xúnhuán/ *v* circle, circulate 4145

训练 /xùnliàn/ *v* train 1143

迅速 /xùnsù/ *adv* rapidly 1028

Y

压 /yā/ *v* press 1468

压力 /yālì/ *n* pressure 1190

压迫 /yāpò/ v oppress 4548

呀 /ya/ part [sentence final particle] 0293

呀 /yā/ interj [interjection expressing surprise] ah, oh 0546

呀 /yā/ ono [the sound of a creak] 3135

鸭 /yā/ n duck 4088

牙 /yá/ n tooth 2618

牙齿 /yáchǐ/ n tooth 4477

雅 /yǎ/ adj elegant, refined 2501

烟 /yān/ n smoke; cigarette 1073

延长 /yáncháng/ v extend, renew 4985

延伸 /yánshēn/ v extend, stretch 4564

延续 /yánxù/ v continue, last 4109

严 /yán/ adj strict, stern; (air- or water-) tight 2031

严格 /yángé/ adj strict 1502

严峻 /yánjùn/ adj severe, serious, stern, grim 4907

严厉 /yánlì/ adj severe, stern 3101

严肃 /yánsù/ adj serious, solemn 1891

严重 /yánzhòng/ adj severe, serious 0673

言 /yán/ n speech, word 1027

岩 /yán/ n rock, cliff 3341

沿 /yán/ prep along 2836

沿海 /yánhǎi/ place along the coast, coastal 3498

沿着 /yánzhe/ prep along 2960

研究 /yánjiù/ v do research, study 0232

研究 /yánjiù/ n research 2596

研究生 /yánjiùshēng/ n graduate, postgraduate 2817

研究所 /yánjiùsuǒ/ n research institute 2285

研制 /yánzhì/ v develop 4609

盐 /yán/ n salt 3304

颜色 /yánsè/ n colour 2236

眼 /yǎn/ n eye 0898

眼 /yǎn/ clas [measure word for the action of look or glance]; [measure word for wells] 1616

眼光 /yǎn'guāng/ n eye, sight; foresight 2226

眼睛 /yǎnjīng/ n eye 0736

眼镜 /yǎnjìng/ n glasses, spectacles 4126

眼泪 /yǎnlèi/ n tear 2435

眼里 /yǎnli/ place in one's eyes, in one's view 2870

眼前 /yǎnqián/ place before one's eyes; the present 2121

眼神 /yǎnshén/ n expression or emotion shown in one's eyes 3472

眼下 /yǎnxià/ time at present, now, for the time being 4940

眼中 /yǎnzhōng/ place in one's eyes 3810

演 /yǎn/ v perform, play, show 2139

演出 /yǎnchū/ v perform, put on a show 1493

演讲 /yǎnjiǎng/ n speech, lecture 3100

演习 /yǎnxí/ v hold (military) exercises, manoeuvre 3521

演员 /yǎnyuán/ n actor or actress 1567

宴会 /yànhuì/ n banquet, dinner party 4638

扬 /yáng/ v raise; spread 3241

羊 /yáng/ n sheep 1868

阳 /yáng/ adj positive; Yang (positive) 2394

阳光 /yángguāng/ n sunshine 1777

洋 /yáng/ adj foreign 2481

仰 /yǎng/ v look up, face up, raise one's head 4988

养 /yǎng/ v keep, raise (animals, etc.); provide for, support (a family); give birth to; develop (a habit); rest, maintain 1133

养成 /yǎngchéng/ v cultivate, acquire, develop 4888

养老 /yǎnglǎo/ v provide for the elderly; live out one's life in retirement 3975

样 /yàng/ clas [measure word for some material objects] type, sort 1244

样 /yàng/ n appearance; sample 1677

样子 /yàngzi/ n look, appearance, manner 0830

腰 /yāo/ n waist 2085

邀 /yāo/ v invite 4511

邀请 /yāoqǐng/ v invite 1910

摇 /yáo/ v shake, rock, wave, wag 3164

摇头 /yáotóu/ v shake one's head 4513

遥远 /yáoyuǎn/ adj far away, remote, distant 3392

咬 /yǎo/ v bite 2140

药 /yào/ n medicine, drug 1127

药品 /yàopǐn/ n medicine, drug 3904

药物 /yàowù/ n medication, drug 3538

要求 /yāoqiú/ v ask for, request, demand 0424

要求 /yāoqiú/ n requirement, request 0738

要 /yào/ v want; order 0020

要么 /yàome/ conj (either . . .) or 3737

要是 /yàoshi/ conj if, in case 2673

爷 /yé/ n [usually taking the suffix 儿] father, grandfather; [used as a polite term of address for an old man] uncle 2065

爷爷 /yéye/ n (paternal) grandpa 2409

也 /yě/ adv also 0017

也 /yě/ conj [as in 既 . . . 也] and also, (not) either 0301

也好 /yěhǎo/ part may as well 2480

也就是说 /yějiùshìshuō/ idiom that is to say, namely 2535

也许 /yěxǔ/ adv perhaps 0645

野 /yě/ adj wild; rough, rude; unruly 4734

业 /yè/ n trade, line of business; profession, occupation; estate, property; undertaking 2927

业绩 /yèjī/ n performance; achievement 4093

业务 /yèwù/ n business; professional work 1256

业余 /yèyú/ adj spare-time; amateur 3692

叶 /yè/ n leaf; part of a historical period 2959

页 /yè/ clas page 3006

夜 /yè/ time night 1478

夜 /yè/ clas night 2151

夜里 /yèlí/ time night 3576

夜晚 /yèwǎn/ time night 3953

一 /yī/ num one, a, an 0003

一般 /yìbān/ adv generally, as a rule 0392

一半 /yíbàn/ num half 1445

一边 /yìbiān/ adv at the same time, simultaneously 1124

一边 /yìbiān/ loc one side 4982

一部分 /yíbùfen/ num a part of 1882

一带 /yídài/ n area, region, part 4289

一旦 /yídàn/ conj once, in case 1336

一道 /yídào/ adv together 4220

一定 /yídìng/ adv certainly 0254

一定 /yídìng/ adj definite, regular; given, certain; fixed, specified 0766

一度 /yídù/ adv once, on one occasion, for a time 4170

一方面 /yìfāngmiàn/ conj on the one hand, while 1913

一共 /yígòng/ adv altogether, in all 4845

一级 /yìjí/ adj first rate, first class, first degree 3247

一块 /yíkuài/ adv together 2726

一块儿 /yíkuàir/ adv together 5004

一流 /yìliú/ adj first rate, first class 3591

一路 /yílù/ adv all the way 3041

一律 /yílǜ/ adv all, with no exception 3833

一面 /yímiàn/ adv [as in 一面 . . . 一面 . . . , equivalent of 一边 . . . 一边 . . .] simultaneously, at the same time 1934

一起 /yìqǐ/ adv together 0252

一切 /yíqiè/ pron everything, all 0366

一日 /yírì/ time one day 2838

一生 /yìshēng/ n all one's life 1460

一时 /yìshí/ adv for the moment, temporarily, for a short while 1977

一手 /yìshǒu/ adv single-handedly, all along, all by oneself 4078

一同 /yìtóng/ adv together 4283

一向 /yíxiàng/ adv all along, always 3226

一些 /yìxiē/ num some 0115

一行 /yìxíng/ n group, delegation 4037

一样 /yíyàng/ aux [usually occurring in 像 . . . 一样] like 0402

一样 /yíyàng/ adj same 0432

一再 /yízài/ adv repeatedly 2917

一直 /yìzhí/ adv straight (in a straight line); always, all along 0240

一致 /yízhì/ adj identical; unanimous; consistent 1417

衣 /yī/ n clothes, clothing 2291

衣服 /yīfu/ n clothes, dress 0981

医 /yī/ n medical science, medicine; doctor, physician 3710

医疗 /yīliáo/ n medicine, medical treatment 2238

医生 /yīshēng/ n doctor 0920

医学 /yīxué/ n medicine, medical science 1863

医药 /yīyào/ n medicine 3756

医院 /yīyuàn/ n hospital 0635

依 /yī/ prep according to, by 3161

依旧 /yījiù/ adv as before, still 4280

依据 /yījù/ n basis, foundation, evidence 3001

依靠 /yīkào/ v depend on, rely on 2212

依赖 /yīlài/ v depend on, count on 3621

依然 /yīrán/ adv still 1381

仪器 /yíqì/ n instrument, apparatus 4997

仪式 /yíshì/ n ceremony 2108

宜 /yí/ adj suitable 4219

移 /yí/ v move, remove; change 2403

移动 /yídòng/ v move 3069

移民 /yímín/ n migrant, immigrant, emigrant; immigration 3183

遗产 /yíchǎn/ n heritage, inheritance, legacy 3156

遗憾 /yíhàn/ adj sorry, pitiful, regretful 2203

遗址 /yízhǐ/ n ancient ruins 2906

疑问 /yíwèn/ n doubt; query 4226

乙 /yǐ/ n [used for the second of enumerated items] second 3025

已 /yǐ/ adv already 0123

已经 /yǐjīng/ adv already 0101

以 /yǐ/ prep by means of, with, in (some way); according to; because of 0077

以 /yǐ/ conj in order to, so as to 1348

以便 /yǐbiàn/ conj so that, in order to 3987

以此 /yǐcǐ/ adv hereby, by this, with this 4574

以后 /yǐhòu/ loc after; afterwards 0248

以及 /yǐjí/ conj and, as well as, along with 0383

以来 /yǐlái/ time since (a previous event) 0742

以前 /yǐqián/ time before 0593

以上 /yǐshàng/ loc above; more than 0662

以外 /yǐwài/ loc beyond, outside; other than 1924

以往 /yǐwǎng/ time before, the past 2372

以为 /yǐwéi/ v think, believe 0875

以下 /yǐxià/ loc below, following, as follows 1623

椅子 /yǐzi/ *n* chair 4032

义 /yì/ *n* meaning, sense; justice, righteousness 2779

义务 /yìwù/ *n* obligation, duty; volunteer, voluntary 2860

亿 /yì/ *num* 100 million 3107

艺术 /yìshù/ *n* art 0492

艺术家 /yìshùjiā/ *n* artist 2832

议论 /yìlùn/ *v* remark on, comment on 3218

亦 /yì/ *adv* also 1970

异 /yì/ *adj* different; strange, unusual 4117

异常 /yìcháng/ *adj* unusual 4160

抑制 /yìzhì/ *v* restrain, refrain 3960

译 /yì/ *v* translate 4016

易 /yì/ *adj* easy 2695

意 /yì/ *n* meaning, idea; intention, desire 1230

意见 /yìjiàn/ *n* opinion, comment; objection, complaint 0627

意识 /yìshí/ *n* consciousness 0854

意识 /yìshí/ *v* be conscious of, be aware of, realise 4304

意思 /yìsi/ *n* meaning, idea, opinion; trace, hint; gift, token of gratitude, etc. 0621

意外 /yìwài/ *adj* unexpected 2499

意味着 /yìwèizhe/ *v* mean, imply 2142

意义 /yìyì/ *n* meaning, significance 0514

意志 /yìzhì/ *n* will 2922

因 /yīn/ *prep* because of, as a result of, according to 0407

因此 /yīncǐ/ *conj* as such, so, therefore, as a result 0389

因而 /yīn'ér/ *conj* so, therefore, hence 2284

因素 /yīnsù/ *n* element, factor 1099

因为 /yīnwèi/ *conj* because 0099

阴 /yīn/ *adj* (of weather) overcast; negative; Yin (negative) 3015

阴影 /yīnyǐng/ *n* shadow, shade; blight, spectre 4589

音 /yīn/ *n* sound; news 2955

音乐 /yīnyuè/ *n* music 1051

银 /yín/ *n* silver 2953

银行 /yínháng/ *n* bank 0755

银子 /yínzi/ *n* silver; money 4874

引 /yǐn/ *v* cause, make; guide, lead; quote, cite 1823

引导 /yǐndǎo/ *v* guide, lead 2666

引发 /yǐnfā/ *v* trigger, evoke 3323

引进 /yǐnjìn/ *v* introduce from elsewhere, import; bring in 2631

引起 /yǐnqǐ/ *v* evoke, give rise to, lead to 0717

饮 /yǐn/ *v* drink 4353

饮料 /yǐnliào/ *n* drink 4855

饮食 /yǐnshí/ *n* food and drink, diet 3602

印 /yìn/ *v* print 3056

印象 /yìnxiàng/ *n* impression 1301

应 /yīng, yìng/ *v* ought to, should; answer, respond, echo; comply with 0361

应当 /yīngdāng/ *v* should, ought to 0992

应该 /yīnggāi/ *v* ought to, should 0196

应有 /yīngyǒu/ *adj* proper, due, deserved 4456

应付 /yìngfu/ *v* handle, deal with; do something perfunctorily, make do 3814

应用 /yìngyòng/ *v* use, apply 2220

英雄 /yīngxióng/ *n* hero 1459

婴儿 /yīng'ér/ *n* infant, baby 4232

迎 /yíng/ *v* welcome; go to meet; move against 2688

迎接 /yíngjiē/ *v* meet, welcome, usher in 3219

营 /yíng/ *n* camp; battalion 2290

营养 /yíngyǎng/ *n* nutrition 2921

营业 /yíngyè/ *v* do business, be open 4274

营造 /yíngzào/ *v* build, construct 4834

赢 /yíng/ *v* win, gain; beat 1524

赢得 /yíngdé/ *v* win 3520

影 /yǐng/ *n* shadow, reflected image; trace; film 3423

影片 /yǐngpiàn/ *n* film, movie 3231

影视 /yǐngshì/ *n* film and video 4092

影响 /yǐngxiǎng/ *v* influence 0333

影响 /yǐngxiǎng/ *n* influence, impact 4325

影子 /yǐngzi/ *n* shadow 4223

硬 /yìng/ *adj* hard 1848

硬 /yìng/ *adv* obstinately, stubbornly; (do something) mechanically in spite of difficulties 3661

哟 /yo/ *interj* [interjection expressing surprise] oh, well 3249

拥抱 /yōngbào/ *v* embrace, hug 4773

拥护 /yōnghù/ *v* support, advocate 4496

拥有 /yōngyǒu/ *v* have, possess, own 0985

永 /yǒng/ *adv* forever 2945

永恒 /yǒnghéng/ *adj* eternal, everlasting 4282

永远 /yǒngyuǎn/ *adv* forever 0910

勇 /yǒng/ *adj* brave, courageous 4572

勇敢 /yǒnggǎn/ *adj* brave 3657

勇气 /yǒngqì/ *n* courage 2506

涌 /yǒng/ *v* gush, surge; rush 2986

用 /yòng/ *v* use 0068

用不着 /yòngbuzháo/ *idiom* no need; have no use for 4373

用品 /yòngpǐn/ *n* articles for use, appliance 4580

用人 /yòngrén/ *v* employ, make use of personnel 4619

用于 /yòngyú/ *v* use in, use for 2335

优 /yōu/ *adj* excellent, fine 4165

优点 /yōudiǎn/ *n* merit, strength, advantage 3870

优美 /yōuměi/ *adj* beautiful, graceful 3978

优势 /yōushì/ *n* advantage, strength 1354

优秀 /yōuxiù/ *adj* excellent 1098

幽默 /yōumò/ *adj* humorous 2575

悠久 /yōujiǔ/ *adj* of long standing 4568

尤其 /yóuqí/ *adv* especially 0639

由 /yóu/ *prep* by, from 0154

由此 /yóucǐ/ *adv* from this, hereby; hence 2994

由于 /yóuyú/ *prep* due to 0327

犹如 /yóurú/ *v* be just like, as if 4512

犹豫 /yóuyù/ *adj* hesitant 4075

邮票 /yóupiào/ *n* stamp 4031

油 /yóu/ *n* oil, petrol, gas 1531

游 /yóu/ *v* swim; travel around 1411

游客 /yóukè/ *n* tourist 3505

游戏 /yóuxì/ *n* game 2184

游行 /yóuxíng/ *v* parade, march 3918

游泳 /yóuyǒng/ *v* swim 2908

友 /yǒu/ *n* friend 2983

友好 /yǒuhǎo/ *adj* friendly 2163

友谊 /yǒuyì/ *n* friendship 2856

有 /yǒu/ *v* have, there be 0009

有的 /yǒude/ *pron* some 0408

有的是 /yǒudeshì/ *idiom* have plenty of, there's no lack of 4124

有点 /yǒudiǎn/ *adv* somewhat, a bit 1269

有关 /yǒuguān/ *v* have something to do with 0451

有关 /yǒuguān/ *prep* concerning, related to 2741

有力 /yǒulì/ *adj* powerful 2420

有利 /yǒulì/ *adj* advantageous, beneficial 2651

有利于 /yǒulìyú/ *v* be beneficial to, be helpful to 2690

有名 /yǒumíng/ *adj* famous 3293

有钱 /yǒuqián/ *adj* rich, wealthy 4842

有趣 /yǒuqù/ *adj* interesting 3079

有人 /yǒurén/ *pron* someone 0391

有时 /yǒushí/ *adv* sometimes 1288

有时候 /yǒushíhou/ *adv* sometimes 2483

有所 /yǒusuǒ/ *adv* somewhat, slightly 1632

有限 /yǒuxiàn/ *adj* limited 2296

有效 /yǒuxiào/ *adj* effective, valid 1379

有些 /yǒuxiē/ *pron* some 0384

有益 /yǒuyì/ *adj* beneficial, good 4116

有意 /yǒuyì/ *adv* intentionally, deliberately 4695

有意思 /yǒuyìsi/ *idiom* interesting 3787

又 /yòu/ *adv* again, once again 0046

又 /yòu/ *conj* [as in 既 . . . 又] (both . . .) and 0620

右 /yòu/ *loc* right 1337

幼儿园 /yòu'éryuán/ *n* kindergarten 4581

诱惑 /yòuhuò/ *v* entice, tempt 4454

于 /yú/ *prep* [indicating time, location, direction, etc.] in, at 0095

于是 /yúshì/ *conj* thereupon, and so, then 0486

予以 /yǔyǐ/ *v* give, bestow 3351

余 /yú/ *num* [following a number] more than, over 0800

鱼 /yú/ *n* fish 0885

娱乐 /yúlè/ *n* entertainment, recreation 2665

愉快 /yúkuài/ *adj* cheerful, joyful, happy 2465

舆论 /yúlùn/ *n* public opinion 2324

与 /yǔ/ *prep* [indicating involvement or relationship] with 0088

与 /yǔ/ *conj* and 0117

与此同时 /yǔcǐtóngshí/ *conj* meanwhile 3205

与其 /yǔqí/ *conj* [used in pair with 不如 or 毋宁 etc.] rather than, better than 3831

宇宙 /yǔzhòu/ *n* universe 2640

雨 /yǔ/ *n* rain 1406

语 /yǔ/ *n* language, word 1212

语气 /yǔqì/ *n* tone, manner of speaking; (subjunctive, imperative, etc.) mood 4577

语文 /yǔwén/ *n* language, (specifically) Chinese (as a school subject) 4650

语言 /yǔyán/ *n* language 0994

玉 /yù/ *n* jade 1678

玉米 /yùmǐ/ *n* sweetcorn 3991

育 /yù/ *v* give birth; raise, keep; educate 4951

预备 /yùbèi/ *v* prepare, get ready 4256

预测 /yùcè/ *v* forecast 3560

预防 /yùfáng/ *v* prevent, secure against 3196

预计 /yùjì/ *v* estimate, expect 4410

预料 /yùliào/ *v* anticipate, expect 4412

预算 /yùsuàn/ *n* budget 4046

欲 /yù/ *v* desire, want, wish; (be) about to 2056

欲望 /yùwàng/ *n* desire 2659

遇 /yù/ *v* meet with, encounter 2242

遇到 /yùdào/ *v* encounter, meet, come across, run into 1005

遇见 /yùjiàn/ *v* meet 4978

愈 /yù/ *adv* [as in 愈 . . . 愈 . . .] the more (the more . . .) 3171

元 /yuán/ *clas* [Chinese currency unit] yuan 0205

员工 /yuángōng/ *n* staff, personnel, employee 2133

园 /yuán/ *n* garden 2437

原 /yuán/ *adj* former, original 1170

原 /yuán/ *adv* [short form of 原来, meaning often implied in the past tense] originally, formerly 1667

原本 /yuánběn/ adv originally, formerly 3124

原来 /yuánlái/ adv [meaning often implied in the past tense] originally, formerly; so, as a matter of fact 0911

原来 /yuánlái/ adj original, former 1276

原谅 /yuánliàng/ v forgive 4668

原料 /yuánliào/ n raw material 3743

原始 /yuánshǐ/ adj primitive, primeval; (of data) original, first-hand 3245

原先 /yuánxiān/ adv originally, formerly 4321

原因 /yuányīn/ n cause, reason 0441

原有 /yuányǒu/ adj old, originally existing 3923

原则 /yuánzé/ n principle 0810

圆 /yuán/ adj round 2848

圆满 /yuánmǎn/ adj satisfactory, successful, happy 4906

援助 /yuánzhù/ v provide help, aid or support 3404

源 /yuán/ n source 2132

远 /yuǎn/ adj far 0454

远远 /yuǎnyuǎn/ adv by far; far away 2154

怨 /yuàn/ v blame; complain 4263

院 /yuàn/ n courtyard; academy, institute, hospital 1265

院长 /yuànzhǎng/ n [head of a hospital, school, faculty, college or university, etc.] director, dean, president 1803

院子 /yuànzi/ n yard, courtyard 3705

愿 /yuàn/ v hope, wish; will, be willing to 1007

愿望 /yuànwàng/ n wish 2447

愿意 /yuànyì/ v be willing to 0554

约 /yuē/ adv approximately, about 0670

约定 /yuēdìng/ v agree on, arrange, fix 4833

约束 /yuēshù/ v bind, restrain 4727

月 /yuè/ n moon; month 0138

月亮 /yuèliang/ n moon 4523

钥匙 /yàoshi/ n key 3905

阅读 /yuèdú/ v read 3759

跃 /yuè/ v leap, jump 3622

越 /yuè/ adv [as in 越 . . . 越 (the more . . .) the more 0347

越来越 /yuèláiyuè/ adv more and more 0604

越是 /yuèshì/ adv [as in 越是 . . . 越是 . . .] the more (. . . the more) 3785

云 /yún/ n cloud 1566

允许 /yǔnxǔ/ v permit, allow 1489

运 /yùn/ v transport 1719

运动 /yùndòng/ n motion, movement; sports, exercise; (political) campaign 0883

运动 /yùndòng/ v move; do sports activities 1901

运动会 /yùndònghuì/ n sports meeting, games 3935

运动员 /yùndòngyuán/ n athlete, sportsman 1957

运气 /yùnqi/ n luck 4857

运输 /yùnshū/ v transport 2255

运行 /yùnxíng/ v move, be in motion; run, operate 2733

运用 /yùnyòng/ v use, apply 1779

运作 /yùnzuò/ v operate 3925

Z

杂 /zá/ adj mixed, varied, miscellaneous 4979

杂志 /zázhì/ n magazine 2035

砸 /zá/ v smash 2533

灾 /zāi/ n disaster, calamity 4913

灾难 /zāinàn/ n disaster 3417

栽 /zāi/ v plant; frame; fall 4719

载 /zǎi, zài/ v record; carry (in a vehicle) 2915

再 /zài/ adv again 0087

再次 /zàicì/ adv once again 1357

再度 /zàidù/ adv again, once more 3985

再说 /zàishuō/ v put off for future decision 2648

再也 /zàiyě/ adv [occurring in negative sentences] ever again 3932

在 /zài/ prep [indicating location or time, etc.] at, in 0004

在 /zài/ v be available or present; exist; consist in 1829

在 /zài/ adv [preceding a verb to indicate an event in progress] 3984

在场 /zàichǎng/ v be present, be at the scene 4206

在内 /zàinèi/ aux including, included 3136

在于 /zàiyú/ v lie in, consist in, depend on 1448

在座 /zàizuò/ v be present 4610

咱 /zán/ pron [including the addressee] we, us 1210

咱们 /zánmen/ pron [including the addressee(s)] we 0540

暂时 /zànshí/ adj temporary 2671

赞成 /zànchéng/ v support, approve, be in favour of 2744

赞赏 /zànshǎng/ v appreciate 4950

赞同 /zàntóng/ v approve of, endorse, be in favour of 4895

脏 /zāng/ adj dirty 3271

遭 /zāo/ v [sometimes written as 遭到] suffer, encounter 2804

遭到 /zāodào/ v suffer; encounter, meet with 2266

遭受 /zāoshòu/ v suffer 3402

早 /zǎo/ adj early 0320

早晨 /zǎochén/ time early morning 2304

早就 /zǎojiù/ adv for a long time, long ago, early 1755

早日 /zǎorì/ *adv* at an earlier date, soon 4847

早上 /zǎoshang/ *time* (early) morning 2356

早已 /zǎoyǐ/ *adv* for a long time, long ago; already 1735

造 /zào/ *v* make, build; make up 1640

造成 /zàochéng/ *v* cause, result in 0656

造型 /zàoxíng/ *n* shape, moulding 4296

则 /zé/ *conj* [indicating cause, condition, contrast, etc.] then 0368

责任 /zérèn/ *n* responsibility 0655

责任感 /zérèngǎn/ *n* sense of duty 4867

怎 /zěn/ *pron* how, why 2701

怎么 /zěnme/ *pron* how 0129

怎么样 /zěnmeyàng/ *pron* how 1156

怎样 /zěnyàng/ *pron* how 0752

增 /zēng/ *v* increase 4070

增加 /zēngjiā/ *v* increase 0691

增强 /zēngqiáng/ *v* enhance, strengthen 2305

增长 /zēngzhǎng/ *v* grow, increase 1024

咋 /zǎ/ *pron* how, why 3286

扎 /zā, zhā/ *v* tie or bind (with a string or ribbon); prick; plunge into 2419

炸 /zhá, zhà/ *v* fry; explode 2191

摘 /zhāi/ *v* pick, pluck, take off; make a summary 3138

窄 /zhǎi/ *adj* narrow 4787

债 /zhài/ *n* debt 4752

沾 /zhān/ *v* be stained with; touch, touch on 3963

展 /zhǎn/ *n* exhibition, display 4242

展开 /zhǎnkāi/ *v* unfold, launch, set off; spread 2012

展览 /zhǎnlǎn/ *v* exhibit, put on display 3611

展示 /zhǎnshì/ *v* demonstrate, reveal, open up before one's eyes 2246

展现 /zhǎnxiàn/ *v* unfold, present 3385

占 /zhàn/ *v* take; take up, occupy 0583

占据 /zhànjù/ *v* occupy, take up 4153

占领 /zhànlǐng/ *v* occupy 2390

占有 /zhànyǒu/ *v* have, possess; occupy, hold 3140

战 /zhàn/ *v* fight 1543

战场 /zhànchǎng/ *n* battlefield 2602

战斗 /zhàndòu/ *v* fight, combat 2026

战略 /zhànlüè/ *n* strategy 1078

战胜 /zhànshèng/ *v* beat, defeat, triumph over; overcome, surmount 2761

战士 /zhànshì/ *n* soldier, fighter 1655

战术 /zhànshù/ *n* tactic 4133

战线 /zhànxiàn/ *n* battle line; front 4808

战役 /zhànyì/ *n* (military) campaign 3712

战友 /zhànyǒu/ *n* comrade in arms, fellow soldier 4584

战争 /zhànzhēng/ *n* war 0597

站 /zhàn/ *v* stand 0376

站 /zhàn/ *n* station, (bus) stop 1644

站 /zhàn/ *clas* [measure word for sections of a bus or railway journey] stop 3640

张 /zhāng/ *clas* [measure word for flat objects and things with a flat surface, and also for bows and mouths] 0216

章 /zhāng/ *clas* chapter 1345

章 /zhāng/ *n* seal, stamp; badge 3050

长 /zhǎng/ *v* grow, develop; increase 2039

长大 /zhǎngdà/ *v* grow up 2362

涨 /zhǎng, zhàng/ *v* (of prices, rivers, etc.) rise; swell 3163

掌 /zhǎng/ *n* palm 4044

掌声 /zhǎngshēng/ *n* applause 2366

掌握 /zhǎngwò/ *v* grasp, master 1181

丈 /zhàng/ *clas* [measure term for length in Chinese local unit] zhang (equivalent of ten chi, or about 3.33 metres) 4938

丈夫 /zhàngfu/ *n* husband 0995

仗 /zhàng/ *n* battle 3545

帐 /zhàng/ *n* account, account book; bill; (mosquito) net 2036

帐篷 /zhàngpéng/ *n* tent 4822

账 /zhàng/ *n* account, account book; bill 2792

障碍 /zhàng'ài/ *n* barrier, obstacle 2539

招 /zhāo/ *n* move, trick 2449

招 /zhāo/ *v* beckon; enrol, recruit; provoke; confess 3384

招呼 /zhāohū/ *v* call; greet 4396

着 /zhāo/ *n* move (in chess), step, trick 0355

着 /zháo/ *v* touch (the ground, land); catch (cold); (fire) be lit, catch fire; succeed in 1297

着急 /zháojí/ *adj* anxious, worried 2591

找 /zhǎo/ *v* look for 0180

找到 /zhǎodào/ *v* find 0813

召开 /zhāokāi/ *v* convene (a conference or meeting), hold 1527

照 /zhào/ *v* shine, beam, light up; reflect, mirror 1512

照 /zhào/ *prep* according to; in the direction of 4491

照顾 /zhàogù/ *v* take care of, look after 1817

照片 /zhàopiàn/ *n* photo 1042

照样 /zhàoyàng/ *adv* all the same 4320

折 /zhé/ *v* break, bend, fold; convert to 3958

折磨 /zhémó/ *v* torture 4401

哲学 /zhéxué/ *n* philosophy 1992

者 /zhě/ *suf* [suffix for nouns denoting persons] -ist, -er 0271

这 /zhè/ pron this 0011

这边 /zhèbian/ pron this side, this way, over here 2582

这儿 /zhèr/ pron here 0703

这个 /zhège/ pron this 0051

这里 /zhèlǐ/ pron here 0178

这么 /zhème/ pron so, such, like this 0175

这时 /zhèshí/ pron at this time 1207

这些 /zhèxiē/ pron these 0104

这样 /zhèyàng/ pron this (kind of, sort of); so 0081

着 /zhe/ aux [aspect marker indicating a durative or ongoing situation] 0027

针 /zhēn/ n pin, needle; stitch; injection 3937

针对 /zhēnduì/ prep at, against, for 2565

珍贵 /zhēnguì/ adj precious 3492

珍惜 /zhēnxī/ v treasure, value, cherish 3886

真 /zhēn/ adv really 0221

真 /zhēn/ adj real, true, genuine 0523

真诚 /zhēnchéng/ adj sincere, true 3104

真的 /zhēnde/ adv really 2147

真理 /zhēnlǐ/ n truth 2300

真实 /zhēnshí/ adj true, real, authentic 1287

真是 /zhēnshì/ adv really, actually; [equivalent of 真是的, expressing dissatisfaction] well, really 2944

真相 /zhēnxiàng/ n truth; the actual situation or facts 3879

真正 /zhēnzhèng/ adv really, truly, genuinely 0840

真正 /zhēnzhèng/ adj genuine, true, real 1166

阵 /zhèn/ clas [measure word for a short period of time or action] gust, spell 2158

阵 /zhèn/ n (military) front, field; battle array 3022

阵地 /zhèndì/ n position, front 2954

镇 /zhèn/ n town, township 2043

震动 /zhèndòng/ v shake, quake, vibrate; shock 4198

震惊 /zhènjīng/ v shock, astonish 3863

争 /zhēng/ v contend for, vie for; argue 1534

争夺 /zhēngduó/ v scramble for, contend for, contest 3888

争论 /zhēnglùn/ v argue, debate 3262

争取 /zhēngqǔ/ v strive for, fight for 1588

征 /zhēng/ v levy; solicit 4346

挣 /zhèng, zhēng/ v earn; struggle to get free 2162

挣扎 /zhēngzhá/ v struggle 4405

挣钱 /zhèngqián/ v earn money 4110

睁 /zhēng/ v open (eyes) 4010

整 /zhěng/ adj whole, entire 1893

整 /zhěng/ v put in order; punish 3141

整顿 /zhěngdùn/ v rectify 3857

整个 /zhěnggè/ adj whole, entire, all 0414

整理 /zhěnglǐ/ v sort 2724

整齐 /zhěngqí/ adj neat, tidy 4838

整体 /zhěngtǐ/ n whole, entirety, overall 2034

整天 /zhěngtiān/ adv all day long 3277

整整 /zhěngzhěng/ adj whole, full 3786

正 /zhèng/ adv just, precisely; just (in progress) 0174

正 /zhèng/ adj principal (as opposed to vice-); straight, upright; right (side); regular (shape) 1424

正常 /zhèngcháng/ adj normal, regular 0870

正当 /zhèngdāng/ adj proper 4570

正好 /zhènghǎo/ adv just (in time); as it happens, exactly 1734

正确 /zhèngquè/ adj correct 1103

正式 /zhèngshì/ adj formal, official 1036

正是 /zhèngshì/ v be exactly 0887

正义 /zhèngyì/ n justice 3281

正在 /zhèngzài/ adv be under way, be in progress 1281

证 /zhèng/ n certificate, papers; proof, evidence 2509

证据 /zhèngjù/ n evidence, proof 2237

证明 /zhèngmíng/ v prove 0906

证券 /zhèngquàn/ n securities, stock 4540

证实 /zhèngshí/ v confirm, prove 3198

证书 /zhèngshū/ n certificate, diploma 4472

政 /zhèng/ n government, politics 3608

政策 /zhèngcè/ n policy 0558

政府 /zhèngfǔ/ n government 0233

政权 /zhèngquán/ n regime; power 2657

政治 /zhèngzhì/ n politics 0308

政治家 /zhèngzhìjiā/ n politician, statesman 4596

之 /zhī/ aux [archaic equivalent of structural particle 的] 0084

之 /zhī/ pron it, him, her, them 3475

之后 /zhīhòu/ loc after, afterwards 0231

之际 /zhījì/ loc at the time when . . . 3438

之间 /zhījiān/ loc between 0275

之类 /zhīlèi/ pron and so on, and the like 2276

之内 /zhīnèi/ loc within 2578

之前 /zhīqián/ loc before 0653

之上 /zhīshàng/ loc above 3461

之所以 /zhīsuǒyǐ/ conj [as in 之所以 . . . 是因为] the reason that . . . 2015

之外 /zhīwài/ loc outside; except 1236

之下 /zhīxià/ loc under, below 1756

之一 /zhīyī/ pron one of 0568

之中 /zhīzhōng/ loc in, inside, within 0930

支 /zhī/ clas [measure word used for long and inflexible objects such as pens, arrows, cigarettes]; [measure word for troops and fleets]; [measure word for songs and melodies]; [measure word for brightness of electric bulbs, equivalent of watt] 0793

支撑 /zhīchēng/ v prop up, support; sustain, hold 3523

支持 /zhīchí/ v support 0538

支队 /zhīduì/ n division, detachment 4335

支付 /zhīfù/ v pay, make a payment 3731

支援 /zhīyuán/ v support, aid 2984

知 /zhī/ v know 0364

知道 /zhīdào/ v know 0090

知名 /zhīmíng/ adj renowned, well known 4028

知识 /zhīshí/ n knowledge 0555

知识分子 /zhīshifènzi/ n intellectual 2303

执 /zhí/ v hold, grasp 3618

执行 /zhíxíng/ v implement, carry out 1286

直 /zhí/ adv straight, directly; keep (doing something), continuously 0842

直 /zhí/ adj straight; straightforward, frank 3294

直到 /zhídào/ prep until, up to 2802

直接 /zhíjiē/ adj direct 0520

值 /zhí/ v be worth; be on duty 2161

值得 /zhíde/ v deserve, be worth 1150

职 /zhí/ n post, position, appointment 2863

职工 /zhígōng/ n staff, staff member, worker 1341

职务 /zhíwù/ n post, position 2490

职业 /zhíyè/ n occupation, profession 1377

职责 /zhízé/ n responsibility, duty 3844

植物 /zhíwù/ n plant 3154

止 /zhǐ/ v stop, end 2822

只 /zhǐ/ adv only 0071

只 /zhī/ clas [measure word for one of a pair, birds and some animals, or boats, boxes, etc.] 0479

只不过 /zhǐbúguò/ adv merely 2502

只好 /zhǐhǎo/ adv have to, have no alternative but to 1292

只是 /zhǐshì/ adv merely, only 1896

只是 /zhǐshì/ conj except that, but 3204

只要 /zhǐyào/ conj if 0485

只有 /zhǐyǒu/ conj only if 1160

只有 /zhǐyǒu/ adv only 4981

纸 /zhǐ/ n paper 1482

指 /zhǐ/ v mean, refer to; point to 0536

指标 /zhǐbiāo/ n target; quota 2923

指出 /zhǐchū/ v point out 0978

指导 /zhǐdǎo/ v guide, direct 1533

指定 /zhǐdìng/ v name, designate, assign, appoint 3861

指挥 /zhǐhuī/ v command, direct; (music) conduct 1770

指挥 /zhǐhuī/ n command, direction; commander; (music) conductor 4974

指示 /zhǐshì/ n directive, instruction 2581

指责 /zhǐzé/ v criticise, accuse 3039

至 /zhì/ v arrive, reach 0382

至今 /zhìjīn/ adv until now, so far 1565

至少 /zhìshǎo/ adv at least 0927

至于 /zhìyú/ prep as regards 1633

志 /zhì/ n ambition, aspiration; will; records 2275

制 /zhì/ v make, manufacture 1183

制定 /zhìdìng/ v draw up, make, set forth 1491

制度 /zhìdù/ n (political or administrative) system, institution 0578

制约 /zhìyuē/ v constrain, condition, govern 4306

制造 /zhìzào/ v make, manufacture 1542

制止 /zhìzhǐ/ v stop, curb, prevent 3887

制作 /zhìzuò/ v make 1919

治 /zhì/ v rule, govern; treat, cure; control, harness; punish 1335

治安 /zhì'ān/ n public order 3753

治理 /zhìlǐ/ v govern; harness 3387

治疗 /zhìliáo/ v treat 1983

质 /zhì/ n quality; substance 3540

质量 /zhìliàng/ n quality 1017

秩序 /zhìxù/ n order 2176

致 /zhì/ v cause, result in; send, deliver (a speech) 1652

致使 /zhìshǐ/ v cause, result in 4562

智 /zhì/ n wisdom 4384

智慧 /zhìhuì/ n wisdom 1938

智力 /zhìlì/ n intelligence 3372

置 /zhì/ v put, place; buy 3319

中 /zhōng/ loc in, within 0030

中等 /zhōngděng/ adj medium, medium-sized 4694

中间 /zhōngjiān/ loc middle, between 1087

中年 /zhōngnián/ n middle age 4809

中午 /zhōngwǔ/ time noon 1915

中心 /zhōngxīn/ n centre 0581

中学 /zhōngxué/ n middle school, secondary school, high school 1398

中央 /zhōngyāng/ n middle, centre; central authorities 0541

中医 /zhōngyī/ n Chinese medicine; herb doctor 4038

终 /zhōng/ adv finally 3663

终身 /zhōngshēn/ n all one's life, lifelong 4810

终于 /zhōngyú/ adv finally, at last 0678

钟 /zhōng/ n clock, bell 1209

种 /zhǒng/ clas [indicating species] kind, type 0029

种 /zhòng/ v plant 3482

种植 /zhòngzhí/ v plant 4351

种子 /zhǒngzi/ n seed 4425

众 /zhòng/ adj numerous 2407

众多 /zhòngduō/ num numerous, many 2181

众人 /zhòngrén/ n everyone, crowd 3604

重 /zhòng/ adj heavy 0726

重大 /zhòngdà/ adj great, major, important, significant 1038

重点 /zhòngdiǎn/ n emphasis, focus point 1359

重点 /zhòngdiǎn/ adj key, major 3781

重视 /zhòngshì/ v take something seriously, attach importance to 0974

重要 /zhòngyào/ adj important, vital 0171

重要性 /zhòngyàoxìng/ n importance 3874

州 /zhōu/ n prefecture; state; [often used as part of place names in China] 2401

周 /zhōu/ clas week; cycle 1659

周 /zhōu/ adj considerate, thoughtful; careful 3394

周 /zhōu/ time week 4713

周边 /zhōubiān/ loc periphery, vicinity, neighbouring, surrounding 4798

周末 /zhōumò/ time weekend 3450

周年 /zhōunián/ clas full year, anniversary 2455

周围 /zhōuwéi/ loc around, round 1184

粥 /zhōu/ n gruel, porridge, congee 4134

株 /zhū/ clas [measure word for plants] 4665

诸多 /zhūduō/ num a lot of 3988

猪 /zhū/ n pig, hog 1700

竹 /zhú/ n bamboo 2928

逐步 /zhúbù/ adv step by step, gradually 2257

逐渐 /zhújiàn/ adv gradually 1666

主 /zhǔ/ adj main, primary, principal 0997

主持 /zhǔchí/ v preside over 2014

主持人 /zhǔchírén/ n (TV or radio) presenter, host; (of meeting) chairperson 2718

主导 /zhǔdǎo/ adj leading, predominant 4735

主动 /zhǔdòng/ adj on one's own initiative, active 1392

主观 /zhǔguān/ adj subjective 4980

主管 /zhǔguǎn/ v take charge of, head 2574

主角 /zhǔjué/ n leading role 3233

主力 /zhǔlì/ n main force, backbone 3309

主人 /zhǔrén/ n master; host; owner 2195

主任 /zhǔrèn/ n director 0751

主题 /zhǔtí/ n theme, keynote 2077

主席 /zhǔxí/ n chairman, chairperson 0499

主要 /zhǔyào/ adj main, major 0466

主要 /zhǔyào/ adv mainly, primarily, principally 0512

主义 /zhǔyì/ n doctrine, -ism 2045

主意 /zhǔyì/ n idea 2445

主张 /zhǔzhāng/ n advocacy, proposition 2774

主张 /zhǔzhāng/ v advocate, maintain, argue for 3053

煮 /zhǔ/ v cook, boil 2962

住 /zhù/ v live, stay 0200

住房 /zhùfáng/ n house, housing 2685

住院 /zhùyuàn/ v be hospitalised 4095

住宅 /zhùzhái/ n residence 3800

助 /zhù/ v help, aid, assist 3615

助理 /zhùlǐ/ n assistant 4485

注 /zhù/ v annotate; pour, inject; concentrate 4021

注册 /zhùcè/ v register 3656

注定 /zhùdìng/ v be doomed, be destined 4559

注意 /zhùyì/ v pay attention to; take notice of, note 0461

注重 /zhùzhòng/ v lay stress on, take pains with 3060

驻 /zhù/ v be stationed 0948

祝 /zhù/ v wish 3722

祝贺 /zhùhè/ v congratulate 4254

著 /zhù/ v write 2691

著名 /zhùmíng/ adj famous, well known 0809

著作 /zhùzuò/ n book, writing, work 2902

抓 /zhuā/ v grab, grasp; arrest 0544

抓紧 /zhuājǐn/ v grasp firmly; pay close attention; hurry 4301

抓住 /zhuāzhù/ v grab, grip; catch hold of; catch; seize (an opportunity) 1202

专 /zhuān/ adv specially, specifically 2504

专家 /zhuānjiā/ n expert, specialist 0803

专门 /zhuānmén/ adv specifically, for a particular purpose, occasion, etc. 1465

专门 /zhuānmén/ adj special, specialised 2897

专业 /zhuānyè/ n speciality, specialised field of study, major 0953

砖 /zhuān/ n brick 3841

转 /zhuǎn, zhuàn/ v change, shift; pass on; rotate, resolve; turn 0669

转变 /zhuǎnbiàn/ v transform, change 2360

转化 /zhuǎnhuà/ v transform, change into 3348

转换 /zhuǎnhuàn/ v change, switch, convert, transform 4623

转身 /zhuǎnshēn/ v turn round 3652

转向 /zhuǎnxiàng/ v change direction 2937

转移 /zhuǎnyí/ v transfer, shift, move 2189

传 /zhuàn/ n biography 3282

赚 /zhuàn/ v earn, make a profit 1889

赚钱 /zhuànqián/ v make money 4683

庄 /zhuāng/ n village, hamlet, farm; manor; place of business 3425

装 /zhuāng/ v pack, load; fix, install; pretend; play the role of 0895

装备 /zhuāngbèi/ n equipment 3706

状 /zhuàng/ n condition; form; plaint 2348

状况 /zhuàngkuàng/ n condition, state of affairs 1290

状态 /zhuàngtài/ n state of affairs, condition 0947

撞 /zhuàng/ v bump against, collide; run into 1982

追 /zhuī/ v chase, pursue; court, woo 1346

追究 /zhuījiù/ v enquire into, take action against, penalise 4510

追求 /zhuīqiú/ v seek, pursue; court, woo 0975

准 /zhǔn/ v allow, permit 1334

准 /zhǔn/ adj accurate; quasi- 2849

准备 /zhǔnbèi/ v prepare, get ready 0337

准确 /zhǔnquè/ adj accurate, exact 2202

准则 /zhǔnzé/ n norm, rule, criterion 4432

捉 /zhuō/ v clutch, seize; catch, capture 4547

桌 /zhuō/ n table, desk 2208

桌子 /zhuōzi/ n table, desk 2920

琢磨 /zhuómó, zuómo/ v carve and polish, polish and refine; think over, ponder 3823

着手 /zhuóshǒu/ v set about, start 4347

诸询 /zīxún/ v consult 2939

姿态 /zītài/ n posture, manner; attitude, stance 3903

资 /zī/ n money, capital, investment; endowment; qualifications 4238

资本 /zīběn/ n capital; advantage 2007

资本主义 /zīběnzhǔyì/ n capitalism 3539

资产 /zīchǎn/ n asset 2062

资格 /zīgé/ n qualification 1873

资金 /zījīn/ n fund, capital 1139

资料 /zīliào/ n data, material 1144

资源 /zīyuán/ n resource 0950

资助 /zīzhù/ v support, sponsor, finance 4308

滋味 /zīwèi/ n taste 3946

子 /zǐ/ n son, child 0511

子 /zi/ suf [nominal suffix to form a disyllabic word] 1449

子女 /zǐnǚ/ n child, children 2186

仔细 /zǐxì/ adj careful 1912

紫 /zǐ/ adj purple, violet 3773

字 /zì/ n (Chinese) character 0329

自 /zì/ prep from 0287

自 /zì/ pron self 2456

自从 /zìcóng/ prep since 2660

自动 /zìdòng/ adj automatic 3627

自豪 /zìháo/ adj proud 3734

自己 /zìjǐ/ pron self 0043

自觉 /zìjué/ adj conscious, conscientious; on one's own initiative 2547

自然 /zìrán/ adv naturally 1188

自然 /zìrán/ adj natural 1254

自然 /zìrán/ n nature 1795

自杀 /zìshā/ v commit suicide 3269

自身 /zìshēn/ pron self, oneself 1587

自我 /zìwǒ/ pron oneself, self 1250

自信 /zìxìn/ v be confident 3919

自行车 /zìxíngchē/ n bicycle, bike 2298

自由 /zìyóu/ adj free 0841

自愿 /zìyuàn/ adv voluntarily 4446

自治 /zìzhì/ n autonomy, self-governing 4450

自治区 /zìzhìqū/ n autonomous region 2415

宗教 /zōngjiào/ n religion 1676

宗旨 /zōngzhǐ/ n aim, goal 4539

综合 /zōnghé/ adj comprehensive, synthetic 1902

总 /zǒng/ adv always; anyway, certainly; sooner or later 0524

总 /zǒng/ adj overall, total; general, chief 0744

总部 /zǒngbù/ n headquarters 2682

总裁 /zǒngcái/ n president, CEO (chief executive officer) 3160

总结 /zǒngjié/ v summarise, sum up 1840

总经理 /zǒngjīnglǐ/ n general manager 2239

总理 /zǒnglǐ/ n premier 0912

总是 /zǒngshì/ adv always 0919

总数 /zǒngshù/ n total amount, sum 4385

总体 /zǒngtǐ/ adj overall, total 2867

总统 /zǒngtǒng/ n president (of a country) 0849

总之 /zǒngzhī/ conj in sum, in a word 2697

走 /zǒu/ v walk; leave 0085

走过 /zǒuguò/ v cross, go through, walk past 4066

走路 /zǒulù/ v walk, go on foot 4154

走私 /zǒusī/ v smuggle 4360

租 /zū/ v rent, hire 3031

足 /zú/ adj enough, adequate, sufficient 1591

足够 /zúgòu/ adj enough, sufficient 2521

足球 /zúqiú/ n football 1737

族 /zú/ n race; group 2642

阻止 /zǔzhǐ/ v prevent, stop 3553

组 /zǔ/ clas group; set 1949

组 /zǔ/ n group 1959

组长 /zǔzhǎng/ n group leader 4747

组成 /zǔchéng/ v form, make up, constitute; consist of 1494

组合 /zǔhé/ v assemble, combine 4560

组建 /zǔjiàn/ v put together, set up 4413

组织 /zǔzhī/ n organisation 0475

组织 /zǔzhī/ v organise 0823

祖国 /zǔguó/ n motherland 1637

钻 /zuān, zuàn/ v get into, get through; dig into; bore or drill (a hole) 2373

嘴 /zuǐ/ n mouth 1015

嘴巴 /zuǐba/ n mouth 4136

嘴里 /zuǐli/ place in mouth 3067

最 /zuì/ adv [superlative degree] most 0058

最初 /zuìchū/ adj initial, first 3042

最低 /zuìdī/ adj lowest, minimum 3660

最好 /zuìhǎo/ adv had better, would better 3867

最后 /zuìhòu/ adj final, last 0227

最佳 /zuìjiā/ adj best, optimal 2652

最近 /zuìjìn/ time recently 0781

最为 /zuìwéi/ adv most 3227

最新 /zuìxīn/ adj latest 3437

最终 /zuìzhōng/ adv finally, eventually 1388

最终 /zuìzhōng/ adj final, ultimate 3527

罪 /zuì/ n crime, offence; guilt; suffering 1788

罪犯 /zuìfàn/ n criminal 4653

醉 /zuì/ v be drunk 2460

尊 /zūn/ v respect 4068

尊敬 /zūnjìng/ v respect 4255

尊严 /zūnyán/ n dignity 3133

尊重 /zūnzhòng/ v respect, value 1268

遵守 /zūnshǒu/ v abide by, observe 3883

昨天 /zuótiān/ time yesterday 1302

左 /zuǒ/ loc left 1224

左右 /zuǒyòu/ num [following a quantifier] about, or so 0952

作 /zuò/ v do 0262

作出 /zuòchū/ v make 1352

作风 /zuòfēng/ n style 3181

作家 /zuòjiā/ n writer 0913

作品 /zuòpǐn/ n work (of art) 0589

作为 /zuòwéi/ v as, take as, regard as 0356

作为 /zuòwéi/ prep as 1430

作业 /zuòyè/ n assignment, homework 2485

作用 /zuòyòng/ n action, effect; role, function 0427

作战 /zuòzhàn/ v fight, conduct military operations 1943

作者 /zuòzhě/ n author 1122

坐 /zuò/ v sit 0279

坐下 /zuòxià/ v sit down 3924

座 /zuò/ clas [measure word used for mountains, buildings, bridges, structures, and statues, etc.] 0471

座位 /zuòwèi/ n seat 4527

做 /zuò/ v do, make 0076

做出 /zuòchū/ v make, put out 1219

做到 /zuòdào/ v accomplish, achieve, manage to do something 1518

做法 /zuòfǎ/ n practice, measure 1776

做饭 /zuòfàn/ v cook 4617

做好 /zuòhǎo/ v do well 2101

做人 /zuòrén/ v conduct oneself, behave; be an upright or decent person 3620

做事 /zuòshì/ v act, work, do one's work 4155

Part of speech index

Frequency rank **Simplified Chinese** /Pinyin/ Part of speech code gloss

Function words

Auxiliaries

0001 **的** /de/ [structural particle used after an attribute]

0005 **了** /le/ [aspect marker indicating realisation of a situation]

0027 **着** /zhe/ [aspect marker indicating a durative or ongoing situation]

0036 **地** /de/ [structural particle introducing an adverbial modifier]

0044 **得** /de/ [structural particle used after a verb that introduces a complement showing effect]

0053 **来** /lái/ [preceding a verb to indicate the intended or suggested action]

0073 **等** /děng/ et cetera

0075 **过** /guo/ [aspect marker indicating experience]

0084 **之** /zhī/ [archaic equivalent of structural particle 的]

0113 **所** /suǒ/ [particle preceding a verb to form a nominal structure]

0402 **一样** /yíyàng/ [usually occurring in 像 . . . 一样 like

0487 **来说** /láishuō/ [equivalent of 来讲, interpreting a topic from a particular viewpoint]

0871 **的话** /dehuà/ [particle used at the end of a clause (. . . 的话) to express a condition] if

0902 **等等** /děngděng/ et cetera, and so on

1164 **似的** /sìde/ seem, as if

1174 **般** /bān/ same as, just like

1927 **而言** /éryán/ [as in 就 . . . 而 言] as far as . . . is concerned

3136 **在内** /zàinèi/ including, included

4300 **来讲** /láijiǎng/ [equivalent of 来说 from one's viewpoint

Classifiers (measure words)

0008 **个** /gè/ clas [generalised measure word used for nouns without a specific measure term]

0029 **种** /zhǒng/ [indicating species] kind, type

0054 **次** /cì/ [measure word indicating number of repetitions or count of actions or events] times

0091 **天** /tiān/ [measure word for time] day

0092 **位** /wèi/ [measure word for respectable people]

0132 **家** /jiā/ [measure word for families or businesses]

0157 **条** /tiáo/ [measure word for things of a long and thin shape (e.g. string and river), pieces of writing (e.g. news, suggestions and regulations), or human life]

0167 **点** /diǎn/ [measure word for point, item, etc.]; [measure word for small quantities]

0192 **名** /míng/ [measure word for persons in general]

0203 **岁** /suì/ year (of age)

0205 **元** /yuán/ [Chinese currency unit] yuan

0216 **张** /zhāng/ [measure word for flat objects and things with a flat surface, and also for bows and mouths]

0219 **件** /jiàn/ [measure word for clothes, furniture, affairs, etc.] item, article

0256 **句** /jù/ [measure word for sentences, poems or spoken words] word, sentence

0281 **间** /jiān/ [measure word for rooms]

0307 **块** /kuài/ [measure word for thick pieces] lump; [spoken equivalent of the Chinese currency unit 元] yuan

0309 **些** /xiē/ some, an amount of

0310 **段** /duàn/ section, part; length (of time or distance); paragraph

0315 **下** /xià/ [measure word for counting actions] one stroke, (do) once

0322 **场** /cháng, chǎng/ [measure word for processes or courses of occurrence such as rain, snow, illness, etc.] period, spell; [measure word for or recreational or sports activities] show, match

0381 **片** /piàn/ [measure word for flat and thin pieces] slice; [with — as in 一片 used for a vast expanse of something such as land and water]; [measure word for scene, sound, atmosphere, speech, intention, etc.]

0412 **部** /bù/ [measure word for machines and vehicles, etc.]; [measure word for books and films, etc.]

0437 份 /fèn/ [measure word for meals, gifts, newspapers, etc.] portion, part, share

0440 项 /xiàng/ [measure word for items stipulated, planned, enumerated or for an account of facts or events]

0460 米 /mǐ/ [standard measure term] metre

0471 座 /zuò/ [measure word used for mountains, buildings, bridges, structures and statues, etc.]

0479 只 /zhī/ [measure word for one of a pair, birds and some animals, or boats, boxes, etc.]

0526 号 /hào/ [measure word for workmen]; kind, sort

0547 套 /tào/ [measure word for a group of associated things] set; suit; suite

0565 步 /bù/ pace; step

0595 类 /lèi/ [measure word for a class of similar persons or things] category, kind, sort

0613 批 /pī/ batch, lot, group

0617 道 /dào/ [measure word for long and narrow objects, doors, orders, questions, dishes in a meal, and steps in a process, etc.]

0651 台 /tái/ [measure word for machines, and also performances, etc.]

0672 分 /fēn/ minute; [Chinese monetary unit] fen; mark, score; [partitive measure for one-tenth of the whole]

0735 届 /jiè/ [measure word used for regular conferences, meetings, graduating classes, sports games, etc.]

0768 篇 /piān/ [measure word for essays and papers] piece (of writing)

0791 口 /kǒu/ [measure word for people in a family or village, and also for pigs, etc.]; [measure word for tool or instrument with an edge such as a sword]; [measure word for the amount held in mouth] mouthful

0793 支 /zhī/ [measure word used for long and inflexible objects such as pens, arrows, cigarettes]; [measure word for troops and fleets]; [measure word for songs and melodies]; [measure word for brightness of electric bulbs, equivalent of watt]

0796 分钟 /fēnzhōng/ minute

0867 本 /běn/ [measure word for books, etc.]

0923 层 /céng/ layer, tier; floor, storey

0924 辆 /liàng/ [measure word for vehicles]

0970 点儿 /diǎnr/ [measure word that often follows numeral 一] a little, a bit

0977 封 /fēng/ [measure word for letters, telegrams, etc.]

0983 公里 /gōnglǐ/ kilometre, km

1013 级 /jí/ [measure word for levels, grades and ranks, etc.]; [measure word for stairs, and steps, etc.]

1035 群 /qún/ [measure word for people or things gathered, also for some birds and animals] crowd, flock, herd

1049 年 /nián/ year

1140 会儿 /huìr/ [usually following the numeral 一] a moment, a while

1206 番 /fān/ [measure word for a course of actions and events]; [measure word indicating species] kind; [measure word indicating multiplication] times, -fold

1231 颗 /kē/ [measure word for small roundish objects such as grains]

1243 头 /tóu/ [measure word for some animals such as pigs and cattle, also for garlic]

1244 样 /yàng/ [measure word for some material objects] type, sort

1249 回 /huí/ [measure word for actions and events] times; [measure word for old-style Chinese novels] chapter

1296 声 /shēng/ [measure word for sound, shout, cry, laugh, yell, etc.]

1331 里 /lǐ/ [measure word for distance in Chinese local unit] li (0.5 km)

1345 章 /zhāng/ chapter

1369 笔 /bǐ/ [measure word for handwritings or drawings]; [measure word for a sum of money or a transaction]

1416 股 /gǔ/ [measure word for a stream of strength, water, air or smell, and also for long narrow things]

1472 倍 /bèi/ (two, three, etc.) -fold; times

1473 面 /miàn/ [measure word for something with a flat surface such as a mirror and flag]

1547 架 /jià/ [measure word for machines and instruments resting on a stand such as airplanes, pianos, cameras, etc.]

1551 根 /gēn/ [measure word for long and slender objects]

1610 期 /qī/ [measure word for things arranged by periods] issue (of a periodical)

1616 眼 /yǎn/ [measure word for the action of look or glance]; [measure word for wells]

1617 处 /chù/ [measure word for places occupied]

1658 幅 /fú/ [measure word for pictures, paintings, calligraphies, maps and cloth, etc.)

1659 周 /zhōu/ week; cycle

1669 对 /duì/ pair, couple

1741 下子 /xiàzi/ [measure word for occurrences of an action or event]; [occurring in the fixed expression 一下子 "suddenly"]

1751 所 /suǒ/ [measure word for houses, schools and hospitals, etc.]

1758 轮 /lún/ round (of competitions and talks, etc.); [measure word for the sun and the full moon]

1759 系列 /xìliè/ series

1767 卷 /juǎn, juàn/ [measure word for things made into the shape of a cylinder] roll; [measure word for book] volume

1816 辈子 /bèizi/ [typically occurring with 一 one] all one's life, lifetime

1845 遍 /biàn/ [measure word for the course of actions] time; once through

1852 堆 /duī/ pile, heap

1914 圈 /quān/ circle, round

1926 度 /dù/ [measure word for temperature, angle, electricity, etc.] degree; kwh

1939 枚 /méi/ [measure word for small objects such as medals, badges, stamps, and also for round-shaped objects like missiles]

1948 吨 /dūn/ ton

1949 组 /zǔ/ group; set

2046 盘 /pán/ [measure word for food contained in a plate]; [measure word for objects of shallow, and usually circular, almost flat shape

such as tapes] coil; [measure word for a game of chess, etc.]

2092 杯 /bēi/ [measure word for drinks] cup, mug, glass

2093 曲 /qǔ/ [measure word for tunes, songs and melodies, etc.]

2136 门 /mén/ [measure word for subjects of study]; [measure word for cannons]

2151 夜 /yè/ night

2158 阵 /zhèn/ [measure word for a short period of time or action] gust, spell

2169 斤 /jīn/ [measure term for weight in Chinese local unit] jin (half a kilo)

2209 顿 /dùn/ [measure word for regular meals]; [measure word for unpleasant events such as criticising, abusing, reprimanding, etc.]

2210 首 /shǒu/ [measure word for songs and poems]

2228 亩 /mǔ/ [measure term for area of land in Chinese local unit] mu (equal to 0.165 acres)

2370 户 /hù/ [measure word for households]

2384 棵 /kē/ [measure word for plants]

2454 毛 /máo/ [measure term for the Chinese currency, less formal than 角] mao (one-tenth of yuan), ten cents

2455 周年 /zhōunián/ full year, anniversary

2491 趟 /tàng/ [measure word for a return trip]; [measure word for a single trip of train]

2513 身 /shēn/ [measure word for clothes] suit; [preceded by the numeral 一 as a temporary measure for things covering somebody like water, mud, sweat, etc.]

2627 碗 /wǎn/ [measure word for food contained in a bowl] bowl

2720 听 /tīng/ [measure word for stuff contained in a tin or can] tin, can

2721 公斤 /gōngjīn/ kilo, kilogram

2780 平方米 /píngfāngmǐ/ square metre

2797 艘 /sōu/ [measure word for boats and ships, etc.]

2819 线 /xiàn/ [measure word for slim things such as rays and hopes]

2837 双 /shuāng/ pair

3006 页 /yè/ page

3092 丝 /sī/ [measure word for tiny bits] a thread of, a trace of

3285 行 /háng/ [measure word for things arranged in a line or row] line; row

3313 团 /tuán/ [measure word for objects made into the shape of a ball] a ball of

3426 刻 /kè/ quarter (of an hour)

3449 幕 /mù/ [measure word for plays] act; scene

3474 节 /jié/ [measure word for a section of things joined together such as coaches of a train and sections of a text]; [measure word for a period of class time]

3609 角 /jiǎo/ [measure term for the Chinese currency] jiao (one-tenth of yuan), ten cents

3640 站 /zhàn/ [measure word for sections of a bus or railway journey] stop

3641 路 /lù/ [measure word for groups of people] route

3677 副 /fù/ [measure word for objects forming a set] pair, set; [measure word for one's facial expression]

3678 起 /qǐ/ [measure word for cases, incidents, accidents, etc.]

3720 平方公里 /píngfānggōnglǐ/ square kilometre

3809 队 /duì/ [measure word for a group of people arranged in a line or file]

3850 班 /bān/ [measure word for a group of people] class, squad, team; [measure word for regular transport services]

3851 册 /cè/ [measure word for books] copy

3852 桶 /tǒng/ [measure word] pail, bucket, barrel

4050 克 /kè/ [measure term for weight] gram

4051 集 /jí/ [measure word for TV plays, movies and books, etc.] episode, part, volume

4190 扇 /shàn/ [measure word for doors, windows, etc.]

4297 朵 /duǒ/ [measure word for flowers]

4298 刀 /dāo/ [measure word for meat] a cut of; [measure word for action of cutting with a knife]

4393 瓶 /píng/ [measure word for drink contained in a bottle] a bottle of

4436 排 /pái/ [measure word for a line of persons or things] a line of, a row of

4437 厘米 /límǐ/ [measure term for length] centimetre, cm

4492 伙 /huǒ/ [measure word for a crowd of people] a crowd of, a band of

4543 顶 /dǐng/ [measure word for objects with a top such as hats, caps and sedan chairs]

4544 栋 /dòng/ [measure word for houses and buildings]

4602 匹 /pǐ/ [measure word for horses and mules, etc.]; [measure word for bolts of cloth]

4603 寸 /cùn/ [measure term for length in Chinese local unit] Chinese inch, cun (equivalent of one-thirtieth of a metre)

4664 尺 /chǐ/ [measure word for length in Chinese local unit] Chinese foot, chi (equivalent of ten cun or one-third of a metre)

4665 株 /zhū/ [measure word for plants]

4666 串 /chuàn/ [measure word for things growing or attached together] string, bunch, cluster

4711 袋 /dài/ [measure word for things contained in a bag, packet, sachet, etc.]

4712 拳 /quán/ [measure word for actions of hitting with one's fist]

4938 丈 /zhàng/ [measure term for length in Chinese local unit] zhang (equivalent of ten chi, or 3.33 metres)

4975 滴 /dī/ [measure word for a tiny amount of liquid] drop

Conjunctions

0016 和 /hé/ and

0049 而 /ér/ and, yet

0061 但 /dàn/ but

0082 可 /kě/ but, yet

0099 因为 /yīnwéi/ because

0102 并 /bìng/ and, besides

0117 与 /yǔ/ and

0122 如果 /rúguǒ/ if

0155 但是 /dànshì/ but

0156 所以 /suǒyǐ/ so, therefore

0185 而且 /érqiě/ (not only . . .) but also

0223 或 /huò/ or

0274 就 /jiù/ [as in 一 . . . 就 . . .] (no sooner . . .) than, at once

0300 虽然 /suīrán/ although

0301 也 /yě/ [as in 既 . . . 也] and also, (not) either

0318 及 /jí/ and

0367 或者 /huòzhě/ or

0368 则 /zé/ [indicating cause, condition, contrast, etc.] then

0369 同时 /tóngshí/ at the same time, simultaneously; besides, moreover

0383 以及 /yǐjí/ and, as well as, along with

0389 因此 /yīncǐ/ as such, so, therefore, as a result

0404 可是 /kěshì/ but

0465 不过 /búguò/ only; but

0485 只要 /zhǐyào/ if

0486 于是 /yúshì/ thereupon, and so, then

0491 既 /jì/ since, now that; as well as

0570 而是 /érshì/ but, rather

0576 不仅 /bùjǐn/ not only

0620 又 /yòu/ [as in 既 . . . 又] (both . . .) and

0695 然而 /rán'ér/ however

0745 那么 /nàme/ then

0805 尽管 /jǐnguǎn/ although, despite

0851 并且 /bìngqiě/ and

0876 还是 /háishì/ or

0908 另外 /lìngwài/ in addition, by the way

0909 不管 /bùguǎn/ no matter (what, how, etc.)

0954 若 /ruò/ if

0972 即使 /jíshǐ/ even if

1048 看来 /kànlái/ it appears, it looks as if

1109 无论 /wúlùn/ no matter (what, how)

1160 只有 /zhǐyǒu/ only if

1255 虽 /suī/ although, though

1319 否则 /fǒuzé/ otherwise

1336 一旦 /yídàn/ once, in case

1348 以 /yǐ/ in order to, so as to

1373 那 /nà/ then, in that case

1405 既然 /jìrán/ since, now that

1437 不但 /búdàn/ not only (. . . but also . . .), as well as

1495 从而 /cóng'ér/ thus, so

1592 且 /qiě/ (both . . .) and; even, furthermore

1880 此外 /cǐwài/ besides, in addition

1895 结果 /jiéguǒ/ as a result, consequently

1913 一方面 /yìfāngmiàn/ on the one hand, while

1921 如 /rú/ if, in case of; as, as if

2015 之所以 /zhīsuǒyǐ/ [as in 之所以 . . . 是因为] the reason that . . .

2268 跟 /gēn/ and

2284 因而 /yīn'ér/ so, therefore, hence

2321 接着 /jiēzhe/ then, next

2339 及其 /jíqí/ and (its, their)

2525 可见 /kějiàn/ it can be seen

2534 甚至 /shènzhì/ so much so that, so far as to

2560 假如 /jiǎrú/ if, in the event of

2593 另一方面 /lìng yìfāngmiàn/ on the other hand

2673 要是 /yàoshi/ if, in case

2697 总之 /zǒngzhī/ in sum, in a word

2788 或是 /huòshì/ or

2810 不论 /búlùn/ no matter (what, who, how, etc.), irrespective of

3204 只是 /zhǐshì/ except that, but

3205 与此同时 /yǔcǐtóngshí/ meanwhile

3248 哪怕 /nǎpà/ even if, even though

3299 不然 /bùrán/ otherwise, or

3327 乃至 /nǎizhì/ even

3328 即便 /jíbiàn/ even if

3530 何况 /hékuàng/ let alone, needless to say; moreover, besides

3696 除非 /chúfēi/ unless

3737 要么 /yàome/ (either . . .) or

3831 与其 /yǔqí/ [used in pair with 不如 or 毋宁, etc.] rather than, better than

3832 万一 /wànyī/ just in case

3899 就算 /jiùsuàn/ granted that, even if

3987 以便 /yǐbiàn/ so that, in order to

4369 不如 /bùrú/ might as well, not so much as

4465 虽说 /suīshuō/ although, though

4631 接下来 /jiēxiàlái/ after that, and then, next

4844 就是 /jiùshì/ [as in 就是 . . . 也] even if

Interjections

0341 啊 /ā, á, ǎ/ [interjection expressing surprise, admiration, etc.] oh

0546 呀 /yā/ [interjection expressing surprise] ah, oh

0820 嗯 /ēn, ńg, ňg, ǹg/ [interjection used for questioning, surprise, disapproval, or agreement] well, eh, hey, m-hm, uh-huh

0946 哎 /āi/ [interjection expressing surprise, disapproval, reminder, etc.]

1675 哦 /ò/ [interjection expressing realisation] ah

1935 唉 /āi, ài/ [interjection expressing sadness, disappointment, weariness, etc.] alas, oh, well; [as a response to calling, etc.]

2635 哼 /hng/ [interjection expressing disapproval] humph

2855 噢 /ō/ [interjection expressing mental realisation] oh

2996 喂 /wèi/ hello, hey

3249 哟 /yo/ [interjection expressing surprise] oh, well

3495 哈 /hā/ [interjection expressing satisfaction] ha

3595 嘿 /hēi/ hey, why

3869 哎呀 /āiyā/ [interjection expressing wonder, shock or complaint] ah, my god, damn

4848 哎哟 /āiyō/ [particle expressing astonishment or pain] hey, oh, ouch

Direction and locality words

0015 上 /shàng/ up, on, in

0030 中 /zhōng/ in, within

0059 里 /lǐ/ in, inside

0064 下 /xià/ under, below

0067 后 /hòu/ behind; after, later

0121 前 /qián/ before; in front of

0231 之后 /zhīhòu/ after, afterwards

0235 内 /nèi/ inside, within

0236 外 /wài/ outside

0248 以后 /yǐhòu/ after; afterwards

0275 之间 /zhījiān/ between

0439 起 /qǐ/ [usually occurring with 从 as in 从 . . . 起] starting from

0653 之前 /zhīqián/ before

0662 以上 /yǐshàng/ above; more than

0734 东 /dōng/ east

0873 面前 /miànqián/ before, in front of

0930 之中 /zhīzhōng/ in, inside, within

0931 里面 /lǐmian/ inside, in

0960 西 /xī/ west

1012 北 /běi/ north

1068 上面 /shàngmian/ on top of, above, over; aforesaid

1087 中间 /zhōngjiān/ middle, between

1184 周围 /zhōuwéi/ around, round

1224 左 /zuǒ/ left

1236 之外 /zhīwài/ outside; except

1337 右 /yòu/ right

1361 附近 /fùjìn/ nearby, (in the) vicinity

1428 内部 /nèibù/ inside, within

1521 南 /nán/ south

1572 旁边 /pángbiān/ side

1593 旁 /páng/ beside, by

1623 以下 /yǐxià/ below, following, as follows

1693 东北 /dōngběi/ northeast

1756 之下 /zhīxià/ under, below

1924 以外 /yǐwài/ beyond, outside; other than

2308 西部 /xībù/ west, western part

2550 内外 /nèiwài/ inside and outside; home and abroad

2578 之内 /zhīnèi/ within

2636 西北 /xīběi/ northwest

2735 上下 /shàngxià/ up and down, high and low; about, approximately

3106 前后 /qiánhòu/ in front and behind; before and after, around; from beginning to end

3358 南部 /nánbù/ southern part, south

3438 之际 /zhījì/ at the time when . . .

3461 之上 /zhīshàng/ above

3496 里边 /lǐbian/ inside, within

3497 底下 /dǐxià/ below, under

3698 北部 /běibù/ north, northern part

3835 里头 /lǐtou/ inside

3901 东部 /dōngbù/ east, eastern part

3934 东南 /dōngnán/ southeast

4030 南北 /nánběi/ north and south, from south to north

4079 身后 /shēnhòu/ behind somebody; after one's death

4171 外部 /wàibù/ outside, exterior

4522 背后 /bèihòu/ behind, at the back

4742 外边 /wàibian/ outside

4798 周边 /zhōubiān/ periphery, vicinity, neighbouring, surrounding

4982 一边 /yìbiān/ one side

Numerals and quantifiers

0003 一 /yī/ one, a, an

0033 两 /liǎng/ two

0052 三 /sān/ three

0062 几 /jǐ/ several; how much

0069 多 /duō/ many, much, numerous

0080 二 /èr/ two

0115 一些 /yìxiē/ some

0128 四 /sì/ four

0152 十 /shí/ ten

0172 五 /wǔ/ five

0238 半 /bàn/ half

0257 许多 /xǔduō/ many, plenty of

0286 八 /bā/ eight

0314 很多 /hěnduō/ very many, a large number or amount of

0332 六 /liù/ six

0375 百 /bǎi/ 100

0388 七 /qī/ seven

0433 万 /wàn/ 10,000

0560 九 /jiǔ/ nine

0666 千 /qiān/ 1,000

0667 数 /shù/ several

0800 余 /yú/ [following a number] more than, over

0951 俩 /liǎ/ the two of, both

0952 左右 /zuǒyòu/ [following a quantifier] about, or so

1001 大量 /dàliàng/ a great deal of, plenty of

1445 一半 /yíbàn/ half

1849 头 /tóu/ first

1882 一部分 /yíbùfèn/ a part of

1979 好几 /hǎojǐ/ several, quite a few, many a

2006 部分 /bùfen/ part of

2016 大部分 /dàbùfen/ a large part of, the majority of

2071 多数 /duōshù/ most, the majority

2181 众多 /zhòngduō/ numerous, many

2224 大多数 /dàduōshù/ most, the majority

2423 无数 /wúshù/ countless, innumerable

2434 少数 /shǎoshù/ a small number of; minority

2713 零 /líng/ zero

2770 好多 /hǎoduō/ a good deal, a lot

3082 若干 /ruògān/ a number of, several; how many, how much

3107 亿 /yì/ 100 million

3250 大批 /dàpī/ large quantities

3439 绝大多数 /juédàduōshù/ vast majority

3499 首 /shǒu/ first

3700 来 /lái/ [following a round number to indicate approximation] a bit over

3788 丝毫 /sīháo/ [normally occurring in negative sentences] at all, least

3988 诸多 /zhūduō/ a lot of

4422 数十 /shùshí/ tens of, dozens of

Onomatopoeias

3135 呀 /yā/ [the sound of a creak]

4338 哈 /hā/ [usually reduplicated to indicate the sound of laughing]

4392 嘿嘿 /hēihēi/ [sound of laughing]

Particles

0019 了 /le/ [sentence final particle indicating change of state or current relevance]

0089 呢 /ne/ [particle used at the end of a question or declarative sentence to indicate mood]

0116 吗 /ma/ [question tag]

0119 吧 /ba/ [modal particle indicating a suggestion or request; marking a question requesting confirmation, or a pause after alternatives]

0222 啊 /a/ [modal particle showing affirmation, approval or consent]

0293 呀 /ya/ [sentence final particle]

0378 啦 /la/ [sentence final particle combining 了 and 啊]

0531 嘛 /ma/ [sentence final modal particle indicating that something is obvious or expressing a hope, advice, etc.]

1529 哪 /na/ [sentence final particle similar to 啊, following words ending with the consonant n]

1966 么 /me/ [interrogative particle]

1967 呃 /e/ [particle used for a pause or to express wonder or admiration] er, oh

2216 而已 /éryǐ/ [sentence final particle, equivalent of 罢了] nothing more, that is all

2480 也好 /yěhǎo/ may as well

2710 哇 /wa/ [sentence final particle replacing 啊 where the preceding word ending with the vowel u or ao]

3690 呐 /na/ [sentence final particle, especially following words ending with the consonant n]

4071 呗 /bei/ [sentence final particle indicating something obvious or expressing resignation]

4689 罢了 /bàle/ [sentence final particle, equivalent of 而已] nothing more, merely, only

Prefixes

0047 第 /dì/ [numeral prefix forming ordinal numbers]

1093 前 /qián/ ex-, former

1636 小 /xiǎo/ [usually preceding a family name or given name as a title of address to show affection]

1736 阿 /ā/ [nominal prefix used before a personal name for endearment]

2616 初 /chū/ [prefix preceding a numeral to indicate dates on the lunar calendar, and also for grades or years in the junior high school]

4912 老 /lǎo/ [used as an affix preceding or following the surname of a person or a numeral to indicate affection or familiarity, or to indicate the order of birth of the children in a family]

Prepositions

0004 在 /zài/ [indicating location or time, etc.] at, in

0022 对 /duì/ for, to, with regard to

0034 把 /bǎ/ [ba-structure preposing the object]

0042 从 /cóng/ from

0057 被 /bèi/ [passive marker]

0060 给 /gěi/ to

0065 为 /wèi/ [introducing purpose, reason, beneficiary, etc.] for, because of

0077 以 /yǐ/ by means of, with, in (some way); according to; because of

0088 与 /yǔ/ [indicating involvement or relationship] with

0095 于 /yú/ [indicating time, location, direction, etc.] in, at

0100 向 /xiàng/ [indicating direction] to, towards

0130 比 /bǐ/ [used for comparison] than

0145 和 /hé/ [indicating relationship or comparison] with

0154 由 /yóu/ by, from

0181 跟 /gēn/ [indicating relationship, involvement or comparison] with

0198 当 /dāng/ just at (time or place)

0202 将 /jiāng/ [equivalent of the object preposer 把]

0207 为了 /wèile/ for the sake of; in order to

0212 同 /tóng/ [indicating relationship, involvement, comparison] with

0287 自 /zì/ from

0292 就 /jiù/ regarding, as far as . . . is concerned

0299 通过 /tōngguò/ by means of, through, via

0327 由于 /yóuyú/ due to

0342 往 /wǎng/ towards

0359 对于 /duìyú/ regarding, as to, for, about

0365 连 /lián/ [as in 连 . . . 都(也) . . .] even

0407 因 /yīn/ because of, as a result of, according to

0457 按 /àn/ according to

0528 关于 /guānyú/ about, regarding, pertaining to

0530 经过 /jīngguò/ through, by; via; as a result of

0543 据 /jù/ according to

0549 根据 /gēnjù/ according to

0767 到 /dào/ to (a place); up until (time)

0795 按照 /ànzhào/ according to

0835 随着 /suízhe/ along with

0844 除了 /chúle/ besides, in addition to; except

0900 经 /jīng/ through, by means of; by way of, via

1283 朝 /cháo/ towards; facing

1315 除 /chú/ except, besides

1430 作为 /zuòwéi/ as

1633 至于 /zhìyú/ as regards

1712 凭 /píng/ by, (taking) as the basis

1907 随 /suí/ along with

2565 针对 /zhēnduì/ at, against, for

2660 自从 /zìcóng/ since

2741 有关 /yǒuguān/ concerning, related to

2802 直到 /zhídào/ until, up to

2836 沿 /yán/ along

2960 沿着 /yánzhe/ along

3161 依 /yī/ according to, by

4189 每当 /měidāng/ whenever, every time

1516 **国外** /guówài/ abroad

1618 **当中** /dāngzhōng/ in the middle or centre; among

1639 **现场** /xiànchǎng/ scene (of event or incident), site, spot

1660 **东方** /dōngfāng/ east; the East

1789 **门口** /ménkǒu/ doorway, gate

1853 **手里** /shǒuli/ in hand, at hand

1875 **手中** /shǒuzhōng/ in hand

2121 **眼前** /yǎnqián/ before one's eyes; the present

2138 **地下** /dìxià/ underground

2223 **北方** /běifāng/ north

2474 **海外** /hǎiwài/ overseas

2566 **空中** /kōngzhōng/ in the air

2661 **村里** /cūnli/ in the village

2702 **内地** /nèidì/ inland

2798 **屋里** /wūli/ indoors, in the house or room

2820 **城里** /chéngli/ in town or city

2870 **眼里** /yǎnli/ in one's eyes, in one's view

2930 **外地** /wàidì/ non-local place

2931 **家中** /jiāzhōng/ at home

3067 **嘴里** /zuǐli/ in mouth

3115 **南方** /nánfāng/ south

3314 **深处** /shēnchù/ depth; deepest or most distant part

3498 **沿海** /yánhǎi/ along the coast, coastal

3546 **街头** /jiētóu/ street, street corner

3610 **境内** /jìngnèi/ within borders (of a country or province, etc.); internal, domestic

3721 **门前** /ménqián/ in front of the door or gate

3810 **眼中** /yǎnzhōng/ in one's eyes

3880 **西南** /xīnán/ southwest

3952 **门外** /ménwài/ outside the door

4052 **本地** /běndì/ [as opposed to 外地] local place

4053 **室内** /shìnèi/ indoor

4667 **路边** /lùbiān/ roadside

4765 **乡下** /xiāngxia/ country, countryside

4824 **窗外** /chuāngwài/ out of the window

4880 **体内** /tǐnèi/ inside the body

4939 **市区** /shìqū/ city proper, town, city; downtown

4966 **郊区** /jiāoqū/ suburbs, outskirts

Suffixes

0111 **们** /men/ [plural marker for pronouns and some animate nouns]

0182 **儿** /ér, r/ [nonsyllabic suffix for retroflection, especially in the Beijing dialect]

0271 **者** /zhě/ [suffix for nouns denoting persons] -ist, -er

0825 **性** /xìng/ [nominal suffix indicating a specified quality or property]

1000 **家** /jiā/ [nominal suffix indicating a specialist in a particular field] -ist, -ian

1050 **式** /shì/ type, style

1200 **型** /xíng/ model, type

1449 **子** /zi/ [nominal suffix to form a disyllabic word]

1699 **化** /huà/ [verb suffix] -ise, -ify

1729 **界** /jiè/ the circle or world of

4080 **热** /rè/ craze, fad

4284 **器** /qì/ [nominal suffix following a verb indicating the related device or instrument]

Time words

0094 **现在** /xiànzài/ now

0144 **今天** /jīntiān/ today

0273 **当时** /dāngshí/ then, at that time

0311 **过去** /guòqù/ (in the) past, before

0331 **后来** /hòulái/ afterwards

0422 **目前** /mùqián/ currently, at the present time

0518 **今年** /jīnnián/ this year

0559 **晚上** /wǎnshang/ (in the) evening

0593 **以前** /yǐqián/ before

0596 **每天** /měitiān/ every day

0742 **以来** /yǐlái/ since (a previous event)

0764 **下午** /xiàwǔ/ (in the) afternoon

0765 **现** /xiàn/ now

0780 **现代** /xiàndài/ modern times

0781 **最近** /zuìjìn/ recently

0811 **当年** /dāngnián, dàngnián/ in those days, past; that very year, current year

0891 **去年** /qùnián/ last year

1002 **未来** /wèilái/ the future

1019 **明天** /míngtiān/ tomorrow

1063 **每年** /měinián/ every year

1095 **如今** /rújīn/ nowadays, today

1107 **期间** /qījiān/ period of time, course

1302 **昨天** /zuótiān/ yesterday

1363 **春** /chūn/ spring

1364 **今后** /jīnhòu/ from now on, hereafter, in future

1474 **上午** /shàngwǔ/ (in the) morning

1478 **夜** /yè/ night

1492 **古代** /gǔdài/ ancient times

1679 **将来** /jiānglái/ future

1732 **平时** /píngshí/ in normal times

1854 **秋** /qiū/ autumn, fall; a period of (troubled) time

1908 **夏** /xià/ summer

1915 **中午** /zhōngwǔ/ noon

2047 **当天** /dàngtiān/ the same day

2078 **今** /jīn/ today, now

2264 **当初** /dāngchū/ at the beginning, in the first place

2277 **春天** /chūntiān/ spring

2292 **当代** /dāngdài/ the present age

2304 **早晨** /zǎochén/ early morning

2315 **当前** /dāngqián/ currently, presently

2325 **今日** /jīnrì/ today

2356 **早上** /zǎoshang/ (early) morning

2357 夏天 /xiàtiān/ summer

2372 以往 /yǐwǎng/ before, the
past

2402 明年 /míngnián/ next year

2457 冬天 /dōngtiān/ winter

2458 春节 /chūnjié/ Spring Festival
(Chinese New Year)

2459 白天 /báitiān/ day, daytime

2540 近年来 /jìnniánlái/ in recent
years

2703 今晚 /jīnwǎn/ tonight

2758 当今 /dāngjīn/ today,
nowadays

2838 一日 /yírì/ one day

3116 凌晨 /língchén/ early
morning before dawn,
small hours

3261 此后 /cǐhòu/ hence, hereafter

3450 周末 /zhōumò/ weekend

3508 冬 /dōng/ winter

3547 上次 /shàngcì/ last time

3576 夜里 /yèlǐ/ night

3811 年底 /niándǐ/ the end of the
year

3881 秋天 /qiūtiān/ autumn

3953 夜晚 /yèwǎn/ night

4054 近日 /jìnrì/ recently, in the
past or next few days

4253 冬季 /dōngjì/ winter

4299 瞬间 /shùnjiān/ instant,
moment

4340 清晨 /qīngchén/ early
morning

4394 会儿 /huìr/ [preceded by the
demonstrative pronoun 这
or 那] (at this or that)
moment

4545 从前 /cóngqián/ before, in
the past

4713 周 /zhōu/ week

4714 深夜 /shēnyè/ late at night,
far into the night

4715 往后 /wǎnghòu/ from now
on, afterwards

4766 夏季 /xiàjì/ summer

4767 后期 /hòuqī/ late stage, late
period

4825 下次 /xiàcì/ next time

4881 前夕 /qiánxì/ (on) the eve of

4882 生前 /shēngqián/ during
one's lifetime, before one's
death

4940 眼下 /yǎnxià/ at present, now,
for the time being

Lexical words

Adjectives

0025 大 /dà/ big, large

0028 好 /hǎo/ good, well

0055 多 /duō/ many, much,
plentiful

0066 小 /xiǎo/ small, little

0106 高 /gāo/ tall, high

0112 新 /xīn/ new

0140 全 /quán/ whole, entire,
complete

0147 老 /lǎo/ old, veteran

0171 重要 /zhòngyào/ important,
vital

0173 长 /cháng/ long

0184 女 /nǚ/ female, woman

0227 最后 /zuìhòu/ final, last

0258 少 /shǎo/ few, rare

0272 难 /nán/ difficult

0296 副 /fù/ deputy, associate,
vice-

0298 不同 /bùtóng/ different

0320 早 /zǎo/ early

0326 完全 /wánquán/ complete,
whole

0358 快 /kuài/ fast, quick

0362 近 /jìn/ near

0401 成功 /chénggōng/ successful

0409 强 /qiáng/ strong, powerful,
better

0414 整个 /zhěnggè/ whole, entire,
all

0425 另 /lìng/ other, another

0432 一样 /yíyàng/ same

0438 对 /duì/ right, correct;
opposite (in direction)

0454 远 /yuǎn/ far

0466 主要 /zhǔyào/ main, major

0468 男 /nán/ male, man

0481 清楚 /qīngchǔ/ clear

0495 满 /mǎn/ full

0504 低 /dī/ low

0505 基本 /jīběn/ basic

0520 直接 /zhíjiē/ direct

0523 真 /zhēn/ real, true, genuine

0532 红 /hóng/ red; popular

0569 容易 /róngyì/ easy

0585 高兴 /gāoxìng/ happy, joyous

0598 清 /qīng/ clear

0608 深 /shēn/ deep

0612 全部 /quánbù/ all, whole, full,
entire, total

0628 不少 /bùshǎo/ a good few

0633 白 /bái/ white

0643 突然 /tūrán/ sudden

0673 严重 /yánzhòng/ severe,
serious

0687 年轻 /niánqīng/ young

0701 困难 /kùnnán/ difficult

0702 非 /fēi/ non-

0708 差 /chà/ short of; poor, not
up to standard; wrong

0719 晚 /wǎn/ late

0726 重 /zhòng/ heavy

0733 共同 /gòngtóng/ common

0743 具体 /jùtǐ/ concrete, specific

0744 总 /zǒng/ overall, total;
general, chief

0754 黑 /hēi/ black; dark

0760 简单 /jiǎndān/ simple, easy

0766 一定 /yídìng/ definite, regular;
given, certain; fixed,
specified

0777 安全 /ānquán/ safe, secure

0792 所谓 /suǒwèi/ so-called

0804 健康 /jiànkāng/ healthy

0809 著名 /zhùmíng/ famous, well
known

0829 认真 /rènzhēn/ earnest,
serious

0838 不行 /bùxíng/ won't do, no
good, poor

0841 自由 /zìyóu/ free

0855 紧张 /jǐnzhāng/ nervous,
strained

0860 忙 /máng/ busy

0863 巨大 /jùdà/ huge

0868 热 /rè/ hot

0870 正常 /zhèngcháng/ normal,
regular

0872 积极 /jījí/ active; positive

0874 初 /chū/ elementary, just beginning; first

0878 科学 /kēxué/ scientific

0897 坏 /huài/ bad

0903 错 /cuò/ wrong, mistaken

0926 平 /píng/ flat, level, even; calm; average, common

0933 矛盾 /máodùn/ contradictory

0936 明 /míng/ bright, light, clear; open, overt, explicit

0944 旧 /jiù/ old, used

0958 双 /shuāng/ double; even (as opposed to odd)

0971 够 /gòu/ enough, sufficient

0993 明显 /míngxiǎn/ obvious, notable, clear

0997 主 /zhǔ/ main, primary, principal

1006 不错 /búcuò/ not bad, pretty good; correct, right

1011 充分 /chōngfèn/ full, abundant, ample, sufficient

1026 全面 /quánmiàn/ all-around, overall

1036 正式 /zhèngshì/ formal, official

1037 长期 /chángqī/ long-term

1038 重大 /zhòngdà/ great, major, important, significant

1043 古 /gǔ/ ancient, old

1058 伟大 /wěidà/ great

1071 急 /jí/ anxious; annoyed; urgent; hurried

1082 强烈 /qiángliè/ intense, strong

1086 特殊 /tèshū/ special

1097 短 /duǎn/ short, brief

1098 优秀 /yōuxiù/ excellent

1103 正确 /zhèngquè/ correct

1113 黄 /huáng/ yellow; pornographic

1117 死 /sǐ/ dead

1120 丰富 /fēngfù/ rich, abundant, plentiful

1126 稳定 /wěndìng/ stable

1132 复杂 /fùzá/ complicated

1142 必要 /bìyào/ necessary

1166 真正 /zhēnzhèng/ genuine, true, real

1170 原 /yuán/ former, original

1176 假 /jiǎ/ fake, false; artificial

1179 普通 /pǔtōng/ common, ordinary

1204 根本 /gēnběn/ basic, fundamental

1211 热情 /rèqíng/ enthusiastic, cordial, warm

1220 美丽 /měilì/ beautiful

1227 漂亮 /piàoliang/ beautiful, pretty, handsome; brilliant, remarkable

1238 幸福 /xìngfú/ happy, blessed

1240 特别 /tèbié/ special, particular

1254 自然 /zìrán/ natural

1259 痛苦 /tòngkǔ/ painful

1260 满意 /mǎnyì/ satisfied, satisfactory

1262 深刻 /shēnkè/ profound

1263 唯一 /wéiyī/ [equivalent of 惟一] only

1276 原来 /yuánlái/ original, former

1287 真实 /zhēnshí/ true, real, authentic

1303 危险 /wēixiǎn/ dangerous

1317 香 /xiāng/ fragrant, sweet-scented; sound (sleep); appetising, (eat) with relish

1325 方 /fāng/ square

1329 明确 /míngquè/ clear-cut, explicit, unequivocal

1366 苦 /kǔ/ bitter; hard (times), tough

1367 彻底 /chèdǐ/ thorough

1379 有效 /yǒuxiào/ effective, valid

1380 良好 /liánghǎo/ good

1392 主动 /zhǔdòng/ on one's own initiative, active

1397 民主 /mínzhǔ/ democratic

1404 实际 /shíjì/ practical, actual

1417 一致 /yízhì/ identical; unanimous; consistent

1424 正 /zhèng/ principal (as opposed to vice-); straight, upright; right (side); regular (shape)

1432 次 /cì/ inferior

1436 先进 /xiānjìn/ advanced

1440 国有 /guóyǒu/ state-owned

1441 久 /jiǔ/ long (time); of a specified duration

1442 合理 /hélǐ/ reasonable, rational

1444 轻 /qīng/ light

1457 美好 /měihǎo/ happy, glorious, good, beautiful

1461 美 /měi/ beautiful, pretty

1476 普遍 /pǔbiàn/ common, widespread

1488 快乐 /kuàilè/ happy

1502 严格 /yángé/ strict

1530 成熟 /chéngshú/ mature

1536 绿 /lǜ/ green

1544 乱 /luàn/ messy, in disorder; confused

1545 特 /tè/ special, unusual

1570 坚决 /jiānjué/ firm, resolute, determined

1582 方便 /fāngbiàn/ convenient

1583 高级 /gāojí/ high quality; high grade, advanced; senior, high level

1591 足 /zú/ enough, adequate, sufficient

1603 广泛 /guǎngfàn/ extensive

1621 富 /fù/ rich, wealthy

1622 平衡 /pínghéng/ balanced

1630 及时 /jíshí/ in time

1631 穷 /qióng/ poor

1649 麻烦 /máfán/ troublesome

1650 差不多 /chàbuduō/ almost the same; just about right; more or less

1665 顺利 /shùnlì/ smooth, successful

1673 广大 /guǎngdà/ vast, broad, extensive

1674 突出 /tūchū/ outstanding, prominent

1690 平等 /píngděng/ equal

1691 独立 /dúlì/ independent

1697 冷 /lěng/ cold

1698 细 /xì/ thin, fine; exquisite; careful

1707 软 /ruǎn/ soft

1727 不足 /bùzú/ insufficient, inadequate

1728 乐 /lè/ happy, joyful

1743 可以 /kěyǐ/ not bad, pretty good; passable

1749 奇怪 /qíguài/ strange

1762 贵 /guì/ expensive

1763 激烈 /jīliè/ intense, fierce

1772 安 /ān/ calm, at ease

1773 牛 /niú/ [a popular compliment among young people] great, excellent, matchless

1790 激动 /jīdòng/ excited

1793 慢 /màn/ slow

1794 聪明 /cōngmíng/ clever, smart, witty

1799 文明 /wénmíng/ civilised, civil

1811 单 /dān/ single, solitary; odd

1834 公开 /gōngkāi/ open, public

1842 强大 /qiángdà/ strong, powerful

1848 硬 /yìng/ hard

1861 公共 /gōnggòng/ public

1879 大型 /dàxíng/ large scale

1891 严肃 /yánsù/ serious, solemn

1892 完整 /wánzhěng/ complete, intact

1893 整 /zhěng/ whole, entire

1894 名 /míng/ famous, renowned

1902 综合 /zōnghé/ comprehensive, synthetic

1912 仔细 /zǐxì/ careful

1920 活 /huó/ living, alive; lively; movable, flexible

1944 理想 /lǐxiǎng/ ideal, desirable

1954 宽 /kuān/ wide, broad; well off

1968 蓝 /lán/ blue

1969 贫困 /pínkùn/ poor, impoverished

1976 相同 /xiāngtóng/ identical, same, common

1984 错误 /cuòwù/ wrong, mistaken

1997 紧 /jǐn/ tight

2004 行 /xíng/ OK, all right

2005 公平 /gōngpíng/ fair

2022 暗 /àn/ dark, unclear

2030 合适 /héshì/ suitable

2031 严 /yán/ strict, stern; (air- or water-) tight

2051 轻松 /qīngsōng/ light, relaxed

2052 热烈 /rèliè/ warm, cordial; lively, enthusiastic

2057 厉害 /lìhài/ intense, severe; harsh, stern; fierce, terrible

2058 空 /kōng, kòng/ empty, hollow; blank; vacant

2124 随便 /suíbiàn/ casual, careless; informal

2125 亲 /qīn/ close, intimate

2126 深入 /shēnrù/ thorough, deep, in depth

2144 干 /gān/ dry

2152 青 /qīng/ blue, green, cyan

2163 友好 /yǒuhǎo/ friendly

2164 相当 /xiāngdāng/ matching, commensurate with; suitable, appropriate; considerable

2165 恶 /è/ bad, evil, wicked; fierce

2173 厚 /hòu/ thick

2174 落后 /luòhòu/ backward, outdated, behind the times

2175 平均 /píngjūn/ average, mean

2192 熟 /shú, shóu/ ripe; (food) cooked, done; familiar; skilled; sound (sleep)

2202 准确 /zhǔnquè/ accurate, exact

2203 遗憾 /yíhàn/ sorry, pitiful, regretful

2204 灵 /líng/ effective; quick-minded

2234 累 /lèi/ tired, weary

2235 发达 /fādá/ developed, advanced; flourishing

2247 热闹 /rènao/ busy, bustling with noise and excitement

2248 新鲜 /xīnxiān/ fresh

2256 独特 /dútè/ unique

2267 统一 /tǒngyī/ unified, uniform; centralised

2282 密切 /mìqiē/ close

2295 生 /shēng/ raw; unripe; unfamiliar; alive, living

2296 有限 /yǒuxiàn/ limited

2306 同样 /tóngyàng/ same

2320 可怕 /kěpà/ frightful, terrible

2338 恐怖 /kǒngbù/ horrible, terrifying

2349 精 /jīng/ clever, shrewd; refined; exquisite; adept, skilled

2367 上述 /shàngshù/ above mentioned

2371 另外 /lìngwài/ another, other, extra

2375 日常 /rìcháng/ daily

2376 艰难 /jiānnán/ difficult, hard

2377 神秘 /shénmì/ mysterious

2393 便宜 /piányi/ cheap, inexpensive

2394 阳 /yáng/ positive; Yang (positive)

2405 沉重 /chénzhòng/ heavy; serious

2406 神 /shén/ magic, miraculous; smart; supernatural

2407 众 /zhòng/ numerous

2420 有力 /yǒulì/ powerful

2431 清醒 /qīngxǐng/ sober, clear-headed

2441 温暖 /wēnnuǎn/ warm

2442 齐 /qí/ neat, even; all ready

2443 出色 /chūsè/ remarkable, brilliant

2465 愉快 /yúkuài/ cheerful, joyful, happy

2466 详细 /xiángxì/ detailed

2481 洋 /yáng/ foreign

2482 合法 /héfǎ/ lawful, legal

2499 意外 /yìwài/ unexpected

2500 可惜 /kěxī/ pitiful

2501 雅 /yǎ/ elegant, refined

2521 足够 /zúgòu/ enough, sufficient

2523 干净 /gānjìng/ clean

2524 集中 /jízhōng/ concentrated, focused; centralised

2545 弱 /ruò/ weak

2546 怪 /guài/ strange

2547 自觉 /zìjué/ conscious, conscientious; on one's own initiative

2575 幽默 /yōumò/ humorous

2576 奇 /qí, jī/ strange; odd (number)

2591 着急 /zháojí/ anxious, worried

2592 通 /tōng/ unblocked, open, through; (of writing) smooth

2611 平静 /píngjìng/ calm, tranquil

2612 客观 /kèguān/ objective

2613 公正 /gōngzhèng/ just, fair, impartial

2632 舒服 /shūfú/ comfortable; (physically) well

2633 亲切 /qīnqiè/ amiable, kind, intimate

2634 不利 /búlì/ unfavourable, harmful

2651 有利 /yǒulì/ advantageous, beneficial

2652 最佳 /zuìjiā/ best, optimal

2656 私人 /sīrén/ private, personal

2669 相反 /xiāngfǎn/ opposite, contrary

2670 破 /pò/ broken, worn out; lousy

2671 暂时 /zànshí/ temporary

2672 当 /dàng/ appropriate

2694 亮 /liàng/ bright, light; enlightened

2695 易 /yì/ easy

2696 难得 /nándé/ rare

2711 精彩 /jīngcǎi/ brilliant, splendid, wonderful

2734 寒 /hán/ cold

2749 辉煌 /huīhuáng/ splendid, glorious

2750 单纯 /dānchún/ simple

2751 敏感 /mǐngǎn/ sensitive

2765 协调 /xiétiáo/ matching, coordinated, in keeping

2768 广 /guǎng/ wide, broad, extensive

2783 响 /xiǎng/ loud; noisy

2784 干脆 /gāncuì/ straightforward, clear-cut

2785 适当 /shìdàng/ suitable, proper

2786 密 /mì/ thick, dense; close, intimate; secret

2787 巧 /qiǎo/ opportune, by chance; skilful, clever

2808 可爱 /kě'ài/ lovely

2809 关键 /guānjiàn/ key, crucial, critical

2827 个别 /gèbié/ very few

2828 大胆 /dàdǎn/ bold, courageous, daring

2847 对外 /duìwài/ external, foreign

2848 圆 /yuán/ round

2849 准 /zhǔn/ accurate; quasi-

2850 类似 /lèisì/ similar

2867 总体 /zǒngtǐ/ overall, total

2879 傻 /shǎ/ foolish

2880 闲 /xián/ free, idle

2881 净 /jìng/ clean; net

2897 专门 /zhuānmén/ special, specialised

2898 混乱 /hùnluàn/ confused

2899 喜 /xǐ/ happy, delighted, joyful

2941 故意 /gùyì/ deliberate, intentional

2942 生动 /shēngdòng/ vivid, lively

2943 大规模 /dàguīmó/ large scale

2967 顺 /shùn/ smooth, without a hitch

2973 灰 /huī/ grey

2989 臭 /chòu/ stinking, smelly; disgraceful, discredited

2990 不满 /bùmǎn/ dissatisfied, discontented, resentful

2991 秘密 /mìmì/ secret

2992 善 /shàn/ virtuous, good; kind, friendly

3015 阴 /yīn/ (of weather) overcast; negative; Yin (negative)

3016 古老 /gǔlǎo/ ancient, old, time-honoured

3017 坚定 /jiāndìng/ firm, steadfast

3018 清晰 /qīngxī/ clear, distinct

3019 便 /biàn/ convenient; informal, ordinary

3020 同一 /tóngyī/ same, identical

3040 花 /huā/ coloured; flowery, fancy; (of eyes) blurred

3042 最初 /zuìchū/ initial, first

3062 私 /sī/ personal, private; illicit

3074 相应 /xiāngyìng/ corresponding, relevant

3079 有趣 /yǒuqù/ interesting

3101 严厉 /yánlì/ severe, stern

3102 灿烂 /cànlàn/ bright; brilliant

3103 冷静 /lěngjìng/ calm

3104 真诚 /zhēnchéng/ sincere, true

3105 不良 /bùliáng/ bad, harmful

3148 紧急 /jǐnjí/ urgent

3149 实 /shí/ solid, firm; true, real, actual

3150 善良 /shànliáng/ kind-hearted, good and honest

3168 繁荣 /fánróng/ prosperous, booming

3169 过分 /guòfèn/ excessive, too much

3201 不幸 /búxìng/ unfortunate, unlucky

3202 老实 /lǎoshí/ honest

3203 艰苦 /jiānkǔ/ difficult, hard

3224 明白 /míngbái/ clear, explicit; sensible

3225 荣 /róng/ proud; glorious; prosperous

3243 饱 /bǎo/ full

3244 光 /guāng/ used up; (of surface) smooth, polished; bare, naked

3245 原始 /yuánshǐ/ primitive, primeval; (of data) original, firsthand

3246 陌生 /mòshēng/ strange, unfamiliar

3247 一级 /yìjí/ first rate, first class, first degree

3271 脏 /zāng/ dirty

3272 平常 /píngcháng/ ordinary, common

3273 失望 /shīwàng/ disappointed

3274 兴奋 /xīngfèn/ excited

3275 完美 /wánměi/ perfect, flawless

3293 有名 /yǒumíng/ famous

3294 直 /zhí/ straight; straightforward, frank

3295 富裕 /fùyù/ affluent, well off

3296 佳 /jiā/ good, excellent

3297 不安 /bù'ān/ uneasy

3298 浪漫 /làngmàn/ romantic

3326 相似 /xiāngsì/ similar

3353 光荣 /guāngróng/ glorious, honoured, proud

3354 纯 /chún/ pure

3356 系统 /xìtǒng/ systematic

3357 良 /liáng/ good

3389 辛苦 /xīnkǔ/ hard, painstaking

3390 骄傲 /jiāo'ào/ proud; arrogant

3391 显著 /xiǎnzhù/ remarkable, outstanding

3392 遥远 /yáoyuǎn/ far away, remote, distant

3393 随意 /suíyì/ random, arbitary; voluntary, as one pleases

3394 周 /zhōu/ considerate, thoughtful; careful

3410 好看 /hǎokàn/ good-looking, beautiful

3413 黑暗 /hēi'àn/ dark

3433 瘦 /shòu/ thin, bony; (of clothes) tight; (of meat) lean

3434 静 /jìng/ quiet; still, motionless

3435 和谐 /héxié/ harmonious, in harmony

3436 虚 /xū/ empty; false; virtual; in poor health; timid

3437 最新 /zuìxīn/ latest

3460 碎 /suì/ broken

3489 宝贵 /bǎoguì/ valuable, precious

3490 坚强 /jiānqiáng/ firm, strong

3491 绝 /jué/ superb, matchless; uncompromising; desperate; exhausted

3492 珍贵 /zhēnguì/ precious

3493 孤独 /gūdú/ lonely

3525 绝对 /juéduì/ absolute

3526 耐心 /nàixīn/ patient

3527 最终 /zuìzhōng/ final, ultimate

3561 免费 /miǎnfèi/ free, free of charge

3563 浅 /qiǎn/ shallow; simple, easy; (of colour) light, pale

3564 浓 /nóng/ thick, dense; strong

3588 欢乐 /huānlè/ joyous, cheerful

3589 惨 /cǎn/ miserable, awful, tragic

3590 母 /mǔ/ female

3591 一流 /yìliú/ first rate, first class

3626 可靠 /kěkào/ reliable

3627 自动 /zìdòng/ automatic

3628 稳 /wěn/ steady; certain

3629 滑 /huá/ slippery, smooth; crafty

3630 灵活 /línghuó/ flexible, elastic

3631 烂 /làn/ rotten, festering; overcooked; lousy, messy

3657 勇敢 /yǒnggǎn/ brave

3658 封建 /fēngjiàn/ feudal

3659 尴尬 /gān'gà/ embarrassed, embarrassing

3660 最低 /zuìdī/ lowest, minimum

3691 粗 /cū/ thick; coarse, rough; (of voice) husky; rude

3692 业余 /yèyú/ spare-time; amateur

3693 温 /wēn/ warm

3694 疯 /fēng/ insane, crazy

3695 杰出 /jiéchū/ outstanding, distinguished

3733 乐观 /lèguān/ optimistic

3734 自豪 /zìháo/ proud

3735 固定 /gùdìng/ fixed

3736 迟 /chí/ late

3770 安静 /ānjìng/ quiet

3771 胖 /pàng/ fat, stout, obese

3772 愤怒 /fènnù/ angry, indignant

3773 紫 /zǐ/ purple, violet

3774 甜 /tián/ sweet

3775 无比 /wúbǐ/ matchless, unsurpassed, immeasurable

3776 精神 /jīngshén/ lively, vigorous, smart, cute

3777 典型 /diǎnxíng/ typical

3778 不对 /búduì/ wrong, incorrect

3779 无奈 /wúnài/ having no choice, utterly helpless

3780 脆弱 /cuìruò/ frail, fragile

3781 重点 /zhòngdiǎn/ key, major

3786 整整 /zhěngzhěng/ whole, full

3824 松 /sōng/ loose, slack, relaxed; soft and crisp

3825 横 /héng, hèng/ horizontal; unruly

3826 散 /sǎn/ loose; leisurely; scattered, dispersive

3827 盲目 /mángmù/ blind

3828 残酷 /cánkù/ cruel

3829 爱国 /àiguó/ patriotic

3830 温柔 /wēnróu/ gentle and soft, amiable

3864 暖 /nuǎn/ warm

3865 惊讶 /jīngyà/ surprised, astonished

3866 惊人 /jīngrén/ astonishing, amazing

3896 庞大 /pángdà/ enormous, huge

3923 原有 /yuányǒu/ old, originally existing

3926 无限 /wúxiàn/ unlimited, boundless

3927 漫长 /màncháng/ very long, endless

3928 鲜明 /xiānmíng/ bright; distinct; striking

3939 平凡 /píngfán/ common, ordinary

3977 临时 /línshí/ temporary

3978 优美 /yōuměi/ beautiful, graceful

3979 雄 /xióng/ male; heroic

3980 伤心 /shāngxīn/ sad

3981 可怜 /kělián/ pitiful, poor

3982 疯狂 /fēngkuáng/ crazy, mad

3983 惟一 /wéiyī/ [equivalent of 惟一] only, sole

4019 怒 /nù/ angry, indignant

4022 糊涂 /hútu/ muddled, confused; blurred

4023 湿 /shī/ wet, sodden

4024 实在 /shízài/ real; honest and trustworthy

4025 难受 /nánshòu/ unwell; unhappy

4026 寂寞 /jìmò/ lonely

4027 好奇 /hàoqí/ curious

4028 知名 /zhīmíng/ renowned, well known

4058 得意 /déyì/ proud (of oneself), complacent

4072 薄 /báo, bó/ thin; small, meagre

4073 光明 /guāngmíng/ bright

4074 古典 /gǔdiǎn/ classical

4075 犹豫 /yóuyù/ hesitant

4076 旺 /wàng/ prosperous, flourishing, brisk; (of fire) blazing

4077 神奇 /shénqí/ magical, mystical, miraculous

4112 高尚 /gāoshàng/ noble, lofty

4113 恶劣 /èliè/ bad, vile, abominable

4114 顽强 /wánqiáng/ indomitable; tenacious

4115 模糊 /móhu/ vague, faint, blurred

4116 有益 /yǒuyì/ beneficial, good

4117 异 /yì/ different; strange, unusual

4138 官方 /guānfāng/ official, of or from the government

4159 沉默 /chénmò/ silent

4160 异常 /yìcháng/ unusual

4161 活泼 /huópō/ lively

4162 了不起 /liǎobuqǐ/ amazing, terrific

4163 神圣 /shénshèng/ holy, divine, sacred

4164 幸运 /xìngyùn/ lucky, fortunate

4165 优 /yōu/ excellent, fine

4166 素 /sù/ plain

4216 偏 /piān/ slanting, leaning; prejudiced, biased

4217 棒 /bàng/ terrific, superb

4218 悲哀 /bēi'āi/ sad, grieved, sorrowful

4219 宜 /yí/ suitable

4277 动人 /dòngrén/ moving, touching

4278 尖锐 /jiānruì/ sharp, penetrating, piercing

4279 肯定 /kěndìng/ affirmative, positive; definite, sure

4281 倒霉 /dǎoméi/ having bad luck

4282 永恒 /yǒnghéng/ eternal, everlasting

4318 繁华 /fánhuá/ flourishing and bustling, busy

4319 短暂 /duǎnzàn/ short, brief, transient

4364 妙 /miào/ wonderful

4365 谨慎 /jǐnshèn/ cautious, prudent

4366 合格 /hégé/ qualified

4367 邪 /xié/ evil, weird

4368 残 /cán/ disabled; incomplete; remnant

4414 好吃 /hǎochī/ tasty, delicious; edible

4415 鲜 /xiān/ fresh; (of colour) bright; (of food) tasty

4416 广阔 /guǎngkuò/ wide, broad, vast

4417 笨 /bèn/ stupid

4418 不易 /búyì/ not easy, difficult

4419 贤 /xián/ virtuous and able; [used as part of a term of respect]

4456 应有 /yīngyǒu/ proper, due, deserved

4460 贫穷 /pínqióng/ poor, impoverished

4461 细致 /xìzhì/ delicate, fine; careful

4462 消极 /xiāojí/ passive, inactive

4463 低下 /dīxià/ low (status)

4464 吉 /jí/ lucky

4508 现有 /xiànyǒu/ currently existing

4516 深厚 /shēnhòu/ deep, profound

4517 高大 /gāodà/ tall; lofty

4518 狂 /kuáng/ mad, crazy; conceited, arrogant; unrestrained, wild

4519 长远 /chángyuǎn/ long-term

4568 悠久 /yōujiǔ/ of long standing

4570 正当 /zhèngdāng/ proper

4571 猛 /měng/ ferocious, hard

4572 勇 /yǒng/ brave, courageous

4573 丰 /fēng/ abundant, plentiful; good-looking

4624 酸 /suān/ sour, tart; pedantic

4625 天真 /tiānzhēn/ naive, innocent

4626 废 /fèi/ waste, useless; disused, abandoned

4627 可笑 /kěxiào/ funny, ridiculous

4628 豪华 /háohuá/ luxurious

4629 单一 /dānyī/ single

4630 俗 /sú/ vulgar

4690 痛快 /tòngkuài/ delighted, jolly; straightforward; to one's heart's content

4691 扁 /biǎn/ flat

4692 天然 /tiānrán/ natural

4693 绝望 /juéwàng/ desperate

4694 中等 /zhōngděng/ medium, medium-sized

4731 活跃 /huóyuè/ active, lively

4732 被动 /bèidòng/ passive

4733 安定 /āndìng/ stable

4734 野 /yě/ wild; rough, rude; unruly

4735 主导 /zhǔdǎo/ leading, predominant

4736 困惑 /kùnhuò/ perplexed, puzzled

4737 满足 /mǎnzú/ satisfied

4787 窄 /zhǎi/ narrow

4788 寒冷 /hánlěng/ cold

4790 透明 /tòumíng/ transparent

4791 巨 /jù/ huge, enormous

4792 孤 /gū/ lonely, solitary

4793 孝 /xiào/ filial

4838 整齐 /zhěngqí/ neat, tidy

4839 初步 /chūbù/ preliminary, initial, tentative

4840 清洁 /qīngjié/ clean

4841 缓慢 /huǎnmàn/ slow

4842 有钱 /yǒuqián/ rich, wealthy

4843 形象 /xíngxiàng/ vivid

4903 淡 /dàn/ bland, tasteless, mild; (of colour) pale; (of business) slack; indifferent

4904 舒适 /shūshì/ comfortable, cosy

4905 反 /fǎn/ reverse, wrong in direction; [used as a prefix] anti-, counter-

4906 **圆满** /yuánmǎn/ satisfactory, successful, happy

4907 **严峻** /yánjùn/ severe, serious, stern, grim

4908 **烦恼** /fánnǎo/ vexed, worried, upset

4909 **现行** /xiànxíng/ current, in effect, in operation

4962 **崇高** /chónggāo/ lofty, high

4968 **平安** /píng'ān/ safe and sound

4969 **反动** /fǎndòng/ reactionary

4979 **杂** /zá/ mixed, varied, miscellaneous

4980 **主观** /zhǔguān/ subjective

4991 **尖** /jiān/ pointed; shrill; sharp, acute

4992 **懒** /lǎn/ lazy

Adverbs

0006 **不** /bù/ no, not

0013 **就** /jiù/ [used for emphasis] just; then; at once

0017 **也** /yě/ also

0023 **还** /hái/ still, yet

0024 **都** /dōu/ all

0038 **很** /hěn/ very

0046 **又** /yòu/ again, once again

0058 **最** /zuì/ [superlative degree] most

0071 **只** /zhǐ/ only

0083 **更** /gèng/ [comparative degree] more

0087 **再** /zài/ again

0093 **才** /cái/ just

0101 **已经** /yǐjīng/ already

0107 **没有** /méiyǒu/ not

0118 **没** /méi/ not

0123 **已** /yǐ/ already

0131 **将** /jiāng/ [indicating a future happening] will, be going to

0150 **却** /què/ but

0151 **太** /tài/ too, excessively; very

0174 **正** /zhèng/ just, precisely; just (in progress)

0217 **非常** /fēicháng/ very, unusually

0221 **真** /zhēn/ really

0240 **一直** /yìzhí/ straight (in a straight line); always, all along

0243 **特别** /tèbié/ especially, particularly

0251 **先** /xiān/ first, earlier

0252 **一起** /yìqǐ/ together

0254 **一定** /yídìng/ certainly

0263 **然后** /ránhòu/ afterwards, then

0276 **当然** /dāngrán/ of course, naturally, only natural

0285 **便** /biàn/ [similar to 就] soon afterwards, just

0321 **比较** /bǐjiào/ comparatively, relatively

0328 **别** /bié/ [negative imperative] don't, had better not

0339 **其实** /qíshí/ actually

0347 **越** /yuè/ [as in 越 . . . 越] (the more . . .) the more

0357 **曾** /céng/ [referring to something that happened previously] once

0392 **一般** /yìbān/ generally, as a rule

0417 **相** /xiāng/ each other

0430 **甚至** /shènzhì/ even

0448 **不要** /búyào/ [negative imperative] don't

0449 **十分** /shífēn/ very, fully

0455 **不断** /búduàn/ unceasingly, always

0476 **仍** /réng/ still

0482 **刚** /gāng/ just, barely; just now

0512 **主要** /zhǔyào/ mainly, primarily, principally

0524 **总** /zǒng/ always; anyway, certainly; sooner or later

0533 **未** /wèi/ [archaic] not (yet)

0539 **较** /jiào/ [preceding an adjective or adverb to form a comparison] relatively

0552 **全** /quán/ all, fully

0557 **首先** /shǒuxiān/ first, first of all

0562 **几乎** /jīhū/ almost, nearly

0604 **越来越** /yuèláiyuè/ more and more

0610 **极** /jí/ extremely

0615 **并** /bìng/ [typically occurring in negation] actually, definitely

0639 **尤其** /yóuqí/ especially

0645 **也许** /yěxǔ/ perhaps

0670 **约** /yuē/ approximately, about

0678 **终于** /zhōngyú/ finally, at last

0688 **大** /dà/ greatly, a lot

0693 **常** /cháng/ often, usually

0720 **挺** /tǐng/ very, rather

0721 **共** /gòng/ all together

0722 **曾经** /céngjīng/ [referring to something that happened previously]

0737 **倒** /dào/ [indicating unexpectedness, contrast or concession] but

0761 **经常** /jīngcháng/ often, frequently

0773 **过** /guò/ excessively, unduly, too

0784 **似乎** /sìhū/ apparently

0794 **更加** /gèngjiā/ more, further

0824 **仍然** /réngrán/ still

0840 **真正** /zhēnzhèng/ really, truly, genuinely

0842 **直** /zhí/ straight, directly; keep (doing something), continuously

0848 **重新** /chóngxīn/ again; anew, afresh

0904 **仅** /jǐn/ just, only

0910 **永远** /yǒngyuǎn/ forever

0911 **原来** /yuánlái/ [meaning often implied in the past tense] originally, formerly; so, as a matter of fact

0916 **立即** /lìjí/ immediately

0919 **总是** /zǒngshì/ always

0927 **至少** /zhìshǎo/ at least

0928 **实际上** /shíjìshàng/ actually, in fact, as a matter of fact

0955 **刚刚** /gānggāng/ just now, a short while ago; barely, just

0959 **相当** /xiāngdāng/ very, quite, considerably

0967 **根本** /gēnběn/ [usually in negative sentences] at all; radically, thoroughly

0969 **确实** /quèshí/ truly, really

1004 **刚才** /gāngcái/ just now, a moment ago

1028 **迅速** /xùnsù/ rapidly

1039 **实在** /shízài/ indeed, really

1041 **快** /kuài/ fast, quickly; soon

1044 **本来** /běnlái/ originally

1055 **进一步** /jínyībù/ further

1084 **反正** /fǎnzhèng/ anyway

1110 **往往** /wǎngwǎng/ often, frequently

1121 **大概** /dàgài/ roughly

1124 **一边** /yìbiān/ at the same time, simultaneously

1135 **不再** /búzài/ no longer

1146 **分别** /fēnbié/ respectively, separately

1151 **始终** /shǐzhōng/ from beginning to end, all along, always

1161 **很快** /hěnkuài/ quickly, soon

1180 **常常** /chángcháng/ often, frequently

1188 **自然** /zìrán/ naturally

1213 **到底** /dàodǐ/ to the end; at last, finally; after all; [used for emphasis]

1228 **还是** /háishì/ still, yet; [indicating a preferred alternative]

1232 **乱** /luàn/ at random, arbitrarily, disorderly

1241 **肯定** /kěndìng/ certainly, for sure

1269 **有点** /yǒudiǎn/ somewhat, a bit

1277 **慢慢** /mànman/ slowly

1281 **正在** /zhèngzài/ be under way, be in progress

1282 **互相** /hùxiāng/ each other

1288 **有时** /yǒushí/ sometimes

1292 **只好** /zhǐhǎo/ have to, have no alternative but to

1304 **竟** /jìng/ [expressing unexpectedness] actually

1305 **难以** /nányǐ/ hard to, difficult to; hardly

1326 **从来** /cónglái/ always, all along

1349 **边** /biān/ [as in 边 . . . 边 . . . indicating simultaneous progression of two events] while

1357 **再次** /zàicì/ once again

1381 **依然** /yīrán/ still

1388 **最终** /zuìzhōng/ finally, eventually

1413 **究竟** /jiūjìng/ [used for emphasis] actually, exactly

1458 **连** /lián/ continuously, repeatedly

1465 **专门** /zhuānmén/ specifically, for a particular purpose, occasion, etc.

1481 **相互** /xiānghù/ each other, mutually

1510 **绝对** /juéduì/ absolutely

1513 **同样** /tóngyàng/ likewise, similarly, by the same token

1514 **恐怕** /kǒngpà/ (I'm) afraid (that)

1519 **亲自** /qīnzì/ in person, personally, (do) oneself

1520 **均** /jūn/ all, with no exception

1554 **显然** /xiǎnrán/ clearly, obviously

1565 **至今** /zhìjīn/ until now, so far

1571 **毕竟** /bìjìng/ after all

1578 **非** /fēi/ not; simply (must)

1595 **好好** /hǎohǎo/ all out, good

1604 **纷纷** /fēnfēn/ one after another

1605 **难道** /nándào/ [used to reinforce a rhetorical question]

1606 **反而** /fǎn'ér/ instead, on the contrary

1607 **必** /bì/ must, certainly

1613 **颇** /pō/ quite, rather

1632 **有所** /yǒusuǒ/ somewhat, slightly

1654 **简直** /jiǎnzhí/ simply

1666 **逐渐** /zhújiàn/ gradually

1667 **原** /yuán/ [short form of 原来, meaning often implied in the past tense] originally, formerly

1692 **到处** /dàochù/ everywhere, in all places

1708 **重** /chóng/ again, once more

1709 **天天** /tiāntiān/ every day; day by day

1721 **大约** /dàyuē/ approximately, about

1722 **仅仅** /jǐnjǐn/ only, merely

1734 **正好** /zhènghǎo/ just (in time); as it happens, exactly

1735 **早已** /zǎoyǐ/ for a long time, long ago; already

1755 **早就** /zǎojiù/ for a long time, long ago, early

1774 **多么** /duōme/ [used in exclamations] how; [occurring in a clause of concession to indicate an unspecified high degree] however, (no matter) how

1780 **马上** /mǎshàng/ at once, immediately

1785 **居然** /jūrán/ [expressing surprise] unexpectedly, actually

1800 **忽然** /hūrán/ suddenly

1835 **本** /běn/ originally, formerly

1867 **基本上** /jīběnshàng/ basically, in the main

1881 **尚** /shàng/ still, yet

1896 **只是** /zhǐshì/ merely, only

1897 **千万** /qiānwàn/ [usually occurring in negative imperatives] be sure to, must

1922 **从此** /cóngcǐ/ since then, after that

1923 **连续** /liánxù/ continuously, in succession

1934 **一面** /yímiàn/ [as in 一面 . . . 一面 . . . , equivalent of 一边 . . . 一边 . . .] simultaneously, at the same time

1945 先后 /xiānhòu/ one after another, successively

1955 接着 /jiēzhe/ follow, carry on

1970 亦 /yì/ also

1977 一时 /yìshí/ for the moment, temporarily, for a short while

1978 就要 /jiùyào/ (be) about to

2032 绝 /jué/ [usually occurring in negative sentences] definitely, absolutely; extremely; by (no) means

2059 赶紧 /gǎnjǐn/ hurriedly

2082 光 /guāng/ only, alone

2083 凡 /fán/ [equivalent of 凡是] all (that meets the specified requirements); altogether

2095 不用 /búyòng/ need not

2096 随时 /suíshí/ at any time

2102 竟然 /jìngrán/ unexpectedly, actually

2127 不必 /búbì/ need not, no need

2128 确 /què/ indeed, really

2145 立刻 /lìkè/ at once, immediately

2146 不得不 /bùdébù/ have to

2147 真的 /zhēnde/ really

2153 尽量 /jìnliàng/ as far as possible, to the greatest extent

2154 远远 /yuǎnyuǎn/ by far; far away

2193 的确 /díquè/ indeed, really

2257 逐步 /zhúbù/ step by step, gradually

2269 单 /dān/ only, alone

2297 随后 /suíhòu/ soon afterwards

2307 渐渐 /jiànjiàn/ gradually

2340 快速 /kuàisù/ fast, at high speed, rapidly

2350 深 /shēn/ deeply, profoundly

2363 极大 /jídà/ enormously; greatly

2378 必然 /bìrán/ necessarily, inevitably

2421 偏 /piān/ simply, wilfully, deliberately

2422 即将 /jíjiāng/ (be) about to, soon

2432 大大 /dàdà/ greatly

2433 相对 /xiāngduì/ relatively

2467 尽快 /jìnkuài/ as soon as possible

2468 微 /wēi/ slightly

2483 有时候 /yǒushíhou/ sometimes

2484 稍 /shāo/ slightly, a little

2502 只不过 /zhǐbúguò/ merely

2503 无疑 /wúyí/ undoubtedly

2504 专 /zhuān/ specially, specifically

2505 皆 /jiē/ all

2548 高度 /gāodù/ highly

2549 无 /wú/ not

2577 向前 /xiàngqián/ forward

2594 从小 /cóngxiǎo/ since childhood, from an early age

2595 极为 /jíwéi/ extremely

2614 果然 /guǒrán/ sure enough, as expected

2615 仿佛 /fǎngfó/ as though, apparently

2674 全都 /quándōu/ all, with no exception

2712 反复 /fǎnfù/ repeatedly, again and again

2726 一块 /yíkuài/ together

2752 同时 /tóngshí/ at the same time, at once

2769 莫 /mò/ not, do not

2789 紧 /jǐn/ tightly, closely; (rain, firing, etc.) heavily

2811 甚 /shèn/ very, quite

2829 大力 /dàlì/ vigorously, greatly

2830 略 /lüè/ slightly; briefly

2851 其次 /qícì/ next, secondly

2852 日益 /rìyì/ day by day

2853 更为 /gèngwéi/ even more, all the more

2854 尚未 /shàngwèi/ not yet

2882 极其 /jíqí/ extremely

2883 特 /tè/ specially, especially

2884 绝不 /juébù/ never

2900 或许 /huòxǔ/ perhaps

2901 大多 /dàduō/ mostly

2917 一再 /yízài/ repeatedly

2944 真是 /zhēnshì/ really, actually; [equivalent of 真是的, expressing dissatisfaction] well, really

2945 永 /yǒng/ forever

2993 赶快 /gǎnkuài/ hurriedly, quickly

2994 由此 /yóucǐ/ from this, hereby; hence

2995 并非 /bìngfēi/ actually not

3041 一路 /yílù/ all the way

3063 不仅仅 /bùjǐnjǐn/ not merely, more than

3080 紧紧 /jǐnjǐn/ tightly, closely

3123 顿 /dùn/ suddenly, immediately

3124 原本 /yuánběn/ originally, formerly

3125 不能不 /bùnéngbù/ have to, cannot but

3151 岂 /qǐ/ [used formally in rhetorical questions] how can it be possible that . . .

3170 另 /lìng/ in addition; separately

3171 愈 /yù/ [as in 愈 . . . 愈 . . .] the more (the more . . .)

3206 渐 /jiàn/ gradually

3226 一向 /yíxiàng/ all along, always

3227 最为 /zuìwéi/ most

3276 通常 /tōngcháng/ usually

3277 整天 /zhěngtiān/ all day long

3300 大声 /dàshēng/ loudly

3329 事先 /shìxiān/ beforehand, in advance

3355 偶然 /ǒurán/ incidentally, by chance; occasionally

3395 精心 /jīngxīn/ with utmost care; meticulously

3414 痛 /tòng/ bitterly; severely, thoroughly

3494 深深 /shēnshēn/ deeply, profoundly

3531 凡是 /fánshì/ [equivalent of 凡] all (that meets the specified requirements)

3532 回头 /huítóu/ [colloquial] later

3533 先是 /xiānshì/ previously, originally, first

3534 实 /shí/ really, truly

3565 格外 /géwài/ especially, exceptionally

3592 独 /dú/ alone; solely, only

3593 当场 /dāngchǎng/ on the spot

3594 轻易 /qīngyì/ easily, readily; lightly, rashly

3632 陆续 /lùxù/ in turn, successively

3661 硬 /yìng/ obstinately, stubbornly; (do something) mechanically in spite of difficulties

3662 处处 /chùchù/ everywhere

3663 终 /zhōng/ finally

3664 从来不 /cóngláibù/ never

3697 从不 /cóngbù/ [equivalent of 从来不] never

3738 好 /hǎo/ very, rather

3739 四处 /sìchù/ everywhere, all round

3782 决 /jué/ extremely, most; [usually in negative sentences] absolutely, at all

3783 许 /xǔ/ about, approximately; perhaps

3784 恰恰 /qiàqià/ exactly, just

3785 越是 /yuèshì/ [as in 越是 . . . 越是 . . .] the more (. . . the more)

3833 一律 /yílǜ/ all, with no exception

3834 互 /hù/ mutually, each other

3867 最好 /zuìhǎo/ had better, would better

3868 不已 /bùyǐ/ endlessly, incessantly

3894 极了 /jíle/ extremely

3895 频繁 /pínfán/ frequently, often

3897 毫不 /háobù/ not at all

3898 顿时 /dùnshí/ suddenly; immediately, at once

3900 故 /gù/ on purpose, deliberately; pretentiously

3929 偷偷 /tōutōu/ stealthily, secretly

3930 大都 /dàdū/ mostly, for the most part

3931 偶尔 /ǒu'ěr/ occasionally

3932 再也 /zàiyě/ [occurring in negative sentences] ever again

3933 不时 /bùshí/ from time to time

3984 在 /zài/ [preceding a verb to indicate an event in progress]

3985 再度 /zàidù/ again, once more

3986 过于 /guòyú/ excessively, too much

4029 单独 /dāndú/ alone

4078 一手 /yìshǒu/ single-handedly, all along, all by oneself

4118 时刻 /shíkè/ at any moment, constantly

4119 明明 /míngmíng/ clearly, obviously, undoubtedly

4120 未必 /wèibì/ not necessarily

4121 尽可能 /jìnkěnéng/ as far as possible

4122 从未 /cóngwèi/ never (before)

4167 不禁 /bùjīn/ can't help (doing something)

4168 复 /fù/ again

4169 较为 /jiàowéi/ relatively, comparatively, more

4170 一度 /yídù/ once, on one occasion, for a time

4220 一道 /yīdào/ together

4221 从中 /cóngzhōng/ from it, therefrom

4280 依旧 /yījiù/ as before, still

4283 一同 /yìtóng/ together

4316 透 /tòu/ really, completely, thoroughly

4317 紧密 /jǐnmì/ closely

4320 照样 /zhàoyàng/ all the same

4321 原先 /yuánxiān/ originally, formerly

4322 特意 /tèyì/ specially

4323 俱 /jù/ all

4324 起码 /qǐmǎ/ at least

4370 临时 /línshí/ temporarily, for the time being

4371 匆匆 /cōngcōng/ hastily, hurriedly, in a hurry

4420 独自 /dúzì/ alone

4421 相继 /xiāngjì/ in succession; one after another

4446 自愿 /zìyuàn/ voluntarily

4520 必定 /bìdìng/ surely

4521 无非 /wúfēi/ only, nothing but, no more than

4574 以此 /yǐcǐ/ hereby, by this, with this

4575 似 /sì/ apparently, as if

4606 拼命 /pīnmìng/ desperately

4632 白 /bái/ in vain, for nothing; free of charge

4633 净 /jìng/ all, all the time; only, merely

4634 无意 /wúyì/ inadvertently, accidentally

4635 猛 /měng/ suddenly, abruptly; vigorously, fiercely

4695 有意 /yǒuyì/ intentionally, deliberately

4696 偏偏 /piānpiān/ wilfully, just, unluckily; contrary to what is expected

4697 宁 /nìng/ (would) rather

4738 稍微 /shāowēi/ slightly, a little

4739 难怪 /nán'guài/ no wonder

4740 当即 /dāngjí/ at once, immediately

4741 更是 /gèngshì/ even more, especially

4794 悄悄 /qiāoqiāo/ quietly

4795 甭 /béng/ don't, needn't

4796 全力 /quánlì/ with all one's strength, all out, sparing no effort

4797 随之 /suízhī/ along with it, following it; accordingly

4845 一共 /yígòng/ altogether, in all

4846 立 /lì/ immediately, instantly

4847 早日 /zǎorì/ at an earlier date, soon

4911 每 /měi/ every time, on each occasion

4963 **不大** /búdà/ not very; not often

4981 **只有** /zhǐyǒu/ only

5004 **一块儿** /yíkuàir/ together

Idiomatic and formulaic expressions

1956 **没什么** /méishénme/ [idiomatic expression] nothing serious, it's nothing, it's all right

2155 **事实上** /shìshíshàng/ in fact

2535 **也就是说** /yějiùshìshuō/ that is to say, namely

2675 **可不** /kěbu/ [same as 可不是 or 可不是吗] sure enough, exactly

3081 **比如说** /bǐrúshuō/ for example, say

3330 **是的** /shìde/ yes

3699 **对了** /duìle/ right, correct, that's it; by the way

3740 **各种各样** /gèzhǒnggèyàng/ various, of all kinds

3741 **你好** /nǐhǎo/ hello

3787 **有意思** /yǒuyìsi/ interesting

4123 **没关系** /méiguānxi/ it doesn't matter, it's all right, never mind

4124 **有的是** /yǒudeshì/ have plenty of, there's no lack of

4172 **无所谓** /wúsuǒwèi/ be indifferent; make no difference

4173 **受不了** /shòubuliǎo/ (somebody) cannot endure, (something) be intolerable

4222 **无论如何** /wúlùnrúhé/ anyhow, at any rate, by all means, whatever happens

4373 **用不着** /yòngbuzháo/ no need; have no use for

4569 **不好意思** /bùhǎoyìsi/ feel embarrassed, find it embarrassing

4636 **实事求是** /shíshìqiúshì/ seek truth from facts, be practical and realistic

4637 **说不定** /shuōbudìng/ maybe, perhaps

Nouns

0014 **人** /rén/ person, human, man

0048 **年** /nián/ year

0072 **问题** /wèntí/ question, problem, issue

0078 **时** /shí/ time when ...

0103 **时候** /shíhou/ when, time when ...

0105 **国** /guó/ country, nation

0108 **事** /shì/ matter, thing

0114 **社会** /shèhuì/ society

0125 **话** /huà/ word, talk, utterance

0126 **世界** /shìjiè/ world

0135 **国家** /guójiā/ country

0138 **月** /yuè/ moon; month

0142 **时间** /shíjiān/ time

0149 **孩子** /háizi/ child, children

0153 **地方** /dìfang, dìfāng/ place, space, room; locality (in relation to central administration)

0158 **钱** /qián/ money

0161 **经济** /jīngjì/ economy

0162 **公司** /gōngsī/ (business) company

0163 **文化** /wénhuà/ culture

0165 **关系** /guānxì/ relation, relationship; connections, ties

0176 **情况** /qíngkuàng/ situation, condition, circumstance

0187 **点** /diǎn/ dot, point

0189 **企业** /qǐyè/ business establishment, enterprise

0193 **方面** /fāngmiàn/ aspect, respect, side

0206 **水** /shuǐ/ water

0208 **东西** /dōngxi/ stuff, thing

0210 **地** /dì/ earth, ground, field

0214 **历史** /lìshǐ/ history

0215 **家** /jiā/ home; family, household

0228 **人民** /rénmín/ (the) people

0229 **手** /shǒu/ hand

0233 **政府** /zhèngfǔ/ government

0234 **先生** /xiānsheng/ Mr; mister, sir

0237 **人们** /rénmen/ people

0241 **书** /shū/ book

0244 **记者** /jìzhě/ reporter, journalist

0246 **头** /tóu/ head; end

0253 **国际** /guójì/ international

0260 **大学** /dàxué/ university

0261 **心** /xīn/ heart; mind; core, centre

0265 **事情** /shìqíng/ matter, thing

0278 **学校** /xuéxiào/ school

0294 **学生** /xuésheng/ student

0297 **路** /lù/ road; distance

0303 **朋友** /péngyou/ friend

0304 **市场** /shìchǎng/ market

0308 **政治** /zhèngzhì/ politics

0312 **地区** /dìqū/ area, region, district

0313 **思想** /sīxiǎng/ thought, idea

0316 **精神** /jīngshén/ spirit, mind, mental state; essence; vigour, vitality

0329 **字** /zì/ (Chinese) character

0334 **领导** /lǐngdǎo/ leader, leadship

0338 **电话** /diànhuà/ telephone, telephone call

0340 **车** /chē/ car, vehicle; cart

0344 **城市** /chéngshì/ city

0345 **办法** /bànfǎ/ method, means

0350 **技术** /jìshù/ technology

0354 **身** /shēn/ body

0355 **着** /zhāo/ move (in chess), step, trick

0374 **个人** /gèrén/ individual

0380 **方式** /fāngshì/ way, pattern or style of doing things

0385 **环境** /huánjìng/ environment

0386 **老师** /lǎoshī/ teacher

0390 **结果** /jiéguǒ/ result, outcome

0393 **方** /fāng/ side, party; square; direction

0400 **会议** /huìyì/ meeting

0403 **能力** /nénglì/ ability, capability

0405 **机会** /jīhuì/ opportunity

0406 同志 /tóngzhì/ comrade; [more recent usage] someone who is homosexual

0410 民族 /mínzú/ nationality

0411 天 /tiān/ day; sky, air; heaven; time of day; weather

0415 过程 /guòchéng/ process, course of actions

0418 家庭 /jiātíng/ family

0420 条件 /tiáojiàn/ condition

0423 人员 /rényuán/ staff, personnel

0427 作用 /zuòyòng/ action, effect; role, function

0429 金 /jīn/ gold, golden; metal; money

0435 人类 /rénlèi/ human being, mankind, man

0441 原因 /yuányīn/ cause, reason

0443 边 /biān/ side; edge

0446 感觉 /gǎnjué/ feeling

0450 部队 /bùduì/ army, troops

0452 父亲 /fùqīn/ father

0456 儿子 /érzi/ son

0459 面 /miàn/ face, surface; side; (wheat) flour

0462 年代 /niándài/ a decade of a century; years, time

0463 世纪 /shìjì/ century

0473 门 /mén/ door, gate

0475 组织 /zǔzhī/ organisation

0477 处 /chù/ place; department

0483 母亲 /mǔqīn/ mother

0484 代表 /dàibiǎo/ representative, delegate

0488 内容 /nèiróng/ content

0489 山 /shān/ mountain, hill

0492 艺术 /yìshù/ art

0496 女人 /nǚrén/ woman

0498 干部 /gànbù/ cadre

0499 主席 /zhǔxí/ chairman, chairperson

0501 对方 /duìfāng/ the opposite side or party, counterpart

0502 生命 /shēngmìng/ life

0507 传统 /chuántǒng/ tradition

0509 农民 /nóngmín/ peasant, farmer

0510 时代 /shídài/ age, times; a period in one's life

0511 子 /zǐ/ son, child

0513 男人 /nánrén/ man

0514 意义 /yìyì/ meaning, significance

0515 队 /duì/ team; queue

0516 单位 /dānwèi/ (working or administrative) unit, institution; unit (of measurement)

0517 军 /jūn/ army

0521 党 /dǎng/ (political) party

0525 水平 /shuǐpíng/ level (of achievement, etc.)

0529 行为 /xíngwéi/ action, behaviour

0534 部门 /bùmén/ department

0541 中央 /zhōngyāng/ middle, centre; central authorities

0545 脸 /liǎn/ face, cheek

0553 基础 /jīchǔ/ base, basis

0555 知识 /zhīshí/ knowledge

0558 政策 /zhèngcè/ policy

0563 小时 /xiǎoshí/ hour

0566 报 /bào/ newspaper

0571 经验 /jīngyàn/ experience

0572 身体 /shēntǐ/ (human) body, health

0573 妈妈 /māma/ mama, mum

0575 计划 /jìhuá/ plan

0577 方法 /fāngfǎ/ method, way

0578 制度 /zhìdù/ (political or administrative) system, institution

0579 气 /qì/ air; breath; gas

0581 中心 /zhōngxīn/ centre

0586 信 /xìn/ letter, mail

0588 同学 /tóngxué/ (fellow) classmate, student

0589 作品 /zuòpǐn/ work (of art)

0590 时期 /shíqī/ a particular period of time (especially in history)

0594 法律 /fǎlǜ/ law

0597 战争 /zhànzhēng/ war

0599 利益 /lìyì/ benefit

0600 病 /bìng/ illness, ailment

0603 楼 /lóu/ building

0605 力量 /lìliàng/ strength, power

0611 项目 /xiàngmù/ project, item

0616 城 /chéng/ town, city; city wall

0619 目标 /mùbiāo/ target, goal

0621 意思 /yìsi/ meaning, idea, opinion; trace, hint; gift, token of gratitude, etc.

0622 群众 /qúnzhòng/ the masses

0625 故事 /gùshì/ story

0627 意见 /yìjiàn/ opinion, comment; objection, complaint

0629 区 /qū/ area, district

0630 行 /xíng/ trip; behaviour

0634 酒 /jiǔ/ wine, alcohol

0635 医院 /yīyuàn/ hospital

0636 地位 /dìwèi/ status, position

0640 电 /diàn/ electricity, power; telegram, cable

0641 省 /shěng/ province

0644 报告 /bàogào/ report

0647 产品 /chǎnpǐn/ product

0648 事业 /shìyè/ cause, career, undertaking

0650 青年 /qīngnián/ youth, young people

0655 责任 /zérèn/ responsibility

0657 态度 /tàidu/ attitude

0658 电影 /diànyǐng/ movie

0663 文学 /wénxué/ literature

0664 信息 /xìnxī/ information

0668 妇女 /fùnǚ/ woman

0674 妈 /mā/ ma, mum

0675 人物 /rénwù/ personage, distinguished individual; characters in literary works

0679 理论 /lǐlùn/ theory

0680 革命 /gémìng/ (political) revolution

0684 象 /xiàng/ elephant; image, shape

0685 父母 /fùmǔ/ father and mother, parent

0689 海 /hǎi/ sea

0690 性 /xìng/ property, disposition; sex

0696 电视 /diànshì/ television, TV

0700 市 /shì/ city, town; market

0705 风 /fēng/ wind

0707 双方 /shuāngfāng/ both parties, the two sides

0709 结构 /jiégòu/ structure

0711 教授 /jiàoshòu/ professor

0715 农村 /nóngcūn/ countryside, rural area

0718 汽车 /qìchē/ automobile, motor vehicle, car

0723 和平 /hépíng/ peace

0724 规定 /guīdìng/ regulation, stipulation, provision

0727 女儿 /nǚ'ér/ daughter

0728 目的 /mùdì/ purpose, aim, end

0729 情 /qíng/ feeling, passion, sentiment; condition, situation

0731 首 /shǒu/ head

0736 眼睛 /yǎnjīng/ eye

0738 要求 /yāoqiú/ requirement, request

0739 爸爸 /bàba/ dad, father

0740 价值 /jiàzhí/ value

0741 文 /wén/ script, language; essay, writing

0747 比赛 /bǐsài/ competition, contest, match, game

0749 部分 /bùfen/ part

0751 主任 /zhǔrèn/ director

0755 银行 /yínháng/ bank

0756 梦 /mèng/ dream

0762 系 /xì/ (academic) department; system, series

0771 底 /dǐ/ bottom, base; end (of month or year); draft copy, duplicate copy for file; background

0774 现象 /xiànxiàng/ appearance; phenomenon

0776 标准 /biāozhǔn/ standard, criterion

0778 小说 /xiǎoshuō/ novel, story

0787 心理 /xīnlǐ/ mentality, psychology

0788 林 /lín/ woods, forest

0790 脚 /jiǎo/ foot, feet; foot (of walls, mountains)

0797 文章 /wénzhāng/ article, essay

0798 新闻 /xīnwén/ news

0801 口 /kǒu/ mouth, opening, entrance; cut, hole

0802 程度 /chéngdù/ degree, level, extent

0803 专家 /zhuānjiā/ expert, specialist

0806 声 /shēng/ sound, noise; voice

0810 原则 /yuánzé/ principle

0814 声音 /shēngyīn/ sound, noise; voice

0815 菜 /cài/ food; dish, course; vegetable

0821 系统 /xìtǒng/ system

0822 感情 /gǎnqíng/ feeling

0826 土地 /tǔdì/ land

0827 任务 /rènwù/ task, mission

0828 代 /dài/ generation; historical period, dynasty

0830 样子 /yàngzi/ look, appearance, manner

0831 农业 /nóngyè/ agriculture

0832 工程 /gōngchéng/ engineering, project

0833 成绩 /chéngjī/ result, academic performance; achievement

0834 老人 /lǎorén/ the aged, old people

0839 节目 /jiémù/ programme; item of performance

0845 县 /xiàn/ county

0846 人才 /réncái/ talented person, talent, qualified personnel

0849 总统 /zǒngtǒng/ president (of a country)

0850 军队 /jūnduì/ army, troops

0852 方向 /fāngxiàng/ direction

0853 形式 /xíngshì/ form

0854 意识 /yìshí/ consciousness

0856 科技 /kējì/ science and technology

0857 社会主义 /shèhuìzhǔyì/ socialism

0858 村 /cūn/ village

0861 事实 /shìshí/ fact

0862 女性 /nǚxìng/ female, woman

0864 会 /huì/ meeting, conference; [also as 会儿] moment

0866 集团 /jítuán/ group

0877 消息 /xiāoxi/ news

0879 船 /chuán/ boat, ship

0880 机构 /jīgòu/ organisation, institution

0883 运动 /yùndòng/ motion, movement; sports, exercise; (political) campaign

0884 事件 /shìjiàn/ event, affair

0885 鱼 /yú/ fish

0888 兴趣 /xìngqù/ interest

0889 阶段 /jiēduàn/ stage

0890 厂 /chǎng/ factory

0894 人生 /rénshēng/ (human) life

0898 眼 /yǎn/ eye

0899 饭 /fàn/ food, meal

0901 商品 /shāngpǐn/ goods, commodity, article, item

0905 现实 /xiànshí/ reality

0912 总理 /zǒnglǐ/ premier

0913 作家 /zuòjiā/ writer

0917 飞机 /fēijī/ airplane

0918 龙 /lóng/ dragon

0920 医生 /yīshēng/ doctor

0921 名字 /míngzì/ name

0922 班 /bān/ class, team; shift, duty; squad

0932 街 /jiē/ street

0934 人口 /rénkǒu/ population

0937 线 /xiàn/ line; thread

0938 委员会 /wěiyuánhuì/ committee

0941 美元 /měiyuán/ US dollar

0942 观众 /guānzhòng/ spectator, audience

0943 书记 /shūjì/ (party) secretary

0947 状态 /zhuàngtài/ state of affairs, condition

0950 资源 /zīyuán/ resource

0953 专业 /zhuānyè/ speciality, specialised field of study, major

0956 工人 /gōngrén/ worker

0961 师 /shī/ teacher; person with a particular professional skill; division

0965 收入 /shōurù/ income, revenue

0966 位置 /wèizhi/ position, location

0973 工业 /gōngyè/ industry

0976 动物 /dòngwù/ animal

0981 衣服 /yīfu/ clothes, dress

0982 图 /tú/ picture, drawing, chart, diagram, graph

0986 官 /guān/ official, officer

0990 军事 /jūnshì/ military affairs

0991 团 /tuán/ something with a round shape, ball, wad; group; regiment; [short form for 共青团] the League

0994 语言 /yǔyán/ language

0995 丈夫 /zhàngfu/ husband

0998 日子 /rìzi/ date; day, time; life

1008 马 /mǎ/ horse

1015 嘴 /zuǐ/ mouth

1016 诗 /shī/ poem, poetry

1017 质量 /zhìliàng/ quality

1022 形象 /xíngxiàng/ image

1023 办公室 /bàngōngshì/ office

1027 言 /yán/ speech, word

1029 网 /wǎng/ net; web, internet

1031 房 /fáng/ room

1034 观念 /guānniàn/ idea, notion, view

1040 女子 /nǚzǐ/ woman

1042 照片 /zhàopiàn/ photo

1046 姑娘 /gūniáng/ girl

1051 音乐 /yīnyuè/ music

1059 特点 /tèdiǎn/ characteristic (feature)

1060 房子 /fángzi/ house

1062 力 /lì/ power, strength

1064 范围 /fànwéi/ range, scope

1066 儿童 /értóng/ child, children

1072 学院 /xuéyuàn/ college

1073 烟 /yān/ smoke; cigarette

1074 商业 /shāngyè/ business, commerce

1075 兵 /bīng/ soldier

1076 材料 /cáiliào/ material

1077 火 /huǒ/ fire

1078 战略 /zhànlüè/ strategy

1088 教师 /jiàoshī/ teacher

1090 道理 /dàolǐ/ reason

1091 世 /shì/ the world; lifetime; era, age

1099 因素 /yīnsù/ element, factor

1104 手段 /shǒuduàn/ means, method; measure, step; trick

1111 店 /diàn/ shop, store; inn

1112 人家 /rénjiā/ household, family

1114 光 /guāng/ light, brightness; glory, honour

1115 老板 /lǎobǎn/ boss

1116 学者 /xuézhě/ scholar

1118 电脑 /diànnǎo/ computer

1122 作者 /zuòzhě/ author

1125 合同 /hétóng/ contract

1127 药 /yào/ medicine, drug

1128 歌 /gē/ song

1136 外国 /wàiguó/ foreign country

1137 警察 /jǐngchá/ police

1138 狗 /gǒu/ dog

1139 资金 /zījīn/ fund, capital

1144 资料 /zīliào/ data, material

1147 体育 /tǐyù/ sport; physical education, PE

1148 建筑 /jiànzhù/ architecture; building

1152 权 /quán/ power, authority; right

1154 河 /hé/ river

1155 价格 /jiàgé/ price

1162 花 /huā/ flower

1163 小姐 /xiǎojie/ miss; young lady; [more recent usage] waitress; prostitute

1167 爱情 /àiqíng/ love

1168 民 /mín/ the people; civilian

1169 事儿 /shìr/ business, matter, affair

1171 队伍 /duìwǔ/ ranks, line, procession, parade; contingent

1172 神 /shén/ god

1173 领域 /lǐngyù/ domain, area, field

1177 部 /bù/ part, section; department; ministry

1185 妻子 /qīzi/ wife

1187 肉 /ròu/ meat

1189 墙 /qiáng/ wall

1190 压力 /yālì/ pressure

1191 网络 /wǎngluò/ network

1197 词 /cí/ word, term; speech, statement; [a kind of Chinese poetry]

1198 速度 /sùdù/ speed

1201 报纸 /bàozhǐ/ newspaper

1205 夫人 /fūrén/ lady; Mrs; wife

1209 钟 /zhōng/ clock, bell

1212 语 /yǔ/ language, word

1214 措施 /cuòshī/ measure

1215 建议 /jiànyì/ suggestion, proposal

1216 局 /jú/ bureau, office; state of affairs

1217 工 /gōng/ work, labour; industry; project

1221 同时 /tóngshí/ meanwhile, the moment

1225 贡献 /gòngxiàn/ contribution

1229 情绪 /qíngxù/ feeling, emotion; mood, sentiment, morale; moodiness

1230 意 /yì/ meaning, idea; intention, desire

1233 贸易 /màoyì/ trade

1237 腿 /tuǐ/ leg

1242 女孩 /nǚhái/ girl

1245 反应 /fǎnyìng/ reaction; response

1247 习惯 /xíguàn/ habit

1248 戏 /xì/ drama, play, show

1256 业务 /yèwù/ business; professional work

1264 兄弟 /xiōngdì/ brother

1265 院 /yuàn/ courtyard; academy, institute, hospital

1270 机关 /jīguān/ organ, office

1271 对象 /duìxiàng/ target, object; boy or girl friend

1272 道路 /dàolù/ road

1273 共产党 /gòngchǎndǎng/ Communist Party

1278 关键 /guānjiàn/ key, crux

1279 血 /xuè/ blood

1280 体制 /tǐzhì/ institutional system, structure

1289 空间 /kōngjiān/ space, room

1290 状况 /zhuàngkuàng/ condition, state of affairs

1293 形势 /xíngshì/ situation

1294 利 /lì/ advantage; benefit, profit, gain

1295 法 /fǎ/ law; method, way, how-to

1298 床 /chuáng/ bed

1299 草 /cǎo/ grass; straw

1300 效果 /xiàoguǒ/ effect, (positive) result

1301 印象 /yìnxiàng/ impression

1306 讲话 /jiǎnghuà/ speech, talk

1307 量 /liàng/ quantity, amount, capacity

1311 粮食 /liángshí/ foodstuff, grain, cereals

1312 工资 /gōngzī/ salary, wage, pay

1313 读者 /dúzhě/ reader

1314 史 /shǐ/ history

1320 交通 /jiāotōng/ traffic

1321 权力 /quánlì/ power, authority

1322 权利 /quánlì/ right

1327 观点 /guāndiǎn/ point of view, viewpoint, opinion

1328 前面 /qiánmian/ front; ahead

1330 大会 /dàhuì/ congress, assembly, meeting

1338 看法 /kànfǎ/ opinion, view; unfavourable view

1339 文字 /wénzì/ character, script, writing; style of writing; word

1340 下面 /xiàmian/ the following, below; next; lower level

1341 职工 /zhígōng/ staff, staff member, worker

1342 心情 /xīnqíng/ feeling, state of mind, mood

1343 道德 /dàodé/ morals, morality, ethics

1344 男子 /nánzǐ/ man, male

1350 雪 /xuě/ snow

1353 鸡 /jī/ chicken

1354 优势 /yōushì/ advantage, strength

1358 物质 /wùzhì/ substance, matter; material

1359 重点 /zhòngdiǎn/ emphasis, focus point

1360 命运 /mìngyùn/ fate

1362 铁路 /tiělù/ railway

1368 设备 /shèbèi/ equipment

1375 票 /piào/ ticket

1376 球 /qiú/ ball

1377 职业 /zhíyè/ occupation, profession

1382 日 /rì/ day; the sun

1383 年龄 /niánlíng/ age

1384 动作 /dòngzuò/ movement, motion, action

1385 物 /wù/ thing

1389 太阳 /tàiyáng/ the sun

1390 客人 /kèren/ guest

1391 家长 /jiāzhǎng/ parent; head of a family

1398 中学 /zhōngxué/ middle school, secondary school, high school

1399 田 /tián/ field, farmland

1400 牌 /pái/ cards; brand; (number) plate

1406 雨 /yǔ/ rain

1407 规模 /guīmó/ scale, size

1408 官员 /guānyuán/ official

1414 行业 /hángyè/ trade, industry, profession

1415 爸 /bà/ dad, father

1418 后面 /hòumian/ rear, back

1419 地球 /dìqiú/ the earth, the globe

1425 学术 /xuéshù/ scholarly learning

1429 生意 /shēngyì/ business, trade

1433 部长 /bùzhǎng/ minister; head of department

1434 想法 /xiǎngfǎ/ idea, opinion

1446 需要 /xūyào/ need

1447 距离 /jùlí/ distance

1450 理由 /lǐyóu/ reason

1453 功能 /gōngnéng/ function

1454 成员 /chéngyuán/ member

1459 英雄 /yīngxióng/ hero

1460 一生 /yìshēng/ all one's life

1462 身份 /shēnfèn/ identity

1466 机 /jī/ machine

1469 全球 /quánqiú/ the whole world

1470 星 /xīng/ star

1471 产业 /chǎnyè/ industry

1477 小学 /xiǎoxué/ primary school

1482 纸 /zhǐ/ paper

1483 校长 /xiàozhǎng/ headmaster; president, chancellor

1484 集体 /jítǐ/ collective

1496 文件 /wénjiàn/ document

1497 经历 /jīnglì/ experiences

1498 素质 /sùzhì/ inner quality, making

1503 刀 /dāo/ knife

1504 科学 /kēxué/ science

1505 出口 /chūkǒu/ exit; export

1506 土 /tǔ/ earth, soil

1507 经理 /jīnglǐ/ manager

1508 末 /mò/ end, tip; minor details; powder

1511 性格 /xìnggé/ disposition, nature, personality

1515 敌人 /dírén/ enemy

1522 号 /hào/ date; number; size

1523 枪 /qiāng/ gun, rifle

1531 油 /yóu/ oil, petrol, gas

1532 角度 /jiǎodù/ angle, viewpoint

1537 色 /sè/ colour; countenance, look; type; female charm

1538 文明 /wénmíng/ civilisation; manners

1539 大陆 /dàlù/ mainland, continent

1540 功 /gōng/ merit, achievement; skill

1546 皇帝 /huángdì/ emperor

1555 桥 /qiáo/ bridge

1556 题 /tí/ title; topic, subject; problem (in exam)

1557 体系 /tǐxì/ system

1560 病人 /bìngrén/ sick person, patient

1561 案 /àn/ (legal or criminal) case; proposal; long narrow table

1566 云 /yún/ cloud

1567 演员 /yǎnyuán/ actor or actress

1568 奖 /jiǎng/ prize, award

1573 室 /shì/ room

1574 话题 /huàtí/ topic, subject

1579 树 /shù/ tree

1584 广告 /guǎnggào/ advertisement, advert

1585 婚姻 /hūnyīn/ marriage, matrimony

1586 说法 /shuōfa/ statement, argument; wording, version

1590 卫生 /wèishēng/ hygiene, sanitation, public health

1594 模式 /móshì/ mode, pattern; way

1596 损失 /sǔnshī/ loss

1597 外面 /wàimian/ outside

1598 皮 /pí/ skin; leather; peel (of fruit)

1599 人士 /rénshì/ person, personage, public figure

1608 课 /kè/ class; subject, course; lesson

1609 成果 /chéngguǒ/ result, outcome, achievement

1612 现代化 /xiàndàihuà/ modernisation

1614 成就 /chéngjiù/ accomplishment, achievement

1615 协议 /xiéyì/ agreement

1624 方案 /fāng'àn/ scheme, plan

1625 气氛 /qìfēn/ atmosphere

1626 年轻人 /niánqīngrén/ young people

1637 祖国 /zǔguó/ motherland

1638 工厂 /gōngchǎng/ factory

1642 统计 /tǒngjì/ statistics

1644 站 /zhàn/ station, (bus) stop

1645 博士 /bóshì/ doctor, PhD

1651 数字 /shùzì/ number, figure

1655 战士 /zhànshì/ soldier, fighter

1656 保险 /bǎoxiǎn/ insurance

1657 特色 /tèsè/ characteristic, unique feature

1668 领导人 /lǐngdǎorén/ leader

1676 宗教 /zōngjiào/ religion

1677 样 /yàng/ appearance; sample

1678 玉 /yù/ jade

1683 规律 /guīlǜ/ law, rule; regularity

1684 分子 /fènzi, fēnzǐ/ member of a class or group; numerator (in a fractional number); molecule

1694 岸 /àn/ bank

1700 猪 /zhū/ pig, hog

1701 命令 /mìnglìng/ order, command

1702 面积 /miànjī/ (surface) area

1703 危机 /wēijī/ crisis

1704 市长 /shìzhǎng/ mayor

1705 手机 /shǒujī/ mobile phone, cell phone

1710 老百姓 /lǎobǎixìng/ ordinary people; civilians

1711 实际 /shíjì/ reality

1714 队员 /duìyuán/ team member

1715 宫 /gōng/ palace

1716 民间 /mínjiān/ among the people, folk

1717 需求 /xūqiú/ demand

1730 立场 /lìchǎng/ stand, position

1733 考试 /kǎoshì/ examination, test, quiz

1737 足球 /zúqiú/ football

1738 文艺 /wényì/ literature and art

1739 基地 /jīdì/ base

1740 实力 /shílì/ strength

1744 房间 /fángjiān/ room

1745 小孩 /xiǎohái/ child

1750 将军 /jiāngjūn/ (army) general

1757 大事 /dàshì/ a major event; the overall situation

1764 概念 /gàiniàn/ concept

1765 计算机 /jìsuànjī/ computer

1766 背景 /bèijǐng/ background

1775 武器 /wǔqì/ weapon

1776 做法 /zuòfǎ/ practice, measure

1777 阳光 /yángguāng/ sunshine

1781 灯 /dēng/ lamp, light

1782 信心 /xìnxīn/ confidence

1786 工作 /gōngzuò/ job, work

1787 货 /huò/ goods

1788 罪 /zuì/ crime, offence; guilt; suffering

1795 自然 /zìrán/ nature

1796 冠军 /guànjūn/ champion

1797 把握 /bǎwò/ grasp, confidence, certainty, probability

1801 机场 /jīchǎng/ airport

1802 乡 /xiāng/ township; country, countryside

1803 院长 /yuànzhǎng/ [head of a hospital, school, faculty, college or university, etc.] director, dean, president

1804 行政 /xíngzhèng/ administration

1805 甲 /jiǎ/ [used for the first of enumerated items] first; shell

1812 茶 /chá/ tea

1813 鸟 /niǎo/ bird

1814 命 /mìng/ life; fate, destiny; order

1815 内心 /nèixīn/ heart

1824 饭店 /fàndiàn/ hotel, restaurant

1825 电视台 /diànshìtái/ television station

1827 科 /kē/ branch of study; division, section

1828 米 /mǐ/ rice

1836 屋 /wū/ house, room

1837 体 /tǐ/ body; style; system

1838 大学生 /dàxuéshēng/ college or university student

1843 外交 /wàijiāo/ diplomacy

1844 电子 /diànzǐ/ electronics

1850 司机 /sījī/ driver, chauffeur

1851 情感 /qínggǎn/ feeling, emotion

1862 哥哥 /gēge/ elder brother

1863 医学 /yīxué/ medicine, medical science

1864 协会 /xiéhuì/ association, society

1865 同事 /tóngshì/ colleague

1868 羊 /yáng/ sheep

1869 空气 /kōngqì/ air

1870 女士 /nǚshì/ lady

1871 食品 /shípǐn/ foodstuff, food

1872 海洋 /hǎiyáng/ ocean

1873 资格 /zīgé/ qualification

1874 核心 /héxīn/ core

1883 天气 /tiānqì/ weather

1884 教学 /jiàoxué/ teaching

1885 少年 /shàonián/ teenager, early youth

1886 天下 /tiānxià/ land under heaven, the world; the country

1898 居民 /jūmín/ resident, inhabitant; citizen

1899 关 /guān/ customs; barrier, obstacle; pass

1903 势力 /shìlì/ power, force

1904 对手 /duìshǒu/ opponent; competitor

1905 石 /shí/ rock, stone

1906 金融 /jīnróng/ finance

1925 科学家 /kēxuéjiā/ scientist

1936 好处 /hǎochù/ benefit, good

1937 不久 /bùjiǔ/ soon, before long, soon after

1938 智慧 /zhìhuì/ wisdom

1946 活 /huó/ work; job

1947 头发 /tóufā/ hair

1957 运动员 /yùndòngyuán/ athlete, sportsman

1958 国民党 /guómíndǎng/ Kuomintang, nationalist party

1959 组 /zǔ/ group

1960 进程 /jìnchéng/ process

1961 哥 /gē/ elder brother

1962 设施 /shèshī/ facility

1971 方针 /fāngzhēn/ policy, directive

1972 记忆 /jìyì/ memory

1973 理 /lǐ/ reason; natural science (in relation to humanities)

1974 士兵 /shìbīng/ soldier

1975 媒体 /méitǐ/ media

1985 通知 /tōngzhī/ note, notice, announcement

1986 数量 /shùliàng/ quantity, amount

1987 风格 /fēnggé/ style

1988 武 /wǔ/ martial arts

1992 哲学 /zhéxué/ philosophy

1993 形 /xíng/ shape, form

1994 风险 /fēngxiǎn/ risk

1998 公园 /gōngyuán/ park

1999 台 /tái/ platform, stage; desk, table; (TV or radio) station

2000 猫 /māo/ cat

2001 价 /jià/ price

2002 目光 /mùguāng/ sight, vision; gaze

2007 资本 /zīběn/ capital; advantage

2008 地震 /dìzhèn/ earthquake

2009 交 /jiāo/ an act of falling over; friendship, acquaintance

2017 客 /kè/ guest; customer

2018 局面 /júmiàn/ situation, aspect

2019 舞台 /wǔtái/ stage; arena

2020 堂 /táng/ hall, room

2023 脑 /nǎo/ brain, head

2033 笔 /bǐ/ pen

2034 整体 /zhěngtǐ/ while, entirety, overall

2035 杂志 /zázhì/ magazine

2036 帐 /zhàng/ account, account book; bill; (mosquito) net

2037 礼 /lǐ/ gift; courtesy; ceremony

2042 石头 /shítou/ rock, stone

2043 镇 /zhèn/ town, township

2044 成本 /chéngběn/ cost

2045 主义 /zhǔyì/ doctrine, -ism

2053 姐姐 /jiějie/ older sister

2060 道 /dào/ road, path; method, way; line

2061 比例 /bǐlì/ proportion, ratio

2062 资产 /zīchǎn/ asset

2063 开始 /kāishǐ/ beginning, start

2064 心灵 /xīnlíng/ internal spirit, heart, soul, mind

2065 爷 /yé/ [usually taking the suffix 儿] father, grandfather; [used as a polite term of address for an old man] uncle

2072 场 /chǎng/ field, court; ground

2073 板 /bǎn/ board, plank

2074 局长 /júzhǎng/ chief of a bureau

2075 鬼 /guǐ/ ghost, spook

2076 虎 /hǔ/ tiger

2077 主题 /zhǔtí/ theme, keynote

2084 全体 /quántǐ/ all, whole

2085 腰 /yāo/ waist

2086 路线 /lùxiàn/ route, line; itinerary

2087 味 /wèi/ taste, smell

2088 财产 /cáichǎn/ wealth, property

2089 思维 /sīwéi/ (way of) thinking, (line of) thought, mind

2090 市民 /shìmín/ city resident; citizen

2091 客户 /kèhù/ client, customer

2097 金牌 /jīnpái/ gold medal

2098 角色 /juésè/ role, part

2103 鞋 /xié/ shoe

2104 人民币 /rénmínbì/ Chinese currency, RMB

2105 奶奶 /nǎinai/ (paternal) grandmother

2106 夫妻 /fūqī/ man and wife, couple

2107 小组 /xiǎozǔ/ group

2108 仪式 /yíshì/ ceremony

2115 错 /cuò/ fault, mistake

2116 错误 /cuòwù/ mistake, error

2117 工具 /gōngjù/ tool

2118 锅 /guō/ pot, pan, wok

2119 岛 /dǎo/ island

2120 机制 /jīzhì/ mechanism

2129 火车 /huǒchē/ train

2130 费用 /fèiyòng/ expense, charge

2131 教训 /jiàoxùn/ lesson

2132 源 /yuán/ source

2133 员工 /yuángōng/ staff, personnel, employee

2134 层次 /céngcì/ level, layer, hierarchy

2135 选手 /xuǎnshǒu/ (selected) contestant, player

2148 画 /huà/ drawing, painting

2149 老婆 /lǎopo/ [informal] wife

2150 案件 /ànjiàn/ case

2156 图书馆 /túshūguǎn/ library

2157 导演 /dǎoyǎn/ (film) director

2166 妹妹 /mèimei/ younger sister

2167 结论 /jiélùn/ conclusion

2168 校 /xiào/ school

2176 秩序 /zhìxù/ order

2177 市场经济 /shìchǎngjīngjì/ market economy

2178 带 /dài/ ribbon, belt; zone, area

2182 湖 /hú/ lake

2183 大人 /dàrén/ adult, grown-up

2184 游戏 /yóuxì/ game

2185 福 /fú/ good fortune, happiness, blessing

2186 子女 /zǐnǚ/ child, children

2194 希望 /xīwàng/ hope

2195 主人 /zhǔrén/ master; host; owner

2196 婚 /hūn/ marriage

2205 认识 /rènshí/ understanding, knowledge, awareness

2206 井 /jǐng/ well

2207 法院 /fǎyuàn/ court of law

2208 桌 /zhuō/ table, desk

2214 写作 /xiězuò/ writing

2217 牛 /niú/ ox, cow, cattle; beef

2218 委员 /wěiyuán/ committee member

2219 人数 /rénshù/ number of people

2225 程序 /chéngxù/ procedure; (computer) programme

2226 眼光 /yǎnguāng/ eye, sight; foresight

2227 大门 /dàmén/ gate, (main) entrance

2236 颜色 /yánsè/ colour

2237 证据 /zhèngjù/ evidence, proof

2238 医疗 /yīliáo/ medicine, medical treatment

2239 总经理 /zǒngjīnglǐ/ general manager

2240 势 /shì/ power, influence; momentum, tendency; situation

2241 代表团 /dàibiǎotuán/ delegation

2249 根 /gēn/ root

2250 杯 /bēi/ cup, mug, glass

2251 洞 /dòng/ hole, cavity, cave

2252 老太太 /lǎotàitai/ old lady

2253 厅 /tīng/ hall, foyer, lounge; [a provincial-level government department] department

2254 生态 /shēngtài/ ecology

2258 星期 /xīngqī/ week

2259 性质 /xìngzhì/ nature, character

2260 时刻 /shíkè/ moment; timetable

2261 区域 /qūyù/ region, area

2262 负责人 /fùzérén/ person in charge, director

2263 红色 /hóngsè/ red

2270 决定 /juédìng/ decision

2271 生活 /shēnghuó/ life

2272 精力 /jīnglì/ energy, vigour

2273 编辑 /biānjí/ editor; editing

2274 服装 /fúzhuāng/ clothing, garment, wear

2275 志 /zhì/ ambition, aspiration; will; records

2283 腐败 /fǔbài/ corruption

2285 研究所 /yánjiùsuǒ/ research institute

2286 铁 /tiě/ iron

2287 公路 /gōnglù/ road, highway

2288 趋势 /qūshì/ trend, tendency

2289 卡 /kǎ/ card

2290 营 /yíng/ camp; battalion

2291 衣 /yī/ clothes, clothing

2298 自行车 /zìxíngchē/ bicycle, bike

2299 期 /qī/ a period of time, phase, stage; schedule time

2300 真理 /zhēnlǐ/ truth

2301 表面 /biǎomiàn/ surface, outside

2302 负担 /fùdān/ burden, load

2303 知识分子 /zhīshifènzi/ intellectual

2309 理想 /lǐxiǎng/ ideal, dream

2310 情形 /qíngxíng/ circumstance, situation

2311 解放军 /jiěfàngjūn/ liberation army (specifically referring to the Chinese army known as the People's Liberation Army), the PLA; PLA soldier

2312 武装 /wǔzhuāng/ arms

2313 军人 /jūnrén/ serviceman, soldier

2322 食物 /shíwù/ food

2323 公 /gōng/ public; official business; father-in-law

2324 舆论 /yúlùn/ public opinion

2341 冰 /bīng/ ice

2342 太太 /tàitai/ Mrs, madam, lady; wife

2343 个体 /gètǐ/ individual; unit

2344 沟 /gōu/ ditch, channel, trench

2345 诗人 /shīrén/ poet, bard

2346 男性 /nánxìng/ male

2347 群体 /qúntǐ/ group

2348 状 /zhuàng/ condition; form; plaint

2351 蛋 /dàn/ egg

2352 所在 /suǒzài/ place, locus, whereabouts

2353 少数民族 /shǎoshùmínzú/ ethnic minority

2354 前提 /qiántí/ premise

2355 夫妇 /fūfù/ a (married) couple

2364 家乡 /jiāxiāng/ hometown

2365 空军 /kōngjūn/ air force

2366 掌声 /zhǎngshēng/ applause

2368 患者 /huànzhě/ patient

2369 旗 /qí/ flag, banner

2379 情景 /qíngjǐng/ scene, sight, situation

2380 规则 /guīzé/ rule

2381 公民 /gōngmín/ citizen

2382 青少年 /qīngshàonián/ adolescent, teenager

2383 姐 /jiě/ elder sister

2395 弟弟 /dìdi/ younger brother

2396 科研 /kēyán/ (scientific) research

2397 森林 /sēnlín/ forest

2398 大街 /dàjiē/ avenue, street

2399 人群 /rénqún/ crowd (of people)

2400 财政 /cáizhèng/ finance

2401 州 /zhōu/ prefecture; state; [often used as part of place names in China]

2408 商店 /shāngdiàn/ shop, store

2409 爷爷 /yéye/ (paternal) grandpa

2410 脑子 /nǎozi/ brain, mind

2411 脑袋 /nǎodài/ head

2412 生物 /shēngwù/ living thing; biology

2413 色彩 /sècǎi/ colour

2414 娘 /niáng/ mother, mum

2415 自治区 /zìzhìqū/ autonomous region

2416 场面 /chǎngmiàn/ scene, spectacle

2417 剑 /jiàn/ sword

2418 大师 /dàshī/ great master

2424 例子 /lìzi/ example, case

2425 规划 /guīhuà/ scheme, plan

2426 律师 /lǜshī/ lawyer

2435 眼泪 /yǎnlèi/ tear

2436 团长 /tuánzhǎng/ head of a delegation or troupe; regimental commander

2437 园 /yuán/ garden

2438 男孩 /nánhái/ boy

2444 生日 /shēngrì/ birthday

2445 主意 /zhǔyì/ idea

2446 商场 /shāngchǎng/ shopping mall

2447 愿望 /yuànwàng/ wish

2448 毒品 /dúpǐn/ drug

2449 招 /zhāo/ move, trick

2450 出版社 /chūbǎnshè/ press, publisher, publishing company

2451 人格 /réngé/ personality, character; integrity

2452 品牌 /pǐnpái/ brand

2453 心态 /xīntài/ state of mind, mindset

2469 馆 /guǎn/ [house for business or public service such as tea house, hotel, library, museum or embassy] hall, house

2470 木 /mù/ wood

2471 前途 /qiántú/ future, prospect

2472 寺 /sì/ temple

2473 贷款 /dàikuǎn/ loan

2485 作业 /zuòyè/ assignment, homework

2486 年级 /niánjí/ grade, year

2487 特征 /tèzhēng/ characteristic

2488 青春 /qīngchūn/ youth, youthfulness

2489 大哥 /dàgē/ eldest brother; [also used as a polite address for a man of about one's own age]

2490 职务 /zhíwù/ post, position

2506 勇气 /yǒngqì/ courage

2507 地面 /dìmiàn/ ground

2508 街道 /jiēdào/ street

2509 证 /zhèng/ certificate, papers; proof, evidence

2510 魅力 /mèilì/ charm

2511 股票 /gǔpiào/ share, stock

2512 消费者 /xiāofèizhě/ consumer

2526 节 /jié, jiē/ festival, holiday; section, division; node, joint; critical juncture

2527 高中 /gāozhōng/ high school

2528 来源 /láiyuán/ source

2529 头脑 /tóunǎo/ brain, head

2530 软件 /ruǎnjiàn/ software

2536 疾病 /jíbìng/ disease, illness

2537 华人 /huárén/ Chinese

2538 事务 /shìwù/ affairs

2539 障碍 /zhàng'ài/ barrier, obstacle

2551 首都 /shǒudū/ capital

2552 利润 /lìrùn/ profit

2553 天地 /tiāndì/ heaven and earth; world

2554 小子 /xiǎozi/ boy, young fellow; [derogatory] bloke; chap

2561 文物 /wénwù/ cultural relic

2562 论文 /lùnwén/ paper, dissertation, thesis

2563 灵魂 /línghún/ soul

2564 个性 /gèxìng/ individuality, (individual) character

2579 品种 /pǐnzhǒng/ variety, assortment

2580 广场 /guǎngchǎng/ square

2581 指示 /zhǐshì/ directive, instruction

2584 对话 /duìhuà/ dialogue

2586 试验 /shìyàn/ test, experiment

2596 研究 /yánjiù/ research

2597 机器 /jīqì/ machine

2598 泥 /ní/ mud

2599 小伙子 /xiǎohuǒzi/ young man

2600 数据 /shùjù/ data

2601 司令 /sīlìng/ commander

2602 战场 /zhànchǎng/ battlefield

2603 表情 /biǎoqíng/ (facial) expression

2604 团体 /tuántǐ/ group, organisation, society

2605 艾滋病 /àizībìng/ AIDS

2606 好事 /hǎoshì/ good deed; good thing; [sometimes used ironically] bad deed

2607 差距 /chājù/ disparity, gap

2608 骨 /gǔ, gú/ bone

2617 宿舍 /sùshè/ dormitory

2618 牙 /yá/ tooth

2619 后果 /hòuguǒ/ consequence

2620 财富 /cáifù/ wealth

2621 氏 /shì/ person surnamed; family, clan

2622 食 /shí/ food, meal; animal feed; eclipse

2623 父 /fù/ father

2624 人性 /rénxìng/ human nature, humanity

2625 柳 /liǔ/ willow

2626 百姓 /bǎixìng/ [also written as 老百姓] common people, civilian

2637 年纪 /niánjì/ age

2638 糖 /táng/ sugar, sweets

2639 蔬菜 /shūcài/ vegetable

2640 宇宙 /yǔzhòu/ universe

2641 舞蹈 /wǔdǎo/ dance

2642 族 /zú/ race; group

2643 佛 /fó/ Buddha

2653 表 /biǎo/ watch; form, table

2654 气候 /qìhòu/ climate

2655 本质 /běnzhì/ essence; true nature

2657 政权 /zhèngquán/ regime; power

2658 妻 /qī/ wife

2659 欲望 /yùwàng/ desire

2665 娱乐 /yúlè/ entertainment, recreation

2667 就业 /jiùyè/ employment

2676 汤 /tāng/ soup

2677 大小 /dàxiǎo/ size

2678 石油 /shíyóu/ oil

2679 鼻子 /bízi/ nose

2680 传说 /chuánshuō/ legend

2681 宝 /bǎo/ treasure

2682 总部 /zǒngbù/ headquarters

2683 明星 /míngxīng/ star

2684 企业家 /qǐyèjiā/ entrepreneur

2685 住房 /zhùfáng/ house, housing

2698 耳朵 /ěrduo/ ear

2699 焦点 /jiāodiǎn/ focus

2700 景 /jǐng/ scene, sight, view

2714 味道 /wèidào/ taste, flavour

2715 功夫 /gōngfū/ kung fu, martial arts; workmanship, skill

2716 条约 /tiáoyuē/ treaty

2717 公安 /gōng'ān/ police

2718 主持人 /zhǔchírén/ (TV or radio) presenter, host; (of meeting) chairperson

2719 黄金 /huángjīn/ gold

2727 发现 /fāxiàn/ finding, discovery

2728 事物 /shìwù/ thing

2729 秘书 /mìshū/ secretary

2730 会计 /kuàijì/ accountant; accounting

2731 境界 /jìngjiè/ realm, level or extent reached

2732 悲剧 /bēijù/ tragedy

2736 汗 /hàn/ perspiration, sweat

2737 毛病 /máobìng/ fault, shortcoming, defect; ailment, illness

2738 人间 /rénjiān/ human world, the world

2739 学会 /xuéhuì/ professional or academic association, society

2740 官兵 /guānbīng/ officers and men (in the army)

2753 可能 /kěnéng/ possibility, chance

2754 肚子 /dùzi/ stomach, belly

2755 手术 /shǒushù/ (surgical) operation

2756 大使 /dàshǐ/ ambassador

2757 摄影 /shèyǐng/ photography

2771 本 /běn/ root, origin, foundation, basis; edition, version

2772 亲戚 /qīnqī/ relative

2773 玻璃 /bōlí/ glass

2774 主张 /zhǔzhāng/ advocacy, proposition

2775 标志 /biāozhì/ sign, symbol

2776 公众 /gōngzhòng/ the public

2777 沙 /shā/ sand

2778 绿色 /lǜsè/ green; (of food) organic

2779 义 /yì/ meaning, sense; justice, righteousness

2781 会谈 /huìtán/ talks

2790 数学 /shùxué/ mathematics, maths

2791 宾馆 /bīn'guǎn/ guesthouse, hotel

2792 账 /zhàng/ account, account book; bill

2793 稿 /gǎo/ script, manuscript, contribution

2794 交易 /jiāoyì/ deal, transaction

2795 女孩子 /nǚháizi/ girl

2796 耳 /ěr/ ear

2812 地点 /dìdiǎn/ venue, location, place

2813 狼 /láng/ wolf

2814 答案 /dá'àn/ answer

2815 决心 /juéxīn/ determination, resolution

2816 教练 /jiàoliàn/ coach

2817 研究生 /yánjiùshēng/ graduate, postgraduate

2818 目 /mù/ eye; list

2825 全球化 /quánqiúhuà/ globalisation

2831 媳妇 /xífù/ daughter-in-law; wife

2832 艺术家 /yìshùjiā/ artist

2833 权益 /quányì/ rights and interests

2834 镜头 /jìngtóu/ (camera) lens; scene, shot (in a movie, etc.)

2835 激情 /jīqíng/ enthusiasm; passion, fervour

2856 友谊 /yǒuyì/ friendship

2857 秘密 /mìmì/ secret

2858 评论 /pínglùn/ comment; review

2859 基层 /jīcéng/ grassroots, basic level, lower level; base

2860 义务 /yìwù/ obligation, duty; volunteer, voluntary

2861 海军 /hǎijūn/ navy

2862 类型 /lèixíng/ kind, type

2863 职 /zhí/ post, position, appointment

2864 活力 /huólì/ vigour, vitality

2865 暴力 /bàolì/ violence

2866 泪 /lèi/ tear

2868 司 /sī/ department (in a ministry); firm, company

2878 买卖 /mǎimài/ buying and selling, (business) transaction, deal

2885 队长 /duìzhǎng/ team leader, captain

2886 号码 /hàomǎ/ number

2887 老虎 /lǎohǔ/ tiger

2888 美女 /měinǚ/ beauty

2889 君 /jūn/ monarch; [used as a formal title of addressing a man] Mr

2890 情节 /qíngjié/ plot; circumstances

2891 画面 /huàmiàn/ (picture) image; (video) frame

2892 德 /dé/ virtue; moral character

2902 著作 /zhùzuò/ book, writing, work

2903 顾客 /gùkè/ customer

2904 毒 /dú/ poison; drug

2905 声明 /shēngmíng/ statement

2906 遗址 /yízhǐ/ ancient ruins

2907 空 /kōng, kòng/ air, sky; empty space, blank space; spare time, free time

2918 水果 /shuǐguǒ/ fruit

2919 化学 /huàxué/ chemistry

2920 桌子 /zhuōzi/ table, desk

2921 营养 /yíngyǎng/ nutrition

2922 意志 /yìzhì/ will

2923 指标 /zhǐbiāo/ target; quota

2924 待遇 /dàiyù/ treatment; remuneration

2925 夫 /fū/ husband; manual labourer

2926 思路 /sīlù/ line of thought, thinking

2927 业 /yè/ trade, line of business; profession, occupation; estate, property; undertaking

2928 竹 /zhú/ bamboo

2929 粮 /liáng/ grain; food

2946 题目 /tímù/ title, topic, subject; question in examination

2947 圈 /quān, juàn/ circle, ring; fold, sty

2948 盘 /pán/ plate, dish; tray; (chess) board

2949 学问 /xuéwèn/ scholarly learning

2950 电台 /diàntái/ transmitter-receiver, transceiver; radio station

2951 丝 /sī/ silk, thread

2952 效率 /xiàolǜ/ efficiency

2953 银 /yín/ silver

2954 阵地 /zhèndì/ position, front

2955 音 /yīn/ sound; news

2956 代价 /dàijià/ price, cost

2957 轨道 /guǐdào/ orbit; track

2958 天空 /tiānkōng/ sky

2959 叶 /yè/ leaf; part of a historical period

2968 科学院 /kēxuéyuàn/ academy of sciences

2969 大爷 /dàyé/ grandpa, elder uncle; [often used as a respectful term of an elderly man, equivalent of 老大爷] uncle

2970 脾气 /píqì/ disposition, temperament

2971 家属 /jiāshǔ/ family member

2972 岗位 /gǎngwèi/ post, position

2974 途径 /tújìng/ means, pathway

2975 农场 /nóngchǎng/ farm

2976 事故 /shìgù/ accident

2977 儿女 /érnǚ/ children

2978 和尚 /héshang/ monk

2979 陆 /lù/ land

2980 国民 /guómín/ national, citizen

2981 校园 /xiàoyuán/ campus

2982 家族 /jiāzú/ clan, family

2983 友 /yǒu/ friend

2997 通讯 /tōngxùn/ communication, telecommunication; correspondence, news report

2998 党员 /dǎngyuán/ Party member

2999 浪 /làng/ wave

3000 县城 /xiànchéng/ county seat, county town

3001 依据 /yījù/ basis, foundation, evidence

3002 社 /shè/ society, club; agency

3003 额 /é/ amount, volume; forehead

3004 权威 /quánwēi/ authority

3005 外国人 /wàiguórén/ foreigner

3021 屋子 /wūzi/ house

3022 阵 /zhèn/ (military) front, field; battle array

3023 监狱 /jiānyù/ prison, jail

3024 家伙 /jiāhuo/ guy, fellow; tool, weapon

3025 乙 /yǐ/ [used for the second of enumerated items] second

3026 黑色 /hēisè/ black

3043 马路 /mǎlù/ road, highway

3044 款 /kuǎn/ money, fund; pattern, style

3045 风景 /fēngjǐng/ scenery

3046 例 /lì/ example, case

3047 手续 /shǒuxù/ formalities, procedure

3048 棋 /qí/ chess, board game

3049 渠道 /qúdào/ channel

3050 章 /zhāng/ seal, stamp; badge

3051 场所 /chǎngsuǒ/ place, venue

3052 术 /shù/ way, practice; (surgical) operation

3054 实验 /shíyàn/ experiment, test

3064 报道 /bàodào/ (news) report

3065 决议 /juéyì/ resolution, motion

3066 环节 /huánjié/ link

3068 窗口 /chuāngkǒu/ window

3083 瓶 /píng/ bottle

3084 俱乐部 /jùlèbù/ club

3085 根本 /gēnběn/ base, root, fundamental, core

3086 角 /jiǎo/ corner; horn; angle, cape

3087 场合 /chǎnghé/ occasion

3088 地质 /dìzhì/ geology

3089 基因 /jīyīn/ gene

3090 细节 /xìjié/ detail

3091 姐妹 /jiěmèi/ sister

3100 演讲 /yǎnjiǎng/ speech, lecture

3108 庙 /miào/ temple

3109 伙伴 /huǒbàn/ partner (for an activity); pal, mate

3110 人体 /réntǐ/ human, human body

3111 可能性 /kěnéngxìng/ possibility, chance

3112 大楼 /dàlóu/ building

3113 局势 /júshì/ situation

3126 流 /liú/ flow, stream of water or air, current

3127 来信 /láixìn/ (incoming) letter

3128 高度 /gāodù/ height

3129 户 /hù/ family, household; door; (bank) account

3130 动力 /dònglì/ drive, motivation; power

3131 公安局 /gōng'ānjú/ public security bureau, police station

3132 版 /bǎn/ edition; (of newspaper) page

3133 尊严 /zūnyán/ dignity

3134 小时候 /xiǎoshíhou/ (in) one's childhood

3152 物理 /wùlǐ/ physics

3153 花园 /huāyuán/ garden

3154 植物 /zhíwù/ plant

3155 厕所 /cèsuǒ/ toilet, WC

3156 遗产 /yíchǎn/ heritage, inheritance, legacy

3157 档案 /dàng'àn/ files, archive

3158 名义 /míngyì/ name

3159 机遇 /jīyù/ opportunity, favourable circumstances

3160 总裁 /zǒngcái/ president, CEO (chief executive officer)

3172 帽子 /màozi/ hat, cap; label

3173 机械 /jīxiè/ machinery

3174 学位 /xuéwèi/ (academic) degree

3175 大地 /dàdì/ earth, ground

3176 画家 /huàjiā/ painter

3177 坑 /kēng/ hole, pit

3178 典型 /diǎnxíng/ typical example, exemplar

3179 房屋 /fángwū/ house

3180 人心 /rénxīn/ public feeling, public sentiment

3181 作风 /zuòfēng/ style

3182 决策 /juécè/ policy decision; decision making

3183 移民 /yímín/ migrant, immigrant, emigrant; immigration

3184 劲儿 /jìnr/ strength; drive, vigour, zeal

3185 面子 /miànzi/ face, reputation; sensibilities

3186 尾 /wěi/ tail; end

3207 布 /bù/ cloth

3208 师傅 /shīfu/ master worker, teacher; [used as a respectful term of address for a skilled worker, or as a polite form of address for a stranger]

3209 博物馆 /bówùguǎn/ museum

3210 怀 /huái/ (in) one's arms, bosom; mind

3211 上帝 /shàngdì/ God

3212 戏剧 /xìjù/ drama, play

3213 同胞 /tóngbāo/ fellow countryman, compatriot

3214 差异 /chāyì/ difference

3228 脖子 /bózi/ neck

3229 上级 /shàngjí/ higher authorities, superior; upper level

3230 洪水 /hóngshuǐ/ flood

3231 影片 /yǐngpiàn/ film, movie

3232 料 /liào/ material; (animal) feed

3233 主角 /zhǔjué/ leading role

3234 双手 /shuāngshǒu/ both hands

3235 福利 /fúlì/ welfare, benefit

3251 苹果 /píngguǒ/ apple

3252 车站 /chēzhàn/ (bus or railway) station

3253 口号 /kǒuhào/ slogan

3254 季节 /jìjié/ season

3255 奖金 /jiǎngjīn/ bonus

3256 梦想 /mèngxiǎng/ dream, dream hope; vain hope

3257 村民 /cūnmín/ villager

3258 台阶 /táijiē/ step; [figuratively] way out

3259 岁月 /suìyuè/ time; years (of one's life)

3260 纪录 /jìlù/ record

3278 叔叔 /shūshu/ uncle; [also used as a polite term of address for men of one's parents' age]

3279 奇迹 /qíjī/ miracle

3280 列车 /lièchē/ train

3281 正义 /zhèngyì/ justice

3282 传 /zhuàn/ biography

3283 同行 /tóngháng/ peer; profession

3284 老年人 /lǎoniánrén/ old people, the aged

3301 窗 /chuāng/ window

3302 笑话 /xiàohuà/ joke

3303 山区 /shānqū/ mountain area

3304 盐 /yán/ salt

3305 逻辑 /luóji/ logic

3306 经费 /jīngfèi/ funding

3307 潮 /cháo/ tide; moist

3308 酒店 /jiǔdiàn/ hotel

3309 主力 /zhǔlì/ main force, backbone

3310 才能 /cáinéng/ talent

3311 初中 /chūzhōng/ junior high school, secondary school

3312 名称 /míngchēng/ name

3331 大夫 /dàifu/ doctor, physician

3332 阶级 /jiējí/ (social) class

3333 邻居 /línjū/ neighbour

3334 沙漠 /shāmò/ desert

3335 垃圾 /lājī/ rubbish, waste, trash; junk

3336 纪律 /jìlǜ/ discipline

3337 党委 /dǎngwěi/ Party committee

3338 时机 /shíjī/ opportunity, time, moment

3339 差别 /chābié/ difference

3340 货物 /huòwù/ goods

3341 岩 /yán/ rock, cliff

3342 联邦 /liánbāng/ federation, commonwealth

3343 理性 /lǐxìng/ reason

3359 篮球 /lánqiú/ basketball

3360 记录 /jìlù/ record; (of meeting) minutes

3361 母 /mǔ/ mother, parent

3362 故乡 /gùxiāng/ hometown, native place

3363 劲 /jìn/ [often as 劲儿] strength; effort; drive, vigour, zeal; interest, relish

3364 信念 /xìnniàn/ faith, belief

3365 难题 /nántí/ difficult problem

3366 胡同 /hútóng/ lane, alley

3367 技巧 /jìqiǎo/ skill, technique

3368 规矩 /guīju/ rule, custom; manners

3369 气质 /qìzhì/ temperament; quality

3370 论坛 /lùntán/ forum, tribune

3371 当局 /dāngjú/ the authorities

3372 智力 /zhìlì/ intelligence

3373 尸体 /shītǐ/ body, corpse

3374 董事长 /dǒngshìzhǎng/ chairperson of the board (of directors)

3375 首脑 /shǒunǎo/ head (of state or government); summit (meeting)

3376 彩 /cǎi/ colour, coloured

3377 古人 /gǔrén/ ancient people

3396 力气 /lìqì/ strength

3397 煤 /méi/ coal

3398 军官 /jūnguān/ (military) officer

3399 景象 /jǐngxiàng/ scene, sight

3400 力度 /lìdù/ dynamism, vigour, strength

3401 荣誉 /róngyù/ honour

3415 鸡蛋 /jīdàn/ (chicken) egg

3416 顾问 /gùwèn/ adviser, consultant

3417 灾难 /zāinàn/ disaster

3418 倾向 /qīngxiàng/ trend, tendency

3419 奶 /nǎi/ milk; breast

3420 爹 /diē/ dad, father

3421 大厅 /dàtīng/ hall

3422 亲 /qīn/ parent, next of kin, relative; marriage

3423 影 /yǐng/ shadow, reflected image; trace; film

3424 家人 /jiārén/ family member

3425 庄 /zhuāng/ village, hamlet, farm; manor; place of business

3440 皮肤 /pífū/ skin

3441 地址 /dìzhǐ/ address

3442 粉 /fěn/ powder

3443 阶层 /jiēcéng/ social stratum

3444 能量 /néngliàng/ energy

3445 峰 /fēng/ peak

3446 民众 /mínzhòng/ populace, people

3447 老爷 /lǎoye/ lord, master; [equivalent of 姥爷] (maternal) grandfather; something old and worn out

3448 基 /jī/ base, foundation

3462 面貌 /miànmào/ appearance, feature; outlook, look

3463 领袖 /lǐngxiù/ leader

3464 旅客 /lǚkè/ passenger

3465 产量 /chǎnliàng/ output

3466 模样 /múyàng/ appearance, look; [used to indicate approximation] about

3467 温度 /wēndù/ temperature

3468 商人 /shāngrén/ business people, merchant

3469 地理 /dìlǐ/ geography

3470 浑身 /húnshēn/ all over

3471 白色 /báisè/ white colour

3472 眼神 /yǎnshén/ expression or emotion shown in one's eyes

3473 镜 /jìng/ mirror; glasses

3500 咖啡 /kāfēi/ coffee

3501 蛇 /shé/ snake

3502 流域 /liúyù/ river basin, valley

3503 经典 /jīngdiǎn/ classics

3504 标题 /biāotí/ title, heading

3505 游客 /yóukè/ tourist

3506 金钱 /jīnqián/ money

3507 价值观 /jiàzhíguān/ values, value judgement

3518 通信 /tōngxìn/ correspondence, communication

3528 威 /wēi/ power, prestige, honour

3529 恐惧 /kǒngjù/ fear, dread

3535 碗 /wǎn/ bowl

3536 卫星 /wèixīng/ satellite

3537 武术 /wǔshù/ martial arts

3538 药物 /yàowù/ medication, drug

3539 资本主义 /zīběnzhǔyì/ capitalism

3540 质 /zhì/ quality; substance

3541 孙子 /sūnzi/ grandson, grandchild

3542 身子 /shēnzi/ body; pregnancy

3543 财务 /cáiwù/ finance

3544 仙 /xiān/ immortal being

3545 仗 /zhàng/ battle

3566 礼物 /lǐwù/ gift, present

3567 成分 /chéngfèn/ ingredient, element

3568 亲人 /qīnrén/ family, relative

3569 品质 /pǐnzhì/ quality

3570 少女 /shàonǚ/ young girl

3571 听众 /tīngzhòng/ audience

3572 现状 /xiànzhuàng/ status quo, present conditions

3573 前景 /qiánjǐng/ prospect, outlook

3574 基金 /jījīn/ fund

3596 江 /jiāng/ river

3597 能源 /néngyuán/ energy

3598 胸 /xiōng/ chest, bosom; mind

3599 度 /dù/ degree (of intensity), extent; capacity; limit

3600 航空 /hángkōng/ aviation, by air

3601 墓 /mù/ tomb, grave

3602 饮食 /yǐnshí/ food and drink, diet

3603 纠纷 /jiūfēn/ dispute

3604 众人 /zhòngrén/ everyone, crowd

3605 法庭 /fǎtíng/ court

3606 工商 /gōngshāng/ industry and commerce

3607 库 /kù/ warehouse, store room, bank

3608 政 /zhèng/ government, politics

3633 京剧 /jīngjù/ Beijing opera

3634 炮 /pào/ cannon, gun; firecracker

3635 箭 /jiàn/ arrow

3636 气息 /qìxī/ flavour, taste; smell, odour; breath

3637 玩具 /wánjù/ toy

3638 高手 /gāoshǒu/ master hand, top player

3639 农 /nóng/ agriculture, farming

3655 伤亡 /shāngwáng/ casualties

3665 血液 /xuèyè/ blood

3666 本事 /běnshi/ [equivalent of 本领] ability, skill

3667 地图 /dìtú/ map

3668 阿姨 /āyí/ (maternal side) aunt, auntie; [also used as a polite term of address for a woman of one's parents' age]

3669 草原 /cǎoyuán/ grassland, prairie

3670 屁股 /pìgu/ buttocks, bottom; end, butt

3671 物品 /wùpǐn/ article, item

3672 幻想 /huànxiǎng/ fantasy, illusion, delusion

3673 果 /guǒ/ fruit

3674 大姐 /dàjiě/ eldest sister, elder sister; [also used as a polite term of address for a women of one's own age] big sister, sister

3675 手法 /shǒufǎ/ technique, skill, way; trick

3676 病毒 /bìngdú/ virus

3701 节日 /jiérì/ holiday, festival

3702 啤酒 /píjiǔ/ beer

3703 胃 /wèi/ stomach

3704 心脏 /xīnzàng/ heart

3705 院子 /yuànzi/ yard, courtyard

3706 装备 /zhuāngbèi/ equipment

3707 税 /shuì/ tax, duty

3708 大队 /dàduì/ brigade

3709 笑容 /xiàoróng/ smile

3710 医 /yī/ medical science, medicine; doctor, physician

3711 财 /cái/ wealth, fortune

3712 战役 /zhànyì/ (military) campaign

3713 笑声 /xiàoshēng/ laughter

3714 当事人 /dāngshìrén/ person or party involved

3715 题材 /tícái/ subject matter, material

3716 贵族 /guìzú/ noble, aristocrat, peer

3717 潜力 /qiánlì/ potential, potentiality

3718 婚礼 /hūnlǐ/ wedding

3719 名单 /míngdān/ (name) list

3742 派 /pài/ side, faction, group, school

3743 原料 /yuánliào/ raw material

3744 礼貌 /lǐmào/ politeness, courtesy; manner

3745 水泥 /shuǐní/ cement

3746 乡村 /xiāngcūn/ village, countryside

3747 领土 /lǐngtǔ/ territory

3748 瓜 /guā/ melon

3749 论 /lùn/ theory; view, opinion

3750 初期 /chūqī/ initial stage, early days

3751 华侨 /huáqiáo/ overseas Chinese

3752 结局 /jiéjú/ ending, final upshot

3753 治安 /zhì'ān/ public order

3754 分歧 /fēnqí/ difference, divergence

3755 电视剧 /diànshìjù/ TV play

3756 医药 /yīyào/ medicine

3764 旅 /lǚ/ trip

3768 冲动 /chōngdòng/ impulse

3789 工程师 /gōngchéngshī/ engineer

3790 神经 /shénjīng/ nerve

3791 沙发 /shāfā/ sofa

3792 积极性 /jījíxìng/ enthusiasm, initiative, zeal

3793 大妈 /dàmā/ (paternal) aunt; [also used in northern dialects as a polite term of address for a woman of one's parents' age]

3794 鲜花 /xiānhuā/ (fresh) flowers

3795 歌曲 /gēqǔ/ song

3796 出路 /chūlù/ way out, solution

3797 象征 /xiàngzhēng/ emblem, symbol, token

3798 车辆 /chēliàng/ vehicle

3799 厂长 /chǎngzhǎng/ factory manager, director

3800 住宅 /zhùzhái/ residence

3801 形态 /xíngtài/ shape, form

3802 借口 /jièkǒu/ excuse

3803 体力 /tǐlì/ physical strength

3804 氛围 /fēnwéi/ ambience, atmosphere, aura

3805 老大 /lǎodà/ eldest child (in a family); number one, leader of a team

3806 策略 /cèlüè/ strategy

3807 硕士 /shuòshì/ master's degree

3808 窝 /wō/ nest

3836 窗户 /chuānghù/ window

3837 厨房 /chúfáng/ kitchen

3838 课程 /kèchéng/ course

3839 旅馆 /lǚguǎn/ guesthouse, hotel

3840 人力 /rénlì/ manpower

3841 砖 /zhuān/ brick

3842 觉 /jiào, jué/ sleep; sense

3843 细胞 /xìbāo/ cell

3844 职责 /zhízé/ responsibility, duty

3845 风暴 /fēngbào/ storm

3846 年度 /niándù/ year

3847 派出所 /pàichūsuǒ/ local police station

3848 难度 /nándù/ (degree of) difficulty

3849 心目 /xīnmù/ mind

3870 优点 /yōudiǎn/ merit, strength, advantage

3871 区别 /qūbié/ difference

3872 雷 /léi/ thunder; mine

3873 骆驼 /luòtuó/ camel

3874 重要性 /zhòngyàoxìng/ importance

3875 风光 /fēngguāng/ scene, scenery, view

3876 节奏 /jiézòu/ rhythm; tempo; pace

3877 处长 /chùzhǎng/ head of department

3878 格局 /géjú/ pattern, setup, layout

3879 真相 /zhēnxiàng/ truth; the actual situation or facts

3902 教室 /jiàoshì/ classroom

3903 姿态 /zītài/ posture, manner; attitude, stance

3904 药品 /yàopǐn/ medicine, drug

3905 钥匙 /yàoshi/ key

3906 神话 /shénhuà/ fairy tale, myth

3907 小事 /xiǎoshì/ trivial matter, triviality

3908 开发区 /kāifāqū/ development district

3909 弹 /dàn/ bullet, bomb

3910 念头 /niàntou/ thought, idea

3911 殿 /diàn/ palace hall

3912 使命 /shǐmìng/ mission

3913 小孩子 /xiǎoháizi/ child

3914 世人 /shìrén/ (common) people, the world

3935 运动会 /yùndònghuì/ sports meeting, games

3936 费 /fèi/ fee, expense

3937 针 /zhēn/ pin, needle; stitch; injection

3938 电梯 /diàntī/ elevator, lift, escalator

3940 协定 /xiédìng/ agreement

3941 宣言 /xuānyán/ declaration, manifesto

3942 行人 /xíngrén/ pedestrian

3943 坦克 /tǎnkè/ tank

3944 名牌 /míngpái/ famous brand or make

3945 历程 /lìchéng/ course, process

3946 滋味 /zīwèi/ taste

3947 毕业生 /bìyèshēng/ graduate

3948 爱心 /àixīn/ love, affection

3949 人文 /rénwén/ humanities

3950 人事 /rénshì/ personnel affairs

3951 诗歌 /shīgē/ poetry, poem

3966 信仰 /xìnyǎng/ belief, faith

3989 钢 /gāng/ steel

3990 国王 /guówáng/ king

3991 玉米 /yùmǐ/ sweetcorn

3992 是非 /shìfēi/ right and wrong; dispute

3993 大众 /dàzhòng/ the public, the people

3994 情报 /qíngbào/ intelligence, information

3995 高潮 /gāocháo/ high tide, upsurge; climax; orgasm

3996 线索 /xiànsuǒ/ clue

3997 学历 /xuélì/ academic qualification

3998 轿车 /jiàochē/ car

3999 平民 /píngmín/ civilians, ordinary people

4000 打算 /dǎsuàn/ plan

4001 步伐 /bùfá/ pace, step

4002 都市 /dūshì/ city, metropolis

4003 大厦 /dàshà/ building, mansion

4004 实验室 /shíyànshì/ lab, laboratory

4005 通道 /tōngdào/ passage, passageway; aisle

4006 内涵 /nèihán/ meaning, connotation

4031 邮票 /yóupiào/ stamp

4032 椅子 /yǐzi/ chair

4033 电报 /diànbào/ telegram, telegraph, cable

4034 家具 /jiājù/ furniture

4035 身材 /shēncái/ stature, figure, build

4036 日报 /rìbào/ daily (newspaper)

4037 一行 /yìxíng/ group, delegation

4038 中医 /zhōngyī/ Chinese medicine; herb doctor

4039 共和国 /gònghéguó/ republic

4040 书法 /shūfǎ/ calligraphy; handwriting

4041 老家 /lǎojiā/ native place, hometown

4042 课题 /kètí/ research topic, (research) project

4043 江湖 /jiānghú/ rivers and lakes; the wide world; itinerant entertainer, quack

4044 掌 /zhǎng/ palm

4045 等级 /děngjí/ class, grade, rank

4046 预算 /yùsuàn/ budget

4047 谷 /gǔ/ grain, cereal; valley

4048 首相 /shǒuxiàng/ prime minister

4049 老鼠 /lǎoshǔ/ rat, mouse

4057 过渡 /guòdù/ transition, interim

4067 聚会 /jùhuì/ gathering, meeting, party

4081 高原 /gāoyuán/ plateau, highland

4082 手指 /shǒuzhǐ/ finger

4083 工夫 /gōngfū/ time; effort; workmanship, skill; [equivalent of 功夫 kung fu, martial arts

4084 美术 /měishù/ art, fine arts, painting

4085 黄色 /huángsè/ yellow; pornography

4086 摩托车 /mótuōchē/ motorcycle, motorbike

4087 蓝色 /lánsè/ blue

4088 鸭 /yā/ duck

4089 高考 /gāokǎo/ college entrance examination

4090 时尚 /shíshàng/ fashion, vogue

4091 兵力 /bīnglì/ troops, military strength; strength

4092 影视 /yǐngshì/ film and video

4093 业绩 /yèjī/ performance; achievement

4111 全部 /quánbù/ all, everything, entirety, totality

4125 平原 /píngyuán/ plain

4126 眼镜 /yǎnjìng/ glasses, spectacles

4127 坡 /pō/ slope

4128 矿 /kuàng/ ore; mine

4129 步骤 /bùzhòu/ step, move

4130 土壤 /tǔrǎng/ soil

4131 面孔 /miànkǒng/ face

4132 脸色 /liǎnsè/ complexion, look; facial expression

4133 战术 /zhànshù/ tactic

4134 粥 /zhōu/ gruel, porridge, congee

4135 壁 /bì/ wall

4136 嘴巴 /zuǐba/ mouth

4137 潮流 /cháoliú/ tide; trend

4139 股市 /gǔshì/ stock market

4140 超市 /chāoshì/ supermarket, superstore

4141 投资 /tóuzī/ investment

4142 泪水 /lèishuǐ/ tear, teardrop

4174 食堂 /shítáng/ canteen, dining hall

4175 晚会 /wǎnhuì/ evening, evening party

4176 码头 /mǎtóu/ harbour, dock, wharf, pier

4177 生气 /shēngqì/ life, vigour, vitality

4178 学说 /xuéshuō/ theory, doctrine

4179 书籍 /shūjí/ (a general term for) books

4180 信号 /xìnhào/ signal

4181 赛 /sài/ match, game, competition

4182 水面 /shuǐmiàn/ water, water surface

4183 高层 /gāocéng/ high level, high tier; high-rise (building)

4184 虫 /chóng/ insect; worm

4185 钢铁 /gāngtiě/ steel, iron

4186 金额 /jīn'é/ amount

4187 大气 /dàqì/ atmosphere; heavy breath

4188 火车站 /huǒchēzhàn/ railway station

4215 审美 /shěnměi/ good taste; appreciation of beauty, aesthetics

4223 影子 /yǐngzi/ shadow

4224 工会 /gōnghuì/ trade union

4225 口袋 /kǒudài/ bag, pocket

4226 疑问 /yíwèn/ doubt; query

4227 铜 /tóng/ copper

4228 牌子 /páizi/ sign, plate; brand

4229 墨 /mò/ ink, China ink, ink stick

4230 地步 /dìbù/ degree, extent, plight

4231 边界 /biānjiè/ boundary, border

4232 婴儿 /yīng'ér/ infant, baby

4233 刊物 /kānwù/ publication, magazine, journal

4234 生理 /shēnglǐ/ physiology

4235 计 /jì/ idea, plan; gauge, metre

4236 级别 /jíbié/ level, rank, scale

4237 散文 /sǎnwén/ prose

4238 资 /zī/ money, capital, investment; endowment; qualifications

4239 眉 /méi/ eyebrow

4240 兄 /xiōng/ elder brother; [preceded by a surname to be used as a courtesy term of address between male friends]

4241 举 /jǔ/ act, move

4242 展 /zhǎn/ exhibition, display

4243 全身 /quánshēn/ the whole body, all over

4244 法官 /fǎguān/ judge

4245 敌 /dí/ enemy

4246 灯光 /dēngguāng/ light, lighting

4247 家园 /jiāyuán/ home, homestead, homeland

4248 出租车 /chūzūchē/ taxi

4249 名人 /míngrén/ celebrity

4250 良心 /liángxīn/ conscience

4251 理念 /lǐniàn/ idea, philosophy

4252 空调 /kōngtiáo/ air conditioner

4262 代理 /dàilǐ/ agent, agency; (computing) proxy

4285 姓名 /xìngmíng/ full name

4286 乒乓球 /pīngpāngqiú/ table tennis

4287 车间 /chējiān/ workshop

4288 口气 /kǒuqì/ tone, manner of speaking

4289 一带 /yídài/ area, region, part

4290 物资 /wùzī/ goods and materials, supplies

4291 老子 /lǎozi/ [informal] father; [referring to the speaker to take advantage of the addressee] I, me

4292 时光 /shíguāng/ time; period of time

4293 点儿 /diǎnr/ point, spot, dot

4294 大海 /dàhǎi/ sea

4295 困境 /kùnjìng/ predicament, plight, dilemma

4296 造型 /zàoxíng/ shape, moulding

4325 影响 /yǐngxiǎng/ influence, impact

4326 级 /jí/ level, rank, grade; step; degree

4327 碑 /bēi/ monument

4328 伤 /shāng/ injury, wound

4329 胡子 /húzi/ beard, moustache, whiskers

4330 舅舅 /jiùjiu/ (maternal) uncle

4331 实质 /shízhì/ essence, substance, crux

4332 记载 /jìzǎi/ record

4333 岗 /gǎng/ post; sentry post; hillock, mound

4334 档 /dàng/ files, archive

4335 支队 /zhīduì/ division, detachment

4336 电视机 /diànshìjī/ television (set)

4337 车子 /chēzi/ vehicle, car

4374 姓 /xìng/ surname, last name

4375 日记 /rìjì/ diary

4376 公元 /gōngyuán/ the Christian era, AD

4377 流氓 /liúmáng/ rogue, hoodlum, rascal, gangster

4378 地主 /dìzhǔ/ landlord, landowner, squire; host

4379 痕迹 /hénjì/ track, trace

4380 魂 /hún/ soul; spirit, mood

4381 歌声 /gēshēng/ singing

4382 屏幕 /píngmù/ screen

4383 谈 /tán/ talk

4384 智 /zhì/ wisdom

4385 总数 /zǒngshù/ total amount, sum

4386 文人 /wénrén/ man of letters, scholar

4387 海湾 /hǎiwān/ gulf, bay

4388 尿 /niào/ urine, pee

4389 谜 /mí/ puzzle, mystery; riddle

4390 心理学 /xīnlǐxué/ psychology

4391 熊 /xióng/ bear

4423 留学生 /liúxuéshēng/ overseas student, returned student

4424 肩 /jiān/ shoulder

4425 种子 /zhǒngzi/ seed

4426 学费 /xuéfèi/ tuition fees

4427 话剧 /huàjù/ (stage) play

4428 课堂 /kètáng/ classroom

4429 大自然 /dàzìrán/ nature

4430 局部 /júbù/ part, locality

4431 **风气** /fēngqì/ general mood; atmosphere; common practice

4432 **准则** /zhǔnzé/ norm, rule, criterion

4433 **含义** /hányì/ meaning, implication

4434 **处境** /chǔjìng/ (difficult) position, plight

4435 **绘画** /huìhuà/ drawing, painting

4450 **自治** /zìzhì/ autonomy, self-governing

4466 **卡车** /kǎchē/ truck, lorry

4467 **物价** /wùjià/ price

4468 **猴子** /hóuzi/ monkey

4469 **地带** /dìdài/ zone, region

4470 **环** /huán/ ring; link

4471 **塑料** /sùliào/ plastics

4472 **证书** /zhèngshū/ certificate, diploma

4473 **角落** /jiǎoluò/ corner

4474 **村子** /cūnzi/ village

4475 **谈话** /tánhuà/ talk

4476 **穷人** /qióngrén/ the poor, poor people

4477 **牙齿** /yáchǐ/ tooth

4478 **肌肉** /jīròu/ muscle

4479 **报刊** /bàokān/ newspapers and periodicals, the press

4480 **工地** /gōngdì/ construction site

4481 **肚** /dù, dǔ/ stomach, belly; tripe

4482 **视野** /shìyě/ field of view, vision

4483 **陵** /líng/ hill, mound; tomb

4484 **玩意** /wányì/ [often taking the suffix 儿] toy, plaything; thing

4485 **助理** /zhùlǐ/ assistant

4486 **空白** /kòngbái/ blank space; gap

4487 **女生** /nǚshēng/ girl student

4488 **老头** /lǎotóu/ [disrespectful] old man, old chap

4489 **本能** /běnnéng/ instinct

4490 **坏人** /huàirén/ bad people, villain, evildoer

4523 **月亮** /yuèliang/ moon

4524 **服务员** /fúwùyuán/ attendant, waiter, waitress

4525 **名** /míng/ name; fame

4526 **箱子** /xiāngzi/ box, suitcase

4527 **座位** /zuòwèi/ seat

4528 **金属** /jīnshǔ/ metal

4529 **驴** /lǘ/ donkey

4530 **心思** /xīnsī/ idea; thinking, thought

4531 **价钱** /jiàqián/ price

4532 **学员** /xuéyuán/ learner, student

4533 **报社** /bàoshè/ newspaper, press

4534 **导师** /dǎoshī/ tutor, supervisor

4535 **心眼** /xīnyǎn/ heart, mind; cleverness; tolerance

4536 **现金** /xiànjīn/ cash

4537 **皇家** /huángjiā/ royal family, imperial family

4538 **婆** /pó/ woman; matron; mother-in-law; grandma

4539 **宗旨** /zōngzhǐ/ aim, goal

4540 **证券** /zhèngquàn/ securities, stock

4541 **头儿** /tóur/ head, chief, superior

4542 **边境** /biānjìng/ border, frontier

4576 **盆** /pén/ basin, tub; pot, bowl

4577 **语气** /yǔqì/ tone, manner of speaking; (subjunctive, imperative, etc.) mood

4578 **尾巴** /wěiba/ tail

4579 **书店** /shūdiàn/ bookstore

4580 **用品** /yòngpǐn/ articles for use, appliance

4581 **幼儿园** /yòu'éryuán/ kindergarten

4582 **树木** /shùmù/ tree

4583 **摊** /tān/ stand, stall, vendor's booth

4584 **战友** /zhànyǒu/ comrade in arms, fellow soldier

4585 **境** /jìng/ border, boundary; condition, circumstance

4586 **高峰** /gāofēng/ peak, summit

4587 **包袱** /bāofu/ burden, weight (on one's mind); a bundle wrapped in cloth

4588 **成人** /chéngrén/ adult

4589 **阴影** /yīnyǐng/ shadow, shade; blight, spectre

4590 **钢琴** /gāngqín/ piano

4591 **内阁** /nèigé/ cabinet

4592 **网站** /wǎngzhàn/ website

4593 **存款** /cúnkuǎn/ deposit (in a bank), savings

4594 **股东** /gǔdōng/ stockholder, shareholder

4595 **生涯** /shēngyá/ career

4596 **政治家** /zhèngzhìjiā/ politician, statesman

4597 **例外** /lìwài/ exception

4598 **举动** /jǔdòng/ act, movement, conduct, behaviour

4599 **新人** /xīnrén/ new face, new people; newly wed, bride and bridegroom; people of a new age or a new generation

4600 **蚂蚁** /mǎyǐ/ ant

4638 **宴会** /yànhuì/ banquet, dinner party

4639 **面包** /miànbāo/ bread

4640 **饺子** /jiǎozi/ dumpling

4641 **裤子** /kùzi/ trousers

4642 **本领** /běnlǐng/ [equivalent of 本事] ability, skill

4643 **镜子** /jìngzi/ mirror

4644 **西瓜** /xīguā/ watermelon

4645 **形状** /xíngzhuàng/ shape

4646 **日期** /rìqī/ date

4647 **骨干** /gǔgàn/ backbone, mainstay

4648 **大脑** /dànǎo/ brain

4649 **功课** /gōngkè/ schoolwork, homework; school subject

4650 **语文** /yǔwén/ language, (specifically) Chinese (as a school subject)

4651 **老年** /lǎonián/ old age

4652 岭 /líng/ ridge; mountain range

4653 罪犯 /zuìfàn/ criminal

4654 味儿 /wèir/ taste, flavour

4655 态 /tài/ form, appearance; state

4656 麦 /mài/ wheat

4657 起点 /qǐdiǎn/ starting point

4658 警方 /jǐngfāng/ police

4659 谱 /pǔ/ chart, list; music score; a fair amount of confidence, idea; spectrum

4660 臂 /bì, bei/ arm

4661 民警 /mínjǐng/ (civilian) police

4662 外汇 /wàihuì/ foreign exchange, foreign currency

4670 竞赛 /jìngsài/ contest, competition, race

4688 失误 /shīwù/ error, mistake

4698 盒 /hé/ box

4699 会场 /huìchǎng/ meeting place, conference site

4700 商 /shāng/ trade, commerce, business

4701 肩膀 /jiānbǎng/ shoulder

4702 家门 /jiāmén/ gate of one's house, one's home; family

4703 乐趣 /lèqù/ joy, pleasure

4704 反响 /fǎnxiǎng/ repercussion, echo; impact, effect

4705 户口 /hùkǒu/ household registration, registered residence

4706 往事 /wǎngshì/ past events, the past

4707 股份 /gǔfèn/ share, stock

4708 公主 /gōngzhǔ/ princess

4709 厂家 /chǎngjiā/ manufacturer

4710 名气 /míngqì/ fame, reputation

4743 气象 /qìxiàng/ meteorology, weather; scene

4744 集 /jí/ collection, album; market, country fair; set, group

4745 棉花 /miánhuā/ cotton

4746 胳膊 /gēbo/ arm

4747 组长 /zǔzhǎng/ group leader

4748 边缘 /biānyuán/ edge, margin, brink

4749 季 /jì/ season; quarter

4750 香烟 /xiāngyān/ cigarette; smoke from burning incense

4751 蝴蝶 /húdié/ butterfly

4752 债 /zhài/ debt

4753 神情 /shénqíng/ look, facial expression

4754 仓库 /cāngkù/ warehouse

4756 车队 /chēduì/ motorcade, a queue of wagons or carts; fleet, vehicle service brigade

4757 豆 /dòu/ bean

4758 纹 /wén/ stria, line

4759 青年人 /qīngniánrén/ young people

4760 婆婆 /pópo/ husband's mother, mother-in-law; old woman

4761 年头 /niántóu/ year; days, times; long time

4762 修养 /xiūyǎng/ culture, cultivation, self-possession

4763 活儿 /huór/ work, job

4779 睡眠 /shuìmián/ sleep

4789 喜悦 /xǐyuè/ happiness, joy

4799 行李 /xínglǐ/ baggage, luggage

4800 嗓子 /sǎngzi/ throat

4801 班长 /bānzhǎng/ class monitor, captain; squad leader

4802 缺点 /quēdiǎn/ shortcoming, weakness, defect

4803 狮子 /shīzi/ lion

4804 骨头 /gútou/ bone; moral character; bitterness

4805 收获 /shōuhuò/ result, reward, gains; harvest

4806 彩色 /cǎisè/ colour

4807 技能 /jìnéng/ skill

4808 战线 /zhànxiàn/ battle line; front

4809 中年 /zhōngnián/ middle age

4810 终身 /zhōngshēn/ all one's life, lifelong

4811 脚步 /jiǎobù/ footstep

4812 帽 /mào/ hat, cap

4813 君子 /jūnzi/ gentleman, man of honour

4814 令 /lìng/ order, command, decree

4815 餐馆 /cānguǎn/ restaurant

4816 上司 /shàngsī/ superior

4817 望远镜 /wàngyuǎnjìng/ telescope, binoculars

4818 话语 /huàyǔ/ what is said, words

4819 模特 /mótè/ [often taking the suffix 儿] model

4820 天堂 /tiāntáng/ heaven, paradise

4821 图案 /tú'àn/ design, pattern

4822 帐篷 /zhàngpéng/ tent

4823 籍 /jí/ record; native place; membership; nationality

4849 表现 /biǎoxiàn/ behaviour

4850 晚饭 /wǎnfàn/ supper, dinner

4851 餐厅 /cāntīng/ dining hall, dining room

4852 气温 /qìwēn/ temperature

4853 小朋友 /xiǎopéngyou/ children

4854 客厅 /kètīng/ sitting room, reception room

4855 饮料 /yǐnliào/ drink

4856 犯人 /fànrén/ convict, prisoner

4857 运气 /yùnqi/ luck

4858 葡萄 /pútao/ grape

4859 旗帜 /qízhì/ banner, flag; [figuratively] one's stand or position

4860 国防 /guófáng/ national defence

4861 河流 /héliú/ river

4862 导弹 /dǎodàn/ missile

4863 动机 /dòngjī/ motive, motivation

4864 废话 /fèihuà/ nonsense

4865 琴 /qín/ [general term for some stringed musical instruments such as piano, violin] instrument, qin

4866 身影 /shēnyǐng/ figure, silhouette

4867 责任感 /zérèngǎn/ sense of duty

4868 棉 /mián/ cotton

4869 名片 /míngpiàn/ (business) card

4870 期限 /qīxiàn/ deadline, time limit, term

4871 公寓 /gōngyù/ flat, apartment

4872 短期 /duǎnqī/ short term

4873 唇 /chún/ lip

4874 银子 /yínzi/ silver; money

4875 男朋友 /nánpéngyou/ boyfriend

4876 王国 /wángguó/ kingdom

4877 伦理 /lúnlǐ/ ethics, moral principles

4878 貌 /mào/ appearance, look

4913 灾 /zāi/ disaster, calamity

4914 雾 /wù/ fog, mist

4915 醋 /cù/ vinegar; jealousy

4916 教材 /jiàocái/ teaching materials

4917 处分 /chǔfèn/ disciplinary action, punishment

4918 不是 /bùshi/ fault, blame

4919 柜台 /guìtái/ counter

4920 性别 /xìngbié/ gender, sex

4921 血管 /xuèguǎn/ vein

4922 胆 /dǎn/ gall, gall bladder; guts, nerve, courage

4923 核 /hé/ pit, stone; nucleus

4924 陆军 /lùjūn/ army, land force

4925 玩笑 /wánxiào/ joke

4926 大桥 /dàqiáo/ (grand) bridge

4927 限度 /xiàndù/ limit, limitation

4928 部位 /bùwèi/ position, place, area

4929 息 /xī/ (bank) interest; breath; news

4930 介绍 /jièshào/ introduction

4931 坏事 /huàishì/ bad thing, evil deed

4932 场景 /chǎngjǐng/ scene

4933 文凭 /wénpíng/ diploma, certificate, academic credentials

4934 童年 /tóngnián/ childhood

4935 火山 /huǒshān/ volcano

4936 古城 /gǔchéng/ ancient city

4937 父子 /fùzǐ/ father and son

4964 变化 /biànhuà/ change

4965 学期 /xuéqī/ term, semester

4970 保护 /bǎohù/ protection

4971 星星 /xīngxing/ star

4972 水稻 /shuǐdào/ (paddy) rice

4973 草地 /cǎodì/ grass, meadow, lawn

4974 指挥 /zhǐhuī/ command, direction; commander; (music) conductor

4983 牛奶 /niúnǎi/ milk

4984 海关 /hǎiguān/ customs

4993 生产 /shēngchǎn/ production

4994 外语 /wàiyǔ/ foreign language

4995 护士 /hùshi/ nurse

4996 科长 /kēzhǎng/ section chief

4997 仪器 /yíqì/ instrument, apparatus

4998 讲座 /jiǎngzuò/ lecture

4999 红旗 /hóngqí/ red flag

Verb

0002 是 /shì/ be

0009 有 /yǒu/ have, there be

0012 说 /shuō/ say, speak, tell

0020 要 /yào/ want; order

0021 到 /dào/ go to, reach, arrive

0031 能 /néng/ can

0035 会 /huì/ can, know how to do

0039 看 /kàn, kān/ look, view; look after

0040 去 /qù/ go

0050 出 /chū/ out; produce; happen

0056 想 /xiǎng/ think

0063 来 /lái/ come

0068 用 /yòng/ use

0070 可以 /kěyǐ/ may, can

0074 没有 /méiyǒu/ have not, there be not

0076 做 /zuò/ do, make

0079 让 /ràng/ give way; let, make; allow

0085 走 /zǒu/ walk; leave

0090 知道 /zhīdào/ know

0097 为 /wéi/ be, act as

0098 工作 /gōngzuò/ work, do a job

0109 发展 /fāzhǎn/ develop

0110 成 /chéng/ become, turn into; succeed

0120 打 /dǎ/ beat, hit, strike; play; typewrite

0124 使 /shǐ/ [often used in serial verb constructions] make, cause, enable

0127 生活 /shēnghuó/ live

0133 像 /xiàng/ look like, resemble; look as if

0134 叫 /jiào/ name, call; shout; order (somebody to do something); order (meal, taxi, etc.)

0136 起 /qǐ/ get up, rise; up

0137 吃 /chī/ eat

0139 开始 /kāishǐ/ begin, start

0141 完 /wán/ finish, be over; (use) up

0143 起来 /qǐlái/ get up, rise; [following a verb to indicate the beginning of a situation] start to; [following a verb to indicate completedness or effectiveness]

0146 听 /tīng/ listen

0148 可能 /kěnéng/ might (happen)

0160 认为 /rènwéi/ think, believe

0164 问 /wèn/ ask

0166 觉得 /juéde/ think, feel

0169 出来 /chūlái/ come out

0170 进行 /jìnxíng/ go on, last; be under way; carry on, carry out, perform

0177 写 /xiě/ write

0180 找 /zhǎo/ look for

0183 讲 /jiǎng/ speak, tell

0186 开 /kāi/ open; operate, drive (car), turn on (light); start (business); hold (meeting, party, etc.); (water) boil; write (cheque); (flower) blossom

0190 进 /jìn/ enter; advance

0191 没 /méi/ have not, there be not

0194 拿 /ná/ hold; take

0196 应该 /yīnggāi/ ought to, should

0197 发现 /fāxiàn/ find

0200 住 /zhù/ live, stay

0201 见 /jiàn/ see, meet

0204 带 /dài/ carry, bring, take

0211 看到 /kàndào/ see

0213 干 /gàn/ work, do (a job)

0218 回 /huí/ return; reply; decline (invitation)

0224 无 /wú/ have no, there be no

0226 成为 /chéngwéi/ become

0230 爱 /ài/ love, like

0232 研究 /yánjiù/ do research, study

0239 死 /sǐ/ die

0242 放 /fàng/ put, place; let go, let off; lay aside; show, play (movies, etc.)

0245 谈 /tán/ talk

0247 需要 /xūyào/ need

0249 发生 /fāshēng/ happen, take place

0250 出现 /chūxiàn/ appear

0255 如 /rú/ like, as, as if; such as

0259 希望 /xīwàng/ hope, wish for

0262 作 /zuò/ do

0264 必须 /bìxū/ must, have to

0266 买 /mǎi/ buy

0268 请 /qǐng/ please (do something); ask (somebody to do something); invite

0269 办 /bàn/ do

0270 教育 /jiàoyù/ educate

0277 学 /xué/ learn, study

0279 坐 /zuò/ sit

0280 告诉 /gàosù/ tell

0284 下 /xià/ come down; alight; rain, snow; get off (from class, work, etc.); give (order, definition, conclusion, etc.); play (chess)

0288 搞 /gǎo/ do

0289 过 /guò/ cross (road); spend (holiday, etc.); go beyond (time); go through; exceed

0291 活动 /huódòng/ move about for exercise

0302 发 /fā/ send out, give out, distribute

0305 得到 /dédào/ get

0306 受 /shòu/ receive; be subject to, suffer; endure, bear

0317 参加 /cānjiā/ take part in, participate; join

0319 就是 /jiùshì/ [emphasising that something is precisely or exactly what is stated] be exactly

0324 送 /sòng/ deliver; give as a gift; see off; escort

0325 变 /biàn/ change

0330 能够 /nénggòu/ be able to, be capable of

0333 影响 /yǐngxiǎng/ influence

0335 得 /dé, děi/ get, gain; must, have to; need

0337 准备 /zhǔnbèi/ prepare, get ready

0346 管理 /guǎnlǐ/ manage

0348 下来 /xiàlái/ come down, descend

0349 解决 /jiějué/ solve (a problem), settle (a dispute)

0351 学习 /xuéxí/ learn, study

0352 当 /dāng, dàng/ work as; regard as

0353 喜欢 /xǐhuān/ like, enjoy

0356 作为 /zuòwéi/ as, take as, regard as

0360 生 /shēng/ give birth to, bear; become (rusty, ill, etc.); light (a fire)

0361 应 /yīng, yìng/ ought to, should; answer, respond, echo; comply with

0363 决定 /juédìng/ decide

0364 知 /zhī/ know

0370 提出 /tíchū/ raise (an issue), propose, suggest

0371 了解 /liǎojiě/ get to know, understand

0376 站 /zhàn/ stand

0377 算 /suàn/ calculate; regard as

0379 给 /gěi/ give

0382 至 /zhì/ arrive, reach

0387 笑 /xiào/ laugh, smile

0394 包括 /bāokuò/ include, comprise

0395 分 /fēn/ divide, separate, differentiate; distribute

0396 继续 /jìxù/ continue

0397 回来 /huílái/ return

0398 表示 /biǎoshì/ express

0399 跑 /pǎo/ run

0416 改革 /gǎigé/ reform

0419 穿 /chuān/ wear, put on; bore a hole; cross

0421 认识 /rènshí/ know, understand; recognise

0424 要求 /yāoqiú/ ask for, request, demand

0426 进入 /jìnrù/ enter, get into

0428 敢 /gǎn/ dare

0431 掉 /diào/ drop

0434 拉 /lā/ pull

0436 表现 /biǎoxiàn/ manifest, show; behave

0442 建设 /jiànshè/ build, construct

0444 管 /guǎn/ manage, run, administer; take care (of), care about

0445 感到 /gǎndào/ feel

0447 入 /rù/ enter

0451 有关 /yǒuguān/ have something to do with

0453 怕 /pà/ be afraid, fear

0458 接受 /jiēshòu/ accept

0461 注意 /zhùyì/ pay attention to; take notice of, note

0467 存在 /cúnzài/ exist

0469 建立 /jiànlì/ establish, set up

0470 靠 /kào/ depend upon; be due to; lean against; come up to

0472 努力 /nǔlì/ strive to, try one's best to; make efforts to

0474 相信 /xiāngxìn/ believe, trust, be convinced

0478 介绍 /jièshào/ introduce

0490 跟 /gēn/ follow

0493 产生 /chǎnshēng/ arise, generate

0494 反 /fǎn/ oppose, combat; reverse; turn against

0497 卖 /mài/ sell

0500 生产 /shēngchǎn/ produce

0503 具有 /jùyǒu/ possess, have

0508 提高 /tígāo/ raise, improve

0519 喝 /hē/ drink

0527 令 /lìng/ order, command; cause, make

0536 指 /zhǐ/ mean, refer to; point to

0537 保护 /bǎohù/ protect

0538 支持 /zhīchí/ support

0542 提供 /tígòng/ provide, supply

0544 抓 /zhuā/ grab, grasp; arrest

0548 受到 /shòudào/ come in for

0550 下去 /xiàqù/ go down, descend

0551 形成 /xíngchéng/ form, make

0554 愿意 /yuànyì/ be willing to

0556 合作 /hézuò/ cooperate, collaborate

0564 变化 /biànhuà/ change

0574 即 /jí/ is; that is

0580 选择 /xuǎnzé/ choose, select

0582 改变 /gǎibiàn/ change, alter

0583 占 /zhàn/ take; take up, occupy

0584 考虑 /kǎolǜ/ think over, consider

0591 定 /dìng/ set, fix, decide; subscribe to (newspapers and periodicals, etc.)

0592 实现 /shíxiàn/ realise, fulfil, achieve

0601 接 /jiē/ put together, join; receive, answer (call, letter, etc.); meet, pick up (somebody); extend, connect; catch (a ball, etc.)

0602 获得 /huòdé/ obtain

0607 读 /dú/ read

0609 处理 /chǔlǐ/ handle, deal with; take disciplinary action against; dispose of, sell at a reduced price

0614 达 /dá/ attain, reach; amount to

0618 完成 /wánchéng/ complete, accomplish

0623 变成 /biànchéng/ become, turn into

0624 结束 /jiéshù/ be over, end, terminate

0626 理解 /lǐjiě/ understand, apprehend

0631 出去 /chūqù/ go out

0632 帮助 /bāngzhù/ help, assist

0637 说话 /shuōhuà/ speak, talk

0638 达到 /dádào/ reach, attain, be up to

0642 投资 /tóuzī/ invest

0646 动 /dòng/ move; arouse; change; use

0649 报道 /bàodào/ report

0652 服务 /fúwù/ serve

0654 行 /xíng/ be all right; travel

0656 造成 /zàochéng/ cause, result in

0659 过来 /guòlái/ come over; manage to do something

0660 花 /huā/ spend

0661 使用 /shǐyòng/ use

0665 离开 /líkāi/ leave, depart

0669 转 /zhuǎn, zhuàn/ change, shift; pass on; rotate, resolve; turn

0671 帮 /bāng/ help, assist, do somebody a favour

0676 留 /liú/ remain, stay; reserve, save for future use; leave behind

0677 无法 /wúfǎ/ be unable to, can't

0681 面对 /miànduì/ face, confront

0682 换 /huàn/ change; exchange

0683 行动 /xíngdòng/ act, take action; move about

0686 加 /jiā/ add, increase; put in

0691 增加 /zēngjiā/ increase

0692 坚持 /jiānchí/ insist, persist, stick to

0694 收 /shōu/ receive, collect; accept

0697 明白 /míngbái/ realise, understand

0698 离 /lí/ leave, be away

0699 发表 /fābiǎo/ publish, issue

0704 保持 /bǎochí/ keep, maintain

0706 取得 /qǔdé/ acquire, obtain, achieve; reach (an agreement)

0710 好像 /hǎoxiàng/ seem, look like, look as if

0712 同意 /tóngyì/ agree

0713 举行 /jǔxíng/ hold (meeting, etc.)

0714 来到 /láidào/ come to

0716 弄 /nòng/ play with; do, get (ready)

0717 引起 /yǐnqǐ/ evoke, give rise to, lead to

0725 利用 /lìyòng/ make use of, exploit

0730 提 /tí/ carry; put forward, raise; mention, ask; lift; promote

0732 记 /jì/ keep in mind, memorise, remember; take note, write down

0746 过去 /guòqu/ go over, pass by; [used as verb complement in a resultative construction to indicate result]

0748 飞 /fēi/ fly

0750 联系 /liánxì/ contact, get in touch

0753 玩 /wán/ play, amuse oneself

0757 分析 /fēnxī/ analyse

0758 控制 /kòngzhì/ control

0759 带来 /dàilái/ bring

0769 派 /pài/ send, dispatch

0770 调查 /diàochá/ investigate, look into

0772 想到 /xiǎngdào/ think of

0775 落 /luò/ fall, drop; lower; fall behind

0779 创造 /chuàngzào/ create

0782 改 /gǎi/ change, revise, modify

0783 称 /chēng/ call; say, state; weigh

0785 安排 /ānpái/ arrange, schedule

0786 采取 /cǎiqǔ/ adopt, carry out (policies, course of action, etc.); take (actions, measures)

0789 回答 /huídá/ reply, answer, respond

0799 成立 /chénglì/ establish, set up

0808 经营 /jīngyíng/ run a business, engage in (a business activity)

0812 冲 /chōng/ dash against, rush; rinse, flush; develop (a film)

0813 找到 /zhǎodào/ find

0816 说明 /shuōmíng/ explain

0817 懂 /dǒng/ understand

0818 反对 /fǎnduì/ oppose, object to, fight against

0819 讨论 /tǎolùn/ discuss

0823 组织 /zǔzhī/ organise

0836 加强 /jiāqiáng/ reinforce, intensify

0837 拍 /pāi/ clap, pat, strike; take (a picture), shoot (a film)

0843 来自 /láizì/ come from

0847 教 /jiào/ teach

0859 看见 /kànjiàn/ see

0865 背 /bēi, bèi/ carry on one's back; learn by heart

0869 杀 /shā/ kill

0875 以为 /yǐwéi/ think, believe

0881 跳 /tiào/ jump

0882 倒 /dǎo, dào/ fall, collapse; (business) close down; reverse, swap; dump (rubbish); move backwards; pour (tea)

0886 采访 /cǎifǎng/ interview

0887 正是 /zhèngshì/ be exactly

0892 负责 /fùzé/ be in charge of; be responsible for

0893 充满 /chōngmǎn/ be full of, be filled with

0895 装 /zhuāng/ pack, load; fix, install; pretend; play the role of

0896 比如 /bǐrú/ take, for example

0906 证明 /zhèngmíng/ prove

0907 培养 /péiyǎng/ train, foster, rear, develop, cultivate

0915 保证 /bǎozhèng/ guarantee

0925 开发 /kāifā/ develop, open up, exploit

0929 唱 /chàng/ sing

0935 是否 /shìfǒu/ whether (or not)

0939 反映 /fǎnyìng/ reflect, mirror; report

0940 承认 /chéngrèn/ admit

0945 关心 /guānxīn/ care for, be concerned about

0948 驻 /zhù/ be stationed

0949 解释 /jiěshì/ explain

0957 回到 /huídào/ come back, go back, return to

0962 尽 /jìn, jǐn/ exhaust; do one's best; give priority to

0964 睡 /shuì/ sleep

0968 不可 /bùkě/ cannot

0974 重视 /zhòngshì/ take something seriously, attach importance to

0975 追求 /zhuīqiú/ seek, pursue; court, woo

0978 指出 /zhǐchū/ point out

0979 道 /dào/ [archaic, usually following communication verbs such as 说, 笑, 喊 and 叫] say, talk, speak

0980 哭 /kū/ cry, sob, weep

0984 借 /jiè/ borrow, lend; take advantage of, make use of

0985 拥有 /yōngyǒu/ have, possess, own

0988 试 /shì/ test, try

0989 回去 /huíqù/ return, go back

0992 应当 /yīngdāng/ should, ought to

0996 画 /huà/ draw, paint (a picture)

0999 留下 /liúxià/ leave behind, remain

1003 毕业 /bìyè/ graduate

1005 遇到 /yùdào/ encounter, meet, come across, run into

1007 愿 /yuàn/ hope, wish; will, be willing to

1009 结婚 /jiéhūn/ marry

1010 交 /jiāo/ hand in, submit, deliver

1020 欢迎 /huānyíng/ welcome

1021 交流 /jiāoliú/ exchange, interchange

1024 增长 /zēngzhǎng/ grow, increase

1025 强调 /qiángdiào/ emphasise, stress

1030 加上 /jiāshàng/ add, include

1032 开放 /kāifàng/ open, open up; (flower) blossom

1033 关注 /guānzhù/ follow (an issue) closely with interest

1045 发挥 /fāhuī/ bring into play, give play to

1047 感 /gǎn/ feel

1052 停 /tíng/ stop

1053 结合 /jiéhé/ combine, integrate; be united in wedlock

1054 竞争 /jìngzhēng/ compete, rival

1057 立 /lì/ stand; erect, set up; establish

1061 超过 /chāoguò/ surpass, exceed

1065 求 /qiú/ beg, request, strike for, seek

1067 洗 /xǐ/ wash

1069 任 /rèn/ appoint, occupy or take up a post; give free rein to

1070 回家 /huíjiā/ go home, come home

1079 听说 /tīngshuō/ hear of, be told

1080 上 /shàng/ go up, ascend; board; leave for; go ahead; be engaged in (class, work, etc.); serve (tea, food, etc.)

1081 恢复 /huīfù/ resume, renew; recover, restore

1083 挂 /guà/ hang

1085 肯定 /kěndìng/ be certain; affirm

1089 包 /bāo/ pack, wrap; assure, guarantee; undertake the whole thing; hire

1092 批评 /pīpíng/ criticise

1096 实行 /shíxíng/ implement, carry out, bring into effect

1101 忘 /wàng/ forget

1102 失去 /shīqù/ lose

1105 翻 /fān/ open (a book); turn over; look through; get over, cross; translate

1106 吃饭 /chīfàn/ eat (a meal)

1108 断 /duàn/ break

1119 见到 /jiàndào/ see

1123 检查 /jiǎnchá/ check up, examine, inspect

1129 退 /tuì/ move back, retreat; return, refund; withdraw; (of tide) recede

1130 活 /huó/ live, survive

1131 合 /hé/ shut; suit, agree; combine; add up to

1133 养 /yǎng/ keep, raise (animals, etc.); provide for, support (a family); give birth to; develop (a habit); rest, maintain

1134 烧 /shāo/ burn; cook, have a fever

1141 摆 /bǎi/ put, place, arrange; put on (airs); sway

1143 训练 /xùnliàn/ train

1145 属于 /shǔyú/ belong to, be classified as

1149 宣布 /xuānbù/ announce, declare

1150 值得 /zhíde/ deserve, be worth

1153 参与 /cānyù/ participate, take part in, be involved in

1157 喊 /hǎn/ call, shout, yell

1158 推 /tuī/ push

1159 发出 /fāchū/ send out; give out

1165 设计 /shèjì/ design

1175 劳动 /láodòng/ work; do physical labour

1178 进步 /jìnbù/ make progress

1181 掌握 /zhǎngwò/ grasp, master

1182 实施 /shíshī/ implement, carry out

1183 制 /zhì/ make, manufacture

1186 扩大 /kuòdà/ enlarge, expand

1192 斗争 /dòuzhēng/ struggle, fight; strive for

1193 建 /jiàn/ establish; construct, build

1194 确定 /quèdìng/ determine, fix

1195 听到 /tīngdào/ hear

1196 销售 /xiāoshòu/ sell

1199 通 /tōng/ open up by poking; understand, know; connect, communicate; lead to

1202 抓住 /zhuāzhù/ grab, grip; catch hold of; catch; seize (an opportunity)

1203 感受 /gǎnshòu/ sense, feel

1208 抱 /bào/ hold in arms

1218 待 /dāi, dài/ stay; wait for; deal with, treat; entertain

1219 做出 /zuòchū/ make, put out

1222 选 /xuǎn/ choose

1223 调整 /tiáozhěng/ adjust

1226 调 /diào, tiáo/ transfer, shift; adjust, turn; harmonise

1234 接触 /jiēchù/ contact, expose to

1235 担心 /dānxīn/ worry

1239 胜利 /shènglì/ win victory

1246 投入 /tóurù/ throw (oneself) into (work); put into (operation)

1252 促进 /cùjìn/ promote, advance

1253 属 /shǔ/ belong, be

1257 显得 /xiǎnde/ appear, seem, look

1258 记得 /jìde/ remember

1261 够 /gòu/ reach

1266 骂 /mà/ scold, tell off; call names, curse; condemn

1267 传 /chuán/ pass on, spread; hand down

1268 尊重 /zūnzhòng/ respect, value

1275 进去 /jìnqù/ go in

1284 流 /liú/ flow

1285 排 /pái/ arrange, line, put in order; exclude, discharge

1286 执行 /zhíxíng/ implement, carry out

1291 举 /jǔ/ lift, raise; enumerate, give (an example)

1297 着 /zháo/ touch (the ground, land); catch (cold); (fire) be lit, catch fire; succeed in

1308 创作 /chuàngzuò/ create (especially literary works), write

1309 拒绝 /jùjué/ refuse, reject, decline

1310 体现 /tǐxiàn/ embody, show

1316 死亡 /sǐwáng/ die

1318 存 /cún/ exist; deposit; accumulate; check (luggage), leave something with someone

1323 向 /xiàng/ side with, be partial to, favour

1324 打开 /dǎkāi/ open

1332 取 /qǔ/ get, take, fetch

1333 吹 /chuī/ blow, puff; play (flute, etc.); boast; (lovers) break up, (plan, etc.) fall through

1334 准 /zhǔn/ allow, permit

1335 治 /zhì/ rule, govern; treat, cure; control, harness; punish

1346 追 /zhuī/ chase, pursue; court, woo

1347 信 /xìn/ believe, believe in

1351 满足 /mǎnzú/ satisfy

1352 作出 /zuòchū/ make

1355 破坏 /pòhuài/ wreck, destroy, damage

1356 吸引 /xīyǐn/ attract

1365 把 /bǎ/ guard; hold

1370 宣传 /xuānchuán/ propagate, publicise, promote

1371 导致 /dǎozhì/ cause, lead to, result in

1372 交往 /jiāowǎng/ associate with, consort with

1378 犯 /fàn/ commit (crime, mistake, etc.); violate, offend (rule, etc.); have a recurrence of (illness, bad habit, etc.)

1386 该 /gāi/ should, ought to

1387 实践 /shíjiàn/ practise

1394 考 /kǎo/ take an examination, test or quiz, test

1395 表达 /biǎodá/ express, voice (one's opinion)

1396 冲突 /chōngtū/ conflict, clash with

1402 望 /wàng/ have a look; hope

1403 旅游 /lǚyóu/ travel, take a tour, go sightseeing

1409 享受 /xiǎngshòu/ lead a life of pleasure; enjoy (rights, benefits, etc.)

1410 消费 /xiāofèi/ consume

1411 游 /yóu/ swim; travel around

1412 了 /liǎo/ finish, settle; [occurring in the structure of verb + 得/不 + 了 to express possibility]

1420 开展 /kāizhǎn/ develop, launch (a campaign), carry out

1421 处于 /chǔyú/ be (in a certain state, position or condition)

1422 感谢 /gǎnxiè/ thank, be grateful, express gratitude

1423 表明 /biǎomíng/ make known or clear; state clearly; show

1426 符合 /fúhé/ accord with, be in keeping with

1427 打电话 /dǎdiànhuà/ make a telephone call

1431 加入 /jiārù/ join, become a member; add (in)

1435 思考 /sīkǎo/ think, ponder over, reflect on

1438 减少 /jiǎnshǎo/ reduce, lessen, decrease

1439 评价 /píngjià/ evaluate, assess

1443 念 /niàn/ read aloud; think of, miss; attend school

1448 在于 /zàiyú/ lie in, consist in, depend on

1451 统一 /tǒngyī/ unify, unite; standardise

1452 闹 /nào/ make noise or disturbance; give vent to (anger, etc.); be troubled with; go in for

1456 寻找 /xúnzhǎo/ look for, seek

1463 进来 /jìnlái/ come in

1464 伤 /shāng/ injure, hurt; do harm to

1467 寄 /jì/ send, post; check (luggage), leave with

1468 压 /yā/ press

1475 费 /fèi/ expend; consume too much, be wasteful

1479 戴 /dài/ put on, wear

1480 失败 /shībài/ fail, be defeated

1485 访问 /fǎngwèn/ visit, pay a visit (to)

1486 解放 /jiěfàng/ liberate; emancipate

1487 生存 /shēngcún/ subsist, live

1489 允许 /yǔnxǔ/ permit, allow

1490 抢 /qiǎng/ rob, loot; snatch, grab; vie for; rush

1491 制定 /zhìdìng/ draw up, make, set forth

1493 演出 /yǎnchū/ perform, put on a show

1494 组成 /zǔchéng/ form, make up, constitute; consist of

1499 代表 /dàibiǎo/ represent, stand for, act on one's behalf

1500 放弃 /fàngqì/ give up, quit

1501 修 /xiū/ repair, mend, fix; build; trim, prune

1509 熟悉 /shúxī/ be familiar with

1512 照 /zhào/ shine, beam, light up; reflect, mirror

1517 从事 /cóngshì/ go in for, be engaged in

1518 做到 /zuòdào/ accomplish, achieve, manage to do something

1524 赢 /yíng/ win, gain; beat

1525 登 /dēng/ ascend, mount, climb; board; print, publish

1526 改造 /gǎizào/ change, transform, reform, reclaim; remodel, convert

1527 召开 /zhāokāi/ convene (a conference or meeting), hold

1528 出版 /chūbǎn/ publish

1533 指导 /zhǐdǎo/ guide, direct

1534 争 /zhēng/ contend for, vie for; argue

1535 结 /jié, jiē/ form; settle; tie, knit, knot; bear (fruit)

1541 估计 /gūjì/ estimate

1542 制造 /zhìzào/ make, manufacture

1543 战 /zhàn/ fight

1548 查 /chá/ look up, consult; check, examine; investigate, look into

1549 维护 /wéihù/ defend, safeguard; uphold, maintain

1550 适应 /shìyìng/ suit; adapt to

1552 联合 /liánhé/ join forces, unite, band together; combine

1553 盖 /gài/ cover; build (a house); affix (a seal); surpass

1558 读书 /dúshū/ read, study; attend school

1559 负 /fù/ bear; take (responsibility); fail; lose (a match)

1562 兼 /jiān/ hold (different posts) concurrently

1563 监督 /jiāndū/ supervise, control

1564 显示 /xiǎnshì/ show

1569 观察 /guānchá/ observe

1575 关 /guān/ close, shut; turn off; concern, involve; shut in, lock up; (business) close down

1576 等 /děng/ wait

1577 鼓励 /gǔlì/ encourage

1580 含 /hán/ keep in mouth; contain, include

1847 需 /xū/ need, require

1855 团结 /tuánjié/ unite

1856 进攻 /jìn'gōng/ attack, take the offensive

1857 牺牲 /xīshēng/ sacrifice

1858 练 /liàn/ practise

1859 围 /wéi/ gather round; wrap round; surround, enclose

1860 回忆 /huíyì/ recall, recollect, bring to mind

1866 对待 /duìdài/ treat

1876 配合 /pèihé/ coordinate, cooperate

1877 陪 /péi/ accompany, escort

1878 乘 /chéng/ ride, travel by; take advantage of; multiply

1887 吓 /xià, hè/ frighten, scare; threaten

1888 缺 /quē/ lack; be absent, be missing

1889 赚 /zhuàn/ earn, make a profit

1890 培训 /péixùn/ train

1901 运动 /yùndòng/ move; do sports activities

1909 出发 /chūfā/ start out

1910 邀请 /yāoqǐng/ invite

1911 观 /guān/ watch, look at

1916 放心 /fàngxīn/ rest assured, feel relieved, set one's mind at rest

1917 恨 /hèn/ hate

1918 获 /huò/ win, obtain, reap

1919 制作 /zhìzuò/ make

1928 逼 /bī/ force, press; close in on

1929 害怕 /hàipà/ be afraid, be scared

1930 出生 /chūshēng/ be born

1931 配 /pèi/ match; deserve; fit; mix; join

1932 欣赏 /xīnshǎng/ appreciate, enjoy

1933 涉及 /shèjí/ involve, concern, cover

1940 忘记 /wàngjì/ forget

1941 构成 /gòuchéng/ constitute, comprise

1942 救 /jiù/ save, rescue

1943 作战 /zuòzhàn/ fight, conduct military operations

1950 混 /hùn/ mix, confuse; muddle along

1951 供 /gōng, gòng/ supply, offer; confess; enshrine

1952 举办 /jǔbàn/ conduct, hold

1953 为主 /wéizhǔ/ give priority to, form the main part

1963 经历 /jīnglì/ experience, live through

1964 搭 /dā/ build, put up; travel by; come into contact

1965 产 /chǎn/ produce, yield; reproduce

1980 抽 /chōu/ draw, take out

1981 答应 /dāying/ answer, reply; agree, promise

1982 撞 /zhuàng/ bump against, collide; run into

1983 治疗 /zhìliáo/ treat

1989 挑 /tiāo, tiǎo/ carry on a pole, shoulder; choose, select; push up, stir up

1990 嫁 /jià/ marry, take as husband

1991 维持 /wéichí/ maintain, keep; continue, last; sustain

1995 挤 /jǐ/ squeeze, press, push; crowd

1996 夺 /duó/ seize, take by force; contend for

2003 发言 /fāyán/ make a speech, make a statement, take the floor

2010 躺 /tǎng/ lie, recline

2011 脱 /tuō/ take off (clothes, shoes, etc.); shed, come off

2012 展开 /zhǎnkāi/ unfold, launch, set off; spread

2013 懂得 /dǒngde/ understand

2014 主持 /zhǔchí/ preside over

2021 除 /chú/ remove, get rid of; divide

2024 据说 /jùshuō/ it is said that

2025 避免 /bìmiǎn/ avoid, avert

2026 战斗 /zhàndòu/ fight, combat

2027 发动 /fādòng/ start, launch; mobilise

2028 体会 /tǐhuì/ know (through learning or by experience)

2029 降 /jiàng/ drop, fall, decline, decrease, lower

2039 长 /zhǎng/ grow, develop; increase

2040 剩下 /shèngxià/ remain, be left over

2041 挑战 /tiǎozhàn/ challenge

2048 逃 /táo/ escape, flee, run away

2049 攻击 /gōngjī/ attack

2050 提到 /tídào/ mention

2054 拖 /tuō/ drag, haul; delay, put off; mop (the floor)

2055 付出 /fùchū/ pay, give . . . as a price

2056 欲 /yù/ desire, want, wish; (be) about to

2067 隔 /gé/ separate; be apart; partition

2068 赛 /sài/ compete; surpass

2069 批准 /pīzhǔn/ approve

2070 离婚 /líhūn/ divorce

2079 叫做 /jiàozuò/ be called

2080 创新 /chuàngxīn/ innovate, be creative

2081 兴 /xīng/ prevail, be in fashion; promote; permit; allow

2094 居 /jū/ live, reside; rank

2099 选举 /xuǎnjǔ/ elect

2100 提醒 /tíxǐng/ remind

2101 做好 /zuòhǎo/ do well

2109 骑 /qí/ ride (a bike, horse, etc.); straddle

2110 睡觉 /shuìjiào/ go to bed, sleep

2111 上班 /shàngbān/ go to work

2112 答 /dá/ answer, reply

2113 消失 /xiāoshī/ disappear

2114 集 /jí/ gather, collect; centre on

2122 抬 /tái/ lift, raise; carry

2123 斗 /dòu/ fight; contend with

2139 演 /yǎn/ perform, play, show

2140 咬 /yǎo/ bite

2141 限制 /xiànzhì/ restrict

2142 意味着 /yìwèizhe/ mean, imply

2143 树 /shù/ set, set up; uphold

2493 计算 /jìsuàn/ calculate, compute

2494 吸收 /xīshōu/ absorb, draw; enrol, recruit

2495 防止 /fángzhǐ/ prevent

2496 会见 /huìjiàn/ meet with (somebody who is paying a visit for official business)

2497 汇报 /huìbào/ report

2498 加快 /jiākuài/ quicken, expedite, speed up

2514 打算 /dǎsuàn/ plan, intend

2515 绕 /rào/ move around, make a detour; wind, make (wire, cable, etc.) into a coil or ball

2516 批判 /pīpàn/ criticise

2517 害 /hài/ do harm to; suffer from (illness); cause trouble to

2518 减 /jiǎn/ subtract, minus; reduce, cut

2519 摆脱 /bǎituō/ get rid of, break away from

2520 恋 /liàn/ love, feel attached to

2522 列 /liè/ list, itemise

2531 跨 /kuà/ step across, stride, step forward; overarch

2532 修改 /xiūgǎi/ revise, amend

2533 砸 /zá/ smash

2541 到达 /dàodá/ arrive, reach

2542 提前 /tíqián/ advance (to an earlier date or time); do something in advance or ahead of time

2543 为止 /wéizhǐ/ until, up to; that's all for ...

2544 似 /sì/ seem, appear

2555 踢 /tī/ kick

2556 少 /shǎo/ be short, lack; [usually in imperatives] stop, quit

2557 保留 /bǎoliú/ keep, retain

2558 超 /chāo/ exceed, surpass, go beyond; overtake

2559 插 /chā/ insert, plug

2567 补充 /bǔchōng/ add; complement; replenish

2568 伸 /shēn/ stretch, extend

2569 企图 /qǐtú/ attempt

2570 炒 /chǎo/ stir fry; speculate, drive up (value or price through manipulation)

2571 居住 /jūzhù/ live, reside, inhabit

2572 思 /sī/ think

2573 碰到 /pèngdào/ come across, meet with

2574 主管 /zhǔguǎn/ take charge of, head

2583 奋斗 /fèndòu/ strive, struggle

2585 连 /lián/ join, link, connect

2587 创 /chuàng/ achieve, set (a record)

2588 砍 /kǎn/ chop, cut

2589 公布 /gōngbù/ announce, publicise

2590 进展 /jìnzhǎn/ make progress

2609 判断 /pànduàn/ judge

2610 拍摄 /pāishè/ take (a picture), shoot (a film)

2628 听见 /tīngjiàn/ hear

2629 摔 /shuāi/ fall; break, cause to fall and break; throw, fling

2630 出身 /chūshēn/ come from (a particular family background)

2631 引进 /yǐnjìn/ introduce from elsewhere, import; bring in

2644 埋 /mái/ cover up, bury

2645 交换 /jiāohuàn/ change, exchange

2646 掏 /tāo/ take out, produce (from pocket)

2647 报 /bào/ report; announce; recompense, reclaim; repay (one's kindness); revenge

2648 再说 /zàishuō/ put off for future decision

2649 发行 /fāxíng/ publish, issue, release, distribute

2650 期待 /qīdài/ look forward to, long for

2662 参观 /cānguān/ visit

2663 碰 /pèng/ touch

2664 接待 /jiēdài/ receive (a guest)

2666 引导 /yǐndǎo/ guide, lead

2668 推出 /tuīchū/ present, introduce

2686 扣 /kòu/ button up, buckle; deduct; detain

2687 盯 /dīng/ stare, keep an eye on

2688 迎 /yíng/ welcome; go to meet; move against

2689 爆炸 /bàozhà/ explode

2690 有利于 /yǒulìyú/ be beneficial to, be helpful to

2691 著 /zhù/ write

2692 签 /qiān/ sign

2693 出于 /chūyú/ start from, stem from; come out of

2704 同情 /tóngqíng/ show pity or compassion

2705 订 /dìng/ book, order, reserve; draw up, conclude; subscribe; staple

2706 出席 /chūxí/ attend

2707 送给 /sònggěi/ give

2708 喝酒 /hējiǔ/ drink (alcohol)

2709 回国 /huíguó/ return to one's country

2723 偷 /tōu/ steal

2724 整理 /zhěnglǐ/ sort

2725 显 /xiǎn/ show, display; be apparent or obvious

2733 运行 /yùnxíng/ move, be in motion; run, operate

2742 疼 /téng/ ache, have a pain, hurt; love dearly

2743 吵 /chǎo/ quarrel, have a row

2744 赞成 /zànchéng/ support, approve, be in favour of

2745 聚 /jù/ gather together

2746 渴望 /kěwàng/ be eager to, long for

2747 到来 /dàolái/ arrive

2748 承受 /chéngshòu/ bear, endure

2759 微笑 /wēixiào/ smile

2760 浪费 /làngfèi/ waste

2761 战胜 /zhànshèng/ beat, defeat, triumph over; overcome, surmount

2762 攻 /gōng/ attack; specialise in

2763 记住 /jìzhù/ remember

2764 舞 /wǔ/ dance; wield

2766 建成 /jiànchéng/ complete, finish building

2767 联 /lián/ ally, join

2782 带有 /dàiyǒu/ have, carry, bear

2799 侵略 /qīnlüè/ invade

2800 临 /lín/ face, overlook; be present; be about to

2801 防 /fáng/ prevent, guard against; defend

2803 消除 /xiāochú/ eliminate, remove

2804 遭 /zāo/ [sometimes written as 遭到] suffer, encounter

2805 分布 /fēnbù/ distribute, spread

2806 来看 /láikàn/ judge from

2807 看出 /kànchū/ make out, see, find

2821 推广 /tuīguǎng/ popularise, promote

2822 止 /zhǐ/ stop, end

2823 拨 /bō/ move; dial (a phone number); allocate

2824 交谈 /jiāotán/ talk, converse

2826 拉开 /lākāi/ draw open; space out

2839 亮 /liàng/ get light, show, reveal; shine; lift (one's voice)

2840 统治 /tǒngzhì/ rule over, reign; dominate

2841 欠 /qiàn/ owe; lack, be short

2842 缺少 /quēshǎo/ lack, be short of

2843 捧 /pěng/ hold (in both hands); give somebody a boost

2844 取消 /qǔxiāo/ cancel

2845 重复 /chóngfù/ repeat

2846 奔 /bēn, bèn/ rush, run quickly; head for; approach

2871 例如 /lìrú/ take . . . for example

2872 忍 /rěn/ bear, endure, stand, put up with

2873 善于 /shànyú/ be good at

2874 办事 /bànshì/ attend to (a matter); act

2875 对付 /duìfu/ deal with, cope with; make do with

2876 冲击 /chōngjī/ charge, attack, assault; lash

2877 露 /lù, lòu/ show, reveal

2893 比 /bǐ/ compare; match, liken to

2894 切 /qiē/ cut, carve

2895 生气 /shēngqì/ be angry

2896 踏 /tà/ step on

2908 游泳 /yóuyǒng/ swim

2909 克服 /kèfú/ overcome

2910 跪 /guì/ kneel down, fall to one's knees

2911 保存 /bǎocún/ preserve; save (a computer file, etc.)

2912 消灭 /xiāomiè/ perish, eliminate

2913 记录 /jìlù/ record, put down

2914 富有 /fùyǒu/ be wealthy; be rich in

2915 载 /zǎi, zài/ record; carry (in a vehicle)

2916 上网 /shàngwǎng/ get on the internet, go online

2932 接到 /jiēdào/ receive, get

2933 违反 /wéifǎn/ violate

2934 袭击 /xíjī/ assault, hit; surprise

2935 放松 /fàngsōng/ relax; loosen

2936 体验 /tǐyàn/ experience

2937 转向 /zhuǎnxiàng/ change direction

2938 名叫 /míngjiào/ be called

2939 咨询 /zīxún/ consult

2940 能否 /néngfǒu/ whether or not one can

2961 剩 /shèng/ leave over, remain

2962 煮 /zhǔ/ cook, boil

2963 否定 /fǒudìng/ negate

2964 添 /tiān/ add

2965 商 /shāng/ discuss, consult

2966 喜 /xǐ/ like, be fond of

2984 支援 /zhīyuán/ support, aid

2985 踩 /cǎi/ step on, tread on

2986 涌 /yǒng/ gush, surge; rush

2987 流动 /liúdòng/ flow, surge

2988 返回 /fǎnhuí/ return

3007 比较 /bǐjiào/ compare

3008 患 /huàn/ suffer from, fall ill with, catch

3009 须 /xū/ must, have to

3010 如同 /rútóng/ like, as

3011 挨 /āi, ái/ be next to; get close to; suffer, endure

3012 探讨 /tàntǎo/ explore, approach, investigate

3013 呈现 /chéngxiàn/ show, appear

3014 前往 /qiánwǎng/ go to, leave for

3027 热爱 /rè'ài/ love

3028 握 /wò/ hold, grasp

3029 生长 /shēngzhǎng/ grow

3030 透 /tòu/ penetrate, pass through; reveal, let out

3031 租 /zū/ rent, hire

3032 评 /píng/ comment, review; judge, appraise; choose

3033 不见 /bújiàn/ disappear, miss; not meet

3034 去世 /qùshì/ die, pass away

3035 呈 /chéng/ assume (shape, colour, property, etc.); submit, present

3036 确保 /quèbǎo/ ensure, make sure

3037 表 /biǎo/ express, show

3038 打断 /dǎduàn/ interrupt, cut short

3039 指责 /zhǐzé/ criticise, accuse

3053 主张 /zhǔzhāng/ advocate, maintain, argue for

3055 签订 /qiāndìng/ sign (an agreement, contract and treaty, etc.)

3056 印 /yìn/ print

3057 探 /tàn/ explore; visit; stretch forward

3058 惊 /jīng/ surprise, shock

3059 损害 /sǔnhài/ harm

3060 注重 /zhùzhòng/ lay stress on, take pains with

3061 露出 /lùchū/ show, reveal

3069 移动 /yídòng/ move

3070 填 /tián/ fill; fill in, complete (a form)

3071 拆 /chāi/ dismantle, take apart, pull down

3072 夹 /jiā/ hold between, put in between; carry under one's arm; mingle, mix

3073 发起 /fāqǐ/ initiate, sponsor, launch

3075 前来 /qiánlái/ come over

3076 附 /fù/ enclose, attach

3077 否认 /fǒurèn/ deny

3078 不能 /bùnéng/ can't

3093 贯彻 /guànchè/ implement, carry out

3094 捞 /lāo/ take something out of water, fish for; gain, get (money or benefits) by improper means

3095 提倡 /tíchàng/ advocate, promote

3096 独立 /dúlì/ be independent

3097 禁止 /jìnzhǐ/ prohibit, ban

3098 闯 /chuǎng/ rush, dash; break in

3099 推荐 /tuījiàn/ recommend

3117 喜爱 /xǐ'ài/ like, love

3118 罚 /fá/ penalise, punish

3119 诞生 /dànshēng/ be born

3120 加大 /jiādà/ increase, enlarge

3121 得知 /dézhī/ learn, hear, get to know

3122 承诺 /chéngnuò/ undertake, promise

3137 围绕 /wéirào/ revolve around; surround

3138 摘 /zhāi/ pick, pluck, take off; make a summary

3139 不顾 /búgù/ have no regard for, neglect

3140 占有 /zhànyǒu/ have, possess; occupy, hold

3141 整 /zhěng/ put in order; punish

3142 怀 /huái/ cherish, keep in mind; be pregnant

3143 聊天 /liáotiān/ chat

3144 学会 /xuéhuì/ learn

3145 当作 /dàngzuò/ treat as, regard as

3146 响 /xiǎng/ sound, make a sound, (of applause) break out, (of telephone) ring

3147 庆 /qìng/ celebrate

3162 习惯 /xíguàn/ be used to, be accustomed to

3163 涨 /zhǎng, zhàng/ (of prices, rivers, etc.) rise; swell

3164 摇 /yáo/ shake, rock, wave, wag

3165 暴露 /bàolù/ expose, reveal

3166 吐 /tǔ, tù/ spit, disgorge; vomit, throw up

3167 得以 /déyǐ/ be able to

3187 对 /duì/ answer; counter; be directed at; compare; suit, agree; match

3188 扶 /fú/ support or hold with hand

3189 积累 /jīlěi/ accumulate

3190 敲 /qiāo/ knock, tap; strike; fleece

3191 描写 /miáoxiě/ describe, portray

3192 进口 /jìnkǒu/ import

3193 蒙 /mēng, méng/ deceive, take in; be shocked; make a wild guess; cover

3194 服 /fú/ take (medicine); be convinced, obey

3195 拼 /pīn/ piece together, join; spell; go all out

3196 预防 /yùfáng/ prevent, secure against

3197 讲究 /jiǎngjiù/ be careful about; strive for

3198 证实 /zhèngshí/ confirm, prove

3199 受伤 /shòushāng/ hurt, be wounded, be injured

3200 命 /mìng/ command, order

3215 请问 /qǐngwèn/ [used as a polite expression when asking for information] may I ask . . .

3216 搁 /gē/ place, put; put aside

3217 保卫 /bǎowèi/ guard, defend

3218 议论 /yìlùn/ remark on, comment on

3219 迎接 /yíngjiē/ meet, welcome, usher in

3220 动员 /dòngyuán/ mobilise

3221 联络 /liánluò/ get or keep in contact or liaison

3222 传来 /chuánlái/ (news, sound, etc.) come

3223 超越 /chāoyuè/ surmount, surpass; overtake

3236 扫 /sǎo/ sweep (away), brush; pass quickly, glance

3237 灭 /miè/ (of fire, light) go off; extinguish, put out, wipe out

3238 脱离 /tuōlí/ leave, separate; break away from, divorce

3239 出门 /chūmén/ go out, be away from home

3240 调动 /diàodòng/ transfer, shift, move; bring . . . into play

3241 扬 /yáng/ raise; spread

3242 判 /pàn/ sentence; judge

3262 争论 /zhēnglùn/ argue, debate

3263 藏 /cáng/ hide

3264 抄 /chāo/ copy

3265 深入 /shēnrù/ penetrate deeply, go deep into

3266 喂 /wèi/ feed

3267 寻求 /xúnqiú/ seek, look for

3268 退出 /tuìchū/ withdraw, drop out of

3269 自杀 /zìshā/ commit suicide

3270 开车 /kāichē/ drive (a car)

3287 度过 /dùguò/ pass, spend (time)

3288 想像 /xiǎngxiàng/ imagine

3289 告别 /gàobié/ leave, say goodbye to

3290 感染 /gǎnrǎn/ infect; affect

3291 决 /jué/ decide; (of a dam or dyke) burst

3292 施 /shī/ impose, exert, carry out; use, apply; give, bestow

3315 刮 /guā/ scrape; shave; (of wind) blow

3316 上课 /shàngkè/ (of students) attend class; (of teachers) give a lesson

3317 带领 /dàilǐng/ lead, guide

3318 警告 /jǐnggào/ warn

3319 置 /zhì/ put, place; buy

3320 包装 /bāozhuāng/ pack, wrap up

3321 看待 /kàndài/ regard, view

3322 杀人 /shārén/ commit manslaughter, murder, kill

3323 引发 /yǐnfā/ trigger, evoke

3324 食 /shí/ eat

3325 没事 /méishì/ be free; it's nothing, it's all right

3344 客气 /kèqì/ be polite; be courteous; act politely; be modest

3345 采购 /cǎigòu/ purchase; do shopping

3346 刻 /kè/ cut, carve, inscribe

3347 考验 /kǎoyàn/ try, test, put to test

3348 转化 /zhuǎnhuà/ transform, change into

3349 撤 /chè/ remove; withdraw, evacuate, retreat

3350 承包 /chéngbāo/ contract

3351 予以 /yǔyǐ/ give, bestow

3352 讨厌 /tǎoyàn/ dislike, hate

3378 登记 /dēngjì/ register; check in (at hotel, etc.)

3379 回头 /huítóu/ turn round

3380 打听 /dǎtīng/ ask about, enquire

3381 撒 /sā, sǎ/ sprinkle, spray, scatter, spread; cast, let go, let out; spill

3382 锁 /suǒ/ lock (up)

3383 寻 /xún/ look for, seek

3384 招 /zhāo/ beckon; enrol, recruit; provoke; confess

3385 展现 /zhǎnxiàn/ unfold, present

3386 启动 /qǐdòng/ start, initiate

3387 治理 /zhìlǐ/ govern; harness

3388 花钱 /huāqián/ spend money

3402 遭受 /zāoshòu/ suffer

3403 动手 /dòngshǒu/ set out, start; use hand (to fight or touch)

3404 援助 /yuánzhù/ provide help, aid or support

3405 安 /ān/ fix, install, set up; be contented

3406 赶上 /gǎnshàng/ catch up with

3407 扯 /chě/ pull; tear (off, into pieces); chat

3408 打工 /dǎgōng/ work (especially referring to doing odd jobs or manual labour)

3409 履行 /lǚxíng/ fulfil

3411 设置 /shèzhì/ set, set up

3412 透露 /tòulù/ reveal, disclose

3427 收拾 /shōushí/ sort out, put in order

3428 闪 /shǎn/ flash, flicker; dodge

3429 痛 /tòng/ hurt, ache, pain

3430 跌 /diē/ fall; (price) drop

3431 办理 /bànlǐ/ handle

3432 描述 /miáoshù/ describe, depict

3451 危害 /wēihài/ endanger, jeopardise

3452 呼吸 /hūxī/ breathe

3453 部署 /bùshǔ/ dispose, deploy

3454 抵 /dǐ/ reach, arrive; balance, be equal to; make up for; resist

3455 迷 /mí/ bewilder, confuse; be fascinated by

3456 播 /bō/ sow, seed; broadcast

3457 抗 /kàng/ resist, fight; refuse, defy

3458 期望 /qīwàng/ expect, look forward to

3459 拜 /bài/ worship, pay respect; visit

3476 翻译 /fānyì/ translate

3477 不如 /bùrú/ be not as good as, be inferior to

3478 献 /xiàn/ offer, present; dedicate

3479 办公 /bàn'gōng/ handle official business; open, work (in office)

3480 拔 /bá/ pull up, pull out

3481 庆祝 /qìngzhù/ celebrate

3482 种 /zhòng/ plant

3483 架 /jià/ put up, set up; support

3484 泡 /pào/ steep, soak; dawdle

3485 顺 /shùn/ obey, yield to; put something in order

3486 嫌 /xián/ dislike, mind

3487 撑 /chēng/ prop up, support; open (an umbrella, etc.); overfill; pole (a boat)

3488 分开 /fēnkāi/ separate

3510 巩固 /gǒnggù/ consolidate, strengthen

3511 逛 /guàng/ stroll

3512 随 /suí/ follow, comply with; allow one to do as one likes

3513 哼 /hēng/ hum

3514 丧失 /sàngshī/ lose

3515 乐 /lè/ be amused; find pleasure in, enjoy, be happy

3516 询问 /xúnwèn/ enquire, question

3517 熬 /áo/ endure, get through; cook, boil

3519 回避 /huíbì/ evade, avoid, bypass

3520 赢得 /yíngdé/ win

3521 演习 /yǎnxí/ hold (military) exercises, manoeuvre

3522 访 /fǎng/ visit, call on

3523 支撑 /zhīchēng/ prop up, support; sustain, hold

3524 回报 /huíbào/ return, repay

3548 蹲 /dūn/ crouch, squat

3549 感觉 /gǎnjué/ feel

3550 清 /qīng/ clear up; settle

3551 染 /rǎn/ catch (a disease), addict; dye

3552 捡 /jiǎn/ pick up

3553 阻止 /zǔzhǐ/ prevent, stop

3554 留学 /liúxué/ study abroad

3555 交代 /jiāodài/ hand over; explain, make clear; confess

3556 供应 /gōngyìng/ supply, serve (a meal)

3557 关怀 /guānhuái/ care for

3558 放到 /fàngdào/ put (something at a particular place)

3559 确认 /quèrèn/ confirm

3560 预测 /yùcè/ forecast

3562 试图 /shìtú/ attempt, try

3577 赔 /péi/ compensate, make good (one's loss); lose in business, sustain a loss

3578 报复 /bàofù/ retaliate, pay back, put it across

3579 检验 /jiǎnyàn/ test, check, verify

3580 抛 /pāo/ throw, toss, fling; leave behind

3581 加速 /jiāsù/ accelerate; expedite, speed up

3582 凑 /còu/ put together, come together; move closer

3583 审查 /shěnchá/ examine, look through

3584 收购 /shōugòu/ purchase, buy

3585 上市 /shàngshì/ put (goods and shares, etc.) on the market

3586 消 /xiāo/ disappear, cause to disappear

3587 违法 /wéifǎ/ break the law, be against the law, be illegal

3611 展览 /zhǎnlǎn/ exhibit, put on display

3612 发明 /fāmíng/ invent

3613 觉 /jué/ feel; become aware

3614 记载 /jìzǎi/ record, write down

3615 助 /zhù/ help, aid, assist

3616 建造 /jiànzào/ build, construct

3617 散 /sǎn, sàn/ fall apart, come loose; break up, disperse; spread, distribute

3618 执 /zhí/ hold, grasp

3619 叹 /tàn/ sigh

3620 做人 /zuòrén/ conduct oneself, behave; be an upright or decent person

3621 依赖 /yīlài/ depend on, count on

3622 跃 /yuè/ leap, jump

3623 讨 /tǎo/ ask for, beg; take (as wife)

3624 辞职 /cízhí/ resign, quit

3625 禁 /jìn, jīn/ prohibit, ban; endure

3642 开玩笑 /kāiwánxiào/ play a joke, make fun of

3643 率领 /shuàilǐng/ lead

3644 采 /cǎi/ pick, gather; mine

3645 干涉 /gānshè/ meddle in

3646 投降 /tóuxiáng/ surrender, give in

3647 怪 /guài/ blame

3648 侵犯 /qīnfàn/ violate, infringe

3649 崇拜 /chóngbài/ worship, adore

3650 留给 /liúgěi/ leave, set aside for

3651 兴奋 /xīngfèn/ be excited

3652 转身 /zhuǎnshēn/ turn round

3653 当成 /dàngchéng/ take for, regard as

3654 善 /shàn/ be good at; be apt to

3656 注册 /zhùcè/ register

3679 尝 /cháng/ taste

3680 烤 /kǎo/ roast, bake, toast; get warm or dry by the fire

3681 过年 /guònián/ celebrate the New Year

3682 沉 /chén/ sink, submerge

3683 设想 /shèxiǎng/ imagine

3684 收回 /shōuhuí/ take back, recover; withdraw

3685 推行 /tuīxíng/ carry out, push on with

3686 尝试 /chángshì/ try, attempt

3687 考上 /kǎoshàng/ be admitted by examination, pass

3688 看上去 /kànshàngqù/ look, appear

3689 释放 /shìfàng/ set free, release

3722 祝 /zhù/ wish

3723 改进 /gǎijìn/ improve

3724 牵 /qiān/ lead, lead along

3725 帮忙 /bāngmáng/ help

3726 纠正 /jiūzhèng/ correct, rectify

3727 测 /cè/ measure, gauge

3728 伸手 /shēnshǒu/ hold out one's hand; ask for

3729 对抗 /duìkàng/ resist, act against, withstand

3730 塑造 /sùzào/ shape, mould; portray (literary characters)

3731 支付 /zhīfù/ pay, make a payment

3732 捐 /juān/ donate, contribute

3757 处 /chǔ/ be in; get along; sentence, punish

3758 下班 /xiàbān/ get off work

3759 阅读 /yuèdú/ read

3760 如下 /rúxià/ as follows

3761 盼 /pàn/ expect, long for, look forward to

3762 抗议 /kàngyì/ protest

3763 策划 /cèhuá/ plot, plan

3765 示 /shì/ show

3766 识 /shí/ know

3767 免 /miǎn/ excuse from, waive, exempt; dismiss; avoid

3769 评估 /pínggū/ evaluate, assess

3812 旅行 /lǚxíng/ travel

3813 惹 /rě/ provoke, cause, make; offend, get on one's nerves

3814 应付 /yìngfu/ handle, deal with; do something perfunctiorily, make do

3815 协助 /xiézhù/ assist, help

3816 抵抗 /dǐkàng/ resist

3817 停留 /tíngliú/ (stop and) stay; remain

3818 视为 /shìwéi/ deem, view as

3819 收费 /shōufèi/ charge

3820 伸出 /shēnchū/ stretch out, extend

3821 舍 /shě/ abandon, give up, part with

3822 清理 /qīnglǐ/ clear, sort out

3823 琢磨 /zhuómó, zuómo/ carve and polish, polish and refine; think over, ponder

3853 练习 /liànxí/ practise

3854 概括 /gàikuò/ recapitulate, summarise, generalise

3855 布置 /bùzhì/ fix up, arrange, decorate; assign (work, homework, etc.)

3856 包含 /bāohán/ contain, include

3857 整顿 /zhěngdùn/ rectify

3858 收集 /shōují/ gather, collect

3859 问道 /wèndào/ ask

3860 迁 /qiān/ move

3861 指定 /zhǐdìng/ name, designate, assign, appoint

3862 抬头 /táitóu/ raise one's head, look up; hold one's head high; gain ground

3863 震惊 /zhènjīng/ shock, astonish

3882 反抗 /fǎnkàng/ resist, revolt, rebel

3883 遵守 /zūnshǒu/ abide by, observe

3884 观看 /guānkàn/ watch, see, view

3885 树立 /shùlì/ set up, establish

3886 珍惜 /zhēnxī/ treasure, value, cherish

3887 制止 /zhìzhǐ/ stop, curb, prevent

3888 争夺 /zhēngduó/ scramble for, contend for, contest

3889 被迫 /bèipò/ be compelled to, be forced to

3890 迷信 /míxìn/ have blind faith in

3891 可谓 /kěwèi/ it may well be said, so to speak

3892 点头 /diǎntóu/ nod

3893 摄 /shè/ take (a photograph)

3915 火 /huǒ/ get angry, be annoyed

3916 磨 /mó/ wear; rub; grind, polish; pester; dawdle

3917 分裂 /fēnliè/ split up, break apart

3918 游行 /yóuxíng/ parade, march

3919 自信 /zìxìn/ be confident

3920 高于 /gāoyú/ be higher than, be above

3921 解除 /jiěchú/ remove, relieve

3922 相处 /xiāngchǔ/ get along

3924 坐下 /zuòxià/ sit down

3925 运作 /yùnzuò/ operate

3954 浮 /fú/ float

3955 堵 /dǔ/ stop up, block

3956 施工 /shīgōng/ be under construction

3957 报名 /bàomíng/ sign up, enrol

3958 折 /zhé/ break, bend, fold; convert to

3959 喷 /pēn/ spurt, squirt, spray, sprinkle

3960 抑制 /yìzhì/ restrain, refrain

3961 忽视 /hūshì/ neglect, overlook

3962 防御 /fángyù/ defend, guard against

3963 沾 /zhān/ be stained with; touch, touch on

3964 惯 /guàn/ be accustomed to; be in the habit of; spoil (a child)

3965 等到 /děngdào/ wait until

3967 回归 /huíguī/ return

3968 始 /shǐ/ begin, start

3969 发布 /fābù/ issue, release, announce; promulgate

3970 度 /dù/ spend, pass (time)

3971 扮演 /bànyǎn/ play the role of, act as

3972 派出 /pàichū/ send

3973 任命 /rènmìng/ appoint

3974 讲述 /jiǎngshù/ talk about, tell

3975 养老 /yǎnglǎo/ provide for the elderly; live out one's life in retirement

3976 竞选 /jìngxuǎn/ run for (an office)

4008 失业 /shīyè/ become unemployed, be out of work

4009 称赞 /chēngzàn/ praise, speak well of

4010 睁 /zhēng/ open (eyes)

4011 欺骗 /qīpiàn/ deceive, cheat

4012 活跃 /huóyuè/ be active, make . . . active

4013 烫 /tàng/ scald, burn; iron, press; have one's hair permed

4014 流传 /liúchuán/ spread, circulate, pass down

4015 飞行 /fēixíng/ fly, make a flight

4016 译 /yì/ translate

4017 提起 /tíqǐ/ mention

4018 心想 /xīnxiǎng/ think

4020 布 /bù/ arrange, deploy; announce, declare

4021 注 /zhù/ annotate; pour, inject; concentrate

4055 松 /sōng/ loosen, unfasten

4056 割 /gē/ cut

4059 忍不住 /rěnbuzhù/ cannot help but

4060 包围 /bāowéi/ surround, encircle

4061 罢 /bà/ stop, cease; dismiss; [used as a resultative verb complement indicating completion] finish

4062 盛 /chéng/ fill (a bowl, etc.) with; hold, contain

4063 积 /jī/ accumulate, collect

4064 谢 /xiè/ thank; (of flowers) wither

4065 购物 /gòuwù/ do shopping

4066 走过 /zǒuguò/ cross, go through, walk past

4068 尊 /zūn/ respect

4069 收藏 /shōucáng/ collect

4070 增 /zēng/ increase

4094 号召 /hàozhào/ call for

4095 住院 /zhùyuàn/ be hospitalised

4096 服从 /fúcóng/ obey; be subordinate to

4097 小心 /xiǎoxīn/ be careful, take care; guard against

4098 燃烧 /ránshāo/ burn

4099 冻 /dòng/ freeze

4100 违背 /wéibèi/ violate, go against, be contrary to

4101 返 /fǎn/ return, go back

4102 促使 /cùshǐ/ impel, spur on, prompt

4103 干扰 /gānrǎo/ disturb

4104 委托 /wěituō/ entrust

4105 奉献 /fèngxiàn/ dedicate, devote, consecrate

4106 审 /shěn/ try; examine, review

4107 传递 /chuándì/ transmit, communicate, pass

4108 享有 /xiǎngyǒu/ enjoy (rights, etc.)

4109 延续 /yánxù/ continue, last

4110 挣钱 /zhèngqián/ earn money

4143 扛 /káng/ carry on one's shoulder, shoulder

4144 呼 /hū/ exhale, breathe; shout; call

4145 循环 /xúnhuán/ circle, circulate

4146 打架 /dǎjià/ fight

4147 瞪 /dèng/ stare at

4148 计 /jì/ count, calculate, number; haggle over

4149 写信 /xiěxìn/ write (a letter)

4150 鼓 /gǔ/ rouse, pluck up (encourage); bulge

4151 跟踪 /gēnzōng/ follow one's tracks, tail

4152 面向 /miànxiàng/ face

4153 占据 /zhànjù/ occupy, take up

4154 走路 /zǒulù/ walk, go on foot

4155 做事 /zuòshì/ act, work, do one's work

4156 继 /jì/ continue, follow

4157 认可 /rènkě/ approve of, accept

4158 敬 /jìng/ respect; offer politely

4191 扑 /pū/ rush at; throw oneself into, be bent on; flap

4192 披 /pī/ drape over one's shoulders

4193 飘 /piāo/ flutter or float (in the air)

4194 晓得 /xiǎode/ know

4195 挡 /dǎng/ keep off; block

4196 晒 /shài/ dry in the sun; sunbathe

4197 形容 /xíngróng/ describe

4198 震动 /zhèndòng/ shake, quake, vibrate; shock

4199 规划 /guīhuà/ plan

4200 往来 /wǎnglái/ contact, exchange visits; travel between

4201 射击 /shèjī/ shoot, fire

4202 赔偿 /péicháng/ compensate

4203 修建 /xiūjiàn/ build

4204 佩服 /pèifú/ admire

4205 抵达 /dǐdá/ arrive

4206 在场 /zàichǎng/ be present, be at the scene

4207 得出 /déchū/ obtain (results, conclusions, etc.)

4208 认同 /rèntóng/ identify with, accept, approve

4209 备 /bèi/ get ready; prepare against; be available, be equipped with

4210 回顾 /huígù/ look back, review

4211 下令 /xiàlìng/ give an order

4212 放开 /fàngkāi/ let go, release

4213 击 /jī/ hit, strike

4214 分为 /fēnwéi/ divide into

4254 祝贺 /zhùhè/ congratulate

4255 尊敬 /zūnjìng/ respect

4256 预备 /yùbèi/ prepare, get ready

4257 道歉 /dàoqiàn/ apologise

4258 递 /dì/ hand over, pass

4259 洒 /sǎ/ spray, sprinkle; spill

4260 愁 /chóu/ worry

4261 提问 /tíwèn/ ask questions; (teacher) put a question to

4263 怨 /yuàn/ blame; complain

4264 来往 /láiwǎng/ come and go, travel between; contact, associate with

4265 象征 /xiàngzhēng/ stand for, symbolise, signify

4266 耽误 /dānwù/ delay

4267 说服 /shuōfú/ convince, persuade

4268 伴 /bàn/ accompany

4269 提升 /tíshēng/ promote

4270 开门 /kāimén/ open the door, open

4271 惩罚 /chéngfá/ punish, penalise

4272 死去 /sǐqù/ die

4273 排除 /páichú/ exclude; remove, clear away

4274 营业 /yíngyè/ do business, be open

4275 安置 /ānzhì/ find a suitable place for, arrange for, help somebody to settle down; install, fix

4276 干活 /gànhuó/ work

4301 抓紧 /zhuājǐn/ grasp firmly; pay close attention; hurry

4302 代替 /dàitì/ substitute, replace

4303 聚集 /jùjí/ assemble, gather

4304 意识 /yìshí/ be conscious of, be aware of, realise

4305 膨胀 /péngzhàng/ expand, inflate

4306 制约 /zhìyuē/ constrain, condition, govern

4307 轮 /lún/ take turns

4308 资助 /zīzhù/ support, sponsor, finance

4309 抢救 /qiǎngjiù/ rescue, save

4310 取代 /qǔdài/ replace, take the place of

4311 分成 /fēnchéng/ divide into

4312 暗示 /ànshì/ suggest, imply

4313 划分 /huáfēn/ divide

4314 挖掘 /wājué/ dig, excavate; tap (potentials, talents, etc.)

4315 亏 /kuī/ lose money (in business); owe; treat unfairly

4341 通知 /tōngzhī/ notify, inform, give notice

4342 决心 /juéxīn/ pledge, resolve, be determined to

4343 羡慕 /xiànmù/ admire, envy

4554 叙述 /xùshù/ give an account of, tell about

4555 下岗 /xiàgǎng/ stand down; be laid off

4556 更新 /gèngxīn/ update, renew

4557 定位 /dìngwèi/ position, set on; locate

4558 响起 /xiǎngqǐ/ sound, make a sound, break out

4559 注定 /zhùdìng/ be doomed, be destined

4560 组合 /zǔhé/ assemble, combine

4561 淘汰 /táotài/ eliminate (through selection or competition); become obsolete

4562 致使 /zhìshǐ/ cause, result in

4563 散发 /sànfā/ distribute, circulate; give off, emit

4564 延伸 /yánshēn/ extend, stretch

4565 融 /róng/ melt, thaw; fuse, mix together

4566 赖 /lài/ rely, depend; go back on one's word; hold on in a place

4567 开拓 /kāituò/ open, open up

4604 消化 /xiāohuà/ digest

4605 催 /cuī/ urge, rush, chase up

4607 分工 /fēn'gōng/ divide up the work

4608 奖励 /jiǎnglì/ reward

4609 研制 /yánzhì/ develop

4610 在座 /zàizuò/ be present

4611 忍受 /rěnshòu/ bear, tolerate, put up with

4612 挺 /tǐng/ straighten up, stiffen; endure

4613 考核 /kǎohé/ examine, appraise, assess

4614 伴随 /bànsuí/ accompany, follow

4615 特有 /tèyǒu/ be unique to or characteristic of

4616 排名 /páimíng/ rank

4617 做饭 /zuòfàn/ cook

4618 弥补 /míbǔ/ make up, compensate, remedy

4619 用人 /yòngrén/ employ, make use of personnel

4620 勒 /lēi, lè/ tighten; strangle; rein in (the horse)

4621 接收 /jiēshōu/ receive

4622 关闭 /guānbì/ close, shut; (of business) close down

4623 转换 /zhuǎnhuàn/ change, switch, convert, transform

4668 原谅 /yuánliàng/ forgive

4669 接见 /jiējiàn/ receive, see

4671 建议 /jiànyì/ suggest, propose, advise

4672 缩 /suō/ shrink, contract; withdraw, draw back

4673 漏 /lòu/ leak; be missing

4674 宣告 /xuān'gào/ declare, proclaim

4675 耍 /shuǎ/ play, play with

4676 吞 /tūn/ swallow, bolt, devour

4677 夸张 /kuāzhāng/ exaggerate

4678 判决 /pànjué/ pass verdict, pronounce, judge

4679 超出 /chāochū/ be beyond or outside, exceed

4680 出差 /chūchāi/ be on a business trip

4681 忽略 /hūlüè/ neglect, ignore

4682 重建 /chóngjiàn/ reconstruct, rebuild

4683 赚钱 /zhuànqián/ make money

4684 升起 /shēngqǐ/ rise, ascend

4685 休 /xiū/ rest, take (leave); stop, cease

4686 乃 /nǎi/ be

4687 流血 /liúxuè/ bleed, shed blood

4716 吊 /diào/ hang, suspend (in the air); lift (with a rope); condole with; revoke

4717 晃 /huǎng, huàng/ dazzle; flash past; shake, jerk, sway

4718 对立 /duìlì/ be opposed

4719 栽 /zāi/ plant; frame; fall

4720 损 /sǔn/ damage, harm; lose; deride, be sarcastic

4721 融合 /rónghé/ merge, mix together

4722 搞好 /gǎohǎo/ do well, do a good job of

4723 上车 /shàngchē/ board, go aboard

4724 赏 /shǎng/ award, bestow (a reward); feast one's eyes on; appreciate

4725 倾 /qīng/ lean, bend; pour out

4726 外出 /wàichū/ go out, be away

4727 约束 /yuēshù/ bind, restrain

4728 命名 /mìngmíng/ name

4729 得罪 /dézuì/ offend

4755 参谋 /cānmóu/ give advice

4768 洗澡 /xǐzǎo/ bathe, take a bath or shower

4769 适用 /shìyòng/ apply

4770 迈 /mài/ stride, take a step

4771 请求 /qǐngqiú/ request, ask

4772 启发 /qǐfā/ enlighten, inspire, illuminate

4773 拥抱 /yōngbào/ embrace, hug

4774 打交道 /dǎjiāodào/ deal with; hang out with; work with

4775 参考 /cānkǎo/ consult, make reference to

4776 发育 /fāyù/ grow, develop (physically or mentally)

4777 困扰 /kùnrǎo/ perplex, puzzle, bother

4778 向往 /xiàngwǎng/ yearn for, look forward to, dream of

4780 低头 /dītóu/ hang (one's) head; give in, submit, bend, bow

4781 出售 /chūshòu/ sell

4782 毁灭 /huǐmiè/ destroy, perish

4783 审判 /shěnpàn/ try, bring to trial

4784 共有 /gòngyǒu/ total; share, have in common

4785 视察 /shìchá/ inspect

4786 处罚 /chǔfá/ punish, penalise

4826 夺取 /duóqǔ/ seize, capture; strive for, win

4827 思索 /sīsuǒ/ think deeply, ponder

4828 缩小 /suōxiǎo/ reduce; shrink

Character frequency index

Frequency rank **Simplified Chinese** [Traditional Chinese] /*Pinyin*/ (Optional HSK Level) List of headwords in word frequency index containing the character and word frequency ranks

0001 的 [的] /*de, dí, dì*/ (1) 的0001 有的0408 目的0728
的话0871 别的0963 似的1164 真的2147 的确2193
是的3330 有的是4124

0002 一 [一] /*yī*/ (1) 一0003 一些0115 一直0240
一起0252 一定0254 一切0366 一般0392 一样0402
一样0432 之一0568 一定0766 进一步1055 一边1124
唯一1263 一旦1336 一致1417 一半1445 统一1451
一生1460 一部分1882 一方面1913 一面1934 一时1977
统一2267 另一方面2593 一块2726 一日2838 一再2917
同一3020 一路3041 一向3226 一级3247 一流3591
万一3832 一律3833 惟一3983 一行4037 一手4078
一度4170 一道4220 同一4283 一带4289 单一4629
一共4845 一边4982 一块儿5004

0003 是 [是] /*shì*/ (1) 是0002 但是0155 就是0319
可是0404 于是0486 而是0570 还是0876 正是0887
总是0919 是否0935 还是1228 算是1670 只是1896
也就是说2535 要是2673 或是2788 真是2944 只是3204
是的3330 凡是3531 先是3533 越是3785 是非3992
有的是4124 实事求是4636 更是4741 就是4844
不是4918

0004 了 [了] /*le, liǎo*/ (1) 了0005 了0019 为了0207
了解0371 除了0844 了1412 对了3699 极了3894
了不起4162 受不了4173 罢了4689

0005 不 [不] /*bù*/ (1) 不0006 不同0298 不要0448
不断0455 不过0465 不仅0576 不少0628 不行0838
不管0909 不可0968 不错1006 不再1135 不但1437
差不多1650 不足1727 不得1810 不久1937 不用2095
不必2127 不得不2146 对不起2358 只不过2502
不利2634 可不2675 不论2810 绝不2884 不满2990
不见3033 不仅仅3063 不能3078 不良3105 不能3125
不顾3139 不幸3201 不安3297 不然3299 不如3477
从来不3664 从不3697 不对3778 不已3868 毫不3897
不时3933 忍不住4059 了不起4162 不禁4167 受不
了4173 不如4369 用不着4373 不易4418
来不及4497 不止4499 不好意思4569 说不定4637
不是4918 不大4963

0006 在 [在] /*zài*/ (1) 在0004 现在0094 存在0467
实在1039 正在1281 在于1448 在1829 所在2352
在内3136 在3984 实在4024 在场4206 处在4408
在座4610

0007 人 [人] /*rén*/ (1) 人0014 人民0228 人们0237
别人0372 个人0374 有人0391 人员0423 人类0435

女人0496 男人0513 人物0675 人家0807 老人0834
人才0846 人生0894 人口0934 工人0956 人家1112
夫人1205 客人1390 敌人1515 病人1560 人士1599
年轻人1626 领导人1668 人人2038 人民币2104
本人2137 大人2183 主人2195 人数2219 负责人2262
军人2313 他人2314 诗人2345 人群2399 人格2451
华人2537 人性2624 私人2656 主持人2718 人间2738
外国人3005 人体3110 人心3180 老年人3284 杀人3322
古人3377 家人3424 商人3468 亲人3568 众人3604
做人3620 当事人3714 人力3840 惊人3866 世人3914
行人3942 人文3949 人事3950 名人4249 动人4277
文人4386 穷人4476 坏人4490 成人4588 新人4599
用人4619 青年人4759 犯人4856

0008 有 [有] /*yǒu*/ (1) 有0009 没有0074 没有0107
所有0290 有些0384 有人0391 有的0408 有关0451
具有0503 拥有0985 只有1160 有点1269 有时1288
有效1379 国有1440 有所1632 有限2296 有力2420
有时候2483 有利2651 有利于2690 有关2741 带有2782
富有2914 有趣3079 占有3140 有名3293 有意思3787
原有3923 享有4108 有益4116 有的是4124 应有4456
现有4508 特有4615 有意4695 共有4784 有钱4842
只有4981

0009 我 [我] /*wǒ*/ (1) 我0007 我们0026 自我1250

0010 这 [這] /*zhè*/ (1) 这0011 这个0051 这样0081
这些0104 这么0175 这里0178 这儿0703 这时1207
这边2582

0011 个 [個] /*gè*/ (1) 个0008 这个0051 那个0220
个人0374 整个0414 哪个1778 个体2343 个性2564
个别2827

0012 他 [他] /*tā*/ (1) 他0010 他们0041 其他0323
他人2314

0013 大 [大] /*dà*/ (1) 大0025 大家0199 大学0260
大0688 巨大0863 大量1001 重大1038 伟大1058
大概1121 扩大1186 大会1330 大陆1539 广大1673
大约1721 大事1757 大学生1838 强大1842 大型1879
大部分2016 大人2183 大多数2224 大门2227 长大2362
极大2363 大街2398 大师2418 大大2432 大哥2489
大小2677 大使2756 大胆2828 大力2829 大多2901
大规模2943 大爷2969 大楼3112 加大3120 大地3175
大批3250 大声3300 大夫3331 大厅3421 绝大
多数3439 大姐3674 大队3708 大妈3793 老大3805
庞大3896 大都3930 大众3993 大厦4003 大气4187

大海4294 大自然4429 高大4517 大脑4648 大桥4926
不大4963

0014 上 [上] /shàng/ (1) 上0015 晚上0559 以上0662
实际上0928 加上1030 上面1068 上1080 上午1474
上去1685 上来1723 马上1780 基本上1867 上班2111
事实上2155 上学2170 上升2188 早上2356 上述2367
上下2735 上网2916 上帝3211 上级3229 上课3316
赶上3406 之上3461 上次3547 上市3585 考上3687
看上去3688 碰上4509 上车4723 上司4816

0015 来 [來] /lái/ (1) 来0053 来0063 起来0143 出来0169
后来0331 下来0348 回来0397 来说0487 越来越0604
过来0659 来到0714 以来0742 带来0759 来自0843
原来0911 未来1002 本来1044 看来1048 原来1276
从来1326 进来1463 将来1679 上来1723 来源2528
近年来2540 到来2747 来看2806 前来3075 来信3127
传来3222 从来不3664 来3700 往来4200 来往4264
来讲4300 来临4358 来不及4497 接下来4631

0016 要 [要] /yào/ (1) 要0020 重要0171 需要0247
要求0424 不要0448 主要0466 只要0485 主要0512
要求0738 必要1142 需要1446 就要1978 要是2673
要么3737 重要性3874

0017 们 [們] /men/ (1) 我们0026 他们0041 们0111
你们0179 人们0237 它们0535 咱们0540 她们0567

0018 说 [說] /shuō/ (1) 说0012 来说0487 说话0637
小说0778 说明0816 听说1079 说法1586 据说2024
说道2463 也就是说2535 再说2648 传说2680
比如说3081 学说4178 说服4267 虽说4465
说不定4637

0019 到 [到] /dào/ (1) 到0021 看到0211 得到0305
感到0445 受到0548 达到0638 来到0714 到0767
想到0772 找到0813 回到0957 遇到1005 见到1119
听到1195 到底1213 做到1518 收到1589 到处1692
提到2050 遭到2266 赶到2464 到达2541 碰到2573
到来2747 直到2802 接到2932 放到3558 等到3965

0020 就 [就] /jiù/ (1) 就0013 就0274 就0292 就是0319 成
就1614 早就1755 就要1978 也就是说2535
就业2667 就算3899 就是4844 就算4910

0021 为 [為] /wèi, wéi/ (1) 为0065 为0097 因为0099
认为0160 为了0207 成为0226 为什么0267 作为0356
行为0529 以为0875 作为1430 称为1653 为主1953
为止2543 极为2595 更为2853 为何3114 最为3227
视为3818 较为4169 分为4214 为首4345 称之为4409
列为4953 变为4961

0022 会 [會] /huì, kuài/ (1) 会0035 社会0114 会议0400
机会0405 社会主义0857 会0864 委员会0938 会儿1140
大会1330 协会1864 体会2028 开会2293 会见2496
会计2730 学会2739 会谈2781 学会3144 运动会3935
聚会4067 晚会4175 工会4224 会儿4394 宴会4638
会场4699 误会5001

0023 地 [地] /de, dì/ (1) 地0036 地方0153 地0210
地区0312 地位0636 土地0826 当地1056 地球1419
基地1739 地震2008 地下2138 地面2507 天地2553
内地2702 地点2812 外地2930 阵地2954 地质3088
大地3175 地址3441 地理3469 地图3667 本地4052
地步4230 地主4378 地带4469 工地4480 草地4973

0024 和 [和] /hé, hè/ (1) 和0016 和0145 和平0723
和尚2978 和谐3435 共和国4039

0025 以 [以] /yǐ/ (1) 可以0070 以0077 所以0156
以后0248 以及0383 以前0593 以上0662 以来0742
以0875 难以1305 以1348 以下1623 可以1743
以外1924 之所以2015 加以2211 以往2372 得以3167
予以3351 以便3987 以此4574

0026 出 [出] /chū/ (1) 出0050 出来0169 出现0250
提出0370 出去0631 指出0978 发出1159 做出1219
作出1352 演出1493 出口1505 出版1528 突出1674
出发1909 出生1930 付出2055 出国2392 出色2443
出版社2450 出身2630 推出2668 出于2693 出席2706
看出2807 露出3061 出门3239 退出3268 杰出3695
出路3796 伸出3820 派出所3847 派出3972 得出4207
出租车4248 超出4679 出差4680 外出4726 出售4781

0027 对 [對] /duì/ (1) 对0022 对于0359 对0438 对方0501
面对0681 反对0818 对象1271 绝对1510 对1669
对待1866 对手1904 对不起2358 相对2433 针对2565
对话2584 对外2847 对付2875 对3187 绝对3525
对了3699 对抗3729 不对3778 对比4442 对立4718

0028 时 [時] /shí/ (1) 时0078 时候0103 时间0142
当时0273 同时0369 时代0510 小时0563 时期0590
那时1018 这时1207 同时1221 有时1288 及时1630
平时1732 此时1900 一时1977 随时2096 时刻2260
有时候2483 暂时2671 同时2752 小时候3134 与此
同时3205 时机3338 顿时3898 不时3933 临时3977
时尚4090 时刻4118 时光4292 临时4370

0029 家 [家] /jiā/ (1) 家0132 国家0135 大家0199 家0215
家庭0418 家里0587 专家0803 人家0807 作家0913
家1000 回家1070 人家1112 家长1391 科学家1925
家乡2364 企业家2684 艺术家2832 家中2931 家属2971
家族2982 家伙3024 画家3176 家人3424 家具4034
老家4041 家园4247 皇家4537 政治家4596 家门4702
厂家4709

0030 也 [也] /yě/ (1) 也0017 也0301 也许0645 也好2480
也就是说2535 再也3932

0031 你 [你] /nǐ/ (1) 你0018 你们0179 你好3741

0032 生 [生] /shēng/ (1) 生活0127 先生0234 发生0249
学生0294 生0360 产生0493 生产0500 生命0502
人生0894 医生0920 生意1429 一生1460 生存1487
卫生1590 大学生1838 出生1930 生态2254 生活2271
生2295 生物2412 生日2444 研究生2817 生气2895
生动2942 生长3029 诞生3119 陌生3246 毕业生3947

生气4177 生理4234 留学生4423 女生4487 生涯4595
生前4882 生病4891 生育4949 生产4993

0033 中 [中] /zhōng, zhòng/ (1) 中0030 其中0343
中央0541 中心0581 之中0930 中间1087 心中1251
中学1398 集中1600 当中1618 手中1875 中午1915
集中2524 高中2527 空中2566 家中2931 初中3311
眼中3810 中医4038 从中4221 中等4694 中年4809

0034 得 [得] /de, dé, děi/ (1) 得0044 觉得0166
得到0305 得335 获得0602 取得0706 值得1150
显得1257 记得1258 使得1647 不得1810 懂得2013
不得不2146 难得2696 得知3121 得以3167 赢得3520
得意4058 晓得4194 得出4207 得罪4729

0035 多 [多] /duō/ (1) 多0055 多0069 许多0257
很多0314 多少0413 差不多1650 多么1774 多数2071
众多2181 大多数2224 好多2770 大多2901 绝大
多数3439 诸多3988 多久4879

0036 子 [子] /zǐ, zi/ (1) 孩子0149 儿子0456 子0511
样子0830 日子0998 女子1040 店子1060 妻子1185
男子1344 子1449 分子1684 下子1741 辈子1816
电子1844 子女2186 知识份子2303 脑子2410 例子2424
小子2554 小伙子2599 鼻子2679 肚子2754 女孩子2795
桌子2920 屋子3021 帽子3172 面子3185 脖子3228
孙子3541 身子3542 院子3705 小孩子3913 椅子4032
影子4223 牌子4228 老子4291 胡子4329 车子4337
种子4425 猴子4468 村子4474 箱子4526 饺子4640
裤子4641 镜子4643 嗓子4800 狮子4803 君子4813
银子4874 父子4937

0037 后 [後] /hòu/ (1) 后0067 最后0227 之后0231
以后0248 然后0263 来来331 今后1364 后面1418
先后1945 落后2174 随后2297 后果2619 前后3106
此后3261 身后4079 后悔4397 背后4522 往后4715
后者4764 后期4767

0038 那 [那] /nà/ (1) 那0037 那么0195 那个0220
那些0295 那样0506 那里0561 那么0745 那儿0987
那时1018 那1373 那天1401 那边1806

0039 过 [過] /guo, guò/ (1) 过0075 过0289 通过0299
过去0311 过程0415 不过0465 经过0530 过来0659
过去0746 过773 超过1061 通过1627 经过2278
只不过2502 过分3169 度过3287 过年3681 过于3986
过渡4057 走过4066 透过4730

0040 自 [自] /zì/ (1) 自己0043 自0287 自由0841
来自0843 自然1188 自我1250 自然1254 亲自1519
自身1587 各自1746 自然1795 自行车2298 自治区2415
自2456 自觉2547 自从2660 自杀3269 自动3627
自豪3734 自信3919 独自4420 大自然4429 自愿4446
自治4450

0041 好 [好] /hǎo, hào/ (1) 好0028 好像0710 只好1292
良好1380 美好1457 好好1595 正好1734 好处1936
好几1979 做好2101 友好2163 也好2480 好事2606

好多2770 好看3410 好3738 你好3741 最好3867
好奇4027 好吃4414 不好意思4569 搞好4722

0042 能 [能] /néng/ (1) 能0031 可能0148 能够0330
能力0403 功能1453 可能2753 能否2940 不能3078
可能性3111 不能3125 才能3310 能量3444 能源3597
尽可能4121 本能4489 技能4807

0043 么 [麼] /me/ (1) 什么0045 怎么0129 这么0175
那么0195 为什么0267 那么0745 怎么样1156 多么1774
没什么1956 么1966 要么3737

0044 可 [可] /kě/ (1) 可以0070 可0082 可能0148
可是0404 不可0968 可以1743 可怕2320 可惜2500
可见2525 可不2675 可能2753 可爱2808 可能性3111
可靠3626 可谓3891 可怜3981 尽可能4121 认可4157
可笑4627

0045 下 [下] /xià/ (1) 下0064 下0284 下0315 下来0348 下
去0550 下午0764 留下0999 下面1340 以下1623
下子1741 之下1756 天下1886 剩下2040 地下2138
下降2332 上下2735 底下3497 下班3758 如下3760
坐下3924 下令4211 低下4463 下岗4555 接下来4631
乡下4765 下次4825 眼下4940

0046 年 [年] /nián/ (1) 年0048 年代0462 今年0518
青年0650 年轻0687 当年0811 去年0891 年1049
每年1063 年龄1383 年轻人1626 少年1885 青少年2382
明年2402 周年2455 年级2486 近年来2540 年纪2637
老年人3284 过年3681 年底3811 年度3846 老年4651
青年人4759 年头4761 中年4809 童年4934

0047 发 [發] /fā/ (1) 发展0109 发现0197 发生0249
发0302 发表0699 开发0925 发挥1045 发出1159
出发1909 头发1947 发言2003 发动2027 爆发2180
发达2235 发行2649 发现2727 发起3073 引发3323
发明3612 沙发3791 开发区3908 发布3969 发射4352
散发4563 启发4772 发育4776

0048 学 [學] /xué/ (1) 大学0260 学0277 学校0278
学生0294 学习0351 同学0588 文学0663 科学0878
学院1072 学者1116 中学1398 学术1425 小学1477
科学1504 大学生1838 医学1863 教学1884 科学家1925
哲学1992 上学2170 学会2739 数学2790 化学2919
学问2949 科学院2968 学会3144 学位3174 留学3554
学历3997 学说4178 心理学4390 留学生4423 学费4426
学员4532 学期4965 开学4976

0049 还 [還] /hái, huán/ (1) 还0023 还是0876 还是1228

0050 都 [都] /dōu, dū/ (1) 都0024 首都2551 全都2674
大都3930 都市4002

0051 事 [事] /shì/ (1) 事0108 事情0265 故事0625
事业0648 事实0861 事件0884 军事0990 事儿1169
从事1517 大事1757 同事1865 事实上2155 事务2538
好事2606 事物2728 办事2874 事故2976 没事3325
事先3329 董事长3374 本事3666 当事人3714 小事3907
人事3950 做事4155 实事求是4636 往事4706 坏事4931

0052 去 [去] /qù/ (1) 去0040 过去0311 下去0550
出去0631 过去0746 去年0891 回去0989 失去1102
进去1275 上去1685 去世3034 看上去3688
死去4272

0053 成 [成] /chéng/ (1) 成0110 成为0226 成功0401
形成0551 完成0618 变成0623 造成0656 成立0799
成绩0833 成员1454 组成1494 成熟1530 成果1609
成就1614 成长1718 构成1941 成本2044 达成2319
赞成2744 建成2766 成分3567 当成3653 分成4311
成人4588 养成4888

0054 天 [天] /tiān/ (1) 天0091 今天0144 天0411
每天0596 明天1019 昨天1302 那天1401 天天1709
天气1883 天下1886 当天2047 春天2277 夏天2357
冬天2457 白天2459 天地2553 天空2958 聊天3143
整天3277 秋天3881 天真4625 天然4692 天堂4820

0055 着 [著] /zhe, zhāo, zháo, zhuó/ (1) 着0027
着0355 随着0835 着1297 接着1955 意味着2142
接着2321 着急2591 沿着2960 着手4347 用不着4373
睡着4515 顺着4601

0056 方 [方] /fāng/ (1) 地方0153 方面0193 方式0380
方0393 对方0501 方法0577 双方0707 方向0852
西方0914 方1325 方便1582 方案1624 东方1660
一方面1913 方针1971 北方2223 另一方面2593
平方米2780 南方3115 平方公里3720 官方4138
警方4658

0057 现 [現] /xiàn/ (1) 现在0094 发现0197 出现0250
表现0436 实现0592 现0765 现象0774 现代0780
现实0905 体现1310 现代化1612 现场1639 发现2727
呈现3013 展现3385 现状3572 现有4508 现金4536
表现4849 现行4909

0058 面 [面] /miàn/ (1) 方面0193 面0459 面对0681
面前0873 里面0931 全面1026 上面1068 前面1328
下面1340 后面1418 面1473 外面1597 面临1602
面积1702 见面1768 一方面1913 一面1934 局面2018
表面2301 场面2416 地面2507 另一方面2593 画面2891
面子3185 面貌3462 面孔4131 面向4152 水面4182
面包4639

0059 作 [作] /zuò/ (1) 工作0098 作0262 作为0356
作用0427 合作0556 作品0589 作家0913 作者1122
创作1308 作出1352 动作1384 作为1430 工作1786
制作1919 作战1943 写作2214 操作2478 作业2485
著作2902 当作3145 作风3181 运作3925

0060 里 [裏, 里] /lǐ/ (1) 里0059 这里0178 心里0522
那里0561 家里0587 里面0931 公里0983 哪里1014
里1331 手里1853 村里2661 屋里2798 城里2820
眼里2870 嘴里3067 里边3496 夜里3576 平方公里3720
里头3835

0061 没 [沒] /méi, mò/ (1) 没有0074 没有0107 没0118
没0191 没什么1956 没事3325 没关系4123 没法4372

0062 经 [經] /jīng/ (1) 已经0101 经济0161 经过0530
经验0571 曾经0722 经常0761 经营0808 经0900
经历1497 经理1507 经历1963 市场经济2177
总经理2239 经过2278 经费3306 经典3503 神经3790

0063 国 [國] /guó/ (1) 国0105 国家0135 国际0253
国内0763 外国1136 国有1440 国外1516 祖国1637
国民党1958 出国2392 回国2709 国民2980 外国人3005
爱国3829 国王3990 共和国4039 国防4860 王国4876

0064 看 [看] /kàn, kān/ (1) 看0039 看到0211 看见0859
看来1048 看法1338 来看2806 看出2807 看待3321
好看3410 看上去3688 观看3884 看望4831

0065 开 [開] /kāi/ (1) 开始0139 开0186 离开0665
开发0925 开放1032 打开1324 开展1420 召开1527
公开1834 展开2012 开始2063 开会2293 拉开2826
开车3270 分开3488 开玩笑3642 开发区3908 放开4212
开门4270 开口4402 开辟4493 开拓4567 开学4976

0066 行 [行] /xíng, háng/ (1) 进行0170 行为0529
行0630 行0654 行动0683 举行0713 银行0755 不行0838
实行1096 执行1286 行业1414 行政1804 行2004
自行车2298 流行2429 发行2649 运行2733 同行3283
行3285 履行3409 推行3685 旅行3812 游行3918
行人3942 飞行4015 一行4037 行李4799 现行4909

0067 小 [小] /xiǎo/ (1) 小0066 小时0563 小说0778
小姐1163 小学1477 小1636 小孩1745 小组2107
小子2554 从小2594 小伙子2599 大小2677 小时候3134
小事3907 小孩子3913 小心4097 缩小4828 小朋友4853

0068 于 [於] /yú/ (2) 于0095 由于0327 对于0359
于是0486 关于0528 终于0678 属于1145 处于1421
在于1448 至于1633 等于1832 位于2245 用于2335
有利于2690 出于2693 善于2873 高于3920 过于3986
基于4339 敢于4892

0069 当 [當] /dāng, dàng/ (1) 当0198 当时0273
当然0276 当0352 当年0811 相当0959 应当0992
当地1056 当中1618 当天2047 相当2164 当初2264
当代2292 当前2315 当2672 当今2758 适当2785
当作3145 当局3371 当场3593 当成3653 当事人3714
每当4189 正当4570 当即4740

0070 心 [心] /xīn/ (1) 心0261 心里0522 中心0581
心理0787 关心0945 担心1235 心中1251 心情1342
信心1782 内心1815 核心1874 放心1916 心灵2064
心态2453 决心2815 人心3180 精心3395 耐心3526
心脏3704 心目3849 爱心3948 伤心3980 心想4018
小心4097 良心4250 决心4342 心理学4390 心思4530
心眼4535

0071 而 [而] /ér/ (1) 而0049 而且0185 而是0570
然而0695 从而1495 反而1606 而言1927 而已2216
因而2284

0072 之 [之] /zhī/ (1) 之0084 之后0231 之间0275
之一0568 之前0653 之中0930 之外1236 之下1756

之所以2015 之类2276 之内2578 总之2697 之际3438
之上3461 之3475 称之为4409 随之4797

0073 用 [用] /yòng/ (1) 用0068 作用0427 使用0661
利用0725 采用1611 运用1779 不用2095 费用2130
应用2220 用于2335 用不着4373 用品4580 用人4619
适用4769

0074 同 [同] /tóng/ (1) 同0212 不同0298 同时0369
同志0406 同学0588 同意0712 共同0733 合同1125
同时1221 同样1513 同事1865 相同1976 同样2306
同情2704 同时2752 如同3010 同一3020 与此同时3205
同胞3213 同行3283 胡同3366 认同4208 一同4283
赞同4895

0075 种 [種] /zhǒng, zhòng/ (1) 种0029 品种2579
种3482 各种各样3740 种植4351 种子4425

0076 道 [道] /dào/ (1) 知道0090 道0617 报道0649
道0979 道理1090 道路1272 道德1343 难道1605 道2060
说道2463 街道2508 味道2714 轨道2957 渠道3049
报道3064 问道3859 通道4005 一道4220 道歉4257
打交道4774

0077 然 [然] /rán/ (1) 然后0263 当然0276 虽然0300
突然0643 然而0695 仍然0824 自然1188 自然1254
依然1381 既然1405 显然1554 居然1785 自然1795
忽然1800 竟然2102 必然2378 果然2614 不然3299
偶然3355 大自然4429 天然4692

0078 前 [前] /qián/ (1) 前0121 目前0422 以前0593
之前0653 面前0873 前1093 前面1328 眼前2121
当前2315 前进2330 前提2354 前途2471 提前2542
向前2577 前往3014 前来3075 前后3106 前景3573
门前3721 从前4545 前夕4881 生前4882

0079 问 [問] /wèn/ (1) 问题0072 问0164 访问1485
学问2949 请问3215 顾问3416 询问3516 问道3859
疑问4226 提问4261 问候4977

0080 实 [實] /shí/ (1) 其实0339 实现0592 事实0861
现实0905 实际上0928 确实0969 实在1039 实行1096
实施1182 真实1287 实践1387 实际1404 实际1711
实力1740 事实上2155 落实2479 实验3054 实1149
证实3198 老实3202 实3534 实验室4004 实在4024
实质4331 实事求是4636

0081 所 [所] /suǒ/ (1) 所0113 所以0156 所有0290
所谓0792 有所1632 所1751 之所以2015 研究所2285
所在2352 场所3051 厕所3155 派出所3847 无所谓4172

0082 点 [點] /diǎn/ (1) 点0167 点0187 点儿0970
特点1059 有点1269 观点1327 重点1359 焦点2699
地点2812 重点3781 优点3870 点头3892 点儿4293
起点4657 缺点4802

0083 长 [長] /cháng, zhǎng/ (1) 长0173 增长1024
长期1037 家长1391 部长1433 校长1483 市长1704
成长1718 院长1803 长2039 局长2074 长大2362
团长2436 队长2885 生长3029 董事长3374 厂长3799

处长3877 漫长3927 长远4519 组长4747 班长4801
延长4985 科长4996

0084 动 [動] /dòng/ (1) 活动0291 动0646 行动0683
运动0883 动物0976 劳动1175 动作1384 主动1392
推动1706 激动1790 感动1826 运动1901 运动员1957
发动2027 生动2942 流动2987 移动3069 动力3130
动员3220 调动3240 启动3386 动手3403 自动3627
冲动3768 运动会3935 震动4198 动人4277 动摇4445
带动4448 举动4598 被动4732 动机4863 反动4969

0085 想 [想] /xiǎng/ (1) 想0056 思想0313 想到0772
想法1434 想起1643 想象1809 理想1944 理想2309
梦想3256 想像3288 幻想3672 设想3683 心想4018
回想4890

0086 些 [些] /xiē/ (1) 这些0104 一些0115 那些0295
些0309 有些0384 某些1731 哪些2722

0087 起 [起] /qǐ/ (1) 起0136 起来0143 一起0252 起0439
引起0717 想起1643 对不起2358 发起3073 起3678
提起4017 了不起4162 起码4324 掀起4411 兴起4505
响起4558 起点4657 升起4684 起草4900

0088 从 [從] /cóng/ (1) 从0042 从来1326 从而1495
从事1517 从此1922 从小2594 自从2660 从来不3664
从不3697 服从4096 从未4122 从中4221 从前4545

0089 样 [樣] /yàng/ (1) 这样0081 一样0402 一样0432 那
样0506 怎样0752 样子0830 怎么样1156 样1244
同样1513 样1677 同样2306 模样3466 各种各样3740
照样4320

0090 两 [兩] /liǎng/ (1) 两0033 两者4438

0091 进 [進] /jìn/ (1) 进行0170 进0190 进入0426
进一步1055 进步1178 促进1252 进去1275 先进1436
进来1463 进攻1856 进程1960 推进2281 前进2330
进展2590 引进2631 进口3192 改进3723

0092 她 [她] /tā/ (1) 她0032 她们0567

0093 分 [分] /fēn/ (1) 分0395 十分0449 分0672 部分0749
分析0757 分钟0796 充分1011 分别1146 分子1684
分配1688 一部分1882 部分2006 大部分2016 知识
分子2303 分布2805 过分3169 分开3488 成分3567
分歧3754 分裂3917 分为4214 分成4311 划分4313
分离4349 分工4607 处分4917

0094 很 [很] /hěn/ (1) 很0038 很多0314 很快1161

0095 理 [理] /lǐ/ (1) 管理0346 处理0609 理解0626
理论0679 心理0787 总理0912 道理1090 合理1442
理由1450 经理1507 理想1944 理1973 总经理2239
真理2300 理想2309 理2462 整理2724 物理3152
理性3343 治理3387 办理3431 地理3469 清理3822
生理4234 理念4251 代理4262 心理学4390 助理4485
伦理4877

0096 主 [主] /zhǔ/ (1) 主要0466 主席0499 主要0512
主任0751 社会主义0857 主0997 主动1392 民主1397
为主1953 主持2014 主义2045 主题2077 主人2195

主意2445 主管2574 主持人2718 主张2774 主张3053
主角3233 主力3309 资本主义3539 地主4378
公主4708 主导4735 主观4980

0097 定 [定] /dìng/ (1) 一定0254 决定0363
定0591 规定0724 一定0766 肯定1085 稳定1126
确定1194 肯定1241 制定1491 决定2270
认定2334 规定2385 否定2963 坚定3017
固定3735 指定3861 协定3940 肯定4279
必定4520 定位4557 注定4559 说不定4637
安定4733 约定4833

0098 工 [工] /gōng/ (1) 工作0098 工程0832 工人0956
工业0973 工1217 工资1312 职工1341 工厂1638
工作1786 工具2117 员工2133 加工2279 打工3408
工商3606 工程师3789 施工3956 工夫4083 工会4224
工地4480 分工4607

0099 意 [意] /yì/ (1) 注意0461 意义0514 愿意0554
意思0621 意见0627 同意0712 意识0854 意1230
满意1260 生意1429 意味着2142 主意2445 意外2499
意志2922 故意2941 随意3393 有意思3787 得意4058
意识4304 特意4322 玩意4484 不好意思4569
无意4634 有意4695

0100 把 [把] /bǎ/ (1) 把0034 把1365 把握1797

0101 情 [情] /qíng/ (1) 情况0176 事情0265 情0729
感情0822 爱情1167 热情1211 情绪1229 心情1342
情感1851 情形2310 情景2379 表情2603 同情2704
激情2835 情节2890 情报3994 神情4753

0102 如 [如] /rú/ (1) 如果0122 如0255 如何0373
如此0606 比如0896 如今1095 如1921 假如2560
例如2871 如同3010 比如说3081 不如3477
如下3760 无论如何4222 不如4369 譬如4403
犹如4512

0103 正 [正] /zhèng/ (1) 正0174 真正0840 正常0870
正是0887 正式1036 反正1084 正确1103 真正1166
正在1281 正1424 正好1734 公正2613 正义3281
纠正3726 正当4570

0104 全 [全] /quán/ (1) 全0140 完全0326 全0552
全部0612 安全0777 全面1026 全球1469 全体2084
全都2674 全球化2825 全部4111 全身4243 全力4796

0105 最 [最] /zuì/ (1) 最0058 最后0227 最近0781
最终1388 最佳2652 最初3042 最为3227 最新3437
最终3527 最低3660 最好3867

0106 但 [但] /dàn/ (1) 但0061 但是0155 不但1437

0107 儿 [兒] /ér, r/ (1) 儿0182 儿子0456 这儿0703
女儿0727 点儿0970 那儿0987 儿童1066 哪儿1100
会儿1140 事儿1169 儿女2977 劲儿3184 婴儿4232
点儿4293 会儿4394 头儿4541 幼儿园4581 味儿4654
活儿4763 一块儿5004

0108 外 [外] /wài/ (1) 外0236 另外0908 外国1136
之外1236 国外1516 外面1597 外交1843 此外1880

以外1924 另外2371 海外2474 意外2499 内外2550
对外2847 外地2930 外国人3005 格外3565 门外3952
外部4171 例外4597 外汇4662 外出4726 外边4742
窗外4824 外语4994

0109 高 [高] /gāo/ (1) 高0106 提高0508 高兴0585
高级1583 高中2527 高度2548 高度3128 高手3638
高于3920 高潮3995 高原4081 高考4089 高尚4112
高层4183 高大4517 高峰4586 崇高4962

0110 什 [什] /shén, shí/ (1) 什么0045 为什么0267
没什么1956

0111 间 [間] /jiān, jiàn/ (1) 时间0142 之间0275 间0281
中间1087 期间1107 空间1289 民间1716 店间1744
人间2738 车间4287 瞬间4299

0112 力 [力] /lì/ (1) 能力0403 努力0472 力量0605
力1062 压力1190 权力1321 实力1740 势力1903
精力2272 有力2420 魅力2510 大力2829 活力2864
暴力2865 动力3130 主力3309 智力3372 力气3396
力度3400 潜力3717 体力3803 人力3840 兵力4091
全力4796 无力4956

0113 明 [明] /míng/ (1) 明白0697 说明0816 证明0906
明936 明显0993 明天1019 明确1329 表明1423
文明1538 聪明1794 文明1799 明年2402 明星2683
声明2905 明白3224 发明3612 鲜明3928 光明4073
明明4119 透明4790 明确5002

0114 本 [本] /běn/ (1) 本0282 基本0505 本0867
根本0967 本来1044 根本1204 本身1274 本1835
基本上1867 资本2007 成本2044 本人2137 本质2655
本2771 根本3085 原本3124 资本主义3539 本事3666
本地4052 本能4489 本领4642

0115 法 [法] /fǎ/ (1) 办法0345 方法0577 法律0594
无法0677 法1295 看法1338 想法1434 说法1586
做法1776 法院2207 合法2482 违法3587 法庭3605
手法3675 书法4040 法官4244 没法4372

0116 话 [話] /huà/ (1) 话0125 电话0338 说话0637
的话0871 讲话1306 打电话1427 话题1574 谈话1808
对话2584 笑话3302 神话3906 话剧4427 谈话4475
话语4818 废话4864

0117 者 [者] /zhě/ (1) 记者0244 者0271 或者0367
学者1116 作者1122 读者1313 患者2368 消费者2512
两者4438 后者4764

0118 部 [部] /bù/ (1) 部0412 部队0450 干部0498
部门0534 全部0612 部分0749 部1177 内部1428
部长1433 一部分1882 部分2006 大部分2016 西部2308
总部2682 俱乐部3084 南部3358 部署3453 北部3698
东部3901 全部4111 外部4171 局部4430 部位4928

0119 女 [女] /nǚ/ (1) 女0184 女人0496 妇女0668
女儿0727 女性0862 女子1040 女孩1242 女士1870
子女2186 女孩子2795 美女2888 儿女2977 少女3570
女生4487

0120 等 [等] /děng/ (1) 等0073 等等0902 等1576
平等1690 等于1832 等待2329 等到3965 等级4045
中等4694

0121 业 [業] /yè/ (1) 企业0189 事业0648 农业0831
专业0953 工业0973 毕业1003 商业1074 业务1256
职业1377 行业1414 产业1471 作业2485 就业2667
企业家2684 业2927 业余3692 毕业生3947 失业4008
业绩4093 营业4274 创业4504

0122 老 [老] /lǎo/ (1) 老0147 老师0386 老人0834
老板1115 老百姓1710 老婆2149 老太太2252 老虎2887
古老3016 老实3202 老年人3284 老爷3447 老大3805
养老3975 老家4041 老鼠4049 老子4291 老头4488
老年4651 老4912

0123 已 [已] /yǐ/ (1) 已经0101 已0123 早已1735
而已2216 不已3868

0124 重 [重] /chóng, zhòng/ (1) 重要0171
严重0673 重0726 重新0848 重视0974 重大1038
尊重1268 重点1359 重1708 沉重2405 重复2845
注重3060 重点3781 重要性3874 重建4682

0125 公 [公] /gōng/ (1) 公司0162 公里0983 办公
室1023 公开1834 公共1861 公园1998 公平2005
公路2287 公2323 公民2381 公布2589 公正2613
公安2717 公斤2721 公众2776 公安局3131
办公3479 平方公里3720 公认4362 公元4376
公主4708 公寓4871

0126 其 [其] /qí/ (1) 其0188 其他0323 其实0339
其中0343 尤其0639 其他1374 及其2339 其次2851
极其2882 其余3575 与其3831

0127 因 [因] /yīn/ (1) 因为0099 因此0389
因0407 原因0441 因素1099 因而2284
基因3089

0128 文 [文] /wén/ (1) 文化0163 文学0663 文0741
文章0797 文字1339 文件1496 文明1538 文艺1738
文明1799 文物2561 论文2562 人文3949 散文4237
文人4386 语文4650 文凭4933

0129 知 [知] /zhī/ (1) 知道0090 知0364 知识0555
通知1985 知识分子2303 得知3121 知名4028
通知4341

0130 给 [給] /gěi, jǐ/ (1) 给0060 给0379 给予1753
交给1784 送给2707 留给3650 供给4941

0131 与 [與] /yǔ, yù/ (2) 与0088 与0117 参与1153
与此同时3205 与其3831

0132 己 [己] /jǐ/ (1) 自己0043 己2869

0133 次 [次] /cì/ (1) 次0054 再次1357 次1432 层次2134
其次2851 上次3547 下次4825

0134 关 [關] /guān/ (1) 关系0165 有关0451 关于0528 关
心0945 关注1033 机关1270 关键1278 关1575
相关1664 关1899 有关2741 关键2809 关怀3557
没关系4123 关闭4622 海关4984

0135 只 [只] /zhī, zhǐ/ (1) 只0071 只0479 只要0485
只有1160 只好1292 只是1896 只不过2502 只是3204
只有4981

0136 民 [民] /mín/ (1) 人民0228 民族0410 农民0509
民1168 民主1397 民间1716 居民1898 国民党1958
市民2090 人民币2104 少数民族2353 公民2381
国民2980 移民3183 村民3257 民众3446 平民3999
民警4661

0137 三 [三] /sān/ (1) 三0052

0138 又 [又] /yòu/ (1) 又0046 又0620

0139 头 [頭] /tóu, tou/ (1) 头0246 头1243 头1849
头发1947 石头2042 头脑2529 镜头2834 回头3379
回头3532 街头3546 里头3835 抬头3862 点头3892
念头3910 码头4176 老头4488 摇头4513 头儿4541
年头4761 低头4780 骨头4804

0140 比 [比] /bǐ/ (1) 比0130 比较0321 比赛0747
比如0896 比例2061 相比2215 比2893 比较3007
比如说3081 无比3775 对比4442

0141 手 [手] /shǒu/ (1) 手0229 手段1104 手机1705
手里1853 手中1875 对手1904 选手2135 手术2755
手续3047 双手3234 动手3403 高手3638 手法3675
伸手3728 一手4078 手指4082 着手4347 握手4546

0142 别 [别] /bié/ (1) 特别0243 别0328 别人0372
别的0963 分别1146 特别1240 个别2827 告别3289
差别3339 区别3871 级别4236 性别4920 区别4986

0143 第 [第] /dì/ (1) 第0047

0144 回 [回] /huí/ (1) 回0218 回来0397 回答0789
回到0957 回去0989 回家1070 回1249 回忆1860
回国2709 返回2988 回头3379 回避3519 回报3524
回头3532 收回3684 回归3967 回顾4210 回想4890

0145 活 [活] /huó/ (1) 生活0127 活动0291 活1130
活1920 活1946 生活2271 活力2864 灵活3630
活跃4012 活泼4161 干活4276 活跃4731
活儿4763

0146 体 [體] /tǐ/ (1) 身体0572 具体0743 体育1147
体制1280 体现1310 集体1484 体系1557 体1837
媒体1975 体会2028 整体2034 全体2084 个体2343
群体2347 团体2604 总体2867 体验2936 人体3110
尸体3373 体力3803 体内4880

0147 位 [位] /wèi/ (1) 位0092 单位0516 地位0636
位置0966 位于2245 岗位2972 学位3174 座位4527
定位4557 部位4928

0148 做 [做] /zuò/ (1) 做0076 做出1219 做到1518
做法1776 叫做2079 做好2101 做人3620 做事4155
做饭4617

0149 水 [水] /shuǐ/ (1) 水0206 水平0525 水果2918
洪水3230 水泥3745 泪水4142 水面4182 水稻4972

0150 无 [無] /wú/ (2) 无0224 无法0677 无论1109
毫无2230 无数2423 无疑2503 无2549 无比3775

无奈3779 无限3926 无所谓4172 无论如何4222
无非4521 无意4634 无力4956

0151 化 [化] /huà/ (1) 文化0163 变化0564 现代化1612
化1699 化1760 全球化2825 化学2919 转化3348
消化4604 变化4964

0152 打 [打] /dǎ, dá/ (1) 打0120 打开1324 打电话1427
打击1648 打破2361 打算2514 打断3038 打听3380
打工3408 打算4000 打架4146 打仗4552 打交道4774
打扮5000

0153 代 [代] /dài/ (1) 年代0462 代表0484 时代0510
现代0780 代0828 古代1492 代表1499 现代化1612
代1662 代表团2241 当代2292 代价2956 交代3555
代理4262 代替4302 取代4310

0154 机 [機] /jī/ (1) 机会0405 机构0880 飞机0917
机关1270 机1466 危机1703 手机1705 计算机1765
机场1801 司机1850 机制2120 机器2597 机遇3159
机械3173 时机3338 电视机4336 动机4863

0155 表 [表] /biǎo/ (1) 表示0398 表现0436 代表0484
发表0699 表达1395 表明1423 代表1499 表演1680
代表团2241 表面2301 表情2603 表2653 表3037
表现4849 表扬4883

0156 电 [電] /diàn/ (1) 电话0338 电0640 电影0658
电视0696 电脑1118 打电话1427 电视台1825
电子1844 电台2950 电视剧3755 电梯3938 电报4033
电视机4336

0157 题 [題] /tí/ (1) 问题0072 题1556 话题1574
主题2077 题目2946 难题3365 标题3504 题材3715
课题4042

0158 相 [相] /xiāng/ (1) 相0417 相信0474 相当0959
互相1282 相互1481 相关1664 相同1976 相当2164
相比2215 相对2433 相反2669 相应3074 相似3326
真相3879 相处3922 首相4048 相继4421

0159 见 [見] /jiàn/ (1) 见0201 意见0627 看见0859
见到1119 见面1768 会见2496 可见2525 听见2628
不见3033 接见4669 遇见4978

0160 先 [先] /xiān/ (1) 先生0234 先0251 首先0557
先进1436 先后1945 事先3329 先是3533
原先4321

0161 名 [名] /míng/ (1) 名0192 著名0809 名字0921
名1894 名叫2938 名义3158 有名3293 名称3312
名单3719 名牌3944 报名3957 知名4028 名人4249
姓名4285 名4525 排名4616 名气4710 命名4728
名片4869

0162 果 [果] /guǒ/ (1) 如果0122 结果0390 效果1300
成果1609 结果1895 果然2614 后果2619 水果2918
苹果3251 果3673

0163 几 [幾] /jǐ, jī/ (1) 几0062 几乎0562 好几1979

0164 性 [性] /xìng/ (2) 性0690 性0825 女性0862
性格1511 性质2259 男性2346 个性2564 人性2624

可能性3111 理性3343 积极性3792 重要性3874
性别4920

0165 将 [將] /jiāng, jiàng/ (1) 将0131 将0202 将来1679
将军1750 即将2422

0166 常 [常] /cháng/ (1) 非常0217 常0693 经常0761
正常0870 常常1180 日常2375 平常3272 通常3276
异常4160

0167 被 [被] /bèi/ (1) 被0057 被迫3889 被动4732

0168 新 [新] /xīn/ (1) 新0112 新闻0798 重新0848
创新2080 新鲜2248 最新3437 更新4556 新人4599

0169 少 [少] /shǎo, shào/ (1) 少0258 多少0413
不少0628 至少0927 减少1438 少年1885 少数民族2353
青少年2382 少数2434 少2556 缺少2842 少女3570

0170 应 [應] /yīng, yìng/ (1) 应该0196 应0361 应当0992
反应1245 适应1550 答应1981 应用2220 相应3074
供应3556 应付3814 应有4456

0171 场 [場] /chǎng, cháng/ (1) 市场0304 场0322
现场1639 立场1730 机场1801 场2072 市场经济2177
场面2416 商场2446 广场2580 战场2602 农场2975
场所3051 场合3087 当场3593 在场4206 会场4699
场景4932

0172 真 [真] /zhēn/ (1) 真0221 真0523 认真0829
真正0840 真正1166 真实1287 真的2147 真理2300
真是2944 真诚3104 真相3879 天真4625

0173 军 [軍] /jūn/ (2) 军0517 军队0850 军事0990
将军1750 冠军1796 解放军2311 军人2313 空军2365
海军2861 军官3398 陆军4924

0174 向 [向] /xiàng/ (1) 向0100 方向0852 向1323
向前2577 转向2937 一向3226 倾向3418 面向4152
向往4778

0175 才 [才] /cái/ (1) 才0093 人才0846 刚才1004
才能3310

0176 身 [身] /shēn/ (1) 身0354 身体0572 本身1274
身边1455 身份1462 自身1587 身2513 出身2630
浑身3470 身子3542 转身3652 身材4035 身后4079
全身4243 终身4810 身影4866

0177 合 [合] /hé/ (1) 合作0556 结合1053 合同1125
合1131 符合1426 合理1442 联合1552 适合1833
配合1876 综合1902 合适2030 合法2482 场合3087
合格4366 组合4560 融合4721

0178 目 [目] /mù/ (1) 目前0422 项目0611 目标0619
目的0728 节目0839 目光2002 目2818 题目2946
盲目3827 心目3849

0179 此 [此] /cǐ/ (2) 此0225 因此0389 如此0606
此外1880 此时1900 从此1922 彼此2066 由此2994
与此同时3205 此后3261 以此4574

0180 认 [認] /rèn/ (1) 认为0160 认识0421 认真0829
承认0940 认2160 认识2205 认定2334 否认3077
确认3559 认可4157 认同4208 公认4362

0181 总 [總] /zǒng/ (1) 总0524 总0744 总统0849
总理0912 总是0919 总结1840 总经理2239 总部2682
总之2697 总体2867 总裁3160 总数4385

0182 再 [再] /zài/ (1) 再0087 不再1135 再次1357
再说2648 一再2917 再也3932 再度3985

0183 干 [幹] /gān, gàn/ (1) 干0213 干部0498 干2144
干净2523 干脆2784 若干3082 干吗3509 干涉3645
干扰4103 干活4276 骨干4647

0184 结 [結] /jié/ (1) 结果0390 结束0624 结构0709
结婚1009 结合1053 结1535 总结1840 团结1855
结果1895 结论2167 结局3752

0185 口 [口] /kǒu/ (1) 口0791 口0801 人口0934
出口1505 门口1789 窗口3068 进口3192 口号3253
借口3802 口袋4225 口气4288 开口4402 户口4705

0186 解 [解] /jiě/ (1) 解决0349 了解0371 理解0626
解释0949 解放1486 解1581 解放军2311 解除3921

0187 产 [產] /chǎn/ (1) 产生0493 生产0500 产品0647 共产党1273 产业1471 产1965 资产2062 财产2088
遗产3156 产量3465 破产4885 生产4993

0188 世 [世] /shì/ (1) 世界0126 世纪0463 世1091
去世3034 世人3914

0189 平 [平] /píng/ (1) 水平0525 和平0723 平0926
平衡1622 平等1690 平时1732 公平2005 平均2175
平静2611 平米2780 平常3272 平方公里3720
平凡3939 平民3999 平原4125 平安4968

0190 完 [完] /wán/ (1) 完141 完全0326 完成0618
完整1892 完善2280 完美3275

0191 书 [書] /shū/ (1) 书0241 书记0943 读书1558
图书馆2156 秘书2729 书法4040 书籍4179 证书4472
书店4579

0192 感 [感] /gǎn/ (1) 感到0445 感觉0446 感情0822
感1047 感受1203 感谢1422 感动1826 情感1851
敏感2751 感染3290 感觉3549 感激4550 责任感4867

0193 二 [二] /èr/ (1) 二0080

0194 放 [放] /fàng/ (1) 放0242 开放1032 解放1486
放弃1500 放心1916 解放军2311 放松2935 放到3558
释放3689 放开4212

0195 加 [加] /jiā/ (1) 参加0317 加0686 增加0691
更加0794 加强0836 加上1030 加入1431 加以2211
加工2279 加快2498 加大3120 加速3581

0196 门 [門] /mén/ (1) 门0473 部门0534 专门1465
门口1789 门2136 大门2227 专门2897 出门3239
门前3721 门外3952 开门4270 家门4702

0197 员 [員] /yuán/ (1) 人员0423 委员会0938 官员1408
成员1454 演员1567 队员1714 运动员1957 员工2133
委员2218 党员2998 动员3220 服务员4524 学员4532

0198 政 [政] /zhèng/ (1) 政府0233 政治0308
政策0558 行政1804 财政2400 政权2657 政3608
政治家4596

0199 气 [氣] /qì/ (1) 气0579 气氛1625 空气1869
天气1883 气2179 勇气2506 气候2654 生气2895
脾气2970 客气3344 气质3369 力气3396 气息3636
生气4177 大气4187 口气4288 风气4431 语气4577
名气4710 气象4743 气温4852 运气4857

0200 信 [信] /xìn/ (1) 相信0474 信0586 信息0664 信1347
信任1748 信心1782 来信3127 信念3364 通信3518
迷信3890 自信3919 信仰3966 写信4149 信号4180

0201 走 [走] /zǒu/ (1) 走0085 走过4066 走路4154
走私4360

0202 今 [今] /jīn/ (1) 今天0144 今年0518 如今1095
今后1364 至今1565 今2078 今日2325 今晚2703
当今2758

0203 更 [更] /gèng/ (1) 更0083 更加0794 更为2853
更新4556 更是4741

0204 并 [並] /bìng/ (2) 并0102 并0615 并且0851
并非2995

0205 教 [教] /jiāo, jiào/ (1) 教育0270 教授0711 教0847
教师1088 宗教1676 教学1884 教训2131 教练2816
教室3902 教材4916

0206 内 [內] /nèi/ (1) 内0235 内容0488 国内0763
内部1428 内心1815 内外2550 之内2578 内地2702
在内3136 境内3610 内涵4006 室内4053 内阁4591
体内4880

0207 系 [系] /xì, jì/ (1) 关系0165 联系0750 系0762
系统0821 体系1557 系列1759 系统3356 没关系4123

0208 记 [記] /jì/ (1) 记者0244 记0732 书记0943
记得1258 忘记1940 记忆1972 记住2763 记录2913
记录3360 登记3378 记载3614 记载4332 日记4375

0209 反 [反] /fǎn/ (1) 反0494 反对0818 反映0939
反正1084 反应1245 反而1606 相反2669 反复2712
违反2933 反抗3882 反省4359 反响4704 反4905
反动4969

0210 它 [它] /tā/ (1) 它0086 它们0535 其它1374

0211 使 [使] /shǐ/ (1) 使0124 使用0661 即使0972
使得1647 大使2756 使命3912 促使4102 致使4562

0212 入 [入] /rù/ (2) 进入0426 入0447 收入0965
投入1246 加入1431 深入2126 陷入2391 深入3265
列入4355

0213 车 [車] /chē/ (1) 车0340 汽车0718 火车2129
自行车2298 车站3252 开车3270 列车3280
车辆3798 轿车3998 摩托车4086 火车站4188
出租车4248 车间4287 车子4337 卡车4466 上车4723
车队4756

0214 提 [提] /tí/ (1) 提出0370 提高0508 提供0542
提0730 提到2050 提醒2100 前提2354 提前2542
提倡3095 提起4017 提问4261 提4269

0215 接 [接] /jiē/ (1) 接受0458 直接0520 接0601
接触1234 接近1628 接着1955 接着2321 接待2664

接到2932 迎接3219 连接4553 接收4621 接下来4631 接见4669

0216 通 [通] /tōng/ (1) 通过0299 普通1179 通1199 交通1320 通过1627 通知1985 沟通2440 通2592 通讯2997 通常3276 通信3518 通道4005 通知4341

0217 由 [由] /yóu/ (2) 由0154 由于0327 自由0841 理由1450 由此2994

0218 度 [度] /dù/ (1) 制度0578 态度0657 程度0802 速度1198 角度1532 度1926 高度2548 高度3128 度过3287 力度3400 温度3467 度3599 年度3846 难度3848 度3970 再度3985 一度4170 限度4927

0219 任 [任] /rèn/ (1) 任何0336 责任0655 主任0751 任务0827 任1069 担任1695 信任1748 任命3973 责任感4867

0220 社 [社] /shè/ (1) 社会0114 社会主义0857 出版社2450 社3002 报社4533

0221 受 [受] /shòu/ (2) 受0306 接受0458 受到0548 感受1203 享受1409 承受2748 受伤3199 遭受3402 难受4025 受不了4173 深受4459 忍受4611

0222 让 [讓] /ràng/ (1) 让0079

0223 思 [思] /sī/ (1) 思想0313 意思0621 思考1435 思维2089 思绪2572 思路2926 有意思3787 心思4530 不好意思4569 思索4827

0224 立 [立] /lì/ (1) 建立0469 成立0799 立即0916 立1057 独立1691 立场1730 立刻2145 设立2336 独立3096 树立3885 对立4718 立4846

0225 难 [難] /nán/ (1) 难0272 困难0701 难以1305 难道1605 艰难2376 难得2696 难题3365 灾难3417 难度3848 难受4025 难免4514 难怪4739

0226 特 [特] /tè/ (1) 特别0243 特点1059 特殊1086 特别240 特1545 特色1657 独特2256 特征2487 特2883 特意4322 特有4615 模特4819

0227 西 [西] /xī/ (1) 东西0208 西方0914 西0960 西部2308 西北2636 西南3880 西瓜4644

0228 原 [原] /yuán/ (1) 原因0441 原则0810 原来0911 原1170 原来1276 原1667 原本3124 原始3245 草原3669 原料3743 原有3923 高原4081 平原4125 原先4321 原谅4668

0229 处 [處] /chǔ, chù/ (1) 处0477 处理0609 处于1421 处1617 到处1692 好处1936 深处3314 处处3662 四处3739 处7573757 处长3877 相处3922 处在4408 处境4434 处罚4786 处分4917

0230 日 [日] /rì/ (1) 日子0998 日1382 今日2325 日常2375 生日2444 一日2838 日益2852 节日3701 日报4036 近日4054 日记4375 日期4646 早日4847

0231 管 [管] /guǎn/ (2) 管理0346 管0444 尽管0805 不管0909 主管2574 血管4921

0232 制 [制] /zhì/ (2) 制度0578 控制0758 制1183 体制1280 制定1491 制造1542 制作1919 机制2120 限制2141 制止3887 抑制3960 制约4306 研制4609

0233 物 [物] /wù/ (1) 人物0675 动物0976 物质1358 物1385 食物2322 生物2412 文物2561 事物2728 物理3152 植物3154 博物馆3209 货物3340 药物3538 礼物3566 物品3671 购物4065 刊物4233 物资4290 物价4467

0234 边 [邊] /biān/ (1) 边0443 一边1124 边1349 身边1455 旁边1572 那边1806 这边2582 里边3496 边界4231 边境4542 路边4667 外边4742 边缘4748 周边4798 一边4982

0235 各 [各] /gè/ (1) 各0096 各自1746 各种各样3740

0236 报 [報] /bào/ (1) 报0566 报告0644 报道0649 报纸1201 汇报2497 报2647 报道3064 回报3524 报复3578 报名3957 情报3994 电报4033 日报4036 报刊4479 报社4533

0237 展 [展] /zhǎn/ (1) 发展0109 开展1420 展开2012 展示2246 进展2590 展现3385 展览3611 展4242

0238 市 [市] /shì/ (1) 市场0304 城市0344 市0700 市长1704 市民2090 市场经济2177 上市3585 都市4002 股市4139 超市4140 市区4939

0239 路 [路] /lù/ (1) 路0297 道路1272 铁路1362 路线2086 公路2287 思路2926 一路3041 马路3043 路3641 出路3796 走路4154 路4667

0240 该 [該] /gāi/ (1) 应该0196 该0283 该1386

0241 听 [聽] /tīng/ (1) 听0146 听说1079 听到1195 听见2628 听2720 打听3380 听众3571 听4896

0242 变 [變] /biàn/ (1) 变0325 变化0564 改变0582 变成0623 转变2360 变为4961 变化4964

0243 界 [界] /jiè/ (1) 世界0126 界1729 境界2731 边界4231

0244 战 [戰] /zhàn/ (2) 战争0597 战略1078 战1543 战士1655 作战1943 战斗2026 挑战2041 战场2602 战胜2761 战役3712 战术4133 战友4584 战线4808

0245 队 [隊] /duì/ (1) 部队0450 队0515 军队0850 队伍1171 队员1714 队长2885 大队3708 队3809 支队4335 车队4756

0246 办 [辦] /bàn/ (1) 办0269 办法0345 办公室1023 举办1952 办事2874 办理3431 办公3479

0247 候 [候] /hòu/ (1) 时候0103 有时候2483 气候2654 小时候3134 问候4977

0248 交 [交] /jiāo/ (1) 交1010 交流1021 交通1320 交往1372 交给1784 外交1843 交2009 交换2645 交易2794 交谈2824 交代3555 打交道4774

0249 觉 [覺] /jué, jiào/ (1) 觉得0166 感觉0446 睡觉2110 自觉2547 感觉3549 觉3613 觉3842

0250 件 [件] /jiàn/ (1) 件0219 条件0420 事件0884 文件1496 案件2150 软件2530

0251 直 [直] /zhí/ (1) 一直0240 直接0520 直0842 简直1654 直到2802 直3294

0252 条 [條] /tiáo/ (1) 条0157 条件0420 条约2716

0253 四 [四] /sì/ (1) 四0128 四处3739

0254 期 [期] /qī/ (1) 时期0590 长期1037 期间1107 期1610 星期2258 期2299 期待2650 期望3458 初期3750 日期4646 后期4767 期限4870 短期4872 学期4965

0255 论 [論] /lùn/ (1) 理论0679 讨论0819 无论1109 结论2167 辩论2244 论2294 舆论2324 论文2562 不论2810 评论2858 议论3218 争论3262 论坛3370 论3749 无论如何4222 谈论4449

0256 怎 [怎] /zěn/ (1) 怎么0129 怎样0752 怎么样1156 怎2701

0257 像 [像] /xiàng/ (1) 像0133 好像0710 想像3288

0258 带 [帶] /dài/ (1) 带0204 带来0759 带2178 带有2782 带领3317 一带4289 带动4448 地带4469

0259 品 [品] /pǐn/ (2) 作品0589 产品0647 商品0901 食品1871 毒品2448 品牌2452 品种2579 品质3569 物品3671 药品3904 用品4580 品4836

0260 快 [快] /kuài/ (1) 快0358 快1041 很快1161 快乐1488 快速2340 愉快2465 尽快2467 加快2498 赶快2993 痛快4690

0261 太 [太] /tài/ (1) 太0151 太阳1389 老太太2252 太太2342

0262 呢 [呢] /ne/ (1) 呢0089

0263 利 [利] /lì/ (1) 利益0599 利用0725 胜利1239 利1294 权利1322 顺利1665 利润2552 不利2634 有利2651 有利于2690 福利3235

0264 风 [風] /fēng/ (1) 风0705 风格1987 风险1994 风景3045 作风3181 风暴3845 风光3875 风气4431

0265 量 [量] /liáng, liàng/ (2) 力量0605 大量1001 质量1017 量1307 数量1986 尽量2153 商量2221 能量3444 产量3465 衡量4455 较量4829

0266 非 [非] /fēi/ (1) 非常0217 非0702 非1578 并非2995 除非3696 是非3992 无非4521

0267 月 [月] /yuè/ (1) 月0138 岁月3259 月亮4523

0268 十 [十] /shí/ (1) 十0152 十分0449 数十4422

0269 资 [資] /zī/ (2) 投资0642 资源0950 资金1139 资料1144 工资1312 资格1873 资本2007 资产2062 资本主义3539 投资4141 资4238 物资4290 资助4308

0270 东 [東] /dōng/ (1) 东西0208 东0734 东方1660 东北1693 东部3901 东南3934 股东4594

0271 每 [每] /měi/ (1) 每0159 每天0596 每年1063 每当4189 每4911

0272 建 [建] /jiàn/ (1) 建设0442 建立0469 建筑1148 建1193 建议1215 建成2766 建造3616 封建3658 修建4203 组建4413 建议4671 重建4682

0273 保 [保] /bǎo/ (2) 保护0537 保持0704 保证0915 保险1656 保障1754 保1769 保留2557 保存2911 确保3036 保卫3217 保密4500 保护4970

0274 决 [決] /jué/ (1) 解决0349 决定0363 坚决1570 决定2270 决心2815 决议3065 决策3182 决3291 决3782 决心4342 判决4678

0275 往 [往] /wǎng/ (1) 往0342 往往1110 交往1372 以往2372 前往3014 往来4200 来往4264 往事4706 往后4715 向往4778

0276 神 [神] /shén/ (1) 精神0316 神1172 神秘2377 神2406 眼神3472 精神3776 神经3790 神话3906 神奇4077 神圣4163 神情4753

0277 至 [至] /zhì/ (2) 至0382 甚至0430 至少0927 至今1565 至于1633 甚2534 乃至3327

0278 住 [住] /zhù/ (1) 住0200 抓住1202 居住2571 住店2685 记住2763 住宅3800 忍不住4059 住院4095

0279 强 [強] /qiáng, qiǎng/ (2) 强0409 加强0836 强调1025 强烈1082 强大1842 增强2305 坚强3490 顽强4114 强迫4886

0280 命 [命] /mìng/ (2) 生命0502 革命0680 命运1360 命令1701 命1814 命3200 使命3912 任命3973 拼命4606 命名4728

0281 告 [告] /gào/ (1) 告诉0280 报告0644 广告1584 告1819 告别3289 警告3318 宣告4674

0282 流 [流] /liú/ (1) 交流1021 流1284 流行2429 流动2987 流3126 流域3502 一流3591 流传4014 潮流4137 流氓4377 流血4687 河流4861

0283 司 [司] /sī/ (2) 公司0162 司机1850 司令2601 司2868 上司4816

0284 清 [清] /qīng/ (1) 清楚0481 清0598 清醒2431 清晰3018 清3550 清理3822 清晨4340 清洁4840

0285 指 [指] /zhǐ/ (1) 指0536 指出0978 指导1533 指挥1770 指示2581 指标2923 指责3039 指定3861 手指4082 指挥4974

0286 区 [區] /qū/ (2) 地区0312 区0629 区域2261 自治区2415 山区3303 区别3871 开发区3908 市区4939 郊区4966 区别4986

0287 师 [師] /shī/ (1) 老师0386 师0961 教师1088 大师2418 律师2426 师傅3208 工程师3789 导师4534

0288 美 [美] /měi/ (2) 美元0941 美丽1220 美好1457 美1461 美女2888 完美3275 优美3978 美术4084 审美4215

0289 数 [數] /shǔ, shù/ (1) 数0667 数字1651 数量1986 多数2071 人数2219 大多数2224 少数民族2353 无数2423 少数2434 数据2600 数学2790 绝大多数3439 总数4385 数十4422

0290 声 [聲] /shēng/ (1) 声0806 声音0814 声1296 掌声2366 声明2905 大声3300 笑声3713 歌声4381

0291 望 [望] /wàng/ (1) 希望0259 望1402 希望2194 愿望2447 欲望2659 渴望2746 失望3273 期望3458 绝望4693 望远镜4817 看望4831

0292 亲 [親] /qīn/ (1) 父亲0452 母亲0483 亲自1519 亲2125 亲切2633 亲戚2772 亲3422 亲人3568

0293 爱 [愛] /ài/ (1) 爱0230 爱情1167 恋爱2427 可爱2808 热爱3027 喜爱3117 爱国3829 爱心3948

0294 求 [求] /qiú/ (1) 要求0424 要求0738 追求0975 求1065 需求1717 寻求3267 实事求是4636 请求4771

0295 义 [義] /yì/ (1) 意义0514 社会主义0857 主义2045 义2779 义务2860 名义3158 正义3281 资本主义3539 含义4433

0296 始 [始] /shǐ/ (1) 开始0139 始终1151 开始2063 原始3245 始3968

0297 传 [傳] /chuán, zhuàn/ (2) 传统0507 传1267 宣传1370 传播2461 传说2680 传来3222 传3282 流传4014 传递4107 传达4498

0298 谈 [談] /tán/ (1) 谈0245 谈判1619 谈话1808 会谈2781 交谈2824 谈4383 谈论4449 谈话4475

0299 术 [術] /shù/ (1) 技术0350 艺术0492 学术1425 手术2755 艺术家2832 术3052 武术3537 美术4084 战术4133

0300 孩 [孩] /hái/ (1) 孩子0149 女孩1242 小孩1745 男孩2438 女孩子2795 小孩子3913

0301 改 [改] /gǎi/ (1) 改革0416 改变0582 改782 改造1526 改善1783 修改2532 改进3723

0302 领 [領] /lǐng/ (1) 领导0334 领域1173 领导人1668 领747 占领2390 带领3317 领袖3463 率领3643 领土3747 本领4642

0303 金 [金] /jīn/ (2) 金0429 资金1139 金融1906 金牌2097 黄金2719 奖金3255 金钱3506 基金3574 金额4186 金属4528 现金4536

0304 吃 [吃] /chī/ (1) 吃0137 吃饭1106 好吃4414

0305 形 [形] /xíng/ (2) 形成0551 形式0853 形象1022 形势1293 形1993 情形2310 形态3801 形容4197 形状4645 形象4843

0306 叫 [叫] /jiào/ (1) 叫0134 叫做2079 名叫2938

0307 安 [安] /ān/ (1) 安全0777 安排0785 安1772 公安2717 公安局3131 不安3297 安3405 治安3753 安静3770 安置4275 安装4348 安定4733 平安4968 安慰4990

0308 友 [友] /yǒu/ (1) 朋友0303 友2163 友谊2856 友2983 战友4584 小朋友4853 男朋友4875

0309 视 [視] /shì/ (1) 电视0696 重视0974 视1726 电视台1825 电视剧3755 视为3818 忽视3961 影视4092 电视机4336 视野4482 视察4785 歧视4837

0310 象 [象] /xiàng/ (2) 象0684 现象0774 形象1022 对象1271 印象1301 想象1809 景象3399 象征3797 象征4265 气象4743 形象4843

0311 观 [觀] /guān/ (1) 观众0942 观念1034 观点1327 观察1569 观1911 客观2612 参观2662 价值观3507 乐观3733 观看3884 主观4980

0312 识 [識] /shí/ (1) 认识0421 知识0555 意识0854 认识2205 知识份子2303 识3766 意识4304

0313 讲 [講] /jiǎng/ (1) 讲0183 讲话1306 演讲3100 讲究3197 讲述3974 来讲4300 讲座4998

0314 何 [何] /hé/ (1) 任何0336 如何0373 何1094 为何3114 何况3530 无论如何4222

0315 色 [色] /sè/ (1) 色1537 特色1657 角色2098 颜色2236 红色2263 色彩2413 出色2443 绿色2778 黑色3026 白色3471 黄色4085 蓝色4087 脸色4132 彩色4806

0316 程 [程] /chéng/ (2) 过程0415 程度0802 工程0832 进程1960 程式2225 工程师3789 课程3838 历程3945

0317 院 [院] /yuàn/ (1) 医院0635 学院1072 院1265 院长1803 法院2207 科学院2968 院子3705 住院4095

0318 收 [收] /shōu/ (1) 收0694 收入0965 收到1589 吸收2494 收拾3427 收购3584 收回3684 收费3819 收集3858 收藏4069 接收4621 收获4805

0319 及 [及] /jí/ (2) 及0318 以及0383 及时1630 涉及1933 及其2339 来不及4497

0320 近 [近] /jìn/ (1) 近0362 最近0781 附近1361 接近1628 近年来2540 近日4054 靠近4404

0321 或 [或] /huò/ (1) 或0223 或者0367 或是2788 或许2900

0322 影 [影] /yǐng/ (1) 影响0333 电影0658 摄影2757 影片3231 影3423 影视4092 影子4223 影响4325 阴影4589 身影4866

0323 百 [百] /bǎi/ (1) 百0375 老百姓1710 百姓2626

0324 服 [服] /fú/ (1) 服务0652 衣服0981 服装2274 舒服2632 克服2909 服3194 服从4096 佩服4204 说服4267 服务员4524

0325 式 [式] /shì/ (2) 方式0380 形式0853 正式1036 式1050 模式1594 仪式2108

0326 许 [許] /xǔ/ (1) 许多0257 也许0645 允许1489 许1807 或许2900 许3783

0327 字 [字] /zì/ (1) 字0329 名字0921 文字1339 数位1651 签字4507

0328 光 [光] /guāng/ (2) 光1114 阳光1777 目光2002 光2082 眼光2226 光3244 光荣3353 风光3875 光明4073 灯光4246 时光4292

0329 统 [統] /tǒng/ (2) 传统0507 系统0821 总统0849 统一1451 统计1642 统一2267 统治2840 系统3356

0330 深 [深] /shēn/ (1) 深0608 深刻1262 深入2126 深2350 深入3265 深处3314 深深3494 深受4459 深厚4516 深夜4714

0331 计 [計] /jì/ (1) 计划0575 设计1165 估计1541 统计1642 计算机1765 计算2493 会计2730 计4148 计4235 预计4410

0332 吗 [嗎] /ma/ (1) 吗0116 干吗3509

0333 单 [單] /dān/ (1) 单位0516 简单0760 单1811 单2269 单纯2750 名单3719 单独4029 单一4629

0334 跟 [跟] /gēn/ (1) 跟0181 跟0490 跟2268 跟踪4151

0335 白 [白] /bái/ (1) 白0633 明白0697 白天2459 明白3224 白色3471 空白4486 白4632

0336 吧 [吧] /ba, bā/ (1) 吧0119

0337 治 [治] /zhì/ (1) 政治0308 治1335 治疗1983 自治区2415 统治2840 治理3387 治安3753 自治4450 政治家4596

0338 整 [整] /zhěng/ (1) 整个0414 调整1223 完整1892 整1893 整体2034 整理2724 整3141 整天3277 整整3786 整顿3857 整齐4838

0339 死 [死] /sǐ/ (1) 死0239 死1117 死亡1316 死去4272

0340 花 [花] /huā/ (1) 花0660 花1162 花3040 花园3153 花钱3388 鲜花3794 棉花4745

0341 商 [商] /shāng/ (1) 商品0901 商业1074 商量2221 商店2408 商场2446 商2965 商人3468 工商3606 商4700

0342 算 [算] /suàn/ (1) 算0377 算是1670 计算机1765 计算2493 打算2514 就算3899 打算4000 预算4046 就算4910

0343 步 [步] /bù/ (1) 步0565 进一步1055 进步1178 逐步2257 步伐4001 步骤4129 地步4230 脚步4811 初步4839

0344 眼 [眼] /yǎn/ (1) 眼睛0736 眼0898 眼1616 眼前2121 眼光2226 眼泪2435 眼里2870 眼神3472 眼中3810 眼镜4126 心眼4535 眼下4940

0345 必 [必] /bì/ (1) 必须0264 必要1142 必1607 不必2127 必然2378 未必4120 必定4520

0346 导 [導] /dǎo/ (1) 领导0334 导致1371 指导1533 领导人1668 导演2157 引导2666 导师4534 主导4735 导弹4862

0347 调 [調] /diào, tiáo/ (1) 调查0770 强调1025 调整1223 调1226 协调2765 调动3240 空调4252

0348 钱 [錢] /qián/ (1) 钱0158 花钱3388 金钱3506 挣钱4110 价钱4531 赚钱4683 有钱4842

0349 际 [際] /jì/ (2) 国际0253 实际上0928 实际1404 实际1711 之际3438

0350 务 [務] /wù/ (1) 服务0652 任务0827 业务1256 职务2490 事务2538 义务2860 财务3543 服务员4524

0351 五 [五] /wǔ/ (1) 五0172

0352 万 [萬] /wàn/ (1) 万0433 千万1897 万一3832

0353 持 [持] /chí/ (1) 支持0538 坚持0692 保持0704 持续1771 维持1991 主持2014 持2333 主持人2718

0354 张 [張] /zhāng/ (1) 张0216 紧张0855 主张2774 主张3053 夸张4677

0355 容 [容] /róng/ (1) 内容0488 容易0569 容1841 笑容3709 形容4197

0356 越 [越] /yuè/ (2) 越0347 越来越0604 超越3223 越是3785

0357 准 [准] /zhǔn/ (1) 准备0337 标准0776 准1334 批准2069 准确2202 准2849 准则4432

0358 城 [城] /chéng/ (1) 城市0344 城0616 城里2820 县城3000 古城4936

0359 团 [團] /tuán/ (1) 集团0866 团0991 团结1855 代表团2241 团长2436 团体2604 团3313

0360 根 [根] /gēn/ (1) 根据0549 根本0967 根本1204 根1551 根2249 根本3085

0361 包 [包] /bāo/ (1) 包括0394 包1089 包装3320 承包3350 包含3856 包围4060 包袱4587 面包4639

0362 历 [曆] /lì/ (1) 历史0214 经历1497 经历1963 历程3945 学历3997

0363 满 [滿] /mǎn/ (1) 满0495 充满0893 满意1260 满足1351 不满2990 满足4737 圆满4906

0364 运 [運] /yùn/ (1) 运动0883 命运1360 运1719 运用1779 运动1901 运动员1957 运输2255 运行2733 运作3925 运动会3935 幸运4164 运气4857

0365 造 [造] /zào/ (2) 造成0656 创造0779 改造1526 制造1542 造1640 建造3616 塑造3730 造型4296 营造4834

0366 空 [空] /kōng, kòng/ (1) 空间1289 空气1869 空2058 空军2365 空中2566 空2907 天空2958 航空3600 空调4252 空白4486 空4947

0367 元 [元] /yuán/ (1) 元0205 美元0941 公元4376

0368 写 [寫] /xiě/ (1) 写0177 写作2214 描写3191 写信4149

0369 转 [轉] /zhuǎn, zhuàn/ (2) 转0669 转移2189 转变2360 转向2937 转化3348 转身3652 转换4623 旋转4893

0370 找 [找] /zhǎo/ (1) 找0180 找到0813 寻找1456

0371 男 [男] /nán/ (1) 男0468 男人0513 男子1344 男性2346 男孩2438 男朋友4875

0372 取 [取] /qǔ/ (1) 取得0706 采取0786 取1332 争取1588 取消2844 取代4310 夺取4826 听取4896

0373 精 [精] /jīng/ (1) 精神0316 精力2272 精2349 精彩2711 精心3395 精神3776

0374 究 [究] /jiù/ (1) 研究0232 究竟1413 研究所2285 研究2596 研究生2817 讲究3197 追究4510

0375 山 [山] /shān/ (1) 山0489 山区3303 火山4935

0376 言 [言] /yán/ (1) 语言0994 言1027 而言1927 发言2003 宣言3941

0377 啊 [啊] /ā, á, ǎ, a/ (1) 啊0222 啊0341

0378 且 [且] /qiě/ (1) 而且0185 并且0851 且1592

0379 科 [科] /kē/ (1) 科技0856 科学0878 科学1504 科1827 科学家1925 科研2396 科学院2968 科长4996

0380 片 [片] /piàn/ (1) 片0381 照片1042 影片3231
名片4869

0381 济 [濟] /jì/ (1) 经济0161 市场经济2177

0382 半 [半] /bàn/ (1) 半0238 一半1445

0383 远 [遠] /yuǎn/ (1) 远0454 永远0910 远远2154
遥远3392 长远4519 望远镜4817

0384 便 [便] /biàn, pián/ (1) 便0285 方便1582 随便2124
便宜2393 便3019 即便3328 以便3987

0385 考 [考] /kǎo/ (1) 考虑0584 考1394 思考1435
考察1682 考试1733 考验3347 考上3687 高考4089
考核4613 参考4775

0386 失 [失] /shī/ (2) 失去1102 失败1480 损失1596
消失2113 失2233 失望3273 丧失3514 失业4008
失误4688

0387 况 [況] /kuàng/ (1) 情况0176 状况1290 何况3530

0388 组 [組] /zǔ/ (1) 组织0475 组织0823 组成1494
组1949 组1959 小组2107 组建4413 组合4560 组长4747

0389 连 [連] /lián/ (1) 连0365 连1458 连续1923 连2585
连接4553

0390 基 [基] /jī/ (1) 基本0505 基础0553 基地1739
基本上1867 基层2859 基因3089 基3448 基金3574
基于4339

0391 早 [早] /zǎo/ (1) 早0320 早已1735 早就1755
早晨2304 早上2356 早日4847

0392 确 [確] /què/ (1) 确实0969 正确1103 确定1194
明确1329 确2128 的确2193 准确2202 确保3036
确认3559 明确5002

0393 级 [級] /jí/ (1) 级1013 高级1583 年级2486
上级3229 一级3247 阶级3332 等级4045 级别4236
级4326

0394 请 [請] /qǐng/ (1) 请0268 邀请1910 申请2213
请问3215 请求4771

0395 设 [設] /shè/ (1) 建设0442 设计1165 设备1368
设1672 设施1962 设立2336 设置3411 设想3683

0396 海 [海] /hǎi/ (1) 海0689 海洋1872 海外2474
海军2861 沿海3498 大海4294 海湾4387 海关4984

0397 乐 [樂] /lè, yuè/ (1) 音乐1051 快乐1488 乐1728
娱乐2665 俱乐部3084 乐3515 欢乐3588 乐观3733
乐趣4703

0398 议 [議] /yì/ (2) 会议0400 建议1215 协议1615
决议3065 议论3218 抗议3762 建议4671

0399 火 [火] /huǒ/ (1) 火1077 火车2129 火3915
火车站4188 火山4935

0400 争 [爭] /zhēng/ (2) 战争0597 竞争1054 斗争1192
争1534 争取1588 争3262 争夺3888

0401 照 [照] /zhào/ (1) 按照0795 照片1042 照1512
照顾1817 照样4320 照4491

0402 病 [病] /bìng/ (1) 病0600 病人1560 疾病2536
爱滋病2605 毛病2737 病毒3676 生病4891

0403 离 [離] /lí/ (1) 离开0665 离0698 距离1447 离婚2070
脱离3238 分离4349

0404 类 [類] /lèi/ (2) 人类0435 类0595 之类2276
类似2850 类型2862

0405 极 [極] /jí/ (1) 极0610 积极0872 极大2363
极为2595 极其2882 积极性3792 极了3894
消极4462

0406 断 [斷] /duàn/ (2) 不断0455 断1108 判断2609
打断3038

0407 达 [達] /dá/ (2) 达0614 达到0638 表达1395
发达2235 达成2319 到达2541 抵达4205 传达4498

0408 较 [較] /jiào/ (1) 比较0321 较0539 比较3007
较为4169 较量4829

0409 热 [熱] /rè/ (1) 热0868 热情1211 热烈2052
热闹2247 热爱3027 热4080

0410 首 [首] /shǒu/ (1) 首先0557 首0731 首2210
首都2551 首脑3375 首3499 首相4048 为首4345

0411 规 [規] /guī/ (2) 规定0724 规模1407 规律1683
规则2380 规定2385 规划2425 大规模2943 规矩3368
规划4199

0412 集 [集] /jí/ (1) 集团0866 集体1484 集中1600
集2114 集中2524 收集3858 集4051 聚集4303 集4744

0413 校 [校] /xiào, jiào/ (1) 学校0278 校长1483 校2168
校园2981

0414 众 [眾] /zhòng/ (2) 群众0622 观众0942 众多2181
众2407 公众2776 民众3446 听众3571 众人3604
大众3993

0415 球 [球] /qiú/ (1) 球1376 地球1419 全球1469
足球1737 全球化2825 篮球3359 乒乓球4286

0416 节 [節] /jié, jiē/ (1) 节目0839 春节2458 节2526
情节2890 环节3066 细节3090 季节3254 节3474
节日3701 节奏3876 节约4987

0417 专 [專] /zhuān/ (2) 专家0803 专业0953 专门1465
专2504 专门2897

0418 共 [共] /gòng/ (1) 共0721 共同0733 共产党1273 公
共1861 共和国4039 共有4784 一共4845

0419 权 [權] /quán/ (3) 权1152 权力1321 权利1322
政权2657 权益2833 权威3004

0420 却 [卻] /què/ (2) 却0150

0421 兴 [興] /xìng, xīng/ (1) 高兴0585 兴趣0888 兴2081
兴奋3274 兴奋3651 兴起4505

0422 研 [研] /yán/ (1) 研究0232 研究所2285 科研2396
研究2596 研究生2817 研制4609

0423 据 [據] /jù/ (2) 据0543 根据0549 据说2024
证据2237 资料2600 依据3001 占据4153

0424 房 [房] /fáng/ (1) 房1031 房子1060 房间1744
住房2685 房屋3179 厨房3837

0425 选 [選] /xuǎn/ (2) 选择0580 选1222 选举2099
选手2135 竞选3976 挑选4894

0426 台 [台] /tái/ (2) 台0651 电视台1825 台1999
舞台2019 电台2950 台阶3258 柜台4919

0427 史 [史] /shǐ/ (1) 历史0214 史1314

0428 切 [切] /qiē/ (1) 一切0366 密切2282 亲切2633
切2894

0429 农 [農] /nóng/ (1) 农民0509 农村0715 农业0831
农场2975 农3639

0430 备 [備] /bèi/ (1) 准备0337 设备1368 具备2328
装备3706 备4209 预备4256

0431 格 [格] /gé/ (2) 价格1155 严格1502 性格1511
资格1873 风格1987 人格2451 格外3565 格局3878
合格4366

0432 功 [功] /gōng/ (2) 成功0401 功能1453 功1540
功夫2715 功课4649

0433 千 [千] /qiān/ (1) 千0666 千万1897

0434 质 [質] /zhì/ (2) 质量1017 物质1358 素质1498
性质2259 本质2655 地质3088 气质3369 质3540
品质3569 实质4331

0435 客 [客] /kè/ (1) 客人1390 客2017 客户2091
客观2612 顾客2903 客气3344 旅客3464 游客3505
客厅4854

0436 落 [落] /luò/ (2) 落0775 落后2174 落实2479
角落4473

0437 哪 [哪] /nǎ, na/ (1) 哪0464 哪里1014 哪儿1100
哪1529 哪个1778 哪些2722 哪怕3248

0438 价 [價] /jià/ (2) 价值0740 价格1155 评价1439
价2001 代价2956 价值观3507 物价4467
价钱4531

0439 响 [響] /xiǎng/ (1) 影响0333 响2783 响3146
影响4325 响起4558 反响4704

0440 则 [則] /zé/ (2) 则0368 原则0810 否则1319
规则2380 准则4432

0441 念 [念] /niàn/ (1) 观念1034 念1443 概念1764
纪念2374 信念3364 念头3910 理念4251

0442 参 [參] /cān/ (1) 参加0317 参与1153 参观2662
参谋4755 参考4775

0443 段 [段] /duàn/ (1) 段0310 阶段0889 手段1104

0444 育 [育] /yù/ (1) 教育0270 体育1147 发育4776
生育4949 育4951

0445 欢 [歡] /huān/ (1) 喜欢0353 欢迎1020 欢乐3588

0446 证 [證] /zhèng/ (2) 证明0906 保证0915 证据2237
证2509 证实3198 证书4472 证券4540

0447 党 [黨] /dǎng/ (2) 党0521 共产党1273 国民党1958
党员2998 党委3337

0448 示 [示] /shì/ (1) 表示0398 显示1564 展示2246
指示2581 示3765 暗示4312

0449 士 [士] /shì/ (2) 人士1599 博士1645 战士1655
女士1870 士兵1974 硕士3807 护士4995

0450 企 [企] /qǐ/ (2) 企业0189 企图2569 企业家2684

0451 易 [易] /yì/ (1) 容易0569 贸易1233 易2695
交易2794 轻易3594 不易4418

0452 需 [需] /xū/ (1) 需要0247 需要1446 需求1717
需1847

0453 随 [隨] /suí/ (2) 随着0835 随1907 随时2096
随便2124 随后2297 随意3393 随3512 伴随4614
随之4797

0454 标 [標] /biāo/ (2) 目标0619 标准0776 标志2775
指标2923 标题3504

0455 习 [習] /xí/ (1) 学习0351 习惯1247 习惯3162
演习3521 练习3853

0456 消 [消] /xiāo/ (1) 消息0877 消费1410 消失2113
消费者2512 消除2803 取消2844 消灭2912 消3586
消极4462 消耗4551 消化4604

0457 息 [息] /xī/ (1) 信息0664 消息0877 休息1742
气息3636 息4929

0458 装 [裝] /zhuāng/ (1) 装0895 服装2274 武装2312
包装3320 装备3706 安装4348

0459 举 [舉] /jǔ/ (1) 举行0713 举1291 举办1952
选举2099 举4241 举动4598

0460 医 [醫] /yī/ (1) 医院0635 医生0920 医学1863
医疗2238 医3710 医药3756 中医4038

0461 底 [底] /dǐ/ (2) 底0771 到底1213 彻底1367
底下3497 年底3811

0462 注 [注] /zhù/ (1) 注意0461 关注1033 注重3060
注册3656 注4021 注定4559

0463 轻 [輕] /qīng/ (1) 年轻0687 轻1444 年轻人1626
轻松2051 轻易3594 减轻4395

0464 青 [青] /qīng/ (1) 青年0650 青2152 青少年2382
青春2488 青年人4759

0465 谁 [誰] /shéi/ (1) 谁0168

0466 呀 [呀] /ya, yā/ (1) 呀0293 呀0546 呀3135
哎呀3869

0467 支 [支] /zhī/ (1) 支持0538 支0793 支援2984
支撑3523 支付3731 支队4335

0468 晚 [晚] /wǎn/ (1) 晚上0559 晚0719 今晚2703
夜晚3953 晚会4175 晚饭4850

0469 官 [官] /guān/ (2) 官0986 官员1408 官兵2740
军官3398 官方4138 法官4244

0470 具 [具] /jù/ (2) 具有0503 具体0743 工具2117
具2201 具备2328 玩具3637 家具4034

0471 演 [演] /yǎn/ (1) 演出1493 演员1567
表演1680 演2139 导演2157 演讲3100 演习3521
扮演3971

0472 府 [府] /fǔ/ (1) 政府0233

0473 土 [土] /tǔ/ (2) 土地0826 土1506 领土3747
土壤4130

0474 紧 [緊] /jǐn/ (1) 紧张0855 紧1997 赶紧2059
紧2789 紧紧3080 紧急3148 抓紧4301 紧密4317

0475 态 [態] /tài/ (1) 态度0657 状态0947 生态2254 心态2453 形态3801 姿态3903 态4655

0476 够 [夠] /gòu/ (1) 能够0330 够0971 够1261 足够2521

0477 妈 [媽] /mā/ (1) 妈妈0573 妈0674 大妈3793

0478 突 [突] /tū/ (1) 突然0643 冲突1396 突出1674 突破2190

0479 局 [局] /jú/ (1) 局1216 局面2018 局长2074 局势3113 公安局3131 当局3371 结局3752 格局3878 局部4430

0480 线 [線] /xiàn/ (2) 线0937 路线2086 线2819 线索3996 战线4808

0481 技 [技] /jì/ (1) 技术0350 科技0856 技巧3367 技能4807

0482 八 [八] /bā/ (1) 八0286

0483 费 [費] /fèi/ (2) 消费1410 费1475 费用2130 消费者2512 浪费2760 经费3306 免费3561 收费3819 费3936 学费4426

0484 号 [號] /hào, háo/ (1) 号0526 号1522 号码2886 口号3253 号召4094 信号4180

0485 刚 [剛] /gāng/ (1) 刚0482 刚刚0955 刚才1004

0486 推 [推] /tuī/ (1) 推1158 推动1706 推进2281 推出2668 推广2821 推荐3099 推行3685

0487 即 [即] /jí/ (2) 即0574 立即0916 即使0972 即将2422 即便3328 当即4740

0488 笑 [笑] /xiào/ (1) 笑0387 微笑2759 笑话3302 开玩笑3642 笑容3709 笑声3713 可笑4627 玩笑4925

0489 存 [存] /cún/ (2) 存在0467 存1318 生存1487 保存2911 存款4593

0490 引 [引] /yǐn/ (2) 引起0717 吸引1356 引1823 引进2631 引导2666 引发3323

0491 喜 [喜] /xǐ/ (1) 喜欢0353 喜2899 喜2966 喜爱3117 喜悦4789

0492 留 [留] /liú/ (1) 留0676 留下0999 保留2557 留学3554 留给3650 停留3817 留学生4423

0493 势 [勢] /shì/ (2) 形势1293 优势1354 势力1903 势2240 趋势2288 局势3113

0494 马 [馬] /mǎ/ (1) 马1008 马上1780 马路3043

0495 双 [雙] /shuāng/ (1) 双方0707 双0958 双2837 双手3234

0496 复 [複] /fù/ (1) 恢复1081 复杂1132 反复2712 重复2845 报复3578 复4168 答复4945

0497 足 [足] /zú/ (1) 满足1351 足1591 不足1727 足球1737 足够2521 满足4737

0498 严 [嚴] /yán/ (2) 严重0673 严格1502 严肃1891 严2031 严厉3101 尊严3133 严峻4907

0499 终 [終] /zhōng/ (2) 终于0678 始终1151 最终1388 最终3527 终3663 终身4810

0500 站 [站] /zhàn/ (1) 站0376 站1644 车站3252 站3640 火车站4188 网站4592

0501 养 [養] /yǎng/ (1) 培养0907 养1133 营养2921 养老3975 修养4762 养成4888

0502 尽 [盡] /jǐn, jìn/ (2) 尽管0805 尽0962 尽量2153 尽快2467 尽可能4121

0503 投 [投] /tóu/ (2) 投资0642 投入1246 投1725 投降3646 投资4141

0504 联 [聯] /lián/ (1) 联系0750 联合1552 联2767 联络3221 联邦3342

0505 母 [母] /mǔ/ (1) 母亲0483 父母0685 母3361 母3590

0506 岁 [歲] /suì/ (1) 岁0203 岁月3259

0507 志 [志] /zhì/ (1) 同志0406 杂志2035 志2275 标志2775 意志2922

0508 游 [遊] /yóu/ (1) 旅游1403 游1411 游戏2184 游泳2908 游客3505 游行3918

0509 拿 [拿] /ná/ (1) 拿0194

0510 革 [革] /gé/ (2) 改革0416 革命0680

0511 音 [音] /yīn/ (1) 声音0814 音乐1051 音2955

0512 买 [買] /mǎi/ (1) 买0266 购买2331 买卖2878

0513 害 [害] /hài/ (2) 害怕1929 厉害2057 伤害2222 害2517 损害3059 危害3451

0514 显 [顯] /xiǎn/ (2) 明显0993 显得1257 显然1554 显示1564 显2725 显著3391

0515 待 [待] /dāi, dài/ (2) 待1218 对待1866 等待2329 期待2650 接待2664 待遇2924 看待3321

0516 另 [另] /lìng/ (2) 另0425 另外0908 另外2371 另一方面2593 另3170

0517 红 [紅] /hóng/ (1) 红0532 红色2263 红旗4999

0518 除 [除] /chú/ (1) 除了0844 除1315 除2021 消除2803 除非3696 解除3921 排除4273

0519 续 [續] /xù/ (1) 继续0396 持续1771 连续1923 手续3047 陆续3632 延续4109

0520 境 [境] /jìng/ (2) 环境0385 境界2731 境内3610 困境4295 处境4434 边境4542 境4585

0521 愿 [願] /yuàn/ (1) 愿意0554 愿1007 愿望2447 自愿4446

0522 群 [群] /qún/ (2) 群众0622 群1035 群体2347 人群2399

0523 飞 [飛] /fēi/ (1) 飞0748 飞机0917 飞行4015

0524 初 [初] /chū/ (1) 初0874 当初2264 初2616 最初3042 初中3311 初期3750 初步4839

0525 采 [採] /cǎi/ (2) 采取0786 采访0886 采用1611 采购3345 采3644

0526 未 [未] /wèi/ (2) 未0533 未来1002 尚未2854 未必4120 从未4122

0527 仅 [僅] /jǐn/ (2) 不仅0576 仅0904 仅仅1722 不仅仅3063

0528 父 [父] /fù/ (1) 父亲0452 父母0685 父2623
父子4937

0529 送 [送] /sòng/ (1) 送0324 送给2707

0530 族 [族] /zú/ (1) 民族0410 少数民族2353 族2642
家族2982 贵族3716

0531 责 [責] /zé/ (1) 责任0655 负责0892 负责人2262
指责3039 职责3844 谴责4354 责任感4867

0532 村 [村] /cūn/ (1) 农村0715 村0858 村里2661
村民3257 乡村3746 村子4474

0533 排 [排] /pái/ (1) 安排0785 排1285 排除4273 排4436
排名4616

0534 苦 [苦] /kǔ/ (1) 痛苦1259 苦1366 艰苦3203
辛苦3389

0535 北 [北] /běi/ (1) 北1012 东北1693 北方2223
西北2636 北部3698 南北4030

0536 曾 [曾] /céng, zēng/ (2) 曾0357 曾经0722

0537 差 [差] /chā, chà, chāi/ (1) 差0708 差不多1650
差距2607 差异3214 差别3339 出差4680

0538 批 [批] /pī/ (1) 批0613 批评1092 批准2069
批判2516 大批3250

0539 低 [低] /dī/ (1) 低0504 降低2388 最低3660
低下4463 低头4780

0540 查 [查] /chá/ (1) 调查0770 检查1123 查1548
审查3583

0541 夫 [夫] /fū/ (1) 丈夫0995 夫人1205 夫妻2106
夫妇2355 功夫2715 夫2925 大夫3331 工夫4083

0542 古 [古] /gǔ/ (2) 古1043 古代1492 古老3016
古人3377 古典4074 古城4936

0543 围 [圍] /wéi/ (1) 范围1064 周围1184 围1859
围绕3137 氛围3804 包围4060

0544 创 [創] /chuàng/ (2) 创造0779 创作1308 创新2080
创2587 创业4504

0545 诉 [訴] /sù/ (1) 告诉0280

0546 约 [約] /yuē/ (2) 约0670 大约1721 条约2716
制约4306 约束4727 约定4833 节约4987

0547 语 [語] /yǔ/ (1) 语言0994 语1212 语气4577
语文4650 话语4818 外语4994

0548 值 [值] /zhí/ (2) 价值0740 值得1150 值2161
价值观3507

0549 护 [護] /hù/ (2) 保护0537 维护1549 护4447
拥护4496 保护4970 护士4995

0550 破 [破] /pò/ (1) 破坏1355 破1818 突破2190
打破2361 破2670 破产4885

0551 绝 [絕] /jué/ (2) 拒绝1309 绝对1510 绝2032
绝不2884 绝大多数3439 绝3491 绝对3525 绝望4693

0552 料 [料] /liào/ (2) 材料1076 资料1144 料3232
原料3743 预料4412 塑料4471 饮料4855

0553 营 [營] /yíng/ (2) 经营0808 营2290 营养2921
营业4274 营造4834

0554 令 [令] /lìng/ (2) 令0527 命令1701 司令2601
下令4211 令4814

0555 错 [錯] /cuò/ (1) 错0903 不错1006 错误1984
错2115 错误2116

0556 帮 [幫] /bāng/ (1) 帮助0632 帮0671 帮忙3725

0557 食 [食] /shí/ (1) 粮食1311 食品1871 食物2322
食2622 食3324 饮食3602 食堂4174

0558 您 [您] /nín/ (1) 您0209

0559 班 [班] /bān/ (1) 班0922 上班2111 下班3758
班3850 班长4801

0560 米 [米] /mǐ/ (1) 米0460 米1828 平方米2780
玉米3991 厘米4437

0561 案 [案] /àn/ (2) 案1561 方案1624 案件2150
答案2814 档案3157 图案4821

0562 纪 [紀] /jì/ (1) 世纪0463 纪念2374 年纪2637
纪录3260 纪律3336

0563 份 [份] /fèn/ (2) 份0437 身份1462 股份4707

0564 倒 [倒] /dǎo, dào/ (1) 倒0737 倒0882 倒霉4281

0565 层 [層] /céng/ (1) 层0923 层次2134 基层2859
阶层3443 高层4183

0566 星 [星] /xīng/ (1) 星1470 星期2258 明星2683
卫星3536 星星4971

0567 委 [委] /wěi/ (2) 委员会0938 委员2218 党委3337
委托4104

0568 兵 [兵] /bīng/ (1) 兵1075 士兵1974 官兵2740
兵力4091

0569 艺 [藝] /yì/ (1) 艺术0492 文艺1738 艺术家2832

0570 脑 [腦] /nǎo/ (2) 电脑1118 脑2023 脑子2410
脑袋2411 头脑2529 首脑3375 大脑4648

0571 职 [職] /zhí/ (2) 职工1341 职业1377 职务2490
职2863 辞职3624 职责3844

0572 周 [周, 週] /zhōu/ (1) 周围1184 周1659 周年2455
周3394 周末3450 周4713 周边4798

0573 致 [致] /zhì/ (2) 导致1371 一致1417 致1652
细致4461 致使4562

0574 派 [派] /pài/ (1) 派0769 派3742 派出所3847
派出3972

0575 项 [項] /xiàng/ (2) 项0440 项目0611

0576 布 [佈] /bù/ (1) 宣布1149 公布2589 分布2805
布3207 布置3855 发布3969 布4020

0577 织 [織] /zhī/ (1) 组织0475 组织0823

0578 称 [稱] /chēng, chèn/ (2) 称0783 称为1653
名称3312 称赞4009 称之为4409

0579 击 [擊] /jī/ (2) 打击1648 攻击2049 冲击2876
袭击2934 射击4201 击4213

0580 故 [故] /gù/ (1) 故事0625 故意2941 事故2976
故乡3362 故3900

0581 图 [圖] /tú/ (1) 图0982 图书馆2156 企图2569
试图3562 地图3667 图案4821

0582 居 [居] /jū/ (2) 居然1785 居民1898 居2094 居住2571 邻居3333

0583 划 [劃] /huá, huà/ (1) 计划0575 划2229 规划2425 策划3763 规划4199 划分4313

0584 按 [按] /àn/ (2) 按0457 按照0795

0585 画 [畫] /huà/ (1) 画0996 画2148 画面2891 画家3176 绘画4435

0586 广 [廣] /guǎng/ (1) 广告1584 广泛1603 广大1673 广播1686 广场2580 广2768 推广2821 广阔4416

0587 块 [塊] /kuài/ (1) 块0307 一块2726 一块儿5004

0588 怕 [怕] /pà/ (1) 怕0453 恐怕1514 害怕1929 可怕2320 哪怕3248

0589 坐 [坐] /zuò/ (1) 坐0279 坐下3924

0590 副 [副] /fù/ (2) 副0296 副3677

0591 似 [似] /sì/ (1) 似乎0784 似的1164 似2544 类似2850 相似3326 似4575

0592 增 [增] /zēng/ (1) 增加0691 增长1024 增强2305 增4070

0593 乎 [乎] /hū/ (2) 几乎0562 似乎0784

0594 章 [章] /zhāng/ (1) 文章0797 章1345 章3050

0595 赛 [賽] /sài/ (1) 比赛0747 赛2068 赛4181 竞赛4670

0596 验 [驗] /yàn/ (1) 经验0571 试验2586 体验2936 实验3054 考验3347 检验3579 实验室4004

0597 助 [助] /zhù/ (1) 帮助0632 援助3404 助3615 协助3815 资助4308 助理4485

0598 负 [負] /fù/ (2) 负责0892 负1559 负责人2262 负担2302 欺负4944

0599 句 [句] /jù/ (1) 句0256

0600 武 [武] /wǔ/ (2) 武器1775 武1988 武装2312 武术3537

0601 饭 [飯] /fàn/ (1) 饭0899 吃饭1106 饭店1824 做饭4617 晚饭4850

0602 须 [須] /xū/ (1) 必须0264 须3009

0603 继 [繼] /jì/ (1) 继续0396 继承2477 继4156 相继4421

0604 希 [希] /xī/ (1) 希望0259 希望2194

0605 评 [評] /píng/ (1) 批评1092 评价1439 评论2858 评3032 评估3769

0606 型 [型] /xíng/ (2) 型1200 大型1879 类型2862 典型3178 典型3777 造型4296

0607 石 [石] /shí/ (2) 石1905 石头2042 石油2678

0608 读 [讀] /dú/ (1) 读0607 读者1313 读书1558 阅读3759

0609 虽 [雖] /suī/ (1) 虽然0300 虽1255 虽说4465

0610 试 [試] /shì/ (1) 试0988 考试1733 试验2586 试图3562 尝试3686 测试4946

0611 酒 [酒] /jiǔ/ (1) 酒0634 喝酒2708 酒店3308 啤酒3702

0612 依 [依] /yī/ (2) 依然1381 依靠2212 依据3001 依3161 依赖3621 依旧4280

0613 独 [獨] /dú/ (2) 独立1691 独特2256 独立3096 孤独3493 独3592 单独4029 独自4420

0614 承 [承] /chéng/ (2) 承认0940 承担1671 继承2477 承受2748 承诺3122 承包3350

0615 模 [模] /mó/ (2) 规模1407 模式1594 大规模2943 模样3466 模糊4115 模特4819

0616 冲 [沖] /chōng, chòng/ (2) 冲0812 冲突1396 冲击2876 冲动3768

0617 构 [構] /gòu/ (2) 结构0709 机构0880 构成1941

0618 察 [察] /chá/ (2) 警察1137 观察1569 考察1682 视察4785

0619 刻 [刻] /kè/ (1) 深刻1262 立刻2145 时刻2260 刻3346 刻3426 时刻4118

0620 简 [簡] /jiǎn/ (1) 简单0760 简直1654

0621 环 [環] /huán/ (2) 环境0385 环节3066 循环4145 环4470

0622 久 [久] /jiǔ/ (1) 久1441 不久1937 悠久4568 多久4879

0623 六 [六] /liù/ (1) 六0332

0624 访 [訪] /fǎng/ (1) 采访0886 访问1485 访3522

0625 般 [般] /bān/ (1) 一般0392 般1174

0626 朋 [朋] /péng/ (1) 朋友0303 小朋友4853 男朋友4875

0627 斗 [鬥] /dòu, dǒu/ (2) 斗争1192 战斗2026 斗2123 奋斗2583

0628 假 [假] /jiǎ, jià/ (1) 假1176 假如2560

0629 换 [換] /huàn/ (1) 换0682 交换2645 转换4623

0630 拉 [拉] /lā/ (1) 拉0434 拉开2826

0631 室 [室] /shì/ (2) 办公室1023 室1573 教室3902 实验室4004 室内4053

0632 黑 [黑] /hēi/ (1) 黑0754 黑色3026 黑暗3413

0633 林 [林] /lín/ (2) 林0788 森林2397

0634 效 [效] /xiào/ (2) 效果1300 有效1379 效率2952

0635 益 [益] /yì/ (2) 利益0599 权益2833 日益2852 有益4116

0636 座 [座] /zuò/ (1) 座0471 座位4527 在座4610 讲座4998

0637 富 [富] /fù/ (1) 丰富1120 富1621 财富2620 富有2914 富裕3295

0638 担 [擔] /dān, dàn/ (2) 担心1235 承担1671 担任1695 负担2302

0639 角 [角] /jiǎo, jué/ (1) 角度1532 角色2098 角3086 主角3233 角3609 角落4473

0640 卖 [賣] /mài/ (1) 卖0497 买卖2878

0641 细 [細] /xì/ (1) 细1698 仔细1912 详细2466 细节3090 细胞3843 细致4461

0642 搞 [搞] /gǎo/ (1) 搞0288 搞好4722

0643 充 [充] /chōng/ (2) 充满0893 充分1011 补充2567

0644 景 [景] /jǐng/ (2) 背景1766 情景2379 景象2700
风景3045 景象3399 前景3573 场景4932

0645 速 [速] /sù/ (2) 迅速1028 速度1198 快速2340
加速3581

0646 优 [優] /yōu/ (2) 优秀1098 优势1354 优点3870
优美3978 优4165

0647 妇 [婦] /fù/ (2) 妇女0668 夫妇2355 媳妇2831

0648 激 [激] /jī/ (2) 激烈1763 激动1790 刺激2318
激情2835 感激4550

0649 王 [王] /wáng/ (2) 国王3990 王国4876

0650 律 [律] /lǜ/ (2) 法律0594 规律1683 律师2426
纪律3336 一律3833

0651 油 [油] /yóu/ (2) 油1531 石油2678

0652 靠 [靠] /kào/ (2) 靠0470 依靠2212 可靠3626
靠近4404 靠4663

0653 状 [狀] /zhuàng/ (2) 状态0947 状况1290 状2348
现状3572 形状4645

0654 器 [器] /qì/ (1) 武器1775 机器2597 器4284
仪器4997

0655 婚 [婚] /hūn/ (2) 结婚1009 婚姻1585 离婚2070
婚2196 婚礼3718

0656 源 [源] /yuán/ (2) 资源0950 源2132 来源2528
能源3597

0657 急 [急] /jí/ (1) 急1071 着急2591 紧急3148

0658 伤 [傷] /shāng/ (2) 伤1464 伤害2222 受伤3199
伤亡3655 伤心3980 伤4328

0659 药 [藥] /yào/ (1) 药1127 药物3538 医药3756
药品3904

0660 止 [止] /zhǐ/ (2) 停止1830 防止2495 为止2543
止2822 禁止3097 阻止3553 制止3887 不止4499

0661 省 [省] /shěng, xǐng/ (1) 省0641 反省4359

0662 警 [警] /jǐng/ (2) 警察1137 警告3318 警方4658
民警4661

0663 乡 [鄉] /xiāng/ (2) 乡1802 家乡2364 故乡3362
乡村3746 乡下4765

0664 善 [善] /shàn/ (2) 改善1783 完善2280 善于2873
善2992 善良3150 善3654

0665 讨 [討] /tǎo/ (1) 讨论0819 探讨3012 讨厌3352
讨3623

0666 银 [銀] /yín/ (1) 银行0755 银2953 银子4874

0667 爸 [爸] /bà/ (1) 爸爸0739 爸1415

0668 坚 [堅] /jiān/ (1) 坚持0692 坚决1570 坚定3017
坚强3490

0669 跑 [跑] /pǎo/ (1) 跑0399

0670 夜 [夜] /yè/ (1) 夜1478 夜2151 夜里3576 夜晚3953
深夜4714

0671 积 [積] /jī/ (2) 积极0872 面积1702 积累3189
积极性3792 积4063

0672 属 [屬] /shǔ/ (2) 属于1145 属1253 家属2971
金属4528

0673 网 [網] /wǎng/ (2) 网1029 网路1191 上网2916
网站4592

0674 抓 [抓] /zhuā/ (2) 抓0544 抓住1202 抓紧4301

0675 户 [戶] /hù/ (1) 客户2091 户2370 户3129 窗户3836
户口4705

0676 素 [素] /sù/ (2) 因素1099 素质1498 素4166

0677 馆 [館] /guǎn/ (1) 图书馆2156 馆2469 宾馆2791
博物馆3209 旅馆3839 餐馆4815

0678 介 [介] /jiè/ (1) 介绍0478 介绍4930

0679 剧 [劇] /jù/ (2) 悲剧2732 戏剧3212 京剧3633
电视剧3755 话剧4427

0680 血 [血] /xiě, xuè/ (2) 血1279 血液3665 流血4687
血管4921

0681 仍 [仍] /réng/ (2) 仍0476 仍然0824

0682 适 [適] /shì/ (1) 适应1550 适合1833 合适2030
适当2785 适用4769 舒适4904

0683 顺 [順] /shùn/ (2) 顺利1665 顺2967 顺3485
顺着4601

0684 招 [招] /zhāo/ (2) 招2449 招3384 招呼4396

0685 票 [票] /piào/ (1) 票1375 股票2511 邮票4031

0686 险 [險] /xiǎn/ (1) 危险1303 保险1656 风险1994

0687 味 [味] /wèi/ (2) 味2087 意味着2142 味道2714
滋味3946 味儿4654

0688 著 [著] /zhù/ (2) 著名0809 著2691 著作2902
显著3391

0689 压 [壓] /yā/ (2) 压力1190 压1468 压迫4548

0690 午 [午] /wǔ/ (1) 下午0764 上午1474 中午1915

0691 春 [春] /chūn/ (1) 春1363 春天2277 春节2458
青春2488

0692 背 [背] /bēi, bèi/ (2) 背0865 背景1766 违背4100
背后4522

0693 防 [防] /fáng/ (2) 防止2495 防2801 预防3196
防御3962 国防4860

0694 获 [獲] /huò/ (2) 获得0602 获1918 收获4805

0695 席 [席] /xí/ (2) 主席0499 出席2706

0696 供 [供] /gōng, gòng/ (2) 提供0542 供1951
供应3556 供给4941

0697 列 [列] /liè/ (2) 系列1759 列2522 列车3280
列入4355 列为4953

0698 楼 [樓] /lóu/ (1) 楼0603 大楼3112

0699 顾 [顧] /gù/ (1) 照顾1817 顾2386 顾客2903
不顾3139 顾问3416 回顾4210

0700 七 [七] /qī/ (1) 七0388

0701 菜 [菜] /cài/ (1) 菜0815 蔬菜2639

0702 歌 [歌] /gē/ (1) 歌1128 歌曲3795 诗歌3951
歌声4381

0703 既 [既] /jì/ (2) 既0491 既然1405

0704 否 [否] /fǒu/ (2) 是否0935 否则1319 能否2940 否定2963 否认3077

0705 答 [答] /dā, dá/ (1) 回答0789 答应1981 答2112 答案2814 答复4945

0706 退 [退] /tuì/ (1) 退1129 退休2430 退出3268

0707 杀 [殺] /shā/ (2) 杀0869 自杀3269 杀人3322

0708 练 [練] /liàn/ (1) 训练1143 练1858 教练2816 练习3853

0709 乱 [亂] /luàn/ (1) 乱1232 乱1544 混乱2898

0710 草 [草] /cǎo/ (1) 草1299 草原3669 起草4900 草地4973

0711 铁 [鐵] /tiě/ (2) 铁路1362 铁2286 钢铁4185

0712 占 [占] /zhàn/ (1) 占0583 占领2390 占有3140 占据4153

0713 密 [密] /mì/ (2) 密切2282 密2786 秘密2857 秘密2991 紧密4317 保密4500

0714 挥 [揮] /huī/ (2) 发挥1045 指挥1770 挥4441 指挥4974

0715 阶 [階] /jiē/ (2) 阶段0889 台阶3258 阶级3332 阶层3443

0716 修 [修] /xiū/ (2) 修1501 修改2532 修建4203 修养4762

0717 困 [困] /kùn/ (1) 困难0701 贫困1969 困境4295 困惑4736 困扰4777 困4989

0718 施 [施] /shī/ (2) 实施1182 措施1214 设施1962 施工3956

0719 遇 [遇] /yù/ (1) 遇到1005 遇2242 待遇2924 机遇3159 遇见4978

0720 厂 [廠] /chǎng/ (1) 厂0890 工厂1638 厂长3799 厂家4709

0721 穿 [穿] /chuān/ (1) 穿0419

0722 店 [店] /diàn/ (1) 店1111 饭店1824 商店2408 酒店3308 书店4579

0723 犯 [犯] /fàn/ (2) 犯1378 犯罪1822 侵犯3648 罪犯4653 犯人4856

0724 策 [策] /cè/ (2) 政策0558 决策3182 策划3763 策略3806

0725 置 [置] /zhì/ (2) 位置0966 置3319 设置3411 布置3855 安置4275

0726 吸 [吸] /xī/ (2) 吸引1356 吸2197 吸收2494 呼吸3452 吸烟4440 吸毒4958

0727 追 [追] /zhuī/ (2) 追求0975 追1346 追究4510

0728 例 [例] /lì/ (1) 比例2061 例子2424 例如2871 例3046 例外4597

0729 南 [南] /nán/ (1) 南1521 南方3115 南部3358 西南3880 东南3942 南北4030

0730 皇 [皇] /huáng/ (2) 皇帝1546 皇家4537

0731 脸 [臉] /liǎn/ (1) 脸0545 脸色4132

0732 牌 [牌] /pái/ (2) 牌1400 金牌2097 品牌2452 名牌3944 牌子4228

0733 甚 [甚] /shèn/ (3) 甚至0430 甚至2534 甚2811

0734 衣 [衣] /yī/ (1) 衣服0981 衣2291

0735 坏 [壞] /huài/ (1) 坏0897 破坏1355 坏人4490 坏事4931

0736 判 [判] /pàn/ (2) 谈判1619 批判2516 判断2609 判3242 判决4678 审判4783

0737 姐 [姐] /jiě/ (1) 小姐1163 姐姐2053 姐2383 姐妹3091 大姐3674

0738 树 [樹] /shù/ (1) 树1579 树2143 树立3885 树木4582

0739 烈 [烈] /liè/ (2) 强烈1082 激烈1763 热烈2052

0740 玩 [玩] /wán/ (1) 玩0753 玩具3637 开玩笑3642 玩意4484 玩笑4925

0741 停 [停] /tíng/ (1) 停1052 停止1830 停留3817

0742 股 [股] /gǔ/ (3) 股1416 股票2511 屁股3670 股市4139 股东4594 股份4707

0743 超 [超] /chāo/ (2) 超过1061 超2558 超越3223 超市4140 超出4679

0744 庭 [庭] /tíng/ (1) 家庭0418 法庭3605

0745 黄 [黃] /huáng/ (1) 黄1113 黄金2719 黄色4085

0746 配 [配] /pèi/ (2) 分配1688 配合1876 配1931

0747 河 [河] /hé/ (1) 河1154 河流4861

0748 钟 [鐘] /zhōng/ (1) 分钟0796 钟1209

0749 掉 [掉] /diào/ (1) 掉0431

0750 华 [華] /huá/ (3) 华人2537 华侨3751 繁华4318 豪华4628

0751 戏 [戲] /xì/ (2) 戏1248 游戏2184 戏剧3212

0752 右 [右] /yòu/ (1) 左右0952 右1337

0753 劳 [勞] /láo/ (1) 劳动1175

0754 闻 [聞] /wén/ (1) 新闻0798 闻2243

0755 敢 [敢] /gǎn/ (1) 敢0428 勇敢3657 敢于4892

0756 罪 [罪] /zuì/ (3) 罪1788 犯罪1822 罪犯4653 得罪4729

0757 胜 [勝] /shèng/ (1) 胜利1239 胜1724 战胜2761

0758 板 [板] /bǎn/ (1) 老板1115 板2073

0759 临 [臨] /lín/ (2) 面临1602 临2800 临时3977 来临4358 临时4370

0760 舞 [舞] /wǔ/ (1) 舞台2019 舞蹈2641 舞2764 跳舞4439

0761 预 [預] /yù/ (1) 预防3196 预测3560 预算4046 预备4256 预计4410 预料4412

0762 良 [良] /liáng/ (2) 良好1380 不良3105 善良3150 良3357 良心4250

0763 街 [街] /jiē/ (1) 街0932 大街2398 街道2508 街头3546

0764 拍 [拍] /pāi/ (1) 拍0837 拍摄2610

0765 财 [財] /cái/ (3) 财产2088 财政2400 财富2620 财务3543 财3711

0766 竟 [竟] /jìng/ (2) 竟1304 究竟1413 毕竟1571 竟然2102

0767 阳 [陽] /yáng/ (1) 太阳1389 阳光1777 阳2394

0768 余 [餘] /yú/ (2) 余0800 其余3575 业余3692

0769 园 [園] /yuán/ (1) 公园1998 园2437 校园2981 花园3153 家园4247 幼儿园4581

0770 货 [貨] /huò/ (2) 货1787 货物3340

0771 啦 [啦] /la/ (1) 啦0378

0772 温 [溫] /wēn/ (2) 温暖2441 温度3467 温3693 温柔3830 气温4852

0773 套 [套] /tào/ (2) 套0547

0774 赶 [趕] /gǎn/ (2) 赶1620 赶紧2059 赶到2464 赶快2993 赶上3406

0775 杂 [雜] /zá/ (1) 复杂1132 杂志2035 杂4979

0776 慢 [慢] /màn/ (1) 慢慢1277 慢1793 缓慢4841

0777 笔 [筆] /bǐ/ (1) 笔1369 笔2033

0778 宣 [宣] /xuān/ (2) 宣布1149 宣传1370 宣言3941 宣告4674

0779 某 [某] /mǒu/ (2) 某0480 某些1731

0780 朝 [朝] /cháo, zhāo/ (1) 朝1283

0781 烟 [煙] /yān/ (2) 烟1073 吸烟4440 抽烟4549 香烟4750

0782 短 [短] /duǎn/ (1) 短1097 短暂4319 短期4872

0783 略 [略] /lüè/ (2) 战略1078 侵略2799 略2830 策略3806 忽略4681

0784 奇 [奇] /qí, jī/ (1) 奇怪1749 奇2576 奇迹3279 好奇4027 神奇4077

0785 礼 [禮] /lǐ/ (1) 礼2037 礼物3566 婚礼3718 礼貌3744

0786 船 [船] /chuán/ (1) 船0879

0787 率 [率] /lǜ, shuài/ (2) 率1761 效率2952 率领3643

0788 堂 [堂] /táng/ (1) 堂2020 食堂4174 课堂4428 天堂4820

0789 左 [左] /zuǒ/ (1) 左右0952 左1224

0790 课 [課] /kè/ (1) 课1608 上课3316 课程3838 课题4042 课堂4428 功课4649

0791 败 [敗] /bài/ (2) 失败1480 腐败2283 败2404

0792 卫 [衛] /wèi/ (2) 卫生1590 保卫3217 卫星3536

0793 范 [範] /fàn/ (2) 范围1064

0794 微 [微] /wēi/ (2) 微2468 微笑2759 稍微4738

0795 咱 [咱] /zán/ (1) 咱们0540 咱1210

0796 括 [括] /kuò/ (2) 包括0394 概括3854

0797 呼 [呼] /hū/ (2) 呼吸3452 呼4144 招呼4396

0798 谢 [謝] /xiè/ (1) 感谢1422 谢谢1646 谢4064

0799 灵 [靈] /líng/ (1) 心灵2064 灵2204 灵魂2563 灵活3630

0800 旅 [旅] /lǚ/ (1) 旅游1403 旅客3464 旅3764 旅行3812 旅馆3839

0801 抗 [抗] /kàng/ (2) 抗3457 对抗3729 抗议3762 抵抗3816 反抗3882

0802 爷 [爺] /yé/ (2) 爷2065 爷爷2409 大爷2969 老爷3447

0803 皮 [皮] /pí/ (2) 皮1598 皮肤3440

0804 互 [互] /hù/ (1) 互相1282 相互1481 互3834

0805 协 [協] /xié/ (3) 协议1615 协会1864 协调2765 协助3815 协定3940

0806 楚 [楚] /chǔ/ (1) 清楚0481

0807 露 [露] /lù, lòu/ (2) 露2877 露出3061 暴露3165 透露3412

0808 材 [材] /cái/ (2) 材料1076 题材3715 身材4035 教材4916

0809 毒 [毒] /dú/ (3) 毒品2448 毒2904 病毒3676 吸毒4958

0810 冷 [冷] /lěng/ (1) 冷1697 冷静3103 寒冷4788

0811 脚 [腳] /jiǎo/ (1) 脚0790 脚步4811

0812 肯 [肯] /kěn/ (2) 肯定1085 肯定1241 肯1791 肯定4279

0813 普 [普] /pǔ/ (2) 普通1179 普遍1476

0814 限 [限] /xiàn/ (2) 限制2141 有限2296 无限3926 限4453 期限4870 限度4927

0815 遗 [遺] /yí/ (3) 遗憾2203 遗址2906 遗产3156

0816 县 [縣] /xiàn/ (2) 县0845 县城3000

0817 编 [編] /biān/ (2) 编2231 编辑2273

0818 喝 [喝] /hē, hè/ (1) 喝0519 喝酒2708

0819 销 [銷] /xiāo/ 销售1196 销4952

0820 怀 [懷] /huái/ (3) 怀疑1663 怀3142 怀3210 关怀3557

0821 救 [救] /jiù/ (2) 救1942 抢救4309

0822 彩 [彩] /cǎi/ (1) 色彩2413 精彩2711 彩3376 彩色4806

0823 洋 [洋] /yáng/ (2) 海洋1872 洋2481

0824 录 [錄] /lù/ (1) 记录2913 纪录3260 记录3360 录4495

0825 恶 [惡] /è, ě/ (3) 恶2165 恶劣4113

0826 掌 [掌] /zhǎng/ (1) 掌握1181 掌声2366 掌4044

0827 私 [私] /sī/ (2) 私人2656 私3062 走私4360

0828 散 [散] /sǎn, sàn/ (1) 散3617 散步3826 散文4237 散发4563

0829 亮 [亮] /liàng/ (1) 漂亮1227 亮2694 亮2839 月亮4523

0830 痛 [痛] /tòng/ (1) 痛苦1259 痛3414 痛3429 痛快4690

0831 雨 [雨] /yǔ/ (1) 雨1406

0832 疑 [疑] /yí/ (2) 怀疑1663 无疑2503 疑问4226

0833 木 [木] /mù/ (2) 木2470 树木4582

0834 维 [維] /wéi/ (2) 维护1549 维持1991 思维2089

0835 训 [訓] /xùn/ (2) 训练1143 培训1890 教训2131

0836 熟 [熟] /shú, shóu/ (1) 熟悉1509 成熟1530 熟2192

0837 秘 [秘] /mì/ (2) 神秘2377 秘书2729 秘密2857
秘密2991

0838 肉 [肉] /ròu/ (1) 肉1187 肌肉4478

0839 梦 [夢] /mèng/ (2) 梦0756 梦想3256

0840 弟 [弟] /dì/ (1) 兄弟1264 弟弟2395

0841 诗 [詩] /shī/ (2) 诗1016 诗人2345 诗歌3951

0842 架 [架] /jià/ (2) 架1547 架3483 打架4146

0843 休 [休] /xiū/ (1) 休息1742 退休2430 休4685
休闲4835

0844 借 [借] /jiè/ (1) 借0984 借口3802

0845 封 [封] /fēng/ (1) 封0977 封建3658 封闭4457

0846 香 [香] /xiāng/ (1) 香1317 香烟4750

0847 纸 [紙] /zhǐ/ (1) 报纸1201 纸1482

0848 毕 [畢] /bì/ (2) 毕业1003 毕竟1571 毕业生3947

0849 鱼 [魚] /yú/ (1) 鱼0885

0850 缺 [缺] /quē/ (2) 缺乏1689 缺1888 缺少2842
缺点4802

0851 忙 [忙] /máng/ (1) 忙0860 帮忙3725

0852 异 [異] /yì/ (2) 差异3214 异4117 异常4160

0853 娘 [娘] /niáng/ (1) 姑娘1046 娘2414

0854 升 [升] /shēng/ (2) 升1839 上升2188 提升4269
升起4684

0855 束 [束] /shù/ (1) 结束0624 约束4727

0856 康 [康] /kāng/ (1) 健康0804

0857 守 [守] /shǒu/ (2) 守1720 遵守3883

0858 绍 [紹] /shào/ (1) 介绍0478 介绍4930

0859 跳 [跳] /tiào/ (1) 跳0881 跳舞4439

0860 探 [探] /tàn/ (2) 探索2232 探讨3012 探3057

0861 免 [免] /miǎn/ (2) 避免2025 免费3561 免3767
难免4514

0862 遍 [遍] /biàn/ (1) 普遍1476 遍1845

0863 脱 [脫] /tuō/ (1) 脱2011 摆脱2519 脱离3238

0864 九 [九] /jiǔ/ (1) 九0560

0865 阵 [陣] /zhèn/ (2) 阵2158 阵地2954 阵3022

0866 惊 [驚] /jīng/ (2) 惊3058 震惊3863 惊讶3865
惊人3866

0867 执 [執] /zhí/ (2) 执行1286 执3618

0868 攻 [攻] /gōng/ (2) 进攻1856 攻击2049 攻2762

0869 贵 [貴] /guì/ (1) 贵1762 宝贵3489 珍贵3492
贵族3716

0870 毛 [毛] /máo/ (1) 毛2454 毛病2737

0871 握 [握] /wò/ (2) 掌握1181 把握1797 握3028
握手4546

0872 迎 [迎] /yíng/ (1) 欢迎1020 迎2688 迎接3219

0873 健 [健] /jiàn/ (1) 健康0804

0874 词 [詞] /cí/ (1) 词1197

0875 哥 [哥] /gē/ (1) 哥哥1862 哥1961 大哥2489

0876 旧 [舊] /jiù/ (1) 旧0944 依旧4280

0877 款 [款] /kuǎn/ (2) 贷款2473 款3044 存款4593

0878 补 [補] /bǔ/ (2) 补1821 补充2567 弥补4618

0879 曲 [曲] /qǔ, qū/ (3) 曲2093 歌曲3795

0880 福 [福] /fú/ (1) 幸福1238 福2185 福利3235

0881 危 [危] /wēi/ (1) 危险1303 危机1703 危害3451

0882 误 [誤] /wù/ (1) 错误1984 误2116 耽误4266
失误4688 误会5001

0883 监 [監] /jiān/ (3) 监督1563 监狱3023

0884 龙 [龍] /lóng/ (2) 龙0918

0885 奖 [獎] /jiǎng/ (2) 奖1568 奖金3255 奖励4608

0886 伙 [夥] /huǒ/ (2) 小伙子2599 家伙3024 伙伴3109
伙4492

0887 陆 [陸] /lù/ (2) 大陆1539 陆2979 陆续3632
陆军4924

0888 忘 [忘] /wàng/ (1) 忘1101 忘记1940

0889 克 [克] /kè/ (1) 克服2909 坦克3943 克4050

0890 虑 [慮] /lǜ/ (2) 考虑0584

0891 央 [央] /yāng/ (2) 中央0541

0892 翻 [翻] /fān/ (1) 翻1105 翻译3476

0893 概 [概] /gài/ (1) 大概1121 概念1764 概括3854

0894 威 [威] /wēi/ (3) 威胁1629 权威3004 威3528

0895 归 [歸] /guī/ (3) 归1601 回归3967

0896 睡 [睡] /shuì/ (1) 睡0964 睡觉2110 睡着4515
睡眠4779

0897 静 [靜] /jìng/ (1) 平静2611 冷静3103 静3434
安静3770

0898 唱 [唱] /chàng/ (1) 唱0929

0899 沉 [沉] /chén/ (2) 沉重2405 沉3682 沉默4159

0900 控 [控] /kòng/ (2) 控制0758 控4361

0901 鼓 [鼓] /gǔ/ (2) 鼓励1577 鼓4150

0902 授 [授] /shòu/ (1) 教授0711

0903 渐 [漸] /jiàn/ (2) 逐渐1666 渐渐2307 渐3206

0904 永 [永] /yǒng/ (1) 永远0910 永2945 永恒4282

0905 付 [付] /fù/ (2) 付出2055 付2327 对付2875
支付3731 应付3814

0906 幸 [幸] /xìng/ (1) 幸福1238 不幸3201 幸运4164

0907 累 [累] /lèi, lěi, léi/ (1) 累2234 积累3189

0908 野 [野] /yě/ (2) 视野4482 野4734

0909 嘴 [嘴] /zuǐ/ (1) 嘴1015 嘴里3067 嘴巴4136

0910 播 [播] /bō/ (1) 广播1686 传播2461 播3456

0911 版 [版] /bǎn/ (2) 出版1528 出版社2450 版3132

0912 挺 [挺] /tǐng/ (1) 挺0720 挺4612

0913 趣 [趣] /qù/ (2) 兴趣0888 有趣3079 乐趣4703

0914 盘 [盤] /pán/ (2) 盘2046 盘2948

0915 努 [努] /nǔ/ (1) 努力0472

0916 顶 [頂] /dǐng/ (2) 顶1641 顶4543

0917 懂 [懂] /dǒng/ (1) 懂0817 懂得2013

0918 骨 [骨] /gǔ, gú/ (2) 骨 2608 骨干 4647 骨头 4804

0919 寻 [尋] /xún/ (2) 寻找 1456 寻求 3267 寻 3383

0920 巨 [巨] /jù/ (2) 巨大 0863 巨 4791

0921 测 [測] /cè/ (2) 预测 3560 测 3727 猜测 4897
测试 4946

0922 牛 [牛] /niú/ (1) 牛 1773 牛 2217 牛奶 4983

0923 托 [托] /tuō/ (2) 托 2317 摩托车 4086 委托 4104

0924 沙 [沙] /shā/ (2) 沙 2777 沙漠 3334 沙发 3791

0925 尚 [尚] /shàng/ (3) 尚 1881 尚未 2854 和尚 2978
时尚 4090 高尚 4112

0926 屋 [屋] /wū/ (1) 屋 1836 屋里 2798 屋子 3021
房屋 3179

0927 稳 [穩] /wěn/ (2) 稳定 1126 稳 3628

0928 挑 [挑] /tiāo, tiǎo/ (2) 挑 1989 挑战 2041 挑选 4894

0929 含 [含] /hán/ (2) 含 1580 包含 3856 含义 4433

0930 述 [述] /shù/ (2) 上述 2367 描述 3432
讲述 3974 叙述 4554

0931 降 [降] /jiàng/ (2) 降 2029 下降 2332 降低 2388
投降 3646

0932 弱 [弱] /ruò/ (2) 弱 2545 脆弱 3780

0933 印 [印] /yìn/ (2) 印象 1301 印 3056

0934 松 [松] /sōng/ (2) 轻松 2051 放松 2935 松 3824
松 4055

0935 扬 [揚] /yáng/ (1) 扬 3241 表扬 4883

0936 怪 [怪] /guài/ (2) 奇怪 1749 怪 2546 怪 3647
难怪 4739

0937 尊 [尊] /zūn/ (2) 尊重 1268 尊严 3133 尊 4068
尊敬 4255

0938 谓 [謂] /wèi/ (2) 所谓 0792 可谓 3891 无所谓 4172

0939 恐 [恐] /kǒng/ (2) 恐怕 1514 恐怖 2338 恐惧 3529

0940 田 [田] /tián/ (2) 田 1399

0941 弄 [弄] /nòng/ (2) 弄 0716

0942 嘛 [嘛] /ma/ (1) 嘛 0531

0943 培 [培] /péi/ (3) 培养 0907 培训 1890

0944 射 [射] /shè/ (2) 射 2159 射击 4201 发射 4352

0945 检 [檢] /jiǎn/ (1) 检查 1123 检验 3579

0946 征 [征] /zhēng/ (2) 特征 2487 象征 3797 象征 4265
征 4346

0947 雪 [雪] /xuě/ (1) 雪 1350

0948 审 [審] /shěn/ (3) 审查 3583 审 4106 审美 4215
审判 4783

0949 端 [端] /duān/ (2) 端 1831

0950 英 [英] /yīng/ (1) 英雄 1459

0951 择 [擇] /zé/ (2) 选择 0580

0952 移 [移] /yí/ (2) 转移 2189 移 2403 移动 3069
移民 3183

0953 旁 [旁] /páng/ (1) 旁边 1572 旁 1593

0954 迷 [迷] /mí/ (2) 迷 3455 迷信 3890

0955 础 [礎] /chǔ/ (1) 基础 0553

0956 姓 [姓] /xìng/ (1) 老百姓 1710 姓 1846 百姓 2626
姓名 4285 姓 4374

0957 拥 [擁] /yōng/ (2) 拥有 0985 拥护 4496 拥抱 4773

0958 枪 [槍] /qiāng/ (2) 枪 1523

0959 摆 [擺] /bǎi/ (1) 摆 1141 摆脱 2519

0960 登 [登] /dēng/ (2) 登 1525 登记 3378

0961 暴 [暴] /bào/ (3) 暴力 2865 暴露 3165 风暴 3845

0962 轮 [輪] /lún/ (2) 轮 1758 轮 4307

0963 篇 [篇] /piān/ (1) 篇 0768

0964 祖 [祖] /zǔ/ (1) 祖国 1637

0965 洗 [洗] /xǐ/ (1) 洗 1067 洗澡 4768

0966 弹 [彈] /dàn, tán/ (2) 弹 3909 导弹 4862 弹 5003

0967 典 [典] /diǎn/ (1) 典型 3178 经典 3503 典型 3777
古典 4074

0968 若 [若] /ruò/ (3) 若 0954 若干 3082

0969 索 [索] /suǒ/ (3) 探索 2232 线索 3996 思索 4827

0970 云 [雲] /yún/ (1) 云 1566

0971 域 [域] /yù/ (3) 领域 1173 区域 2261 流域 3502

0972 智 [智] /zhì/ (3) 智慧 1938 智力 3372 智 4384

0973 纷 [紛] /fēn/ (2) 纷纷 1604 纠纷 3603

0974 透 [透] /tòu/ (2) 透 3030 透露 3412 透 4316
透过 4730 透明 4790 渗透 4957

0975 暗 [暗] /àn/ (2) 暗 2022 黑暗 3413 暗示 4312

0976 丝 [絲] /sī/ (2) 丝 2951 丝 3092 丝毫 3788

0977 绿 [綠] /lǜ/ (1) 绿 1536 绿色 2778

0978 亡 [亡] /wáng/ (3) 死亡 1316 伤亡 3655 亡 4451

0979 秀 [秀] /xiù/ (2) 优秀 1098

0980 禁 [禁] /jìn, jīn/ (2) 禁止 3097 禁 3625 不禁 4167

0981 震 [震] /zhèn/ (3) 地震 2008 震惊 3863 震动 4198

0982 帝 [帝] /dì/ (2) 皇帝 1546 上帝 3211

0983 献 [獻] /xiàn/ (2) 贡献 1225 献 3478 奉献 4105

0984 额 [額] /é/ (3) 额 3003 金额 4186

0985 德 [德] /dé/ (2) 道德 1343 德 2892

0986 硬 [硬] /yìng/ (2) 硬 1848 硬 3661

0987 奋 [奮] /fèn/ (2) 奋斗 2583 兴奋 3274 兴奋 3651

0988 宝 [寶] /bǎo/ (2) 宝 2681 宝贵 3489

0989 奶 [奶] /nǎi/ (1) 奶奶 2105 奶 3419 牛奶 4983

0990 鲜 [鮮] /xiān, xiǎn/ (2) 新鲜 2248 鲜花 3794
鲜明 3928 鲜 4415

0991 博 [博] /bó/ (3) 博士 1645 博物馆 3209 赌博 4899

0992 减 [減] /jiǎn/ (2) 减少 1438 减 2518 减轻 4395

0993 释 [釋] /shì/ (2) 解释 0949 释放 3689

0994 秋 [秋] /qiū/ (1) 秋 1854 秋天 3881

0995 竞 [競] /jìng/ (2) 竞争 1054 竞选 3976 竞赛 4670

0996 荣 [榮] /róng/ (2) 繁荣 3168 荣 3225 光荣 3353
荣誉 3401

0997 醒 [醒] /xǐng/ (2) 提醒 2100 醒 2316 清醒 2431

0998 麻 [麻] /má/ (1) 麻烦 1649

0999 尤 [尤] /yóu/ (1) 尤其 0639

1000 雄 [雄] /xióng/ (2) 英雄1459 雄3979

1001 厚 [厚] /hòu/ (2) 厚2173 深厚4516

1002 软 [軟] /ruǎn/ (2) 软1707 软件2530

1003 茶 [茶] /chá/ (1) 茶1812

1004 烧 [燒] /shāo/ (1) 烧1134 燃烧4098

1005 盖 [蓋] /gài/ (2) 盖1553 覆盖4830

1006 售 [售] /shòu/ (3) 销售1196 出售4781

1007 针 [針] /zhēn/ (2) 方针1971 针对2565 针3937

1008 汽 [汽] /qì/ (1) 汽车0718

1009 童 [童] /tóng/ (2) 儿童1066 童年4934

1010 敌 [敵] /dí/ (2) 敌人1515 敌4245

1011 默 [默] /mò/ (2) 幽默2575 沉默4159

1012 核 [核] /hé/ (3) 核心1874 考核4613 核4923

1013 折 [折] /zhé/ (2) 折3958 折磨4401

1014 姑 [姑] /gū/ (1) 姑娘1046

1015 夏 [夏] /xià/ (1) 夏1908 夏天2357 夏季4766

1016 绩 [績] /jī/ (1) 成绩0833 业绩4093

1017 逐 [逐] /zhú/ (2) 逐渐1666 逐步2257

1018 灯 [燈] /dēng/ (1) 灯1781 灯光4246

1019 镇 [鎮] /zhèn/ (3) 镇2043

1020 输 [輸] /shū/ (1) 输1687 运输2255

1021 签 [簽] /qiān/ (2) 签2692 签订3055 签字4507

1022 妻 [妻] /qī/ (2) 妻子1185 夫妻2106 妻2658

1023 闹 [鬧] /nào/ (2) 闹1452 热闹2247

1024 挂 [掛] /guà/ (1) 挂1083

1025 零 [零] /líng/ (1) 零2713

1026 辩 [辯] /biàn/ (3) 辩1798 辩论2244

1027 丰 [豐] /fēng/ (1) 丰富1120 丰4573

1028 惯 [慣] /guàn/ (1) 习惯1247 习惯3162 惯3964

1029 促 [促] /cù/ (2) 促进1252 促使4102

1030 宫 [宮] /gōng/ (3) 宫1715

1031 避 [避] /bì/ (2) 避免2025 回避3519 避4494

1032 损 [損] /sǔn/ (2) 损失1596 损害3059 损4720

1033 厅 [廳] /tīng/ (2) 厅2253 大厅3421 餐厅4851
客厅4854

1034 途 [途] /tú/ (2) 前途2471 途径2974

1035 虚 [虛] /xū/ (2) 虚3436

1036 谋 [謀] /móu/ (3) 谋4356 参谋4755

1037 贫 [貧] /pín/ (3) 贫困1969 贫穷4460

1038 混 [混] /hùn, hún/ (2) 混1950 混乱2898

1039 鸡 [雞] /jī/ (1) 鸡1353 鸡蛋3415

1040 均 [均] /jūn/ (2) 均1520 平均2175

1041 驻 [駐] /zhù/ (3) 驻0948

1042 汉 [漢] /hàn/ (1)

1043 刀 [刀] /dāo/ (1) 刀1503 刀4298

1044 附 [附] /fù/ (1) 附近1361 附3076

1045 床 [床] /chuáng/ (1) 床1298

1046 染 [染] /rǎn/ (2) 污染2387 感染3290 染3551

1047 杯 [杯] /bēi/ (1) 杯2092 杯2250

1048 伟 [偉] /wěi/ (1) 伟大1058

1049 妹 [妹] /mèi/ (1) 妹妹2166 姐妹3091

1050 固 [固] /gù/ (2) 巩固3510 固定3735

1051 购 [購] /gòu/ (2) 购买2331 采购3345 收购3584
购物4065

1052 哈 [哈] /hā/ (1) 哈3495 哈4338

1053 夺 [奪] /duó/ (2) 夺1996 争夺3888 夺取4826

1054 宗 [宗] /zōng/ (3) 宗教1676 宗旨4539

1055 抢 [搶] /qiǎng/ (2) 抢1490 抢救4309

1056 载 [載] /zǎi, zài/ (3) 载2915 记载3614 记载4332

1057 残 [殘] /cán/ (3) 残酷3828 残4368

1058 赞 [贊] /zàn/ (2) 赞成2744 称赞4009 赞同4895
赞赏4950

1059 圆 [圓] /yuán/ (1) 圆2848 圆满4906

1060 抽 [抽] /chōu/ (1) 抽1980 抽烟4549

1061 届 [屆] /jiè/ (2) 届0735

1062 岸 [岸] /àn/ (2) 岸1694

1063 摄 [攝] /shè/ (3) 拍摄2610 摄影2757 摄3893

1064 触 [觸] /chù/ (2) 接触1234

1065 启 [啟] /qǐ/ (2) 启动3386 启发4772

1066 顿 [頓] /dùn/ (1) 顿2209 顿3123 整顿3857
顿时3898

1067 沿 [沿] /yán/ (2) 沿2836 沿着2960 沿海3498

1068 抱 [抱] /bào/ (1) 抱1208 抱怨4357 拥抱4773

1069 析 [析] /xī/ (2) 分析0757

1070 圈 [圈] /quān, juàn/ (2) 圈1914 圈2947

1071 哎 [哎] /āi/ (2) 哎0946 哎呀3869 哎哟4848

1072 粮 [糧] /liáng/ (2) 粮食1311 粮2929

1073 舍 [舍] /shě, shè/ (1) 宿舍2617 舍3821

1074 映 [映] /yìng/ (2) 反映0939

1075 序 [序] /xù/ (2) 秩序2176 程序2225

1076 旗 [旗] /qí/ (2) 旗2369 旗帜4859 红旗4999

1077 浪 [浪] /làng/ (2) 浪费2760 浪2999 浪漫3298

1078 伴 [伴] /bàn/ (3) 伙伴3109 伴4268 伴随4614

1079 距 [距] /jù/ (2) 距离1447 差距2607

1080 劲 [勁] /jìn/ (2) 劲儿3184 劲3363

1081 迹 [跡] /jī/ (2) 奇迹3279 痕迹4379

1082 盛 [盛] /chéng, shèng/ (3) 盛4062

1083 享 [享] /xiǎng/ (2) 享受1409 享有4108

1084 融 [融] /róng/ (2) 金融1906 融4565 融合4721

1085 镜 [鏡] /jìng/ (2) 镜头2834 镜3473 眼镜4126
镜子4643 望远镜4817

1086 丽 [麗] /lì/ (2) 美丽1220

1087 壮 [壯] /zhuàng/ (3)

1088 蛋 [蛋] /dàn/ (1) 蛋2351 鸡蛋3415

1089 净 [淨] /jìng/ (1) 干净2523 净2881 净4633

1090 胡 [胡] /hú/ (2) 胡同3366 胡子4329

1091 悲 [悲] /bēi/ (2) 悲剧2732 悲哀4218

1092 宽 [寬] /kuān/ (2) 宽1954

1093 赏 [賞] /shǎng/ (3) 欣赏1932 赏4724 赞赏4950

1094 操 [操] /cāo/ (1) 操作2478 操4452

1095 替 [替] /tì/ (2) 替1696 代替4302

1096 扩 [擴] /kuò/ (2) 扩大1186

1097 码 [碼] /mǎ/ (2) 号码2886 码头4176 起码4324

1098 迫 [迫] /pò/ (2) 被迫3889 压迫4548 强迫4886

1099 末 [末] /mò/ (3) 末1508 周末3450

1100 偏 [偏] /piān/ (2) 偏2421 偏偏4216 偏偏4696

1101 筑 [築] /zhù/ (2) 建筑1148

1102 墙 [牆] /qiáng/ (1) 墙1189

1103 冰 [冰] /bīng/ (2) 冰2341

1104 藏 [藏] /cáng, zàng/ (2) 藏3263 收藏4069

1105 桥 [橋] /qiáo/ (1) 桥1555 大桥4926

1106 炸 [炸] /zhà, zhá/ (3) 炸2191 爆炸2689 轰炸4363

1107 季 [季] /jì/ (2) 季节3254 冬季4253 季4749
夏季4766

1108 俗 [俗] /sú/ (2) 俗4630

1109 纯 [純] /chún/ (3) 单纯2750 纯3354

1110 耳 [耳] /ěr/ (2) 耳朵2698 耳2796

1111 幕 [幕] /mù/ (3) 幕3449 荧幕4382

1112 睛 [睛] /jīng/ (1) 眼睛0736

1113 哭 [哭] /kū/ (1) 哭0980

1114 虎 [虎] /hǔ/ (2) 虎2076 老虎2887

1115 辈 [輩] /bèi/ (3) 辈子1816

1116 恋 [戀] /liàn/ (2) 恋爱2427 恋2520

1117 佛 [佛] /fó, fú/ (2) 仿佛2615 佛2643

1118 穷 [窮] /qióng/ (2) 穷1631 贫穷4460 穷人4476

1119 阴 [陰] /yīn/ (1) 阴3015 阴影4589

1120 聚 [聚] /jù/ (3) 聚2745 聚会4067 聚集4303

1121 陈 [陳] /chén/ (3)

1122 隐 [隱] /yǐn/ (3)

1123 潮 [潮] /cháo/ (3) 潮3307 高潮3995 潮流4137

1124 贴 [貼] /tiē/ (2) 贴1752

1125 灾 [災] /zāi/ (2) 灾难3417 灾4913

1126 遭 [遭] /zāo/ (2) 遭到2266 遭2804 遭受3402

1127 烦 [煩] /fán/ (1) 麻烦1649 烦4887 烦恼4908

1128 弃 [棄] /qì/ (2) 放弃1500 弃4458 抛弃4506

1129 忽 [忽] /hū/ (1) 忽然1800 忽视3961 忽略4681

1130 辆 [輛] /liàng/ (1) 辆0924 车辆3798

1131 嗯 [嗯] /ēn, ńg, ňg, ǹg/ (1) 嗯0820

1132 毫 [毫] /háo/ (2) 毫无2230 丝毫3788 毫不3897

1133 摇 [搖] /yáo/ (2) 摇3164 动摇4445 摇头4513

1134 欲 [欲] /yù/ (2) 欲2056 欲望2659

1135 予 [予] /yǔ, yù/ (3) 给予1753 予以3351 赋予4832

1136 灭 [滅] /miè/ (2) 消灭2912 灭3237 毁灭4782

1137 拜 [拜] /bài/ (2) 拜3459 崇拜3649

1138 汇 [匯] /huì/ (3) 汇报2497 外汇4662

1139 齐 [齊] /qí/ (1) 齐2442 整齐4838

1140 宜 [宜] /yí/ (1) 便宜2393 宜4219

1141 卷 [卷] /juǎn, juàn/ (2) 卷1767

1142 侵 [侵] /qīn/ (2) 侵略2799 侵犯3648

1143 键 [鍵] /jiàn/ (2) 关键1278 关键2809

1144 玉 [玉] /yù/ (2) 玉1678 玉米3991

1145 餐 [餐] /cān/ (2) 餐馆4815 餐厅4851

1146 兄 [兄] /xiōng/ (2) 兄弟1264 兄4240

1147 凭 [憑] /píng/ (3) 凭1712 文凭4933

1148 凡 [凡] /fán/ (2) 凡2083 凡是3531 平凡3939

1149 闭 [閉] /bì/ (2) 闭2359 封闭4457 关闭4622

1150 敬 [敬] /jìng/ (2) 敬4158 尊敬4255

1151 巧 [巧] /qiǎo/ (2) 巧2787 技巧3367

1152 窗 [窗] /chuāng/ (1) 窗口3068 窗3301 窗户3836
窗外4824

1153 庆 [慶] /qìng/ (2) 庆3147 庆祝3481

1154 诚 [誠] /chéng/ (2) 真诚3104

1155 络 [絡] /luò/ (3) 网络1191 联络3221

1156 俩 [倆] /liǎ/ (1) 俩0951

1157 彻 [徹] /chè/ (2) 彻底1367 贯彻3093

1158 爆 [爆] /bào/ (3) 爆发2180 爆炸2689 爆4898

1159 绪 [緒] /xù/ (2) 情绪1229

1160 唯 [唯] /wéi/ (2) 唯一1263

1161 繁 [繁] /fán/ (2) 繁荣3168 频繁3895 繁华4318

1162 措 [措] /cuò/ (2) 措施1214

1163 忆 [憶] /yì/ (2) 回忆1860 记忆1972

1164 桌 [桌] /zhuō/ (1) 桌2208 桌子2920

1165 冬 [冬] /dōng/ (1) 冬天2457 冬3508 冬季4253

1166 刺 [刺] /cì/ (2) 刺激2318 讽刺4943

1167 召 [召] /zhāo/ (2) 召开1527 号召4094

1168 丈 [丈] /zhàng/ (2) 丈夫0995 丈4938

1169 逃 [逃] /táo/ (2) 逃2048

1170 婆 [婆] /pó/ (3) 老婆2149 婆4538 婆婆4760

1171 唐 [唐] /táng/

1172 纳 [納] /nà/

1173 偷 [偷] /tōu/ (2) 偷2723 偷偷3929

1174 寒 [寒] /hán/ (1) 寒2734 寒冷4788

1175 航 [航] /háng/ (2) 航空3600

1176 仪 [儀] /yí/ (2) 仪式2108 仪器4997

1177 珍 [珍] /zhēn/ (2) 珍贵3492 珍惜3886

1178 订 [訂] /dìng/ (2) 订2705 签订3055

1179 忍 [忍] /rěn/ (2) 忍2872 忍不住4059 忍受4611

1180 泪 [淚] /lèi/ (2) 眼泪2435 泪2866 泪水4142

1181 甲 [甲] /jiǎ/ (3) 甲1805

1182 貌 [貌] /mào/ (2) 面貌3462 礼貌3744 貌4878

1183 疗 [療] /liáo/ (3) 治疗1983 医疗2238

1184 盾 [盾] /dùn/ (2) 矛盾0933

1185 迅 [迅] /xùn/ (2) 迅速1028

1186 伍 [伍] /wǔ/ (2) 队伍1171

1187 斤 [斤] /jīn/ (1) 斤2169 公斤2721

1188 闲 [閑] /xián/ (2) 闲2880 休闲4835

1189 符 [符] /fú/ (2) 符合1426

1190 吹 [吹] /chuī/ (1) 吹1333

1191 幅 [幅] /fú/ (2) 幅1658

1192 抵 [抵] /dǐ/ (3) 抵3454 抵抗3816 抵达4205

1193 勇 [勇] /yǒng/ (2) 勇气2506 勇敢3657 勇4572

1194 喊 [喊] /hǎn/ (1) 喊1157

1195 龄 [齡] /líng/ (2) 年龄1383

1196 叶 [葉] /yè/ (2) 叶2959

1197 碰 [碰] /pèng/ (1) 碰到2573 碰2663 碰上4509

1198 矛 [矛] /máo/ (2) 矛盾0933

1199 缓 [緩] /huǎn/ (3) 缓慢4841

1200 骗 [騙] /piàn/ (2) 骗2199 欺骗4011

1201 袋 [袋] /dài/ (2) 脑袋2411 口袋4225 袋4711

1202 波 [波] /bō/ (3)

1203 殊 [殊] /shū/ (2) 特殊1086

1204 涉 [涉] /shè/ (3) 涉及1933 干涉3645

1205 粉 [粉] /fěn/ (2) 粉3442 粉碎4350

1206 腿 [腿] /tuǐ/ (1) 腿1237

1207 贸 [貿] /mào/ (2) 贸易1233

1208 狗 [狗] /gǒu/ (2) 狗1138

1209 乘 [乘] /chéng/ (2) 乘1878

1210 裁 [裁] /cái/ (3) 总裁3160

1211 缩 [縮] /suō/ (2) 缩4672 缩小4828

1212 炮 [炮] /pào/ (2) 炮3634

1213 扎 [紮] /zā, zhā/ (2) 扎2419 挣扎4405

1214 淡 [淡] /dàn/ (2) 淡4903

1215 徒 [徒] /tú/ (3)

1216 悉 [悉] /xī/ (2) 熟悉1509

1217 猪 [豬] /zhū/ (1) 猪1700

1218 滑 [滑] /huá/ (2) 滑3629

1219 卡 [卡] /kǎ/ (1) 卡2289 卡车4466

1220 漫 [漫] /màn/ (3) 浪漫3298 漫长3927

1221 泥 [泥] /ní/ (2) 泥2598 水泥3745

1222 洞 [洞] /dòng/ (2) 洞2251

1223 废 [廢] /fèi/ (3) 废4626 废话4864

1224 巴 [巴] /bā/ (2) 嘴巴4136 尾巴4578

1225 违 [違] /wéi/ (2) 违反2933 违法3587 违背4100

1226 荒 [荒] /huāng/ (3)

1227 横 [橫] /héng, hèng/ (3) 横3825

1228 隔 [隔] /gé/ (2) 隔2067

1229 冒 [冒] /mào/ (1) 冒2171

1230 箱 [箱] /xiāng/ (2) 箱子4526

1231 障 [障] /zhàng/ (3) 保障1754 障碍2539

1232 胆 [膽] /dǎn/ (2) 大胆2828 胆4922

1233 磨 [磨] /mó/ (2) 琢磨3823 磨3916 折磨4401

1234 估 [估] /gū/ (2) 估计1541 评估3769

1235 滋 [滋] /zī/ (2) 艾滋病2605 滋味3946

1236 厉 [厲] /lì/ (2) 厉害2057 严厉3101

1237 缘 [緣] /yuán/ (3) 边缘4748

1238 钢 [鋼] /gāng/ (1) 钢3989 钢铁4185 钢琴4590

1239 稿 [稿] /gǎo/ (3) 稿2793

1240 蓝 [藍] /lán/ (1) 蓝1968 蓝色4087

1241 漂 [漂] /piāo, piǎo, piào/ (1) 漂亮1227

1242 铺 [鋪] /pū, pù/ (2) 铺2428

1243 摸 [摸] /mō/ (2) 摸1792

1244 绕 [繞] /rào/ (2) 绕2515 围绕3137

1245 伸 [伸] /shēn/ (2) 伸2568 伸手3728 伸出3820
    延伸4564

1246 圣 [聖] /shèng/ (3) 神圣4163

1247 辞 [辭] /cí/ (3) 辞职3624

1248 晨 [晨] /chén/ (1) 早晨2304 凌晨3116 清晨4340

1249 陪 [陪] /péi/ (2) 陪1877

1250 租 [租] /zū/ (1) 租3031 出租车4248

1251 倍 [倍] /bèi/ (1) 倍1472

1252 申 [申] /shēn/ (2) 申请2213

1253 拔 [拔] /bá/ (2) 拔3480

1254 羊 [羊] /yáng/ (1) 羊1868

1255 奔 [奔] /bēn, bèn/ (3) 奔2846

1256 亏 [虧] /kuī/ (3) 亏4315

1257 毁 [毀] /huǐ/ (3) 毁2389 毁灭4782

1258 旦 [旦] /dàn/ (3) 一旦1336

1259 泛 [泛] /fàn/ (2) 广泛1603

1260 跃 [躍] /yuè/ (2) 跃3622 活跃4012 活跃4731

1261 骂 [罵] /mà/ (2) 骂1266

1262 暖 [暖] /nuǎn/ (1) 温暖2441 暖3864

1263 惜 [惜] /xī/ (2) 可惜2500 珍惜3886

1264 糊 [糊] /hú/ (2) 糊涂4022 模糊4115

1265 猛 [猛] /měng/ (3) 猛4571 猛4635

1266 疾 [疾] /jí/ (3) 疾病2536

1267 寄 [寄] /jì/ (1) 寄1467

1268 江 [江] /jiāng/ (1) 江3596 江湖4043

1269 昨 [昨] /zuó/ (1) 昨天1302

1270 拒 [拒] /jù/ (2) 拒绝1309 拒4954

1271 倾 [傾] /qīng/ (3) 倾向3418 倾4725

1272 撤 [撤] /chè/ (3) 撤3349

1273 讯 [訊] /xùn/ (2) 通讯2997

1274 艰 [艱] /jiān/ (2) 艰难2376 艰苦3203

1275 庄 [莊] /zhuāng/ (2) 庄3425

1276 鸟 [鳥] /niǎo/ (2) 鸟1813

1277 孤 [孤] /gū/ (3) 孤独3493 孤4792

1278 兼 [兼] /jiān/ (3) 兼1562

1279 湖 [湖] /hú/ (1) 湖2182 江湖4043

1280 潜 [潛] /qián/ (2) 潜力3717

1281 罚 [罰] /fá/ (3) 罚3118 惩罚4271 处罚4786

1282 番 [番] /fān/ (3) 番1206

1283 灰 [灰] /huī/ (2) 灰2973

1284 薄 [薄] /báo, bó/ (2) 薄4072

1285 聊 [聊] /liáo/ (2) 聊2492 聊天3143

1286 鬼 [鬼] /guǐ/ (2) 鬼2075

1287 污 [污] /wū/ (2) 污染2387

1288 档 [檔] /dàng/ (3) 档案3157 档4334

1289 剩 [剩] /shèng/ (1) 剩下2040 剩2961

1290 狂 [狂] /kuáng/ (3) 疯狂3982 狂4518

1291 刑 [刑] /xíng/

1292 励 [勵] /lì/ (2) 鼓励1577 奖励4608

1293 库 [庫] /kù/ (3) 库3607 仓库4754

1294 督 [督] /dū/ (3) 监督1563

1295 患 [患] /huàn/ (3) 患者2368 患3008

1296 誉 [譽] /yù/ 荣誉3401

1297 坛 [壇] /tán/ 论坛3370

1298 恢 [恢] /huī/ (2) 恢复1081

1299 瓜 [瓜] /guā/ (2) 瓜3748 西瓜4644

1300 牙 [牙] /yá/ (2) 牙2618 牙齿4477

1301 衡 [衡] /héng/ (3) 平衡1622 衡量4455

1302 佳 [佳] /jiā/ (3) 最佳2652 佳3296

1303 税 [稅] /shuì/ (3) 税3707

1304 贯 [貫] /guàn/ (2) 贯彻3093

1305 辑 [輯] /jí/ (3) 编辑2273 逻辑3305

1306 援 [援] /yuán/ (2) 支援2984 援助3404

1307 贡 [貢] /gòng/ (2) 贡献1225

1308 沟 [溝] /gōu/ (3) 沟2344 沟通2440

1309 洁 [潔] /jié/ (3) 清洁4840

1310 延 [延] /yán/ (2) 延续4109 延伸4564 延长4985

1311 径 [徑] /jìng/ (3) 途径2974

1312 欣 [欣] /xīn/ (3) 欣赏1932

1313 岛 [島] /dǎo/ (2) 岛2119

1314 搬 [搬] /bān/ (1) 搬1634

1315 币 [幣] /bì/ (2) 人民币2104

1316 冠 [冠] /guàn/ (2) 冠军1796

1317 瞧 [瞧] /qiáo/ (2) 瞧1635

1318 赢 [贏] /yíng/ (1) 赢1524 赢得3520

1319 雅 [雅] /yǎ/ (3) 雅2501

1320 暂 [暫] /zàn/ (2) 暂时2671 短暂4319

1321 焦 [焦] /jiāo/ (3) 焦点2699

1322 媒 [媒] /méi/ 媒体1975

1323 恰 [恰] /qià/ (3) 恰恰3784

1324 陷 [陷] /xiàn/ (3) 陷入2391

1325 堆 [堆] /duī/ (2) 堆1852

1326 忧 [憂] /yōu/

1327 勤 [勤] /qín/ (3)

1328 赖 [賴] /lài/ (3) 依赖3621 赖4566

1329 鞋 [鞋] /xié/ (1) 鞋2103

1330 腐 [腐] /fǔ/ (2) 腐败2283

1331 饮 [飲] /yǐn, yìn/ (3) 饮食3602 饮4353 饮料4855

1332 锅 [鍋] /guō/ (2) 锅2118

1333 扫 [掃] /sǎo/ (2) 扫3236

1334 尾 [尾] /wěi/ (2) 尾3186 尾巴4578

1335 恨 [恨] /hèn/ (2) 恨1917

1336 刊 [刊] /kān/ (3) 刊物4233 报刊4479

1338 阿 [阿] /ā/ (2) 阿1736 阿姨3668

1339 盟 [盟] /méng/ (3)

1340 扶 [扶] /fú/ (2) 扶3188

1341 妙 [妙] /miào/ (2) 妙4364

1342 丢 [丢] /diū/ (1) 丢1681

1343 荡 [蕩] /dàng/

1344 祝 [祝] /zhù/ (1) 庆祝3481 祝3722 祝贺4254

1345 阻 [阻] /zǔ/ (3) 阻止3553

1346 幽 [幽] /yōu/ 幽默2575

1347 乏 [乏] /fá/ (2) 缺乏1689

1348 浓 [濃] /nóng/ (2) 浓3564

1349 拖 [拖] /tuō/ (2) 拖2054

1350 偶 [偶] /ǒu/ (3) 偶然3355 偶尔3931

1351 颗 [顆] /kē/ (2) 颗1231

1352 扣 [扣] /kòu/ (3) 扣2686

1353 仿 [仿] /fǎng/ (2) 仿佛2615

1354 诸 [諸] /zhū/ 诸多3988

1355 臣 [臣] /chén/

1356 碎 [碎] /suì/ (2) 碎3460 粉碎4350

1357 洪 [洪] /hóng/ (3) 洪水3230

1358 斯 [斯] /sī/ (3)

1359 京 [京] /jīng/ (2) 京剧3633

1360 壁 [壁] /bì/ (2) 壁4135

1361 挖 [挖] /wā/ (2) 挖1713 挖掘4314

1362 描 [描] /miáo/ (2) 描写3191 描述3432 描绘4955

1363 挣 [掙] /zhèng, zhēng/ (3) 挣2162 挣钱4110 挣扎4405

1364 侧 [側] /cè/ (3)

1365 尖 [尖] /jiān/ (2) 尖锐4278 尖4991

1366 搭 [搭] /dā/ (2) 搭1964

1367 拼 [拼] /pīn/ (2) 拼3195 拼命4606

1368 豆 [豆] /dòu/ (2) 豆4757

1369 撞 [撞] /zhuàng/ (2) 撞1982

1370 凉 [涼] /liáng/ (1)

1371 呆 [呆] /dāi/ (2) 呆1820

1372 腰 [腰] /yāo/ (2) 腰2085

1373 惨 [慘] /cǎn/ (3) 惨3589

1374 宾 [賓] /bīn/ (2) 宾馆2791

1375 递 [遞] /dì/ (2) 传递4107 递4258

1376 践 [踐] /jiàn/ (1) 实践1387

1377 怒 [怒] /nù/ (2) 愤怒3772 怒4019

1378 迟 [遲] /chí/ (1) 迟3736

1379 宿 [宿] /sù, xiǔ/ (1) 宿舍2617

1380 丧 [喪] /sàng/ (3) 丧失3514

1381 挤 [擠] /jǐ/ (1) 挤1995

1382 慰 [慰] /wèi/ (2) 安慰4990

1383 矿 [礦] /kuàng/ (2) 矿4128

1384 陶 [陶] /táo/

1385 雷 [雷] /léi/ (2) 雷3872

1386 锁 [鎖] /suǒ/ (3) 锁3382

1387 允 [允] /yǔn/ (2) 允许1489

1388 酸 [酸] /suān/ (1) 酸4624

1389 逼 [逼] /bī/ (2) 逼1928

1390 稍 [稍] /shāo/ (2) 稍2484 稍微4738

1391 炼 [煉] /liàn/ (1) 锻炼2326

1392 粗 [粗] /cū/ (2) 粗3691

1393 裂 [裂] /liè/ (3) 分裂3917

1394 宁 [寧] /nìng, níng/ (3) 宁4697

1395 植 [植] /zhí/ (2) 植物3154 种植4351

1396 脏 [臟] /zāng, zàng/ (1) 脏3271 心脏3704

1397 拨 [撥] /bō/ (3) 拨2823

1398 辛 [辛] /xīn/ (1) 辛苦3389

1399 莫 [莫] /mò/ (3) 莫2769

1400 棋 [棋] /qí/ (3) 棋3048

1401 返 [返] /fǎn/ (3) 返回2988 返4101

1402 轰 [轟] /hōng/ (3) 轰炸4363

1403 烂 [爛] /làn/ (3) 灿烂3102 烂3631

1404 摩 [摩] /mó/ (3) 摩托车4086

1405 戴 [戴] /dài/ (1) 戴1479

1406 截 [截] /jié/ (3)

1407 综 [綜] /zōng/ (2) 综合1902

1408 邀 [邀] /yāo/ (2) 邀请1910 邀4511

1409 氛 [氛] /fēn/ (3) 气氛1625 氛围3804

1410 骑 [騎] /qí/ (1) 骑2109

1411 奉 [奉] /fèng/ (3) 奉献4105

1412 浮 [浮] /fú/ (2) 浮3954

1413 肥 [肥] /féi/ (2)

1414 抬 [抬] /tái/ (1) 抬2122 抬头3862

1415 插 [插] /chā/ (2) 插2559

1416 井 [井] /jǐng/ (2) 井2206

1417 岗 [崗] /gǎng/ (3) 岗位2972 岗4333 下岗4555

1418 亿 [億] /yì/ (1) 亿3107

1419 滚 [滾] /gǔn/ (2) 滚4344

1420 腾 [騰] /téng/ (3)

1421 饱 [飽] /bǎo/ (1) 饱3243

1422 竹 [竹] /zhú/ (2) 竹2928

1423 峰 [峰] /fēng/ (3) 峰3445 高峰4586

1424 胸 [胸] /xiōng/ (2) 胸3598

1425 瓶 [瓶] /píng/ (1) 瓶3083 瓶4393

1426 仰 [仰] /yǎng/ (2) 信仰3966 仰4988

1427 幼 [幼] /yòu/ (3) 幼儿园4581

1428 吓 [嚇] /xià, hè/ (2) 吓1887

1429 耐 [耐] /nài/ (2) 耐心3526 耐4501

1430 闪 [閃] /shǎn/ (2) 闪3428

1431 哲 [哲] /zhé/ (2) 哲学1992

1432 赔 [賠] /péi/ (2) 赔3577 赔偿4202

1433 豪 [豪] /háo/ (3) 自豪3734 豪华4628

1434 鼻 [鼻] /bí/ (2) 鼻子2679

1435 猜 [猜] /cāi/ (2) 猜2172 猜测4897

1436 君 [君] /jūn/ 君2889 君子4813

1437 柔 [柔] /róu/ (3) 温柔3830

1438 叔 [叔] /shū/ (2) 叔叔3278

1439 戒 [戒] /jiè/

1440 册 [冊] /cè/ (2) 注册3656 册3851

1441 肩 [肩] /jiān/ (2) 肩4424 肩膀4701

1442 罢 [罷] /bà/ (3) 罢4061 罢了4689

1443 驾 [駕] /jià/ (1) 驾驶4400

1444 肃 [肅] /sù/ (2) 严肃1891

1445 址 [址] /zhǐ/ (2) 遗址2906 地址3441

1446 纵 [縱] /zòng/ (3)

1447 虫 [蟲] /chóng/ (2) 虫4184

1448 孙 [孫] /sūn/ (3) 孙子3541

1449 犹 [猶] /yóu/ (3) 犹豫4075 犹如4512

1450 奏 [奏] /zòu/ (3) 节奏3876

1451 碗 [碗] /wǎn/ (1) 碗2627 碗3535

1452 尝 [嘗] /cháng/ (2) 尝3679 尝试3686

1453 牵 [牽] /qiān/ (2) 牵3724

1454 账 [賬] /zhàng/ (3) 账2792

1455 扭 [扭] /niǔ/ (2) 扭4444

1456 旋 [旋] /xuán/ (3) 旋转4893

1457 捕 [捕] /bǔ/ (2)

1458 坦 [坦] /tǎn/ (3) 坦克3943

1459 署 [署] /shǔ/ (3) 部署3453

1460 邮 [郵] /yóu/ (1) 邮票4031

1461 牲 [牲] /shēng/ (2) 牺牲1857

1462 纠 [糾] /jiū/ (2) 纠纷3603 纠正3726

1463 叹 [歎] /tàn/ (3) 叹3619

1464 跨 [跨] /kuà/ (2) 跨2531

1465 舒 [舒] /shū/ (1) 舒服2632 舒适4904

1466 润 [潤] /rùn/ (3) 利润2552

1467 宇 [宇] /yǔ/ (3) 宇宙2640

1468 塞 [塞] /sāi, sài, sè/ (3) 塞2200

1469 嫁 [嫁] /jià/ (3) 嫁1990

1470 趋 [趨] /qū/ (3) 趋势2288

1471 碍 [礙] /ài/ (3) 障碍2539

1472 尔 [爾] /ěr/ (2) 偶尔3931

1473 邻 [鄰] /lín/ (2) 邻居3333

1474 愈 [愈] /yù/ (3) 愈3171

1475 忠 [忠] /zhōng/ (3)

1476 袭 [襲] /xí/ (3) 袭击2934

1477 揭 [揭] /jiē/ (3)

1478 宋 [宋] /sòng/ (3)

1479 阔 [闊] /kuò/ (2) 广阔4416

1480 啥 [啥] /shà/ (3) 啥1393

1481 哼 [哼] /hēng, hng/ (2) 哼2635 哼3513

1482 埋 [埋] /mái/ (2) 埋 2644

1483 梁 [梁] /liáng/ (2)

1484 劝 [勸] /quàn/ (2) 劝 2187

1485 债 [債] /zhài/ (3) 债 4752

1486 糖 [糖] /táng/ (1) 糖 2638

1487 聪 [聰] /cōng/ (2) 聪明 1794

1488 扰 [擾] /rǎo/ (2) 干扰 4103 困扰 4777

1489 轨 [軌] /guǐ/ (3) 轨道 2957

1490 籍 [籍] /jí/ (3) 书籍 4179 籍 4823

1491 渡 [渡] /dù/ (2) 过渡 4057 渡 4884

1492 颜 [顏] /yán/ (1) 颜色 2236

1493 篮 [籃] /lán/ (1) 篮球 3359

1494 饰 [飾] /shì/ (3)

1495 崇 [崇] /chóng/ (2) 崇拜 3649 崇高 4962

1496 症 [症] /zhèng/ (3)

1497 蒙 [蒙] /méng, mēng/ (3) 蒙 3193

1498 脆 [脆] /cuì/ (2) 干脆 2784 脆弱 3780

1499 凝 [凝] /níng/ (3)

1500 尘 [塵] /chén/ (3)

1501 栏 [欄] /lán/

1502 仗 [仗] /zhàng/ (3) 仗 3545 打仗 4552

1503 猫 [貓] /māo/ (2) 猫 2000

1504 涂 [塗] /tú/ (2) 糊涂 4022 涂 4398

1505 泡 [泡] /pào/ (3) 泡 3484

1506 涨 [漲] /zhǎng, zhàng/ (2) 涨 3163

1507 览 [覽] /lǎn/ (1) 展览 3611

1508 谷 [穀] /gǔ/ (3) 谷 4047

1509 踏 [踏] /tà/ (3) 踏 2896

1510 怨 [怨] /yuàn/ (3) 怨 4263 抱怨 4357

1511 屈 [屈] /qū/ (3)

1512 塑 [塑] /sù/ (2) 塑造 3730 塑料 4471

1513 赚 [賺] /zhuàn/ (3) 赚 1889 赚钱 4683

1514 译 [譯] /yì/ (1) 翻译 3476 译 4016

1515 汗 [汗] /hàn/ (2) 汗 2736

1516 频 [頻] /pín/ 频繁 3895

1517 耗 [耗] /hào/ (3) 消耗 4551

1518 姻 [姻] /yīn/ (2) 婚姻 1585

1519 墓 [墓] /mù/ (3) 墓 3601

1520 敏 [敏] /mǐn/ (3) 敏感 2751

1521 询 [詢] /xún/ (3) 咨询 2939 询问 3516

1522 魂 [魂] /hún/ (3) 灵魂 2563 魂 4380

1523 剑 [劍] /jiàn/ (3) 剑 2417

1524 牢 [牢] /láo/ (3)

1525 钻 [鑽] /zuān, zuàn/ (2) 钻 2373

1526 欺 [欺] /qī/ (2) 欺骗 4011 欺负 4944

1527 慧 [慧] /huì/ (3) 智慧 1938

1528 彼 [彼] /bǐ/ (3) 彼此 2066

1529 煤 [煤] /méi/ (2) 煤 3397

1530 愤 [憤] /fèn/ (2) 愤怒 3772

1531 晓 [曉] /xiǎo/ (2) 晓得 4194

1532 贪 [貪] /tān/ 贪 4959

1533 嫌 [嫌] /xián/ (3) 嫌 3486

1534 拳 [拳] /quán/ (3) 拳 4712

1535 悠 [悠] /yōu/ (2) 悠久 4568

1536 棉 [棉] /mián/ (2) 棉花 4745 棉 4868

1537 爬 [爬] /pá/ (1) 爬 1661

1538 稀 [稀] /xī/ (3)

1539 迁 [遷] /qiān/ 迁 3860

1540 俱 [俱] /jù/ (2) 俱乐部 3084 俱 4323

1541 悄 [悄] /qiāo/ (2) 悄悄 4794

1542 帐 [帳] /zhàng/ (3) 帐 2036 帐篷 4822

1543 寺 [寺] /sì/ (2) 寺 2472

1544 杆 [桿] /gān/ (2)

1545 仔 [仔] /zǐ, zǎi/ (2) 仔细 1912

1546 胞 [胞] /bāo/ (3) 同胞 3213 细胞 3843

1547 漠 [漠] /mò/ (2) 沙漠 3334

1548 幻 [幻] /huàn/ (3) 幻想 3672

1549 疼 [疼] /téng/ (1) 疼 2742

1550 朵 [朵] /duǒ/ (2) 耳朵 2698 朵 4297

1551 仙 [仙] /xiān/ 仙 3544

1552 诺 [諾] /nuò/ (2) 承诺 3122

1553 涌 [湧] /yǒng/ (3) 涌 2986

1554 刷 [刷] /shuā/ (2)

1555 箭 [箭] /jiàn/ (2) 箭 3635

1556 摊 [攤] /tān/ (3) 摊 4583

1557 欠 [欠] /qiàn/ (2) 欠 2841

1558 隆 [隆] /lóng/

1559 肚 [肚] /dù, dǔ/ (2) 肚子 2754 肚 4481

1560 胁 [脅] /xié/ (3) 威胁 1629

1561 勃 [勃] /bó/ (3)

1562 孔 [孔] /kǒng/ (2) 面孔 4131

1563 盆 [盆] /pén/ (2) 盆 4576

1564 惑 [惑] /huò/ (2) 诱惑 4454 困惑 4736

1565 颇 [頗] /pō/ (2) 颇 1613

1566 帽 [帽] /mào/ (1) 帽子 3172 帽 4812

1567 燃 [燃] /rán/ (2) 燃烧 4098

1568 鉴 [鑒] /jiàn/ (3)

1569 吵 [吵] /chǎo/ (2) 吵 2743

1570 狱 [獄] /yù/ (3) 监狱 3023

1571 夹 [夾] /jiā/ (2) 夹 3072

1572 柜 [櫃] /guì/ (3) 柜台 4919

1573 贷 [貸] /dài/ (3) 贷款 2473

1574 甘 [甘] /gān/ (3)

1575 呈 [呈] /chéng/ (3) 呈现 3013 呈 3035

1576 飘 [飄] /piāo/ (2) 飘 4193

1577 喂 [喂] /wèi/ (1) 喂 2996 喂 3266

1578 翼 [翼] /yì/

1579 珠 [珠] /zhū/ (2)

1580 盗 [盜] /dào/ (2)

1581 辉 [輝] /huī/ (2) 辉煌2749

1582 阅 [閱] /yuè/ (2) 阅读3759

1583 拆 [拆] /chāi/ (2) 拆3071

1584 割 [割] /gē/ (2) 割4056

1585 详 [詳] /xiáng/ (2) 详细2466

1586 吐 [吐] /tǔ, tù/ (2) 吐3166

1587 狠 [狠] /hěn/ (3)

1588 寿 [壽] /shòu/ (3)

1589 眉 [眉] /méi/ (3) 眉4239

1590 醉 [醉] /zuì/ (2) 醉2460

1591 擦 [擦] /cā/ (1) 擦2439

1592 偿 [償] /cháng/ (3) 赔偿4202

1593 吉 [吉] /jí/ 吉4464

1594 姿 [姿] /zī/ (3) 姿态3903

1595 森 [森] /sēn/ (2) 森林2397

1596 慈 [慈] /cí/

1597 岩 [岩] /yán/ (3) 岩3341

1598 添 [添] /tiān/ (2) 添2964

1599 朗 [朗] /lǎng/ (2)

1600 串 [串] /chuàn/ (3) 串4666

1601 亚 [亞] /yà/ (3)

1602 躲 [躲] /duǒ/ (2) 躲2198

1603 琴 [琴] /qín/ (3) 钢琴4590 琴4865

1604 雕 [雕] /diāo/ (3)

1605 贩 [販] /fàn/

1606 铜 [銅] /tóng/ (2) 铜4227

1607 挨 [挨] /āi, ái/ (2) 挨3011

1608 筹 [籌] /chóu/

1609 凶 [凶] /xiōng/ (3)

1610 氏 [氏] /shì/ (3) 氏2621

1611 窝 [窩] /wō/ 窝3808

1612 池 [池] /chí/ (2)

1613 御 [禦] /yù/ (3) 防御3962

1614 巡 [巡] /xún/

1615 赴 [赴] /fù/ 赴2337

1616 梯 [梯] /tī/ (2) 电梯3938

1617 驶 [駛] /shǐ/ (3) 驾驶4400

1618 抑 [抑] /yì/ (3) 抑制3960

1619 脉 [脈] /mài/ (2)

1620 掩 [掩] /yǎn/ (3)

1621 郎 [郎] /láng/ (2)

1622 枚 [枚] /méi/ 枚1939

1623 液 [液] /yè/ (2) 血液3665

1624 尺 [尺] /chǐ/ (2) 尺4664

1625 麦 [麥] /mài/ (2) 麦4656

1626 伏 [伏] /fú/

1627 遥 [遙] /yáo/ (3) 遥远3392

1628 跌 [跌] /diē/ (2) 跌3430

1629 夸 [誇] /kuā/ (3) 夸4407 夸张4677

1630 弯 [彎] /wān/ (2)

1631 踪 [蹤] /zōng/ 跟踪4151

1632 霸 [霸] /bà/

1633 喷 [噴] /pēn/ (2) 喷3959

1634 浅 [淺] /qiǎn/ (1) 浅3563

1635 畅 [暢] /chàng/ (3)

1636 丑 [醜] /chǒu/ (3)

1637 汤 [湯] /tāng/ (1) 汤2676

1638 乃 [乃] /nǎi/ 乃至3327 乃4686

1639 朱 [朱] /zhū/ (3)

1640 扑 [撲] /pū/ (2) 扑4191

1641 盲 [盲] /máng/ (3) 盲目3827

1642 劫 [劫] /jié/

1643 撑 [撐] /chēng/ (3) 撑3487 支撑3523

1644 亦 [亦] /yì/ (2) 亦1970

1645 悟 [悟] /wù/ (2) 悟4901

1646 嘿 [嘿] /hēi/ (2) 嘿3595 嘿嘿4392

1647 苍 [蒼] /cāng/ (3)

1648 袖 [袖] /xiù/ (2) 领袖3463

1649 臭 [臭] /chòu/ (2) 臭2989

1650 填 [填] /tián/ (2) 填3070

1651 锋 [鋒] /fēng/

1652 哇 [哇] /wa, wā/ (2) 哇2710

1653 柳 [柳] /liǔ/ (3) 柳2625

1654 赤 [赤] /chì/ (3)

1655 恒 [恆] /héng/ 永恒4282

1656 傻 [傻] /shǎ/ (2) 傻2879

1657 储 [儲] /chú/

1658 饿 [餓] /è/ (1) 饿2475

1659 悬 [懸] /xuán/ (3)

1660 甜 [甜] /tián/ (2) 甜3774

1661 厌 [厭] /yàn/ (2) 讨厌3352

1662 湿 [濕] /shī/ (2) 湿4023

1663 凌 [淩] /líng/ 凌晨3116

1664 咬 [咬] /yǎo/ (2) 咬2140

1665 夕 [夕] /xì/ 前夕4881

1666 宴 [宴] /yàn/ (1) 宴会4638

1667 庙 [廟] /miào/ (2) 庙3108

1668 敲 [敲] /qiāo/ (2) 敲3190

1669 紫 [紫] /zǐ/ (2) 紫3773

1670 丁 [丁] /dīng/ (3)

1671 鼠 [鼠] /shǔ/ (2) 老鼠4049

1672 撒 [撒] /sā, sǎ/ (2) 撒3381

1673 缝 [縫] /féng, fèng/ (3)

1674 堪 [堪] /kān/

1675 妥 [妥] /tuǒ/ (3)

1676 吨 [噸] /dūn/ (2) 吨1948

1677 捐 [捐] /juān/ 捐3732

1678 阁 [閣] /gé/ 内阁 4591

1679 冻 [凍] /dòng/ (2) 冻 4099

1680 宅 [宅] /zhái/ (3) 住宅 3800

1681 酷 [酷] /kù/ (3) 残酷 3828

1682 炒 [炒] /chǎo/ (3) 炒 2570

1683 锐 [銳] /ruì/ (2) 尖锐 4278

1684 吞 [吞] /tūn/ (3) 吞 4676

1685 牺 [犧] /xī/ (2) 牺牲 1857

1686 哀 [哀] /āi/ (3) 悲哀 4218

1687 枝 [枝] /zhī/ (3)

1688 邪 [邪] /xié/ 邪 4367

1689 猴 [猴] /hóu/ (2) 猴子 4468

1690 押 [押] /yā/ (3)

1691 昏 [昏] /hūn/ (2)

1692 勾 [勾] /gōu/ (3)

1693 绘 [繪] /huì/ 绘画 4435 描绘 4955

1694 葬 [葬] /zàng/

1695 衰 [衰] /shuāi/ (3)

1696 辱 [辱] /rǔ/ (3)

1697 匆 [匆] /cōng/ (3) 匆匆 4371

1698 奴 [奴] /nú/ (3)

1699 振 [振] /zhèn/ (3)

1700 旨 [旨] /zhǐ/ 宗旨 4539

1701 赌 [賭] /dǔ/ 赌博 4899

1702 诞 [誕] /dàn/ (3) 诞生 3119

1703 扮 [扮] /bàn/ (2) 扮演 3971 打扮 5000

1704 伪 [偽] /wěi/

1705 炉 [爐] /lú/ (3)

1706 柱 [柱] /zhù/ (3)

1707 渴 [渴] /kě/ (1) 渴望 2746

1708 炎 [炎] /yán/

1709 笼 [籠] /lóng, lǒng/ (3)

1710 聘 [聘] /pìn/

1711 肠 [腸] /cháng/ (2)

1712 猎 [獵] /liè/ (3)

1713 循 [循] /xún/ (3) 循环 4145

1714 疏 [疏] /shū/

1715 泳 [泳] /yǒng/ (1) 游泳 2908

1716 墨 [墨] /mò/ (2) 墨 4229

1717 劣 [劣] /liè/ (3) 恶劣 4113

1718 覆 [覆] /fù/ 覆盖 4830

1719 漏 [漏] /lòu/ (2) 漏 4673

1720 慎 [慎] /shèn/ (3) 谨慎 4365

1721 坡 [坡] /pō/ (2) 坡 4127

1722 怖 [怖] /bù/ (3) 恐怖 2338

1723 瓦 [瓦] /wǎ/ (3)

1724 诱 [誘] /yòu/ 诱惑 4454

1725 狼 [狼] /láng/ (2) 狼 2813

1726 仁 [仁] /rén/

1727 械 [械] /xiè/ (2) 机械 3173

1728 恩 [恩] /ēn/

1729 页 [頁] /yè/ (1) 页 3006

1730 棒 [棒] /bàng/ (3) 棒 4217

1731 抛 [拋] /pāo/ (3) 抛 3580 抛弃 4506

1732 佩 [佩] /pèi/ (3) 佩服 4204

1733 裤 [褲] /kù/ (2) 裤子 4641

1734 摔 [摔] /shuāi/ (2) 摔 2629

1735 贺 [賀] /hè/ (2) 祝贺 4254

1736 桃 [桃] /táo/ (3)

1737 郁 [鬱] /yù/

1738 鸣 [鳴] /míng/ (3)

1739 挡 [擋] /dǎng/ (2) 挡 4195

1740 悔 [悔] /huǐ/ (2) 后悔 4397

1741 州 [州] /zhōu/ 州 2401

1742 泉 [泉] /quán/

1743 姨 [姨] /yí/ (2) 阿姨 3668

1744 胀 [脹] /zhàng/ (3) 膨胀 4305

1745 碑 [碑] /bēi/ (2) 碑 4327

1746 魔 [魔] /mó/

1747 憾 [憾] /hàn/ (3) 遗憾 2203

1748 摘 [摘] /zhāi/ (2) 摘 3138

1749 倡 [倡] /chàng/ (2) 提倡 3095

1750 逢 [逢] /féng/ (2) 逢 4942

1751 拟 [擬] /nǐ/

1752 皆 [皆] /jiē/ 皆 2505

1753 殿 [殿] /diàn/ (3) 殿 3911

1754 削 [削] /xiāo, xuē/ (3)

1755 董 [董] /dǒng/ 董事长 3374

1756 扔 [扔] /rēng/ (2) 扔 2265

1757 愁 [愁] /chóu/ (3) 愁 4260

1758 祸 [禍] /huò/

1759 剪 [剪] /jiǎn/ (2)

1760 胃 [胃] /wèi/ (2) 胃 3703

1761 腹 [腹] /fù/

1762 晶 [晶] /jīng/

1763 躺 [躺] /tǎng/ (1) 躺 2010

1764 役 [役] /yì/ 战役 3712

1765 瘦 [瘦] /shòu/ (2) 瘦 3433

1766 坑 [坑] /kēng/ (3) 坑 3177

1767 拓 [拓] /tuò/ 开拓 4567

1768 怜 [憐] /líng/ (2) 可怜 3981

1769 伦 [倫] /lún/ (2) 伦理 4877

1770 茫 [茫] /máng/

1771 饼 [餅] /bǐng/ (2)

1772 弥 [彌] /mí/ 弥补 4618

1773 剂 [劑] /jì/

1774 娱 [娛] /yú/ (3) 娱乐 2665

1775 盐 [鹽] /yán/ (2) 盐 3304

1776 唤 [喚] /huàn/ (3)

1777 乙 [乙] /yǐ/ (3) 乙 3025

1778 吊 [吊] /diào/ (2) 吊 4716

1779 浑 [渾] /hún/ (3) 浑身 3470

1780 盼 [盼] /pàn/ (2) 盼 3761

1781 驱 [驅] /qū/

1782 迈 [邁] /mài/ (2) 迈 4770

1783 寸 [寸] /cùn/ (2) 寸 4603

1784 熊 [熊] /xióng/ (2) 熊 4391

1785 斜 [斜] /xié/ (2)

1786 腔 [腔] /qiāng/ (3)

1787 亩 [畝] /mǔ/ (2) 亩 2228

1788 郊 [郊] /jiāo/ (2) 郊区 4966

1789 塔 [塔] /tǎ/ (2)

1790 牧 [牧] /mù/ (3)

1791 垂 [垂] /chuí/ (3)

1792 稻 [稻] /dào/ (2) 水稻 4972

1793 抚 [撫] /fǔ/

1794 拐 [拐] /guǎi/ (2)

1795 屏 [屏] /píng/ 屏幕 4382

1796 杰 [傑] /jié/ 杰出 3695

1797 盒 [盒] /hé/ (2) 盒 4698

1798 悦 [悅] /yuè/ (3) 喜悦 4789

1799 脾 [脾] /pí/ (2) 脾气 2970

1800 踢 [踢] /tī/ (1) 踢 2555

1801 梅 [梅] /méi/ (3)

1802 遵 [遵] /zūn/ (2) 遵守 3883

1803 闯 [闖] /chuǎng/ (2) 闯 3098

1804 吁 [籲] /xū, yù/

1805 披 [披] /pī/ (2) 披 4192

1806 歧 [歧] /qí/ 分歧 3754 歧视 4837

1807 臂 [臂] /bì, bei/ 臂 4660

1808 斥 [斥] /chì/ (3)

1809 掘 [掘] /jué/ 挖掘 4314

1810 尸 [屍] /shī/ 尸体 3373

1811 祥 [祥] /xiáng/

1812 搜 [搜] /sōu/ (3)

1813 惠 [惠] /huì/

1814 轿 [轎] /jiào/ 轿车 3998

1815 滴 [滴] /dī/ (2) 滴 4975

1816 蓄 [蓄] /xù/

1817 谊 [誼] /yí/ (1) 友谊 2856

1818 衷 [衷] /zhōng/ (3)

1819 疲 [疲] /pí/ (2)

1820 逆 [逆] /nì/

1821 徐 [徐] /xú/

1822 堵 [堵] /dǔ/ (2) 堵 3955

1823 顽 [頑] /wán/ (3) 顽强 4114

1824 蹈 [蹈] /dǎo, dào/ (3) 舞蹈 2641

1825 胎 [胎] /tāi/

1826 耕 [耕] /gēng/ (3)

1827 肤 [膚] /fū/ (2) 皮肤 3440

1828 奈 [奈] /nài/ (3) 无奈 3779

1829 羽 [羽] /yǔ/ (2)

1830 仓 [倉] /cāng/ (3) 仓库 4754

1831 傲 [傲] /ào/ (2) 骄傲 3390

1832 赋 [賦] /fù/ 赋予 4832

1833 肝 [肝] /gān/ (2)

1834 丛 [叢] /cóng/ (3)

1835 卧 [臥] /wò/ (3)

1836 璃 [璃] /lí/ (2) 玻璃 2773

1837 捞 [撈] /lāo/ (2) 捞 3094

1838 扇 [扇] /shàn/ (2) 扇 4190

1839 胖 [胖] /pàng/ (2) 胖 3771

1840 渠 [渠] /qú/ (2) 渠道 3049

1841 拾 [拾] /shí/ (1) 收拾 3427

1842 秩 [秩] /zhì/ (2) 秩序 2176

1843 抄 [抄] /chāo/ (2) 抄 3264

1844 掏 [掏] /tāo/ (2) 掏 2646

1845 邦 [邦] /bāng/ (3) 联邦 3342

1846 尿 [尿] /niào/ (2) 尿 4388

1847 硕 [碩] /shuò/ (2) 硕士 3807

1848 舰 [艦] /jiàn/ (3)

1849 李 [李] /lǐ/ (1) 行李 4799

1850 鸭 [鴨] /yā/ (3) 鸭 4088

1851 逝 [逝] /shì/ (3)

1852 谱 [譜] /pǔ/ 谱 4659

1853 椅 [椅] /yǐ/ (1) 椅子 4032

1854 慌 [慌] /huāng/ (2)

1855 跪 [跪] /guì/ (2) 跪 2910

1856 捧 [捧] /pěng/ (2) 捧 2843

1857 忌 [忌] /jì/

1858 框 [框] /kuāng/

1859 诊 [診] /zhēn/ (3)

1860 锦 [錦] /jǐn/

1861 洒 [灑] /sǎ/ (2) 洒 4259

1862 慨 [慨] /kài/

1863 灌 [灌] /guàn/ (3)

1864 榜 [榜] /bǎng/ (2)

1865 惩 [懲] /chéng/ 惩罚 4271

1866 慕 [慕] /mù/ (2) 羡慕 4343

1867 伯 [伯] /bó/ (2)

1868 凤 [鳳] /fèng/

1869 愉 [愉] /yú/ (1) 愉快 2465

1870 寂 [寂] /jì/ (3) 寂寞 4026

1871 捉 [捉] /zhuō/ (2) 捉 4547

1872 砖 [磚] /zhuān/ (3) 砖 3841

1873 剥 [剝] /bō/ (3)

1874 苗 [苗] /miáo/ (3)

1875 逻 [邏] /luó/ (3) 逻辑3305

1876 玻 [玻] /bō/ (2) 玻璃2773

1877 叙 [敘] /xù/ (3) 叙述4554

1878 履 [履] /lǚ/ 履行3409

1879 伐 [伐] /fá/ 步伐4001

1880 砍 [砍] /kǎn/ (2) 砍2588

1881 朴 [樸] /pǔ/ (2)

1882 粒 [粒] /lì/ (2)

1883 盈 [盈] /yíng/

1884 谨 [謹] /jǐn/ (3) 谨慎4365

1885 锻 [鍛] /duàn/ (1) 锻炼2326

1886 煌 [煌] /huáng/ (3) 辉煌2749

1887 肿 [腫] /zhǒng/ (3)

1888 耀 [耀] /yào/ (3)

1889 孕 [孕] /yùn/

1890 拦 [攔] /lán/ (2) 拦4967

1891 歪 [歪] /wāi/ (2)

1892 厨 [廚] /chú/ (2) 厨房3837

1893 滩 [灘] /tān/ (3)

1894 杨 [楊] /yáng/

1895 棵 [棵] /kē/ (1) 棵2384

1896 厦 [廈] /shà/ 大厦4003

1897 秦 [秦] /qín/

1898 绳 [繩] /shéng/ (2)

1899 堡 [堡] /bǎo/

1900 泄 [泄] /xiè/

1901 兰 [蘭] /lán/ (3)

1902 斑 [斑] /bān/

1903 桶 [桶] /tǒng/ (2) 桶3852

1904 搁 [擱] /gē/ (2) 搁3216

1905 辅 [輔] /fǔ/ (1)

1906 罗 [羅] /luó/

1907 涵 [涵] /hán/ 内涵4006

1908 棚 [棚] /péng/ (3)

1909 催 [催] /cuī/ (2) 催4605

1910 乳 [乳] /rǔ/

1911 裕 [裕] /yù/ (3) 富裕3295

1912 叛 [叛] /pàn/

1913 糟 [糟] /zāo/ (2)

1914 莲 [蓮] /lián/

1915 挽 [挽] /wǎn/ (3)

1916 艇 [艇] /tǐng/

1917 谅 [諒] /liàng/ (1) 原谅4668

1918 舌 [舌] /shé/ (2)

1919 蔬 [蔬] /shū/ (2) 蔬菜2639

1920 宙 [宙] /zhòu/ (3) 宇宙2640

1921 魅 [魅] /mèi/ 魅力2510

1922 旺 [旺] /wàng/ 旺4076

1923 祭 [祭] /jì/

1924 杜 [杜] /dù/

1925 刮 [刮] /guā/ (1) 刮3315

1926 泼 [潑] /pō/ (2) 活泼4161

1927 券 [券] /quàn/ 证券4540

1928 粹 [粹] /cuì/

1929 柴 [柴] /chái/ (2)

1930 趟 [趟] /tàng/ (2) 趟2491

1931 帅 [帥] /shuài/

1932 纹 [紋] /wén/ (3) 纹4758

1933 瓷 [瓷] /cí/ (3)

1934 淋 [淋] /lín/ (3)

1935 痕 [痕] /hén/ (3) 痕迹4379

1936 遣 [遣] /qiǎn/

1937 菌 [菌] /jūn, jùn/ (2)

1938 烤 [烤] /kǎo/ (2) 烤3680

1939 暑 [暑] /shǔ/ (2)

1940 淘 [淘] /táo/ (3) 淘汰4561

1941 儒 [儒] /rú/

1942 乌 [烏] /wū/

1943 艳 [豔] /yàn/ (3)

1944 戚 [戚] /qī/ (2) 亲戚2772

1945 胶 [膠] /jiāo/ (3)

1946 港 [港] /gǎng/ (2)

1947 秒 [秒] /miǎo/ (2)

1948 荷 [荷] /hé/

1949 誓 [誓] /shì/

1950 贤 [賢] /xián/ (3) 贤4419

1951 膀 [膀] /bǎng/ (2) 肩膀4701

1952 歉 [歉] /qiàn/ (2) 道歉4257

1953 雾 [霧] /wù/ (2) 雾4914

1954 泊 [泊] /bó, pō/

1955 筋 [筋] /jīn/ (3)

1956 懒 [懶] /lǎn/ (2) 懒4992

1957 娃 [娃] /wá/

1958 囊 [囊] /náng/

1959 浩 [浩] /hào/

1960 兽 [獸] /shòu/ (3)

1961 蛇 [蛇] /shé/ (2) 蛇3501

1962 契 [契] /qì/

1963 辟 [辟] /pì, bì/ (2) 开辟4493

1964 辨 [辨] /biàn/

1965 糕 [糕] /gāo/ (2)

1966 啡 [啡] /fēi/ (1) 咖啡3500

1967 荐 [薦] /jiàn/ (3) 推荐3099

1968 郑 [鄭] /zhèng/

1969 灿 [燦] /càn/ (3) 灿烂3102

1970 赠 [贈] /zèng/ (3)

1971 咳 [咳] /ké/ (1)

1972 肺 [肺] /fèi/ (2)

1973 绵 [綿] /mián/

1974 晰 [晰] /xī/ (3) 清晰3018

1975 磁 [磁] /cí/ (1)

1976 骄 [驕] /jiāo/ (2) 骄傲3390

1977 驳 [駁] /bó/

1978 廉 [廉] /lián/

1979 巾 [巾] /jīn/ (2)

1980 攀 [攀] /pān/ (3)

1981 侦 [偵] /zhēn/

1982 趁 [趁] /chèn/ (2)

1983 绸 [綢] /chóu/

1984 狮 [獅] /shī/ (2) 狮子4803

1985 昂 [昂] /áng/

1986 寓 [寓] /yù/ (3) 公寓4871

1987 芳 [芳] /fāng/

1988 雇 [雇] /gù/ (3)

1989 壳 [殼] /ké/ (3)

1990 塌 [塌] /tā/ (3)

1991 薪 [薪] /xīn/

1992 谐 [諧] /xié/ 和谐3435

1993 咖 [咖] /kā/ (1) 咖啡3500

1994 湾 [灣] /wān/ 海湾4387

1995 吴 [吳] /wú/ (3)

1996 溢 [溢] /yì/

1997 呐 [吶] /na, nà/ (1) 呐3690

1998 旱 [旱] /hàn/ (3)

1999 搏 [搏] /bó/

2000 浴 [浴] /yù/ (3)

2001 缴 [繳] /jiǎo/

2002 桑 [桑] /sāng/

2003 抖 [抖] /dǒu/ (2)

2004 亭 [亭] /tíng/ (3)

2005 脖 [脖] /bó/ (2) 脖子3228

2006 卜 [蔔] /bo, bǔ/ (2)

2007 雀 [雀] /què/

2008 垃 [垃] /lā/ (2) 垃圾3335

2009 筒 [筒] /tǒng/ (3)

2010 厕 [廁] /cè/ (2) 厕所3155

2011 畏 [畏] /wèi/

2012 窃 [竊] /qiè/

2013 煮 [煮] /zhǔ/ (2) 煮2962

2014 炭 [炭] /tàn/

2015 滥 [濫] /làn/ (3)

2016 蜜 [蜜] /mì/ (2)

2017 拘 [拘] /jū/

2018 丹 [丹] /dān/

2019 驼 [駝] /tuó/ (3) 骆驼3873

2020 愧 [愧] /kuì/ (3)

2021 勒 [勒] /lēi, lè/ 勒4620

2022 挫 [挫] /cuò/ (3)

2023 圾 [圾] /jī/ (2) 垃圾3335

2024 铃 [鈴] /líng/ (2)

2025 烫 [燙] /tàng/ (2) 烫4013

2026 巷 [巷] /xiàng/ (3)

2027 堤 [堤] /dī/ (3)

2028 骚 [騷] /sāo/ (3)

2029 艘 [艘] /sōu/ (3) 艘2797

2030 嫂 [嫂] /sǎo/ (3)

2031 链 [鏈] /liàn/

2032 惹 [惹] /rě/ (2) 惹3813

2033 鞭 [鞭] /biān/

2034 匹 [匹] /pǐ/ (2) 匹4602

2035 竭 [竭] /jié/ (3)

2036 掠 [掠] /lüè/ (3)

2037 宰 [宰] /zǎi/

2038 壶 [壺] /hú/ (2)

2039 笨 [笨] /bèn/ (2) 笨4417

2040 伞 [傘] /sǎn/ (2)

2041 勉 [勉] /miǎn/ (3)

2042 舟 [舟] /zhōu/

2043 逮 [逮] /dǎi/ (3)

2044 掀 [掀] /xiān/ (2) 掀起4411

2045 裙 [裙] /qún/ (2)

2046 踩 [踩] /cǎi/ (2) 踩2985

2047 枯 [枯] /kū/ (3)

2048 傅 [傅] /fù/ (1) 师傅3208

2049 衔 [銜] /xián/

2050 叉 [叉] /chā, chá, chǎ/ (2)

2051 兔 [兔] /tù/ (2)

2052 婴 [嬰] /yīng/ (3) 婴儿4232

2053 庞 [龐] /páng/ 庞大3896

2054 纤 [纖] /xiān/ (2)

2055 愚 [愚] /yú/ (3)

2056 苏 [蘇] /sū/ (1)

2057 逛 [逛] /guàng/ (2) 逛3511

2058 澡 [澡] /zǎo/ (1) 洗澡4768

2059 蒸 [蒸] /zhēng/ (3)

2060 庸 [庸] /yōng/

2061 僵 [僵] /jiāng/ (3)

2062 罐 [罐] /guàn/ (2)

2063 蝶 [蝶] /dié/ (3) 蝴蝶4751

2064 携 [攜] /xié/

2065 衫 [衫] /shān/ (2)

2066 韵 [韻] /yùn/

2067 脊 [脊] /jí/

2068 喻 [喻] /yù/

2069 乒 [乒] /pīng/ (2) 乒乓球4286

2070 撕 [撕] /sī/ (2) 撕 4399

2071 涯 [涯] /yá/ 生涯 4595

2072 窄 [窄] /zhǎi/ (2) 窄 4787

2073 逗 [逗] /dòu/ (2)

2074 鼎 [鼎] /dǐng/

2075 谦 [謙] /qiān/ (2)

2076 钩 [鈎] /gōu/ (3)

2077 顷 [頃] /qǐng/ (3)

2078 魄 [魄] /pò/

2079 膜 [膜] /mó/

2080 睁 [睜] /zhēng/ (2) 睁 4010

2081 乒 [乒] /pāng/ (2) 乒乓球 4286

2082 擅 [擅] /shàn/

2083 峻 [峻] /jùn/ 严峻 4907

2084 苹 [蘋] /píng/ (1) 苹果 3251

2085 酱 [醬] /jiàng/ (2)

2086 歇 [歇] /xiē/ (2)

2087 咽 [咽] /yàn/ (2)

2088 蹲 [蹲] /dūn/ (2) 蹲 3548

2089 嗓 [嗓] /sǎng/ (2) 嗓子 4800

2090 恳 [懇] /kěn/ (2)

2091 妄 [妄] /wàng/

2092 衬 [襯] /chèn/ (2)

2093 晴 [晴] /qíng/ (1)

2094 扁 [扁] /biǎn/ (2) 扁 4691

2095 晒 [曬] /shài/ (2) 晒 4196

2096 狭 [狹] /xiá/

2097 蜂 [蜂] /fēng/ (2)

2098 叠 [疊] /dié/ (2)

2099 芒 [芒] /máng/

2100 哨 [哨] /shào/ (3)

2101 矮 [矮] /ǎi/ (1)

2102 捡 [撿] /jiǎn/ (2) 捡 3552

2103 鹅 [鵝] /é/ (2)

2104 甩 [甩] /shuǎi/ (2) 甩 4443

2105 鹰 [鷹] /yīng/

2106 啤 [啤] /pí/ (1) 啤酒 3702

2107 醋 [醋] /cù/ (2) 醋 4915

2108 坊 [坊] /fāng, fáng/

2109 巩 [鞏] /gǒng/ (2) 巩固 3510

2110 翅 [翅] /chì/ (2)

2111 嚷 [嚷] /rǎng/ (2)

2112 铅 [鉛] /qiān/ (1)